UNIVERSITY CASEBOOK SERIES

EDITORIAL BOARD

ROBERT C. CLARK
DIRECTING EDITOR
Distinguished Service Professor and Austin Wakeman Scott
Professor of Law and Former Dean
Harvard University

DANIEL A. FARBER
Sho Sato Professor of Law and Director, Environmental Law Program
University of California at Berkeley

OWEN M. FISS
Sterling Professor of Law
Yale University

SAMUEL ISSACHAROFF
Bonnie and Richard Reiss Professor of Constitutional Law
New York University

HERMA HILL KAY
Barbara Nachtrieb Armstrong Professor of Law and
Former Dean of the School of Law
University of California, Berkeley

HAROLD HONGJU KOH
Dean and Gerard C. & Bernice Latrobe Smith Professor of
International Law
Yale University

SAUL LEVMORE
Dean and William B. Graham Professor of Law
University of Chicago

THOMAS W. MERRILL
Professor of Law
Yale University

ROBERT L. RABIN
A. Calder Mackay Professor of Law
Stanford University

CAROL M. ROSE
Gordon Bradford Tweedy Professor of Law & Organization, Emerita
Yale University
Lohse Chair in Water and Natural Resources
University of Arizona

DAVID L. SHAPIRO
Professor of Law, Emeritus
Harvard University

KATHLEEN M. SULLIVAN
Stanley Morrison Professor of Law and
Former Dean of the School of Law
Stanford University

BANKRUPTCY

PROPERTY OF US ARMY LEGAL SERVICES AGENCY

EIGHTH EDITION

by

WILLIAM D. WARREN
University of California, Los Angeles

DANIEL J. BUSSEL
University of California, Los Angeles

FOUNDATION PRESS
2009

THOMSON REUTERS

This publication was created to provide you with accurate and authoritative information concerning the subject matter covered; however, this publication was not necessarily prepared by persons licensed to practice law in a particular jurisdiction. The publisher is not engaged in rendering legal or other professional advice and this publication is not a substitute for the advice of an attorney. If you require legal or other expert advice, you should seek the services of a competent attorney or other professional.

Nothing contained herein is intended or written to be used for the purposes of 1) avoiding penalties imposed under the federal Internal Revenue Code, or 2) promoting, marketing or recommending to another party any transaction or matter addressed herein.

© 1985, 1989, 1993, 1995, 1999, 2002 FOUNDATION PRESS
© 2006 THOMSON REUTERS/FOUNDATION PRESS
© 2009 By THOMSON REUTERS/FOUNDATION PRESS
     195 Broadway, 9th Floor
     New York, NY 10007
     Phone Toll Free 1–877–888–1330
     Fax (212) 367–6799
     foundation-press.com
Printed in the United States of America

ISBN 978–1–59941–658–8

PREFACE TO THE EIGHTH EDITION

This EIGHTH EDITION of BANKRUPTCY is published under the extraordinary circumstances of the "Great Recession" of 2008-2009. A residential real estate bubble-burst quickly led to a crisis in sub-prime mortgage lending markets, then a general credit crisis, and, ultimately, in Fall 2008, into a global financial panic the likes of which has not been seen since the 1930s. Within the last year, three major investment banks, Bear Stearns, Lehman Brothers and Merrill Lynch, collapsed or were forced to merge over weekends, the world's largest insurer AIG, a sprawling financial services supermarket, was effectively nationalized after receiving $180 billion in government bailout funds (without any Congressional action), and global banking giants such as Citibank and Bank of America received huge injections of capital from the Treasury and the Federal Reserve that may yet result in their *de facto* nationalization. Thus far into the crisis the United States government has pumped an estimated $3 trillion into the financial system through a bewildering set of interventions ranging from direct infusions of loans and equity capital into banks, to credit facilities for the purchase of commercial paper and other suddenly illiquid securities, the AIG bailout, guarantees of money market funds and bank deposits, and more. The deregulatory model for financial services that has dominated public policy for a generation is in ruins.

Financial panic, and depressed real estate, stock and bond values pushed the already fragile American economy into deep recession, and, unsurprisingly, played a significant role is shifting control of the federal government to the Democratic Party. The domestic automobile sector is in the throes of a massive government-funded restructuring, now being implemented in part through the government-orchestrated Chapter 11 filing of Chrysler. The even more complex and extraordinary restructuring of General Motors, involving not only the Treasury and investors with many more billions at stake, but also thousands of dealers and suppliers, hundreds of thousands of retirees, and a huge, largely-unionized workforce, seems just around the next corner.

The crisis seems likely to transform bankruptcy law, as well as the banking, insurance, auto, and a host of other, industries. On the business side, the prepackaged bankruptcies and quick section 363 sales in Chapter 11 that came into vogue in the 1990s and early 2000s depended upon financial markets awash in liquidity. On the consumer side, the political and social consensus driving the crackdown on consumer debtors embodied in the 2005 BAPCPA amendments has evaporated, as the American middle class experienced a wrenching decline in its home values and retirement accounts amidst the most severe unemployment in a generation. Our crystal ball is as cloudy as all others with respect to how these forces will reshape bankruptcy law yet again, though reshape it they (and other forces) surely will. What is clear, however, is that the bankruptcy courts will continue to be the front-line responders struggling to find new (necessarily imperfect) solutions to critical social and economic problems as they emerge. It is this leading edge role in dealing with crisis that makes bankruptcy work and study so challenging, now more than ever.

As always, our "bankruptcy" colleagues on this law faculty, Kenneth Klee, Lynn LoPucki and (an adoptive bankruptcy colleague from the world of empirical analysis) Dr. Joseph Doherty, are an invaluable resource and make UCLA School of Law the very best place to do academic work in this field. Lynn LoPucki has emerged as the preeminent empiricist on business bankruptcy issues in legal academia. His wide-ranging and enormous body of empirical work is now an indispensible part of any comprehensive introduction to bankruptcy law. We are especially grateful for his generosity in permitting us to quote and cite that work on topics ranging from venue, to sales, to reorganization practice, to asset protection trusts and to transnational bankruptcy. Ken Klee's nationally and internationally prominent role in bankruptcy legislation, law practice at the highest level, and academic writing and lecturing, have made him a leading voice in all aspects of bankruptcy policy, scholarship and practice for a generation. His recently published book, BANKRUPTCY AND THE SUPREME COURT (LEXIS-NEXIS 2008), promises to be a classic of the field. We feel privileged to be in this company every day.

James A. Field, UCLA School of Law Class of 2009, provided excellent research and editing assistance for this EIGHTH EDITION. Our administrative assistant, Tal Grietzer, prepared a camera-ready manuscript of these materials through the miracle of modern desk-top publishing. His skill and care made timely publication of this EIGHTH EDITION possible, and we thank him again for his unstinting efforts in our cause.

William D. Warren

Daniel J. Bussel

Los Angeles, California
May 2009

ACKNOWLEDGMENTS

We gratefully acknowledge the permission extended to reprint excerpts from the following works:

Douglas G. Baird, *The New Face of Chapter 11*, 12 Am.Bankr.Instit.L. Rev. 69, 80-81 (2004). Reprinted by permission of the author and the American Bankruptcy Institute.

Walter Blum & Stanley Kaplan, *The Absolute Priority Doctrine in Corporate Reorganizations*, 41 U.Chi. L.Rev. 651, 656-657 (1974). Reprinted by permission of the authors and the University of Chicago Law Review.

Richard Broude, *Cramdown and Chapter 11 of the Bankruptcy Code: The Settlement Imperative*, 39 Bus.Law. 441, 448-449 (1984). Copyright © 1984 by the American Bar Association. All rights reserved. Reprinted by permission of the American Bar Association and its Section of Corporation, Banking and Business Law.

Daniel J. Bussel, *Power, Authority, and Precedent in Interpreting the Bankruptcy Code*, 41 UCLA L.Rev. 1063, 1071-1075, 1094 (1994). Originally published in 41 UCLA Law Review 1063. Copyright © 1994, The Regents of the University of California. All rights reserved.

Daniel J. Bussel & Edward A. Friedler, *The Limits on Assuming and Assigning Executory Contracts*, 74 Am. Bankr. L.J. 321 (2000). Reprinted by permission of the authors and the American Bankruptcy Law Journal.

COLLIER ON BANKRUPTCY, ¶1129.06 [1][c] (15th ed. rev. 2000). Reprinted with the permission of Matthew Bender & Company, Inc., a member of the LexisNexis Group.

Vern Countryman, *Executory Contracts in Bankruptcy: Part I*, 57 Minn.L.Rev. 439, 460 (1973). Reprinted by permission of the Minnesota Law Review.

Chaim J. Fortgang & Lawrence P. King, *The 1978 Bankruptcy Code: Some Wrong Policy Decisions*, 56 N.Y.U. L.Rev. 1148, 1165-1166 (1981). Reprinted by permission of the authors and the New York University Law Review.

Delmar Karlen, *Exemptions From Execution*, 22 Bus.Law. 1167, 1169 (1967). Copyright © 1967 by the American Bar Association. All rights reserved. Reprinted by permission of the American Bar Association and its Section of Corporation, Banking and Business Law.

Kenneth N. Klee, *Cram Down II*, 64 Am. Bankr. L.J. 229, 244 (1990). Reprinted by permission of the author and the American Bankruptcy Law Journal.

Louis E. Levinthal, *The Early History of Bankruptcy Law*, 66 U.Pa.L.Rev. 223, 224-225 (1918). Copyright © 1918 by the University of Pennsylvania Law Review. Reprinted by permission of the University of Pennsylvania Law Review.

Lynn M. LoPucki, *Courting Failure*, pp. 104-106 (2005). Published by The University of Michigan Press. Reprinted by permission of the author.

Lynn M. LoPucki and Joseph W. Doherty, *Bankruptcy Fire Sales*, 106 Mich.L.Rev. 1, 44-45 (2007). Reprinted by permission of the authors from Michigan Law Review. Copyright © 2007 by Lynn M. LoPucki and Joseph W. Doherty.

Lynn M. LoPucki, *The Death of Liability*, 106 Yale L.J. 32-34 (1996). Reprinted by permission of the author and The Yale Law Journal Company and Fred B. Rothman & Company from The Yale Law Journal Vol. 106, pages 32-34.

Lynn M. LoPucki & William C. Whitford, *Bargaining Over Equity's Share in the Bankruptcy Reorganization of Large, Publicly Held Companies*, 139 U.Pa.L.Rev. 125, 149, 194-195 (1990). Copyright © 1990 by the University of Pennsylvania Law Review. Reprinted by permission of the authors and the University of Pennsylvania Law Review.

National Bankruptcy Conference, *Reforming the Bankruptcy Code*, p. 124 (Rev.ed. 1997). Reprinted by permission of the National Bankruptcy Conference.

Charles Jordan Tabb, *The Law of Bankruptcy*, p. 431 (Foundation Press 1997). Reprinted by permission of the author and the Foundation Press.

Jay L. Westbrook, *A Functional Analysis of Executory Contracts*, 74 Minn. L.Rev. 227, 243 (1989). Reprinted by permission of the author and the Minnesota Law Review.

SUMMARY OF CONTENTS

Preface iii
Acknowledgments v
Table of Contents ix
Table of Cases xxiii

Chapter 1.
INTRODUCTION TO BANKRUPTCY 1

Chapter 2.
THE BANKRUPTCY ESTATE... 29

Chapter 3.
CLAIMS 77

Chapter 4.
DISCHARGE 129

Chapter 5.
STAYS AND INJUNCTIONS 179

Chapter 6.
EXECUTORY CONTRACTS AND LEASES 229

Chapter 7.
THE AVOIDING POWERS OF THE TRUSTEE 323

Chapter 8.
EQUITABLE SUBORDINATION AND
SUBSTANTIVE CONSOLIDATION 431

Chapter 9.
THE CONSUMER DEBTOR IN CHAPTERS 7 AND 13 465

Chapter 10.
REORGANIZATION IN CHAPTER 11:
OPERATING THE DEBTOR & PROPOSING A PLAN............. 575

Chapter 11.
REORGANIZATION IN CHAPTER 11:
CONFIRMING A PLAN 713

Chapter 12.
THE BANKRUPTCY COURTS 823

Appendix
Selected Official Consumer Bankruptcy Forms 901

Index.. 919

TABLE OF CONTENTS

PREFACE iii
ACKNOWLEDGMENTS v
SUMMARY OF CONTENTS vii
TABLE OF CASES xxiii
APPENDIX: **Selected Official Consumer Bankruptcy Forms** 901
INDEX 919

Chapter 1. INTRODUCTION TO BANKRUPTCY

    A. Consensual and Judicial Liens 1
        1. Introduction 1
        2. Consensual Liens 3
            a. Security Interests in Personal Property 3
                (i) Types of Security Devices 3
                (ii) Creation of the Security Interest 4
                (iii) Perfection and Priorities 5
                (iv) Default 8
            b. Security Interests in Real Property 9
                (i) Introduction 9
                (ii) Types of Security Devices 10
                (iii) Creation of Security Interest 11
                (iv) Perfection and Priorities 12
                (v) Rents 13
                (vi) Foreclosure 13
        3. Judicial Liens 14
            a. Judgment and Execution Liens 14
                (i) Judgment Liens 15
                (ii) Execution Liens 16
            b. Attachment Liens 17
    B. Early Bankruptcy Law 18
    C. Overview of Bankruptcy 20
        1. Introduction 20
        2. Types of Bankruptcy 21
        3. Eligibility for Bankruptcy 23
        4. The Petition in Bankruptcy and the Automatic Stay 24
        5. The Trustee in Bankruptcy 24

6. Meeting of Creditors	26
7. Claims in Bankruptcy	27
8. Distribution of Assets to Unsecured Creditors	27
9. Discharge	28

Chapter 2. THE BANKRUPTCY ESTATE

A. Introduction 29
   1. The *Butner* Doctrine 29
   Butner v. United States 29
   Notes 34
   2. Defining Property of the Estate 35
      a. What Is Included 35
      b. Consequences of Exclusion and Inclusion 35
      c. Turnover 36
      d. Unresolved Issues 38
B. Exempt Property 40
   1. A Perspective 40
   2. The Collection Process 41
   3. Exemption Laws 42
   4. Exemptions in Bankruptcy 43
   5. Retirement Plans 44
   6. Impairment of Exemptions 46
      a. Avoidance of Security Interests under § 522(f)(1)(B) 46
         (i) Personal Finance Companies 46
         (ii) The RAND Study 47
      b. Avoidance of Judicial Liens under § 522(f)(1)(A) 48
         (i) Impairment 48
         Problem 49
         In re Silveira 49
         Notes 54
         (ii) The "Fixing of a Lien" 55
         Problem 56
   7. Prebankruptcy Planning 56
      a. Introduction 56
      b. Homestead Exemption 57
         (i) Section 522(b)(3)(A) 57
         Problem 58
         (ii) Section 522(p) 58
         (iii) Section 522(q) 59
      c. Fraudulent Use of Exemptions 59
   Norwest Bank Nebraska v. Tveten 61
   Hanson v. First National Bank in Brookings 68
   Notes 73
   8. Asset Protection Trusts 74

Chapter 3. CLAIMS

- A. Introduction 77
  1. Terminology 77
  2. Claims Procedures 78
     a. Allowed Claims 78
     Problem 79
     b. Time Limits for Filing Proof of Claim 79
- B. Rights to Payment 80
  1. Legal Rights 80
  In re Piper Aircraft 80
  Notes 85
  Note: Mass Future Claims in Bankruptcy 87
  2. Equitable Rights 93
  In re Ward 93
  Notes 102
- C. Determining the Amount of a Claim 104
- D. Secured Claims 106
  1. Introduction 106
  2. Valuing a Secured Claim 109
     a. Cramdown 109
     Associates Commercial Corporation v. Rash 109
     Notes 116
     b. Redemption 116
  3. Avoiding Liens Under § 506(d) 117
  4. Postfiling Interest on Secured Claims 120
- E. Priority Claims 121
  1. Domestic Support Obligations (DSO) 122
  2. Administrative Expenses 123
  In re Jartran, Inc. 123
  Problem 127

Chapter 4. DISCHARGE

- A. Introduction 129
- B. Denial of Discharge Because of Debtor's Misconduct 130
Problem 131
- C. Nondischargeable Debts 132
  1. Unscheduled Debts 132
  In re Madaj 132
  Notes 136

      2. Domestic Support Obligations (DSO) 137
         a. Section 523(a)(5) 137
         In re Werthen 138
         Note 143
         b. Section 523(a)(15) 143
         Problems 144
      3. Willful and Malicious Injury 145
      Kawaauhau v. Geiger 145
      Notes 149
      Problem 150
      4. Educational Loans 151
         a. The *Brunner* Test 152
            (i)   Second prong 152
            (ii)   Third prong 153
         b. Partial discharge 154
         c. Educational Credit Management Corporation Regulations 154
      5. Fraudulently Incurred Debts 155
      Problem 155
      6. Fraud and Defalcation 156
      7. Credit Card Fraud 156
      American Express Travel Related Services Co, v. Hashemi 158
      Notes 160
      8. Fine, Penalty or Forfeiture 163
         a. Punitive Damages 163
         b. Criminal Penalties 165
         c. Restitution Settlements 166
      9. Taxes 167
      Problem 168

  D. Protection of the Discharge 168
      1. Introduction 168
      2. Discharge Exceptions Procedures 170
      Problems 170

  E. Discrimination Against Debtors 171

In re Majewski 172

Note 174

Toth v. Michigan State Housing Development Authority 174

Notes 177

Chapter 5. STAYS AND INJUNCTIONS

- A. Introduction 179
- B. Applicability of the Stay 180
  - 1. Creditor Processes Stayed 180
  - 2. Parties and Property Protected 181
  - 3. Exceptions to the Stay 182
    - a. Section 362(b) 182
    - **Problem** 183
    - b. Police and Regulatory Power Exception 184
  - 4. Termination of the Stay 185
- C. Effect of Violation of Stay 185
  - 1. Damages 185
    - a. Willful Violation 185
    - b. Meaning of "Individual" 186
  - 2. Void or Voidable? 187
  - *In re Soares* 187
  - **Notes** 196
- D. Secured Claims 197

Johnson v. First National Bank 198

Problem 204

- E. Actions Against Nondebtors 204
  - 1. Co–Defendants in Lawsuits 204
  - *A.H. Robins Co. v. Piccinin* 206
  - **Notes** 211
  - 2. Third Parties Liable to Pay the Debtor's Obligations 213
    - a. Guarantors 213
    - *Credit Alliance Corp. v. Williams* 213
    - **Notes** 215
    - b. Issuers of Letters of Credit 217
    - c. Partners of Bankrupt Partnership 218
    - *Patton v. Bearden* 219
    - **Notes** 221

F. Relief From Automatic Stay for Cause 222
In re Holtkamp 223
Notes 225
Problem 226
G. Prepetition Waiver of Stay 226

Chapter 6. EXECUTORY CONTRACTS AND LEASES

A. Executory Contracts 229
    1. Introduction 229
    2. Decision to Assume or Reject 231
    3. Meaning of "Executory Contract" 232
    Problem 236
    4. Rejection of Licenses of Intellectual Property 237
    Lubrizol Enterprises, Inc. v. Richmond Metal Finishers, Inc. 237
    Notes 241
    5. Contracts Not Assignable Under Nonbankruptcy Law 244
        a. Assumption 244
        In re Catapult Entertainment, Inc. 245
        Notes 253
        b. Assignment 258
        In re Pioneer Ford Sales, Inc. 258
        Notes 263
    6. Enforcement Before Assumption or Rejection 267
    Matter of Whitcomb & Keller Mortgage Co. 267
        Notes 273
B. Leases 274
    1. Rejection by Debtor in Possession as Lessor 274
    Precision Industries, Inc. v. Qualitech Steel SBQ, LLC 276
    Notes 282
    2. Rejection by Debtor in Possession as Lessee 283
    3. Liability for Use of Leased Property Before Rejection and
        Time Limits for Assumption or Rejection 285
        a. Real Estate Leases 285
        Problem 288
        b. When Rejection Occurs 289
        c. Personal Property Leases 290
        d. Time in Which to Assume or Reject 291
    4. Evicting the Debtor in Possession 292
        a. Expiration of Lease 293
        b. Termination Before Expiration of Lease 293

	5. Assumption and Assignment 294
	a. The Perils of Assumption 294
	In re Klein Sleep Products, Inc. 295
	Note 305
	b. Effect of Violation of Use Clause 306
	Matter of U.L. Radio Corp. 306
	Note 311
	In re Standor Jewelers West, Inc. 312
C.	Shopping Center Leases 314

In re Trak Auto Corporation 316

Chapter 7. THE AVOIDING POWERS OF THE TRUSTEE

A.	Preferences.. 323
	1. The Concept of a Preference 323
	Problems 325
	2. Transfer of Debtor's Interest in Property and the "Earmarking" Doctrine 326
	Problems 326
	3. The Preference Period 328
	4. Contemporaneous Exchanges 328
	Problems 329
	5. Ordinary Course Payments 330
	a. Policy Basis of § 547(c)(2) 330
	Problem 333
	Union Bank v. Wolas 334
	Notes 340
	b. Meaning of Ordinary Course under § 547(c)(2) 342
	In re Tolona Pizza Products Corp. 342
	Note 346
	6. The "Subsequent Advance" Rule 346
	Problem 347
	Note: Time of Transfer When Payment Made by Check 347
	Problem 348
	7. Security Interests in Inventory and Accounts Receivable 349
	Problem 351
	8. Other Protected Transfers 351
	Problem 352
	9. Letters of Credit 352
	In re Powerine Oil Co. 354
	Note 358
	10. False Preferences: Delayed Perfection of Liens 360

- B. Setoff 362
  - 1. What Is Setoff? 362
  - *Citizens Bank of Maryland v. Strumpf* 362
  - **Notes** 365
  - **Problem** 367
  - 2. The Improvement in Position Test 368
  - **Problem** 368
- C. Fraudulent Transfers 368
  - 1. Actual Fraud 368
  - 2. Constructive Fraud 373
    - a. Introduction 373
    - b. Religious and Charitable Contributions 374
    - c. Insider Transfers or Obligations under Employment Contracts 376
  - 3. Foreclosures 377
  - *BFP v. Resolution Trust Co.* 377
  - **Notes** 385
  - 4. Corporate Distributions as Fraudulent Transfers 386
  - **Problem** 388
  - *Robinson v. Wangemann* 388
  - **Notes** 390
  - 5. Reasonably Equivalent Value in Corporate Transactions 391
    - **Problem** 391
    - *In re Northern Merchandise, Inc.* 392
    - **Problem** 396
  - 6. Leveraged Buyouts 398
  - **Problem** 398
  - *Bay Plastics, Inc. v. BT Commercial Corp.* 400
  - **Note** 415
    - a. Insolvency 415
    - b. The Innocent Shareholder Defense 416
  - 7. Insider Preferences 420
- D. The Strong-Arm Clause 421
  - 1. Introduction 421
  - 2. Knowledge of the Trustee in Bankruptcy 423
  - *McCannon v. Marston* 423
  - **Notes** 426
  - 3. Property Held by Debtor as Nominee or Trustee. 427

Chapter 8. EQUITABLE SUBORDINATION AND SUBSTANTIVE CONSOLIDATION

A. Equitable Subordination 431
   1. Claims of Insiders 431
      a. Inequitable Conduct 431
      b. Undercapitalization 434
      c. Recharacterization 435
   2. Claims of Noninsiders 436
   Matter of Clark Pipe & Supply Co. 439
   Notes 445
B. Substantive Consolidation 447
In re Owens Corning, Inc. 448
Notes 460

Chapter 9. THE CONSUMER DEBTOR IN CHAPTERS 7 AND 13

A. Introduction to Consumer Bankruptcy 465
   1. Background 466
   2. Private Sector Debt Relief 467
   3. Bankruptcy Relief 468
B. The Consumer Debtor in Chapter 7 before BAPCPA 468
   1. Access to Chapter 7 under the 1978 Code 468
   2. The 1984 Substantial Abuse Test 469
C. BAPCPA 471
   1. Introduction 473
   2. The Means Test 473
      a. General Power to Dismiss 474
      b. Presumption of Abuse 474
      c. Current Monthly Income 477
      d. Debtor's Monthly Expenses 478
      e. Residual Power of Court to Dismiss 482
      f. Safe Harbor 486
   Problems 487
      g. Critique 490
      h. A Chapter 11 Solution for a Consumer Debtor? 492
   3. Debtor's Duties 493

  4. Duties of Debtor's Attorney and U.S. Trustee 495
   a. Attorneys 495
   b. Debt Relief Agencies 496
   Milavetz, Gallop & Milavetz, P.A. v. United States 496
   Notes 502
   c. Advertising 503
   d. U.S. Trustee 503
   e. Audits 504
  5. Mandatory Credit Counseling 505
   a. Credit Counseling 505
   b. Financial Management Instructional Courses 508
D. Chapter 13 as an Alternative for the Consumer Debtor 508
  1. An Overview of Chapter 13 508
  2. Eligibility for Chapter 13 512
  Problems 514
  3. Repeated Discharges and Filings 514
   a. Repeated Discharges 514
   Problem 515
   b. Repetitive Filings under BAPCPA 516
  4. Commencing a Chapter 13 Case 517
  5. Property of the Estate 520
   a. Role of Property of the Estate 520
   b. Conversion to Chapter 7 520
  6. The Plan 521
   a. Domestic Support Obligations 521
   b. Commitment Period 522
   c. Disposable Income 522
    (i) Before BAPCPA 522
    (ii) BAPCPA 525
    (iii) Does BAPCPA work? 528
    Problem 530
   d. Modification of Plan 533
   e. Payments "Outside the Plan" 535
   f. Classification of Unsecured Claims 536
   In re Crawford 537
   Note 541
E. Discharge 541
  1. Complete Payment Discharge 541
  2. Hardship Discharge 543
F. Reaffirmation of Discharged Debts 544
  1. Introduction 544
  2. BAPCPA 545

G. Secured Claims in Personal Property 547
   1. In Chapter 7 547
   Problem 548
   2. In Chapter 13 549
      a. The "Hanging Paragraph" 549
      b. Cramdown 550
      c. Surrender 551
      In re Wright 552
      Notes 556
      d. Interest 557
      e. Refinancing Balances Due on Trade-in Vehicles 558
      Problem 558
   3. Valuation of Collateral 559
   4. Interest Rate 560
H. Secured Claims in Debtor's Residence 561
   1. Modification of Home Mortgages 561
   Nobelman v. American Savings Bank 562
   Notes 566
   Problem 567
   2. Modification of Wholly Unsecured Home Loans 568
   Problem 568
   Notes 568
   3. The 2007 Home Loan Crisis 569
   4. Cure of Defaults 571
   5. Three-to-Five Year Limitation 573

Chapter 10. REORGANIZATION IN CHAPTER 11: OPERATING THE DEBTOR & PROPOSING A PLAN

A. Introduction 575
   1. Rationale of Reorganization 575
   2. Reorganization Under Previous Law 577
   3. The Chapter 11 Approach 582
B. Management and Control 586
   1. Role of Debtor in Possession 586
   2. Appointment of Trustee in Bankruptcy 587
   3. Examiners 588
   4. Creditors' Committees 589

C. Adequate Protection for Undersecured Creditors 591
United Savings Assoc. of Texas v. Timbers of Inwood Forest Assoc., Ltd. 592
Notes 599
Note: Single Asset Real Estate 602
D. Operating the Business From Petition to Confirmation 604
   1. Introduction 604
   2. Use of Deposit Accounts and Other Cash Collateral 604
   Problem 606
   3. Sale or Lease of Property in Ordinary Course 607
   4. Obtaining Credit 608
      a. Critical Vendors 608
      Matter of Kmart Corporation 609
      Notes 613
      Note: Reclamation 614
      b. Rights of Administrative Claimants 615
      General Electric Credit Corp. v. Levin & Weintraub 616
      Notes 620
      Hartford Underwriters Ins. Co. v. Union Planters Bank, N.A. 621
      Note 625
      c. Rights of Prepetition Creditors 626
      d. Cross–Collateralization 628
      Matter of Saybrook Manufacturing Co. 628
      Note 633
   5. Sales Not in Ordinary Course: Partial Liquidation 634
   In re Lionel Corp. 634
   Notes 645
   6. Sales Free and Clear of Interests 648
   In re PW, LLC 648
   Notes 664
   Note: Personal Indentifiable Information 665
   7. Break–Up Fees and Bidding Procedures 666
E. Proposing the Plan 669
   1. Introduction 669
   2. Exclusivity 670
   3. Acceptance of the Plan 672
      a. Solicitation 672
      Century Glove, Inc. v. First American Bank of New York 672
      Note 680
      Note: Prepackaged Bankruptcies 680
      Note: Small Business Cases 681
      b. Trading Claims 682
      In re Figter Limited 682
      Notes 688

4. Impairment of Claims or Interests	690
5. Classification of Claims	692
In re U.S. Truck Co.	693
Note	699
Problem	699
Matter of Greystone III Joint Venture	699
Notes	707

Chapter 11. REORGANIZATION IN CHAPTER 11: CONFIRMING A PLAN

A. Feasibility	713
In re Orfa Corp. of Philadelphia	713
Note	718
B. Treatment of Priority Claims	719
C. Treatment of Secured Claims	720
1. § 1129(b)(2)(A) Standards For Cramdown	720
a. Deferred Cash Payments	720
Till v. SCS Credit Corporation	722
Notes	745
Note: Chapter 12—Family Farmers	746
b. Sale of Property	748
c. Indubitable Equivalence	749
In re Arnold & Baker Farms	749
Notes	756
2. § 1129(b)(1) "Fairness" And Negative Amortization	757
Great Western Bank v. Sierra Woods Group	757
3. The § 1111(b) Election	763
Problem	767
D. Treatment of Unsecured Claims and Ownership Interests	767
1. Best Interests Test	767
2. Absolute Priority Rule	768
Problems	768
3. Inter-Class "Give-Ups"	772
In re Armstrong World Industries, Inc.	772
Notes	781
4. New Value Rule	782
Bank of America v. 203 North LaSalle Street Partnership	788
Notes	807

E. Evolving Norms in Large Chapter 11 Reorganizations 810
　　F. Effect of Confirmation of Plan 815
　　G. Modification of Plan 818

Chapter 12. THE BANKRUPTCY COURTS

　　A. Original Jurisdiction 823
　　　　1. Introduction 823
　　　　2. "Related-to," "Core" and "Non-core" Jurisdiction 825
　　　　In re Toledo 826
　　　　Notes 838
　　　　3. Further Limits on Original Jurisdiction 840
　　　　　　a. Withdrawal of the Reference 841
　　　　　　b. Abstention 841
　　　　　　c. Arbitration 842
　　　　　　d. Sovereign Immunity 844
　　　　　　Central Virginia Community College v. Katz 847
　　　　　　Note 859
　　B. Venue 860
　　　　1. Commencement of the Case 860
　　　　Problem 862
　　　　2. Proceedings in the Case 862
　　C. Appellate Jurisdiction 863
　　D. Right to Jury Trial 868
　　Granfinanciera, S.A. v. Nordberg 869
　　Notes 879
　　E. Transnational Bankruptcy 883
　　In re Maxwell Communication Corporation 885
　　Notes 897

Appendix: SELECTED OFFICIAL CONSUMER BANKRUPTCY FORMS 901

Index 919

TABLE OF CASES

Principal cases are in **bold** type. Non-principal cases are in roman type. References are to Pages.

203 North LaSalle Street Partnership, In re, 126 F.3d 955 (7th Cir. 1997), rev'd on other grounds, 526 U.S. 434 (1999): 867

604 Columbus Ave. Realty Trust, In re, 968 F.2d 1332 (1st Cir. 1992): 446

8th Street Village Limited Partnership, In re, 94 B.R. 993 (N.D.Ill.1988): 599

A. H. Robins Co., In re, 880 F.2d 694 (4th Cir. 1989): 217

A.H. Robins Co. v. Piccinin, 788 F.2d 994 (4th Cir. 1986): 92, 106, **206**, 212, 589

Aberegg, In re, 961 F.2d 1307 (7th Cir. 1992): 536

Addison, In re, 540 F.3d 805 (8th Cir. 2008): 73

Ades & Berg Group Investors, In re, 550 F.3d 240 (2d Cir. 2008): 430

Ahlers, In re, 794 F.2d 388 (8th Cir. 1986): 747, 783, 784, 788

Aiello v. Providian Financial Corp., 239 F.3d 876 (7th Cir. 2001): 186

All Media Properties, Inc., In re, 5 B.R. 126 (Bankr.S.D.Tex.1980): 80

Allegheny Int'l, Inc., In re, 118 B.R. 282 (Bankr.W.D.Pa.1990): 688, 689

Amber's Stores, Inc., In re, 193 B.R. 819 (Bankr.N.D.Tex.1996): 289

American Express Travel Related Services Company, Inc. v. Hashemi, 104 F.3d 1122 (9th Cir. 1996): 157, **158**, 160, 162, 163

American Freight Sys., Inc., In re, 164 B.R. 341 (D.Kan.1994): 843

American HomePatient, In re, 420 F.3d 559 (6th Cir. 2005): 745

American Lumber, In re, 5 B.R. 470 (D.Minn.1980): 437

American Mariner Industries, Inc., In re, 734 F.2d 426 (9th Cir. 1984): 592

American Solar King Corp., In re, 90 B.R. 808 (Bankr.W.D.Tex.1988): 819

Anderson, In re, 397 B.R. 363 (6th Cir. BAP 2008): 506

Ansar, In re, 383 B.R. 344 (Bankr.D.Minn.2008): 503

Apex Express Corp., In re, 190 F. 3d 624 (4th Cir. 1999): 840

Applied Theory Corp., In re, 493 F.3d 82 (2d Cir. 2007): 432

Arch Wireless, Inc., In re, 534 F.3d 76 (3d Cir. 2008): 817

Archer v. Warner, 538 U.S. 314 (2003): 166

Arecibo Community Health Care, Inc. v. Puerto Rico, 270 F.3d 17 (1st Cir. 2001): 859

Armstrong World Industries, Inc., In re, 432 F.3d 507 (3d Cir. 2005): 772, 781

Arnold & Baker Farms, In re, 85 F.3d 1415 (9th Cir. 1996): 749

Arnold Print Works, Inc., In re, 815 F.2d 165 (1st Cir. 1987): 839

Associates Commercial Corporation v. Rash, 520 U.S. 953 (1997): **109**, 116, 117, 559, 560

At Home Corp., In re, 392 F. 3d 1064 (9th Cir. 2004): 290

Atlanta–Stewart Partners, In re, 193 B.R. 79 (Bankr.N.D.Ga.1996): 711

Austin v. Unarco Industries, Inc., 705 F.2d 1 (1st Cir. 1983): 205

Autostyle Plastics, Inc., In re, 269 F.3d 726 (6th Cir. 2001): 435, 436

B&L Oil Co., In re, 782 F.2d 155 (10th Cir. 1986): 366

Baldi v. Samuel Son & Co. Ltd., 548 F.3d 579 (7th Cir. 2008): 435

Baldwin–United Corp., In re, 55 B.R. 885 (Bankr.S.D.Ohio 1985): 105, 106

Ballard, In re, 526 F.3d 634 (10th Cir. 2008): 557

Bank of America v. 203 North LaSalle Street Partnership, 526 U.S. 434 (1999): 782, 788, 807, 808, 809, 810

Barakat, In re, 99 F.3d 1520 (9th Cir. 1996): 709

Barclays Bank PLC v. Homan, BCLC 680 (1993): 899

Barnes v. Whelan, 689 F.2d 193 (D.C.Cir. 1982): 537

Barnhill v. Johnson, 503 U.S. 393 (1992): 348

Bateman, In re, 515 F.3d 272 (4th Cir. 2008): 515

Bay Plastics, Inc. v. BT Commercial Corp., 187 B.R. 315 (Bkrtcy.C.D.Cal.1995): **400**, 416

Baylis, In re, 313 F.3d 9 (1st Cir. 2002): 156

Bear Stearns High Grade Structured Credit Strategies Master Fund Ltd, In re, 389 B.R. 325 (S.D.N.Y.2008): 898

Bear Stearns Securities Corp. v. Gredd, 397 B.R. 1 (S.D.N.Y.2007): 418

Beard v. Braunstein, 914 F.2d 434 (3d Cir. 1990): 840

Table of Cases   XXV

Belisle v. Plunkett, 877 F.2d 512 (7th Cir. 1989):   429, 430

Bell, In re, 194 B.R. 192 (Bankr.S.D.Ill.1996):   422

Ben Cooper, Inc., In re, 896 F.2d 1394 (2d Cir.), cert. granted, 497 U.S. 1023 (1990), cert. denied, 500 U.S. 928 (1991) (after remand):   882, 883

Bermec, In re, 445 F.2d 367 (2d Cir. 1971):   600

Beverages International, Ltd., In re, 50 B.R. 273 (Bankr.D.Mass.1985): 438

Bevill, Bresler & Schulman Asset Mgmt. Corp., In re, 878 F.2d 742 (3d Cir. 1989):   418

BFP v. Resolution Trust Co., 511 U.S. 531 (1994):   377, 385, 386

Billing v. Ravin, Greenberg, & Zackin, P.A., 22 F.3d 1242 (3d Cir. 1994): 839, 881

Bjolmes Realty Trust, In re, 134 B.R. 1000 (Bankr.D.Mass.1991):   787

Bohlen Enterprises, Ltd., In re, 859 F.2d 561 (8th Cir. 1988):   327

Bonner Mall Partnership, In re, 2 F.3d 899 (9th Cir. 1993), cert. dismissed, 513 U.S. 18 (1994):   784, 786, 788, 808

Boodrow, In re, 126 F.3d 43 (2d Cir. 1997):   548

Boston Post Road Limited Partnership, In re, 21 F.3d 477 (2d Cir. 1994): 708

Braniff Airways, Inc., In re, 700 F.2d 935 (5th Cir. 1983):   646

Bronson v. United States, 46 F.3d 1573 (Fed.Cir. 1995):   187

Brown, In re, 303 F.3d 1261 (11th Cir. 2002):   74

Brunner v. New York State Higher Education Services Corp., 831 F.2d 395 (2d Cir. 1987):   151, 152, 154, 155

Bryan Road, LLC, (Bankr.S.D.Fla.2008):   227

Bryson Properties, XVIII, In re, 961 F.2d 496 (4th Cir. 1992):   708

Bugna, In re, 33 F.3d 1054 (9th Cir. 1994):   164

Buncher Co. v. Official Committee of Unsecured Creditors, 229 F.3d 245 (3d Cir. 2000):   390

Burgic, In re, 239 B.R. 406 (9th Cir. BAP 1999):   530

Butner v. United States, 440 U.S. 48 (1979):   1, **29**, 34, 35, 38, 39, 552, 556

Cacioli, In re, 463 F.3d 229 (2d Cir. 2006):   132

Cain, In re, 423 F.3d 617 (6th Cir. 2005):   573

Callicott, In re, 396 B.R. 506 (E.D. Mo.2008):   558

Callister, In re, 15 B.R. 521 (Bankr.D.Utah1981):   600

Canal Place Limited Partnership, Matter of, 921 F.2d 569 (5th Cir. 1991):   599

Capital One Auto Finance v. Osborn, 515 F.3d 817 (8th Cir. 2008):   556, 557

Cardelucci, In re, 285 F.3d 1231(9th Cir. 2002):   120

Carlton Restaurant, Inc., In re, 151 B.R. 353 (Bankr.E.D.Pa.1993):   275

Carpet Center Leasing Co., In re, 991 F.2d 682, amended on reh'g, 4 F.3d 940 (11th Cir. 1993):   601

Cartridge Television, Inc., In re, 535 F.2d 1388 (2d Cir. 1976):   105

Casa Loma Associates, In re, 122 B.R. 814 (Bankr.N.D.Ga.1991):   820

Case v. Los Angeles Lumber Prods. Co., 308 U.S. 106 (1939):   580, 747, 782, 783, 786

Castlerock Properties, In re, 781 F.2d 159 (9th Cir. 1986):   839

Castro, In re, 919 F.2d 107 (9th Cir. 1990):   840

Catapult Entertainment, Inc., In re, 165 F.3d 747 (9th Cir. 1999):   244, **245**, 255, 256, 263, 266

Celotex Corp. v. Edwards, 514 U.S. 300 (1995):   216

Central Virginia Community College v. Katz, 546 U.S. 356 (2006):   **847**, 859

Century Glove, Inc. v. First American Bank of New York, 860 F.2d 94 (3d Cir. 1988):   672, 680, 682

Chateaugay Corp., In re, 108 B.R. 17 (S.D.N.NY 1989):   841

Chemetron Corp. v. Jones, 72 F.3d 341 (3d Cir. 1995):   817

CHG International, Inc., 897 F.2d 1479 (9th Cir. 1990):   340

Christopher, In re, 28 F.3d 512 (5th Cir. 1994):   817

Citizens Bank of Maryland v. Strumpf, 516 U.S. 16 (1995):   362, 365

City of New York v. Exxon Corp., 932 F.2d 1020 (2d Cir. 1991):   841

Clamp–All Corp., In re, 233 B.R. 198 (Bankr.D.Mass.1999):   680

Claremont Acquisition Corp., Inc., In re, 113 F.3d 1029 (9th Cir. 1997):   257, 258

Clark Pipe & Supply Co., Matter of, 893 F.2d 693 (5th Cir. 1990) (on rehearing):   432, 437, **439**, 446

Clay, In re, 35 F.3d 190 (5th Cir. 1994):   883

Cohen v. de la Cruz, 523 U.S. 213 (1998):   164

Colon v. Option One Mortgage Corp., 319 F.3d 912 (7th Cir. 2003):   573

Colonial Surety Company v. Weizman, —F.3d—, 2009 WL 1219508 (1st Cir. 2009): 136

Columbia Gas Sys., In re, 164 B.R. 883 (Bankr.D.Del.1994): 839

Com. v. Fremont Investment & Loan, 897 N.E.2d 548 (Mass. Supp. 2008): 570

Commodity Futures Trading Commission v. Schor, 478 U.S. 833 (1986): 824

Commodity Futures Trading Commission v. Weintraub, 471 U.S. 343 (1986): 586, 588

Commonwealth Oil Refining Co., In re, 596 F.2d 1239 (5th Cir. 1979): 862

Compton Corp., In re, 831 F.2d 586 (5th Cir. 1987): 353

Computer Communications, Inc. v. Codex Corp., 824 F.2d 725 (9th Cir. 1987): 274

Continental Airlines, In re, 91 F.3d 553 (3d Cir. en banc 1996): 867

Cook, In re, 126 B.R. 575 (Bankr.D.S.D.1991): 745, 765

Corland Corp., In re, 967 F.2d 1069 (5th Cir. 1992): 326

Costal Federal Credit Union v. Hardiman, 398 B.R. 161 (E.D.N.C. 2008): 548

Cox, In re, 338 F.3d 1238 (11th Cir. 2003): 154

Cozad, In re, 208 B.R. 495 (10th Cir.BAP 1997): 55

Crawford, In re, 324 F.3d 539 (7th Cir. 2003): 537

Credit Alliance Corp. v. Williams, 851 F.2d 119 (4th Cir. 1988): 213

Curry and Sorensen, Inc., In re, 57 B.R. 824 (9th Cir. BAP 1986): 388

Curry, In re, 362 B.R. 394 (Bankr.N.D.Ill.2007): 516

Cushman, In re, 217 B.R. 470 (Bankr.E.D.Va.1998): 514

Cypresswood Land Partners I, 2009 WL 136021 (Bankr.S.D.Tex.2009): 810

D'Alfonso, In re, 211 B.R. 508 (Bankr.E.D.Pa. 1997): 386

Dana Corp., In re, 367 B.R. 409 (Bankr.S.D.N.Y.2007): 615

Davis v. Aetna Acceptance Co., 293 U.S. 328 (1934): 150

Davis, In re, 989 F.2d 208 (6th Cir. 1993): 566

Dawson, In re, 390 F.3d 1139 (9th Cir. 2004): 186

Dean v. Davis, 242 U.S. 438 (1917): 329

Dean, In re, 537 F.3d 1315 (11th Cir. 2008): 550

Decker v. Advantage Fund Ltd., 362 F.3d 593 (9th Cir. 2004): 388

Dent, In re, 130 B.R. 623 (Bankr.S.D.Ga.1991): 567

Desai, In re, 282 B.R. 527 (Bankr.M.D.Ga.2002): 227

DeSardi, In re, 340 B.R. 790 (Bankr.S.D.Tex.2006): 518

Dewsnup v. Timm, 502 U.S. 410 (1992): 109, 119, 120

Diasonics, Inc. v. Ingalls, 121 B.R. 626 (Bankr.N.D.Fla.1990): 435

Dixon v. Federal National Mortgage Association, 2006 WL 3371500 (S.D.Tex.2006): 516

Drexel Burnam Lambert Group. Inc., In re, 960 F.2d 285 (2d Cir. 1992): 217

Drive Financial Services, L.L.P.v. Jordan, 521 F.3d 343 (5th Cir. 2008): 557

Dumont, In re, 383 B.R. 481 (9th Cir. BAP 2008): 548

Durrett v. Washington Nat'l Ins. Co., 621 F.2d 201 (5th Cir. 1980): 374, 377

Easley v. Pettibone Michigan Corp., 990 F.2d 905 (6th Cir. 1993): 196

Edgeworth, Matter of, 993 F.2d 51 (5th Cir. 1993): 212

Elcona Homes Corp., Matter of, 863 F.2d 483 (7th Cir. 1988): 366

Ellingsworth, In re, 212 B.R. 326 (Bankr.W.D.Mo.1997): 157, 160, 161, 162, 163

Enewally, In re, 368 F.3d 1165 (9th Cir. 2004): 574

Entringer Bakeries Inc., Matter of, 548 F.3d 344 (5th Cir. 2008): 327

Entz–White Lumber and Supply, Inc., In re, 850 F.2d 1338 (9th Cir. 1988): 691

Espinosa v. United Student Aid Funds, 545 F.3d 1193 (9th Cir. 2008): 542

Eurofood IFSC Ltd, 2006 E.C.R. 1-3813: 884, 898

Ewers, In re, 366 B.R. 139 (Bankr.D.Nev 2007): 535

Ezell, In re, 338 B.R. 330 (Bankr.E.D.Tenn.2006): 551, 552

Fairchild Aircraft Corp., In re, 6 F.3d 1119 (5th Cir. 1993): 398

Farrey v. Sanderfoot, 500 U.S. 291 (1991): 55, 56

FBI Distribution Corp., In re, 330 F.3d 36 (1st Cir. 2003): 127

Federal Communications Commission v. NextWave Personal Communications, Inc., 537 U.S. 293 (2003): 177

Fenix Cattle Co. v. Silver (In re Select–A–Seat Corp.), 625 F.2d 290 (9th Cir. 1980): 242

Fidelity Financial Services, Inc. v. Fink, 522 U.S. 211 (1998): 361

Field v. Mans, 516 U.S. 59 (1995): 155

Figter Limited, In re, 118 F.3d 635 (9th Cir. 1997): 682, 688, 689, 781

Findley v. Blinken, 982 F.2d 721 (2d Cir. 1992): 819

Flagstaff Foodservice Corp., In re, 762 F.2d 10 (2d Cir. 1985): 621

Fleet Mortgage Group, Inc. v. Kaneb, 196 F.3d 265 (1st Cir. 1999): 186

Fogel v. Zell, 221 F.3d 955 (7th Cir. 2000): 85

Ford Motor Credit Company v. Dobbins, 35 F.3d 860 (4th Cir. 1994): 601

Ford, In re, 296 B.R. 537 (Bankr.N.D.Ga.2003): 386

Fox, In re, 370 B.R. 639 (Bankr.D.N.J.2007): 476, 477

Frederickson, In re, 545 F.3d 652 (8th Cir. 2008): 530, 531, 532

Fretz, In re, 244 F.3d 1323 (11th Cir. 2001): 168

Frushour, In re, 433 F.3d 393 (4th Cir. 2005): 152

FTC v. Toysmart.com, LLC, 2000 WL 1523287 (D Mass.): 665, 666

Gaglia v. First Federal Savings & Loan Ass'n, 889 F.2d 1304 (3d Cir. 1989): 119

Gardner v. New Jersey, 329 U.S. 565 (1947): 860

Gaylor, In re, 123 B.R. 236 (Bankr.E.D.Mich.1991): 864, 865

GECC v. Future Media Productions, Inc., 536 F.3d 969 (9th Cir. 2008): 691

General Electric Credit Corp. v. Levin & Weintraub, 739 F.2d 73 (2d Cir. 1984): 616, 621

General Oil Distributors, Inc., In re, 20 B.R. 873 (Bankr.E.D.N.Y.1982): 633

Germain v. Connecticut National Bank, 988 F.2d 1323 (2d Cir. 1993): 880, 881

Gerwer, In re, 898 F.2d 730 (9th Cir. 1990): 39

Girodes, In re, 350 B.R. 31 (Bankr.M.D.N.C.2006): 535

Glenn, In re, 760 F.2d 1428 (6th Cir. 1985): 572

Globe Illumination Co., In re, 149 B.R. 614 (Bankr.C.D.Cal.1993): 865

Goldrich, In re, 771 F.2d 28 (2d Cir. 1985): 177

Good Hope Refineries, Inc. v. Benavides, 602 F.2d 998 (1st Cir. 1979): 204

Gossett, In re, 369 B.R. 361 (Bankr.N.D.Ill.2007): 507

Grady v. A.H. Robins Co., 839 F.2d 198 (4th Cir. 1988): 92

Grain Merchants of Indiana, Inc. v. Union Bank & Sav. Co., 408 F.2d 209 (7th Cir. 1969):   350, 351

Grand Eagle Companies, Inc., In re, 288 B.R. 484 (Bankr.N.D.Ohio 2003):   417, 418

Grandote Country Club Co., In re, 252 F.3d 1146 (10th Cir. 2001):   385

Granfinanciera, S.A. v. Nordberg, 492 U.S. 33 (1989):   869, 879, 880, 882

Graupner, In re, 537 F.3d 1295 (11th Cir. 2008):   558

Great Western Bank v. Sierra Woods Group, 953 F.2d 1174 (9th Cir. 1992):   757

Green v. Welsh, 956 F.2d 30 (2d Cir. 1992):   226

Green, In re, 934 F.2d 568 (4th Cir. 1991):   470, 483

Greystone III Joint Venture, Matter of, 995 F.2d 1274 (5th Cir. 1991):   602, **699**, 707, 708, 709, 710

Griffith, In re, 206 F.3d 1389 (11th Cir. en banc 2000):   168

Gruntz, In re, 202 F.3d 1074 (9th Cir. 2000):   183

Gulevsky, In re, 362 F.3d 961 (7th Cir. 2004):   156

Haas, In re, 48 F.3d 1153 (11th Cir. 1995):   168

Hailes, In re, 77 F.3d 873 (5th Cir. 1996):   352

Hallahan, In re, 936 F.2d 1496 (7th Cir. 1991):   880, 881

Handy Andy Home Improvement Centers, Inc., Matter of, 144 F.3d 1125 (7th Cir. 1998):   288

Hanson v. First Bank of South Dakota, 828 F.2d 1310 (8th Cir. 1987):   699

Hanson v. First National Bank in Brookings, 848 F.2d 866 (8th Cir. 1988):   60, **68**, 73

Hartford Underwriters Ins. Co. v. Union Planters Bank, N.A., 530 U.S. 1 (2000):   372, 590, **621**, 625

Haskell L.P., In re, 321 B. R. 1 (Bankr.D.Mass.2005):   282, 283

Havoco of America, Ltd. v. Hill, 197 F.3d 1135 (11th Cir. 1999):   74

Hays & Co. v. Merrill, Lynch, Pierce, Fenner & Smith, Inc., 885 F.2d 1149 (3d Cir. 1989):   843

Hechinger Investment Co. of Delaware, In re, 327 B.R. 537 (D.Del.2005):   881

Hendrix, Matter of, 986 F.2d 195 (7th Cir. 1993):   226

Herby's Food, Inc., Matter of, 2 F.3d 128 (5th Cir. 1993):   434, 435

Table of Cases   xxxi

Herrington v. Davitt, 115 N.E. 476 (N.Y.1917):   544
Hersh v. United States, 553 F.3d 743 (5th Cir. 2008):   502
Heward Brothers, In re, 210 B.R. 475 (Bankr.D.Id.1997):   283
Hilton Land & Cattle Co., In re, 101 B.R. 604 (D.Neb.1989):   746
Holcomb, In re, 380 B.R. 813 (10th Cir. BAP 2008):   516
Holtkamp, In re, 669 F.2d 505 (7th Cir. 1982):   223, 226
Hooker Investments, Inc., In re, 937 F.2d 833 (2d Cir. 1991):   882
Huang, In re, 23 B.R. 798 (9th Cir. BAP 1982):   231
Hyman, In re, 502 F.3d 61 (2d Cir. 2007):   156
In re Johnson, In re, 80 B.R. 953 (Bankr.D.Minn.1987):   186
In re LTV Steel Co., 274 B.R. 278 (Bankr.N.D.Ohio 2001):   463
Integrated Telecom Express, Inc., In re, 384 F.3d 108 (3d Cir. 2004):   485
Ireland, In re, 366 B.R. 27 (Bankr.W.D.Ark.2007):   534
IRFM, Inc., In re, 52 F.3d 228 (9th Cir. 1995):   347
James A. Phillips, Inc., In re, 29 B.R. 391 (S.D.N.Y.1983):   607
James Cable Partners, In re, 27 F.3d 534 (11th Cir. 1994):   244
Jaquith v. Alden, 189 U.S. 78 (1903):   346
Jartran, Inc., In re, 732 F.2d 584 (7th Cir. 1984):   123, 127, 820
Jensen, In re, 946 F.2d 369 (5th Cir. 1991):   880, 881
John Hancock Mutual Life Insurance Co. v. Route 37 Business Park Assoc., 987 F.2d 154 (3d Cir. 1993):   708
Johns–Manville Corp., In re, 517 F.3d 52 (2d Cir. 2008), cert. granted, 77 U.S.L.W. 3358 (2008):   838
Johns–Manville Corp., In re, 801 F.2d 60 (2d Cir. 1986):   587
Johns–Manville Corp., In re, 920 F.2d 121 (2d Cir. 1990):   819
Johnson v. First National Bank, 719 F.2d 270 (8th Cir. 1983):   198
Johnson v. Home State Bank, 501 U.S. 78 (1991):   511, 514
Jones, In re, 2008 WL 5063809 (2d Cir. 2008):   518
Juzwiak, In re, 89 F.3d 424 (7th Cir. 1996):   131
K & M Printing, Inc., In re, 210 B.R. 583 (Bankr.D.Ariz.1997):   820
K.M.C. Co., Inc. v. Irving Trust Co., 757 F.2d 752 (6th Cir. 1985):   446
Kagenveama, In re, 527 F.3d 990 (9th Cir. 2008):   528, 529, 530, 531, 532, 534
Kaiser Steel Corp., In re, 952 F.2d 1230 (10th Cir. 1991):   417

Kalb v. Feuerstein, 308 U.S. 433 (1940):   187

Kane v. Johns–Manville Corp., 843 F.2d 636 (2d Cir. 1988):   88, 89, 90

Kane, In re, 336 B.R. 447 (Bankr.D.Nev.2006):   59

Kawaauhau v. Geiger, 523 U.S. 57 (1998):   **145**, 149

Kelly v. Robinson, 479 U.S. 36 (1986):   165

Kelly, In re, 841 F.2d 908 (9th Cir. 1988):   470

Kemko, Inc., In re, 181 B.R. 47 (Bankr.S.D.Ohio1995):   603

Kennedy v. Medicap Pharmacies, Inc., 267 F.3d 493 (6th Cir. 2001):   102

Kham & Nate's Shoes No. 2, Inc. v. First Bank of Whiting, 908 F.2d 1351 (7th Cir. 1990):   445, 784

Kibbe, In re, 361 B.R. 302 (1st Cir. BAP 2007):   529

Kids World of Am., Inc., In re, 349 B.R. 152 (Bankr.W.D.Ky.2006):   839

Kimbro, In re, 389 B.R. 518 (6th Cir. BAP 2008):   480

Kingston Square Associates, In re, 214 B.R. 713 (Bankr.S.D.N.Y.1997):   463

Klein Sleep Products, Inc., In re, 78 F.3d 18 (2d Cir. 1996):   273, **295**, 305

Kmart Corporation, Matter of, 359 F.3d 866 (7th Cir. 2004):   **609**, 614, 615

Koenig Sporting Goods, Inc., In re, 203 F.3d 986 (6th Cir. 2000):   288

Kontrick v. Ryan, 540 U.S. 443 (2004):   130

Koopmans, In re, 22 B.R. 395 (Bankr.D.Utah 1982):   599

Korhonen, In re, 296 B.R. 492 (Bankr.D.Minn.2003):   154

L & J Anaheim Associates, In re, 995 F.2d 940 (9th Cir. 1993):   711

Lacy, In re, 304 B.R. 439 (D. Colo.2004):   820

Langenkamp v. Culp, 498 U.S. 42 (1990):   879, 882

Lanning, In re, 545 F.3d 1269 (10th Cir. 2008):   529, 530

Lasowski, In re, 384 B.R. 205 (8th Cir. BAP 2008):   474, 526

Lawrence, In re, 279 F.3d 1294 (11th Cir. 2005):   76

Laymon, In re, 958 F.2d 72 (5th Cir. 1992):   121

Lazurus, In re, 478 F.3d 12 (1st Cir. 2007):   361

Leco Enterprises, Inc., In re, 125 B.R. 385 (S.D.N.Y.1991):   839

Lehman, In re, 205 F.3d 1255 (11th Cir. 2000):   54

LeMaire, In re, 898 F.2d 1346 (8th Cir. en banc 1990):   542

Lemelle v. Universal Mfg. Corp., 18 F.3d 1268 (5th Cir. 1994):   86

Levit v. Ingersoll Rand Financial Corp., 874 F.2d 1186 (7th Cir. 1989): 421

Lifschulz Fast Freight, Matter of, 132 F.3d 339 (7th Cir. 1997):   435

Lionel Corp., In re, 722 F.2d 1063 (2d Cir. 1983):   634

Lisanti Foods, Inc., In re, 2006 WL 2927619 (D.N.J. 2006):   462

Litchfield Co. of South Carolina Limited Partnership, 135 B.R. 797 (W.D.N.C.1992):   222

LNC Investments, Inc. v. First Fidelity Bank, 247 B.R. 38 (S.D.N.Y.2000), aff'd sub nom. LNC Investments, Inc. v. National Westminister Bank, 308 F.3d 169 (2d Cir. 2002):   602

Local Loan Co. v. Hunt, 292 U.S. 234 (1934):   35

Lombardo, In re, 370 B.R. 506 (Bankr.E.D.N.Y.2007):   484

Long v. Bullard, 117 U.S. 617 (1886):   108, 109, 117, 118, 119

Long, In re, 519 F.3d 288 (6th Cir. 2008):   557

Lopez, In re, 372 B.R. 40 (9th Cir. BAP 2007):   518, 535

Lowenschuss, In re, 67 F.3d 1394 (9th Cir. 1995):   217

LTV Steel Co., In re, 274 B.R. 278 (Bankr.N.D.Ohio2001):   463

Lubrizol Enterprises, Inc. v. Richmond Metal Finishers, Inc., 756 F.2d 1043 (4th Cir. 1985):   237, 241, 242, 243, 244, 274, 276, 283

Ludford Fruit Prod., Inc., In re, 99 B.R. 18 (Bankr.C.D.Cal.1989):   327

Lumber Exchange Building Ltd. Partnership, Matter of, 968 F.2d 647 (8th Cir. 1992):   708

Lybrook, In re, 951 F.2d 136 (7th Cir. 1991):   520

Lynch v. Johns–Manville Sales Corp., 710 F.2d 1194 (6th Cir. 1983):   204

Madaj, In re, 149 F.3d 467 (6th Cir. 1998):   132, 136

Magness, In re, 972 F.2d 689 (6th Cir. 1992):   264

Majewski, In re, 310 F.3d 653 (9th Cir. 2002):   172, 174

Marrama v. Citizens Bank of Massachusetts, 549 U.S. 365 (2007):   513, 514

Martin Paint Stores, In re, 199 B.R. 258 (Bankr.S.D.N.Y.1996):   312

Maryland v. Antonelli Creditors' Liquidating Trust, 123 F.3d 777 (4th Cir. 1997):   846

Maxwell Communication Corp. plc v. Société Générale PLC, 186 B.R. 807 (S.D.N.Y.1995):   899

Maxwell Communication Corporation, In re, 93 F.3d 1036 (2d Cir. 1996): 884, **885**, 897, 898, 899

Maxwell, In re, 40 B.R. 231 (N.D.Ill.1984): 293

Maya Constr. Co., In re, 78 F.3d 1395 (9th Cir. 1996): 817

Mayo, In re, 2007 WL 1074078 (Bankr.D.Md.2007): 473

Mayo, In re, 322 B.R. 712 (Bankr.D.Vt.2005): 174

McCannon v. Marston, 679 F.2d 13 (3d Cir. 1982): **423**, 426

McKeesport Steel Castings Co., In re, 799 F.2d 91 (3d Cir. 1986): 621

McLaren, In re, 3 F.3d 958 (6th Cir. 1993): 880

Mellon Bank v. Metro Communications, Inc., 945 F.2d 635 (3d Cir. 1991): 396, 398

Mercer, In re, 211 F.3d 214 (5th Cir. 2000): 161, 162

Meza, In re, 467 F.3d 874 (5th Cir. 2006): 534

Milavetz, Gallop & Milavetz, P.A. v. United States, 541 F.3d 785 (8th Cir. 2008): **496**, 503

Miller v. NLVK, LLC, 454 F.3d 899 (8th Cir. 2006): 385

Minges, In re, 602 F.2d 38 (2d Cir. 1979): 231

Minoco Group of Companies, Ltd., In re, 799 F.2d 517 (9th Cir. 1986): 211

Mirant Corp., Matter of, 440 F.3d 238 (5th Cir. 2006): 245

MMH Automotive Group, LLC, In re, 385 B.R. 347 (Bankr.S.D.Fla.2008): 283

Mobile Steel Co., In re, 563 F.2d 692 (5th Cir. 1977): 432

Montgomery Ward Holding Corp., In re, 268 F.3d 205 (3d Cir. 2001): 288

Moody v. Security Pacific Business Credit, Inc., 971 F.2d 1056 (3d Cir. 1992): 416

Moore v. Bay, 284 U.S. 4 (1931): 371

Moses, In re, 256 B.R. 641 (10th Cir. BAP 2000): 327

Mosko, In re, 515 F.3d 319 (4th Cir. 2008): 153

Motorola, Inc. v. Official Committee of Unsecured Creditors (In re Iridium Operating LLC), 478 F.3d 452 (2d Cir. 2007): 781

Mullane v. Central Hanover Bank & Trust Co., 339 U.S. 306 (1950): 91, 816, 817

Munford, Inc., In re, 98 F.3d 604 (11th Cir. 1996): 417

Murel Holding Corp., In re, 75 F.2d 941 (2d Cir. 1935): 599, 600

Murphy, In re, 474 F.3d 143 (4th Cir. 2007):   534

Myers, In re, 491 F.3d 120 (3d Cir. 2007):   196

Mystic Tank Lines Corp., In re, 544 F.3d 524 (3d Cir. 2008):   185

N.C.P. Marketing Group, Inc. v. Big Star Productions, Inc., 129 S.Ct. 1577 (2009) (on certiorari):   255

Nat'l City Bank v. Hotchkiss, 231 U.S. 50 (1913):   329

Nat'l Envtl. Waste Corp., In re, 129 F.3d 1052 (9th Cir. 1997):   196

National Gypsum Co., Matter of, 118 F.3d 1056 (5th Cir. 1997):   843

Natural Gas Distributors LLC, In re, 556 F.3d 247 (4th Cir. 2009):   419

Nelson Co., In re, 959 F.2d 1260 (3d Cir. 1992):   328

Nelson v. Scala, 192 F.3d 32 (1st Cir. 1999):   55

New Valley Corp., In re, 168 B.R. 73 (Bankr.D.N.J.1994):   692

Nobelman v. American Savings Bank, 508 U.S. 324 (1993):   562, 566, 574

Norfolk & Western Railway Company v. Ayers, 538 U.S. 135 (2003):   91

Norquist, In re, 43 B.R. 224 (Bankr.E.D.Wash.1984):   234

Norstan Apparel Shops, Inc., In re, 367 B.R. 68 (Bankr.E.D.N.Y.2007):   417

Northampton Corp., In re, 39 B.R. 955 (Bankr.E.D.Pa.1984):   820

Northern Merchandise, Inc., In re, 371 F.3d 1056 (9th Cir. 2004):   392

Northern Pacific Railway Co. v. Boyd, 228 U.S. 482 (1913):   580, 582, 746

Northern Pipeline Constr. Co. v. Marathon Pipe Line Co., 458 U.S. 50 (1982):   823, 824, 839, 840, 841, 868

Northwest Timberline Enter., In re, 348 B.R. 412 (Bankr.N.D.Tex.2006):   745

Norwest Bank Nebraska v. Tveten, 848 F.2d 871 (8th Cir. 1988):   60, 61, 74

Norwest Bank Worthington v. Ahlers, 485 U.S. 197 (1988):   783

Nys, In re, 446 F.3d 938 (9th Cir. 2006):   152

O'Brien Environmental Energy, Inc., In re, 181 F.3d 527 (3d Cir. 1999):   668

O'Brien, In re, 373 B.R. 503 (Bankr.N.D.Ohio2007):   484

Oca, Inc., Matter of, 552 F.3d 413 (5th Cir. 2008):   868

Official Comm. of Unsecured Creditors for Dornier (North Am.) Ltd., In re, 453 F.3d 225 (4th Cir. 2006):   436

Official Committee of Unsecured Creditors of Cybergenics Corp. v. Chinery (Cybergenics I), 310 F.3d 785 (3d Cir. 2002):   372

Official Committee of Unsecured Creditors of Cybergenics Corp. v. Chinery, (Cybergenics II), 330 F.3d 548 (3d Cir. en banc 2003):   372, 591, 625

Ohio v. Kovacs, 469 U.S. 274 (1985):   104

Omegas Group, Inc., In re, 16 F.3d 1443 (6th Cir. 1994):   429, 430, 626

Oot, In re, 368 B.R. 662 (Bankr.N.D.Ohio2007):   483

Orfa Corp. of Philadelphia, In re, 129 B.R. 404 (Bankr.E.D.Pa.1991): **713**, 721

Orion Pictures Corp., In re, 4 F.3d 1095 (2d Cir. 1993):   840, 841, 883

Orvco, In re, 95 B.R. 724 (9th Cir. BAP 1989):   287

Osborne, In re, 42 B.R. 988 (W.D.Wis.1984):   447

Otero Mills, Inc., In re, 25 B.R. 1018 (D.N.M.1982):   215, 216

Owen v. Owen, 500 U.S. 305 (1991):   48, 49

Owens Corning, Inc., In re, 419 F.3d 195 (3d Cir. 2005):   448, 461, 462

Oxford Royal Mushroom Products, Inc., In re, 45 B.R. 792 (Bankr.E.D.Pa.1985):   235

Pacemaker Diagnostic Clinic of America, Inc. v. Instromedix, Inc., 725 F.2d 537 (9th Cir. 1984):   883

Pacific Express, Inc., In re, 69 B.R. 112 (9th Cir. BAP 1986):   436

Pacific–Atlantic Trading Co., In re, 27 F.3d 401 (9th Cir. 1994):   286

Pacor, Inc. v. Higgins, 743 F.2d 984 (3d Cir. 1984):   838, 839

Page, In re, 18 B.R. 713 (D.D.C.1982):   217

Pajaro Dunes Rental Agency, Inc., In re, 174 B.R. 557 (Bankr.N.D.Cal.1994):   415

Pak, In re, 343 B.R. 239 (Bankr.N.D.Cal.2006):   485

Paradise Valley Country Club, In re, 31 B.R. 613 (D.Colo.1983):   815

Parr Meadows Racing Association, Inc., In re, 880 F.2d 1540 (2d Cir. 1989):   182

Patton v. Bearden, 8 F.3d 343 (6th Cir. 1993):   219, 221, 222

Pearson, In re, 390 B.R. 706 (10th Cir. BAP 2008):   480

Pease, Matter of, 195 B.R. 431 (Bankr.D.Neb.1996):   226

Penn Terra Ltd. v. Department of Environment, 733 F.2d 267 (3d Cir. 1984): 184

Pennsylvania Department of Public Welfare v. Davenport, 495 U.S. 552 (1990): 166

Pennsylvania v. Union Gas Co., 491 U.S. 1 (1989): 845

Penrod, In re, 392 B.R. 835 (9th Cir. BAP 2008): 558

Pepper v. Litton, 308 U.S. 295 (1939): 431, 432

Perez v. Campbell, In re, 402 U.S. 637 (1971): 171, 172

Perfetto, In re, 361 B.R. 27 (Bankr.D.R.I.2007): 477

Perry v. Commerce Loan Co., 383 U.S. 392 (1966): 129

Petur U.S.A. Instrument Co., In re, 35 B.R. 561 (Bankr.W.D.Wash.1983): 231

Phar–Mor, Inc. v. Coopers & Lybrand, 22 F.3d 1228 (3d Cir. 1994): 590

Pine Gate Associates, Ltd., In re, 2 B.C.D. 1478 (Bankr.N.D.Ga.1976): 764, 766

Pioneer Ford Sales, Inc., In re, 729 F.2d 27 (1st Cir. 1984): **258**, 263, 264, 265, 267

Pioneer Investment Services Co. v. Brunswick Associates Limited Partnership, 507 U.S. 380 (1993): 80

Piper Aircraft, In re, 58 F.3d 1573 (11th Cir. 1995): **80**, 86

Potter Material Service, Inc., In re, 781 F.2d 99 (7th Cir. 1986): 783, 786

Powerine Oil Co., In re, 59 F.3d 969 (9th Cir. 1995): **354**, 359

Precision Industries, Inc. v. Qualitech Steel SBQ, LLC, 327 F.3d 537 (7th Cir. 2003): **276**, 282, 283

Prime Motor Inns, Inc., In re, 130 B.R. 610 (S.D.Fla.1991): 218

Prussia Associates, In re, 322 B.R. 572 (Bankr.E.D.Pa.2005): 745

Public Service of New Hampshire, In re, 88 B.R. 521 (Bankr.D.N.H.1988): 670, 671

PW, LLC, In re, 391 B.R. 25 (9th Cir. BAP 2008): **648**, 668, 867

QSI Holdings, Inc. v. Alford, 382 B.R. 731 (W.D. Mich. 2007): 418

Racing Services, Inc., In re, 363 B.R. 911 (8th Cir. BAP 2007): 432

Racing Services, Inc., In re, 540 F.3d 892 (8th Cir. 2008): 324

Rake v. Wade, 508 U.S. 464 (1993): 573, 691

Ramirez, In re, 204 F.3d 595 (5th Cir. 2000): 537

Ransom, In re, 380 B.R. 799 (9th Cir. BAP 2007): 480

Rasmussen, In re, 888 F.2d 703 (10th Cir. 1989): 514

Reed, In re, 247 B.R. 618 (E.D.Pa.2000):   567
Related Asbestos Cases, 23 B.R. 523, In re, 532 (N.D.Cal.1982):   206
Reliable Electric Co. v. Olson, 726 F.2d 620 (10th Cir. 1984):   817
Resorts International, Inc., In re, 181 F.3d 505 (3d Cir. 1999):   417
Rheuban, In re, 128 B.R. 551 (Bankr.C.D.Cal.1991):   864, 865
Riodizio, Inc., In re, 204 B.R. 417 (Bankr.S.D.N.Y.1997):   231, 236
Roach, In re, 824 F.2d 1370 (3d Cir. 1987):   572
Robbins, In re, 964 F.2d 342 (4th Cir. 1992):   225
Roberson, In re, 999 F.2d 1132 (7th Cir. 1993):   151
Robert L. Helms Construction and Development Co., Inc., In re, 139 F.3d 702 (9th Cir. en banc 1998):   236
Roberts Farms, Inc., In re, 652 F.2d 739 (9th Cir. 1981):   867
Roberts v. Picture Butte Municipal Hospital [1998], 227 A.R. 308:   899
Robinson v. Wangemann, 75 F.2d 756 (5th Cir. 1935):   388, 390, 391
Rodriguez de Quijas v. Shearson/American Express, Inc., 490 U.S. 477 (1989):   842
Rosson, Matter of, 545 F.3d 764 (9th Cir. 2008):   514
Ross-Tousey, In re, 2008 WL 5234070 (7th Cir. 2008):   479
Roth Steel Tube Co. v. Comm'r of Internal Revenue, 800 F.2d 625 (6th Cir. 1986):   436
Rubin v. Manufacturers Hanover Trust Co., 661 F.2d 979 (2d Cir. 1981):   396, 398
Rudler, In re, 388 B.R. 433 (1st Cir. BAP 2008):   481
Sanders, In re, 551 F.3d 397 (6th Cir. 2008):   515
Santa Fe Development & Mortgage Corp., In re, 16 B.R. 165 (9th Cir. BAP 1981):   204
Santa Monica Beach Hotel, Ltd., In re, 209 B.R. 722 (9th Cir. BAP 1997):   273
Saxman, In re, 325 F.3d 1168 (9th Cir. 2003):   154
Saybrook Manufacturing Co., Matter of, 963 F.2d 1490 (11th Cir. 1992):   616, 628, 867
Scarborough, In re, 461 F.3d 406 (3d Cir. 2006):   568
Scarpino, In re, 113 F.3d 338 (2d Cir. 1997):   56
Scotia Pacific Co., LLC, In re, 508 F.3d 214 (5th Cir. 2007):   603
Scovis, In re, 249 F.3d 975 (9th Cir. 2001):   514
Selcke v. New England Ins. Co., 995 F.2d 688 (7th Cir. 1993):   843

Table of Cases   xxxix

SemCrude, L.P., In re, 399 B.R. 388 (Bankr.D.Del.2009):   366
Seminole Tribe of Florida v. Florida, 517 U.S. 44 (1996):   845, 846, 860
Shearson/American Express, Inc. v. McMahon, 482 U.S. 220 (1987):   842
Sherman, In re, 223 B.R. 555 (10th Cir. BAP 1998):   386
SI Restructuring, Inc., In re, 532 F.3d 355 (5th Cir. 2008):   433, 434, 436
Silveira, In re, 141 F.3d 34 (1st Cir. 1998):   49
Skaggs, In re, 349 B.R. 594 (Bankr.E.D.Mo.2006):   481
Slaughter, In re, 188 B.R. 29 (Bankr.D.N.D.1995):   536
Smith v. Dowden, 47 F.3d 940 (8th Cir. 1995):   882
Smith v. Household Automotive Finance Corp., 313 B.R. 267 (N.D.Ill.2004):   117
Smith, In re, 201 B.R. 267 (D.Nev.1996):   820
Sniadach v. Family Finance Corp.:   41
Soares, In re, 107 F.3d 969 (1st Cir. 1997):   187, 196
Southeast Co., In re, 868 F.2d 335 (9th Cir. 1989):   690, 691
Southland Corp., In re, 160 F.3d 1054 (1998):   691
Southmark Corp., In re, 193 F.3d 925 (5th Cir. 1999):   839
Spears, In re, 355 B.R. 116 (Bankr.E.D.Wis.2006):   507
Spectrum Info. Tech., Inc., In re, 183 B.R. 360 (Bankr.E.D.N.Y.1995):   843
SPM Manufacturing Corp., In re, 163 B.R. 411 (Bankr.D.Mass.1994):   390, 772
Spookyworld, Inc., In re, 346 F.3d 1 (1st Cir. 2003):   187
St. Jude Medical, Inc. v. Medtronic, Inc., 536 N.W.2d 24 (Minn.App.1995):   668
Standard Brands Paint Co., In re, 154 B.R. 563 (Bankr.C.D.Cal.1993):   865
Standor Jewelers West, Inc., In re, 129 B.R. 200 (9th Cir. 1991):   312
Stone Barn Manhattan LLC, In re, 398 B.R. 359 (Bankr.S.D.N.Y.2008):   288
Summit Investment and Development Corp. v. Leroux, 69 F.3d 608 (1st Cir. 1995):   244, 256, 266, 267
Sunterra Corp., In re, 361 F.3d. 257 (4th Cir. 2004):   244
Superior Stamp & Coin Co., Inc., In re, 223 F.3d 1004 (9th Cir. 2000):   327

Supermercado Gamboa, Inc., Matter of, 68 B.R. 230 (Bankr.D.Puerto Rico 1986):   216

Swan, In re, 368 B.R. 12 (Bankr.N.D.Cal.2007):   533

Swedeland Development Group, Inc., In re, 16 F.3d 552 (3d Cir. 1994):   627

T.F. Stone Co., Inc., In re, 72 F.3d 466 (5th Cir. 1995):   385, 386

Taddeo, In re, 685 F.2d 24 (2d Cir. 1982):   571, 572

Talbert, In re, 344 F.3d 555 (6th Cir. 2003):   119

Tanner, 217 F.3d 1357 (11th Cir. 2000):   569

Telefest, Inc. v. VU-TV, Inc., 591 F.Supp. 1368 (D.N.J. 1984):   396, 397, 398

Telesphere Communications, In re, 148 B.R. 525 (Bankr.N.D.Ill.1992):   287

Telfair v. First Union Mortgage Corp., 216 F.3d 1333 (11th Cir. 2000):   520

Teltronics Services, In re, 29 B.R. 139 (Bankr.E.D.N.Y.1983):   436

Tennessee Chemical Co., In re, 112 F.3d 234 (6th Cir. 1997):   349

Tennessee Student Assistance Corp. v. Hood, 541 U.S. 440 (2004):   846

Texlon Corp., In re, 596 F.2d 1092 (2d Cir. 1979):   633

The Universal Church v. Geltzer, 463 F.3d 218 (2d Cir. 2006):   524

Thinking Machines Corp., In re, 67 F.3d 1021 (1st Cir. 1995):   289, 290

Thomas v. Union Carbide Agricultural Products Co., 473 U.S. 568 (1985):   824

Thompson, In re, 788 F.2d 560 (9th Cir. 1986):   290

Thompson, In re, 894 F.2d 1227 (10th Cir. 1990):   572

Tidewater Finance Co. v. Kenney, 531 F.3d. 312 (4th Cir. 2008):   557

Till v. SCS Credit Corporation, 541 U.S. 465 (2004):   557, 560, 569, **722**, 745

Tinker v. Colwell, 193 U.S. 473 (1904):   149

Tirch, In re, 409 F.3d 677 (6th Cir. 2005):   153, 154

Toibb v. Radloff, 501 U.S. 157 (1991):   493, 582

Toledo, In re, 170 F.3d 1340 (11th Cir. 1999):   **826**, 838, 840

Tolona Pizza Products Corp., In re, 3 F.3d 1029 (7th Cir. 1993):   **342**, 346

Torwico Electronics, In re, 8 F.3d 146 (3d Cir. 1993):   104

Toth v. Michigan State Housing Development Authority, 136 F.3d 477 (6th Cir. 1998): **174**, 177, 178

Toyota Motor Credit Corp. v. John, 2007 WL 2702193 (W.D.La.2007): 550

Trak Auto Corporation, In re, 367 F.3d 237 (4th Cir. 2004): 316

Travelers Indemnity Co. v. Bailey, Sup.Ct. No. 08-295 (argued Mar. 21, 2009): 90

Travellers International AG v. Robinson, 982 F.2d 96 (3d Cir. 1992): 882

Treco, In re, 240 F.3d 148 (2d Cir. 2001): 897

Twyne's Case, 3 Coke 80b, 76 Eng. Rep. 809 (1601): 371

U.L. Radio Corp., Matter of, 19 B.R. 537 (Bankr.N.Y.1982): 306, 312

U.S. Truck Co., In re, 800 F.2d 581 (6th Cir. 1986): 693, 699, 707

UAL Corp., In re, 310 B.R. 373 (Bankr.N.D.Ill.2004): 826

Udell, In re, 18 F.3d 403 (7th Cir. 1994): 93, 102, 103, 104

Unioil, In re, 948 F.2d 678 (10th Cir. 1991): 817

Union Bank v. Wolas, 502 U.S. 151 (1991): 334, 340, 342

United Airlines, Inc. v. US Bank, N.A., 406 F.3d 918 (7th Cir. 2005): 291

United Press International, Inc., In re, 60 B.R. 265 (Bankr.D.C.1986): 671

United Savings Assoc. of Texas v. Timbers of Inwood Forest Assoc., Ltd., 484 U.S. 365 (1988): 592, 599, 602, 603

United States v. Maxwell, 157 F.3d 1099 (7th Cir. 1998): 366

United States v. Nicolet, 857 F.2d 202 (3d Cir. 1988): 185

United States v. Ron Pair Enterprises, Inc., 489 U.S. 235 (1989): 120

United States v. Spicer, 57 F.3d 1152 (D.C.Cir. 1995): 166

United States v. Tabor Court Realty Corp., 803 F.2d 1288 (3d Cir. 1986): 399, 400

United States v. Whiting Pools, Inc., 462 U.S. 198 (1983): 36, 37, 38, 39, 575

W.T. Grant, 4 B.R. 53 (Bankr.S.D.N.Y.1980): 438

Wadsworth, In re, 383 B.R. 330 (Bankr.N.D.Ohio2007): 484

Wagner v. PennWest Farm Credit, ACA, 109 F.3d 909 (3d Cir. 1997): 747

Ward, In re, 194 B.R. 703 (Bankr.D.Mass.1996): **93**, 102, 103

Warren, In re, 512 F.3d 1241 (10th Cir. 2008): 73

Washington, In re, 967 F.2d 173 (5th Cir. 1992): 567

Watman, In re, 301 F.3d 3 (1st Cir. 2002): 372

Weathington, In re, 254 B.R. 895 (6th Cir. BAP 2000): 560

Weber v. U.S., 484 F.3d 154 (2d Cir. 2007): 557

Weinstein, In re, 164 F.3d 677 (1st Cir. 1999): 49, 881

Weitzen, In re, 3 F.Supp. 698 (S.D.N.Y.1933): 226

Wells Fargo Bank v. Desert View Bldg. Supplies, Inc., 475 F.Supp. 693 (D.Nev. 1978), aff'd, 633 F.2d 221 (9th Cir. 1980): 392

Werthen, In re, 329 F.3d 269 (1st Cir. 2003): **138**, 143

West Coast Video Enterprises, Inc., In re, 145 B.R. 484 (Bankr.E.D.Pa.1992): 841

West Electronics, Inc., In re, 852 F.2d 79 (3d Cir. 1988): 244

West, Matter of, 22 F.3d 775 (7th Cir. 1994): 166

Wetmore v. Markoe, 196 U.S. 68 (1904): 137

Whitcomb & Keller Mortgage Co., Matter of, 715 F.2d 375 (7th Cir. 1983): **267**, 273, 274

Whiting-Turner Contracting Co. v. Electric Machinery Enterprises, Inc., 479 F.3d 791 (11th Cir. 2007): 843

Wilkow v. Forbes, Inc., 241 F.3d 552 (7th Cir. 2001): 810

Wilson v. Commonwealth Mortgage Corp. 895 F.2d 123 (3d Cir. 1990): 566

Windsor on the River Associates, Ltd., In re, 7 F.3d 127 (8th Cir. 1993): 710, 711

Wood v. National City Bank, 24 F.2d 661 (2d Cir. 1928): 386

Woodbrook Associates, Matter of, 19 F.3d 312 (7th Cir. 1994): 708, 709, 710

Woodridge North Apts., Ltd., In re, 71 B.R. 189 (Bankr.N.D.Cal.1987): 767

World Health Alternatives, Inc., In re, 344 B.R. 291 (Bankr.D.Del.2006): 781

Wright, In re, 492 F.3d 829 (7th Cir. 2007): 34, **552**, 556, 557

Yale Express System, Inc., In re, 384 F.2d 990 (2d Cir. 1967): 599, 600

Young v. United States, 535 U.S. 43 (2002): 167

Young, Ex parte, 209 U.S. 123 (1908): 846

Young, In re, 148 B.R. 886 (Bankr.D.Minn.1992): 374, 375
Zahn v. Yucaipa Capital Fund, 218 B.R. 656 (D.R.I. 1998): 415
Zerand-Bernal Group, Inc. v. Cox, 23 F.3d 159 (7th Cir. 1994): 838
Zimmer, In re, 313 F.3d 1220 (9th Cir. 2002): 568
Zimmerman v. Continental Airlines, Inc., 712 F.2d 55 (3d Cir. 1983): 842, 843

BANKRUPTCY

*

CHAPTER 1
INTRODUCTION TO BANKRUPTCY

A. CONSENSUAL AND JUDICIAL LIENS

1. INTRODUCTION

Bankruptcy law is federal law. The applicable statute is the Bankruptcy Reform Act of 1978, codified in Title 11 of the United States Code, as subsequently amended. We will refer to the 1978 Act as the Bankruptcy Code, and to the previous law the Bankruptcy Act of 1898 as the Bankruptcy Act. The Bankruptcy Code is supplemented by various provisions in Title 18 of the United States Code relating to bankruptcy crimes and in Title 28 of the United States Code relating to the bankruptcy courts and their jurisdiction. Bankruptcy procedure is also governed by Bankruptcy Rules promulgated under the authority of the Supreme Court of the United States.

Although bankruptcy is federal law, the substantive rights in bankruptcy of debtors and creditors are governed in large part by applicable state law. *Butner v. United States*, 440 U.S. 48 (1979). In order to understand the rights of the creditor in bankruptcy it is essential to understand the various rights and remedies created by state law regarding the collection of a debt from a debtor in default. If the debtor does not voluntarily pay the debt the creditor normally obtains payment by first obtaining an interest, generically referred to as a lien, in the debtor's property. A creditor who has a lien may have the liened property sold and the proceeds of sale applied to payment of the debt. Liens are obtained in three ways: by voluntary grant by the debtor; by judicial action taken by the creditor; or by statute because of the status of the particular creditor. Liens in these three categories are usually referred to respectively as consensual liens, judicial liens and statutory liens.

Consensual liens usually arise at the inception of a credit transaction. They are defined in the Bankruptcy Code as security interests in § 101(51) and may relate to both personal and real property. Article 9 of the Uniform Commercial Code, in effect in all of the states, governs the creation and enforcement of security interests in most forms of personal property. Thus, the law of personal property security interests is substantially uniform throughout the United States. Security interests in real property, arising under mortgages or deeds of trust granted by the debtor, are governed by the real property law of the jurisdiction in which the real property is located. This law varies substantially from state to state.

Judicial liens, defined in § 101(36), are created in the litigation process in which the creditor seeks a money judgment on the debt. They may arise either before or after judgment. After a money judgment has been given by the court the creditor, under the law of all of the states, is entitled to seizure of the debtor's property to pay the debt, subject to certain exemptions which allow the debtor to protect some property from the reach of creditors. Sometimes the seizure is a physical taking of the property. In other cases the seizure is symbolic and occurs by the public filing of a document. In either case the seizure results in the transfer from the debtor to the creditor of an interest in the seized property, and that interest is called a judicial lien. The lien gives to the creditor a secured status akin to that of a creditor holding a security interest. Some creditors may be able to acquire secured status at the inception of the judicial action if the applicable law provides for prejudgment seizure. Prejudgment judicial liens are severely limited in most states, and the grounds for obtaining them vary widely among the various jurisdictions.

Statutory liens, defined in § 101(53), are not consensual and do not depend upon judicial action by the creditor. Rather, they are status liens. Certain creditors, favored by the state, are given the rights of secured creditors even though they did not bargain for security. There are many examples of statutory liens. Among the most common are those that arise in favor of creditors who have performed some service or otherwise gave value which resulted in improvement or other benefit to the property to which the lien applies. Illustrations are the mechanic's and materialman's real property lien in favor of unpaid suppliers of services and goods used to improve the property, and the warehouseman's lien which allows an unpaid storer of goods to retain possession of the goods until the storage charges are paid. A more modern statutory lien that has become pervasive is the tax lien that allows the state or federal government to obtain a lien in all of the property of the taxpayer to secure assessed taxes.

Liens are of paramount importance in bankruptcy. The creditor whose debt is secured by a lien in the debtor's property has absolute priority with respect to that property over other creditors who have no lien or a lien with lower priority. Usually bankrupts are insolvent, i.e., the value of their assets is less than their debts, and, particularly in the case of business debtors, the debtor's property is normally encumbered. The result in many of these cases is that the bulk of the debtor's assets is applied to the payment of secured debts. Much of bankruptcy law is concerned with striking an equitable balance between the rights of secured and unsecured creditors to the debtor's assets. Toward this end bankruptcy law allows some liens that are valid outside bankruptcy to be invalidated in the bankruptcy proceedings, thus demoting the lienholder from the status of secured creditor to that of unsecured creditor. Sometimes bankruptcy law recognizes the validity of a lien but the rights of the lienholder are restricted in some fashion in order to enhance the rights of unsecured creditors.

We summarize below the most essential aspects of state law regarding the creation and enforcement of security interests and judicial liens. Statutory liens are discussed in chapter 7 of the Casebook.

2. Consensual Liens

a. Security Interests in Personal Property

(i) Types of Security Devices

Security interests in personal property can be created in a variety of ways. The earliest and simplest method was the common law pledge, which remained the only form of chattel security until early in the nineteenth century. In a pledge the creditor takes possession of the collateral as security for payment of the debt. A pledge can apply not only to tangible property but also to reified intangibles such as negotiable instruments, investment securities and documents of title. The two most important nonpossessory security interests in personal property—the chattel mortgage and the conditional sale—were developed in the nineteenth century as alternatives to the pledge for situations where it was not convenient or practical for the creditor to remain in possession of the collateral.

The chattel mortgage, validated by statutory law, was modeled on the real property mortgage. The mortgagor, who retained possession of the collateral, conveyed it to the mortgagee as security for payment of the debt owed to the mortgagee. The validating law required, however, that the mortgage be recorded in the public records in order to be valid against third parties.

Under a conditional sale the seller delivered goods to the buyer under a contract of sale that provided that title to the goods remained in the seller until the buyer paid the purchase price. If the price was paid, the sale became absolute by passage of title from the seller to the buyer. If the buyer failed to pay according to the sales contract, the sale was not consummated and the seller could retake the goods to which the seller still had title. The conditional sale device was originally validated by judicial authority but in many states it was later regulated by statute. Although the conditional sale was functionally a security device similar to the chattel mortgage, the conditional seller was treated as owner of the goods rather than as a lienholder.

There were a variety of other security devices based either on assignment of rights by the debtor or retention of title by the creditor under which a creditor could get a nonpossessory security interest in collateral. Before the adoption of the Uniform Commercial Code, each security device was governed by a separate body of law. The result was law that was not only complex but also uncertain because it was often unclear what law governed a given transaction. Article 9 of the Uniform Commercial Code greatly simplified the law by adopting a functional approach to secured transactions. UCC § 9-109(a)(1) states that Article 9 applies to "a transaction, regardless of its form, that creates a security interest in personal property * * *." Thus, all of the pre-Article 9 security devices are now simply Article 9 security interests and are governed by a single law.

(ii) Creation of the Security Interest

Security interest is defined in UCC § 1-201(b)(35) to mean "an interest in personal property * * * which secures payment or performance of an obligation." This definition is broader than the bankruptcy definition of security interest in § 101. The UCC definition includes nonconsensual as well as consensual liens. The Bankruptcy Code definition is limited to consensual liens. Under the UCC security interests in goods can arise under either Article 2, which governs sales, or Article 9, which governs secured transactions. Article 9 security interests are those created "by contract" (UCC § 9-109(a)(1)) and thus are included in the Bankruptcy Code definition. Article 2 security interests are nonconsensual and can arise in favor of either the seller or the buyer.

How do Article 9 security interests arise? UCC § 9-203(a) uses the word "attach" to describe when the security interest is created. A security interest attaches upon the occurrence of three events: (1) value has been given; (2) the debtor has rights in the collateral; and (3) either the debtor has authenticated a security agreement describing the collateral, or the debtor has agreed to the security interest and the collateral is in the possession of the secured party pursuant to that agreement. The three events can occur in any order. For example, suppose a bank and a prospective borrower sign a security agreement under which the bank will make future loans to be secured by "all of the borrower's business equipment whether then owned or subsequently acquired." If the bank makes a loan pursuant to the agreement, a security interest in all of the business equipment owned by the borrower at that time will attach at the time the loan is made. The giving of value (the loan) was the last of the three events to occur. If the borrower subsequently acquires additional business equipment, a security interest in that equipment will attach at the time it is acquired. In this case the obtaining of rights in the collateral by the debtor was the last of the three events to occur. The effect of UCC § 9-203 is to greatly simplify the creation of security interests. It also makes it possible for a lender, by virtue of one security agreement, to secure any loan that it might make in the future by a security interest in any personal property that the debtor owns or may own in the future.

If an Article 9 security interest attaches to the collateral, it continues in the collateral notwithstanding sale or other transfer of the collateral to a third party unless transfer free of the security interest was authorized by the secured party. UCC § 9-315(a)(1). In addition to retaining the security interest in the transferred collateral, the secured party, by virtue of this section, also gets a security interest in identifiable proceeds of the transfer, whether or not the transfer was authorized. Thus, if the debtor sells the collateral for money or exchanges it for other property, the secured party has a security interest in the money or other property received by the debtor. If any proceeds are used to acquire property, the security interest attaches to this property as well. This proceeds rule is very important in cases in which the collateral is property such as inventory or accounts receivable, which by its nature will be disposed of for cash or other property when it is sold or collected by the debtor in the ordinary course of business.

(iii) Perfection and Priorities

Attachment of the security interest means that the lien of the secured party may be enforced against the debtor. But "perfection" of the security interest normally determines whether the security interest will be effective against third parties. Suppose the debtor, after granting a security interest in collateral to Creditor #1, either sells the collateral to Buyer or grants a security interest in the collateral to Creditor #2. In most cases Creditor #1 can have priority over Buyer or Creditor #2 only if the security interest of Creditor #1 was perfected. By requiring perfection the law accommodates the interests of the secured party and creditors of the debtor or other third parties who deal with the collateral. Since these third parties may not know that the debtor's assets are burdened with a security interest, it may be unfair for the secured party to assert rights against them based on the security interest unless some public notice of the security interest has been given. To protect the interests of these third parties the secured party is not allowed, in most cases, to enforce the security interest against these third parties unless the security interest is perfected. UCC § 9-308(a), which defines perfection, states that "a security interest is perfected if it has attached and all of the applicable requirements for perfection * * * have been satisfied." The "applicable requirements" refer to some action by the secured party that gives notice of the security interest, usually possession of the collateral by the secured party or filing in a designated public office of a notice of the secured transaction.

With respect to some kinds of collateral, possession is a common method of perfection; for example, pledges of negotiable instruments or securities. On the other hand, possession cannot be used as a method of perfection if the nature of the collateral does not permit it. This is usually true in the case of intangible property. A common example is the account receivable that is defined in UCC § 9-102(a)(2) as meaning a right to payment for certain specified monetary obligations. In cases in which perfection by possession is not possible, perfection by filing may be necessary. With respect to most types of personal property, possession and filing represent alternative methods of perfection, but perfection by filing is far more common.

The great majority of all secured transactions in personal property represent the financing of the purchase price of "consumer goods," defined in UCC § 9-102(a)(23) as goods "used or bought for use primarily for personal, family or household purposes." The secured party, who may be the seller of the goods or a financial institution that lends the purchase price to the buyer, is secured by a security interest in the goods purchased. With respect to these purchase money security interests in consumer goods, no filing under the UCC is necessary to perfect the security interest. Rather, the security interest is automatically perfected when it attaches. A special rule, however, applies to motor vehicles that are required to be registered under state law. Perfection requires notice of the security interest even in the case of purchase money consumer transactions. Motor vehicles are registered under certificate of title laws that require security interests in the vehicle to be noted on the certificate of title. Perfection under the UCC is accomplished by compliance with the certificate of title law.

With respect to securities, deposit accounts, letters of credit and other financial assets held by financial intermediaries, perfection may also occur by obtaining "control" over the account with the intermediary in which such assets are held. UCC §§ 9-104, 9-105, 9-106, 9-107 and 9-314.

Perfection by filing under the UCC may be accomplished by filing of the security agreement between the secured party and the debtor. This carries forward the practice under the pre-Code chattel mortgage statutes that required filing of the mortgage. But this method is not typical. The normal practice is to file a document or other record known as a financing statement, which is described in UCC § 9-502(a). This document provides very little information. It need only disclose the names of the debtor and the secured party and indicate the collateral involved in the transaction. For example, the financing statement might indicate that the collateral is "business equipment." One cannot, by looking at the financing statement, identify the particular items of business equipment involved, the nature or amount of the debt secured or any other details of the transaction. Thus, the UCC adopts the principle of "notice filing," that is, that the secured party need only give notice that the secured party has, or may obtain in the future, a security interest in the indicated collateral. The burden is on the third party to determine the facts concerning the transaction.

Filing of the financing statement may either precede or follow the attachment of the security interest. In loan transactions it is common for the lender to file before the loan is made. By filing before the transaction is made the lender can be sure that the security interest will be perfected at the same time that it attaches. UCC § 9-308(a) provides that a security interest is perfected when it has attached and the steps required for perfection—in this case filing—have been taken. If the financing statement is filed after attachment, the security interest will become perfected at the time of filing.

If the filing of a financing statement results in perfection of a security interest in collateral, the perfection will automatically carry over for at least 20 days to identifiable proceeds if the collateral is sold or otherwise disposed of by the debtor. In most cases this perfection will continue after the 20-day period without any further act of the secured party. In some cases, however, the secured party must either take possession of the proceeds or file a financing statement with respect to the proceeds in order to obtain perfection after the 20-day period. The perfection rules for proceeds are stated in UCC § 9-315.

Unperfected security interests, although enforceable against the debtor, are given very little protection against the claims of third parties who subsequently acquire property interests in the collateral. UCC § 9-317(a). If a creditor of the debtor acquires a judicial lien in the collateral the judicial lien has priority over the unperfected security interest. Moreover, as we shall see later, an unperfected security interest may be avoided in bankruptcy. An unperfected security interest is also subordinated to the title of most third parties who buy the collateral from the debtor. The only exception is that some buyers who buy with knowledge of the security interest take subject to it.

Suppose Debtor granted competing security interests in the same collateral to secure debts owed to two different creditors. Assume that each creditor perfected by filing a financing statement. There are a number of ways in which the priority between the two creditors might be determined. For example, the rule might be that the first security interest to attach has priority, or the first security interest to be perfected might be given priority. The UCC rejects both these solutions by adopting a rule that gives priority to the creditor who first files a financing statement. UCC § 9-322(a). The effects of this rule are far-reaching and surprising. Suppose, in our example, Creditor #1 and Debtor signed a security agreement in which Debtor granted a security interest in the collateral to secure any loans that Creditor #1 might make to Debtor in the future. Creditor #1 then filed a financing statement relating to the collateral. Later, but before any loan was made by Creditor #1, Debtor borrowed from Creditor #2 on the security of the same collateral. Creditor #2 filed. At that point Creditor #2 had a perfected security interest in the collateral. Creditor #1 had no security interest, perfected or unperfected, in the collateral because

Creditor #1 had not yet made any loan to Debtor. If Creditor #1 then lends money to Debtor, Creditor #1 will at that time take a perfected security interest in the collateral. Because Creditor #1 was the first to file a financing statement, the security interest of Creditor #1 will have priority even though it attached and was perfected after the security interest of Creditor #2 attached and was perfected. This result follows even if Creditor #1 made the loan to Debtor with knowledge of the transaction between Debtor and Creditor #2. There are some exceptions to this rule. One important exception is that security interests perfected by control have priority over security interests perfected by other means even if control is obtained later. Another is that in some circumstances "purchase money" security interests in after-acquired property may have priority over security interests perfected by filing.

(iv) Default

If a debtor in default refuses or is unable to pay, an unsecured creditor can collect the debt only by bringing an action against the debtor and obtaining judgment. The action may be costly and there may be a substantial delay before judgment can be obtained. The secured creditor need not get judgment against the debtor in order to collect the debt and in many cases can obtain payment with either no judicial intervention or after a summary court procedure. UCC § 9-609 states that on the debtor's default the secured party has the right to take possession of the collateral. The secured party can seize the collateral without judicial intervention if the seizure can be accomplished "without breach of the peace." The quoted phrase has been given a very broad interpretation by the courts to exclude seizure in any case in which there is any resistance, verbal as well as physical, or in which the seizure involves a nonconsensual entry on property of the debtor or other person. As a practical matter, self-help seizure is restricted to cases in which the debtor voluntarily gives up possession or in which the collateral is property, such as an automobile, that can be found in some public place while the debtor or other custodian is not present.

If self-help is not possible, the secured party can obtain possession by judicial process in a summary proceeding. State law normally provides a provisional remedy under which the secured party can get immediate possession of the collateral by a judicial seizure. There must be a noticed hearing in which the secured party must establish, usually by affidavit, the probable validity of its claim, but the only litigable issue is whether the debtor is in default. The law normally provides for the posting of a surety bond or other undertaking by the plaintiff to protect the debtor in case of a wrongful seizure. Thus, a secured creditor can normally get possession of the collateral either by self-help or after a quick summary proceeding.

A secured party in possession of the collateral after default is entitled by UCC § 9-610 to "sell, lease, license or otherwise dispose of" the collateral. Normally the collateral is sold in either a public or private sale after notice to the debtor, UCC § 9-611. The proceeds of the sale are applied to the expenses of retaking and sale and satisfaction of the debt, UCC § 9-615. If the proceeds of sale are not sufficient to satisfy the debt, the secured party can usually sue for any deficiency, UCC § 9-615(d).

b. Security Interests in Real Property

The sources of real property security law differ greatly from those of personal property security law. Personal property security law is virtually uniform throughout the nation; moreover, it is conveniently available in Article 9 of the UCC. In contrast, the principles of real property security law are found in a complex mosaic of case and statutory law unique to each state. Hence, the description below is only an approximate generalization from the great body of diverse doctrine in this area. The publication in 1997 of the *Restatement (Third) of Property, Mortgages* offers a welcome synthesis of this body of law.

(i) Introduction

Like the pledge of personal property, the early mortgage of real property involved the creditor's taking possession of the property. The mortgagor (debtor) deeded the property to the mortgagee (creditor) on condition subsequent that if the mortgagor paid the debt by a given day, called the "law day," the mortgagee would reconvey the land to the mortgagor. Under the deed, the mortgagee was entitled to possession and to the crops and rents from the land. In time, the practice developed of leaving the mortgagor in possession with a right in the mortgagee to take possession and obtain payment from the rents and profits upon default.

A mortgagor who failed to repay the debt on the law day lost all interest in the land. Time was of the essence. However, equity intervened to allow mortgagors to redeem their property by paying the debt after the law day. To the present day the debtor's interest under a mortgage is described as the "equity of redemption." Since the intervention of the courts of equity in giving the mortgagor the right to redeem made the mortgagee's rights uncertain, the procedure developed in equity of allowing the mortgagee to request that the court order the mortgagor to redeem by a certain date and, if the mortgagor failed to do so, to foreclose the mortgagor of the right to redeem. The term "foreclosure" has come to mean any method of realizing on the mortgagee's security interest. Since no sale was required in this earliest procedure, and the potential for forfeiture was present, this type of foreclosure, called "strict foreclosure," is prohibited in most states. Foreclosure today requires that the mortgaged land be sold at public sale with any surplus over the mortgagee's debt returned to the mortgagor. Some states by statute allow the mortgagor to redeem for a period after the foreclosure sale from the purchaser at that sale.

(ii) Types of Security Devices

Three types of real property security devices are prevalent in the United States: the mortgage, the deed of trust, and the installment sale contract. For convenience and following common usage, we sometimes refer to the mortgage as the generic security device in real property transactions.

Mortgage. The early mortgage conveyed title to the mortgagee with a right to take possession. Although some states still purport to retain the "title" theory of mortgages, most states have adopted the "lien" theory that views a mortgage transaction as one granting the mortgagee merely a security interest in the land. These jurisdictions have done by case law what UCC § 9-202 has done in personal property secured transactions: whether title is nominally in the mortgagee or not is immaterial; if the transaction is for security, the creditor's only interest is a security interest. Differences between the title and lien theories have been eroded. The modern mortgage is a contract, usually written by the mortgagee, and the law of mortgages today largely concerns the question of the extent to which courts will enforce against mortgagors the terms of the mortgage. These decisions are more influenced by present day views on contracts of adhesion and debtor protection than by conceptual distinctions based on the location of legal title.

Deed of Trust. In this transaction the trustor (debtor) conveys legal title to a trustee in trust for the benefit of the beneficiary (creditor). The probable reason for the growth of the deed of trust was the desire of creditors to supplant the time-consuming requirement of judicial foreclosure with foreclosure by exercise of a private power of sale. An early view was that a conventional mortgage could not contain a power of sale because the power had to be vested in a third party as trustee. Hence, the deed of trust was devised to allow a trustee to sell the property for the benefit of the creditor on default by the trustor. Today, there has been a general assimilation of the deed of trust and the mortgage. Although one device may be more popular in some jurisdictions than in others, the rights of the parties vary only marginally under either. A mortgage may contain an enforceable power of sale and, although the trustee under a deed of trust holds legal title, the rights of the trustor and beneficiary are quite similar to those of the mortgagor and mortgagee.

Installment Sale Contract. Here the seller sells land to the buyer on the condition that title will pass to the buyer only when the buyer has completed the installment payments called for by the contract. In its early usage, the device was advantageous to sellers because default by the buyer resulted in forfeiture of all payments the buyer had made and terminated the buyer's right to possession. Thus, the land contract gave sellers what amounted to strict foreclosure of the buyer's interest: the debtor's interest was cut off without a foreclosure sale. However, the 20th century saw a remarkable case law development that relieved the debtor from forfeiture in defaults on installment contracts and went far toward assimilating the installment sale contract with the mortgage and deed of trust. *Restatement (Third) of Property, Mortgages* § 3.4 (1997) assimilates them completely. Nonetheless, in some states the assimilation has not been complete, and the installment contract remains a special security device of limited usefulness to both sellers and buyers. Sellers may have no expedited method to cut off the buyer's interests akin to foreclosure by exercise of private power of sale. Buyers may have no absolute right to compel a sale to prevent forfeiture of their interests.

(iii) Creation of Security Interest

A security interest in personal property may arise under UCC § 1-201(b)(35) only when there is an obligation to be secured. Similarly, there can be no enforceable real property mortgage if there is no underlying obligation. Hence, in some jurisdictions a gift of a mortgage and note to a donee does not create a right in the donee to enforce the note and mortgage. The *Restatement (Third) of Property, Mortgages* § 1.2 (1997) takes a contrary view. However, a mortgage may be enforceable even though the debtor is not personally liable. This may occur when the mortgagor has been discharged in bankruptcy, when personal liability is barred by anti-deficiency statutes, or when the parties contractually agree to limit liability to the value of the collateral. This latter "nonrecourse" transaction is of growing importance in commercial financing.

Under the UCC, if a transaction results in the creation of a security interest under § 1-201(b)(35), the provisions of Article 9 apply whatever the form of the transaction. At an early date a parallel doctrine had emerged in real property law to the effect that if rights in land were conveyed to secure a debt, the law of mortgages applied to protect the debtor however the transaction was disguised. One of the earliest examples of this rule was the "deed absolute" transaction. If the grantor conveys land to the grantee by an unconditional deed with an oral agreement that if the grantor pays a debt owed to the grantee by a given date the grantee will reconvey, the court will allow proof of the oral agreement and will allow the grantor either to redeem or compel foreclosure by sale. A familiar modern example of a disguised secured transaction is a sale and leaseback. Seller sells land to Buyer for $100,000. Buyer leases the land back to Seller for a rental of $12,000 per year. Seller agrees to repurchase the land in five years for $100,000. Courts see this transaction as a disguised loan transaction and apply mortgage principles to it. Sales with options to repurchase that are the functional equivalent of obligations to repurchase are treated in the same way.

Once a transaction is recognized as being one for security, courts will not enforce terms of a security agreement that give up the debtor's basic rights as a mortgagor, that is, the rights to redemption or foreclosure. For instance, if the parties agree at the time of the credit extension that in order to avoid the expense of foreclosure the mortgagor will place a deed to the land in escrow to be delivered to the mortgagee upon default by the mortgagor, the court will consider this an invalid attempt to waive fundamental rights of a mortgagor. On the other hand, an agreement to waive the mortgagor's rights in foreclosure is enforceable if entered into after the mortgagor is already in default.

(iv) Perfection and Priorities

The mortgagee perfects rights against third-party claimants by recording the mortgage document in the records of the county in which the land is located. But a mortgagee has priority over third parties who know of the mortgage when they acquire their interests even if the mortgage is not recorded. Moreover, unlike the UCC rule under § 9-317, the majority view is that although a good faith purchaser of real property without knowledge of the mortgage takes free of an unrecorded mortgage, a judicial lien creditor whether with or without knowledge does not. Later we will see this distinction between real property security law and personal property security law acknowledged in § 544(a) which grants the trustee in bankruptcy power to avoid unperfected security interests in both real and personal property.

A major problem in real property law is the priority of the mortgagee's future advances against intervening secured interests. Of growing popularity are "open end" mortgages in which the mortgagee has the option but not the obligation to advance additional funds to the mortgagor upon request. Another common use of future advances is the construction mortgage in which funds are advanced by the mortgagee as progress payments conditional on a structure's reaching prescribed stages of completion. The prevailing priority rule distinguishes between future advances made pursuant to commitment and those that are made at the option of the mortgagee, the so-called "optional–obligatory" distinction. Advances made pursuant to commitment take their priority from the date of the commitment. Optional advances relate back to the date of the mortgage only if made by the mortgagee without knowledge of an intervening security interest. Hence, unlike a junior secured party subject to the UCC rule of § 9-322(a), a second mortgagee can be sure that no optional future advance by the first mortgagee will have priority over the second mortgage by notifying the first mortgagee of the second mortgagee's interest.

(v) Rents

In lending on commercial property, mortgagees not only want a security interest in the land but also in the rents arising from leases made by the mortgagor. If the mortgagor is in default, it may be of great importance for the mortgagee to be able to collect the rentals until the property is sold by foreclosure. Commonly, the mortgage will expressly grant the mortgagee rights in the rentals. Real property rents are rights to the payment of money and, as such, have much in common with accounts receivable. A seller who sells goods on credit may assign the buyer's debt, described as an account by UCC § 9-102(a)(2), to a creditor as security for a loan. As we have seen, under Article 9 of the UCC, the creditor may take a perfected security interest in the account as soon as the buyer owes the debt, and the priority of the creditor's interest dates from the time of filing a financing statement. The UCC does not apply to real property rentals (UCC § 9-109(d)(11)).

(vi) Foreclosure

When a debtor is in default under a personal property security agreement, UCC § 9-601(c) provides that the secured party's remedies are cumulative, that is, the secured party may sue to obtain a personal judgment against the debtor, may proceed to foreclose on the collateral, or may do both at the same time. If the secured party forecloses on the collateral, the debtor is liable for any deficiency remaining after the sale. In some states the real property mortgagee's remedies are also cumulative. In others the mortgagee has the option either of suing on the debt or foreclosing on the collateral, but must elect one or the other and cannot do both. In some of the Western states, including California, the mortgagee's only action is to foreclose on the collateral and to ask for a deficiency judgment in that action. This rule is called the "one-action rule."

The traditional method of foreclosing a real property mortgage is the often long and costly process of judicial foreclosure. The mortgagee sues to foreclose; the mortgagor and junior lienholders must be joined; after a hearing the court orders a sale; public sale by a judicial officer follows the requisite statutory notice; the proceeds of the sale are applied to pay the mortgage debt; any surplus goes first to junior lienholders and then to the mortgagor; any deficiency is assessed as a personal judgment against the mortgagor. Frequently, the property is sold to the mortgagee who is entitled to make a "credit bid" at the sale, that is, the amount of the mortgage debt may be credited against the price of the land at the sale.

The protection afforded the mortgagor to ensure that the land will bring a fair price is based on formal compliance with the requirements of the statute. If the sale is regularly conducted with respect to notice and other formal statutory requirements, courts are very unlikely to allow the sale to be challenged as not fetching a high enough price. In contrast, Article 9 of the UCC imposes a general duty on a secured party to sell collateral in a "commercially reasonable" manner. In some instances this may entail selling the property in the manner that a dealer in that kind of property would utilize. The more flexible, result-oriented UCC rules on foreclosure sales were a deliberate reaction to the formalistic approach to foreclosure of real property law.

In about half the states, mortgagees may foreclose by exercise of the power of sale contained in the mortgage. Here, the mortgagee gives notice of default to the mortgagor who usually has a statutory right to cure the default within a few weeks. If the default is not cured, notice of sale is given, and the land is sold at public sale by the mortgagee or, in the case of a deed of trust, by the trustee. The mortgagor has no automatic right to a presale hearing. The mortgagor may contest the existence of default by moving to enjoin the sale. Power of sale foreclosure is much faster and cheaper than judicial foreclosure, and in those states in which it is permitted it has become the most commonly used method of foreclosure. Its major shortcoming is that it cannot resolve disputes between competing interests in the manner that a court decree does in a judicial foreclosure. Unlike non-judicial foreclosure sales under the UCC, the price of proceeding by non-judicial sale against real estate under a private power of sale is usually that the mortgagee forfeits any right to a deficiency judgment.

In a number of states, the mortgagor may redeem property sold at the foreclosure sale by acting within a statutory period that runs from three months in some states to two years in others. In some of these states a junior lienholder can also redeem. The chilling effect that the potential for postsale redemption poses for foreclosure sales has led many other states to provide for no postsale redemption. The Great Depression spawned a number of statutes limiting or prohibiting deficiency judgments. These debtor protection statutes have by and large remained in force.

3. JUDICIAL LIENS

a. Judgment and Execution Liens

A money judgment against a defendant can be collected by a levy (seizure) on property of the defendant and a subsequent sale of that property. Levy and sale are done pursuant to a writ of execution which is usually issued by the clerk of the court upon application of the judgment creditor. The writ orders the levying officer (sheriff, marshal or similar officer) to enforce the judgment by levying on property of the debtor. The property to be levied on is usually identified in instructions to the levying officer signed by the judgment creditor or the creditor's attorney. In this process of judgment and execution of judgment, two types of judicial lien can result. One is a specific lien, called an execution lien, which attaches to the property on which levy is made under the writ of execution. The other is a general lien, called a judgment lien which arises as a result of the judgment itself. It applies to all of the property of the debtor to which a judgment lien can apply. Both liens can arise only after a judgment has been obtained but the execution lien can arise only if a writ of execution also has been obtained.

(i) Judgment Liens

Judgment liens are recognized in a large majority of the states. Historically they applied only to real property, and that continues to be the rule in all but a few jurisdictions. The kinds of interests in real property to which a judgment lien attaches may vary in different jurisdictions. The procedure for obtaining the lien may also vary, but generally the lien attaches to all real property of the judgment debtor in the county in which the judgment is docketed or in which the judgment or an abstract is recorded in the land records. In most states, the lien attaches not only to property of the debtor existing at the time the judgment was docketed or recorded but to after-acquired property as well. Typically, duration of the judgment lien is equal to the life of the judgment, a relatively long period. Ten years or more from the entry of the judgment is common. In most states the lien can be extended beyond the original period by a renewal of the judgment. One of the advantages of a judgment lien is its generality. It allows the judgment creditor to obtain the security of a lien in the debtor's property even though that property has not yet been identified by the creditor.

In a few states the judgment lien attaches to personal property as well as real property. One of the most innovative and sophisticated statutes providing for a judgment lien in personal property is that of California, which became effective in 1983. Cal. Civ. Proc. Code §§ 697.510 to 697.670. It allows a money judgment creditor to obtain a judgment lien in personal property by filing a notice of lien in the office of the Secretary of State. The lien applies only to specified business property: accounts receivable, chattel paper, equipment, farm products, inventory, and negotiable documents of title. These terms are defined in the same way as the comparable terms were defined in the original draft of Article 9. The lien attaches only to property in which an Article 9 security interest could be perfected by filing a financing statement with the Secretary of State. In effect, the statute gives to the judgment creditor the functional equivalent of an Article 9 security interest in the property affected. The filing of the notice of lien is the equivalent of perfection under the UCC. The lien applies both to property owned by the judgment debtor at the time of filing the notice of lien and to property acquired thereafter. In most respects the judgment lien is treated like an Article 9 security interest. As under the UCC, the lien attaches to identifiable cash proceeds of the sale of any property subject to the lien. Noncash proceeds are, in effect, treated as after-acquired property. If noncash proceeds do not fall within one of the enumerated classes of property to which the lien applies, the judgment lien does not attach. The judgment lien continues in property that is disposed of by the judgment debtor, but third parties who would have taken free of a perfected Article 9 security interest in the same property also take free of the judgment lien. Priorities among conflicting judgment liens are governed by a first-to-file rule similar to that governing Article 9 security interests. There is also a first-to-file rule governing conflicts between judgment liens and Article 9 security interests subject to certain exceptions.

(ii) Execution Liens

The method of carrying out levy pursuant to a writ of execution may vary from state to state, and it also varies depending upon the type of property involved. With respect to real property, we have seen that the judgment creditor, by virtue of the judgment, usually can obtain a judgment lien in real property of the debtor. In some states the creditor with a judgment lien can obtain sale of the liened property by judicial foreclosure in proceedings similar to foreclosure of a mortgage. In other states the judgment lienholder obtains sale by levying on the property pursuant to a writ of execution. Levy on real property usually requires the recording by the levying officer in the land records of the writ of execution or a notice of levy. An execution lien arises in the real property when the recording occurs. With respect to tangible personal property in the possession of the debtor, levy usually is done by physical seizure. The levying officer either takes custody by removing the property to a place of safekeeping or, if the property is not portable, by installing a keeper who maintains custody. In some states levy on property that cannot be conveniently moved is done by serving a notice of levy on the debtor or by some public filing. With respect to intangible property that represents an obligation owed to the debtor, such as wages, deposit accounts, accounts receivable and general intangibles, levy is normally done by garnishment. A copy of the writ of execution or a notice of levy is served on the person owing the debt to the judgment debtor. The effect of garnishment is to require the garnishee to make payment of the obligation to the levying officer. A similar procedure is often provided for in the case of levy on tangible property of the debtor which is in the hands of a third party under some claim of right as in the case of a lease or pledge. Within these general categories, the law of the jurisdiction may provide special methods of levy for particular types of property.

Levy on personal property pursuant to a writ of execution gives rise to an execution lien in favor of the judgment creditor, but the time that the lien arises may vary in different jurisdictions. Some states follow the common law rule that delivery of the writ of execution to the levying officer gives rise to an execution lien in the personal property of the debtor covered by the writ. However, this lien is inchoate. If no valid levy is made, either because the levying officer cannot find property of the debtor or because the writ of execution expired before levy was made, the lien lapses. If a valid levy is made, the inchoate lien becomes perfected and dates from the date of delivery of the writ of execution. In other states the rule is that the execution lien arises at the time the levy is made. In some cases the validity of a lien in bankruptcy depends upon the time that the lienholder obtained the lien. For example, a judicial lien obtained within 90 days of bankruptcy while the debtor was insolvent can usually be avoided by the trustee in bankruptcy while a lien obtained more than 90 days before bankruptcy may be indefeasible. Sometimes a creditor has more than one judicial lien in the same property. For example, suppose a judgment creditor obtained a judgment lien in real property of the debtor and later the creditor obtained an execution lien by levying on that real property. The normal result in this case is that the effective date of the execution lien relates back to the date of the earlier judgment lien.

b. Attachment Liens

We have seen that upon default by the debtor a secured creditor may normally get payment by selling the collateral. In most cases little or no judicial intervention is required for the secured creditor to assert rights to the collateral. The creditor's remedy is fast and inexpensive. Consider the rights of an unsecured creditor against a debtor in default. The only remedy of the creditor is to bring an action on the debt. When judgment is eventually recovered it may be satisfied by seizure and sale of property of the debtor, but judgment may be delayed for a long period during which the creditor is subject to substantial risks. An improvident debtor may dissipate assets before judgment can be obtained. A dishonest debtor may conceal property or remove it from the jurisdiction or may dispose of it in order to defraud creditors. An unsecured creditor may obtain protection against these risks by obtaining prejudgment seizure of the debtor's assets. This prejudgment seizure is known as attachment. Do not confuse this term with the same term that is used in the UCC to describe the creation of an Article 9 security interest.

Prejudgment attachment is generally available as a provisional remedy in conjunction with the commencement of the action on the debt. The grounds for obtaining the remedy vary widely from state to state. Attachment may not be available in all kinds of actions. For example, in some states the remedy is restricted to contract claims in which the amount of the claim is readily ascertainable. In most states attachment is allowed only in cases in which the defendant is not resident in the state or in which the defendant is avoiding service of process or in which there is basis for believing that the defendant will conceal assets, remove assets from the state or convey them in fraud of creditors. In some states attachment can be obtained if the action is based on a debt fraudulently contracted by the debtor. In a minority of states attachment is available with respect to certain kinds of claims even in the case of resident defendants and even in the absence of grounds for believing that the defendant will conceal or fraudulently dispose of assets.

Attachment involves a levy on the property of the defendant that is similar to a levy under a writ of execution, although in some cases physical seizure, which is the norm with respect to execution on chattels, is replaced by levy by filing with respect to some kinds of property. An attachment lien arises at the time the levy is made. Attachment is a very drastic remedy since it may allow the debtor to be deprived of the use of property and since it always burdens that property with a lien that may prevent the debtor from freely disposing of the property. The debtor can normally prevent attachment by posting a surety bond, but this requirement may in some cases be just as onerous as attachment itself. Since the remedy is given before a judgment on the claim has been made, serious constitutional issues of taking without due process of law are involved. Because of constitutional law considerations the remedy of attachment has been substantially limited in recent years. The remedy is not normally available unless there has been a judicial determination of the probable validity of the creditor's claim. That determination, however, is normally made in a summary proceeding and can, in some cases, be made ex parte so long as the debtor is given opportunity to promptly challenge the attachment.

B. EARLY BANKRUPTCY LAW

The law of bankruptcy can be traced to the law of various Italian city states of the 14th century, which in turn was based on Roman origins. Some of these principles eventually found their way into the English law and thus into the law of the United States. The concept of bankruptcy viewed historically and comparatively has been described as follows:

> All bankruptcy law, however, no matter when or where devised and enacted, has at least two general objects in view. It aims, first, to secure an equitable division of the insolvent debtor's property among all his creditors, and, in the second place, to prevent on the part of the insolvent debtor conduct detrimental to the interests of his creditors. In other words, bankruptcy law seeks to protect the creditors, first, from one another and, secondly, from their debtor. A third object, the protection of the honest debtor from his creditors, by means of the discharge, is

sought to be attained in some of the systems of bankruptcy, but this is by no means a fundamental feature of the law.

* * *

The laws that have for their object the protection of the creditors from one another seek to prevent any one of the creditors from obtaining more than his proportionate share of the debtor's assets. A special process of collective execution is devised, a process directed against all of the property of the debtor, resorted to for the common benefit and at the common expense of all the creditors.

Louis E. Levinthal, *The Early History of Bankruptcy Law*, 66 U.Pa.L.Rev. 223, 225 (1918).

The most important early English bankruptcy law was the Statute of Bankrupts, 13 Elizabeth, c. 7 (1570). It was directed against fraudulent debtors and was punitive in nature. It applied only to debtors who were merchants and it provided that a debtor who committed an act of bankruptcy "shall be reputed, deemed and taken for a bankrupt." There were various acts of bankruptcy including the debtor's departure from the realm, the debtor's taking refuge in the debtor's house, taking sanctuary and various other acts if the debtor's purpose was to avoid process with the intent of defrauding or hindering creditors. Upon complaint, the Lord Chancellor could appoint a commission of "wise, honest and discreet" persons who were authorized to seize the property of the bankrupt and sell it for the payment, pro rata, of the debts of the bankrupt. The bankrupt remained liable to the extent that creditors were not paid in full. The bankrupt could be imprisoned by the commissioners and, by virtue of a later statute, could be subjected to pillory and the loss of an ear as well. Louis E. Levinthal, *The Early History of English Bankruptcy*, 67 U.Pa.L.Rev. 1, 16–18 (1919). Thus, early English bankruptcy law was designed to protect creditors and to punish debtors who were avoiding the payment of just debts. The Statute of Bankrupts was amended or supplemented by numerous statutes over the years. It was not until the early eighteenth century with the Statutes of 4 Anne, c. 17 (1705), and 10 Anne, c. 15 (1711), that the law allowed discharge of the bankrupt of the debts owing at the time of bankruptcy. Levinthal, *supra* at 18-19.

The Statute of Bankrupts was the bankruptcy law during the colonial period in America. The first federal bankruptcy law, the Bankruptcy Act of 1800, followed closely the Statute of Bankrupts. Other bankruptcy laws were enacted in 1841 and 1867 as emergency legislation in the wake of financial panics. Each of these three laws was repealed shortly after enactment. Agrarian populists opposed federal bankruptcy laws, which they saw as instruments of oppression that allowed bankers to take their land. Financial interests favored these laws as giving them a way to share equally in the assets of insolvent debtors. David A. Skeel, Jr., *Debt's Dominion: A History of Bankruptcy Law in America* 3 (2001). The notion of allowing a debtor to voluntarily choose bankruptcy as a means of finding relief from creditors did not become a part of English bankruptcy law until well into the nineteenth century. Voluntary bankruptcy did not become a part of the American law until the Bankruptcy Act of 1841.

Not until the Bankruptcy Act of 1898 did America have a permanent bankruptcy statute, and this act, as amended on numerous occasions, was the bankruptcy law of the United States until 1979 when the present Bankruptcy Code became effective. The Bankruptcy Act was our first modern bankruptcy statute, and is, in large part, the basis of the Bankruptcy Code. However, during the 19th century, development of the law of corporate reorganization occurred largely outside the Bankruptcy Act by use of equity receiverships principally in cases involving insolvent railroads. Equity receivership law was reformed and codified as part of the Bankruptcy Act during the Great Depression of the 1930s and then reformed again and recodified as modern Chapter 11 in the Bankruptcy Code.

C. OVERVIEW OF BANKRUPTCY

1. INTRODUCTION

We have seen that under the early law bankruptcy was exclusively a creditor's remedy. In modern times bankruptcy is still an important, though little used, creditor's remedy. Some creditors who would receive little or nothing in payment of their claims outside bankruptcy may be able to obtain substantial payment by forcing the debtor into involuntary bankruptcy under § 303. But bankruptcy today is most important as a debtor's remedy, and the overwhelming majority of bankruptcies occur by voluntary act of debtors who are seeking relief from the demands of their creditors.

Outside of bankruptcy, there is often little relief for a debtor who is unable to pay creditors. Creditors with security interests may seize and sell collateral. Other creditors may have obtained, or are threatening to obtain, judicial liens in the debtor's property. Although state law may allow the debtor to protect exempt property from execution or attachment, that law may not apply to some property that the debtor vitally needs. Most debtors that are not natural persons cannot protect any property from creditors under nonbankruptcy law. For debtors beset by creditors, bankruptcy can provide instant and dramatic relief. The paragraphs that follow provide a brief description of the principal characteristics of bankruptcy proceedings. Because involuntary bankruptcy is relatively uncommon, we will deal only with voluntary bankruptcy.

Chapter 1. Introduction to Bankruptcy

The United States is divided into 94 judicial districts. In each district there is a bankruptcy court with one or more bankruptcy judges. There are also United States Trustees, each of whom is assigned to one or more of the judicial districts. They are officials of the United States Department of Justice, whose function it is to supervise the administration of bankruptcy cases. The duties of the United States Trustee are stated in 28 U.S.C. § 586. Judicial districts for Alabama and North Carolina were allowed to remain out of the U.S. Trustee system unless the district elects to be included. In these jurisdictions, a Bankruptcy Administrator is given roughly the same responsibilities as the United States Trustee.

2. TYPES OF BANKRUPTCY

The debtor can choose between two types of bankruptcy. The first, and most simple type, is a bankruptcy liquidation under Chapter 7 of the Bankruptcy Code. In a liquidation bankruptcy all of the property of the debtor owned at the date of bankruptcy becomes part of the bankruptcy estate. § 541. A debtor who is an individual is entitled to exempt certain property from the bankruptcy estate. The exempt property is released to the debtor. The property that may be exempted is in most cases determined by the law of the state of the debtor's domicile and consists of property that is exempt from judicial liens in that state. In some cases the debtor has the option of electing to exempt property listed in § 522(d). The trustee in bankruptcy must also dispose of property in which a lienholder or other person such as a co-owner has a property interest. In some cases the property is released by the trustee. In other cases the property is sold by the trustee and the property interest of the lienholder or other person is satisfied from the proceeds of sale. Any remaining property of the estate is sold by the trustee in bankruptcy and the proceeds are applied to payment of the debts of the debtor and the expenses of the bankruptcy proceedings. A debtor who is an individual normally will be discharged of personal liability on all or most prebankruptcy debts. The ability of an individual to obtain a discharge of prebankruptcy debts is one of the most important characteristics of modern bankruptcy law. The overextended debtor can get a "fresh start" by having personal liability on prebankruptcy debts wiped out while being allowed to retain all exempt property. Liquidating debtors other than individuals, such as corporations and partnerships, have no need for a fresh start. After distributing all its assets to creditors, an insolvent organization can simply be dissolved. Thus, in Chapter 7, only an individual can be discharged. § 727(a)(1). Since 2005, access to Chapter 7 for an individual whose income prior to the bankruptcy exceeded State medians, has been limited by a "means test" that is designed to require individuals who are deemed to have sufficient future income to obtain relief in Chapter 13 rather than Chapter 7.

The second type of bankruptcy is usually referred to as reorganization or rehabilitation bankruptcy and is governed by Chapter 11, Chapter 12, or Chapter 13 of the Bankruptcy Code. Chapter 13 can be used only by a debtor who is "an individual with regular income that owes, on the date of the filing of the petition, noncontingent, liquidated, unsecured debts of less than $336,900 and noncontingent, liquidated, secured debts of less than $1,010,650 * * *." § 109(e). The great advantage of Chapter 13 is that the debtor can get the benefit of discharge without losing nonexempt property. The debtor is required to formulate a plan under which the debtor proposes to pay, in whole or in part, some or all prebankruptcy debts over a period of time which is usually five years. Creditors are paid in accordance with the plan normally from postbankruptcy earnings although the plan could provide for a liquidation of some assets. The plan need not be approved by creditors. If the plan is confirmed by the bankruptcy court, creditors are bound by its terms. § 1327(a). But a plan cannot be confirmed over the objection of a creditor unless certain requirements are met. If the plan does not propose payment in full of unsecured claims, the plan must provide for the payment of all of the debtor's "projected disposable income" for the period of the plan. § 1325(b)(1). In most cases, disposable income means total income received by the debtor less the amount reasonably necessary for the maintenance or support of the debtor and the debtor's dependents. § 1325(b)(2). But for debtors whose incomes exceed state family medians, the calculation of projected disposable income is limited by certain standards that rely on historical earnings statistical medians published by the Internal Revenue Service and the Bureau of the Census § 1325(b)(3) that may not reflect the debtors' actual income and expenses during the plan period. When all payments are completed, the debtor is entitled to a discharge of those debts (with some exceptions) that are provided for in the plan. § 1328(a). Under some circumstances the debtor can obtain a discharge even if payments under the plan have not been completed if the failure to complete the plan is not the fault of the debtor. § 1328(b).

Chapter 11 may be used by both individuals and firms, but it is designed primarily for business firms. It resembles Chapter 13 in that the debtor normally retains its assets and operates its business as a "debtor in possession." The debtor proposes a plan of reorganization under which creditors will be paid, sometimes over a period of time, from assets of the estate or postconfirmation earnings of the debtor. Unlike Chapter 13, confirmation of a plan in Chapter 11 is considered only after it has been voted on by the various classes of creditors and stockholder interests of the debtor. Acceptance by a class is accomplished by a vote of members of the class in specified majorities. Under some circumstances, a plan can be confirmed even though not all classes accept the plan. Other plans that fail to meet certain statutory requirements cannot be confirmed even if all classes accept the plan. Under some circumstances, other parties in interest may propose a reorganization plan. Upon confirmation of the plan, the debtor, whether an individual or an organization, is normally given a discharge of all preconfirmation debts. In return, creditors and stockholder interests have rights that are given to them by the plan. There are various provisions in Chapter 11 designed to protect the interests of creditors and stockholder interests who did not accept the plan.

Chapter 12 was added to the Bankruptcy Code in 1986 to provide for the rehabilitation of "family farmers" defined in § 101(18). Chapter 12 is similar to Chapter 13, but it incorporates some elements of Chapter 11. It is specifically designed to make it easier for family farmers to restructure their debts in bankruptcy while continuing to operate their farms even if they are unable to provide payment in full to their creditors or obtain their consent to a plan..

Chapter 9 of the Bankruptcy Code, which governs the bankruptcy of municipalities, is not discussed in this book.

3. ELIGIBILITY FOR BANKRUPTCY

Under § 301 a voluntary case can be commenced by any "entity that may be a debtor." Section 101(15) defines entity to include "person, estate, trust, [and] governmental unit." It apparently can "include" others because "includes" is not limiting (§ 102(3)), but we are given no guidance as to what those others might be. But not all entities can qualify as debtors. Only a person or a municipality may be a debtor. §§ 101(13), 109(a). "Person" is defined in § 101(41) to include individuals, partnerships and corporations, but not governmental units. "Corporation" is defined in § 101(9) to include some entities that aren't corporations such as limited liability companies, unincorporated associations and business trusts. The effect of this mystifying series of definitions within definitions is that an applicant for voluntary bankruptcy qualifies if either a person or a municipality. The definitions exclude governmental units, other than municipalities, and estates and trusts, unless the trust is a business trust. Thus, the City of New York, but not the State of New York or the United States of America, can go into bankruptcy. Estates and trusts, whose affairs are governed by state courts exercising traditional equity powers, are left to those courts. A business trust, which is undefined in the Bankruptcy Code, qualifies as a "debtor" because it is included in the definition of "corporation" and thus is also included in the definition of "person." Section 109(b) and (d) further limit the persons eligible for bankruptcy. Insurance companies, banks and similar financial institutions may not be debtors. These institutions are regulated by other statutes that provide for insolvency proceedings. Railroads may be debtors under Chapter 11 (§ 109(d)) but not under Chapter 7 (§ 109(b)(1)).

Brokerages, on the other hand, may not reorganize under Chapter 11, but may liquidate under special provisions in Chapter 7. §§ 741 et seq.

Most debtors who file in bankruptcy are insolvent, but insolvency, which is defined in § 101(32), is not necessary. For individuals, access to Chapter 7 bankruptcy may be limited by the "means test" described in chapter 9 of the Casebook.

4. THE PETITION IN BANKRUPTCY AND THE AUTOMATIC STAY

A "voluntary case" as it is called in the Bankruptcy Code, is commenced by the debtor's filing a petition in bankruptcy in the bankruptcy court. § 301. In addition to the petition, the debtor must file various statements and schedules of information including a statement of assets and liabilities with descriptions of each and a list of creditors identified by name and address.

The filing of the petition in bankruptcy results in an automatic stay against a variety of acts that might otherwise be taken against the debtor or with respect to property of the bankruptcy estate. § 362. The automatic stay bars: the commencement or continuation of judicial proceedings against the debtor to recover a prebankruptcy claim; the enforcement of any prebankruptcy judgment against the debtor or against property of the estate; any act to obtain possession of property of the estate or property held by the estate; and any act to create, perfect or enforce any lien against property of the estate. The stay even applies to informal acts to collect a prebankruptcy debt such as dunning letters, telephone calls and the like. There are some exceptions to the very broad scope of the stay, but the stay effectively insulates the debtor from any kind of action to collect prebankruptcy debts. A creditor can get relief from the stay in some cases, but the effect of the stay is to require all collection action to be made through the bankruptcy court. The importance of the automatic stay cannot be overemphasized. Frequently the primary purpose of the filing of a bankruptcy petition is to obtain the benefit of the stay.

5. THE TRUSTEE IN BANKRUPTCY

In a Chapter 7 bankruptcy, the bankruptcy estate is administered by a trustee in bankruptcy who can be either an individual or a corporation. § 321. The duties of the trustee are listed in § 704. The principal role of the trustee is to collect the property of the estate, sell it, and use the proceeds to pay expenses and creditor claims. Collecting the property of the estate sometimes requires the trustee to recover property that was transferred by the debtor prior to bankruptcy in transactions that are avoidable in bankruptcy. The trustee's "avoiding powers" are among the most important aspects of bankruptcy. In asserting these powers the trustee acts primarily for the benefit of unsecured creditors. The trustee also has wide powers of investigation of the financial affairs of the debtor and may oppose discharge of the debtor if the circumstances warrant. The trustee may also examine the validity of claims of creditors and may oppose improper claims. The trustee, who must be a disinterested person, is a fiduciary although the Bankruptcy Code does not specify the nature of the fiduciary relationship. The trustee's duties, particularly those of collecting, holding and disposing of property of the estate, are exercised on behalf of creditors generally, but often the trustee must oppose some creditors to benefit others. Basically the job of the trustee is to maximize the assets available for payment to general unsecured creditors.

Promptly after a Chapter 7 case is commenced, an interim trustee in bankruptcy is appointed by the United States Trustee. In each district there is a panel of persons who are qualified to serve as trustees. The interim trustee is appointed from this panel. § 701. Selection is usually done by a random draw. In most cases, the interim trustee becomes the permanent trustee, and in such cases is referred to as the panel or case trustee.

In Chapter 7 cases, § 326(a) states the maximum compensation that can be paid to the trustee in bankruptcy based on "all moneys" disbursed by the trustee after liquidating assets of the estate. The maximum fee schedule is: 25 percent on the first \$5,000; 10 percent on any amount in excess of \$5,000 but not in excess of \$50,000; 5 percent on any amount in excess of \$50,000 but not in excess of \$1 million; and reasonable compensation not to exceed 3 percent of any amount in excess of \$1 million. In "no-asset" cases the trustee is entitled to only a flat fee of \$60, an amount not increased since 1994. Since the great majority of cases are no-asset, trustees are left hoping for a case with assets to counter balance their no-asset cases. The United States Trustee will serve as trustee in cases in which nobody is willing to serve as interim trustee.

The trustee in bankruptcy, with the court's approval, may employ professional persons such as attorneys and accountants to represent or assist the trustee in carrying out the trustee's duties, and may agree to pay reasonable compensation. §§ 327, 328. The court may also allow the trustee to personally perform the duties of attorney or accountant and to be paid for professional services rendered. § 327(d). Whether compensation is reasonable is to be judged by a variety of factors, § 330(a), including the cost of comparable services in nonbankruptcy cases. Since a large part of the work in administering the bankruptcy estate is done by professionals, the relatively generous payments for professional services allow the trustee's duties to be performed in spite of relatively low trustee's fees. Payments to the trustee and to professionals are administrative expenses that are paid from assets of the estate before payments to any unsecured creditors.

There is a trustee in bankruptcy in a case under Chapter 12 or Chapter 13, but the trustee's duties are somewhat different. The only property of the bankruptcy estate that normally comes into the hands of the trustee is the earnings of the debtor that are the source of the payments under the plan. The primary duty of the trustee is to disburse to creditors payments due under the plan. The trustee is either appointed by the bankruptcy court to serve in the particular case or is a "standing trustee" appointed by the court to act generally in Chapter 12 or Chapter 13 cases filed in the district. Normally, there is no trustee in bankruptcy in a Chapter 11 case. Rather, the debtor continues in possession of its property as a "debtor in possession" that exercises the powers of a trustee in bankruptcy. A trustee in bankruptcy is appointed in a Chapter 11 case only in unusual cases, such as those involving fraud or gross mismanagement by the debtor.

6. MEETING OF CREDITORS

A meeting of creditors, after notice to the debtor and the creditors, must be convened by the United States Trustee within a reasonable time after the filing of the petition in bankruptcy. § 341. The debtor is required to attend. § 343. One of the purposes of the meeting is to allow the creditors to examine the debtor under oath. The principal purposes of the examination are to determine the accuracy of the debtor's statement of assets, whether avoidable transfers of property have occurred, and whether there are any grounds for objecting to the discharge of the debtor. Because the examination may disclose facts that may bear on matters that may subsequently be presented to the bankruptcy court for judicial determination, the bankruptcy judge may not attend the meeting. § 341(c). The presiding officer at the meeting is the United States Trustee.

In a Chapter 7 bankruptcy, the other principal purpose of the meeting of creditors is to elect a permanent trustee in bankruptcy. § 702(b). Election is by the creditors, and voting is done on the basis of the amount of the claims. Not all claims qualify a creditor to vote. Creditors whose claims are secured or that are entitled to priority of payment over general creditors cannot vote on the basis of those claims. Furthermore, claims must be allowable, undisputed, liquidated and fixed. Conflicts of interest are also disqualifying; relatives or affiliates of the debtor as well as creditors with interests materially adverse to those of general creditors can't vote. Election of a trustee is permissible only if creditors holding at least 20% in amount of eligible claims request election. Election requires a majority of the amount of claims voted, and at least 20% of the amount of eligible claims must be voted. The 20% requirement is designed to prevent the election of a trustee in cases in which there is little creditor interest in election. Under previous law it sometimes happened that a trustee was elected by one creditor whose sole purpose was to provide fees for lawyers who would act as counsel for the trustee. If no trustee is elected, the interim trustee serves as trustee. In many Chapter 7 cases the debtor's schedule of assets will indicate that there are no substantial assets available for distribution to creditors. In many of these cases there is no incentive for creditors to file claims or to attend the meeting of creditors. The clerk will notify creditors when no bankruptcy dividend is likely.

7. CLAIMS IN BANKRUPTCY

A claim is the basis for a distribution from the bankruptcy estate. A "proof of claim," which is a written statement setting forth a creditor's claim, is normally filed by the creditor. § 501 and Bankruptcy Rule 3001. Creditor is defined by § 101(10) to mean an entity (which in turn is defined in § 101(15)) holding a claim that arose before the filing of the petition in a voluntary case. Thus, rights against the debtor that arise after bankruptcy are not treated as claims in bankruptcy. There are a few exceptions to this statement.

A claim can be paid only if it is "allowed." Allowance of a claim means simply that it has been recognized by the court as valid in the amount claimed. If there is a dispute concerning a claim, the court must determine whether the claim should be allowed. Section 502 contains detailed provisions governing allowance and disallowance.

Claims are classified as either secured or unsecured. Suppose the debtor owes Bank $20,000 and the debt is secured by a security interest in collateral of the debtor on which there are no other liens. The collateral, because it was owned by the debtor, is part of the bankruptcy estate. § 541(a)(1). If Bank's security interest is valid in bankruptcy, Bank has a secured claim to the extent its claim is covered by value of the collateral. To the extent the claim exceeds the value of the collateral, Bank has an unsecured claim. § 506(a)(1). For example, if the collateral has a value of $30,000, Bank is oversecured and has a secured claim of $20,000; if the collateral has a value of $15,000, Bank is undersecured, and it has a secured claim of $15,000 and an unsecured claim of $5,000. The value of the collateral is determined by the bankruptcy court.

8. DISTRIBUTION OF ASSETS TO UNSECURED CREDITORS

After all priority claims have been paid in their order of priority, distribution is made pursuant to § 726 to the remaining creditors. With some exceptions, these claims are paid on a pro rata basis to the extent of the property available. First to be paid are the ten priority claims set out in § 507(a) in the order of priority prescribed in that provision. The first priority is domestic support obligations, defined in § 101(14A). Second priority is administrative expenses described in § 503. Other priority claims are ranked in an ever-growing list of additional categories by § 507(a)(3)-(10). The most important are certain claims of employees of the debtor that have a fourth and fifth priority and taxes with an eighth priority.

The § 507 priorities also apply to cases under Chapters 11, 12 and 13. Under Chapters 12 and 13, the plan must provide for payment in full of all priority claims, but deferred payment can be made, with interest, over the period of the plan. A Chapter 11 plan must provide for payment in full of all priority claims. Some priority claims must be paid in cash on the effective date of the plan and some can be paid, with interest, over time.

9. DISCHARGE

In a Chapter 7 bankruptcy, a debtor who is an individual will normally receive a discharge from pre-bankruptcy debts. § 727(b). For individuals, the primary purpose of filing a petition in Chapter 7 is to obtain this discharge. In some cases, however, the debtor is not entitled to a discharge. The various grounds for denying a discharge to a debtor in Chapter 7 are set forth in § 727(a). A debtor is not entitled to a discharge if the debtor has received a discharge under Chapter 7 in a case commenced within eight years of the time the current case was commenced. The other grounds stated for denying discharge refer to misconduct by the debtor. This reflects the fact that bankruptcy is an equitable proceeding and that a debtor guilty of certain inequitable conduct should not enjoy the benefit of a discharge. Even in cases in which the debtor is entitled to discharge, not all debts are dischargeable. Discharge is a benefit to the debtor and a concomitant loss to the creditor. While a debtor is generally entitled to a discharge of prepetition debts, in some cases the creditor may have equities that are greater than those of the debtor. In those cases, the law provides that a debt of that creditor is nondischargeable. In effect, that creditor can participate in the distribution of the debtor's property, but, to the extent the creditor's debt has not been satisfied, the creditor will have a claim against the debtor that survives bankruptcy. Debts that are excepted from a Chapter 7 discharge are described in § 523(a). Chapters 11, 12 and 13 have their own discharge provisions. Corporations and partnerships may be discharged in Chapter 11 and Chapter 12, but not in Chapter 7. The Chapter 11 discharge for non-individual debtors is extremely broad and is not subject to the special exceptions to dischargeability applicable under § 523(a). The Chapter 13 discharge available to individuals who successfully complete their debt repayment plans is also broader than the Chapter 7 discharge but its breadth has been significantly eroded over time. § 1328(a).

CHAPTER 2
THE BANKRUPTCY ESTATE

A. INTRODUCTION

Commencing a bankruptcy case creates a bankruptcy estate. Section 541, which defines the estate, applies both to Chapter 7 liquidations and to reorganizations and rehabilitations under Chapters 11, 12 and 13. With respect to cases under Chapters 12 and 13, and Chapter 11 cases involving individual debtors, however, the bankruptcy estate is augmented by earnings and other property acquired by the debtor after commencement of the case but before it is closed. §§ 1115, 1207, 1306. The special treatment of property of the estate in these cases is considered later in the book.

Section 541(a)(1), the basic provision, states that the estate is comprised of "all legal or equitable interests of the debtor in property as of the commencement of the case." The following sections discuss important issues concerning property of the estate.

1. THE *BUTNER* DOCTRINE

What law determines property rights in the debtor's assets, federal bankruptcy law or otherwise applicable state or federal law? The case below (decided under the Bankruptcy Act of 1898) informs that decision, and, accordingly, is fundamental in bankruptcy law. The principle it embodies regarding the proper scope of bankruptcy law will be relevant throughout this course.

Butner v. United States
Supreme Court of the United States, 1979.
440 U.S. 48.

■ Mr. Justice STEVENS delivered the opinion of the Court.

A dispute between a bankruptcy trustee and a second mortgagee over the right to the rents collected during the period between the mortgagor's bankruptcy and the foreclosure sale of the mortgaged property gave rise to the question we granted certiorari to decide. That question is whether the right to such rents is determined by a federal rule of equity or by the law of the State where the property is located.

On May 14, 1973, Golden Enterprises, Inc. (Golden), filed a petition for an arrangement under Chapter XI of the Bankruptcy Act [of 1898]. In those proceedings, the bankruptcy judge approved a plan consolidating various liens on North Carolina real estate owned by Golden. As a result, petitioner acquired a second mortgage securing an indebtedness of $360,000. Petitioner did not, however, receive any express security interest in the rents earned by the property.

On April 18, 1974, the bankruptcy judge granted Golden's motion to appoint an agent to collect the rents and to apply them as directed by the court. The order of appointment provided that the money should be applied to tax obligations, payments on the first mortgage, fire insurance premiums, and interest and principal on the second mortgage. There is no dispute about the collections or payments made pursuant to that order.

The arrangement plan was never confirmed. On February 14, 1975, Golden was adjudicated a bankrupt, and the trustee in bankruptcy was appointed. At that time both the first and second mortgages were in default. The trustee was ordered to collect and retain all rents "to the end that the same may be applied under this or different or further orders of [the bankruptcy] [c]ourt."

After various alternatives were considered, and after the District Court refused to confirm a first sale, the properties were ultimately sold to petitioner on November 12, 1975, for $174,000. That price was paid by reducing the estate's indebtedness to petitioner from $360,000 to $186,000.

As of the date of sale, a fund of $162,971.32 had been accumulated by the trustee pursuant to the February 14 court order that he collect and retain all rents. On December 1, 1975, petitioner filed a motion claiming a security interest in this fund and seeking to have it applied to the balance of the second mortgage indebtedness. The bankruptcy judge denied the motion, holding that the $186,000 balance due to petitioner should be treated as a general unsecured claim.

The District Court reversed. It recognized that under North Carolina law, a mortgagor is deemed the owner of the land subject to the mortgage and is entitled to rents and profits, even after default, so long as he retains possession. But the court viewed the appointment of an agent to collect rents during the arrangement proceedings as tantamount to the appointment of a receiver. This appointment, the court concluded, satisfied the state-law requirement of a change of possession giving the mortgagee an interest in the rents; no further action after the adjudication in bankruptcy was required to secure or preserve this interest.

The Court of Appeals reversed and reinstated the disposition of the bankruptcy judge. The court acknowledged that the agent appointed to collect rents

Chapter 2. The Bankruptcy Estate   31

before the bankruptcy was equivalent to a state-court receivership, but held that the adjudication terminated that relationship. Because petitioner had made no request *during the bankruptcy* for a sequestration of rents or for the appointment of a receiver, petitioner had not, in the court's view, taken the kind of action North Carolina law required to give the mortgagee a security interest in the rents collected after the bankruptcy adjudication. One judge dissented, adopting the position of the District Court.

I.

We did not grant certiorari to decide whether the Court of Appeals correctly applied North Carolina law. Our concern is with the proper interpretation of the federal statutes governing the administration of bankrupt estates. Specifically, it is our purpose to resolve a conflict between the Third and Seventh Circuits on the one hand, and the Second, Fourth, Sixth, Eighth, and Ninth Circuits on the other, concerning the proper approach to a dispute of this kind.

The courts in the latter group regard the question whether a security interest in property extends to rents and profits derived from the property as one that should be resolved by reference to state law. In a few States, sometimes referred to as "title States," the mortgagee is automatically entitled to possession of the property, and to a secured interest in the rents. In most States, the mortgagee's right to rents is dependent upon his taking actual or constructive possession of the property by means of a foreclosure, the appointment of a receiver for his benefit, or some similar legal proceeding. Because the applicable law varies from State to State, the results in federal bankruptcy proceedings will also vary under the approach taken by most of the Circuits.

The Third and Seventh Circuits have adopted a federal rule of equity that affords the mortgagee a secured interest in the rents even if state law would not recognize any such interest until after foreclosure. Those courts reason that since the bankruptcy court has the power to deprive the mortgagee of his state-law remedy, equity requires that the right to rents not be dependent on state-court action that may be precluded by federal law. Under this approach, no affirmative steps are required by the mortgagee-in state or federal court-to acquire or maintain a right to the rents.

II.

We agree with the majority view.

The constitutional authority of Congress to establish "uniform Laws on the subject of Bankruptcies throughout the United States" would clearly encompass a federal statute defining the mortgagee's interest in the rents and profits earned by property in a bankrupt estate. But Congress has not chosen to exercise its power to fashion any such rule. The Bankruptcy Act does include provisions invalidating certain security interests as fraudulent, or as improper preferences over general creditors. Apart from these provisions, however, Congress has generally left the determination of property rights in the assets of a bankrupt's estate to state law.[9]

Property interests are created and defined by state law. Unless some federal interest requires a different result, there is no reason why such interests should be analyzed differently simply because an interested party is involved in a bankruptcy proceeding. Uniform treatment of property interests by both state and federal courts within a State serves to reduce uncertainty, to discourage forum shopping, and to prevent a party from receiving "a windfall merely by reason of the happenstance of bankruptcy." *Lewis v. Manufacturers National Bank,* 364 U.S. 603, 609. The justifications for application of state law are not limited to ownership interests; they apply with equal force to security interests, including the interest of a mortgagee in rents earned by mortgaged property.

The minority of courts which have rejected state law have not done so because of any congressional command, or because their approach serves any identifiable federal interest. Rather, they have adopted a uniform federal approach to the question of the mortgagee's interest in rents and profits because of their perception of the demands of equity. The equity powers of the bankruptcy court play an important part in the administration of bankrupt estates in countless situations in which the judge is required to deal with particular, individualized problems. But undefined considerations of equity provide no basis for adoption of a uniform federal rule affording mortgagees an automatic interest in the rents as soon as the mortgagor is declared bankrupt.

In support of their rule, the Third and Seventh Circuits have emphasized that while the mortgagee may pursue various state-law remedies prior to bank-

---

[9] "The Federal Constitution, Article I, § 8, gives Congress the power to establish uniform laws on the subject of bankruptcy throughout the United States. In view of this grant of authority to the Congress it has been settled from an early date that state laws to the extent that they conflict with the laws of Congress, enacted under its constitutional authority, on the subject of bankruptcies are suspended. While this is true, state laws are thus suspended only to the extent of actual conflict with the system provided by the Bankruptcy Act of Congress. *Sturges v. Crowninshield,* 4 Wheat. 122; *Ogden v. Saunders,* 12 Wheat. 213.

"Notwithstanding this requirement as to uniformity the bankruptcy acts of Congress may recognize the laws of the state in certain particulars, although such recognition may lead to different results in different States. For example, the Bankruptcy Act recognizes and enforces the laws of the states affecting dower, exemptions, the validity of mortgages, priorities of payment and the like. Such recognition in the application of state laws does not affect the constitutionality of the Bankruptcy Act, although in these particulars the operation of the act is not alike in all the states." *Stellwagen v. Clum,* 245 U.S. 605, 613.

ruptcy, the adjudication leaves the mortgagee "only such remedies as may be found in a court of bankruptcy in the equitable administration of the bankrupt's assets." *Bindseil v. Liberty Trust Co.,* 248 F. 112, 114 (CA3 1917). It does not follow, however, that "equitable administration" requires that all mortgagees be afforded an automatic security interest in rents and profits when state law would deny such an automatic benefit and require the mortgagee to take some affirmative action before his rights are recognized. What does follow is that the federal bankruptcy court should take whatever steps are necessary to ensure that the mortgagee is afforded in federal bankruptcy court the same protection he would have under state law if no bankruptcy had ensued. This is the majority view, which we adopt today.

The rule of the Third and Seventh Circuits, at least in some circumstances, affords the mortgagee rights that are not his as a matter of state law. The rule we adopt avoids this inequity because it looks to state law to define the security interest of the mortgagee. At the same time, our decision avoids the opposite inequity of depriving a mortgagee of his state-law security interest when bankruptcy intervenes. For while it is argued that bankruptcy may impair or delay the mortgagee's exercise of his right to foreclosure, and thus his acquisition of a security interest in rents according to the law of many States, a bankruptcy judge familiar with local practice should be able to avoid this potential loss by sequestering rents or authorizing immediate state-law foreclosures. Even though a federal judge may temporarily delay entry of such an order, the loss of rents to the mortgagee normally should be no greater than if he had been proceeding in a state court: for if there is a reason that persuades a federal judge to delay, presumably the same reason would also persuade a state judge to withhold foreclosure temporarily. The essential point is that in a properly administered scheme in which the basic federal rule is that state law governs, the primary reason why any holder of a mortgage may fail to collect rent immediately after default must stem from state law.

III.

Recognizing that the bankruptcy frustrated petitioner's right to take possession of the mortgaged property and thereby to establish his right to rents as a matter of North Carolina law, the Court of Appeals assumed that a request to the bankruptcy judge for sequestration of rents, for the appointment of a receiver, or for permission to proceed with a state-court foreclosure would have satisfied the state-law requirement. Since none of these steps was taken during the bankruptcy, the Court of Appeals held that petitioner had no right to the rents.

The dissenting judge in the Court of Appeals, as well as the District Judge, felt that the action taken during the arrangement proceedings, coupled with informal requests for abandonment of the property during the bankruptcy, was sufficient to comply with North Carolina law. Neither of these judges, however, based his analysis on the federal rule followed in the Third and Seventh Circuits. They merely disagreed with the majority about the requirements of North Carolina law.

In this Court the parties have argued the state-law question at great length, each stressing different aspects of the record. We decline to review the state-law question. The federal judges who deal regularly with questions of state law in their respective districts and circuits are in a better position than we to determine how local courts would dispose of comparable issues.

The judgment is affirmed.

NOTES

1. The *Butner* principle is that the substantive rights of the parties are ordinarily determined by otherwise applicable non-bankruptcy law unless a specific bankruptcy rule or principle alters those rights. This statement of the principle emphasizes two critical limitations on *Butner* that together constitute much of what bankruptcy law is about. First, *Butner* focuses on the *substantive* rights of the parties. Bankruptcy by its very nature substitutes new specialized federal collective procedures for the realization of those substantive rights. In bankruptcy, the *procedural* rights of the parties are necessarily a product of federal bankruptcy law even if non-bankruptcy law determines substantive entitlements. Second, *Butner* is a *default* rule: it does not apply if federal bankruptcy law specifically alters the substantive non-bankruptcy entitlements of the parties. It turns out, of course, that Congress does make myriad substantive choices in the Bankruptcy Code that importantly affect or alter the non-bankruptcy rights of the parties. When it chooses to do so, those substantive bankruptcy law choices preempt otherwise applicable non-bankruptcy law to the contrary. *See* Daniel J. Bussel, *Creditors' Committees as Estate Representatives in Bankruptcy Litigation*, 10 STAN. J.L.B.&F. 28, 34-35 (2004). Nonetheless, the *Butner* principle hovers over all bankruptcy law; woe to bankruptcy lawyers who ignore it by casually assuming that state law no longer governs the rights and liabilities of the parties post-bankruptcy. *See, e.g., In re Wright* at p. 552.

2. Note that the Supreme Court's decision to allocate the specific substantive issue at stake in *Butner*, the scope of the mortgagee's interest in real property rents, to state law proved deeply troublesome, and, ultimately, unsatisfactory. It turned out that there was not only great variation, but also great uncertainty regarding the mortgagee's rights under state law in many jurisdictions, leading to confusion and many conflicting decisions in the bankruptcy courts over the respective rights of the mortgagee and the debtor. Daniel J. Bussel, *Bankruptcy Appellate Reform: Issues and Options*, in NORTON'S ANN.

SURV. OF BANKR. L. 257, 261-62 & n.14 (1995) (noting widespread division of authority). Eventually, in 1994, *Butner* notwithstanding, Congress responded by crafting a uniform federal rule governing rents that extended the mortgagee's security interest to rents as provided by the terms of the mortgage without reference to otherwise applicable non-bankruptcy law. § 552(b)(2). The effect of this amendment is that real property rents are treated as "cash collateral" in bankruptcy cases nationwide without regard to the idiosyncracies of widely varying state real estate law. *See infra* at 604.

2. DEFINING PROPERTY OF THE ESTATE

a. What Is Included

The commencement of a bankruptcy case creates an estate comprised of "all legal or equitable interests of the debtor in property as of the commencement of the case." Hence, the property is that of the debtor as of the commencement of the case, "wherever located and by whomever held." Congress spread the net broadly to take in all the assets of value owned by the debtor when filing occurred. But in the case of an individual who has filed in Chapter 7, an important corollary to § 541(a)(1) is that, as a general rule, property that was acquired by the debtor after commencement of the bankruptcy case is not property of the estate and is not available for the enforced payment of prebankruptcy claims.

The all-inclusive breadth of § 541(a)(1) furthers the time-honored purpose of Chapter 7 of allowing the debtor a "fresh start." *See Local Loan Co. v. Hunt*, 292 U.S. 234 (1934). Prepetition creditors take the debtor's prepetition assets and the debtor is discharged from prepetion claims. The debtor's postpetiton assets are free of the claims of prepetition creditors; the debtor is given "a new opportunity in life and a clear field for future effort, unhampered by the pressure and discouragement of preexisting debt." 292 U.S. at 244.

b. Consequences of Exclusion and Inclusion

It is important to know which assets of the debtor make up property of the bankruptcy estate under § 541(a)(1) for a number of reasons.

The property of the estate constitutes the pool of assets available to satisfy creditors' claims. In Chapter 7 cases, the trustee will liquidate the property of the estate and distribute the proceeds to creditors. Property in the possession of the debtor at the time of filing that is not property of the estate is not subject to the claims of prepetition creditors. For instance, the debtor may have possession of personal property of a third party for safe-keeping or other innocuous reasons at the time of filing. This property is not property of the estate; the debtor has possession but not ownership.

Under Chapters 11 and 13, the debtor may retain its assets during the reorganization (Chapter 11) or rehabilitation (Chapter 13) period, but the debtor's plan must give creditors as much value as they would have received under Chapter 7 liquidation. See § 1129(a)(7)(A)(ii) and § 1325(a)(4). This requires a pro forma calculation of the property of the estate in Chapter 7.

Note that if property is excluded from the estate, that property does not simply disappear. Someone other than the bankruptcy estate will end up with the excluded property and those with competing interests in the property therefore benefit from the exclusion. Congress can effectively prefer some constituents over others by excluding property in which the preferred constituents have an interest from the estate. Thus by excluding from the estate postpetition earnings of an individual debtor in a Chapter 7 case, the interests of the debtor and the fresh-start policy of the Bankruptcy Code are advanced at the cost of creditor recoveries. Creditors fare better in Chapter 13 and, since 2005, individual Chapter 11 cases, by virtue of Congress's redefinition of the property of estate to include postpetition earnings in such cases.

During a bankruptcy case, the automatic stay of § 362(a)(3) protects the property of the estate from the acts of third parties to obtain possession of or exercise control over these assets without the permission of the bankruptcy court. Section 362(a)(4) stays secured claim holders from proceeding against property of the estate. As we see in the following section, the trustee may compel third parties in possession of property of the estate to deliver the property to the trustee.

c. Turnover

At the time a debtor files in bankruptcy, property of the debtor's estate may be in possession of third parties. The trustee must gain possession of this property, unless it is of inconsequential value, to add to the debtor's pool of assets. It may do so through a turnover order under § 542(a), which requires a third party in possession of "property that the trustee may use, sell, or lease under § 363" to deliver that property to the trustee. Subsections (b) and (c) of § 363 empower the trustee to use, sell, or lease "property of the estate." Since these subsections apply only to property of the debtor's estate, the turnover motion fails if it is shown that the property in question is not property of debtor's estate.

In *United States v. Whiting Pools, Inc.*, 462 U.S. 198 (1983), the debtor Whiting Pools, which sold, installed, and serviced swimming pools, was delinquent on its federal taxes to the tune of $92,000. The Internal Revenue Service (IRS) seized Whiting Pools' equipment, vehicles, inventory and office supplies, to be sold for the back taxes pursuant to the procedures set forth in the Internal Revenue Code. The day after the seizure, Whiting Pools filed for reorganization in Chapter 11. The bankruptcy court found that the liquidation value of Whiting's property was at most $35,000 (less than the back taxes) but its estimated going-concern value in the debtor's hands was $162,876 (more than the back taxes).

The IRS moved in the bankruptcy court for relief from the automatic stay of § 362(a) so it could proceed with its nonbankruptcy tax foreclosure sale. Whiting Pools opposed the lifting of the stay and counterclaimed for a turnover order pursuant to § 542(a). The IRS opposed turnover on the ground that under otherwise applicable nonbankruptcy law (here the Internal Revenue Code), Whiting Pool's only interest in the seized property was to redeem the property by paying indebtedness owed on the taxes. Until this was done, the debtor had no substantive entitlement to possession under otherwise applicable nonbankruptcy law and therefore no right to turnover. The Supreme Court nevertheless held that the trustee was entitled to a turnover order. Its Delphic statement on the meaning of § 541(a)(1) was:

> Although these statutes could be read to limit the estate to those "interests of the debtor in property" at the time of the filing of the petition, we view them as a definition of what is included in the estate, rather than as a limitation.

Although the Court's reasoning was obscure, the policy of allowing debtors in Chapter 11 to recover assets seized by a secured creditor that are necessary to reorganize their businesses is consistent with the pro-reorganization policies of the Bankruptcy Code and strikes a balance between the interests of the lienholder in realizing on its collateral and those of other constituents and society in reorganization—at least so long as the lienholder's rights are adequately protected. Merely staying foreclosure accomplishes little in advancing the reorganization effort if the debtor cannot actually regain possession of the seized property and use it in its business. Moreover, as we shall see later in the course, p. 599, the usual balance drawn between the debtor and secured party is that debtor can stave off foreclosure of property that is necessary to effective reorganization by affording the secured party "adequate protection." §§ 361, 362(d). We will see in chapter 10 at p. 575 that the debtor in a case like *Whiting Pools* in order to defeat a motion for relief from stay must also show under § 362(d) that the property it seeks to recover is necessary to an effective reorganization. If there is no reasonable possibility of a successful reorganization or equity in the property, relief from stay should be granted, and, presumably, turnover denied. Thus, until the IRS cuts off Whiting's interest in the property by completing the tax sale and conveying the property to a bona fide purchaser for value, Whiting has a sufficient interest in the seized property from the perspective of bankruptcy law to defer foreclosure and obtain turnover (at least if the repossessed property has an equity value or is essential for an effective reorganization) notwithstanding the fact that Whiting has no such entitlement under otherwise applicable nonbankruptcy law.

Consider how *Whiting Pools* fits together with *Butner* to define the substantive and procedural rights of the parties. The amount of the IRS claim and the value and priority of its security interest in the seized property, substantive rights created by the Internal Revenue Code, are recognized and preserved in the bankruptcy proceeding. But the IRS's right to realize on that claim and lien by following the (highly-favorable-to-the-IRS) collection procedures laid out in the Internal Revenue Code are supplanted by federal bankruptcy procedures, substituting such devices as the automatic stay, the right to seek relief from stay under specified standards, and the right to adequate protection, for the expedited tax sale authorized by the Internal Revenue Code.

In 1984 the phrase "and by whomever held" was added at the end of the introductory paragraph of § 541(a) suggesting Congressional approval of the *Whiting Pools* result. A favorable view of *Whiting Pools* is expressed in Stephen J. Ware, *Security Interests, Repossessed Collateral, and Turnover of Property to the Bankruptcy Estate*, 2 Utah L. Rev. 775 (2002).

d. Unresolved Issues

In Footnotes 14 and 17 of the opinion in *Whiting Pools,* the Court declined to decide two important turnover issues that were not before the court. These issues are discussed in the following two Cases.

Case #1. Bank made a loan to Debtor that was secured by a security interest in the equipment purchased with the proceeds of the loan. Debtor defaulted on the loan and Bank repossessed the equipment pursuant to its rights under the security agreement. Debtor filed in Chapter 7 bankruptcy and Debtor's trustee (T) moved for a turnover order requiring Bank to deliver possession of the equipment to T so that it could liquidate the property and distribute the proceeds among Debtor's unsecured claimants after paying Bank's secured claim. In Footnote 17 of the opinion in *Whiting Pools*, a Chapter 11 case, the Court reserved judgment on whether T would have been entitled to a turnover order in a Chapter 7 liquidation proceeding. Should T be entitled to a turnover order for the equipment in Bank's possession if the unpaid amount of the loan was $10,000 and value of the equipment was $15,000? Recall that § 542(a), together with § 363(b) and (c), allows the trustee to obtain a turnover order to "use, sell, or lease" property of the estate. If your answer is in the affirmative, should T seek a turnover order if the value of the collateral was only $5,000? T is entitled to a turnover order in the case in which the collateral is worth $15,000 but not in the case in which it is worth $5,000. There is no basis in the statute for limiting § 542(a) to Chapter 11 cases. This point is well made in *Gerwer*, discussed below. That section authorizes turnover orders against third parties in possession in cases in which the trustee may "use, sell or lease" the property recovered. The function of a trustee in a Chapter 7 case is to gather the property of the estate, liquidate it and distribute the proceeds to creditors. Pursuant to this function, § 542(a) allows a trustee to recover property of the estate in possession of others and sell it so long as the trustee has the power under § 363 to sell the property recovered. Thus, a Chapter 7 trustee may sell free of the lien of a secured party who has repossessed collateral that is property of the estate under § 363(f)(3), if the debtor has an equity in the property (the value of the collateral exceeds the amount of the debt) and the creditor's security interest is adequately protected under § 363(e). Adequate protection may consist of giving the secured party a lien on the proceeds of the sale to the extent of the debt owed. If the debtor does not have an equity in the collateral held by the secured party, there is no point to the trustee's recovering the property and selling it because there would be no benefit to the estate. All the proceeds of the sale would have to be paid to the secured creditor, with nothing left for unsecured creditors. See the "unless" clause at the end of § 542(a). Under § 554, a Chapter 7 trustee abandons property that has no value to the estate, and the secured party may proceed against the abandoned property under state law (*Butner*) in satisfaction of its claim.

Case #2. Debtor sold real property to Buyer for the price of $100,000. Buyer paid Debtor $20,000 in cash and executed a promissory note for $80,000 payable to Debtor, secured by a mortgage on the land. In a subsequent unrelated transaction, Debtor borrowed $50,000 from Lender and delivered the note to Lender to hold as security for the loan. The transaction in which Lender holds possession of property as security for Debtor's obligation is called a pledge. When Debtor filed in Chapter 7, the trustee (T) sought a turnover order of the note from Lender with the intention of selling the note to enlarge the pool of assets available to Debtor's creditors. In Footnote 14 of *Whiting Pools* the Court refrained from deciding whether a debtor could obtain turnover in a pledge situation. Should a turnover order be granted in this case?

In *In re Gerwer*, 898 F.2d 730 (9th Cir. 1990), there was a pledge of notes as in Case #2. The court concluded that the trustee had the power to obtain turnover of property from the secured creditor in Chapter 7 prior to any default. Judge Noonan said "As written, the statute speaks to the power of the trustee whether the debtor's estate is in reorganization or liquidation." He notes that an earlier edition of *Collier* had opined that turnover should be denied in a pledge case because the estate had no present possessory interest. Noonan finds no requirement in § 542 that the debtor hold a possessory interest.

B. EXEMPT PROPERTY

1. A PERSPECTIVE

In the following sections we explore the large body of complex state and federal law that has grown up around exemptions. Too often in law school courses we look at statutes without reference to their real world context. But now we stand back and examine the effect of current business conditions and practices on exemption laws in the tumultuous first decade of this century. Debtors have long been able to grant security interests in their exempt property that take precedence over their exemptions. Otherwise, debtors would be greatly restricted in obtaining mortgage loans on their homes or financing for their cars. However, given the high loan-to-value ratios that characterized consumer lending in the early 2000s, exemption laws have become almost irrelevant with respect to both home and auto financing, even though homes and cars are the items of exempt property that are of greatest importance to consumer debtors.

Exemptions apply only to a debtor's equity in property, and in much home mortgage and automobile financing large loans and shrinking property values have combined to reduce or obliterate debtors' equity in both homes and cars. With respect to homes, in the first few years of the 21st century, homeowners (encouraged by home lenders) obtained "subprime" first mortgages with minimal down payments and "home equity" loans secured by second mortgages that were based on rapidly inflating home values; when the real estate bubble burst in 2007, many homes were worth far less than the amount of the outstanding mortgages against them. In the heyday of auto loan and lease financing, new car buyers were offered no-down-payment financing for terms as long as seven years. Under such plans buyers never have an equity in the automobile. Moreover, when used car values declined with rising fuel prices and deteriorating economic conditions, the relatively high assumed residual values for the cars securing shorter term auto loans and leases also proved illusory.

When exempt property is subject to security interests, in times of declining property valuations, exemptions—when they are most needed—may have little or no effect. This appears to be true in many cases with respect to both home and car financing, the two largest areas of consumer secured financing. If exemptions are largely inoperative in these two vast areas, the message is clear:

under current conditions exemptions are of significantly reduced importance in bankruptcy.

2. THE COLLECTION PROCESS

The property of a judgment debtor can be seized and sold to satisfy the judgment. We describe the judicial sale process in detail in the introductory chapter on pp. 14–18. Suffice it to say that collection of a debt by judicial process is extremely inefficient, costly and prolonged. First, the creditor must obtain a judgment against the debtor; this entails hiring a lawyer, finding and serving the recalcitrant debtor, obtaining a court date and prevailing at a hearing. Small claims courts offer an abbrieviated, nonlawyer procedure for lesser claims. However the judgment is obtained, whether in ordinary courts or small claims courts, it must be delivered to a judicial officer for levy, usually requiring seizure, of the items of nonexempt property of the judgment debtor described in the writ. After due notice has been given, a judicial auction sale may proceed, often under circumstances (*e.g.*, sale on the courthouse steps) producing bids that may be only a fraction of the replacement value of the property, unless real property, motor vehicles or other items having resale value are involved. Sale by eBay would be much better. In view of this, it is no wonder that creditors strive to take security interests in the debtor's property at the outset of the credit extension that, with respect to personal property, allows creditors the simple, extrajudicial process under UCC Article 9.

A creditor seeking payment of a judgment against an individual often looks to the debtor's wages as the most immediate source of payment. The creditor garnishes the debtor's wages by directing the levying officer to serve a document on the debtor's employer directing payment of the debtor's wages to the levying officer for the benefit of the creditor. Wage garnishment is a powerful collection device that is often onerous to the debtor, and it has been curtailed by both court decisions and legislation. On due process grounds, *Sniadach v. Family Finance Corp.*, 395 U.S. 337 (1969), prejudgment garnishment of wages has been eliminated as a normal creditor's remedy. Postjudgment garnishment has been severely limited legislatively by the Consumer Credit Protection Act, 15 U.S.C. §§ 1671–1677. With some exceptions, such as child and spousal support claims, a creditor can garnish no more than 25 percent of the debtor's disposable earnings. Disposable earnings are defined as wages and similar earnings after deduction of amounts required by law to be withheld such as federal and state income taxes and social security taxes. More severe restrictions apply to debtors with very low incomes. The federal limitations represent the maximum amount of earnings that can be reached by creditors. State law may impose additional restrictions on wage garnishment. *See, e.g.*, Cal. Code Civ. Proc. § 706.051(b) (West 2000), which allows the debtor in some cases to protect any wages "necessary for the support of the judgment debtor or the judgment debtor's family supported in whole or in part by the judgment debtor."

3. EXEMPTION LAWS

Bankruptcy law has traditionally offered the debtor who is granted a discharge in Chapter 7 a fresh start, free of prepetition claims. But in order to achieve the goal of a fresh start, the discharged debtor must be left with enough property to meet the debtor's basic postpetition needs. This protection is gained through state and federal laws that designate certain kinds of property as exempt. We discuss these issues in detail below.

Both state and federal law protect certain property of individuals from claims of creditors. These laws are usually referred to as exemption laws and the protected property is called exempt property. This law is primarily a matter of state law, but there is a major exception: in wage garnishment cases, as noted above, debtors are protected by federal law. Although there is general consensus that individual debtors should be permitted to retain some property as exempt from creditor claims, widely varying state law suggests that there is little consensus on how much or what kinds of property should be exempt.

Outside of bankruptcy and except for wage garnishment, state law is the primary source of protection of a debtor's property from the claims of creditors. However, most pensions and retirement accounts, social security benefits and some other federal payments are exempt from garnishment or attachment under federal law. Although all states provide that some property of the individual debtor is exempt from execution, some allow the debtor to retain little more than the bare necessities of life. Others permit the debtor to retain property of very substantial value.

State exemption laws designate property that may not be seized by a creditor in the judicial debt collection process, but exempt property is not exempt from claims of all creditors. Certain creditors that the state recognizes as having particularly meritorious claims may be able to seize property otherwise exempt. A common example is a claim for spousal or child support. But, as explained above, the gaping hole in debtor protection by exemption laws is that they do not inhibit enforcement of the ubiquitous security interests in homes and durable goods, like cars. Moreover, certain statutory liens apply without respect to exemption laws. For example, the state law may exempt cars, but the exempt status of the automobile would not prevent an unpaid mechanic who performed work on the car from enforcing a mechanic's lien in the car.

Although state exemption statutes vary widely in the types of property that are exempt, the following categories of property are frequently covered: the family residence and household furnishings, the clothing and personal effects of the debtor and the debtor's family, the family car or cars, and the tools and other personal property used in the debtor's occupation. Since insurance on the life of the debtor is an important protection for the debtor's dependents, it is also frequently covered by exemption statutes. Within these categories there are usually dollar limitations on the amount of property that may be exempted. However, there are some glaring exceptions to this rule. For instance, in Florida, Iowa, Kansas, Oklahoma and Texas, there is *no* ceiling on the value of an exempt homestead.

Exempt categories are often ludicrously out-of-date, especially with respect to dollar limits. In a fairly recent expression of legislative views on the definition of "household goods," BAPCPA, largely a product of the late 1990s, speaks of "1 radio," "1 television," "1 VCR," and "1 personal computer and related equipment." § 522(f)(4). And this list is not ten years old.

4. EXEMPTIONS IN BANKRUPTCY

Although state exemption law is important in state proceedings in which a creditor is attempting to enforce a claim against the debtor, it is also commonly invoked in bankruptcy. When a debtor is unable to pay creditors and is faced with immediate or eventual execution against the debtor's property, the typical recourse sought is the protection of the bankruptcy law, with its automatic stay. Under the Bankruptcy Act of 1898, determination of the debtor's assets that were subject to distribution in bankruptcy was made according to the state law of exemptions. The result was a highly nonuniform bankruptcy law. Debtors from states with generous exemption laws were treated far better than debtors from states which granted minimal exemptions to their citizens.

Strong arguments were made in favor of a uniform system of exemptions provided by federal bankruptcy law itself that would override state exemption laws. This view was reflected in early versions of the 1978 Bankruptcy Code, which contained a schedule of exemptions falling between the extremes represented by state law. But opposition to a uniform system arose on the part of creditors who wanted to preserve the law in states that had low exemptions and consumers in states that had more generous ones. The result was the compromise that appears in § 522(b). Pursuant to subsection (b)(1), the debtor may elect either the schedule of federal exemptions under (b)(2), which includes those appearing in subsection (d), or, in the alternative, the state exemptions under subsection (b)(3). But the debtor's right to elect the more favorable schedule has been greatly restricted by § 522(b)(2), which allows any state to opt out of the federal exemptions by enacting a law taking away from its citizens the right to elect the § 522(d) exemptions. Thus, in the 34 opt-out states, each state determines its own schedule of exemptions and debtors are unable to elect the federal exemptions. *Collier on Bankruptcy* ¶ 522.02[1] (15th ed. rev. 2008). An important new qualification on the states' opt-out power is that retirement funds are now exempt under both federal and state law. § 522(b)(3)(C) and (d)(12).

Frequently, a husband and wife in bankruptcy have joint debts and own most of their property jointly. To accommodate this, § 302 provides for the filing of a single petition for relief in bankruptcy by the husband and wife. This is known as a "joint case." Under the Bankruptcy Code, as originally enacted, one spouse could elect the § 522(b) exemptions and the other spouse the § 522(d) exemptions. By that device, it was possible to exempt more property than could be exempted if either system alone was used. In 1984, § 522(b)(1) was amended to prohibit a split election in a joint case.

Insulation of exempt property from claims of creditors with respect to liability on prebankruptcy debts carries over to the postbankruptcy period. § 522(c). In a Chapter 7 case, an individual normally will receive a discharge under § 727(a) that relieves the debtor of personal liability on all prebankruptcy debts. § 727(b). But some debts are not dischargeable in bankruptcy. § 523(a). Section 522(c) applies to those debts. The creditor on a nondischargeable debt is entitled to share in the distribution of assets of the bankruptcy estate, and postbankruptcy assets of the debtor are also liable for payment of that debt. But, in general, exempt property is not available for distribution to creditors in bankruptcy, and by virtue of § 522(c) remains exempt after bankruptcy. An exception is found in § 522(c)(1), as amended by BAPCPA, which provides that notwithstanding nonbankruptcy exemption laws, a debtor's postpetition assets remain liable for domestic support claims (§ 101(10A)). The primary effect of § 522(c) is to allow a debtor who claimed the federal exemptions under § 522(d) to preserve in the postbankruptcy period the status of the exempt property with respect to a claim to enforce the personal liability of the debtor on a nondischargeable debt.

5. RETIREMENT PLANS

A retirement plan may be an individual debtor's most valuable asset. By the eve of passage of BAPCPA, case law had established that qualified employer-sponsored retirement plans were protected from creditors in bankruptcy by federal law. But there was a division of authority as to the exempt status of the hugely popular IRAs in bankruptcy. IRAs are investment accounts that are entirely funded by the contributions of individuals; the funds grow tax-deferred, and the contributions are in some instances deductible. They resemble tax-free bank accounts: the owner may withdraw funds at will, paying only a 10% penalty if withdrawal occurs before the age of 59 ½. IRA funds are taxed as they are distributed; distributions must begin no later than the year the account holder turns 70 ½. By the end of 2003, nearly $3 trillion was invested in IRAs.

Christopher Conkey & Rachel Emma Silverman, *High Court Rules IRAs Untouchable*, Wall St.J., April 5, 2005, at D1.

Exemption of IRAs is an especially important issue because of the use of these plans as repositories for tax-free rollovers from exempt employer-sponsored 401(k) or 403(b) plans when employees change jobs or retire. Some account holders were reluctant to roll their funds over into IRAs as long as the exempt status of IRAs was uncertain.

BAPCPA has boldly reformed the law on exemption of retirement plans in bankruptcy and has done so in a manner that is very favorable to debtors. It permits a debtor to exempt retirement funds "to the extent that those funds are in a fund or account that is exempt from taxation under section 401 [qualified plans], 403 [annuities], 408 [IRAs], 408(A) [Roth IRAs], 414 [hybrid plans], 457 [deferred compensation plans], or 501(a) [employee contribution plans] of the Internal Revenue Code." The specified retirement funds or accounts are exempt in bankruptcy under both the state (§ 522(b)(3)(C)) and the federal (§ 522(d)(12)) exemptions. Among the assets protected under these provisions are the popular defined contribution 401(k) plans, set up by employers, under which employees are allowed to contribute, within certain dollar amount limits, a percentage of their annual pay into investment accounts, with employers sometimes contributing matching amounts; the fund grows tax-deferred. Both the basic IRA (IRC § 408) and the Roth IRA (IRC § 408(A)) are also protected. Section 522(n) places a $1,095,000 dollar cap ($2,190,000 for a married couple filing jointly) on the amount exempted for both IRAs and Roth IRAs, but the amount "may be increased if the interests of justice so require." There is no limitation on funds contributed to or contained in plans provided by the debtor's employer. Section § 522(n) goes even further in excluding from consideration in calculating the $1,095,000 cap funds rolled over into an IRA or Roth IRA from other exempt plans, such as 401(k) and 403(b) plans. It is unusual for an IRA to contain over $1,095,000 without rollovers. Loans made to debtors from their retirement plans are not to be construed as claims or debts (§§ 362(b)(19), 523(a)(18)), and are not dischargeable under § 523(a)(18)). Automatic deductions from a debtor's wages to repay a loan from a retirement plan are not stayed by the debtor's filing (§ 362(b)(19)). All told, BAPCPA is remarkably generous to debtors in safeguarding their retirement funds in bankruptcy.

Funds placed in education IRAs and qualified state tuition programs under IRC § 529 are, under certain conditions, excluded from the debtor's estate by § 541(b)(5) and (6). The maximum annual contribution to educational IRAs is $2,000. To qualify for exclusion, funds in educational IRAs must have been deposited not less than a year before the date of filing, and the exclusion applies only to the extent of $5,475 for contributions made not earlier than 720 days or later than 365 days before filing. The requirements for the exclusion of state tuition accounts under IRC § 529 are similar. These provisions treat educational savings accounts differently from retirement savings accounts by excluding them from the estate rather than exempting them. Funds withheld by employers from employee wages as contributions to the plans exempted by the statute or received by employers from employees for these purposes are excluded from the debtor-employee's estate by § 541(b)(7).

6. IMPAIRMENT OF EXEMPTIONS

a. Avoidance of Security Interests under § 522(f)(1)(B)

(i) Personal Finance Companies

In the early years of the past century the primary source of personal loans was banks. Bank loan officers required detailed financial statements showing income, employment and past credit record. The old saw was that the only people who could qualify for bank loans were those who didn't need them. But lower income individuals needed credit, sometimes desperately, and illegal lending flourished. A reform movement rose to meet the legitimate needs of debtors who couldn't meet bank standards. Out of this ferment grew personal finance companies (often called small loans companies) that offered relatively small loans at rates much higher than those charged by banks. These businesses were licensed under state law and closely regulated. They customarily took security interests in their borrower's personal property such as household goods. These loans were nonpossessory and nonpurchase money; that is, possession of the goods was left with the debtors and the proceeds of the loan were not used to purchase the collateral.

Section 522(f)(1)(B) is directed at the personal loan industry. It allows debtors in bankruptcy to avoid security interests in their exempt property to the extent these liens impair an exemption if the lien is a "nonpossessory, nonpurchase-money security interest in" certain enumerated goods, including household goods, furnishings, and the like, "held primarily for the personal, family, or household use of the debtor." Since most of the enumerated goods are exempt under state laws, the effect of this provision is to deprive personal finance companies of their status as secured creditors in bankruptcy. Why this radical treatment of the highly regulated, closely monitored personal finance industry that was conceived to help low-income debtors? The legislative history of the 1978 Code explains:

> Frequently, creditors lending money to a consumer debtor take a security interest in all of the debtor's belongings, and obtain a waiver by the debtor of his exemptions. In most of these cases, the debtor is unaware of the consequences of the forms he signs. The creditor's ex-

perience provides him with a substantial advantage. If the debtor encounters financial difficulty, creditors often use threats of repossession of all of the debtor's household goods as a means of obtaining payment.

In fact, were the creditor to carry through on his threat and foreclose on the property, he would receive little, for household goods have little resale value. They are far more valuable to the creditor in the debtor's hands, for they provide a credible basis for the threat, because the replacement costs of the goods are generally high. Thus, creditors rarely repossess, and debtors, ignorant of the creditors' true intentions, are coerced into payments they simply cannot afford to make.

The exemption provision allows the debtor, after bankruptcy has been filed, and creditor collection techniques have been stayed, to undo the consequences of a contract of adhesion, signed in ignorance, by permitting the invalidation of nonpurchase money security interests in household goods. Such security interests have too often been used by overreaching creditors. The bill eliminates any unfair advantage creditors have.

H.R. Rep. No. 595. 95th Cong., 2d Sess. at 126-127.

In practice, personal finance companies rarely, if ever, foreclosed on their collateral. They relied primarily on their debtor's earning capacity, and § 522(f)(1)(B) took the position that these companies should not be armed with security interests in a debtor's household goods that were useful only for their in terrorem effect in coercing debtors into payment. The goods were of little worth to creditors on resale but might be of great practical and emotional value to debtors.

(ii) The RAND Study

In BAPCPA, § 522(f)(4) was added to spell out in detail the items of property that qualified as "household goods." At the time of this amendment, Congress ordered the Director of the Executive Office for the United States Trustees (EOUST) to report in two years on "the utilization of the definition of household goods included in section 522(f)(4) of the amended Bankruptcy Code and its impact on debtors and the bankruptcy court." EOUST engaged RAND to do the study. The report, published in 2007, recommended that no changes should be made in the law. But of greater importance is the inescapable inference to be drawn from the study that the traditional personal finance industry, whose abuses are supposedly curbed by § 522(f)(1)(B), *no longer exists*. It was the victim of the credit card.

The first credit cards were issued in volume in the 1960s. Their growth has been phenomenal. At the beginning, credit cards were restricted to middle or upper income groups, but over the years aggressive competition for market share led card issuers to lower their credit standards, sometimes with disastrous results. Direct mail solicitation with low temporary teaser rates (sometimes zero), became standard, as did "pre-approved" card offers, and many consumers have several cards. It is no wonder that a consumer with immediate credit needs would find it much easier to use one of her credit cards, or apply for an additional card, in preference to going to a personal finance company and undergoing a grilling by a cold-eyed loan officer about her credit record.

The RAND study found very little current need for the services of personal finance companies. It concluded that both before and after BAPCPA was enacted, Chapter 7 debtors rarely used BAPCPA-affected goods to secure nonpurchase money loans. And they attempted to use the lien-avoidance provision for these loans even less (in fewer than 1% of filings). The investigators explained that they found so few nonpossessory, nonpurchase money small loans cases that they had difficulty drawing conclusions about the questions they were mandated to study. Anecdotal evidence collected from experienced attorneys confirmed that nonpurchase money loans secured by household goods are rarely seen and that credit cards have preempted the market.

Section 522(f)(1)(B) it turns out is an anachronism.

b. Avoidance of Judicial Liens under § 522(f)(1)(A)

(i) Impairment

Normally in a conflict between a debtor's exemption and a judicial lien in the property of debtor's estate, the exemption prevails. Thus, broadly speaking, the judicial lien cannot "impair" the debtor's exemption. The following cases, problems and notes suggest some of the mind-numbing difficulties arising from the laudable Congressional attempt to come up with a formula for impairment. Under § 522(f)(1)(A) a debtor may avoid the "fixing of" a judicial lien on the debtor's property "to the extent that such lien impairs an exemption to which the debtor would have been entitled" on that property. There is no explanation in the legislative history why the § 522(f)(1) avoiding power is given the debtor beyond the general statement that "[s]ubsection (f) protects the debtor's exemptions, his discharge, and thus his fresh start by permitting him to avoid certain liens on exempt property." H.R.Rep. No. 95-595 at 362. The courts have struggled with the meaning of impairment since enactment of the Code. In *Owen v. Owen*, 500 U.S. 305, 310–311 (1991), the Court said: "To determine the application of § 522(f) they ask not whether the lien impairs an exemption to which the debtor is in fact entitled, but whether it impairs an exemption to which he *would have been* entitled but for the lien itself." The following Problem illustrates the operation of *Owen*.

PROBLEM

In September 2008, a judgment lien was recorded on Debtor's residence, which she had owned for two decades. In January 2009, Debtor recorded a declaration of homestead that under state law created an exemption in the property to the extent of $55,000. However, state law provided that no homestead declaration affects a previously existing mortgage, lien or other encumbrance. When Debtor filed in Chapter 7 in July 2009, she claimed the exemption on the ground that state law provisions excepting preexisting liens were preempted by § 522(f) under the holding in *Owen* because, absent the lien, Debtor would have been entitled to the homestead exemption. What result? The facts are based on *In re Weinstein*, 164 F.3d 677 (1st Cir. 1999).

The *Silveira* case below discusses the division of authority on the meaning of impairment and the 1994 amendment of § 522(f) that resolves the issue in § 522(f)(2).

In re Silveira
United States Court of Appeals, First Circuit, 1998.
141 F.3d 34.

■ STAHL, Circuit Judge.

This bankruptcy appeal requires us to decide the extent to which a Chapter 7 debtor may, pursuant to § 522(f)(1) and (f)(2)(A), avoid the fixing of a judicial lien on the debtor's property, when the market value of the property *exceeds* the sum of (1) all consensual (non-judicial) liens on the property and (2) the amount of the debtor's exempt interest under § 522(d). We hold that, in such a situation, section 522(f)(1) permits the avoidance of the targeted judicial lien only in part, not in its entirety. Because the district court concluded otherwise, we vacate the judgment and remand for further proceedings.

I.

The debtor and appellee in this action, Thomas J. Silveira, owns, as his primary residence, a property that has been stipulated for purposes of this appeal to have a fair market value of $157,000. The property is subject to a mortgage of $117,680. The appellant, East Cambridge Savings Bank ("the Bank"), holds a $209,500 judicial lien * * * on the property.

On May 9, 1995, Silveira filed a voluntary petition under Chapter 7 of the Bankruptcy Code. He claimed an exemption of $15,000 in the property pursuant to § 522(d)(1).[1] Silveira then filed a motion to avoid the Bank's $209,500 judicial lien pursuant to § 522(f)(1) and § 522(f)(2)(A). The bankruptcy court ruled that those provisions permitted the debtor to avoid the Bank's lien in its entirety and thus granted Silveira's motion. The Bank appealed to the district court, arguing that on the facts of this case, § 522(f)(1) & (f)(2)(A) permitted only a *partial* avoidance of its judicial lien. The district court disagreed and entered an order affirming the bankruptcy court's determination. This appeal followed.

II.

The Bankruptcy Code provides every debtor with a personal power to avoid certain types of liens that would impinge upon interests that the debtor would otherwise be entitled to claim as exemptions from the bankruptcy estate. § 522(f)(1). Judicial liens are principal targets for this avoidance power:

> **(f)(1)** ... [T]he debtor may avoid the fixing of a lien on an interest of the debtor in property to the extent that such lien impairs an exemption to which the debtor would have been entitled under [§ 522(b)], if such lien is—
>
> > **(A)** a judicial lien, other than a judicial lien that secures a debt. . ...

In the years leading up to the Bankruptcy Reform Act of 1994 ("1994 Act"), a wide divergence of views developed concerning the circumstances in which a judicial lien could be deemed to "impair" an exemption within the meaning of § 522(f)(1), and the precise extent to which liens causing such impairment could be avoided. *See, e.g.*, 2 David G. Epstein, Steve H. Nickles & James J. White, Bankruptcy § 8-28, at 560 (West 1992) (describing various approaches). In an effort to resolve this discord, Congress included in the 1994 Act an amendment to § 522(f), which added the following new subsection:

> For the purposes of this subsection, a lien shall be considered to impair an exemption to the extent that the sum of—
>
> > **(i)** the lien;
> >
> > **(ii)** all other liens on the property; and

---

[1] As the Supreme Court has explained, "[a]n exemption is an interest withdrawn from the [bankruptcy] estate (and hence from the creditors) for the benefit of the debtor." *Owen v. Owen*, 500 U.S. 305, 308 (1991).

> **(iii)** the amount of the exemption that the debtor could claim if there were no liens on the property;

exceeds the value that the debtor's interest in the property would have in the absence of any liens.

§ 522(f)(2)(A).

In this case, it is undisputed that the sum of the targeted judicial lien ($209,500), all other liens ($117,680) and the amount of the debtor's exemption ($15,000) *exceeds* the (stipulated) value of the debtor's property ($157,000), by $185,180. Thus, the Bank's judicial lien clearly does "impair" an exemption of the debtor within the meaning of § 522(f)(2)(A). The question here concerns the extent of the debtor's power under § 522(f)(1) to alleviate this "impairment."

The district court concluded that once a debtor's power of avoidance is triggered by the fact of an impairment of whatever size, that power permits the debtor to avoid the judicial lien causing the impairment in its entirety. The court thus held that Silveira was entitled to avoid the entire amount of the Bank's $209,500 lien. The Bank now argues that the district court misapplied § 522(f)(1)(A), and that Silveira is in fact entitled to avoid only so much of the Bank's lien as necessary to prevent impairment of the debtor's exemption within the meaning of § 522(f)(2)(A). We agree.

As an initial matter, we find unpersuasive Silveira's argument that the "plain language" of the statute supports the district court's view. On the contrary, the language of the relevant provisions seems to us to support the Bank's position. Section 522(f)(1) permits a debtor to "avoid the fixing of a lien on an interest of the debtor in property *to the extent that* such lien impairs an exemption [of the debtor]." § 522(f)(1) (emphasis added). Section 522(f)(2)(A), similarly, provides that a judicial lien "impair[s] an exemption *to the extent that* "the targeted lien, in combination with other liens and the value of the debtor's exemption, exceeds the value of the debtor's property. § 522(f)(2)(A) (emphasis added). If Congress intended for avoidance of judicial liens to be an "all-or-nothing" matter, one might wonder why the provisions' drafters chose to use the connective phrase "to the extent that," in lieu of the word "if," which obviously would have been a simpler construction. *See In re Furkes*, 65 B.R. 232, 235 (D.R.I.1986) ("The 'to the extent that' clause cannot be seen as some sort of legislative slip of the pen.... [H]ad Congress intended... an all-or-nothing proposition, it would have drafted the statutory language more infrangibly....") The statutory directive that a debtor may avoid a judicial lien "to the extent that" the lien impairs an exemption favors—or is at least readily amenable to—reading the definition of "impairment" in § 522(f)(2)(A) not only as a *condition* of avoidability, but also as a *proportional measure* of the scope of the debtor's avoidance power.

But even if the statute's language does not settle the issue, the debtor's proposed interpretation is unacceptable in view of the statute's intended purposes. Consider the following two hypothetical scenarios:

Hypothetical A: The debtor owns a primary residence with a market value of $100,000, subject to an outstanding mortgage balance of $55,000, a judicial lien of $30,000 (not securing a debt), and no other liens. The debtor is entitled, under § 522(d)(1), to claim an exemption of $15,000 with respect to the property.

Hypothetical B: Same as Hypothetical A, except that the debtor's property is subject to a judicial lien of $30,001 instead of $30,000.

In Hypothetical A, we can see that the sum of the judicial lien ($30,000), other liens ($55,000) and the debtor's exemption ($15,000) does *not* exceed the value of the debtor's property ($100,000). Thus the judicial lien in Hypothetical A does *not* impair the debtor's exemption within the meaning of § 522(f)(2)(A), and the debtor is *not* entitled to avoid any portion of that lien under § 522(f)(1).

In Hypothetical B, however, the sum of the judicial lien ($30,001), other liens ($55,000) and the debtor's exemption ($15,000) *does* exceed the property's value (by $1), and so the targeted judicial lien is deemed under § 522(f)(2)(A) to impair the debtor's exemption. Under Silveira's proposed interpretation, the fact of this impairment requires that the debtor in Hypothetical B be permitted to avoid the $30,001 judicial lien *in its entirety*. Thus, as Silveira would have it, a $1 *increase* in the amount of the (unavoidable) judicial lien in Hypothetical A would result in the debtor's acquiring the power to avoid the lien in full.[4]

We find it difficult to conceive of any reason that would counsel in favor of interpreting § 522(f)(1)(A) and (f)(2)(A) to produce such a result. The district court, in siding with Silveira, suggested that denying debtors the right to avoid *in full* any judicial lien that impairs an exemption would "circumvent" Congress's goal of providing debtors with a "fresh start" after bankruptcy and would thus frustrate the basic purpose of § 522(f)(1). The problem with this argument, however, is that it proves too much.

The implication of the district court's reasoning is that the statute effects a general policy against the fixing of judicial liens with respect to property in which the debtor holds an exempt interest. Clearly, however, the statute cannot be read so broadly. Section 522(f) unquestionably contemplates that in some

---

[4] The debtor in Hypothetical A would also acquire full avoidance power (according to Silveira's approach) if the value of the debtor's property were reduced, or the amount of consensual liens were increased, by $1.

Chapter 2. The Bankruptcy Estate 53

circumstances—see, for example, Hypothetical A above—a judicial lien up to some calculable amount will *not* be deemed to impair the debtor's exemption and hence will not be subject to the debtor's avoidance power. But if, in such a circumstance, the statute would not permit the debtor to avoid any judicial lien *smaller* than that calculable amount, it would seem arbitrary and unfair to permit a creditor to avoid the *entirety* of a judicial lien that was *larger* than that amount. Thus, if § 522(f)(1) would permit the fixing of a $30,000 judicial lien on the facts of Hypothetical A above, then it would border on the absurd not to permit the holder of a $30,001 judicial lien, on otherwise identical facts, to pursue the fixing of its lien *up to* the amount of $30,000.

This reasoning compels an analogous result in this case. Here, the sum of the debtor's exemption ($15,000) and all consensual liens on his property ($117,680) is $24,320 *less* than the value of the property ($157,000); in other words, there is $24,320 of excess equity available. This means that if the Bank's judicial lien here had been for $24,320 or less, that lien would have been absolutely unavoidable under § 522(f)(1), because there would have been no "impairment" within the meaning of § 522(f)(2)(A).[5] The fact that the Bank's actual lien is for more than $24,320 surely provides no reason to place the Bank in a position *worse* than it would have been had its lien originally been limited to that amount. Fairness requires, therefore, that the Bank be permitted to pursue the fixing of its $209,500 judicial lien *up to* the amount of $24,320.

In more intuitive terms, it is obvious that the value of the debtor's property in this case is sufficient to cover the entire amount of the debtor's mortgage ($117,680) plus his claimed exemption ($15,000), with $24,320 of equity to spare. Nothing in § 522(f)(1) or § 522(f)(2) can be read to require that this excess equity be preserved either for the debtor or the bankruptcy estate, rather than being made available for the partial satisfaction of a judicial lien. And, as shown above, the fixing of a judicial lien in an amount equal to this excess equity would not create any impairment of the debtor's $15,000 exemption. See § 522(f)(2)(A). It follows that no legitimate purpose underlying the statute would be served by permitting Silveira to avoid so much of the Bank's lien— $24,320—as could be covered by the excess equity available in the property.

In summary, we apply § 522(f)(1)(A) and § 522(f)(2)(A) to the facts of this case as follows. First, pursuant to § 522(f)(2)(A), we determine that the sum of (i) the targeted judicial lien ($209,500), (ii) all other liens ($117,680), and (iii)

---

[5] That is, the sum of (i) the judicial lien ($24,320), (ii) other liens ($117,680), and (iii) the debtor's exemption ($15,000) would *not* have exceeded the value of the debtor's property ($157,000). See § 522(f)(2)(A).

the amount of the debtor's exemption ($15,000)—which sum equals $342,180—*exceeds* the value that the debtor's property would have in an unencumbered state ($157,000), and exceeds that value by $185,180. Thus, the Bank's judicial lien impairs the debtor's exemption to the extent of $185,180. Because Silveira is entitled to avoid the Bank's lien to the extent of any impairment, Silveira is entitled to avoidance in the amount of $185,180. See § 522(f)(1)(A). The remainder of the Bank's judicial lien, in the amount of $24,320 ($209,500 minus $185,180), is not subject to avoidance by the debtor under § 522(f)(1)(A).[6]

We note that this result follows the approach recently adopted by this Circuit's Bankruptcy Appellate Panel. * * *; *see also* 2 Norton Bankruptcy Law & Practice 2d § 46:23, at 334–35 (Supp.1997) (applying same approach); David G. Carlson, Security Interests on Exempt Property After the 1994 Amendments to the Bankruptcy Code, 4 Am. Bankr.Inst.L.Rev. 57, 65 (1996) (same).

* * *

IV.

The interpretation of § 522(f)(1)(A) and § 522(f)(2)(A) advocated by the Bank is consistent with the text of those provisions, fully vindicates the statute's basic purpose, and averts the unfair consequences that the debtor's interpretation would entail. Because the district court rejected the approach we adopt here, we vacate the judgment below and remand this case for further proceedings consistent with the principles set forth herein.

NOTES

1. Impairment is extensively discussed in Charles Jordan Tabb, *The Law of Bankruptcy* § 9.9 (1997).

2. Arthur and Bertha owned a home valued at $225,000 as tenants in common, subject to a first-priority mortgage securing an obligation of $165,000. Judgment Creditor (JC) obtained a judgment lien on the home in the amount of $53,878. Arthur (but not Bertha) filed in Chapter 7 and sought complete avoidance of the lien. He claimed an exemption of $5,312. On these facts, the court in *In re Lehman*, 205 F.3d 1255 (11th Cir. 2000), opined that strict application of the formula in § 522(f)(2)(A) to these facts would allow Arthur to avoid all of JC's lien: the calculation would be $53,878 plus $165,000 plus $5,312 total $224,190, which exceeds the value of Arthur's interest in the

---

[6] These figures would change, of course, if the actual value of the debtor's property were determined, on remand, to be different from the stipulated value of $157,000.

property, in the absence of liens, of $112,500 by $111,690, an amount greater than all of JC's lien.

The court concluded that this result was "absurd" because it would leave Arthur an equity of $30,000 in the property ($225,000 minus $165,000 equals $60,000, divided in half) that would be entirely free from JC's lien, even though Arthur was entitled to an exemption of only $5,312. In a case in which the debtor owns less than all of the property, the statutory formula yields a fair result only if it is tweaked somewhat. According to the court, a fair result under the facts of this case could be reached if the amount of the mortgage proportional to the debtor's share of the property ($82,500) is used in place of the amount of the mortgage on the whole property ($165,000). This would leave JC with a lien of $24,688 ($30,000 less $5,312) on the property. The court's interpretation of the statute is in accord with *Nelson v. Scala*, 192 F.3d 32 (1st Cir. 1999). *But see In re Cozad*, 208 B.R. 495 (10th Cir.BAP 1997).

(ii) The "Fixing of a Lien"

In *Farrey v. Sanderfoot*, 500 U.S. 291 (1991), the Court was faced with a common fact situation. In a property settlement upon divorce, it is common for one spouse, here Husband, to take the residence and agree to pay the other spouse, Wife, her share of the house's value over a period of time. If all Wife received from Husband was an unsecured note, Husband's subsequent bankruptcy might discharge his debt on the note and leave Wife with nothing. Usually, Wife will demand a security interest in the residence to safeguard her interest. In *Farrey*, Wife did not obtain a consensual security interest in the residence, but the divorce decree granted Wife a lien on the residence to secure Husband's obligation to pay the debt. A few months after the decree was issued, Husband filed in bankruptcy, claimed the residence as exempt property and moved to avoid Wife's judicial lien under § 522(f)(1). Congress could not have intended to allow debtors to avoid liens in a case of this sort, and the 1994 amendments except from avoidance judicial liens securing debts to spouses and children for alimony, maintenance or support.

It is clear that the facts of *Farrey* cried out for relief for Wife, and the Court delivered. It said:

> The statute does not say that the debtor may undo a lien on an interest in property. Rather, the statute expressly states that the debtor may avoid "the fixing" of a lien on the debtor's interest in property. The gerund "fixing" refers to a temporal event. That event—the fastening of a liability—presupposes an object onto which the liability can fasten. The statute defines this pre-existing object as "an interest of the debtor in property." Therefore, unless the debtor had the property interest to which the lien attached at some point *before* the lien attached to that

interest, he or she cannot avoid the fixing of the lien under the terms of § 522(f)(1).

500 U.S. at 296. But Husband countered that he had owned the residence with Wife before the judicial lien attached. No, replied the Court, Husband's current interest in the property came into being at the time of the divorce decree, which both awarded him the residence and affixed Wife's lien to the property. Since he had not owned his current interest in the residence before the judicial lien attached, Husband cannot use § 522(f)(1) to avoid Wife's lien.

PROBLEM

Under New York law, an unsatisfied money judgment automatically becomes a lien on real property thereafter acquired by the judgment debtor in the county in which the judgment has been docketed. Bank obtained a judgment against Debtor for $16,000, which was docketed in 1990 in Monroe County, New York. In 1994, Debtor purchased land in that county valued at $86,000; the judgment was never satisfied. In 1995, Debtor filed in bankruptcy, claimed his $10,000 homestead exemption in the Monroe County land and moved to avoid Bank's judicial lien on that property under § 522(f)(1)(A). Under *Farrey* is Debtor entitled to avoidance? Did Debtor have an interest in the property at the time the lien attached? This Problem is based on the facts of *In re Scarpino*, 113 F.3d 338 (2d Cir. 1997). "Fixing" is discussed in Charles Jordan Tabb, *The Law of Bankruptcy* § 9.8 (1997).

7. PREBANKRUPTCY PLANNING

a. Introduction

What is the proper purpose of state exemption laws and how should they be used in bankruptcy? This question was considered by Delmar Karlen in an article in 22 Bus. Law. 1167 (1967). He made the following statement:

> As a matter of common sense and fairness, it would seem that the governing policy should be that a man ought to pay his just debts and if he fails or refuses to do so, his property and income should be taken by law and devoted to that purpose. The only qualification to this principle would be that the debtor and his family should not be pauperized and thrown on relief; they should be left enough property and income to keep going and to make a fresh start toward solvency.

Id. at 1169.

Some exemption laws may reflect that policy but many do not. The federal Consumer Credit Protection Act, 15 U.S.C. § 1673, prevents wage garnishment of more than 25% of the disposable earnings of the debtor, but it applies alike to a debtor with earnings of $200 a week and one who earns $2,000 a week. In Florida and a few other states, a debtor may exempt equity in the family home whether that equity is worth $1,000 or $1,000,000 or more. Fla.Const. Art. 10, § 4 (West 1995). Moreover, debtors with equal assets may be allowed to retain more or less property depending upon the type of assets held. For example, consider two debtors in California with $70,000 to invest in property. Debtor A chose to invest the $70,000 in investment securities and to pay rent on the family home. Debtor B used the $70,000 to buy a house used as the family home. Debtor A can lose the entire $70,000 of securities if a creditor levies on them. Debtor B can protect all of the $70,000 invested in the family home. Cal.Code Civ.Proc. § 704.730(a)(2) (1987 and 2000 Supp.).

b. Homestead Exemption

A matter of great contention in drafting BAPCPA was the extent to which debtors in bankruptcy should be allowed to exempt the land and buildings that make up their homestead. The homestead exemption, the most basic of exemptions, is intended to protect debtors' homes from being seized by their creditors. Most states place dollar limits on homestead exemptions, which vary widely. But a few, notably Florida and Texas, have *no* limits. In 1997, the *NBRC Report* recommended that state laws should govern the amount of the exemption which should be not less than $20,000 nor more than $100,000. The Report noted that few states exempted more than $100,000 or less than $20,000. *NBRC Rep.* 125 (1997). BAPCPA moved decisively into the field. It laid down rules to determine which state's exemption law applies in bankruptcy, and in some cases limits the amount of a state exemption that can be claimed in bankruptcy.

(i) Section 522(b)(3)(A)

This provision states a general rule that for a debtor in bankruptcy to claim the exemptions of a state the debtor must have lived in that state for 730 days (two years) immediately before filing. But if the debtor has not lived in a single state for that period, the state where the debtor lived for the 180 days before a 730-day period immediately before the debtor filed "or for a larger portion of such 180-day period than in any other place." If the debtor has moved every six months for the three years before filing, the debtor can claim only the exemptions allowed by the state in which the debtor was domiciled during the greater part of the 180-day period before the 730-day period began to run. So if a debtor wishes to use more generous exemptions in another state, she must start her bankruptcy planning at least two years before filing.

PROBLEM

Debtor has lived in State A, which has a $25,000 homestead exemption, for 30 years before retiring and moving to State B, which has a $100,000 exemption and a much better climate, on January 2, 2008. After moving, Debtor sold his home in State A and bought one in State B. On January 2, 2009, Debtor filed in Chapter 7 in State B and claimed a $100,000 exemption in the new home. Under the laws of both states, homestead exemption laws apply only to real property within the state. If Debtor chooses the state exemptions, how much of the value of the residence can Debtor exempt under § 522(b)(3)(A): (a) $100,000 (b) $25,000 (c) $0 or (d) none of the above? See the stand-alone sentence at the end of § 522(b)(3).

(ii) Section 522(p)

Section 522(b)(3)(A) expressly makes that provision subject to § 522(p). Since state homestead exemptions vary widely among the states, debtors may engage in opportunistic behavior to take advantage of these differences by moving to states with larger exemptions. Exemption-shopping became a public scandal when well-known public figures frustrated their creditors by moving to states with unlimited homestead exemptions. Public outrage led to Congressional support for an across-the-broad cap of $125,000 on homestead exemptions. This would exceed the limits in almost all the states but would limit homestead exemptions in Florida and Texas and other states with unlimited exemptions. Debate was heated and threatened to stall enactment of BAPCPA. The battle-cry "Don't mess with Texas" was heard. Finally, as a compromise, subsections 522(p) and (q) were added. Section 522(p) was intended to close the "millionaire's mansion" loophole that allowed rich debtors to move to Florida or Texas, or other states with either no cap on their homestead exemption or a very high cap, and invest a fortune in a sumptious homestead, wholly protected from creditor claims in bankruptcy. Doubtless the intent of § 522(p) was to limit a debtor's homestead exemption to $125,000 (now $136,875), regardless of any higher exemption adopted by state law if the debtor had not owned the homestead or a predecessor homestead in the same state for at least 1,215 days (approximaterly three- and one-third years) before filing in bankruptcy.

However, § 522(p) contains what is apparently a drafting error that threatens to render the measure ineffective in the states that have opted out of the federal exemptions. It provides that the $125,000 cap comes into effect "as a result of [a debtor's] *electing*... to exempt property under State or local law..." The problem of the use of the term "electing" as the triggering event is that in the opt-out states, in which debtors can use only state exemptions, debtors cannot and do not "elect" anything. Since there is no election, nothing happens as the "result of electing." Does this mean that the 1,215-day ownership requirement does not apply to a debtor who has moved to Florida, an opt-out state, leaving the $125,000 cap inapplicable? If so, does this leave the "millionaire loophole" unscathed?

Bankruptcy courts have reached several different results on the issue. In the early going, Judge Bruce Markell's opinion in *In re Kane*, 336 B.R. 447 (Bankr.D.Nev.2006), has gained the largest following. Judge Markell, a well-regarded lawyer and scholar, concluded that Congress could not have intended to leave the loophole wide open in opt-out states and that *Kane* is that rare case in which judicial correction is justified, even under Justice Scalia's severe standards. Hence, in a case like that before the court in *Kane* (in which Nevada, an opt-out state, had a homestead exemption of $350,000) the $125,000 cap applied.

(iii) Section 522(q)

During the years in which BAPCPA was before Congress, corporate scandals were much in the news featuring multimillionaire executives in no-limit states who were on trial for securities law violations, fraud in a fiduciary capacity and the like, and who lived in or were constructing valuable residences that were protected from aggrieved creditors and shareholders by exemption laws. The following tortuous compromise dealing with this kind of case emerged.

Section 522(q) provides that a debtor electing the state exemptions under (b)(3)(A) may not exempt any amount of an interest in property that the debtor uses as a residence or claims as a homestead that exceeds $125,000 (now $136,875) if (i) the debtor has been convicted of a felony under circumstances that demonstrate that the filing of the case was an abuse of the provisions of the Bankruptcy Code, or (ii) the debtor owes a debt arising from violations of securities laws, or fraud in a fiduciary capacity or in connection with securities sales or purchases. Previously, exemption laws have drawn rules for different kinds of property; here the rule is drawn on the basis of the conduct of the debtor: debtors cannot exempt more than $125,000, whatever the state homestead exemption statutes provide, if they have been bad actors, unless under § 522(q)(2), the property is reasonably necessary for the support of the debtor and dependants. Moreover, §§ 727(a)(12) and 1328(h) allow courts to hold up the discharge of a debtor if there is reasonable cause to believe that the debtor has engaged in the reprehensible conduct described in § 522(q).

c. Fraudulent Use of Exemptions

If a debtor contemplating bankruptcy holds substantial property that is not exempt under the state exemption law, is it proper to sell the nonexempt property and use the proceeds to buy property that is exempt? Is it ethical for a lawyer to advise a client contemplating bankruptcy to do so? Is it malpractice if the lawyer does not advise the client that the exemption laws can be used to the client's advantage?

Tveten and *Hanson*, which follow, shed light on these questions. These cases were decided by the same court, the Eighth Circuit, on the same day as companion cases. The debtor in *Tveten* was domiciled in Minnesota; the debtors in *Hanson* were domiciled in South Dakota. At the time the relevant events occurred, the Uniform Fraudulent Conveyance Act (UFCA) was in effect in both states. UFCA § 7 states: "Every conveyance made * * * with actual intent, as distinguished from intent presumed in law, to hinder, delay, or defraud either present or future creditors, is fraudulent as to both present and future creditors." UFCA § 4 provides: "Every conveyance made * * * by a person who is or will be thereby rendered insolvent is fraudulent as to creditors without regard to his actual intent if the conveyance is made... without a fair consideration." Suppose an insolvent debtor was faced with creditors who were about to levy on the debtor's real property. Before levy was made, the debtor conveyed title to the property to a relative without consideration. Under the UFCA, the conveyance is fraudulent under § 4, and, if the purpose of the conveyance was to prevent the levy and thus avoid payment of the debt, the conveyance is fraudulent under § 7 as well. Under UFCA § 9 fraudulent conveyances can be nullified with the effect of returning the conveyed property to the debtor's estate. If a debtor made a fraudulent conveyance before bankruptcy, the trustee in bankruptcy can, if certain conditions are met, nullify the conveyance either on the basis of the state law or under § 548. Fraudulent transfers are discussed at length in chapter 7, *infra*.

The effect of converting nonexempt assets into exempt assets on the eve of bankruptcy is similar to that of a fraudulent transfer. If the exemption is allowed, the ability of creditors to reach assets of the debtor has been frustrated. But the analogy to fraudulent transfer law is imperfect. The public policy of that law in favor of protecting creditors from actions by a debtor that avoid payment of debts collides with another public policy represented by the exemption laws in favor of allowing the debtor to protect certain property from the claims of creditors. How is the conflict to be resolved?

BAPCPA intervened in this dispute by providing in § 522(o) that if a debtor within the 10-year period before filing has fraudulently converted nonexempt property into property that the debtor claims as a homestead, the value of the homestead must be reduced by the amount of the nonexempt property fraudulently transferred. The amendment extends the period of limitations for fraudulent transfer from two years under § 548(a) to 10 years but does not deal with the troublesome substantive issue treated by the following cases with respect to circumstances under which such a conversion is deemed fraudulent.

One of the principal reasons the National Bankruptcy Review Commission recommended a uniform federally prescribed lump-sum $20,000 nonhomestead exemption, *NBRC Rep.* § 1.2.1 & § 1.2.3, was to minimize the need for what has come to be called "prebankruptcy planning." These recommendations would enable the debtor, at the time of bankruptcy, to select any personal property to claim as exempt, so long as the value was under the ceiling. Debtors who are too ill-informed to engage in sophisticated transfers from nonexempt to exempt property on the eve of bankruptcy could enjoy the full measure of their exemptions, free from creditor challenges.

Norwest Bank Nebraska v. Tveten

United States Court of Appeals, Eighth Circuit, 1988.
848 F.2d 871.

■ TIMBERS, Circuit Judge.

Appellant Omar A. Tveten, a physician who owed creditors almost $19,000,000, mostly in the form of personal guaranties on a number of investments whose value had deteriorated greatly, petitioned for Chapter 11 bankruptcy. He had converted almost all of his non-exempt property, with a value of about $700,000, into exempt property that could not be reached by his creditors. The bankruptcy court, on the basis of its findings of fact and conclusions of law, entered an order on February 27, 1987, denying a discharge in view of its finding that Tveten intended to defraud, delay, and hinder his creditors. The district court * * * affirmed the bankruptcy court's order. On appeal, Tveten asserts that his transfers merely constituted astute pre-bankruptcy planning. We hold that the bankruptcy court was not clearly erroneous in inferring fraudulent intent on the part of Tveten. We affirm.

I.

Tveten is a 59-year-old physician in general practice. He is the sole shareholder of Omar A. Tveten, P.A., a professional corporation. He has no dependents. He began investing in various real estate developments. These investments initially were quite successful. Various physician friends of Tveten joined him in organizing a corporation to invest in these ventures. These investments were highly leveraged. The physicians, including Tveten, personally had guaranteed the debt arising out of these investments. In mid–1985, Tveten's investments began to sour. He became personally liable for an amount close to $19,000,000—well beyond his ability to pay. Appellees * * * became creditors of Tveten as a result of his various investment ventures.

Tveten filed a Chapter 11 petition on January 7, 1986. Meanwhile, several creditors already had commenced lawsuits against him. Panuska had obtained a $139,657 judgment against him on October 9, 1985. * * * On the date the Chapter 11 petition was filed, Tveten owed his creditors close to $19,000,000.

Before filing for bankruptcy, Tveten consulted counsel. As part of his pre-bankruptcy planning, he liquidated almost all of his non-exempt property, converting it into exempt property worth approximately $700,000. This was accomplished through some seventeen separate transfers. The non-exempt property he liquidated included land sold to his parents and his brother, respectively, for $70,000 and $75,732 in cash; life insurance policies and annuities with a for-profit company with cash values totalling $96,307.58; his net salary and bonuses of $27,820.91; his Keogh plan and individual retirement fund of $20,487.35; his corporation's profit-sharing plan worth $325,774.51; and a home sold for $50,000. All of the liquidated property was converted into life insurance or annuity contracts with the Lutheran Brotherhood, a fraternal benefit association, which, under Minnesota law, cannot be attached by creditors. Tveten concedes that the purpose of these transfers was to shield his assets from creditors. Minnesota law provides that creditors cannot attach *any* money or other benefits payable by a fraternal benefit association. * * * Unlike most exemption provisions in other states, the Minnesota exemption has no monetary limit. Indeed, under this exemption, Tveten attempted to place $700,000 worth of his property out of his creditors' reach.

Tveten sought a discharge with respect to $18,920,000 of his debts. Appellees objected to Tveten's discharge. In its order of February 27, 1987, the bankruptcy court concluded that, although Tveten's conversion of non-exempt property to exempt property just before petitioning for bankruptcy, standing alone, would not justify denial of a discharge, his inferred intent to defraud would. The bankruptcy court held that, even if the exemptions were permissible, Tveten had abused the protections permitted a debtor under the Bankruptcy Code (the "Code"). His awareness of Panuska's judgment against him and of several pending lawsuits, his rapidly deteriorating business investments, and his exposure to extensive liability well beyond his ability to pay, all were cited by the court in its description of the circumstances under which Tveten converted his property. Moreover, the court concluded that Tveten intended to hinder and delay his creditors. Accordingly, the bankruptcy court denied Tveten a discharge.

Tveten appealed from the bankruptcy court order to the federal district court. * * * [T]he district court affirmed the denial of a discharge, concluding that the bankruptcy court's finding as to Tveten's intent was not clearly erroneous.[3]

The instant appeal followed. Basically, Tveten asserts on appeal that as a matter of law we should reject the factors relied on by the bankruptcy court to infer that Tveten intended to delay, hinder and defraud creditors. We disagree. We affirm.

II.

The sole issue on appeal is whether Tveten properly was denied a discharge in view of the transfers alleged to have been in fraud of creditors.

At the outset, it is necessary to distinguish between (1) a debtor's right to exempt certain property from the claims of his creditors and (2) his right to a discharge of his debts. * * * When the debtor claims a state-created exemption, the scope of the claim is determined by state law. It is well established that under the Code the conversion of non-exempt to exempt property for the purpose of placing the property out of the reach of creditors, without more, will not deprive the debtor of the exemption to which he otherwise would be entitled. *E.g., Ford v. Poston*, 773 F.2d 52, 54 (4th Cir. 1985); * * * *In re Reed*, 700 F.2d 986, 990 (5th Cir. 1983) * * *. Both the House and Senate Reports regarding the debtor's right to claim exemptions state:

> "As under current law, the debtor will be permitted to convert non-exempt property into exempt property before filing a bankruptcy petition. The practice is not fraudulent as to creditors, and permits the debtor to make full use of the exemptions to which he is entitled under the law."

H.R.Rep. No. 595, 95th Cong., 1st Sess. 361 (1977); S.Rep. No. 989, 95th Cong., 2d Sess. 76 (1978). * * * This blanket approval of conversion is qualified, however, by denial of discharge if there was extrinsic evidence of the debtor's intent to defraud creditors.

A debtor's right to a discharge, however, unlike his right to an exemption, is determined by *federal,* not state, law. The Code provides that a debtor may be

---

[3] Before the district court entered its order, the Supreme Court of Minnesota held in a decision entered March 27, 1987, that annuities and life insurance contracts issued by a fraternal benefit society were exempt under Minnesota law, but that these statutory provisions violated the Minnesota Constitution. Accordingly, Tveten no longer will be able to claim these exemptions. Following the opinion of the Supreme Court of Minnesota, Tveten claimed an exemption for his pension in the amount of approximately $200,000. He and his creditors settled this issue before the bankruptcy court. He will retain this property as exempt.

denied a discharge under Chapter 7 if, among other things, he has transferred property "with intent to hinder, delay, or defraud a creditor" within one year before the date of the filing of the petition. § 727(a)(2). Although Tveten filed for bankruptcy under Chapter 11, the proscription against discharging a debtor with fraudulent intent in a Chapter 7 proceeding is equally applicable against a debtor applying for a Chapter 11 discharge. The reason for this is that the Code provides that confirmation of a plan does not discharge a Chapter 11 debtor if "the debtor would be denied a discharge under section 727(a) of this title if the case were a case under Chapter 7 of this title." § 1141(d)(3)(C).

Although the determination as to whether a discharge should be granted or denied is governed by federal law, the standard applied consistently by the courts is the same as that used to determine whether an exemption is permissible, i.e. absent extrinsic evidence of fraud, mere conversion of non-exempt property to exempt property is not fraudulent as to creditors even if the motivation behind the conversion is to place those assets beyond the reach of creditors. * * * *Forsberg v. Security State Bank*, 15 F.2d 499 (8th Cir. 1926).

As the bankruptcy court correctly found here, therefore, the issue in the instant case revolves around whether there was extrinsic evidence to demonstrate that Tveten transferred his property on the eve of bankruptcy with intent to defraud his creditors. The bankruptcy court's finding that there was such intent to defraud may be reversed by us only if clearly erroneous. * * *

There are a number of cases in which the debtor converted non-exempt property to exempt property on the eve of bankruptcy and was granted a discharge because there was no extrinsic evidence of the debtor's intent to defraud. In *Forsberg*, supra, an old decision of our Court, a debtor was granted a discharge despite his trade of non-exempt cattle for exempt hogs while insolvent and in contemplation of bankruptcy. Although we found that the trade was effected so that the debtor could increase his exemptions, the debtor "should [not] be penalized for merely doing what the law allows him to do." 15 F.2d at 501. We concluded that "before the existence of such fraudulent purpose can be properly found, there must appear in evidence some facts or circumstances which are extrinsic to the mere facts of conversion of nonexempt assets into exempt and which are indicative of such fraudulent purpose." Id. at 502. * * *

There also are a number of cases, however, in which the courts have denied discharges after concluding that there was extrinsic evidence of the debtor's fraudulent intent. * * * In *In re Reed*, supra, shortly after the debtor had arranged with his creditors to be free from the payment obligations until the following year, he rapidly had converted non-exempt assets to extinguish one home mortgage and to reduce another four months before bankruptcy, and had diverted receipts from his business into an account not divulged to his creditors.

Chapter 2. The Bankruptcy Estate   65

The Fifth Circuit concluded that the debtor's "whole pattern of conduct evinces that intent." 700 F.2d at 991. The court went further and stated:

> "It would constitute a perversion of the purposes of the Bankruptcy Code to permit a debtor earning $180,000 a year to convert every one of his major nonexempt assets into sheltered property on the eve of bankruptcy with actual intent to defraud his creditors and then emerge washed clean of future obligation by carefully concocted immersion in bankruptcy waters."

Id. at 992.

In most, if not all, cases determining whether discharge was properly granted or denied to a debtor who practiced "pre-bankruptcy planning", the point of reference has been the state exemptions if the debtor was claiming under them. Although discharge was not denied if the debtor merely converted his non-exempt property into exempt property as permitted under state law, the exemptions involved in these cases comported with federal policy to give the debtor a "fresh start"—by limiting the monetary value of the exemptions. This policy has been explicit, or at least implicit, in these cases. In *Forsberg*, supra, for example, we stated that it is not fraudulent for an individual who knows he is insolvent to convert non-exempt property into exempt property, thereby placing the property out of the reach of creditors

> because the statutes granting exemptions have made no such exceptions, and because the policy of such statutes is to favor the debtors, at the expense of the creditors, *in the limited amounts allowed to them, by preventing the forced loss of the home and of the necessities of subsistence,* and because such statutes are construed liberally in favor of the exemption.

Forsberg, supra, 15 F.2d at 501 (emphasis added). * * *

In the instant case, however, the state exemption relied on by Tveten was unlimited, with the potential for unlimited abuse. Indeed, this case presents a situation in which the debtor liquidated almost his entire net worth of $700,000 and converted it to non-exempt property in seventeen transfers on the eve of bankruptcy while his creditors, to whom he owed close to $19,000,000, would be left to divide the little that remained in his estate. Borrowing the phrase used by another court, Tveten "did not want a mere *fresh* start, he wanted a *head start.*" *In re Zouhar*, supra, 10 B.R. at 156 (emphasis in original). His attempt to shield property worth approximately $700,000 goes well beyond the purpose for which exemptions are permitted. Tveten's reliance on his attorney's advice does not protect him here, since that protection applies only to the extent that the reliance was reasonable. * * *

The bankruptcy court, as affirmed by the district court, examined Tveten's entire pattern of conduct and found that he had demonstrated fraudulent intent. We agree. While state law governs the legitimacy of Tveten's exemptions, it is federal law that governs his discharge. Permitting Tveten, who earns over $60,000 annually, to convert all of his major non-exempt assets into sheltered property on the eve of bankruptcy with actual intent to defraud his creditors "would constitute a perversion of the purposes of the Bankruptcy Code." *In re Reed*, supra, 700 F.2d at 992. Tveten still is entitled to retain, free from creditors' claims, property rightfully exempt under relevant state law.

We distinguish our decision in *Hanson v. First National Bank*, decided today. *Hanson* involves a creditor's objection to two of the debtors' claimed exemptions under South Dakota law, a matter governed by state law. The complaint centered on the Hansons' sale, while insolvent, of non-exempt property to family members for fair market value and their use of the proceeds to prepay their preexisting mortgage and to purchase life insurance policies in the limited amounts permissible under relevant state law. The bankruptcy court found no extrinsic evidence of fraud. The district court * * * affirmed. We also affirmed, concluding that the case fell within the myriad of cases which have permitted such a conversion on the eve of bankruptcy.

To summarize:

We hold that the bankruptcy court was not clearly erroneous in inferring fraudulent intent on the part of the debtor, rather than astute pre-bankruptcy planning, with respect to his transfers on the eve of bankruptcy which were intended to defraud, delay and hinder his creditors.

■ ARNOLD, Circuit Judge, dissenting.

The Court reaches a result that appeals to one's general sense of righteousness. I believe, however, that it is contrary to clearly established law, and I therefore respectfully dissent.

Dr. Tveten has never made any bones about what he is doing, or trying to do, in this case. He deliberately set out to convert as much property as possible into a form exempt from attachment by creditors under Minnesota law. Such a design necessarily involves an attempt to delay or hinder creditors, in the ordinary, non-legal sense of those words, but, under longstanding principles embodied both in judicial decisions and in statute, such a purpose is not unlawful. The governing authority in this Court is *Forsberg v. Security State Bank*. There we said:

It is well settled that it is not a fraudulent act by an individual who knows he is insolvent to convert property into exempt property, for the purpose of claiming his exemptions therein, and of thereby placing it out of the reach of his creditors.

* * *

To be sure, if there is extrinsic evidence of fraud, or of a purpose to hinder or delay creditors, discharge may and should be denied, but "extrinsic," in this context, must mean something beyond the mere conversion of assets into exempt form for the purpose of putting them out of the reach of one's creditors. If Tveten had lied to his creditors, like the debtor in *McCormick v. Security State Bank*, or misled them in some way, like the debtor in *In re Reed*, or transferred property for less than fair value to a third party, like the debtor in *Ford v. Poston*, we would have a very different case. There is absolutely no evidence of that sort of misconduct in this record, and the Court's opinion filed today cites none.

One is tempted to speculate what the result would have been in this case if the amount of assets converted had been $7,000, instead of $700,000. Indeed, the large amount of money involved is the only difference I can see between this case and *Forsberg*. It is true that the *Forsberg* opinion referred to "the limited amounts allowed to" debtors by exemptions, 15 F.2d at 501, but whether exemptions are limited in amount is a legislative question ordinarily to be decided by the people's elected representatives, in this case the Minnesota Legislature. Where courts punish debtors simply for claiming exemptions within statutory limits, troubling problems arise in separating judicial from legislative power.

* * *

If there ought to be a dollar limit, and I am inclined to think that there should be, and if practices such as those engaged in by the debtor here can become abusive, and I admit that they can, the problem is simply not one susceptible of a judicial solution according to manageable objective standards. A good statement of the kind of judicial reasoning that must underlie the result the Court reaches today appears in *In re Zouhar*, 10 B.R. 154 (Bankr.D.N.M.1981), where the amount of assets converted was $130,000. The Bankruptcy Court denied discharge, stating, among other things, that "'there is a principle of too much; phrased colloquially, when a pig becomes a hog it is slaughtered.'" *Id.* at 157. If I were a member of the Minnesota Legislature, I might well vote in favor of a bill to place an over-all dollar maximum on any exemption.[3] But sitting as a judge, by what criteria do I determine when this pig

---

[3] There is some irony in the fact that the exemption sought by the debtor in this case, that for benefits under annuities or life-insurance policies issued by fraternal associations, has been held unconstitutional under two provisions of the Minnesota Constitution. One such provision, Article 1, Section 12, provides that "[a] reasonable amount of property shall

becomes a hog? If $700,000 is too much, what about $70,000? Would it matter if the debtor were a farmer, as in *Forsberg,* rather than a physician? (I ask the question because the appellee creditor's brief mentions the debtor's profession, which ought to be legally irrelevant, several times.)

Debtors deserve more definite answers to these questions than the Court's opinion provides. In effect, the Court today leaves the distinction between permissible and impermissible claims of exemption to each bankruptcy judge's own sense of proportion. As a result, debtors will be unable to know in advance how far the federal courts will allow them to exercise their rights under state law.

Where state law creates an unlimited exemption, the result may be that wealthy debtors like Tveten enjoy a windfall that appears unconscionable, and contrary to the policy of the bankruptcy law. I fully agree with Judge Kishel, however, that

> [this] result * * * cannot be laid at [the] Debtor's feet; it must be laid at the feet of the state legislature. Debtor did nothing more than exercise a prerogative that was fully his under law. It cannot be said that his actions have so tainted him or his bankruptcy petition as to merit denial of discharge.

In re Johnson, 80 B.R. 953, 963 (Bankr.D.Minn.1987). I submit that Tveten did nothing more fraudulent than seek to take advantage of a state law of which the federal courts disapprove.

I would reverse this judgment and hold that the debtor's actions in converting property into exempt form do not bar a discharge in bankruptcy.

Hanson v. First National Bank in Brookings
United States Court of Appeals, Eighth Circuit, 1988.
848 F.2d 866.

■ TIMBERS, Circuit Judge.

A creditor bank appeals from a district court order * * * affirming the bankruptcy court's order which rejected the creditor's challenge to the debtors' claimed exemptions. On appeal, the creditor asserts that there was extrinsic evidence establishing the debtors' intent to defraud their creditors. We disagree.

---

be exempt * * *." The Supreme Court of Minnesota has held that the exemption statute involved in the present case is unconstitutional precisely because it contains no dollar limit. So the principle of limitation has been upheld, the debtor has in any event lost the exemption he sought, but he also loses his discharge under today's decision.

We hold that the bankruptcy court was not clearly erroneous in finding no fraudulent intent. We affirm.

I.

On November 30, 1983 appellees Kenneth Hanson and his wife Lucille Hanson (the "Hansons" or "debtors"), residents of South Dakota, filed a voluntary joint bankruptcy petition pursuant to Chapter 7 of the Bankruptcy Code. Appellant First National Bank in Brookings ("First National") is the principal creditor of appellees. The instant appeal arises out of First National's objections to the exemptions claimed by the Hansons.

First National loaned money to the Hansons who were farmers. The Hansons sustained financial problems which led to their default on the loans. Before filing for bankruptcy, the Hansons consulted an attorney. On the advice of counsel, the Hansons had appraised and sold certain of their property which would not be exempt under South Dakota law. They sold to their son, Ronald Hanson, a car, two vans, and a motor home for a total of $27,115, the amount for which the property was appraised. Ronald had purchased the property with money he obtained from a bank loan. The debtors also sold some of their household goods and furnishings to Kenneth's brother, Allen Hanson, for $7,300, the appraised value.

A couple weeks prior to filing their bankruptcy petition, the Hansons used these proceeds to purchase life insurance policies with cash surrender values of $9,977 and $9,978 and, two days before filing their petition had prepaid $11,033 on their homestead real estate mortgage which was held by First National. This property was exempt from their creditors' reach. Under South Dakota law, a debtor may exempt the proceeds of life insurance policies up to a total of $20,000 * * * and he also may exempt his homestead. * * *

First National objected to these exemptions, claiming that the debtors had converted non-exempt property to exempt property on the eve of bankruptcy with intent to defraud their creditors. At the hearing before the bankruptcy court on September 10, 1984, First National asserted that none of the property allegedly sold ever was transferred to the buyers. The debtors testified that the vehicles sold to their son, Ronald, were stored at their home because Ronald still lived with them while he was working part time and attending school part time. Part of the agreement, the debtors testified, included their permission to store the vehicles on their property. While the debtors said they occasionally used the vehicles, they did so only with express permission of their son. Ronald subsequently sold the motor home to a third party. The household goods and furnishings were stored in the Hansons' home, they said, because Allen Hanson, Kenneth's brother, was then living in Anchorage, Alaska, and could not retrieve the property immediately after the sale. First National did not assert, nor does it assert on appeal before us, that the transfers were for less than fair market value. The bankruptcy court from the bench denied First National's motion which objected to the exemptions. The court found that the Hansons had done what was permissible under the law and that their actions did not constitute extrinsic evidence of fraud.

First National appealed to the federal district court * * * [T]he district court affirmed * * * The sole issue on appeal is whether the Hansons should not be allowed to claim their life insurance and homestead exemption as a product of fraudulent conveyances. We affirm.

II.

Under the Bankruptcy Code (the "Code"), a debtor is entitled to exempt certain property from the claims of his creditors. The Code permits a debtor to exempt either under the provisions of the Code itself if not forbidden by state law, § 522(b) & (d), or under the provisions of state law and federal law other than the minimum allowances in the Code. § 522(b)(2). When the debtor claims a state-created exemption, the scope of the claim is determined by state law.

It is well established that under the Code, a debtor's conversion of non-exempt property to exempt property on the eve of bankruptcy for the express purpose of placing that property beyond the reach of creditors, without more, will not deprive the debtor of the exemption to which he otherwise would be entitled. * * * A leading bankruptcy commentator explains that this rule is just because "The result which would obtain if debtors were not allowed to convert property into allowable exempt property would be extremely harsh, especially in those jurisdictions where the exemption allowance is minimal." 3 Collier on Bankruptcy ¶ 522.08[4], at 40 (15th ed.1984). Nevertheless, this rule is not absolute. Where the debtor acts with actual intent to defraud creditors, his exemptions will be denied. Since fraudulent intent rarely is susceptible of direct proof, courts long have accepted extrinsic evidence of fraud. Absent extrinsic evidence of fraud, however, the debtor's mere conversion of non-exempt property to exempt property, even while insolvent, is not evidence of fraudulent intent as to creditors.

The crux of the issue on the instant appeal is whether there was extrinsic evidence to establish that the Hansons transferred the property with intent to defraud their creditors. We may reverse the bankruptcy court's finding as to the debtors' actual intent only if it is clearly erroneous. * * * *In re Cadarette*, 601 F.2d 648, 650 (2d Cir. 1979). * * *

First National asserts here that the Hansons while insolvent committed a "classic badge of fraud" by transferring their property to family members and at the same time retaining the use and enjoyment of that property. First National asserts that the controlling case is *Cadarette,* supra. We disagree.

In *Cadarette,* the debtor, whose business was on the brink of financial collapse, transferred title to his expensive automobile, boat and trailer to his fiancee without consideration three weeks before filing his bankruptcy petition. The district court, reversing the decision of the bankruptcy court, held that the debtor's discharge was denied because of his fraudulent intent to shield his assets from his creditors. The Second Circuit, in affirming the district court, found a number of factors clearly evidencing the debtor's fraudulent intent. The court found significant, among other things, that "someone facing dire financial straits would choose to make a gift of a valuable and highly marketable automobile"; that eight days after the alleged transfer of the car a service charge of $399 was paid not by the alleged new owner but by the debtor, who further depleted his business assets by paying with a company check; that the debtor's fiancee lived only two houses away from him; and that he retained a key to the car and continued to use the car to the same extent as he previously had used it.

We find the instant case quite different from the situation in *Cadarette.* First National does not dispute the fact that the purchasers paid fair market value. The vehicles and household goods were not gifts. Title appears to have been transferred correctly. In the instant case, the debtors had reasonable explanations as to why the property they sold remained on their premises. Of particular significance, their son purchased the vehicles with a bank loan taken in his name and he subsequently resold the motor home to a third party, keeping all of the proceeds himself. The sale to family members, standing on its own, does not establish extrinsic evidence of fraud. * * *

The bankruptcy court found that First National did not establish any indicia of fraud: the Hansons did not borrow money to place into exempt properties; they accounted for the cash they received from the sales; they had a preexisting homestead; and they did not obtain goods on credit, sell them, and then place the money into exempt property. They sold the property for its fair market value and then used this money to take advantage of some of the limited exemptions available under South Dakota law on the advice of counsel.

III.

To summarize:

We hold that the bankruptcy court was not clearly erroneous in finding no fraudulent intent by the Hansons and permitting them to claim their full exemptions. We believe that the instant case falls within the myriad of cases which have permitted such a conversion.

■ ARNOLD, Circuit Judge, concurring.

I agree with the result reached by the Court and with almost all of its opinion. I write separately to indicate some variation in reasoning and also to compare this case with the companion case of *Norwest Bank Nebraska, N.A. v. Tveten*, 848 F.2d 871, also decided today by this panel.

In general, as the Court says, citing *Forsberg v. Security State Bank*, 15 F.2d 499 (8th Cir. 1926), "a debtor's conversion of non-exempt property to exempt property on the eve of bankruptcy for the express purpose of placing that property beyond the reach of creditors, without more, will not deprive the debtor of the exemption to which he would otherwise be entitled." * * * And this is so even if the conversion of property into exempt form takes place while the debtor is insolvent. The result is otherwise, of course, if there is "extrinsic evidence of fraud," * * * but the word "extrinsic" must mean some evidence other than the debtor's purpose to put the property beyond the reach of creditors. Otherwise, the entire *Forsberg* rule would be swallowed up in the exception for "extrinsic fraud."

The Court is entirely correct in holding that there is no extrinsic fraud here. The money placed into exempt property was not borrowed, the cash received from the sales was accounted for, and the property was sold for fair market value. The fact that the sale was to family members, "standing on its own, does not establish extrinsic evidence of fraud."

With all of this I agree completely, but exactly the same statements can be made, just as accurately, with respect to Dr. Tveten's case. So far as I can tell, there are only three differences between Dr. Tveten and the Hansons, and all of them are legally irrelevant: (1) Dr. Tveten is a physician, and the Hansons are farmers; (2) Dr. Tveten attempted to claim exempt status for about $700,000 worth of property, while the Hansons are claiming it for about $31,000 worth of property; and (3) the Minnesota exemption statute whose shelter Dr. Tveten sought had no dollar limit, while the South Dakota statute exempting the proceeds of life-insurance policies * * * is limited to $20,000. The first of these three differences—the occupation of the parties—is plainly immaterial, and no one contends otherwise. The second—the amounts of money involved—is also irrelevant, in my view, because the relevant statute contains no dollar limit, and for judges to set one involves essentially a legislative decision not suitable for the judicial branch. The relevant statute for present purposes is § 522(b)(2)(A), which authorizes debtors to claim exemptions available under "State or local law," and says nothing about any dollar limitations, by contrast to § 522(d), the federal schedule of exemptions, which contains a number of dollar limitations. The third difference—that between the Minnesota and South Dakota statutes—is also legally immaterial, and for a closely related reason. The federal exemption statute, just referred to, simply incorporates state and local exemption laws without regard to whether those laws contain dollar limitations of their own.

The Court attempts to reconcile the results in the two cases by characterizing the question presented as one of fact—whether the conversion was undertaken with fraudulent intent, or with an intent to delay or hinder creditors. In *Tveten*, the Bankruptcy Court found fraudulent intent, whereas in *Hanson* it did not. Neither finding is clearly erroneous, the Court says, so both judgments are affirmed. This analysis collapses upon examination. For in *Tveten* the major indicium of fraudulent intent relied on by the Bankruptcy Court was Dr. Tveten's avowed purpose to place the assets in question out of the reach of his creditors, a purpose that, as a matter of law, cannot amount to fraudulent intent, as the Court's opinion in *Hanson* explicitly states. The result, in practice, appears to be this: a debtor will be allowed to convert property into exempt form, or not, depending on findings of fact made in the court of first instance, the Bankruptcy Court, and these findings will turn on whether the Bankruptcy Court regards the amount of money involved as too much. With all deference, that is not a rule of law. It is simply a license to make distinctions among debtors based on subjective considerations that will vary more widely than the length of the chancellor's foot.

NOTES

1. In *In re Addison*, 540 F.3d 805 (8th Cir. 2008), Debtor owed $1.3 million on a personal guarantee made to Bank, which was pursuing him for payment. On advice of a bankruptcy attorney, shortly before bankruptcy, Debtor transferred money from a nonexempt brokerage account into exempt Roth IRAs for himself and his wife and instructed his wife to use nonexempt funds to pay down their home mortgage, which was on an exempt homestead. In Chapter 7, Debtor claimed both the IRA and his equity in the home as exempt. Trustee objected to these exemptions on grounds of fraud and the BAP agreed; the Eighth Circuit reversed. (i) With respect to the IRA, the court relied on *Hanson* that the conversion of nonexempt property to exempt property on the eve of bankruptcy for the express purpose of placing the property beyond the reach of creditors without evidence of indicia of fraud beyond mere use of the exemptions can not be challenged. (ii) With respect to the homestead, the Trustee invoked § 522(o), enacted in 2005, under which the amount of a state homestead exemption is reduced to the extent the value of the exemption is attributable to nonexempt property that the debtor converted to homestead within ten years of filing in bankruptcy if the conversion was made "with the intent to hinder, delay, or defraud a creditor." The court held that the *Hanson* test applied in this case as well; evidence of fraud beyond mere conversion of nonexempt to exempt property must be found, and there was none in this case.

2. In *In re Warren*, 512 F.3d 1241 (10th Cir. 2008), Debtors, husband and wife, both CPAs, were engaged in litigation with Mathai, which they were unable to resolve. After consulting bankruptcy counsel, they engaged in what the court described as a "frenzy" of activity in the days immediately before filing, consisting of liquidation of their nonexempt property, sometimes at steep discounts, and use of the proceeds to purchase exempt property—life insurance policies, cheap cars, purchase of a new home falling within the homestead exemption, and the like. At the time of filing in Chapter 7, Debtors had only $20 cash on hand. Miffed by the possibility that his claims against Debtors would be discharged, Mathai filed a complaint to prevent them from obtaining a discharge on the grounds that they had transferred and concealed property to "hinder, delay, or defraud" creditors under § 727(a)(2)(A). The court discussed Judge Arnold's "oft quoted" dissent in *Tveten,* and concluded: "[W]e are most reluctant (for the reasons expressed by Judge Arnold) to recognize a conversion of nonexempt assets to exempt assets as fraudulent, and we need not do so to affirm the BAP decision in this case." The bankruptcy court had found glaring irregularities in Debtors' schedules: forgotten transactions and inaccurate reporting that substantially undermined their credibility. This was in contrast to the meticulously accurate list of creditors the Debtors compiled from whose claims Debtors sought discharge.

   3. In *Havoco of America, Ltd. v. Hill*, 197 F.3d 1135 (11th Cir. 1999), the Circuit Court certified to the Florida Supreme Court the question whether the state constitution exempts a Florida homestead acquired by the debtor with nonexempt funds with the specific intent of hindering, delaying or defrauding creditors in violation of state fraudulent conveyance law. In a subsequent opinion in the case, 255 F.3d 1321 (11th Cir. 2001), the court reported that the Florida court answered the question in the affirmative so long as the funds were not obtained through fraud or egregious conduct.

8. ASSET PROTECTION TRUSTS

   Asset protection trusts are used by persons seeking to shelter their assets from their creditors. Several jurisdictions have sought to become havens for these trusts. What is the status of these trusts in bankruptcy? If Settlor grants property to Trustee to hold in trust for Beneficiary and provides that the beneficial interest cannot be voluntarily or involuntarily transferred, the restriction is generally valid under state law and the corpus of the trust is not subject to attachment by Beneficiary's creditors. This is the familiar "spendthrift trust." Section 541(c)(2) provides that this restriction on transfer is enforceable in bankruptcy because it is enforceable under nonbankruptcy law; the effect is that the beneficial interest under the trust is not property of the estate. But if Settlor grants property to Trustee to hold in trust for *Settlor*, state common law has long held that a restriction on transfer is not binding on Settlor's creditors. Historically, settlors could not free their assets from liability to their creditors while retaining a beneficial interest in those assets in this manner. *See In re*

Brown, 303 F.3d 1261 (11th Cir. 2002). Since such a trust is ineffective for asset protection under nonbankruptcy law, it is ineffective in bankruptcy as well. Jurisdictions seeking to become havens for asset protection trusts have principally done so by changing their law to validate spendthrift clauses in self-settled trusts. In these jurisdictions, restrictions against involuntary transfers in self-settled trusts are now valid under the law of the haven state.

In *The Death of Liability*, 106 Yale L.J. 1, 32–34 (1996), Professor Lynn LoPucki describes the use of asset protection trusts:

> More than a half-dozen nations compete for foreign investment by refusing comity with respect to the enforcement of judgments and providing havens for judgment debtors from their foreign creditors. They implement the latter policy principally by validating self-settled spendthrift trusts under which the settlor is a beneficiary. In the United States, such a trust is ineffective against creditors as against public policy. A self-settled spendthrift trust amounts, in essence, to a declaration that one wishes to own one's assets free of the claims of one's judgment creditors—that is, free of liability. One commentator estimates that this offshore trust industry already administers a trillion dollars in assets.
>
> To understand the strategy of removing assets to a spendthrift trust jurisdiction, consider the example of a medical doctor who lives and practices medicine in the United States. Assume that the doctor owns a nonexempt home, a medical practice, and liquid assets in a brokerage account. Each of the three assets is worth approximately one million dollars.... All of the assets are located in the United States.... Through a U.S. lawyer who specializes in such transactions... the doctor establishes a spendthrift trust [in the Cook Islands].... Cook Islands law permits the doctor to serve as the "protector" of the trust assets with the power to remove and replace trustees and to veto investment decisions. Over one aspect of trust management, the doctor retains no control or power of revocation: Whoever is trustee may not expose trust assets to the claims of the doctor's creditors. The standard trust documents also mandate that the trustee ignore instructions made by the doctor under duress, such as an order from a U.S. court that the doctor cause the trust to return assets so that they may be applied to the claim of a creditor.
>
> Once the trust has been established, the doctor deeds his home and transfers ownership of his medical practice into it. Though both are now foreign owned, the home and the medical practice remain physically in the United States. The trust will permit the doctor to use them without charge.... The doctor also transfers the liquid assets... to the Cook Islands trustee, who then proceeds to invest them in accord with non-binding instructions furnished by the doctor.

Although, as Professor LoPucki indicates, the movement toward asset protection trusts began in offshore venues—the Channel Islands, the Cook Islands, the Cayman Islands, and the like—those seeking asset protection no longer need go abroad. Alaska, Delaware, Missouri, Nevada, Oklahoma, Rhode Island, South Dakota, and Utah have become the first United States jurisdictions to permit self-settled spendthrift trusts. These American cousins of the offshore asset protection trust are subject to attack if created with the intent to defraud creditors and, in Delaware, the trusts are not effective against tort creditors. BAPCPA § 548(e) provides for a 10-year look-back provision in place of the two-year period in § 548(a) if the debtor has transferred assets to a self-settled trust for the benefit of the debtor with fraudulent intent, which may be to shelter the assets from any liability that might be incurred for violating securities laws or fraud in a fiduciary capacity or in connection with the purchase or sale of certain securities. Since such acts would likely have been considered fraudulent under the prior law, the only significant change in the law made by BAPCPA is to give trustees eight more years of look-back time to seek out fraud. Thus, efforts by some in Congress to use BAPCPA to abolish outright asset protection trusts in the United States failed. Nevertheless, the trusts, if created with actual intent to hinder, delay and defraud creditors (and what other explanation is there for a self-settled spendthrift trust?) remain vulnerable to fraudulent transfer attack for the period of the extended statute of limitations. *See* p. 373, *infra*. Debtors who defy court orders to repatriate assets held in offshore trusts have been incarcerated for contempt. *See, e.g., In re Lawrence*, 279 F.3d 1294 (11th Cir. 2005).

CHAPTER 3
CLAIMS

A. INTRODUCTION

1. TERMINOLOGY

In the last chapter we defined the property of the estate that is distributed in bankruptcy; in this chapter we examine who receives this property. Only holders of "claims" may receive distributions in bankruptcy. § 726(a). The terms "debt" and "claim" are correlatives. "Debt" is defined in § 101(12) as "liability on a claim." A debtor's obligation to a creditor becomes the creditor's claim when the debtor files in bankruptcy. In addition, under § 727(b) a discharge in bankruptcy "discharges the debtor from all debts" that arose before bankruptcy. Since a debt must be a "liability on a claim," a debtor cannot be discharged from an obligation unless the obligation is on a claim. Thus, the term "claim" serves the dual function of defining the obligations that will receive distributions in bankruptcy and the kinds of obligations that will be discharged.

"Claim" is defined in § 101(5) in very broad terms as any "right to payment, whether or not such right is reduced to judgment, liquidated, unliquidated, fixed, contingent, matured, unmatured, disputed, undisputed, legal, equitable, secured, or unsecured," and also includes a "right to an equitable remedy for breach of performance if such breach gives rise to a right to payment." The breadth of this definition furthers the fresh-start principle: just as the property of the estate is defined broadly to include virtually all the debtor's assets, claim is defined broadly to discharge substantially all obligations of the debtor. Since corporations have no post-bankruptcy life, they are treated differently, as we will see later.

Throughout this chapter, we deal with three kinds of claims:

(1) Secured claims. The debtor's obligation is secured by a lien on the debtor's property that enables the creditor to proceed against this property to satisfy the debt if the debtor defaults. Security interests are common in cases involving the purchase of significant assets. If the debtor defaults, the secured creditor is relieved from the expensive and time-consuming judicial collection procedures. UCC Article 9 offers secured parties extrajudicial procedures for realizing on personal property

collateral; some jurisdictions make similar procedures available for real property mortgages. And, as we saw in the last chapter, secured financing greatly reduces the protection extended to debtors by exemption statutes.

(2) Priority claims. For policy reasons certain unsecured claims are granted priority over other unsecured claims. For instance, domestic support obligations incurred for alimony, maintenance and support of former spouses or children are granted priority status.

(3) Unsecured claims. This is the residual category of claims. Outside bankruptcy, creditors establish their relative priority by the "race to the courthouse" in which the first creditor to impose a judicial lien on an artcle of the debtor's property may satisfy its claim from this property. Some creditors may be paid in full and others may receive nothing. Bankruptcy offers a collective process in which creditors share pro rata the property of the estate without respect to when their claims arose or became due. § 726(b). The automatic stay prevents creditors from seizing the debtor's property before the trustee can make an orderly disposition of the property and distribute the proceeds, pro rata of any nonexempt property.

2. CLAIMS PROCEDURES

a. Allowed Claims

When a debtor files a petition in bankruptcy, she must submit schedules listing the names and addresses of her creditors. Official Form 6. Her creditors will be given notice of the bankruptcy by the clerk of the bankruptcy court. Rule 2002. Since a claim is the basis for a distribution from the bankruptcy estate, a "proof of claim," which is a written statement setting forth a creditor's claim, is usually filed by the creditor having the claim. § 501 and Rule 3001. A claim is entitled to distributions only if it is "allowed." § 726(a). Allowance of a claim means simply that it has been recognized by the court as valid in the amount claimed. In most cases there is no dispute concerning the claim. For that reason § 502(a) provides that a claim, proof of which has been filed, is allowed unless a party in interest objects. If there is an objection, the court must determine whether the claim is allowable. § 502(b).

In Chapter 7, if a creditor fails to file a proof of claim, the claim cannot be allowed under § 502 and cannot share in the distribution of the estate under § 726(a). But claims that are not allowed are nevertheless discharged under § 727(b). This is also true in Chapter 11: under § 1141(d), confirmation of a plan discharges the debtor from any debt that arose before the date of confirmation whether or not proof of claim was filed or the claim was allowed under

§ 502. In Chapter 7 if it appears that there are no assets from which a dividend can be paid to creditors, Rule 2002(e) provides that creditors may be notified that it is unnecessary to file claims.

"Creditor" is defined in § 101(10) to mean an entity holding a claim that arose before the filing of the petition in a voluntary case or before the order for relief in an involuntary case. Thus, if a debtor files in Chapter 7, rights to payment against the debtor that arise after bankruptcy are not claims in bankruptcy. Holders of such postpetition rights to payment against debtors cannot share in the distribution of the estate and their claims are not discharged. Postpetition obligations of the bankruptcy trustee, however, are treated as expense of administration and entitled to priority.

PROBLEM

Donald filed in Chapter 7 bankruptcy but forgot to list one of his creditors, Charles, who did not learn of the case until after the trustee had distributed the property of the estate, the case was closed and Donald was discharged. Donald now is acquiring assets. You may assume that Donald's failure to list Charles on his schedules was a good faith mistake with no fraudulent intent involved. Charles comes to you for advice on how he should proceed against Donald. Is he entitled to recover (a) the full amount of his claim (b) the amount that he would have received had he shared in the distribution of the estate (c) nothing? See § 523(a)(3).

b. Time Limits for Filing Proof of Claim

Cases under Chapters 7, 12 and 13. Creditors whose claims are scheduled by the debtor should receive notice of the commencement of the bankruptcy case, the date of the statutory first meeting of the creditors, and the deadline to file a proof of claim, often called the bar date. Rule 2002. For Chapters 7, 12 and 13, Rule 3002(c) prescribes that this date will be not later than 90 days after "the first date set for the meeting of creditors called under § 341(a)," subject to five stated exceptions. We will not examine the complex body of statutory and case law dealing with the status of tardily filed claims.

Cases under Chapter 11. The 90-day rule of Rule 3002(c) doesn't apply in Chapter 11. Rather, the time within which proofs of claim must be filed is fixed by the court. The bar date may be extended by the court for cause. Rule 3003(c). Late-filed claims under Chapter 11 are governed by Rule 9006(b)(1). In the context of the filing of a proof of claim after a bar date, the rule provides that a bankruptcy court "for cause shown may *** in its discretion *** on motion made after the [bar date] permit [a proof of claim to be filed] where the failure to act was the result of excusable neglect." The Supreme Court has adopted a flexible analysis of the circumstances constituting "excusable neglect." *Pioneer Investment Services Co. v. Brunswick Associates Limited Partnership*, 507 U.S. 380 (1993).

B. RIGHTS TO PAYMENT

1. LEGAL RIGHTS

Although claim is defined to include a right to payment, it is not necessary that there be a present right to receive money. Unmatured claims are specifically covered in the definition of claim. Nor is it necessary that there be any certainty that a right to payment will ever mature. The definition of claim includes contingent claims. A contingent claim is "one which the debtor will be called upon to pay only upon the occurrence or happening of an extrinsic event which will trigger the liability of the debtor to the alleged creditor and if such triggering event or occurrence was one reasonably contemplated by the debtor and creditor at the time the event giving rise to the claim occurred." *In re All Media Properties, Inc.*, 5 B.R. 126, 133 (Bankr.S.D.Tex.1980). For example, the debtor may have guaranteed some performance by X that is due to Y in the future. Does Y have a claim in the bankruptcy of the debtor if the performance by X is not yet due and there is no basis for determining whether X will or will not perform? There are two aspects to the problem: First, if Y has a claim, the court must determine the amount that Y is entitled to receive. Second, if Y has a claim, it is subject to discharge in bankruptcy. Under § 727(b) the debtor is discharged "from all debts that arose before the date of the order for relief." In many cases estimating the amount of a contingent liability is speculative; nonetheless, the contingent claim must be estimated by the court and discharged.

Under the Bankruptcy Code much turns on when a claim arises. The following opinion reviews the contesting authorities on this issue.

In re Piper Aircraft
United States Court of Appeals, Eleventh Circuit, 1995.
58 F.3d 1573.

■ BLACK, Circuit Judge:

This is an appeal by David G. Epstein, as the Legal Representative for the Piper future claimants (Future Claimants), from the district court's order of June 6, 1994, affirming the order of the bankruptcy court entered on December 6, 1993. The sole issue on appeal is whether the class of Future Claimants, as defined by the bankruptcy court, holds claims against the estate of Piper

Aircraft Corporation (Piper), within the meaning of § 101(5) of the Bankruptcy Code. After review of the relevant provisions, policies and goals of the Bankruptcy Code and the applicable case law, we hold that the Future Claimants do not have claims as defined by § 101(5) and thus affirm the opinion of the district court.

I. Factual and procedural background

Piper has been manufacturing and distributing general aviation aircraft and spare parts throughout the United States and abroad since 1937. Approximately 50,000 to 60,000 Piper aircraft still are operational in the United States. Although Piper has been a named defendant in several lawsuits based on its manufacture, design, sale, distribution and support of its aircraft and parts, it has never acknowledged that its products are harmful or defective.

On July 1, 1991, Piper filed a voluntary petition under Chapter 11 of Bankruptcy Code in the United States Bankruptcy Court for the Southern District of Florida. Piper's plan of reorganization contemplated finding a purchaser of substantially all of its assets or obtaining investments from outside sources, with the proceeds of such transactions serving to fund distributions to creditors. On April 8, 1993, Piper and Pilatus Aircraft Limited signed a letter of intent pursuant to which Pilatus would purchase Piper's assets. The letter of intent required Piper to seek the appointment of a legal representative to represent the interests of future claimants by arranging a set-aside of monies generated by the sale to pay off future product liability claims.

On May 19, 1993, the bankruptcy court appointed Appellant Epstein as the legal representative for the Future Claimants. The Court defined the class of Future Claimants to include:

All persons, whether known or unknown, born or unborn, who may, after the date of confirmation of Piper's Chapter 11 plan of reorganization, assert a claim or claims for personal injury, property damages, wrongful death, damages, contribution and/or indemnification, based in whole or in part upon events occurring or arising after the Confirmation Date, including claims based on the law of product liability, against Piper or its successor arising out of or relating to aircraft or parts manufactured and sold, designed, distributed or supported by Piper prior to the Confirmation Date.

This Order expressly stated that the court was making no finding on whether the Future Claimants could hold claims against Piper under § 101(5) of the Code.

On July 12, 1993, Epstein filed a proof of claim on behalf of the Future Claimants in the approximate amount of $100,000,000. The claim was based on statistical assumptions regarding the number of persons likely to suffer, after the confirmation of a reorganization plan, personal injury or property damage caused by Piper's pre-confirmation manufacture, sale, design, distribution or support of aircraft and spare parts. The Official Committee of Unsecured Creditors (Official Committee), and later Piper, objected to the claim on the ground that the Future Claimants do not hold § 101(5) claims against Piper. After a hearing on the objection, the bankruptcy court agreed that the Future Claimants did not hold § 101(5) claims, and, on December 6, 1993, entered an Order Sustaining the Committee's Objection and Disallowing the Legal Representative's Proof of Claim. * * * Epstein, as Legal Representative, then appealed from the bankruptcy court's order. * * * [T]he district court affirmed and accepted the decision of the bankruptcy court. Epstein now appeals from the district court's order, challenging in particular its use of the prepetition relationship test to define the scope of a claim under § 101(5).

II. Discussion

A. Statute

Under the Bankruptcy Code, only parties that hold preconfirmation claims have a legal right to participate in a Chapter 11 bankruptcy case and share in payments pursuant to a Chapter 11 plan. §§ 101(10), 501, 502 (West 1993). In order to determine if the Future Claimants have such a right to participate, we first must address the statutory definition of the term "claim." The Bankruptcy Code defines claim as:

> **(A)** right to payment, whether or not such right is reduced to judgment, liquidated, unliquidated, fixed, contingent, matured, unmatured, disputed, undisputed, legal, equitable, secured, or unsecured; or
>
> **(B)** right to an equitable remedy for breach of performance if such breach gives rise to a right to payment, whether or not such right to an equitable remedy is reduced to judgment, fixed, contingent, matured, unmatured, disputed, undisputed, secured, or unsecured.

§ 101(5). The legislative history of the Code suggests that Congress intended to define the term claim very broadly under § 101(5), so that "all legal obligations of the debtor, no matter how remote or contingent, will be able to be dealt with in the bankruptcy case." H.R.Rep. No. 595, 95th Cong., 2d Sess. 309 (1978), *reprinted in* 1978 U.S.C.C.A.N. 5787, 5963, 6266.

B. Case Law

Since the enactment of § 101(5), courts have developed several tests to determine whether certain parties hold claims pursuant to that section: the accrued state law claim test,[2] the conduct test, and the prepetition relationship test. The bankruptcy court and district court adopted the prepetition relationship test in determining that the Future Claimants did not hold claims pursuant to § 101(5).

Epstein primarily challenges the district court's application of the prepetition relationship test. He argues that the conduct test, which some courts have adopted in mass tort cases,[3] is more consistent with the text, history, and policies of the Code.[4] Under the conduct test, a right to payment arises when the conduct giving rise to the alleged liability occurred. Epstein's position is that any right to payment arising out of the prepetition conduct of Piper, no matter how remote, should be deemed a claim and provided for, pursuant to § 101(5), in this case. He argues that the relevant conduct giving rise to the alleged liability was Piper's prepetition manufacture, design, sale and distribution of allegedly defective aircraft. Specifically, he contends that, because Piper performed these acts prepetition, the potential victims, although not yet identifiable, hold claims under § 101(5) of the Code.

The Official Committee and Piper dispute the breadth of the definition of claim asserted by Epstein, arguing that the scope of claim cannot extend so far as to include unidentified, and presently unidentifiable, individuals with no discernible prepetition relationship to Piper. Recognizing, as Appellees do, that the conduct test may define claim too broadly in certain circumstances, several courts have recognized "claims" only for those individuals with some type of prepetition relationship with the debtor. *See In re: Jensen,* 995 F.2d 925, 929-31

---

[2] The accrued state law claim theory states that there is no claim for bankruptcy purposes until a claim has accrued under state law. The most notable case adopting this approach is the Third Circuit's decision in *In re: M. Frenville Co.,* 744 F.2d 332 (3d Cir.1984), *cert. denied,* 469 U.S. 1160, 105 S.Ct. 911, 83 L.Ed.2d 925 (1985). This test since has been rejected by a majority of courts as imposing too narrow an interpretation on the term claim. * * * We agree with these courts and decline to employ the state law claim theory.

[3] *See, e.g., A.H. Robins Co.,* 839 F.2d at 203 (Dalkon Shield); *In re: Waterman Steamship Corp.,* 141 B.R. 552, 556 (Bankr.S.D.N.Y.1992) (asbestos), *vacated on other grounds,* 157 B.R. 220 (Bankr.S.D.N.Y.1993); *In re: Johns-Manville Corp.,* 36 B.R. 743, 750 (Bankr.S.D.N.Y.1984) (asbestos).

[4] Epstein claims that the prepetition relationship test, by requiring identifiability of claimants, eliminates the words "contingent," "unmatured," "unliquidated," and "disputed" from the statute. He further argues that requiring a prepetition relationship is contrary to the Congressional objective that bankruptcy permit a complete settlement of the affairs of the debtor and a complete discharge and fresh start, as the claims of those persons whose injuries become manifest after the petition is filed could prove a drain on the reorganized debtor's assets for years to come.

(9th Cir. 1993); *In re: Chateaugay Corp.*, 944 F.2d 997, 1003-04 (2d Cir. 1991); *In re: Correct Mfg. Corp.*, 167 B.R. 458, 459 (Bankr.S.D.Ohio 1994). The prepetition relationship test, as adopted by the bankruptcy court and district court, requires "some prepetition relationship, such as contact, exposure, impact, or privity, between the debtor's prepetition conduct and the claimant" in order for the claimant to hold a § 101(5) claim.

Upon examination of the various theories, we agree with Appellees that the district court utilized the proper test in deciding that the Future Claimants did not hold a claim under § 101(5). Epstein's interpretation of "claim" and application of the conduct test would enable anyone to hold a claim against Piper by virtue of their potential future exposure to any aircraft in the existing fleet. Even the conduct test cases, on which Epstein relies, do not compel the result he seeks. In fact, the conduct test cases recognize that focusing solely on prepetition conduct, as Epstein espouses, would stretch the scope of § 101(5). Accordingly, the courts applying the conduct test also presume some prepetition relationship between the debtor's conduct and the claimant. *See A.H. Robins*, 839 F.2d 198, 203 (4th Cir. 1988); *In re Waterman Steamship Corp.*, 141 B.R. 552, 556 (Bankr.S.D.N.Y.).

While acknowledging that the district court's test is more consistent with the purposes of the Bankruptcy Code than is the conduct test supported by Epstein, we find that the test as set forth by the district court unnecessarily restricts the class of claimants to those who could be identified prior to the filing of the petition. Those claimants having contact with the debtor's product post-petition but prior to confirmation also could be identified, during the course of the bankruptcy proceeding, as potential victims, who might have claims arising out of debtor's prepetition conduct.

We therefore modify the test used by the district court and adopt what we will call the "*Piper* test" in determining the scope of the term claim under § 101(5): an individual has a § 101(5) claim against a debtor manufacturer if (i) events occurring before confirmation create a relationship, such as contact, exposure, impact, or privity, between the claimant and the debtor's product; and (ii) the basis for liability is the debtor's prepetition conduct in designing, manufacturing and selling the allegedly defective or dangerous product. The debtor's prepetition conduct gives rise to a claim to be administered in a case only if there is a relationship established before confirmation between an identifiable claimant or group of claimants and that prepetition conduct.[5]

---

[5] This modified test was set forth by the bankruptcy court in a related case, *In re: Piper Aircraft Corp.*, 169 B.R. 766 (Bankr.S.D.Fla.1994). By changing the focal point of the relationship from the petition date to the confirmation date, the test now encompasses those

In the instant case, it is clear that the Future Claimants fail the minimum requirements of the Piper test. There is no preconfirmation exposure to a specific identifiable defective product or any other preconfirmation relationship between Piper and the broadly defined class of Future Claimants. As there is no preconfirmation connection established between Piper and the Future Claimants, the Future Claimants do not hold a § 101(5) claim arising out of Piper's prepetition design, manufacture, sale, and distribution of allegedly defective aircraft.

III. Conclusion

For the foregoing reasons, we hold that the Future Claimants do not meet the threshold requirements of the *Piper* test and, as a result, do not hold claims as defined in § 101(5) of the Bankruptcy Code.

AFFIRMED.

NOTES

1. In *Fogel v. Zell*, 221 F.3d 955 (7th Cir. 2000), the debtor's predecessor, Interpace manufactured and sold defective prestressed concrete pipe to 10,000 end users including the the City of Denver. Interpace was sold to the debtor. By the time of the debtor's bankruptcy in 1991, eight purchasers of Interpace pipe had filed suit against the debtor asserting damages of $300 million. Denver was not among the eight because its Interpace sewer pipes had not yet burst. By the time the pipes did burst (causing $17 million in damages) it was 1997, long after the April 5, 1993 claims bar date fixed by the bankruptcy court in the debtor's case. Chief Judge Posner expressed doubt that Denver held a claim subject to discharge at the time of the bar date:

> Suppose a manufacturer goes bankrupt after a rash of products liability suits. And suppose that ten million people own automobiles manufactured by it that may have the same defect that gave rise to those suits but, so far, only a thousand have had an accident caused by the defect. Would it make any sense to hold that all ten million are tort creditors of the manufacturer * * * ? Does a pedestrian have a contingent claim against the driver of every automobile that might hit him? We are not alone in thinking that the answer to those questions is "no."

* * *

---

with injuries occurring post-petition but pre-confirmation, consistent with the policies underlying the Bankruptcy Code.

There has been, however, understandable pressure to expand the concept of a "claim" in bankruptcy in order to enable a nonarbitrary allocation of limited assets to be made between present and future claimants

* * *

However, mindful of the problem flagged by our automobile hypotheticals, the courts in these cases have suggested various limiting principles. We needn't go through them, for a reason that will appear in a moment; and anyway we greatly doubt that the issue is one that lends itself to governance by formula. It may not be possible to say anything more precise than that if it is reasonable to do so, bearing in mind the cost and efficacy of notice to potential future claimants and the feasibility of estimating the value of their claims before, perhaps long before, any harm giving rise to a matured tort claim has occurred, the bankruptcy court can bring those claimants into the bankruptcy proceeding and make provision for them in the final decree. This "test," if it can be dignified by such a term, would exclude the automobile hypotheticals; given that so far only one of every thousand pipes sold by Interpace have burst, this case may be closer to those hypotheticals than to asbestos and Dalkon Shield.

Id. at 960-962.

2. What are the consequences of the decision in *Piper Aircraft* with respect to the nonbankruptcy remedies of any future victims? This issue was before the court in *Lemelle v. Universal Mfg. Corp.*, 18 F.3d 1268 (5th Cir. 1994), and its resolution shows the great importance of whether the court chooses the Conduct test or the Relationship test in determining the existence of a claim. In *Lemelle* the victims died in a fire in a mobile home manufactured by Debtor before it filed in Chapter 11. The fire occurred two years after Debtor's reorganization plan had been confirmed and a discharge entered. The question was whether the victim's personal representative could bring a wrongful death action against the corporation into which Debtor's reorganized entity had been merged. The court held that the cause of action for wrongful death was not a claim that was discharged in Debtor's bankruptcy; hence, the successor corporation was potentially liable on the wrongful death claim.

> [A]t a minimum, there must be evidence that would permit the debtor to identify, during the course of the bankruptcy proceeding, potential victims and thereby permit notice to these potential victims of the pendency of the proceedings. * * * This record is devoid of any evidence of any pre-petition contact, privity, or other relationship between [Debtor] * * * [and the decedents]. We think the absence of this evidence

precludes a finding * * * that the claims asserted * * * were discharged * * *.

18 F.3d at 1277.

NOTE: MASS FUTURE CLAIMS IN BANKRUPTCY

The Asbestos Cases. Methods of dealing with mass future claims in bankruptcy have been explored by the courts in cases involving mass products liabilities torts. Prototypic cases are those involving claimants exposed to asbestos fibers. Exposure to asbestos may cause asbestosis, a disease of the lungs, lung cancer, and mesothelioma, an asbestos-related cancer of chest and abdominal membranes, as well as other pleural disorders. But these diseases normally have a long incubation period. Symptoms may not appear until many years after asbestos fibers were inhaled by the victim.

In the 1970s and 1980s, thousands of lawsuits were brought against asbestos producers based on injuries caused by asbestos. Many plaintiffs were employees of shipyards and other industries in which workers were exposed to asbestos in their employment. Faced by the prospect of unending personal injury and wrongful death suits, Johns-Manville and UNR Industries, both asbestos producers, filed in Chapter 11 in 1982.

At the time the asbestos producers filed for bankruptcy, many people who had been exposed to asbestos were already suffering from injuries attributable to these products. Others had not developed symptoms of injury but would develop symptoms in the future. What impact would bankruptcy have on the people who would eventually develop symptoms but who were without symptoms at the time of the Chapter 11 filings? To share in a debtor's bankruptcy, one must have a claim under § 101(10). The effect of recognizing or not recognizing a claim in bankruptcy by a person who has inhaled asbestos fibers but who has not yet developed symptoms of injury will differ depending on whether the manufacturer is liquidating in Chapter 7 or reorganizing in Chapter 11.

In Chapter 7, nonrecognition of a claim means that the victim will get no compensation for injury that becomes manifest after bankruptcy because the bankruptcy estate will have been liquidated and distributed to creditors. In Chapter 11, nonrecognition of the claim means that the manufacturer's potential liability is not discharged under § 1141(d)(1)(A). Under that provision, confirmation of a plan of reorganization discharges the debtor from any "debt" that arose before the date of the confirmation of the plan of reorganization. Since "debt" is defined as liability on a claim, § 101(12), if a victim is held to have no claim because symptoms of injury do not develop until after confirmation, the victim is not barred from asserting a cause of action against the reorganized debtor.

As a practical matter it may be impossible to successfully reorganize a business that has massive undischarged future claims hanging over it. Since the asbestos producers desired to stay in business, they chose Chapter 11 reorganization. Thus, it was in their interest that all persons with potential causes of action be classified as holders of claims so that their rights could be terminated by the § 1141 discharge. But it may not be possible to stretch the definition of claim to include all potential claimants. Although the "relationship test" may be sufficiently broad to accord claim status to employees and customers who were exposed to asbestos fibers prepetition, it might not include those exposed afterwards or who were exposed to ambient asbestos without regard to any relationship with its producer or distributor.

Trust for Future Claims. The central question raised by the asbestos cases is how might a successful reorganization occur under these circumstances and on what terms? In the belief that a bankruptcy court's equitable powers might be broad enough to make provision for future claims whether or not they meet the definition of "claim" under § 101, the *Manville* reorganization plan established a trust from which claimants might collect compensatory damages by mediation, arbitration or traditional tort litigation. In confirming the plan, the court in *Kane v. Johns–Manville Corp.*, 843 F.2d 636, 640 (2d Cir. 1988), described the trust fund device as follows:

> The purpose of the Trust is to provide a means of satisfying Manville's ongoing personal injury liability while allowing Manville to maximize its value by continuing as an ongoing concern. To fulfill this purpose, the Plan seeks to ensure that health claims can be asserted only against the Trust and that Manville's operating entities will be protected from an onslaught of crippling lawsuits that could jeopardize the entire reorganization effort. To this end, the parties agreed that as a condition precedent to confirmation of the Plan, the Bankruptcy Court would issue an injunction channeling all asbestos-related personal injury claims to the Trust (the "Injunction"). The Injunction provides that asbestos health claimants may proceed only against the Trust to satisfy their claims and may not sue Manville, its other operating entities, and certain other specified parties, including Manville's insurers. Significantly, the Injunction applies to all health claimants, both present and future, regardless of whether they technically have dischargeable "claims" under the Code. The Injunction applies to any suit to recover "on or with respect to any Claim, Interest or Other Asbestos Obligation." "Claim" covers the present claimants, who are categorized as Class–4 unsecured creditors under the Plan and who have dischargeable "claims" within

the meaning of § 101(4). The future claimants are subject to the Injunction under the rubric of "Other Asbestos Obligation," which is defined by the Plan as asbestos-related health liability caused by pre-petition exposure to Manville asbestos, regardless of when the individual develops clinically observable symptoms. Thus, while the future claimants are not given creditor status under the Plan, they are nevertheless treated identically to the present claimants by virtue of the Injunction, which channels all claims to the Trust.

The Manville Trust, established in 1986 under the *Manville* plan of reorganization, was initially given about $2 billion in assets, which included a substantial amount of Manville's common stock, and the right to receive 20% of Manville's future profits, for payment of claims. The number of claimants greatly exceeded the original estimate and more resources had to be poured into the trust.

The trust device has been used in other future claims cases. In the best known of these, the claimants were women who had used the Dalkon Shield intrauterine device manufactured by A.H. Robins Co. By the middle 1970s, millions of women were using IUDs, and the Dalkon Shield was one of the most prominent of these devices. By the end of the 1970s, hundreds of lawsuits had been brought against Robins for damages for health problems attributed to use of the Dalkon Shield. Some of the suits resulted in multi-million dollar punitive damage awards. Robins faced a problem similar to that of the asbestos producers. Symptoms of injury from use of the Dalkon Shield might not become manifest until passage of a substantial period of time after use of the device had terminated. Beset by negative publicity and fearing that it would not be able to pay the punitive damage awards sure to lie ahead, Robins filed in Chapter 11 in 1985. The Dalkon Shield saga is recounted in Richard B. Sobol, *Bending the Law, The Story of the Dalkon Shield Bankruptcy* (1991) (hereafter cited as "Sobol").

Other prominent examples of use of a trust are: (1) The Dow Corning bankruptcy in which a Chapter 11 plan was confirmed to compensate women injured by breast implants containing Dow Corning silicone gel. The plan set up a trust including $3.2 billion for payments to 175,000 women who had filed claims and an additional 125,000 expected to file in the future. 11 BNA Bankr. L. Rep. 1073 (1999), and (2) the W. R. Grace Chapter 11 plan, entailing payment of $3 billion for asbestos claims, which called for an early 2009 emergence from bankruptcy, was still under challenge by claimants late in 2008. *See*, Peg Brickley, *Claimants Seek to Block Grace's Bankruptcy Exit*, Wall St. J., Oct. 22, 2008, at B7.

Channeling Injunctions. A major purpose of creating a trust to pay future claims is to safeguard the reorganized debtor from postbankruptcy lawsuits by future claimants. As indicated above, in the Manville bankruptcy the bankruptcy court faced the issue squarely by issuing a "channeling" injunction compelling all future claimants to seek compensation solely from the trust rather than from the reorganized debtor. The Second Circuit upheld confirmation of the plan but declined to pass on the validity of the injunction. Part of the bankruptcy court's purpose in enjoining claims against the reorganized debtor was to allow the reorganized debtor to attract investment and generate sufficient profits to meet the requirements of future claimants. Uncertainties about the validity of the injunction have clouded Manville's prospects, and Manville management pressed for new legislation explicitly authorizing courts to issue channeling injunctions. In 1994 Congress generously responded to Manville's entreaties by enacting an elaborate piece of special legislation, § 524(g), that applies only to asbestos claims and validates the injunctions issued in *Manville* and other asbestos cases. It authorizes similar injunctions to be issued in the future in other asbestos cases so long as the debtors in those cases have taken the same precautions to safeguard the rights of victims observed by Manville in its trust/injunction mechanism. The injunctions may even enjoin litigation against third parties (e.g., officers, directors, and insurance companies) if those parties may be liable for the claims or demands made on the debtor. In order to assure that Manville and UNR, "both of which have met and surpassed the standards imposed in this section, will be able to take advantage of the certainty it provides without having to reopen their cases" (Section-by-Section Description § 111, 140 Cong.Rec. H10765 (Oct. 4, 1994)), § 524(g) applies to cases already filed.

Notwithstanding enactment of § 524(g), the *Manville* case continues to pose jurisdictional puzzles for the courts. The Supreme Court is now considering whether the Second Circuit erred in restricting the scope of the *Manville* channeling injunction's release of their third party "direct action" claims against its insurers. *Travelers Indemnity Co. v. Bailey*, Sup.Ct. No. 08-295 (argued Mar. 21, 2009).

A Federal "Global Solution"? Asbestos litigation has transcended the status of merely posing challenging legal issues of management of mass tort claims and assumed the condition of a national crisis, if not scandal. Insurance companies predict that a million asbestos claims would ultimately be filed; according to a RAND study, 600,000 already have, and, although asbestos has not been widely used for more than 30 years, the number of claims increases each year. Shailagh Murray & Kathryn Kranhold, *Unsettling Dust: Asbestos Factions Struggle to Settle Their 30-Year War*, Wall St. J., Oct. 15, 2003, at A1. Labor unions complained that asbestos litigation was closing down businesses and costing jobs. Some studies claim that as many as 60,000 workers have lost jobs as a direct result of asbestos-related bankruptcies. *See* 15 BNA Bankr. L.

Rep. 195-196 (2003). Law firms devoted entirely to representing asbestos claimants have sprung up as courts found liability not just against entities that had manufactured products containing asbestos but also against those using or selling such products. Some individuals brought multiple claims against every conceivable defendant; one brought 62 claims. *See* Michelle J. White, *Why the Asbestos Genie Won't Stay in the Bankruptcy Bottle*, 70 U. Cin. L.Rev. 1319 (2002).

Sick claimants stood by anxiously as an increasing share of litigation proceeds went to claimants with no symptoms of asbestosis or cancer as courts allowed recoveries by those who claimed mental anguish damages resulting from fear of developing cancer caused by work-related exposure to asbestos with no proof of physical manifestation of the claimed emotional distress. *Norfolk & Western Railway Company v. Ayers*, 538 U.S. 135 (2003). Business entities found themselves blindsided by asbestos claims arising from activities of acquired companies that occurred many years before the acquisition. White quotes a RAND study that concluded that only about one-third of compensation expenditures reached the claimants, with the remainder going to administrative expenses and lawyers. White, *supra*, at 1327.

Firms have stampeded into bankruptcy in an attempt to limit their asbestos liability. White counted 48 firms that filed between 1982 and 1999, and an additional 30 firms that filed between 2000 and 2002. *See* White, *supra*, at 1320. Managers, contract creditors and asbestos trial lawyers discovered a community of interest in discharging the debtor firms while establishing a largely insurer funded trust to handle asbestos claims.

Coalitions of interested parties began to lobby Congress for a "global" settlement. A $140 billion trust fund has been proposed, financed by defendants and insurers; the federal government would not contribute. Murray & Kranhold, *supra*, chronicles developments in the effort to persuade Congress to set up such a trust fund, similar to the toxic waste superfund, from which payments would be made to claimants. In recent years Congress has given consideration to a bill under which workers injured from asbestos exposure would receive monetary awards based on the severity of their injury. The largest award of $1.1 million would go to workers with mesothelioma, a deadly form of lung cancer. When the trust fund is set up, all lawsuits alleging injury from asbestos exposure would be barred unless the fund runs out of money. Businesses and insurers would pay into the fund for an estimated 30 years. However, controversy over which industries would have to contribute and how much they would have to contribute prevented enactment

Due Process Requirements. Mullane v. Central Hanover Bank & Trust Co., 339 U.S. 306 (1950), held that before a court can deprive a person of property, due process requires notice and opportunity for hearing; notice by publication may meet this standard if persons to be notified are unknown. Such notice was given in the *Robins* settlement. There the court dealt with the future claims issue by ruling that a woman's claim arose for purposes of bankruptcy law at the time she began use of the Dalkon Shield even though injury might not occur until after the date of confirmation of the *Robins* plan. Sobol, at 113–114. This ruling was upheld in *Grady v. A.H. Robins Co.*, 839 F.2d 198 (4th Cir. 1988), which described future claims as "contingent." A notice of the bar date, which was published widely, said:

> "IF YOU * * * may have used the Dalkon Shield but have not yet experienced an injury * * * and if you wish to assert a claim against [Robins], the United States Bankruptcy Court * * * must receive your claim * * * on or before April 30, 1986 or you will lose the right to make a claim."

Sobol, at 110. Women who had not submitted claims by the bar date were allowed to claim from the trust by showing that they first manifested injury after the bar date and that they lacked knowledge either of the bar date or of the fact that the IUD that she used was a Dalkon Shield. Sobol, at 223. The plan enjoined all persons holding claims from commencing or continuing any action on the claims outside the plan. Given the likelihood that many women either would not see the bar date notice or, if free of symptoms, would not act on it, the *Robins* plan provisions dealing with future claims raise due process concerns. Nevertheless, the *Robins* experience is widely viewed as one of the more successful attempts at managing the problem of mass torts through the Chapter 11 trust/ channeling injunction devices. Georgene Vairo, *Mass Tort Bankruptcies: The Who, The Why and The How*, 78 Am. Bankr. L. J. 93 (2004) (99% of claims resolved without litigation or formal arbitration enabling trust to make pro rata distributions equal to 102% of initial claims and resolve 300,000 claims within 10 years before terminating in 2000).

In order to address the due process issue, some courts dealing with mass torts appointed a legal representative to act in a fiduciary capacity on behalf of future claimants. In mass asbestos cases, § 524(g)(4)(B) now requires such a representative if future "demands" are to be channeled to a § 524(g) trust. Such a representative may file claims, investigate, negotiate, cast votes, and exercise the powers of a creditors' committee. The National Bankruptcy Review Commission Report § 2.1.2 (1997) recommended that that the Bankruptcy Code be amended to require appointment of such legal representatives outside the mass asbestos cases, and commentators, e.g., Alan N. Resnick, *Bankruptcy As a Vehicle For Resolving Enterprise–Threatening Mass Tort Liability*, 148 U. Pa. L. Rev. 2045, 2078 (2000), concur. Both the *NBRC Report* (§ 2.1.4) and Professor Resnick also recommend empowering courts to issue channeling injunctions in appropriate cases to preserve assets for future claimants.

Although courts and litigants are becoming more sure-footed in dealing with future tort claims, the subject will be clouded with doubt until substantial amendments are made to the Bankruptcy Code. The Resnick article cited above is a helpful guide to the formulation of such amendments.

2. EQUITABLE RIGHTS

Claim is defined in § 101(5) to include "a right to an equitable remedy for breach of performance if such breach gives rise to a right to payment." The apparent meaning of the quoted language is that the equitable remedy need not give rise to a right to payment, but the right to the remedy must be based on breach of an obligation to the claimant on which a right to payment could be based. The most common example is a breach of contract that gives rise not only to a legal right to recover damages but also to an equitable right to specific performance of the contract. The definition would appear to mean that the right to obtain the equitable remedy of specific performance is a claim. Under this reading of the quoted language, a debtor could discharge an obligation to make specific performance so long as that was the non-debtor's sole remedy under otherwise applicable nonbankruptcy law. The claimant who loses the remedy for specific performance can have its claim valued under § 502(c)(2) as a right to payment. But the court in *In re Udell*, 18 F.3d 403 (7th Cir. 1994), read the quoted language differently and cast doubt on the dischargeability of specific performance obligations arising out of contracts. *Udell* is critically discussed in the following case.

In re Ward
United States Bankruptcy Court, D. Massachusetts, 1996.
194 B.R. 703.

■ JAMES F. QUEENAN, JR., Bankruptcy Judge.

Seeking to enforce a noncompetition clause in its franchise agreement, The Maids International, Inc. ("Maids") has brought this complaint to enjoin Michael E. Ward and Angela L. Ward (the "Debtors") from owning or operating a maintenance and cleaning service within a fifty mile radius of the franchised territory. Maids contends neither the Debtors' bankruptcy filing nor rejection of their covenant not to compete affects its right to an injunction against the Debtors' competition. I am thus faced with the question of whether Maids' right to injunctive relief is a "claim" within the meaning of the Bankruptcy Code and hence subject to being discharged. * * *

I. Facts

The facts are not in dispute. Maids has developed a system for establishing and operating a household maintenance and cleaning service. Having a principal office in Omaha, Nebraska, Maids franchises its rights in the system to numerous parties throughout the United States.

On April 10, 1989, Maids signed a franchise agreement with a corporation owned and operated by the Debtors named Award Services, Inc. ("Award"). In addition to signing on behalf of Award, the Debtors signed the agreement personally as guarantors of Award's performance thereunder. The agreement also includes the Debtors within the meaning of the term "Franchise", thereby making them jointly responsible with Award. Under the agreement, Maids gave Award the exclusive right to use its system and the name "Maids" in Concord, Massachusetts and in several nearby towns. In return, Award paid Maids $15,900 and obligated itself (and the Debtors) to pay Maids a royalty based on a percentage of its gross sales at rates which range from 4.5% to 7%, depending upon the amount of weekly gross sales. The agreement was for an initial term of five years.

The following provisions of the franchise agreement are of relevance to the present proceeding:

XV. Covenants

. . . . .

C. FRANCHISEE further covenants that for a period of two (2) years after the termination or nonrenewal of the franchise, regardless of the cause of termination, it shall not, either directly or indirectly, for itself, or on behalf of or in conjunction with any other person, persons, partnership or corporation, own, maintain, engage in, or participate in the operation of a maintenance and cleaning service system within a radius of fifty (50) miles of the area designated hereunder or any then existing The Maids Unit Franchise.

. . . . .

E. FRANCHISEE acknowledges that a violation of any covenant in this Paragraph will cause irreparable damage to FRANCHISOR, the exact amount of which may not be subject to reasonable or accurate ascertainment, and therefore, FRANCHISEE does hereby consent that in the event of such violation, FRANCHISOR shall as a matter of right be entitled to injunctive relief to restrain FRANCHISEE, or anyone acting for or on behalf (sic), from violating said covenants, or any of them. Such remedies, however, shall be cumulative and in addition to any other remedies to which FRANCHISOR may then be entitled. FRANCHISEE represents and acknowledges that in the event of the termination of this Agreement for whatever cause, its experience and capabili-

Chapter 3. Claims 95

ties are such that it can obtain employment in business engaged in other lines or of a different nature than that of the operation of a maintenance and cleaning service franchise and that the enforcement of a remedy by way of injunction will not prevent it from earning a livelihood. In the event FRANCHISOR brings suit to enforce any provision hereof, FRANCHISOR shall be entitled to receive, in addition to any relief or remedy granted, the cost of bringing such suit, including reasonable attorney's fees. The covenants set forth in this Paragraph XV shall survive the termination or expiration of this Agreement.

. . . . .

XVIII. Resolution of dispute

Except as to a breach for non-payment of any fee for royalty or advertising as set forth heretofore, any controversy or claim arising out of or relating to this Agreement, or the breach thereof, shall be settled by arbitration conducted in Omaha, Nebraska in accordance with the commercial Arbitration Rules of the American Arbitration Association and judgement upon any award rendered by the Arbitrator may be entered in any court having jurisdiction thereof.

. . . . .

XXVIII. Liability for breach

In the event of any default on the part of either party hereto, in addition to any other remedies of the aggrieved party, the party in default shall pay to the aggrieved party all amounts due and all damages, costs and expenses, including reasonable attorneys fees, incurred by the aggrieved party as a result of any such default.

. . . . .

XXXIII. Equitable relief

Nothing herein contained shall bar the right of either party to obtain injunction relief against threatened conduct that will cause loss or damages under the usual equity rules, including the applicable rules for obtaining preliminary injunctions, provided an appropriate bond against damages be provided.

. . . . .

The franchisee agreement expired on April 9, 1994, the end of its five year term. Thereafter, the Debtors commenced operation of a cleaning service within the franchised territory. They operate the business under the name "Mops" and do not hold themselves out as operating a franchise of Maids.

Maids responded to this competition with a series of legal actions. It first commenced an arbitration proceeding in Omaha with the American Arbitration Association. This was uncontested by the Debtors. On March 31, 1995, the arbitrator awarded Maids damages (including interest) of $29,232. He also ordered the Debtors to cease and desist the ownership or operation of a maintenance and cleaning service until April 9, 1996, within a radius of fifty miles from the franchised area or within a radius of fifty miles from any Maids franchise existing on April 9, 1994. Maids then brought suit in the District Court of Douglas County, Nebraska. On July 20, 1995, that court entered a default judgment against the Debtors in the sum of $61,056. Apparently this was in part a confirmation of the arbitration award. At no time has any court entered an injunction against the Debtors competing, in confirmation of the arbitration award or otherwise. Maids next brought its attack closer to home. On November 1, 1995, it filed suit on the judgment in the District Court of Concord, Massachusetts. That court authorized attachments of the Debtors' residence and bank accounts.

Shortly thereafter, on November 13, 1995, the Debtors filed a petition with this court requesting entry of an order for relief under chapter 7 of the Bankruptcy Code. Undeterred, Maids on January 25, 1996 filed its complaint commencing the present adversary proceeding. In its complaint Maids requested an injunction against the Debtors owning or operating a maintenance and cleaning establishment within a fifty mile radius of the franchised territory. At the same time, Maids filed a motion for a temporary restraining order and asked for an emergency hearing. At the hearing on February 5, 1996, I denied the motion, dismissed the complaint and ordered Maids to file a proof of claim. Maids thereafter filed a proof of claim within the permissible filing period.

II. Validity of debtors' covenant not to compete

* * *

Covenants not to compete are often made by sellers of small businesses, key employees, franchisees and partners. The covenant is generally valid under state law so long as its time period, geographic area and covered activities go no further than what is reasonably necessary to protect the other's business and goodwill. For this reason, the wording of the covenant is usually restricted in time and area, and sometimes in scope of activity. The Debtors' covenant was so restricted. It is valid and enforceable.

III. Maids' injunctive rights as a "claim"

The Debtors are clearly in breach of their covenant not to compete. Breach of the ordinary contract gives rise only to a claim for damages. Maids, however, has the additional right under state law to obtain an injunction against the Debtors' competition, without regard to the provision in the agreement permitting such relief. Although many of the decisions do not reach the issue, engaging instead in what is often a mechanical search for "executoriness," breach of a covenant not to compete presents a question which has proven difficult for the courts: Do the nondebtor's injunctive rights constitute a "claim" so as to be subject to discharge? The Debtors' discharge hinges upon this issue. A discharge in bankruptcy releases a debtor only as to liability on a "debt,"[7] which is defined as "liability on a claim."[8]

The Code defines "claim" as follows:

(A) right to payment, whether or not such right is reduced to judgment, liquidated, unliquidated, fixed, contingent, matured, unmatured, disputed, undisputed, legal, equitable, secured, or unsecured; or

(B) right to an equitable remedy for breach of performance if such breach gives rise to a right to payment, whether or not such right to an equitable remedy is reduced to judgment, fixed, contingent, matured, unmatured, disputed, undisputed, secured, or unsecured.[9]

Maids unquestionably has a "right to an equitable remedy" for breach of the Debtors' covenant. But does the breach also give rise to a "right to payment" within the meaning of the statute? That question is not answered by Maids having obtained a damage judgment. As shall be explained, the damages available for breach of the covenant must be an alternative to an equitable remedy if "a right to payment" is to be present. For all we know, the arbitration award and default judgment Maids obtained were only for damages accrued to the date of the hearings, and did not include the future damages that are an alternative to equitable relief.

The only order issued against the Debtors competing is the arbitrator's cease and desist order. No court has entered an injunction against the competition. Even if one had, it would make no difference on the claim issue. The inclusion of an equitable remedy within the definition of "claim" applies "whether or not such right to an equitable remedy is reduced to judgment...."[10]

* * *

Focussing more on the statutory definition, some courts hold the nondebtor party's injunctive right is not a claim because it is present only if the remedy at law is "inadequate," or only if the threatened harm is "irreparable," concluding from this that the nondebtor has no right to payment within the meaning of the statutory definition. Although these courts are correct in ruling a right to payment must exist under nonbankruptcy law, their holding that there is no right to payment for breach of a covenant not to compete conflicts with the

---

[7] § 524(a).

[8] § 101(12).

[9] § 101(5).

[10] Id.

damage rights of the beneficiary of a covenant as well as with the general standard employed by courts in determining whether a party's remedy at law is adequate. This requires some explanation.

An injunction against breach of the covenant is a grant of specific performance. As a result of the historical separation of courts of law and equity, such an equitable remedy is available only if the remedy at law, typically damages, is "inadequate." Courts take into account a number of factors in determining whether damages are inadequate. Principal among them are difficulty in proving the existence and amount of damages with reasonable certainty, difficulty in collecting a monetary judgment, and uncertainty that the benefits of a monetary judgment would be equivalent to the promised performance.[24] The rule has been stated as follows: "The adequate remedy at law, which will preclude the grant of specific performance of a contract by a court of equity, must be as certain, prompt, complete, and efficient to attain the ends of justice as a decree of specific performance."[25] Put another way, "the remedy at law, in order to exclude a concurrent remedy at equity, must be as complete, as practical and as efficient to the ends of justice and its prompt administration, as the remedy at equity."[26]

Courts thus compare the remedies at law and equity to see which is more effective in serving the ends of justice. Difficulty in fixing damages is only one factor in that equation. In any event, damages need only be difficult, not impossible, to prove for equitable relief to be available. Comparison of the two remedies usually leads to the grant of equitable relief. Doubts as to the adequacy of the remedy at law are resolved in favor of granting equitable relief. In sum, courts look quite favorably upon equitable relief. This has led one author to conclude that the adequate remedy rule is essentially dead.[30]

Loss of future profits is typically a principal element of damages for breach of a covenant not to compete. The evidentiary problems here for Maids and other covenant beneficiaries are obvious. The proof involves futuristic projections which are especially subject to contest. Courts therefore readily grant an injunction for breach of a covenant not to compete. Indeed, the injured party

---

[24] *E.g.*, Arthur L. Corbin, 5A Corbin on Contracts 5A § 1142 (1964); Restatement (Second) of Contracts § 360 (1981).

[25] *National Marking Mach. Co. v. Triumph Mfg. Co.*, 13 F.2d 6, 9 (8th Cir.1926) * * *.

[26] *Walla Walla City v. Walla Walla Water Co.*, 172 U.S. 1, 12, 19 S.Ct. 77, 82, 43 L.Ed. 341 (1898).

[30] Douglas Laycock, *The Death of the Irreparable Injury Rule*, 103 Harv.L.Rev. 688 (1990).

invariably requests injunctive relief because an injunction gives strong assurance he will receive precisely what was bargained for. This avoids the trauma of future injury, the need to prove damages, and problems in collecting a money judgment. The request for equitable relief has historically been regarded as the election of a preferred remedy.

If the beneficiary of a covenant not to compete elects to receive damages for loss of future profits, he gets the lost profits. Lost profits are a proper element of damages for any breach of contract so long as at the time of the contract the breaching party had reason to know they would be the probable result of breach.[34] The Debtors certainly had that knowledge. The purpose of their covenant was to protect Maids' business. Although damages must be established with reasonable certainty,[35] an approximation rather than mathematical accuracy is all that is required.[36] The perceived difficulty in proving lost profits is less present today because of the receptive attitude of modern courts toward proof of sophisticated financial data through expert testimony.[37] The award of damages for lost future profits is now a commonplace remedy for breach of all kinds of contracts.

Maids therefore has the right to obtain either damages for the Debtors' future competition or an injunction against the competition.[39] As a result, in the words of the statute, Maids has a "right to an equitable remedy for breach of performance... [which] breach gives rise to a right to payment...."[40] As an alternative remedy, this right to payment permits a dollar sign to be placed on the equitable remedy, as is done with other claims. Including equitable remedies within the statute's definition of "claim" is therefore supported by a strong bankruptcy policy—equal treatment of similar rights. And because a "claim" is subject to discharge, another important bankruptcy policy is promoted—the policy favoring a debtor's fresh start, unencumbered by past commitments.

In *In re Udell*,[42] the Seventh Circuit came to the opposite conclusion, and in the process added greatly to the confusion in this troubled area of the law. The debtor there had signed an agreement not to compete with his former

---

[34] Restatement (Second) of Contracts § 351 (1981).

[35] *Id.* at § 352 (1981).

[36] *Id.*, cmt. a.

[37] *Id.*

[39] He is also entitled to compensation for any damages already incurred. * * *

[40] § 101(5); see National Bankruptcy Conference, Reforming The Bankruptcy Code 202 (1994), which adopts this view.

[42] 18 F.3d 403 (7th Cir.1994).

employer, Standard Carpetland USA, Inc. The covenant was for three years, commencing on termination of employment, and covered a fifty mile radius from the store where the debtor worked. It further provided: "In the event of [the debtor's] actual or threatened breach of the [covenant], Carpetland shall be entitled to an injunction restraining [the debtor] as well as reimbursement for reasonably [sic] attorneys fees incurred in securing said judgment and stipulated damages in the sum of $25,000." Soon after leaving his employment, the debtor purchased a carpet store which he claimed did not compete in the same market as Carpetland's. He sued Carpetland in state court, seeking past due commissions and other compensation. Contending the debtor had breached his agreement not to compete, Carpetland counterclaimed for damages and an injunction against the debtor operating his new store. The state court issued the requested preliminary injunction. The debtor appealed and then filed a chapter 13 petition. Carpetland moved for relief from the automatic stay in order to pursue the state court litigation.

In approving relief from stay as a proper exercise of discretion, the Seventh Circuit in *Udell* held Carpetland's injunctive rights were not a "claim" and hence were not dischargeable in bankruptcy. Although not finding the statutory definition of claim ambiguous, the court nevertheless looked to the legislative history that accompanied the final version of the definition, which reconciled differences in the House and Senate bills.[45] It saw significance in the following statement made on the floors of both houses of Congress:

> Section 101(4)(B) [now § 101(5)(B)] represents a modification of the House-passed bill to include [sic] the definition of "claim" a right to an equitable remedy for breach of performance if such breach gives rise to a right to payment. This is intended to cause the liquidation or estimation of contingent rights of payment for which there may be an alternative equitable remedy with the result that the equitable remedy will be susceptible to being discharged in bankruptcy. For example, in some States, a judgment for specific performance may be satisfied by an alternative right to payment, in the event performance is refused; in that event the creditor entitled to specific performance would have a "claim" for purposes of proceeding under title 11.

> On the other hand, rights to an equitable remedy for breach of performance with respect to which such breach does not give rise to a right

---

[45] The definition in the Senate bill included only "right to payment", with no reference to an equitable remedy. The House bill referred to an equitable remedy in these words: "right to an equitable remedy for breach of performance if such breach does not give rise to a right to payment. . .." H.R. 8200, 95th Cong. 1st Sess. § 101(4)(B) (1977).

Chapter 3. Claims 101

to payment are not "claims" and would therefore not be susceptible to discharge in bankruptcy.[46]

The *Udell* court constructed a confusing alternative test from this floor statement. It seized on the awkward phrase "with respect to which such breach does not give rise to a right to payment" appearing in the last sentence. Because the phrase arguably modifies "equitable remedy" rather than "breach of performance," the court concluded equitable rights are a claim if payment arises from their exercise. This is opposed to the wording of the statute, which clearly requires that the breach, not the equitable remedy, give rise to a right to payment. And the test makes no sense because equitable remedies are typically designed to provide nonmonetary relief. Having thus created a virtually unpassable test, the court ruled it was flunked by the facts before it because the right to obtain liquidated damages arose from the contract, not from an equitable remedy under it.

The *Udell* court also fashioned another test which, if passed, would make an equitable remedy a claim. It here focussed on the reference in the floor statement to a right to payment being an "alternative" to the equitable remedy. From this the court concluded *all* right to payment must be an alternative to the equitable remedy. Because state courts would enforce the parties' agreement by granting both damages and an injunction, the court ruled an alternative right to payment was not present, so Carpetland's rights failed this test as well. This reasoning ignores Carpetland's right to damages for future loss, which is an alternative to its equitable remedy. The floor statement's reference to a right to payment being an alternative to equitable relief is understandable because the claim for future loss is the monetary equivalent to the right to an injunction against further competition. Nor is there any reason to believe Congress intended that this alternative right to payment be the only right to payment. The statute does not say so. The injured party is obviously entitled to compensation for damages already incurred by the time of trial, as well as to an injunction against future competition. The liquidated damage clause before the court was presumably designed to provide this compensation because the parties also agreed upon an injunction to prevent future loss. *Udell* thus commits the double sin of elevating legislative history above the statute's plain wording and then misunderstanding the legislative history.

The real basis for the *Udell* court's holding emerges from the concurring opinion of Judge Flaum. He thought the majority opinion "dodges this statute's

---

[46] 124 CONG.REC. H11090 (daily ed. Sept. 28, 1978); S17406 (daily ed. Oct. 6, 1978) (statements of Rep. Edwards and Sen. DeConcini).

plain language in an effort to reach a sensible result." To Judge Flaum, and one suspects to the other panel members, discharge in bankruptcy of an injunction against competition is like a bankruptcy discharge of an injunction against trespassing, polluting, stalking or battering. Because he thought the debtor's discharge would have similar "patently absurd consequences," Judge Flaum believed the plain language of the statute should not be followed.

Judge Flaum's reasoning leaves much to be desired as well, quite apart from his willingness to elide what he admits to be the statute's plain wording. The case concerned breach of contract, not trespass, pollution, stalking or battery. Moreover, trespass and the like is prohibited by law, without regard to the existence of an injunction. So a bankruptcy discharge does not terminate the obligation to refrain from such conduct. In the final analysis, the decision in *Udell* comes down to this: The court could not bring itself to equate an injunction against breach of contract with a monetary judgment for breach of contract which is routinely discharged in bankruptcy.

IV. Conclusion

In summary, although the decisions are in disarray, Maids' alternative right to damages from the Debtors' future competition in breach of their covenant not to compete is a "right to payment" within the meaning of the statutory definition of an equitable claim. Hence, under the definition, Maids' injunctive rights constitute a claim. That state courts consider damages inadequate when compared to the equitable remedy of an injunction is beside the point. Although damages for breach of the covenant, particularly damages for lost future profits, are difficult to fix, courts are perfectly capable of doing so. This alternative right to damages fits into the statutory definition of an equitable claim very well. The same breach, a debtor's competition and threat of further competition, "gives rise" to both a damage claim and injunctive rights. The definition imposes no requirement that the claimant elect to receive a monetary payment, that compliance with the injunction require an expenditure of funds, or that the equitable remedy, as opposed to the breach, give rise to a right to payment. Following the statute's plain meaning promotes two fundamental policies of the Bankruptcy Code—the policy favoring a debtor's fresh start and the policy favoring equality among holders of similar rights.

NOTES

1. *Kennedy v. Medicap Pharmacies, Inc.*, 267 F.3d 493 (6th Cir. 2001), adopts the *Udell* interpretation of the statute and holds that the right to equitable relief constitutes a claim only if it is an alternative to a right to payment or if compliance with the equitable order will itself require payment of money. Judge Queenan's well reasoned holding in *Ward* is a minority view.

2. The prototypic case for finding a right to an equitable remedy to be a claim in bankruptcy is specific performance for breach of a contract to convey real estate in which the seller is the debtor in bankruptcy. Even though under state law damages for the breach of a land sale contract is an inadequate remedy because land is unique, strong bankruptcy policies of equality of treatment for creditors and a fresh start for debtors support the conclusion that the buyer's only right in bankruptcy should be a claim for money damages instead of a right to specific performance. National Bankruptcy Conference, *Reforming the Bankruptcy Code* 132 (Rev.ed.1997), takes the view that these bankruptcy policies, on balance, "outweigh any nonbankruptcy policies that support specific performance" of covenants not to compete. But some fact situations regarding noncompete covenants raise difficult problems.

To enjoin former franchisees like Barry Udell from selling carpets or Michael and Angela Ward from providing maintenance and cleaning services seems harsh. There is no indication that their breach of the noncompete covenant threatened their former franchisors' businesses. Thus, without paying very much for the noncompete covenant, their former franchisors would be making it very difficult for them to start over after bankruptcy. But what of the case in which the noncompete covenant was a key element in the sale of a business, the existence of which was essential to protect the good will the buyer was purchasing? For example Likeable Phil, who had built his pricey fish market, "Phil's Phish," on his sparkling personality over the years, sold to Dull Don who was willing to pay three times the value of the tangible assets for the business if Phil would sign an ironclad ten-year, 25–mile noncompete covenant and go away. Phil took the money and ran. Within a year he had lost everything in subprime mortgage loans, filed in Chapter 7, scheduled the noncompete covenant obligation as a debt owing to Don, obtained postpetition financing and opened a fish store down the street from Don which he named "Phresh Phish." You may assume that any claim for damages against Phil would be valueless and that Don's business was sinking fast. Should Don be able to enjoin Phil from proceeding with his new store? phresh start or head start?

3. Toward the end of the opinion in *Ward*, the court discussed Judge Flaum's view in *Udell* that a literal interpretation of the statutory definition of "claim" would result in a "patent absurdity" is apparently based on the intentional tort and criminal examples that he mentions. Here Flaum is on solid ground. It would be absurd to allow a person to avoid having to comply with an injunction or order against such tortious conduct as maintaining a nuisance or such criminal conduct as stalking or battering a victim merely by filing a petition in bankruptcy. Indeed, criminal and regulatory orders obtained by governmental units are specifically excepted from the automatic stay provisions of the Code. § 362(b)(1) and (4). Even money damages arising out of such conduct are generally nondischargeable in Chapter 7 cases. § 523(a)(6). And there is no dispute, generally speaking, that equitable remedies restraining acts that prospectively endanger public health and safety should not be dischargeable.

Most of the litigation in the area of equitable remedies in bankruptcy has arisen from environmental cases in which public health and safety are implicated. *In re Torwico Electronics*, 8 F.3d 146 (3d Cir. 1993), is an example of a case in which a debtor was not required to comply with a state environmental order regarding cleaning up hazardous wastes by filing in bankruptcy, while *Ohio v. Kovacs*, 469 U.S. 274 (1985), shows that circumstances may exist even in environmental cases in which discharge may be appropriate. But *Udell* is a contract case, and here a literal interpretation of § 101 ("claim") would not result in a "patent absurdity." Carpetland has been harmed by Udell's breach (its business is not worth as much as it would have been had Udell not broken the contract), and presumably Udell would have to answer in damages for the breach but for the state law rule that damages are considered to be too speculative in cases of breach of noncompete covenants. David G. Epstein, Steve H. Nickles & James J. White, *Bankruptcy* § 11–2 (1993), views breach of a covenant not to compete as giving the nondebtor "not only a right to equitable injunctive relief but also a right to payment, i.e., [the nondebtor] would have a 'claim'." For an argument that bankruptcy courts are compelled by § 502(c)(2) to monetize equitable remedies, however contingent or unliquidated, so that creditors can be dealt with equally and debtors can be given a fresh start, whatever limitations state law places on remedies available outside bankruptcy, see Jay L. Westbrook, *A Functional Analysis of Executory Contracts*, 74 Minn.L.Rev. 227, 255–57, 277–78 (1989).

C. Determining the Amount of a Claim

Section 502(b) directs the bankruptcy court to determine the amount of each claim in dollars. If the claim is for a fixed amount and the claim is not disputed, the bankruptcy court does not have to act on the claim, for a claim is deemed allowed unless there is an objection to it. § 502(a). But many claims, such as tort claims, may be unliquidated or there may be a dispute concerning the extent to which the debtor is liable. Upon objection, the bankruptcy court must determine whether the claim is valid and its amount in a summary hearing. A personal injury tort or wrongful death claim must be tried in a federal district court rather than in the bankruptcy court. 28 U.S.C. § 157(b)(2)(B) and § 157(b)(5). With respect to personal injury and wrongful death claims, bankruptcy does not affect any right to trial by jury that an individual has under applicable nonbankruptcy law. 28 U.S.C. § 1411. By filing proof of other kinds of claims, the creditor brings itself within the equitable jurisdiction of the bankruptcy court and relinquishes any right to trial by jury with respect to the determination of that claim.

Section 502(c)(1) directs the bankruptcy court to estimate the amount of a contingent or unliquidated claim. This is a major change from pre-Code law. Under the Bankruptcy Act, if liquidation or estimation of a claim "would unduly delay administration of the estate," the claim was not allowable. The impact of this provision on unliquidated claims is illustrated by a well known pre-Code case, *In re Cartridge Television, Inc.*, 535 F.2d 1388 (2d Cir. 1976), in which stockholders of a corporation in liquidation bankruptcy filed proof of claims of about $60 million. The claims were based on alleged fraud by the corporation in the sale of its stock. Under current law, § 510(b) would result in the subordination of such claims. The *Cartridge Television* court reached a comparable result on the ground that liquidation of these claims might have required litigation of several years. Even though the consequence of disallowing the stockholders' claims was to leave them with a worthless claim against an asset-less corporate shell, the court disallowed the claims because they would unduly delay the administration of the estate. Disallowance of claims not otherwise subject to subordination on the ground that litigation would unduly delay administration of the estate results in a windfall to other creditors. Section 502(c) rejects this approach: any contingent or unliquidated claim must be estimated by the court and is subject to discharge.

> No longer will some creditors enjoy a windfall or effectively be denied any recovery based upon the provability or allowability of their claims and the financial status of the debtor after bankruptcy. Equally important, Congress has insured that the debtor will receive a complete discharge of his debts and a real fresh start, without the threat of lingering claims "riding through" the bankruptcy.

In re Baldwin–United Corp., 55 B.R. 885, 898 (Bankr.S.D.Ohio 1985).

The bankruptcy court may determine the amount of an unliquidated claim under § 502(b) itself, or, as we will see with respect to stays and injunctions in chapter 5 of this Casebook, it may modify the automatic stay to allow the creditor to liquidate the claim in a state court. The effect of the state court judgment is to give the creditor a liquidated claim in bankruptcy.

In Chapter 11 cases, the bankruptcy court must determine that the reorganization plan is feasible. In making the feasibility finding, the court may make a preliminary estimation of the amount of claims and reserve final determination of the value of the claim for later. Moreover, claims may be temporarily allowed for the purpose of establishing voting rights in connection with confirmation of a proposed plan. Rule 3018(a). Although the bankruptcy court may not fix the amount of personal injury tort or wrongful death claims for purposes of distribution, it may estimate the claims for purposes of determining the feasibility of a Chapter 11 plan or establishing voting rights. *A.H. Robins Co. v. Piccinin*, 788 F.2d 994 (4th Cir. 1986).

Section 502(c) gives no hint to courts of how they are to go about estimating the amount of contingent or unliquidated claims. *Collier* advises: "In estimating a claim, the bankruptcy court should use whatever method is best suited to the particular circumstances." *Collier on Bankruptcy* ¶ 502.04[2] (15th ed. rev. 2008). In *Baldwin-United*, which involved hundreds of millions of dollars in complicated indemnity and contribution claims, the court noted that "a formal trial on the merits would eviscerate the purpose underlying § 502(c)" and held that a summary two-day hearing which allowed one witness per party met the requirements of due process in estimating the value of these claims. At that hearing the court estimated these claims at $0. 55 B.R. at 899.

D. Secured Claims

1. Introduction

The holder of a secured claim enjoys the top priority in the hierarchy of claims. A secured claim is a right to specific property, the collateral in which the creditor has a security interest; an unsecured claim is a right to what is left in the bankruptcy estate after the secured claims are fully paid. Since it is simple under Article 9 of the Uniform Commercial Code for a creditor to take a security interest in virtually all of a debtor's personal property, now owned and hereafter obtained, there is often nothing left in the estate for unsecured claims.

Some creditors don't take security interests at all because they deal with debtors of such high credit reputation and capacity to repay that security interests in their assets are unnecessary. These lenders reduce credit risks by monitoring their borrowers' activities against a background of covenants in the loan agreement that forbid encumbering or transferring assets, exceeding loan-to-asset ratios, engaging in novel endeavors, and the like. But many creditors, both lenders and sellers, routinely demand security interests. Sellers to consumers usually take security interests in big-ticket goods they sell on credit, such as automobiles and other hard goods. Lenders financing real property sales invariably take mortgages on the property. However, trade creditors (suppliers of goods or services to businesses) often do not take security interests and are, in consequence, subordinated to secured creditors in bankruptcy. Credit card issuers usually do not take security interests in goods purchased by consumers and small businesses by use of credit cards.

Why do we allow a debtor to contract with one creditor to award that creditor a priority over the debtor's other creditors, past and future, however meritorious their claims and whenever they extended credit, by taking a security interest in the debtor's assets? UCC Article 9 not only allows creditors to take security interests in all of a debtor's present and future tangible property, such as inventory or equipment, but also in the debtor's stream of earnings or cash flow, that is, the proceeds of sales of inventory or services from which unsecured creditors such as trade creditors expect to be paid. Although, in theory, voluntary creditors can use caution in dealing with debtors whose assets are or may be covered by security interests, an involuntary creditor like a tort claimant cannot, and may find its judgment debtor judgment-proof because all its assets are subject to security interests. *Compare* Thomas H. Jackson & Anthony T. Kronman, *Secured Financing and Priorities Among Creditors*, 88 Yale L.J. 1143 (1979), supporting secured credit, *with* Lynn LoPucki, *The Unsecured Creditor's Bargain*, 80 Va.L.Rev. 1887 (1994), challenging it.

Enforcing a secured claim in bankruptcy. When a debtor files in bankruptcy, the holder of a secured claim in that debtor's property is automatically stayed by § 362(a)(4) from enforcing the claim by foreclosure or other state law proceedings. The secured party is limited to its rights under the Bankruptcy Code to enforce its security interest. Under § 506(a) a secured party has a secured claim to the extent of the value of its collateral; if the collateral is worth less than the amount of the claim, the secured party has a secured claim to the extent of the value of the collateral and an unsecured claim for the rest of the debt. In Chapter 7 proceedings, the task of the trustee in bankruptcy is (1) to dispose of property of the estate in which there are security interests (§ 725), and (2) to liquidate the remaining assets of the estate and distribute proceeds to claimants according to the priorities set out in § 726.

If a secured creditor is oversecured (the collateral is worth more than the amount of the secured party's claim), the trustee will sell the collateral, pay the secured party the amount of its claim, and distribute the surplus in payment of the unsecured claims. If a creditor is undersecured (its collateral is worth less than the amount of the secured party's claim), all the proceeds of the sale of the collateral must go to the secured party, who will be left with an unsecured claim for any remaining deficiency. Since, in the case of an undersecured claim, the estate will not directly benefit from the trustee's sale of the collateral, the trustee may choose to save expenses by abandoning the property under § 554(a) to the debtor or agreeing to a lifting of the stay under § 362(d). If the property is abandoned or the stay is lifted, the secured party may proceed under state law to foreclose on its collateral; if a deficiency results, the creditor may file an unsecured claim in debtor's bankruptcy for the amount of the deficiency.

Under Chapters 11, 12 and 13, the debtor seeks to avoid liquidation under Chapter 7 by confirming a plan of rehabilitation or reorganization that will allow the debtor to retain most of the property of the estate (including assets subject to security interests) by payment over time of part or all the claims of its creditors. The Code requires that the secured party's economic interest in the value of its collateral be respected throughout. As we will see in detail, the holders of secured claims are entitled to adequate protection of their rights during the preconfirmation period (§ 362(d)(1)) and compensation for the present value of their secured claims under the confirmed plan. §§ 1129(b)(2)(A), 1225(a)(5), and 1325(a)(5).

Effect of discharge on secured claims. If the property of the estate subject to the lien is abandoned to the debtor under § 554, or the stay is lifted under § 362(d) and the debtor is given a discharge under § 727(b), the effect is to discharge the debtor from liability on the debt that is secured by the lien. How does this affect the rights of the lienholder? The theory of discharge has always been that it affects only the personal liability of the debtor. It does not affect the debt itself, which remains unpaid. If third parties are liable on the debt, they remain liable. For example, a surety or other guarantor is liable even though the principal debtor is released as a result of the discharge. Nor is an insurance carrier's liability affected by the discharge of the insured. Similarly, if the debt is secured by property of a third party, that property can be reached to the full extent of the security agreement. This theory of discharge is specifically recognized in § 524(e).

The same rule applies if the discharged debt is secured by a lien in the debtor's property. As we shall see, liens may be modified in connection with confirmation of reorganization plans under Chapters 11, 12 and 13. But, otherwise, the debt and the lien continue to exist after bankruptcy even though the debtor may have been discharged from personal liability to pay the debt and even though the creditor did not file a proof of claim in bankruptcy. This principle was recognized in *Long v. Bullard*, 117 U.S. 617 (1886), a case antedating the Bankruptcy Act of 1898. In that case, Long received a discharge in bankruptcy and retained as exempt property a homestead that was subject to a mortgage in favor of Bullard. Bullard did not file proof of the mortgage debt in the bankruptcy. After bankruptcy, Bullard brought a foreclosure action. Long defended on the ground that the discharge prevented foreclosure under the mortgage. This defense was rejected in the trial court which charged the jury that "there could be no personal recovery against [Long] upon the note, but that the property could be subjected to the payment of the amount due, as the discharge of Long in bankruptcy did not release the lien of the mortgage." The court entered a decree for sale of the property. The Supreme Court of the United States affirmed the decree. Chief Justice Waite stated:

[T]he discharge releases the bankrupt only from debts which were or might have been proved, and * * * debts secured by mortgage or pledge can only be proved for the balance remaining due after deducting the value of the security, unless all claim upon the security is released. Here the creditor neither proved his debt in bankruptcy nor released his lien. Consequently his security was preserved notwithstanding the bankruptcy of his debtor. * * * The dispute in the court below was as to the existence of the lien at the time of the commencement of the proceedings in bankruptcy. That depended entirely on the state laws, as to which the judgment of the state court is final and not subject to review here.

117 U.S. at 620–621. Thus, the oft stated maxim of *Long v. Bullard* is that liens pass through bankruptcy unaffected. In the context of Chapter 7 bankruptcies, the Supreme Court has effectively reaffirmed the traditional *Long v. Bullard* principle under the 1978 Bankruptcy Code in *Dewsnup v. Timm*, p. 119 infra.

2. VALUING A SECURED CLAIM

a. Cramdown

In several bankruptcy contexts courts are required to value secured claims. Section 506(a)'s vague directive to value the claim in the light of the purposes of the valuation and the proposed disposition or use of the property, has led courts to adopt widely disparate methods of determining value. The following case addresses and purports to resolve the long-standing division of authority on valuation methodology. Although it arises under Chapter 13, its interpretation of § 506(a) informs valuation in reorganization cases under Chapters 11 and 12 as well.

Associates Commercial Corporation v. Rash
Supreme Court of the United States, 1997.
520 U.S. 953.

■ Justice GINSBURG delivered the opinion of the Court.

We resolve in this case a dispute concerning the proper application of § 506(a) of the Bankruptcy Code when a bankrupt debtor has exercised the "cram down" option for which Code § 1325(a)(5)(B) provides. Specifically, when a debtor, over a secured creditor's objection, seeks to retain and use the creditor's collateral in a Chapter 13 plan, is the value of the collateral to be determined by (1) what the secured creditor could obtain through foreclosure sale of the property (the "foreclosure-value" standard); (2) what the debtor would have to pay for comparable property (the "replacement-value" standard);

or (3) the midpoint between these two measurements? We hold that § 506(a) directs application of the replacement-value standard.

I.

In 1989, respondent Elray Rash purchased for $73,700 a Kenworth tractor truck for use in his freight-hauling business. Rash made a downpayment on the truck, agreed to pay the seller the remainder in 60 monthly installments, and pledged the truck as collateral on the unpaid balance. The seller assigned the loan, and its lien on the truck, to petitioner Associates Commercial Corporation (ACC).

In March 1992, Elray and Jean Rash filed a joint petition and a repayment plan under Chapter 13 of the Bankruptcy Code (Code). At the time of the bankruptcy filing, the balance owed to ACC on the truck loan was $41,171. Because it held a valid lien on the truck, ACC was listed in the bankruptcy petition as a creditor holding a secured claim. Under the Code, ACC's claim for the balance owed on the truck was secured only to the extent of the value of the collateral; its claim over and above the value of the truck was unsecured. See § 506(a).

To qualify for confirmation under Chapter 13, the Rashes' plan had to satisfy the requirements set forth in § 1325(a) of the Code. The Rashes' treatment of ACC's secured claim, in particular, is governed by subsection (a)(5). Under this provision, a plan's proposed treatment of secured claims can be confirmed if one of three conditions is satisfied: the secured creditor accepts the plan, see § 1325(a)(5)(A); the debtor surrenders the property securing the claim to the creditor, see § 1325(a)(5)(C); or the debtor invokes the so-called "cram down" power, see § 1325(a)(5)(B). Under the cram down option, the debtor is permitted to keep the property over the objection of the creditor; the creditor retains the lien securing the claim, see § 1325(a)(5)(B)(i), and the debtor is required to provide the creditor with payments, over the life of the plan, that will total the present value of the allowed secured claim, i.e, the present value of the collateral, see § 1325(a)(5)(B)(ii). The value of the allowed secured claim is governed by § 506(a) of the Code.

The Rashes' Chapter 13 plan invoked the cram down power. It proposed that the Rashes retain the truck for use in the freight-hauling business and pay ACC, over 58 months, an amount equal to the present value of the truck. That value, the Rashes' petition alleged, was $28,500. ACC objected to the plan and asked the Bankruptcy Court to lift the automatic stay so ACC could repossess the truck. ACC also filed a proof of claim alleging that its claim was fully secured in the amount of $41,171. The Rashes filed an objection to ACC's claim.

The Bankruptcy Court held an evidentiary hearing to resolve the dispute over the truck's value. At the hearing, ACC and the Rashes urged different valuation benchmarks. ACC maintained that the proper valuation was the price the Rashes would have to pay to purchase a like vehicle, an amount ACC's expert estimated to be $41,000. The Rashes, however, maintained that the proper valuation was the net amount ACC would realize upon foreclosure and sale of the collateral, an amount their expert estimated to be $31,875. The Bankruptcy Court agreed with the Rashes and fixed the amount of ACC's secured claim at $31,875; that sum, the court found, was the net amount ACC would realize if it exercised its right to repossess and sell the truck. The Bankruptcy Court thereafter approved the plan, and the United States District Court for the Eastern District of Texas affirmed.

A panel of the Court of Appeals for the Fifth Circuit reversed. On rehearing en banc, however, the Fifth Circuit affirmed the District Court, holding that ACC's allowed secured claim was limited to $31,875, the net foreclosure value of the truck.

In reaching its decision, the Fifth Circuit highlighted, first, a conflict it perceived between the method of valuation ACC advanced, and the law of Texas defining the rights of secured creditors. Tex. Bus. & Com.Code Ann. §§ 9.504(a), (c), 9.505 (1991). In the Fifth Circuit's view, valuing collateral in a federal bankruptcy proceeding under a replacement-value standard—thereby setting an amount generally higher than what a secured creditor could realize pursuing its state-law foreclosure remedy—would "chang[e] the extent to which ACC is secured from what obtained under state law prior to the bankruptcy filing." *In re Rash*, 90 F.3d 1036, 1041 (5th Cir. 1996). Such a departure from state law, the Fifth Circuit said, should be resisted by the federal forum unless "clearly compel[led]" by the Code.

The Fifth Circuit then determined that the Code provision governing valuation of security interests, § 506(a), does not compel a replacement-value approach. Instead, the court reasoned, the first sentence of § 506(a) requires that collateral be valued from the creditor's perspective. And because "the creditor's interest is in the nature of a security interest, giving the creditor the right to repossess and sell the collateral and nothing more[,]. . .. the valuation should start with what the creditor could realize by exercising that right." This foreclosure-value standard, the Fifth Circuit found, was consistent with the other relevant provisions of the Code, economic analysis, and the legislative history of the pertinent provisions. Judge Smith, joined by five other judges, dissented, urging that the Code dictates a replacement-value standard.

Courts of Appeals have adopted three different standards for valuing a security interest in a bankruptcy proceeding when the debtor invokes the cram down power to retain the collateral over the creditor's objection. In contrast to the Fifth Circuit's foreclosure-value standard, a number of Circuits have followed a replacement-value approach.[2] * * * Other courts have settled on the midpoint between foreclosure value and replacement value. *See In re Hoskins*, 102 F.3d 311, 316 (7th Cir. 1996) * * *. We granted certiorari to resolve this conflict among the Courts of Appeals * * * and we now reverse the Fifth Circuit's judgment.

II.

The Bankruptcy Code provision central to the resolution of this case is § 506(a), which states:

> An allowed claim of a creditor secured by a lien on property in which the estate has an interest... is a secured claim to the extent of the value of such creditor's interest in the estate's interest in such property,... and is an unsecured claim to the extent that the value of such creditor's interest... is less than the amount of such allowed claim. Such value shall be determined in light of the purpose of the valuation and of the proposed disposition or use of such property. . ..

Over ACC's objection, the Rashes' repayment plan proposed, pursuant to § 1325(a)(5)(B), continued use of the property in question, i.e., the truck, in the debtor's trade or business. In such a "cram down" case, we hold, the value of the property (and thus the amount of the secured claim under § 506(a)) is the price a willing buyer in the debtor's trade, business, or situation would pay to obtain like property from a willing seller.

Rejecting this replacement-value standard, and selecting instead the typically lower foreclosure-value standard, the Fifth Circuit trained its attention on the first sentence of § 506(a). In particular, the Fifth Circuit relied on these first sentence words: a claim is secured "to the extent of the value of such *creditor's interest* in the estate's interest in such property." The Fifth Circuit read this phrase to instruct that the "starting point for the valuation [is] what the creditor could realize if it sold the estate's interest in the property according to the security agreement," namely, through "repossess[ing] and sell [ing] the collateral."

We do not find in the § 506(a) first sentence words—"the creditor's interest in the estate's interest in such property"—the foreclosure-value meaning advanced by the Fifth Circuit. Even read in isolation, the phrase imparts no

---

[2] * * * By using the term "replacement value," we do not suggest that a creditor is entitled to recover what it would cost the debtor to purchase the collateral brand new. Rather, our use of the term replacement value is consistent with the * * * meaning of fair-market value; by replacement value, we mean the price a willing buyer in the debtor's trade, business, or situation would pay a willing seller to obtain property of like age and condition.

valuation standard: A direction simply to consider the "value of such creditor's interest" does not expressly reveal *how* that interest is to be valued.

Reading the first sentence of § 506(a) as a whole, we are satisfied that the phrase the Fifth Circuit considered key is not an instruction to equate a "creditor's interest" with the net value a creditor could realize through a foreclosure sale. The first sentence, in its entirety, tells us that a secured creditor's claim is to be divided into secured and unsecured portions, with the secured portion of the claim limited to the value of the collateral. * * * To separate the secured from the unsecured portion of a claim, a court must compare the creditor's claim to the value of "such property," i.e., the collateral. That comparison is sometimes complicated. A debtor may own only a part interest in the property pledged as collateral, in which case the court will be required to ascertain the "estate's interest" in the collateral. Or, a creditor may hold a junior or subordinate lien, which would require the court to ascertain the creditor's interest in the collateral. The § 506(a) phrase referring to the "creditor's interest in the estate's interest in such property" thus recognizes that a court may encounter, and in such instances must evaluate, limited or partial interests in collateral. The full first sentence of § 506(a), in short, tells a court what it must evaluate, but it does not say more; it is not enlightening on how to value collateral.

The second sentence of § 506(a) does speak to the *how* question. "Such value," that sentence provides, "shall be determined in light of the purpose of the valuation and of the proposed disposition or use of such property." § 506(a). By deriving a foreclosure-value standard from § 506(a)'s first sentence, the Fifth Circuit rendered inconsequential the sentence that expressly addresses how "value shall be determined."

As we comprehend § 506(a), the "proposed disposition or use" of the collateral is of paramount importance to the valuation question. If a secured creditor does not accept a debtor's Chapter 13 plan, the debtor has two options for handling allowed secured claims: surrender the collateral to the creditor, see § 1325(a)(5)(C); or, under the cram down option, keep the collateral over the creditor's objection and provide the creditor, over the life of the plan, with the equivalent of the present value of the collateral, see § 1325(a)(5)(B). The "disposition or use" of the collateral thus turns on the alternative the debtor chooses—in one case the collateral will be surrendered to the creditor, and in the other, the collateral will be retained and used by the debtor. Applying a foreclosure-value standard when the cram down option is invoked attributes no significance to the different consequences of the debtor's choice to surrender the property or retain it. A replacement-value standard, on the other hand, distinguishes retention from surrender and renders meaningful the key words "disposition or use."

Tying valuation to the actual "disposition or use" of the property points away from a foreclosure-value standard when a Chapter 13 debtor, invoking cram down power, retains and uses the property. Under that option, foreclosure is averted by the debtor's choice and over the creditor's objection. From the creditor's perspective as well as the debtor's, surrender and retention are not equivalent acts.

When a debtor surrenders the property, a creditor obtains it immediately, and is free to sell it and reinvest the proceeds. We recall here that ACC sought that very advantage. If a debtor keeps the property and continues to use it, the creditor obtains at once neither the property nor its value and is exposed to double risks: The debtor may again default and the property may deteriorate from extended use. Adjustments in the interest rate and secured creditor demands for more "adequate protection," § 361, do not fully offset these risks. *See* 90 F.3d, at 1066 (Smith, J., dissenting) ("vast majority of reorganizations fail... leaving creditors with only a fraction of the compensation due them"; where, as here, "collateral depreciates rapidly, the secured creditor may receive far less in a failed reorganization than in a prompt foreclosure") (internal cross–reference omitted) * * *.[3]

Of prime significance, the replacement-value standard accurately gauges the debtor's "use" of the property. It values "the creditor's interest in the collateral in light of the proposed [repayment plan] reality: no foreclosure sale and economic benefit for the debtor derived from the collateral equal to... its [replacement] value." *In re Winthrop Old Farm Nurseries*, 50 F.3d 72, 75 (1st Cir. 1995). The debtor in this case elected to use the collateral to generate an income stream. That actual use, rather than a foreclosure sale that will not take place, is the proper guide under a prescription hinged to the property's "disposition or use." *See ibid*.

The Fifth Circuit considered the replacement-value standard disrespectful of state law, which permits the secured creditor to sell the collateral, thereby obtaining its net foreclosure value "and nothing more." In allowing Chapter 13 debtors to retain and use collateral over the objection of secured creditors, however, the Bankruptcy Code has reshaped debtor and creditor rights in marked departure from state law. *See, e.g.*, Uniform Commercial Code §§ 9-504, 9-505. The Code's cram down option displaces a secured creditor's state-law right to obtain immediate foreclosure upon a debtor's default. That change, ordered by federal law, is attended by a direction that courts look to the

---

[3] On this matter, amici curiae supporting ACC contended: " 'Adequate protection' payments under §§ 361, 362(d)(1) typically are based on the assumption that the collateral will be subject to only ordinary depreciation. Hence, even when such payments are made, they frequently fail to compensate adequately for the usually more rapid depreciation of assets retained by the debtor." Brief for American Automobile Manufacturers Association, Inc., et al. as Amici Curiae 21, n. 9.

"proposed disposition or use" of the collateral in determining its value. It no more disrupts state law to make "disposition or use" the guide for valuation than to authorize the rearrangement of rights the cram down power entails.

Nor are we persuaded that the split-the-difference approach adopted by the Seventh Circuit provides the appropriate solution. Whatever the attractiveness of a standard that picks the midpoint between foreclosure and replacement values, there is no warrant for it in the Code.[5] Section 506(a) calls for the value the property possesses in light of the "disposition or use" in fact "proposed," not the various dispositions or uses that might have been proposed. * * * The Seventh Circuit rested on the "economics of the situation," *In re Hoskins*, 102 F.3d, at 316, only after concluding that the statute suggests no particular valuation method. We agree with the Seventh Circuit that "a simple rule of valuation is needed" to serve the interests of predictability and uniformity. Id., at 314. We conclude, however, that § 506(a) supplies a governing instruction less complex than the Seventh Circuit's "make two valuations, then split the difference" formulation.

In sum, under § 506(a), the value of property retained because the debtor has exercised the § 1325(a)(5)(B) "cram down" option is the cost the debtor would incur to obtain a like asset for the same "proposed... use."[6]

* * *

For the foregoing reasons, the judgment of the Court of Appeals is reversed, and the case is remanded for further proceedings consistent with this opinion.

It is so ordered.

■ Justice STEVENS, dissenting. [Opinion omitted.]

---

[5] As our reading of § 506(a) makes plain, we also reject a ruleless approach allowing use of different valuation standards based on the facts and circumstances of individual cases. *Cf. In re Valenti*, 105 F.3d 55, 62–63 (C.A.2 1997) (permissible for bankruptcy courts to determine valuation standard case-by-case).

[6] Our recognition that the replacement-value standard, not the foreclosure-value standard, governs in cram down cases leaves to bankruptcy courts, as triers of fact, identification of the best way of ascertaining replacement value on the basis of the evidence presented. Whether replacement value is the equivalent of retail value, wholesale value, or some other value will depend on the type of debtor and the nature of the property. We note, however, that replacement value, in this context, should not include certain items. For example, where the proper measure of the replacement value of a vehicle is its retail value, an adjustment to that value may be necessary: A creditor should not receive portions of the retail price, if any, that reflect the value of items the debtor does not receive when he retains his vehicle, items such as warranties, inventory storage, and reconditioning. Nor should the creditor gain from modifications to the property—e.g., the addition of accessories to a vehicle—to which a creditor's lien would not extend under state law.

NOTES

1. In footnote 6 to *Rash*, the Court directs that the replacement value should not include certain enumerated items. How does such a reduced replacement value vary from a wholesale price?

2. How would *Rash* be decided under the amended version of § 506(a)(2) quoted below?

> **(2)** If the debtor is an individual in a case under chapter 7 or 13, such value with respect to personal property securing an allowed claim shall be determined based on the replacement value of such property as of the date of filing the petition without deduction for costs of sale or marketing. With respect to property acquired for personal, family, or household purpose, replacement value shall mean the price a retail merchant would charge for property of that kind considering the age and condition of the property at the time value is determined.

We reserve for chapter 9 on consumer debtors a full discussion of valuation in consumer cases but *Rash*'s result is codified and simplified in the consumer context by § 506(a)(2). Since § 506(a)(2) doesn't apply to cases concerning corporate or partnership debtors or to Chapter 11 or 12 cases, *Rash* (in all its original ambiguity) remains good authority in commercial cases. What guidance does it offer on how to determine the "replacement value" of important types of collateral in business reorganization cases involving inventory or accounts receivable?

3. We will see in detail in chapter 9 on consumer debtors that under BAPCPA the infamous "hanging paragraph" of § 1325(a) arguably simplifies the task of judges in valuing motor vehicles for cramdown purposes by making valuation irrelevant. If the creditor has a purchase money security interest in a motor vehicle purchased for the personal of the debtor within 910 days of bankruptcy, § 506 does not apply and the debtor must pay the full amount of the claim, whatever the value of the motor vehicle securing the claim.

b. Redemption

Assume that Secured Creditor (SC) repossessed defaulting Debtor's car. Debtor filed in Chapter 7 and petitioned to redeem the car under § 722, which allows the Debtor to retain the car free of SC's security interest "by paying the holder of such lien the amount of the allowed secured claim of such holder that is secured by such lien in full at the time of redemption." The wholesale value of the car is $4,400 and the replacement value is $8,900. Debtor contends that the holding in *Rash*, which was a Chapter 13 cramdown case, does not control in a redemption case, and that she should be able to redeem by paying $4,400. She relies on the language in 506(a)(1) emphasized by the Court in *Rash* stating that value is to be determined "in the light of the purpose of the valuation and proposed disposition or use of such property." Should a different rule apply for valuation in redemption cases than for cramdown?

Prior to the enactment of § 506(a)(2) redemption cases had been uniform in holding that wholesale value rather than replacement value should prevail. *See, e.g., Smith v. Household Automotive Finance Corp.*, 313 B.R. 267 (N.D. Ill.2004). Both cramdown and redemption are means of allowing a debtor in default to retain the collateral in which creditor has a security interest. But they differ in several aspects. Cramdown allows the debtor to retain the collateral by paying its present value over time in installments. Redemption requires the debtor to pay the allowed secured claim in full at the time of redemption. The creditor's risk in cramdown is greater; the property is in possession of the debtor and will depreciate; the debtor may default, requiring the creditor to retake the collateral. In redemption, the creditor has no risk; the secured claim in paid in full. Does the fact that the redeeming debtor tenders cash "up front" while the debtor exercising its rights under cramdown pays the secured claim over time justify a different approach to valuation? Is the question moot after enactment of § 506(a)(2) which dictates use of replacement value in individual consumer Chapter 7 cases?

3. AVOIDING LIENS UNDER § 506(d)

Section 506 provides:

> **(d)** To the extent that a lien secures a claim against the debtor that is not an allowed secured claim, such lien is void, unless
>
>> **(1)** such claim was disallowed only under section 502(b)(5) [unmatured domestic support claim] or 502(e) [certain claims for reimbursement or contribution] of this title; or
>>
>> **(2)** such claim is not an allowed secured claim due only to the failure of an entity to file a proof of such claim under section 501 of this title.

Section 506(d) was meant to preserve the rule of *Long v. Bullard*, 117 U.S. 617 (1886). The House Report on the Bankruptcy Reform Act of 1978 states with respect to the original version of § 506(d):

> Subsection (d) permits liens to pass through the bankruptcy case unaffected. However, if a party in interest requests the court to determine and allow or disallow the claim secured by the lien under section 502 and the claim is not allowed, then the lien is void to the extent that the claim is not allowed.

1978 U.S.C.C.A.N. 6313. But on its face § 506(d) states only when a lien is void. Only by negative implication does it indicate that a lien not void under § 506(d) will "pass through the bankruptcy case unaffected." The unstated assumption is that the rule of *Long v. Bullard* governs if the lien is not avoided under § 506(d) and is not avoided by some other provision of the Code. Section 506(d) is illustrated by the hypothetical cases that follow. Assume in each case that the debtor has filed in Chapter 7.

Case #1. Debtor owes Creditor $100,000 secured by a lien on land worth $75,000. If Creditor files a claim in Debtor's bankruptcy, under § 506(a) it would have an allowed secured claim of $75,000 and an allowed unsecured claim for $25,000. Debtor is convinced that property values will increase and wishes to retain ownership of the land. In pursuance of this plan, Debtor files a proceeding to limit or "strip down" Creditor's lien to the value of the land, $75,000, on the ground that under § 506(d) Creditor's lien is void to the extent it is not an allowed secured claim. Since the unless clause is not applicable, literally read, § 506(d) allows the court to strip down the lien to $75,000, the amount of the secured claim. If Debtor can borrow enough money to redeem the land by paying off the remaining amount of the lien, it will gain the advantage of any subsequent increase in the value of the land. Creditor would lose the potential future appreciation that it might have been able to realize under state law that would allow the debtor to redeem property subject to a lien only by paying the full amount of the debt—$100,000.

Case #2. Debtor owes Creditor $100,000 secured by a first lien on land owned by Debtor. Debtor owes Lender $25,000 secured by a second lien on the same land. At the time of bankruptcy the land is worth $100,000. Debtor is willing to reaffirm the $100,000 debt under § 524(c); this would allow Debtor to keep the land as long as the installment payments were made to Creditor. As Debtor reduces the first mortgage debt by payments after bankruptcy or as the value of the land increases, Debtor can build a substantial equity in the land. But for Debtor to receive the full benefit of the reaffirmation with Creditor, it must avoid the second lien in bankruptcy. If the second lien is not avoided, the first $25,000 of any postbankruptcy equity will be captured by Lender. Literally read § 506(d) allows Debtor to void the "underwater" second lien because it had no present value at the time of the bankruptcy and, therefore, does not secure an allowed secured claim. Debtor could then capture all postbankruptcy appreciation upon reaffirming its obligation to Creditor.

Most courts adopted the foregoing literal interpretation of § 506(d), e.g., *Gaglia v. First Federal Savings & Loan Ass'n*, 889 F.2d 1304 (3d Cir. 1989), but the Supreme Court in *Dewsnup v. Timm*, 502 U.S. 410 (1992), rejected this reading of § 506(d) in a case similar to Case #1. In the majority opinion, Justice Blackmun noted that before enactment of the Bankruptcy Code of 1978, liens on property passed through bankruptcy unaffected. *Long v. Bullard*. Under this rule, debtors could not redeem property from a mortgagee unless the debt was paid in full. Congress fully understood this pre-Code rule. The Court found that the new Code did not unambiguously repeal this rule and would not assume that Congress intended to grant to debtors a broad new remedy to strip down liens to the amount of the allowed secured claim as defined in § 506(a). In the view of the majority, all § 506(d) does is avoid liens that secured disallowed claims; that is, if the debtor doesn't legally owe the debt, the lien securing the debt is void. The majority read § 506(d) as though the word "secured" in the phrase "allowed secured claim" were deleted. Thus, after *Dewsnup*, in Case #1, Debtor's attempt to strip down liens would fail. Future appreciation belongs to the secured creditor.

Case #2 involves an attempt by the debtor to "strip off" a junior lien that is totally unsecured ("underwater"). *In re Talbert*, 344 F.3d 555 (6th Cir. 2003), held that the *Dewsnup* reading of § 506(d) applied to this case and strip off of an underwater lien securing an allowed claim was not permissible. The mortgagee's bargain is that a consensual lien remains on the property until payment or foreclosure; until this happens any future increase in the value of the property accrues to the mortgagee.

The majority opinion in *Dewsnup* left most commentators surprised and Justice Scalia sputtering in dissent. Although on a policy basis leaving any future appreciation in the collateral with the secured creditor is, as Justice Scalia conceded, quite defensible, on statutory interpretation grounds the majority opinion is of questionable legitimacy. On its face § 506(d) voids a lien to the extent the claim it secures is not both an "allowed claim" and a "secured claim" under § 506(a). The premise of the majority opinion is that somehow "allowed secured claim" in § 506(d) means something different from the definition of allowed secured claim in § 506(a), a proposition that Justice Scalia derided as the one-subsection-at-a-time technique of statutory interpretation. While the statutory construction technique of looking to pre-Code precedents to decide the meaning of ambiguous provisions is well established, it seems inappropriate in a case involving a provision as clearly stated as § 506(d), using an obviously technical term defined earlier in the very same code section. The Court's assertion that the term "secured claim" may, chameleon like, change meaning in different sections of the Code casts doubt on the meaning of the many provisions of the Code using the term. As we shall see in our consideration of

Chapters 11 and 13, notwithstanding *Dewsnup,* lien stripping plans are confirmable in reorganization cases.

4. POSTFILING INTEREST ON SECURED CLAIMS

Section 502(b) states that the amount of a claim shall be determined by the court "as of the date of the filing of the petition, and shall allow such claim * * * in such amount." Claims for postpetition interest are normally disallowed under § 502(b)(2). Under this general rule a creditor is not entitled to compensation for the delay in payment which results from the bankruptcy proceedings. In a Chapter 7 case, postfiling interest on unsecured claims is allowed only in the rare case in which the debtor is solvent and all claims are paid in full. Section 726(a)(5) states that in that case interest at the "legal rate" is payable from the date of filing of the petition. Legal rate is not defined; several "legal rates" exist. The authorities are split on which legal rate should apply. *See, e.g., In re Cardelucci,* 285 F.3d 1231(9th Cir. 2002) (applying federal judgment rate). There is a special rule, however, for secured claims. Section 506(b) allows an oversecured creditor, to the extent of the value of the collateral, to recover in addition to the secured claim "interest on such claim, and any reasonable fees, costs, or charges provided for under the agreement under which such claim arose."

In the famous "comma" case, *United States v. Ron Pair Enterprises, Inc.,* 489 U.S. 235 (1989), the Supreme Court held that the language quoted above meant that oversecured involuntary secured claims, such as judicial or statutory liens, were also entitled to postpetition interest. The position of the comma between "claim" and "and" showed that no agreement is necessary for recovery of interest; an agreement is needed only for recovery of fees, costs, and charges.

Although § 506(b) awards the oversecured creditor postfiling interest, it is silent on the rate at which the interest is payable, at least after *Ron Pair* which divorces § 506(b)'s reference to "the agreement" from the statutory right to interest. In general, courts have nevertheless continued to apply the contract rate of interest in the case of consensual security interests while necessarily looking to the statutory rate with respect to judicial or statutory liens. *Collier on Bankruptcy,* ¶ 506.04[2][b] (15th ed. rev. 2008). If bankruptcy is seen as essentially a specialized federal procedure for honoring substantive rights created by state law, which is more efficient than the state law race-to-the-courthouse collection system in the case of insolvent debtors, it is appropriate that substantive state law rights be left unaltered to the extent possible under bankruptcy procedures. Under this view, oversecured creditors should earn the same interest rates that they enjoyed under the contract before filing. But if bankruptcy law is seen as having its own redistributive and rehabilitative imperatives, state created substantive rights may have to yield. Both views of bankruptcy law find some support in the Code. Katherine R. Heidt, *Interest Under Section 506(b) of the Bankruptcy Code: The Right, the Rate and the Relationship to Bankruptcy Policy*, 1991 Utah L.Rev. 361.

The tension between recognition of state law substantive rights and applying bankruptcy law notions of equity is manifested in *In re Laymon*, 958 F.2d 72 (5th Cir. 1992). There the court of appeals reviewed an innovative bankruptcy court holding granting to an oversecured consensual creditor the federal judgment rate of interest. It reversed in favor of the contract rate on the ground that this was the prevailing pre-Code law and was not changed by the Code. But the contract called for 10% pre-default interest and 18% post-default interest. Respect for state substantive law would call for awarding the creditor the 18% rate. The court waffled, stating: "Under pre-Code law, courts were 'not required in all cases to apply a contractual default rate of interest * * *.' Most courts took a flexible approach, recognizing situations in which 'the higher rate would produce an inequitable or unconscionable result * * *'." 958 F.2d at 75. It remanded the issue to the bankruptcy court with a vague mandate to examine the equities in deciding what rate to apply.

E. PRIORITY CLAIMS

We have seen that before the final distribution of the bankruptcy estate in a Chapter 7 case the bankruptcy court or the trustee in bankruptcy will already have satisfied secured claims. § 362(d), § 554 and § 725. Section 726(a) states a schedule of priorities for the final distribution of the estate to the holders of unsecured claims.

Unsecured claims are divided into two groups: those entitled to priority under § 507 and those not entitled to priority. Priority claims must be paid in full before any payment is made to nonpriority claims. Priority claims are now divided into ten orders of priority. Claims within any order of priority must be paid in full before any payment is made to a claim in a lower order of priority. If all claims of the same order of priority cannot be fully paid, payment is made pro rata. The § 507 priorities are also recognized in reorganizations under Chapters 11, 12 and 13.

Priority claim status is important because in most liquidation cases there is little or nothing paid to nonpriority claims, and in reorganization cases priority claims must be paid in full in order to confirm reorganization plans under Chapters 11, 12 and 13. Nonpriority claims are paid pro rata, except that certain claims are subordinated by subsections (a)(3) and (a)(4) of § 726. Section 726(a)(4), subordinating fines and penalties (including punitive damage claims), applies both to secured and unsecured claims. If a creditor has a claim described in § 726(a)(4) that is secured by a lien, the claim is not treated as a secured claim. The trustee may avoid the lien under § 724(a). The claim is then paid only if all other unsecured claims are first paid. The rationale is that claims designed to punish the debtor should be disfavored if the effect of enforcement would be to punish other creditors by reducing the amount payable to them.

1. DOMESTIC SUPPORT OBLIGATIONS (DSO)

The first priority is accorded to domestic support obligations. § 507(a)(1)(A). As the drafting of BAPCPA progressed, women's and children's advocates became alarmed that rights to alimony, maintenance and support were being squeezed out by amendments giving automobile financers additional rights, both before and after discharge, by making credit card claims nondischargeable in more transactions, and by not cracking down on reaffirmation of otherwise dischargeable consumer debts. If the position of other creditors was being enhanced by these amendments, that of women and children was being correlatively reduced, particularly with respect to the competition for the debtor's postpetition earnings, usually the only source from which domestic support obligations (DSOs) could be satisfied. Congress responded to these concerns with a panoply of amendments designed to shore up claims for domestic support obligations, both with respect to assets of the debtor's estate and, more importantly, the debtor's postpetition assets. These changes will be discussed in context throughout the book, most extensively in chapter 4 on discharge and chapter 9 on consumer debtors.

Since Chapter 7 debtors have nonexempt assets to distribute to unsecured creditors in only a small percentage of cases, the extraordinary promotion of DSO claims from a seventh priority to a first priority in BAPCPA, ahead of even administrative expense claims (§ 507(a)(2)), may not be as helpful as it appears. Nonetheless, short of awarding such claims lien status, Congress has done all it can to give DSO claimants first call on assets of the estate that are neither exempt nor burdened by security interests. It is difficult to predict how the subordination of administrative expenses to DSOs will play out. Lawyers handling cases with limited assets and substantial DSO claims can expect no compensation from the estate, setting up a potentially interesting set of negotiations between the debtor, the debtor's bankruptcy lawyer and the debtor's former spouse.

The definition of DSOs, found in § 101(14A), expressly covers not only debts in the nature of alimony, maintenance and support that are owed to a spouse, former spouse or child of the debtor but also those owed to a governmental unit. Governments become involved because as a condition to obtaining Temporary Assistance to Needy Families under § 408(a)(3) of the Social Security Act, any child support obligation must be assigned to the state. *Collier on Bankruptcy* ¶ 523.11[8] (15th ed. rev. 2008). Unlike the prior law,

§ 507(a)(1) grants a priority not only to obligations owed to a spouse or child ((a)(1)(A)), but also to governmental units to which such obligations have been assigned ((a)(1)(B)), though subparagraph (1)(B) subordinates obligations owed to governmental units to those owed to spouses or children. These priorities are, in turn, subordinated to certain administrative expenses of a trustee who administers assets available for payment of DSOs. § 507(a)(1)(C). Section 1322(a)(4), added by BAPCPA, provides that if the debtor's repayment plan provides for less than full payment of the § 507(a)(1)(B) governmental priority claims, the plan must have a five-year duration. Considering the large percentage of failure of even three-year plans, such a requirement will make Chapter 13 plans more difficult to carry out.

2. ADMINISTRATIVE EXPENSES

The second priority is administrative expenses allowed under § 503. § 507(a)(2).

In re Jartran, Inc.
United States Court of Appeals, Seventh Circuit, 1984.
732 F.2d 584.

■ CUDAHY, Circuit Judge.

Appellants Reuben H. Donnelley Corporation ("Donnelley") and Sandra C. Tinsley, Inc. ("Tinsley") filed a claim for administrative priority against appellee Jartran, Inc.'s ("Jartran") estate. The bankruptcy judge denied the claim and, on appeal, the district court affirmed. Our appellate jurisdiction was properly invoked * * * and, for the reasons set forth below, we affirm.

The facts are undisputed and can be stated briefly. Jartran is in the business of leasing trucks to consumers nationwide. Pursuant to an agreement dated September 11, 1979 (the "Agreement"), Tinsley, an advertising agency, placed Jartran's orders for classified advertisements in telephone directories (the "Yellow Pages") with Donnelley. Donnelley, in turn, arranged with the Yellow Pages' publishers nationwide for Jartran's ads to appear. Under the Agreement, Tinsley and Jartran were liable to Donnelley for the cost of the advertising. Donnelley was liable to the publishers of the various directories. Although the parties were irrevocably committed to pay for the advertising several months before the ads were to appear,[1] the Agreement provided that Tinsley and Jartran would be billed for the ads only after they were published.

On December 31, 1981, Jartran filed for reorganization under Chapter 11 of the Bankruptcy Code, 11 U.S.C. §§ 1101–1174. At that time, the closing date had passed for many directories which had not yet been published. Appellants claim that the amount owing for ads placed in such directories, $1,311,695.50, should be treated as an administrative expense.[2] As is apparent from our discussion of the law relating to the allowance of administrative expenses, the key fact is that the irrevocable commitment by Jartran, Donnelley and Tinsley to place the ads was made before the filing of the petition in bankruptcy.

Section 503 of the Bankruptcy Code provides as follows:

* * *

(b) After notice and a hearing, there shall be allowed, administrative expenses * * * including—

(1)(A) the actual, necessary costs and expenses of preserving the estate, including wages, salaries or commissions for services rendered after the commencement of the case[.]

It is well settled that expenses incurred by the debtor-in-possession in attempting to rehabilitate the business during reorganization are within the ambit of § 503. * * * Appellants claim that, because the ads involved in the case were not published until after the "commencement of the case" and presumably aid Jartran in its efforts to rejuvenate its business, the cost of those ads should be treated as an administrative expense. As an administrative expense, the fees for the ads would be afforded priority ahead of certain pre-petition creditors.

The policies underlying the provisions of § 503 (and its predecessor, § 64(a)(1) of the Bankruptcy Act) are not hard to discern. If a reorganization is to succeed, creditors asked to extend credit after the petition is filed must be given priority so they will be moved to furnish the necessary credit to enable

---

[1] The date upon which ads were irrevocably placed is referred to in the Agreement and by the parties as the "closing date." On that date, up to six months prior to actual publication, ads could no longer be withdrawn from the directory. Each directory had its own closing date, but Donnelley uniformly billed the advertisers after publication. The Agreement provided that cancellations were effective only with respect to directories for which the closing date had not passed.

[2] Appellants agree that billing for ads published before the petition for reorganization was filed should be treated as non-priority, pre-petition debts. The parties also agree that expenses for ads for which the closing date occurred after the petition was filed are entitled to § 503 priority. * * *

the bankrupt to function. *See In re Mammoth Mart, Inc.*, 536 F.2d 950, 954 (1st Cir. 1976) (Coffin, Chief Judge). Thus, "[w]hen third parties are *induced* to supply goods or services to the debtor-in-possession * * * the purposes of [§ 503] plainly require that their claims be afforded priority." Id. (emphasis added; footnote omitted). Without a provision like § 503, efforts to reorganize would be hampered by the necessity of advance payment for all goods and services supplied to the estate since presumably no creditor would willingly assume the status of a non-priority creditor to a debtor undergoing reorganization.

This involves no injustice to the pre-petition creditors because it is for their benefit that reorganization is attempted. If reorganization successfully rehabilitates the debtor, presumably the pre-petition creditors will be better off than in a liquidation.

* * *

Recognizing the need for careful criteria in granting priority, the court in *Mammoth Mart* established a two part test for determining whether a debt should be afforded administrative priority. Under these criteria a claim will be afforded priority under § 503 if the debt both (1) "arise[s] from a transaction with the debtor-in-possession" and (2) is "beneficial to the debtor-in-possession in the operation of the business." *In re Mammoth Mart, Inc.*, 536 F.2d at 954. This test is, of course, essentially an effort to determine whether the underlying statutory purpose will be furthered by granting priority to the claim in question, and we will apply it in that spirit.

There is no question that the appearance of ads in Yellow Page directories throughout the country is beneficial to Jartran, as a debtor-in-possession, in the operation of its business. After filing the petition in bankruptcy, Jartran continued to place new ads in directories throughout the nation, thus evidencing the importance of Yellow Pages advertising to the success of the Jartran business. Therefore, the only serious question on appeal is whether the district court incorrectly concluded that the claim did not arise from a transaction with the debtor-in-possession.

Stated this simply, we believe that the district court's conclusion was correct: the agreement among the parties was entered into, and the ads were placed without possibility of revocation, before the petition was filed. Appellants urge, however, that the *publication date* rather than the closing date is the key date for § 503 purposes. They argue forcefully that, because the ads were *published* after the petition in bankruptcy was filed, appellants "supplied [consideration] to the debtor-in-possession in the operation of the business." *Mammoth Mart*, 536 F.2d at 954. Appellants support this argument by pointing out that appellants provided additional services after the closing date, and, presumably, after the petition was filed, including "review of advertising copy for correctness, size of advertisement, placement by page and category, accuracy of telephone listings and addresses, review of art work, and response to numerous queries from publishers concerning the advertisements." It was also necessary for Donnelley and Tinsley (presumably after the filing of the petition) to examine the final, published ads to ascertain their correctness. Then, and only then, would Jartran be billed for the advertisements.

We recognize that the services performed by appellants after the closing date, and after the filing of the petition, were significant and of value to Jartran. However, appellants do not allege that Jartran, after the filing of the petition, requested that appellants continue work on ads for which the closing date had passed. Nor is it claimed that Jartran had a duty to take affirmative steps to prevent Donnelley from engaging in post-petition performance. Thus, it was the pre-petition Jartran and not Jartran as debtor-in-possession that *induced* appellants to perform these services. To serve the policy of the priority, inducement of the creditor's performance *by the debtor-in-possession* is crucial to a claim for administrative priority in the context of the furnishing of goods or services to the debtor. * * * Because the closing date occurred before the debtor-in-possession came into existence (through the filing of the Chapter 11 petition), the bankruptcy court in the case before us held that the debtor-in-possession did not induce appellants' performance. * * *

As noted, the reason that *inducement* of the creditor's performance by the debtor-in-possession is crucial to a claim for administrative priority is rooted in the policies that gave rise to the creation of the priority. Thus, administrative priority is granted to post-petition expenses so that third parties will be moved to provide the goods and services necessary for a successful reorganization. * * * In the case before us, no inducement by the debtor-in-possession was required because the liability for the costs of the ads was irrevocably incurred before the petition was filed. This construction of the requirements for the administrative priority provides as full an opportunity as can be furnished for rehabilitation of the debtor. And this approach simply carries out the teaching of the Supreme Court, "that fairness requires that any claims incident to the debtor-in-possession's operation of the business be paid before those for whose benefit the continued operation of the business was allowed." *Mammoth Mart*, 536 F.2d at 954 citing *Reading Co. v. Brown*, 391 U.S. 471, 478 (1968) (first priority for tort claims based upon negligence attributable to debtor-in-possession). It is clear, however, that appellants' claim here arises out of commitments made before the debtor-in-possession came into existence.

Chapter 3. Claims

PROBLEM

Carly had achieved success as merchandising manager of GoodCo, a solvent, well regarded retailer. She agreed to leave her good job at GoodCo and join NewCo as general manager at an annual salary of $500,000, generous fringe benefits, stock options, etc. But NewCo was somewhat shaky financially and she was not finally won over by its blandishments until NewCo agreed to a "golden parachute" deal for her, referred to as the "Retention Agreement," which provided that should Carly's employment terminate without cause following a "Change of Control" she would receive three years' salary plus other benefits, including legal fees and expenses. Two years later, NewCo filed in Chapter 11; during the attempted reorganization Carly continued to work and was paid her prepetition salary. The reorganization failed, the assets were sold and Carly was terminated. She sought an administrative priority under § 503(b)(1)(A) for her claim for severance pay under the Retention Agreement. Carly argued that the severance agreement was implicitly a term of her postpetition employment. The bankruptcy court denied administrative expense status for her claim on the ground that the consideration for the Retention Agreement was entirely performed by Carly at the time she left the employment of GoodCo and joined NewCo; thus the severance pay was earned prepetition. She received reasonable compensation for her postpetition services and may make a prepetition claim for breach of the Retention Agreement. How should the appellate court rule on this case on appeal under the principles set forth in *Jartran*? *See In re FBI Distribution Corp.*, 330 F.3d 36 (1st Cir. 2003).

CHAPTER 4
DISCHARGE

A. INTRODUCTION

This Chapter discusses discharge in Chapter 7 bankruptcy. Chapters 11 and 13 contain separate—and distinctive—discharge provisions, and we will discuss these further in the material dealing with those Chapters. In Chapter 7 the debtor, if an individual, is entitled to a discharge of personal liability on prebankruptcy debts. Liquidating corporations don't need a bankruptcy discharge; after Chapter 7 liquidation, they can dissolve under state law. If individuals did not receive a discharge from prebankruptcy debts, they would be burdened with these debts indefinitely. In return for a discharge, the debtor must make available for distribution to creditors all nonexempt assets. However, in a large percentage of Chapter 7 bankruptcies of individuals, there are no assets available for payment to unsecured creditors. For most individuals the primary purpose of filing in bankruptcy is to obtain a discharge. Section 727(a) provides for the grant of a discharge to debtors, and § 727(b) declares that the effect of a discharge is to free the debtor from all debts that arose before bankruptcy. Other effects of the discharge are stated in § 524, which we will discuss later.

In some cases debtors are not entitled to a discharge. The various grounds for denying a discharge are set forth in § 727(a). Most of the grounds refer to misconduct by the debtor. But an important ground for denying discharge, § 727(a)(8), is not directly related to any misconduct by the debtor. It denies a Chapter 7 discharge if the debtor has previously received a discharge under Chapter 7 in a case commenced within eight years before the date of the filing of the petition. Before BAPCPA the period was six years. The most commonly stated rationale for this rule, which was also part of the Bankruptcy Act, is that given by Justice Clark in *Perry v. Commerce Loan Co.*, 383 U.S. 392, 399 (1966): "The unmistakable purpose of the six-year provision was to prevent the creation of a class of habitual bankrupts—debtors who might repeatedly escape their obligations as frequently as they chose by going through repeated bankruptcy."

Section 727(a)(9) provides that if a debtor has received a Chapter 13 discharge, she cannot receive a subsequent Chapter 7 discharge in a case filed within six years (the six-year period was not changed in this provision) after the

Chapter 13 discharge. The exception to that rule is that if, in the Chapter 13 case, the debtor paid under the plan either all of the unsecured claims or 70% of such claims and proposed the plan in good faith and gave her best effort, she is not barred by the six-year rule in receiving a Chapter 7 discharge.

Even if a debtor is entitled to a discharge in Chapter 7, the discharge may not apply to all of the debts of the debtor. A qualified debtor is generally entitled to the "fresh start" given by a discharge, but Congress determined that some types of creditors holding certain types of claims generally have equities that are greater than those of the debtor. These enumerated types of claims are "nondischargeable." § 523(a). Creditors holding such claims may file a claim in the bankruptcy and can participate in the distribution of the bankruptcy estate, but, to the extent the creditor's claim has not been satisfied, the creditor's claim will survive bankruptcy.

Section 727(c)(1) provides that objection to a discharge of a Chapter 7 debtor may be made by the trustee, a creditor or the U. S. Trustee. Rule 4004(a) requires that the objection must be filed within 60 days after the first date set for the § 341 meeting of creditors, unless the court extends the time to file the objection for cause under Rule 4004(b). As with other statute of limitations type defenses, however, a debtor that fails to timely assert the time-bar issue may waive the defense. *Kontrick v. Ryan*, 540 U.S. 443 (2004).

B. DENIAL OF DISCHARGE BECAUSE OF DEBTOR'S MISCONDUCT

A fresh start by discharge is denied to some debtors that are guilty of inequitable conduct. This policy is detailed in § 727(a). Depriving individual debtors of a discharge in Chapter 7 is a very serious sanction. It leaves debtors with the dismal prospect of having their postpetition assets, including future earnings, subject to seizure under state law to pay the deficiencies remaining on prepetition debts.

Section 727(a)(2) denies a discharge to debtors who, within a year of filing, transfer or conceal their property with "intent to hinder, delay, or defraud" creditors. Perhaps the most common example of this conduct is the foolish attempt of debtors faced with bankruptcy to hide assets by transferring them to relatives for little or no consideration in the belief that the worst that can happen to them is that, if bankruptcy ensues, the property will be brought back into the bankruptcy estate and distributed to creditors. What do such debtors have to lose? Answer: their discharge, if they find themselves in bankruptcy within a year of the transfer. We have a full treatment of fraudulent transfers in chapter 7. Debtors making fraudulent transfers may be smoked out by their response to Question 10 in Official Form 7 (Statement of Financial Affairs) which requires a description of any property transferred out of ordinary course within one year of filing and a statement of the value received and the relationship of the transferee.

If a debtor fails to disclose such a transfer or makes other false statements in the schedules required at the time of filing, the debtor forfeits a discharge under § 727(a)(4)(A) for making a "false oath or account." Section 521(1) requires debtors to file schedules listing creditors, assets, liabilities and other matters, including a statement of the debtor's financial affairs, and the Official Forms for the schedules require that debtors sign a declaration under penalty of perjury that the information given is "true and correct." The false oath ground for denial of discharge addresses one of the most common ploys of dishonest debtors: their failure to disclose assets. Some assets are easy to hide and hard to find. This type of cheating is probably endemic but is sometimes discovered by comparing bullish financial statements made by debtors applying for credit with the meager assets listed on bankruptcy schedules only a few months later. Unless the debtor can satisfactorily describe what happened to the missing assets, § 727(a)(5) denies a discharge to the memory-challenged debtor.

A controversial ground for denial of discharge is that in § 727(a)(3) regarding the debtor's failure to keep records "from which the debtor's financial condition or business transactions might be ascertained." Understandably, the policy of restricting discharges to honest debtors can be implemented only by requiring debtors to come clean with the bankruptcy system. If they can't produce intelligible records so that trustees and creditors can trace their dealings, vital issues concerning their entitlement to receive a discharge may remain unsolved. But judicial determination of what is adequate recordkeeping may be difficult in the extreme. It is an easy case if the debtor is known to have destroyed or concealed relevant records, but what if the debtor is just a sloppy bookkeeper who is the only person who can readily interpret the chicken tracks in her ledgers? See *In re Juzwiak*, 89 F.3d 424 (7th Cir. 1996) (the fact that an accountant could reconstruct debtor's financial records by a painstaking study of the written records supplemented by the debtor's oral explanations was not good enough). Or what if she delegates the record keeping for their partnership to her partner who does a bad job? The following problem is such a case.

PROBLEM

Debtor was a high school graduate working for UPS in 2002 when the real estate business was booming. He decided to stop delivering packages and start making money in real estate. He encountered Parker who appeared to be an experienced real estate operator. In time Debtor and Parker formed a partnership ("D & P"), which, in turn, set up a series of partnerships engaged in purchasing, rehabilitating and managing multi-family rental properties. They prospered—for awhile. Although they had no formal agreement allocating the responsibilities of each partner, Debtor's role evolved as the one who located the properties for acquisition; Parker managed the properties and maintained the partnership financial records. After the real estate bubble burst in 2006, all their properties were foreclosed by unpaid lenders during 2007-2008. These lenders sued Debtor and Parker individually for their liability on deficiency judgments. Debtor filed in Chapter 7 in 2008. Lender objected to Debtor's discharge on the ground that under § 727(a)(3) Debtor had failed to keep records from which his financial condition might be ascertained. Debtor conceded that he had failed to do so but contended that his failure was justified under all the circumstances of the case. Debtor knew nothing about record keeping or financial matters in general, and it was understood that Parker would deal with these matters. In fact, Parker had made a mess of the financial records and absconded before Debtor's filing in bankruptcy. Debtor's description in court of his business activities seemed credible and his honesty was not questioned. How should the the court rule on Lender's objection? See *In re Cacioli*, 463 F.3d 229 (2d Cir. 2006).

C. NONDISCHARGEABLE DEBTS

1. UNSCHEDULED DEBTS

In re Madaj
United States Court of Appeals, Sixth Circuit, 1998.
149 F.3d 467.

■ BATCHELDER, Circuit Judge.

"How sharper than a serpent's tooth it is to have a thankless child!"
WILLIAM SHAKESPEARE, KING LEAR, act I, sc. 4

Before us on appeal are a husband and wife ("the Creditors"), who have felt the bite of their thankless foster child. With his wife, this foster child ("the Debtors") borrowed a substantial sum of money from his foster parents, promising to repay the loan within a few months out of anticipated insurance proceeds from a fire loss. Instead of repaying the loan, however, the Debtors filed a petition in bankruptcy under Chapter 7 and failed to include the foster parents in the list of creditors filed with the petition. Their no-asset case was duly administered, the Debtors eventually obtained a discharge pursuant to § 727, and their case was closed. The Creditors, unaware of the bankruptcy proceeding, and having repeatedly importuned the Debtors to repay the loan according to their promise, filed suit in state court and obtained a judgment against the Debtors for the unpaid balance of the loan.

The Debtors moved to reopen their Chapter 7 proceeding in order to list the debt, claiming that their failure to include it initially had been due to forgetfulness and inadvertence. The Creditors objected to the motion to reopen, claiming that in light of their repeated requests for payment and the Debtors' protests of poverty, the Debtors' memory lapse was not credible, and that the Debtors had failed to list the debt because they intended to defraud the Creditors. The Creditors opposed the reopening of the Chapter 7 proceeding because they believed, and still believe, that an unlisted debt is not discharged, and that the Debtors ought not be permitted to now list this debt and obtain its discharge. The parties agree that if this debt had been timely scheduled, it would have been dischargeable under § 523, and that even if the debt had been listed and a proof of claim had been filed, because this was a no-asset case, there would have been no payment on the debt. The Bankruptcy Court denied the Debtors' motion to reopen, but held that the debt to the Creditors was nonetheless discharged, and the District Court affirmed. The Creditors timely appealed. We now AFFIRM.

* * *

The confusion in the district and circuit courts concerning unlisted Chapter 7 debts in a no-asset case, including the dischargeability of such debts, the effect of an order of discharge on such debts, and the efficacy of reopening a bankruptcy case to include them, is widespread. This confusion is due, in part, to a line of cases that perpetuates the erroneous view that once his case is closed, the debtor must have his case reopened in order to discharge a pre-petition debt not listed in the bankruptcy petition; once the case is reopened, the debtor amends his schedules to list the debt, and the now-scheduled debt is covered by the discharge. But this is not the law.

In a Chapter 7 no-asset case such as this, "reopening the case merely to schedule [an omitted] debt is for all practical purposes a useless gesture." *In re Hunter*, 116 B.R. 3, 5 (Bankr.D.D.C.1990). * * * Under these circumstances, amending the schedule is pointless because, as we shall explain, this debt is discharged and reopening the case and scheduling the debt cannot affect that fact.

The law in this area is counter-intuitive, and requires a careful fitting together of the relevant sections of the Bankruptcy Code and Rules. Because of the confusion in this area, a review of the provisions governing dischargeability of debts and the effect of a discharge in a Chapter 7 proceeding is in order. At the risk of appearing simplistic, we can summarize the relevant provisions as follows:

A discharge under § 727 discharges every prepetition debt, without regard to whether a proof of claim has been filed, unless that debt is specifically excepted from discharge under § 523. Section 523(a)(3) contains the only exceptions for unlisted and unscheduled debts. Section 523(a)(3)(B) excepts from discharge those debts originally incurred by means of fraud, false pretenses, or malicious conduct, as enumerated in §§ 523(a)(2), (4), and (6), (hereinafter "fraudulent" or "fraudulently incurred" debts).

Section 523(a)(3)(A) excepts from discharge all other debts—i.e., debts other than those fraudulent debts specified in § 523(a)(2), (4), or (6)—which are not listed by the debtor in his petition and schedules in time for the creditor to file a timely proof of claim. However, even § 523(a)(3)(A) does not except an unscheduled debt from discharge if the creditor had notice or actual knowledge of the bankruptcy case in time for timely filing of a proof of claim.

In a Chapter 7 no-asset case the court does not set a deadline for the filing of proofs of claim. Rather, the court may notify creditors that there are no assets, that it is not necessary to file claims, and that if sufficient assets become available for payment of a dividend, further notice will be given for filing of claims. See Fed. R. Bankr.P. 2002(e). Therefore, there is no date by which a proof of claim must be filed to be "timely," and whenever a creditor receives notice or knowledge of the bankruptcy, he may file a proof of claim.

The operation of § 523 is obscured somewhat by its convoluted structure, but most of the twists and turns affecting dischargeability have to do with the fraudulent types of debts enumerated in §§ 523(a)(2), (4), and (6).

The statutory language relevant to debts not fraudulently incurred reads as follows:

> A discharge under section 727. . . does not discharge an individual debtor from any debt. . . neither listed nor scheduled. . . in time to permit. . . timely filing of a proof of claim, unless such creditor had notice or actual knowledge of the case in time for such timely filing.

§ 523(a)(3)(A). Thus, § 523(a)(3)(A) excepts a debt from discharge if the debt was not scheduled in time for a timely filing of the proof of claim, *but not if,* despite the debt's not having been scheduled, the creditor nevertheless received notice of the bankruptcy in time to file a timely proof of claim. Put another way, the debt is discharged so long as it is scheduled in time for the creditor to file a proof of claim or the creditor finds out about the bankruptcy case in time to do so. Scheduling the debt enables the bankruptcy court to provide the creditor with notice. Where the creditor, through some other means, finds out about the bankruptcy in time to assert his right to a portion of the proceeds of the estate, there is no reason to except an otherwise dischargeable debt from the effect of the discharge. But where the creditor is not aware of the bankruptcy, he cannot assert his right. Without the exception in § 523(a)(3)(A), the debtor could simply deny his uninformed creditors the opportunity to recover from the bankruptcy estate by omitting their debts from the schedule.

In a Chapter 7 no-asset case, however, the creditors cannot recover from the estate because there is nothing to recover. For this reason, there is no deadline for filing a timely proof of claim in a no-asset case. Technically speaking, therefore, no matter when the creditor learns of the bankruptcy, he is able to file a timely claim. Because § 523(a)(3)(A) excepts the unscheduled debt from discharge "unless such creditor had notice or actual knowledge of the case in time for such timely filing," the moment the creditor receives notice or knowledge of the bankruptcy case, § 523(a)(3)(A) ceases to provide the basis for an exception from discharge. Consequently, the debt is at that point discharged.

The result may seem strange at first blush, but it makes sense when one considers both the type of debt involved and the nature of a no-asset case. Unlike the fraudulent debts covered by §§ 523(a)(2), (4) and (6), the debts excepted from discharge by § 523(a)(3)(A) are not excepted because of their nature, but because an injustice will result if the debt is discharged in a situation where the creditor never had the opportunity to participate in the distribution of the assets of the estate.

Yet, there are no proceeds to be distributed to the creditors in a no-asset case, which renders the notice function served by the scheduling of debts far less important. For precisely this reason, there is no deadline for the filing of proofs of claim in a no-asset case. For the most part, creditors in a no-asset case do not stand to gain by having their debts scheduled, nor do they stand to lose by having their debts omitted from the schedules. Thus, it should come as no surprise that the exception contained in § 523(a)(3)(A)—designed as it is to prevent an ignorant creditor from suffering an unjust loss by having a debt discharged without his knowing it—operates differently in no-asset cases where there is little risk that a creditor will suffer a disadvantage resulting from an unscheduled debt. * * *

In the case before us, it is undisputed that the debt at issue, *had it been timely filed*, would not have been included in any category of debts that are excepted from discharge by § 523. It is undisputed that the Debtors' bankruptcy was a no-asset Chapter 7 case. In order to determine whether the bankruptcy court erred in denying the Debtors' motion to reopen their Chapter 7 case to amend the schedule of debts and in holding that the debt at issue here was nevertheless discharged, we must answer one question: when an otherwise dischargeable debt is omitted from the schedule in a Chapter 7 no-asset case and the debtor receives a discharge, what is the effect of re-opening the case to permit the debtor to schedule the omitted debt?

The answer is "there is no effect." The reason that the reopening has no effect is clear. A debtor cannot change the nature of the debt by failing to list it in his petition and schedules. Section 523(a)(3)(A) excepts from discharge only those debts as to which a timely proof of claim cannot be filed because the debts were not listed and the creditor had neither notice nor actual knowledge of the bankruptcy in time to file a timely a proof of claim. In a no-asset Chapter 7 case, there is no date by which a proof of claim must be filed in order to be "timely." Whenever the creditor receives notice or acquires actual knowledge of the bankruptcy, he may file a proof of claim, that claim will be timely, and the fact that the debts were not listed becomes irrelevant. Section 523(a)(3)(A) simply provides no basis for excepting an unlisted debt from discharge if the creditor has actual knowledge such that he can file a proof of claim. And once the § 727 order of discharge is entered, all of the debtor's prepetition debts are either discharged or they are not discharged; nothing the debtor does after the entry of the order of discharge can change the character of those debts.

If the Creditors before us had acquired knowledge of the bankruptcy prior to the entry of the discharge order, the debt would not have been excepted from discharge because the Creditors had actual knowledge in time to file a proof of claim. Their learning of the bankruptcy after the entry of the discharge order did not transmogrify the debt into one that is excepted from discharge under some provision of the Code other than § 523(a)(3)(A). Whether or not the Debtors reopen their case and amend their schedules to list this debt, there will still be no date by which proofs of claim would have to be filed in order to be timely; because the Creditors have actual knowledge of the bankruptcy, § 523(a)(3)(A) does not except this debt from discharge. Hence, the reopening of the Debtors' Chapter 7 case to permit the amendment of the schedules can have no effect whatsoever. The debt in question, listed or not, is discharged.

For these reasons, the order of the bankruptcy court denying the Debtors' motion to reopen and holding that the debt to the Creditors has been discharged is AFFIRMED.

NOTES

1. Does the view of the court in *Madaj* offer incentive for debtors to intentionally fail to schedule debts? The First Circuit rejected the no-assets-no-notice rule in *Colonial Surety Company v. Weizman*, 2009 WL 1219508 (1st Cir. 2009).

2. *Collier on Bankruptcy* ¶ 523.09[5] (15th ed. rev. 2007) endorses the view that it is unnecessary to reopen a case in order to obtain discharge of an unsche-

duled debt in a no-asset case; however, a bankruptcy court has the discretion to reopen a case to allow a debtor to add a creditor in order to promote the debtor's fresh start by having a complete list of all discharged debts.

2. DOMESTIC SUPPORT OBLIGATIONS (DSO)

a. Section 523(a)(5)

Ex-spouses often incur obligations arising from alimony, maintenance, child support, property settlements, assumption of marital debts, or the like. It has been long-standing bankruptcy policy that dependent spouses and children should receive protection against being deprived of the benefits of support obligations by the discharge of the obligated spouse in bankruptcy. *Wetmore v. Markoe*, 196 U.S. 68 (1904). This policy has been carried forward in the 1978 Bankruptcy Code, and BAPCPA further expanded the protection from discharge of inter-spousal obligations.

Section 523(a)(5) provides that "domestic support obligations" (DSOs) are nondischargeable in Chapters 7, 11, 12 and 13. DSO is defined in § 101(14A) as a debt owing to a spouse, former spouse or child of the debtor or governmental unit that is in the nature of alimony, maintenance or support and that is established by a separation agreement, divorce decree, or property settlement agreement, a court order, or a determination made under nonbankruptcy law by a governmental unit. Support obligations do not qualify as DSOs if they are assigned to a nongovernmental entity unless they are voluntarily assigned for collection. DSOs are often assigned to governmental units as a condition to obtaining Temporary Assistance to Needy Families (formerly Aid to Families with Dependent Children) under § 408(a)(3) of the Social Security Act.

The Code does not define the terms alimony, maintenance or support of spouses or children. State court decrees or settlement agreements may label obligations as alimony, child support or property settlements, and these designations are given weight in determining the nature of the obligation, but they are not conclusive. Section 101(14A)(B) provides that a debt may be held to be one "in the nature of alimony, maintenance, or support * * * whether such debt is expressly so designated."

Under the original version of the 1978 Code, debts relating to marital dissolutions that were essentially support obligations of one kind or another (alimony, maintenance or child or spousal support) were nondischargeable under former § 523(a)(5), but those that merely divided up the assets of the marital estate (property settlements) were dischargeable. This distinction was the subject of much litigation. *Collier* attempts to distill the case law into a series of factors. Among these are: (1) labels are given some weight; (2) if the spouse or children benefited by the payments have a strong need for support, the obligations are nondischargeable; (3) if the obligation terminates on the death or remarriage of the receiving spouse, it is usually nondischargeable; (4) if the term of payments is for a fixed period of time, particularly a short period of time, this tends to show a property settlement that is dischargeable; (5) if the obligation is subject to modification by a court, it looks more like a support obligation and less like a property equalization obligation; and (6) if tax law treats the payments as alimony, maintenance or support, bankruptcy courts may be influenced to follow. *Collier on Bankruptcy* ¶ 523.11[6] (15th ed. rev. 2007).

The following opinion reflects the exasperation of a leading jurist in attempting to distinguish support obligations and property settlements. As we will see, the distinction is still important under BAPCPA.

In re Werthen

United States Court of Appeals, First Circuit, 2003.
329 F.3d 269.

■ BOUDIN, Chief Judge.

Paul Werthen, the debtor in this chapter 7 bankruptcy proceeding, appeals from a judgment of the Bankruptcy Appellate Panel ("BAP") for the First Circuit affirming an order of the bankruptcy court. That order determined that two obligations of Paul to his ex-wife Kathleen Werthen, incurred in their state-court divorce proceeding, were alimony or support rather than property division, and therefore nondischargeable in bankruptcy under § 523(a)(5) (2000). We affirm, conceding the case to be a close one under a badly muddled statute.

Paul and Kathleen were married in 1982 and separated in 1995, when Kathleen filed for divorce. During the marriage, Kathleen was the primary caretaker of the home and the couple's four children. Paul was the primary earner, working full time at Whitman Tool & Die Co. ("Whitman"), his family's business in which he held a considerable equity interest. The Massachusetts Probate and Family Court issued an initial divorce decree on March 7, 2000, and entered an amended judgment together with a supporting memorandum on May 2, 2000.

The picture painted by the state court was not favorable to Paul. He had drinking problems, he physically abused his wife and children during the marriage, and he frustrated Kathleen's efforts to obtain a college degree and a measure of financial independence while strictly limiting her allowance. During the divorce proceedings, he and other family members engaged in obfuscatory tactics or worse, aiming to diminish the award against him. The state court noted these circumstances as supporting a generous award, but they do not by themselves explain which portion of the award was alimony and support.

More pertinent to the level of alimony and support were other findings: that the Werthens were a "middle-to-high income family;" that she would have custody of the children who were still relatively young; that her ability to work was affected by a back injury and limited by her curtailed education; that his past income and the value of his family-company stock were large; and that he had understated income and value to decrease the award. On this last issue, the state court found: "Any which way the Husband could avoid his financial obligations to his wife and children, obfuscate his financial condition, and shrink the marital pool of assets, he tried with all his might."

The final decree awarded Kathleen—under the rubric of "Child Support and Alimony"—one-third of Paul's future bonuses and $450 a week in child support. The former payments are to continue until Paul's death or Kathleen's death or remarriage; and the latter payments are to continue until the youngest child (born in 1989) is emancipated, graduates from college, or reaches the age of twenty-three. Paul does not dispute that these awards are not dischargeable in bankruptcy. The dischargeability issue, which alone concerns us, arises from two items contained in the balance of the state court award.

Under the rubric of "Property Division," the state court awarded Kathleen *inter alia* (1) $222,000, representing 60 percent of the gross bonuses received by Paul in the years 1996-99, reduced to $124,485.84 by amounts in savings accounts already awarded Kathleen (the "past bonus award"); and (2) $611,163.20, representing Kathleen's 40 percent marital share of Paul's 22 percent equity interest in Whitman (the "stock award"). With respect to these two awards, the court structured Paul's payment schedule as yearly installments of $50,000 for nine years beginning in 2000, with the remaining balance due in two separate payments in the tenth and the eleventh years (plus interest on unpaid balances).

On July 28, 2000, less than 90 days after the final judgment, Paul filed a voluntary petition for chapter 7 bankruptcy. In that proceeding Kathleen sought a ruling that the past bonus and stock awards—largely or entirely yet unpaid—were not subject to discharge. Her first claim was based on the above-quoted paragraph (5) of subsection 523(a), which prevents discharge of obligations for alimony or support. Alternatively, she relied on paragraph (15), which prevents discharge of other debts incurred in a divorce—even where not within the scope of paragraph (5)—unless the hardship from such a discharge is outweighed by the interests of the debtor. Kathleen bore the burden of showing that the debts were nondischargeable. * * *

The bankruptcy court held a trial on October 2, 2001, and then ruled in a bench opinion that both the bonus and stock awards were nondischargeable under paragraph (5). Thereafter, the court initially altered its position as to the stock award, raising the possibility that it might instead be separately analyzed under paragraph (15); but in a final written decision, the court returned to its original ruling, holding both the bonus and stock awards to be nondischargeable under paragraph (5). The bankruptcy court treated the issue as one turning on the intent of, but not necessarily the label employed by, the state court judge in making the awards.

To discern this intent, the bankruptcy court invoked a set of factors set forth in *Altavilla v. Altavilla* (*In re Altavilla*), 40 B.R. 938, 941 (Bankr.D. Mass.1984). In viewing the awards as intended "to provide support" for Kathleen and the children rather than as division of property, the court stressed in its final decision Kathleen's otherwise limited resources and earning capacity, the lengthy pay-out period of the two awards, and several other factors. On Paul's appeal, the BAP affirmed, holding that intent was a question of fact and concluding that the bankruptcy court's decision was not plainly wrong. It too mentioned the payment structure and the lack of other assured income to support the family, the future bonus payments being uncertain.

* * * The issue presented is a recurring one with a long history of case-law and legislative development. Unfortunately, the statutory bifurcation in paragraph (5) rests on an unstable assumption.

Paragraph (5) turns upon a supposed distinction between "support" payments for spouse and children (what the statute calls "alimony to, maintenance for, or support of such spouse or child") and other kinds of divorce awards—for example, a division of jointly owned property. A similar distinction is used to determine the federal tax consequences of such payments and may have other effects under state law.[4] But the concepts are not necessarily identical in each context, and we are concerned here only with the meaning of the terms in section 523(a)(5), which is a matter of federal bankruptcy law. * * *

The underlying concept is easy to grasp: support payments are, roughly speaking, what is given to provide for the upkeep of the recipient spouse and children, *see, e.g.,* 4 *Collier,* ¶ 523.11, at 523-81, while other divisions or payments serve different purposes. The central problem is that the two supposedly separate categories overlap because the need for ongoing support will often depend on how much property the less well-off spouse is given outright. Indeed, under Massachusetts law, courts are authorized expressly to award property "[i]n addition to or *in lieu of* a judgment to pay alimony." Mass. Gen. Laws ch. 208, § 34 (2000) (emphasis added).

---

[4] In general, alimony is deductible to the payor and taxable to the payee, 26 U.S.C. §§ 61(a)(8), 62(a)(10) (2000); and in Massachusetts, alimony is modifiable, but property divisions are not * * * .

The federal courts have been unwilling to treat the label applied by the divorce court as controlling for Bankruptcy Code purposes. * * *

Nominally, the critical issue is whether the divorce court judge "intended" a particular award to be for support or for something else. * * * In practice, courts look at a range of factors, including the language used by the divorce court and whether the award seems designed to assuage need, as discerned from the structure of the award and the financial circumstances of the recipients. 4 *Collier,* ¶ 523.11.

Here, as usual in cases worth litigating, the factors do not all line up on one side. One of those helpful to Kathleen is that the award of formal alimony and support to her seems quite limited for an upper middle-class household with several children: $450 per week for the four children (roughly $23,400 per year), plus the evanescent obligation that Paul pay Kathleen one-third of his future "bonuses"—a form of compensation that the state court recognized could easily be manipulated downward within a family company. Kathleen did have real earning capacity but it was capped by her frustrated education, childcare obligations and her back injury.

In this situation, it is no great leap to suppose that $50,000 per year for the next decade, representing the structured pay-out of the past bonus and stock awards, was intended in some measure to close the gap. As the bankruptcy court pointed out, the main pay-out period corresponded roughly to the time in which Kathleen would be supporting the children and would be responsible as well, under the decree, for a portion of their college tuition. That the payment period did not end with anyone's death or exact majority could be a point in Paul's favor, 4 *Collier,* ¶ 523.11[d], at 523-85, but a payout of fixed property in installments is another way to recognize resources available from the payor in fixing support.

The Tenth Circuit took such a view in *Goin v. Rives (In re Goin),* 808 F.2d 1391 (10th Cir. 1987) (*per curiam*). There, a state court awarded the wife $350 per month in child support and the sum of $80,000 to be paid in annual increments of $5,000. The decree said that the $80,000 represented the wife's "one-half interest in certain real estate and stock." *Id.* at 1392. The Tenth Circuit affirmed a finding of nondischargeability, in part because the state decree did not provide for any alimony, and because the bankruptcy court found that $350 a month was insufficient to support both the spouse and the children in conformity with the lifestyle to which they had become accustomed. *Id.* at 1392-93.

Paul's first argument for an out-and-out discharge is the state court's formal division of its assessments into two boxes; but under paragraph (5), payments intended for the support of spouse and child are not dischargeable and the Massachusetts statute quoted above says that an award of property can be made "in lieu" of alimony. Perhaps a more useful point—which Paul does not stress—is that, although $50,000 a year for alimony might not seem outlandish for a man who averaged roughly $150,000 a year during 1996-99, the final catch-up payments in years 10-11 appear to total over $200,000 apart from accrued interest, which does not sound like annual alimony or support outside the world of the super-rich.

Paul also argues in his brief that a precise calculation of Kathleen's income and needs shows that she was well-off without the disputed awards, but Kathleen's own detailed figures and analysis suggest that she was underfunded. Neither the state court nor the bankruptcy court made a systematic assessment of the numbers in terms of "need." Our own assessment suggests that without the awards, Kathleen would be underfunded at least to some extent in relation to her own description of expenses.

Accordingly, we see no basis to disturb the conclusion of the bankruptcy court. Just how much deference is due to its assessment is debatable * * * but there is substantial reason to believe that the state court in some measure intended the property division to assure adequate support for Kathleen and her children. The raw numbers, the uncertainty of future bonus payments, and the lengthy payout period all support this conclusion. The property-division label applied by the court seems most likely to have reflected no more than the mechanical fact that the payments were to come from identified existing resources.

This could be a different case had Paul argued for a remand. A position neither side has taken is that the two disputed awards were partly intended as support and partly as an equitable division of joint property over and above the amount needed for adequate support. Some allocation of the awards between the two categories might reflect the "right" answer; and some courts have so analyzed such problems. * * *

But in this case such a division would be very hard to calculate and would consume more time and lawyer expense—not to speak of the need then to decide the residual paragraph (15) issue. Nor is it clear that the result would better correspond to the "intent" of the state judge who was not completing a bankruptcy schedule but trying to solve a down-to-earth problem of allocating assets and income streams in a divorce. Paul was entitled to make this appeal an all or nothing choice; we see no reason to inject further options that he did not seek. * * *

The larger problem remains that the present statute needs revision. It is no accident that the 1970 Commission on the Bankruptcy Laws of the United States recommended that the line-drawing approach between alimony and property division be abandoned. The competing interests are for Congress to sort out; but a more administrable solution is overdue.

Affirmed.

NOTE

Why didn't Chief Judge Boudin decide *Werthen* under § 523(a)(15), discussed below?

b. Section 523(a)(15)

Until 1994, former § 523(a)(5), which provided that support obligations substantially similar to those now included in the definition of DSOs in § 101(14A) were nondischargeable, was the only provision dealing with the dischargeability of marital claims in the Code. A major shortcoming of § 523(a)(5) is that it requires courts to draw lines in very ambiguous situations. Negotiations surrounding a divorce may result in the debtor undertaking obligations that benefit the nondebtor spouse or child but are, arguably, not for alimony, maintenance or support. The most common example of this is property settlement agreements dividing the marital property between the spouses. Another is "hold harmless" agreements in which the debtor agrees to pay a debt on which both spouses are liable and hold the nondebtor spouse harmless against liability on that debt. But debts for support falling within § 523(a)(5) and debts arising from property settlements or hold harmless agreements falling outside that section may be strongly interrelated: the debtor may be willing to make a more generous property settlement in exchange for lower support payments.

By adding § 523(a)(15) in 1994, Congress showed its dissatisfaction with the existing system that required judges to declare certain kinds of debts relating to marriage dissolution nondischargeable and other (often interdependent) dissolution-related debts dischargeable. After § 523(a)(15), as amended by BAPCPA, a broad array of inter-spousal debts are nondischargeable in Chapter 7. Such obligations are:

> to a spouse, former spouse, or child of the debtor and not of the kind described in paragraph (5) that is incurred by the debtor in the course of a divorce or separation or in connection with a separation agreement, divorce decree or other order of a court of record, or a determination made in accordance with State or territorial law by a governmental unit

What is the breadth of this provision?

PROBLEMS

1. Husband (H) is a lawyer; Wife (W) is a doctor. They decided to dissolve their marriage amicably and to remain good friends. How does § 523(a)(15) apply to the following cases?

a. As part of the dissolution settlement, W agreed to pay H $100,000 in five annual installments in order to equalize the division of their assets. A year after dissolution of the marriage, a recession struck, and the HMO whose members W treated filed in bankruptcy, leaving W with several hundred thousand dollars of worthless claims against the HMO for services rendered to its members for which W was entitled to reimbursement. W had insufficient assets to deal with her creditors and filed in Chapter 7. At the time of dissolution, W and H each had incomes of roughly $150,000 per year, but by the time of W's filing, W had an income of no more than $30,000; H, an insolvency lawyer, had an income that had burgeoned to $400,000 annually. Is W's debt to H nondischargeable? What policy would be furthered by making such a debt nondischargeable?

b. During their marriage, H and W had always shared investment opportunities. After they had reached a property settlement and had a court date set for final dissolution, H told W of an initial public offering of stock that his broker had made available to him in the amount of $100,000 and inquired whether she wished to share his allotment. She agreed to go in on the deal but was short of cash. H lent her $50,000 to purchase her half of the allotment. If W files for Chapter 7 bankruptcy after dissolution of the marriage, will W's debt to H be considered to have been "incurred by the debtor in the course of a divorce" and therefore nondischargeable under § 523(a)(15)? What policy would be furthered by making such a debt nondischargeable?

2. Husband (H) and Wife (W) were both employed at the time of the amicable dissolution of their marriage. In the dissolution settlement, H agreed to assume liability for approximately $25,000 that W owed on her automobile, credit cards and other personal debts. After dissolution, H lost his job and filed in Chapter 13. Which provision applies to H's assumption of W's debts, § 523(a)(5) or (15)? Why does it matter? § 1328(a)(2).

With respect to Problem 2, amendments to § 1328(a)(2) in BAPCPA expanded the kinds of debts that are nondischargeable in Chapter 13 cases, but the expansion does not include debts falling within § 523(a)(15). Since H filed in Chapter 13, the court must work through the traditional analysis of whether his assumption of W's personal debts was in the nature of a support payment within the DSO definition in § 101(14A). In a number of other provisions throughout BAPCPA, special treatment is given DSOs that is not accorded the kinds of debts included in § 523(a)(15), *e.g.*, priority under § 507(a)(1). The issue of whether a dissolution-related debt falls within the DSO definition must be faced with respect to a number of provisions throughout the Code, but § 523(a)(15) operates only with respect to Chapter 7 discharges.

3. WILLFUL AND MALICIOUS INJURY

Section 523(a)(6) makes nondischargeable a debt "for willful and malicious injury by the debtor to another entity or to the property of another entity." Since a discharge in bankruptcy is an equitable remedy for the relief of debtors it may be inequitable to allow discharge in cases in which the debt represents liability for conduct of the debtor involving moral turpitude. This exception from discharge means, for example, that a debtor who assaults a neighbor or deliberately burns down the neighbor's house cannot get absolution in Chapter 7 from the liability resulting from those acts. But not many cases of that kind reach the bankruptcy courts. Most cases of injury to person or property involve a degree of moral culpability by the debtor that is much lower.

To define the line between dischargeability and nondischargeability, the Bankruptcy Code uses two rather imprecise terms: willful and malicious. Most of the litigated cases have fallen into two groups: those involving personal injuries, particularly injuries resulting from automobile accidents caused by the debtor while intoxicated, and those involving conversion of property. The drunken driving issue was resolved by the addition in 1984 of § 523(a)(9) at the behest of Mothers Against Drunken Driving, making such debts nondischargeable. The Supreme Court has spoken on personal injuries in the next case, and we follow that case with material on property conversion.

Kawaauhau v. Geiger
Supreme Court of the United States, 1998.
523 U.S. 57.

- Justice GINSBURG delivered the opinion of the Court.

Section 523(a)(6) of the Bankruptcy Code provides that a debt "for willful and malicious injury by the debtor to another" is not dischargeable. § 523(a)(6). The question before us is whether a debt arising from a medical malpractice judgment, attributable to negligent or reckless conduct, falls within this statutory exception. We hold that it does not and that the debt is dischargeable.

I.

In January 1983, petitioner Margaret Kawaauhau sought treatment from respondent Dr. Paul Geiger for a foot injury. Geiger examined Kawaauhau and admitted her to the hospital to attend to the risk of infection resulting from the injury. Although Geiger knew that intravenous penicillin would have been more effective, he prescribed oral penicillin, explaining in his testimony that he understood his patient wished to minimize the cost of her treatment.

Geiger then departed on a business trip, leaving Kawaauhau in the care of other physicians, who decided she should be transferred to an infectious disease specialist. When Geiger returned, he canceled the transfer and discontinued all antibiotics because he believed the infection had subsided. Kawaauhau's condition deteriorated over the next few days, requiring the amputation of her right leg below the knee.

Kawaauhau, joined by her husband Solomon, sued Geiger for malpractice. After a trial, the jury found Geiger liable and awarded the Kawaauhaus approximately $355,000 in damages.[1] Geiger, who carried no malpractice insurance, moved to Missouri, where his wages were garnished by the Kawaauhaus. Geiger then petitioned for bankruptcy. The Kawaauhaus requested the Bankruptcy Court to hold the malpractice judgment nondischargeable on the ground that it was a debt "for willful and malicious injury" excepted from discharge by § 523(a)(6). The Bankruptcy Court concluded that Geiger's treatment fell far below the appropriate standard of care and therefore ranked as "willful and malicious." Accordingly, the Bankruptcy Court held the debt nondischargeable. * * * In an unpublished order, the District Court affirmed.

A three-judge panel of the Court of Appeals for the Eighth Circuit reversed, and a divided en banc court adhered to the panel's position. Section 523(a)(6)'s exemption from discharge, the en banc court held, is confined to debts "based on what the law has for generations called an intentional tort." On this view, a debt for malpractice, because it is based on conduct that is negligent or reckless, rather than intentional, remains dischargeable.

The Eighth Circuit acknowledged that its interpretation of § 523(a)(6) diverged from previous holdings of the Sixth and Tenth Circuits. We granted certiorari to resolve this conflict and now affirm the Eighth Circuit's judgment.

II.

Section 523(a)(6) of the Bankruptcy Code provides:

"(a) A discharge under Section 727, 1141, 1228(a), 1228(b), or 1328(b) of this title does not discharge an individual debtor from any debt—

. . . .

---

[1] The jury awarded Margaret Kawaauhau $203,040 in special damages and $99,000 in general damages. In addition, the jury awarded Solomon Kawaauhau $18,000 in general damages for loss of consortium and $35,000 for emotional distress.

"(6) for willful and malicious injury by the debtor to another entity or to the property of another entity."

The Kawaauhaus urge that the malpractice award fits within this exception because Dr. Geiger intentionally rendered inadequate medical care to Margaret Kawaauhau that necessarily led to her injury. According to the Kawaauhaus, Geiger deliberately chose less effective treatment because he wanted to cut costs, all the while knowing that he was providing substandard care. Such conduct, the Kawaauhaus assert, meets the "willful and malicious" specification of § 523(a)(6).

We confront this pivotal question concerning the scope of the "willful and malicious injury" exception: Does § 523(a)(6)'s compass cover acts, done intentionally,[3] that cause injury (as the Kawaauhaus urge), or only acts done with the actual intent to cause injury (as the Eighth Circuit ruled)? The words of the statute strongly support the Eighth Circuit's reading.

The word "willful" in (a)(6) modifies the word "injury," indicating that nondischargeability takes a deliberate or intentional *injury*, not merely a deliberate or intentional *act* that leads to injury. Had Congress meant to exempt debts resulting from unintentionally inflicted injuries, it might have described instead "willful acts that cause injury." Or, Congress might have selected an additional word or words, i.e., "reckless" or "negligent," to modify "injury." Moreover, as the Eighth Circuit observed, the (a)(6) formulation triggers in the lawyer's mind the category "intentional torts," as distinguished from negligent or reckless torts. Intentional torts generally require that the actor intend "the *consequences* of an act," not simply "the act itself." Restatement (Second) of Torts § 8A, comment a, p. 15 (1964) (emphasis added).

The Kawaauhaus' more encompassing interpretation could place within the excepted category a wide range of situations in which an act is intentional, but injury is unintended, i.e., neither desired nor in fact anticipated by the debtor. Every traffic accident stemming from an initial intentional act—for example, intentionally rotating the wheel of an automobile to make a left-hand turn without first checking oncoming traffic—could fit the description. A "knowing breach of contract" could also qualify. A construction so broad would be incompatible with the "well-known" guide that exceptions to discharge "should be confined to those plainly expressed." *Gleason v. Thaw*, 236 U.S. 558, 562 (1915).

---

[3] The word "willful" is defined in Black's Law Dictionary as "voluntary" or "intentional." Black's Law Dictionary 1434 (5th ed.1979). Consistently, legislative reports note that the word "willful" in § 523(a)(6) means "deliberate or intentional."

Furthermore, "we are hesitant to adopt an interpretation of a congressional enactment which renders superfluous another portion of that same law." *Mackey v. Lanier Collection Agency & Service, Inc.*, 486 U.S. 825, 837 (1988). Reading § 523(a)(6) as the Kawaauhaus urge would obviate the need for § 523(a)(9), which specifically exempts debts "for death or personal injury caused by the debtor's operation of a motor vehicle if such operation was unlawful because the debtor was intoxicated from using alcohol, a drug, or another substance." § 523(a)(9); see also § 523(a)(12) (exempting debts for "malicious or reckless failure" to fulfill certain commitments owed to a federal depository institutions regulatory agency).

The Kawaauhaus heavily rely on *Tinker v. Colwell*, 193 U.S. 473 (1904), which presented this question: Does an award of damages for "criminal conversation" survive bankruptcy under the 1898 Bankruptcy Act's exception from discharge for judgments in civil actions for "'willful and malicious injuries to the person or property of another'"? Id., at 481. The *Tinker* Court held such an award a nondischargeable debt. The Kawaauhaus feature certain statements in the *Tinker* opinion, in particular: "[An] act is willful... in the sense that it is intentional and voluntary" even if performed "without any particular malice," id., at 485; an act that "necessarily causes injury and is done intentionally, may be said to be done willfully and maliciously, so as to come within the [bankruptcy discharge] exception," id., at 487. See also id., at 487 (the statute exempts from discharge liability for "'a wrongful act, done intentionally, without just cause or excuse'") (quoting from definition of malice in *Bromage v. Prosser*, 4 Barn. & Cress. 247, 107 Eng. Rep. 1051 (K.B.1825)).

The exposition in the *Tinker* opinion is less than crystalline. Counterbalancing the portions the Kawaauhaus emphasize, the *Tinker* Court repeatedly observed that the tort in question qualified in the common law as trespassory. Indeed, it ranked as "trespass *vi et armis*." 193 U.S., at 482, 483. Criminal conversation, the Court noted, was an action akin to a master's "action of trespass and assault... for the battery of his servant," id., at 482. *Tinker* thus placed criminal conversation solidly within the traditional intentional tort category, and we so confine its holding. That decision, we clarify, provides no warrant for departure from the current statutory instruction that, to be nondischargeable, the judgment debt must be "for willful and malicious *injury*."

Subsequent decisions of this Court are in accord with our construction. In *McIntyre v. Kavanaugh*, 242 U.S. 138 (1916), a broker "deprive[d] another of his property forever by deliberately disposing of it without semblance of authority." Id., at 141. The Court held that this act constituted an intentional injury to property of another, bringing it within the discharge exception. But in *Davis v. Aetna Acceptance Co.*, 293 U.S. 328 (1934), the Court explained that not every tort judgment for conversion is exempt from discharge. Negligent or reckless acts, the Court held, do not suffice to establish that a resulting injury is "wilful and malicious." *See id.*, at 332.

Finally, the Kawaauhaus maintain that, as a policy matter, malpractice judgments should be excepted from discharge, at least when the debtor acted recklessly or carried no malpractice insurance. Congress, of course, may so decide. But unless and until Congress makes such a decision, we must follow the current direction § 523(a)(6) provides. * * *

We hold that debts arising from recklessly or negligently inflicted injuries do not fall within the compass of § 523(a)(6). For the reasons stated, the judgment of the Court of Appeals for the Eighth Circuit is

Affirmed.

NOTES

1. Courts have not known what to make of *Tinker v. Colwell*, 193 U.S. 473 (1904), in which Colwell's judgment for $50,000 against Tinker for criminal conversation with his wife was held to be nondischargeable within the willful and malicious exception even though Tinker's act was done without "any particular malice." *Mellinkoff's Dictionary of American Legal Usage* 140 (1992) defines criminal conversation as "the waning civil action for damages for adultery with plaintiff's spouse." The Court in *Kawaauhau* makes clear that *Tinker* is a waning authority, confined, in effect, to its facts.

2. A second group of cases involving conversion of property is an important focus of § 523(a)(6) and has significant commercial importance. There is ample authority for holding that conversion of property can qualify as a "willful and malicious injury" to property under § 523(a)(6). The clearest example is a theft of property by the debtor. But that kind of case is not typical. The most common cases under § 523(a)(6) are those in which the debtor in a secured transaction converts the collateral of the secured party by selling it and spending the proceeds of the sale for the benefit of the debtor or a third party. For example, a finance company has a security interest in the debtor's inventory and any proceeds of the sale of the inventory. Under the security agreement the debtor is required to pay over to the finance company the cash proceeds of any sale of the inventory. If the debtor sells inventory and, in violation of the security agreement, uses the proceeds of the sale to pay other debts of the debtor, there is a clear conversion of property of the finance company. This kind of conversion is sometimes referred to as a "sale out of trust."

The conversion, however, is not necessarily "willful and malicious" as required by § 523(a)(6). Conversion can occur in cases in which the debtor has exercised unauthorized control over somebody else's property without being aware of the fact that the conduct was unlawful. This exercise of control may be willful in the sense that the debtor intended to do the act that constituted the exercise of control. But the act is clearly not "willful and malicious" under § 523(a)(6) if the debtor thought that the exercise of control was lawful. This point was made by Justice Cardozo in *Davis v. Aetna Acceptance Co.*, 293 U.S. 328 (1934). He took the view that, though a sale by a dealer "out of trust" is a conversion, it is not, without more, willful and malicious conduct. "There may be a conversion which is innocent or technical, an unauthorized assumption of dominion without willfulness or malice. * * * There may be an honest, but mistaken belief, engendered by a course of dealing, that powers have been enlarged or incapacities removed. In these and like cases, what is done is a tort, but not a willful or malicious one." 293 U.S. at 332. But cases of innocent conversion of collateral by the debtor are not usually litigated under § 523(a)(6). In the typical litigated case the debtor knows that the use of the cash proceeds of the sale of collateral is a violation of the property rights of the secured party. In those cases the conversion is certainly willful. Is such a conversion necessarily also malicious?

PROBLEM

Corporation borrowed $50,000 from Bank in order to purchase a piece of business equipment. Bank perfected a security interest in the equipment. The security agreement forbids sale of the equipment or its removal from the state in which Corporation's place of business was located without permission of Bank. Debtor, an individual who is the principal stockholder of Corporation, guaranteed payment of the Bank's loan.

A few months after the loan was made, a sudden downturn in Corporation's sales caused a severe cash shortage. In order to raise cash Debtor, acting for Corporation, removed the equipment to another state and sold it to Buyer for $40,000, its fair value. Debtor, knowing that the sale violated Bank's security agreement, told Buyer that the equipment was unencumbered. Bank had no knowledge of the transaction. Corporation's business did not improve, and eventually Corporation filed in bankruptcy. Debtor also filed in bankruptcy at the same time. At that time: (i) Corporation owed $50,000 to Bank, (ii) Corporation was insolvent and all of its assets were encumbered by liens that secured debts (other than Bank's claim) in excess of the value of the assets, and (iii) Debtor was also insolvent and had no nonexempt assets.

Assume that under state law Bank has no right to assert its security interest against Buyer. Is Bank's claim against Debtor for conversion nondischargeable under § 523(a)(6)? Would it matter if Debtor's conversion was done solely for the purpose of raising funds to keep Corporation afloat and all of the $40,000 was invested in Corporation? *See* Charles Jordan Tabb, *The Scope of the Fresh Start in Bankruptcy: Collateral Conversions and the Dischargeability Debate*, 59 Geo. Wash. L. Rev. 56 (1990).

4. EDUCATIONAL LOANS

Federally guaranteed educational loans have played an essential role in making it possible for many students to pay the ever-rising costs of higher education. Most loans are made by private lenders and guaranteed by agencies of the federal government, but a growing number are made through the federal direct loan program. An enduring policy dispute has centered around what to do about educational loans in bankruptcy. The current law—conceived in the 1970s when tuition at most state schools was nominal and was more affordable than today for most families at private schools—provides broadly that educational loans are nondischargeable except in cases of "undue hardship." § 523(a)(8).

A starry-eyed undergraduate receiving a student loan may have no comprehension that she is undertaking a lifetime obligation—there is no statute of limitations—that in default, even under subsidized interest rates, can grow substantially over time and that, under current practices, may be enforced against her at any point during her life by collection agencies to which the Department of Education has outsourced delinquent debts for a commission. Nonetheless, in today's culture, forgoing a college education is not a rational option for students who strive to enter or remain in the middle class.

In justifying the severe attitude that most courts have taken against students seeking discharge in the past, one court stated the prevailing view: "The government is not twisting the arms of potential students. The decision of whether or not to borrow for a college education lies with the individual* * *." *In re Roberson*, 999 F.2d 1132, 1137 (7th Cir. 1993). But times have changed. Given the staggering costs of higher education today, the children of lower and middle income families have no choice but to rely on educational loans. Nevertheless, Congress continues to reject the view that educational loans should be dischargeable; however, as we see below, the Department of Education has offered some amelioration of the debtor's plight.

Section 523(a)(8) provides an exception if nondischargeability of an educational debt "will impose an undue hardship on the debtor and the debtor's dependents." There is no definition in the statute of "undue hardship." Since many debtors are desperate to escape nondischargebility of their educational loans, predictably, a large body of case law has grown around the meaning of these words. Most of the circuits have accepted the three-part test announced in *Brunner v. New York State Higher Education Services Corp.*, 831 F.2d 395 (2d Cir. 1987).

a. The *Brunner* Test

The usual statement of the test is:

(1) that the debtor cannot maintain, based on current income and expenses, a "minimal" standard of living for herself and her dependents if forced to repay the loans;

(2) that additional circumstances exist indicating that this state of affairs is likely to persist for a significant portion on the repayment period of the student loans; and

(3) that the debtor has made good faith efforts to repay the loans.

Most litigation has centered about the meaning of the second and third prongs of *Brunner*.

(i) Second prong

The division of authority focusses on the meaning of "additional circumstances." The following cases demonstrate the competing views:

In re Frushour, 433 F.3d 393 (4th Cir. 2005). At the time of the proceeding, Debtor was in her forties and had a seven-year-old son for whom she received no child support. She had several years of college largely financed by educational loans. She held a number of jobs in the restaurant management field and, later, in tourism. She never made more than $20,000 annually. After the birth of her son she worked out of her home on a self-employed basis for which her annual income never exceeded $11,000. Her expenses exceeded her income, even excluding the modest amounts she paid on her educational loans. The standard for undue hardship adopted by the court was that the required hardship under § 523(a)(8) must be more than the usual hardship that accompanies bankruptcy. Inability to pay one's debts by itself cannot be sufficient; otherwise all bankruptcy litigants would have undue hardship. Only a debtor with exceptional circumstances meets the test, such as illness, disability, lack of useable job skills, or a large number of dependents. The court held that Debtor did not meet the second prong. There was a bitter dissent, noting that the bankruptcy court that saw and heard Debtor found undue hardship.

In re Nys, 446 F.3d 938 (9th Cir. 2006). Debtor is a 51-year old drafting technician who borrowed $30,000 to pay for her education in drafting technology; her obligation has ballooned to $85,000 in accumulated principal and interest. Her monthly income is $2,300 and she claims monthly expenses of $2,295. She sought to have her student loans fully discharged as imposing an undue hardship on her. The court stated the standard to be that undue hardship requires only a showing that the debtor will not be able to maintain a minimal standard of living now and in the future if forced to repay her student loans. It is enough if she shows that her income cannot reasonably be expected to increase and that her inability to make payments will likely persist throughout a substantial portion of the loan's repayment period. Additional circumstances need not be "exceptional," such as serious illness, psychiatric problems or disability of a dependent. It is enough, as debtor claimed in this case, that she is 14 years from retirement, in her career as a drafting technician her income is as high as it will ever be, her house needs substantial repairs, and her car will soon need to be replaced.

Which view best carries out the policies of § 523(a)(8)?

(ii) Third prong

To receive an undue hardship discharge, the debtor must demonstrate a good faith effort to pay her educational loans. Courts are not generous with debtors whose record shows scofflaw tendencies; failure to make payments in the past when the debtor could afford payments is a major demerit. Other typical fact patterns involving good faith are demonstrated in the two following cases:

In re Mosko, 515 F.3d 319 (4th Cir. 2008): Brenda's student loans totalled $57,156; Robert, her husband, had student loans of $63,417. In the three years before they filed in bankruptcy their joint income was $75,546, $78,363 and $64,130 respectively. Brenda earned about $38,000 annually teaching school. Robert had several jobs over the years. For one employer, he worked as a programmer until he learned that he would not receive time-and-a-half for overtime. He was fired from a job at Lowe's because he suffered from daytime sleepiness. He took some online computer courses that he thought might open possibilities of employment. The court concluded that neither spouse demonstrated a good faith effort to obtain employment and maximize income. Brenda should have found summer employment and Robert's medical condition didn't preclude him from part-time work. Moreover, the debtors' expenditures don't indicate a good faith effort to minimize expenses. In the few months before they filed, they spent $1,600 at Circuit City, Best Buy, Amazon.com and Radio Shack; over $3,000 at Sam's Club, Wal-Mart and Kmart; and over $800 on software. Then, too, they failed to make payments on their student loans during a period when their income substantially exceeded their necessary expenses.

In re Tirch, 409 F.3d 677 (6th Cir. 2005): Debtor ran up $84,600 in educational debts in earning degrees in Counseling; interest was accruing at a rate of $558 per month. She worked in counseling positions at salaries ranging from $27,000 to $28,500 from 1999 through 2001, when she stopped working because of illness. She first defaulted on her loans in October 2000 and filed in bankruptcy at some point during that year. Her health problems were substantial. She went on disability benefits at $1,400 per month for 24 months. The court held that she failed to demonstrate a good faith effort to repay her loans.

She had paid only $4,000 on her $84,600 loan even though 20 years had passed since she received her first degree. The case is interesting because of the weight the court gave to her rejection of the ICRP option (see below) that would have allowed her to pay only $183.66 per month for an extended period of years. The court said that Debtor's failure to take advantage of ICRP, while not a per se indication of the lack of good faith, was "probative of her intent." Cases like *Tirch* make it very difficult for a debtor to obtain discharge of an entire educational loan so long as the debtor can pay even a small amount of the debt.

b. Partial discharge

Debtor owes Lender an educational loan of $100,000. Under *Brunner* his circumstances are such that he meets the test for undue hardship under § 523(a)(8); therefore, Debtor qualifies for discharge of the full amount of his loan. However, Lender proposed that Debtor be discharged for only $45,000 of his loans but not for the $55,000 balance, which Debtor could repay without undue hardship. Does § 523(a)(8) empower a bankruptcy court to grant a partial discharge in such a case? Some cases say no, *e.g., In re Cox*, 338 F.3d 1238 (11th Cir. 2003). Others say yes, *e.g., In re Saxman*, 325 F.3d 1168 (9th Cir. 2003), which held that bankruptcy courts may exercise their equitable authority under § 105(a) to partially discharge student loans. Which view is the correct interpretation of § 523(a)(8)? Note that although § 523(a)(2) and (7) include the phrase "to the extent," those words do not appear in § 523(a)(8). Is the emergence of partial discharge a pro-debtor or pro-creditor development? Do partial discharges further the policy objective of § 523(a)(8)?

c. Educational Credit Management Corporation Regulations

The U. S. Department of Education offers its educational loan debtors the option of choosing one of the following repayment plans: (1) the standard 10-year plan; (2) the extended plan (ranging from 12 years for a loan less than $10,000 to 30 years for a loan in excess of $60,000); (3) the graduated 30-year plan; and (4) the William D. Ford Income Contingent Repayment Plan (ICRP), which allows a borrower to remain current on her loan obligation by paying an amount based on income, debt, and family size. *See* 34 C.F.R. § 685.208, § 685.209.

A summary of the ICRP appears in *In re Korhonen*, 296 B.R. 492, 496 (Bankr.D.Minn.2003):

The Income Contingent Repayment Program permits a student loan debtor to pay twenty percent of the difference between his adjusted gross income and the poverty level for his family size, or the amount the debtor would pay if the debt were repaid in twelve years, whichever is less. Under the program, the borrower's monthly repayment amount is adjusted each year to reflect any changes in these factors. The borrower's repayments may be adjusted during the year based on special circumstances. *See* 34 C.F.R. § 685.209(c)(3). At the end of the twenty five year payment period, any remaining loan balance would be cancelled by the Secretary of Education. However, the amount discharged would be taxable income.

Proving undue hardship under *Brunner* was difficult and hardship discharges were few, but the DOE regulations show that the government (like other creditors) would rather have distressed debtors voluntarily pay something on their debts than attempt to involuntarily collect the debt. Hence, these regulations offer debtors a better deal than they would be likely to otherwise obtain in bankruptcy: pay us what you can and you will eventually be discharged. Moreover, because of these regulations, debtors that have some disposable income will have difficulty in showing that they can't pay something under one of the DOE plans.

5. Fraudulently Incurred Debts

A debtor who has engaged in certain kinds of fraudulent conduct such as concealing or transferring assets with intent to hinder or defraud creditors or falsifying information from which the debtor's financial condition might be ascertained may be denied a discharge in bankruptcy. § 727(a)(2) and (3). Debts resulting from a debtor's fraudulent conduct may be nondischargeable under § 523(a)(2).

Section 523(a)(2)(A) provides that debts obtained by "false pretenses, a false misrepresentation, or actual fraud" are nondischargeable but is silent on the degree of reliance required on the part of creditors for nondischargeability. In *Field v. Mans*, 516 U.S. 59 (1995), the Supreme Court addressed this oft-litigated issue and concluded, on facts of exasperating complexity, that the standard for reliance is "justifiable reliance" rather than "reasonable reliance." Thus, the debtor's reliance on a misrepresentation is justifiable so long as the falsity of the representation is not obvious to someone of the debtor's knowledge and intelligence, even though an investigation would have disclosed the falsehood. The debtor's conduct need not conform to the standard of the reasonable person.

PROBLEM

The question of overlap among the various provisions of § 523(a) has arisen in a number of cases. The following facts raise this issue. Debtor orally induced Creditor to pay money on his behalf to a construction project by promising to reimburse Creditor soon after. Debtor knew that he had no realistic prospect of repaying the money, and his statements amounted to a false statement of financial condition. Creditor obtained a judgment against Debtor for the amount of the loan and Debtor filed in Chapter 7. Creditor objected to discharge of the debt. Since § 523(a)(2)(B) has a writing requirement, Creditor relied on § 523(a)(6), which has no such requirement. Is that provision applicable in this case? The facts are based on *In re Gulevsky*, 362 F.3d 961 (7th Cir. 2004).

6. FRAUD AND DEFALCATION

Debts arising from fraud or defalcation while acting in a fiduciary capacity are nondischargeable under § 523(a)(4). It is clear that fraud requires intentional deceit, but courts are divided whether defalcation under the statute includes all misappropriations or failures to account or only those that evince some wrongful conduct. *Collier on Bankruptcy*, ¶ 523.10 (15th ed. rev. 2007), states that some degree of culpability should be required to make a debt nondischargeable as defalcation under the statute. How much? The circuits are in disarray. Although some hold that an innocent mistake can constitute a defalcation, most require some level of wrongful misconduct. After inventorying circuit-level authorities, *In re Hyman*, 502 F.3d 61 (2d Cir. 2007), adopted a standard requiring a showing of conscious behavior or extreme recklessness. This standard does not reach fiduciaries who have failed to account for funds or property for which they were responsible only as a consequence of negligence, inadvertence or similar conduct not shown to be sufficiently culpable. A similar standard was adopted in *In re Baylis*, 313 F.3d 9, 18 (1st Cir. 2002), which held that defalcation requires a degree of fault "closer to fraud, without the necessity of meeting a strict specific intent requirement."

7. CREDIT CARD FRAUD

The growth of credit card debts to financial institutions has been phenomenal. The first bank credit cards were issued in the 1950s. By 1971, VisaUSA had passed the $1 billion mark in transactions per year; it had reached the $1 trillion mark in 2003. Eileen Alt Powell, *Use of "Plastic" Changing Rapidly*, LA Times, Aug. 29, 2003, at C2. Credit cards have been so wildly successful in expanding the volume of consumer credit that they are viewed as posing serious social problems for consumers, particularly in the area of bankruptcy. The recession of 2008-2009 has driven both the Federal Reserve Board and Congress to address these problems. However, our treatment in this section is limited to the discharge issue.

Before credit cards, credit was usually given by the creditor only after a face-to-face meeting with the debtor in which the debtor's creditworthiness was assessed. The creditor had complete control over the amount of the credit extension and could assess the debtor's current financial position. This control is substantially lessened in credit card transactions in which the cardholder may use the card to buy goods or obtain cash advances from merchants or banks other than the issuer of the card. Moreover, cardholders may continue to use (indeed increase usage of) their cards after their financial condition has, unknown to the card issuer, worsened. Card issuers have attempted to reduce these risks by imposing limits on the amount the cardholder can charge on a card and by requiring merchants and others honoring cards to seek approval from the card issuer for amounts exceeding specified amounts. Improved information systems offer vendors and lenders more information about cardholders' accounts through credit card networks like VisaUSA or MasterCard International, but these systems provide information only with respect to the account being charged and not the cardholders' other credit card accounts.

Consumers often obtain very large amounts of approved credit by accepting offers of credit cards from several different issuers. Consumers may receive many unsolicited offers from issuers to accept credit cards with pre-approved lines of credit. A frequent element in personal bankruptcy cases is a large amount of debt owing on a number of credit cards that have been used up to or beyond their credit limits. In some instances the cards have been heavily used during the period immediately before the debtor filed in bankruptcy. Courts often characterize such use as a "credit card spree."

Credit card issuers have invoked § 523(a)(2)(A) to challenge the dischargeability of debts incurred by cardholders. A debtor who contracts a debt intending not to pay the debt is guilty of actual fraud. Credit card issuers maintain that actual fraud is also involved in cases in which the card is used by an insolvent cardholder who could not reasonably have believed that repayment was possible. In resisting nondischargeability motions, cardholders assert that no fraud is present in these cases unless the card issuer can prove that the cardholder did not intend to pay at the time the credit card debt was incurred. Some courts see nondischargeability proceedings as attempts by card issuers to cut losses from abnormal credit risks knowingly created by themselves in order to gain greater market share by issuing large numbers of cards without regard to creditworthiness.

The *Hashemi* case that follows reflects the orthodox view of focusing on the intent of the cardholder. In the Note following *Hashemi*, *Ellingsworth* presents a revisionist approach which calls into question whether there is justifiable reliance on the part of the card issuer.

American Express Travel Related Services Co. v. Hashemi
United States Court of Appeals, Ninth Circuit, 1996.
104 F.3d 1122.

■ KOZINSKI, Circuit Judge.

Appellant didn't leave home without his American Express cards. In fact, he and his family traveled to Europe in style, and charged it all. On his return, appellant owed American Express more than $60,000, the bulk of which represented charges made during the six-week trip. He promptly filed for bankruptcy, and American Express petitioned to have his debt declared nondischargeable under § 523(a)(2)(A), which precludes discharge of debts obtained through "actual fraud." The bankruptcy court denied appellant's request for a jury trial, ruled the debt nondischargeable and ordered appellant to pay American Express $69,793.67 plus interest. The district court affirmed the bankruptcy court's judgment and Dr. Hashemi appeals again. * * *

* * *

* * * [A]ppellant claims the bankruptcy court erred in finding that he defrauded American Express. Section 523(a)(2)(A) precludes discharge of any debt obtained by "false pretenses, a false representation, or actual fraud." In order to establish a debt's nondischargeability under this section, the creditor must show:

(1) the debtor made. . . representations;

(2) that at the time he knew they were false;

(3) that he made them with the intention and purpose of deceiving the creditor;

(4) that the creditor relied on such representations; [and]

(5) that the creditor sustained the alleged loss and damage as the proximate result of the misrepresentations having been made.

* * * These requirements mirror the elements of common law fraud, *see In re Eashai*, 87 F.3d 1082, 1087 (9th Cir. 1996), and the creditor is required to prove each by a preponderance of the evidence. * * * Appellant contends that American Express failed to establish his intent to defraud, that he made no false representations to American Express, and that if any such representations were made, American Express did not justifiably rely on them.

a. *Fraudulent Intent*. "[A] court may infer the existence of the debtor's intent not to pay if the facts and circumstances of a particular case present a picture of deceptive conduct by the debtor." *In re Eashai*, 87 F.3d at 1087. In *In* *re Dougherty*, 84 B.R. 653 (9th Cir. BAP 1988), our Bankruptcy Appellate Panel enumerated twelve factors relevant to determining a debtor's intent.[2] These factors are nonexclusive; none is dispositive, nor must a debtor's conduct satisfy a minimum number in order to prove fraudulent intent. So long as, on balance, the evidence supports a finding of fraudulent intent, the creditor has satisfied this element. * * * We adopted *Dougherty's* twelve-factor test as the law of the circuit in *In re Eashai*, 87 F.3d at 1087–88.

Applying the test set out in *Dougherty* and *Eashai*, as did the bankruptcy court, there is ample evidence to support the finding that appellant intended to defraud American Express. Appellant made nearly 170 charges totaling more than $60,000 during a six-week trip with his family to France. These charges exceeded appellant's annual income and, even before the trip, appellant already owed more than $300,000 in unsecured credit card debt. Appellant did have one major asset when he made the charges—a one-half ownership interest in an eight-unit condominium project. He claims the purpose of his trip was to borrow money from his mother-in-law to support this real estate venture. This does not explain why appellant stayed in France for six weeks, took his wife and two children with him, took a side-trip to the French Riviera, purchased cosmetics, expensive meals and other luxury items, and ultimately charged almost as much on his credit cards as he claims he planned to borrow. Moreover, while appellant was away, the holder of the second mortgage on his condominium project initiated foreclosure proceedings. This should have alerted appellant that he would not be able to repay his debt by selling his interest in the property. Given these facts, the bankruptcy court could reasonably infer that appellant tried to have a last hurrah at American Express's expense.

b. *False Representations*. Appellant also complains that he never made any fraudulent misrepresentations to American Express because American Express extended him an unlimited line of credit. We rejected the identical argument in *In re Anastas*, 94 F.3d 1280 (9th Cir. 1996). Each time a "card holder uses his

---

[2] The factors are: (1) the length of time between the charges and the bankruptcy filing; (2) whether or not an attorney had been consulted concerning the filing of bankruptcy before the charges were made; (3) the number of charges made; (4) the amount of the charges; (5) the financial condition of the debtor at the time the charges were made; (6) whether the charges were above the credit limit of the account; (7) whether the debtor made multiple charges on the same day; (8) whether or not the debtor was employed; (9) the debtor's prospects for employment; (10) the financial sophistication of the debtor; (11) whether there was a sudden change in the debtor's buying habits; and (12) whether the purchases made were luxuries or necessities. * * *

credit card, he makes a representation that he intends to repay the debt. . . . When the card holder uses the card without an intent to repay, he has made a fraudulent representation to the card issuer." Id. at 1285. Because the bankruptcy court found that appellant had no intention of repaying his debt, each time he used his cards he made a fraudulent representation to American Express.

c. *Justifiable Reliance.* "[T]he credit card issuer justifiably relies on a representation of intent to repay as long as the account is not in default and any initial investigations into a credit report do not raise red flags that would make reliance unjustifiable." Id. at 1286. At the time appellant began his spending spree, his account was not in default. In fact, he owed American Express only $227. Moreover, appellant himself testified that he had repaid American Express balances of up to $60,000 "numerous times" before. American Express therefore had no reason to question the good faith of appellant's promise to repay. Because American Express provided ample evidence of each element of common law fraud, the bankruptcy court was fully justified in declaring appellant's debt nondischargeable.

* * *

AFFIRMED AND REMANDED.

NOTES

1. In *In re Ellingsworth*, 212 B.R. 326 (Bankr.W.D.Mo.1997), the court held that even if the cardholders misrepresented their intention to repay, the debt was dischargeable because the card issuer did not make an adequate inquiry into their financial position and could not be found to have justifiably relied on their representation to repay. The court was critical of *Hashemi* and characterized the case as follows:

> A woman walks in one day and says she wants to borrow $60,000 on her signature. She willingly fills out a financial statement which shows that she already has $300,000 in unsecured debt, but she needs these additional funds for a business trip. She also shows one asset, a heavily encumbered apartment building that is being foreclosed. Of course, she promises to repay the loan if one is made to her. Would a bank that makes such a loan be found to have justifiably relied on her promise? Of course not. But, what if, instead, the bank made the loan without bothering to ask her basic information about assets, liabilities, and income? And what if she did not make an express promise to repay the loan? Should this bank be allowed to claim that it justifiably relied on her implied promises to pay? One would think not. However, these are the very facts of a recent bankruptcy opinion [*Hashemi*], except that

rather than a face to face encounter with a bank officer, the debt was incurred through use of a credit card.

212 B.R. at 329.

Ellingsworth involved Debtors who owed over $65,000 in unsecured debts, mostly on 16 credit cards, at the time Issuer offered them a pre-approved card with a $4,000 limit. Debtors used their new card for cash advances after they had "maxed out" on their other cards. When they reached the credit limit, they ceased use of the new card and, without making a single payment on it, filed in bankruptcy. Noting that their monthly obligations far exceeded their income, the court concluded that Debtors knew that they would be unable to repay the $4,000 debt and thus should be considered to have misrepresented their intent to repay.

The Issuer offered Debtors a pre-approved card on the basis of a credit scoring formula that emphasized their history of not defaulting on their debts. Debtors verified by telephone their income and employment. No information was sought about the amount of their liabilities, assets or monthly expenses. A full credit bureau report would have listed their obligations in detail and implied their insolvency. The court concluded that offering a customer a pre-approved credit card without making a full inquiry into the customer's financial status was not justifiable reliance. If Debtors had applied to a bank for an unsecured loan for $4,000 and had revealed their true financial position on their credit application, the bank could not be held to have justifiably relied on Debtors' promise to repay the loan. Why should credit cards be treated differently?

In a far-ranging discussion of the economics of the credit card business, the court conjectured that even with a six percent charge-off rate credit cards are highly profitable because issuers charge high rates and enjoy a vast customer base. The court observed:

> In their eagerness to capture market share, banks spend little time gathering financial information about their potential credit card customers. Prior to a mass mailing, creditors such as [Issuer] obtain lists from credit bureaus with the names of candidates and a "credit score" for each person on the list. These scores relate generally to past card use, whether the candidate pays the minimum monthly balance on current cards, and whether there are any delinquencies or bankruptcies on record. Car loans, medical bills, and mortgages are not included in the credit score, nor are income, job history, marital status, and assets.

212 B.R. at 330-331. *In re Mercer*, 211 F.3d 214 (5th Cir. 2000), agrees that a creditor cannot justifiably rely on a representation if the credit card was pre-approved and no direct financial information was obtained by the issuer.

2. In § 1229 of BAPCPA, Congress reacted to the concerns expressed in *Ellingsworth* with a Sense-of-the-Congress provision noting, gingerly, that "(1) certain lenders may sometimes offer credit to consumers indiscriminately, without taking steps to ensure that consumers are capable of repaying the resulting debt; and in a manner which may encourage certain consumers to accumulate additional debt; and (2) resulting consumer debt may increasingly be a major contributing factor to consumer insolvency." The Board of Governors of the Federal Reserve System was directed to conduct a study of this problem, make a report and issue regulations prescribing additional disclosures for consumers and take any other appropriate action consistent with its statutory authority. What kind of disclosure do you think would help credit card users? What "other appropriate action" should be taken?

3. Credit card issuers significantly gained ground on cardholders on the discharge front in BAPCPA by an amendment to § 523(a)(2)(C) that presumes nondischargeable all consumer debts to a single creditor aggregating more than $550 (formerly $1,225) incurred on or within 90 (formerly 60) days of filing if for "luxury goods or services." § 523(a)(2(C)(i)(I). The quoted term "does not include goods or services reasonably necessary for the support or maintenance of the debtor or a dependent of the debtor." § 523(a)(2(C)(ii)(II). There is no positive definition of "luxury;" the extent to which goods and services not reasonably necessary for support or maintenance should be deemed luxury goods or services is not clear. Cash advances aggregating more than $825 (formerly $1,225) obtained on or within 70 (formerly 60) days before filing are presumed nondischargeable, but only if made in an open end credit transaction, which is the kind of transaction used for cash advances on credit cards. So long as the loan transaction is an extension of consumer credit, that is, the loan was obtained for a personal, family or household purpose, there are no limits on the use of the loan proceeds. Thus, the original, sensible concept that card issuers deserve some protection against the excesses of "credit card sprees" that allow debtors to acquire expensive "luxury goods" on the eve of bankruptcy, now, as amended, potentially applies to the huge volume of consumer sales transactions made by use of credit cards within three months before filing and cash advances made pursuant to credit cards 70 days before filing. This provision enhances the procedural advantage enjoyed by credit card issuers described in the following Note.

4. Since *Hashemi* and *Ellingsworth*, a number of cases have been decided on the nondischargeability problem, roughly divided between the views of these two cases, with no clear pattern prevailing. *See In re Mercer*, 246 F.3d 391 (5th Cir. 2001), in which there were *three* views on the issue within the *en banc* court itself. The National Bankruptcy Review Commission Report viewed the law governing the dischargeability of credit card debts as chaotic and unfair.

Chapter 4. Discharge   163

NBRC Rep. at 180–196. Creditors are increasingly challenging discharge of credit card debts on the basis of fraud. Impoverished debtors lack the resources to litigate the issue, and the law is so unsettled that it is difficult for debtors to avail themselves of the remedy offered by § 523(d) to force creditors to pay costs and attorney's fees in cases in which the creditors' challenge to discharge fails "if the court finds that the position of the creditor was not substantially justified." This is true because in the muddle of conflicting case law on the subject creditors can find some legal justification for almost any position they may take. *NBRC Rep.* at 193.

5. Some consumers abuse credit cards: They apply for cards from multiple grantors with similar credit limits, thereby greatly amplifying their capacity to obtain more credit than they can repay. When their cards are maxed out, they apply for additional cards from other grantors. They continue to use their cards after their credit position has weakened, including heavy use in the period immediately before bankruptcy. These practices are well known to credit card issuers; why do they tolerate them? In the early years of credit cards, information systems were so primitive that information about consumer use was virtually unobtainable. Even after the arrival of electronic data retrieval, timely information was difficult and expensive to obtain. This is no longer true; new technology allows lenders to get *daily* reports on their customers from the major credit bureaus. Ron Lieber, *Careful, Your Bank Is Watching*, Wall St. J., July 22, 2003, at D1, notes that credit grantors can receive daily reports on when customers are applying for new credit cards or new loans, when their credit cards are maxed out, how much credit they are using, and whether they have fallen behind on insurance premiums or other bills. How does this greatly enhanced monitoring capacity on the part of card issuers affect your views on *Hashemi, Ellingsworth* and the Commission Report, which proposed allowing debtors to discharge credit card debts that did not exceed the debtor's credit limit unless the debts were incurred within 30 days of bankruptcy?

8. FINE, PENALTY OR FORFEITURE

a. Punitive Damages

"Claim" is a very broad term designed to encompass virtually all rights to payment without regard to the identity of the entity having the right to payment or the reason why the law creates the right. Some rights to payment are created in order to punish the person against whom the right can be asserted. Examples are causes of action for punitive damages in a tort case or for treble damages under the antitrust laws. Another example is a civil penalty imposed by a state or the United States under the tax laws. These rights to payment are specially treated under the Bankruptcy Code. If an insolvent debtor is in Chapter 7, and the holder of a punitive right to payment is entitled to pro rata distribution of the estate along with holders of compensatory rights of payment, the punitive claim would in effect be paid from the pockets of other creditors rather than from the pocket of the debtor. This inequity is prevented by § 726(a)(4), which subordinates a punitive and multiple damage claim or a claim for a "fine, penalty or forfeiture" to the extent the claim is not "compensation for actual pecuniary loss suffered by the holder of such claim." The result is that punitive damages claimants seldom receive anything from the bankruptcy estate. Hence, unless punitive damages debts are nondischargeable under § 523, a Chapter 7 filing effectively defeats these claims in most cases.

The circuits are divided over the issue of whether punitive damages are made nondischargeable by § 523(a). Courts agreed that § 523(a)(6) ("any debt * * * for willful and malicious injury by the debtor to another entity or to the property of another entity") clearly encompassed punitive damages. *See, e.g., In re Bugna*, 33 F.3d 1054 (9th Cir. 1994). But § 523(a)(2)(A) ("any debt * * * for money, property, services * * * to the extent obtained by * * * fraud") is drafted in a manner that led some courts to hold that the portion of a damages award rendered nondischargeable is limited to the value of the "money, property, services." Hence, the amount of the damages award allocable to punitive damages remains dischargeable. This view gained some support from the maxim that, in order to protect the debtor's interest in a fresh start, exceptions from discharge should be narrowly construed. Other courts, in the belief that Congress could not have intended such a distinction, held that all liability arising from the fraud, whether in the form of compensatory or punitive damages, should be nondischargeable. The interest in giving debtors a fresh start applies to honest debtors and not perpetrators of fraud.

The issue was resolved in *Cohen v. de la Cruz*, 523 U.S. 213 (1998), which involved the following facts: a landlord fraudulently overcharged his tenants $31,382 in excess rents; pursuant to the provisions of the state consumer fraud act, judgment was entered for the amount of the excess rents and treble damages. The landlord filed in bankruptcy and contended that only the compensatory portion of the damages award was nondischargeable. The Court held that once it is established that property has been obtained by fraud, any claim arising therefrom—punitive as well as compensatory—is nondischargeable. The issue decided in *Cohen*, whether the scope of the discharge is broad enough to encompass punitive damage claims, does not affect other creditors holding dischargeable claims, but it does bear on other creditors with nondischargeable claims who must compete for payment out of the debtor's future earnings and after-acquired property.

b. Criminal Penalties

The status of rights to payment arising out of criminal proceedings is not completely clear. A crime may be punished by a judgment of the court providing for a fine or imprisonment or both. If a fine is imposed, the judgment represents a right to payment in favor of the state against the criminal. If the fine is not paid the judgment usually may be satisfied by imprisonment in lieu of payment. The state law might also provide that the judgment may be enforced in the same manner as a civil judgment. *See, e.g.* Cal. Penal Code § 1214(a) (West 2004). Thus, the obligation to pay a fine imposed in a criminal proceeding would seem to fall within the definition of "debt" in § 101(12). In any event it is clear under § 523(a)(7) that an obligation to pay a fine imposed in a criminal proceeding is not dischargeable in bankruptcy.

Conviction of a crime may give rise to other rights to payment that have some similarity to fines but which also differ in that they are payable for the benefit of someone other than the state. For example, if the crime resulted in an injury or loss to a victim, the culprit may be ordered to make restitution to the victim. Normally, the restitution is payable to the state for the benefit of the victim. Does the restitution order give status to the state as a creditor having a claim in bankruptcy if the culprit files a petition in bankruptcy? Is the obligation to make restitution a debt? If it is a debt, is it made nondischargeable by § 523(a)(7)? These questions were considered in *Kelly v. Robinson*, 479 U.S. 36 (1986). Debtor pleaded guilty to larceny resulting from wrongful receipt of welfare benefits. She was sentenced to a suspended prison term and was then placed on probation. As a condition to probation, she was ordered to make restitution of the welfare benefits in monthly installments over the probation period. Three months later she filed a petition in Chapter 7 bankruptcy. She listed the restitution obligation as a debt. The State of Connecticut, which was entitled to receive the restitution payments, did not file a claim in the bankruptcy and did not oppose discharge. It took the position that discharge did not affect the restitution debt. Debtor was granted a discharge, but the bankruptcy court held that the restitution obligation was excepted from discharge under § 523(a)(7).

The Second Circuit reversed the bankruptcy court's determination that the restitution obligation was excepted from discharge. It held that the obligation was a debt under § 101(12) and that § 523(a)(7) did not apply because the restitution order was intended as "compensation for actual pecuniary loss" of the State of Connecticut. The Supreme Court reversed. It relied on the fact that under the Bankruptcy Act fines, forfeitures and obligations to pay restitution were not allowable claims and thus were not subject to discharge. The Supreme Court also relied on a "fundamental policy against federal interference with state criminal prosecutions." 479 U.S. at 47. To allow discharge of an obligation to pay restitution in a criminal case could interfere with the ability of the state courts to choose the best combination of imprisonment, fine or restitution to further the rehabilitative and deterrent goals of the state criminal justice system. In the Court's view the phrase "compensation for actual pecuniary loss" does not apply to restitution orders because compensation of the victim for loss is only an incidental result of a restitution order. The primary function of the order is to carry out the penal goals of the state. In the course of the opinion the Court expressed "serious doubts" whether criminal penalties were debts within § 101(12), but found it unnecessary to decide the issue.

The doubt about whether criminal penalties were debts were removed in *Pennsylvania Department of Public Welfare v. Davenport*, 495 U.S. 552 (1990), in which the Court held that a restitution obligation imposed as a condition of probation in a state criminal action is a debt for bankruptcy purposes and was dischargeable in Chapter 13 under § 1328(a), which did not except fines or penalties from discharge. Congress moved with rare alacrity in adding § 1328(a)(3), which excepted from discharge any debt for criminal restitution. In 1994, § 1328(a)(3) was amended to include criminal fines.

c. Restitution Settlements

Restitution settlements are common in fraud and embezzlement cases. How are these agreements treated in bankruptcy? Debtor embezzled $100,000 while working as Creditor's bookkeeper. Creditor demanded restitution but Debtor had already spent the money. Ultimately a settlement was reached in which Debtor executed a note to Creditor for $75,000, in consideration for which Creditor executed a general release and covenant not to sue Debtor for any obligations other than her obligation as maker of the note. When Debtor filed in Chapter 7 a few months later, Creditor contended that the debt on the note was nondischargeable under § 523(a)(4). On these facts, the court in *Matter of West*, 22 F.3d 775 (7th Cir. 1994), held the debt to be dischargeable on the ground that the obligation was based on the note rather than on the fraudulent conduct that gave rise to the note. The court relied on the fact that Creditor had given Debtor a full release; in the view of the court, the release extinguished the underlying debt based on the embezzlement. In *United States v. Spicer*, 57 F.3d 1152 (D.C.Cir. 1995), another full release case, the court disagreed on the ground that the settlement obligation was wholly attributable to Debtor's admittedly fraudulent conduct. The Supreme Court resolved the issue in *Archer v. Warner*, 538 U.S. 314 (2003), in which the Court concluded that the settlement debt arose out of fraud and was nondischargeable.

9. TAXES

Congress has balanced the "fresh start" policy of bankruptcy law against the government's insatiable need for tax revenue. We shall not delve into the complex rules regarding the dischargeability of the numerous varieties of taxes. A brief treatment of the income tax demonstrates how the Bankruptcy Code balances the policies of discharge against those of protection of the public fisc. Before 1966, tax debt was not dischargeable in bankruptcy; the IRS could allow unpaid taxes to accumulate and, limited only by the statute of limitations, collect these taxes from the debtor's bankruptcy estate. By the time of the 1978 Act, a compromise had been reached in which only tax debts for which the return was due three years or less before the petition was filed were nondischargeable. This forced the IRS to act within the three-year period to assess the taxes and obtain a lien that would be nondischargeable in bankruptcy for tax debts without respect to the three-year lookback provision. Under the current law this policy is implemented by § 523(a)(1)(A), which excepts from discharge income taxes, among others, for which a priority is given under § 507(a)(8), meaning income taxes for which returns were due within three years of the debtor's bankruptcy. Section 523(a)(1)(B) excepts from discharge taxes whenever due for which the debtor either filed no return or filed a return late and within two years of bankruptcy. Hence, a debtor who has not been filing returns cannot avoid nondischargeability by filing shortly before bankruptcy.

In *Young v. United States*, 535 U.S. 43 (2002), the Court held that the three-year lookback period is tolled during the pendency of a debtor's Chapter 13 case. Although § 507(a)(8) says nothing about tolling, the Court held that equitable tolling is appropriate when a debtor files a Chapter 13 case during the three-year lookback period, thereby precluding the IRS from proceeding to collect the tax, owing to the automatic stay of § 362. A tax loophole would result if a debtor remains in Chapter 13 until the three-year period has run on an unpaid tax and then voluntarily dismisses the case and files in Chapter 7. By equitably tolling the three-year lookback period while the debtor was in bankruptcy, the Court closed the loophole. BAPCPA codified the tolling period for cases in which collection was stayed in a prior bankruptcy proceeding, plus 90 days. § 507(a)(8) (hanging paragraph).

Controversy has surrounded the meaning of § 523(a)(1)(C), which excepts from discharge taxes whenever due "with respect to which the debtor made a fraudulent return or willfully attempted in any manner to evade or defeat such a tax." How would you apply this provision to the facts in the following Problem?

PROBLEM

The IRS contended that Debtor's income tax for which a return was due more than three years before bankruptcy was nondischargeable under § 523(a)(1)(C) in each of the following situations. In each case, Debtor filed a timely and accurate return but, although she was fully aware of her legal obligation, did not pay the tax.

Case #1. Debtor did not pay the tax because she had no money beyond that required to support her and her family at a subsistence level.

Case #2. Debtor did not pay the tax because she needed the money to keep her business going. She chose to use the money to buy supplies and pay her employees. By this choice she was able to avoid closing the business and impoverishing her employees.

Case #3. Debtor used the money to buy a residence with her husband as tenants in the entirety. Under relevant state law, assets held in tenancy in the entirety are exempt from levy without a judgment against both owners.

Debtor contended that the tax claims were dischargeable in all three cases because, under the literal wording of § 523(a)(1)(C), the phrase "attempted in any manner to evade or defeat such tax" does not imply attempts to evade or defeat *payment* of the tax. Since mere nonpayment of taxes should not make taxes nondischargeable under § 523(a)(1)(C), the language of the statute must require the debtor to engage in affirmative acts other than nonpayment of taxes in order to establish the exception. This view was taken by *In re Haas*, 48 F.3d 1153 (11th Cir. 1995). But in *In re Griffith*, 206 F.3d 1389 (11th Cir. *en banc* 2000), the Eleventh Circuit overruled *Haas*, and reinterpreted the quoted language to mean: (1) mere nonpayment of taxes is insufficient to establish the § 523(a)(1)(C) exception; but (2) tax debts are nondischargeable if the debtor engages in affirmative acts seeking to evade or defeat the collection of taxes. How would you apply this test to the three cases? What if the debtor had failed to file a return? *See In re Fretz*, 244 F.3d 1323 (11th Cir. 2001).

D. PROTECTION OF THE DISCHARGE

1. INTRODUCTION

Under § 727 the debtor in a Chapter 7 case is granted a discharge from all prebankruptcy debts. But the effect of the discharge may be limited because specific debts described in § 523 are excepted from the discharge. As we have seen, the issue of whether a particular debt is or is not dischargeable in many cases cannot be determined except by a fact-finding process. Suppose a creditor who has a prebankruptcy claim waits until after the bankruptcy case has been

Chapter 4. Discharge 169

closed and then brings an action on the claim in a state court. This was a frequent scenario under the Bankruptcy Act before 1970. Under that regime, if the claim of the creditor had been discharged in bankruptcy, the discharge was simply an affirmative defense to a subsequent state court action brought by the creditor. A debtor who had just gone through bankruptcy might not have the resources to bear the litigation expenses involved in asserting the defense. Or, the debtor might erroneously believe that there was no need to defend because the debt had already been discharged. If the debtor did not assert the defense it was waived, and any subsequent judgment was conclusive on the question of liability. Thus, a creditor was sometimes able to get a judgment on a discharged debt even in cases in which there was no doubt about dischargeability.

Even if the debtor defended the state court action, the question of whether the claim was or was not discharged was determined by the state court rather than the bankruptcy court. In the state court the creditor sometimes found a forum more favorable to debt collection than to the bankruptcy policy of providing a fresh start for debtors. But apart from any question of bias, determination of dischargeability in the state court may have been less efficient than having the bankruptcy court determine all matters regarding the bankruptcy in the original bankruptcy proceedings. Moreover, uniform application of bankruptcy policies was not furthered by state court adjudication of these questions.

In some cases a creditor was able to collect a discharged debt without resort to judicial process. A creditor dealing with an unsophisticated debtor could sometimes induce payment by misrepresentations about the effect of discharge or by simply dunning the debtor or threatening to take legal action. In 1970 the Bankruptcy Act was amended to address some of the problems just outlined. These provisions were modified and expanded and became part of the Bankruptcy Code as § 524(a)(1) and (2) and § 523(c). *See* Charles Jordan Tabb, *The Law of Bankruptcy* § 10.30 (1997).

The National Bankruptcy Review Commission found that creditor misconduct in violation of the discharge injunction of § 524(a)(2) was so widespread that it recommended in § 1.3.2, *NBRC Rep.* at 161:

> An additional subsection should be added to section 524 to provide that the court shall grant judgment in favor of an individual who has received a discharge under section 727, 1141, 1228, or 1328 of this title for costs and attorney's fees, plus treble damages, from a creditor who threatens, files suit, or otherwise seeks to collect any debt that was discharged in bankruptcy and was not the subject of an agreement in accordance with subsections (c) and (d) of section 524.

Congress did not respond to the Commission's recommendation in BAPCPA but did amend § 524 to add one mildly pro-consumer provision and one sensible pro-creditor provision. Section 524(i) provides that the willful failure on the part of a creditor to credit payments received under a confirmed plan (this includes plans under Chapters 11, 12 and 13) is a violation of the injunction under § 524(a)(2), but only if this failure "caused material injury to the debtor." Section 524(j) addresses concerns that home mortgage lenders have about how to deal with debtors who have been discharged but who remain on property subject to their still enforceable mortgage. Do such lenders violate § 524(a)(2) if they send the debtor notices requesting payments and explaining the consequences if the debtor falls behind in her payments? Section 524(j) provides a safe harbor that allows home mortgage lenders to deal with discharged debtors in the ordinary manner to induce them to keep their payments current, that is threaten or conduct foreclosures. Certainly mortgagees can communicate with debtors about the consequences of falling into default.

2. DISCHARGE EXCEPTIONS PROCEDURES

Section 523(c)(1) provides that exceptions to discharge falling within § 523(a)(2) (false representations, etc.), § 523(a)(4) (defalcation), and § 523(a)(6) (willful and malicious injury) may only be determined by the bankruptcy court. These grounds for exception to discharge are the most commonly litigated and for uniformity these challenges should be heard as part of the bankruptcy case by judges familiar with bankruptcy procedures. Section 523(c)(1) requires the creditor to request determination of the dischargeability of the debt in these cases and under Rule 4007(c) this request must be timely so that the issue can be decided as part of the bankruptcy case.

The determination of the other exceptions to discharge set out in § 523(a), such as taxes (§ 523(a)(1)) or educational loans (§ 523(a)(8)), may be made by state or nonbankruptcy federal courts, as well as by bankruptcy courts. For instance, if Lender files a claim in Debtor's bankruptcy on an educational loan obligation Debtor may either (i) file a complaint to have the dischargeability of the Lender's claim determined in the bankruptcy court or (ii) leave it to Lender to raise the issue of the exception to discharge. If Lender does not and Debtor receives a discharge, Lender may sue Debtor on the claim in a state court. Debtor may raise her discharge as a defense and the determination of whether the exception to discharge applies will be made by the state court. However, we will see in the Problems below that in such a case Lender is taking a chance of violating § 524(a).

PROBLEMS

1. Debtor owed $4,000 to Finance Co. on an unsecured loan. Debtor filed in bankruptcy and scheduled the debt to Finance Co. Debtor received a § 727(b)

discharge. Finance Co. did not file a bankruptcy claim or otherwise take part in the bankruptcy because Debtor had no nonexempt assets and Finance Co. had received notice pursuant to Rule 2002(e) that it was unnecessary to file a claim. After the bankruptcy case was closed Finance Co. brought an action on the loan debt in a state court. Debtor pleaded the discharge in bankruptcy. Finance Co. alleged that the loan was obtained by Debtor by written fraudulent statements concerning Debtor's financial condition and was therefore nondischargeable under § 523(a)(2). Debtor moved for summary judgment. What result? § 523(c)(1); Bankruptcy Rule 4007(c). Can Finance Co. be cited for contempt? § 524(a)(2).

2. Assume the facts in Problem 1 except for the following changes: The loan was an educational loan described in § 523(a)(8) and the creditor was a university. In the state court, Debtor alleged that repayment of the loan would impose an undue hardship. Can the state court dispose of the case? Could the bankruptcy court dispose of the case after Debtor's bankruptcy case has been closed? § 350(b) and Bankruptcy Rule 4007(a) and (b).

3. Suppose in Problem 1 that Debtor did not answer Finance Co.'s complaint and Finance Co. was given a default judgment in the state court proceeding. Finance Co. then garnished Debtor's wages to pay the judgment. What are the rights of Debtor? § 524(a)(1) and (2).

4. Suppose in Problem 1 that Finance Co. took no legal action against Debtor. Instead, it obtained voluntary repayment of the debt by Debtor by convincing Debtor that the debt was not discharged in bankruptcy because of Debtor's fraudulent statements. What are Debtor's rights? § 524(a)(2) and (f).

E. DISCRIMINATION AGAINST DEBTORS

Perez v. Campbell, 402 U.S. 637 (1971), involved an Arizona statute that suspended the debtor's driver license for nonpayment of a judgment for damages resulting from an automobile accident. The statute specifically provided that a discharge in bankruptcy of the judgment debt did not relieve the judgment debtor from the effects of the statute. The Arizona statute was based on a uniform act adopted in most states. A divided Court held that the statute was unconstitutional under the Supremacy Clause. The majority opinion described the issue as "whether a state statute that protects judgment creditors from 'financially irresponsible persons' is in conflict with a federal statute that gives discharged debtors a new start 'unhampered by the pressure and discouragement of preexisting debt.'" 402 U.S. at 649. The majority opinion saw the principal purpose of the statute to be the protection of the public from "financial hardship which may result from the use of automobiles by financially irresponsible persons." *Id.* at 644. It stated that the "sole emphasis of the [statute] is one of providing leverage for the collection of damages from drivers who either admit that they are at fault or are adjudged negligent." *Id.* at 646–647.

Perez may merely be an example of invalidation of an indirect attempt to force payment of a discharged debt. But from this case there has developed a broader policy prohibiting certain kinds of discrimination against bankrupts. The policy is embodied in § 525. Subsection (a) relates to action by governmental units (§ 101(27)). It codifies the result of *Perez*, but the focus of the provision is against discrimination rather than coercion to pay a discharged debt. It expands protection substantially beyond *Perez* in protecting the debtor from loss of employment as a result of bankruptcy. The reason for this provision is obvious. The most dramatic frustration of the fresh start that discharge gives the debtor is to deny the debtor employment that may be vital to that fresh start. In 1984, Subsection (b) of § 525 was added. By virtue of that amendment a bankrupt is now protected from discrimination in employment by private as well as public employers.

In re Majewski

United States Court of Appeals, Ninth Circuit, 2002.
310 F.3d 653.

■ SCHROEDER, Chief Judge:

Debtor Norman Majewski incurred large medical expenses at the hospital where he was employed, and he did not pay them. After repayment negotiations failed, he told the hospital he intended to file for bankruptcy, and the hospital fired him before he did so. The trustee in Majewski's bankruptcy, William Leonard, now contends that the firing violated the bankruptcy code provision barring termination of an individual who "is or has been" a bankruptcy debtor "solely because" the individual is or has been a debtor in bankruptcy. § 525(b).

The bankruptcy court dismissed the trustee's claim against the hospital for violation of the statute, holding that the statute did not protect persons who had not yet filed for bankruptcy. The district court affirmed. We affirm as well.

The anti-discrimination provision of the bankruptcy code provides:

> No private employer may terminate the employment of, or discriminate with respect to employment against, an individual who is or has been a debtor under this title, or an individual associated with such debtor, solely because such debtor
>
> **(1)** is or has been a debtor under this title; * * *

§ 525(b). In this appeal, Leonard contends that we should interpret the provision of subparagraph 1 liberally to apply to debtors before they file a bankruptcy petition. * * *

The bankruptcy provision at issue in this case forbids firing an employee solely because that person "is or has been" a debtor. § 525(b). At the time the hospital fired Majewski, he was not, and had not been, a debtor in bankruptcy. The bankruptcy statutes therefore did not forbid the hospital from firing him. We reject Leonard's proposed reading of the statute, which is both inconsistent with the statute's text and incompatible with its purpose.

Bankruptcy's fresh start comes at the cost of actually filing a bankruptcy petition, turning one's assets over to the court and repaying debts that can be paid. One is not entitled to the law's protections, including employment security and the automatic stay of litigation, before being bound by its other consequences. We therefore affirm the bankruptcy court's dismissal of Leonard's action against the hospital.

AFFIRMED.

REINHARDT, Circuit Judge, dissenting:

Norman Majewski was hospitalized at St. Rose Dominican Hospital, and incurred substantial medical expenses. He later went to work for St. Rose, but in three years was unable to earn enough to discharge his medical debt. He then advised his employer that he intended to file for bankruptcy, but before he could actually file a formal petition, he was summarily fired.

Despite Congressional intent to enact legislation banning precisely such retaliation, the majority's opinion gives employers free license to punish an employee's good-faith efforts to become a protected debtor. Indeed, under today's holding, an employer may take advantage of a debtor's honesty by eliminating his most likely means to financial recovery. The majority adopts an unnaturally rigid and formalistic construction of the Bankruptcy Code that contravenes Congress's clear intent: to insulate debtors from unfair employment practices directly tied to their attempts to get a "fresh start." Accordingly, I respectfully dissent.

* * *

Bankruptcy is not only for companies like Enron and Worldcom. Individual employees have the same right to seek bankruptcy protection as large corporations and Congress has determined that they should be able to do so without fear of losing their livelihood as a result. Section 525(b) was enacted to protect the Majewskis of the world from the sort of direct retaliatory discrimination encountered here, and to ensure that individuals are able to receive the same fresh start as some of our less deserving corporate predators. A worker like Majewski should not be stripped of his rights either because his employer succeeds in firing him before he can get his papers on file in bankruptcy court, or because this court is afraid of encouraging him to avail himself of a remedy that Congress intended be available to him. The majority's unduly narrow construction of the Bankruptcy Code unjustly undoes an important part of the protections that Congress intended to offer working people. For that reason, I dissent.

NOTE

"[T]his Court finds the reasoning set forth by Judge Reinhardt in his dissent in [*Majewski*] to be sound and consistent with the legislative intent of § 525." *In re Mayo*, 322 B.R. 712 (Bankr.D.Vt.2005).

Do you agree?

Toth v. Michigan State Housing Development Authority
United States Court of Appeals, Sixth Circuit, 1998.
136 F.3d 477.

■ ALAN E. NORRIS, Circuit Judge.

Plaintiff Sue Toth appeals from the district court's grant of summary judgment to the Michigan State Housing Development Authority and two of its officers in an action alleging discrimination in violation of § 525(a) of the Bankruptcy Code. She contends that the denial of her application for a low income home improvement loan based upon a recent discharge in bankruptcy was contrary to the language of § 525(a) of the Code. Plaintiff further claims that the violation of § 525(a) gives rise to a 42 U.S.C. § 1983 claim. Because we conclude that § 525(a) does not forbid consideration of a prior bankruptcy in post-discharge credit arrangements with state entities, we affirm.

I.

Plaintiff received a discharge in bankruptcy in June 1995. Several months later, she applied to the Michigan State Housing Development Authority ("MSHDA") for a home improvement loan. That agency administers a home improvement loan program of the United States Department of Housing and Urban Development designed to assist eligible low income participants. Thereafter, in November 1995, MSHDA notified plaintiff that her loan application had been denied due to the agency's policy of requiring at least three years to lapse after the date of a bankruptcy discharge before a loan application will be processed.

Plaintiff filed suit in February 1996 in United States District Court for the Western District of Michigan alleging that MSHDA and two of its officials

Chapter 4. Discharge 175

unlawfully discriminated against her in violation of § 525(a) of the Bankruptcy Code. She sued the two officials, James Logue III, executive director of MSHDA, and Robert Brown, manager of MSHDA's home improvement loan program, in both their official and individual capacities. Plaintiff contended that § 525(a) prohibits a state's denial of a low-interest home improvement loan based solely upon a prior discharge in bankruptcy, and that the violation of § 525(a) gave rise to a cause of action under 42 U.S.C § 1983.

The parties consented to the exercise of jurisdiction by a magistrate judge, who issued the district court's opinion and order holding that the court had jurisdiction over the case notwithstanding the Eleventh Amendment, and granted defendants' motion for summary judgment on the merits.

II.

The primary issue raised by this appeal is whether the denial by MSHDA of a home improvement loan solely because the applicant had been discharged in bankruptcy within three years of the loan application violates § 525(a) of the Bankruptcy Code. Plaintiff asserts that the strictures of § 525(a) apply to the home improvement loan program operated by the Michigan agency to prohibit implementation of the agency's policy to deny her a loan based solely upon her prior discharge in bankruptcy. We disagree.

A.

Section 525(a) provides:

(a) ... a governmental unit may not deny, revoke, suspend, or refuse to renew a license, permit, charter, franchise, *or other similar grant to*, condition such a grant to, *discriminate with respect to such a grant* against, deny employment to, terminate the employment of, or discriminate with respect to employment against, a person that is or has been a debtor under this title, or another person with whom such debtor has been associated, *solely because* such debtor is or has been a debtor under this title, has been insolvent before the commencement of the case under this title, or during the case but before the debtor is granted or denied a discharge, or has not paid a debt that is dischargeable in the case under this title.

To the extent that it may apply to the circumstances of this case, § 525(a) prohibits a governmental entity from denying a "license, permit, charter, franchise, or other similar grant" or discriminating "with respect to such a grant" solely on the basis that the person seeking such a boon has been a bankrupt.

B.

One could, of course, argue that the scope of § 525(a)'s "other similar grant" language should be construed broadly, relying upon the general policy underlying bankruptcy, that a debtor should be able to have a "fresh start," to preclude conduct that would frustrate that policy. However, the courts of appeals that have approached the question have read the statute's reach narrowly, focusing upon the specific language of the statute. See, *e.g., Watts v. Pennsylvania Hous. Fin. Co.*, 876 F.2d 1090, 1093–94 (3d Cir. 1989); *In re Goldrich*, 771 F.2d 28, 30 (2d Cir. 1985). *Watts* involved an emergency mortgage assistance program designed by the State of Pennsylvania to prevent imminent mortgage foreclosures by providing for loans to distressed borrowers in the form of direct payments to their mortgage lenders, keeping their mortgages current. When plaintiff borrowers filed for bankruptcy, the program suspended these payments for the duration of the Bankruptcy Code's automatic stay. Plaintiffs contended this suspension violated § 525(a). In response, the court of appeals noted that a loan from the Pennsylvania program simply was not a "license, permit, charter [or] franchise," and that since those terms "are in the nature of indicia of authority from a governmental unit to. . . pursue some endeavor," the term "similar grant" should be given the same meaning. *Watts*, 876 F.2d at 1093. Similarly, the court in *In re Goldrich* concluded that § 525(a) did not prohibit consideration of prior bankruptcies in credit decisions, since "the language of section 525 may not properly be stretched so far beyond its plain terms." *Goldrich*, 771 F.2d at 29. We agree with the analysis employed by our sister courts.

The items enumerated in the statute—licenses, permits, charters, and franchises—are benefits conferred by government that are unrelated to the extension of credit. They reveal that the target of § 525(a) is government's role as a gatekeeper in determining who may pursue certain livelihoods. It is directed at governmental entities that might be inclined to discriminate against former bankruptcy debtors in a manner that frustrates the "fresh start" policy of the Bankruptcy Code, by denying them permission to pursue certain occupations or endeavors. The intent of Congress incorporated into the plain language of § 525(a) should not be transformed by employing an expansive understanding of the "fresh start" policy to insulate a debtor from all adverse consequences of a bankruptcy filing or discharge. A reckoning of an applicant's financial responsibility is an essential part of any lender's evaluation of a post-discharge application for a loan or extension of credit.

Accordingly, the district court correctly concluded that plaintiff failed to make out a case of discrimination under § 525(a), since that section does not include within its purview either the extension of credit by home loan programs

Chapter 4. Discharge

of the nature involved in this case, or the specific conduct of defendants about which plaintiff complains.

* * *

The judgment of the district court is affirmed.

NOTES

1. The court cites *In re Goldrich*, 771 F.2d 28 (2d Cir. 1985), as one of the cases supporting its view that § 525(a) should be read narrowly. In that case Debtor defaulted on a student loan guaranteed by an agency of New York State that has a statute providing that no student in default under a guaranteed student loan is eligible for another guaranteed loan so long as the default is not cured. The court held that a grant of credit is not included in the phrase "license, permit, charter, franchise, or other similar grant" appearing in § 525(a). In 1994, § 525(c) was added which, according to the Section-by-Section Description § 313, 140 Cong. Rec. H10771 (Oct 4, 1994), was intended to overrule *Goldrich* because it "gave an unduly narrow interpretation to Code section 525." If the interpretation of § 525(a) in *Goldrich* was too narrow, why is the interpretation of § 525(a) in *Toth* not also unduly narrow?

2. The most spectacular use of § 525(a) occurred in *Federal Communications Commission v. NextWave Personal Communications, Inc.*, 537 U.S. 293 (2003), in which billions of dollars of worth of broadband wireless spectrum licenses were in issue. In this case, NextWave, the debtor, was awarded exclusive licenses for broadband personal communications services by the Federal Communications Commission (FCC) pursuant to a set of auction procedures designed to limit the spectrum licenses to "small businesses." In accordance with FCC regulations, NextWave made a small downpayment on the purchase price and signed promissory notes for the balance to be paid in installments, secured by a security interest in NextWave's rights in the licenses. The licenses recited that they were conditioned on compliance with terms of the installment plan and failure to comply with these conditions would result in automatic cancellation of the licenses. When NextWave had difficulty in obtaining financing for its operations, the FCC suspended the installment payments schedule pending NextWave's adoption of restructuring options. When NextWave saw that it would be unable to restructure within the deadline set by the FCC, it sought to obtain further extensions of the deadline from the Commission and courts, to no avail. NextWave filed in Chapter 11 in June 1998 and suspended payments to all creditors, including the FCC, pending confirmation of a reorganization plan.

The FCC objected to the proposed Chapter 11 plan on the ground that NextWave's licenses had been cancelled automatically when the company missed its first payment deadline in October 1998, after NextWave filed in Chapter 11. NextWave contended that the FCC's cancellation of the licenses violated § 525(a). The Court agreed with NextWave, holding that the case fell squarely within the language of § 525(a): a governmental unit, the FCC, revoked licenses of the the debtor, NextWave, solely because the debtor had not paid a dischargeable debt. The fact that the FCC may have had a valid regulatory motive for the cancellation is irrelevant; there is no regulatory exception to § 525(a). *Id.* at 302.

In his dissent, Justice Breyer criticized the result in this case as inconsistent with the purpose of § 525, which was to prevent discrimination against persons on account of their status as bankrupts. Granted that a state or federal governmental unit should not be able to deny or revoke a license solely because a person has filed in bankruptcy, § 525(a) was intended to protect debtors from discriminatory license terminations. But that's not this case. There was no discrimination against NextWave based on its status as a bankrupt, rather NextWave lost its license because it didn't pay a debt secured by the licenses at issue. This has nothing to do with discrimination based on bankruptcy. He urged that the language of the statute be interpreted in conformity with the statute's purposes, and he suggested some interpretations that would reach that goal. He cited *Toth* as being consistent with his views about a more limited view of the statute.

CHAPTER 5
STAYS AND INJUNCTIONS

A. INTRODUCTION

Stays and injunctions in bankruptcy arise principally under two sections of the Bankruptcy Code: Section 105 allows a bankruptcy court to "issue any order, process, or judgment that is necessary or appropriate to carry out the provisions of this title." Under § 105 the bankruptcy court has wide discretion to issue injunctions to facilitate the bankruptcy process. Under § 362(a) the filing of a petition in bankruptcy operates as a stay against a variety of acts affecting the debtor, property of the debtor, property of the estate or property held by the estate. This stay is known as the automatic stay.

> The automatic stay is one of the fundamental debtor protections provided by the bankruptcy laws. It gives the debtor a breathing spell from his creditors. It stops all collection efforts, all harassment, and all foreclosure actions. It permits the debtor to attempt a repayment or re-organization plan, or simply to be relieved of the financial pressures that drove him into bankruptcy.
>
> The automatic stay also provides creditor protection. Without it, certain creditors would be able to pursue their own remedies against the debtor's property. Those who acted first would obtain payment of the claims in preference to and to the detriment of other creditors. Bankruptcy is designed to provide an orderly liquidation procedure under which all creditors are treated equally. A race of diligence by creditors for the debtor's assets prevents that.

H. Rep. No. 95–595, 1978 U.S.C.C.A.N. 6296–6297.

This oft-quoted passage from the legislative history justifies the automatic stay of § 362 as a fundamental protection for both debtors (safeguard against dismembering the bankrupt's estate) and creditors (insuring ratable distribution). Evidence of the importance of the automatic stay is the extraordinary volume of litigation regarding its scope, effect, and duration.

The automatic stay pervades bankruptcy law and we refer to it throughout this Casebook. The overview of bankruptcy in chapter 1 presented a very brief description of the automatic stay intended to allow students to understand references to it in chapters 2 through 4. In this chapter we offer a more detailed treatment of the stay, but important issues concerning stays and injunctions are raised in context in other chapters of the book as well. Under state law the property of a defaulting debtor may be seized by unsecured creditors in an unruly "race of diligence" to obtain judicial liens on the debtor's assets; the first person to obtain a lien on the property prevails to the exclusion of other creditors. Liquidation bankruptcy offers debtors respite from seizure of their assets under state law and assures unsecured creditors ratable distribution of the debtor's estate. The automatic stay is the instrument that protects the debtor, its assets and its creditors from creditor collection activity during the bankruptcy case.

B. APPLICABILITY OF THE STAY

1. CREDITOR PROCESSES STAYED

The date of filing a petition in bankruptcy is the Prime Meridian of bankruptcy law. As we have seen, this date is important in determining what is property of the estate (§ 541) and which claims are discharged (§ 727(b)). It also governs the applicability of the automatic stay (§ 362(a)). The rules are relatively simple: all proceedings to collect prepetition claims are stayed if these claims are against the debtor, the property of the debtor or the property of the estate; the stay is automatic, no injunction need be sought, and it is immediately binding on all persons and entities, whether they have notice of the bankruptcy petition or not. An important function of the automatice stay is to funnel all collection proceedings through the bankruptcy court. We pose a series of basic questions that are intended to illustrate these general principles.

Problem 1.

What creditor processes are stayed by § 362(a)? In each of the following questions, assume that Debtor filed a petition in Chapter 7 bankruptcy on July 1. The inquiry in each case is whether Creditor's conduct violated § 362(a) and, if so, which, if any, paragraph or paragraphs of subsection (a) was violated .

Question #1. Creditor held a perfected security interest in Debtor's equipment that secured a promissory note on which Debtor defaulted on May 1. Creditor gave Debtor appropriate notice that the equipment would be sold on July 10 pursuant to Article 9 of the UCC. Although Creditor learned of Debtor's bankruptcy filing, it proceeded to sell the property on July 10 at a nonjudicial sale conducted by Creditor.

Question #2. Same facts as Question #1 except that Creditor notified Debtor that the sale would be held on July 2. At the time the sale was held, Creditor knew nothing of Debtor's status as a debtor in bankruptcy.

Chapter 5. Stays and Injunctions

Question #3. On July 1, Creditor held a judgment against Debtor that was duly recorded in the land records of the county where the land owned by the Debtor is located. Hence, Creditor has a valid judicial lien on the property, indefeasible in bankruptcy. On July 15, Creditor obtained a writ of execution ordering the appropriate judicial officer to foreclose on the land. No further action was taken.

Question #4. Creditor performed successful surgery on Debtor who still owed Creditor $10,000 on July 1 for the procedure. Creditor was outraged to learn of Debtor's bankruptcy and had his assistant call the ungrateful Debtor at least once a day in the period following July 1, demanding payment of his fee. The calls became more irate each day.

Question #5. Same facts as Question above except that Creditor called Debtor and told her that he would no longer perform services for her until she paid her bill.

Question #6. On June 29, Creditor repossessed Debtor's automobile in which Creditor held a validly perfected security interest. Debtor was clearly in default and Creditor complied with all requirements for a valid repossession. On July 10, while Creditor was still in possession of the car, Debtor's trustee in bankruptcy demanded that Creditor return the vehicle, in which under the law of the jurisdiction the Debtor held legal title until its ownership rights were cut off by a resale by Creditor. Creditor refused.

2. PARTIES AND PROPERTY PROTECTED

Problem 2.

What parties and property are protected by the stay? Same instructions as those for Problem 1 above.

Question #1. Debtor borrowed $1,000 from Creditor who insisted that Guarantor co-sign the note evidencing the obligation. When Debtor defaulted on the note, Creditor, with full knowledge of Debtor's bankruptcy, brought suit on the note on July 10 against Guarantor to collect the amount of the note. Under the law of the state, if Guarantor pays the note it has a right of action for reimbursement against Debtor.

Question #2. Creditor, a lender who deals in the sub-prime market, prefers to lend money to debtors who have recently filed in bankruptcy because these debtors cannot receive a discharge in Chapter 7 in a case filed within eight years of their prior discharge. On July 15, Creditor lent $1,000 to Debtor who missed her first payment on the loan that was due on August 15. Creditor immediately filed suit against Debtor for a money judgment. Under § 362(c)(2), the stay was still in effect because the case was not closed.

Question #3. Same facts as in Question #2 except that in connection with its suit on the postpetition claim, Creditor attached property in Debtor's possession that she had owned at the time of bankruptcy.

Question #4. Section 541(a)(6) provides that earnings of a debtor for services performed postpetition are not property of the estate. On July 1, Creditor held a prepetition claim of $1,000. Knowing that Debtor's deposit account was entirely made up of postpetition earnings of Debtor, Creditor attached the account on July 20 in an attempt to collect the debt.

3. EXCEPTIONS TO THE STAY

a. Section 362(b)

The sweep of the automatic stay under § 362(a) is so broad and its impact so great that over the years numerous interests have sought and obtained exceptions; these are enumerated in § 362(b). Most of these are specific to the needs of the parties seeking relief and need not concern us, *e.g.*, § 362(b)(3) allows secured creditors to maintain perfection of security interests by an act such as filing a UCC continuation statement during the stay; § 362(b)(9) was significantly broadened to allow tax authorities during the stay to conduct tax audits, make demands for tax returns, and make certain assessments for tax liabilities and issue notice and demand for payment of these assessments; and § 362(b)(18) was added allowing for the creation or perfection of ad valorem tax liens during the stay. This last amendment resolves an issue that illustrates the inexorable law of unintended consequences that faces all statutory drafters. In *In re Parr Meadows Racing Association, Inc.*, 880 F.2d 1540 (2d Cir. 1989), the court held that § 362(a)(4), staying "any act to create, perfect, or enforce any lien against property of the estate," precluded local government units from imposing liens for ad valorem property taxes that became due after the petition in bankruptcy. *Id.* at 1544. Local government tax authorities were shocked to learn that the operation of the stay deprived them of the priority over mortgages that they enjoyed under nonbankruptcy law and relegated them to the status of unsecured claimants for the amount of taxes owed. Their cries were heard and § 362(b)(18) resulted.

The amendments to § 362 in BAPCPA go beyond merely correcting oversights in the original statute and move toward limiting the automatic stay in order to enable favored groups of creditors to proceed against debtors unhindered by the stay. For instance, Wall Street has obtained special exemption from the automatic stay for a broad range of financial instruments, swaps and derivitives. § 362(b)(6), (7), (17) & (27). The stay is likewise limited to preclude bankruptcy from interfering with rights of spouses and children to receive domestic support payments from debtor spouses, *e.g.*, § 362(b)(2)(C). Other examples are the provisions strengthening the rights of secured creditors and landlords, *e.g.* § 362(b)(22), which excepts from the stay the continuation of eviction proceedings involving residential property if the landlord has obtained a judgment for possession before the tenant filed in bankruptcy. Under § 362(h), the stay is terminated if the debtor who has retained possession of personal property subject to a security interest or lease without the consent of the creditor fails to redeem (§ 722) the property or reaffirm the contract (§ 524(c)) within statutory time limits.

Limitations on the stay are used to deal with the abuse of repeated filings: § 362(c)(3)(A) provides that if an individual debtor has had a prior case dismissed in the preceding one-year period, the automatic stay in the second case terminates "with respect to the debtor" within 30 days after filing unless the debtor can rebut a heavy presumption that her case was not filed in good faith. But, as we point out in our discussion of repetitive filings in chapter 9, *infra*, case law has predominately held that the statute is a failure because it does not terminate the stay with respect to the property of the debtor's estate. If two or more cases have been pending within the previous year, there is no stay at all in the second case unless the bad faith presumption described in the preceding sentence is rebutted. § 362(c)(4). If a court finds that the transfer of real property or multiple bankruptcy filings affecting real property is part of a scheme to defraud creditors, the court order may be recorded and is binding *in rem* in any bankruptcy case affecting the property within the next two years, (§ 362(d)(4)), and in such a case, the automatic stay does not apply to actions to enforce a lien or security interest for a period of two years after entry of the order. § 362(b)(20).

Section 362(b)(1) states the obvious: a debtor cannot avoid criminal proceedings by filing in bankruptcy. But what if the purpose of the criminal proceeding is to collect a debt?

PROBLEM

Debtor was delinquent in his child support payments and filed in bankruptcy. When his former wife stopped receiving the payments, she complained to the district attorney in an effort to make Debtor resume payments. As a result, criminal charges were brought in state court against Debtor for his dereliction. After his conviction, Debtor requested the bankruptcy court to declare the state criminal proceedings void as a violation of the automatic stay. Are state criminal proceedings excepted from the application of the automatic stay even if the prosecution is motivated by the complaining witness's desire to collect a debt? *See In re Gruntz*, 202 F.3d 1074 (9th Cir. 2000).

b. Police and Regulatory Power Exception

The major exception to § 362(a) is the police and regulatory power exception of § 362(b)(4), which allows a governmental unit to invoke legal process against a debtor in bankruptcy to prevent or stop violations of fraud, environmental protections, consumer protection, safety, or similar police or regulatory laws, or to fix damages for violation of such laws. Clearly, filing bankruptcy cannot be a license to avoid compliance with all manner of generally applicable environmental, zoning, safety, criminal, antitrust and licensing statutes and regulations. Unfortunately, the current wording of § 362(b)(4) was carelessly cobbled together in 1998 in the dying days of the 105th Congress. The ostensible purpose of the 1998 amendment was to expand the § 362(b)(4) exception to exempt agencies having authority under an international convention prohibiting chemical weapons. Since it is unimaginable that any bankruptcy judge would find chemical weapons inspections and regulations precluded by the automatic stay in any event, the chemical weapons provision is of no import. But, courts have struggled with the meaning of the 1998 redraft of § 362(b)(4).

Section 362(b)(4) exempts from the automatic stay actions or proceedings of governmental units or organizations "to enforce such governmental unit's or organization's police and regulatory power, including the enforcement of a judgment *other than a money judgment*, obtained in an action or proceeding by the governmental unit's or organization's police or regulatory power." The money judgment exclusion from the police and regulatory power exception is intended to prevent governmental units from using their police and regulatory powers to gain preferential treatment at the expense of other creditors in bankruptcy. The governmental unit may obtain a judgment against the debtor but cannot enforce it. The distinction is between the governmental unit acting as a regulator, which is exempted from the stay, and acting as a creditor, which is not.

Environmental cases have often raised § 362(b)(4) issues. Two oft-cited Third Circuit cases are informative. In *Penn Terra Ltd. v. Department of Environment*, 733 F.2d 267 (3d Cir. 1984), Debtor was a coal mining company that had violated state environmental laws. It entered into a prepetition consent decree requiring it to remedy some of these violations, but filed in Chapter 7 and went out of business before any work had been done. After Debtor filed, the state brought an action in a state court to compel Debtor to comply with the consent decree. The state court's order compelling Debtor to clean up the environmental hazard was challenged by Debtor as a violation of the automatic stay, but the Third Circuit held that the order was not enforcement of a money judgment within § 362(b)(4). The court explained that it was the enforcement of a money judgment by seizure or an attempt to seize a debtor's property that is proscribed by the automatic stay. *Query:* How could Debtor comply with the order other than to use whatever remained of the assets of the estate to pay for the work?

In *United States v. Nicolet*, 857 F.2d 202 (3d Cir. 1988), the Environmental Protection Agency incurred costs in abating an environmental hazard on land owned by Debtor. It filed suit in a state court against Debtor for reimbursement of these costs before Debtor filed in Chapter 11. The question before the court was whether the EPA could continue its suit after Debtor filed. The court held that the suit was by a governmental unit to enforce its police or regulatory power, a proceeding expressly exempt from the automatic stay under § 362(b)(4). Thus, the case may proceed to trial so that damages, if any, may be fixed. It was the intent of Congress that proceedings like this should be exempt from the automatic stay up to and including entry of a monetary judgment. On similar facts, *In re Mystic Tank Lines Corp.*, 544 F.3d 524 (3d Cir. 2008), followed *Nicolet*.

4. TERMINATION OF THE STAY

Termination of the stay is governed by § 362(c). If the stay is of an act against property of the estate, the stay terminates when the property ceases to be property of the estate. With respect to any other act, the stay terminates when the bankruptcy case is closed or dismissed or the debtor is granted or denied a discharge, whichever occurs first. Under § 362(d) the bankruptcy court may lift the stay or grant other relief from the stay.

C. EFFECT OF VIOLATION OF STAY

1. DAMAGES

a. Willful Violation

Section 362(k)(1) is strong medicine. It provides that an individual injured by "any willful violation of a stay provided by this section *shall* recover actual damages, including costs and attorneys' fees, and, in appropriate circumstances, may recover punitive damages." Given the potential liability for not only costs and attorneys' fees but also punitive damages, creditors must take care to establish procedures to deal with bankruptcy notices concerning their debtors.

Under Rule 1007(a)(1), when a debtor files in bankruptcy she must supply the court with the names and addresses of her creditors, and notice of the filing is sent to these addresses. But addresses supplied by the debtor may be the addresses to which she was required to send her monthly payments, so-called "lockbox" accounts that did nothing but process payments, and creditors, such as banks and retailers, complained that they should not be penalized for violating the automatic stay in such cases until they received actual notice of the bankruptcy. BAPCPA added § 342(f) and (g) that allow creditors to protect themselves in such cases by filing with any bankruptcy court a notice of address that must be used by all bankruptcy courts in notifying that entity. If the creditor has filed the prescribed notice of bankruptcy with the court, no notice to a creditor at a different address is effective until it is "brought to the attention" of such creditor. § 342(g)(1). No monetary penalty may be imposed on a creditor for acts violating the stay committed before the creditor is given an effective notice. § 342(g)(2).

The circuits are divided on whether "actual damages" in § 362(k) includes emotional distress. The Seventh Circuit in *Aiello v. Providian Financial Corp.*, 239 F.3d 876, 880 (7th Cir. 2001), saw the protection of the automatic stay as primarily financial in character and required proof of financial loss in order to claim emotional distress damages. Other circuits have disagreed. The Ninth Circuit in *In re Dawson*, 390 F.3d 1139 (9th Cir. 2004), ruled that damages for emotional distress may be recovered if it is established that the individual debtor suffered significant harm as a result of the violation of the stay. No proof of pecuniary loss is required and the debtor may prove entitlement to damages even in the absence of corroborating evidence if the debtor in fact suffered significant emotional harm and the circumstances surrounding the violation make it obvious that a reasonable person would suffer significant emotional harm. *See also Fleet Mortgage Group, Inc. v. Kaneb*, 196 F.3d 265 (1st Cir. 1999).

The majority of courts hold that in order to demonstrate a violation of § 362(k)(1), the debtor has the burden of establishing, by a preponderance of the evidence, that the creditor knew of the automatic stay and intended the actions that constitute the violation. No proof of specific intent on the part of the creditor to violate the stay is required. *See, e.g., In re Johnson*, 501 F.3d 1163 (10th Cir. 2007).

b. Meaning of "Individual"

Section 362(k) allows an "individual" injured by a willful violation of the stay to recover damages. The term "individual," although not defined in the Bankruptcy Code, is consistently used in the Code to refer to natural persons in contrast to legal entities such as corporations and partnerships. Examples are § 109(e) and § 101(30) ("individual with regular income"), which limit the use of Chapter 13 to natural persons, and § 101(18) ("family farmer"), which distinguishes between farmers who are individuals and those that are corporations or partnerships. A similar distinction is made in § 101(31) ("insider"). Under § 101(41), "person" includes individual, partnership, and corporation.

Thus, the literal meaning of § 362(k) is that a corporation or partnership that is in bankruptcy is not entitled to the cause of action provided by that section.

Nonetheless, some courts have refused to draw a distinction between natural persons and other debtors in § 362(k). Currently the circuits are divided on the issue with four holding that the term "individual" does not include corporations and two holding that it does. The authorities are marshaled in *In re Spookyworld, Inc.*, 346 F.3d 1 (1st Cir. 2003). Majority view courts point out that corporations are free to petition bankruptcy courts to award damages for automatic stay violations pursuant to their § 105(a) power, a practice that was routine prior to the enactment of § 362(k). See *Spookyworld*, 346 F.3d at 8.

2. VOID OR VOIDABLE?

Another long-standing division of authority concerns whether acts in violation of the automatic stay are void or voidable. In *Kalb v. Feuerstein*, 308 U.S. 433, 438 (1940), the Court, in construing the effect of a stay under a prior bankruptcy statute, held a postpetition state court real property foreclosure to be "not merely erroneous but * * * beyond its power, void, and subject to collateral attack." The Bankruptcy Code does not directly speak to the issue. Some courts believe that § 362(d), which empowers courts to annul the stay, undermines *Kalb*: if an act in violation of the stay is a nullity, how can it be subsequently ratified by annulment of the stay? See a discussion of this view in *Bronson v. United States*, 46 F.3d 1573 (Fed.Cir. 1995) (a strong holding that acts violating the stay are voidable). The confines of the automatic stay and the consequences of the void/voidable distinction are discussed in the following case.

In re Soares
United States Court of Appeals, First Circuit, 1997.
107 F.3d 969.

■ SELYA, Circuit Judge.

"[T]he dead tree gives no shelter." T.S. Eliot, *The Waste Land, I, The Burial of the Dead* (1922). Like a shade tree, the automatic stay which attends the initiation of bankruptcy proceedings, § 362(a), must be nurtured if it is to retain its vitality. This appeal, which pits a Chapter 13 debtor bent on saving his home against a creditor bent on enforcing its rights under a mortgage, raises issues which touch upon the degree of judicial protection that the automatic stay invites. These issues are whether the automatic stay precludes a state court from undertaking ministerial acts after a bankruptcy filing; if not, what acts are exempt under that rubric; whether a bankruptcy court may grant retroactive relief from the automatic stay; and if so, what legal standard it should apply in prescribing such an anodyne.

I. Laying the foundation

We begin by retracing the labyrinthine corridors through which this litigation has passed. In 1990 the debtor, Napoleon G. Soares, purchased a home in Brockton, Massachusetts. He executed a $70,000 promissory note to the Brockton Credit Union (BCU) and secured the note by a first mortgage on the real estate. After sustaining injuries in a motorcycle accident, Soares lagged in his monthly payments. BCU grew restive and commenced foreclosure proceedings in the state superior court. Soares did not file an answer. On March 22, 1995, BCU sent a letter to the clerk of court seeking an order of default and a judgment authorizing foreclosure. Two days later Soares filed a bankruptcy petition, thus triggering the automatic stay. He immediately gave notice to BCU, but neither party alerted the state court. On April 10, with the stay still firmly in place, a judge of that court issued the requested default order. One week later, she authorized the entry of a foreclosure judgment.

Soares missed some post-petition mortgage payments. On June 14, 1995, BCU, without apprising the bankruptcy court of the orders previously obtained in the state proceedings, filed a motion seeking relief from the automatic stay. The debtor's then-counsel, Gerard Williamson, neglected to oppose BCU's motion. The bankruptcy court granted the unopposed motion on June 29 (the same day, coincidentally, that Soares, unbeknownst to the judge, paid the post-petition arrearage). The court subsequently refused to entertain a belated objection filed by Williamson.

When Soares missed his November payment, BCU activated the state court judgment. At the ensuing foreclosure sale, held on November 29, BCU itself bid in the mortgaged premises and paid approximately $14,200 in overdue municipal taxes to clear the title. Soares thereafter sought relief in the state court on the ground that the foreclosure judgment had been issued in contravention of the automatic stay. The court denied the motion, saying that its post-petition actions had been "ministerial" and that any error was harmless.

Soares' unsuccessful foray apparently rang warning bells for BCU, which asked the bankruptcy court to clarify whether the June 29 order (lifting the automatic stay) ratified the earlier state court judgment. BCU served this so-called clarification motion on the attorney, Williamson, but not on Soares. In a margin order entered on February 9, 1996, Judge Kenner addressed the question of retroactivity for the first time and vacated the automatic stay retroactive to March 24, 1995, "such that the [state] judgment and movant's foreclosure shall not be deemed to have violated the automatic stay."

Less than three weeks later Soares, through newly retained counsel, filed a motion to reconsider both the February 9 order and the original grant of relief from the automatic stay. Judge Kenner denied the reconsideration motion on the merits and also denied a companion motion to void the foreclosure sale. The judge advanced three reasons for having lifted the automatic stay retroactively on February 9. First, because BCU "had done everything right," it would be inequitable to upset its expectations. Second, because the foreclosure had wiped out junior lienholders, it would be too complicated to "unscramble the egg." Third, because Soares could not immediately repay the funds that BCU had expended to clear title to the property, the economic realities favored ratification of the foreclosure.

Soares appealed. The district court temporarily stayed further proceedings (blocking both a planned eviction and a possible resale of the property). Eventually, however, the district court—although finding that BCU had neglected its responsibility to apprise the state tribunal of Soares' bankruptcy (an error which it termed "harmless")—determined that the retroactive lifting of the automatic stay did not constitute an abuse of discretion.

Soares again appealed. We enlarged the earlier stay on condition that Soares make monthly payments to BCU for use and occupancy of the premises (to be credited against the mortgage indebtedness, should Soares prevail on appeal).

II. Discussion

To the extent that the threshold inquiries in this case involve questions of statutory interpretation, we exercise plenary review.[4] * * * From this vantage point we first address the purported exemption for "ministerial acts," as it is only necessary to reach the retroactivity question if a violation of the automatic stay in fact occurred.

A. The Nature of the State Court's Actions.

The parties clash head-on in respect to classification of the state court's actions. The debtor claims that the state court order and judgment transgressed the automatic stay. The creditor claims that these entries, though occurring post-petition, were purely ministerial and, thus, not offensive to the stay. The debtor has the better argument.

Section 362(a)(1) of the Bankruptcy Code provides that the filing of a bankruptcy petition stays the commencement or continuation of all nonbankruptcy judicial proceedings against the debtor. Here, the state court default order eventuated more than two weeks *after* Soares filed for bankruptcy and the foreclosure judgment one week later. The issue, then, is whether these entries contravened the mandate of section 362(a)(1). BCU asserts that they did not

---

[4] A different standard of review applies to the bankruptcy court's discretionary decision to lift the automatic stay retroactively. We review that ruling for abuse of discretion. * * *

because the stay was not in effect when the creditor requested the state court to act and because the state court's actions, when taken, constituted ministerial acts.

The creditor's first assertion is mere buzznacking. The focus here is whether or not the state court's actions, when effected, transgressed the automatic stay. The date on which the creditor asked the state court to act, while material to an assessment of the creditor's good faith (which is not seriously questioned here), does not bear on whether the activities themselves constituted the forbidden continuation of a judicial proceeding.

BCU's second assertion is more substantial. Ministerial acts, even if undertaken in a state judicial proceeding subsequent to a bankruptcy filing, do not fall within the proscription of the automatic stay. * * * But the state court's actions in this case cannot properly be characterized as ministerial.

A ministerial act is one that is essentially clerical in nature. *See Black's Law Dictionary* 996 (6th ed. 1990). Thus, when an official's duty is delineated by, say, a law or a judicial decree with such crystalline clarity that nothing is left to the exercise of the official's discretion or judgment, the resultant act is ministerial. *See United States ex rel. McLennan v. Wilbur*, 283 U.S. 414, 420 (1931) (indicating that a duty is ministerial if "the obligation to act [is] peremptory, and plainly defined"); *Neal v. Regan*, 587 F.Supp. 1558, 1562 (N.D.Ind.1984) (describing a ministerial act as "one which "the law prescribes and defines... with such precision as to leave nothing to the exercise of discretion or judgment'") (citation omitted). Such acts can usefully be visualized as the antithesis of judicial acts, inasmuch as the essence of a judicial act is the exercise of discretion or judgment. *See Black's Law Dictionary*, supra, at 846.

Virtually by definition, a judicial proceeding does not conclude until the judicial function is completed, that is, until the judicial decision is made. *See, e.g., Bidermann*, 21 F.3d at 528 (holding that the judicial function is completed "at the moment the judge direct[s] entry of judgment"). Frequently, routine scrivening, such as recordation or entry on the docket, follows on the heels of a judicial decision. Such actions—taken in obedience to the judge's peremptory instructions or otherwise precisely defined and nondiscretionary—are ministerial and, consequently, do not themselves violate the automatic stay even if undertaken after an affected party files for bankruptcy. *See, e.g., Knightsbridge Dev.*, 884 F.2d at 148 (suggesting that merely recording a previously decided award would be a "clerical act" and therefore would not infract the automatic stay); *In re Capgro Leasing Assocs.*, 169 B.R. 305, 315–16 (Bankr.E.D.N.Y.1994) (stating that "entry of a judgment will constitute a "ministerial act' where the judicial function has been completed and the clerk has merely to perform the rote function of entering the judgment upon the court's docket"). By the same token, however, acts undertaken in the course of carrying out the core judicial function are not ministerial and, if essayed after bankruptcy filing, will be deemed to violate the automatic stay.

Bidermann captures this distinction. There, the district judge ruled *ora sponte* and endorsed the motion papers. The defendant then sought refuge in bankruptcy. The Second Circuit held the clerk's subsequent, post-petition entry of the judgment on the docket to be ministerial (and, therefore, unaffected by the automatic stay). Other cases are to the same effect. *See Heikkila v. Carver (In re Carver)*, 828 F.2d 463, 464 (8th Cir. 1987) (holding that a "routine certification" by the clerk, entered post-petition, did not transgress the automatic stay); *Capgro Leasing*, 169 B.R. at 315–16 (holding the clerk's entry of judgment on the docket to be ministerial when, prior to the bankruptcy filing, the court had ordered summary judgment). A parallel line of cases reinforces the notion that the compendium of ministerial acts excludes those involving deliberation, discretion, or judicial involvement. *See, e.g., Ellis v. Consolidated Diesel Elec. Corp.*, 894 F.2d 371, 372–73 (10th Cir. 1990) (invalidating a judicial decision that granted summary judgment two weeks after a bankruptcy filing); *Knightsbridge Dev.*, 884 F.2d at 148 (voiding an arbitration award because the bulk of the panel's deliberations occurred after the stay arose); *Ellison v. Northwest Eng'g Co.*, 707 F.2d 1310, 1311 (11th Cir. 1983) (holding that while the automatic stay was in effect a court could not render a decision in a case which had been briefed and argued pre-petition).

This line of demarcation makes perfectly good sense. The statutory proviso which gives rise to the automatic stay says what it means and means what it says. * * * Confining the exemption for ministerial acts to those actions which are essentially clerical, as opposed to judicial, honors this principle because such an interpretation comports precisely with the text of section 362(a)(1). In the bargain, this interpretation also facilitates the statute's due administration.

Silhouetted against this legal landscape, it is readily apparent that the state court's actions in ordering a default and directing the entry of a judgment possess a distinctly judicial, rather than a ministerial, character. The record is totally barren of any evidence that the state court judge decided to grant BCU's request prior to the date of the bankruptcy filing, and all visible signs point in the opposite direction. The judge did not enter the default order until more than two weeks after Soares sought the protection of the bankruptcy court and she did not direct the entry of a judgment authorizing foreclosure until another week had elapsed. Moreover, the judge indicated after the fact that she waited to confirm Soares' nonmilitary status before directing the entry of judgment. This indicates deliberativeness and a concomitant willingness to exercise discretion.

Nor does the fact that the judge later characterized her entry of the foreclosure judgment as "ministerial" require a different result. An appellate court is not bound by a trial judge's unsupported description, * * * and we are aware of no reason why that salutary principle would not apply with equal vigor to our assessment of a state court's actions when the underlying question relates to the effect of those actions *under federal law*. Hence, we decline to adopt the label that the state court judge chose in hindsight to affix to her activities.

We summarize succinctly. Because the decision which animated the entry of the order and judgment occurred after the stay was in force, those actions continued the state judicial proceeding within the meaning of section 362(a)(1). Consequently, the actions violated the automatic stay. Given this infraction, we now must assess the availability of a retroactive cure.

B. The Operation of the Automatic Stay.

We subdivide this part of our discussion into four segments. In each segment, our comments reflect our awareness that bankruptcy courts traditionally pay heed to equitable principles. * * *

1. The Nature of the Stay. The automatic stay is among the most basic of debtor protections under bankruptcy law. * * * It is intended to give the debtor breathing room by "stop[ping] all collection efforts, all harassment, and all foreclosure actions." H.R. Rep. No. 95–595, at 340 (1977). * * *

The stay springs into being immediately upon the filing of a bankruptcy petition: "[b]ecause the automatic stay is exactly what the name implies—'automatic'—it operates without the necessity for judicial intervention." *Sunshine Dev., Inc. v. FDIC*, 33 F.3d 106, 113 (1st Cir. 1994). It remains in force until a federal court either disposes of the case, see § 362(c)(2), or lifts the stay, *see id.* § 362(d)-(f). This respite enables debtors to resolve their debts in a more orderly fashion, *see In re Siciliano*, 13 F.3d 748, 750 (3d Cir. 1994), and at the same time safeguards their creditors by preventing "different creditors from bringing different proceedings in different courts, thereby setting in motion a free-for-all in which opposing interests maneuver to capture the lion's share of the debtor's assets." *Sunshine Dev.*, 33 F.3d at 114; *see generally* 3 *Collier on Bankruptcy* ¶ 362.03 (15th rev. ed. 1996).

In order to secure these important protections, courts must display a certain rigor in reacting to violations of the automatic stay. * * * The circuits are split on whether actions taken in derogation of the automatic stay are merely "voidable" or, more accurately, "void." Some courts characterize unauthorized postpetition proceedings as "voidable." * * * Other courts—a majority, insofar as we can tell—call such actions "void," but recognize that equitable considerations may alter some outcomes. * * *

Our earlier opinions—which we today reaffirm—align us with the majority view. * * * This semantic difference has practical consequences because the characterization of an infringing action as "void" or "voidable" influences the burden of going forward. Treating an action taken in contravention of the automatic stay as void places the burden of validating the action after the fact squarely on the shoulders of the offending creditor. In contrast, treating an action taken in contravention of the automatic stay as voidable places the burden of challenging the action on the offended debtor. We think that the former paradigm, rather than the latter, best harmonizes with the nature of the automatic stay and the important purposes that it serves. *See generally* 3 *Collier on Bankruptcy*, supra, ¶ 362.11[1] & n.1 (observing that most courts hold violations void and terming this the better view).

2. The Availability of Retroactive Relief. While the automatic stay is significant, it is not an immutable article of faith. Indeed, the Bankruptcy Code, § 362(d), expressly authorizes courts to lift it in particular situations. Whether this statutory authorization encompasses retroactive relief is not entirely clear. We previously hinted that a court may set aside the automatic stay retroactively in an appropriate case. *See Smith Corset Shops*, 696 F.2d at 976–77. We now confirm *Smith's* adumbration, holding that § 362(d) permits bankruptcy courts to lift the automatic stay retroactively and thereby validate actions which otherwise would be void.

Section 362(d) confers upon courts discretionary power in certain circumstances to terminate, annul, modify, or place conditions upon the automatic stay.[6] In drafting the law, Congress chose to include both the power to terminate the stay and the power to annul it. When construing this language, we must try to give independent meaning to each word. * * * The only plausible distinction between the two verbs in this context is that terminating the stay blunts it prospectively, from the moment the court's order enters, whereas annulling the stay erases it retrospectively, as of some date prior to the entry of the court's order (reaching as far back as the date when the debtor filed the bankruptcy petition, if the court so elects).

---

[6] The statute provides in pertinent part:

On request of a party in interest and after notice and a hearing, the court shall grant relief from the stay. . ., such as by terminating, annulling, modifying, or conditioning such stay—

> (1) for cause, including the lack of adequate protection of an interest in property of such party in interest;. . ..

Seen from this perspective, Congress' grant of a power of annulment is meaningful only if the court may thereby validate actions taken *before* the date on which the court rules. On any other construction, annulment lacks any independent significance; it merely replicates termination. It follows, therefore, that section 362(d) authorizes retroactive relief from the automatic stay. * * *

3. The Limiting Principle. Recognizing the discretionary authority of bankruptcy courts to relieve creditors and other interested parties retroactively from the operation of the automatic stay tells us nothing about the yardstick by which attempts to secure such relief should be measured. We turn next to this inquiry.

Once again, the overarching purpose of the automatic stay informs our analysis. Because the stay is a fundamental protection for all parties affected by the filing of a petition in bankruptcy, it should not be dismantled without good reason. * * * Undoing the stay retroactively should require a measurably greater showing. Congress intended the stay to afford debtors breathing room and to assure creditors of equitable distribution. *See* H.R.Rep. No. 95–595, supra, at 340. If retroactive relief becomes commonplace, creditors—anticipating post facto validation—will be tempted to pursue claims against bankrupts heedless of the stay, leaving debtors with no choice but to defend for fear that post-petition default judgments routinely may be resuscitated.

We believe that Congress created the automatic stay to ward off scenarios of this sort. Thus, if congressional intent is to be honored and the integrity of the automatic stay preserved, retroactive relief should be the long-odds exception, not the general rule. In our view, only a strict standard will ensure the accomplishment of these objectives. * * * We conclude, therefore, that although courts possess a limited discretion to grant retroactive relief from the automatic stay, instances in which the exercise of that discretion is justified are likely to be few and far between.

We do not suggest that we can write a standard that lends itself to mechanical application. Each case is sui generis and must be judged accordingly. But, while it is not practical to anticipate and catalogue the varied circumstances in which retroactive relief from the automatic stay may be warranted, some examples may be helpful.

When a creditor inadvertently violates the automatic stay in ignorance of a pending bankruptcy, courts sometimes have afforded retroactive relief. *See, e.g., In re Jones*, 63 F.3d 411, 412–13 (5th Cir. 1995) (affirming retroactive validation of a foreclosure sale where the mortgagee had no notice of the bankruptcy filing); * * *. By like token, debtors who act in bad faith may create situations that are ripe for retroactive relief. * * *

These examples—a creditor's lack of notice or a debtor's bad faith— clearly do not exhaust the possibilities. But they illustrate that a rarely dispensed remedy like retroactive relief from the automatic stay must rest on a set of facts that is both unusual and unusually compelling. The case law echoes this conclusion. * * *

4. Applying the Standard. Having constructed the limiting principle, we now consider whether the bankruptcy court erred in validating the foreclosure judgment which had been obtained in violation of the automatic stay. We conclude that no proper predicate existed for doing so and that the bankruptcy court therefore abused its discretion in ordering retroactive relief. * * *

Contrary to BCU's importunings, it is the creditor's knowledge, not the state court's nescience, that is relevant to the question at hand. Bankruptcy law forbids creditors from continuing judicial proceedings against bankrupts, see § 362(a)(1), and, accordingly, it is the creditor's obligation to inform other courts of the situation * * *. Here, both BCU's knowledge and its failure to act are undisputed; the debtor immediately notified BCU of the bankruptcy filing, but BCU kept quiet and permitted the superior court to proceed in ignorance of the stay. We are reluctant to reward creditors who, despite notice of a bankruptcy filing, fail for no discernible reason to notify courts in which they have initiated proceedings of the changed circumstances.

The other facts are no more conducive to the bestowal of retroactive relief. The creditor was represented by counsel throughout and does not claim that it misapprehended the effect of the filing. The bankruptcy court made no finding that Soares acted in bad faith, and, at any rate, the record does not contain any basis for such a finding. The procedural errors committed by both parties, such as BCU's failure to serve Soares with the so-called clarification motion and Soares' failure to lodge timely objections at various points in the proceedings, seemingly cancel each other out. And BCU's entreaty that the equities favor retroactive relief rings unmistakably hollow; though BCU expended funds to clear title and maintain the property after foreclosing, this financial hardship is the natural consequence of its own failure to abide by the terms of the automatic stay. Thus, it is unredressable. *See K–Mart Corp. v. Oriental Plaza, Inc.*, 875 F.2d 907, 916 (1st Cir. 1989) (declining to deny permanent injunctive relief which would require substantial demolition of an expensive structure where "appellant's wound, deep as it appears, was self-inflicted"). In the last analysis, BCU is the author of its own misfortune.

III. Conclusion

To sum up, we hold that the state court's post-petition issuance of a foreclosure judgment violated the automatic stay; that bankruptcy courts ordinarily must hold those who defile the automatic stay to the predictable consequences of their actions and can grant retroactive relief only sparingly and in compelling circumstances; and that, because this case involves no sufficiently unusual circumstances, the bankruptcy court abused its discretion ingranting retroactive relief from the automatic stay.[7]

In an abundance of caution, we note that our review is confined to the order granting the so-called clarification motion and the retroactive relief awarded therein. Although Soares may ask the bankruptcy court to reconsider its decision to lift the automatic stay, BCU can request a new foreclosure judgment in the state court unless and until the bankruptcy court reinstates the stay. For our part, we need go no further.

Reversed and remanded.

NOTES

1. Why was it important whether the judge's entry of the foreclosure judgment in *Soares* was ministerial? What is a ministerial act?

2. What is the court's view of the functional difference between void or voidable with respect to actions taken in violation of the stay? Can a void act be cured or validated? See § 362(d).

3. In *Soares*, the court's standard for granting retroactive annulment requires "compelling circumstances" or "unusual circumstances." The court in *In re Myers*, 491 F.3d 120 (3d Cir. 2007), relies on *Soares* in its holding that actions taken in violation of the automatic stay are ratifiable by annulment of the stay, but adopts a standard for granting relief of whether the debtor engaged in a "bad faith filing." Under this view, the bankruptcy court has wide discretion in balancing the equities on a case by case basis to determine whether the debtor engaged in inequitable, unreasonable or dishonest behavior. Other courts have taken this view as well, *see, e.g., In re Nat'l Envtl. Waste Corp.*, 129 F.3d 1052 (9th Cir. 1997).

4. In *Easley v. Pettibone Michigan Corp.*, 990 F.2d 905, 909 (6th Cir. 1993), the court found the term "void" to be so indeterminate as to be almost useless as a guide to courts and rejected the voidness rule. The same courts that embrace the voidness rule readily recognize exceptions to it based on the equities in the case. The *Easley* court scrapped the void/voidable terminology:

> We think that "invalid" is a more appropriate adjective to use when defining an action taken against a debtor during the duration of the automatic stay. Like the word "void," "invalid" describes something that

---

[7] We recognize the difficulties that attend the undoing of the foreclosure sale and the restoration of the pre-petition status quo, but that problem cannot in and of itself justify overlooking BCU's unexcused violation of the automatic stay. * * *

is without legal force or effect. However, something that is invalid is not incurable, in contrast to a void action which is incapable of being ratified.

D. SECURED CLAIMS

The automatic stay functions differently for secured creditors than for unsecured creditors. In liquidation bankruptcy secured creditors are entitled to the value of their secured claims. The stay gives the trustee time to sell the collateral and turn the proceeds over to the secured creditor. If the proceeds of the sale exceed the amount of the secured claim, the excess is available for distribution to the unsecured creditors when the case closes. If the trustee sees no likelihood of there being equity in the collateral, any sale by the trustee would be entirely for the benefit of the secured creditor and not worth incurring the expenses of a sale. In such a case it may abandon the property to the debtor under § 554(a), subject to the secured creditor's security interest. In rehabilitation or reorganization bankruptcy, the stay may allow the debtor to retain the property if it is necessary for an effective reorganization.

Section 362(a) stays any act of a prepetition secured creditor to enforce its security interest in property of the estate or of the debtor. Accordingly, a creditor having an UCC Article 9 security interest in personal property is barred by the stay from availing itself of its rights under UCC § 9-609 to repossess by either self-help or judicial process. If the creditor is a pledgee or has retaken possession of the collateral before the debtor's petition, it may not realize on the collateral by either a judicial sale or nonjudicial creditor's sale under the UCC after the petition. If sale of the collateral had already been completed before the petition, the debtor has no right under the UCC to redeem and the stay is inapplicable because the property sold is no longer either property of the estate or of the debtor.

The real property secured creditor is stayed from foreclosing its mortgage by either judicial action or extrajudicial process, which usually would be exercise of a power of sale. The creditor must halt its judicial action or extrajudicial proceeding at any stage of the foreclosure process as soon as the debtor's petition is filed. However, if the foreclosure sale is completed before the petition and the debtor has no right to redeem under the law of the jurisdiction, the real property does not become property of the bankruptcy estate, and the stay is inapplicable.

Much litigation concerns the effect of § 362 on the debtor's right to redeem from the foreclosure sale of real property when the petition was filed after the sale but before the expiration of a statutory redemption period. In that case, the bankruptcy estate includes the debtor's right to redeem the property. Was § 362 intended to halt the running of the time for redemption and other limitation periods? The following case discusses the effect of § 105(a), § 108(b), and § 362 on the mortgagor's right of redemption.

Johnson v. First National Bank

United States Court of Appeals, Eighth Circuit, 1983.
719 F.2d 270.

■ Ross T. Roberts, District Judge.

This case presents a troublesome question concerning whether a bankruptcy court possesses the authority to toll or suspend the running of a statutory redemption period created by state law in connection with real estate mortgage foreclosures.

The First National Bank of Montevideo ("First National") appeals from an order of the District Court for the District of Minnesota. That District Court order affirmed a bankruptcy court order which enjoined First National from taking further action to foreclose a lien on certain real estate, and stayed the expiration of the redemption period allowed by Minnesota law. For the reasons set forth below we reverse the judgment of the district court, and remand for further proceedings consistent with this opinion.

The relevant facts are undisputed. Curtis H. Johnson and Gloria Jean Johnson ("debtors") are the principal officers and shareholders of Oak Farms, Inc., and Oak Farms Service Co., both Minnesota corporations engaged in agricultural business pursuits. In 1978 Oak Farms, Inc. executed a mortgage on certain parcels of real estate located in Yellow Medicine and Lac qui Parle counties, Minnesota, to secure a $300,000 promissory note in favor of First National. In 1979, Oak Farms, Inc., Oak Farms Service Co., and the Johnsons executed a second mortgage to First National on the same property to secure nineteen additional promissory notes totaling approximately $650,000. Each mortgage contained a clause allowing First National to sell the mortgaged property at public auction in the event of default.

Following the debtor's default in September of 1980, First National commenced foreclosure proceedings. A sheriff's auction was held on October 31, 1980, in conformity with the requirements of Minnesota statutes. At that auction First National purchased the mortgaged property for the sum of $566,355.34.

Minn. Stat. § 580.23(2) provides that a mortgagor shall have twelve months following the sale of real estate within which to redeem the property by paying the sale price plus interest from the date of the sale. In this instance that redemption period would have expired on or about October 31, 1981. Approximately three weeks prior to the expiration date, however, without having redeemed the property, the debtors filed a joint petition for reorganization under Chapter 11 of the Bankruptcy Code (the "Code"), and an adversary complaint alleging, in part, that they had substantial equity in the mortgaged property and were entitled to an order staying the expiration of the redemption period.

At a hearing convened before the bankruptcy court on October 16, 1981, Curtis Johnson testified that he estimated the value of the mortgaged property at $2,720,000 and that the encumbrances against the property totaled $2,043,000. Based upon Johnson's testimony, on October 20, 1981, the bankruptcy judge found that "an exigency exists, and that the debtors have substantial equity in [the] real property." Upon these findings, he enjoined First National from taking any further action to foreclose the property and ordered that the running of the statutory redemption period be stayed until further order or until the bankruptcy cases concerning the property were closed, all pursuant to 11 U.S.C. § 105. On March 17, 1982, the district court affirmed the bankruptcy court's order.

* * *

The issue as to whether the broad powers granted the bankruptcy court by § 105(a)—to "issue any order * * * necessary or appropriate to carry out the provision of [the Code]"—empowers the court to suspend the running of a statutory period of redemption in a matter of first impression among the circuit courts. An examination of the reported decisions of those district courts and bankruptcy courts which have considered the matter reveals a wide divergence of opinion.

Section 2(a)(15) of the Bankruptcy Act, from which § 105(a) is derived, allowed a bankruptcy court to issue such orders as might be necessary to prevent the defeat or impairment of its jurisdiction and to protect the integrity of the bankruptcy estate. * * * Although § 105(a) is in certain respects broader in scope than its predecessor, the general equitable powers granted to the bankruptcy court by the statute are not unlimited, particularly in instances where property rights created and defined by state law are involved. * * *

* * * [I]t follows that, absent a specific grant of authority from Congress or exceptional circumstances, a bankruptcy court may not exercise its equitable powers to create substantive rights which do not exist under state law. * * * To conclude otherwise, and thus to hold that a bankruptcy court may, as a matter of course, suspend the running of a statutory period of redemption pursuant to § 105(a), would be to enlarge the debtor's property rights beyond those specifically set forth by the Minnesota legislature and by Congress in § 108(b). Despite the broad equitable powers bestowed by § 105(a), we therefore find ourselves in agreement with those courts which have held that § 105(a) may not be invoked to toll or suspend the running of a statutory period of redemption absent fraud, mistake, accident, or erroneous conduct on the part of the foreclosing officer. * * *

Although the bankruptcy court here did not purport to create a uniform rule that the redemption period is tolled whenever a petition in bankruptcy is filed, we cannot agree with the district court that the bankruptcy court's order was a proper exercise of its equitable authority to deal with a "particular, individualized problem" under the standards outlined above. The bankruptcy court, after hearing certain evidence, found only "that an exigency exists, and that the debtors have substantial equity" in the property. One might well anticipate that in many instances the debtor will indeed enjoy substantial equity in the property in question. It is precisely this concern, however, which the Minnesota legislature addressed by providing for a one-year period of redemption. As will be developed in detail below, whatever "exigency" may be said to have existed due to the timing of the expiration of that period was susceptible to alleviation by the specific provisions of § 108(b). There is no claim that First National or any other party was guilty of any wrongdoing which adversely affected the debtors' ability to redeem the property within the statutory period. "[E]quity is available to protect property rights of the innocent debtor from the wrongful acts of other persons; however, equity does not extend to situations in which the debtor is simply unable to make the required payment within the prescribed time." *In re Headley*, [13 B.R. 295, 297 (Bankr.D.Colo.1981).] Nor have the debtors identified any federal interest which would * * * justify interference with clearly expressed state law and thwart First National's reasonable expectation that, upon expiration of the redemption period, it would obtain full title to the property. Given these circumstances, we hold that the bankruptcy court erred in ordering that the running of the statutory period of redemption be stayed pursuant to § 105(a).

Although the district court rested its decision solely upon § 105(a), the potential application of two other statutes—namely, § 362(a) and § 108(b)—has been briefed and argued on appeal by the parties. Since an appellate court is entitled to affirm a district court's judgment on grounds other than those relied upon by the district court, * * * a complete disposition of the present appeal therefore requires us to determine whether the decision below may be sustained by virtue of either of these two statutes.

Courts which have considered the present question under § 362(a) and § 108(b) have been virtually unanimous in concluding that, upon the filing of a petition in bankruptcy by a debtor, one of the two sections operates to stay the expiration of a statutory redemption period. The courts are in sharp disagreement, however, as to which section is the fount of such authority, and as to the extent of the relief granted. One line of cases * * * stands for the proposition that the automatic stay provisions of § 362(a) should be liberally construed to suspend the running of a statutory period of redemption. Other decisions, holding to the contrary with respect to § 362(a), have instead found that § 108(b) is the sole applicable statute, and that its automatic extension of a redemption period provides the only relief available. * * * We conclude that the latter group of cases more accurately construe the language and legislative history of the two sections.

Preliminary to an examination of § 362(a), it is important to identify the debtors' remaining interest in mortgaged property following a foreclosure sale, and to determine whether that interest constitutes property of the bankruptcy estate. It is long-settled under Minnesota law that foreclosure extinguishes the mortgage and that the purchaser at the foreclosure sale acquires a vested right to become the absolute owner of the property upon expiration of the redemption period, or, in lieu thereof, to receive the payment of the purchase price plus interest. * * * The mortgagor, on the other hand, retains only the equity of redemption, plus the rights to possessions, rents, and profits of the property during the period of redemption. Accordingly, it is only the right of redemption, rather than the property itself, which passes into the bankruptcy estate if the redemption period has not expired at the time the bankruptcy petition is filed. * * *

Section 362(a) prohibits the "commencement or continuation * * * of a judicial, administrative, or other proceeding," the "enforcement" of a judgment obtained prior to bankruptcy, or any other "act" to obtain possession of property of the estate or to create, perfect, or enforce any lien against property of the estate. The fundamental purposes of the automatic stay imposed by § 362(a) against such actions are two-fold: to provide the debtor with a breathing spell from the collection efforts of creditors, and to protect creditors by insuring that the assets of the estate will not be dissipated in a number of different proceedings. * * * Although a stay under the circumstances involved here would be consistent with these broad policies, we are of the view that § 362(a) cannot be read to stay the mere running of a statutory time period.

We respectfully disagree with those courts which have held that an automatic transfer of property, following the expiration of a period of redemption, constitutes either an "act" or "proceeding," or the "enforcement" of a right, within the meaning of § 362(a). * * * That Congress intended § 362(a) to prohibit only certain types of *affirmative actions* is evidenced by its use of the terms referenced above and by a corresponding failure to use terms which appropriately describe the suspension or extension of a statutory time period. * * * It is also instructive to note that although Congress did not, in § 362(a), specifically empower the bankruptcy court to suspend the running of a statutory period of redemption, it had no difficulty expressing such authority when it amended § 203 of the Bankruptcy Act in 1935 to provide for the tolling of statutory redemption periods in cases involving the reorganization of family farming operations.

Section 362(a) was designed to codify, in a single section, the scattered provisions of the Act and the former Bankruptcy Rules which governed the stay of various actions. 2 *Collier on Bankruptcy* ¶ 362.01 at 362–5 (15th ed.1983). The clear majority of cases decided under the prior provisions relating to automatic stays held that the filing of a petition in bankruptcy did not toll or extend the running of a statutory period of redemption. * * * If we assume, as it is proper to do, that Congress acts with knowledge of existing law, * * * it follows that, absent a clear manifestation of contrary intent, a newly-enacted or revised statute is presumed to be harmonious with existing law and its judicial construction. * * * This presumption is especially valid where, as in the present case, the language of the statute under consideration is substantially identical to that of the previous statutes. * * * We conclude, therefore, that § 362(a) does not operate to toll or suspend the running of the one-year statutory period of redemption created by Minn. Stat. § 580.23(2).

The opposite result has been reached in jurisdictions which require that some affirmative action be taken by a creditor or by a third party in order to transfer full title to property upon the expiration of the period of redemption. * * * Under the statutory scheme adopted by Minnesota, however, once the sheriff's certificate is issued to the successful bidder following the foreclosure sale, no further proceedings are required to vest absolute title to the property in the holder of the sheriff's certificate, assuming the debtor takes no steps to redeem the property.[10] * * * First National, as purchaser at the foreclosure sale, thus had the right to expect either full title upon the expiration of the redemption period or, in lieu thereof, payment of the full purchase price plus accrued interest. Even accepting the debtors' argument that § 362(a) is designed in part to preserve the status quo as of the date of the petition in bankruptcy, their right remains only to redeem the property within the period established by statute. To hold that § 362(a) operates as an automatic stay of the running of the statutory period of redemption would be to enlarge property rights created by state law, a result we view as unjustified by the language of § 362(a) and as unintended by Congress.

Our conclusion regarding § 362(a) is also based in part upon the presence in the Code of § 108(b). That latter section, derived from § 11(e) of the Act, provides that where the debtor "may file any pleading, demand, notice, or proof

---

[10] It may also be noted that apparently Minnesota law contains no provision for extension of the statutory period of redemption.

of claim or loss, cure a default, or perform any other similar act," and the period for so doing has not expired as of the filing of the petition in bankruptcy, the trustee is given until the end of such period, "including any suspension of such period occurring on or after the commencement of the case," or 60 days, whichever is later, to perform that act. The relationship between § 362(a) and § 108(b) was treated at length in *Bank of Commonwealth v. Bevan*, [13 B.R. 989 (E.D.Mich.1981).] the case which underlies the district court's opinion below and one of the few cases to consider all three statutes involved in this controversy (i.e., §§ 362(a), 108(b), and 105(a)). In *Bevan*, the mortgagor filed a petition for reorganization under Chapter 11 of the Code following foreclosure of the mortgaged property. The bankruptcy court subsequently entered an order pursuant to § 362(a), indefinitely extending the statutory redemption period. In reviewing the bankruptcy court's order the district court noted that, unlike the language of § 362(a), which does not appear to affect the running of specific time periods, § 108(b) explicitly grants the trustee additional time in which to perform an act such as that of redemption. Reading the two sections together, the court held that the automatic stay provisions of § 362(a) do not override the extension of time provision contained in § 108(b). "While a stay tolling the running of the statutory period would give the debtor greater protection than that contemplated by § 108," the court reasoned, "where one section of the Bankruptcy Code explicitly governs an issue, another section should not be interpreted to cause an irreconcilable conflict." Id., at 994. Thus, the court concluded:

> "An interpretation of § 362(a) as an indefinite stay of the statutory period of redemption would render § 108(b) superfluous. If § 362(a) automatically stays the running of the statutory right to redeem until the stay is lifted pursuant to § 362(c) or (d), the pertinent time allotments of § 108(b) are completely extraneous as statutory time periods designed to control the trustee's activity. Moreover, if § 362(a) is interpreted to provide for the automatic stay of time periods for an indefinite amount of time, then subsections (a) and (b) of § 108, which define minimum and maximum time periods for the trustee to act, directly conflict with § 362(a)."

A number of other courts have agreed * * * as does the leading authority in the field, see 4 *Collier on Bankruptcy*, ¶ 541.07[3] at 541–30 (15th ed 1983).

Given our conclusion that the bankruptcy court lacked authority under either § 105(a) or § 362(a), to stay indefinitely the expiration of the statutory period of redemption, it becomes apparent that the only extension of time available to the debtors was that provided by the express terms of § 108(b). Since their petition in bankruptcy was filed on October 8, 1981, some three weeks prior to the expiration of the one-year statutory period of redemption, the debtors had sixty days from the former date, or until December 8, 1981, within which to redeem the mortgaged property. That sixty-day period having passed without the debtors redeeming the property, full title vested automatically in First National in accordance with Minnesota law.

The decision of the district court is reversed and the case is remanded to the district court for further proceedings consistent with this opinion.

PROBLEM

On November 1, Debtor filed a petition in bankruptcy under Chapter 11. On June 1 of that year Debtor had obtained an option under which Debtor had the right to purchase a tract of real property for $100,000 at any time before December 1. At the time Debtor filed in bankruptcy the option had not yet been exercised. Does Debtor, as debtor in possession, have any right to exercise the option on or after December 1? Does § 108(b) apply? *See Good Hope Refineries, Inc. v. Benavides*, 602 F.2d 998 (1st Cir. 1979); *In re Santa Fe Development & Mortgage Corp.*, 16 B.R. 165 (9th Cir. BAP 1981); *Collier on Bankruptcy* ¶ 108.03[1] (15th ed. rev. 2008).

E. ACTIONS AGAINST NONDEBTORS

1. CO–DEFENDANTS IN LAWSUITS

Section 362(a)(1) applies to actions and other proceedings against the debtor. It does not apply to actions or proceedings against anybody other than the debtor. But § 105(a) gives the bankruptcy court broad authority to "issue any order, process, or judgment that is necessary or appropriate to carry out the provisions of this title." Can § 105(a) be used to provide relief to anyone other than the debtor?

Lynch v. Johns–Manville Sales Corp., 710 F.2d 1194 (6th Cir. 1983), concerns that problem. Thousands of personal-injury actions had been brought against two major asbestos manufacturers, Johns–Manville and Unarco. While the cases were pending, Johns–Manville and Unarco filed in bankruptcy under Chapter 11. As a result, all of these actions were stayed by § 362(a)(1) and relief from the stay under § 362(d) was not available. Since an asbestos victim does not normally know the identity of the manufacturer of the asbestos that caused the injury, the practice is for the victim to file an action in which all available asbestos manufacturers are joined as co-defendants. Thus, in the actions against Johns–Manville and Unarco there were other defendants, and some were not in bankruptcy. Since the nonbankrupt defendants are not covered by § 362(a)(1), the pending actions, although stayed so far as Johns–

Manville and Unarco were concerned, could continue against the nonbankrupt defendants. Some of these defendants asked the bankruptcy court to use its equity powers to stay continuation of these actions against them. Their arguments were summarized in *Lynch* as follows:

> Particularly, the solvent co-defendants conjecture that a continuation of proceedings in the absence of J–M and Unarco will result in multiple and piecemeal litigation on a scale heretofore unknown in the history of American jurisprudence; initial litigation would transpire in the state and federal forums and then duplicative litigation would issue in the respective bankruptcy forums for indemnity or contribution thereby adversely impacting upon valuable judicial resources and generating a risk of inadequate and conflicting adjudications. Additionally the solvent co-defendants assert that the automatic stay of. . . § 362 precludes discovery upon J–M and Unarco thereby seriously compromising their ability to successfully defend pending actions.

710 F.2d at 1199. The court denied relief and gave the following response to the arguments stated above:

> Confronting these arguments, it is initially observed that any duplicative or multiple litigation which may occur is a direct by-product of bankruptcy law. As such, the duplication, to the extent that it may exist, is congressionally created and sanctioned. More importantly, however, any benefits which may derive to the solvent co-defendants from a stay are clearly outweighed by the countervailing interests of the plaintiffs. As the First Circuit has cogently observed:
>
>> In a number of those [asbestos] cases, plaintiffs and crucial witnesses are dying. We are not persuaded that the hardship to defendants of having to go forward on this appeal without Unarco, or the interests of judicial economy in avoiding relitigation of the issues, are strong enough to justify forcing plaintiff and a number of other plaintiffs to wait until bankrupt defendants are successfully reorganized in order to be able to pursue their claims.

[*Austin v. Unarco Industries, Inc.*, 705 F.2d 1, 5 (1st Cir. 1983).] The First Circuit's implicit concern that time is of the essence in the prosecution of asbestos cases is further amplified by the unknown and potentially unlimited duration of the stay which, to successfully avoid duplicative litigation, must necessarily issue until reorganization is effected:

> A "temporary" stay which was keyed to the resolution of the pending "relief-from-stay" petitions in the bankruptcy courts could, indeed, become one of nearly "indefinite," or, at least, unpredictable duration. These plaintiffs should not be thus denied a forum in which to pursue

their claims against those defendants who remain unshielded by the bankruptcy laws. *In re Related Asbestos Cases*, [23 B.R. 523, 532 (N.D.Cal.1982)].

710 F.2d at 1199.

Although courts have generally been unwilling to use § 105(a) to protect the interest of a nondebtor, actions against nondebtors have been stayed in a number of Chapter 11 cases on the ground that reorganization of the debtor could be jeopardized by continuation of an action against a third party that affects the debtor. An example is the following much cited case.

A.H. Robins Co. v. Piccinin
United States Court of Appeals, Fourth Circuit, 1986.
788 F.2d 994.

■ DONALD RUSSELL, Circuit Judge:

Confronted, if not overwhelmed, with an avalanche of actions filed in various state and federal courts throughout the United States by citizens of this country as well as of foreign countries seeking damages for injuries allegedly sustained by the use of an intrauterine contraceptive device known as a Dalkon Shield, the manufacturer of the device, A.H. Robins Company, Incorporated (Robins) filed its petition under Chapter 11 of the Bankruptcy Code in August, 1985.

The device, which is the subject of these suits, had been developed in the 1960's by Dr. Hugh Davis at the Johns Hopkins Hospital in Baltimore, Maryland. In mid–1970 Robins acquired all patent and marketing rights to the Dalkon Shield and engaged in the manufacture and marketing of the device from early 1971 until 1974, when it discontinued manufacture and sale of the device because of complaints and suits charging injuries arising allegedly out of the use of the device. The institution of Dalkon Shield suits did not, however, moderate with the discontinuance of manufacture of the device, since Robins did not actually recall the device until 1984. By the middle of 1985, when the Chapter 11 petition was filed the number of such suits arising out of the continued sale and use of the Dalkon Shield device earlier put into the stream of commerce by Robins had grown to 5,000. More than half of these pending cases named Robins as the sole defendant; a co-defendant or co-defendants were named in the others. Prior to the filing, a number of suits had been tried and, while Robins had prevailed in some of the actions, judgments in large and burdensome amounts had been recovered in others. Many more had been settled.[4] Moreover, the costs of defending these suits both to Robins and to its insurance carrier had risen into the millions. A large amount of the time and energies of Robins' officers and executives was also being absorbed in preparing material for trial and in attending and testifying at depositions and trials. The problems arising out of this mounting tide of claims and suits precipitated this Chapter 11 proceeding.

The filing of the Chapter 11 petition automatically stayed all suits against Robins itself under section 362(a) of the Bankruptcy Code * * *. But a number of plaintiffs in suits where there were defendants other than Robins, sought to sever their actions against Robins and to proceed with their claims against the co-defendant or co-defendants. Robins responded to the move by filing an adversary proceeding in which it named as defendants the plaintiffs in eight such suits pending in various state and federal courts. In that proceeding, the debtor sought (1) declaratory relief adjudging that the debtor's products liability policy with Aetna Casualty and Insurance Company (Aetna) was an asset of the estate in which all the Dalkon Shield plaintiffs and claimants had an interest and (2) injunctive relief restraining the prosecution of the actions against its co-defendants. * * *

At the hearing on the motion for a preliminary injunction, a number of defendants as well as the Committee constituted by the court to represent Dalkon Shield Claimants appeared by counsel. At the commencement of the hearing the defendant Piccinin, a plaintiff in one of the Dalkon Shield actions which Robins sought to stay, filed through her attorney a written motion to dismiss as against her. No other defendant filed a motion in response to the motion for a preliminary injunction. After receiving certain testimony, admitting various records, and hearing arguments of parties, the district court granted Robins' request for a preliminary injunction.

In his order granting the preliminary injunction, the district judge found (1) that continuation of litigation in the civil actions threatened property of Robins' estate, burdened and impeded Robins' reorganization effort, contravened the public interest, and rendered any plan of reorganization futile; (2) that this burden on Robins' estate outweighed any burden on the Dalkon claimants caused by enjoining their civil actions; and (3) that all remaining insurance coverage in favor of the debtor under its liability policy issued by Aetna was property of the Robins' Chapter 11 estate. The district judge then held that all actions for damages that might be satisfied from proceeds of the Aetna insur-

---

[4] * * * A recent article in the Nat.L.J., p. 10, (March 17, 1986), states that by mid 1985, Robins, along with its insurer, Aetna Casualty & Surety Company, "had paid roughly $517 million for 25 trial judgments and 9,300 settlements since the first verdict in 1975."

ance policy were subject to the stay pursuant to § 362(a)(3) and enjoined further litigation in the eight civil actions, pursuant to § 362(a)(1), (3) as supplemented by § 105. * * *

I.

The initial question in the appeal of the first issue relates to the court's jurisdiction to grant a stay or injunction of suits in other courts against co-defendants of the debtor or of third parties; none of the parties herein contest the jurisdiction of the bankruptcy court to stay actions against the debtor itself in any court. Jurisdiction over suits involving co-defendants or third-parties may be bottomed on two statutory provisions of the Bankruptcy Act itself as well as on the general equitable powers of the court. The first of these statutory grants of jurisdiction is found in section 362 * * *.

[Section 362](a)(1) is generally said to be available only to the debtor, not third party defendants or co-defendants. * * * However, as the Court in *Johns–Manville Sales Corp.*, 26 B.R. 405, 410 (S.D.N.Y.1983) remarked, * * * "there are cases [under § 362(a)(1)] where a bankruptcy court may properly stay the proceedings against non-bankrupt co-defendants" but, it adds, that in order for relief for such non-bankrupt defendants to be available under § 362(a)(1), there must be "unusual circumstances" and certainly "'[s]omething more than the mere fact that one of the parties to the lawsuit has filed a Chapter 11 bankruptcy must be shown in order that proceedings be stayed against non-bankrupt parties.'" This "unusual situation," it would seem, arises when there is such identity between the debtor and the third-party defendant that the debtor may be said to be the real party defendant and that a judgment against the third-party defendant will in effect be a judgment or finding against the debtor. An illustration of such a situation would be a suit against a third-party who is entitled to absolute indemnity by the debtor on account of any judgment that might result against them in the case. To refuse application of the statutory stay in that case would defeat the very purpose and intent of the statute. * * *

But [§ 362](a)(1), which stays actions against the debtor and arguably against those whose interests are so intimately intertwined with those of the debtor that the latter may be said to be the real party in interest, is not the only part of section 362 providing for an automatic stay of proceedings. Subsection (a)(3) directs stays of any action, *whether against the debtor or third-parties,* to obtain possession or to exercise control over property of the debtor. A key phrase in the construction and application of this section is, of course, "property" as that term is used in the Act. Section 541(a)(1) * * * provides that the "estate is comprised of all the following property, wherever located * * * all legal or equitable interests of the debtor in property as of the commencement of the case." * * *

Under the weight of authority, insurance contracts have been said to be embraced in this statutory definition of "property." *In re Davis*, 730 F.2d 176, 184 (5th Cir. 1984). For example, even the right to cancel an insurance policy issued to the debtor has uniformly been held to be stayed under section 362(a)(3). * * * A products liability policy of the debtor is similarly within the principle: it is a valuable property of a debtor, particularly if the debtor is confronted with substantial liability claims within the coverage of the policy in which case the policy may well be, as one court has remarked in a case like the one under review, "the most important asset of [i.e., the debtor's] estate," *In re Johns–Manville Corp.*, 40 B.R. 219, 229 (S.D.N.Y.1984). Any action in which the judgment may diminish this "important asset" is unquestionably subject to a stay under this subsection. Accordingly actions "related to" the bankruptcy proceedings against the insurer or against officers or employees of the debtor who may be entitled to indemnification under such policy or who qualify as additional insureds under the policy are to be stayed under section 362(a)(3).

The statutory power of the bankruptcy court to stay actions involving the debtor or its property is not, however, limited to section 362(a)(1) and (a)(3). It has been repeatedly held that § 105 which provides that the bankruptcy court "may issue any order, process, or judgment that is necessary or appropriate to carry out the provisions of this title," "empowers the bankruptcy court to enjoin parties other than the bankrupt" from commencing or continuing litigation. *In re Otero Mills, Inc.*, 25 B.R. 1018, 1020 (D.N.M.1982). * * *

[In *In re Johns–Manville Corp.*, 40 B.R. 219 (S.D.N.Y.1984),] the Court phrased somewhat fuller the circumstances when section 105 may support a stay:

> In the exercise of its authority under § 105, the Bankruptcy Court may use its injunctive authority to "protect the integrity of a bankrupt's estate and the Bankruptcy Court's custody thereof and to preserve to that Court the ability to exercise the authority delegated to it by Congress" [citing authority]. Pursuant to the exercise of that authority the Court may issue or extend stays to enjoin a variety of proceedings [including discovery against the debtor or its officers and employees] which will have an adverse impact on the Debtor's ability to formulate a Chapter 11 plan.

40 B.R. at 226.

Beyond these statutory powers under section 362 and section 105 to enjoin other actions whether against the debtor or third-parties and in whatsoever court, the bankruptcy court under its comprehensive jurisdiction as conferred by [28 U.S.C.] § 1334 has the "inherent power of courts under their general equity powers and in the efficient management of the dockets to grant relief" to grant a stay. * * * In exercising such power the court, however, must "weigh competing interests and maintain an even balance" and must justify the stay "by clear and convincing circumstances outweighing potential harm to the party against whom it is operative." * * *

* * * In the three situations in which the defendants have challenged the injunction granted by the district judge * * * the only defendants other than the debtor, are the two Robins, Dr. Frederick A. Clark, Jr., Dr. Hugh J. Davis, and the debtor's insurer Aetna. So far as the suits against the two Robins and Dr. Clark, those defendants were entitled to indemnification by the debtor under the corporate by-laws and the statutes of Virginia, the State of debtor's incorporation, and were, in addition, additional insureds under the debtor's insurance policy. Dr. Davis was the beneficiary of an express contract of indemnification on the part of Robins and was, under a compromise agreement with Robins and Aetna, an additional insured under Robins' insurance policy. The *Manville* court had granted a preliminary injunction in favor of defendants in the same position as these defendants, as we have seen, on facts similar to those here, finding that the requirements of possible irreparable harm "had been satisfied by the showing * * * [that the suits against the defendants would represent] an immediate and irreparable impact on the pool of insurance assets, of the existence of sufficiently serious questions going to the merits," and of the tipping in the defendants' favor in the hardships in a balancing of the debtor's and the plaintiffs'. That court had previously disposed of the public interest being weighted in the debtor's favor: "Indeed, this Court finds the goal of removing all obstacles to plan formulation eminently praiseworthy and supports every lawful effort to foster this goal while protecting the due process rights of all constituencies." 26 B.R. at 428.

II.

The district court in this case applied the test for a grant of preliminary injunctive relief * * *. It found, as had the Johns–Manville courts, that irreparable harm would be suffered by the debtor and by the defendants since any of these suits against these co-defendants, if successful, would reduce and diminish the insurance fund or pool represented in Aetna's policy in favor of Robins and thereby affect the property of the debtor to the detriment of the debtor's creditors as a whole. The likelihood of success by the debtor under these circumstances appeared indisputable. The hardships which would be suffered irreparably by the debtor and by its creditors generally in permitting these plaintiffs to secure as it were a preference in the distribution of the insurance pool herein to which all creditors were entitled, together with the unquestioned public interest in promoting a viable reorganization of the debtor can be said to outweigh any contrary hardship to the plaintiffs. Such was the finding in the *Manville* cases and that finding does not appear unreasonable here.

The appellants, however, suggest that the record is insufficient to support such findings by the district judge. We disagree. The record is not extensive but it includes every fact considered by the courts in the *Manville* cases to be necessary for their decision. The rights of Dr. Davis, Dr. Clark and the two Robins to indemnity and their status as additional insureds under Robins' insurance policy are undisputed on the record. That there are thousands of Dalkon Shield actions and claims pending is a fact established in the record and the limited fund available under Robins' insurance policy is recognized in the record. It seems incontestable that, if the suits are permitted to continue and discovery allowed, any effort at reorganization of the debtor will be frustrated, if not permanently thwarted. It is obvious from the record that if suits are permitted to proceed against indemnitees on claims on which the indemnitees are entitled to indemnity by Robins, either a binding judgment against the debtor will result or * * * inconsistent judgments will result, calling for the exercise of the court's equitable powers. In our opinion, the record was thus more than adequate to support the district court's grant of injunctive relief. Certainly, the district court did not commit an abuse of discretion in granting the injunction herein.

The appellants add a final complaining note that the district judge stated in his decision that the "Conclusions of Law" made by him should apply "with equal force to all defendants similarly situated who are brought to the attention of the court." This is little different, however, from the language of the court in the *Manville* cases in which there was a broad, general injunction against all present or future suits.

In summary, we have no difficulty in sustaining the grant of a preliminary injunction herein. We are sustained in this conclusion by the fact, recognized by the district judge on the record, that any Dalkon Shield plaintiff may at any time petition for the vacation of the stay as it affects his or her suit and he or she is entitled to a hearing on such petition. Actually, there is one such petition pending and the district judge has agreed to set a hearing on that petition. * * *

NOTES

1. In *In re Minoco Group of Companies, Ltd.*, 799 F.2d 517 (9th Cir. 1986), Minoco owned insurance policies that covered claims by directors and officers for indemnification for legal expenses and judgments arising from their activities as directors and officers. The policies covered claims made through July 1, 1984. The policies were prepaid, but they allowed either Minoco or the insurers to cancel at any time upon 30 days notice. Minoco filed in Chapter 11 in September 1983. Two months later the insurers cancelled the policies. Minoco brought an action seeking a declaratory judgment that cancellation of the policies was automatically stayed by § 362(a). The court held that § 362(a)(3) applied. The court explained:

> The reasoning of the Fourth Circuit in *A.H. Robins* applies to this case with full force. For the purposes of the automatic stay, we see no significant distinction between a liability policy that insures the debtor against claims by *consumers* and one that insures the debtor against claims by *officers and directors.* In either case, the insurance policies protect against diminution of the value of the estate. As the Fourth Circuit understood, liability policies meet the fundamental test of whether they are 'property of the estate' because the debtor's estate is worth more with them than without them. *See* Jackson, *Translating Assets and Liabilities to the Bankruptcy Forum*, 14 J.Legal Stud. 73, 99 (1985). Accordingly, cancellation of the insurance policies by First State was automatically stayed by section 362(a)(3).

799 F.2d at 519.

2. Assume the common case in which Debtor has a liability policy with Insurer to pay personal injury and property damages claims stemming from Debtor's use of an automobile up to a limit of $500,000? Debtor negligently injured Plaintiff who sued Debtor and Insurer for $200,000. Debtor filed in Chapter 7 and Debtor and Insurer sought to stay Plaintiff's suit under § 362(a)(3) and § 105(a) on the ground that the insurance policy was property of Debtor's estate. Should Plaintiff's suit against Insurer be enjoined? *Matter of Edgeworth*, 993 F.2d 51 (5th Cir. 1993), held in a comparable case that the insurance proceeds were not property of the estate because they were entirely payable to Plaintiff; Debtor has no right to receive and keep any of the proceeds. Liability insurance policies differ from those covering collision and fire insurance in which the proceeds go to Debtor as beneficiary and inure to the creditors of the estate. The court distinguished the facts in this Note from those of cases like *Piccinin* in which liability insurance proceeds would be exhausted by the claims of the many plaintiffs if the proceeds were not marshaled in a bankruptcy proceeding.

2. THIRD PARTIES LIABLE TO PAY THE DEBTOR'S OBLIGATIONS

a. Guarantors

Credit Alliance Corp. v. Williams

United States Court of Appeals, Fourth Circuit, 1988.
851 F.2d 119.

■ WILKINSON, Circuit Judge:

* * *

I.

On February 22, 1980, Penn Hook Coal Co. signed a three year conditional sales contract note with Croushorn Equipment Co. for the purchase of a John Deere wheel loader. Croushorn assigned Penn Hook's note to Credit Alliance Corp. and Gary Williams and Malcolm C. Williams executed a guaranty of Penn Hook's obligation in favor of Credit Alliance.

Penn Hook subsequently defaulted on its obligation. On January 14, 1981, Credit Alliance filed suit in the United States District Court for the Southern District of New York against Penn Hook and the guarantors, Gary and Malcolm Williams. Credit Alliance sought judgment in the amount of $54,018.07, the balance due on the note after crediting the proceeds realized from the sale of the collateral, plus attorneys' fees, interest, and costs. Defendants failed to respond to the summons and complaint, and on March 4, 1981, Penn Hook petitioned for bankruptcy under Chapter 11 of the Bankruptcy Code in the District Court for the Western District of Virginia. On April 15, 1981, the District Court for the Southern District of New York entered a default judgment in the amount of $62,866.70 against the three defendants.

On October 5, 1984, Credit Alliance instituted garnishment proceedings against Penn Hook and the guarantors in the Western District of Virginia. The matter was referred to the bankruptcy court which held that the automatic stay provision of the Bankruptcy Code, § 362, rendered void the default judgment against the debtor and the non-debtor guarantors, entered after Penn Hook petitioned for bankruptcy. The district court reversed the decision of the bankruptcy court with respect to the guarantors, and held that Credit Alliance's claim against Gary Williams and Malcolm Williams was not stayed or void. Guarantor Gary Williams now appeals.

II.

Appellant seeks to invoke the automatic stay provision of § 362 to invalidate the New York judgment entered against him in his capacity as guarantor of the now bankrupt debtor's note with Credit Alliance.

The plain language of § 362, however, provides only for the automatic stay of judicial proceedings and enforcement of judgments "against the debtor or the property of the estate." * * *

Nothing in § 362 suggests that Congress intended that provision to strip from the creditors of a bankrupt debtor the protection they sought and received when they required a third party to guaranty the debt. Congress knew how to extend the automatic stay to non-bankrupt parties when it intended to do so. Chapter 13, for example, contains a narrowly drawn provision to stay proceedings against a limited category of individual cosigners of consumer debts. *See* § 1301(a). No such protection is provided to the guarantors of Chapter 11 bankrupts by § 362(a). * * *

Guarantors of debtors proceeding in bankruptcy under Chapter 11 are limited to claims for reimbursement or contribution to the extent allowed under § 502(e) or subrogation to the rights of the creditor under § 509. This scheme protects the assured creditor "to the extent that a surety or codebtor is not permitted to compete with the creditor he has assured until the assured party's claim has been paid in full." 124 Cong.Rec. H11089 (Sept. 28, 1978) (statement of Rep. Edwards). A reading of § 362 restricting a creditor's ability to proceed against its guarantor would eliminate the protection of assured creditors contemplated by the Bankruptcy Code.

A.H. Robins Co. v. Piccinin, 788 F.2d 994 (4th Cir. 1986), is not to the contrary. We recognized in *Robins* that in "unusual circumstances" a court, pursuant to § 362, may properly stay proceedings against non-bankrupt codefendants of the bankrupt debtor. Such unusual circumstances might arise where "there is such identity between the debtor and the third-party defendant that the debtor may be said to be the real party defendant and that a judgment against the third-party defendant will in effect be a judgment or finding against the debtor," id. at 999, or where proceedings against non-debtor codefendants would reduce or diminish "the property of the debtor [such as the debtor's insurance fund or pool] to the detriment of the debtor's creditors as a whole." Id. at 1008.

There is nothing "unusual" about this guaranty agreement that would permit the guarantor, Williams, to invoke the statutory protection of § 362 or that would permit us to stay the enforcement of the New York judgment against him on equitable grounds. *See A.H. Robins*, 788 F.2d at 1000. It is unnecessary to stay proceedings or void the judgment against the nonbankrupt guarantor to protect Penn Hook or to prevent the dissipation of its assets, since neither Penn Hook nor its estate is jeopardized by the judgment against Williams. "The very purpose of a guaranty is to assure the [creditor] that in the event the [debtor] defaults, the [creditor] will have someone to look to for reimbursement." *Rojas v. First Bank National Ass'n*, 613 F.Supp. 968, 971 (E.D.N.Y.1985). The purpose of the guaranty would be frustrated by interpreting § 362 so as to stay Credit Alliance's action against the non-bankrupt guarantor when the defaulting debtor petitioned for bankruptcy. * * *

We conclude that the judgment against Gary Williams is valid and enforceable. The judgment of the district court is therefore

Affirmed.

NOTES

1. *In re Otero Mills, Inc.*, 25 B.R. 1018 (D.N.M.1982), involved the use of § 105(a) with respect to a guaranty. Otero executed two promissory notes for a total principal amount of $650,000 in favor of Bank. The obligation of Otero to pay the notes was guaranteed by Dugan, a stockholder and the president of Otero. Otero defaulted on the notes and filed in Chapter 11. Dugan did not file in bankruptcy. Bank brought an action in state court against Dugan on the guaranty and obtained judgment. The bankruptcy court issued an injunction pursuant to § 105(a) against enforcement of the judgment against Dugan, but it allowed Bank to domesticate the judgment in states in which Dugan had assets. Bank appealed to the district court, which affirmed.

The district court held that an injunction could issue only if there was proof that irreparable harm to the bankruptcy estate would result from enforcement of the judgment. Otero argued that irreparable harm would result because Otero's reorganization plan would require Dugan to contribute assets to the reorganized corporation. The bankruptcy court found that if Bank were allowed to reach Dugan's property the ability of Otero to implement its reorganization plan would be impaired.

Since in most cases, a personal guarantor of the debt of a corporation is a principal stockholder, it is likely that an argument such as that made in *Otero* will be made routinely in any instance in which the guarantor might contribute assets to the reorganization. What about the potential for harm to Bank? If Otero is unable to pay Bank and Dugan is allowed to divert assets to Otero that otherwise would be paid to Bank under the guaranty, Bank will be injured if Dugan has insufficient assets to pay Bank after contributing to the reorganization.

A debt that is secured by a personal guaranty can be compared to a debt secured by a lien in property of the debtor. If a debt is secured by a lien in property of the debtor, the creditor does not have an unqualified right to resort to the collateral when the debtor goes into bankruptcy. The secured creditor can be stayed from enforcing the lien if the collateral is necessary to the Chapter 11 reorganization and the secured claim is adequately protected.

Does the same analysis apply to a personal guaranty? If resort to the guaranty will jeopardize the reorganization it may be proper to enjoin enforcement of the guaranty so long as the creditor's claim is adequately protected. The bankruptcy court in *Otero* recognized that Bank had a right to adequate protection of its claim and found that Bank was adequately protected. The loan was secured by assets of Debtor and Bank apparently stipulated that it was adequately protected "until at least August 26, 1982." The bankruptcy court indicated that it would consider lifting the stay when Bank was no longer adequately protected. Lack of adequate protection as a basis for relief from the automatic stay is considered in chapter 10.

2. In *Matter of Supermercado Gamboa, Inc.*, 68 B.R. 230 (Bankr.D. Puerto Rico 1986), the court indicated that it would require a clear showing that making the nondebtor guarantor pay would have a detrimental impact on the debtor's reorganization before it would stay action against the guarantor. The court said, "I believe the more relaxed approach initiated in *In re Otero Mills, Inc.*, * * * and its progeny is simply bad law." 68 B.R. at 234. In *Supermercado* the court rejected the contention that the creditor's suit against the guarantor indirectly involved property of the estate and was stayed by § 362 because the guarantor might claim indemnity against the bankruptcy estate. It should not make any difference whether the guarantor had paid the creditor and had a claim for indemnity against the estate or the creditor remained unpaid and had its original claim. *Otero* is criticized in Howard C. Buschman, III, and Sean P. Madden, *The Power and Propriety of Bankruptcy Court Intervention in Actions Between Nondebtors*, 47 Bus.Law. 913 (1992).

3. The courts are divided on the extent to which injunctions against non-debtors are permissible on the ground that they are necessary to protect the debtor's ability to formulate a reorganization plan. For an exhaustive analysis of the subject, see Ralph Brubaker, *Bankruptcy Injunctions and Complex Litigation: A Critical Reappraisal of Non–Debtor Releases in Chapter 11 Reorganizations*, 1997 U. Ill. L.Rev. 959 (1997). He cites a number of cases permitting injunctions in such cases. *Id.* at 1055, n.363. In *Celotex Corp. v. Edwards*, 514 U.S. 300 (1995), the Supreme Court found that the bankruptcy court had jurisdiction to temporarily stay a non-debtor from execution on a supersedeas bond that could impede the debtor's ability to reorganize. Professor Brubaker distinguishes between temporary injunctions and permanent ones that amount to extinction of the non-debtor's rights; he finds no statutory basis for the latter in the Code. Brubaker, *supra*, at 1077 *et seq*. The issue of the permissible scope of such permanent injunctions (sometimes referred to as "third party releases") under Chapter 11 reorganization plans has sharply divided the Courts of Appeals for 30 years. *Compare In re Lowenschuss*, 67 F.3d 1394, 1401-1402 (9th Cir. 1995), *cert. den.* 517 U.S. 1243 (1996), with *In re Drexel Burnam Lambert Group. Inc.*, 960 F.2d 285 (2d Cir. 1992) and *In re A. H. Robins Co.*, 880 F.2d 694 (4th Cir. 1989).

b. Issuers of Letters of Credit

There are three principal consensual security devices that can be used to assure payment of a debt. First, the debtor can grant the creditor a security interest in property of the debtor. Second, a third party can guarantee payment of the debt by either a personal guaranty or by providing collateral to secure payment of the debt. Third, the debtor can obtain a standby letter of credit from a bank for the benefit of the creditor. The bank that issues the letter of credit obligates itself to pay the creditor the amount of the debt if certain conditions stated in the letter of credit are met. The conditions usually require the creditor to demand payment from the bank and to provide a certificate or other evidence that the debt is due and has not been paid. In most cases the debtor grants a security interest in property to the issuing bank or obtains a third-party guarantee to secure the debtor's obligation to reimburse the bank in the event the bank pays the creditor under the letter of credit.

A creditor dealing with a debtor with adequate collateral may have a choice of security devices. The creditor may obtain a security interest in the debtor's collateral, or the creditor may induce the debtor to cause a bank to issue a letter of credit for the benefit of the creditor. In the latter case, assume that the bank obtains a security interest in the debtor's property as security for its right of reimbursement. If the debtor is unable to pay the debt and files in bankruptcy, what are the rights of the creditor in each of the two cases? If the creditor was granted a security interest in the debtor's collateral, § 362(a)(4) stays any act by the creditor to enforce the security interest. If, instead, a letter of credit was issued to the creditor, does § 362(a) prevent the creditor from obtaining payment from the bank under the letter of credit? This issue was presented in *In re Page*, 18 B.R. 713 (D.D.C.1982). In that case the bankruptcy court enjoined payment of a letter of credit issued for the benefit of a creditor of a Chapter 11 debtor. In the opinion of the bankruptcy court, payment under the letter of credit would violate § 362(a)(3) and (4). On appeal, the district court reversed the bankruptcy court. Judge Gesell stated:

> With respect to § 362(a)(3), cashing the letter of credit will not divest the estate of property since neither the letter of credit nor its

proceeds are property of the estate under the Bankruptcy Code. Section 541 defines property of the estate as "all legal or equitable interests of the debtor" (subject to various limitations not relevant in this case). In issuing the letter of credit the Bank entered into an independent contractual obligation to pay [the beneficiary of the letter of credit] out of its own assets. Although cashing the letter will immediately give rise to a claim by the Bank against the debtors pursuant to the latter's indemnification obligations, that claim will not divest the debtors of any property since any attempt to enforce that claim would be subject to an automatic stay pursuant to § 362(a)(4).

Nor would cashing the letter of credit "create, perfect or enforce" a lien in the property securing the debtors' obligation to indemnify the Bank. The Bank's liens on property of the debtors to secure the letter of credit arrangement were created prior to the initiation of Chapter 11 proceedings and remain valid in bankruptcy whether or not the letter of credit is cashed. * * *

It is uncontested that the Bank's liens were perfected prior to the Chapter 11 filing. Appellees acknowledge that the "security interest in favor of First National Bank was perfected when the Letter of Credit was initially provided." * * * Since the liens have already been perfected and the Bank is under a contractual obligation to fund the letter of credit, the Bank has perfected liens valid in a Chapter 11 proceeding. Since perfected liens already exist cashing of the letter of credit cannot have the effect of either creating or perfecting a lien.

Cashing of the letter of credit is not an act to "enforce" a lien. The Bank will, of course, have a claim against the debtors under the indemnification agreement once the letter of credit is funded. But the filing of the Chapter 11 petition automatically stays any attempt to enforce that claim. Funding of the letter is therefore not an act to "enforce" a lien.

18 B.R. at 715–716. This statement of the law is generally accepted. See also *In re Prime Motor Inns, Inc.*, 130 B.R. 610 (S.D.Fla.1991).

c. Partners of Bankrupt Partnership

Partners of a general partnership are personally liable to pay the debts and obligations of the partnership. Revised Uniform Partnership Act § 306. In addition to having liability to partnership creditors, a partner is obliged to contribute toward the losses sustained by the partnership according to the partner's share in the profits. Revised Uniform Partnership Act § 401(b). Under § 807 of the Act, the assets of the partnership include the contributions of the partners necessary for the payment of all the liabilities of the partnership. Thus, the right of the partnership to obtain contribution from the partners is property of the bankruptcy estate under § 541(a)(1) if the partnership is in bankruptcy. Suppose a partnership has filed for relief under Chapter 11, but the partners of the firm have not filed in bankruptcy. If, after bankruptcy, a prepetition creditor of the partnership brings an action against a partner to enforce the claim, can the bankruptcy court use § 105(a) to enjoin the action? This issue was raised in the case that follows.

Patton v. Bearden
United States Court of Appeals, Sixth Circuit, 1993.
8 F.3d 343.

■ KENNEDY, Circuit Judge.

In this contract case for royalties allegedly due, defendants Richard Bearden, Robert Bearden, and J.M. Bearden, individually and d/b/a Bearden Fish Farms (collectively referred to as "the Beardens") appeal the grant of summary judgment for Nicolas M. Patton, the plaintiff. The Beardens assert the following errors: * * * (3) the judgment against the Beardens violated the automatic bankruptcy stay of claims against the Bearden & Sons Fish Farm partnership. For the reasons stated below, we affirm.

Patton developed a process for a catfish breading mix and in 1982 entered into a licensing agreement with Anthony Pizzolato. This licensing agreement granted Pizzolato the exclusive right to produce Patton's breading mix. Subsequently, Pizzolato granted a sub-license for the breading mix to Richard Bearden, Robert Bearden and J.M. Bearden, individually and d/b/a Bearden Farms.

After production commenced, the Beardens issued several royalty checks directly to Patton as provided by the sub-license agreement. After the payments were sent to Patton, Patton then divided up the royalties between Pizzolato and himself. However, a dispute arose between Patton on the one hand and Pizzolato and the Beardens on the other regarding the production costs of the breading mix. Consequently, the Beardens stopped selling Patton's breading mix and contracted for a similar breading mix made by a different manufacturer and stopped making royalty payments to Patton.

In accord with the licensing agreement, Pizzolato and Patton settled their disagreement, regarding the production costs of the mix, by arbitration. As a result of this arbitration, Pizzolato assigned any rights he had to royalty payments from the Beardens to Patton.

Patton, the assignee, filed this action against the Beardens, individually and d/b/a Bearden Fish Farms, to recover unpaid royalties allegedly due under the sub-license agreement in the United States District Court for the Western

Division of Tennessee. Patton then moved for summary judgment. * * * The District Court * * * granted Patton summary judgment.

Finally, the Beardens filed a Notice of Bankruptcy indicating that Bearden & Sons Fish Farms d/b/a Bearden Farms, a partnership, had filed for chapter 11 reorganization. The Beardens argued that Richard Bearden, Robert Bearden and J.M. Bearden were partners of Bearden & Sons Fish Farm and that entry of judgment against the individuals, who are the partners of the debtor-partnership, violated the automatic stay of § 362.

The District Court rejected this argument because the automatic stay does not protect a partner of a partnership. * * *

The District Court concluded that the automatic stay of claims against the debtor-partnership did not protect the Beardens. We agree that defendants' mere status as general partners does not entitle them to protection under the automatic stay of the debtor-partnership. * * *

The automatic stay provision of the Bankruptcy Code, § 362(a)(1) stays an "action or proceeding against the debtor that was or could have been commenced before the commencement of the case under this title, or to recover a claim against the debtor that arose before the commencement of the case under this title. . . ." Clearly, § 362(a)(1) stays any actions against the *debtor*. The Beardens argue the stay should be extended to protect non-debtor partners, merely because of their partner status.

Under chapter 11, a partnership may file a petition in bankruptcy even though its partners have not. This Court sees no reason to ignore the formal distinctions between the partners and the partnership in this case. Because the partners are jointly and severally liable, Patton's action operates against individual assets of the partners, not partnership assets. Indeed, "[t]he stay of § 362 is extremely broad in scope. . . and should apply to almost any type of formal or informal action against the debtor or the property of the estate. . . . [The stay] does not extend, however, to separate legal entities such as corporate affiliates, *partners in debtor partnerships* or to codefendants in pending litigation." 2 *Collier on Bankruptcy* ¶ 362.04 (15th ed.1993) (emphasis added).

Some courts have held that the debtor's stay may be extended to non-bankrupt parties in "unusual circumstances." * * * Such circumstances usually include when the debtor and the non-bankrupt party are closely related or the stay contributes to the debtor's reorganization. It should be noted that such extensions, although referred to as extensions of the automatic stay, were in fact injunctions issued by the bankruptcy court after hearing and the establishment of unusual need to take this action to protect the administration of the bankruptcy estate.

Even if we were to adopt the unusual circumstances test, the bankruptcy court would first need to extend the automatic stay under its equity jurisdiction pursuant to § 105. Moreover, the Beardens have not brought forth any evidence of unusual circumstances which would justify extending the automatic stay to their protection.

Under § 362(a)(3), filing a chapter 11 petition stays "any act to obtain possession of property of the estate or of property from the estate or to exercise control over property of the estate." The Beardens argue that the partnership is entitled to compel contributions from the partners for partnership debt. This chose in action constitutes partnership property, and under § 541(a), this power to compel contributions became the property of the estate upon the filing of the bankruptcy petition and may be enforced against the partners to the extent of any deficiency in the debtor's property. The Beardens argue that § 362(a)(3) prevents the prosecution of the action against them because this action is "an act to obtain possession of property of the estate or to exercise control over property of the estate," and any proceeding against the general partners would necessarily impair the debtor's right to compel contribution from its partners, thus interfering with the debtor's property.

The court in *In re Litchfield Co. of South Carolina Limited Partnership*, 135 B.R. 797 (W.D.N.C.1992), adopted the argument urged by the defendants. However, in *Litchfield*, the partner promised to devote assets to the reorganizational efforts and testified that entry of the judgment could render the partner insolvent or impair his ability to pay the debtor's creditors if liquidation ensued. *Id.*, at 801; *see also In re Marley Orchards Income Fund I, Limited Partnership*, 120 B.R. 566 (Bankr.E.D.Wash.1990) (Court refused to extend the automatic stay to general partners of a debtor-partnership under § 362(a)(3) absent evidence of a potential deficiency in partnership assets.).

In the present case, the defendants do not even allege that the judgments here will render them insolvent or impair their ability to help with reorganizational efforts. Rather, the Beardens merely rely on their status as general partners to urge extension of the automatic stay for their benefit.

Thus, even if a debtor-partnership may under unusual circumstances seek an injunction prohibiting action against its partners, requests for such relief can only be presented to the bankruptcy court.

For the reasons stated above, we AFFIRM the District Court's decision

NOTE

Patton represents the prevailing view that § 362 should not be stretched to protect partners against partnership creditors. Partners have had somewhat better success in seeking a § 105(a) injunction on the ground that allowing suits against them will irreparably harm the partnership's attempt to reorganize. Factors that courts have considered in § 105(a) cases are whether general partners' plans to contribute capital to the reorganized entity would be frustrated by allowing creditor suits against them and whether partners' efforts to defend themselves against creditors would divert their attention from the reorganization.

Litchfield, discussed in *Patton*, is an example of the use of § 105 in conjunction with § 362(a)(3) in a partnership reorganization case. In that case a limited partnership had a general partner that was itself a partnership having two general partners (Partners). The limited partnership (Debtor) filed in Chapter 11 after a workout plan failed owing to Bank's refusal to agree to a stretchout and lowering of interest rate on its debt. Before Debtor filed, Bank had brought an action on its debt in state court against Debtor and Partners. Debtor's other creditors were unwilling to agree to a reorganization plan if Bank was able to recover against Partners. Debtor elicited an agreement from Partners to make their property available to help in funding the plan and filed a complaint seeking to stay Bank's suit against Partners.

The court affirmed the bankruptcy court's grant of a stay under § 362(a)(3) and an injunction under § 105(a). Under the state law in question, a partnership had a right to compel its partners to contribute to it if necessary to pay its debts. The court held that this right is property of the partnership's estate in bankruptcy, and a suit by a partnership creditor against a partner is stayed under § 362(a)(3) because it is an act to obtain possession of property of the estate or to exercise control over property of the estate. The bankruptcy court properly exercised its discretion to enjoin the action of Bank against Partners under § 105(a) because of the likelihood of irreparable harm that would result were Bank allowed to recover from Partners. A judgment by Bank against Partners would block a successful reorganization because their assets, already pledged to the plan, were essential to success of the plan which called for paying all creditors in full over an extended period of time. With the injunction, the court believed Debtor had a reasonable likelihood of a successful reorganization.

F. RELIEF FROM AUTOMATIC STAY FOR CAUSE

Relief from the automatic stay pursuant to § 362(d) is an issue of great importance that has been heavily litigated. Earlier in this chapter we briefly considered the issue as it relates to secured creditors in liquidation bankruptcy. Later in chapters 9 and 10 we will consider the issue in greater detail as it relates to secured creditors in rehabilitation and reorganization proceedings. In the present section we deal with but a limited part of the issue. We examine when a claimant barred by the automatic stay of § 362 is entitled to relief from the stay to allow a lawsuit pending against the debtor to proceed to judgment.

In re Holtkamp

United States Court of Appeals, Seventh Circuit, 1982.
669 F.2d 505.

■ BAUER, Circuit Judge.

Defendants-appellants Charles Holtkamp and Holtkamp Farms, Inc. (collectively Holtkamp) appeal from an order of the bankruptcy court lifting an automatic stay and permitting a pending civil action to proceed. We affirm.

The pending civil action was a personal injury suit initiated by plaintiff-appellee Ronald E. Littlefield in 1979 and set for trial in May 1980. Five days before the trial was scheduled to begin, Holtkamp filed voluntary bankruptcy petitions under Chapter 11 of the Bankruptcy Code designating Littlefield's personal injury claim as an unsecured debt. The personal injury suit was stayed automatically pursuant to § 362(a). Littlefield immediately filed adversary proceedings in the bankruptcy court seeking an emergency hearing to lift the stay. Holtkamp had only three hours notice of this hearing. The bankruptcy court granted Littlefield's request to permit the personal injury suit to proceed to judgment, but prohibited Littlefield from attempting to collect any judgment he might receive. After a jury trial, a $5,025,000 judgment was entered in Littlefield's favor.

Holtkamp contends that the modification of the automatic stay arising under § 362 constitutes reversible error because it contravenes the express provisions of the statute. * * *

I.

Section 362(d) provides for relief from the automatic stay "for cause, including the lack of adequate protection of an interest in property of such party in interest." Since the statute commits the decision of whether to lift the stay to the discretion of the bankruptcy judge, his decision may be overturned only upon a showing of abuse of discretion. * * *

Citing no authority to support his contention, Holtkamp argues that § 362(d) applies only to secured creditors and, thus, has no relevance to Littlefield's unsecured claim. He maintains that Congress intended the automatic stay provisions to be broadly applied to cover all situations not specifically exempted by the statute and asserts that because none of the enumerated exceptions in § 362(d) apply here the lifting of the stay is contrary to both the spirit and the policy of the new Code. Holtkamp maintains that by permitting the litigation to proceed Littlefield, as an unsecured creditor, has improved his position at the expense of other creditors.

Holtkamp's contention that § 362(d) applies only to secured creditors is not supported by the statutory language or case-law. Subsection (d) grants relief from the automatic stay, under certain conditions, to "a party in interest." Had Congress intended the section to apply only to secured creditors, it undoubtedly would have so stated. Further, nothing in the legislative history implies that Congress intended the restrictive application Holtkamp urges. Moreover, although the scope of subsection (d) is an issue of first impression in this Circuit, courts from other jurisdictions have applied subsection (d) in analogous situations. Thus, previously filed actions involving unsecured creditors have been allowed to continue despite the automatic stay provisions in § 362(a). * * *

While we agree that Congress intended that the automatic stay have broad application, the legislative history to § 362 clearly indicates that Congress recognized that the stay should be lifted in appropriate circumstances. It states:

> [I]t will often be more appropriate to permit proceedings to continue in their place of origin, when no great prejudice to the bankruptcy estate would result, in order to leave the parties to their chosen forum and to relieve the bankruptcy court from many duties that may be handled elsewhere.

* * * S.Rep. No. 989, 95th Cong., 2d Sess. 50.

Holtkamp's claim that permitting the trial to go forward enabled Littlefield to gain a superior position over other creditors is belied by the facts. Holtkamp argues that by obtaining a judgment Littlefield can now enforce that judgment by securing a lien against Holtkamp's property. This contention is erroneous, for the bankruptcy's court's order expressly prohibited Littlefield from attempting to enforce his judgment. Allowing the pending action to proceed merely determined Holtkamp's liability but did not change Littlefield's status in relation to other creditors. * * *

Indeed, contrary to Holtkamp's assertion that the order of the bankruptcy court frustrated the policy of the Code, the lifting of the stay in this case is in complete harmony with the Code's policy of quickly and efficiently formulating plans for repayment and reorganization. The purpose of the automatic stay is to preserve what remains of the debtor's insolvent estate and to provide a systematic equitable liquidation procedure for all creditors, secured as well as unsecured * * * thereby preventing a "chaotic and uncontrolled scramble for the debtor's assets in a variety of uncoordinated proceedings in different courts." *In re Frigitemp Corp.*, 8 B.R. 284, 289 (S.D.N.Y.1981).

However, where, as here, the pending action is neither connected with nor interfering with the bankruptcy proceeding, the automatic stay in no way fosters Code policy. * * * Allowing the civil action to go forward did not jeopardize Holtkamp's bankrupt estate because his insurance company assumed full financial responsibility for defending that litigation. On the other hand, the interests of judicial economy militated in favor of permitting the suit to go forward, for the trial date had been set and witnesses, including Littlefield who is a quadriplegic and several out of state witnesses, had been subpoenaed. Additionally, determination of the issues in the personal injury action did not require the expertise of the bankruptcy court. Under these circumstances, the lifting of the stay was proper. * * *

NOTES

1. A portion of the legislative history with respect to § 362 follows:

> The lack of adequate protection of an interest in property of the party requesting relief from the stay is one cause for relief, but is not the only cause. [A] desire to permit an action to proceed to completion in another tribunal may provide another cause. Other causes might include the lack of any connection with or interference with the pending bankruptcy case. For example, a divorce or child custody proceeding involving the debtor may bear no relation to the bankruptcy case. In that case, it should not be stayed. A probate proceeding in which the debtor is the executor or administrator of another's estate usually will not be related to the bankruptcy case, and should not be stayed. Generally, proceedings in which the debtor is a fiduciary, or involving postpetition activities of the debtor, need not be stayed because they bear no relationship to the purpose of the automatic stay, which is debtor protection from his creditors. The facts of each request will determine whether relief is appropriate under the circumstances.

H.Rep. No. 95–595, 1978 U.S.C.C.A.N. 6300.

2. The statement in the above-quoted legislative history that "a desire to permit an action to proceed to completion in another tribunal" may be a cause for lifting the stay has proved prophetic. A strong body of authority has developed to the effect that a plaintiff in a nonbankruptcy proceeding against the debtor may have the stay lifted if it is ordered or stipulated that the plaintiff will use the nonbankruptcy forum only to liquidate the claim and not to satisfy any judgment obtained from the assets of the estate. The factors a court should consider in deciding whether cause has been shown under § 362(d)(1) are stated in *In re Robbins*, 964 F.2d 342, 345 (4th Cir. 1992):

(1) whether the issues in the pending litigation involve only state law, so the expertise of the bankruptcy court is unnecessary; **(2)** whether modifying the stay will promote judicial economy and whether there would be greater interference with the bankruptcy case if the stay were not lifted because matters would have to be litigated in bankruptcy court; and **(3)** whether the estate can be protected properly by a requirement that creditors seek enforcement of any judgment through the bankruptcy court.

PROBLEM

Plaintiff sued Debtor in a state court in tort for negligence. The claim against Debtor was fully covered by Debtor's liability insurance. Before trial Debtor filed a petition in Chapter 7 and listed Plaintiff as an unsecured creditor with an unliquidated claim. Plaintiff did not attempt to obtain relief from the automatic stay to pursue the tort claim against Debtor under the *Holtkamp* doctrine. Debtor received a discharge, which applied to the debt on the tort claim. When Debtor was discharged, the automatic stay expired under § 362(c)(2)(C) and, at the same time, the discharge operated "as an injunction against the commencement or continuation of an action * * * to collect, recover or offset any such debt as a personal liability of the debtor." § 524(a)(2). Plaintiff wishes to continue the state court tort action against Debtor for the purpose of recovering against Debtor's insurer. § 524(e). Does § 524(a)(2) prohibit Plaintiff from continuing the state court action? If Plaintiff were to obtain a judgment in the action, would the judgment be void under § 524(a)(1)? See *Green v. Welsh*, 956 F.2d 30 (2d Cir. 1992); *Matter of Hendrix*, 986 F.2d 195 (7th Cir. 1993).

G. PREPETITION WAIVER OF STAY

We began this chapter by reciting what is perhaps the most quoted piece of legislative history on any provision of the Bankruptcy Code: "The automatic stay is one of the fundamental debtor protections provided by the bankruptcy laws." H. Rep. No. 95–595, 1978 U.S.C.C.A.N. 6296. It has long been the law that debtors cannot waive the right to file for bankruptcy in the future. *In re Weitzen*, 3 F.Supp. 698 (S.D.N.Y.1933). Many assume that this anti-waiver view carries over to such a fundamental debtor protection as the automatic stay as well, and some courts have held that prepetition waivers of the automatic stay are unenforceable per se as undermining the carefully drawn statutory scheme of the Bankruptcy Code, e.g., *Matter of Pease*, 195 B.R. 431 (Bankr.D.Neb.1996). But an increasing number of courts are enforcing these waivers in varying degrees, *e.g., In re Bryan Road, LLC,* (Bankr.S.D.Fla.2008). How can this be?

The real estate recession of the 1980's chastened secured lenders who had agreed in workout agreements to give defaulting debtors another chance, only to be met with subsequent defaults leading to a Chapter 11 filing on the part of the debtors who then strenuously resisted foreclosure for protracted periods by reliance on the automatic stay. Although they had doubts about the enforceability of waiver-of-stay clauses, lenders began to demand waivers on a routine basis as a part of the consideration for workout deals with real property developers: if the debtor can't meet its obligations under the workout agreement, the lender claims the right to foreclose immediately upon postpetition default. No more stalling.

To the surprise of most lawyers and academics, some courts began to enforce these clauses, and this view is gathering strength. *See* Daniel B. Bogart, *Games Lawyers Play: Waivers of the Automatic Stay in Bankruptcy and the Single Asset Loan Workout,* 43 UCLA L.Rev. 1117, 1127 n.20 (1996) ("Interviews with many attorneys indicate what might be deemed amazement at courts' enforcement of these provisions. This reaction is also found in published materials in bar journals and the like.") Some scholars have found merit in waiver clauses, *e.g.,* Marshall E. Tracht, *Contractual Bankruptcy Waivers: Reconciling Theory, Practice and Law*, 82 Cornell L.Rev. 301 (1997).

Some courts have taken a middle view in holding that although waiver-of-stay clauses are not self-executing, they may be weighed as a factor in the court's decision whether to lift the automatic stay for cause under § 362(d), *e.g., In re Desai*, 282 B.R. 527 (Bankr.M.D.Ga.2002), a single-asset case in which, in the context of a consensual plan in a previous case, debtor agreed not to oppose a motion for relief from the stay by the secured creditor if debtor defaulted and filed in bankruptcy again. The court held that such waivers are not self-executing and that in deciding whether a stay should be granted based on the waiver several factors should be considered: the sophistication of the party making the waiver; the consideration for the waiver, including the creditor's risk and the length of time the waiver covers; whether other parties are affected, including unsecured creditors and junior lienholders; the feasibility of the debtor's plan; and whether the debtor has any equity in the property.

In *Bryan Road, supra,* Bank agreed to reschedule foreclosure for a period of time during which Debtor hoped to refinance. In exchange, Debtor agreed to forbear protection of the automatic stay if it later filed in bankruptcy. The refinancing effort failed, and when Debtor subsequently filed in bankruptcy immediately before Bank's scheduled foreclosure, the court held that the forbearance agreement was enforceable against Debtor. The existence of the enforceable stay relief agreement constituted "cause" under § 362(d)(1) for grant of Bank's motion for relief from the automatic stay. The court emphasized that Debtor had been represented throughout by experienced bankruptcy counsel who was "fully capable of understanding the implications of the Forbearance Agreement." 382 B.R. at 849.

The National Bankruptcy Review Commission has taken a strong position in opposition to any prepetition agreement by a debtor that waives, terminates, restricts, conditions, or otherwise modifies "any rights or defenses provided by" the Bankruptcy Code. *NBRC Rep.* at 478. "The ability of one creditor to negotiate privately with the debtor for special treatment in bankruptcy runs counter to the principle of equitable treatment and could have significant distributional consequences for all other creditors." *Id.* at 481.

CHAPTER 6
EXECUTORY CONTRACTS AND LEASES

A. EXECUTORY CONTRACTS

1. INTRODUCTION

Suppose a contract for a sale of goods with Buyer to pay at the time of delivery. What are the rights and obligations of the parties if either goes into bankruptcy before delivery (and payment) is due? This question can arise in a Chapter 7 case as well as in all types of reorganization cases, but typically the issue arises in Chapter 11 cases and we assume Chapter 11 filing in this discussion. Suppose Seller is the debtor in bankruptcy. Because "claim" is defined in § 101 in very broad terms to include any right to enforce an obligation of the debtor so long as breach of that obligation gives rise to a right to payment, Buyer has a claim in the bankruptcy even though the claim is unmatured. But it is not possible to know at the time of bankruptcy whether this claim will ever ripen into a right to payment. Bankruptcy is not treated as an automatic repudiation of the obligations of the debtor. If Seller continues its business as debtor in possession, Seller in many cases would want to perform the contract and obtain payment as though bankruptcy had not occurred. If Seller is able to perform and the contract is favorable to Seller, Seller will normally want to perform the contract. If the contract is unfavorable, Seller will want to refuse to perform.

Section 365 governs this situation. It allows the trustee in bankruptcy (including a debtor in possession), subject to approval of the bankruptcy court, to "assume or reject any executory contract or unexpired lease of the debtor." § 365(a).

Fundamental to the treatment of executory contracts under § 365 is the notion that an unperformed contract is a "package deal" that must be assumed or rejected in its entirety. If the bankruptcy trustee wishes to retain the benefit of the agreement or lease for the estate, the estate must accept the burden of performance in accordance with the original terms of the contract. In our sale of goods example, the trustee must deliver the goods to earn the sale price. What the trustee cannot do is demand Buyer's future performance (payment) without binding the estate to the perform its obligations as Seller (delivery).

229

If the trustee decides to have the estate perform the contract (in order to gain the benefit of a favorable agreement), the contract must be assumed. The effect of assumption is to convert the obligations of Seller under the contract into obligations of the bankruptcy estate. After assumption, if the debtor in possession fails to perform in compliance with the contract, Buyer has a right to payment of an administrative expense for damages for breach of contract.

If the trustee decides not to perform under the contract, the contract must be rejected. "Reject" is perhaps an inapt word to express the intent of § 365(a) and the courts sometimes have given the word surprising interpretations. Rejection can best be understood as the opposite of assumption. It is a formal declaration not to assume the contract. Rejection is treated by § 365(g) as a breach of Seller's contract because rejection means that Seller's obligations under the contract will not be performed. Buyer has a prepetition claim in bankruptcy for breach of contract and is released from the obligation to render any further performance under the contract. § 502(g).

The following cases illustrate the advantages § 365(a) gives to the bankruptcy estate.

Case #1. On February 1, Seller and Buyer agreed to a sale of goods at $20 a unit with delivery and payment to be made on April 1. On March 1, Buyer filed a Chapter 11 petition. Because similar goods can be purchased from another supplier for $15 a unit Buyer, as debtor in possession, seeks to reject the contract.

Case #2. Under the same contract described in Case #1, Seller rather than Buyer filed a Chapter 11 petition in bankruptcy under Chapter 11. Seller can sell the goods to others for $25 a unit. Seller, as debtor in possession, seeks to reject the contract.

Assume that nonpriority creditors in each case will receive less than the full amount of their claims. If Buyer is allowed to reject in Case #1, the bankruptcy estate will normally benefit because the goods can be bought more cheaply from another supplier. If Seller is allowed to reject in Case #2, the estate will normally benefit because the goods can be sold at a higher price to other buyers. In either case the nonbankrupt party to the contract is entitled to damages for breach of contract. If damages are measured only by a $5 per unit loss of bargain in each case, there is a net benefit to the estate because the claim will be paid at less than face amount and the estate will receive a full $5 per unit benefit in the substitute transactions. If the nonbankrupt party has damages in addition to the $5 per unit loss of bargain, the estate may or may not benefit from rejection, depending upon the amount of the additional damages and the extent to which payment of claims is discounted below 100% of face amount.

The National Bankruptcy Review Commission proposed several changes in § 365 and related provisions. Among these are recommendations to replace the concept of "rejection" with "election to breach," which the Commission describes as "a common-sense clarification," and "assumption" with "election to perform," a concept parallel to "election to breach." *NBRC Rep.* at 459–465. We will comment on the substantive consequences of these recommendations at appropriate places in this Chapter.

2. DECISION TO ASSUME OR REJECT

A trustee or debtor in possession must obtain the court's approval in order to assume or reject a contract. § 365(a). The statute is silent on what standards a court should apply in granting its approval. The prevailing view, which accords great deference to the decision of the trustee, is that the trustee's decision to assume or reject because of belief that there is a business advantage in doing so must be accepted by the court unless it is shown that the decision was made in bad faith or in abuse of discretion. *In re Minges*, 602 F.2d 38 (2d Cir. 1979). This is similar to the business judgment rule of corporation law which protects directors from liability when decisions made by them on matters entrusted to their business judgment turn out badly. Ordinarily the trustee should reject a contract if the trustee believes that the estate's costs of taking over the debtor's remaining burdens exceed the value of the nondebtor party's remaining performance.

Occasionally courts refuse to go along with the trustee's business judgment either because the contract is not "burdensome" or because the cost of rejection to the nondebtor party is disproportionate to the benefit to the estate—the "balancing of equities" rule. These rules are discussed in Jesse M. Fried, *Executory Contracts and Performance Decisions in Bankruptcy*, 46 Duke L.J. 517, 540–544 (1996). Under the burdensomeness test a trustee would not be allowed to reject a contract on the ground that although performance of the original contract would increase the value of the estate, the estate could make more money devoting its resources to another contract. Under the balancing test, if rejection would benefit the bankruptcy estate only slightly but would destroy the nondebtor's business, the court may withhold its approval. In *In re Chi-Feng Huang*, 23 B.R. 798, 801 (9th Cir. BAP 1982), the court held that it is "proper for the court to refuse to authorize rejection of a lease or executory contract where the party whose contract is to be rejected would be damaged disproportionately to any benefit that would be derived by the general creditors of the estate * * *." In *In re Petur U.S.A. Instrument Co.*, 35 B.R. 561 (Bankr.W.D.Wash.1983), the court would not allow rejection of a licensing agreement because the rejection threatened to ruin the nondebtor's profitable business. Unpersuaded, the court in *In re Riodizio, Inc.*, 204 B.R. 417, 425 n.9

(Bankr.S.D.N.Y.1997), declared "Section 365 does not require any balancing of the equities." The National Bankruptcy Conference recommends replacing the business judgment standard with an "interest-of-the-estate" test that would give less deference to the judgment of the trustee. Reforming the Bankruptcy Code 126 (Rev.ed.1997).

Section 365(g) treats the rejection of a contract as a prepetition breach, and as a result the damages for the breach to the nondebtor party are considered a prepetition claim. This claim of the nondebtor party will be treated like other prepetition claims, and the nondebtor will receive only a ratable share of the assets of the estate available to general creditors. These pro-rata "bankruptcy dollars" can be pretty small. Estimates are that 80% of liquidation cases yield no distribution to general creditors, and in the cases in which there is a payout creditors often receive a small fraction of their claims. Even in reorganization cases involving the largest corporations the payout rate often doesn't exceed 50%. Professor Fried argues that under the present ratable share rule, trustees have too much incentive to reject and proposes reforms that would limit the rights of trustees to reject value producing contracts, that is, cases in which rejection makes the estate better off but makes the other party worse off by a greater amount.

3. MEANING OF "EXECUTORY CONTRACT"

The term "executory contract" is not defined in the Bankruptcy Code and may not be definable, except in an arbitrary way. Long ago Professor Williston counseled against the use of the terms "executed contract" and "executory contract" on the ground that they were vague and misleading. He stated: "All contracts to a greater or lesser extent are executory. When they cease to be so, they cease to be contracts." *Williston on Contracts* § 14 (1920). More recently, Professor Jay Westbrook has said with respect to § 365(a):

> It is obvious that a contract must be executory to be assumed or rejected, if the term is used in its ordinary sense to mean merely that aspects of the contract were not fully performed or satisfied on Bankruptcy Day. But if executoriness had such a simple meaning, the requirement would be trivial. The trustee need not, and could not, assume or reject a contract fully performed a year before bankruptcy—nor would anyone dream of doing so. Speaking of a "nonexecutory" contract in that sense is like discussing a sunset after dark.

Jay L. Westbrook, *A Functional Analysis of Executory Contracts*, 74 Minn.L.Rev. 227, 243 (1989). The courts, however, treat the adjective "executory" in § 365 as a limitation on the contracts to which the section applies. In this regard the courts have been strongly influenced by a definition of executory contract proposed by Professor Vern Countryman in *Executory Contracts in*

Bankruptcy: Part I, 57 Minn.L.Rev. 439, 460 (1973). He states that an executory contract is:

> [A] contract under which the obligation of both the bankrupt and the other party to the contract are so far unperformed that the failure of either to complete performance would constitute a material breach excusing the performance of the other.

Countryman defined executory contract as requiring performance due on both sides because he believed that it furthered the purpose for which the trustee is given the option to assume or reject. This purpose is to benefit the estate. If the creditor has already performed, the estate has already received the full benefit, and rejection would have no function for it would change neither the creditor's claim nor the estate's liability. According to Countryman, assumption would in no way benefit the estate and would convert the debtor's obligation on the contract into an administrative expense. If the debtor has performed, rejection would not be a breach and assumption would add nothing to its right to have the other party perform.

Under the Countryman definition a contract cannot be "executory" under § 365(a) if either the debtor or the other party to the contract has fully performed its obligations under the contract. The following Case #3 and Case #4 are examples.

> **Case #3.** Seller and Buyer agree to a sale of goods with payment to be made six months after delivery of the goods. After Seller delivers the goods but before payment is due, either Seller or Buyer files in Chapter 11 bankruptcy.

If Seller is the bankrupt in Case #3, the right to payment of the price of the goods from Buyer is property of the bankruptcy estate that can be enforced by the debtor in possession. Buyer has a claim in bankruptcy if there was a breach of contract with respect to Seller's performance, such as breach of warranty. There is no reason for § 365 to apply because assumption or rejection of the contract can't affect the rights of Buyer or the estate. Seller has fully performed. A decision to assume or not to assume can't relate to performance that has already occurred.

If Buyer is the bankrupt in Case #3, Seller has a claim in bankruptcy for the price of the goods. Since the only obligation of Buyer under the contract was to pay money, there is no need for § 365. The estate already has the goods and cannot obtain any benefit through § 365.

Under the Countryman definition, § 365(a) cannot be applied to Case #3, and that is the right result. But that result should follow even if the word "executory" were deleted from § 365(a). Assumption or rejection is irrelevant in Case #3.

Case #4. On February 1, Seller and Buyer agreed to a sale of goods with delivery to be made on April 1. Buyer paid Seller the price of the goods at the time the agreement was signed as required by the agreement. On March 1, before the time for Seller's performance, either Buyer or Seller filed a petition in bankruptcy under Chapter 11.

Under the Countryman definition, § 365(a) cannot be applied to Case #4 because Buyer has fully performed. If Buyer is the bankrupt, there is no obligation that the debtor in possession can assume or reject. The right of the bankruptcy estate to receive goods from Seller can be enforced by the debtor in possession. Section 365 is irrelevant. The Countryman definition produces the right result, but it is not necessary. The analysis is the same as in Case #3 if Buyer is the bankrupt.

But suppose Seller is the bankrupt in Case #4 and the contract is unfavorable to Seller. Why shouldn't the debtor in possession be able to reject the contract under § 365? The case is essentially the same as Case #2 and there is no apparent reason to treat Case #4 differently. What happens if Case #4 is excluded from § 365(a)? Seller's filing in bankruptcy does not oblige the bankruptcy estate to perform the contract. The estate hasn't agreed to perform it. If the contract isn't assumed the estate has no liability on the contract. But if the contract isn't performed, Buyer should have a claim in bankruptcy for damages. Even if § 365(a) is held not to apply, the result should be the same as if the contract had been rejected under § 365(a). Thus, the Countryman definition does not affect nonperformance of the contract, but that definition would prevent assumption of the contract. Although, in most cases, performance by the estate will not benefit the estate if Buyer has prepaid, there may be cases in which the estate might suffer loss by reneging on the obligation. The Countryman definition prevents the trustee or debtor in possession from avoiding such a loss by assuming the contract.

Several courts have questioned whether assumption or rejection by the trustee should depend upon performance or nonperformance by the nonbankrupt party. In *In re Norquist*, 43 B.R. 224 (Bankr.E.D.Wash.1984), the debtor was a partner in a firm of doctors carrying on a medical practice. The debtor withdrew from the firm and, upon withdrawal, was bound by a covenant not to compete with the firm for two years in the city in which the firm's practice was carried on. As debtor in possession, the debtor wanted to avoid the burden of the covenant by rejecting the partnership agreement. The court said with respect to the Countryman test, "The logic of this approach escapes me. I believe that the requirement of a remaining material obligation on the part of the nondebtor serves no useful purpose. It eliminates from the category of executory contracts some obligations which may prove extremely burdensome and, in some cases, obligations which may be prohibitive to the reorganization efforts of the debtor." 43 B.R. at 227. In *In re Oxford Royal Mushroom Products, Inc.*, 45 B.R. 792 (Bankr.E.D.Pa.1985), Judge Goldhaber concluded that an executory contract is one that requires substantial performance by either party to the contract other than the payment of money.

Although the Countryman definition is widely cited by almost all of the courts that have decided § 365 cases, the use of that definition has been severely criticized. The primary attack began in Professor Westbrook's article cited above and in two articles by Michael T. Andrew: *Executory Contracts in Bankruptcy: Understanding "Rejection,"* 59 U.Colo.L.Rev. 845 (1988), and *Executory Contracts Revisited: A Reply to Professor Westbrook*, 62 U.Colo.L.Rev. 1 (1991). These articles have been very influential and they contend that "executoriness" of a contract should not be a precondition to assuming or rejecting a contract under § 365(a).

The National Bankruptcy Conference, Reforming the Bankruptcy Code 124 (Rev.ed.1997), explains:

> The terms used in section 365, especially "rejection" and "executory contract," should be retired from use, as they carry the accumulated baggage of too many erroneous preconceptions. A fundamental change of mind set is necessary. This will be difficult to accomplish unless these terms are replaced by others conveying more precisely that the decision facing the trustee is whether to perform the contract as an administrative expense, or breach it and pay in bankruptcy dollars (absent equitable remedies). Also, the trustee, acting in the interest of the estate, should be free to decide not to perform future contractual obligations without first having to show that the contract is "executory." The trustee must determine either to perform or breach, according to whichever is better calculated to achieve the maximum economic net value for the estate. An inquiry into whether the contract is "executory" is beside the point.

The National Bankruptcy Review Commission agreed. It recommended that "all references to 'executory' be deleted from § 365 and related provisions, and that 'executoriness' be eliminated as a prerequisite to the trustee's election to assume or breach a contract." *NBRC Rep.* at 472. The Report explains on p. 475:

> A growing case law trend de-emphasizes a strict analysis of the term "executory" in favor of a "functional" analysis, an approach articulated by Professor Jay Westbrook, Michael Andrew, and others. Using a functional analysis, a court does not consider remaining mutual material performance but instead considers the goals that assumption or rejection were expected to accomplish: enhancement of the estate. * * *

[A] few courts taking the functional approach have declined to make the threshold finding of executoriness at all and simply have focused on whether the estate would be benefited by performance or breach.

PROBLEM

On May 1 Seller sold Buyer an option to buy real property from Seller for the price of $200,000 at any time within the following six months. Buyer paid $5,000 for the option. Although market conditions caused the value of the property to rise, Buyer's business faltered and it filed in Chapter 11 on September 1. Buyer as Debtor in Possession sought to exercise the option contract in order to resell the property to another purchaser for $250,000. Is the option contract an executory contract that can be lost if not assumed by the estate? Or is the option simply an asset of Buyer's bankruptcy estate that can be exercised in accordance with its terms? Jay L. Westbrook, *A Functional Analysis of Executory Contracts*, 74 Minn.L.Rev. 227, 316 (1989); Michael T. Andrew, *Executory Contracts Revisited: A Reply to Professor Westbrook*, 62 U.Colo.L.Rev. 1, 32 (1991). *See In re Robert L. Helms Construction and Development Co., Inc.*, 139 F.3d 702, 706 (9th Cir. *en banc* 1998), in which the court held that an option was not an executory contract and therefore remained an asset of the bankruptcy estate notwithstanding the debtor's rejection of all its executory contracts. With respect to option contracts "[t]he question thus becomes: At the time of filing, does each party have something it must do to avoid materially breaching the contract? Typically, the answer is no; the optionee commits no breach by doing nothing." Compare *In re Riodizio, Inc.*, 204 B.R. 417, 424 (Bankr.S.D.N.Y.1997), which held a stock option to be an executory contract because "each party must perform under the Warrant to obtain the benefits under the contingent bilateral contract of sale." If you agree with the *Helms Construction* view, what result if the bankrupt is the Seller/Optionor and the option price is unfavorable to Seller? Would Seller be precluded from rejecting its obligation to deliver the land for a below-market price?

4. REJECTION OF LICENSES OF INTELLECTUAL PROPERTY

Lubrizol Enterprises, Inc. v. Richmond Metal Finishers, Inc.
United States Court of Appeals, Fourth Circuit, 1985.
756 F.2d 1043.

■ JAMES DICKSON PHILLIPS, Circuit Judge:

The question is whether Richmond Metal Finishers (RMF), a bankrupt debtor in possession, should have been allowed to reject as executory a technology licensing agreement with Lubrizol Enterprises (Lubrizol) as licensee. The bankruptcy court approved rejection pursuant to § 365(a) * * * but the district court reversed on the basis that within contemplation of § 365(a), the contract was not executory * * *. We reverse and remand for entry of judgment in conformity with that entered by the bankruptcy court.

I.

In July of 1982, RMF entered into the contract with Lubrizol that granted Lubrizol a nonexclusive license to utilize a metal coating process technology owned by RMF. RMF owed the following duties to Lubrizol under the agreement: (1) to notify Lubrizol of any patent infringement suit and to defend in such suit; (2) to notify Lubrizol of any other use or licensing of the process, and to reduce royalty payments if a lower royalty rate agreement was reached with another licensee; and (3) to indemnify Lubrizol for losses arising out of any misrepresentation or breach of warranty by RMF. Lubrizol owed RMF reciprocal duties of accounting for and paying royalties for use of the process and of cancelling certain existing indebtedness. The contract provided that Lubrizol would defer use of the process until May 1, 1983, and in fact, Lubrizol has never used the RMF technology.

RMF filed a petition for bankruptcy pursuant to Chapter 11 of the Bankruptcy Code on August 16, 1983. As part of its plan to emerge from bankruptcy, RMF sought, pursuant to § 365(a), to reject the contract with Lubrizol in order to facilitate sale or licensing of the technology unhindered by restrictive provisions in the Lubrizol agreement. On RMF's motion for approval of the rejection, the bankruptcy court properly interpreted § 365 as requiring it to undertake a two-step inquiry to determine the propriety of rejection: first, whether the contract is executory; next, if so, whether its rejection would be advantageous to the bankrupt.

Making that inquiry, the bankruptcy court determined that both tests were satisfied and approved the rejection. But, as indicated, the district court then reversed that determination on the basis that neither test was satisfied and disallowed the rejection. This appeal followed.

II.

We conclude initially that, as the bankruptcy court ruled, the technology licensing agreement in this case was an executory contract, within contemplation of § 365(a). Under that provision a contract is executory if performance is due to some extent on both sides. * * * This court has recently adopted Professor Countryman's more specific test for determining whether a contract is "executory" in the required sense. * * * This issue is one of law that may be freely reviewed by successive courts.

Applying that test here, we conclude that the licensing agreement was at the critical time executory. RMF owed Lubrizol the continuing duties of notifying Lubrizol of further licensing of the process and of reducing Lubrizol's royalty rate to meet any more favorable rates granted to subsequent licensees. By their terms, RMF's obligations to give notice and to restrict its right to license its process at royalty rates it desired without lowering Lubrizol's royalty rate extended over the life of the agreement, and remained unperformed. Moreover, RMF owed Lubrizol additional contingent duties of notifying it of suits, defending suits and indemnifying it for certain losses.

The unperformed, continuing core obligations of notice and forbearance in licensing made the contract executory as to RMF. In *Fenix Cattle Co. v. Silver (In re Select–A–Seat Corp.)*, 625 F.2d 290, 292 (9th Cir. 1980), the court found that an obligation of a debtor to refrain from selling software packages under an exclusive licensing agreement made a contract executory as to the debtor notwithstanding the continuing obligation was only one of forbearance. Although the license to Lubrizol was not exclusive, RMF owed the same type of unperformed continuing duty of forbearance arising out of the most favored licensee clause running in favor of Lubrizol. Breach of that duty would clearly constitute a material breach of the agreement.

Moreover, the contract was further executory as to RMF because of the contingent duties that RMF owed of giving notice of and defending infringement suits and of indemnifying Lubrizol for certain losses arising out of the use of the technology. Contingency of an obligation does not prevent its being executory under § 365. See *In re Smith Jones, Inc.*, 26 B.R. 289, 292 (Bankr.D.Minn.1982) (warranty obligations executory as to promisor); *In re O.P.M. Leasing Services, Inc.*, 23 B.R. 104, 117 (Bankr.S.D.N.Y.1982) (obligation to defend infringement suits makes contract executory as to promisor). Until the time has expired during which an event triggering a contingent duty may occur, the contingent obligation represents a continuing duty to stand ready to perform if the contingency occurs. A breach of that duty once it was triggered by the contingency (or presumably, by anticipatory repudiation) would have been material.

Because a contract is not executory within the meaning of § 365(a) unless it is executory as to both parties, it is also necessary to determine whether the licensing agreement was executory as to Lubrizol. * * * We conclude that it was.

Lubrizol owed RMF the unperformed and continuing duty of accounting for and paying royalties for the life of the agreement. It is true that a contract is not executory as to a party simply because the party is obligated to make payments of money to the other party. * * * Therefore, if Lubrizol had owed RMF nothing more than a duty to make fixed payments or cancel specified indebtedness under the agreement, the agreement would not be executory as to Lubrizol. However, the promise to account for and pay royalties required that Lubrizol deliver written quarterly sales reports and keep books of account subject to inspection by an independent Certified Public Accountant. This promise goes beyond a mere debt, or promise to pay money, and was at the critical time executory. See *Fenix Cattle,* 625 F.2d at 292. Additionally, subject to certain exceptions, Lubrizol was obligated to keep all license technology in confidence for a number of years.

Since the licensing agreement is executory as to each party, it is executory within the meaning of § 365(a), and the district court erred as a matter of law in reaching a contrary conclusion.*

III.

There remains the question whether rejection of the executory contract would be advantageous to the bankrupt. * * * Courts addressing that question must start with the proposition that the bankrupt's decision upon it is to be accorded the deference mandated by the sound business judgment rule as generally applied by courts to discretionary actions or decisions of corporate directors. * * *

As generally formulated and applied in corporate litigation the rule is that courts should defer to—should not interfere with—decisions of corporate directors upon matters entrusted to their business judgment except upon a finding of bad faith or gross abuse of their "business discretion." Transposed to the bankruptcy context, the rule as applied to a bankrupt's decision to reject an

---

* We disagree with the district court's characterization of the transaction as effectively a completed sale of property. If an analogy is to be made, licensing agreements are more similar to leases than to sales of property because of the limited nature of the interest conveyed. Congress expressly made leases subject to rejection under § 365 in order to "preclude any uncertainty as to whether a lease is an executory contract" under § 365. 2 Collier on Bankruptcy ¶ 365.02 (L.King 15th ed.1984).

executory contract because of perceived business advantage requires that the decision be accepted by courts unless it is shown that the bankrupt's decision was one taken in bad faith or in gross abuse of the bankrupt's retained business discretion.

* * *

Here, the bankruptcy judge had before him evidence not rebutted by Lubrizol that the metal coating process subject to the licensing agreement is RMF's principal asset and that sale or licensing of the technology represented the primary potential source of funds by which RMF might emerge from bankruptcy. The testimony of RMF's president, also factually uncontested by Lubrizol, indicated that sale or further licensing of the technology would be facilitated by stripping Lubrizol of its rights in the process and that, correspondingly, continued obligation to Lubrizol under the agreement would hinder RMF's capability to sell or license the technology on more advantageous terms to other potential licensees. On the basis of this evidence the bankruptcy court determined that the debtor's decision to reject was based upon sound business judgment and approved it.

On appeal the district court simply found to the contrary that the debtor's decision to reject did not represent a sound business judgment. The district court's determination rested essentially on two grounds: that RMF's purely contingent obligations under the agreement were not sufficiently onerous that relief from them would constitute a substantial benefit to RMF; and that because rejection could not deprive Lubrizol of all its rights to the technology, rejection could not reasonably be found beneficial. We conclude that in both of these respects the district court's factual findings, at odds with those of the bankruptcy court, were clearly erroneous and cannot stand.

A

In finding that the debtor's contingent obligations were not sufficiently onerous that relief from them would be beneficial, the district court could only have been substituting its business judgment for that of the debtor. There is nothing in the record from which it could be concluded that the debtor's decision on that point could not have been reached by the exercise of sound (though possibly faulty) business judgment in the normal process of evaluating alternative courses of action. If that could not be concluded, then the business judgment rule required that the debtor's factual evaluation be accepted by the court, as it had been by the bankruptcy court. * * *

B

On the second point, we can only conclude that the district court was under a misapprehension of controlling law in thinking that by rejecting the agreement the debtor could not deprive Lubrizol of all rights to the process. Under

§ 365(g), Lubrizol would be entitled to treat rejection as a breach and seek a money damages remedy; however, it could not seek to retain its contract rights in the technology by specific performance even if that remedy would ordinarily be available upon breach of this type of contract. *See In re Waldron*, 36 B.R. 633, 642 n.4 (Bankr.S.D.Fla.1984). Even though § 365(g) treats rejection as a breach, the legislative history of § 365(g) makes clear that the purpose of the provision is to provide only a damages remedy for the non-bankrupt party. * * * For the same reason, Lubrizol cannot rely on provisions within its agreement with RMF for continued use of the technology by Lubrizol upon breach by RMF. Here again, the statutory "breach" contemplated by § 365(g) controls, and provides only a money damages remedy for the non-bankrupt party. Allowing specific performance would obviously undercut the core purpose of rejection under § 365(a), and that consequence cannot therefore be read into congressional intent.

IV.

Lubrizol strongly urges upon us policy concerns in support of the district court's refusal to defer to the debtor's decision to reject or, preliminarily, to treat the contract as executory for § 365(a) purposes. We understand the concerns, but think they cannot control decision here.

It cannot be gainsaid that allowing rejection of such contracts as executory imposes serious burdens upon contracting parties such as Lubrizol. Nor can it be doubted that allowing rejection in this and comparable cases could have a general chilling effect upon the willingness of such parties to contract at all with businesses in possible financial difficulty. But under bankruptcy law such equitable considerations may not be indulged by courts in respect of the type of contract here in issue. Congress has plainly provided for the rejection of executory contracts, notwithstanding the obvious adverse consequences for contracting parties thereby made inevitable. Awareness by Congress of those consequences is indeed specifically reflected in the special treatment accorded to union members under collective bargaining contracts * * * and to lessees of real property, see § 365(h). But no comparable special treatment is provided for technology licensees such as Lubrizol. They share the general hazards created by § 365 for all business entities dealing with potential bankrupts in the respects at issue here.

The judgment of the district court is reversed and the case is remanded for entry of judgment in conformity with that entered by the bankruptcy court.

NOTES

1. In *Lubrizol,* the difference of opinion between Judge Phillips and Judge Warriner, the District Court judge whose judgment was reversed, reflects a fundamental disagreement about the nature of rejection under § 365. Judge Warriner assumed that the only effect of rejection was to relieve RMF of future performance under the contract. In Judge Warriner's view, the only significant executory performance was that of defending Lubrizol in infringement suits. Since RMF had already granted to Lubrizol the right to use the technology, RMF couldn't take back that right by rejecting the contract. Judge Warriner saw the licensing agreement as the grant of a property right. One analogy is the conveyance of real property under a warranty deed. The grantor conveys title to the grantee and covenants to defend the grantee against any suits that question the grantee's title. If the grantor goes into bankruptcy after conveying the property the grantor might reject the executory obligation to defend the grantee's title, but no court would hold that the grantor can rescind the conveyance of the property. A closer analogy is that of a real property lease. A lease is a type of executory contract but it is separately treated in § 365. If a lessor goes into bankruptcy, the lessor can, by rejecting the lease, relieve itself of executory duties under the lease such as providing heat, utilities, repair services and the like, but it cannot take away from the lessee the right to possession of the premises granted by the lease. § 365(h). Judge Warriner's view is consistent with the policy that underlies § 365(h). The view of Judge Phillips is not.

Judge Phillips apparently differentiates between a contract right and a property right, and places licenses in the first category. Suppose X conveyed to Y ownership of intellectual property such as a patent or a copyright. X also agreed to defend Y against infringement suits. This case is like that of the warranty deed discussed above. Even Judge Phillips would not allow X to rescind Y's ownership by rejecting under § 365. But suppose X had licensed to Y the right to use the patent or copyright and further covenanted to license no other. *Select–A–Seat* which is discussed in *Lubrizol* involved this sort of exclusive license. In that case the Ninth Circuit treated the case as involving an executory contract because the bankrupt licensor had an unperformed obligation to refrain from licensing others. The court recognized that the bankrupt could not use § 365 to prevent the licensee from using the intellectual property, but the court allowed the bankrupt to convert the exclusive license into a nonexclusive license by rejecting the contract, i.e. repudiating its obligation not to license others. The court argued that the obligation not to license others was like the obligation of a lessor under § 365(h) with respect to heat and utilities discussed above; either obligation can be rejected by the debtor in possession under § 365. In our opinion, the lease case is not a valid analogy to the exclusive license case. The grant of an exclusive license to use intellectual property is the practical equivalent of an outright transfer of intellectual property. A principal reason for expressing a transfer of intellectual property as an exclusive license rather than a sale is that the price is normally not a fixed amount that can be determined at the inception of the transaction. Rather, it is usually calculated by a formula based on the income that will be generated by the intellectual property over the life of the property. Expression of the price as a license fee that varies with the eventual economic value of the property is a more convenient way of setting up the transaction. In *Select–A–Seat* there was an additional reason. The transaction had to take the form of an exclusive license because exclusivity was geographical. The exclusive license applied to all but five areas of the world in which others had been granted licenses. But with respect to the areas of the world to which the exclusive license applied the licensor had no residual rights. It had granted everything to the licensee. *Select–A–Seat* is more like the conveyance of real property by warranty deed discussed above. It is meaningless to say that the contract by which the real property was conveyed is executory because the bankrupt had an unperformed obligation not to convey the real property to somebody else. The bankrupt has already disposed of the real property. In our opinion the same analysis should apply to an exclusive license which effectively disposes of the intellectual property. The licensor has already fully performed. There is nothing left to repudiate.

Select–A–Seat was bad enough. *Lubrizol* is worse. *Lubrizol* treats rejection as a strange variety of contract rescission that enables the debtor in possession to nullify rights already granted, and in return gives to the licensee damages for the wrongful nullification. In *Lubrizol* the court concedes that allowing debtors to take back the right to use a technology "could have a general chilling effect on the willingness * * * to contract at all with businesses in possible financial difficulty." 756 F.2d at 1048. Experience in high-technology fields is that important technology is often developed by small, unseasoned companies that are candidates for bankruptcy. It is common for these start-up companies to grant licenses to more established firms to develop marketable products based on the licensed technology. The licensed companies may invest large sums of money that would be lost if the licensor's bankruptcy allows the licensee to be deprived of its right to exploit the technology. The "Intellectual Property Protection Act" was introduced in Congress in 1987 and enacted in 1988. Its sponsors were an industry coalition of the largest high-technology companies. This Act overturns *Lubrizol* with respect to intellectual property by adding subsection (n) to § 365, which allows licensees to retain rights in intellectual property conveyed to them before the licensor's bankruptcy.

2. The National Bankruptcy Review Commission recommended that § 365 be amended to provide that rejection is merely a breach of a contract and does not nullify, rescind or "vaporize" the contract or terminate the rights of the parties. It is not an avoiding power that enables a trustee to retrieve property already transferred. The effect of rejection in most cases is merely that the nondebtor party is entitled to recover money damages, paid ratably with other

general creditors, and the creditor's claim is discharged. *Lubrizol* led the list of cases disapproved. *NBRC Rep.* at 460–463.

5. CONTRACTS NOT ASSIGNABLE UNDER NONBANKRUPTCY LAW

a. Assumption

Suppose Corporation entered into a three-year employment contract with Executive at $250,000 per year. Two years remained on the contract when Corporation filed a petition in bankruptcy under Chapter 11. Corporation continued to operate the business as debtor in possession. The debtor in possession can replace Executive with a competent person who will work for less than $250,000 per year. Executive will probably not be able to find a position elsewhere at a salary that high. The debtor in possession can, with the approval of the bankruptcy court, reject the contract. § 365(a). Executive has a claim in bankruptcy for breach of contract. § 365(g) and § 502(g). But the damages of Executive are limited by § 502(b)(7).

Suppose, instead, that the debtor in possession wishes to assume Executive's contract, but Executive doesn't want to work for a company that is in bankruptcy. Can the debtor in possession assume the contract if Executive is unwilling? Outside of bankruptcy, Executive could be held to the employment contract. The contract is not specifically enforceable, but Executive could be held liable for damages for refusing to perform or in an appropriate case Corporation might be able to obtain an injunction against Executive's employment by somebody else. But Corporation couldn't assign the contract to a third party without consent of Executive. If Corporation files in bankruptcy are the rights of Executive and Corporation changed? This question is dealt with by § 365(c)(1). Subsection (c)(1)(A) has been amended twice. As originally enacted it read, "applicable law excuses a party, other than the debtor, to such contract or lease from accepting performance from or rendering performance to *the trustee or an assignee of such contract or lease * * *.*" (Emphasis added.) In 1984 the words in italics were changed to "an entity other than the debtor or the debtor in possession or an assignee of such contract or lease." In 1986 "or an assignee of such contract or lease" was deleted from the 1984 version. What were these amendments intended to achieve?

Catapult Entertainment, which follows, interprets the 1986 version of § 365(c)(1)(A) as posing a "hypothetical test." Three other Circuits take this view: *In re West Electronics, Inc.*, 852 F.2d 79 (3d Cir. 1988); *In re Sunterra Corp.*, 361 F.3d 257 (4th Cir. 2004), and *In re James Cable Partners*, 27 F.3d 534 (11th Cir. 1994). The First Circuit adopted the competing "actual test" favored by most bankruptcy courts and commentators in *Summit Investment and Development Corp. v. Leroux*, 69 F.3d 608 (1st Cir. 1995). The Fifth Circuit concurred in *Matter of Mirant Corp.*, 440 F.3d 238 (5th Cir. 2006). BAPCPA failed to clear up this long-running dispute that has such important consequences, particularly in the field of intellectual property.

In re Catapult Entertainment, Inc.

United States Court of Appeals, Ninth Circuit, 1999.
165 F.3d 747.

■ FLETCHER, CIRCUIT JUDGE.

Appellant Stephen Perlman ("Perlman") licensed certain patents to appellee Catapult Entertainment, Inc. ("Catapult"). He now seeks to bar Catapult, which has since become a Chapter 11 debtor in possession, from assuming the patent licenses as part of its reorganization plan. Notwithstanding Perlman's objections, the bankruptcy court approved the assumption of the licenses and confirmed the reorganization plan. The district court affirmed the bankruptcy court on intermediate appeal. Perlman appeals that decision. We are called upon to determine whether, in light of § 365(c)(1) of the Bankruptcy Code, a Chapter 11 debtor in possession may assume certain nonexclusive patent licenses over a licensor's objection. We conclude that the bankruptcy court erred in permitting the debtor in possession to assume the patent licenses in question.

I.

Catapult, a California corporation, was formed in 1994 to create an online gaming network for 16-bit console videogames. That same year, Catapult entered into two license agreements with Perlman, wherein Perlman granted to Catapult the right to exploit certain relevant technologies, including patents and patent applications.

In October 1996, Catapult filed for reorganization under Chapter 11 of the Bankruptcy Code. Shortly before the filing of the bankruptcy petition, Catapult entered into a merger agreement with Mpath Interactive, Inc. ("Mpath"). This agreement contemplated the filing of the bankruptcy petition, followed by a reorganization via a "reverse triangular merger" involving Mpath, MPCAT Acquisition Corporation ("MPCAT"), and Catapult. Under the terms of the merger agreement, MPCAT (a wholly-owned subsidiary of Mpath created for this transaction) would merge into Catapult, leaving Catapult as the surviving entity. When the dust cleared, Catapult's creditors and equity holders would have received approximately $14 million in cash, notes, and securities; Catapult, in turn, would have become a wholly-owned subsidiary of Mpath. The relevant third party creditors and equity holders accepted Catapult's reorganization plan by the majorities required by the Bankruptcy Code.

On October 24, 1996, as part of the reorganization plan, Catapult filed a motion with the bankruptcy court seeking to assume some 140 executory contracts and leases, including the Perlman licenses. Over Perlman's objection, the bankruptcy court granted Catapult's motion and approved the reorganization plan. The district court subsequently affirmed the bankruptcy court. * * * *

II.

Section 365 of the Bankruptcy Code gives a trustee in bankruptcy (or, in a Chapter 11 case, the debtor in possession) the authority to assume, assign, or reject the executory contracts and unexpired leases of the debtor, notwithstanding any contrary provisions appearing in such contracts or leases. See § 365(a) & (f). This extraordinary authority, however, is not absolute. Section 365(c)(1) provides that, notwithstanding the general policy set out in § 365(a):

> **(c)** The trustee may not assume or assign any executory contract or unexpired lease of the debtor, whether or not such contract or lease prohibits or restricts assignment of rights or delegation of duties, if
>
> **(1)(A)** applicable law excuses a party, other than the debtor, to such contract or lease from accepting performance from or rendering performance to an entity other than the debtor or the debtor in possession, whether or not such contract or lease prohibits or restricts assignment of rights or delegation of duties; and
>
> **(B)** such party does not consent to such assumption or assignment. . . ..

Our task, simply put, is to apply this statutory language to the facts at hand and determine whether it prohibits Catapult, as the debtor in possession, from assuming the Perlman licenses without Perlman's consent.

While simply put, our task is not so easily resolved; the proper interpretation of § 365(c)(1) has been the subject of considerable disagreement among courts and commentators. On one side are those who adhere to the plain statutory language, which establishes a so-called "hypothetical test" to govern the assumption of executory contracts. * * * *In re West Elec., Inc.*, 852 F.2d 79, 83 (3d Cir. 1988) * * *. On the other side are those that forsake the statutory language in favor of an "actual test" that, in their view, better accomplishes the intent of Congress. See *Institut Pasteur v. Cambridge Biotech Corp.*, 104 F.3d 489, 493 (1st Cir. 1997). . . .[2] Although we have on two occasions declined to choose between these competing visions, today we hold that we are bound by

---

[2] The weight of lower court authority appears to favor the "actual test." * * * *

the plain terms of the statute and join the Third and Eleventh Circuits in adopting the "hypothetical test."

III.

We begin, as we must, with the statutory language.... The plain language of § 365(c)(1) "link[s] nonassignability under 'applicable law' together with a prohibition on assumption in bankruptcy." 1 DAVID G. EPSTEIN, STEVE H. NICKLES & JAMES J. WHITE, BANKRUPTCY § 5–15 at 474 (1992). In other words, the statute by its terms bars a debtor in possession from *assuming* an executory contract without the nondebtor's consent where applicable law precludes *assignment* of the contract to a third party. The literal language of § 365(c)(1) is thus said to establish a "hypothetical test": a debtor in possession may not assume an executory contract over the nondebtor's objection if applicable law would bar assignment to a hypothetical third party, even where the debtor in possession has no intention of assigning the contract in question to any such third party.

Before applying the statutory language to the case at hand, we first resolve a number of preliminary issues that are either not disputed by the parties, or are so clearly established as to deserve no more than passing reference. First, we follow the lead of the parties in assuming that the Perlman licenses are executory agreements within the meaning of § 365. Second, it is well-established that § 365(c)'s use of the term "trustee" includes Chapter 11 debtors in possession. Third, our precedents make it clear that federal patent law constitutes "applicable law" within the meaning of § 365(c), and that nonexclusive[3] patent licenses are "personal and assignable only with the consent of the licensor." *Everex*, 89 F.3d at 680.

When we have cleared away these preliminary matters, application of the statute to the facts of this case becomes relatively straightforward:

> **(c)** *Catapult* may not assume... the *Perlman licenses*,... if

---

[3] One of the two Perlman licenses began its life as an exclusive license. Perlman in a sworn declaration stated that, pursuant to its terms, the license has since become nonexclusive. Because Catapult has not offered any rebuttal evidence, and because neither party raised the issue in connection with the issues raised in this appeal, we will assume that the Perlman licenses are nonexclusive. Accordingly, we express no opinion regarding the assignability of exclusive patent licenses under federal law, and note that we expressed no opinion on this subject in *Everex*. See *Everex*, 89 F.3d at 679 ("Federal law holds a nonexclusive patent license to be personal and nonassignable....") (emphasis added).

> **(1)(A)** *federal patent* law excuses *Perlman* from accepting performance from or rendering performance to an entity other than *Catapult*. . .; and
>
> **(B)** *Perlman* does not consent to such assumption. . ..

11 U.S.C. § 365(c) (substitutions in italics).

Since federal patent law makes nonexclusive patent licenses personal and nondelegable, § 365(c)(1)(A) is satisfied. Perlman has withheld his consent, thus satisfying § 365(c)(1)(B). Accordingly, the plain language of § 365(c)(1) bars Catapult from assuming the Perlman licenses.

IV.

Catapult urges us to abandon the literal language of § 365(c)(1) in favor of an alternative approach, reasoning that Congress did not intend to bar debtors in possession from assuming their own contracts where no assignment is contemplated. In Catapult's view, § 365(c)(1) should be interpreted as embodying an "actual test": the statute bars assumption by the debtor in possession only where the reorganization in question results in the nondebtor actually having to accept performance from a third party. Under this reading of § 365(c), the debtor in possession would be permitted to assume any executory contract, so long as no assignment was contemplated. Put another way, Catapult suggests that, as to a debtor in possession, § 365(c)(1) should be read to prohibit assumption and assignment, rather than assumption or assignment.

Catapult has marshalled considerable authority to support this reading. The arguments supporting Catapult's position can be divided into three categories: (1) the literal reading creates inconsistencies within § 365; (2) the literal reading is incompatible with the legislative history; and (3) the literal reading flies in the face of sound bankruptcy policy. Nonetheless, we find that none of these considerations justifies departing from the plain language of § 365(c)(1).

A.

Catapult first argues that a literal reading of § 365(c)(1) sets the statute at war with itself and its neighboring provisions. Deviation from the plain language, contends Catapult, is necessary if internal consistency is to be achieved. We agree with Catapult that a court should interpret a statute, if possible, so as to minimize discord among related provisions. *See* 2A NORMAN J. SINGER, SUTHERLAND STATUTORY CONSTRUCTION § 46.06 (5th ed. 1992) ("A statute should be construed so that effect is given to all its provisions, so that no part will be inoperative or superfluous, void or insignificant, and so that one section will not destroy another unless the provision is the result of obvious mistake or error."). However, the dire inconsistencies cited by Catapult turn out, on closer analysis, to be no such thing.

Catapult, for example, singles out the interaction between § 365(c)(1) and § 365(f)(1) as a statutory trouble spot. *See In re Catron*, 158 B.R. at 636 (exploring apparent conflict between subsections (c)(1) and (f)(1)); *In re Cardinal Indus.*, 116 B.R. at 976–77 (same). Subsection (f)(1) provides that executory contracts, once assumed, may be assigned notwithstanding any contrary provisions contained in the contract *or applicable law*:

> **(f)(1)** Except as provided in subsection **(c)** of this section, notwithstanding a provision in an executory contract or unexpired lease of the debtor, *or in applicable law*, that prohibits, restricts, or conditions the assignment of such contract or lease, the trustee may assign such contract or lease under paragraph **(2)** of this subsection. . . .

§ 365(f)(1) (emphasis added).

The potential conflict between subsections (c)(1) and (f)(1) arises from their respective treatments of "applicable law." The plain language of subsection (c)(1) bars assumption (absent consent) whenever "applicable law" would bar assignment. Subsection (f)(1) states that, *contrary provisions in applicable law notwithstanding*, executory contracts may be assigned. Since assumption is a necessary prerequisite to assignment under § 365, see § 365(f)(2)(A), a literal reading of subsection (c)(1) appears to render subsection (f)(1) superfluous. In the words of the Sixth Circuit, "[S]ection 365(c), the recognized exception to 365(f), appears at first to resuscitate in full the very anti-assignment 'applicable law' which 365(f) nullifies." *In re Magness*, 972 F.2d 689, 695 (6th Cir. 1992) (Guy, J., concurring). Faced with this dilemma, one district court reluctantly concluded that the "[c]onflict between subsections (c) and (f) of § 365 is inescapable." *See In re Catron*, 158 B.R. at 636.

Subsequent authority, however, suggests that this conclusion may have been unduly pessimistic. The Sixth Circuit has credibly reconciled the warring provisions by noting that "each subsection recognizes an 'applicable law' of markedly different scope." Subsection (f)(1) states the broad rule–a law that, as a general matter, "prohibits, restricts, or conditions the assignment" of executory contracts is trumped by the provisions of subsection (f)(1). Subsection (c)(1), however, states a carefully crafted exception to the broad rule–where applicable law does not merely recite a general ban on assignment, but instead more specifically "excuses a party. . . from accepting performance from or rendering performance to an entity" different from the one with which the party originally contracted, the applicable law prevails over subsection (f)(1). In other words, in determining whether an "applicable law" stands or falls under § 365(f)(1), a court must ask why the "applicable law" prohibits assignment. Only if the law prohibits assignment on the rationale that the identity of the contracting party is material to the agreement will subsection (c)(1) rescue it.[4] We agree with the Sixth and Eleventh Circuits that a literal reading of subsection (c)(1) does not inevitably set it at odds with subsection (f)(1).

Catapult next focuses on the internal structure of § 365(c)(1) itself. According to Catapult, the literal approach to subsection (c)(1) renders the phrase "or the debtor in possession" contained in § 365(c)(1)(A) superfluous.[5] In the words of one bankruptcy court, "[i]f the directive of Section 365(c)(1) is to prohibit assumption whenever applicable law excuses performance relative to any entity other than the debtor, why add the words 'or debtor in possession?' The [hypothetical] test renders this phrase surplusage." *In re Hartec*, 117 B.R. at 871–72.

A close reading of § 365(c)(1), however, dispels this notion. By its terms, subsection (c)(1) addresses two conceptually distinct events: assumption and assignment. The plain language of the provision makes it clear that each of these events is contingent on the nondebtor's separate consent. Consequently, where a nondebtor consents to the assumption of an executory contract, subsection (c)(1) will have to be applied a second time if the debtor in possession wishes to assign the contract in question. On that second application, the relevant question would be whether "applicable law excuses a party from accepting performance from or rendering performance to an entity other than. . . *the debtor in possession*." § 365(c)(1)(A) (emphasis added). Consequently, the phrase "debtor in possession," far from being rendered superfluous by a literal reading of subsection (c)(1), dovetails neatly with the disjunctive language that opens subsection (c)(1): "The trustee may not assume *or* assign. . . ." § 365(c) (emphasis added); *cf. In re Catron*, 158 B.R. at 636 (rejecting argument that

---

[4] We note that, in the instant case, the federal law principle against the assignability of nonexclusive patent licenses is rooted in the personal nature of a nonexclusive license–the identity of a licensee may matter a great deal to a licensor. See In re CFLC, 89 F.3d at 679 (explaining rationale behind federal law rule against assignability).

[5] The phrase in question was added by Congress in 1984, replacing an earlier formulation focusing on the "trustee or an assignee":

> (1)(A) applicable law excuses a party, other than the debtor, to such contract or lease from accepting performance from or rendering performance to an entity other than the trustee or an assignee of such contract or lease *the debtor or the debtor in possession*, whether or not such contract or lease prohibits or restricts assignment of rights or delegation of duties.

§ 365(c)(1)(A) (prior language stricken through).

literal reading of § 365(c) makes "or assign" superfluous insofar as assumption is a prerequisite to assignment).

A third potential inconsistency identified by Catapult relates to § 365(c)(2). According to Catapult, a literal reading of subsection (c)(1) renders subsection (c)(2) a dead letter. Subsection (c)(2) provides:

> **(c)** The trustee may not assume or assign any executory contract or unexpired lease of the debtor, whether or not such contract or lease prohibits or restricts assignment of rights or delegation of duties, if
>
>> **(2)** such contract is a contract to make a loan, or extend other debt financing or financial accommodations, to or for the benefit of the debtor, or to issue a security of the debtor. . . .

§ 365(c)(2). According to Catapult, the contracts encompassed by subsection (c)(2) are all nonassignable as a matter of applicable state law. As a result, a literal reading of subsection (c)(1) would seem to snare and dispose of every executory contract within subsection (c)(2)'s scope. Perlman, however, persuasively rebuts this argument, noting that even if the state law governing the assignability of loan agreements and financing contracts is relatively uniform today, Congress by enacting subsection (c)(2) cemented nationwide uniformity in the bankruptcy context, effectively ensuring creditors that these particular contracts would not be assumable in bankruptcy. Put another way, it is the national uniformity of applicable state law that has rendered subsection (c)(2) superfluous, not the terms of subsection (c)(1).

In any event, subsection (c)(1) does not completely swallow up subsection (c)(2). Subsection (c)(1) by its terms permits assumption and assignment of executory loan agreements *so long as the nondebtor consents.* See § 365(c)(1)(B). Subsection (c)(2), in contrast, bans assumption and assignment of such agreements, *consent of the nondebtor notwithstanding. See Transamerica Commercial Fin. Corp. v. Citibank, N.A. (In re Sun Runner Marine, Inc.),* 945 F.2d 1089, 1093 (9th Cir. 1991) ("Section 365(c)(2) unambiguously prohibits the assumption of financial accommodation contracts, regardless of the consent of the non-debtor party."); 2 WILLIAM L. NORTON, JR., NORTON BANKRUPTCY LAW AND PRACTICE 2D § 39:19 ("[T]he correct view is that executory credit contracts may not be assumed in bankruptcy regardless of the desires of the parties."). Accordingly, contrary to Catapult's assertion, subsection (c)(1) does not necessarily catch upriver all the fish that would otherwise be netted by subsection (c)(2). Once again, the "inconsistency" identified by Catapult proves evanescent under close scrutiny. We see no reason why these two provisions cannot happily coexist.[6]

We conclude that the claimed inconsistencies are not actual and that the plain language of § 365(c)(1) compels the result Perlman urges: Catapult may not assume the Perlman licenses over Perlman's objection. Catapult has not demonstrated that, in according the words of subsection (c)(1) their plain meaning, we do violence to subsection (c)(1) or the provisions that accompany it.

B.

Catapult next urges that legislative history requires disregard of the plain language of § 365(c)(1). First off, because we discern no ambiguity in the plain statutory language, we need not resort to legislative history.

We will depart from this rule, if at all, only where the legislative history clearly indicates that Congress meant something other than what it said. Here, the legislative history unearthed by Catapult falls far short of this mark. The legislative history behind § 365(c) was exhaustively analyzed by the bankruptcy court in *In re Cardinal Industries*, 116 B.R. at 978–80. Its discussion makes it clear that there exists no contemporaneous legislative history regarding the current formulation of subsection (c)(1). *Id.* at 978 ("[T]here is no authoritative legislative history for BAFJA as enacted in 1984."). Catapult, however, argues that the language as ultimately enacted in 1984 had its genesis in a 1980 House amendment to an earlier Senate technical corrections bill. The amendment was accompanied by "a relatively obscure committee report." 1 DAVID G. EPSTEIN, STEVE H. NICKLES & JAMES J. WHITE, BANKRUPTCY § 5–15 (1992). In explaining the amendment, the report stated:

> This amendment makes it clear that the prohibition against a trustee's power to assume an executory contract does not apply where it is the debtor that is in possession and the performance to be given or received under a personal service contract will be the same as if no petition had been filed because of the personal service nature of the contract.

In re Cardinal Indus., 116 B.R. at 979 (quoting H.R.Rep. No. 1195, 96th Cong., 2d Sess. § 27(b) (1980)). However, since the report relates to a different

---

[6] Catapult also advances what it claims is a fourth inconsistency by contrasting the plain language of § 365(c)(1) with the provisions of § 365(e)(1), which nullifies "ipso facto" clauses. In rejecting this contention, it is enough to note that § 365(e)(2)(A) expressly revives "ipso facto" clauses in precisely the same executory contracts that fall within the scope of § 365(c)(1).

proposed bill, predates enactment of § 365(c)(1) by several years, and expresses at most the thoughts of only one committee in the House, we are not inclined to view it as the sort of clear indication of contrary intent that would overcome the unambiguous language of subsection (c)(1).

C.

Catapult makes the appealing argument that, as a leading bankruptcy commentator has pointed out, there are policy reasons to prefer the "actual test." See 3 LAWRENCE P. KING, COLLIER ON BANKRUPTCY § 365.06[1][d][iii] (15th ed. revised) (arguing that sound bankruptcy policy supports the actual test). That may be so, but Congress is the policy maker, not the courts.

Policy arguments cannot displace the plain language of the statute; that the plain language of § 365(c)(1) may be bad policy does not justify a judicial rewrite. And a rewrite is precisely what the actual test requires. The statute expressly provides that a debtor in possession "may not assume *or* assign" an executory contract where applicable law bars assignment and the nondebtor objects. § 365(c)(1) (emphasis added). The actual test effectively engrafts a narrow exception onto § 365(c)(1) for debtors in possession, providing that, as to them, the statute only prohibits assumption and assignment, as opposed to assumption or assignment. *See In re Fastrax*, 129 B.R. at 277 (admitting that, by adopting the actual test, the court reads the word "assume" out of subsection (c) with respect to debtors in possession).

V.

Because the statute speaks clearly, and its plain language does not produce a patently absurd result or contravene any clear legislative history, we must "hold Congress to its words." Accordingly, we hold that, where applicable nonbankruptcy law makes an executory contract nonassignable because the identity of the nondebtor party is material, a debtor in possession may not assume the contract absent consent of the nondebtor party. A straightforward application of § 365(c)(1) to the circumstances of this case precludes Catapult from assuming the Perlman licenses over Perlman's objection. Consequently, the bankruptcy court erred when it approved Catapult's motion to assume the Perlman licenses, and the district court erred in affirming the bankruptcy court.

REVERSED.

NOTES

1. Consider the following passages from Daniel J. Bussel and Edward A. Friedler, *The Limits on Assuming and Assigning Executory Contracts*, 74 Am. Bankr. L.J. 321 (2000):

Section 365 gets off on the wrong foot by equating assumption and assignment notwithstanding sharp policy distinctions between the two. Assumption involves performance of the agreement by and to the bankruptcy estate. Assignment involves performance by and to a third party and a release of the bankruptcy estate from further liability. Assignment does not merely substitute the bankruptcy estate as a successor to the prebankruptcy debtor–it allows the bankruptcy estate greater rights than those held by the prebankruptcy debtor, that is, the additional right to assign an otherwise nonassignable agreement. Yet § 365 appears to authorize assignment and limit assumption as if the two involved the same balance of interests. Most bankruptcy courts and a few higher courts have sought to repair the damage by decoupling the two, finding that a nonassignable contract outside of bankruptcy was nonassumable only where under the particular circumstances the assumption would amount to a forbidden assignment under otherwise applicable law. This "actual test" yields correct results from the point of view of bankruptcy policy and allows results in bankruptcy to effectively mirror the results outside of bankruptcy.

But most courts of appeals have followed the literal language of § 365(c) to the conclusion that the bankruptcy estate loses the rights of the prebankruptcy debtor to valuable contracts that would not be assignable under otherwise applicable law even when no assignment is contemplated, and the nondebtor party to the contract, under nonbankruptcy law, could not refuse the performance that is actually offered. Under this "hypothetical test" contracts governed by § 365(c)(1) become one of the very few instances where the debtor's valuable rights against nondebtors are legally forfeited simply because of a bankruptcy filing. This kind of forfeiture is generally inconsistent with current bankruptcy policy as indicated by provisions invalidating the *ipso facto* or "bankruptcy default" clauses that commonly resulted in such forfeitures under the Bankruptcy Act of 1898. §§ 365(e)(1), 541(c)(1) and 545(1).

* * *

[The] hypothetical test flies in the face of (i) the pro-reorganization policy of the Code, (ii) the policy that bankruptcy entitlements should generally mirror nonbankruptcy entitlements subject to the exigencies of the collective bankruptcy proceeding itself, and (iii) principles favoring equal treatment of creditors with similar nonbankruptcy law entitlements. It could not be what the Congress that enacted the Bankruptcy Reform Act of 1978 and the two subsequent amendments to § 365(c)(1) intended.

* * *

Most nonbankruptcy law regulating assignment of contract rights does not flatly prohibit or authorize assignment. Only a few types of contracts are always, or never, assignable under nonbankruptcy law. Contracts governed by nonbankruptcy law that does not flatly prohibit assignment cannot fit within the framework of the hypothetical test because it is impossible to know in the abstract whether or not such an agreement is assignable under otherwise applicable law. The answer otherwise applicable law gives to the question "Is it assignable?" is "It depends upon particular facts and circumstances." In order to determine if a contract could be assigned to some hypothetical third party under an applicable law that allows assignment under certain conditions, it is necessary to know whether the proposed assignee meets those conditions. If there is no proposed assignee, this is impossible to do and the hypothetical test completely breaks down. The literal "hypothetical" construction of § 365(c) when applied to contracts assignable only under particular circumstances is simply incoherent. Only contracts subject to a flat ban on assignment fail the § 365(c) test whether construed literally as a hypothetical test or as an actual test.

* * *

[T]he purpose of § 365(c)(1) is to simply preserve the nonbankruptcy law consent requirement in the few instances that nonbankruptcy law requires consent as a condition to assignment, and not to impose an independent and higher bankruptcy law bar to assumption or assignment. Given the function of § 365(c)(1), and its relationship to § 365(f), it is error to construe § 365(c)(1) to preclude assumption of an executory contract by a Chapter 11 debtor in possession. . . .. There is no nonbankruptcy law that requires express consent to the continued performance or receipt of performance of the original contracting party. Section 365(c)(1) simply has no application in the case of assumption of an executory contract or lease by the debtor in possession.

Two Supreme Court Justices have recently expressed interest in resolving the division in authorities over this issue. *N.C.P. Marketing Group, Inc. v. Big Star Productions, Inc.*, 129 S.Ct. 1577 (2009) (on certiorari) (statement of Justices Kennedy and Breyer in connection with denial of certiorari).

2. Even if the "actual test" rejected in *Catapult Entertainment* is the correct interpretation of § 365(c)(1), non-debtor parties to contracts that fall under § 365(c)(1) have argued that they are entitled to enforce ipso facto clauses in such agreements. These ipso facto clauses are extremely common and they provide that the contract is terminated upon the bankruptcy of a party to the agreement. The effect of accepting this argument is equivalent to denying the debtor-in-possession the right to assume the contract—it frees the non-debtor party from any obligation to perform for or accept performance from the debtor in the event of bankruptcy. Non-debtors argue that even if § 365(c)(1) imposes an "actual test," the plain language of § 365(e)(2), which is an exception to the general rule that such ipso facto clauses are invalid in bankruptcy, imposes a *Catapult Entertainment*-style "hypothetical test." Originally, § 365(c)(1) and § 365(e)(2) were strictly parallel, the apparent notion being that there would be no harm in allowing an ipso facto clause to operate in the case of a contract that could not be assumed without the consent of the non-debtor pursuant to § 365(c)(1). In 1984 and 1986 when Congress amended § 365(c)(1) in the manner described in the introductory note before *Catapult Entertainment* and arguably created the textual basis for the "actual test" interpretation of § 365(c)(1), § 365(e)(2) was left untouched. The language of the two sections is therefore no longer parallel and to the extent that the "actual test" interpretation of § 365(c)(1) critically depends upon the 1984 and 1986 amendments, the "actual test" may not apply to § 365(e)(2). In *Summit Investment and Development Corp. v. Leroux*, 69 F.3d 608 (1st Cir. 1995), the Court in an opinion by Judge Cyr (a former bankruptcy judge) nevertheless found that § 365(c) and § 365(e) were necessarily parallel in scope and were both properly construed as imposing an "actual test":

> Given the interrelated concerns addressed by sections 365(c) and 365(e)(2), however, we think Congress contemplated in 1984 that section 365(e)(2) would permit a debtor or a debtor in possession to avoid *automatic termination* of his executory contract rights under the section 365(e)(2)(A) exception. Were this not so, an absurd result would eventuate: there would be no contractual right left for a debtor or debtor in possession to *assume* under section 365(c)(1) because it would already have been terminated automatically under section 365(e). * * *

3. Under contract law an assignor remains liable on the assigned contract or lease unless the non-assigning party consents to a release. This rule of contract law is preempted by the Bankruptcy Code–§ 365(k) provides that assignment relieves the trustee and the estate from any liability occurring after assignment. The non-assigning party finds protection in the requirement under § 365(f)(2) that a contract or lease may be assigned only if the debtor assumes the contract or lease and the assignee provides adequate assurance of future performance, whether or not the contract or lease is in default.

Section 365(b)(1) precludes a debtor from assuming an executory contract or lease in default until the debtor has cured the default or provided adequate assurance that it will promptly do so. Certain kinds of defaults are excepted from the cure requirement by § 365(b)(2). The most important of these are those stemming from "bankruptcy clauses" or "ipso facto" clauses which declare the debtor in default upon filing in bankruptcy. These clauses are rendered inoperative by § 365(b)(2)(A)-(C) and (e)(1).

Under the 1994 version of § 365(b)(2), the cure condition to assumption did not apply to a default that is a breach of a provision relating to

> **(D)** the satisfaction of any penalty rate or provision relating to a default arising from any failure by the debtor to perform nonmonetary obligations under the executory contract or unexpired lease.

This provision might have been viewed as intended to make it easier for debtors to assume contracts and leases by resolving two separate issues. First, contracts and leases often provide for a higher rate of interest after a default; under (D) debtors can cure without paying the default rate. Second, there may be defaults in the performance of nonmonetary obligations that may be impossible to cure; under (D) no cure of these defaults is required. *Collier on Bankruptcy* ¶ 365.05[4] (15th ed. rev. 2008). However, the first authoritative decision on this provision, *In re Claremont Acquisition Corp., Inc.*, 113 F.3d 1029 (9th Cir. 1997), rejected this broad interpretation and held that (D) is limited to excusing debtors from having to pay penalties. The court reached this result by holding that "penalty" modified both "rate" and "provision"; hence, the debtor is excused from curing defaults of nonmonetary obligations only to the extent of penalties that the contract imposes for the default. An example would be a clause calling for the payment of a specified sum as a penalty for breach of a nonmonetary obligation.

The severe consequences of this holding are seen in *Claremont* which involved an attempt on the part of Debtor, an auto dealer, to assume and assign a General Motors franchise. The GM dealer agreement contained a provision terminating a franchise for failure to operate the business for seven consecutive days; Debtor had failed to operate the dealership for two weeks prior to filing. The District Court held that this was a nonmonetary obligation which need not be cured under § 365(b)(2)(D). The Ninth Circuit, in the belief that this provision was intended by Congress only to relieve debtors of obligations to pay penalties, held (i) Debtor was not excused from its obligation to cure because the exception in (D) did not apply to Debtor's default; and (ii) since the default could not be cured, the contract could not be assumed and assigned. *See* Charles Jordan Tabb, *The Law of Bankruptcy* 614–615 (1997) (discussing the consequences of an incurable default). The *Claremont* holding is particularly devastating for debtors who had leased their places of business under long-term commercial leases which commonly provide for lease termination whenever the tenant ceases operation (in the vernacular, "goes dark") at the leased premises.

BAPCPA codified *Claremont* by adding "penalty" before "provision." But the amended version of § 365(b)(1)(A) carves out an important exception with respect to unexpired real property leases: the trustee need not cure defaults that relate to breach of nonmonetary obligations in real property leases if it is impossible to do so. However, the trustee must begin performing all nonmonetary obligations under the lease at or after the time of assumption. Moreover, if a lessor of nonresidential real property suffers any pecuniary losses as a result of the debtor's failure to perform its nonmonetary obligations under the lease, these losses must be compensated as part of the cure. The effect of these two amendments is to reverse *Claremont* as to real property leases but to uphold its result as to personal property leases and executory contracts other than unexpired leases of real property. Under § 365(b)(2)(D), those debtors with personal property leases and other executory contracts may not be permitted to assume and assign their agreements if they have committed an incurable nonmonetary default.

b. Assignment

Subsections 365(c) and (f) read like Joseph Heller's *Catch–22*. Subsection (f) seems to embody a special bankruptcy "pro-assignment" policy. Section 365(f)(1) allows the trustee to assign an executory contract notwithstanding a provision in the contract or in "applicable law" prohibiting the assignment. But a contract cannot be assigned unless it has been assumed. § 365(f)(2)(A). And what kind of contracts cannot be assumed? Those which "applicable law" makes non-assignable. In short, the debtor can assign non-assignable agreements, but only if it can assume them—which it cannot if they are non-assignable. Both provisions refer to "applicable law" that may prohibit assignment without consent of both parties to the contract. Section 365(c)(1) says that the "applicable law" is controlling while § 365(f)(1) allows assignment notwithstanding that law. Since § 365(c)(1) controls § 365(f)(1) there is great confusion concerning the meaning of § 365(f)(1).

Pioneer Ford, which follows, interprets § 365(c)(1)(A) as originally enacted. It also discusses the relationship between § 365(c)(1)(A) and § 365(f)(1) and how they can be harmonized.

In re Pioneer Ford Sales, Inc.
United States Court of Appeals, First Circuit, 1984.
729 F.2d 27.

■ BREYER, Circuit Judge.

The Ford Motor Company appeals a federal district court decision allowing a bankrupt Ford dealer (Pioneer Ford Sales, Inc.) to assign its Ford franchise over Ford's objection to a Toyota dealer (Toyota Village, Inc.). The district court decided the case on the basis of a record developed in the bankruptcy court. The bankruptcy court had approved the transfer, which ran from Pioneer to Fleet National Bank (Pioneer's principal secured creditor) and then to Toyota Village. Fleet sought authorization for the assignment because Toyota Village will pay $10,000 for the franchise and buy all parts and accessories in Pioneer's inventory at fair market value (about $75,000); if the franchise is not assigned, Ford will buy only some of the parts for between $45,000 and $55,000. Thus, the assignment will increase the value of the estate. Fleet is the appellee here.

The issue that the case raises is the proper application of § 365(c)(1)(A), an exception to a more general provision, § 365(f)(1), that allows a trustee in bankruptcy (or a debtor in possession) to assign many of the debtor's executory contracts even if the contract itself says that it forbids assignment. The exception at issue reads as follows:

> **(c)** The trustee [or debtor in possession] may not assume or assign an executory contract * * * of the debtor, whether or not such contract * * * prohibits assignment if—
>
> **(1)(A)** applicable law excuses [the other party to the contract] from accepting performance from * * * an assignee * * * whether or not [the] * * * contract * * * prohibits * * * assignment.

The words "applicable law" in this section mean "applicable non-bankruptcy law." * * * Evidently, the theory of this section is to prevent the trustee from assigning (over objection) contracts of the sort that contract law ordinarily makes nonassignable, i.e. contracts that cannot be assigned when the contract itself is silent about assignment. At the same time, by using the words in (1)(A) "whether *or not* the contract prohibits assignment," the section prevents parties from using contractual language to prevent the trustee from assigning contracts that (when the contract is silent) contract law typically makes assignable. Id. Thus, we must look to see whether relevant nonbankruptcy law would allow Ford to veto the assignment of its basic franchise contract "whether or not" that basic franchise contract itself specifically "prohibits assignment."

The nonbankruptcy law to which both sides point us is contained in Rhode Island's "Regulation of Business Practices Among Motor Vehicle Manufacturers, Distributors and Dealers" Act, R.I.Gen.Laws § 31-5.1-4(C)(7). It states that

> [N]o dealer * * * shall have the right to * * * assign the franchise * * * without the consent of the manufacturer, except that such consent shall not be unreasonably withheld.

The statute by its terms, allows a manufacturer to veto an assignment where the veto is reasonable but not otherwise. The statute's language also indicates that it applies "whether or not" the franchise contract itself restricts assignment. Thus, the basic question that the case presents is whether Ford's veto was reasonable in terms of the Rhode Island law.

Neither the district court nor the bankruptcy court specifically addressed this question. Their failure apparently arose out of their belief that § 365(c)(1)(A) refers only to traditional personal service contracts. But in our view they were mistaken. The language of the section does not limit its effect to personal service contracts. It refers generally to contracts that are not assignable under nonbankruptcy law. State laws typically make contracts for personal services nonassignable (where the contract itself is silent); but they make other sorts of contracts nonassignable as well. *See, e.g.*, N.Y. State Finance Law § 138 (1974) (making certain government contracts unassignable); N.Y. General Municipal Law § 109 (1977) (same); N.C.Gen.Stat. § 147–62 (1978) (same). The legislative history of § 365(c) says nothing about "personal services." To the contrary, it speaks of letters of credit, personal loans, and leases—instances in which assigning a contract may place the other party at a significant disadvantage. The history thereby suggests that (c)(1)(A) has a broader reach.

The source of the "personal services" limitation apparently is a bankruptcy court case, *In re Taylor Manufacturing, Inc.*, 6 B.R. 370 (Bankr.N.D. Ga.1980), which other bankruptcy courts have followed. The *Taylor* court wrote that (c)(1)(A) should be interpreted narrowly, in part because it believed that (c)(1)(A) conflicted with another section, (f)(1), which states in relevant part:

> Except as provided in subsection (c) * * *, notwithstanding a provision * * * in applicable law that prohibits * * * the assignment of [an executory] contract * * * the trustee may assign [it] * * *.

As a matter of logic, however, we see no conflict, for (c)(1)(A) refers to state laws that prohibit assignment "whether or not" the contract is silent, while (f)(1) contains no such limitation. Apparently (f)(1) includes state laws that prohibit assignment only when the contract is *not* silent about assignment; that is to say, state laws that enforce contract provisions prohibiting assignment. *See* 1 Norton, Bankruptcy Law and Practice § 23.14. These state laws are to be ignored. The section specifically excepts (c)(1)(A)'s state laws that forbid assignment even when the contract *is* silent; they are to be heeded. Regardless, we fail to see why a "conflict" suggests that (c)(1)(A) is limited to "personal services."

The *Taylor* court cites 2 Collier on Bankruptcy § 365.05 and the Commission Report, H.R.Doc. No. 93–137, 93rd Cong., 1st Sess. 199 (1973), in support. Both of these sources speak of personal services. However, they do not say that (c)(1)(A), was intended to be *limited* to personal services. Indeed, since it often is difficult to decide whether or not a particular duty can be characterized by the label "personal service," it makes sense to avoid this question and simply look to see whether state law would, or would not, make the duty assignable where the contract is silent. Thus, the Fifth Circuit has found no reason for limiting the scope of (c)(1)(A) to personal service contracts. *In re Braniff Airways, Inc.*, 700 F.2d 935, 943 (5th Cir. 1983). Fleet concedes in its brief that "the exception to assignment [of § 365(c)(1)(A)] is not limited to personal services contracts." We therefore reject the district court's conclusion in this respect.

Although the district court did not explicitly decide whether Ford's veto was reasonable, it decided a closely related question. Under other provisions of § 365 a bankruptcy court cannot authorize assignment of an executory contract if 1) the debtor is in default, unless 2) there is "adequate assurance of future performance," § 365(b)(1)(C). Pioneer is in default, but the bankruptcy and district courts found "adequate assurance." For the sake of argument, we shall assume that this finding is equivalent to a finding that Ford's veto of the assignment was unreasonable. And, we shall apply a "clearly erroneous" standard in reviewing the factual element in this lower court finding. Fed.R.Civ.P. 52. On these assumptions, favorable to Fleet, we nonetheless must reverse the district court, for, in our view, any finding of unreasonableness, based on this record, is clearly erroneous.

Our review of the record reveals the following critical facts. First, in accordance with its ordinary business practice and dealer guidelines incorporated into the franchise agreement, Ford would have required Toyota Village, as a dealer, to have a working capital of at least $172,000, of which no more than half could be debt. Toyota Village, however, had a working capital at the end of 1981 of $37,610; and its net worth was $31,747. Although the attorney for Fleet at one point in the bankruptcy proceedings said Toyota Village could borrow some of the necessary capital from a bank, he made no later reference to the point, nor did he ever specifically state how much Toyota Village could borrow. Since the tax returns of Toyota Village's owner showed gross income of $27,500 for 1981, there is no reason to believe that the owner could readily find the necessary equity capital.

Second, at a time when Japanese cars have sold well throughout the United States, Toyota Village has consistently lost money. * * *

At the same time, the record contains no significant evidence tending to refute the natural inference arising from these facts. The bankruptcy court mentioned five factors that it said showed that Toyota Village gave "adequate assurance" that it could do the job.

(1) Toyota Village was an established dealership.

(2) Toyota Village was "located within 500 yards of the present Ford dealership."

(3) Toyota Village had a proven track record for selling cars.

(4) Toyota Village was willing and able to pay $15,000 that Pioneer still owed Ford.

(5) The owner and sole stockholder of Toyota Village testified that he was willing and able to fulfill the franchise agreement.

The first of these factors (dealer experience), while favoring Toyota Village, is weak, given the record of continuous dealership losses. The second (location) proves little, considering that Pioneer went bankrupt at the very spot. The third (track record) cuts against Toyota Village, not in its favor, for its track record is one of financial loss. The fourth (willingness to pay a $15,000 debt that Pioneer owed Ford) is relevant, but it shows, at most, that Toyota Village *believed* it could make a success of the franchise. The fifth (ability to act as franchisee) is supported by no more than a simple statement by the owner of Toyota Village that he could do the job.

We do not see how the few positive features about Toyota Village that the record reveals can overcome the problem of a history of losses and failure to meet Ford's capital requirements. In these circumstances, Ford would seem perfectly reasonable in withholding its consent to the transfer. Thus, Rhode Island law would make the franchise unassignable.

* * *

One might still argue that under Rhode Island law the only "reasonable" course of action for Ford is to allow the transfer and then simply terminate Toyota Village if it fails to perform adequately. This suggestion, however, overlooks the legal difficulties that Ford would have in proving cause for termination under the Rhode Island "Regulation of Business Practices Among Motor Vehicle Manufacturers, Distributors and Dealers" Act. R.I.Gen.Laws § 31–5.1–4(D)(2). The very purpose of the statute—protecting dealer reliance—suggests that it ought to be more difficult for a manufacturer to terminate a dealer who has invested in a franchise than to oppose the grant of a franchise to one who has not. In any event, the law does not suggest a manufacturer is "unreasonable" in objecting to a transfer unless he would have "good cause" to terminate the transferee. And, to equate the two standards would tend to make the "unreasonable" provision superfluous. Thus, we conclude that the Rhode Island law would make the franchise unassignable on the facts here revealed. Therefore, neither the bankruptcy court nor the district court had the power to authorize the transfer.

* * *

For these reasons, the judgment of the district court is
Reversed.

NOTES

1. The result in this case is full of irony. Surely the relevant Rhode Island statute was enacted to protect auto dealers from onerous anti-assignment provisions imposed by manufacturers in their agreements. It is a pro-assignment statute. And yet because the legislature acted to limit contractual anti-assignment clauses in these franchise agreements, the franchise in *Pioneer Ford* is rendered non-assignable. Had there been no such statute then any anti-assignment clause in the agreement would have been unenforceable in toto.

2. Section 365 is ambiguous on the assignability of otherwise non-assignable contracts in bankruptcy. Under § 365(f)(1) the trustee may assign an executory contract "notwithstanding a provision * * * in applicable law, that prohibits, restricts, or conditions the assignment * * *." Subsection (f)(1) is subject to subsection (c) which states that the trustee may not assign if "applicable law excuses a party, other than the debtor, * * * from accepting performance from or rendering performance to * * * an entity other than the debtor or the debtor in possession." This suggests that there are some contracts that are nonassignable under nonbankruptcy law that can be assigned in bankruptcy in spite of that law (§ 365(f)(1)) and some contracts that are nonassignable under nonbankruptcy law that can't be assigned in bankruptcy. § 365(c)(1)(A). This was the basis of the lower court's conclusion in *Pioneer Ford* that § 365(c)(1)(A) was meant to apply only to personal service contracts and that all other contracts nonassignable under nonbankruptcy law fall under § 365(f)(1).

On appeal, the First Circuit harmonized the two provisions in a different way. It held that (c)(1)(A) applies to cases in which the nonbankruptcy law forbids assignment regardless of whether the contract specifically forbids assignment, while (f)(1) applies to cases in which assignment is prohibited only because the nonbankruptcy law enforces a contract provision that specifically forbids assignment. In other words some contracts, such as personal service contracts, are nonassignable regardless of whether the contract specifically forbids assignment. They cannot be assigned in bankruptcy. A contract such as the nonexclusive patent license in *Catapult Entertainment* falls in this category because assignment without approval of the licensor is forbidden by federal patent law. Other contracts are nonassignable only if the contract specifically forbids assignment. They can be assigned in bankruptcy. The basis of this analysis is the presence in § 365(c) of the phrase "whether or not such contract

*** prohibits or restricts assignment" and the absence of that phrase in subsection (f)(1). In *Pioneer Ford,* (c)(1)(A) applied because the Rhode Island statute prevented assignment without consent of Ford Motor Company regardless of what the contract provided.

3. The *Pioneer Ford* reconciliation of § 365(c) and (f) is criticized in Daniel J. Bussel & Edward A. Friedler, *The Limits on Assuming and Assigning Executory Contracts*, 74 Am. Bankr. L.J. 321 (2000):

> While *Pioneer Ford*'s reconciliation of subsections (c) and (f) parses the statute cleverly, the policy and legislative intent supporting such a distinction are either obscure or nonexistent. *Pioneer Ford* invites state legislatures to override bankruptcy's pro-assignment policy to protect favored constituencies, thereby undermining the uniformity and coherence of federal bankruptcy law on an *ad hoc* and state-by-state basis. And from the perspective of nonbankruptcy policy, there is no apparent justification for giving priority to statutory restrictions on assignment over bargained-for restrictions on assignment that would be clearly enforceable under otherwise applicable law. Nonbankruptcy policy does not give greater weight to statutory restrictions on alienation than to contractual restrictions. Indeed, under state law parties can almost always override statutory restrictions on alienation by agreement.
>
> The court in *In re Magness*, 972 F.2d 689 (6th Cir. 1992), states that *Pioneer Ford* erred in limiting § 365(f) to cases in which there are contractual provisions prohibiting assignment. "There is simply nothing in the language of § 365(f) which supports the limitation read into it by that court." 972 F.2d at 695. If *Pioneer Ford* narrowed the scope of "applicable law" in § 365(f), *Magness* appeared to narrow the scope of these words in § 365(c) to situations in which the common law would permit the nondebtor party to refuse to accept performance from a proposed assignee, even in the absence of an express anti-assignment agreement. *Magness* held a Chapter 7 debtor's "golf membership" in a country club to be nonassignable as a "personal contract" under Ohio common law. The judge writing the majority opinion (a respected former law school dean who was an avid golfer) rhapsodized on the unique relationship created by golf club memberships. Quieting any possible reservations we might have had on the issue, he stated that the memberships "were not in any way commercial" (gulp) and "[t]hey create personal relationships among individuals who play golf, who are waiting to play golf, who eat together, swim and play together." 972 F.2d at 696. To allow a trustee in bankruptcy to confer this idyllic status on the highest bidder was unthinkable, even though no riff-raff need apply because under club rules no one could become a golf member without being a social (nongolf) club member.

Bussel and Friedler, *supra*, reject the holding and reasoning of *Pioneer Ford*. They argue that nonbankruptcy law restrictions on assignment fall into four categories, and that § 365(f) overrides such restrictions in all but those instances where the restriction forbids all assignments without the consent of the nondebtor party:

Accordingly, under modern law, there are virtually no absolute prohibitions on assignment of contract rights. A few contract rights are conclusively presumed assignable (the first category). Most other contract rights are rebuttably presumed assignable, that is they are assignable unless the party resisting assignment can point to valid contractual restrictions or partial statutory or common law restrictions on assignment that apply under the circumstances of the particular case (the second and third categories). These contracts are "somewhat assignable." In a few instances, however, there are contract rights that are presumed nonassignable absent the express consent on the non-assigning party (the fourth category).

Section 365(c)(1) is directed at preserving the consent requirement for the fourth category of contract rights. Section 365(f) overrides otherwise applicable law restricting assignment for the second and third categories. If the assignor is in bankruptcy, the protection for the non-assigning party against material alteration of rights or duties is found in the requirement that the assuming debtor or trustee or any assignee provide adequate assurance of future performance. [§ 365(b)(1)(C), (f)(2)(B)]. The requirements of cure and adequate assurance of future performance replace the conditions under which most "somewhat assignable" contracts could be assigned outside of bankruptcy. Most law limiting contract assignments does so to protect the non-assigning party from adverse material changes on account of performance by or to an assignee. Requiring prophylactic court findings of cure and adequate assurance of future performance meets this important policy concern.

If we understand the limited purpose of § 365(c)(1) to be to preserve the consent requirement in the few instances that nonbankruptcy law requires consent as a condition to assignment, it becomes clear that all contractual and most statutory and common law limitations on assignability are overridden by the pro-assignment policy embodied in § 365(f). Only in those few instances where otherwise applicable law presumes complete nonassignability absent express consent does § 365(c)(1) apply.

This reading of § 365(c) also has the virtue of making sense of the language of § 365(c)(1)(B) which limits the § 365(c)(1)(A) restriction on assumption to cases where the nondebtor "party does not consent to such assumption or assignment." This language is a clear textual indication that the purpose of § 365(c)(1) is to simply preserve the nonbankruptcy law consent requirement in the few instances that nonbankruptcy law requires consent as a condition to assignment, and not to impose an independent and higher bankruptcy law bar to assumption or assignment.

74 Am. Bankr. L.J. at 336-337. The recommendation of the National Bankruptcy Conference in Reforming the Bankruptcy Code 140 (Rev.ed.1997) is that any contract, other than a personal service or credit extension contract, should be assignable so long as adequate assurance of future performance is provided. "The present bankruptcy policy of enforcing nonbankruptcy case law or statutory law prohibitions, restrictions, or conditions on the assignment of a contract or delegation of performance duties thereunder should not be continued."

4. In portions of *Summit Investment and Development Corp. v. Leroux*, not mentioned in the discussion of that case in Note 2 following the *Catapult* opinion, the Court dealt with the problem of the enforcement of statutory bankruptcy termination provisions applicable to executory contracts. Contractual bankruptcy termination provisions ("ipso facto clauses") are invalidated by § 365(e). The First Circuit in *Summit* refused to recognize any distinction between statutory and contractual provisions in the case of bankruptcy termination provisions. In *Summit*, the executory contract at issue was a limited partnership agreement. The debtor in bankruptcy was a general partner with certain management rights under this agreement. The relevant state law, the Massachusetts Limited Partnership Act, provided that in the absence of any contractual provision to the contrary, the general partner's interest was terminated upon the bankruptcy of one of the general partners. The partnership agreement itself provided likewise. The First Circuit held the partnership agreement nevertheless assumable by the debtor in possession and the provisions of both the contract and state law ousting the debtor as general partner unenforceable under § 365(e). After reviewing the plain language of § 365(e) and noting the absence of any legislative history supporting the contractual—statutory distinction, the Court wrote:

> We are left, then, with no rationale which would warrant the categorical conclusion that Congress recognized a State interest sufficiently compelling to outweigh the important rehabilitative policies that section 365(e) was designed to serve. Nor has Summit suggested a sound basis for concluding that Congress considered statutory ipso facto provisions a lesser impediment to chapter 11 rehabilitation efforts than contractual ipso facto clauses.

69 F.3d at 611.

Chapter 6. Executory Contracts and Leases

Is there a sound basis for distinguishing state mandated anti-assignment statutes (enforceable under *Pioneer Ford*) from state mandated bankruptcy termination statutes (unenforceable under *Summit*)?

6. ENFORCEMENT BEFORE ASSUMPTION OR REJECTION

We have seen what the rights of the parties are under executory contracts if the debtor (i) rejects, (ii) assumes or (iii) assumes and assigns. But in Chapter 11 reorganizations a debtor in possession may be allowed a considerable period of time in which to decide whether to reject or assume. In this section we examine the rights of the parties during this hiatus. Section 365(d)(2) provides that in a Chapter 11 case the debtor's decision whether to reject or assume may be made "at any time before the confirmation of a plan," but allows the nondebtor party to request that the court fix an earlier time within which the debtor must decide. Since the debtor in possession may not be able to decide whether to assume before its plan of reorganization is formulated, courts have usually been reluctant to force a premature decision. Until the debtor in possession has assumed, an executory contract is not enforceable against the estate. But is it enforceable against the nondebtor party? If the debtor in possession enforces it against the nondebtor party, has the contract been assumed? The following case is a leading case on these questions.

Matter of Whitcomb & Keller Mortgage Co.

United States Court of Appeals, Seventh Circuit, 1983.
715 F.2d 375.

■ JAMESON, District Judge.

This is an appeal from an order of the district court affirming a decision of the bankruptcy court allowing the debtor, Whitcomb & Keller Mortgage Co., Inc., Appellee, to reject an executory contract with Data–Link Systems, Inc., Appellant, and classifying Data–Link as a general unsecured creditor in the Whitcomb & Keller bankruptcy proceeding for the sum of $12,954.63. We affirm.

I. Factual and procedural background

Whitcomb & Keller, a mortgage banker whose business included servicing mortgage accounts for investors, executed an executory contract with Data–Link, whereby, for a fee, Data–Link was to provide computer services to update and maintain Whitcomb & Keller's customer accounts. The contract provided that upon termination of the contract, Data–Link would return all master files and other occupational data relating to Whitcomb & Keller upon payment in full of any outstanding balance.

On October 27, 1980, Whitcomb & Keller filed for relief under Chapter 11 of the Bankruptcy Code. The bankruptcy court approved Whitcomb & Keller as a debtor in possession. At the time Whitcomb & Keller filed its bankruptcy petition, it owed Data–Link $12,954.63 for computer services previously rendered. Data–Link's claim for that amount was listed in the bankruptcy schedule as a general unsecured claim. Data–Link continued providing computer services, and Whitcomb & Keller paid for all services provided during the administration of the estate.

During the course of the bankruptcy, Whitcomb & Keller determined that it should sell its mortgage servicing contract assets. On February 26, 1981, the bankruptcy court found the bids of Milliken Mortgage Company and Unity Savings Association to be the best for the sale of the assets. As the district court found, on March 4, 1981, Data–Link discontinued computer services to Whitcomb & Keller, paralyzing it, and precipitated the filing of an application for a temporary restraining order and preliminary injunction. Over Data–Link's objections, the bankruptcy court entered an order enjoining Data–Link from terminating the computer services, and the services were resumed.

On March 5, 1981, Data–Link filed its answer which included a counterclaim requesting the bankruptcy court either (1) to declare that Whitcomb & Keller, by its application requesting the court to enforce the executory contract and by its continued receipt of the benefits of the executory contract, had assumed the executory contract, or (2) to require Whitcomb & Keller to decide whether to assume or reject the executory contract within a specified period of time before the confirmation of the plan. After a hearing on March 9, 1981, the bankruptcy court took the matter under advisement and continued the restraining order in effect.

On March 12, 1981, Unity Savings informed the bankruptcy court that Data–Link refused to give either Whitcomb & Keller or Unity Savings essential information stored in the master data base, thereby preventing Unity Savings from purchasing the servicing contract assets. Data–Link contended that the restraining order did not require it to provide Unity Savings with test tapes of information stored in the master data base but only to provide computer services to Whitcomb & Keller. Following a hearing on March 16, 1981, the bankruptcy court directed Data–Link to cooperate and turn over test tapes to expedite the sale of Whitcomb & Keller's mortgage servicing assets. The parties stipulated that any right, lien or other interest Data–Link might have would attached to proceeds of the sale of Whitcomb & Keller's assets. Whitcomb & Keller paid Data–Link in full for all charges relating to the preparation of the master data base.

On April 8, 1981, the bankruptcy court found that Whitcomb & Keller had not assumed the executory contract. The court found further that Whitcomb & Keller had remained current on its post-petition debts and that Data–Link was adequately protected, in that any right, lien or other interest that it might have would attach to the proceeds of the sale of Whitcomb & Keller's assets. Accordingly, the bankruptcy court denied Data–Link's request to require Whitcomb & Keller to assume or reject the executory contract prior to the confirmation of the plan.

Also on April 8, 1981, Whitcomb & Keller requested authority to reject the executory contract. Data–Link objected, and the matter was set for trial. On April 24 the court confirmed the second amended plan of reorganization. Data–Link filed a proof of claim on April 30, asserting priority for the pre-petition claim of $12,954.63.

On July 10, 1981, a trial was held in bankruptcy court on Whitcomb & Keller's request for authority to reject the executory contract. By order dated April 15, 1982, the court found that Whitcomb & Keller had not assumed the executory contract and that the language of the contract did not give rise to an equitable lien or warehouseman's lien on the information stored in Data–Link's computer. Accordingly, the bankruptcy court concluded that (1) Whitcomb & Keller was entitled to reject the executory contract, and (2) Data–Link's prepetition debt of $12,954.63 incurred under the executory contract was an unsecured claim. On appeal the district court affirmed the decision of the bankruptcy court.

II. Contentions on appeal

Data–Link contends that:

(1) neither the debtor in possession nor the bankruptcy court had authority to enforce the executory contract unless the contract was assumed by the debtor;

(2) because of the essential nature of the services provided under the contract, the bankruptcy court should have specified a period of time within which Whitcomb & Keller was required to decide whether to assume or reject the contract;

(3) Whitcomb & Keller continued receiving benefits from the executory contract and should have been required to assume its burdens; and

(4) Whitcomb & Keller's request for an order prohibiting Data–Link from terminating computer services and the bankruptcy court's restraining orders constituted an assumption by Whitcomb & Keller of the executory contract.

III. Authority to enforce executory contract pending acceptance or rejection

Acceptance and rejection of executory contracts are governed by Section 365 of the Bankruptcy Code. Section 365(d)(2) provides: In a case under Chapter 9, 11 or 13 of this title, the trustee may assume or reject an executory contract or unexpired lease of the debtor at any time before the confirmation of a plan, but the court, on request of any party to such contract or lease, may order the trustee to determine within a specified period of time whether to assume or reject such contract or lease.[3]

In *In re American National Trust*, 426 F.2d 1059, 1064 (7 Cir. 1970), this court held that a trustee in a reorganization proceeding "is entitled to a reasonable time to make a careful and informed evaluation as to possible burdens and benefits of an executory contract," quoting from 6 Collier on Bankruptcy (14th Ed.) 576–80.

The executory contract between Data–Link and Whitcomb & Keller was in effect on October 27, 1980, when Whitcomb & Keller filed its bankruptcy petition. The contract remained in effect until Whitcomb & Keller made its decision to assume or reject the contract. Before Whitcomb & Keller made its decision, however, Data–Link ceased providing essential computer services. Whitcomb & Keller then applied for the restraining order, as it had a right to do. Similarly, the bankruptcy court had the authority to preserve the status quo until Whitcomb & Keller made its decision.[4] The district court held that the bankruptcy court did not err in issuing the restraining order. We agree.

IV. Requiring debtors in possession to assume or reject executory contract

Data–Link contends that because of the essential nature of the service it provided under the contract, the bankruptcy court, pursuant to Section 365 of

---

[3] The policy behind § 365(d)(2) was summarized by the bankruptcy court in its April 8, 1981, order as follows:

Since a debtor is in limbo until confirmation of a plan, it is understandably difficult to commit itself to assuming or rejecting a contract much before the time for confirmation of a plan. Thus, the code allows for the debtor to provide for assumption or rejection of the executory contracts in its plan. This procedure insures that the debtor is not in the precarious position of having assumed a contract relying on confirmation of a particular plan, only to find the plan to have been rejected.

[4] The Bankruptcy Code provides a sufficient legal basis for a bankruptcy court to issue an injunction or restraining order in appropriate situations. Section 105(a) empowers a bankruptcy court to issue any order that is necessary or appropriate to carry out the provisions of the Code.

the Bankruptcy Code, § 365(d)(2), should have specified a period of time within which Whitcomb & Keller was required to decide whether to assume or reject the executory contract. The parties had, of course, stipulated that the computer services were essential and that the information stored in the computer included information essential to the sale of Whitcomb & Keller's accounts. Data–Link argues that time for further inquiry into the benefits and burdens of the contract was not needed.

Data–Link interprets the purpose of § 365(d) too narrowly. It is not enough that the trustee or debtor in possession recognize that the services provided under the contract are essential. Rather, § 365(d) allows the trustee or debtor in possession a reasonable time within which to determine whether adoption or rejection of the executory contract would be beneficial to an effective reorganization. *In re American National Trust, supra*, 426 F.2d at 1064 (interpreting § 516(1) (repealed 1979), predecessor to § 365).

The bankruptcy court addressed this issue in its order of April 8, 1981. After discussing the purpose of allowing the trustee a reasonable time to make its decision, the court noted that Data–Link was adequately protected because (1) Whitcomb & Keller had paid for all services received during the administration of its estate, and (2) the parties had stipulated that any right, lien or other interest that Data–Link might have would attach to the proceeds of the sale of Whitcomb & Keller's assets. Accordingly, the court exercised its discretion under § 365(d) in denying Data–Link's request to require Whitcomb & Keller "to assume or reject the contract forthwith." We find no abuse of the bankruptcy court's discretion.

V. Receipt of benefits and assumption of burdens

Data–Link next contends that a finding that Keller assumed the contract is necessary to avoid the inequitable result of allowing Whitcomb & Keller to derive the benefits of the contract without assuming its burdens.

In the first place, it may be noted that general principles governing contractual benefits and burdens do not always apply in the bankruptcy context. The purpose of the Bankruptcy Code is to "suspend the normal operation of rights and obligations between the debtor and his creditors." *Fontainebleau Hotel Corp. v. Simon*, 508 F.2d 1056, 1059 (5 Cir. 1975). Moreover, successful reorganization under Chapter 11 depends on relieving the debtor of burdensome contracts and pre-petition debts so that "additional cash flow thus freed is used to meet current operating expenses." H.R.Rep. No. 595, 95th Cong., 1st Sess. 221 (1977). The post-petition services provided by Data–Link were operating expenses which Whitcomb & Keller paid in full. But merely providing such services did not alter Data–Link's position as a general unsecured creditor on its pre-petition claim. * * *

The cases upon which appellant relies are factually distinguishable. Here it is undisputed that Whitcomb & Keller paid in full for all services rendered during the administration of the estate, including the preparation of the data base tape. The only alleged breach of the executory contract relates to the indebtedness owed by Whitcomb & Keller when the petition was filed. Data–Link suffered no harm nor prejudice through the continued utilization of its computer services. Rather it presumably earned a profit from the continued use.[5] We agree with district court that Whitcomb & Keller's utilization of the computer services during the administration of the estate did not support a finding that Whitcomb & Keller assumed the contract or that Data–Link was entitled to a priority.

VI. Requirements for assumption of executory contracts

Finally, Data–Link contends that Whitcomb & Keller's "application for the enforcement of this essential executory contract and the Bankruptcy Court's mandatory order thereon (that Data–Link must perform) constituted an assumption with Court approval."

Under § 365(a) the trustee or debtor in possession, "*subject to the court's approval,* may assume or reject any executory contract * * *." § 365(a) (emphasis added). Interpreting similar language in [the Bankruptcy Act] * * * this court declared: "'Assumption or adoption of the contract can only be affected through an express order of the judge.'" [*In re American National Trust, supra*, 426 F.2d at 1064] (quoting 6 Collier on Bankruptcy 576–80 (14th ed.)). No such order issued in the present case. Neither the bankruptcy court nor Whitcomb & Keller exhibited any intention of assuming the contract when the court enjoined Data–Link's termination of services. We will not infer such intention. Instead, we find the order was directed solely toward maintaining the status quo—a permissible purpose well within the bankruptcy court's power, as we have noted.

VII. Conclusion

We find no abuse of the bankruptcy court's discretion. We agree with the bankruptcy court and the district court that (1) Whitcomb & Keller did not assume the executory contract; but rather (2) was entitled to and did reject the contract; and (3) Data–Link's pre-petition claim of $12,954.63 is an unsecured claim.

Affirmed.

---

[5] As the district court noted, Whitcomb & Keller in effect "assumed the burdens as it received the benefits during the administration of the estate. If Whitcomb & Keller had continued to receive the services of Data–Link during the administration of the estate and not paid for them, the law clearly states that that indebtedness would be entitled to priority status. However, that is not the case here."

NOTES

1. If Debtor assumes an executory contract, the contract becomes a postpetition obligation of the estate and Nondebtor is entitled to an administrative expense priority for its performance according to the terms of the contract. This issue is discussed in detail in *In re Klein Sleep Products, Inc., infra*. In this Note we consider the estate's liability to Nondebtor if Nondebtor continues to perform during the gap period and Debtor eventually rejects. In *Whitcomb & Keller* we saw that Debtor's acceptance of Nondebtor's postpetition performance is not assumption of the executory contract. Hence, the extent to which Nondebtor is entitled to an administrative expense priority is governed by benefit conferred on the estate by Nondebtor's performance. § 503(b)(1)(A). The benefit-to-the-estate standard may be difficult to apply in some cases.

Suppose Debtor, a developer, contracted with Nondebtor to serve as project manager in construction of a hotel in 1997. Nondebtor was to provide security services at the construction site. Debtor agreed to indemnify Nondebtor against suits brought against Nondebtor in the performance of its duties under the contract; the indemnification agreement specifically included attorney's fees and expenses. After construction money dried up, Debtor filed in Chapter 11 and asked Nondebtor to continue to perform security services. In the course of doing so, Nondebtor was sued by a subcontractor for allegedly allowing spoliation of certain building materials. Nondebtor spent $125,000 in successfully defending against this claim. When Debtor eventually rejected the prepetition contract, Nondebtor requested administrative expense treatment for the $125,000 postpetition indemnity claim. Debtor opposed the request on the ground that the contract calling for indemnification was not assumed and the debt incurred by Nondebtor in defending the claim did not "directly and substantially" benefit the estate under § 503(b)(1)(A). Neither Debtor nor Nondebtor referred to indemnity when Nondebtor was asked to continue. Nondebtor can show that indemnity agreements are common in situations like this and will testify that it wouldn't have undertaken to continue without indemnity. Should Nondebtor receive administrative expense priority for the $125,000? See *In re Santa Monica Beach Hotel, Ltd.*, 209 B.R. 722 (9th Cir. BAP 1997). Should Nondebtor's legitimate expectations be a factor in this case?

2. The National Bankruptcy Review Commission has proposed that the law governing compensation for the performance of the nondebtor during the gap period before the debtor's election to reject be changed to focus on damage to the nondebtor rather than on benefit to the estate. It recommends in *NBRC Rep.* at 465 that a court be authorized to order the nondebtor (i) to continue to perform during the gap period, and (ii) to provide protection of the nondebtor's interests during that period. Compensation awarded to the nondebtor would be based on ordinary contract principles. "Whatever compensation would be awarded to the nondebtor party under similar nonbankruptcy circumstances should be its allowed administrative claim for postpetition performance or breach." *NBRC Rep.* at 468. The current standard of actual benefit to the estate would be abandoned.

3. There are major risks to nondebtor parties to executory contracts who take unilateral actions with respect to their relationship with the debtor prior to rejection. *Computer Communications, Inc. v. Codex Corp.*, 824 F.2d 725 (9th Cir. 1987), is a leading case in point. The debtor CCI entered into a restated four-year Joint Marketing and Development Agreement (JMDA) relating to complex telecommunications equipment, software and related services with Codex two days before filing under Chapter 11. Codex terminated the agreement asserting its rights under the contract's ipso facto clause were enforceable because the JMDA was a nonassignable agreement that could not be assumed. Unlike Data–Link in *Whitcomb & Keller,* CCI did not seek to enjoin the termination. Instead it found itself with a substantial new asset: its damage claim against Codex based on a violation of the automatic stay. In upholding a $5 million judgment in favor of the debtor, the Ninth Circuit wrote : "Even if Codex had a valid reason for terminating the Agreement, it still was required to petition the court for relief from the automatic stay. . ... We need not reach t[he] question [whether the JMDA could be assumed, and, if so, whether it could nevertheless be terminated under the ipso facto clause], however, because we hold that even if § 365(e)(2) allowed Codex to terminate the contract, § 362 automatically stayed termination." 824 F.2d at 730.

B. LEASES

1. REJECTION BY DEBTOR IN POSSESSION AS LESSOR

The rejection of executory contracts allows the debtor in possession or trustee to avoid the burden on the bankruptcy estate of performing contracts that are not beneficial to the estate and gives to the nondebtor party a claim in bankruptcy for breach of contract damages. The predominant view, notwithstanding *Lubrizol*, is that it *does not* allow the debtor in possession to rescind the contract and to take back performance already granted. Thus, if the debtor granted a patent license or a franchise, the debtor in possession can refuse to perform unperformed obligations under the license agreement or franchise agreement, but should not be able to take away from the nonbankrupt party the right to use the patent or the right to operate the franchise.

A similar analysis applies to land sale contracts in which the debtor is the vendor. Land sale contracts are sometimes used as a substitute for the more common installment note secured by a mortgage, particularly in the case of the sale of a home to a low income buyer. Under the contract, the real property title passes to the buyer only when the buyer has made all of the installment payments required by the contract. If the seller were to file in Chapter 11 and the transaction were treated as an executory contract that could be rejected, the debtor in possession would presumably not be required to give the buyer a deed to the property. Some cases decided under the Bankruptcy Act reached that result, but under the Bankruptcy Code the buyer's property interest, which amounts to equitable title to the real property, is protected by § 365(i). The seller, as debtor in possession, can refuse to perform collateral obligations under the contract, but must deliver a deed to the real property as required by the contract if the nondebtor buyer makes all the payments.

In cases involving bankrupt landlords of real property, § 365(h) gives to the lessee rights comparable those of a buyer under a land sale contract. The landlord, as debtor in possession, can refuse to perform collateral obligations such as providing heat, utilities, property maintenance and the like, but the debtor in possession cannot deprive the lessee of the leasehold itself. Under § 365(h)(1) the lessee is given an option to treat the lease as terminated for material breach and assert a claim for damages in the bankruptcy or to remain in possession under the lease. As in the case of the land sale buyer, the lessee exercising its option to remain in possession can recover damages resulting from the failure to perform collateral services, but recovery can be had only by deducting those damages from rent due under the lease. § 365(h)(1)(B). For example, if the landlord is required under the lease to keep the property in good repair, the lessee can cause any required repair to be made and can deduct the cost of the repair from the rent.

What rights does the lessee who remains in possession under a rejected lease have, in addition to the essential right to remain in possession for the duration of the rejected lease? The issue has sometimes been posed in terms of whether rejection by the debtor-landlord terminates the lease, leaving the lessee with nothing but this essential right. *In re Carlton Restaurant, Inc.*, 151 B.R. 353 (Bankr.E.D.Pa.1993), cited in the Section-by-Section Description § 205, 140 Cong. Rec. H10767 (1994), took the view that the debtor-landlord's rejection does terminate the lease and leaves the lessee with only its "personal rights to possession." Therefore, the lessee cannot assign its right to another. Congress disapproved this narrow view and in 1994 added § 365(h)(1)(A) which provides:

> * * * the lessee may retain its rights under such lease (including rights such as those relating to the amount and timing of payment of rent and other amounts payable by the lessee and any right of use, possession, quiet enjoyment, subletting, assignment, or hypothecation) that

are in or appurtenant to the real property for the balance of the term of such lease * * *.

After this amendment, the lessee's rights under a rejected lease are very similar to those before rejection and it is questionable whether a debtor-landlord gains much from rejection beyond limiting the lessee's remedies for post-rejection breaches to an offset against rentals.

The effect of rejection of a personal property lease by the lessor is not clear. Rejection raises an issue similar to that in the technology licensing cases. The result in *Lubrizol* has been reversed by § 365(n), but the rationale of the case could be used to deprive the personal property lessee of the right to continue use of the property under the lease. We disagree with *Lubrizol* and would allow the lessee to retain the right to use the property. We see no policy reason to differentiate between real property and personal property leases in this respect. Nevertheless, the legislative decision to limit the statutory safe harbors to real property leases and intellectual property licenses might be viewed as creating a contrary inference with respect to personal property leases.

The vast real estate finance industry was rudely jolted by the following decision, handed down by one of the most prestigious commercial courts in the land.

Precision Industries, Inc. v. Qualitech Steel SBQ, LLC
United States Court of Appeals, Seventh Circuit, 2003.
327 F.3d 537.

■ ILANA DIAMOND ROVNER, Circuit Judge.

In this case of first impression at the circuit level, we are asked to reconcile two distinct provisions of the Bankruptcy Code: § 363(f), which authorizes the sale of a debtor's property free of any "interest" other than the estate's, and § 365(h), which protects the rights of the lessee when the debtor rejects a lease of estate property. The bankruptcy court in this case construed a sale order issued pursuant to section 363(f) to extinguish the possessory rights bestowed by a lease of the estate's land. The district court disagreed, reasoning that sections 363(f) and 365(h) conflict and that the more specific terms of the latter provision concerning leaseholds trump those of the former, in this way preserving the lessee's possessory interest even after a section 363(f) sale. We reverse, concluding that under the plain terms of section 363(f), the sale order extinguished the lessee's possessory interest.

I.

The debtors in the underlying bankruptcy proceedings—Qualitech Steel Corporation and Qualitech Steel Holdings Corporation (collectively, "Qualitech")—owned and operated a steel mill on a 138-acre tract of land in Pittsboro, Indiana. Before it entered bankruptcy, Qualitech had entered into two related agreements with appellees Precision Industries, Inc. and Circo Leasing Co., LLC (collectively, "Precision"). A detailed supply agreement executed on June 29, 1998, provided that Precision would construct a supply warehouse at Qualitech's Pittsboro facility and operate it for a period of ten years so as to provide on-site, integrated supply services for Qualitech. The second agreement, a land lease executed on February 25, 1999, specified that Qualitech would lease to Precision the property underlying the warehouse for a period of ten years. In exchange for nominal rent of $1 per year, the lease granted Precision exclusive possession of the warehouse and any other improvements or fixtures it installed on the land for the term of the lease; and in the event of an early termination or default under either the lease or the supply agreement, Precision had the right to remove all improvements and fixtures from the property. Assuming no default, Qualitech had the right at the end of the lease term to purchase the warehouse, its fixtures, and other improvements for $1. In accordance with the two agreements, Precision built and stocked a warehouse on the leased property and Qualitech began purchasing goods from Precision. The lease was never recorded.

Heavily in debt, Qualitech filed a Chapter 11 bankruptcy petition on March 22, 1999. On June 30, 1999, substantially all of Qualitech's assets were sold at auction for a credit bid of $180 million to a group of senior pre-petition lenders that held the primary mortgage on the Pittsboro property. On August 13, 1999, at the conclusion of a noticed hearing, the bankruptcy court entered an order approving the sale (hereinafter, the "Sale Order"). Precision, which had notice of the hearing, did not object to the Sale Order. That order directed Qualitech to convey its assets to the pre-petition lenders—referred to in the Sale Order collectively as the "purchaser"—"free and clear of all liens, claims, encumbrances, and *interests*," except for specifically enumerated liens, pursuant to section 363(f), among other provisions of the Code. All persons and entities holding interests other than those expressly preserved in the Sale Order were barred from asserting those interests against the purchaser. The pre-petition senior lenders subsequently transferred their interest in the purchased assets to newly-formed Qualitech Steel SBQ, LLC ("New Qualitech"), which assumed the rights of the purchaser under the Sale Order and took title to the Pittsboro property. The Sale Order also reserved for the purchaser the debtor's right to assume and assign executory contracts pursuant to § 365. Although the sale closed on or about August 26, 1999 without assumption of either the lease or the supply agreement with Precision, negotiations toward that end continued and the parties extended the deadline for assumption on four occasions. Those negotiations did not prove successful, however, with the result that Precision's lease and supply agreement were *de facto* rejected.

By December 3, 1999, Precision had completely vacated and padlocked the warehouse. Shortly thereafter, New Qualitech, without Precision's knowledge or consent, hired a locksmith and changed the locks on the building. New Qualitech's takeover of the warehouse led to a dispute over whether Precision's possessory interest in the leased property, pursuant to section 365(h), survived the bankruptcy sale. Finding itself locked out of the warehouse, Precision filed a diversity suit in the district court contending that New Qualitech was guilty of trespass, conversion, wrongful eviction, breach of an implied contract, and estoppel. New Qualitech in turn asked the district court to refer Precision's complaint—which was premised on the notion that Precision retained a possessory interest in the warehouse under the lease—to the bankruptcy court, and New Qualitech also filed a request with the bankruptcy court asking it to clarify that the Sale Order had extinguished Precision's possessory interest. The district court obliged New Qualitech by referring Precision's complaint to the bankruptcy court, and that court in turn resolved the matter of Precision's possessory interest in New Qualitech's favor.

Based on the terms of both section 363(f) and the Sale Order itself, the bankruptcy court determined that New Qualitech had obtained title to Qualitech's property free and clear of any possessory rights that Precision otherwise might have enjoyed under its lease. In relevant part, the court held that Precision's possessory interest was among those interests extinguished by the Sale Order. * * * New Qualitech filed a timely notice of appeal from the district court's decision. * * *

II.

Our task in this appeal is straightforward. We must decide whether a sale order issued under section 363(f), which purports to authorize the transfer of a debtor's property "free and clear of all liens, claims, encumbrances, and interests," operates to extinguish a lessee's possessory interest in the property, or whether the terms of section 365(h) operate to preserve that interest. This is, of course, a question of law, making our review of the district court's decision de novo. * * *

As in all statutory interpretation cases, we begin with the statutory language. * * * Statutory terms or words will be construed according to their ordinary, common meaning unless they are specifically defined by the statute or the statutory context requires a different definition. * * * We must also have in mind our obligation to construe the two statutory provisions at issue in this case in such a way as to avoid conflicts between them, if such a construction is possible and reasonable. * * *

Section 363 generally provides for the use, sale, or lease of property belonging to the bankruptcy estate. As relevant here, subsections (b) and (c) permit the trustee of a bankruptcy estate to sell estate property either within the normal course of a debtor's business (in which case the sale may take place without prior notice and a hearing) or outside the normal course of business (in which case, as here, notice and hearing are mandatory). Subsection (f) makes clear that the property, under specified conditions, may be sold unencumbered of interests held by others:

> The trustee may sell property under subsection (b) or (c) of this section free and clear of *any interest* in such property of an entity other than the estate, only if—
>
> (1) applicable nonbankruptcy law permits sale of such property free and clear of such interest;
>
> (2) such entity consents;
>
> (3) such interest is a lien and the price at which such property is to be sold is greater than the aggregate value of all liens on such property;
>
> (4) such interest is in bona fide dispute; or
>
> (5) such entity could be compelled, in a legal or equitable proceeding, to accept a money satisfaction of such interest.

(Emphasis ours.) Finally, subsection (e) provides that "on request of an entity that has an interest in property... proposed to be... sold... by the trustee, the court, with or without a hearing, shall prohibit or condition such... sale... as is necessary to provide adequate protection of such interest." We note that although section 363(f) refers to the powers and obligations of the "trustee," these are powers and obligations which, in a Chapter 11 case, inure to the debtor-in-possession. *See* § 1107(a). * * *

Because Precision's right to possess the property as a lessee qualifies as an interest for purposes of section 363(f), the statute on its face authorized the sale of Qualitech's property free and clear of that interest. Although the statute conditions such a sale on the satisfaction of one of five conditions, the parties before us do not dispute that at least one of those conditions was satisfied.[3] On the contrary, both parties to the appeal proceed from the premise that section

---

[3] New Qualitech asserts in its opening brief that "[p]utting aside the issue of whether § 365(h) somehow trumps a § 363(f) sale, it is not disputed that the Debtor was authorized to sell the property free and clear of Precision's unrecorded lease." Precision does not take issue with this assertion in its response brief. Accordingly, we shall assume, as New Qualitech asserts, that one or more of the statutory criteria were met and that a sale of the property free and clear of Precision's possessory interest as a lessee was permissible.

363(f) standing alone permits the sale of estate property free and clear of a lessee's possessory interest.

Where the parties lock horns is on whether the terms of section 365(h) conflict with and override those of section 363(f). Section 365 generally provides the trustee (and here, the debtor-in-possession, *see* § 1107(a)) with the right to reject executory contracts, a power that serves to relieve the debtor of contractual obligations that are unduly burdensome. * * * However, insofar as lessees of the estate's property are concerned, the power of rejection is limited so as to preclude eviction of the lessee. In relevant part, section 365(h)(1)(A)(ii) provides:

> If the trustee rejects an unexpired lease of real property under which the debtor is the lessor and—
>
> . . .
>
> (ii) if the term of such lease has commenced, the lessee may retain its rights under such lease. . . that are in or appurtenant to the real property for the balance of the term of such lease and for any renewal or extension of such rights to the extent that such rights are enforceable under applicable non-bankruptcy law.

The terms of section 365(h) thus allow a lessee to remain in possession of estate property notwithstanding the debtor-in-possession's decision to reject the lease. In this way, the statute strikes a balance between the respective rights of the debtor-lessor and its tenant: the lessee retains the right to possess the property for the remainder of the term it bargained for, while the rejection frees the debtor-lessor of other burdensome obligations that it assumed under the lease (as, for example, the duty to provide services to the lessee). * * *

The district court, following the lead of other lower courts, concluded that the limitations imposed by section 365(h) vis à vis rejection of leases necessarily conflict with and override the debtor-in-possession's ability to sell estate property free and clear of a lessee's possessory interest. But for the reasons that follow, we conclude that the terms of section 365(h) do not supersede those of section 363(f).

First, the statutory provisions themselves do not suggest that one supersedes or limits the other. Notably, sections 363 and 365 both contain cross-references indicating that certain of their provisions are subject to other statutory mandates. *See* §§ 363(d), 365(a). But nowhere in either section 363(f) or section 356(h) is there a similar cross-reference indicating that the broad right to sell estate property free of "any interest" is subordinate to the protections that section 365(h) accords to lessees. The omission suggests that Congress did not intend for the latter section to limit the former. * * *

Second, the plain language of section 365(h)(1)(A) suggests that it has a limited scope. By its own terms, that subsection applies "[i]f the trustee [or debtor-in-possession] *rejects* an unexpired lease of real property...." (Emphasis supplied.) Here what occurred in the first instance was a sale of the property that Precision was leasing rather than a rejection of its lease. Granted, if the Sale Order operated to extinguish Precision's right to possess the property—as we conclude it did—then the effect of the sale might be understood as the equivalent of a repudiation of Precision's lease. *See In re Taylor*, 198 B.R. 142, at 166 (Bankr.D.S.C.1996) ("[t]o allow a sale free and clear of a leasehold interest pursuant to § 363... would effectively provide a debtor with means of dispossessing the lessee"). But nothing in the express terms of section 365(h) suggests that it applies to any and all events that threaten the lessee's possessory rights. Section 365(h) instead focuses on a specific type of event—the rejection of an executory contract by the trustee or debtor-in-possession—and spells out the rights of parties affected by that event. It says nothing at all about sales of estate property, which are the province of section 363. The two statutory provisions thus apply to distinct sets of circumstances. * * *

Third, section 363 itself provides for a mechanism to protect the rights of parties whose interests may be adversely affected by the sale of estate property. As noted above, section 363(e) directs the bankruptcy court, on the request of any entity with an interest in the property to be sold, to "prohibit or condition such... sale... as is necessary to provide adequate protection of such interest." Because a leasehold qualifies as an "interest" in property for purposes of section 363(f), a lessee of property being sold pursuant to subsection (f) would have the right to insist that its interest be protected. "Adequate protection" does not necessarily guarantee a lessee's continued possession of the property, but it does demand, in the alternative, that the lessee be compensated for the value of its leasehold—typically from the proceeds of the sale. * * * Lessees like Precision are therefore not without recourse in the event of a sale free and clear of their interests. They have the right to seek protection under section 363(e), and upon request, the bankruptcy court is obligated to ensure that their interests are adequately protected.

With these points in mind, it is apparent that the two statutory provisions can be construed in a way that does not disable section 363(f) vis à vis leasehold interests. Where estate property under lease is to be sold, section 363 permits the sale to occur free and clear of a lessee's possessory interest—provided that the lessee (upon request) is granted adequate protection for its interest. Where the property is not sold, and the debtor remains in possession thereof but chooses to reject the lease, section 365(h) comes into play and the lessee retains the right to possess the property. So understood, both provisions may be given full effect without coming into conflict with one another and without disregarding the rights of lessees.

We are persuaded that it is both reasonable and correct to interpret and reconcile sections 363(f) and 365(h) in this way. It is consistent with the express terms of each provision, and it avoids the unwelcome result of reading a limitation into section 363(f) that the legislature itself did not inscribe onto the statute. Congress authorized the sale of estate property free and clear of "*any* interest," not "any interest *except* a lessee's possessory interest." The interpretation is also consistent with the process of marshaling the estate's assets for the twin purposes of maximizing creditor recovery and rehabilitating the debtor, which are central to the Bankruptcy Code. * * * Thus, section 363(f), as we interpret that provision, permitted the bankruptcy court to allow the sale of Qualitech's Pittsboro property unencumbered by Precision's possessory interest as a lessee. Precision neither objected to the sale nor sought the protection that was available under section 363(e). Its possessory interest was extinguished by the sale.

III.

As the sale of Qualitech's property terminated Precision's possessory interest in the property as a lessee, we REVERSE the district court's judgment to the contrary.

NOTES

1. The holding of the principal case is that if debtor-lessor *rejects* an unexpired real estate lease the lessee has a right to retain possession under § 365(h)(1)(A)(ii), but if the debtor-lessor *sells* the leased premises free and clear of the interests of others under § 365(f), the right of the lessee to remain in possession is cut off and the lessee's only remedy is to seek adequate protection under § 363(e). Since the option to sell or reject lies with the debtor-lessor, is not sale of the leased premises free and clear of the lessee's interest a *de facto* rejection of the lease?

2. The court in *In re Haskell L.P.*, 321 B. R. 1 (Bankr.D.Mass.2005), rejected *Qualitech* on the ground that under the sale-rejection distinction "the provisions of § 365(h) would be eviscerated." 321 B. R. at 10. This is the view of Michael S. Baxter, *Section 363 Sales Free and Clear of Interests: Why the Seventh Circuit Erred in Precision Industries v. Qualitech Steel*, 59 Bus. Law. 475 (2004), a withering critique of *Qualitech*. The author points out the "potentially devastating consequences" of this decision in the common transaction in which a lessee enters into a long-term real estate lease (the lease in *Haskell* was 99 years) and constructs an expensive building on the premises. The lender advancing the construction financing takes a security interest in the lease as security for its advances. Both the lessee and the lender rely on the lengthy term of the lease and § 365(h) as protection against the lessor's bankruptcy.

3. While conceding that the "vast majority of lower court cases" are contrary to *Qualitech*, the court in *In re MMH Automotive Group, LLC*, 385 B.R. 347, 363 (Bankr.S.D.Fla.2008), holds that the case is correct as a matter of statutory interpretation, and that the adequate protection requirement is sufficient protection for the lessee. But how could a court arrive at a form of adequate protection under § 363(e) for sale of the premises free of the lessee's interest in a case like *Haskell* in which the lessee might have had a right to possession for decades under § 365(h)? In that case the lessee successfully contended that only continuation of the lessee's right to possession for the remaining term of the lease would constitute adequate protection because its losses cannot be quantified. If the required adequate protection mimics § 365(h) rights, then *Qualitech* is simply a trap for unwary lessees who fail to lodge a timely demand for adequate protection, right?

4. Section 365(n) extends licensees rights similar to those extended by § 365(h) to lessees of real property How would *Qualitech* affect the rights of a licensee of intellectual property in case the debtor-licensor sells the property free and clear under § 363(f)?

2. REJECTION BY DEBTOR IN POSSESSION AS LESSEE

In the previous section we saw that if a land sale contract vendor files in bankruptcy, § 365(i) treats the transaction, in effect, as a secured transaction rather than as an executory contract. Section 365(i) allows the vendee to remain in possession, make the required installment payments and, upon completion, receive a deed from the vendor. Although no comparable statutory provision applies to cases in which the bankruptcy debtor is the vendee, caselaw holds that the transaction should be treated as a security interest rather than an executory contract for this purpose as well. *See, e.g., In re Heward Brothers*, 210 B.R. 475 (Bankr.D.Id.1997) (marshaling the authorities).

If a land sale contract were treated as an executory contract, the debtor-vendee could be compelled to elect whether to assume or reject. Rejection as the concept was understood in *Lubrizol*, p. 237, would result in forfeiture of the vendee's equitable interest in the real property notwithstanding the vendor's receipt of prior installment payments, even if the value of the property were substantially greater than the present value of the future installment payments due the vendor. If on the other hand the vendee-debtor were to assume the contract in order to preserve its equity in the property, it must cure all payments in default and give adequate assurance that it will perform the remainder of the contract as written. Modification of the rights of the nondebtor vendor under Chapter 11 would be virtually precluded. But if the transaction is characterized as a secured transaction, as we shall see, a Chapter 11 plan can both preserve the debtor's equity in the property and modify the nondebtor-vendor's rights significantly, even though the debtor remains in possession of the property without the vendor's consent. The *Restatement of Property (Third) Mortgages* § 3.4(b) provides: "A contract for deed creates a mortgage." One of the reasons given for the Restatement rule is the harsh bankruptcy treatment of the vendee if the transaction were viewed as an executory contract rather than a secured transaction.

As is true with respect to executory contracts, a trustee in bankruptcy or debtor in possession may reject an unwanted lease or assume a favorable lease. § 365(a). Rejection of a lease under which the debtor is lessee is a breach of the lease giving the landlord a claim in bankruptcy for damages. § 365(g) and § 502(g). The landlord is entitled to a bankruptcy claim to the extent that it could have recovered compensatory damages under otherwise applicable law. In the case of a lease of real property, however, although the amount of the landlord's bankruptcy claim can be no more than the actual damages under nonbankruptcy law, the claim is further limited by § 502(b)(6).

That provision is best understood through an example. Suppose the debtor was the lessee under a 10-year lease of real property, and that the debtor files in bankruptcy at the end of the first year of the lease. At the time of filing the debtor occupies the leased premises, but it subsequently rejects the lease and turns over the premises. The landlord asserts a damage claim under § 365(g) for its actual damages including loss of future rent. Under § 502(b)(6) the landlord can recover no more than one year of future rent, or rent for 15% of the remaining term, whichever is greater. Since 15% of the remaining term of nine years is 1.35 years, the landlord's claim is limited to 1.35 years of rent. If the lease had had a shorter term, say five years, 15% of the remaining term of four years would be 0.6 years. In that case the landlord could claim up to a maximum of one year of rent. The second limitation of § 502(b)(6) applies only to long-term leases. It means that in no event can the landlord claim more than three years of rent. If the term of the lease had been 25 years, 15% of the remaining term of 24 years is 3.6 years. In that case the landlord's claim cannot exceed three years of rent. In addition to its capped claim for future rent, the landlord is entitled to a claim in bankruptcy for any unpaid rent due at the time of the filing and may have a right to payment of an administrative expense for postpetition rent for the period before the lease is rejected.

Section § 502(b)(6) reflects a certain skepticism over landlords' future rent claims. Damages under unfavorable long-term leases can be asserted to be very high, especially if the debtor's bankruptcy occurs at a time when real estate markets are greatly (and perhaps artificially and temporarily) depressed. In a liquidation, if damages are not limited they might so overwhelm other unsecured claims as to effectively deprive anyone but the landlord of any recovery from the estate. In a reorganization, the landlord's uncapped damage claim might be a great impediment to the ability of the debtor to confirm and carry out the plan. These practical difficulties are compounded by the difficulty of assessing future market conditions in order to calculate the damages. Particularly in cases involving long-term leases, a landlord might well receive a windfall if given full damages based on estimates and projections. Finally, the fact that bankruptcy courts do not discount future obligations to present value in calculating claims would lead to greatly inflated claims under long-term leases but for the § 502(b)(6) limitation.

3. LIABILITY FOR USE OF LEASED PROPERTY BEFORE REJECTION AND TIME LIMITS FOR ASSUMPTION OR REJECTION

In many cases, a landlord wants to be rid of a lessee that is in bankruptcy. The landlord-tenant relationship can be greatly complicated by the intervention of bankruptcy with its attendant tangle of legal rules. Before the Bankruptcy Code a landlord could often avoid these complications by a clause in the lease that allowed termination of the lease when the lessee went into bankruptcy. Even under the old Bankruptcy Act, however, courts would sometimes refuse to enforce these "ipso facto" or "bankruptcy termination" clauses. Section 365(e) has made clear in all cases that a lease can be assumed notwithstanding an ipso facto clause in the lease. Moreover, § 365(f) allows a lease to be assigned notwithstanding a clause in the lease prohibiting or restricting assignment.

a. Real Estate Leases

What are the rights and obligations of the landlord and the bankruptcy estate before the debtor's lease is either rejected or assumed under § 365? Before 1984, the general rule was that the estate was liable only for the reasonable value of the occupancy of the leased premises. There was authority stretching back to the 1898 Bankruptcy Act that, if the trustee in bankruptcy did not occupy the leased premises, no compensation was due to the landlord during a reasonable period taken by the trustee to decide whether to reject or assume the lease. The rationale was that there was no benefit to the estate if the trustee did not occupy the leased premises, even though the bankruptcy stay precluded the landlord from obtaining possession and reletting the premises prior to rejection of the lease. This doctrine when carried forward into cases filed under the Bankruptcy Code and coupled with § 365(d)(2), which allowed the debtor in possession in a Chapter 11 case to elect to assume or reject at any time before confirmation of the plan of reorganization, placed landlords in an unfavorable position. Premises might stand vacant for months while the debtor pondered whether to reject or assume. If the ultimate decision was to reject, the lessor received no compensation. If the debtor occupied the premises, the landlord received rent at reasonable value, an uncertain amount measured by current market rents that might be less than the rent provided for by the lease. The landlord's only legal recourse was to request the court to order the lessee to determine within a specified period of time whether to assume or reject. This state of the law resulted in landlords having to incur legal expenses in litigating the value of occupancy and in obtaining orders compelling the lessee to assume or reject. It meant that landlords might receive no income from the rental property for a period of time during which they had to continue making mortgage and tax payments. Sometimes the landlord's only practical course of action was to attempt to buy a prompt rejection from the debtor in possession. Landlords thought that under the Bankruptcy Code the pendulum had swung too far in favor of the debtor in possession.

The Leasehold Management Bankruptcy Amendments Act formed an important part of the 1984 amendments to the Bankruptcy Code and changed the relative bargaining positions of landlords and commercial tenants in Chapter 11 cases. These amendments apply to all leases of "nonresidential real property," which is generally understood to exclude leases of real property that is used by the debtor as his or her residence as well as personal property leases.

The key amendment is § 365(d)(3) which requires the debtor in possession to "timely perform all the obligations of the debtor * * * arising from and after the order for relief under any unexpired lease of nonresidential real property, until such lease is assumed or rejected * * *." Under a literal reading of this provision, the bankruptcy estate is liable for the rent called for by the lease and other payments, like common area charges in shopping centers, until rejection, regardless of whether the premises are occupied during the period before rejection, and the payments must be made at the time called for by the lease. The landlord need not fall within § 503(b)(1) for the allowance of administrative expenses in order to be entitled to the rent. The court may give the debtor in possession, for cause, a 60–day grace period after the petition during which payments may be postponed so long as all payments falling due within that period are made by the end of the period. The reason for the grace period is to allow the debtor in possession sufficient time to evaluate the situation and to arrange for payment. No more arguments about the fair value of the premises. Until rejection, the bankruptcy estate must pay the rent required by the lease even though it may be above market rates. While not all cases have interpreted § 365(d)(3) literally, the dominant view is that the statute means what it says, at least if the bankruptcy estate is administratively solvent. *In re Pacific–Atlantic Trading Co.*, 27 F.3d 401 (9th Cir. 1994).

Some courts go even further and apply the statute literally even in the case of an administratively insolvent estate in which the effect of strict compliance with § 365(d)(3) is to give the landlord's administrative rent claim a priority in payment over other administrative claims. This issue was addressed in *In re Orvco*, 95 B.R. 724 (9th Cir. BAP 1989), as follows:

> Great Western next argues that because section 365(d)(3) requires that the trustee "timely" perform the obligations of the debtor, it is entitled to immediate payment of its claim, without regard to the amount owing other administrative claimants. In other words, Great Western seeks a super-administrative status for its claim. We don't believe the statute supports such a reading.
>
> Although section 365(d)(3) calls for "timely" performance of the debtor's lease obligations, there is no indication that Congress intended to grant landlords some type of super-priority status. Accordingly, most courts addressing the issue have held that where there are insufficient funds in the estate to satisfy all administrative claims, a landlord is only entitled to its pro rata share with the other allowed administrative claimants. * * *
>
> [W]e agree with the *Dieckhaus* court that:
>
>> The enactment of section 365(d)(3) reflects a policy choice comparable to that of section 331. Congress clearly envisioned that debtor-tenants would "pay their rent, common area, and other charges on *time* pending the trustee's assumption or rejection of the lease." In light of this strong expression of legislative intent, I must conclude that a non-residential lessor's administrative expense claim arising under section 365(d)(3) should be paid immediately unless the trustee establishes good cause for withholding the payment.
>
> 73 B.R. at 973 (citations omitted) (emphasis in original). Because the record indicates that there may not be sufficient funds in the estate to pay all administrative claimants in full, the bankruptcy court did not err in deferring payment on Great Western's claim pending a determination of the amount of the claim and the ability of the Debtor to pay all administrative claimants.

95 B.R. at 728.

However, in *In re Telesphere Communications*, 148 B.R. 525 (Bankr.N.D. Ill.1992), although the court conceded that *Orvco* represents the majority view on this issue, it held that the requirement of "timely performance" in § 365(d)(3) mandates immediate and full payment of each rental payment when due.

Several courts of appeal have also found that the requirement of timely payment of rent is not subject to pro rata reduction in the case in which rent is due in advance and the lease terminated by rejection before the prepaid period has elapsed. In *In re Koenig Sporting Goods, Inc.*, 203 F.3d 986 (6th Cir. 2000), the debtor was obligated to pay $8500 in rent monthly in advance on the first day of each month. Debtor rejected the lease, vacated the premises and turned them back to the landlord on December 2. The court held that the December rent payment that was due in full on December 1 constituted an administrative obligation of the estate and would not be prorated. *See also In re Montgomery Ward Holding Corp.*, 268 F.3d 205 (3d Cir. 2001); contra *In re Stone Barn Manhattan LLC*, 398 B.R. 359 (Bankr.S.D.N.Y.2008) (discussing authorities).

PROBLEM

Assume that property taxes on leased commercial real estate are billed to the lessor as owner, and the lease requires the lessee to reimburse the lessor for the amounts paid by the lessor; reimbursement payment must be made at the time the lessor bills the lessee. In *In re Montgomery Ward Holding Corp.*, 268 F.3d 205 (3d Cir. 2001), lessor billed the lessee for back taxes after the lessee had filed in bankruptcy but before the lease was rejected. The lessee argued that § 365(d)(3) should not be read to cover the amounts accrued over past years merely because the lessor chose to bill the lessee for these after the lessee's filing; such amounts should be treated as prepetition unsecured claims. The court held that the entire amount for which the lessee was billed fell under § 365(d)(3) as obligations of the debtor arising under a lease after the order of relief (the "billing" test). It recognized that its view leaves room for strategic behavior on the part of lessors. In an earlier case, *Matter of Handy Andy Home Improvement Centers, Inc.*, 144 F.3d 1125 (7th Cir. 1998), Judge Posner adopted an "apportionment" test that treats obligations for past taxes as arising when those taxes were due and not when the lessor bills lessee for them. Admitting that the broad wording of § 365(d)(3) gave him some difficulties, he declared that "statutory language like other language should be read in context * * * When context is disregarded, silliness results." 144 F.3d at 1128. To him, § 365(d)(3) required the lessee to pay the full rent under the lease for every day the lessee continued occupancy until rejection, but tax debts for prior years relate to an earlier period and were no different from its debts to trade creditors that arose prepetition. Such debts should be treated as sunk costs (treat "bygones as bygones") and the lessee should be allowed to continue to operate as long as it yields net economic benefit. Which court has the better interpretation of the statute?

b. When Rejection Occurs

Since a lessee is liable for rent called for by the lease for the period after filing until it rejects the lease, large sums of money may ride on how quickly a lessee can jettison an expensive lease. Under Bankruptcy Rule 9014 the debtor must obtain court approval for assumption or rejection of a lease under § 365(a) by filing a motion in the bankruptcy court. Notice and opportunity for hearing must be afforded the landlord before the court rules on the motion. The cases have divided on whether the effective date of the lessee's rejection is the motion filing date or the date of court approval. In the first court of appeals decision in point, *In re Thinking Machines Corp.*, 67 F.3d 1021 (1st Cir. 1995), the court adopted the date-of-approval view. In that case the lessee occupied only a fraction of the leased space after August 17, the date it filed in Chapter 11. On September 13 it filed a motion to reject and the court approved the motion on October 4. The difference between the rental due on the motion filing date and on the date of court approval was more than $200,000.

Lessee contended that the motion filing date was the proper date of rejection on two grounds: (i) When the Bankruptcy Code makes judicial approval a condition precedent to a trustee's action, it usually says "the trustee, after notice and a hearing" (e.g., § 363(b)(1)), but § 365(a) merely says "the trustee, subject to the court's approval." (ii) Use of the date of court approval departs from Chapter 11 policy in that it burdens the scarce resources of bankruptcy estates with unnecessary expenses, here, $200,000. The court rejected these arguments and held that when the Bankruptcy Code made court approval obligatory for the first time (under the Bankruptcy Act a trustee, acting alone, could reject a lease), Congress intended to involve bankruptcy courts more actively in the decisional process and increased involvement is better served by viewing judicial approval as a condition precedent to the effectiveness of a rejection instead of as a condition subsequent. "We see no reason for allowing a trustee to substitute his voice for that of the court. The trustee may sing all he wants, but it is the court that must call the tune. Cf. W.A. Mozart, Le Nozze di Figaro, Act 1, sc.2 (1786) (Figaro's Aria)." 67 F.3d at 1026.

The court added, however, that bankruptcy courts, as courts of equity, may enter retroactive orders of approval in cases in which the balance of equities favors this result. It made no effort to spell out what circumstances might justify retroactivity. The court in *In re Amber's Stores, Inc.*, 193 B.R. 819 (Bankr.N.D.Tex.1996), expressly relied on this dictum in a case in which the lessee, a month before filing, vacated and turned over the keys to landlord. Lessee served an emergency motion to reject on the lessor on the date of its Chapter 11 petition. It filed this motion with the court three days after its petition; the court approved the motion the same day, effective the date of the petition. It held that retroactive rejection of the lease was justified by the equities of the case.

In *In re At Home Corp.*, 392 F. 3d 1064 (9th Cir. 2004), citing *Thinking Machines*, the Ninth Circuit affirmed a bankruptcy court's decision approving rejection of a real property lease as of the date of the filing of the Chapter 11 debtor's motion to reject basing this exercise of its equitable discretion on the debtor's prompt action seeking rejection, that the debtor was not occupying the premises and that the landlord's opposition was based solely on its desire to claim $1 million in administrative rent notwithstanding the lack of any delay in its ability to repossess the premises.

c. Personal Property Leases

Section 365(d)(3) does not apply to personal property leases or to leases of residential real property. With respect to the rights of the lessor when a debtor in possession as lessee rejects a personal property lease, Judge (now Supreme Court Justice) Anthony Kennedy stated in *In re Thompson*, 788 F.2d 560, 563 (9th Cir. 1986):

> When a lease is ultimately rejected but its interim continuance was an actual and necessary cost and expense of the estate, the allowable administrative expense is valued not according to the terms of the lease * * * but under an objective worth standard that measures the fair and reasonable value of the lease. * * * The rent reserved in the lease is presumptive evidence of fair and reasonable value * * * but the presumption may be rebutted by demonstrating that the reasonable worth of the lease differs from the contract rate * * *.
>
> The actual value or benefit conferred on the debtor is not the object of the reasonable worth inquiry. * * * Rather, the fair and reasonable value of the lease upon the open market must control. * * * Fair market value may be determined by expert testimony if, in the discretion of the trial court, it is warranted in the circumstances of a particular case. * * * The debtor's experience and his testimony regarding his actual use of the equipment and the value the equipment conferred upon him would seem in most cases irrelevant, though testimony such as whether the leased equipment operated as promised might bear upon the question whether the equipment was still marketable and acceptable in the industry generally, a matter that in turn would bear upon fair market value. * * * Equating reasonableness with fair market value provides a neutral estimate of the value of the leased property and is therefore the fairest measure of compensation for all concerned. Furthermore, it avoids self-serving testimony by a debtor on the benefit, or lack of benefit, he has experienced.

Personal property lessors were dissatisfied with this state of the law and pressed for the inclusion of personal property leases in § 365(d)(3) so that lessees in bankruptcy would have to make timely payments of contract rentals. They failed, and the tortured compromise that emerged in 1994 was a package of amendments that added § 365(b)(2)(D) and § 365(d)(10), and amended § 363(e). Under § 365(d)(10), the debtor-lessee must make, on a timely basis, rental payments called for by the lease that come due 60 days or more after the petition *unless* the debtor can convince the court "based on the equities of the case" that the amount of payments should be less or the time of making the payments should be delayed. The statute is silent on what the debtor's liability is for the rentals due during the first 60 days after the petition. However, § 363(e) was amended to provide that the lessor is entitled to adequate protection of its interest under an unexpired lease of personal property. Curiously, its right to adequate protection under § 363(e) is "to the exclusion of such property being subject to an order to grant relief from the stay under section 362."

It is not clear that the position of personal property lessors has been appreciably strengthened by these amendments. What a debtor-lessee will be required to pay and when it will be required to pay it seem completely discretionary with the court, with a sort of presumption that the time and amount of payments called for by the lease will control unless the debtor can rebut the presumption, perhaps by showing that current payment of contract rent is too great a burden on the reorganization effort. Note that secured lenders are most certainly not entitled to interim loan payments in accordance with their loan agreements during the pendency of a bankruptcy case. Courts can and do recharacterize personal property leases as secured loans when the lessor fails to retain a meaningful reversionary interest in the leased property either because the lease exhausts the useful economic life of the property or because the lessee has the obligation or option to acquire the property at the expiration of the lease. Section 365(d)(10) makes the power to recharacterize personal property leases as secured loans even more important.

Note that leases of commercial aircraft and related equipment and vessels are a special case in Chapter 11 cases. Under § 1110, unless such a lease is assumed within 60 days of the order for relief, lessors may exercise all their rights under their lease agreement, such rights being "not limited or otherwise affected by any other provision of this title or by any power of the court." *See United Airlines, Inc. v. US Bank, N.A.*, 406 F.3d 918 (7th Cir. 2005).

d. Time in Which to Assume or Reject

Before 1984, there were two rules with respect to the amount of time allowed to a trustee or debtor in possession to decide whether to reject or assume an executory contract or unexpired lease of the debtor. In Chapter 7 cases

§ 365(d)(1) applied. If a decision is not made within 60 days after the order for relief, the contract or lease is rejected. The bankruptcy court, for cause, may give the trustee additional time. In Chapter 11 cases, § 365(d)(2) applied. The debtor in possession could defer the decision until the time of confirmation of the plan of reorganization unless the bankruptcy court orders the debtor in possession to make an earlier decision. In 1984, § 365(d)(1) and (2) were amended so that they no longer apply to leases of nonresidential real property. Section 365(d)(4), added in 1984, governs leases of nonresidential real property and applies to a bankruptcy case under any chapter of the Bankruptcy Code.

BAPCPA significantly amended § 365(d)(4), requiring the written consent of the lessor to extend the time within which a debtor in possession may assume, assume and assign, or reject an unexpired lease of nonresidential real property beyond seven months after the commencement of a voluntary chapter 11 case, unless the lessor consents in writing. Absent a court order, the debtor-lessee has until the earlier of (1) 120 days (about 4 months) after the order for relief is entered or (2) the date the confirmation order is entered, to assume, assume and assign or reject its leases of nonresidential real property. For cause, the court can extend the 120-day period by 90 days (about 3 months). After the court grants that first 90-day extension, however, it cannot further extend the assumption/rejection period without the consent of the lessor.

These amendments seem likely to change the course of many Chapter 11 cases, particularly cases involving large numbers of retail outlets, where a debtor often seeks to postpone the decision on what to do with its store leases until the very end of the case or at least until it determines the size of the reorganized entity or is able to operate through critical selling seasons, often the Christmas season. Absent striking a deal with their landlords, those debtors may be forced to prematurely assume or reject their leases of nonresidential real property. Premature rejection may result in unnecessary store closures and impair reorganization. Premature assumption may result in potentially catastrophic administrative liabilities in the event the reorganization fails.

4. EVICTING THE DEBTOR IN POSSESSION

One of the objectives of the 1984 amendments was to aid landlords in evicting lessees of nonresidential real property when their leases had terminated either before or after commencement of the case. To this end, § 362(b)(10), § 365(c)(3) and § 541(b)(2) were all added. A lease can terminate "by expiration of the stated term of such lease" and § 362(b)(10) and § 541(b)(2) apply to leases that terminate in that way. A lease can also be "terminated under applicable nonbankruptcy law" and § 365(c)(3) applies to termination in that way. Thus, the Code makes a distinction between expiration of a lease and termination for cause before the expiry date. Sections 362(b)(10) and § 541(b)(2) apply to cases in which expiration occurs either before or after commencement of the case. Section 365(c)(3) applies to cases in which termination prior to the lease's expiry date occurs before commencement of the case.

a. Expiration of Lease

Suppose that under a five-year lease of nonresidential real property expiring on July 1, 2010 the lessee was not entitled to renew at the end of the term. A few months before the expiry date the landlord informed the lessee that the landlord had found another tenant and that the lessee was required to quit the premises on the expiration date. On June 15, 2010, while still in possession of the premises, the lessee filed a petition in bankruptcy under Chapter 11. On July 1, 2010 the lessee, as debtor in possession, informed the landlord that it refused to quit the premises. If this case had arisen before 1984, the landlord could not have evicted the debtor in possession without first obtaining a bankruptcy court order. Under § 362(a)(3) there is an automatic stay against "any act to obtain possession * * * of property from the estate." The landlord must request relief from the stay under § 362(d). This is changed by § 362(b)(10) which provides that the automatic stay does not apply. Section 362(b)(10) allows the landlord to bring an eviction action in state court without first seeking relief from stay.

Under § 541(a)(1) the lease became property of the estate when the lessee filed in bankruptcy on June 15, 2010 and, under § 541(b)(2), it ceased to be property of the estate on July 1, 2010 when the lease expired. Section 541(b)(2) may be redundant. The same result can be obtained without it. On July 1, 2010 the debtor in possession had no rights under the lease under § 365(a) because that provision applies only to unexpired leases.

b. Termination Before Expiration of Lease

Suppose a five-year lease that restricts the use of the premises to the sale of merchandise at retail. Six months after the commencement of the lease the lessee's retail business failed and, acting without the landlord's consent or knowledge, the lessee converted the business to a restaurant. Under the terms of the lease, violating the use covenant constituted a default justifying termination upon notice from the landlord and otherwise applicable law does not allow for reinstatement or cure after notice has been given. Assume that upon discovering the facts shortly after the restaurant opened, the landlord duly notified the lessee that the lease was terminated because of breach of the use covenant. The lessee then files in Chapter 11. What are the rights of the debtor in possession and the landlord in the demised premises?

The debtor in possession cannot assume the lease if, before the lessee filed in bankruptcy, the lease terminated under state law. *In re Maxwell*, 40 B.R. 231 (N.D.Ill.1984). If the lease has been terminated it is not be property of the estate because the debtor had no "legal or equitable interest" at the time of filing. § 541(a)(1). Section 541(b)(2) does not apply because termination of the lease occurred before its expiry date. Section 365(c)(3) applies but it does not affect the result. If the lease has been fully and finally terminated under the state law, the lease cannot be assumed. Section 365(c)(3) is not only redundant, it is confusing as well. A lease of residential real property or a personal property lease that was terminated before filing would also not be assumable under the previous law. To the extent § 365(c)(3) applies specifically to nonresidential real property, one could argue that the negative inference is that other terminated leases or contracts can be assumed. This is not so.

If the landlord brings an action in a state court to evict the debtor in possession, the lessor has violated § 362(a)(3), and § 362(b)(10) does not apply because termination did not occur because of "expiration of the stated term of the lease." Why is § 362(b)(10) limited to cases of expiration? There is not likely to be any question about whether termination is valid if the lease's expiry date has passed. But whether a lease has been terminated for cause before its expiry date depends upon facts that may be disputed. If termination is for violation of a use clause, it is necessary to determine whether the new use conflicts with use permitted under the lease. If a use clause is arbitrary or unreasonable a court may find that the lease may not be terminated for violation of the clause. For example, if a lease restricts use of the premises to operation of a French restaurant it does not necessarily follow that operation of an Italian restaurant allows the lessor to terminate for violation of the use clause. A court would have to look at the context in which the clause was adopted to determine whether it is reasonable to enforce it. If there is no interest of the landlord that is affected by the kind of food served in the restaurant, the violation is innocuous and termination should not be allowed. If there is doubt about whether termination is valid, it is proper to have that determination made by the bankruptcy court before permitting the landlord to exercise its rights under state law. Limiting § 362(b)(10) to cases of lease expiration carries out that policy.

5. ASSUMPTION AND ASSIGNMENT

a. The Perils of Assumption

If you were advising a debtor in possession or bankruptcy trustee, what concerns would you have about assuming a long-term commercial real estate lease before confirmation of a reorganization plan? Consider the following case.

In re Klein Sleep Products, Inc.
United States Court of Appeals, Second Circuit, 1996.
78 F.3d 18.

■ CALABRESI, Circuit Judge:

The liquidation provisions of the Bankruptcy Code contained in § 726 distribute a pro-rata share of a debtor's estate to each unsecured creditor so that similarly situated creditors may be treated alike. This pro-rata rule does not, however, always lead to an equitable distribution of the estate. When one claimant is a landlord holding a long-term lease, its single unsecured claim for twenty or thirty years of future rent could devour so much of the debtor's estate that only crumbs could be left for the other unsecured creditors. Recognizing the potentially distorting effect of claims arising out of long-term leases, Congress capped unsecured claims for future rent at one year. § 502(b)(6). This allows landlords to recover some of their losses from a bankrupt tenant, but sees to it that their recovery will not crowd out the claims of competing creditors.

Bankruptcy law also aims to avoid liquidation altogether when that is possible. Although the Code offers no magical potion to restore a debtor's financial health, it does provide some useful medicine designed to help a debtor get back on its feet and heading towards convalescence. It does this by allowing a debtor to attempt to reorganize rather than fold and by creating incentives for creditors to continue to do business with the debtor while reorganization proceeds. The Code does this, at least in part, by assuring these post-bankruptcy creditors that, if the debtor fails to rehabilitate itself and winds up in liquidation, they can move to the front of the distributive line, ahead of the debtor's pre-bankruptcy creditors. Special priority is therefore accorded to expenses incurred under new contracts with the debtor, as "administrative expenses" of the estate. The same priority is given to expenses arising under pre-existing contracts that the debtor "assumes"—contracts whose benefits and burdens the debtor decides, with the bankruptcy court's approval, are worth retaining.

These two competing bankruptcy policies—promoting parity among creditors and yet granting priority to the claims of creditors who continue to do business with an insolvent debtor—collide in the case before us. After entering bankruptcy, Klein Sleep (the debtor) assumed, with court approval, the unexpired lease it had with Nostas Associates (its landlord). Some eighteen months later, when it became apparent that the reorganization had failed, the newly appointed bankruptcy trustee decided to "reject" the lease. The landlord then sought to recover the future rent that was due under the lease. The bankruptcy court held, and the district court agreed, that Nostas was entitled to recover as an administrative expense only the rent that had come due before the trustee rejected the lease. Beyond that, Nostas could recover as a general unsecured claim only one year's worth of the rent coming due after rejection.

Two questions arise on appeal. We must first decide whether the future rent gives rise to a general unsecured claim that receives no priority or whether it is, instead, an administrative expense entitled to priority. If it is an administrative expense, we must then determine whether the claim is nonetheless capped at a year's worth of rent by § 502(b)(6).

Our task would be far easier if Congress had answered these questions explicitly in the Code, but unfortunately it left its intentions ambiguous. In order to resolve this ambiguity, we turn first to the various provisions of the Code that discuss the timing and priority of claims. Since we do not find an unmistakable Code directive, however, we also seek guidance from the practice prevailing under the Code's predecessor, the Bankruptcy Act. Adhering to that practice, we hold that damages arising from future rent under an assumed lease must be treated as an administrative expense, and we therefore reverse in part.

The conclusion we reach seems on its face to be unduly favorable to landlords. But it may in fact do no more than recognize the existence of a default rule, which the bankruptcy court can use in encouraging landlords and tenants alike to renegotiate leases in bankruptcy so as to treat all the parties, including general unsecured creditors, equitably.

I. Facts

Nostas Associates, the landlord, appeals from a judgment of the United States District Court * * *, affirming the bankruptcy court's order—which assigned administrative priority to Nostas's claims for past rent accruing under a commercial lease, allowed another year's worth of future rent as a general unsecured claim, and disallowed any recovery for the rest. Before entering bankruptcy, Klein Sleep, Inc. had leased a store from Nostas in Paramus, New Jersey. Shortly after filing for Chapter 11 relief in June 1991, Klein Sleep (acting as debtor-in-possession) assumed the lease with the approval of the bankruptcy court pursuant to § 365, and accordingly cured all rental arrears to that point. Klein Sleep continued to pay rent through October 1992. By January 1993, however, it had become clear that the reorganization had failed so completely that liquidating the firm's assets would not cover even the administrative expenses of the estate. On January 29, 1993, Klein Sleep's newly appointed Chapter 11 trustee, who was assigned the task of liquidating the estate, rejected the lease and surrendered possession of the store to Nostas.

Nostas argued to the bankruptcy court, to the district court, and now to us on appeal that Klein Sleep's court-approved lease assumption converted *all* liability under the lease into administrative expenses that warrant a first priority in repayment under § 507(a)(1) (providing that administrative expenses, as defined by § 503(b), are first in the order of repayment of claims and expenses). Under this theory, Nostas seeks administrative expense status for rent arrearages from November 1992 through January 1993, [and] for future rent accruing after January 1993 * * *.

The bankruptcy court * * * allowed Nostas's claims in the following order of priority: (1) Super-priority administrative expense status for rent during the liquidation period, from December 1, 1992, through January 29, 1993 (approximately $18,000, of which 100% will be paid upon distribution of the estate), as "burial expenses" of winding up the estate; (2) priority administrative expense status for rent during the pre-liquidation period, from November 1, 1992, through December 1, 1992 (approximately $6800, of which approximately 85% will be paid upon distribution of the estate); and (3) general unsecured claim status for future damages arising after the trustee rejected the lease (approximately $80,000[2] or one year's future rent as limited by § 502(b)(6), of which nothing will be paid upon distribution of the estate). * * *

* * * Relying primarily on this court's decision in *Trustees of Amalgamated Insurance Fund v. McFarlin's, Inc.*, 789 F.2d 98, 101 (2d Cir. 1986) * * * the district court held that:

> benefit to the estate as required by section 503(b)(1)(A) must be shown for damages arising from the subsequent rejection of an assumed lease to be afforded administrative priority, even if the expenses are considered post-petition expenses under section 365(g)(2)(A). Because the post-surrender damages incurred by Nostas in the instant case conferred no benefit upon Klein Sleep, those expenses are not entitled to administrative priority status.

* * *

II. Discussion

A. Administrative Expense Status

According to § 503(b)(1)(A), "the actual, necessary costs and expenses of preserving the estate" constitute administrative expenses entitled to priority status upon distribution of the estate. The crux of Nostas's argument is that a trustee's or debtor-in-possession's assumption of an unexpired lease transforms *all* liability under the lease, including damages that stem from a subsequent rejection of the lease, into administrative expenses. There is strong bankruptcy

---

[2] Because Nostas relet the premises beginning on July 1, 1993, it claimed the entire rent due under the Klein Sleep lease from January 29, 1993 through June 30, 1993 (totalling approximately $38,000), plus the difference between the rent it would have collected under the remainder of the Klein Sleep lease (approximately $215,000) and the rent due under the new lease (approximately $157,000), for a total claim of $96,000 in post-rejection rent.

court precedent directly on point that supports this proposition. *See, e.g.,* * * * 2 COLLIER ON BANKRUPTCY ¶ 365.08[01], at 365–65 (15th ed. 1995) ("[A] trustee must proceed cautiously in electing whether to assume or reject since an assumption will have the effect of making the expenses and liabilities incurred expenses of administration.").

Multech, the seminal case on this issue, offers the following rationale for this rule:

> By defining the time at which a rejection of an assumed contract or lease constitutes a breach, § 365(g) clearly indicates that the act of assumption creates an administrative expense obligation of the particular proceedings in which the contract or lease was assumed. Consequently, if a lease is assumed in Chapter 11 proceedings, the liabilities flowing from the rejection of that lease will ever after be regarded as a Chapter 11 administrative expense.

47 B.R. at 750 (footnote omitted).

Citing our decision in *McFarlin's*, however, the district court declined to follow *Multech* and its progeny. The court stated that our decision in *McFarlin's* established that expenses fall within § 503(b)(1)(A) if they arise out of a transaction between the debtor and the creditor, and "'only to the extent that the consideration supporting the claimant's right to payment was both supplied to and beneficial to the debtor-in-possession in the operation of the business.'" *McFarlin's*, 789 F.2d at 101 (quoting *In re Mammoth Mart, Inc.*, 536 F.2d 950, 953 (1st Cir. 1976)). It then asserted that Klein Sleep derived actual benefit not from its *assumption* of the lease, but only from its *occupation* of the leased premises.

Once the trustee gave the store back to Nostas, the court reasoned, Klein Sleep received no further benefit from the lease. As a result, the damages it sought for future rent did not meet the prerequisites for administrative expense status under § 503(b)(1)(A). * * *

At first glance, the bankruptcy court's approach has much to recommend it. By denying administrative expense status for all future rent under an assumed lease, the court followed our stated policy that priorities in bankruptcy should be narrowly construed and sparingly granted. *McFarlin's*, 789 F.2d at 100. And, the bankruptcy court's relegation of Nostas to the ranks of the unsecured creditors furthered this fundamental policy—based on the notion that individual creditors, whenever possible, should be prevented from seizing a disproportionate share of the estate—in a second way as well. Once future rent is treated merely as an unsecured claim, it is clearly capped by § 502(b)(6) at one year's worth of unpaid rent. As a result, the rent claims cannot absorb all the assets of the estate, no matter how long the lease.

Yet this approach has several deficiencies. First, it relies on an unduly narrow view of the benefit conferred on an estate when a trustee assumes an unexpired lease. Second, it does not adequately account for the Code's timing provisions, which explicitly provide that claims arise "postpetition," and therefore during the administration of the estate, if they are based on breaches of assumed leases. And finally, even if these two considerations did not resolve the matter, the district court's approach does not accord with prior practice under the Bankruptcy Act (practice which, in cases of ambiguity, stands as a decisive guidepost for interpreting today's Bankruptcy Code). Bankruptcy Act practice strongly directs us to treat the entire liability resulting from breach of an assumed lease as a cost of administering the estate.

1. Benefit

* * *

The trustee argues that any inquiry as to "benefit" is foreclosed by the district court's factual finding that Klein Sleep did not benefit from its assumption of the lease. The opposite, however, is true: the bankruptcy court's earlier decision to let Klein Sleep assume the unexpired lease—a decision that was not appealed—precluded a subsequent finding that assuming the lease did not benefit Klein Sleep. That decision required a judicial finding—up-front—that it was in the best interests of the estate (and the unsecured creditors) for the debtor to assume the lease, pursuant to § 365(a). It is the same kind of finding that the bankruptcy court is required to make with regard to all *new* contracts entered into by the trustee without prior court approval during the administration of the estate in order for those contracts to qualify for priority pursuant to § 503(b). Compare *In re Orion Pictures Corp.*, 4 F.3d 1095, 1099 (2d Cir. 1993) ("[A] bankruptcy court reviewing a trustee's or debtor-in-possession's decision to assume or reject an executory contract [pursuant to § 365] should examine a contract and the surrounding circumstances and apply its best 'business judgment' to determine if it would be beneficial or burdensome to the estate to assume it.") with *Mammoth Mart*, 536 F.2d at 954 (granting administrative expense status to postpetition claim only if consideration "was both supplied to and beneficial to the debtor-in-possession in the operation of the business").

As one bankruptcy court has explained:

> By requiring the court to determine the reasonable necessity of the newly entered contract under § 503(b), Congress has insured some judicial control over the determination of what executory contracts will be granted administrative expense priority. The Code, in order to streamline reorganization procedure, allows a debtor in possession to enter into contracts in the ordinary course of business without seeking court approval. Thus, contracts initially entered into during reorganiza-

tion, unlike contracts assumed during reorganization, will not have undergone court scrutiny. By limiting automatic administrative expense treatment under § 365(g) to assumed contracts, and by requiring initially entered contracts to qualify under § 503(b) in order to be granted an administrative expense priority, Congress has insured both similar treatment and similar procedural safeguards for these fundamentally similar obligations. * * *

In short, we decline to find that Klein Sleep did not benefit by assuming its lease simply because the lease was no longer profitable at the time it stopped displaying mattresses on the premises. Such a holding would mean that any post-bankruptcy contract, entered into for the benefit of a bankrupt's estate, would cease to be entitled to priority the moment the deal turned sour. When the debtor-in-possession assumed the lease, it retained the right to occupy the leased premises immediately and in the future. Its ability to assign this immediate right of possession, as well as its ability to assign the future right of possession under the lease, had a present value at the time of assumption. Acquisition of those rights clearly constituted a benefit to the estate even if, later, the benefit turned to dust.

2. Timing

The Code's timing provisions also tilt in favor of Nostas's position that all future rent is an administrative expense. In allowing and assigning priority to claims arising from unexpired leases, the Code distinguishes between leases that have been assumed, and those that have not. Section 502(g) of the Code clearly instructs us that claims arising from *unassumed* leases are to be allowed as general unsecured claims. Section 502(g) has no analogue that tells us what to do with claims arising from *assumed* leases. But because § 502(g) limits its reach to unassumed leases, it is reasonable to infer that assumed leases are to be treated differently. Since it would be absurd to suppose that such leases would not qualify as claims at all, it follows that they must be considered administrative expenses of the estate. * * *

This inference is further supported by § 365(g), which fixes the time at which a debtor's rejection of an unexpired lease is deemed to constitute a breach of the lease. When a debtor rejects an unassumed lease, breach is deemed to occur at the time the bankruptcy petition was filed. § 365(g)(1). If the lease has been assumed, however, breach is deemed to occur whenever the lease is later rejected. § 365(g)(2)(A).⁵ According to the Code's legislative history, the purpose of § 365(g) is to treat claims arising from unassumed leases "as prepetition claims." H.R.REP. NO. 595, 95th Cong., 2d Sess. 349 (1977); S.REP. NO. 989, 95th Cong., 2d Sess. 63 (1978). But the only way in which prepetition claims are treated differently from postpetition claims is that the former are classified as general claims, whereas the latter—arising, for example, from torts committed by the estate in bankruptcy, or from contracts entered into by the trustee or debtor-in-possession—are entitled to administrative expense priority. It would seem to follow that rejection of an assumed lease—that is, breach of contract committed by the trustee or debtor-in-possession while administering the estate—gives rise to a debt entitled to the same administrative expense priority.

The timing provisions of the Code were not, however, directly designed to answer the question we are asking today, and so we are hesitant to read too much into them. Indeed, because all of our previous discussion has essentially required us to read between the lines of Congress's directives, we conclude that the Bankruptcy Code, though it clearly leans in favor of administrative status for assumed leases, is still ambiguous. When that is the case, we are required to turn for further guidance to the prior practice under the Bankruptcy Act.

3. Practice Under the Bankruptcy Act

Were we writing on a clean slate, we might perhaps be persuaded by the district court's analysis—though, as we have discussed above, we think that the structure of the Code favors the landlord's position. We are not, however, permitted to start from scratch. In *Dewsnup v. Timm*, 502 U.S. 410 (1992), the Supreme Court declined to resolve de novo an ambiguous interrelationship between certain Bankruptcy Code provisions, where accepted pre-Code bankruptcy practice existed. The Court stated:

> When Congress amends the bankruptcy laws, it does not write "on a clean slate.". . . Furthermore, this Court has been reluctant to accept arguments that would interpret the Code, however vague the particular language under consideration might be, to effect a change in pre-Code practice that is not the subject of at least some discussion in the legislative history.

502 U.S. at 419 (citation omitted).

---

⁵ When a reorganization case is converted to a liquidation proceeding after the lease has been assumed but before it is rejected, breach is deemed to have occurred immediately before the conversion. § 365(g)(2)(B).

In the case before us, an ambiguity arguably exists as to whether claims arising from the rejection of assumed contracts by definition meet the "actual and necessary" requirements of § 503(b)(1)(A) and hence automatically enjoy administrative expense priority under § 507(a)(1). * * * Nostas and amicus argue, however, that the pre-Code practice was to grant administrative status automatically to all claims arising from the subsequent rejection of an assumed executory contract—and, therefore, that any ambiguity must be resolved in favor of granting administrative expense status.

* * *

Absent a clear Code directive, or legislative history that directly addresses the issue and reaches a contrary result, the rule of construction set forth in *Dewsnup* dictates that Nostas's claim for post-rejection rental damages should be governed by Bankruptcy Act practice. That practice strongly supports the conclusion that Nostas's claim was entitled to administrative expense status. This result, moreover, agrees with our earlier analysis that the Code's timing provisions, together with the rules governing "benefit," indicate that all future rent accruing under an assumed lease is entitled to the status of an administrative expense. Accordingly, we so hold.

B. The § 502(b)(6) Cap on Damages for Future Rent

Because it determined that Nostas's claim was not an administrative expense, the district court never reached the issue of whether § 502(b)(6) limits Nostas's claim arising from the assumed leases to one year's worth of future rent. Since we conclude that such future rent is an administrative expense, we must now decide whether § 502(b)(6) caps the rent.

Section 502(b)(6) requires a court to allow a claim except to the extent that it exceeds one year's rent due under the lease.[6] This cap is designed to prevent a

---

[6] Section 502(b)(6) provides, more fully, that the bankruptcy court shall allow a lessor's claim for damages arising from the termination of a lease of real property, except to the extent that the claim exceeds

> (A) the rent reserved by such lease, without acceleration, for the greater of one year, or 15 percent, not to exceed three years, of the remaining term of such lease, following the earlier of—
>
> (i) the date of the filing of the petition; and
>
> (ii) the date on which such lessor repossessed, or the lessee surrendered, the leased property; plus
>
> (B) any unpaid rent due under such lease, without acceleration, on the earlier of such dates. . . .

Because in the case before us § 502(b)(6) operates to limit rent claims to one year—rather than fifteen percent of all future rent capped at three years—we refer to this section as imposing a "one-year cap."

landlord's single unsecured claim—which, depending on the length of the lease, may be enormous—to elbow aside the other unsecured creditors. The trustee argues that "[t]he policy underlying Code § 502(b)(6) applies equally to claims arising under leases that have been assumed and those that have not." Indeed, because the drafters of the Code took such care to prevent a monstrous *unsecured* claim from swallowing up the estate, it might seem odd not only to give an analogous type of claim priority over unsecured creditors, but also to allow such a claim in its entirety, merely because it arose from an assumed lease.

Sensible as this policy argument might be, we do not find the Code ambiguous on this point. Section 502, which contains the cap on future rent, applies only to "a claim or interest, proof of which is filed under section 501." § 502(a). Section 501 prescribes the method for filing proofs of prepetition claims against the debtor and certain postpetition claims that are deemed to have arisen prepetition. It does not apply to administrative expenses payable by the debtor, which must be requested pursuant to § 503. See also id. § 507 (referring to "expenses and claims"). And because § 502 does not apply to administrative expenses, it cannot cap future rent due under an assumed lease.

The legislative history of § 502(b)(6) confirms that, at least on this score, Congress said what it meant. H.R.REP. NO. 595, 95th Cong., 2d Sess. 353 (1977); S.REP. NO. 989, 95th Cong., 2d Sess. 63 (1978) (stating that § 502(b)(6) "does not apply to limit administrative expense claims for use of the leased premises to which the landlord is otherwise entitled"); see also *Multech*, 47 B.R. at 751 (explaining that the policy of preventing landlord's unsecured claim from crowding out other unsecured creditors "is no longer germane in the case of an assumed contract or lease, since the resulting obligations and liabilities are elevated to a priority status and no longer fall in the class of general unsecured creditors"); *In re Johnston, Inc.*, 164 B.R. at 555 (stating that § 502(b)(6) does not limit administrative expense claims); 2 COLLIER ON BANKRUPTCY ¶ 365.08, at 365–67 (15th ed. 1995) ("[T]he limitation upon the amount of an allowed claim arising from breach of a lease in section 502(b)(6) of the Code does not apply to leases assumed and thereafter rejected in the case.")

* * *

III. Conclusion

It would surely have been better if Congress had spelled out its intentions as to assumed leases in the Code, rather than leaving it up to the courts to clean up the ambiguities. But, under the circumstances, clean them up we must. The trustee complains that the rule we pick—a rule that accords administrative priority to claims for all future rent under an assumed lease—is overly generous to landlords, since it gives them a lion's share of estates upon liquidation. While that may seem to be the case, we doubt that it will work out that way in practice. Under the rule we adopt, bankruptcy courts will rarely find that assuming liability for all future rent under a long-term lease is in the best interests of the estate—including the interest of the general creditors—unless the rental terms are highly advantageous. They will therefore block assumption of such leases except in unusual cases. As a result, landlords will find themselves with unsecured claims capped at one year's worth of future rent.

This may also seem undesirable, especially since in some such cases the tenant properly wishes to continue the rental. But this too is not quite the end of the story, for bankruptcy courts may have another option open to them. Faced with the unattractive choice of either requiring a bankrupt tenant to reject its long-term lease (and thereby possibly dooming the reorganization to failure) or letting it assume the lease (and leaving the general creditors with a paltry recovery should liquidation ensue), one bankruptcy court suggested that it could instead put off the decision on whether or not to assume a long-term lease. It could delay, the court stated, until the moment of confirmation, when the debtor's chances of rehabilitation would finally be clear. *See In re Monica Scott*, 123 B.R. 990, 993 (Bankr.D.Minn.1991). ("Unless the Congress addresses this situation, cause will undoubtedly be found to exist, as a matter of course, for extending to confirmation the time to assume or reject significant leases in Chapter 11 cases."), *id.* n.8 (citing § 365(d)(4), which permits bankruptcy courts to extend the 60–day assumption/rejection period "for cause"). The uncertainty engendered by such an approach would give the bankruptcy court significant leverage over both tenant and landlord, and might well lead to a renegotiation of the long-term lease. The tenant who wishes to retain control over the premises has an interest—arising out of fear that the court will force rejection of the original lease—in renegotiating the lease, though perhaps for a shorter term. The landlord also has an interest in renegotiating the lease to escape the limbo between assumption and rejection. In such circumstances the landlord might well prefer to recover some guaranteed amount of future rent, as an administrative expense, under a new contract rather than risk having the lease rejected and the recovery limited to a fractional share of one year's worth of future rent, as an unsecured claim, under the pre-existing contract.[7]

None of this is before us today. But we do note that the rule that we enunciate may not be quite as rigid as it looks. It may well operate, like so many other default rules in contract law, only as a backdrop against which the

---

[7] In either event, of course, the landlord is entitled to recover as an administrative expense the rent due while the debtor and the bankruptcy court debate whether to assume the lease. § 365(d)(3).

parties—here the landlord and tenant—can renegotiate to reach a satisfactory, middle solution.

* * *

For the reasons stated above, we hold that claims for future rent arising out of assumed leases are administrative expenses of the debtor's estate, regardless of whether they are subsequently rejected, and that they are not capped at a year's worth of unpaid rent by § 502(b)(6). We reach this conclusion in light of the prior practice under the Bankruptcy Act, the timing provisions of the Code, and an understanding that debtors generally benefit from court-approved assumptions of executory contracts and unexpired leases.

Reversed to the extent that the court disallowed Nostas's claim for future rent as an administrative expense, and remanded for further proceedings consistent with this opinion.

NOTE

Section 503(b)(7) overruled that portion of *Klein Sleep* that held that the lessor was entitled to an unlimited administrative expense claim. Under the amendment, a lessor with respect to a nonresidential real property lease that was previously assumed and then rejected will have an administrative expense claim for future rent capped at an amount equal to the rent "[f]or the period of 2 years following the later of the rejection date or the date of actual turnover of the premises. . . ." Damages for "going dark" and penalties are expressly excluded from the administrative claim. Mitigation principles will apply only to the extent that the lessor actually receives rent from a nondebtor. It is not entirely clear whether future rent claims based on rents due more than two years after rejection may be asserted as administrative claims to the extent that the cap is not otherwise exhausted.

Section 503(b)(7) also reversed that portion of *Klein Sleep* that held that the § 502(b)(6) cap does not apply to these claims, although the cap will apply on a more limited basis. It applies to the lessor's claim for future rent in excess of the capped administrative claim: "[t]he claim for remaining sums due for the balance of the term of the lease shall be a claim under section 502(b)(6)."

These amendments to some degree mitigate the effects of the new 7-month time limit on nonconsensual extensions of the time for assumption or rejection, by limiting the economic consequences of rejecting previously assumed leases. Still the consequences remain severe: the landlord under such a lease will retain its cure payments, its postpetition administrative rent, hold a second-priority administrative claim for up to 2 years future rent, and hold an unsecured, albeit capped, claim for the balance under § 502(b)(6).

b. Effect of Violation of Use Clause

Matter of U.L. Radio Corp.
United States Bankruptcy Court, S.D. New York, 1982.
19 B.R. 537.

■ JOHN J. GALGAY, Bankruptcy Judge.

Debtor, U.L. Radio Corp., has moved for an order, pursuant to Bankruptcy Code section 365(f), authorizing it to assume its lease ("Lease") with Jemrock Realty Company ("Jemrock"), the landlord, and authorizing U.L. Radio to assign the Lease to Just Heaven Restaurant, Ltd. ("Just Heaven"). U.L. Radio operates the leasehold as a television sales and service store. Just Heaven, the prospective assignee, will operate the premises as a small bistro. Jemrock opposes such an assignment, citing a use clause in the Lease which provides that the lessee shall use the premises only for television service and sale of electrical appliances. Jemrock asserts that the assignment of the Lease to Just Heaven would unlawfully modify the Lease by violating the use clause. Such modification, Jemrock avers, is not permitted under section 365 without the landlord's consent, which consent Jemrock withholds.

* * * The Court grants debtor's motion to assume and assign the Lease to Just Heaven.

I. Background

On September 17, 1979, the debtor entered into the Lease with Jemrock for a store located at 2656 Broadway, New York, New York. The store is located in a building which is also occupied by a grocery store, a Chinese restaurant, a liquor store, and 170 apartments. The term of the Lease is for ten years. The rent required to be paid is as follows: $9,600 per year from November 1, 1979, to October 31, 1982; $10,800 from November 1, 1982, to October 31, 1985; and $12,000 from November 1, 1985 to October 31, 1989. Paragraph 43 of the rider to the Lease provides that the tenant may assign the Lease with the written consent of the Landlord, which consent is not to be unreasonably withheld.

On May 20, 1981, the debtor filed an original petition under Chapter 11 of the Bankruptcy Code and continues to operate its business as debtor in possession. * * * The debtor intends to propose a liquidation plan of reorganization. The debtor is current in the payment of rent and related charges required by the terms of the Lease and is not in default of any of the Lease terms.

In furtherance of its intention to liquidate all of its assets and to propose a plan of reorganization, the debtor, subject to the approval of this Court, entered into an assignment of the Lease to Just Heaven. The proposed assignment provides, *inter alia,* that Just Heaven will pay to the debtor as consideration for the assignment as follows: for the period commencing three months after this Court's approval of the assignment to October 31, 1988, the sum of $2,000 per month. Such payments will fund a plan paying unsecured creditors 100 percent of their claims. Rockwell International, the largest creditor, recommends the assignment.

The president of Just Heaven has executed a personal guarantee for the payment of rent in favor of the landlord for the first two years of the assignment, together with a statement that her net worth exceeds $50,000.

The Lease provides * * * that "any noise emanating from said premises shall be deemed a breach of the terms and conditions of this Lease." Just Heaven has allocated $20,000 for construction, including soundproofing. David Humpal St. James, Vice President and Secretary as well as a director and a shareholder of Just Heaven, is a noted interior designer including the design of commercial restaurants. His design work has involved soundproofing. * * *

II. Issues

Two issues confront this Court:

(1) Have the provisions of section 365, regarding assumption and assignment of leases, been satisfied?

(2) Can deviation from a use clause prevent the assignment of a lease, when the assumption and assignment otherwise comport with the requirements of section 365?

III. Assumption and assignment under section 365

Code section 365 governs the assumption and assignment of executory contracts, providing broad authority to a trustee or debtor in possession to assume and assign an unexpired lease. * * *

Assignment of a lease, which is at issue here, must comply with section 365(f).

* * *

Subsection (f)(1) "partially invalidates restrictions on assignment of contracts or leases by the trustee to a third party." House Report at 349; Senate Report at 59 * * *. Subsection (f)(2) "imposes two restrictions on assignment by the trustee: (1) he must first assume the contract or lease, subject to all the restrictions found in the section; and (2) adequate assurance of future performance must be provided to the other contracting party." House Report at 349;

Senate Report at 59.[1] Finally, subsection (f)(3) "invalidates contractual provisions that permit termination or modification in the event of an assignment, as contrary to the policy of this subsection." House Report at 349; Senate Report at 59.

* * *

B. Adequate Assurance of Future Performance

The second requirement of assignment under section 365(f)(2) is adequate assurance of future performance ("adequate assurance"). * * * The phrase "adequate assurance of future performance" is not found in the Bankruptcy Act.

* * * In the legislative history of section 365(b), Congress while discussing assumption under section 365(b) and the bankruptcy clause under section 365(f), provided this explanation of adequate assurance:

> If a trustee is to assume a contract or lease, the courts will have to insure that the trustee's performance under the contract or lease gives the other contracting party the full benefit of the bargain.

House Report at 348; Senate Report at 59.

Beyond equating adequate assurance with the full benefit of the bargain, Congress offers no definition of adequate assurance except in the case of real property leases in shopping centers. [See Bankruptcy Code § 365(b)(3).] The Lease at issue here is not located in a shopping center. Congress described a shopping center as "often a carefully planned enterprise, and though it consists of numerous individual tenants, the center is planned as a single unit, often subject to a master lease or financing agreement." House Report at 348. The building in which U.L. Radio is located is primarily a residential apartment building, with a liquor store, a grocery store, a restaurant, and U.L. Radio on the first floor. Thus the specific provisions of adequate assurance in the shopping center case do not apply to the assignment at issue here. * * *

* * * Adequate assurance of future performance are not words of art, but are to be given practical, pragmatic construction. What constitutes "adequate assurance" is to be determined by factual conditions. * * * The broad authorization of the trustee or debtor to assume or assign unexpired leases, notwithstanding anti-assignment or bankruptcy clauses, prompted the admonition from Congress that the courts must "be sensitive to the rights of the nondebtor party to * * * unexpired leases." House Report at 348; Senate Report at 59.

---

[1] Code section 365(f) does not state which party must provide assurance. However, since Code section 365(k) relieves the debtor-assignor of liability under the lease after assignment, it is sensible that the assignee must provide the assurance of performance.

The phrase "adequate assurance of future performance" was adopted from Uniform Commercial Code section 2–609. *Report of the Commission on Bankruptcy Laws of the United States* (1973). U.C.C. section 2–609 provides that a party with reasonable grounds for insecurity regarding another party's performance may demand "adequate assurance." * * * Regarding adequate assurance under an assignment pursuant to section 365(f)(2), the Court in *In re Lafayette Radio Electronics Corp.*, 9 B.R. 993 [, 998] (Bankr.E.D.N.Y.1981), stated, "[T]he Court's primary focus will be on the ability of [the assignee] to comply with the financial obligations under the agreement."

In *In re Pin Oaks Apartments*, 7 B.R. 364 (Bankr.S.D.1980), the Court found that changes in financial provisions of a lease, a percentage rental clause and a sublease provision which protected that rental clause, precluded a finding that adequate assurance had been provided because of the drastic effect the changes would have on rentals received.

Thus, the primary focus of adequate assurance is the assignee's ability to satisfy financial obligations under the lease. In this case, the president of the assignee has executed a personal guarantee of the payment of rent in favor of the landlord for the first two years of the assignment, together with a statement that her net worth exceeds $50,000. The assignee has budgeted $20,000 for construction, enhancing the chances of success of the assignee's enterprise. The assignee will have operating capital of an additional $30,000. * * * Upon these facts, the Court rules that adequate assurance of future financial performance has been provided by the assignee.

IV. Use clause

However, adequate assurance of future financial performance is not the complete statutory requirement; adequate assurance of future performance is. The financial capability of an assignee may be sufficient for a finding of adequate assurance under an executory sales contract or a similar commercial transaction. In a landlord-tenant relationship, more than an assignee's ability to comply with the financial provisions of a lease may be required. More particularly, will compliance with a use clause be required in order to provide adequate assurance?

Congress indicates that adequate assurance will give the landlord the full benefit of his bargain. In its case-by-case determination of those factors, beyond financial assurance, which constitute the landlord's bargain, the Court will generally consider the provisions of the lease to be assigned. * * *

However, it is equally clear that, by requiring provision of adequate assurance under section 365, i.e., the lessor's receipt of the full benefit of his bargain, Congress did not require the Court to assure literal fulfillment by the lessee of each and every term of the bargain. * * * Section 365, by its own terms, empowers the court to render unenforceable bankruptcy clauses and anti-assignment clauses which permit modification or termination of a lease for filing in bankruptcy or assignment of the lease. § 365(e), (f)(3). Section 365(k) relieves the estate of liability for future breaches of a lease after assignment, notwithstanding lease provisions to the contrary. * * *

The Court in *In re Pin Oaks Apartments* argued that court authority to abrogate lease provisions extends only to those provisions expressly stated by Congress:

> If Congress intended to give this Court or the trustee the power to abrogate any contractual rights between a debtor and non-debtor contracting party other than anti-assignment and "ipso facto" [i.e. bankruptcy] clauses, it would have expressly done so.

7 B.R. at 367.

Such a narrow view of court authority is not supported by the statute or the legislative history. First, such a narrow view would frustrate the express policy of Congress favoring assignment. Under the *Pin Oaks* reasoning, lessors could employ very specific use clauses to prevent assignment and thus circumvent the Code. Section 365(f), in broad language, empowers the Court to authorize assignment of an unexpired lease and invalidate any lease provision which would terminate or modify the lease because of the assignment of that lease. § 365(f)(1), (3). Any lease provision, not merely one entitled "anti-assignment clause", would be subject to the court's scrutiny regarding its anti-assignment effect. The court could render unenforceable any provision whose sole effect is to restrict assignment, "as contrary to the policy of [subsection (f)(3)]." House Report at 349; Senate Report at 59. * * *

* * *

Thus, provision of adequate assurance of future performance does not require an assignee's literal compliance with each and every term of the lease. The court may permit deviations from strict enforcement of any provision including a use clause. * * *

One commentator suggested that the court render completely invalid any use clause in a non-shopping center lease because: (1) "the lessor is seeking to protect his tenant mix with the lease provision, and the Code does not require the court to provide such protection"; and (2) a use clause "invalidly conditions assignment." Fogel, Executory Contracts and Unexpired Leases in the Bankruptcy Code, 64 Minn.L.Rev. 341, 364 (1980). * * * The Court rejects this "*per se* unenforceable" reading of a use clause.

However, the Court will not go to the other extreme and adopt the "insubstantial" breach or disruption standard for non-shopping center cases that is applicable only to shopping center leases. The insubstantial breaches and disruptions language of section 365(b)(3) clearly reflects an attempt to limit the effect of what was understood—and feared—to be the more expansive authority conferred by the balance of [s]ection 365(a). * * * The Court's authority to waive strict enforcement of lease provisions in the non-shopping center cases will permit deviations which would exceed those permitted in the shopping center cases. * * *

Within the range between unenforceability of a use clause and insubstantial breaches of a use clause, the Code provides no specific standard by which to measure permissible deviations in use. Whatever standard is applied must serve the policy aims of Congress.

Section 365 expresses a clear Congressional policy favoring assumption and assignment. Such a policy will insure that potential valuable assets will not be lost by a debtor who is reorganizing his affairs or liquidating assets for distribution to creditors. * * * To prevent an assignment of an unexpired lease by demanding strict enforcement of a use clause, and thereby contradict clear Congressional policy, a landlord or lessor must show that actual and substantial detriment would be incurred by him if the deviation in use was permitted.

In this case, the contemplated deviation in use is from an appliance store to a small bistro. The building in which the unexpired leasehold is located already contains a restaurant, a laundry, and a liquor store. The landlord has failed to demonstrate any actual and substantial detriment which he would incur if the proposed deviation in use is permitted. The Court also notes that the contemplated use, along with the planned soundproofing, will have no adverse effect on other tenants in the building. Thus, this Court rules that the use clause may not be enforced so as to block assignment of this lease to Just Heaven. The fact that Jemrock withholds its consent to the proposed assignment will not prevent the assignment. * * *

Congress, in section 365, has stated a general policy favoring assignment. Balanced against this general policy is the requirement that the non-debtor contracting party receive the full benefit of his bargain. Jemrock Realty will receive the full benefit of its bargain under the proposed assignment of the leasehold from U.L. Radio to Just Heaven. No defaults exist under the lease. The lease has properly been assumed and Just Heaven has provided adequate assurance of future performance. The landlord has shown no actual or substantial detriment to him from the proposed assignment. The statutory requirements have been satisfied. The assignment is authorized.

NOTE

In a non-shopping center case, Debtor's lease restricted use to the sale of hardware, paint and related items. Upon Debtor's liquidation, the highest bidder for the remaining 12–year term of the lease was a ladies clothing outlet. The court relied on *U.L. Radio* to approve the assignment over the objections of the lessor and another tenant of the lessor in the same building which also sold ladies clothing. The court held that the other tenant had no standing to object: "Section 365 aims to ensure that the landlord receives the benefit of his bargain, and looks, therefore, to the prejudice to the landlord. It does not deal with a third party's benefit of its own bargain with the landlord * * *." *In re Martin Paint Stores*, 199 B.R. 258, 264 (Bankr.S.D.N.Y.1996).

In re Standor Jewelers West, Inc.

United States Bankruptcy Appellate Panel, Ninth Circuit, 1991.
129 B.R. 200.

■ JONES, Bankruptcy Judge:

* * *

On June 1, 1990 Debtor Standor Jewelers West, Inc. filed a voluntary petition for relief under Chapter 11 of the Bankruptcy Code. At the time, Debtor operated four retail jewelry stores including a store leased at the South Coast Plaza Mall in Costa Mesa, California. On July 30, 1990 Debtor sought to assume and assign the lease for its South Coast Plaza Store (the "Lease") and to sell the assets of the South Coast Plaza Store free and clear of liens, with liens to attach to proceeds, to Sterling, Inc., an Ohio corporation ("Sterling"). South Coast Plaza objected to the assumption and assignment of the Lease because of debtor's alleged refusal to provide it with "adequate assurances" that it would comply with a provision in the Lease requiring the lessee to remit to the landlord 75% of the appreciation in value of the Lease as a condition to the landlord's consent to any assignment. * * *

The bankruptcy court held that, even if the provision of the Lease allocating 75% of the value of the leasehold to the landlord as a condition of the assignment was valid under state law, that provision constituted a restriction on transfer of the lease which was preempted by and invalid pursuant to § 365(f). * * *

* * * In order to facilitate the assignment of unexpired leases, § 365(f)(1) renders unenforceable provisions in a lease which condition or in any way restrict the assignment of the lease:

> . . . notwithstanding a provision in an. . . unexpired lease of the debtor, or in applicable law, that prohibits, restricts, or conditions the assignment of such contract or lease, the trustee may assign such contract or lease. . ..

* * * The legislative history of § 365(f) states that contractual provisions that modify the terms of a lease upon assignment are invalid, as contrary to the rehabilitative policies of the Bankruptcy Code. * * *

In *In re National Sugar Refining Co.*, 21 B.R. 196 (Bankr.S.D.N.Y.1982) the court invalidated provisions in a lease which required the debtor to transfer a portion of the purchase price to the lessor.[3] South Coast Plaza attempts to distinguish *National Sugar Refining* by claiming that the court in that case misunderstood that it must first determine whether the provision validly allocated the ownership interest under state law. South Coast Plaza contends that in the instant case, the bankruptcy court erred by not initially determining who owns the property at issue: the 75% of the appreciated leasehold estate. In order to do so, South Coast Plaza argues that the court must refer to state law and the language of the Lease.

Under applicable California law, parties to a commercial lease are permitted to condition assignment of that lease upon payment to the landlord of some or all of any consideration the tenant receives upon assignment in excess of the rent provided in the lease. * * * However, the bankruptcy court rejected this reasoning and found *National Sugar Refining* controlling, concluding that because the Lease is an asset of the estate pursuant to § 541, restrictions on its transfer are invalid pursuant to § 365(f).

In *In re Howe*, 78 B.R. 226 (Bankr.S.D.1987) the court struck down a provision in an executory contract which provided that the vendor would consent to an assignment if the debtor paid a 4% assumption fee. The court stated:

---

[3] The provision under review in *National Sugar Refining,* is virtually identical in effect to Sections 10.01(e) of the Debtor's lease with South Coast Plaza.

The court in *National Sugar Refining* stated:

The clear language of Section 36.01 of the Lease prohibits [the Debtor] from assigning the Lease without [the landlord's] consent. Section 36.02 of the Lease, which applies only to consensual assignment, provides that as a condition precedent to obtaining [the landlord's] consent to an assignment, [the Debtor] must offer to surrender the premises to [the landlord]. If [the Debtor's] offer to surrender is refused by [the landlord]... [the landlord] has the right to request the profits realized by [the Debtor] upon an assignment.

21 B.R. at 198.

Compare: Paragraph 10.01(e) states in pertinent part:

As a condition to Landlord's consent to any assignment or subletting, Landlord shall be entitled to receive, in the case of an assignment, 75% of all consideration given, directly or indirectly by the assignee to tenant for tenant's leasehold interest hereunder. (Emphasis added.)

It is clear from the language of the contract that [vendor's] consent to assignment is directly conditioned on its receipt of the four percent assumption fee. . . . Therefore, Section 365(f)(1) governs this matter and precludes enforcement of the four percent assumption fee required in the contract for the deed.

78 B.R. at 230. The court further added that to the extent the 4% assumption fee represented "an attempt by the vendor to extract any profit realized upon the assignment of the contract. . . [S]uch a purpose would frustrate the Congressional policy of assisting the debtor in realizing the equity in all his or her assets. . . [and] would result in a windfall to the vendor" in contravention of Congressional policy. Id. at 230 n.7.

We find this reasoning persuasive. In this case, enforcement of § 10.01(b) and (e) of the Lease will favor the Landlord by conditioning and restricting assignment of the Lease. Consequently, the enforcement of the allocation provision in § 10.01(e) would adversely affect the ability of the debtor in its rehabilitation effort in contravention of § 365(f).

VI. Conclusion

Pursuant to § 365(f) of the Bankruptcy Code, a provision which conditions or restricts the ability of a debtor to fully realize the economic value of its lease upon assignment is invalid. Accordingly, the bankruptcy court order denying South Coast Plaza's claim to 75% of the appreciated value of the leasehold estate upon assignment is Affirmed.

C. Shopping Center Leases

The shopping center industry feared that the general assignment privileges of Chapter 11 lessees threatened to destroy the identity and integrity of shopping centers. Accordingly, they sponsored § 365(b)(3) which sets forth special standards for adequate assurance of future performance in the assumption and assignment of shopping center leases. The Bankruptcy Code does not define "shopping center," but the House Report tells us what Congress had in mind.

A shopping center is often a carefully planned enterprise, and though it consists of numerous individual tenants, the center is planned as a single unit, often subject to a master lease or financing agreement. Under these agreements, the tenant mix in a shopping center may be as important to the lessor as the actual promised rental payments, because certain mixes will attract higher patronage of the stores in the center, and thus a higher rental for the landlord from those stores that are subject to a percentage of gross receipts rental agreement. Thus, in order to assure a landlord of his bargained for exchange, the court would have to consider such factors as the nature of the business to be conducted by the trustee or his assignee, whether that business complies with the requirements of any master agreement, whether the kind of business proposed will generate gross sales in an amount such that the percentage rent specified in the lease is substantially the same as what would have been provided by the debtor, and whether the business proposed to be conducted would result in a breach of other clauses in master agreements relating, for example, to tenant mix and location.

1978 U.S.C.C.A.N., p. 6305.

Before amendment in 1984, § 365(b)(3) provided as follows:

(3) For the purposes of paragraph (1) of this section, adequate assurance of future performance of a lease of real property in a shopping center includes adequate assurance—

(A) of the source of rent and other consideration due under such lease;

(B) that any percentage rent due under such lease will not decline substantially;

(C) that assumption or assignment of such lease will not breach substantially any provision, such as a radius, location, use, or exclusivity provision, in any other lease, financing agreement, or master agreement relating to such shopping center; and

(D) that assumption or assignment of such lease will not disrupt substantially any tenant mix or balance in such shopping center.

The word "substantially" in subparagraphs (C) and (D) caused difficulty to shopping center lessors, because it made it possible for a bankruptcy court to permit some assignments that in fact violated agreement terms and tenant mixes. In the amended version of these subparagraphs the word "substantially" was deleted, thus requiring strict compliance by the assuming lessee or assignee of every term of the agreement and barring even minor alterations in the tenant mix. Second, the following was added to subparagraph (A): "and in the case of an assignment, that the financial condition and operating performance of the proposed assignee and its guarantors, if any, shall be similar to the financial condition and operating performance of the debtor and its guarantors, if any, as of the time the debtor became the lessee under the lease." Thus, under this amendment, not only the financial condition of the assignee and any guarantors must pass muster but also their "operating performance" must meet the level of the original lessee at the time it became the lessee.

The 1984 amendments restrict even more than did the 1978 Code the capacity of courts to deal with adequate assurance with respect to shopping center leases on a flexible case-by-case approach. They appear to require strict enforcement of restrictive use clauses against potential assignees. They pose financial and performance standards that will make it more difficult to find qualified assignees. In short, they limit severely the Chapter 11 lessee's ability to assume or assign its shopping center lease and, thereby, to realize on what might be a valuable asset. In so doing they frustrate the original Congressional intent of allowing leases to be preserved and assigned as valuable property of the estate in order to aid in the lessee's reorganization. Hence, in the case of shopping center leases Congress weighed the interest of landlords and the other tenants in the integrity of the center more heavily than the lessee's interest in rehabilitation. In 2006, approximately 75% of all non-automotive retail trade in the country was conducted in shopping centers. International Council of Shopping Centers, Scope USA (2006) <http://www.icsc.org/srch/rsrch/scope/current/UnitedStates06.pdf>.

Accordingly, the shopping center amendments constitute a major limitation of the rights of Chapter 11 lessees to assign leases. The following case shows the extent of the shopping center industry's victory.

In re Trak Auto Corporation

United States Court of Appeals, Fourth Circuit, 2004.
367 F.3d 237.

■ MICHAEL, CIRCUIT JUDGE:

A Chapter 11 debtor-tenant sought to assign its shopping center lease in contravention of a provision that limits use of the premises to the sale of auto parts. The bankruptcy and district courts approved the assignment, and the lessor and owner of the shopping center appeals. We are asked to resolve the conflict between § 365(f)(1), which generally allows a debtor to assign its lease notwithstanding a provision restricting assignment, and § 365(b)(3)(C), which specifically requires a debtor-tenant in a shopping center to assign its lease subject to any provision restricting use of the premises. We hold that § 365(b)(3)(C), the more specific provision, controls in this case. As a result, we reverse and remand.

I.

Trak Auto Corporation (Trak Auto) is a retailer of auto parts and accessories that once operated 196 stores in Virginia, eight other states, and the District of Columbia. On July 5, 2001, in the Eastern District of Virginia, Trak Auto filed a petition under Chapter 11 of the Bankruptcy Code and continued in business as debtor in possession. As part of its effort to reorganize, Trak Auto obtained court approval to close its stores in four states, Illinois, Indiana, Michigan, and Wisconsin. Thereafter, Trak Auto sought to assume and assign certain of its leases of retail space where stores had been closed. One of these leases (the West Town lease or the lease) is at West Town Center, a shopping center in Chicago. Trak Auto's lessor and the owner of the shopping center is West Town Center LLC (West Town), the appellant. The West Town lease contains explicit use restrictions. Section 1.1(L) limits "PERMITTED USES" to the "[s]ale at retail of automobile parts and accessories and such other items as are customarily sold by Tenant at its other Trak Auto stores." J.A. 579. In section 8.1 Trak Auto "covenants... to use the Leased Premises only as a Trak Auto Store and for the Uses provided in Section 1.1(L)." J.A. 588.

Trak Auto engaged a real estate firm to advertise the availability of the West Town lease and to solicit bids. Of the bids received, none came from an auto parts retailer. The high bidder was A & E Stores, Inc. (A & E), an apparel merchandiser that offered $80,000 to buy out the lease. If A & E obtains the lease, it will open a Pay Half store on the premises, selling brand name family apparel at discount prices.

In a motion filed in the bankruptcy court, Trak Auto sought an order authorizing it to assume the West Town lease and to assign it to A & E. West Town, Trak Auto's lessor, objected on two grounds. First, West Town argued that the proposed assignment would breach the lease provision limiting use to the sale of auto parts and accessories. According to West Town, this use provision was enforceable under § 365(b)(3)(C) (West Town did not rely on the lease restriction that said the premises could be used "only as a Trak Auto Store.") Second, West Town argued that the assignment would disrupt its shopping center's tenant mix in violation of § 365(b)(3)(D). Trak Auto responded that the use restrictions in the lease were unenforceable anti-assignment provisions under § 365(f)(1) and that an assignment to A & E would not, as a matter of fact, disrupt the tenant mix.

The bankruptcy court held an evidentiary hearing and made the following factual findings, which we accept. The West Town shopping center is in an urban area (Chicago) where only fifty-nine percent of the population own cars. The shopping center is surrounded by competing shopping areas not owned by West Town. The twenty-five tenants in West Town Center include clothing stores, food vendors, a K-Mart, a laundromat, a travel agency, a bank, a cash advance (or small loan) agency, an adult entertainment outlet, and a public library branch. Trak Auto was the shopping center's only auto parts retailer, but there are seven auto parts retailers within three miles of the center. After announcing its factual findings, the bankruptcy court issued its conclusions. First, the court concluded that the lease's use restrictions amounted to anti-assignment provisions that were prohibited by § 356(f)(1) of the Bankruptcy Code. Second, the court concluded that West Town did not present sufficient evidence to support a finding that assignment of the lease to A & E would disrupt the tenant mix at West Town Center. Based on these conclusions, the bankruptcy court entered an order granting Trak Auto's motion to assume the West Town lease and, in turn, to assign it to A & E.

West Town filed a notice of appeal to the district court, and the bankruptcy court stayed its order pending appeal. The district court affirmed, and West Town then appealed to our court. We have also granted a stay. On October 7, 2003, three weeks before oral argument, West Town filed a motion to dismiss its own appeal as moot, arguing that its lease to Trak Auto had expired by its own terms on September 30, 2003. We deferred a ruling on the motion, which we take up now. * * *

III.

Today's substantive issue requires us to deal with the conflict between two provisions in § 365 of the Bankruptcy Code dealing with the assignment of a lease by a debtor (or trustee). Section 365(b)(3)(C) specifically requires a debtor-tenant at a shopping center to assign its store lease subject to any provision restricting the use of the premises. On the other hand, § 365(f)(1) generally allows a debtor to assign its lease notwithstanding a provision restricting assignment. In this case, the bankruptcy court permitted Trak Auto to assign its shopping center lease to the highest bidder, refusing to enforce the restriction that required the premises to be used for the retail sale of auto parts and accessories. The district court affirmed. The legal issue is dispositive of this appeal, and we (like the district court) review the bankruptcy court's legal conclusions de novo. We hold that § 365(b)(3)(C) controls in this case. This means that the bankruptcy court erred in permitting Trak Auto to assign its lease to an apparel merchandiser that would not honor the use restriction. Our analysis follows.

Section 365(a) allows a Chapter 11 debtor to assume an unexpired lease. § 365(a). The debtor may, in turn, assign the lease if the assignee provides "adequate assurance of future performance." *Id.* § 365(f)(2)(B). When a debtor-tenant in a shopping center seeks to assign its lease, the "adequate assurance of future performance" must include specific assurances that are spelled out in the Code. Most important to this case, there must be adequate assurance that assignment of a shopping center lease "is subject to all the provisions thereof, including (but not limited to) provisions such as a radius, location, use, or exclusivity provision, and will not breach any such provision contained in any other lease, financing agreement, or master agreement relating to such shopping center." *Id.* § 365(b)(3)(C). Section 365(f)(1), on the other hand, contains a general provision that prohibits the enforcement in bankruptcy of anti-assignment clauses in leases. This section allows a debtor to assign a lease "notwithstanding a provision... that prohibits, restricts, or conditions... assignment." *Id.* § 365(f)(1). Again, we must decide whether Congress intends, notwithstanding § 365(f)(1), for a debtor's assignee to provide adequate assurance that it will comply with use restrictions in a shopping center lease, such as the restriction here that limits the use of the space to the sale of auto parts and accessories.

We begin our inquiry with a look at the interesting history of Congress's efforts to protect shopping center landlords in § 365(b)(3) of the Bankruptcy Code. Congress has been interested in the financial well-being of shopping centers since at least the late 1970s. Specifics, such as the importance of a carefully selected tenant mix, have not escaped Congress's attention. The House Judiciary Committee discussed the tenant mix subject in a 1977 report:

A shopping center is often a carefully planned enterprise, and though it consists of nuemrous [sic] individual tenants, the center is planned as a single unit, often subject to a master lease or financing agreement. Under these agreements, the tenant mix in a shopping center may be as important to the lessor as the actual promised rental payments, because certain mixes will attract higher patronage of the stores in the center.

H.R.Rep. No. 95-595, at 348 (1977), U.S.Code Cong. & Admin.News 1977 at 5963, 6305. To maintain proper tenant mix, that is, store variety, shopping center landlords have routinely placed use restrictions in leases. Before 1978 the bankruptcy of a shopping center tenant with a use restriction did not present an inordinate problem for a landlord; the typical lease provided that the landlord could terminate the lease if the tenant went bankrupt. The termination option allowed the landlord to engage a new tenant that would contribute to an acceptable mix of stores. *See* Jeffrey S. Battershall, *Commercial Leases and Section 365 of the Bankruptcy Code,* 64 Am. Bankr. L.J. 329, 329 (1990). With the enactment of the Bankruptcy Reform Act of 1978 (the 1978 Act), however, landlords "were no longer able to regain control of the leased property in the event of bankruptcy, and the lease routinely became part of the debtor's estate to be administered" in the bankruptcy. *Id.* at 330. *See* § 365(e). Still, shopping center landlords were able to persuade Congress that they needed special protection, which Congress attempted to write into the 1978 Act. The 1978 legislation provided that a debtor-tenant could not assign its shopping center lease unless there was adequate assurance that "assignment of [the] lease [would] not breach *substantially* any provision, such as a radius, location, use, or exclusivity provision, *in any other* lease, financing agreement, or master agreement relating to such shopping center." § 365(b)(3) (1982) (emphases added).

Shopping center landlords soon realized that the 1978 provisions did not provide them with sufficient protection against debtor-tenant lease assignments that were being made in breach of use (and other) restrictions, with the approval of bankruptcy courts. For example, debtors avoided the 1978 provisions by convincing bankruptcy courts that an assignment would not "breach substantially" a use, radius, location, or exclusivity provision in another lease. *See id.* § 365(b)(3)(C) (1982). And, debtors were able to convince courts that even though an assignment would breach a use provision in the lease sought to be assigned, the assignment could proceed because the 1978 Act only prevented assignment if *some other* lease or agreement relating to the shopping center would be breached. *See id.* Shopping center landlords were, as a result, able to convince Congress that bankruptcy courts were too often "creating new [shopping center] leases by changing essential lease terms to facilitate assignments" by debtor-tenants. 130 Cong. Rec. S8891 (daily ed. June 29, 1984) (statement of Sen. Hatch), *reprinted in* 1984 U.S.C.C.A.N. 590, 600. Congress was told that this practice of avoiding use restrictions was creating problems with tenant mix in affected shopping centers. These locations were losing their balance-of-merchandise drawing card, which was a threat to overall sales revenues in the shopping center sector of the economy. *See* Battershall, *supra*, at 334-35.

Congress responded in 1984 by amending the shopping center provisions in the Bankruptcy Code. Among other things, § 365(b)(3)(C) was amended to delete the word "substantially" from the provision previously requiring that assignment of a shopping center lease must not "breach substantially" certain restrictions. This section was also amended to provide that any assigned shopping center lease would remain subject to all of the provisions of the lease and not just the provisions of "any other lease" relating to the center. Again, the amended provision that we interpret today provides: "adequate assurance of future performance of a lease of real property in a shopping center includes adequate assurance. . . that assumption or assignment of such lease is subject to all the provisions thereof, including (but not limited to) provisions such as a radius, location, use, or exclusivity provision." § 365(b)(3).

This background brings us to the matter of resolving the conflict between § 365(f)(1), a general provision that permits lease assignment notwithstanding anti-assignment clauses, and § 365(b)(3)(C), a more specific provision that requires the assignee of a shopping center lease to honor a clause restricting the use of the premises. For guidance in sorting out the conflict, we turn to the canons of statutory construction. When two provisions in a statute are in conflict, "a specific [provision] closely applicable to the substance of the controversy at hand controls over a more generalized provision." *Sigmon Coal Co. v. Apfel*, 226 F.3d 291, 302 (4th Cir. 2000) (internal quotation marks and citation omitted). *See also* Norman J. Singer, 2A Sutherland Statutes and Statutory Construction § 46:05 (6th ed.2000). Under this canon, § 365(b)(3)(C) controls because it speaks more directly to the issue, that is, whether a debtor-tenant assigning a shopping center lease must honor a straightforward use restriction. This construction is consistent with "the purpose[ ] Congress sought to serve." *Norfolk Redevelopment & Hous. Auth. v. Chesapeake & Potomac Tel. Co.,* 464 U.S. 30, 36 (1983) (internal quotation marks and citation omitted). Congress's purpose is clear from the history (recited above) that culminated in the 1984 shopping center amendments to the Bankruptcy Code and from the language of § 365(b)(3)(C) after those amendments. Specifically, when a shopping center lease is assigned in bankruptcy, Congress's purpose in § 365(b)(3)(C) is to preserve the landlord's bargained-for protections with respect to premises use and other matters that are spelled out in the lease with the debtor-tenant. *In re Ames Dep't Stores, Inc.,* 121 B.R. 160, 165 n.4 (Bankr.S.D.N.Y.1990). We therefore hold that because A & E does not propose to take the West Town lease subject to the specific restriction limiting use of the premises to the sale of auto parts and accessories, Trak Auto's motion to assume and assign the lease must be denied. * * *

Our decision to block Trak Auto's lease assignment is not an attempt on our part to water down one of the important purposes of Chapter 11. That purpose is to give business debtors with some prospects the opportunity to reorganize, revive their operations, and continue in existence. The assumption and assignment of leases can be an important part of this effort. *See In re Shangra-La, Inc.,* 167 F.3d 843, 849 (4th Cir. 1999). Shopping center leases are in a special category, however, because Congress has made it more difficult for debtor-tenants to assign these leases in Chapter 11. This special protection for shopping center landlords, as spelled out in § 365(b)(3)(C), dictates the result in today's case. But this does not mean that § 365(f)(1) can never be used to invalidate a clause prohibiting or restricting assignment in a shopping center lease. *But see In re Joshua Slocum Ltd.,* 922 F.2d 1081, 1090 (3d Cir. 1990) (concluding that § 365(b)(3) (1982) rendered § 365(f)(1) inapplicable to shopping center leases). A shopping center lease provision designed to prevent any assignment whatsoever might be a candidate for the application of § 365(f)(1). For example, Senator Hatch, in explaining the 1984 amendment to § 365(b)(3)(C), said that the "amendment is not intended to enforce requirements to operate under a specified trade name." 130 Cong. Rec. S8891 (daily ed. June 29, 1984), *reprinted in* 1984 U.S.C.C.A.N. 590, 600. Senator Hatch's comment suggests that Congress did not intend to make § 365(f)(1) completely inapplicable to shopping center leases. Of course, the issue of when § 365(f)(1) might apply is a subject for some future case.

IV.

In conclusion, we deny West Town's motion to dismiss this appeal as moot. On the merits, we hold that because A & E does not propose to take the West Town lease subject to the restriction limiting premises use to the retail sale of auto parts and accessories, Trak Auto's motion in bankruptcy court to assume and assign the lease must be denied under § 365(b)(3)(C). * * *

CHAPTER 7
THE AVOIDING POWERS OF THE TRUSTEE

A. PREFERENCES

1. THE CONCEPT OF A PREFERENCE

Since an insolvent debtor cannot pay all unsecured creditors in full, transfer of property of the debtor to pay or secure the obligations of some creditors "prefers" those creditors at the expense of others. "Transfer," defined in § 101(54), includes payments in cash or in kind or the grant of a security interest in the debtor's property. Some transfers are involuntary, for example, creation of a judicial lien in the debtor's property under a writ of execution or attachment. For the most part, the obtaining of an advantage by one creditor over another in this manner is valid (indeed encouraged) under nonbankruptcy law. State debt collection law is characterized by a race of diligence among creditors. The first to obtain an interest in the debtor's property is paid in full to the extent of that interest.

In a bankruptcy liquidation secured claims are satisfied first. Then unsecured claims are paid according to a system of priorities stated in § 507. With some exceptions stated in § 726, unsecured claims without priority are paid pro rata. This scheme of distribution cannot be altered by the debtor or creditors after bankruptcy commences. The debtor's property becomes property of the estate under the control of the bankruptcy court, and creditors are prohibited by the automatic stay from taking any action under nonbankruptcy law to obtain payment of their claims. § 362. But the distribution contemplated by the Bankruptcy Code can be frustrated by transactions occurring before bankruptcy. For example, an unsecured creditor who would receive ten cents on the dollar in the impending bankruptcy of the debtor might try to avert that result by obtaining a judicial lien in the debtor's property before the debtor can file the petition in bankruptcy. Or, the debtor might voluntarily favor a particular unsecured creditor by paying its debt in some measure greater than ten cents on the dollar.

Section 547 is designed to avoid certain prebankruptcy transfers the effect of which would be to frustrate the bankruptcy distribution scheme. These transfers are known as voidable preferences. The five elements of a voidable preference are set forth in § 547(b). To be avoided the transfer must be to or for the benefit of a creditor, on account of antecedent debt, while the debtor was insolvent, within 90 days of the bankruptcy filing (one year for "insiders") and enable the preferred creditor to receive more than it would otherwise be entitled to in a Chapter 7 liquidation. Subsection § 547(c) insulates from avoidance certain transfers that meet the elements of voidable preference under subsection (b), but that are deemed not to violate the policy that § 547 is designed to carry out. Section 547(b)(3) provides that the debtor must be insolvent at the time of the transfer. Section 547(f) creates a presumption that the debtor was insolvent during the 90 days immediately preceding the date of filing of the petition in bankruptcy. Accordingly, if the recipient of the preference fails to rebut the presumption, this element of the preference cause of action is deemed satisfied. If the presumption is rebutted, however, the trustee must prove insolvency by a preponderance of the evidence. With respect to § 547(c) defenses, the burden of proof is on the recipient of the preference who is seeking to make out an affirmative defense to liability, § 547(g).

If the trustee in bankruptcy avoids a preferential transfer under § 547(b), the result is that the property transferred to the creditor can be recovered for the benefit of the estate. § 550(a). Creditors may, with court approval, avoid a transfer on behalf of the estate if the trustee (or debtor-in-possession) consents or unjustifiably refuses to pursue the claim. *See In re Racing Services, Inc.*, 540 F.3d 892 (8th Cir. 2008). If the preference involved payment of a debt in cash, the trustee is entitled to recover an equivalent amount, which then becomes part of the bankruptcy estate. § 541(a)(3). Suppose the preference occurred when the creditor obtained a lien in the debtor's property to secure the debt either by voluntary act of the debtor, as in the case of a security interest, or against the will of the debtor, as in the case of a judicial lien. Avoidance of a preferential lien usually means that the creditor's lien is nullified, and, if the lien is in property of the estate, the effect of nullification is to increase the value of the estate in the amount of the nullified lien.

The effect of avoidance of a preferential lien may be more complex if there is more than one lien in the property. Assume Blackacre is property of the bankruptcy estate and is worth $150,000. Blackacre is burdened by two liens that are both valid outside of bankruptcy. The first lien is held by Creditor A who is owed $100,000 and the second is held by Creditor B who is also owed $100,000. Because the value of Blackacre is less than the amount of debt secured by the liens, Blackacre has no value to the bankruptcy estate unless one or both of the liens can be avoided in bankruptcy. Because Creditor A, as senior lienor, is entitled to full payment from the proceeds of a foreclosure sale of Blackacre before Creditor B receives anything, Creditor B's lien is worth only $50,000. Make a final assumption: the lien of Creditor A is avoidable under § 547(b) while the lien of Creditor B is indefeasible in bankruptcy.

If the lien of Creditor A were nullified, the effect would be to benefit Creditor B because Creditor B's lien becomes the only lien in Blackacre. Before nullification, the junior lien of Creditor B had a value of $50,000; after nullification, it has a value of $100,000. Nullification also increases the value of the estate's interest in Blackacre from zero to $50,000. But the purpose of allowing the trustee to avoid preferential transfers is to benefit the estate, i.e., to increase the value of the estate for the benefit of creditors with unsecured claims who are paid from property of the estate. If avoidance of the $100,000 lien of Creditor A means that the lien is nullified, the avoidance results in a benefit of only $50,000 to the estate. Shifting the benefit from one lien creditor to another lien creditor does not carry out the purpose of preference law to benefit the estate. Section 551 addresses that problem by providing that the "transfer avoided * * * is preserved for the benefit of the estate." The "transfer avoided" is Creditor A's lien. That lien is automatically "preserved," that is, it is artificially treated as though it had not been nullified. Section 551 treats the lien as having been taken away from Creditor A and given to the bankruptcy estate. In effect, the bankruptcy estate is subrogated to the rights of Creditor A with respect to the avoided lien. Thus, by virtue of § 551, Creditor B's status as holder of a junior lien is not changed by the avoidance of Creditor A's lien. Creditor B is entitled to receive only $50,000, the value of the junior lien before the avoidance occurred. The remaining $100,000 value of Blackacre originally held by Creditor A by virtue of its avoidable lien is retained by the bankruptcy estate.

PROBLEMS

1. On May 1, Smith was indebted to Jones on an overdue unsecured loan made the previous year. On that date Smith paid Jones cash equal to the amount due on the loan. At the time of payment Smith had other unpaid debts that exceeded her assets. On July 15, Smith filed a petition in bankruptcy under Chapter 7.

(a) Is the trustee in bankruptcy entitled to recover from Jones the amount received from Smith? § 547(b) and § 550(a). Does it matter whether Jones knew of Smith's financial condition when Jones received payment? Who has the burden of proving that Smith was insolvent? § 101 ("insolvent") and § 547(f) and (g)?

(b) Suppose that on May 1 Smith had not paid the loan and that Jones on that date had obtained a prejudgment attachment lien on business property of Smith with a value exceeding the amount due on the loan. At the time of filing in bankruptcy on July 15, Smith's assets included the property on which Jones had an attachment lien. What are the rights of the trustee in bankruptcy? § 547(b) and § 101(54) ("transfer").

2. Bank made a one-year loan of $10,000 to Debtor on September 1, 2007, and to secure the loan Debtor granted Bank a security interest in equipment owned by Debtor. Bank promptly perfected by filing a financing statement. On September 1, 2008 Debtor paid Bank $10,000 plus interest in discharge of the debt. Debtor filed a petition in bankruptcy on November 1, 2008. Debtor was insolvent on September 1, 2008 and at all times thereafter. Assume that the value of the equipment was greater than the payment made to Bank and that there were no other security interests or liens in the equipment superior to the security interest of Bank. Can the transfer be avoided by the trustee in bankruptcy under § 547(b)? What is the effect of § 547(b)(5)? Would the outcome of the case be different if Bank had been undersecured at the time it received payment from Debtor?

2. TRANSFER OF DEBTOR'S INTEREST IN PROPERTY AND THE "EARMARKING" DOCTRINE

Section 547(b) allows the trustee to avoid only transfers of property of the debtor's estate. Questions have arisen over the applicability of § 547(b) when creditors of the debtor have been paid from funds supplied by third parties. The following Problems explore these issues. *Collier on Bankruptcy* at ¶ 547.03[2], 547-21 (15th ed. rev. 2008) states the guiding principle to be: "The fundamental inquiry is whether the transfer diminished or depleted the debtor's estate."

PROBLEMS

In each of the following Problems, you may assume that the transfer would have been preferential under § 547 if there had been a transfer of an interest of the debtor in the property.

1. D's obligation to C was guaranteed by Guarantor. The contract of guaranty allowed Guarantor to seek reimbursement from D for any payments made on its behalf but granted Guarantor no security interest in D's assets to secure D's reimbursement obligation. When D defaulted on its obligation, Guarantor paid C. May D's trustee in bankruptcy avoid the transfer to C? *In re Corland Corp.*, 967 F.2d 1069 (5th Cir. 1992), held that payments on the guaranty were not property of the estate because the funds came from Guarantor and not from D. In view of the fact that D became liable to reimburse Guarantor for the amount of its payment, do you agree with the holding in *Corland*?

2. D owes C1, C2 and C3 $10,000 each. D obtains a loan from Bank and directs Bank to disburse the loan proceeds by making direct payments of D's debts to C1, C2 and C3. Is there a preference in this case? Has there been a depletion of D's estate?

3. D obtains a loan from Bank of $30,000 for the specific purpose of paying its debts to C1, C2 and C3. Pursuant to agreement with D, Bank disburses the loan proceeds by depositing them in D's account in Bank on July 1, and D pays the three creditors by checks drawn on the account on July 2. Has there been a depletion of D's estate?

Some courts recognize what is called the "earmarking" doctrine and hold that there is no preference in Problem 3 even though while the funds were in D's account D clearly had the power to divert the funds to purposes other than payment to the three creditors and the funds were subject to D's creditors. These courts purport to cut through form to substance and focus on the reality that functionally the transactions in Problems 2 and 3 are the same. In *In re Superior Stamp & Coin Co., Inc.*, 223 F.3d 1004 (9th Cir. 2000), the court justified its holding that there was no preference in a case resembling Problem 3 by stating that even though D was given the *power* to divert the funds it did not have the *right* to do so; hence, D never had *control* of the funds. But are Problems 2 and 3 the same? The earmarking doctrine is controversial. *See, e.g., In re Bohlen Enterprises*, Ltd., 859 F.2d 561 (8th Cir. 1988) (questioning the doctrine). What policy is served by protecting the preferred creditors (C1, C2 and C3) in cases like Problem 3 at the expense of other creditors of D? *See In re Moses*, 256 B.R. 641, 647 (10th Cir. BAP 2000) ("[A]pplication of the earmarking doctrine * * * serves to *prefer* the old creditor, the creditor who was likely clamoring for payment. * * * Such a preference is the essence of what § 547(b) was enacted to prevent."); *In re Ludford Fruit Prod., Inc.*, 99 B.R. 18, 21 (Bankr.C.D.Cal.1989) ("Common sense is stretched to the breaking point when a court finds that funds loaned to a debtor, even for the specified purpose of paying an existing creditor, do not become property of the debtor.")

The premise on which the earmarking doctrine rests in cases like Problem 3 is the fiction that payment passing through the debtor's account is not "really" the debtor's funds. However shaky this premise, most courts have accepted this extension of the earmarking doctrine beyond the guarantor cases. Why should it matter—so the argument goes—if the debtor wishes to make sure payment goes to the old creditor by having it routed through her account? Either way the debtor's estate is not diminished. The decisions require that the new creditor and debtor agree that the new loan proceeds are used to pay a particular creditor. *Matter of Entringer Bakeries Inc.*, 548 F.3d 344 (5th Cir. 2008); *Collier on Bankruptcy* ¶ 547.03[2], 547-28 (15th ed. 2008). See Christopher W. Frost, *Earmarking Payments—Refinancing or Payments on Antecedent Debt*, 28 Bankr. L. Ltr., No. 4 (Apr. 2008), for a review of the case law.

3. THE PREFERENCE PERIOD

Under § 547(b)(4) a transfer cannot be a voidable preference unless it occurs within what can be called the "preference period." If the transferee is an insider, defined in § 101(31), the preference period is the one year before the date of the filing of the petition in bankruptcy. If the transferee is not an insider, the preference period is the 90 days before the filing of the petition. The same standards for avoidance apply to both insiders and other transferees. The only difference is that the preference period for insiders is longer. We consider the question of preferences to insiders in connection with the material on fraudulent transfers later in this chapter.

There is some confusion concerning how the preference period is calculated. For example, in the case of the 90–day period, the language of the statute suggests that you count back from the date of the petition 90 calendar days excluding the date of the filing of the petition. Thus, if a petition is filed on June 1, the preference period would start on March 3. The statutory period is controlled by Bankruptcy Rule 9006(a), which is identical to Federal Rule of Civil Procedure 6(a), and the meaning of the rule is not completely clear. It provides that "the day of the act, event, or default from which the designated period of time begins to run shall not be included" but the last day of the period shall be included unless it is a Saturday, Sunday or a legal holiday. In that case the period is extended until the next day that is not a Saturday, Sunday or legal holiday.

The court in *In re Nelson Co.*, 959 F.2d 1260 (3d Cir. 1992), held that the "event" referred to in Rule 9006(a) is the filing of the petition not the transfer, and said:

> Our research indicates that no other court of appeals has yet to address this issue in a published opinion. The majority view of district courts and bankruptcy courts faced with the necessity of calculating the 90–day preferential period do so by calculating backward from the date of the filing of the petition in bankruptcy. * * * A minority of courts have calculated the 90–day period from the date of the transfer.

959 F.2d at 1266 n.6.

4. CONTEMPORANEOUS EXCHANGES

One element of a voidable preference is that the transfer be "for or on account of an antecedent debt." § 547(b)(2). Thus, if an insolvent buyer buys goods and pays for them at the time of sale by transferring money or other property to the seller, there is no preference because the buyer's obligation to pay for the goods and the transfer of the buyer's property to satisfy the obligation arise contemporaneously. But suppose there is a short delay between the time the obligation is incurred and the payment of the obligation. Does the short delay make the debt antecedent? The issue was considered by the Supreme Court in the case of *Dean v. Davis*, 242 U.S. 438 (1917). On September 3 the debtor obtained a loan from Dean on the debtor's promise to secure the loan by a mortgage on all of his property. The proceeds of the loan were used by the debtor to pay a debt owed to a bank. The mortgage was executed on September 10 and recorded the next day. Within a few days a petition for involuntary bankruptcy was filed against the debtor. The trustee in bankruptcy brought an action to set aside the mortgage. Both the district court and the court of appeals held that the mortgage was voidable as a fraudulent conveyance. The court of appeals also held that the mortgage could be avoided as a preference under § 60b of the Bankruptcy Act. The Supreme Court, in reversing the court of appeals on the latter point stated:

> The mortgage was not voidable as a preference under § 60b. Preference implies paying or securing a pre-existing debt of the person preferred. The mortgage was given to secure Dean for a substantially contemporary advance. The bank, not Dean, was preferred. The use of Dean's money to accomplish this purpose could not convert the transaction into a preferring of Dean, although he knew of the debtor's insolvency.

242 U.S. at 443.

Section 547(c)(1) codifies this holding of the Supreme Court: if the parties intend a contemporaneous exchange of a loan for a mortgage and the transfer of the debtor's property represented by the mortgage is delayed only a short time, the exchange is substantially contemporaneous and the mortgage cannot be avoided. Does this analysis apply to the Problems that follow?

PROBLEMS

1. Bank made an unsecured demand loan to Debtor on the morning of April 1. Bank believed that Debtor was financially sound. Later that day Bank received a credit report indicating that Debtor was in financial difficulty and might be insolvent. Bank immediately talked to Debtor who acknowledged the truth of the credit report. When Bank demanded immediate repayment of the loan, Debtor offered instead to secure the loan by a mortgage on real property worth more than the amount of the loan. Bank agreed, and the mortgage was executed on the evening of April 1 and recorded the next day. If Debtor was insolvent on April 1 and filed a petition in bankruptcy on June 1, can the mortgage be avoided as a preference? § 547(b) and § 547(c)(1). *Nat'l City Bank v. Hotchkiss*, 231 U.S. 50 (1913).

2. On April 1, Bank loaned $10,000 to Debtor by crediting that amount to Debtor's checking account. The loan agreement signed on that day provided that the $10,000 would be used to buy certain described equipment in which Debtor granted a security interest to Bank. Bank filed a financing statement covering equipment of Debtor on April 1. On April 7, Debtor bought the equipment described in the loan agreement. On June 20, Debtor filed a petition in bankruptcy. Under § 547(e)(2) and (3), when did a transfer of property of Debtor occur? If Debtor was insolvent on April 1 and at all times thereafter, can Bank's security interest be avoided under § 547(b)? Is avoidance prevented under § 547(c)(1)? Is avoidance prevented under § 547(c)(3)? Would your answers be different if Debtor had acquired the equipment on April 30?

5. ORDINARY COURSE PAYMENTS

a. Policy Basis of § 547(c)(2)

Preference law reflects the oft-stated, though inconsistently followed, policy in favor of equal treatment of creditors. Justification for taking away from the preferred creditor an advantage that was lawfully obtained under nonbankruptcy law was often expressed in terms of unfair conduct by the debtor and the preferred creditor. We can find this notion as far back as the 16th century *Case of Bankrupts*, in which the court stated "* * * there ought to be an equal distribution * * * but if, after the debtor becomes a bankrupt, he may prefer one * * * and defeat and defraud many other poor men of their true debts, it would be unequal and unconscionable, and a great defect in the law * * *." 76 Eng. Rep. 441, 473 (K.B. 1584). The court was referring to the conduct of the debtor in that case, but in some cases the preferred creditor, because of a special relationship to the debtor, is able to obtain an advantage not obtainable by others.

The characterization of preference in terms of unconscionability or fraud has had an important influence on the development of preference law. The classic preference situation is that of a privileged creditor—perhaps an insider—with knowledge of and influence over the affairs of the debtor who, seeing that the debtor is sinking in insolvency, obtains payment from the debtor before the debacle becomes manifest. But the typical preference situation today, more often than not, does not fit this classic pattern. A debtor in trouble may try to hide insolvency and often succeeds for an extended period of time. The debtor pays bills as long as possible hoping that somehow the crisis will pass. Many, if not most, creditors who are paid shortly before bankruptcy are not taking advantage of any special status that they have and indeed may not be aware that the debtor is in any financial difficulty. Is there any basis for treating differently the creditor who takes payment of a debt knowing that other creditors will go unpaid and the creditor who receives payment without knowledge that it is being preferred over the others?

This distinction was made in the Bankruptcy Act. Under Bankruptcy Act § 60b a preferential transfer could be avoided by the trustee only if the creditor had at the time when the transfer was made "reasonable cause to believe that the debtor [was] insolvent." Under this standard the preferred creditor could lose the preference only if the creditor was on notice of the fact that receipt of property of the debtor would prejudice the rights of other creditors. Under the Bankruptcy Act preferential transfers resulting from judicial liens obtained against insolvent debtors within the four-month period before filing of the petition were separately treated by § 67a and were nullified. Although it was not necessary to prove that the creditor had reasonable cause to believe that the debtor was insolvent at the time the lien was obtained, any creditor who obtains a judicial lien is not an innocent recipient of payment of a debt. Debtors who allow their property to be subjected to judicial liens are frequently in financial difficulty, and judicial seizure of a debtor's property is often followed by bankruptcy. Thus, under the Bankruptcy Act a creditor whose preference was avoided usually had received notice that an advantage over other creditors was being obtained.

The Commission on the Bankruptcy Laws of the United States recommended to Congress that proof of "reasonable cause to believe" be eliminated as a requirement for the avoidance of a preference. The recommendation was adopted in § 547(b). The reasons for this change have been described as follows:

> The Commission on the Bankruptcy Laws of the United States, in its report submitted to Congress, was first to recommend the elimination of this requirement. During the congressional hearings that were held both on the bill prepared by the Commission and a companion bill, there was testimony critical of the former requirement. The criticism was twofold. First, it was said that reasonable cause to believe was an unnecessary burden to impose upon the trustee in bankruptcy. Invariably, the transferee alleged that he did not know or have reason to know that the debtor was insolvent, thus creating a litigable issue in every case, with the burden of proof resting on the trustee in bankruptcy. As a result, many preferential transfers were not avoided, thereby undermining a basic tenet of the bankruptcy law—equitable distribution of a debtor's assets among its unsecured creditors. Second, it was said that the requirement had no logical basis in the law of voidable preferences. The main elements of a preference were set forth in section 60a: (1) a transfer of the debtor's property, (2) made within four months before bankruptcy, (3) for an antecedent debt, (4) at a time when the debtor was

insolvent, and (5) the effect of which was to permit the transferee to receive a greater portion of its debt than other creditors in the same class would receive. When one reviewed these elements, an intention on the part of the debtor, or intention or knowledge on the part of the creditor, seemed to be irrelevant factors.

Chaim J. Fortgang & Lawrence P. King, *The 1978 Bankruptcy Code: Some Wrong Policy Decisions*, 56 N.Y.U.L.Rev. 1148, 1165–1166 (1981).

In spite of the difficulties that the reasonable-cause-to-believe requirement may have caused, it also performed a useful function. Normally, in the 90–day period before bankruptcy, the debtor has paid many unsecured debts of a recurring nature as they become due. An individual debtor, for example, pays utility bills and credit card debts, and may be paying for previously rendered personal services such as those of doctors and dentists. A business debtor normally purchases inventory and supplies, as well as services of employees and other suppliers, on short-term unsecured credit which may call for payment for various periods of time ranging from 10 or 20 days to as long as six months. Under the Bankruptcy Act, preferential payments of this kind were not voidable because the creditor normally would not have any cause to believe that the debtor was insolvent. But under the Code, if the debtor is insolvent when payment is made, all payments become potential preferences if the debtor goes into bankruptcy within 90 days. Is that a desirable result?

One vital goal of any commercial law regime is certainty and finality of transactions. If large numbers of ordinary commercial transactions are subject to being upset by later legal proceedings, all such transactions become more expensive. There is general consensus in favor of avoiding preferences made in out-of-the-ordinary transactions in which a creditor seeks, and is given, favored treatment by a debtor in obvious financial difficulty. It is not so clear that transactions by an insolvent debtor in paying debts as they mature should be avoided solely because an incidental result is that the creditor that received payment was preferred over others who did not have the good fortune of being paid before bankruptcy. If a doctrine designed to obtain equality for all creditors interferes with normal commercial practices and significantly adds to the cost of ordinary commercial transactions, the cost of the equality may be too high.

In the Bankruptcy Code, Congress attempted to alleviate the effects of dropping the reasonable-cause-to-believe requirement by adopting § 547(c)(2). The purpose of that section was to insulate from avoidance preferential transfers resulting from certain ordinary course transactions of the type outlined above. As originally adopted, § 547(c)(2) read as follows:

(c) The trustee may not avoid under this section a transfer—

(2) to the extent that such transfer was—

(A) in payment of a debt incurred in the ordinary course of business or financial affairs of the debtor and the transferee;

(B) made not later than 45 days after such debt was incurred;

(C) made in the ordinary course of business or financial affairs of the debtor and the transferee; and

(D) made according to ordinary business terms;

From 1984 to 2005 § 547(c)(2), was virtually identical to this provision except for the deletion of subparagraph (B), which required that payment be no more than 45 days after the debt was incurred. Pre–1984 § 547(c)(2) was effective in excluding from avoidance many ordinary course payments, but the 45-day provision in subparagraph (B) was deleted from the Code at the instance of participants in the commercial paper market and certain trade creditors who commonly dealt in 60-day or 90-day obligations. The effect of the deletion of the 45-day requirement has proved far broader than remedying an artificial distinction between certain types of commercial paper and certain trade creditors, as suggested by the following problem and case. In BAPCPA, § 547(c)(2) was materially amended by making new subparagraphs (A) and (B) (former paragraphs (C) and (D) shown above) disjunctive rather than conjunctive. We discuss this important change *infra* at 341-346.

PROBLEM

Five years ago Debtor Corporation borrowed $400,000 from Bank to be used for working capital. The loan was unsecured. It bore interest payable monthly and had a maturity of 90 days. It was the understanding of the parties that the loan would be renewed at maturity from time to time for additional 90-day periods if the financial situation of Debtor was satisfactory to Bank. The loan was regularly renewed over the years and was increased from time to time as the business of Debtor expanded. At the most recent maturity date, the outstanding principal balance was $950,000. Shortly before the maturity date, Bank examined the financial affairs of Debtor and discovered that Debtor had suffered grave financial reversals during the previous 90 days. In fact, Bank determined that Debtor was not paying some of its creditors and was probably insolvent at that time. Bank requested that the loan be repaid at the due date, but Debtor was unable to pay. Bank and Debtor then entered into the following transaction on the due date of the loan: Debtor paid the monthly interest of about $11,500 and repaid $450,000 of the principal. Bank renewed the loan for its unpaid principal amount of $500,000 for an additional 90–day period, but the interest rate was increased substantially. The affairs of Debtor continued to decline. Debtor failed to make any further interest payments to Bank. Two months after the renewal, Debtor filed a petition in bankruptcy under Chapter 7. The trustee in bankruptcy brought an action against Bank to recover the $450,000 and $11,500 payments that Debtor had made to Bank when the loan was renewed. Is the trustee entitled to recover under § 547?

The following case elaborates the Supreme Court's views on the policy justification for preference law.

Union Bank v. Wolas
Supreme Court of the United States, 1991.
502 U.S. 151.

■ Justice STEVENS delivered the opinion of the Court.

Section 547(b) of the Bankruptcy Code authorizes a trustee to avoid certain property transfers made by a debtor within 90 days before bankruptcy. The Code makes an exception, however, for transfers made in the ordinary course of business, § 547(c)(2). The question presented is whether payments on long-term debt may qualify for that exception.

On December 17, 1986, ZZZZ Best Co., Inc. (Debtor) borrowed seven million dollars from petitioner, Union Bank (Bank).[1] On July 8, 1987, the Debtor filed a voluntary petition under Chapter 7 of the Bankruptcy Code. During the preceding 90–day period, the Debtor had made two interest payments totalling approximately $100,000 and had paid a loan commitment fee of about $2,500 to the Bank. After his appointment as trustee of the Debtor's

---

[1] The Bankruptcy Court found that the Bank and Debtor executed a revolving credit agreement on December 16, 1986, in which the Bank agreed to lend the Debtor $7 million in accordance with the terms of a promissory note to be executed and delivered by the Debtor. * * * On December 17, 1986, the Debtor executed and delivered to the Bank a promissory note in the principal sum of $7 million. The promissory note provided that interest would be payable on a monthly basis and would accrue on the principal balance at a rate of .65% per annum in excess of the Bank's reference rate.

estate, respondent filed a complaint against the Bank to recover those payments pursuant to § 547(b).

The Bankruptcy Court found that the loans had been made "in the ordinary course of business or financial affairs" of both the Debtor and the Bank, and that both interest payments as well as the payment of the loan commitment fee had been made according to ordinary business terms and in the ordinary course of business. As a matter of law, the Bankruptcy Court concluded that the payments satisfied the requirements of § 547(c)(2) and therefore were not avoidable by the trustee. The District Court affirmed the Bankruptcy Court's summary judgment in favor of the Bank.

Shortly thereafter, in another case, the Court of Appeals held that the ordinary course of business exception to avoidance of preferential transfers was not available to long-term creditors. *In re CHG International, Inc.*, 897 F.2d 1479 (C.A.9 1990). In reaching that conclusion, the Court of Appeals relied primarily on the policies underlying the voidable preference provisions and the state of the law prior to the enactment of the 1978 Bankruptcy Code and its amendment in 1984. Thus, the Ninth Circuit concluded, its holding in *CHG International, Inc.* dictated a reversal in this case. The importance of the question of law decided by the Ninth Circuit, coupled with the fact that the Sixth Circuit had interpreted § 547(c)(2) in a contrary manner * * * persuaded us to grant the Bank's petition for certiorari. * * *

I.

We shall discuss the history and policy of § 547 after examining its text. In subsection (b), Congress broadly authorized bankruptcy trustees to "avoid any transfer of an interest of the debtor in property" *if* five conditions are satisfied and *unless* one of seven exceptions defined in subsection (c) is applicable. In brief, the five characteristics of a voidable preference are that it (1) benefit a creditor; (2) be on account of antecedent debt; (3) be made while the debtor was insolvent; (4) be within 90 days before bankruptcy; and (5) enable the creditor to receive a larger share of the estate than if the transfer had not been made. Section 547 also provides that the debtor is presumed to have been insolvent during the 90-day period preceding bankruptcy. § 547(f). In this case, it is undisputed that all five of the foregoing conditions were satisfied and that the interest and loan commitment fee payments were voidable preferences unless excepted by subsection (c)(2).

The most significant feature of subsection (c)(2) that is relevant to this case is the absence of any language distinguishing between long-term debt and short-term debt. * * *

Instead of focusing on the term of the debt for which the transfer was made, subsection (c)(2) focuses on whether the debt was incurred, and payment made, in the "ordinary course of business or financial affairs" of the debtor and transferee. Thus, the text provides no support for respondent's contention that § 547(c)(2)'s coverage is limited to short-term debt, such as commercial paper or trade debt. Given the clarity of the statutory text, respondent's burden of persuading us that Congress intended to create or to preserve a special rule for long-term debt is exceptionally heavy. As did the Ninth Circuit, respondent relies on the history and the policies underlying the preference provision.

II.

The relevant history of § 547 contains two chapters, one of which clearly supports, and the second of which is not inconsistent with, the Bank's literal reading of the statute. Section 547 was enacted in 1978 when Congress overhauled the Nation's bankruptcy laws. The section was amended in 1984. For purposes of the question presented in this case, the original version of § 547 differed in one significant respect from the current version: it contained a provision that the ordinary course of business exception did not apply unless the payment was made within 45 days of the date the debt was incurred. That provision presumably excluded most payments on long-term debt from the exception. In 1984 Congress repealed the 45-day limitation but did not substitute a comparable limitation. * * *

Respondent contends that this amendment was intended to satisfy complaints by issuers of commercial paper[10] and by trade creditors[11] that regularly extended credit for periods of more than 45 days. Furthermore, respondent continues, there is no evidence in the legislative history that Congress intended to make the ordinary course of business exception available to conventional long-term lenders. Therefore, respondent argues, we should follow the analysis of the Ninth Circuit and read § 547(c)(2) as protecting only short-term debt payments. * * *

We need not dispute the accuracy of respondent's description of the legislative history of the 1984 amendment in order to reject his conclusion. For even

---

[10] Because payments to a commercial paper purchaser within 90 days prior to bankruptcy may be preferential transfers under § 547(b), a purchaser could be assured that the payment would not be avoided under the prior version of § 547(c)(2) only if the commercial paper had a maturity of 45 days or less. Commercial issuers thus complained that the 45-day limitation lowered demand for commercial paper with a maturity in excess of 45 days. * * *

[11] Trade creditors stated that normal payment periods in many industries exceeded 45 days and complained that the arbitrary 45-day limitation in § 547(c)(2) deprived these trade creditors of the protection of the ordinary course of business exception to the trustee's power to avoid preferential transfers. * * *

if Congress adopted the 1984 amendment to redress particular problems of specific short-term creditors, it remains true that Congress redressed those problems by entirely deleting the time limitation in § 547(c)(2). The fact that Congress may not have foreseen all of the consequences of a statutory enactment is not a sufficient reason for refusing to give effect to its plain meaning. * * *

Respondent also relies on the history of voidable preferences prior to the enactment of the 1978 Bankruptcy Code. The text of the preference provision in the earlier Bankruptcy Act did not specifically include an exception for payments made in the ordinary course of business. The courts had, however, developed what is sometimes described as the "current expense" rule to cover situations in which a debtor's payments on the eve of bankruptcy did not diminish the net estate because tangible assets were obtained in exchange for the payment. * * * Without such an exception, trade creditors and other suppliers of necessary goods and services might have been reluctant to extend even short-term credit and might have required advance payment instead, thus making it difficult for many companies in temporary distress to have remained in business. Respondent argues that Congress enacted § 547(c)(2) in 1978 to codify that exception, and therefore the Court should construe § 547(c)(2) as limited to the confines of the current expense rule.

This argument is not compelling for several reasons. First, it is by no means clear that § 547(c)(2) should be construed as the statutory analogue of the judicially crafted current expense rule because there are other exceptions in § 547(c) that explicitly cover contemporaneous exchanges for new value.[13] Those provisions occupy some (if not all) of the territory previously covered by the current expense rule. Nor has respondent directed our attention to any extrinsic evidence suggesting that Congress intended to codify the current expense rule in § 547(c)(2).

The current expense rule developed when the statutory preference provision was significantly narrower than it is today. To establish a preference under the Bankruptcy Act, the trustee had to prove that the challenged payment was made at a time when the creditor had "reasonable cause to believe that the debtor [was] insolvent." 11 U.S.C. § 96(b) (1976 ed.). When Congress rewrote the preference provision in the 1978 Bankruptcy Code, it substantially enlarged the trustee's power to avoid preferential transfers by eliminating the reasonable

---

[13] Thus, for example, § 547(c)(1) exempts a transfer to the extent that it was a "contemporaneous exchange for new value given to the debtor," and § 547(c)(4) exempts a transfer to a creditor "to the extent that, after such transfer, such creditor gave new value to or for the benefit of the debtor * * *."

cause to believe requirement for transfers made within 90 days of bankruptcy and creating a presumption of insolvency during that period. * * * At the same time, Congress created a new exception for transfers made in the ordinary course of business, § 547(c)(2). This exception was intended to "leave undisturbed normal financial relations, because it does not detract from the general policy of the preference section to discourage unusual action by either the debtor or his creditors during the debtor's slide into bankruptcy." H.R.Rep. No. 95–595, at 373.

In light of these substantial changes in the preference provision, there is no reason to assume that the justification for narrowly confining the "current expense" exception to trade creditors before 1978 should apply to the ordinary course of business exception under the 1978 Code. Instead, the fact that Congress carefully reexamined and entirely rewrote the preference provision in 1978 supports the conclusion that the text of § 547(c)(2) as enacted reflects the deliberate choice of Congress.[15]

III.

The Bank and the trustee agree that § 547 is intended to serve two basic policies that are fairly described in the House Committee Report. The Committee explained:

> "A preference is a transfer that enables a creditor to receive payment of a greater percentage of his claim against the debtor than he would have received if the transfer had not been made and he had participated in the distribution of the assets of the bankrupt estate. The purpose of the preference section is two-fold. First, by permitting the trustee to avoid prebankruptcy transfers that occur within a short period before bankruptcy, creditors are discouraged from racing to the courthouse to dismember the debtor during his slide into bankruptcy. The protection thus afforded the debtor often enables him to work his way out of a difficult financial situation through cooperation with all of his creditors. Second, and more important, the preference provisions facilitate the prime bankruptcy policy of equality of distribution among cred-

---

[15] Indeed, the House Committee Report concludes its discussion of the trustee's avoidance powers with the observation that the language in the preference section of the earlier Bankruptcy Act was "hopelessly complex" and had been "subject to varying interpretations. The bill undoes the numerous amendments that have been heaped on section 60 during the past 40 years, and proposes a unified and coherent section to deal with the problems created by prebankruptcy preferential transfers." H.R.Rep. No. 95–595, p. 179 (1977). Respondent's assumption that § 547(c)(2) was intended to preserve pre-existing law is at war with this legislative history.

itors of the debtor. Any creditor that received a greater payment than others of his class is required to disgorge so that all may share equally. The operation of the preference section to deter "the race of diligence' of creditors to dismember the debtor before bankruptcy furthers the second goal of the preference section—that of equality of distribution."

Id., at 177-178.

As this comment demonstrates, the two policies are not entirely independent. On the one hand, any exception for a payment on account of an antecedent debt tends to favor the payee over other creditors and therefore may conflict with the policy of equal treatment. On the other hand, the ordinary course of business exception may benefit all creditors by deterring the "race to the courthouse" and enabling the struggling debtor to continue operating its business.

Respondent places primary emphasis, as did the Court of Appeals, on the interest in equal distribution. * * * When a debtor is insolvent, a transfer to one creditor necessarily impairs the claims of the debtor's other unsecured and undersecured creditors. By authorizing the avoidance of such preferential transfers, § 547(b) empowers the trustee to restore equal status to all creditors. Respondent thus contends that the ordinary course of business exception should be limited to short-term debt so the trustee may order that preferential long-term debt payments be returned to the estate to be distributed among all of the creditors.

But the statutory text—which makes no distinction between short-term debt and long-term debt—precludes an analysis that divorces the policy of favoring equal distribution from the policy of discouraging creditors from racing to the courthouse to dismember the debtor. Long-term creditors, as well as trade creditors, may seek a head start in that race. Thus, even if we accept the Court of Appeals' conclusion that the availability of the ordinary business exception to long-term creditors does not directly further the policy of equal treatment, we must recognize that it does further the policy of deterring the race to the courthouse and, as the House Report recognized, may indirectly further the goal of equal distribution as well. Whether Congress has wisely balanced the sometimes conflicting policies underlying § 547 is not a question that we are authorized to decide.

IV.

In sum, we hold that payments on long-term debt, as well as payments on short-term debt, may qualify for the ordinary course of business exception to the trustee's power to avoid preferential transfers. We express no opinion, however, on the question whether the Bankruptcy Court correctly concluded that the Debtor's payments of interest and the loan commitment fee qualify for the ordinary course of business exception, § 547(c)(2). In particular, we do not decide whether the loan involved in this case was incurred in the ordinary course of the Debtor's business and of the Bank's business, whether the payments were made in the ordinary course of business, or whether the payments were made according to ordinary business terms. These questions remain open for the Court of Appeals on remand.

The judgment of the Court of Appeals is reversed and the case is remanded for further proceedings consistent with this opinion.

It is so ordered.

■ Justice SCALIA, concurring.

I join the opinion of the Court, including Parts II and III, which respond persuasively to legislative-history and policy arguments made by respondent. It is regrettable that we have a legal culture in which such arguments have to be addressed (and are indeed credited by a Court of Appeals), with respect to a statute utterly devoid of language that could remotely be thought to distinguish between long-term and short-term debt. Since there was here no contention of a "scrivener's error" producing an absurd result, the plain text of the statute should have made this litigation unnecessary and unmaintainable.

NOTES

1. The Court in *Wolas* does not rest its decision solely on the plain meaning of § 547(c)(2) but finds a policy justification for its decision as well. We explain in the introduction to this section that preference law is based on the creditor equality principle. However, § 547(c)(2) can be repugnant to the creditor equality principle in some cases. The fact that payments are made in ordinary course does not detract from the reality that they may deplete the debtor's estate for the benefit of the creditor receiving payment. If we can understand the basis for the § 547(c)(2) exception, it will be easier to decide whether it should apply to long-term debts. The *CHG International* case read § 547(c)(2) as restricted to short-term credit, thus making it consistent with the creditor equality principle. The court in that case said: "The rationale for both the old 'current expense' rule and for the section 547(c)(2) exception is the same: the payment does not diminish the estate, is not for antecedent debt, and allows the debtor to remain in business." 897 F.2d at 1483. The value given by the creditor and the payment made by the debtor soon after are viewed as a single transaction. Thus, the payment does not harm the other creditors. But this rationale requires that § 547(c)(2) be restricted to short-term trade debt. Section 547(c)(1) protects suppliers selling for cash; § 547(c)(2) protects those selling for short-term credit. In neither instance is the estate truly depleted. If

§ 547(c)(2) is to be justified as applying only to transactions that don't in substance deplete the estate, it cannot accommodate long-term credit.

2. Justice Stevens justifies including long-term debt within the purview of § 547(c)(2) by identifying a second policy basis for preference law: to deter the race of diligence among creditors to dismember the debtor. If preference law can be relied on to reverse transfers made on the eve of bankruptcy, creditors will be less motivated to dismember a debtor who is in financial trouble. He states that § 547(c)(2) is consistent with this second policy basis. "[T]he ordinary course of business exception may benefit all creditors by deterring the 'race to the courthouse' and enabling the struggling debtor to continue operating its business." 502 U.S. at 161. Presumably, Justice Stevens is suggesting that the lure of possibly receiving a nonavoidable transfer in the ordinary course will encourage creditors who might otherwise take aggressive collection activity to desist. Viewed in this way, § 547(c)(2) deters a race of diligence.

We question, however, whether a rule making ordinary course payments nonrecoverable actually discourages collection. How many creditors faced with a sinking debtor will knowingly defer collection activity in the hope that (i) the debtor will voluntarily pay the patient creditor before filing bankruptcy, and (ii) such payment will later be found by a court to fall within the uncertain scope of the § 547(c)(2) ordinary course exception? On the other hand, how many arguably "racing" creditors (those with knowledge of the debtor's looming insolvency) who successfully collect payments within the preference period will assert the § 547(c)(2) defense and force the trustee to litigate these issues when they become preference defendants? If preferences generally become harder to recover because defendants routinely can create litigable issues under a broad ordinary course exception, then finding ways to receive preferences in the form of voluntary transfers from the debtor becomes even more attractive to creditors, not less. Commentators have thus questioned Justice Stevens's incentive rationale for the ordinary course exception. *See* Charles Jordan Tabb, *The Law of Bankruptcy* § 6.18 (1997).

3. The Court quotes the brief reference to § 547(c)(2) in the House Report, which said that the provision was intended to "leave undisturbed normal financial relations, because it does not detract from the general policy of the preference section to discourage unusual action by either the debtor or his creditors during the debtor's slide into bankruptcy." But the issue is whether payment by an insolvent debtor to a creditor holding a large long-term debt is payment in ordinary course. Although we know of no empirical evidence on the subject, we suspect that a very high percentage of payments made to creditors within the 90–day preference period are payments made in the good faith exercise of the debtor's business judgment concerning how to stay afloat. The debtor is more likely to pay creditors on whom the debtor is dependent and to defer payment to other creditors. There are costs associated with allowing bankruptcy trustees to upset completed transactions. Uncertainty about finality of payment is a disincentive on the part of credit grantors to deal with businesses in distress. In the introductory material to this section we suggest the view that preference law should balance the interest of creditor equality against the cost of upsetting normal transactions. The cost of creditor equality may sometimes be too high. Omitting the reasonable-cause-to-believe test in the Bankruptcy Code gave trustees greater power to upset normal transactions. Clearly § 547(c)(2) was intended to fill part of the gap left by this omission; it has a legitimate role to play in moderating the costs of preference law. The decision to include long-term debt in § 547(c)(2) may be right on policy grounds as well as under the plain meaning rule so long as the payment of the long term debt is in fact in the ordinary course. The meaning of "ordinary course" in this context was left open in *Wolas*.

b. Meaning of Ordinary Course under § 547(c)(2)

Courts have had no end of trouble in deciding what transfers § 547(c)(2) should protect. *Wolas* told us only that payments on long-term debt may qualify for the ordinary course of business exception, but offered no guidance on what ordinary course means. BAPCPA amended § 547(c)(2) to allow the preferred creditor to defend on either the ground that the payment was in the ordinary course of business affairs of the parties *or* was in accordance with ordinary business terms. Formerly, as we see in *Tolona Pizza*, the defense required that both elements be satisfied to make out the defense. We include the case for its much cited holding on the meaning of ordinary course of business.

In re Tolona Pizza Products Corp.
United States Court of Appeals, Seventh Circuit, 1993.
3 F.3d 1029.

■ POSNER, Circuit Judge.

When, within 90 days before declaring bankruptcy, the debtor makes a payment to an unsecured creditor, the payment is a "preference," and the trustee in bankruptcy can recover it and thus make the creditor take pot luck with the rest of the debtor's unsecured creditors. § 547. But there is an exception if the creditor can show that the debt had been incurred in the ordinary course of the business of both the debtor and the creditor, § 547(c)(2)(A); that the payment, too, had been made and received in the ordinary course of their businesses, § 547(c)(2)(B); and that the payment had been "made according to ordinary business terms." § 547(c)(2)(C). The first two requirements are easy to understand: *of course* to defeat the inference of preferential treatment the debt must have been incurred in the ordinary course of business of both debtor and creditor and the payment on account of the debt must have been in the ordinary course as well. But what does the third requirement—that the payment have been "made according to ordinary business terms"—add? And in particular does it refer to what is "ordinary" between this debtor and this creditor, or what is ordinary in the market or industry in which they operate? The circuits are divided on this question * * *.

Tolona, a maker of pizza, issued eight checks to Rose, its sausage supplier, within 90 days before being thrown into bankruptcy by its creditors. The checks, which totaled a shade under $46,000, cleared and as a result Tolona's debts to Rose were paid in full. Tolona's other major trade creditors stand to receive only 13 cents on the dollar under the plan approved by the bankruptcy court, if the preferential treatment of Rose is allowed to stand. Tolona, as debtor in possession, brought an adversary proceeding against Rose to recover the eight payments as voidable preferences. The bankruptcy judge entered judgment for Tolona. The district judge reversed. He thought that Rose did not, in order to comply with § 547(c)(2)(C), have to prove that the terms on which it had extended credit to Tolona were standard terms in the industry, but that if this was wrong the testimony of Rose's executive vice-president, Stiehl, did prove it. The parties agree that the other requirements of § 547(c)(2) were satisfied.

Rose's invoices recited "net 7 days," meaning that payment was due within seven days. For years preceding the preference period, however, Tolona rarely paid within seven days; nor did Rose's other customers. Most paid within 21 days, and if they paid later than 28 or 30 days Rose would usually withhold future shipments until payment was received. Tolona, however, as an old and valued customer (Rose had been selling to it for fifteen years), was permitted to make payments beyond the 21-day period and even beyond the 28-day or 30-day period. The eight payments at issue were made between 12 and 32 days after Rose had invoiced Tolona, for an average of 22 days; but this actually was an improvement. In the 34 months before the preference period, the average time for which Rose's invoices to Tolona were outstanding was 26 days and the longest time was 46 days. Rose consistently treated Tolona with a degree of leniency that made Tolona (Stiehl conceded on cross-examination) one of a "sort of exceptional group of customers of Rose... fall[ing] outside the common industry practice and standards."

It may seem odd that paying a debt late would ever be regarded as a preference to the creditor thus paid belatedly. But it is all relative. A debtor who has entered the preference period—who is therefore only 90 days, or fewer, away from plunging into bankruptcy—is typically unable to pay all his outstanding debts in full as they come due. If he pays one and not the others, as happened here, the payment though late is still a preference to that creditor, and is avoidable unless the conditions of § 547(c)(2) are met. One condition is that payment be in the ordinary course of both the debtor's and the creditor's business. A late payment normally will not be. It will therefore be an avoidable preference.

This is not a dryly syllogistic conclusion. The purpose of the preference statute is to prevent the debtor during his slide toward bankruptcy from trying to stave off the evil day by giving preferential treatment to his most importunate creditors, who may sometimes be those who have been waiting longest to be paid. Unless the favoring of particular creditors is outlawed, the mass of creditors of a shaky firm will be nervous, fearing that one or a few of their number are going to walk away with all the firm's assets; and this fear may precipitate debtors into bankruptcy earlier than is socially desirable. * * *

From this standpoint, however, the most important thing is not that the dealings between the debtor and the allegedly favored creditor conform to some industry norm but that they conform to the norm established by the debtor and the creditor in the period before, preferably well before, the preference period. That condition is satisfied here—if anything, Rose treated Tolona more favorably (and hence Tolona treated Rose less preferentially) before the preference period than during it.

But if this is all that the third subsection of 547(c)(2) requires, it might seem to add nothing to the first two subsections, which require that both the debt and the payment be within the ordinary course of business of both the debtor and the creditor. For, provided these conditions are fulfilled, a "late" payment really isn't late if the parties have established a practice that deviates from the strict terms of their written contract. But we hesitate to conclude that the third subsection, requiring conformity to "ordinary business terms," has no function in the statute. We can think of two functions that it might have. One is evidentiary. * * * If the debtor and creditor dealt on terms that the creditor testifies were normal for them but that are wholly unknown in the industry, this casts some doubt on his (self-serving) testimony. Preferences are disfavored, and subsection C makes them more difficult to prove. The second possible function of the subsection is to allay the concerns of creditors that one or more of their number may have worked out a special deal with the debtor, before the preference period, designed to put that creditor ahead of the others in the event of bankruptcy. It may seem odd that allowing late payments from a debtor would be a way for a creditor to make himself more rather than less assured of repayment. But such a creditor does have an advantage during the preference period, because he can receive late payments then and they will still be in the ordinary course of business for him and his debtor.

The functions that we have identified, combined with a natural reluctance to cut out and throw away one-third of an important provision of the Bankruptcy Code, persuade us that the creditor must show that the payment he received was made in accordance with the ordinary business terms in the industry. But this does not mean that the creditor must establish the existence of some single, uniform set of business terms, as Tolona argues. * * * Not only is it difficult to identify the industry whose norm shall govern (is it, here, the sale of sausages to makers of pizza? The sale of sausages to anyone? The sale of anything to makers of pizza?), but there can be great variance in billing practices within an industry. Apparently there is in this industry, whatever exactly "this industry" is; for while it is plain that neither Rose nor its competitors enforce payment within seven days, it is unclear that there is a standard outer limit of forbearance. It seems that 21 days is a goal but that payment as late as 30 days is generally tolerated and that for good customers even longer delays are allowed. The average period between Rose's invoice and Tolona's payment during the preference period was only 22 days, which seems well within the industry norm, whatever exactly it is. The law should not push businessmen to agree upon a single set of billing practices; antitrust objections to one side, the relevant business and financial considerations vary widely among firms on both the buying and the selling side of the market.

We conclude that "ordinary business terms" refers to the *range* of terms that encompasses the practices in which firms similar in some general way to the creditor in question engage, and that only dealings so idiosyncratic as to fall outside that broad range should be deemed extraordinary and therefore outside the scope of subsection C. * * * Stiehl's testimony brought the case within the scope of "ordinary business terms" as just defined. Rose and its competitors pay little or no attention to the terms stated on their invoices, allow most customers to take up to 30 days to pay, and allow certain favored customers to take even more time. There is no single set of terms on which the members of the industry have coalesced; instead there is a broad range and the district judge plausibly situated the dealings between Rose and Tolona within it. These dealings are conceded to have been within the normal course of dealings between the two firms, a course established long before the preference period, and there is no hint either that the dealings were designed to put Rose ahead of other creditors of Tolona or that other creditors of Tolona would have been surprised to learn that Rose had been so forbearing in its dealings with Tolona.

Tolona might have argued that the district judge gave insufficient deference to the bankruptcy judge's contrary finding. The district judge, and we, are required to accept the bankruptcy judge's findings on questions of fact as long as they are not clearly erroneous. * * * But since Tolona did not argue that the district judge had applied an incorrect standard of review, we need not decide whether the district judge overstepped the bounds. Which is not to say that he did. While he did not intone the magic words "clear error," he may well have believed that the record as a whole left no doubt that Tolona's dealings with Rose were within the broad band of accepted practices in the industry. It is true that Stiehl testified that Tolona was one of an exceptional group of Rose's customers with whom Rose's dealings fell outside common industry practice. But the undisputed evidence concerning those dealings and the practices of the industry demonstrates that payment within 30 days is within the outer limits of normal industry practices, and the payments at issue in this case were made on average in a significantly shorter time.

The judgment reversing the bankruptcy judge and dismissing the adversary proceeding is

AFFIRMED.

■ FLAUM, Circuit Judge, dissenting. [opinion omitted]

NOTE

Tolona Pizza minimizes the inquiry that a court must make into "ordinary business terms," and BAPCPA goes further by giving the creditor the option of proving *either* that payment was made in ordinary course of the debtor's business *or* that it was made according to ordinary business terms. Is this is a good change? Under what circumstances should a trustee be able to claw back payments in the ordinary course between debtor and creditor that are on terms that are not customary in the industry? Why should extraordinary payments as between debtor and creditor be shielded from avoidance so long as made in accordance with ordinary business terms?

6. THE "SUBSEQUENT ADVANCE" RULE

Section 547(c)(4) creates a "shelter" rule in situations in which a creditor subsequently advances new value after receiving a payment on account of past debt that would otherwise be an avoidable preference. This subsection is designed for, and of special importance in, the case of running accounts between the debtor and its suppliers. In general, suppliers advance trade credit only up to a preset credit limit. As payments are received, commonly fresh credit is extended; this fresh credit ordinarily would not have been extended in the absence of the payment. Keeping these running accounts alive is of great importance to almost all businesses and especially distressed ones. Prior law permitted the creditor to offset all payments and advances made during the preference period in determining the creditor's net preference liability. *Jaquith v. Alden*, 189 U.S. 78 (1903) (adopting the so-called "net result rule"). Section 547(c)(4) is framed in somewhat narrower terms, limiting recovery of prior preferential payments to the extent that the preferred creditor has made subsequent unsecured advances. Applying this narrower "subsequent advance" rule, raises tricky problems, including the issue of repayment of subsequent advances with transfers that are themselves avoidable preferences. *See* Charles Jordan Tabb, *The Law of Bankruptcy* § 6.20 (1997).

PROBLEM

Day 1. Creditor ships $100 in goods to Debtor.

Day 15. Debtor pays Creditor $100 for the Day 1 shipment.

Day 30. Creditor ships $125 in goods to Debtor.

Day 45. Debtor pays Creditor $125 for the Day 30 shipment.

Day 60. Creditor ships $150 in goods to Debtor.

Day 80. Debtor pays Creditor $150 for the Day 60 shipment.

Day 90. Bankruptcy petition is filed.

Assume that Creditor's shipments are on unsecured credit and that all of Debtor's payments would be avoidable were it not for § 547(c)(4). Which, if any, payments made by Debtor may be avoided under § 547(c)(4)? See *In re IRFM, Inc.*, 52 F.3d 228 (9th Cir. 1995).

> One commentator has explained:
>
>> If the debtor has made payments for goods or services that the creditor supplied on unsecured credit after an earlier preference, *and if these subsequent payments are themselves voidable as preferences* (or on any other ground), then under section 547(c)(4)(B) the creditor should be able to invoke those unsecured credit extensions as a defense to the recovery of the *earlier* voidable preference. On the other hand, the debtor's subsequent payments might not be voidable on any other ground and not voidable under section 547, because the goods and services were given C.O.D. rather than on a credit, or because the creditor has a defense under section 547(c)(1), (2), or (3). In this situation, the creditor may keep his payments but has no section 547(c)(4) defense to the trustee's action to recover the earlier preference. In either event, the creditor gets credit only once for goods and services later supplied.
>
> Vern Countryman, *The Concept of a Voidable Preference in Bankruptcy*, 38 Vand.L.Rev. 713, 788 (1985) (emphasis added and footnotes omitted) * * *.

NOTE: TIME OF TRANSFER OF PAYMENT BY CHECK

If a debtor gives a check to a creditor and the check is paid, the result is a "transfer of an interest of the debtor in property" under Section 547(b). When exactly does the transfer occur? Under the date-of-delivery view, the transfer occurs when the check is delivered to the creditor so long as the check is paid by the bank on which it was drawn within a reasonable time. Under the date-of-honor view, the transfer occurs when the check is honored, that is, paid by the drawee bank.

Time of transfer is important both under § 547(b) and § 547(c). Under § 547(b)(4) the transfer must occur within the preference period. If a check is delivered to the creditor before the start of the preference period and is paid after the start of the period, under the delivery rule there cannot be a voidable preference, while under the honor rule § 547(b)(4) is satisfied. The Supreme Court in *Barnhill v. Johnson*, 503 U.S. 393 (1992), held that for the purpose of § 547(b)(4) transfer occurs on the date the drawee bank honors the check.

PROBLEM

In *Barnhill* the Court noted that the Courts of Appeal had been unanimous in holding that the delivery rule prevailed in § 547(c) cases and made clear that it was not deciding that issue. Do you believe the policies involved in deciding when a transfer takes place under § 547(c) are sufficiently different from those under § 547(b) to justify having different rules for the determining the time of transfer with respect to checks under each subsection? How would you decide the following case?

Debtor was a struggling borrower that "paid when it could." With growing reluctance, Supplier continued to ship ingredients essential for Debtor to continue its manufacturing business. Supplier delivered a $25,000 shipment on March 1. On March 18, Debtor ordered an additional shipment, but Supplier refused to make any more shipments until "I see your money" in payment of the March 1 shipment. On March 20, Supplier received by overnight mail Debtor's check for $25,000; on March 21, Supplier delivered the new order invoiced at $30,000; on March 22, the $25,000 check was honored. Debtor filed in bankruptcy on April 3, and Debtor's trustee sought to recover the $25,000 payment as a preference; Supplier defended under § 547(c)(4). Debtor relied on *Barnhill* to assert that the $30,000 shipment could not be offset against Debtor's $25,000 payment under § 547(c)(4) because the check had not transferred property of Debtor to Supplier until March 22, the date of its honor; hence, the preference was subsequent to the shipment. Supplier contended that the $25,000 payment took place on March 20 when the check was delivered; hence, the $30,000 shipment on March 21 was subsequent to the payment and could be setoff against it. Supplier argued that the purpose of § 547(c)(4) is to encourage creditors to continue to deal with troubled debtors; this purpose was better served by allowing Supplier to rely on delivery of Debtor's check rather than having to wait for the check to clear. Who has the better argument? *See, e.g., In re Tennessee Chemical Co.*, 112 F.3d 234 (6th Cir. 1997).

7. SECURITY INTERESTS IN INVENTORY AND ACCOUNTS RECEIVABLE

The battle over the validity of floating liens in bankruptcy was the cause celebre of commercial law in the years immediately after enactment of the UCC. The bankruptcy bar had stood by, largely ignored, while Article 9 was drafted to give every advantage to the secured creditor: abrogation of the prohibition on the debtor's retention of unrestricted dominion over collateral in § 9-205; automatic future advance and after-acquired property clauses in § 9-204; first-to-file priority rule in § 9-322; notice filing in § 9-502. Taken together, these provisions allowed the secured party to take a security interest in all of a debtor's personal property now owned or thereafter acquired to secure both present and future advances. If the floating lien were upheld in bankruptcy, there would be nothing left in a debtor's estate to distribute among unsecured trade creditors who had provided goods and services to the failed debtor.

But bankruptcy counsel believed that the drafters of the 1962 version of Article 9, none of whom was experienced in the nether world of bankruptcy law, had painted themselves into a corner, and that security interests in inventory acquired and accounts that arose during the preference period were potentially voidable as preferences. This view if accepted could have severely affected the inventory and accounts financing industry. And these lawyers had a solid basis for their opinion because the time of transfer for security interests in bankruptcy is the time of perfection of the security interest, not its attachment. § 547(e).

Suppose Debtor, an appliance retailer, signed a security agreement on February 1 granting a security interest to Bank to secure a loan made at the same time. The collateral was all of Debtor's inventory then owned or thereafter acquired. Bank immediately filed a financing statement covering inventory. Under Article 9 the security interest attached, with respect to any item of inventory, when all of the following conditions were met: (1) there was an authenticated security agreement; (2) Bank gave value to Debtor; and (3) Debtor had rights in the item of inventory. § 9-203(b). The first two conditions were satisfied on February 1 when the loan was made and the agreement signed. The third condition was satisfied at various times. With respect to inventory owned on February 1 it was satisfied on that date. With respect to after-acquired inventory it was satisfied when the inventory was acquired. Section 9-308(a) states that a security interest is perfected when it has attached and when all of the applicable steps required for perfection have been taken. The step normally taken to perfect a security interest in inventory is the filing of a financing statement. Thus, under Article 9 whenever Debtor acquired an item of inventory after February 1, a security interest in that item attached and was perfected. Filing of the financing statement occurred on February 1 but perfection with respect to the inventory covered by the financing statement could not occur until the inventory was acquired.

Suppose in our example that Debtor's inventory completely turned over every 60 days and that Debtor filed in bankruptcy on December 1. Under this assumption, all inventory on hand at the date of bankruptcy had been acquired during the preference period. Assume further that Bank did not make additional loans to Debtor after February 1 and that the original loan was unpaid at the date of bankruptcy. Under Article 9 the security interest of Bank in inventory at the date of bankruptcy attached and was perfected during the preference period and secured a debt that arose on February 1. Under Bankruptcy Act § 60a(2) (now found in § 547(e)), the apparent result was that the transfer of Debtor's property represented by the security interest was made when the security interest attached and was perfected during the preference period. Thus, if Debtor was insolvent at the time of the transfer, the security interest was voidable as a preferential transfer under Bankruptcy Act § 60b.

For our purposes, it is enough to say that in *Grain Merchants of Indiana, Inc. v. Union Bank & Sav. Co.*, 408 F.2d 209 (7th Cir. 1969), the court, in a highly unorthodox reading of the law, upheld the validity of floating lien security interests in inventory and accounts in bankruptcy. The reasoning of this opinion was sufficiently troublesome to drive all parties to resolve the issue by a compromise amendment to the Bankruptcy Code. This provision is now § 547(c)(5). It was drafted against a background that assumed the following: accounts receivable and inventory normally turn over within a short period of time; it is likely that at the date of bankruptcy some receivables or inventory on hand had been acquired by the debtor within the 90-day period; since a security interest in this new collateral was, by virtue of § 547(e)(3), a transfer to the secured party when it was acquired by the debtor, there might have been a voidable preference under § 547(b) if the debtor was insolvent at the time. Section 547(c)(5), set out below, is a limited exemption from this rule.

> (c) The trustee may not avoid under this section a transfer—
>
> > (5) that creates a perfected security interest in inventory or a receivable or the proceeds of either, except to the extent that the aggregate of all such transfers to the transferee caused a reduction, as of the date of the filing of the petition and to the prejudice of other creditors holding unsecured claims, of any amount by which the debt secured by such security interest exceeded the value of all security interests for such debt on the later of

(A)(i) with respect to a transfer to which subsection (b)(4)(A) of this section applies, 90 days before the date of the filing of the petition; or

(ii) with respect to a transfer to which (b)(4)(B) of this section applies, one year before the date of the filing of the petition; or

(B) the date on which new value was first given under the security agreement creating such security interest;

PROBLEM

How does § 547(c)(5) work? Secured Party is secured by all accounts receivable of Debtor, now owned or thereafter acquired. At the beginning of the 90-day period the debt was $100,000 and at the date of bankruptcy the debt was $90,000; at the beginning of the 90-day period there were $60,000 in receivables. During the 90-day period Debtor increased its receivables so that on the date of bankruptcy they amounted to $70,000. The test is stated in terms of the amount of the reduction of the amount by which the debt exceeded the value of the security interest from the beginning of the 90-day period to the date of bankruptcy.

(a) What result would it give in this case?

(b) What result if Secured Party's $100,000 debt was secured by $120,000 in account receivables at the beginning of the 90-day period and $70,000 in receivables on the date of bankruptcy all obtained by Debtor within the 90-day period?

Section 547(c)(5) is a variation of the substitution theory, which was one of the more persuasive bases of the *Grain Merchants* decision. It provides, in effect, that it is not important whether the items making up the mass of inventory or accounts receivable at bankruptcy were identical to the items making up the mass at the beginning of the 90-day period so long as the volume has not changed. Within that limitation any new item that came into existence within the 90-day period is treated as a substitute for an item that was disposed of by the debtor during the same period. Note the extreme difficulty in applying this net "improvement in position" test to a constantly fluctuating inventory (which may include raw materials and work in progress as well as finished goods) in constantly fluctuating market conditions.

8. OTHER PROTECTED TRANSFERS

The equality-of-distribution premise of preference law gives way to strong policy concerns protecting payments made for domestic support obligations.

These are obligations owed to spouses or children in the nature of alimony, maintenance or support. § 101(14A). This definition includes debts owed to governmental units that have acquired such rights in exchange for assistance provided to families. Thus, spouses, children and governmental units providing assistance don't have to give back alimony or child support payments received within the preference period from debtors who file in bankruptcy. Section 547(c)(7) precludes recovery of such payments as preferences.

Section 547(c)(8) provides a small transactions exception for payments made on debts that are "primarily consumer debts." If the "aggregate value of all property that constitutes or is affected by such transfer is less than $600," the property cannot be recovered as preferences. BAPCPA appropriately added a comparable provision excepting property of less than $5,000 (now $5,475) made in payment of debts that are "not primarily consumer debts." § 547(c)(9). Recovering preferences in these small-potatoes cases consumes judicial resources better devoted to more important matters. Moreover, creditor recipients of such small transfers commonly find it un-economic to defend the trustee's action regardless of the merits. Although § 547(c)(8) and (9) function as jurisdictional minimums, § 547(g) frames them as affirmative defenses rather than an element in the trustee's case in chief.

PROBLEM

Insolvent Debtor made payments of $500 to Bank on her overdue credit card debt on the first day of each month from January through July. She filed in Chapter 7 bankruptcy on July 15, and her trustee in bankruptcy sought to recover $1,500 from Bank as a voidable preference. Bank relied on § 547(c)(8) in its contention that trustee should recover nothing. Does that provision allow the trustee to aggregate all sums paid during the 90–day period to the same creditor? *See In re Hailes*, 77 F.3d 873 (5th Cir. 1996).

9. LETTERS OF CREDIT

As we saw on pp. 217 if Applicant obtains a letter of credit from Issuer Bank to support performance of its obligation to Beneficiary, Applicant's bankruptcy does not affect Beneficiary's right to proceed against Issuer on its independent undertaking under the letter of credit, unimpeded by the automatic stay of § 362. This is an end devoutly to be desired by any obligee, so much so that sometimes clients come to believe that obtaining a letter of credit fully insulates them from the risks attending the bankruptcy of their obligors. But under preference law this view may not be true in certain situations.

In the common case there is no preference because the letter of credit is given for contemporaneous consideration. Usually a letter of credit is issued at the inception of a credit sale transaction. To assure payment, the seller requires the buyer to obtain a letter of credit obliging the issuing bank to pay the sale price if the buyer doesn't pay when it becomes due. To induce the bank to issue the letter of credit, the buyer grants the bank a security interest in the buyer's property to secure the buyer's obligation to reimburse the bank if the bank is required to pay the seller. The letter of credit transaction is a substitute for a secured transaction between the seller and buyer. After the letter of credit is issued, the seller delivers the goods to the buyer. If the buyer doesn't pay and files in bankruptcy, the seller obtains payment from the bank. The bank has a secured claim in bankruptcy. There is no preference to either the seller or the bank in this kind of case. Although the security interest granted to the bank is a transfer of property by the buyer for the benefit of the seller, it is not a preference to the seller because the transfer is not on account of an antecedent debt. Rather, it is a contemporaneous exchange for new value by the seller. The seller obligates itself to make a credit sale of goods to the buyer in exchange for issuance of the letter of credit. There is no preference to the bank because the security interest does not secure an antecedent debt owed to the bank. The transfer of property to the bank is contemporaneous exchange for new value by the bank, the bank's issuance of the letter of credit.

The result may be different if the letter of credit is given to the creditor for antecedent consideration. Suppose that Debtor, an insolvent company, owed Creditor $500,000 and Creditor was pressing Debtor for payment. When it became convinced that Debtor was unable to pay at that time, Creditor accepted a letter of credit issued by Bank for $500,000 payable to Creditor a year later if Debtor had not paid Creditor its debt by that time. In order to induce Bank to issue the letter of credit, Debtor granted Bank a security interest in its property to secure its obligation to reimburse Bank for any payment Bank has to make on the letter of credit to Creditor. Debtor failed to pay its obligation to Creditor within the one-year deadline and Bank paid Creditor the amount owing on the letter of credit. Debtor filed in bankruptcy and its assets were liquidated. Bank received full payment from Debtor's estate on its secured claim. Debtor's trustee brought an action against Creditor to recover the amount paid to Bank on the secured claim on the ground that Creditor had received a voidable preference.

If Debtor had granted Creditor a security interest in its property rather than a letter of credit, there clearly would have been an avoidable preference: there would be a transfer of an interest in Debtor's property for the benefit of a creditor for the account of an antecedent debt made while Debtor was insolvent. The use by Debtor of a letter of credit does not change this result. The court in *In re Compton Corp.*, 831 F.2d 586 (5th Cir. 1987), held that there was a preferential transfer to Creditor even though Debtor transferred no property to

Creditor. There is no requirement that the transfer of Debtor's property be to Creditor. A transfer of Debtor's property "to or for the benefit of" Creditor is sufficient under § 547(b)(1). Since the transfer was made on account of the past-due debt to Creditor, § 547(b)(2) is satisfied as well. Thus there was a voidable preference to Creditor. However, there was no preference to the Bank because the transfer of the security interest to the Bank was a contemporaneous exchange for new value by Bank, the Bank's undertaking on the letter of credit.

Sometimes determining the recipient of a voidable preference is not easy, particularly in a triangular standby letter of credit relationship, like that in the following case. The Note following the case questions the court's solution.

In re Powerine Oil Co.
United States Court of Appeals, Ninth Circuit, 1995.
59 F.3d 969.

■ KOZINSKI, Circuit Judge.

Can an unsecured creditor be better off when the debtor defaults rather than paying off the debt? Yes: Law can be stranger than fiction in the Preference Zone.

I.

Powerine Oil Company (the debtor here) obtained a $250.6 million line of credit from a syndicate consisting of several banks and insurance companies; the loan was secured by most of Powerine's personal property. The security agreement provided that the collateral would serve as security for all letters of credit that "have been, or are in the future, issued on the account of Debtor."

Koch Oil Company thereafter agreed to sell crude oil to Powerine. To secure Powerine's obligation, it designated Koch as beneficiary of two irrevocable standby letters of credit issued by First National Bank of Chicago, one of the lenders covered by the security agreement. The letters, which were to expire in April 1984, totaled approximately $8.7 million, an amount at all times sufficient to cover the cost of the oil Koch sold to Powerine.

In January and February 1984, Koch billed Powerine $3.2 million for oil it had delivered in December and January. Powerine eventually paid this amount but, unfortunately for Koch, it also filed a chapter 11 bankruptcy petition less than 90 days later. The Committee of Creditors Holding Unsecured Claims (the

Committee) eventually brought an action to recover the payment, claiming it was a preference under § 547(b).[1]

The bankruptcy court held that the transfer was protected by the "contemporaneous exchange for new value" exception of § 547(c)(1) and granted Koch's motion for summary judgment. The Bankruptcy Appellate Panel (BAP) affirmed on a different ground: It held that the payment wasn't a preference because it didn't enable Koch to recover more than it would in a chapter 7 liquidation. Even if Powerine hadn't made the $3.2 million transfer, the BAP reasoned, Koch would have been paid in full because it would have drawn on First National's letters of credit.

II.

Bankruptcy Code section 547(b) sets forth the five elements of a preferential transfer. The parties dispute only whether the last element—section 547(b)(5)—was satisfied here. Under this provision, the Committee must prove that Koch "received more than it would [have] if the case were a chapter 7 liquidation case, the transfer had not been made, and [Koch] received payment of the debt to the extent provided by the provisions of the Code." 4 Collier on Bankruptcy ¶ 547.08, at 547–45 (Lawrence P. King ed., 15th ed. 1995).

Whether section 547(b)(5)'s requirements have been met turns in part on the status of the creditor to whom the transfer was made. Pre-petition payments to a fully secured creditor generally "will not be considered preferential because the creditor would not receive more than in a chapter 7 liquidation." Id. at 547–47. With respect to unsecured creditors, however, the rule is quite different: "[A]s long as the distribution in bankruptcy is less than one-hundred percent, *any* payment 'on account' to an unsecured creditor during the preference period will enable that creditor to receive more than he would have received in liquidation had the payment not been made." *In re Lewis W. Shurtleff, Inc.*, 778 F.2d 1416, 1421 (9th Cir. 1985).

Vis-a-vis Powerine, Koch was an unsecured creditor as it didn't hold any security interest in Powerine's property. *See* 11 U.S.C. § 506(a). Because most of Powerine's assets on the date it filed for bankruptcy were subject to the lien

---

[1] Pursuant to Powerine's reorganization plan, any preferential transfers recovered for the estate will be divided equally between secured and unsecured creditors. The full amount of the January and February payments was $8.5 million, but only $3.2 million was paid more than 45 days after delivery. We agree with the BAP that Powerine incurred its debts on the date Koch delivered the oil, not (as Koch argues) the first date the exact amount of the debt could be determined. Accordingly, $3.2 million of the transfer wasn't covered by the "ordinary course of business" exception under the version of § 547(c)(2) in effect at the time of the transfer. * * *

held by the secured creditors, Powerine's unsecured creditors could expect to receive much less than one-hundred cents on the dollar in a chapter 7 liquidation. Consequently, Powerine's $3.2 million pre-petition payment enabled Koch to recover more than it would have in a chapter 7 liquidation, and it was therefore a preference.

The BAP came to the contrary conclusion by focusing on the fact that Koch could have drawn down the letters of credit, had Powerine not paid it directly. Since Koch would have recovered the full amount owed to it (albeit from First National) had Powerine defaulted, the BAP reasoned that the $3.2 million payment wasn't a preference.

Courts have long held, however, that the key factor in determining whether a payment is a preference is the "percentage[ ]... [creditors'] claims are entitled to draw out of the *estate of the bankrupt*." *Swarts v. Fourth Nat'l Bank*, 117 F. 1, 7 (8th Cir. 1902) (emphasis added). Thus, the relevant inquiry focuses "not on whether a creditor may have recovered all of the monies owed by the debtor *from any source whatsoever*, but instead upon whether the creditor would have received less than a 100% payout" from the debtor's estate. *Id.* * * * That Koch had recourse against a third party in case the debtor defaulted thus has no bearing on this issue.

The BAP nonetheless invoked a "rule of reason" to avoid what it viewed as an inequitable result. Koch's right to collect under the letters could be taken into account, the BAP held, because the letters of credit had expired by the time the Committee initiated its preference action. Koch was thus left far worse off because Powerine paid its bill rather than defaulting. The BAP recognized that a creditor's "rights against a surety are not relevant to whether a transfer is preferential so long as those rights are still in place after the preference action is commenced." It concluded, however, that "when that right of action against the surety no longer exists, it is incumbent upon the court to measure the net recovery that the transferee would have obtained from the surety had the transfer not been made." The BAP cited no authority for this proposition and we construe it to have been an exercise of its equitable powers.

Although bankruptcy courts are sometimes referred to as courts of equity, the Supreme Court has reminded us that "whatever equitable powers remain in the bankruptcy courts must and can only be exercised within the confines of the Bankruptcy Code." *Norwest Bank Worthington v. Ahlers*, 485 U.S. 197, 206 (1988). Equity may not be invoked to defeat clear statutory language, nor to reach results inconsistent with the statutory scheme established by the Code. * * * Because the statutory language here provides no basis for the BAP's "rule of reason," we conclude that it was error to consider the right to draw on third-party letters of credit in deciding whether Koch had received a preference.

III.

Having determined that Powerine's $3.2 million payment to Koch was preferential under section 547(b), we must next determine whether any of section 547(c)'s exceptions apply. Placing heavy reliance on *In re Fuel Oil Supply & Terminaling, Inc.*, 837 F.2d 224 (5th Cir. 1988), Koch contends the payment it received is protected by the "contemporaneous exchange for new value" exception of § 547(c)(1).[3] In *Fuel Oil*, the debtor paid one of its unsecured creditors within 90 days of filing for bankruptcy. Like Koch, the creditor was the beneficiary of two letters of credit securing payment if the debtor defaulted. The issuing banks "held a security interest in [debtor]'s assets which at all times was equal to or in excess of [debtor]'s obligation to [the creditor]." *Id.* at 228.

The Fifth Circuit held that the payment was protected by the contemporaneous exchange for new value exception, reasoning that, when the debtor paid the creditor, the banks' exposure under the letters of credit was reduced by a corresponding amount. The banks' contingent reimbursement claim against the debtor's assets was thereby released, giving the debtor new value. "This outcome is consistent with the principle underlying § 547(c)(1)," the Fifth Circuit noted, "because the release of the debtor's collateral offsets the transfer to the creditor, thereby resulting in no depletion to the debtor's estate." *Id.* * * *

Unlike the banks in *Fuel Oil Supply*, which were fully secured, however, First National was only partially secured. When Powerine filed for bankruptcy, it had $282 million in secured debt and assets of only $66 million. Nor did First National have first claim on the security because the loan agreement provided that Powerine's debts would be secured "equally without preference or priority of any one over the other."

Only a portion of First National's contingent reimbursement claim was thus secured by the blanket lien. When Powerine paid Koch directly, First National's exposure under the letters of credit was reduced by a corresponding amount, and its contingent claim against Powerine's assets was thereby released, but only to the extent the claim was secured. Thus, Powerine received new value equal to the amount of the secured portion of First National's reimbursement claim. * * * As to the unsecured portion of First National's claim, however, Powerine didn't receive new value; the bank couldn't release a

---

[3] Section 547(c)(1) provides:

The trustee may not avoid under this section a transfer. . . to the extent that such transfer was—(A) intended by the debtor and the creditor to or for whose benefit such transfer was made to be a contemporaneous exchange for new value given to the debtor; and (B) in fact a substantially contemporaneous exchange.

security interest in Powerine's assets it didn't in fact have. The contemporaneous exchange for new value exception therefore doesn't protect Koch's $3.2 million payment to the extent First National's reimbursement claim was unsecured.

* * *

We are unable to determine on this record how much of First National's contingent reimbursement claim against Powerine was secured. We therefore remand for the bankruptcy court to determine what portion of the $3.2 million payment may be recovered from Koch.

REVERSED and REMANDED.

■ FARRIS, Circuit Judge, dissenting:

Bankruptcy courts sit as courts of equity, but they may not avoid the plain language of a statute. * * * We must decide whether the Bankruptcy Appellate Panel's interpretation of § 547(b)(5) is plausible.

Section 547(b)(5) states: [T]he trustee may avoid any transfer of an interest of the debtor in property—

> .. . . . .
>
> **(5)** that enables such creditor to receive more than such creditor would receive if
>
>> **(A)** the case were a case under chapter 7 of this title;
>>
>> **(B)** the transfer had not been made; and
>>
>> **(C)** such creditor received payment of such debt to the extent provided by the provisions of this title.

The plain language of the statute does not limit consideration to funds from Powerine's estate. Under a hypothetical chapter 7 liquidation, it could have collected from First National as "provided by the provisions of this title." In its opinion, the BAP ruled that "[n]othing in title 11 would prevent a draw down on the credits here at issue had Powerine filed bankruptcy without paying Koch."

In my opinion, the BAP's decision does not avoid the plain language of section 547(b)(5). I respectfully dissent.

NOTE

Koch, Powerine, and First Chicago entered into this triangular standby letter of credit relationship on the understanding that Powerine would pay Koch for the oil Koch provided and if Powerine could not or would not pay Koch directly then First Chicago would honor the letter of credit and seek reimbursement from Powerine. The point of this entirely sensible business relationship was to shift the credit risk of Powerine's insolvency from Koch to First Chicago, presumably because First Chicago was better positioned than Koch to assess and monitor Powerine's creditworthiness. As the Ninth Circuit holds in Part III of its opinion, the payment by Powerine to Koch had the effect of depleting the bankruptcy estate within the preference period in order to satisfy an unsecured claim. But the parties had agreed by entering into the standby letter of credit that the risk of non-payment of this unsecured obligation was First Chicago's risk, not Koch's. From a functional point of view the payment to Koch, by eliminating a partially unsecured contingent reimbursement obligation to First Chicago, benefited First Chicago, not Koch, which otherwise would have simply drawn on the standby letter of credit. In short, the true beneficiary of the payment to Koch (the preference sought to be recovered) was First Chicago, not Koch. Nevertheless, the Ninth Circuit in *Powerine Oil* authorizes recovery of the preference from Koch, which left Koch with an unsecured claim against now-bankrupt Powerine. Koch, which bargained to shift this credit risk to First Chicago is left without any recourse against First Chicago. And to add insult to Koch's injury, First Chicago retains the benefit of the preference it indirectly received, and pursuant to the stipulation referred to in footnote 1, First Chicago as one of the stipulating secured lenders also receives a pro rata portion of half of the money recovered from Koch!

After *Powerine Oil*, the safest way to structure this triangular relationship from Koch's perspective is as a commercial letter of credit. Under the terms of a commercial letter of credit, First Chicago would have had to honor a draft under the letter of credit upon Koch's presentation of documents evidencing the shipment of the oil. Standby letters of credit are generally favored over commercial letters because they are less cumbersome to administer and are thought to achieve the same effective shifting of credit risk from beneficiary to issuing bank. As a result the standby letter of credit is a commonplace and valuable tool in commercial transactions. There is no apparent reason why the Bankruptcy Code should require parties to use commercial letters in these situations when they would otherwise prefer to use standby letters.

In *Powerine Oil,* the Ninth Circuit follows the "plain meaning" of § 547(b) to a result it concedes is "stranger than fiction" in the face of clear policy considerations to the contrary and in the absence of any evidence that Congress ever considered the application of the statutory text to standby letters of credit. Is it really so plain that this is the meaning of § 547(b)? If so, was it nevertheless appropriate to use "equitable considerations" or a "rule of reason" (as the bankruptcy appellate panel did) in order to reach a more sensible result?

10. FALSE PREFERENCES: DELAYED PERFECTION OF LIENS

We have already dealt with the problem of a secured creditor who makes a loan to a debtor in what is a secured transaction but in which there is some delay between the time the loan is made and the time that the security interest attaches. Since the attaching of the security interest is a transfer of property of the debtor on account of the antecedent loan debt, there is a prima facie voidable preference if the other elements of § 547(b) are present. If the delay is very short, the security interest may, under some circumstances, be saved by § 547(c)(1). If the loan is made to enable the debtor to acquire the collateral which secures the loan debt, the security interest may be saved if there is compliance with § 547(c)(3). In these cases the problem arises because of a delay in the creation of the security interest.

A problem that is superficially similar but of an entirely different legal category arises when the making of the loan and the creation of the security interest are contemporaneous, but there is a delay between the creation, i.e. attachment, of the security interest and the perfection of the security interest. There is no true preference in these cases because the transfer of the security interest to the creditor is not on account of an antecedent debt. Rather, the problem of delayed perfection is the evil of the secret lien. The classic case is that of a debtor in financial difficulty who wants to conceal from general creditors the true state of its financial condition. The debtor obtains an emergency loan from a creditor and grants to that creditor a mortgage on real property or a security interest in personal property to secure the loan. The property involved might well be most of the debtor's previously unencumbered assets. If public notice of the transaction were given by recording of the mortgage or filing a financing statement with respect to the security interest, the result might be that other creditors will be deterred from giving the debtor further unsecured credit because of the absence of unencumbered assets. To avoid this result the creditor might be induced not to record the mortgage or file the financing statement.

Essentially, the issue is one of fraud on creditors, not whether a transfer for antecedent consideration prefers one creditor over another. Usually an unrecorded real property mortgage has priority over a creditor who subsequently levies on the property. The holder of an unperfected security interest in personal property takes a greater risk by not promptly perfecting because an unperfected Article 9 security interest does not have priority over a subsequent judicial lien. But in either case the creditor can protect the lien by promptly perfecting at the first sign that other creditors may either levy on assets of the debtor or file a petition for involuntary bankruptcy against the debtor. In the classic case, the creditor is an insider with access to information that provides some assurance that the creditor will have sufficient advance notice of facts to allow the creditor to perfect in time.

It is understandable that there should be a policy against secret liens, and such a policy was expressed in the Bankruptcy Act. However, the preferences approach used in the Bankruptcy Act to address the evil was unusual. Instead of dealing with the problem directly as a case of fraud on creditors, the Bankruptcy Act discouraged secret liens by treating a lien as effective at the time it was perfected rather than when it was actually created. Hence, if the creditor gave value at the time the security interest was created but did not perfect until later, the effect was that the lien was treated as having been for an antecedent debt. This technique of turning secret liens into false preferences was carried over into the Bankruptcy Code. The relevant provision is § 547(e)(2). The meaning of § 547(e)(2) is clarified in § 547(e)(1), which defines the term "perfected" and in § 547(e)(3), which states that a transfer cannot occur before the debtor has rights in the property transferred.

Although former § 547(e)(2) was intended to eliminate the evils of the secret lien, unfortunately, it could also ensnare a hapless secured creditor who, through no fault of its own, was unable to perfect within the pre-BAPCPA 10–day grace period. This is particularly true in cases involving motor vehicles for which a security interest must be noted on a certificate of title issued by a state agency. Unhappy with the harsh results in cases in which perfection was delayed beyond 10 days, several states attempted to deal with the problem by making special rules for security interests in motor vehicles by providing that if proper documentation is presented to the relevant state agency within a given period of time (usually from 15 to 30 days) after the security interest has attached, the security interest is deemed to have been perfected at the time it attached. Courts divided over whether the extended relation-back period under the state statute could prevail over the 10–day period in former § 547(e)(2). The Supreme Court resolved the issue in *Fidelity Financial Services, Inc. v. Fink*, 522 U.S. 211 (1998), by holding that the time period provided in § 547(e)(2) trumped any more expansive relation-back period under state law. In BAPCPA, the periods in § 547(e)(2)(A), (B) and (C) for refinancing transactions and in § 547(c)(3)(b) for purchase money transactions are extended to 30 days. These amendments should ameliorate the difficulties posed for secured creditors by the *Fink* analysis.

Creditors that nevertheless inadvertently fail to perfect within 30 days are unlikely to find solace in the contemporaneous exchange for value test of § 547(c)(1). *See In re Lazurus*, 478 F.3d 12 (1st Cir. 2007). In that case, Chief Judge Boudin explains: "Congress has been laboring for many years to devise and refine a specific, largely mechanical test to govern security interests in the context of antecedent debt. The contemporaneousness test was added late in the day to address a much broader generic problem—ordinary exchange of goods for check or credit payment—where recording and other perfection devices do not exist. The test was assuredly not meant to override the specific 10-day [now 30-day] requirement." 478 F.3d at 19.

B. SETOFF

1. WHAT IS SETOFF?

Citizens Bank of Maryland v. Strumpf
Supreme Court of the United States, 1995.
516 U.S. 16.

■ Justice SCALIA delivered the opinion of the Court.

We must decide whether the creditor of a debtor in bankruptcy may, in order to protect its setoff rights, temporarily withhold payment of a debt that it owes to the debtor in bankruptcy without violating the automatic stay imposed by § 362(a).

I.

On January 25, 1991, when respondent filed for relief under Chapter 13 of the Bankruptcy Code, he had a checking account with petitioner, a bank conducting business in the State of Maryland. He also was in default on the remaining balance of a loan of $5,068.75 from the bank. Under § 362(a), respondent's bankruptcy filing gave rise to an automatic stay of various types of activity by his creditors, including "the setoff of any debt owing to the debtor that arose before the commencement of the [bankruptcy case] against any claim against the debtor." § 362(a)(7).

On October 2, 1991, petitioner placed what it termed an "administrative hold" on so much of respondent's account as it claimed was subject to setoff—that is, the bank refused to pay withdrawals from the account that would reduce the balance below the sum that it claimed was due on respondent's loan. Five days later, petitioner filed in the Bankruptcy Court, under § 362(d), a "Motion for Relief from Automatic Stay and for Setoff." Respondent then filed a motion to hold petitioner in contempt, claiming that petitioner's administrative hold violated the automatic stay established by § 362(a).

The Bankruptcy Court ruled on respondent's contempt motion first. It concluded that petitioner's "administrative hold" constituted a "setoff" in violation of § 362(a)(7) and sanctioned petitioner. Several weeks later, the Bankruptcy Court granted petitioner's motion for relief from the stay and authorized petitioner to set off respondent's remaining checking account balance against the unpaid loan. By that time, however, respondent had reduced the checking account balance to zero, so there was nothing to set off.

The District Court reversed the judgment that petitioner had violated the automatic stay, concluding that the administrative hold was not a violation of § 362(a). The Court of Appeals reversed. "[A]n administrative hold," it said, "is tantamount to the exercise of a right of setoff and thus violates the automatic stay of § 362(a)(7)." 37 F.3d [at] 158. We granted certiorari.

II.

The right of setoff (also called "offset") allows entities that owe each other money to apply their mutual debts against each other, thereby avoiding "the absurdity of making A pay B when B owes A." *Studley v. Boylston Nat. Bank*, 229 U.S. 523, 528 (1913). Although no federal right of setoff is created by the Bankruptcy Code, 11 U.S.C. § 553(a) provides that, with certain exceptions, whatever right of setoff otherwise exists is preserved in bankruptcy. Here it is undisputed that, prior to the bankruptcy filing, petitioner had the right under Maryland law to set off the defaulted loan against the balance in the checking account. It is also undisputed that under § 362(a) respondent's bankruptcy filing stayed any exercise of that right by petitioner. The principal question for decision is whether petitioner's refusal to pay its debt to respondent upon the latter's demand constituted an exercise of the setoff right and hence violated the stay.

In our view, petitioner's action was not a setoff within the meaning of § 362(a)(7). Petitioner refused to pay its debt, not permanently and absolutely, but only while it sought relief under § 362(d) from the automatic stay. Whether that temporary refusal was otherwise wrongful is a separate matter—we do not consider, for example, respondent's contention that the portion of the account subjected to the "administrative hold" exceeded the amount properly subject to setoff. All that concerns us here is whether the refusal *was a setoff*. We think it was not, because—as evidenced by petitioner's "Motion for Relief from Automatic Stay and for Setoff"—petitioner did not purport permanently to reduce respondent's account balance by the amount of the defaulted loan. A requirement of such an intent is implicit in the rule followed by a majority of jurisdictions addressing the question, that a setoff has not occurred until three steps have been taken: (i) a decision to effectuate a setoff, (ii) some action accomplishing the setoff, and (iii) a recording of the setoff. * * * But even if state law were different, the question whether a setoff *under § 362(a)(7)* has occurred is a matter of federal law, and other provisions of the Bankruptcy Code would lead us to embrace the same requirement of an intent permanently to settle accounts.

Section 542(b) of the Code, which concerns turnover of property to the estate, requires a bankrupt's debtors to "pay" to the trustee (or on his order) any "debt that is property of the estate and that is matured, payable on demand, or payable on order. . . *except to the extent that such debt may be offset under section 553 of this title against a claim against the debtor.*" § 542(b) (emphasis added). Section 553(a), in turn, sets forth a general rule, with certain exceptions, that any right of setoff that a creditor possessed prior to the debtor's filing for bankruptcy is not affected by the Bankruptcy Code. It would be an odd construction of § 362(a)(7) that required a creditor with a right of setoff to do immediately that which § 542(b) specifically excuses it from doing as a general matter: pay a claim to which a defense of setoff applies.

Nor is our assessment of these provisions changed by the fact that § 553(a), in generally providing that nothing in the Bankruptcy Code affects creditors' prebankruptcy setoff rights, qualifies this rule with the phrase "[e]xcept as otherwise provided in this section and in sections 362 and 363." This undoubtedly refers to § 362(a)(7), but we think it is most naturally read as merely recognizing that provision's restriction upon *when* an *actual setoff* may be effected—which is to say, not during the automatic stay. When this perfectly reasonable reading is available, it would be foolish to take the § 553(a) "except" clause as indicating that § 362(a)(7) requires immediate payment of a debt subject to setoff. That would render § 553(a)'s general rule that the Bankruptcy Code does not affect the right of setoff meaningless, for by forcing the creditor to pay *its* debt immediately, it would divest the creditor of the very thing that supports the right of setoff. Furthermore, it would, as we have stated, eviscerate § 542(b)'s exception to the duty to pay debts. It is an elementary rule of construction that "the act cannot be held to destroy itself." *Texas & Pacific R. Co. v. Abilene Cotton Oil Co.*, 204 U.S. 426, 446 (1907).

Finally, we are unpersuaded by respondent's additional contentions that the administrative hold violated § 362(a)(3) and § 362(a)(6). Under these sections, a bankruptcy filing automatically stays "any act to obtain possession of property of the estate or of property from the estate or to exercise control over property of the estate," § 362(a)(3), and "any act to collect, assess, or recover a claim against the debtor that arose before the commencement of the case under this title," § 362(a)(6). Respondent's reliance on these provisions rests on the false premise that petitioner's administrative hold took something from respondent, or exercised dominion over property that belonged to respondent. That view of things might be arguable if a bank account consisted of money belonging to the depositor and held by the bank. In fact, however, it consists of nothing more or less than a promise to pay, from the bank to the depositor * * *; and petitioner's temporary refusal to pay was neither a taking of possession of respondent's property nor an exercising of control over it, but merely a refusal to perform its promise. In any event, we will not give

§§ 362(a)(3) or (6) an interpretation that would proscribe what § 542(b)'s "except[ion]" and § 553(a)'s general rule were plainly intended to permit: the temporary refusal of a creditor to pay a debt that is subject to setoff against a debt owed by the bankrupt.

The judgment of the Court of Appeals for the Fourth Circuit is reversed.

NOTES

1. The Court states that the act of setoff is not complete until three steps have been taken: (i) the decision to exercise the right, (ii) some action that accomplishes the setoff, and (iii) some record evidencing that the right of setoff has been exercised. What is the action that "accomplishes the setoff"? It is no more than a bookkeeping transaction. The bank debits (reduces) the debtor's deposit account (the bank's debt to the debtor) in the amount of the setoff and credits (reduces) the debtor's loan account (the debtor's debt to the bank) in the same amount. The bookkeeping entries merely reflect the bank's unilateral determination that each of the mutual debts has been reduced by the amount of the setoff. If the bank does not set off, but simply places a hold on (freezes) the account, the bank continues to recognize its debt to the debtor but refuses to pay the debt by allowing withdrawals from the account by check or otherwise. In both setoff and freezing, the debtor loses the use of the deposit account and the bank retains the money. But there are some differences between setoff and freezing. For example, if the deposit account bears interest, a setoff will terminate the running of interest on both the deposit account and the loan from the time of, and to the extent of, the setoff. A freezing of the account allows interest to run on both debts. But differences of this kind may be of minor importance. As a practical matter, the principal benefits of setoff can be obtained by the bank by freezing the account and the burden on the debtor is essentially the same in either case.

2. As the Court points out, the Bankruptcy Code does not create the right to set off mutual debts, but § 553 brings the state law doctrine of setoff into bankruptcy. The traditional policy basis for setoff is to avoid "the absurdity of making A pay B when B owes A." Outside bankruptcy, this policy may make sense but in bankruptcy it produces results that fly in the face of the equality-of-distribution rule that is posited as the backbone of preference law. Suppose Debtor in *Strumpf* owed Bank $20,000 and had a balance of $10,000 in its deposit account in Bank when it filed in bankruptcy. Its nonexempt assets were valued at $20,000, including the deposit account balance, and it owed ten other creditors $20,000 apiece. The doctrine of setoff allows Bank to take the full $10,000 balance of the account as an offset to its claim for $20,000, while the other creditors receive distributions of $1,000 each. The right of setoff is accorded the same favorable treatment as a security interest, and § 506(a) recognizes that a claim subject to setoff under § 553 is a secured claim to the extent of the setoff right.

3. Courts distinguish between setoff that involves mutual debts arising out of different transactions and "recoupment" that involves netting of debts and credits to determine net liability on a single transaction. Under this doctrine, "recoupment" does not require relief from the automatic stay and is not subject to the other limitations of § 553. Determining whether debts and credits arise out of the same or different transactions, however, can be subject to considerable dispute. *See, e.g., In re B&L Oil Co.*, 782 F.2d 155 (10th Cir. 1986) (finding overpayments under oil division order may be recouped against obligations arising from postpetition shipments).

4. Section 553's "mutuality" requirement can be an important limitation on creditor setoff rights when the creditor has relationships with multiple related entities. If those entities are not guarantors, or otherwise co-liable, on each others' debts so-called "triangular" setoffs may be prohibited. *Matter of Elcona Homes Corp.*, 863 F.2d 483 (7th Cir. 1988) (Posner, J.), involved a bank, a manufacturer and a dealer that used "retail proceeds" financing. The wholesale price of mobile homes manufactured by the debtor was payable by the dealer out of the proceeds of its retail sale to the consumer. Typically, the homes were sold under installment sales contracts negotiated by the dealer with the consumer and assigned to the bank which then remitted the loan proceeds equal to the wholesale price of the home directly to the debtor-manufacturer rather than to the dealer. After the manufacturer filed for bankruptcy, the bank tried to set off its obligation to remit proceeds of an assigned installment contract against other obligations that the debtor happened to owe the bank. The court held that this was only permissible if the bank had the right under state law to discharge its obligation to the dealer by remitting directly to the debtor-manufacturer, rather than to the dealer. *In re SemCrude, L.P.*, 399 B.R. 388 (Bankr.D.Del.2009), went further in limiting triangular setoff in bankruptcy notwithstanding an apparent state law right to make the setoff. Chevron had claims against two debtor affiliates for $13.5 million, but owed a third debtor affiliate $1.4 million. The court refused to allow setoff by Chevron, notwithstanding contractual provisions in the agreements, presumably enforceable under state law, allowing setoffs of the obligations of one debtor affiliate against payments owed another affiliate on the ground that the debts for which setoff was being sought were not mutual debts within the meaning of § 553. A different variation on the problem is when the creditor operates through multiple entities and wishes to set off claims against the debtor against the debtor's rights against the creditor's affiliate. *United States v. Maxwell*, 157 F.3d 1099 (7th Cir. 1998), following the weight of authority that the United States was a unitary entity,

allowed the United States Small Business Administration to set off its claim based on a loan to the debtor against monies due the debtor from the United States Navy on the basis that the United States government was a single entity whose claims and obligations vis-à-vis the debtor were properly subject to set off. Almost every person and business in the United States has many relationships with various agencies of the United States that collectively buy, sell, tax, regulate, subsidize and employ to the tune of 30% of GDP. Given this, the unitary theory of government in setoff cases amounts to an important erosion of the equality of distribution principle.

PROBLEM

1. Debtor, a wholesaler, sold goods to Retailer on unsecured credit for a price of $10,000. The goods sold to Retailer had been acquired by Debtor from Manufacturer at a price of $8,000 on unsecured credit. When Manufacturer demanded payment from Debtor of the $8,000 price of the goods, Debtor was unable to pay. Debtor offered to assign, as security for the debt, Debtor's right to receive payment from Retailer. Manufacturer refused after determining that Debtor was insolvent. After Manufacturer explained the situation to Retailer, the claim of Manufacturer against Debtor was assigned to Retailer who paid Manufacturer $4,000 for it. Shortly thereafter, Debtor filed in Chapter 7 bankruptcy. The trustee in bankruptcy demanded payment from Retailer of the $10,000 price of the goods purchased from Debtor. Retailer asserted a right to set off against the $10,000 owed to Debtor the $8,000 claim against Debtor acquired from Manufacturer. As a matter of policy, should the setoff be allowed? Assume that all of the bankruptcy estate will be consumed by secured and priority claims so that nothing will be available to pay ordinary unsecured claims such as the claim assigned to Retailer. Is the setoff permissible? § 553(a)(2).

2. Debtor owed Bank $20,000 on a past-due loan. Debtor's checking account was also overdrawn by more than $1,000. When Bank demanded payment of both debts, Debtor was unable to pay because of insolvency. Debtor told Bank that bankruptcy was imminent. Debtor offered to pay the loan by conveying to Bank the title to Blackacre, a small lot that was Debtor's only unencumbered asset of substantial value. Bank refused the offer but urged Debtor to sell Blackacre before going into bankruptcy. Bank reasonably assumed that Debtor would deposit the proceeds of sale in Debtor's checking account with Bank because Debtor had no other bank account. Debtor sold Blackacre and deposited the $15,000 proceeds in Debtor's account with Bank. Shortly thereafter, Debtor filed in bankruptcy. At the date of bankruptcy, Debtor's account with Bank had a credit balance of $13,500. The trustee in bankruptcy and Bank both claim the $13,500 balance in Debtor's bank account. Who wins? Would your answer differ if Debtor had not had the conversation with Bank described above and Debtor simply sold Blackacre and deposited the proceeds in the checking account? § 553(a)(3).

2. THE IMPROVEMENT IN POSITION TEST

PROBLEM

On January 2, 90 days before Debtor's bankruptcy, Debtor owed Bank $10,000 on an unsecured demand promissory note. On that date Debtor's checking account had a $1,000 balance. On March 20, Debtor deposited a check for $15,000 in the checking account. The deposit was made in the ordinary course of business and with the expectation that the proceeds of the check would be available for withdrawal when the check was collected. The check was collected on March 25 and as a result Debtor's credit balance exceeded $15,000. Checks of Debtor were paid by Bank after that date. On March 29, Bank learned that Debtor was in serious financial difficulty, but before that date Bank had had no notice of that fact. Bank immediately demanded payment of the note. Debtor could not pay and, on March 30, Bank exercised its setoff rights given by state law by debiting Debtor's checking account $10,300, the amount then due under the note. After the setoff Debtor's account was reduced to $2,000. On April 2, Debtor filed in Chapter 7 bankruptcy. On March 29 and at all times thereafter, Debtor was insolvent. May the trustee in bankruptcy recover, under § 553(b), any part of the setoff? If Bank had not set off before bankruptcy it would have been able to assert its entire $10,300 setoff in the bankruptcy. § 506(a). Section 553(a) recognizes the right of setoff "except as otherwise provided in this section." Section 553(b)(1) is a limitation on § 553(a) but it applies only to a setoff "on or within 90 days before the date of the filing of the petition." Thus, a postbankruptcy setoff is not affected by § 553(b). What is the policy basis for reducing the rights of creditors that exercise setoff rights within 90 days before bankruptcy while preserving for the benefit of the creditor the value of unexercised setoff rights postbankruptcy?

C. FRAUDULENT TRANSFERS

1. ACTUAL FRAUD

Fact Situation. Debtor owned a residence valued at $100,000. While driving, she negligently collided with Plaintiff's car and badly injured him. Since Debtor carried only the legal minimum of liability insurance for personal injuries, she feared that she might lose her residence if sued by Plaintiff. On the day after the collision, she deeded her residence to her mother for no consideration; her mother recorded the deed. Debtor continued to live in the residence. Plaintiff sued Debtor for damages and obtained a judgment for $1 million.

State Law. American law, following English precedents, traditionally gave persons in the position of Plaintiff remedies in such cases. The most recent codification of fraudulent transfer law, which has been adopted by most states, is the Uniform Fraudulent Transfer Act (UFTA). In the case above, the transfer of the residence depleted the Debtor's assets from which Plaintiff could satisfy his judgment. Under UFTA § 4(a)(1), the transfer was made "with actual intent to hinder, delay, or defraud any creditor of the debtor," and Plaintiff can avoid the transfer to the extent necessary to satisfy his claim (§ 7(a)(1)) or, if he has obtained a judgment, as Plaintiff has in this case, move immediately to levy execution on the asset transferred or its proceeds (§ 7(b)). The effect is to treat the residence that was fraudulently transferred as though it remained Debtor's property.

Federal Law. Assume that in the fact situation above, before Plaintiff could levy on the residence, Debtor filed in Chapter 7 bankruptcy.

Section 548 provides:

> **(a)(1)** The trustee may avoid any transfer * * * of an interest of the debtor in property, or any obligation * * * incurred by the debtor, that was made or incurred on or within 2 years before the date of filing of the petition, if the debtor voluntarily or involuntarily
>
> > **(A)** made such transfer or incurred such obligation with actual intent to hinder, delay, or defraud any entity to which the debtor was or became, on or after the date that such transfer was made or such obligation was incurred, indebted; or

* * *

Section 550 provides:

(a) Except as otherwise provided in this section, to the extent that a transfer is avoided under section 544 [or] * * * 548 * * * of this title, the trustee may recover, for the benefit of the estate, the property transferred, or, if the court so orders, the value of such property from—

> **(1)** the initial transferee of such transfer or the entity for whose benefit such transfer was made; or
>
> **(2)** any immediate or mediate transferee of such initial transferee.

* * *

Thus, § 548(a)(1)(A) allows the bankruptcy trustee to avoid fraudulent transfers, such as the one in the case above, of property by Debtor to her mother made with actual intent to hinder, delay, or defraud creditors. Section 550(a) allows the trustee to recover the residence from Debtor's mother "for the benefit of the estate," and § 541(a)(3) provides that the property recovered regains its status as property of Debtor's estate available for distribution to claimants. The similarities between UFTA and the fraudulent transfer provisions of the Bankruptcy Code, such as § 548(a)(1)(A), are obvious and intentional. The UFTA was drafted after enactment of the Bankruptcy Code in 1978, and the drafters of UFTA strove to make that statute compatible with the fraudulent transfer provisions in the Code.

But there are significant differences. First, in bankruptcy, Plaintiff loses his right under the UFTA to satisfy his in personam judgment out of Debtor's property fraudulently transferred, and the judgment is discharged. Section 550(a) provides that the trustee may recover property fraudulently transferred for the benefit of the estate. Thus, Debtor's filing in bankruptcy relegates Plaintiff to the status of a creditor with an unsecured claim who shares pro rata in the property transferred with the other general creditors. Since in Chapter 11 cases there usually is no trustee, under § 1107(a) the debtor in possession exercises the trustee's rights to proceed under § 550(a). Later in this section we will consider whether courts may authorize creditors' committees to bring avoidance proceedings under § 550(a) when debtors in possession lack incentive to do so.

Another difference is that § 548(a) allows trustees to avoid only fraudulent transfers made within two years of filing in bankruptcy, but the statute of limitations for a transfer avoidable under UFTA § 4(1)(a) is four years pursuant to UFTA § 9(a). Given the complexities of some bankruptcy cases, empowering the trustee to overturn transactions occurring as far back as four years before the debtor's filing may be of great importance to the trustee. But how does a trustee in bankruptcy operating under the federal Bankruptcy Code take advantage of the four-year state law UFTA statute of limitation? The answer lies in § 544(b)(1), which gives a trustee in bankruptcy derivative rights of creditors under the UFTA.

Section 544

(b) * * * [T]he trustee may avoid any transfer of an interest of the debtor in property * * * that is voidable under applicable law by a creditor holding an unsecured claim that is allowable * * *.

Section 550(a) allows the trustee to set aside any transfer avoidable under § 544. Since UFTA § 4(a) is "applicable law" under § 544, the trustee may take the rights under § 4(a)(1) of any actual creditor holding an unsecured claim at the time of bankruptcy without regard to whether the claim arose before or after the transfer. With these derivative rights, the trustee can set aside the transfer. Hence, in any actual fraud case, the trustee can fall back on the UFTA four-year reach-back provision because there will always be at least one unpaid creditor at the time of bankruptcy.

In the celebrated case of *Moore v. Bay*, 284 U.S. 4 (1931) (Holmes, J.), the Court held that the action of a trustee in avoiding a transfer is not just for the benefit of creditors who would have been able to set aside the transfer under state law, nor is the avoidance power limited to the amount of such creditors' claims, rather the entire transfer is set aside for the benefit of the estate, *i.e.*, for the benefit of all creditors with unsecured claims in the bankruptcy. The principle of *Moore v. Bay* can have dramatic effects and is applicable to cases brought under either § 544(a) or 548. Assume that the debtor made a transfer of property worth $1,000,000 and that under state law one creditor, with a claim of $100, can avoid the transfer because some duty to that creditor had not been performed. Assume that no other creditor has a right under the state law to attack the transfer, that under the state law the creditor with the $100 claim is entitled to have the claim paid from the property transferred, and that the transfer is otherwise valid. The effect in bankruptcy, if the $100 claim still exists, is that (i) the entire $1,000,000 transfer is voidable by the trustee under § 544(b); (ii) the estate receives the benefit of the avoidance; and (iii) the creditor who, prebankruptcy, had the state law right to avoid the transfer will lose that right and will receive only its pro rata share of the (enhanced) estate in accordance with its rights under bankruptcy law.

What is Actual Intent to Hinder, Delay, or Defraud? Courts have struggled for centuries to decide this illusive issue. Sometimes it is obvious, as in the fact situation at the beginning of the section in which a debtor attempts to shield her assets from her creditors by transferring them to a relative for nominal or no consideration. But in other cases it is not so clear. Given the practical difficulty of obtaining direct evidence of the debtor's intent, few cases turn on such proof. Instead, looking to the circumstances surrounding the transfer, courts have identified several objective indicia that, taken together, strongly indicate fraudulent intent. These indicia have been referred to as the "badges of fraud" from the time of *Twyne's Case*, 3 Coke 80b, 76 Eng. Rep. 809 (1601). These indicia include: (1) insider relationships between the parties; (2) retention of possession, benefit or use of the property; (3) the lack or inadequacy of consideration for the transfer; (4) the financial condition of the party sought to be charged both before and after the transaction at issue; (5) the existence or cumulative effect of the pattern or series of transactions or course of conduct after the incurring of debt, onset of financial difficulties, or pendency or threat of suits by creditors; (6) the general chronology of events and transactions under inquiry; and (7) an attempt by the debtor to keep the transfer a secret. *See* UFTA § 4(b). How many of these criteria apply to the fact situation at the beginning of the section? In *In re Watman*, 301 F.3d 3 (1st Cir. 2002), the court added a 21st century indicium: "The shifting of assets by the debtor to a corporation wholly controlled by him is another badge of fraud." 301 F.3d at 8.

Who Can Sue to Set Aside the Transfer? In recent years disagreement has arisen on this basic question. Section 550(a) allows trustees to recover property fraudulently transferred under § 548(a), and this power may be exercised by the debtor in possession in Chapter 11 cases. § 1107(a). Section 544(b) also refers only to trustees. But in some situations the transfers may have been made by the management of the debtor now serving as debtor in possession and in other cases the debtor in possession may be attempting to negotiate a plan with the recipients of the alleged fraudulent transfer; in neither instance does the debtor in possession have much incentive to prosecute an avoidance claim. Seeing the debtor in possession dragging its heels, creditors may wish to take matters in their own hands. The accepted remedy has been for the creditors' committee to ask the court to permit it to pursue recovery for the benefit of the estate. This practice was accepted by courts pre-1978 and carried on under the new Code even though there is no specific authorization under § 544(b) or § 550, both of which refer to only trustees and debtors in possession.

A bombshell was exploded by *Official Committee of Unsecured Creditors of Cybergenics Corp. v. Chinery (Cybergenics I)*, 310 F.3d 785 (3d Cir. 2002), in which a Third Circuit panel decreed that the holding in *Hartford Underwriters Ins. Co. v. Union Planters Bank, N.A.*, 530 U.S. 1 (2000) (reprinted at p. 621), compelled a "plain meaning" reading of § 544(b) that precluded creditors' committees from bringing fraudulent transfer actions. In footnote 5 of *Hartford Underwriters*, the Court had left open the issue before the *Cybergenics* I court. The Third Circuit, besieged by demands from academics and other amici for a rehearing, reversed the panel in *Official Committee of Unsecured Creditors of Cybergenics Corp. v. Chinery, (Cybergenics II)*, 330 F.3d 548 (3d Cir. *en banc* 2003). The majority held that the equitable power of a bankruptcy court gave it the power to craft a remedy when the Code's "envisioned scheme breaks down." 330 F.3d at 553. A vigorous dissenting opinion saw the case as a simple instance of interpreting the wording of an unambiguous statute, the meaning of which is plain; if Congress had intended to allow creditors' committees to pursue fraudulent transfers, it would have expressly said so in the statute. But the law of fraudulent transfers is of little help to defrauded creditors if there is no one with the incentive to enforce it, and even critics of *Cybergenics II* have difficulty articulating any policy basis for denying standing to bring such suits in appropriate circumstances. *See* Daniel J. Bussel, *Creditors' Committees as Estate Representatives in Bankruptcy Litigation*, 10 Stan. J. L. Bus. & Fin. 28 (2004).

Section 548(e). BAPCPA added § 548(e) to deal with asset protection trusts. In the last section of chapter 2, we explain how these are used to shelter assets from creditors in and out of bankruptcy. During the drafting process, critics of these devices urged that the legislation that finally became BAPCPA should do away with them. This was not done. About the only change that § 548(e) made in pre-BAPCPA law was to extend the two-year look-back period in § 548(a) to ten years.

2. CONSTRUCTIVE FRAUD

a. Introduction

"Constructive fraud" is an oxymoron; fraud generally connotes some degree of evil intent. Professor Tabb observes:

> The promulgation of the [Uniform Fraudulent Conveyance Act] in 1918 marked a watershed in the evolution of fraudulent conveyance law. The objectification of the law, developed over the centuries by courts through the invocation of "badges of fraud" as a means of inferring actual fraudulent intent, was given formal recognition. For the first time, proof of certain specified facts conclusively established that the transfer at issue was a fraudulent conveyance, irrespective of the actual subjective intention of the debtor. This type of fraudulent conveyance has come to be known as *constructive* fraud.

Charles Jordan Tabb, *The Law of Bankruptcy* 423 (1997).

Constructive fraud is a basis for avoidance under both UFTA § 4(a)(2) and § 548(a)(1)(B) of the Bankruptcy Code. Under the latter provision, a trustee can avoid a transfer or obligation by proving (A) that the debtor received less than reasonably equivalent value in exchange for the transfer or obligation, and, (B) that on the date the transfer was made or the obligation was incurred, the debtor was either (i) insolvent or was rendered insolvent by the transfer or obligation, (ii) was engaged in or was about to engage in business or a transaction for which any property remaining with the debtor was unreasonably small capital, or (iii) intended to incur debts beyond the debtor's ability to pay as the debts matured. Dean Robert C. Clark's aphorism sums it up: insolvent debtors must "be just before [they] are generous." *The Duties of the Corporate Debtor to Its Creditors*, 90 Harv.L.Rev. 505, 510 (1977). The metaphor sometimes invoked is that an insolvent debtor holds property in trust for its creditors.

The drafters of the UFCA in 1918 could not possibly have imagined the impact that their modest-appearing constructive fraud provisions would have on common business transactions involving corporate distributions, mergers and acquisitions, guaranties and foreclosures. As we shall see, no lawyer can give competent counsel in these areas without having a good grasp of the law of fraudulent transfers. In order to predict whether a transfer or obligation will stand up in a subsequent bankruptcy, transaction planners must address two inherently fact-intensive, often difficult, issues: whether the transferor or obligor will receive reasonably equivalent value and whether this person is, or will be rendered, insolvent at the time of the transfer. In the following materials we will examine the meaning of these terms.

The rationale of § 548(a)(1)(B) is that a transfer of property by an insolvent debtor for less than reasonably equivalent value is unfair to creditors having claims at the time of the transfer because those creditors are being deprived of assets that would otherwise be available for payment of the debts owed to them. Gratuitous transfers are obviously subject to avoidance under this provision, but sale transactions may also be avoided. If a sale is made at a bargain price to an insider, the debtor may intend to confer a benefit on the buyer. If that is so, the debtor has made a gratuitous transfer to the buyer to the extent the price received is less than the price that would have been received in an arms-length transaction.

If the debtor is not trying to favor the buyer, the interests of the debtor and creditors coincide. There is no advantage to either the debtor or the creditors if the property is not sold for the best price possible. Thus, if the debtor and the buyer arrive at a price in an arms-length uncoerced transaction, that price should represent reasonably equivalent value or at least the best evidence of that value. Opinion concerning what price the property might have brought if it had been sold in a hypothetical transaction involving a different buyer or seller or both may be an unreliable guide to value. Some courts, however, have second-guessed the price received in forced sale scenarios. The most notorious example of this is the *Durrett* case, discussed later at p. 377.

b. Religious and Charitable Contributions

Bruce and Nancy Young were active church members who made annual contributions to the church in furtherance of their religious beliefs. When they filed in Chapter 7 bankruptcy in 1992, their trustee successfully challenged a $13,450 contribution made by them in the year preceding their bankruptcy on the ground of constructive fraud under § 548(a)(1)(B); the Youngs did not receive reasonably equivalent value from the church in exchange for their gift. *In re Young*, 148 B.R. 886 (Bankr.D.Minn.1992). This set in motion a series of events that culminated in passage of the "Religious Liberty and Charitable Donation Protection Act of 1998." After the bankruptcy court opinion, trustees in other cases began to challenge tithes by insolvent debtors, and the attention of the religious and bankruptcy communities was drawn to this issue. When the case was before the Eighth Circuit, the Justice Department filed a brief in favor of the trustee. In the 18 months between oral argument and the final decision in

In re Young, 82 F.3d 1407 (8th Cir. 1996), Congress enacted the Religious Freedom Restoration Act (RFRA), 42 U.S.C. § 2000bb. In a move that was described by headline writers as "divine intervention," President Clinton ordered the Department of Justice to pull its *Young* brief and campaigned as a protector of religious freedom, highlighting the issue in one of the TV debates with Senator Dole. Mary Jo Newborn Wiggins, *A Statute of Disbelief?: Clashing Ethical Imperatives in Fraudulent Transfer Law*, 48 S.C.L.Rev. 771, 774 n.25 (1997).

In *Young*, the Eighth Circuit held that although the debtors' donation was an avoidable transfer under § 548(a)(2) (now § 548(a)(1)(B)), recovery from the church would substantially burden the debtors' free exercise of religion and was not justified by a compelling governmental interest; hence, the church won under RFRA. But in *City of Boerne v. Flores*, 521 U.S. 507 (1997), the Supreme Court held the RFRA unconstitutional insofar as it sought to preempt on free exercise grounds state law that was otherwise consistent with the First Amendment, reopening the possibility that tithes could be avoided as fraudulent transfers under state law notwithstanding RFRA and *Young*. Religious indignation at this turn of events resulted in prompt enactment of the "Religious Liberty and Charitable Donation Protection Act" in 1998 by the unanimous vote of both houses of Congress. Although the impetus for this law came from religious groups, Congress included all charities to head off constitutional objections to the Act based on the First Amendment's establishment of religion clause.

This measure added § 548(a)(2), which allows individuals to make contributions to qualified religious or charitable entities without fear of avoidance as constructive fraud under § 548 so long as (i) the contribution does not exceed 15% of the debtor's gross annual income for the year in which the transfer is made (there is no limit on the number of such contributions), or (ii) even if it does exceed that amount, the contribution is consistent with the practices of the debtor in making charitable contributions in the past. Section 544(b) was amended to prevent the trustee from using state fraudulent transfer law to avoid these transfers.

Presumably, charities around the nation are rejoicing that they can broaden their solicitations to include a group never before thought to be promising targets—insolvents on the eve of bankruptcy. Astonishingly, on the face of the statute, debtors can clean out their entire estate on the eve of bankruptcy by making gifts of up to 15% of their incomes to each of several qualified donees until their money runs out, without offending the constructive fraud provisions of § 548. Any state law action to recover a contribution to a qualified charity as a fraudulent transfer is preempted by the debtor's filing bankruptcy.

What is left of fraudulent transfer law in the area of charitable giving? The statute speaks only of transfers; obligations to make charitable gifts in the future (the familiar charitable pledge) could still be set aside under § 548's constructive fraud provisions. Since the actual intent fraud provision of § 548(a)(1)(A) is unchanged, presumably a debtor who engages in the abusive conduct described above would face a challenge under this provision, as well as the threat of being barred from discharge by § 727(a)(2). Interestingly, the Act makes no reference to preference law and if payment of a pledge within 90 days of bankruptcy can be characterized as a transfer to a creditor on account of antecedent debt, the payment is arguably avoidable as a preference.

Professor Klee has made an empirical survey of both Chapter 7 and Chapter 13 cases since the Religious Liberty Act and suggests that fraudulent transfer law in practice is not much changed. Before the Act, *de facto* tithes and other charitable gifts were rarely recovered except in cases where the giving appeared fraudulent or abusive or not consistent with the debtor's past practices. After the Act, tithing is *de jure* protected except in cases where the gifts are actually fraudulent and trustees, and bankruptcy courts are likely to view apparently abusive giving not consistent with past practices as actual fraud. Kenneth N. Klee, *Tithing and Bankruptcy*, 75 Am. Bankr. L. J. 157 (2001). Klee suggests that the real effect of the Religious Liberty Act is not in fraudulent transfer law but in Chapter 13 cases since the statute now expressly includes charitable giving as a living expense reducing the net disposable income available for debt repayment. *Id.*, at 192. By including substantial amounts of giving in their Chapter 13 plan budgets, debtors can reduce their obligations to creditors, standing Dean Clark's aphorism on its head: Chapter 13 now presumes one can be generous before being just. *See infra* chapter 9.

c. Insider Transfers or Obligations under Employment Contracts

BAPCPA adopts a fraudulent transfer approach to excessive compensation for insider employees. Section 548(a)(1) is amended to address the issue by allowing the trustee to recover such payments or avoid such obligations made to insiders under employment contracts by showing (i) that the services rendered by the employee were not reasonably equivalent value for the transfers or obligations, § 548(a)(1)(B)(i), and (ii) that the transfers or obligations were not made "in ordinary course of business," § 548(a)(1)(B)(ii)(IV). The novelty of the amendment is that the trustee can prove constructive fraud without proof of the insolvency of the debtor. Before this amendment, constructive fraud in fraudulent transfer law was present only when the debtor made transfers or incurred obligations that diminished the assets of the debtor to the prejudice of the creditors of the debtor. Generally speaking, creditors are prejudiced only when a debtor, who is insolvent at the time of the transfer or obligation, or is rendered insolvent thereby, doesn't receive reasonably equivalent value from the transferee or obligee. § 548(a)(1)(B)(ii)(I).

It is not clear what, if any, effect this amendment will have. First, the trustee will have a difficult task in proving that the compensation called for by an employment contract, viewed at the time of making the contract, is so excessive that the employee's services would not amount to reasonably equivalent value. Salaries of executives vary widely: the appropriate level of executive compensation is much debated as are the theories of how the level should be determined. Even if the trustee makes this proof, it must still prove that the payments or obligations were not in ordinary course of business. Presumably this means the debtor's course of business. Would the trustee's case fail if the debtor routinely overpaid all its executives? Nell Hennessey, Marcia Goldstein, Scott Cohen & Matthew Weinstein, *Employee Benefits and Executive Compensation Provisions in the New Bankruptcy Act*, BNA Bankruptcy Law Reporter, Vol. 17, No. 19 (2005), conclude that since most employment contracts can be treated as arguably in the ordinary course of a company's business, the amendment will have little effect. They point out that, perversely, the most vulnerable contracts may be those made with bankruptcy turnaround professionals. Transfers not made in ordinary course of the debtor's business is a new concept in contructive fraudulent transfer law.

3. FORECLOSURES

One of the more heated controversies in fraudulent transfer law arose from the holding in *Durrett v. Washington Nat'l Ins. Co.*, 621 F.2d 201 (5th Cir. 1980), which decided for the first time that a regularly conducted, noncollusive foreclosure sale of real estate, valid under state mortgage foreclosure statutes, could be set aside in bankruptcy as a fraudulent transfer if the amount paid by the foreclosure sale buyer was found by a bankruptcy court to be less than reasonably equivalent value. The Supreme Court resolved this controversy in the following case.

BFP v. Resolution Trust Co.
Supreme Court of the United States, 1994.
511 U.S. 531.

■ Justice SCALIA delivered the opinion of the court.

This case presents the question whether the consideration received from a noncollusive, real estate mortgage foreclosure sale conducted in conformance with applicable state law conclusively satisfies the Bankruptcy Code's requirement that transfers of property by insolvent debtors within one year prior to the filing of a bankruptcy petition be in exchange for "a reasonably equivalent value." § 548(a)(2).

I.

Petitioner BFP is a partnership, formed by Wayne and Marlene Pedersen and Russell Barton in 1987, for the purpose of buying a home in Newport Beach, California, from Sheldon and Ann Foreman. Petitioner took title subject to a first deed of trust in favor of Imperial Savings Association (Imperial) to secure payment of a loan of $356,250 made to the Pedersens in connection with petitioner's acquisition of the home. Petitioner granted a second deed of trust to the Foremans as security for a $200,000 promissory note. Subsequently, Imperial, whose loan was not being serviced, entered a notice of default under the first deed of trust and scheduled a properly noticed foreclosure sale. The foreclosure proceedings were temporarily delayed by the filing of an involuntary bankruptcy petition on behalf of petitioner. After the dismissal of that petition in June 1989, Imperial's foreclosure proceeding was completed at a foreclosure sale on July 12, 1989. The home was purchased by respondent Paul Osborne for $433,000.

In October 1989, petitioner filed for bankruptcy under Chapter 11 of the Bankruptcy Code. Acting as a debtor in possession, petitioner filed a complaint in Bankruptcy Court seeking to set aside the conveyance of the home to respondent Osborne on the grounds that the foreclosure sale constituted a fraudulent transfer under § 548 of the Code. Petitioner alleged that the home was actually worth over $725,000 at the time of the sale to Osborne. Acting on separate motions, the Bankruptcy Court ... granted summary judgment in favor of Imperial. The Bankruptcy Court found, *inter alia*, that the foreclosure sale had been conducted in compliance with California law and was neither collusive nor fraudulent.... [T]the District Court affirmed.... A divided bankruptcy appellate panel affirmed the Bankruptcy Court's entry of summary judgment for Imperial.... [T]the panel majority held that a "non-collusive and regularly conducted nonjudicial foreclosure sale... cannot be challenged as a fraudulent conveyance because the consideration received in such a sale establishes 'reasonably equivalent value' as a matter of law."

Petitioner sought review of both decisions in the Court of Appeals for the Ninth Circuit, which consolidated the appeals. The Court of Appeals affirmed. *In re BFP*, 974 F.2d 1144 (1992). BFP filed a petition for certiorari, which we granted.

II.

Section 548 of the Bankruptcy Code sets forth the powers of a trustee in bankruptcy (or, in a Chapter 11 case, a debtor in possession) to avoid fraudulent transfers. It permits to be set aside not only transfers infected by actual fraud but certain other transfers as well—so-called constructively fraudulent transfers. The constructive fraud provision at issue in this case applies to transfers by insolvent debtors. It permits avoidance if the trustee can establish (1) that the debtor had an interest in property; (2) that a transfer of that interest occurred within one year of the filing of the bankruptcy petition; (3) that the debtor was insolvent at the time of the transfer or became insolvent as a result thereof; and (4) that the debtor received "less than a reasonably equivalent value in exchange for such transfer." § 548(a)(2)(A).[Now § 548(a)(1)(B)(i)] It is the last of these four elements that presents the issue in the case before us.

Section 548 applies to any "transfer," which includes "foreclosure of the debtor's equity of redemption." § 101(54). Of the three critical terms "reasonably equivalent value," only the last is defined: "value" means, for purposes of § 548, "property, or satisfaction or securing of a... debt of the debtor," § 548(d)(2)(A). The question presented here, therefore, is whether the amount of debt (to the first and second lienholders) satisfied at the foreclosure sale (viz., a total of $433,000) is "reasonably equivalent" to the worth of the real estate conveyed.

The Courts of Appeals have divided on the meaning of those undefined terms. In *Durrett v. Washington Nat. Ins. Co.,* 621 F.2d 201 (1980), the Fifth Circuit, interpreting a provision of the old Bankruptcy Act analogous to § 548(a)(2), held that a foreclosure sale that yielded 57% of the property's fair market value could be set aside, and indicated in dicta that any such sale for less than 70% of fair market value should be invalidated. *Id.*, at 203-204. This "*Durrett* rule" has continued to be applied by some courts under § 548 of the new Bankruptcy Code. *** In *In re Bundles,* 856 F.2d 815, 820 (1988), the Seventh Circuit rejected the *Durrett* rule in favor of a case-by-case, "all facts and circumstances" approach to the question of reasonably equivalent value, with a *rebuttable* presumption that the foreclosure sale price is sufficient to withstand attack under § 548(a)(2). In this case the Ninth Circuit, agreeing with the Sixth Circuit, see *In re Winshall Settlor's Trust,* 758 F.2d 1136, 1139 (CA6 1985), adopted the position first put forward in *In re Madrid,* 21 B.R. 424 (Bkrtcy.App.Pan. CA9 1982), affirmed on other grounds, 725 F.2d 1197 (CA9 1984), that the consideration received at a noncollusive, regularly conducted real estate foreclosure sale constitutes a reasonably equivalent value under § 548(a)(2)(A).[now § 548(a)(1)(B)(i)] The Court of Appeals acknowledged that it "necessarily part[ed] from the positions taken by the Fifth Circuit in *Durrett*... and the Seventh Circuit in *Bundles.*" 974 F.2d, at 1148.

In contrast to the approach adopted by the Ninth Circuit in the present case, both *Durrett* and *Bundles* refer to fair market value as the benchmark against which determination of reasonably equivalent value is to be measured. In the context of an otherwise lawful mortgage foreclosure sale of real estate,[3] such reference is in our opinion not consistent with the text of the Bankruptcy Code. The term "fair market value," though it is a well-established concept, does not appear in § 548. In contrast, § 522, dealing with a debtor's exemptions, specifically provides that, for purposes of that section, "'value' means fair market value as of the date of the filing of the petition." § 522(a)(2). "Fair market value" also appears in the Code provision that defines the extent to which indebtedness with respect to an equity security is not forgiven for the purpose of determining whether the debtor's estate has realized taxable income. § 346(j)(7)(B). Section 548, on the other hand, seemingly goes out of its way to avoid that standard term. It might readily have said "received less than fair market value in exchange for such transfer or obligation," or perhaps "less than a reasonable equivalent of fair market value." Instead, it used the (as far as we are aware) entirely novel phrase "reasonably equivalent value." "[I]t is generally presumed that Congress acts intentionally and purposely when it includes particular language in one section of a statute but omits it in another," *Chicago v. Environmental Defense Fund*, 511 U.S. 328, 338 (1994), and that presumption is even stronger when the omission entails the replacement of standard legal terminology with a neologism. One must suspect the language means that fair market value cannot—or at least cannot *always*—be the benchmark.

That suspicion becomes a certitude when one considers that market value, as it is commonly understood, has no applicability in the forced-sale context; indeed, it is the very *antithesis* of forced-sale value. "The market value of. . . a piece of property is the price which it might be expected to bring if offered for sale in a fair market; not the price which might be obtained on a sale at public auction or a sale forced by the necessities of the owner, but such a price as would be fixed by negotiation and mutual agreement, after ample time to find a purchaser, as between a vendor who is willing (but not compelled) to sell and a purchaser who desires to buy but is not compelled to take the particular. . . piece of property." Black's Law Dictionary 971 (6th ed. 1990). In short, "fair market value" presumes market conditions that, by definition, simply do not obtain in the context of a forced sale. * * *

---

[3] We emphasize that our opinion today covers only mortgage foreclosures of real estate. The considerations bearing upon other foreclosures and forced sales (to satisfy tax liens, for example) may be different.

Neither petitioner, petitioner's *amici,* nor any federal court adopting the *Durrett* or the *Bundles* analysis has come to grips with this glaring discrepancy between the factors relevant to an appraisal of a property's market value, on the one hand, and the strictures of the foreclosure process on the other. Market value cannot be the criterion of equivalence in the foreclosure-sale context. The language of § 548(a)(2)(A) ("received less than a reasonably equivalent value in exchange") requires judicial inquiry into whether the foreclosed property was sold for a price that approximated its worth at the time of sale. An appraiser's reconstruction of "fair market value" could show what similar property would be worth if it did not have to be sold within the time and manner strictures of state-prescribed foreclosure. But property that *must* be sold within those strictures is simply *worth less.* No one would pay as much to own such property as he would pay to own real estate that could be sold at leisure and pursuant to normal marketing techniques. And it is no more realistic to ignore that characteristic of the property (the fact that state foreclosure law permits the mortgagee to sell it at forced sale) than it is to ignore other price-affecting characteristics (such as the fact that state zoning law permits the owner of the neighboring lot to open a gas station). Absent a clear statutory requirement to the contrary, we must assume the validity of this state-law regulatory background and take due account of its effect. "The existence and force and function of established institutions of local government are always in the consciousness of lawmakers and, while their weight may vary, they may never be completely overlooked in the task of interpretation." *Davies Warehouse Co. v. Bowles*, 321 U.S. 144, 154 (1944).

There is another artificially constructed criterion we might look to instead of "fair market price." One might judge there to be such a thing as a "reasonable" or "fair" forced-sale price. Such a conviction must lie behind the *Bundles* inquiry into whether the state foreclosure proceedings "were calculated... to return to the debtor-mortgagor his equity in the property." 856 F.2d, at 824. And perhaps that is what the courts that follow the *Durrett* rule have in mind when they select 70% of fair market value as the outer limit of "reasonably equivalent value" for forecloseable property (we have no idea where else such an arbitrary percentage could have come from). The problem is that such judgments represent policy determinations that the Bankruptcy Code gives us no apparent authority to make. How closely the price received in a forced sale is likely to approximate fair market value depends upon the terms of the forced sale—how quickly it may be made, what sort of public notice must be given, etc. But the terms for foreclosure sale are not *standard.* They vary considerably from State to State, depending upon, among other things, how the particular State values the divergent interests of debtor and creditor. To specify a federal "reasonable" foreclosure-sale price is to extend federal bankruptcy law well beyond the traditional field of fraudulent transfers, into realms of policy where it has not ventured before. Some sense of history is needed to appreciate this.

The modern law of fraudulent transfers had its origin in the Statute of 13 Elizabeth, which invalidated "covinous and fraudulent" transfers designed "to delay, hinder or defraud creditors and others." 13 Eliz., ch. 5 (1570). English courts soon developed the doctrine of "badges of fraud": proof by a creditor of certain objective facts (for example, a transfer to a close relative, a secret transfer, a transfer of title without transfer of possession, or grossly inadequate consideration) would raise a rebuttable presumption of actual fraudulent intent. See *Twyne's Case,* 3 Coke Rep. 80b, 76 Eng.Rep. 809 (K.B. 1601); O. Bump, Fraudulent Conveyances: A Treatise upon Conveyances Made by Debtors to Defraud Creditors 31-60 (3d ed. 1882). Every American bankruptcy law has incorporated a fraudulent transfer provision; the 1898 Act specifically adopted the language of the Statute of 13 Elizabeth. Bankruptcy Act of July 1, 1898, ch. 541, § 67(e), 30 Stat. 564-565.

The history of foreclosure law also begins in England, where courts of chancery developed the "equity of redemption"—the equitable right of a borrower to buy back, or redeem, property conveyed as security by paying the secured debt on a later date than "law day," the original due date. The courts' continued expansion of the period of redemption left lenders in a quandary, since title to forfeited property could remain clouded for years after law day. To meet this problem, courts created the equitable remedy of foreclosure: after a certain date the borrower would be forever foreclosed from exercising his equity of redemption. This remedy was called strict foreclosure because the borrower's entire interest in the property was forfeited, regardless of any accumulated equity. See G. Glenn, 1 Mortgages 3-18, 358-362, 395-406 (1943); G. Osborne, Mortgages 144 (2d ed. 1970). The next major change took place in 19th-century America, with the development of foreclosure by sale (with the surplus over the debt refunded to the debtor) as a means of avoiding the draconian consequences of strict foreclosure. *Id.*, at 661-663; Glenn, *supra*, at 460-462, 622. Since then, the States have created diverse networks of judicially and legislatively crafted rules governing the foreclosure process, to achieve what each of them considers the proper balance between the needs of lenders and borrowers. All States permit judicial foreclosure, conducted under direct judicial oversight; about half of the States also permit foreclosure by exercising a private power of sale provided in the mortgage documents. * * * Foreclosure laws typically require notice to the defaulting borrower, a substantial lead time before the commencement of foreclosure proceedings, publication of a notice of sale, and strict adherence to prescribed bidding rules and auction procedures. Many States require that the auction be conducted by a government official, and some forbid the property to be sold for less than a specified fraction of a mandatory presale fair-market-value appraisal. * * * When these procedures have been followed, however, it is "black letter" law that mere inadequacy of the foreclosure sale price is no basis for setting the sale aside, though it may be set aside (*under state foreclosure law,* rather than fraudulent transfer law) if the price is so low as to "shock the conscience or raise a presumption of fraud or unfairness." *Gelfert v. National City Bank of N.Y.,* 313 U.S. 221, 232 (1941).

Fraudulent transfer law and foreclosure law enjoyed over 400 years of peaceful coexistence in Anglo-American jurisprudence until the Fifth Circuit's unprecedented 1980 decision in *Durrett.* To our knowledge no prior decision had ever applied the "grossly inadequate price" badge of fraud under fraudulent transfer law to set aside a foreclosure sale. To say that the "reasonably equivalent value" language in the fraudulent transfer provision of the Bankruptcy Code requires a foreclosure sale to yield a certain minimum price beyond what state foreclosure law requires, is to say, in essence, that the Code has adopted *Durrett* or *Bundles.* Surely Congress has the power pursuant to its constitutional grant of authority over bankruptcy, U.S. Const., Art. I, § 8, cl. 4, to disrupt the ancient harmony that foreclosure law and fraudulent conveyance law, those two pillars of debtor-creditor jurisprudence, have heretofore enjoyed. But absent clearer textual guidance than the phrase "reasonably equivalent value"—a phrase entirely compatible with pre-existing practice—we will not presume such a radical departure.[7]

---

[7] We are unpersuaded by petitioner's argument that the 1984 amendments to the Bankruptcy Code codified the *Durrett* rule. Those amendments expanded the definition of "transfer" to include "foreclosure of the debtor's equity of redemption," 11 U.S.C. § 101(54) (1988 ed., Supp. IV), and added the words "voluntarily or involuntarily" as modifiers of the term "transfer" in § 548(a). The first of these provisions establishes that foreclosure sales fall within the general definition of "transfers" that may be avoided under several statutory provisions, including (but not limited to) § 548. See § 522(h) (transfers of exempt property), § 544 (transfers voidable under state law), § 547 (preferential transfers), § 549 (postpetition transfers). The second of them establishes that a transfer may be avoided as fraudulent even if it was against the debtor's will. See *In re Madrid,* 725 F.2d 1197, 1199 (CA9 1984) (preamendment decision holding that a foreclosure sale is not a "transfer" under § 548). Neither of these consequences has any bearing upon the meaning of "reasonably equivalent value" in the context of a foreclosure sale.

Nor does our reading render these amendments "superfluous," as the dissent contends, *post,* at 1770. Prior to 1984, it was at least open to question whether § 548 could be used to invalidate even a *collusive* foreclosure sale, see *Madrid, supra,* at 1204 (Farris, J., concurring). It is no superfluity for Congress to clarify what had been at best unclear, which is what it did here by making the provision apply to involuntary as well as voluntary transfers and by including foreclosures within the definition of "transfer." See *infra,* at 1765-1766.

Federal statutes impinging upon important state interests "cannot... be construed without regard to the implications of our dual system of government.... [W]hen the Federal Government takes over... local radiations in the vast network of our national economic enterprise and thereby radically readjusts the balance of state and national authority, those charged with the duty of legislating [must be] reasonably explicit." Frankfurter, Some Reflections on the Reading of Statutes, 47 Colum.L.Rev. 527, 539-540 (1947). It is beyond question that an essential state interest is at issue here: We have said that "the general welfare of society is involved in the security of the titles to real estate" and the power to ensure that security "inheres in the very nature of [state] government." *American Land Co. v. Zeiss,* 219 U.S. 47, 60 (1911). Nor is there any doubt that the interpretation urged by petitioner would have a profound effect upon that interest: The title of every piece of realty purchased at foreclosure would be under a federally created cloud. (Already, title insurers have reacted to the *Durrett* rule by including specially crafted exceptions from coverage in many policies issued for properties purchased at foreclosure sales. * * * To displace traditional state regulation in such a manner, the federal statutory purpose must be "clear and manifest," *English v. General Elec. Co.,* 496 U.S. 72, 79 (1990). * * * Otherwise, the Bankruptcy Code will be construed to adopt, rather than to displace, pre-existing state law. * * * For the reasons described, we decline to read the phrase "reasonably equivalent value" in § 548(a)(2) to mean, in its application to mortgage foreclosure sales, either "fair market value" or "fair foreclosure price" (whether calculated as a percentage of fair market value or otherwise). We deem, as the law has always deemed, that a fair and proper price, or a "reasonably equivalent value," for foreclosed property, is the price in fact received at the foreclosure sale, so long as all the requirements of the State's foreclosure law have been complied with.

This conclusion does not render § 548(a)(2) superfluous, since the "reasonably equivalent value" criterion will continue to have independent meaning (ordinarily a meaning similar to fair market value) outside the foreclosure context. Indeed, § 548(a)(2) will even continue to be an exclusive means of invalidating some foreclosure sales. Although *collusive* foreclosure sales are likely subject to attack under § 548(a)(1), which authorizes the trustee to avoid transfers "made... with actual intent to hinder, delay, or defraud" creditors, that provision may not reach foreclosure sales that, while not intentionally fraudulent, nevertheless fail to comply with all governing state laws. * * * Any irregularity in the conduct of the sale that would permit judicial invalidation of the sale under applicable state law deprives the sale price of its conclusive force under § 548(a)(2)(A), and the transfer may be avoided if the price received was not reasonably equivalent to the property's actual value at the time of the sale

Chapter 7. The Avoiding Powers of the Trustee   385

(which we think would be the price that would have been received if the foreclosure sale had proceeded according to law).

* * *

For the foregoing reasons, the judgment of the Court of Appeals for the Ninth Circuit is

Affirmed.

■   Justice SOUTER, with whom Justice BLACKMUN, Justice STEVENS, and Justice GINSBURG join, dissenting. [Opinion omitted.]

NOTES

1. In dissent, Justice Souter gleefully noted that Justice Scalia, the prince of the plain meaning rule, had taken liberties with the meaning of a statute clear to any "ordinary speaker of English." Ouch! He pointed out the absurdity that under the majority's test a peppercorn paid at a noncollusive and procedurally regular foreclosure sale must be treated as the reasonably equivalent value of a California beachfront estate (the property involved in *BFP*). And, indeed, in *In re T.F. Stone Co., Inc.*, 72 F.3d 466 (5th Cir. 1995), the court relied on *BFP* to hold that a regularly conducted, noncollusive tax sale for $325 was a sale "for present fair equivalent value" under § 549(c) even though the buyer resold the property a few months later for $39,500! *See also In re Grandote Country Club Co.*, 252 F.3d 1146 (10th Cir. 2001) (refusing to upset tax sale under Colorado fraudulent transfer law).

2. Section 549(a) allows the trustee to avoid postpetiton transfers of property of the estate unless they were authorized, subject to an exception under § 549(c) affording protection to good faith purchasers of real property without knowledge of the commencement of the case and for "present fair equivalent value." In *Miller v. NLVK, LLC*, 454 F.3d 899 (8th Cir. 2006), the court refused to follow *T.F. Stone* in extending *BFP*'s safe harbor for buyers at prepetition foreclosure sales to cases involving postpetition foreclosure sales avoidable under § 549(c). The *Miller* court remanded for a factual finding on whether the payment of $3,847 in satisfaction of past due homeowners' association assessments in the context of a postpetition foreclosure sale constituted "present fair value equivalent value" for the transfer of a condominium worth up to $650,000 subject to senior liens subject to senior liens of at least $463,000, noting that one pre-*BFP* court had found that 73% of fair market value did not rise to the level of "present fair equivalent value." Id. at 903. Query whether "present fair equivalent value" under § 549(c) (unauthorized postpetition transfer) differs in meaning from "reasonably equivalent value" under § 548(a) (prepetition constructively fraudulent transfer).

3. The scope of *BFP* is in dispute in the lower courts. *See, e.g., In re Ford*, 296 B.R. 537 (Bankr.N.D.Ga.2003) (rejecting *T.F. Stone's* holding that *BFP* applies to § 549(c)); *In re D'Alfonso*, 211 B.R. 508 (Bankr.E.D.Pa.1997) (refusing to extend *BFP* to tax sales). The Court emphasized that its opinion covers only mortgage foreclosures of real estate, but its forced-sale rationale would seem to apply as well to foreclosures of personal property collateral under the UCC and, as noted above, *T.F. Stone* applied it to local government tax sales. 511 U.S. at 537 n.3. Uniform Fraudulent Transfer Act § 3(b) adopts the irrebuttable presumption rule that was later accepted by the Court in *BFP* with respect to § 548, and the UFTA applies both to real and personal property foreclosures. Courts have generally limited *BFP* to situations where the transfer involved forced sale at public auction pursuant to statutes requiring an opportunity for competitive bidding. *In re Sherman*, 223 B.R. 555 (10th Cir. BAP 1998) (finding tax sale in which competitive bidding was not permitted to be a constructively fraudulent transfer).

4. CORPORATE DISTRIBUTIONS AS FRAUDULENT TRANSFERS

We have seen that a gratuitous transfer by an insolvent debtor is a fraudulent transfer even if there is no fraudulent intent by the debtor. An insolvent person who gives away property that is subject to levy by creditors is disposing of the property unfairly. The debtor is transferring economic value to the transferee that in equity belongs to creditors. The protection of this interest of creditors is recognized in other areas of the law as well. Corporation law protects creditors of corporations by limiting the extent to which dividends and other distributions can be made to stockholders. A dividend, although not a gift, is gratuitous in the sense that it is a transfer of property for which no value is received in exchange. Limitations on dividends and other distributions to stockholders are analogous to limitations found in fraudulent transfer law on transfers by debtors, and they cover distributions made by both solvent and insolvent corporations.

A distribution by a corporation to its stockholders might violate both the corporation law and the fraudulent transfer law. Or, it might not be prohibited by the corporation law, but it may fall within the fraudulent transfer law. If the distribution violates both laws, the remedy provided by one law may differ from the remedy provided by the other. The relationship between the corporation law and the law of fraudulent transfers was noted by Judge Learned Hand in *Wood v. National City Bank*, 24 F.2d 661, 662–663 (2d Cir. 1928) as follows:

> [Plaintiff] depends upon the fact that the directors have paid, and the defendants received, dividends when the corporation was insolvent. Merely because this impairs the capital stock, it is commonly regarded as a wrong to creditors on the directors' part, and it is often made such

by statute. We may, without discussion, assume that it would be a wrong in the case at bar. Even so, it is primarily only the wrong of those who commit it, like any other tort, and innocent participants are not accomplices to its commission. Hence it has been settled, at least for us, that when the liability is based merely on the depletion of the capital, a stockholder must be charged with notice of that fact. * * *

* * *

However, there is quite another theory, and quite another liability, if the payments not only impair the capital, but are taken out of assets already too small to pay the existing debts. The situation then strictly is not peculiar to corporation law, but merely an instance of a payment from an insolvent estate. Since, as we have said, a stockholder is a donee, he receives such payments charged with whatever trust they were subject to in the hands of the corporation. In that situation it can indeed be said with some truth that the corporate assets have become a "trust fund." * * * Hence it has never been doubted, so far as we can find, at least in any federal court, that if the dividends are paid in fraud of creditors the stockholder is so liable.

Judge Hand distinguished between dividends paid by an insolvent corporation and dividends paid by a solvent corporation that merely impair capital, stating that the former case is governed by fraudulent transfer law. But even the second case may be covered by the UFTA.

If payment of a dividend violates UFTA § 4(a)(2)(i), can the dividend be recovered from a stockholder who received it in good faith and without knowledge that it was unlawfully paid? California Corporations Code § 506(a), for example, limits liability to a stockholder who receives any distribution prohibited by the Corporations Code "with knowledge of facts indicating the impropriety thereof." Similar provisions are found in some other corporation statutes. Provisions of this kind reflect the fact that in many cases stockholders are passive investors who would not normally have any basis for determining whether a distribution was lawful or not. Quite apart from the practical difficulty of recovering relatively small amounts from large numbers of stockholders, it may be unfair to force disgorgement of payments innocently received and already spent. But UFTA § 8 does not recognize innocent receipt of a gratuitous fraudulent transfer as a defense. Thus, there may be a conflict between corporation law and fraudulent transfer law with respect to available remedies. California Corporations Code § 506(d) resolves the conflict in favor of the UFTA. It states that "nothing contained in this section affects any liability which any shareholder may have under [the UFTA]." The question of the relationship between corporation law and fraudulent transfer law is addressed by Robert C.

Clark, *Corporate Law* 88–89 (1986) (arguing fraudulent transfer law should preempt dividend rules of corporation laws).

PROBLEM

Debtor Corporation, while insolvent, issued stock to Defendant in order to raise capital. Defendant paid $100,000 for the shares and shortly thereafter sold them for more than that amount. When Debtor filed in Chapter 7 bankruptcy, its Trustee filed a complaint in bankruptcy court to avoid the issuance of the stock as a fraudulent transfer because Debtor did not receive reasonably equivalent value. On similar facts, the Ninth Circuit affirmed the bankruptcy court's dismissal of Trustee's claim on the ground that "unissued stock is not an interest of the debtor corporation in property; it is merely equity in the corporation itself." *Decker v. Advantage Fund Ltd.*, 362 F.3d 593, 596 (9th Cir. 2004). An earlier decision had explained: "Since an action directed at recovery of corporate stock could only effect equitable ownership of the corporation and would not restore property to the estate or avoid an estate obligation, then it is not a transfer subject to question under Section 548." *In re Curry and Sorensen, Inc.*, 57 B.R. 824, 829 (9th Cir. BAP 1986). Do you agree with this analysis?

Robinson v. Wangemann
United States Court of Appeals, Fifth Circuit, 1935.
75 F.2d 756.

■ FOSTER, Circuit Judge.

This is an appeal from a judgment affirming an order of the referee allowing a claim against the estate of Reichardt–Abbott Company, Inc., bankrupt, based on a note given by the corporation in payment for shares of its own stock purchased by it.

The facts are not in dispute. In October, 1922, Arthur Wangemann, who was its president and a large stockholder in Wangemann–Reichardt Company, Inc., sold 500 shares of its own stock owned by him to the corporation at $110 per share, a total of $55,000, to be paid for on or before January 1, 1923. The purchase was authorized by a meeting of stockholders and the company's note, due January 1, 1923, bearing 7 per cent interest from October 1, 1922, was delivered to him in payment. At that time the corporation was solvent and its surplus in cash, over and above its liabilities, was more than $55,000. The note, due January 1, 1923, was not paid. From time to time, renewal notes were issued and the debt was reduced to $35,000. The name of the corporation was changed to Reichardt–Abbott Company, Inc., and under that name it was adjudicated bankrupt. Its assets are not sufficient to pay creditors in full. The claim of appellee is based on one of the renewal notes for $30,000, due January 1, 1933, and four notes each for $500, given in payment of interest on said note, together with interest on all the said notes. Appellee holds said notes as executrix under his will and sole legatee of Arthur Wangemann.

The referee held that the corporation had the right to purchase its own stock, * * * that the transaction was in good faith, and, as the corporation had sufficient surplus out of which the stock could have been paid for at the time it was purchased, without prejudice to creditors, appellee was entitled to prove her claim and participate equally with the other creditors in the distribution of the assets.

It may be conceded that if Arthur Wangemann had received cash for his stock at the time he relinquished it the transaction would have been valid, but that is not the case here presented.

* * * Arthur Wangemann loaned no money to the corporation. The note he accepted for his stock did not change the character of the transaction nor did the renewals have that effect. A transaction by which a corporation acquires its own stock from a stockholder for a sum of money is not really a sale. The corporation does not acquire anything of value equivalent to the depletion of its assets, if the stock is held in the treasury, as in this case. It is simply a method of distributing a proportion of the assets to the stockholders. The assets of a corporation are the common pledge of its creditors, and stockholders are not entitled to receive any part of them unless creditors are paid in full. When such a transaction is had, regardless of the good faith of the parties, it is essential to its validity that there be sufficient surplus to retire the stock, without prejudice to creditors, at the time payment is made out of assets. In principle, the contract between Wangemann and the corporation was executory until the stock should be paid for in cash. It is immaterial that the corporation was solvent and had sufficient surplus to make payment when the agreement was entered into. It is necessary to a recovery that the corporation should be solvent and have sufficient surplus to prevent injury to creditors when the payment is actually made. This was an implied condition in the original note and the renewals accepted by Arthur Wangemann.

As the assets of the bankrupt are not sufficient to pay the creditors in full and there is no surplus out of which the note could be paid, appellee, who is in no better position than the original holder of the notes, cannot be permitted to share with the other unsecured creditors in the distribution of the assets of the bankrupt estate. She may be permitted to file her claim, but it is subordinate to the claims of the other creditors. * * *

Reversed and remanded for further proceedings not inconsistent with this opinion.

NOTES

1. In *In re SPM Manufacturing Corp.*, 163 B.R. 411 (Bankr.D.Mass.1994), the court said: "*Robinson v. Wangemann* is a policy statement that redemption debt must come behind general creditors in bankruptcy because of the priority creditors enjoy in bankruptcy over stockholders." 163 B.R. at 415.

2. As the court in *Robinson* recognized, the purchase by a corporation of its own shares is simply a distribution of assets of the corporation to the stockholder selling the shares. It is economically indistinguishable from the payment of a dividend, except that a dividend is a general distribution paid pro rata to all holders of the same class of stock while in a purchase of shares the distribution is limited to the selling stockholder. Repurchased stock, sometimes known as "treasury stock" because it is held in the corporation's treasury, may retain the status of issued stock until it is cancelled. Since it can be resold it might resemble an asset, but corporations can usually issue additional shares without first repurchasing those already issued; hence, repurchased shares are no more an asset than authorized but unissued shares. Indeed, both California, Cal.Corp.Code § 510(a), and the Revised Model Business Corporation Act § 6.31(a), eliminate the concept of treasury stock by providing that repurchased stock reverts to the status of authorized but unissued stock. William L. Cary & Melvin A. Eisenberg, *Cases and Materials on Corporations* 1388 (7th ed.1995). Dean Clark admonishes:

> Remember that there is never "fair consideration," in the sense meant by the [Uniform Fraudulent Conveyance Act] when a corporation makes a distribution to shareholders, because the corporation receives nothing the creditors could levy on or, if they did levy on it (as in the case of repurchased stock) nothing that would have value in their hands equivalent to the assets transferred to the shareholders. That is, from the creditor's perspective, distributions clearly reduce or deplete the "estate of the debtor."

Robert C. Clark, *Corporate Law* 638, n.9 (1986). In *Buncher Co. v. Official Committee of Unsecured Creditors*, 229 F.3d 245 (3d Cir. 2000), the court likened the purchase by a limited partnership of the shares of some of its limited partners to a stock redemption by a corporation and held that the limited partnership received no value.

The similarity between the payment of a dividend and the purchase of the corporation's shares is reflected in corporation statutes that impose similar restrictions on the ability of the corporation to make either kind of distribution. For example we have seen that Model Business Corporation Act § 1.40(6) defines "distribution" to include "a purchase, redemption, or other acquisition of shares."

3. In *Robinson* the corporation had sufficient assets to allow it to lawfully pay cash for the shares at the date of purchase. If the parties choose to have the then solvent corporation pay for the shares by giving its promissory note instead of cash, why should the enforceability of the note depend upon the financial condition of the corporation at the time the note is paid? The statutory response to this issue varies among the states.

Section 166 of the California Corporations Code follows the rationale of *Robinson* by stating that "the time of any distribution by purchase or redemption of shares shall be the date cash or property is transferred by the corporation, whether or not pursuant to a contract of an earlier date * * *." An exception to this rule is provided for the case in which the corporation purchases its shares by issuing to the seller a debt obligation that is an investment security of a type commonly traded in the securities markets. In that case the distribution occurs when the corporation acquires the purchased shares. What is the rationale for applying one rule to the case in which the corporation pays with a simple promissory note and a different rule when the corporation pays with a debenture that is an investment security?

The Model Act is contrary to the California statute and to most prior case law. It provides that the validity of a distribution by purchase, redemption or other acquisition of a corporation's shares shall be measured "as of the earlier of (i) the date money or other property is transferred or debt incurred by the corporation or (ii) the date the shareholder ceases to be a shareholder with respect to the acquired shares." § 6.40(e)(1). Section 6.40(f) goes further by stating: "A corporation's indebtedness to a shareholder incurred by reason of a distribution made in accordance with this section is at parity with the corporation's indebtedness to its general, unsecured creditors except to the extent subordinated by agreement."

5. REASONABLY EQUIVALENT VALUE IN CORPORATE TRANSACTIONS

PROBLEM

Corporation's obligation to Bank was secured by stock of Subsidiary, whose stock was wholly owned by Corporation. When Corporation defaulted on its loan to Bank, Corporation and Bank negotiated a transaction whereby Subsidiary's stock was released from Bank's security interest, Bank loaned Subsidiary $2 million, and Bank was granted a security interest in Subsidiary's assets. On the same day as the new loan was made, Subsidiary paid Corporation as a dividend $2 million, and Corporation paid $2 million to Bank in partial payment of Corporation's prior debt to Bank. Subsidiary was solvent when the deal was made but, owing to the large amount of debt it incurred, began to experience cash flow problems thereafter and sank into insolvency. Subsidiary filed in Chapter 7 within one year of the $2 million loan transaction.

(a) Can Subsidiary's trustee avoid Bank's security interest in Subsidiary's assets? Avoid Subsidiary's obligation to repay the debt? *See Wells Fargo Bank v. Desert View Bldg. Supplies, Inc.*, 475 F.Supp. 693 (D.Nev. 1978), *aff'd*, 633 F.2d 221 (9th Cir. 1980). *See* § 548(a)(1)(B).

(b) Can Subsidiary's trustee proceed against Corporation on the ground that the dividend was a fraudulent conveyance? A violation of the state corporation laws?

In re Northern Merchandise, Inc.
United States Court of Appeals, Ninth Circuit, 2004.
371 F.3d 1056.

■ WARDLAW, Circuit Judge:

Frontier Bank ("Frontier") appeals a decision of the Bankruptcy Appellate Panel ("BAP") affirming in part the bankruptcy court's summary judgment in favor of Ronald G. Brown, Chapter 7 Trustee ("Trustee"), in the Trustee's action alleging that Frontier received a fraudulent transfer from Chapter 7 Debtor Northern Merchandise, Inc. ("Debtor"). Specifically, Frontier challenges the BAP's ruling that Debtor did not receive reasonably equivalent value under 11 U.S.C. § 548(a)(1)(B) in exchange for a security interest it granted to Frontier and, thus, Frontier was not protected under 11 U.S.C. § 548(c). * * * Reviewing the bankruptcy court's decision to grant summary judgment de novo * * * we reverse.

I. Background

In 1997, Debtor, a company that sold general merchandise to grocery stores, was incorporated by Paul Weingartner, Gary David, and Paul Benjamin. In February 1998, Frontier loaned $60,000 to the newly formed company. The loan was evidenced by a promissory note in the amount of $60,000, secured by a commercial financing agreement granting Frontier a security interest in Debtor's inventory, chattel paper, accounts, equipment, and general intangibles. The security interest was later perfected by the filing of a Uniform Commercial Code financing statement on February 24, 1998.

In October 1998, Debtor sought a second loan of $150,000 from Frontier to provide Debtor with working capital. Frontier refused to give such a loan to Debtor after determining that Debtor's financial performance did not support an additional direct loan to the company. However, Frontier agreed to loan $150,000 (the "October Loan") to Paul Weingartner, Paul Benjamin, and

Stephen Comer, Debtor's shareholders (collectively, "Shareholders"), whose credit warranted such a loan.[1] Frontier understood that the Shareholders would, in turn, allow Debtor to utilize the money to fund its business operations. In fact, the loan transaction was structured so that Frontier deposited the proceeds of the October Loan directly into Debtor's checking account. However, while the funds themselves were transferred directly from Frontier to Debtor, the transaction was documented as a loan to Shareholders, who then turned the funds over to Debtor. The October Loan was evidenced by a promissory note in favor of Frontier executed by Shareholders. However, on the same day that Shareholders entered into the October Loan with Frontier, Debtor executed a commercial security agreement granting Frontier a security interest in its inventory, chattel paper, accounts, equipment, and general intangibles.

On March 5, 1999, Debtor ceased doing business, leaving approximately $875,000 in unsecured debt. At the time, Debtor had approximately $400,000 worth of inventory. Debtor transferred the $400,000 worth of inventory to Benjamin News Group, a company owned by shareholder Paul Benjamin, for $125,000.[2] On March 19, 1999, Benjamin News Group paid Frontier, not Debtor, the $125,000, which amount was credited to the October Loan. The remaining $25,000 due on the October Loan was paid to Frontier by the Safeway Corporation from the proceeds of prior sales of inventory to the Safeway Corporation.

On March 22, 1999, creditors filed an involuntary Chapter 7 petition against Debtor, and a trustee was appointed. Debtor scheduled assets of $4,116.17 and debts of $875,847.32. On February 9, 2001, Trustee filed a complaint against Frontier, and thereafter a motion for partial summary judgment, arguing that the grant of the security interest and the $125,000 transfer were fraudulent conveyances under 11 U.S.C. § 548(a). The bankruptcy court granted the motion for summary judgment, holding that a fraudulent conveyance had occurred. On appeal before the BAP, Frontier argued, *inter* alia, that the bankruptcy court erred in finding a fraudulent conveyance because (1) Debtor received reasonably equivalent value for the security interest * * * The BAP ruled in favor of Trustee * * *.

II. Reasonably equivalent value

11 U.S.C. § 548(a)(1) provides:

---

[1] Shareholders were also officers and/or directors of Debtor.

[2] Trustee filed a fraudulent conveyance action against Benjamin News Group and ultimately recovered $45,000.

> The trustee may avoid any transfer of an interest of the debtor in property, or any obligation incurred by the debtor, that was made or incurred on or within one year before the date of the filing of the petition, if the debtor voluntarily or involuntarily... received less than a reasonably equivalent value in exchange for such transfer or obligation.

It is well settled that "reasonably equivalent value can come from one other than the recipient of the payments, a rule which has become known as the indirect benefit rule." *Harman v. First Am. Bank (In re Jeffrey Bigelow Design Group, Inc.)*, 956 F.2d 479, 485 (4th Cir. 1992). For example, in *Rubin v. Manufacturers Hanover Trust Co.*, the court explained:

> a debtor may sometimes receive "fair" consideration even though the consideration given for his property or obligation goes initially to a third person... although transfers solely for the benefit of third parties do not furnish fair consideration... the transaction's benefit to the debtor need not be direct; it may come indirectly through benefit to a third person.... If the consideration given to the third person has ultimately landed in the debtor's hands, or if the giving of the consideration to the third person otherwise confers an economic benefit upon the debtor, then the debtor's net worth has been preserved, and [the statute] has been satisfied—provided, of course, that the value of the benefit received by the debtor approximates the value of the property or obligation he has given up.

661 F.2d 979, 991-92 (2d Cir. 1981) (internal quotation marks and citations omitted).

Jeffrey Bigelow is such an example. In Jeffrey Bigelow, shareholders of a debtor entered into a line of credit agreement with First American Bank for $1,000,000. Although the shareholders were the makers of the line of credit, "only the debtor received the draws and all payments were made directly from the debtor to First American." *Id.* Subsequently, "the debtor executed a note for $1,000,000 to [the shareholders] with substantially the same terms as the line of credit between First American and [the shareholders]." *Id.* As the debtor directly repaid First American, its liability on the note to the shareholders likewise decreased. *Id.* Holding that the payments made by the debtor on the shareholders' line of credit did not constitute fraudulent conveyances, the Fourth Circuit reasoned:

> [T]he proper focus is on the net effect of the transfers on the debtor's estate, the funds available to the unsecured creditors. As long as the unsecured creditors are no worse off because the debtor, and consequently the estate, has received an amount reasonably equivalent to what it paid, no fraudulent transfer has occurred.

Id. at 484. Because it was "apparent that the transfers [had] not resulted in the depletion of the bankruptcy estate," but rather "served simply as repayment for money received," the Fourth Circuit held that "no fraudulent transfer occurred." *Id.* at 485.

As *Jeffrey Bigelow* illustrates, the primary focus of Section 548 is on the net effect of the transaction on the debtor's estate and the funds available to the unsecured creditors. *See id.* ("the focus is whether the net effect of the transaction has depleted the bankruptcy estate"); *see also Nordberg v. Republic Nat'l Bank (In re Chase & Sanborn Corp.),* 51 B.R. 739, 740 (Bankr.S.D.Fla.1985) ("the indirect benefit cases are bottomed upon the ultimate impact to the debtor's creditors"); *Rubin,* 661 F.2d at 992 ("decisions in [indirect benefit cases] turn on the statutory purpose of conserving the debtor's estate for the benefit of creditors."). Trustee contends that Debtor's grant of the security interest to Frontier resulted in a $150,000 loss to Debtor's estate and thus the funds available to the unsecured creditors. Trustee reasons that because the transfer of $150,000 from Shareholders to Debtor was technically a capital contribution, rather than a loan, Debtor was under no legal obligation to grant a security interest to Frontier. Therefore, Trustee argues, Debtor would have been justified to not grant the security interest to Frontier, which would have resulted in an additional $150,000 in Debtor's estate.

We reject this formalistic view. Although Debtor was not a party to the October loan, it clearly received a benefit from that loan. In fact, Frontier deposited the $150,000 proceeds of the October Loan directly into Debtor's checking account. Because Debtor benefited from the October Loan in the amount of $150,000, its grant of a security interest to Frontier to secure Shareholder's indebtedness on that loan, which totaled $150,000, resulted in no net loss to Debtor's estate nor the funds available to the unsecured creditors. To hold otherwise would result in an unintended $150,000 windfall to Debtor's estate. Accordingly, Debtor received reasonably equivalent value in exchange for the security interest it granted to Frontier. * * *

IV. Conclusion

For the foregoing reasons, the BAP erred in holding that Debtor did not receive reasonably equivalent value under § 548(a)(1)(B) in exchange for the security interest it granted to Frontier and that Frontier was not protected under § 548(c).

REVERSED.

PROBLEM

Holding, Inc. acquired all the stock of Galaxy Pictures, a old line film studio that produced and distributed films for theatrical release as well as television. Its earnings came from distribution fees from its new films and licensing fees from its large library of classic motion pictures and TV films. In January 2008, Holding initiated discussions with Bank for a loan.

a. Holding offered Bank a security interest in the stock of Galaxy Pictures as security for the loan. Bank rejected this proposal and declared that it would not make the loan to Holding unless Galaxy Pictures guaranteed the loan and secured its guarantee with a security interest in all Galaxy's assets. Why does Bank prefer a security interest in Galaxy's assets instead of its stock?

b. Bank would advance the money to Holding only if Galaxy guaranteed Holding's obligation to repay Bank and granted a security interest to Bank in its assets to secure its guarantee. Galaxy complied and Bank advanced the funds to Holding in January; Holding used the funds to pay some debts that had nothing to do with Galaxy. Unfortunately, 2008 was a disastrous year for both Holding and Galaxy, which produced several over-budget box office bombs, and word went out that Galaxy might have to sell its film library piecemeal to survive. On this news, Galaxy's creditors forced it into involuntary bankruptcy in early December. Holding defaulted on its loan to Bank. Galaxy's trustee sought to avoid both Galaxy's obligation to Bank under the guarantee and Bank's security interest in Galaxy's assets on the ground that Galaxy did not receive reasonably equivalent value from Bank for either the obligation or the security interest. You may assume that Galaxy was insolvent at all times during 2008. Should Trustee prevail?

c. Would your answer change if Galaxy had been solvent during the first six months of 2008? *See* § 548(a)(1)(B)(ii).

d. Would your answer change if Holding had used the proceeds of the loan to purchase the stock of Globe Theaters, Inc., which owned a chain of theaters where Galaxy's films would be shown? See *Telefest, Inc. v. VU-TV, Inc.*, 591 F.Supp. 1368 (D.N.J. 1984); *Mellon Bank v. Metro Communications, Inc.*, 945 F.2d 635 (3d Cir. 1991), discussed below.

The court in *Rubin v. Manufacturers Hanover Trust Co.*, 661 F.2d 979 (2d Cir. 1981), recognized that subsidiaries of a debtor may receive reasonably equivalent value for their guaranties even if the benefit derived from the guaranties was indirect. The court, however, went on to hold that the benefit had to be quantified and compared to the amount of the obligations incurred or the property transferred under the guaranty. In *Telefest* the court did not require quantification of the benefit received for the guaranty. The debtor, VU–TV, was engaged in the business of distributing TV programming to TV stations and cable companies. VU–TV was a wholly-owned subsidiary of CATV. MHT, a bank, loaned money to CATV to enable CATV to acquire the capital stock of San Antonio, a cable television company. As security for this loan and other loans made by MHT to any of the three affiliated corporations, CATV, VU–TV and San Antonio executed cross-corporate guaranties under which each corporation guaranteed the obligation of each other corporation and each corporation granted to MHT a security interest in the assets of the corporation to secure payment of its obligations and the obligations of each other corporation. In the bankruptcy of VU–TV a security interest in assets of VU–TV to secure VU–TV's guaranty of the loan obligation of CATV to MHT was challenged as a fraudulent transfer on the ground that VU–TV did not receive fair consideration under UFCA § 4. The court stated:

> I am satisfied that it was intended that a benefit would flow to VU–TV through the loans to CATV and San Antonio ultimately guaranteed by VU–TV. In April, 1982, when MHT was considering whether or not to extend a $300,000 loan to CATV for the purchase of San Antonio, MHT certainly regarded CATV and VU–TV as having an identity of interest. An internal memo * * * evidences what MHT has consistently argued, i.e. that it always regarded VU–TV and its parent in tandem in its dealing with these companies. Such an outlook is relevant in considering whether the transferee of a conveyance acted in good faith. * * *
>
> Even more important than good faith in considering whether fair consideration passed is the nature of the transferor's business and its relationship with its parent. It is clear * * * that VU–TV was devoted to providing programming for cable television companies * * *. Monies loaned to VU–TV's parent to purchase a cable television system or for other moves directed toward expansion would most probably provide an additional and obviously secure market for VU–TV. The consideration for VU–TV's guarantee of the loans of its parent and sister companies may not have been a direct benefit, but it was a specific enough benefit for a reasonable trier of fact to conclude that fair consideration inhered in the conveyance.
>
> In any event, the notion that a benefit accrues to a subsidiary only when there is a direct flow of capital to that entity the result of its guarantee of a loan to its parent is inhibitory of contemporary financing practices, which recognize that cross-guarantees are often needed because of the unequal abilities of interrelated corporate entities to collateralize loans.

591 F.Supp. at 1378–1379.

The analysis in *Telefest* is supported by *Mellon Bank v. Metro Communications, Inc.*, 945 F.2d 635 (3d Cir. 1991), a case involving facts somewhat similar to those in *Telefest*. The court stated that a synergistic business relationship between the parent, which received the loan, and the subsidiary, which guaranteed the loan debt, was a substantial indirect benefit to the subsidiary. That benefit, along with the subsidiary's enhanced ability to borrow working capital resulting from the relationship, could amount to reasonably equivalent value for the guaranty. Another case taking the view that an indirect benefit may constitute reasonably equivalent value is *In re Fairchild Aircraft Corp.*, 6 F.3d 1119 (5th Cir. 1993). In that case, debtor, an airplane manufacturer, wished to keep an affiliate, a small airline, in business so that it would eventually buy airplanes from the debtor, which expected to make a profit of $800,000 for each airplane sold. In pursuance of this objective, the debtor agreed with a fuel supplier to pay for fuel that supplier delivered to the affiliate in order to keep its planes flying. The airline failed before buying any of the debtor's aircraft, although it did lease three. Nonetheless, the court, citing *Rubin* and *Mellon Bank*, held that the debtor had received reasonably equivalent value for its payments (amounting to $432,381) to the supplier that enabled the airline to stay in business. The economic benefit must, according to the court, be determined at the time the investment is made, not later when the deal turns sour.

6. LEVERAGED BUYOUTS

A person may want to buy a corporation but lacks the money or collateral necessary to finance the purchase. If the corporation has unencumbered assets, it may be possible to use those assets to provide most of the capital necessary to make the purchase. Doing so, however, may violate fraudulent transfer law with serious consequences if the acquired firm subsequently files in bankruptcy. Corporate acquisitions in which assets of the acquired firm are encumbered require careful attention to the fraudulent transfer issues raised by the transaction.

PROBLEM

Case #1. Shareholder agrees to sell the stock of Target Corporation to Acquirer who is unable to pay for the stock out of its own assets. Acquirer offers Shareholder a security interest in the stock of Target to secure the unpaid amount of the purchase price. Shareholder isn't interested in this because under the absolute priority rule debt must be paid before equity and creditors of Target would come ahead of Shareholder in any liquidation. Shareholder will sell on credit only if it can have a security interest in Target's assets. Acquirer agrees, and Target grants Shareholder a security interest in Target's assets to secure Acquirer's debt to Shareholder. This rudimentary transaction is what used to be called "bootstrap financing" and is potentially a constructively fraudulent transfer under § 548(a)(1)(B)(i) because Target does not receive "reasonably equivalent value" for its transfer of the security interest; in fact it receives no value, all the benefit flows to Acquirer and Shareholder. Thus, if the transfer rendered Target insolvent or left it with unreasonably small capital to engage in business and Target filed in bankruptcy, the trustee of Target may avoid the security interest under § 548.

Case #2. Same facts, except that instead of Shareholder financing the deal Acquirer borrows money from Bank to buy the stock from Shareholder and causes Target to grant Bank a security interest in its assets to secure the loan. Bank advances the loan proceeds to Acquirer who pays Shareholder for the stock. Again, this is a potentially fraudulent transaction because Target granted Bank a security interest in its assets and got nothing that its creditors could reach in return. The value went to Acquirer and Shareholder. If the insolvency test of § 548(a)(1)(B)(ii)(I) is met, Target's trustee may avoid the security interest under § 548.

Case #3. Same facts. But Bank is wise to the problem posed by Case #2 transaction, and loan officers are taught to be sure that the loan proceeds go to the entity that grants Bank the security interest. The transaction is structured so that the loan goes to Target which grants Bank a security interest in its assets. Target then reloans the money to Acquirer, an acquisition entity without significant assets, and Acquirer uses the money to pay Shareholder for the stock in Target. Now Bank believes that it is safe; it received a security interest in Target's assets and gave hard cash to Target in exchange. What Target does with the loan proceeds is its own business. Surely this meets the requirements of "reasonably equivalent value" under § 548(a)(1)(B)(i).

When *United States v. Tabor Court Realty Corp.*, 803 F.2d 1288 (3d Cir. 1986) (often referred to by its district court title, "*Gleneagles*"), held that under the facts of Case #3 Bank was the recipient of a fraudulent transfer, the ancient law of fraudulent transfers became required reading for mergers and acquisitions lawyers throughout the land. The court invalidated Bank's security interest as a fraudulent transfer on the ground that although Bank had given value to Target at the time it received the security interest, the money "merely passed through" Target to Acquirer and ultimately to the shareholders of Target. Acquirer's note to Target was worthless because Acquirer had virtually no assets other than the stock of now insolvent Target; hence, Target's loan to

Acquirer was a fraudulent transfer. Bank countered by insisting that there were two separate transactions, first, its loan to Target and, second, Target's loan to Acquirer. Bank gave good value to Target and what Target chose to do with the proceeds of the loan was a decision that should not affect the legitimacy of Bank's security interest. The court rejected this argument; since Bank knew the purpose of the loan, the two transactions were in fact "part of one integrated transaction."

Gleneagles was a case that concerned the liability of the lender in a leveraged buyout situation. The following opinion considers the liability of the old stockholders whose interest was bought out under the LBO. Judge Bufford is a well known law teacher and scholar.

Bay Plastics, Inc. v. BT Commercial Corp.

United States Bankruptcy Court, C.D. California, 1995.
187 B.R. 315.

■ SAMUEL L. BUFFORD, Bankruptcy Judge.

I. Introduction

The debtor has brought this adversary proceeding against the selling shareholders of a leveraged buyout ("LBO") to recover the funds that they received in the buyout transaction. While the action was also brought against the bank that financed the transaction, the bank has settled. The Court grants summary judgment to the debtor on the undisputed facts.

The Court holds that the transaction may be avoided as a constructive fraudulent transfer under the California version of the Uniform Fraudulent Transfer Act ("UFTA"), on which the debtor relies pursuant to Bankruptcy Code § 544(b), and that in consequence the debtor is entitled to recover against the selling shareholders. The Court finds that the transaction rendered the debtor insolvent, and that the sellers did not act in good faith.

II. Facts

The Court finds that the following facts are undisputed. Defendants Bob Younger, Abner Smith and Paul Dodson ("the selling shareholders") formed debtor Bay Plastics, Inc. ("Bay Plastics") in 1979 to manufacture polyvinyl chloride ("PVC") plastic pipe for water well casings and turf irrigation. Bay Plastics filed this bankruptcy case on January 25, 1990.

A. The Buyout

Because they were nearing retirement, on October 31, 1988 (fifteen months before this bankruptcy filing) the selling shareholders sold their Bay Plastics stock to Milhous Corporation ("Milhous") for $3.5 million in cash plus $1.8 million in deferred payments.[2] Milhous did not acquire the Bay Plastics stock directly. Instead, it caused its subsidiary Nicole Plastics to form its own subsidiary, BPI Acquisition Corp. ("BPI"), to take ownership of the Bay Plastics stock. Formally, the parties to the stock sale transaction were ultimately BPI and the selling shareholders.

The sale was unexceptional. The difficulty lay in the financing of the purchase. Milhous put no money of its own, or even any money that it borrowed, into this transaction. Instead, it caused Bay Plastics to borrow approximately $3.95 million from defendant BT Commercial Corp. ("BT") (a subsidiary of Bankers Trust), and then caused Bay Plastics to direct that $3.5 million of the loan be disbursed to BPI. BPI in turn directed that the $3.5 million be paid directly to the selling shareholders in substantial payment for their stock. Thus, at the closing, $3.5 million of the funds paid into escrow by BT went directly to the selling shareholders.

As security for its $3.95 million loan, BT received a first priority security interest in essentially all of the assets of Bay Plastics. In consequence, BT has received all of the proceeds of debtor's assets in this bankruptcy case, and nothing is left for unsecured or even for administrative creditors.

The financing also provided a revolving credit facility for working capital, in addition to the payment for the LBO, up to a total loan of $7 million.[4] A total of just over $4 million was owing to BT at the time of the bankruptcy filing, according to the debtor's schedules. Thus most of the debt (all but approximately $500,000) owing to BT at the time of the filing resulted from the LBO.

The selling shareholders were not in the dark about the financing. On October 25, 1988 they and their attorney met with Milhous representatives in Los Angeles to finalize the deal. While the Milhous representatives provided rather little information about the Milhous finances, they did disclose the details of the BT secured loan to Bay Plastics to finance the stock purchase. In addition, the selling shareholders received a projected post-transaction balance sheet, which showed a balance of $250,000 in equity only because of the addition to the

---

[2] Apparently the deferred payments have not been made. All but $100,000 of the deferred payments were designated as compensation for a non-competition agreement.

[4] While working capital advances were authorized up to $3.35 million, the Court has received no evidence on whether such advances were actually made.

asset side of the ledger the sum of $2,259,270 in goodwill. Both the selling shareholders and their attorney were experienced in LBOs, and the selling shareholders discussed this feature of the transaction, and their exposure on a fraudulent transfer claim, with their attorney on that date. With this information in hand, Younger, Smith and Dodson approved the terms of the sale.

In contrast to the selling shareholders, the industry did not know about the LBO character of the transaction until a number of months later. Shintech Corp., a creditor at the time of the transaction (and continuously thereafter), did not learn of it until ten months later, in August, 1989.

B. The Shintech Debt

Some three months before the LBO, on July 22, 1988, Bay Plastics entered into a requirements contract with Shintech to supply PVC resin. Shintech agreed under the contract to supply up to 2.6 million pounds of PVC resin per month on payment terms of 30 days after shipment. To induce Shintech to enter into this contract, Bay Plastics granted Shintech a security interest in all its assets, and the shareholders gave personal guaranties. This arrangement stood in the way of the BT transaction.

In consequence, the selling shareholders, their attorney, and Milhous representatives met with Shintech in late October, 1988 (after Milhous had disclosed to the selling shareholders the terms of the LBO), to arrange a new deal with Shintech. The parties to the LBO persuaded Shintech of Milhous' good credit, and induced Shintech to release both its security interest and the guaranties.[5] However, they did not disclose the LBO character of the transaction, and Shintech did not learn of this until ten months later.

The impact of this transaction on the balance sheet of Bay Plastics was dramatic. Immediately after the transaction, its balance sheet showed tangible assets of approximately $7 million, and liabilities of approximately $9 million. Only the addition of almost $2.26 million in goodwill, which had not appeared on prior balance sheets, and for which no explanation has been provided, permitted the balance sheet to show a modest shareholder equity of $250,000. But for the newly discovered goodwill, there would have been a net deficiency of some $2 million. In contrast, immediately before the transaction Bay Plastics had assets of $6.7 million and liabilities of $5.6 million, and a net equity of $1.1 million.

Bay Plastics was unable to service this overload of debt, and filed its bankruptcy petition fifteen months later. According to the debtor's schedules, at the

---

[5] In consequence of giving up its security and its guaranties, Shintech now holds more than 99% of the unsecured debt in this case.

time of filing its two principal creditors were BT and Shintech: it owed approximately $4 million in secured debt to BT, and $3.5 million in unsecured debt to Shintech. No other creditor was owed more than $20,000.

III. Discussion

The Bankruptcy Code gives a trustee the power to avoid a variety of kinds of prepetition transactions. Such transactions include preferential payments to creditors (§ 547), fraudulent transfers (§ 548), the fixing of statutory liens (§ 545), and setoffs (§ 553). A debtor in possession in a chapter 11 case has all of the rights (except the right to compensation) and the powers of a trustee under chapter 11. This includes the right to exercise the avoiding powers. Bankruptcy Code § 1107(a).

However, the debtor is unable to use the fraudulent transfer provision of the Bankruptcy Code (§ 548) in this case, because it is only applicable to transfers made or obligations incurred on or within one year before the date of the filing of the petition. § 548(a). Where state law provides a similar avoiding power to a creditor, on the other hand, Bankruptcy Code § 544(b)[7] permits a trustee (or a debtor in possession) to stand in the shoes of the creditor and to assert the same cause of action. *Kupetz v. Wolf*, 845 F.2d 842, 845 (9th Cir. 1988). Trustees and debtors in possession routinely utilize this provision to make fraudulent transfer claims under applicable state law, which typically provides a statute of limitations of four to seven years. *See, e.g.*, Cal.Civ.Code § 3439.09 (West Supp.1995). Thus the debtor has brought this adversary proceeding under § 544(b) and the UFTA as adopted in California.

A. Fraudulent Transfer Law

The purpose of fraudulent transfer law is to prevent a debtor from transferring away valuable assets in exchange for less than adequate value, if the transfer leaves insufficient assets to compensate honest creditors. * * *

Modern fraudulent transfer law traces its origins to a statute of Elizabeth enacted in 1570. This statute provided that a conveyance made "to the End, Purpose and Intent to delay, hinder or defraud creditors" is voidable. Courts often relied on circumstantial "badges of fraud" to presume fraudulent intent. *See, e.g.*, Twyne's Case, 76 Eng.Rep. 809, 810–14 (1601). The English law of fraudulent conveyance passed into the common law in the United States. This law was revised and codified by the National Conference of Commissioners on

---

[7] Section 544(b) provides:

The trustee may avoid any transfer of an interest of the debtor in property or any obligation incurred by the debtor that is voidable under applicable law by a creditor holding an unsecured claim. . . .

Uniform State Laws ("NCCUSL") in 1918, when it promulgated the Uniform Fraudulent Conveyance Act ("UFCA"). The UFCA was adopted by California in 1939, and by a number of other states on various dates.

The NCCUSL rewrote the UFCA and promulgated it as the UFTA in 1984. California adopted its version of the UFTA, which is applicable in this case, in 1986. Bankruptcy Code § 548 contains a similar fraudulent transfer provision.[9]

1. The Species of Fraudulent Transfer

A transfer or conveyance is fraudulent if it is (1) an intentional fraudulent transfer, i.e., a transfer made with the intent to defeat, hinder or delay creditors; or (2) a transfer that is constructively fraudulent because the debtor is in financial distress. There are three kinds of financial distress that make a transaction a fraudulent transfer: (a) a transfer while a debtor is insolvent or that renders a debtor insolvent; (b) a transfer that leaves a debtor undercapitalized or nearly insolvent (i.e., with insufficient assets to carry on its business); (c) a transfer when the debtor intends to incur debts beyond its ability to pay. See UFTA §§ 4, 5; UFCA § 4; Bankruptcy Code § 548(a). Constructive fraudulent transfer law applies without regard to intent (except the intent to incur debts in the last alternative). * * *

In this adversary proceeding the debtor relies on the first two varieties of constructive fraudulent transfer, and is entitled to prevail if either cause of action is upheld. The Court addresses only the first (a transfer that renders the debtor insolvent), because it finds that the debtor is entitled to prevail on this cause of action.

2. Fraudulent Transfer Resulting in Insolvency

The UFTA [§ 5(a)], adopted in California effective for transactions after January 1, 1987, provides in relevant part:

> A transfer made or obligation incurred by a debtor is fraudulent as to a creditor whose claim arose before the transfer was made or the obligation was incurred if the debtor made the transfer or incurred the obligation without receiving a reasonably equivalent value in exchange for the transfer or obligation and the debtor was insolvent at the time or the debtor became insolvent as a result of the transfer or obligation.

Cal.Civ.Code § 3439.05 (West Supp.1995).

---

[9] The Bankruptcy Code and its predecessor the Bankruptcy Act of 1898 have traditionally included their own fraudulent transfer provisions, because a number of states did not adopt the UFCA, and some have not yet adopted the UFTA.

3. Application of Fraudulent Transfer Law to LBOs

a. General

The basic structure of an LBO involves a transfer of corporate ownership financed primarily by the assets of the corporation itself.[11] Typically the corporation borrows the funds, secured by the assets of the corporation, and advances them to the purchasers, who use the funds to pay the purchase price to the selling shareholders. *Kathryn v. Smyser, Going Private and Going Under: Leveraged Buyouts and the Fraudulent Conveyance Problem*, 63 Ind.L.J. 781, 784–85 (1988). LBOs have two essential features:

> First, the purchaser acquires the funds necessary for the acquisition through borrowings secured directly or indirectly by the assets of the company being acquired. Second, the lender who provides such funds is looking primarily to the future operating earnings of the acquired company and/or to the proceeds from future sales of assets of the company, rather than to any other assets of the purchasers, to repay the borrowings used to effect the acquisition.

Id., at 785. LBO investors thus generally consider cash flow, the money available for working capital and debt service, as the most important factor in assessing a potential buyout candidate.

The application of fraudulent transfer law to LBOs has generated considerable debate among courts and commentators. LBOs were a popular form of consensual corporate takeover in the 1980's. They fell into disuse at the end of that decade for economic reasons. However, the use of the LBO as an acquisition device has recently become popular again. See Laura Jereski, *'Recaps' Are Secret Fuel for Leveraged Buyouts*, Wall St.J., July 25, 1995, at C1.

The LBO dates back long before the 1980's. In earlier years, it was known as a "bootstrap acquisition." Some of these transactions were invalidated as fraudulent conveyances. * * *

* * *

B. Trustee's Prima Facie Case

After having explored the applicable statutes and governing case law, the Court is now in position to apply this law to the facts of the instant case.

The Court notes at the outset that this case is not determined by the Ninth Circuit case law as set forth in *Lippi v. City Bank*, 955 F.2d 599 (9th Cir. 1992),

---

[11] While LBOs have frequently been used by management to buy out existing shareholders and take over the ownership of a business, management is not an essential party to an LBO. Indeed, in this case the purchaser was an outside third party.

and *Kupetz v. Wolf*, 845 F.2d 842 (9th Cir. 1988). Those cases both involved a fraudulent transfer attack on behalf of subsequent creditors. This case, in contrast, is brought for the principal benefit of a creditor existing at the time of the transaction, which holds more than 99% of the outstanding unsecured debt.

We begin with the elements of the cause of action under the UFTA § 5, as adopted in California, for a constructive fraudulent transfer rendering the debtor insolvent. The elements of a cause of action under this statute are as follows: the debtor (1) made a transfer or incurred an obligation, (2) without receiving a reasonably equivalent value in exchange, (3) which rendered the debtor insolvent (or the debtor was already insolvent),[22] and (4) which is attacked by a pre-transaction creditor.

1. Transfer or Obligation

The selling shareholders do not dispute that, in making the BT loan, the debtor made a transfer or incurred an obligation. In fact, the debtor did both. The debtor undertook the $3.95 million obligation to BT, it transferred a security interest in essentially all of its assets to BT, and it transferred $3.5 million ultimately to the selling shareholders. Thus the first element of the cause of action is satisfied.

2. Lack of Reasonably Equivalent Value

The selling shareholders likewise do not contest whether the debtor received reasonably equivalent value for the BT loan. However, this element is not apparent on its face.

Nominally, BT's transaction was only with Bay Plastics. It lent the $3.95 million *to the debtor*, the debtor promised to repay the loan, and the debtor gave a first priority security interest in essentially all of its assets to secure the repayment. If this were the transaction, creditors likely would have no grounds for complaint, and it would not be vulnerable to fraudulent transfer attack.

However, the foregoing structure obscures the reality of the transaction. The selling shareholders' transaction was formally with Milhous, and eventual-

---

[22] The definitions of insolvency under the various fraudulent transfer statutes differ. The UFCA adopts the "equity" or "cash flow" test of insolvency, under which a debtor is insolvent if the present fair salable value of the debtor's assets is less than the amount required to pay existing debts as they become due. UFCA § 2(a). The Bankruptcy Code § 101(32)(A) adopts the balance sheet definition of insolvency, under which a debtor is insolvent if the debtor's liabilities exceed the debtor's assets. § 101(32)(A). Under the UFTA, a debtor is insolvent if the debtor's liabilities exceed the debtor's assets (the balance sheet definition), and the debtor is presumed to be insolvent if the debtor is generally not paying his or her debts as they become due (the equity or cash flow test). UFTA § 2(a), (c).

ly with BPI, the new owner of Bay Plastics. BPI purchased their stock, and arranged for their payment with funds that Bay Plastics borrowed from BT. Before Bay Plastics received the funds, it directed that $3.5 million be transferred to its incoming parent, BPI, and BPI in turn directed that the funds be paid out for the stock purchase. Thus in substance $3.5 million of the funds that Bay Plastics borrowed from BT went to pay for the stock of the selling shareholders, rather than to Bay Plastics.

This raises the question whether the Court should collapse the various transactions in this case into one integrated transaction. Under *Lippi* this turns on whether, from the perspective of the selling shareholders, the transaction appeared to be a straight sale without an LBO. *Lippi*, 955 F.2d at 612. If, in contrast, there is evidence that the parties knew or should have known that the transaction would deplete the assets of the company, the Court should look beyond the formal structure. *Id*. In *Kupetz* the Ninth Circuit found it improper to collapse the transactions where the selling shareholders had no knowledge of the LBO character of the transaction, and there were no pre-transaction creditors.

In this case, in contrast, the selling shareholders had full knowledge that this was an LBO. The Milhous representatives informed them of this at the October 25 meeting before the transaction was finalized, and it was disclosed in the financial projections provided at that time. In addition, the selling shareholders discussed this feature with their legal counsel on October 25, and specifically discussed their exposure to a fraudulent transfer claim. Both the selling shareholders and their legal counsel were familiar with leveraged buyouts, because they had done others previously, and they knew the fraudulent transfer risks.

This knowledge of the selling shareholders distinguishes this case from both *Kupetz* (where the selling shareholders did not know or have reason to know of the LBO) and from *Lippi* (where the evidence was disputed). Instead, this case is like *In re Richmond Produce Co.*, 151 B.R. 1012 (Bankr.N.D.Cal.1993), *United States v. Tabor Court Realty Corp.*, 803 F.2d 1288 (3d Cir. 1986), and *Wieboldt Stores, Inc. v. Schottenstein*, 94 B.R. 488 (N.D.Ill.1988), where the transaction was collapsed because of the knowledge of the selling shareholders.

In addition, because Shintech qualifies as a pre-transaction creditor, the Court does not need to reach the issue of the knowledge of the LBO feature of the transaction by the selling shareholders: this is material to whether the transaction's various parts should be collapsed only when challenged by post-transaction creditors.

Thus, in this case the Court finds it appropriate to collapse the various pieces of this transaction into one integral transaction, in which the funds went to the selling shareholders, not to Bay Plastics or to its new parent BPI. The loan obligation, in contrast, was undertaken by Bay Plastics, which also provided the security for the loan.

Bay Plastics received no reasonably equivalent value for the security interest in all of its assets that it gave to BT in exchange for BT's funding of the stock sale. Under California law, reasonable equivalence must be determined from the standpoint of creditors. *Hansen v. Cramer*, 39 Cal.2d 321 (1952) (applying rule to "fair consideration" under predecessor statute) * * *. The Ninth Circuit has adopted the same view in interpreting the California version of the UFTA. * * * Payment of funds to a parent corporation prevents a transaction from satisfying the "reasonably equivalent value" requirement. A financially healthy entity may give away its assets as it pleases so long as there remains enough to pay its debts. A financially distressed donor, however, may not be so generous.

From the debtor's perspective, it is apparent that the $450,000 that Bay Plastics presumably received (the $3.95 million loan less the $3.5 million paid to the selling shareholders) is not reasonably equivalent to the $3.95 million obligation that it undertook. *Cf. Shape, Inc. v. Midwest Engineering (In re Shape, Inc.)*, 176 B.R. 1, 3 (Bankr.D.Me.1994) (payment of $70,000 for stock worth more than $1.5 million lacks reasonably equivalent value). Thus Bay Plastics did not receive reasonably equivalent value for the loan obligation and security interest that it granted to BT.

3. Insolvency of the Debtor

The third element of the fraudulent transfer cause of action at issue in this litigation is that the transaction rendered the debtor insolvent, if it was not so already. In this case the Court finds the evidence undisputed that the LBO rendered the debtor insolvent.

Insolvency is defined in California Civil Code § 3439.02(a) (West Supp.1995): "A debtor is insolvent if, at fair valuations, the sum of the debtor's debts is greater than all of the debtor's assets." UFTA § 2(a) is essentially the same. These statutes adopt the balance sheet test for insolvency: a debtor is insolvent if the liabilities exceed the assets.

The usual starting point for determining the sufficiency of assets is the balance sheet, particularly if the balance sheet is prepared according to generally accepted accounting principles consistently applied. * * * However, these principles do not control a court's decision regarding the solvency of an entity. * * *

The valuation of assets for insolvency purposes is based on "a fair valuation." This differs from a balance sheet, where most assets apart from publicly traded stocks and bonds are carried at historic cost, rather than current market value. The values of assets must be updated in light of subsequent use and market conditions: in accounting parlance, they must be "marked to market."

In addition, a balance sheet may include intangible assets such as goodwill[24] that may have no liquidation or going concern value, and which thus must be deleted in evaluating the solvency of an entity. Goodwill cannot be sold to satisfy a creditor's claim. Thus, in a liquidation bankruptcy case it must be disregarded in determining solvency of the debtor at the time of an LBO.

Nominally, Bay Plastic's corporate balance sheet showed the debtor to be solvent after the LBO. But this resulted only from the addition of $2.26 million of goodwill to the asset side of the balance sheet. Bay Plastics had not previously carried any goodwill on its balance sheets.

The parties to this litigation have accepted the debtor's balance sheet immediately after the LBO as a fair presentation of the debtor's financial status, with the exception of goodwill. Thus the Court is relieved of the burden of marking to market the debtor's assets. However, the trustee contends that the goodwill of $2.26 million that first appeared at that time must be deleted in determining the debtor's solvency.

The Court finds that the balance sheet must be adjusted by deleting the unamortized goodwill of $2.26 million. It was not carried on the balance sheet before the LBO, and in any case it could not be sold to satisfy a creditor's claim. † † † This is a liquidation case, where goodwill has no other value. This downward adjustment left Bay Plastics with a negative net worth of approximately $2 million immediately after the LBO. For fraudulent transfer purposes, it was rendered insolvent by the transaction.

---

[24] Goodwill is generally understood to represent the value of intangible factors that are expected to translate into greater than normal earning power. In addition to the advantageous relationship that a business enjoys with its customers, goodwill also includes advantageous relationships with employees, suppliers, lenders and others. * * *

Because goodwill has no independent market or liquidation value, generally accepted accounting principles require that goodwill be written off over a period of time. In acquisition accounting, going concern value in excess of asset value is treated as goodwill. Dictionary of Finance & Investment Terms 157 (2d ed. 1987).

Goodwill frequently appears on a balance sheet after the sale of a business, where it represents the excess of the purchase price over the net value of the other assets purchased. * * * It appears that this may be the explanation for the appearance of goodwill on the debtor's balance sheet in this case.

Indeed, this is exactly the type of transaction that poses the extreme risk of an LBO. No Milhous entity put any funds or assets at risk in the investment at all. In consequence of the structure of the transaction, all of the risks of the enterprise were placed on its creditors. Milhous retained only the right to reap the benefits if the business was sufficiently profitable to avoid bankruptcy.[25]

4. Attack by a Pre–Transaction Creditor

The final element of the cause of action for fraudulent transfer rendering a debtor insolvent is that the transaction must be attacked by a pre-transaction creditor. This element is satisfied in this case.

Shintech, the principal unsecured creditor in this case, which holds more than 99% of the unsecured debt, is the pre-existing creditor. It was secured until this transaction, and in addition it held guaranties from each of the selling shareholders. In this transaction the selling shareholders and Milhous induced it to relinquish its security and guaranties to permit the transaction to be consummated. Although knowing the LBO character of the transaction, both the selling shareholders and Milhous failed to disclose this feature to Shintech.

* * *

C. Application of Fraudulent Transfer Law to LBOs

The Court finds it appropriate to apply fraudulent transfer law to an LBO. An LBO is different, not just in degree, but in character from the ordinary business and investment transactions engaged in by a corporation's management. An LBO is not a routine business transaction that should normally be given deference by the courts. It is not a corporate investment in a new venture, new equipment or property. Indeed, an LBO normally does not affect the business of the corporation at all: it only changes the ownership and adds a large layer of secured debt. Rather, an LBO is an investment of corporate assets, by borrowing against them, for the *personal* benefit of both old and new equity owners. Thus, the application of fraudulent transfer law to LBOs does not limit corporate entrepreneurial decisions.

Since an LBO reduces the availability of unencumbered assets, the buyout depletes estate assets available to pay creditors' claims. As the Ninth Circuit has stated:

---

[25] In such a transaction there is a danger that the selling shareholders will be paid more than their stock is worth. With nothing at risk if the business is not sufficiently profitable, the purchaser has less incentive to make sure that the price is not excessive. Absent fraudulent transfer law, there is nothing to deter the buyers, sellers and bank from imposing all of the risks of loss on the creditors, as they did in this case.

Existing unsecured creditors are vulnerable in [an LBO]. From their perspective, a pledge of the company's assets as collateral to finance the purchase of the company reduces the assets to which they can look for repayment.

Kupetz, 845 F.2d at 846; *accord, Moody v. Security Pacific Business Credit, Inc.*, 971 F.2d 1056, 1073 (3d Cir. 1992). An LBO is attractive to the sellers, the buyers and the lender because it shifts most of the risk of loss to other creditors of the corporation. *Mellon Bank v. Metro Communications, Inc.*, 945 F.2d 635 (3d Cir. 1991). The acquired corporation receives little or nothing in exchange for the debt that it incurs.

From a creditor's point of view, an LBO is indistinguishable from a distribution or a gift to shareholders. The harm is quite like the harm imposed on creditors by donative transfers to third parties, which is one of the most traditional kinds of fraudulent transfers.[30] If the value of the security interest given by the corporation does not exceed the shareholders' equity as shown on the balance sheet (after suitable revisions to mark the assets to market and to eliminate intangible assets of dubious value), there is usually no substantial harm to creditors. Indeed, typical corporate distribution statutes permit the payment of dividends in such circumstances, to the extent of the balance sheet equity. *See, e.g.,* Cal.Corp.Code § 166 (West Supp.1995). If the price paid to selling shareholders is higher, however, there may be insufficient assets remaining to satisfy creditors.

The vice of an LBO lies in the fact that the selling shareholders are paid indirectly with assets from the corporation itself, rather than by the purchasers. In effect, in an LBO the shareholders are paid with a corporate dividend or distribution. An LBO enables the selling shareholders to liquidate their equity interests, which are otherwise subordinate to general unsecured claims, without first paying creditors, which a normal liquidation would require. The selling shareholders in the transaction in effect disregard the status of the corporation as a separate entity for their benefit, but insist on respect of the corporation's separate status when it comes to creditors' claims (apart from those of the lender providing the funds for the transaction).

The possible detriment to creditors is exacerbated if the corporation's cash flow is not sufficient to service the loan. The bank eventually proceeds to foreclose on the corporation's assets and sells them at foreclosure prices, and

---

[30] David Epstein and his co-authors state: "[The creditors] are harmed just as much as if the debtor had given away the equity in its assets as a gift." Epstein, [Bankruptcy], § 6–52 at 69.

leaves nothing for other creditors. Such foreclosure is frequently interrupted by the filing of a bankruptcy case. So it happened in this case.

Most courts that have considered the issue have decided that fraudulent transfer law should apply to LBOs. * * * In fact, despite the reservations expressed in *Kupetz, supra*, and, 629 F.Supp. 175 (C.D.Cal.1985), there appears to be no published opinion to *Credit Managers Ass'n of Southern California v. Federal Co.*the contrary.[31]

It does not follow, however, that the fraudulent transfer analysis of an LBO will result in a recovery for the benefit of the bankruptcy estate. In both *Moody* and *Mellon Bank* the Third Circuit upheld the transactions at issue against the fraudulent transfer attack. In *Lippi*, similarly, the Ninth Circuit ruled in favor of some of the defendants, and remanded for further consideration as to the remainder.

Should all LBO's be exposed to fraudulent transfer challenge? Certainly not. Under this Court's analysis, two kinds of LBO's ordinarily escape fraudulent transfer attack. This includes many, if not most, LBOs.[32]

First, in a legitimate LBO, in which the assets mortgaged by a corporation to support an LBO do not exceed the net equity of the business (after appropriate adjustments), the transaction will not make the corporation insolvent, at least according to the balance sheet test.[34] If in addition it has sufficient projected cash flow to pay its debts as they come due, the cash flow solvency test

---

[31] *But see Kaiser Steel Corp. v. Pearl Brewing Co. (In re Kaiser Steel Corp.)*, 952 F.2d 1230 (10th Cir.1991), where the court held that the trustee could not recover from selling shareholders of a publicly traded corporation because their payments constituted non-avoidable "settlement payments" under Bankruptcy Code § 546(e).

[32] In *Credit Managers Association v. Federal Co.*, 629 F.Supp. 175, 179 (C.D.Cal.1985), a district judge in this district stated, "it is not at all clear that fraudulent conveyance law is broadly applicable to [LBOs]." That court relied substantially on Baird & Jackson, [38 Vand.L.Rev. 829 (1985)] Ten years of court decisions and scholarly commentary since that decision have helped to refine the application of fraudulent transfer law to LBOs. Even the *Credit Managers* court, however, apparently would permit pre-transaction creditors, such as exist in this case, to attack an LBO.

[34] It makes sense to limit legitimate LBOs to transactions that do not leave a corporation insolvent. In a perfect world (as typically assumed by economists), an LBO would never run afoul of this rule, because the price paid for the stock would be the net equity in the firm. Baird & Jackson, [38 Vand.L.Rev.] at 851. Such an LBO would place the corporation on the verge of insolvency, but not beyond. In the real world, some LBOs leave corporations insolvent, perhaps because of imperfect information about the value of the corporation's stock.

is met, also. This leaves an LBO exposed to fraudulent transfer attack only if the margin of equity is too thin to support the corporation's business.

A second kind of LBO also escapes fraudulent transfer attack, even though it leaves the subject corporation insolvent. If the cash flow is sufficient to make the debt payments, the transaction also is unassailable. This ordinarily turns on two factors: the degree of risk of default undertaken in the first instance, and the degree to which projected economic developments impacting the business are not overly optimistic. These LBOs escape fraudulent transfer attack either because of good financial projections or because of good luck: either factor is sufficient.

The Court's view of the proper application of fraudulent transfer law to LBO's does not make the selling shareholders the guarantors of the success of the LBO. A legitimate LBO, as described supra, shifts the risk of failure off their shoulders. As to subsequent creditors, they should not be required to shoulder the risk if the failure is caused by outside forces not reasonably foreseeable at the time of the transaction. *Moody v. Security Pacific Business Credit, Inc.*, 971 F.2d 1056, 1073 (3d Cir. 1992) (failure caused by increased competition rather than lack of capital) * * *.

However, an LBO that is leveraged beyond the net worth of the business is a gamble. A highly leveraged business is much less able to weather temporary financial storms, because debt demands are less flexible than equity interest. The risks of this gamble should rest on the shoulders of the shareholders (old and new), not those of the creditors: the shareholders enjoy the benefits if the gamble is successful, and they should bear the burdens if it is not. This, after all, is the role of equity owners of a corporation. The application of fraudulent transfer law to LBOs shifts the risks of an LBO transaction from the creditors, who are not parties to the transaction, back to the old and new shareholders who bring about such transactions. As Sherwin states:

> These parties, who are directly involved as the principal engineers and beneficiaries of the buyout, should bear the risk of negative consequences if the transaction does not in fact comply with the standards for creditor protection set out in the fraudulent conveyance statutes. . . . They should be accountable to creditors for the benefits diverted from the corporation if they knew or should have known. . . of facts the court determines to establish a constructive fraud against creditors.

Sherwin, [72 Minn.L.Rev.] at 519.

How long should selling shareholders be exposed to the risk that an LBO will go bad? There is a traditional answer to this question: until the statute of limitations runs. Perhaps there should be a shorter statute of limitations for

LBOs than the four to seven years that is common under the UFTA. This is a decision for the legislature to make.

The Court perceives no unfairness in imposing the risks of an overleveraged LBO on the old and new shareholders who undertake the risks, rather on the creditors who do not intend to do so. Indeed, it is the selling shareholders who are ordinarily least worthy of sympathy in an LBO. As Epstein states:

> In the beginning of the transaction they are below existing creditors. In the end, they "cash out" and march off over the heads of the existing creditors. It is a neat trick of legal magic that allows the shareholders to subordinate, unilaterally, the creditors' claims.

2 Epstein, [Bankruptcy], at 74.

D. Good Faith Defense

The selling shareholders claim that they acted in good faith, and that this is a defense to the fraudulent transfer claim. From the earliest fraudulent transfer statutes, a good faith transferee for value has enjoyed an affirmative defense to the cause of action. *See, e.g.*, 13 Stat.Eliz. ch. 5, § 6 (1570). However, this defense has been greatly restricted in recent statutes.

The UFTA, including California's version thereof, provides a complete defense to an intentional fraudulent transfer for a transferee who took "in good faith and for a reasonably equivalent value." UFTA § 8(a); * * *. This defense is not available for a constructive fraudulent conveyance, and thus is not applicable in this adversary proceeding.

A second good faith provision is contained in UFTA § 8(d) and the California Civil Code, which provide:

> Notwithstanding voidability of a transfer or an obligation under this chapter, a good faith transferee or obligee is entitled, *to the extent of the value given the debtor* for the transfer or obligation, to the following:
>
> **(1)** A lien on or a right to retain any interest in the asset transferred.
>
> **(2)** Enforcement of any obligation incurred.
>
> **(3)** A reduction in the amount of the liability on the judgment.

UFCA § 8(d) * * * (emphasis added).[36]

In this case the selling shareholders gave up their shares of stock in the debtor in exchange for their payment of $3.5 million. However, this provision is

---

[36] Bankruptcy Code § 548(c) provides a transferee with a similar defense to a fraudulent conveyance claim to the extent of the value given to the debtor if such transferee acted in good faith.

not applicable in this case, because the shareholders did not transfer their shares or give any other value *to the debtor*. The shares went to BPI, the new parent corporation of Bay Plastics, and from there to Milhous. The debtor itself received neither shares nor money. This did not constitute "value given the debtor", within the meaning of UFTA § 8(d) or California Civil Code § 3439.08(d). Thus the good faith defense fails.

IV. Conclusion

Having found no triable issue of material fact, the Court concludes that the trustee is entitled to a summary judgment setting aside the constructive fraudulent transfer in this case to the selling shareholders. After having collapsed the series of transactions into a single transaction, the Court finds that in substance the selling shareholders received payment for their shares that was secured by the assets of debtor, and that this transaction defrauded an existing creditor. The payment to the selling shareholders is thus avoidable under UFTA § 5, as adopted in California in California Civil Code § 3439.05, which in turn is incorporated in Bankruptcy Code § 544(b).

NOTE

Under the court's reasoning, would BT's security interest have been subject to avoidance had it not settled with the trustee? Would Bay Plastic's obligation be avoidable as well, leaving BT without even an unsecured claim in Bay Plastic's bankruptcy? If this case had been brought under § 548, would § 548(c) have been of any help to BT? Were Bay Plastic's $3.5 million obligation to BT avoided, the effect would be to increase Bay Plastic's equity by that amount, giving the acquirer, BPI, a huge windfall. Would a better result be to subordinate BT's claim to that of Shintech and the other creditors under the broad powers given courts under § 105(a) or the principles of equitable subordination pursuant to § 510(c) that we will discuss in the next chapter? *See In re Pajaro Dunes Rental Agency, Inc.*, 174 B.R. 557 (Bankr.N.D.Cal.1994). For a comprehensive treatment of the remedial issues raised by fraudulent transfer avoidance of leveraged buyouts see Robert J. White, *Leveraged Buyouts and Fraudulent Conveyance Laws Under the Bankruptcy Code—Like Oil and Water, They Just Don't Mix*, 1991 Ann.Surv.Am.L. 357. *See also Zahn v. Yucaipa Capital Fund*, 218 B.R. 656, 664 (D.R.I. 1998) (permitting avoidance recovery to be shared between plan proponent and unsecured creditors).

a. Insolvency

However sophisticated the structure of the LBO transaction, one must assume that a bankruptcy court may look through the form of the transaction and conclude that the target corporation did not receive reasonably equivalent value.

Given this possibility, lenders and selling stockholders are never really safe in an LBO transaction (until the statute of limitations has run) unless the target corporation can pass all the solvency tests prescribed by § 548(a)(1)(B)(ii) and any applicable under state law in bankruptcy through § 544(b). The "bankruptcy" test of insolvency is found in § 101(32) ("insolvent") ("the sum of such entity's debts is greater than all of such entity's property, at a fair valuation"). This test must be contrasted with the "equity" test, which finds insolvency when a debtor is unable to pay debts as they become due, that is often applicable under state fraudulent transfer laws. UFTA § 2. A functionally similar test is found in the "unreasonably small capital" requirement of § 548(a)(1)(B)(ii)(II) and UFTA § 5.

Since, as *Bay Plastics* points out, the expectation in LBOs is usually that the acquisition debt is to be paid out of the earnings of the acquired company, it is fair to say that the key inquiry that courts make about the solvency of the acquired company is whether it is left with the ability to generate sufficient profits after paying its debts (including acquisition-related debt) to sustain operations. From this, courts reason that a business debtor is left with adequate capital only when its projected cash flow is sufficient to meet its reasonably foreseeable obligations, particularly those arising from the LBO transaction. The best judicial discussion of the issue is found in *Moody v. Security Pacific Business Credit, Inc.*, 971 F.2d 1056 (3d Cir. 1992). *See* Bruce A. Markell, *Toward True and Plain Dealing: A Theory of Fraudulent Transfers Involving Unreasonably Small Capital*, 21 Ind.L.Rev. 469 (1988).

As the court explains in *Moody*, the equity test of insolvency and the unreasonably small capital test are not identical. The latter test requires that after the transfer the debtor have a reasonable likelihood of continuing to meet its obligations. Immediately after an LBO, a debtor can be solvent under the equity test in that it is able to pay its debts then coming due but still can be left with unreasonably small capital because its projected cash flow in the future may be insufficient to meet its future obligations. If the target company fails because of unforeseen adverse changes in its business, a court may uphold the LBO if its cash flow projections were reasonable at the time made. Of course, cash flow projections cannot rely on historical data alone; they must contain some margin for error regarding economic trends, interest rate fluctuations, and the like.

b. The Innocent Shareholder Defense

Section 548(c) extends protection against avoidance to transferees or obligees who take for value and in good faith. On the face of it, this provision should not protect selling stockholders from having to disgorge in cases like *Bay Plastics*, in which the court has "collapsed" the transaction, because the transfer is treated as a corporate distribution to the selling stockholders for which they gave no value to the debtor corporation. Nevertheless, some courts have conceived an "innocent shareholder" defense that absolves selling stockholders from having to disgorge if they can distance themselves from the LBO transaction. Michael L. Cook, et al., *The Judicially Created "Innocent Shareholder" Defense to Constructive Fraudulent Transfer Liability in Failed Leveraged Buyouts*, 43 S.C.L.Rev. 777 (1992).

The courts are divided on parameters of the judge-made innocent shareholder defense. In recent years judicial attention has turned to § 546(e), which offers a safe harbor against exercise by the trustee of the avoiding powers in certain commodity and securities transactions:

Notwithstanding [the avoiding powers] the trustee may not avoid a transfer that is a margin payment ... or *settlement payment*, as defined in section 101 or 741 of this title, made by or to (or for the benefit of) a commodity broker, forward contract merchant, stockbroker, *financial institution*, financial participant, or securities clearing agency, ...

Apparently the provision was enacted to alleviate the concern of Congress about upsetting transactions in the public commodities and security markets. The fear was that those markets would be disrupted by a major bankruptcy that might result in the avoidance of settled securities transactions. The case that focused attention on § 546(e) was *In re Kaiser Steel Corp.*, 952 F.2d 1230 (10th Cir. 1991), that involved an LBO in which the old stockholders cashed out by selling their stock to investors through a financial intermediary that distributed the proceeds of the sale to brokers holding the accounts of the selling stockholders. The issue was whether the distribution of the proceeds of the sale of the stock to the old stockholders through financial intermediaries was a settlement payment within § 546(e). The court held that it was and that the old stockholders were protected against the trustee's avoiding powers because there had been a settlement payment through a financial institution.

In re Munford, Inc., 98 F.3d 604 (11th Cir. 1996), took another view and held that LBO payments received by selling stockholders were not covered by § 546(e) because the financial institutions involved never acquired a beneficial interest in the property transferred; they were merely conduits. *In re Resorts International, Inc.*, 181 F.3d 505 (3d Cir. 1999), rejected *Munford* as reading into § 546(e) a beneficial interest requirement that is not justified by the plain wording of the statute. The court endorsed *Kaiser Steel*.

The current state of case law on § 546(e) divides on the issue whether the statute should apply to transactions like private LBOs or should be reserved for settlements involving publicly traded securities in which the securities clearance and settlement system is involved. *In re Grand Eagle Companies, Inc.*, 288 B.R. 484 (Bankr.N.D.Ohio 2003) and *In re Norstan Apparel Shops, Inc.*, 367

B.R. 68 (Bankr.E.D.N.Y.2007), take the view that § 546(e) should not apply to LBOs of private companies. The court in *Grand Eagle* says that applying to § 546(e) to private transactions "would, essentially, convert that statutory provision into a blanket transactional cleansing mechanism for any entity savvy enough to funnel payments for the purchase and sale of privately held stock through a financial institution." 288 B.R. at 494.

The contrary view is stated in *QSI Holdings, Inc. v. Alford*, 382 B.R. 731 (W.D. Mich. 2007), an LBO case, which reaches a result closely resembling that disparaged in the quotation above. According to the court, the plain meaning of the statute is that the § 546(e) exemption applies even when the securities are privately held and the centralized clearance system is not involved. The breadth of the statute makes such an interpretation possible and the court states that the majority of district court cases support this view.

It is not clear why Congress would wish to insulate selling shareholders in private LBO transactions by an exemption from the trustee's avoiding powers so long as they run their transaction through a financial institution. The definition of "settlement payment" in § 741(8) ends with "or any other similar payment commonly used in the *securities trade*." If the purpose of § 546(e) is to protect the securities markets from disruptions caused by major bankruptcies, that purpose is in no way advanced by its application to private transactions like that in *QSI*. Granting safe harbor in such cases allows the parties to immunize common transactions against the avoiding powers on no cogent policy basis, unless there is actual fraud in the transaction under § 548(a)(1)(A). *See* Christopher W. Frost, *Settlement Payments and the Safe Harbor of Section 546(e)*, 28 Bankr. L. Ltr. No. 5 (May 2008).

c. Special Defenses for Counterparties to Swaps, Derivatives, Repurchase Agreements and Other Financial Contracts

Over the last 20 years, there has been unceasing pressure from Wall Street to protect innovative financial engineering products from bankruptcy generally and in particular from bankruptcy's automatic stay and avoiding powers. See p. 182. Section 546(e) which even under its narrowest interpretation shields financial institutions operating in established securities and publicly commodities markets from avoidance liability (except in certain cases of actual fraud, *see Bear Stearns Securities Corp. v. Gredd*, 397 B.R. 1 (S.D.N.Y.2007), is the acorn from which has sprung a mighty oak whose interrelated branches include special protections not only for those dealing in traditional securities and commodities markets, but a welter of specialized provisions relating to repurchase agreements and reverse purchase agreements (functionally, loans secured by marketable securities, *see In re Bevill, Bresler & Schulman Asset Mgmt. Corp.*, 878 F.2d 742, 743 (3d Cir. 1989)), swaps, options, and futures. See §§ 101(22), (22A), (25), (26), (38), (38A), (38B), (46), (47), (49), (51A),

(53A)-(53C), 546(g), 546(j), 548(d)(2)(D), 555, 556, 559-562. The gist of all of these provisions is that those who deal in these complex financial instruments are entitled to enforce the terms of their contracts, including any "master netting agreement" under which they are issued, in accordance with otherwise applicable nonbankruptcy law and without regard to the automatic stay, avoiding powers and other aspects of bankruptcy law. A full examination of how these complex financial instruments operate outside bankruptcy law, and the implications that various bankruptcy law doctrines pose for these instruments, are outside the scope of this course. Compare Note 5, p. 462, discussing treatment of securitizations in the context of substantive consolidation. So long as these special protections were confined exclusively to the realm of high finance, they coexisted, albeit in some cases uneasily, with traditional bankruptcy law which governed the rights and liabilities of those in traditional commercial relationships.

In 2005, however, under further pressure from Wall Street to ensure that bankruptcy law would not adversely affect traders in the ever expanding dominion of these new financial instruments, BAPCPA radically expanded the definition of "swap agreement" in ways that potentially divorce the special bankruptcy protections afforded "swap agreements" under § 546(g) from the common understanding of "swap" and potentially opens up this special exemption from avoiding power liability to those in a wide variety of traditional commercial relationships with a bankruptcy debtor. *In re National Gas Distributors LLC*, 369 B.R. 884 (Bankr.E.D.N.C.2007), was an early attempt to reconcile the BAPCPA amendment to the definition of "swap agreement" with the traditional understanding of the scope of the avoiding powers. The bankruptcy court found that an ordinary supply contract contemplating the physical delivery of natural gas in fixed quantities at a fixed price and time that was not traded in the financial markets was not a "swap agreement" under the seemingly all encompassing post-2005 definition.

The Fourth Circuit reversed and remanded, *In re Natural Gas Distributors LLC*, 556 F.3d 247 (4th Cir. 2009), finding no statutory requirement that a "swap agreement" be a contract of a type that is traded in financial markets or not involve the physical delivery of the commodity at issue. Acknowledging that "the potpourri of agreements included in the term 'swap agreement' barely distinguish any major commercial contract from a swap agreement" and that the bankruptcy court on remand faced an "imperfect statute" with little in the way of case authority or marketplace definitions to look to for guidance, the Fourth Circuit nevertheless did not provide a definition for the bankruptcy court to apply, noting that to qualify as a commodity forward contract an agreement had to at a minimum involve sale of a commodity in the future at a fixed price, fixed quantity and fixed time. "Thus, insofar as our holding precludes the bankruptcy court from requiring, in defining a 'commodity forward agreement' that the contract be traded in a market or on an exchange or that it not involve physical delivery of the commodity, our holding does not define that instrument or hold that the contracts in this case are commodity forward agreements. We leave that to further legal and factual development on remand." 556 F.3d at 260-261.

7. INSIDER PREFERENCES

A classic form of preference is one in which an insider creditor receives payment or security from an insolvent corporation that is sinking into bankruptcy. "Insider" is broadly defined in § 101(31). With respect to corporations, the term includes affiliates, officers, directors, and persons in control. These persons may have superior information about the financial position of the corporation and may also have the power to cause the corporation to make the payment or grant the security more than 90 days before the the corporation files in bankruptcy. Section 547(b)(4)(B) addresses this issue by fixing a one year reach-back period for insider preferences.

A familiar insider preference issue involves guarantees by insiders of loans made to the debtor corporation. Lenders are often reluctant to lend to smaller corporations unless the owners personally guarantee the loan. How does the Code deal with the following cases?

Case #1. CEO is the president of and principal stockholder in Ajax Corporation. Bank made a loan to Ajax, which CEO guaranteed. On May 1, CEO caused Ajax, then insolvent, to repay the loan to Bank. Upon payment, CEO was released from the guarantee. After Ajax filed in bankruptcy on July 1, Trustee proceeded under § 550(a) against CEO to avoid the payment that Ajax made to Bank. Can Trustee recover the money from either Bank or CEO? Yes, it may recover from either one. Under § 547(b)(1), the payment was preferential with respect to both Bank and CEO as it was "to" Bank and "for the benefit of" CEO. Under § 550(a)(1), the trustee may recover the money from either Bank (the initial transferee) or CEO (the entity for whose benefit the transfer was made).

Case #2. If the loan had been repaid on February 1, instead of May 1, can Trustee recover from CEO? Yes, the payment was made within the one-year reach-back period under § 547(4)(B) that applies to insiders.

Case #3. Under the same facts, can Trustee recover from Bank? Prior to 1989, the traditional view was that since Bank is not an insider, no preference occurs because the 90-day reach-back period of § 547(b)(4)(A) applies. Thus, 90 days after the date of the payment, Banks understood that they were protected from a preference challenge even though the debtor was insolvent at the time of the payment.

Levit v. Ingersoll Rand Financial Corp., 874 F.2d 1186 (7th Cir. 1989) (the case is often referred to by the name of the debtor "*Deprizio*"), a seminal decision, held that the plain meaning of § 550(a)(1) was that both an insider and noninsider "initial transferee" had liability for insider preferences. A firestorm ensued on the part of lenders. One of the strongest forces in moving the Bankruptcy Reform Act of 1994 through Congress was creditor dislike of *Levit.*

The 1994 Reform Act added subsection § 550(c):

(c) If a transfer made between 90 days and one year before the filing of the petition—

(1) is avoided under section 547(b) of this title; and

(2) was made for the benefit of a creditor that at the time of such transfer was an insider;

the trustee may not recover under subsection (a) from a transferee that is not an insider.

Subsequent to the enactment of § 550(c), a division of authority developed over whether trustees could avoid security interests granted to noninsider transferees even if they could not recover payments since the avoidance of security interests (as opposed to the recovery of payments) was governed by § 547, not § 550(c). BAPCPA closed the remaining loophole by adding § 547(i):

If the trustee avoids under subsection (b) a transfer made between 90 days and 1 year before the date of filing of the petition, by the debtor to an entity that is not an insider for the benefit of a creditor that is an insider, such transfer shall be considered to be avoided under this section only with respect to the creditor that is an insider.

D. THE STRONG-ARM CLAUSE

1. INTRODUCTION

a. Section 544(a)(1)

This provision arms the trustee with the powers of a hypothetical lien creditor under state law. Any actual knowledge that the trustee or creditors may have is irrelevant. Its principal application is to empower trustees to avoid unperfected security interests in personal property. We have seen that under bankruptcy law secured claims are prior to unsecured claims, thus a creditor holding a security interest in all the debtor's personal property, now owned or thereafter acquired, can clean out the estate, leaving the unsecured creditors with nothing. UCC Article 9 enables creditors to take security interests in all the personal property, tangible or intangible, that a debtor owns or will acquire in the future. The major weapon that trustees can use to attack Article 9 security interests is the strong arm clause of § 544(a)(1), which allows for invalidation of unperfected security interests in personal property.

Perfection under Article 9 is usually done by filing an appropriate financing statement; trustees assiduously examine the filing documentation in search of errors. The effect of avoiding a security interest in bankruptcy is to relegate the secured creditor to the status of an unsecured creditor who will share with the other general creditors.

In re Bell, 194 B.R. 192, 195 (Bankr.S.D.Ill.1996), explains the application of § 544(a)(1):

> Section 544(a)(1) provides that a bankruptcy trustee acquires, as of the commencement of a case, the status of a hypothetical judicial lien creditor and "may avoid" any lien or encumbrance on property of the debtor that is voidable by such a creditor under state law. Under this provision, federal and state law work in tandem. First, the substance of the trustee's rights as judicial lien creditor—primarily the priority of his claim in relation to other interests in the property—is determined by reference to state law. If the trustee has priority over a third party's interest under state law, federal law prescribes the consequence. Under § 544(a)(1), the trustee may entirely avoid the inferior third-party interest in the property, and the third party is left with only an unsecured claim against the debtor's estate. * * *

Sections 546(b) and 362(b)(3) allow perfection after bankruptcy to defeat the rights of the trustee under § 544(a)(1) in cases in which the applicable nonbankruptcy law gives retroactive effect to the perfection. An example is UCC § 9-317(e). If a purchase money security interest is perfected by filing within 20 days of the debtor's taking of possession of the collateral, the security interest is good in bankruptcy even if the debtor goes into bankruptcy before the filing is made.

b. Section 544(a)(3)

Subsection 544(a)(3) arms trustees with the powers of a bona fide purchaser of real estate. This provision is important because of a discontinuity between the UCC (governing personal property) and most states' real property law. Although judicial lien creditors defeat unperfected security interests in personalty, in most states an unrecorded mortgage on real property has priority over a subsequent judicial lien. But an unrecorded mortgage is normally not enforceable against a subsequent bona fide purchaser of the real property. By virtue of § 544(a)(3), unrecorded mortgages are invalidated in bankruptcy if under the nonbankruptcy law they are subject to the rights of a bona fide purchaser of the real property. "Purchaser" means any voluntary transferee including an encumbrancer (§ 101(43)). "Transfer" is defined in § 101(54). In this way, the holder of an unrecorded mortgage is put on the same footing as the holder of an unperfected UCC security interest. But, as we shall see, in solving this particular problem, § 544(a)(3) creates other discontinuities in the treatment of real and personal property in bankruptcy.

2. KNOWLEDGE OF THE TRUSTEE IN BANKRUPTCY

Although the strong arm clause is primarily directed at secret liens, its language also covers other obligations or transfers of the debtor that are voidable by bona fide purchasers of real property or judicial lienholders. The case that follows is illustrates the limits of the strong arm clause. .

McCannon v. Marston

United States Court of Appeals, Third Circuit, 1982.
679 F.2d 13.

■ GIBBONS, Circuit Judge:

* * *

On March 19, 1973, Miriam H. McCannon entered into an agreement with a partnership doing business as The Drake Hotel (the debtor) for the sale of a condominium apartment and of a certain percentage of the common areas in that hotel. * * *

Pursuant to the agreement, McCannon paid a deposit of $500 toward the purchase price of $17,988. She began residence in the apartment in April of 1975 and resides there presently. The bankruptcy court found, however, that "[f]or a variety of reasons, settlement on the property has never taken place." *In re Hotel Associates, Inc.*, 10 B.R. 668, 669 (Bankr.E.D.Pa.1981). McCannon never recorded her agreement for sale.

In November of 1979, the debtor filed a petition under Chapter 11 of the Code. McCannon filed a complaint in February of 1981 seeking relief from the automatic stay imposed by Section 362 of the Code and requesting specific performance of the agreement to purchase the apartment. Holding that the trustee, as a bona fide purchaser without regard to any knowledge on his part, may avoid McCannon's interest in the property pursuant to Pennsylvania law and to Section 544(a)(3) of the Code, the bankruptcy court granted the trustee's motion for judgment at the close of the plaintiff's case. * * * The district court affirmed the bankruptcy court's judgment, employing the same interpretation of Section 544 * * *. This appeal followed.

* * * At issue in this case is the interrelationship of [§ 544(a)(3)] concerning the rights of transferees of real property and the prepositional phrase [in the introductory clause of § 544(a)], "without regard to any knowledge of the trustee or of any creditor," an interrelationship of state and federal law.

The law of Pennsylvania considers a purchaser under a written agreement for the sale of real property to be the equitable owner of that property. * * * After reviewing the contract, we find no fault with the conclusion of the bankruptcy court that McCannon acquired such an equitable interest * * *.

Pennsylvania law gives subsequent purchasers of real property priority over the rights of prior purchasers if the subsequent purchasers are bona fide purchasers for value without notice. Record notice defeats the claims of a subsequent purchaser. McCannon's equitable interest was unrecorded. However, in Pennsylvania, clear and open possession of real property generally constitutes constructive notice to subsequent purchasers of the rights of the party in possession. Such possession, even in the absence of recording, obliges any prospective subsequent purchaser to inquire into the possessor's claimed interests, equitable or legal, in that property. * * * Thus in Pennsylvania the rights of a subsequent purchaser do not take priority over those of one in clear and open possession of real property.

The bankruptcy and district courts, however, concluded that any notice which might be imputed to the trustee from possession is irrelevant because of the language of the above-quoted prepositional phrase in Section 544: "without regard to any knowledge of the trustee or of any creditor." Equating "knowledge" with "notice," both courts ruled that the trustee assumes the powers of a bona fide purchaser without notice, whether or not a transferee has given the rest of the world actual or constructive notice by possession.[2]

Although the word "knowledge" is not defined in the Code and the legislative history of its inclusion is scant, in our view Congress cannot have intended such an interpretation. Once a transferee of real property in Pennsylvania has given all potential subsequent purchasers actual or constructive notice of an interest in that property, nothing else need be done to protect against claims of future purchasers. According to the bankruptcy and district courts, however, nothing can be done to protect against the claims of a future trustee in bankruptcy who assumes the role of a hypothetical bona fide purchaser without actual knowledge. The trustee, under that interpretation of Section 544, has been clothed not only with the rights of a bona fide purchaser, but has been granted as well a substantial additional mantle of power not available to any actual

---

[2] The reasoning of the bankruptcy and district courts would apparently allow a trustee to avoid even the interests of those who had given proper record notice.

subsequent purchaser in Pennsylvania. Such a conclusion is not to be lightly inferred.

That the words "without regard to any knowledge" were not meant by Congress to nullify all state law protections of holders of equitable interests is suggested both by the history of its inclusion in the statutory language and by other language within Section 544(a)(3). The reference to the trustee's or creditors' knowledge appears to have originated out of a concern that actual knowledge might affect the trustee's status as a hypothetical judicial lien creditor. In a draft bankruptcy act prepared in 1973 by the Commission on Bankruptcy Laws of the United States, a note by the Commission explained that the trustee's status as hypothetical lien creditor should not be affected by any knowledge which he, personally, or any or all creditors may have. Report of the Commission on the Bankruptcy Laws of the United States, H.R.Doc. No. 93-137, Part II, 93rd Cong., 1st Sess. 160-61 & n.3 (1973). The note referred to an article by Professor Vern Countryman criticizing cases construing both the "strong arm" provision of the former Bankruptcy Act, Section 70(c), and Article 9 of the Uniform Commercial Code, holding that a trustee with actual knowledge of unperfected security interests could not avoid those interests despite his status as hypothetical lien creditor. *See* Countryman, *The Use of State Law in Bankruptcy Cases,* 47 N.Y.U.L.Rev. 631, 652-55 (1972). In 1977 Congress first provided the trustee with the status of bona fide purchaser of real property. At that time it inserted the clarification regarding the trustee's actual knowledge. * * *

Viewed in the context of this history, congressional desire to disregard the trustee's knowledge of the debtor's previous transactions with various claimants is appropriately understood to respond to the Article 9 problems referred to by Professor Countryman, rather than to obliterate the rights of equitable owners in possession of real property. Further evidence that the latter result was not intended by Congress is found in the language of Section 544(a)(3). Congress was careful to modify the status of bona fide purchasers by inserting the words "against whom applicable law permits such transfer to be perfected." As explained in statements made by Representative Edwards of California and Senator DeConcini of Arizona, sponsors of the proposed Code:

> Section 544(a)(3) modifies similar provisions contained in the House bill and Senate amendment so as not to require a creditor to perform the impossible in order to perfect his interest. Both the lien creditor test in section 544(a)(1), and the bona fide purchaser test in section 544(a)(3) should not require a transferee to perfect a transfer against an entity with respect to which applicable law does not permit perfection.

124 Cong.Rec.H. 11097 (daily ed. Sept. 28, 1978); 124 Cong.Rec.S. 17413 (daily ed. October 6, 1978). Such solicitude for transferees subject to laws not

permitting perfection as to certain purchasers is not consistent with an interpretation of Section 544(a) that would ignore constructive notice under governing state law when a trustee was appointed.

One further point of dispute must be addressed. The trustee argues that the circumstances of McCannon's possession, as the occupant of one of many condominium apartments, a number of which were leased, are not constructive notice obliging a subsequent purchaser to inquire as to her interests. The only Pennsylvania cases cited, however, find no obligation to inquire in circumstances where the grantor was both record owner and in possession and where the one in possession was sharing possession with the record owner. * * * We believe that were the Pennsylvania Supreme Court asked to consider whether a subsequent purchaser *of a condominium building* had a duty to make inquiry as to the rights of persons in possession of apartments in that building, it would hold that such possession provides constructive notice, as a matter of law, no different than in the case of possession of a single family home.

* * *

NOTES

1. The court in *McCannon* refers to an article by Professor Countryman in which he discussed a dispute under Bankruptcy Act § 70c with respect to the status of unperfected Article 9 security interests of which the trustee or all creditors of the debtor had knowledge before bankruptcy. Under the 1962 Official Text of the UCC, which was in effect at the time, an unperfected security interest was subordinated to the rights of a subsequent judicial lienholder only if the lienholder at the time the lien arose did not have knowledge of the security interest. One point of view, supported by a few judicial decisions, was that an unperfected Article 9 security interest could not be avoided under § 70c if either the person who eventually became trustee or all of the actual creditors in the bankruptcy had knowledge of the security interest before bankruptcy. The issue was resolved against this view in states adopting the 1972 Official Text of the UCC which gave a subsequent judicial lien creditor priority regardless of knowledge, but in states which retained the 1962 Official Text the issue remained open. The issue was finally resolved in favor of avoidance by the trustee in all states by the language in the introductory clause of § 544(a), "without regard to any knowledge of the trustee or of any creditor."

A trustee in bankruptcy in a Chapter 7 case would usually not have knowledge of an unrecorded real property mortgage at the time of bankruptcy because at that time the person who eventually becomes trustee would not be acquainted with the debtor's activities. But in Chapter 11 cases the opposite is true because the debtor normally takes the powers of the trustee in bankruptcy as debtor in possession. § 1107(a). The quoted language of the introductory clause of § 544(a) makes clear that a debtor in possession may avoid an unrecorded mortgage executed by that debtor before bankruptcy if a bona fide purchaser could take free of the unrecorded mortgage.

2. An amendment in 1984 added the phrase "and has perfected such transfer," which now appears in § 544(a)(3). Under the laws of some states a bona fide purchaser of real property defeats the rights of a previous transferee of an interest in the property who has not recorded the interest only if the bona fide purchaser records before the prior transferee records. Before the amendment it was not entirely clear whether § 544(a)(3) would invalidate an unrecorded transfer of real property under statutes of this kind. For example, it could be argued that a postbankruptcy recording of the previously unrecorded transfer cut off the rights of the trustee if it was assumed that the hypothetical § 544(a)(3) bona fide purchaser did not record. §§ 546(b) and 362(b)(3). This argument was rejected in a number of cases. The amendment disposed of this ambiguity in § 544(a)(3) by adopting the view expressed by these cases.

3. PROPERTY HELD BY DEBTOR AS NOMINEE OR TRUSTEE.

Section 541(a)(1) includes in property of the estate "all legal or equitable interests of the debtor in property." How does that section apply to property of which the debtor is the nominal or legal owner but with respect to which the debtor has no beneficial interest? Suppose, for example, that David, an experienced investor, from time to time has invested money of members of his family and some close personal friends who are not sophisticated about investments. For example, Aunt Minnie gave him $40,000 to invest, Cousin Harry gave him $25,000 and George, his next door neighbor, gave him $35,000. With that money David bought 100 shares of stock for $15,000, he bought Blackacre, a vacant lot, for $50,000, and he loaned $35,000 to Roe who gave him a promissory note to evidence the debt. The promissory note is secured by a second mortgage on Whiteacre, which is Roe's residence. For convenience the stock was registered in the name of David, the deed to Blackacre was in the name of David and the promissory note was made payable to David. The mortgage on Whiteacre states that it is given to secure the promissory note payable to David who is named as mortgagee. The deed to Blackacre and the mortgage on Whiteacre were duly recorded. David signed documents clearly indicating that the transactions were made for the benefit of Minnie, Harry and George and that they hold undivided interests in the stock, Blackacre and the promissory note proportionate to the investments made by them, i.e., 40%, 25% and 35% respectively.

Suppose David goes into bankruptcy. Does any of the property held by David as a result of the $100,000 investment become part of the estate? Section

541(a)(1) is somewhat ambiguous. David does not have any beneficial interest in the property; he acted solely as an agent. But he is the holder of the note and is the record owner of the stock and Blackacre. It should be clear that, without more, the nominal ownership of David is not sufficient to divest Minnie, Harry and George of their beneficial ownership. Bankruptcy Act § 70a, which is the predecessor of 541(a), gave to the trustee "the title of the bankrupt." Since David had only bare legal title, under the Bankruptcy Act, the trustee got nothing more. The same result should follow under § 541(a)(1). In any event, 541(d) clearly supports that conclusion.

Can Minnie, Harry and George be divested of their property by virtue of § 541(a)(3) and § 544(a)? Although § 541(a)(1) gives David's legal title to the bankruptcy estate it does not affect the claims of beneficial ownership of Minnie, Harry and George. But how about 544(a)? That provision gives to the trustee in bankruptcy the rights and powers of a judicial lien creditor with respect to all the property held by David and of a bona fide purchaser of the real property. The trustee could argue that the equitable title of the beneficial owners can be avoided to the extent the holder of a judicial lien in personal property or a bona fide purchaser of real property could have taken the property free of the interests of those owners.

The stock is clearly personal property. The note is also personal property even though it is secured by a real property mortgage. The mortgage has no independent significance. It is an interest in real property, but that interest is a security interest that simply follows ownership of the note which is personal property. Thus, avoidance depends upon whether a judicial lien would defeat the interest of the owner of the note. In the absence of a statute specifically giving priority, a judicial lien is not effective against property not beneficially owned by the debtor. Thus, the normal result would be that the bankruptcy estate cannot keep the stock and the promissory note free of the claims of beneficial owners. But a bona fide purchaser of Blackacre from David would normally defeat the unrecorded equitable title of Minnie, Harry, and George. Could the trustee therefore avoid those interests under § 544(a)(3)? Does § 541(d) change that result?

Before amendment of § 541(d) in 1984, the reference in § 541(d) was to "subsection (a) of this section" rather than the present "subsection (a)(1) or (2) of this section."

The Senate Report on the Bankruptcy Code contained the following statement regarding the original version of § 541(d).

> [541(d)] confirms the current status under the Bankruptcy Act of bona fide secondary mortgage market transactions as the purchase and sale of assets. Mortgages or interests in mortgages sold in the secondary

market should not be considered as part of the debtor's estate. To permit the efficient servicing of mortgages or interests in mortgages the seller often retains the original mortgage notes and related documents, and the purchaser records under State recording statutes the purchaser's ownership of the mortgages or interests in mortgages purchased. [§ 541(d)] makes clear that the seller's retention of the mortgage documents and the purchaser's decision not to record do not impair the asset sale character of secondary mortgage market transactions. The committee notes that in secondary mortgage market transactions the parties may characterize their relationship as one of trust, agency, or independent contractor. The characterization adopted by the parties should not affect the [status] in bankruptcy of bona fide secondary mortgage market purchases and sales.

Sen.Rep. No. 95–989, 1978 U.S.C.C.A.N. 5869–5870.

The court in *Belisle v. Plunkett*, 877 F.2d 512 (7th Cir. 1989), a case similar to the hypothetical case above, saw no conflict between § 541(d) and § 544(a)(3) and held that avoidance of unrecorded interests in real property under the latter should be permitted even though the debtor had defrauded the investors. In that case the beneficial interests of defrauded investors in Virgin Islands real property titled in the debtor's name was avoided and the investors were left with only unsecured claims against the insolvent debtor. Other courts have relied upon § 541(d) to limit the scope of the strong-arm power in this context.

If the decision in *In re Omegas Group, Inc.*, 16 F.3d 1443 (6th Cir. 1994), is followed, the complexities encountered in *Belisle* in attempting to reconcile § 541(d) with § 544(a) with respect to constructive trusts and the odd discontinuity between treatment of real and personal property are avoided completely. In a sweeping holding the *Omegas* court decided that a constructive trust recognized in a bankruptcy case does not give the claimant an equitable interest in fraudulently obtained property "as of the commencement of the case" and, therefore, § 541(d) cannot apply to exclude the property from the debtor's estate. A constructive trust is merely a remedy for unjust enrichment. "Because a constructive trust, unlike an express trust, is a remedy, it does not exist until a plaintiff obtains a judicial decision finding him to be entitled to a judgment 'impressing' defendant's property or assets with a constructive trust. Therefore, a creditor's claim of entitlement to a constructive trust is not an 'equitable interest' in the debtor's estate existing prepetition, excluded from the estate under § 541(d)." 16 F.3d at 1451.

But what if under state law a constructive trust is deemed to have come into existence at the time the property was fraudulently obtained? Although in *Omegas* the state law was not entirely clear on this subject, the court gave it short shrift: "The equities of bankruptcy are not the equities of the common law. Constructive trusts are anathema to the equities of bankruptcy since they take from the estate, and thus directly from competing creditors and not from the offending debtor." *Id.* at 1452. The court concluded that the defrauded creditor merely has a claim that it may be able to show is nondischargeable under § 523(a)(2)(A). It failed to point out that Debtor is a corporation in Chapter 7 that cannot be discharged and that the hapless claimant would be left with a nondischargeable claim against a corporate shell. In a world-weary mode, the court observed that in most bankruptcies there are creditors who, for good reason or bad, believe they have been defrauded, and the claimant in this case is just one of a crowd.

Both *Plunkett* and *Omegas* are criticized in Andrew Kull, *Restitution in Bankruptcy: Reclamation and Constructive Trust*, 72 Am. Bankr. L. J. 265 (1998). *See also In re Ades & Berg Group Investors*, 550 F.3d 240 (2d Cir. 2008).

CHAPTER 8.
EQUITABLE SUBORDINATION AND SUBSTANTIVE CONSOLIDATION

A. EQUITABLE SUBORDINATION

1. CLAIMS OF INSIDERS

a. Inequitable Conduct

In accordance with equitable traditions, bankruptcy courts may "sift the circumstances surrounding any claim" in order to avoid unfairness in distributing the assets of the estate among claimants. *Pepper v. Litton*, 308 U.S. 295, 308 (1939). In that seminal case on inequitable conduct, Litton was the dominant stockholder of Debtor against which he asserted a claim of $30,000 for accumulated salary, dating back at least five years. When Pepper brought an action against Debtor for an accounting of royalties, Litton moved to prevent Pepper from reaching Debtor's property: he obtained a judgment against Debtor for the amount of his claim and levied on Debtor's property. But not until Pepper subsequently levied her judgment on Debtor's property did Litton cause the property to be sold. He purchased at the sale for $3,200, and swiftly transferred the property to a new corporation that he controlled. Two days later, Litton caused Debtor to file in bankruptcy. The Supreme Court subordinated Litton's claim to that of Pepper. It concluded:

> * * * Litton allowed his salary claims to lie dormant for years and sought to enforce them only when his debtor corporation was in financial difficulty. Then he used them so that the rights of another creditor were impaired. Litton as an insider utilized his strategic position for his own preferment to the damage of Pepper. Litton as the dominant influence over [Debtor] used his power not to deal fairly with the creditors of that company but to manipulate its affairs in such a manner that when one of its creditors came to collect her just debt the bulk of the assets had disappeared into another Litton company. Litton, though a fiduciary, was enabled by astute legal maneuvering to acquire most of the assets of the company not for cash or other consideration of value to

creditors but for bookkeeping entries representing at best merely Litton's appraisal of the worth of Litton's services over the years.

308 U.S. at 311.

Following *Pepper v. Litton*, bankruptcy courts may depart from the basic rule of equality of distribution to subordinate particular claims and interests to others in the exercise of their equitable powers. The great bulk of equitable subordination cases in bankruptcy concern the activities of fiduciaries or "insiders" (§ 101(31)), usually the affiliates, officers, directors, or controlling stockholders of corporations. Their dealings are closely scrutinized to make sure they are not unfair to other creditors. Even if those dealings do not give rise to affirmative liability to the estate for breach of duty, they may provide a basis for the equitable subordination of their claims and interests.

The Bankruptcy Act made no specific reference to equitable subordination. Bankruptcy Code § 510(c)(1) merely authorizes the court to subordinate claims and interests "under principles of equitable subordination." The statute does not state who can be the moving party in seeking subordination of a claim. Since equitable subordination claims do not belong to the estate like those for fraudulent transfers or voidable preferences, some cases have held that creditors may prosecute equitable subordination actions against other creditors without first obtaining consent of the court. *In re Racing Services, Inc.*, 363 B.R. 911 (8th Cir. BAP 2007). But see *In re Applied Theory Corp.*, 493 F.3d 82 (2d Cir. 2007) (creditors' committee must seek court approval before bringing an equitable subordination action against a creditor.)

In giving meaning to the undefined phrase "equitable subordination," the post-Code case law has relied on a set of principles announced by the court in *In re Mobile Steel Co.*, 563 F.2d 692 (5th Cir. 1977), a Bankruptcy Act case. Under this case equitable subordination is appropriate if the creditor (i) has engaged in inequitable conduct, (ii) the misconduct has resulted in injury to the creditors of the bankrupt or conferred an unfair advantage on the claimant, and (iii) the subordination is not inconsistent with the provisions of the Bankruptcy Act. Although the scope of "inequitable conduct" cannot be precisely delineated, the court in *In re Clark Pipe & Supply Co.*, 893 F.2d 693 (5th Cir. 1990), reprinted *infra*, states that it encompasses (i) fraud, illegality and breach of fiduciary duties, (ii) undercapitalization, and (iii) the claimant's use of the debtor corporation as a mere instrumentality or alter ego. Under *Mobile Steel* there can be no equitable subordination of a claim without some degree of inequitable conduct on the part of the claim holder.

Recharacterization, which does not necessarily require misconduct, is conceptually different from equitable subordination, but is also sometimes relied on to subordinate or disallow insider claims. It is not unusual for the moving parties to allege undercapitalization and inequitable conduct and concurrently seek recharacterization in a single case to see which of these alternative theories finds judicial favor on the facts of the case. Each of these theories will be discussed in the light of the following hypothetical:

> Insiders are officers, directors and the largest shareholders of Debtor which was suffering in the credit crunch of 2008. In April 2008 Insiders loaned Debtor $1 million after other financial options fell through and took a security interest in Debtor's property to secure the indebtedness. Debtor continued to have cash flow problems and sought financing from banks; when none was forthcoming, Insiders lent Debtor an additional $2.5 million in November 2008, and again took a security interest in Debtor's property. After Debtor's financial condition continued to deteriorate, it filed in Chapter 11. After obtaining court authorization, the unsecured creditors' committee brought an adversary proceeding against Insiders, seeking to subordinate their claims to the status of unsecured creditors. If Insider's security interests are upheld, the unsecured creditors will receive only a small dividend on their claims.

The 1970 Commission on the Bankruptcy Laws of the United States recommended adoption of a new bankruptcy statute that became the 1978 Bankruptcy Code. Section 4–406(a)(2) of the Commission's proposed statute subordinated "any claim, whether secured or unsecured, of any principal officer, director or affiliate of a debtor, or of any member of the immediate family of such officer, director, or affiliate." Under this provision, Insiders would have been automatically subordinated in cases like that above. However, this recommendation was not adopted in the Bankruptcy Code. Section 510(c) reflects the rejection by Congress of automatic subordination of insider claims. The rationale is that insiders may deal honestly and fairly with their firms and should not be discouraged by the automatic subordination doctrine from lending money to them. *See* Robert C. Clark, *The Duties of the Corporate Debtor to its Creditors*, 90 Harv.L.Rev. 505, 538 (1977).

The hypothetical above is based on *In re SI Restructuring, Inc.*, 532 F.3d 355 (5th Cir. 2008), in which the unsecured creditors' committee convinced the bankruptcy court that Insiders were guilty of inequitable conduct with respect to the November loan in that they presented it to Debtor's board as the only option available, at the "eleventh hour," as a *fait accompli*. Insiders told the board that they must approve the loan or the company "collapses tomorrow," and in doing so, Insiders took unfair advantage. The Fifth Circuit reversed on the ground that unsecured creditors as a class were not harmed. The November loan was real money that was used to pay current unsecured creditors, and therefore unsecured creditors as a class were not harmed when Insiders obtained security for their loans. The fact that some unsecured creditors were paid and others were not does not amount to inequitable conduct on the part of Insiders.

Patricia A. Redmond, *Not All Loans Are Created Equal: Equitable Subordination and Prepetition Insider Lending After SI Restructuring*, 27 Am. Bankr. Inst. J. 22 (2008), argues that *SI Restructuring* is an important decision. Faced with the specter of equitable subordination or recharacterization, insiders have been less likely to loan their companies funds that are needed to stave off bankruptcy. On facts like those in that case, subordination or recharacterization had become almost automatic in some courts. She sees the holding as heralding a resurgence of a policy that favors the rehabilitation of companies outside bankruptcy.

Change the facts in the hypothetical to these:

Insiders did not perfect their security interests until a month before the company filed in bankruptcy and some unsecured creditors advanced credit without knowing of Insiders' security interests.

One of the oldest abuses of secured transactions is for a creditor to deliberately postpone public filing or recordation of its security interest. Prospective creditors may be more willing to extend unsecured credit if they believe that all of a debtor's assets are unencumbered. The secured creditor has the best of both worlds; the debtor is able to obtain more credit because new creditors see only unencumbered assets, but the secured creditor can move in and perfect (outside the applicable preference period) by filing if the debtor is failing. Even if the Insiders' late-perfected security interests are not avoidable as preferences, this may be inequitable conduct justifying subordination of Insiders' claims. *See Matter of Herby's Food, Inc.*, 2 F.3d 128 (5th Cir. 1993).

b. Undercapitalization

Hypothetical. Insider was the controlling stockholder of Debtor, a wholesale enterprise. Two years after Debtor opened its business the economy slowed and Insider found that the proceeds from the sales to customers had become inadequate to allow Debtor to acquire necessary inventory and meet its payroll. In order to allow Debtor to stay in business until the economy improved, Insider made periodic cash advances to Debtor to help it meet its needs. These advances were carried on Debtor's books as loans from Insider. Debtor paid interest on these loans from time to time but it never repaid any part of the principal. In effect to keep Debtor in business, Insider provided working capital for Debtor denominated as loans rather than equity capital. When Insider finally gave up on Debtor and put it into Chapter 11, the unsecured creditors' committee sought to have Insider's claims subordinated to those of the unsecured creditors. The theory advanced by the committee was that Debtor was grossly undercapitalized and that Insider's advances were capital contributions and not true loans. How strong is this case for either subordination based on undercapitalization or recharacterization, as discussed below? See *Herby's Food, supra,* and *Diasonics, Inc. v. Ingalls,* 121 B.R. 626 (Bankr.N.D.Fla.1990).

Recognizing undercapitalization as an independent ground for subordination is challenged in *Matter of Lifschulz Fast Freight,* 132 F.3d 339, 346 (7th Cir. 1997).

> So what is wrong with undercapitalization in itself? The trustee argues that "insufficient capital leads to financing the operation with secured debt, and that exposes unsecured commercial creditors to a greater risk of loss." Quite so. But again, where is the wrong? Creditors extend credit voluntarily to a debtor. The debtor owes no duties to the creditor beyond those it promises in its contract (and beyond whatever common and statutory law may apply). A debtor decidedly does not owe a fiduciary duty to a creditor. * * * And a debtor is just as surely not obliged to be the lender's insurer. A lender will not offer a loan to a borrower unless the rate of return justifies the risk of default or underpayment. The same is true for the sub-class of lenders called trade creditors, for prudent business people assess the risk of default before allowing customers to pay for goods or services on credit. The higher that risk, the more interest (or collateral) the lender will demand. If a firm is poorly capitalized, and thus less likely to repay than a better capitalized firm in the same line of business, the lender may require more security or more interest. But that a highly leveraged company exposes its creditors to serious risks is no new fact of commerce. Creditors are free to lend elsewhere. If they choose to lend to a company that then loses their investment, they cannot go to the bankruptcy court and cry misconduct.

Thus, the court in *Lifschultz* places undercapitalization in commercial context and finds that within this context subordination should not be based on undercapitalization alone. Judge Posner defines the term as merely "excessive leverage." *Baldi v. Samuel Son & Co. Ltd.,* 548 F.3d 579 (7th Cir. 2008). *Lifschultz* recognizes the importance of insider contributions to closely held businesses and is reluctant to find a basis for subordination, with its harsh consequences, unless proof of misconduct is clear. Subordination should not be undertaken lightly, but insider transactions are to be closely scrutinized for inequitable conduct. *Lifschultz* requires "undercapitalization-plus" to justify equitable subordination.

c. Recharacterization

As indicated in the hypothetical above, the same facts might be analyzed as giving rise to both undercapitalization and recharacterization. But the two are conceptually different. In *In re Autostyle Plastics, Inc.,* 269 F.3d 726 (6th Cir.

2001), the court distinguished between equitable subordination and recharacterization of debt as equity: In equitable subordination, the remedy is subordination of a creditor's claim to that of another creditor only to the extent necessary to offset the injury suffered by the other creditor. In recharacterization, the purported creditor has no legitimate claim; it has only an ownership interest and is subordinate to all claims under the rule that debt has priority over equity. *Autostyle* concedes that some courts intermix the two doctrines in that similar factors are relied on to show each status.

For determining whether a debt should be recharacterized as equity, the court cited a number of factors set out in *Roth Steel Tube Co. v. Comm'r of Internal Revenue,* 800 F.2d 625 (6th Cir. 1986). Among these are: (1) the absence of notes or other instruments of indebtedness with stated payment schedules and interest rates is evidence that no loan was intended; (2) if expectation of payment depends solely on the success of the borrower's business, the transaction is likely a capital contribution; (3) inadequacy of capitalization is evidence that the advances are capital contributions; (4) if stockholders make advances in proportion to their respective stock ownership, an equity contribution is indicated; (5) absence of security is evidence of capital contributions; (6) debtor's inability to obtain outside financing tends to show a capital contribution; and (7) use of advances as working capital to meet daily operating needs of debtor is evidence of bona fide indebtedness.

A familiar form versus substance debate has been joined over the issue of recharacterization. Some courts disclaim power to recharacterize advances properly documented as loans as capital contributions in the absence of inequitable conduct. *See In re SI Restructuring, Inc.*, 532 F.3d 355 (5th Cir. 2008); *In re Pacific Express, Inc.*, 69 B.R. 112 (9th Cir. BAP 1986). Other courts insist that a bankruptcy court is not bound by the parties' labels and can independently determine whether a given advance was "truly a loan or was instead a capital contribution." *In re Official Comm. of Unsecured Creditors for Dornier (North Am.) Ltd.*, 453 F.3d 225, 231-33 (4th Cir. 2006).

2. CLAIMS OF NONINSIDERS

When a business debtor files in bankruptcy, a relationship between the debtor and its dominant creditor, usually a secured lender, that allows the lender to exert control over the business decisions of the debtor, may form the basis for an attempt by the trustee to convince the bankruptcy court that the claim of the lender should be subordinated to the claims of other creditors. The following quotation from *In re Teltronics Services*, 29 B.R. 139, 170–171 (Bankr. E.D.N.Y.1983), raises some of the difficulties facing creditors who exert control over their debtors:

The general rule that a creditor is not a fiduciary of his debtor is not without exception. In the rare circumstance where a creditor exercises such control over the decision-making processes of the debtor as amounts to a domination of its will, he may be held accountable for his actions under a fiduciary standard. * * * Accordingly, several commentators have admonished creditors to avoid becoming overly involved in the debtor's management:

Where the creditor controls the corporate debtor by voting control of its stock, dominant influence in its management or ability otherwise to control its business affairs, the creditor may have a fiduciary duty to its corporate debtor.

* * *

... [W]henever a creditor interferes in the business affairs of a financially troubled corporate debtor, it risks the possibility that such interference may provide a basis for the equitable adjustment of its claims against the debtor, the imposition of statutory liability or the imposition of liabilities at common law.

Douglas–Hamilton, *Creditor Liabilities Resulting from Improper Interference with the Management of a Financially Troubled Debtor*, 31 Bus.Law. 343, 352, 365 (1975).

... [O]nce the creditor is not satisfied with simply insulating himself from the risk of loss of capital and interest, and instead insists upon affirmative participation in the entrepreneurial effort being financed ... he has entered into a relationship whose expected extraordinary economic benefit justifies the requirement of special obligations.

* * *

With affirmative conduct thus has come voluntary assumption of duty, and the fact that the creditor's motives are not altruistic will strengthen arguments for the imposition of liability.

Bartlett & Lapatin, *The Status of a Creditor as a Controlling Person*, 28 Mercer L. Rev. 639, 655–57 (1977).

While it is possible for a creditor to be cast in the role of fiduciary, several cases illustrate the difficulty in demonstrating that the claimant so dominated the will of the debtor to the detriment of the other creditors that his claim should be relegated to inferior status. In affirming the subordination of a claim asserted by a creditor bank, the district court in *In re American Lumber*, 5 B.R. 470, 478 (D.Minn.1980) [discussed below in *Clark Pipe*] found "overwhelming" evidence that the bank purposefully manipulated the bankrupt's operations in a manner detrimental to the debtor's unsecured creditors. Among the indicia of control deemed sufficient to manifest a complete domination of will were the following: (1) the bank had the right to a controlling interest in debtor's stock pledged as collateral in the event of default in certain loan obligations; (2) the bank, which was the debtor's sole source of credit, placed the debtor within its coercive powers by refusing to honor the debtor's payroll checks, and by foreclosing on its security interests in the debtor's only source of ready cash, to wit, its accounts receivable and contract rights; and (3) the bank forced compliance with its wishes by imposing such harsh measures on the debtor as: forcing termination of most employees, requiring drastic reduction of officers' salaries, coercing execution of security agreements on the debtor's only remaining assets, and determining which creditors were to be paid by the debtor.

* * *

In the *W.T. Grant* case, 4 B.R. 53 (Bankr.S.D.N.Y.1980), the objectants sought to have the claims of creditor banks subordinated where it was alleged that the banks influenced several of the debtor's key financial decisions. Judge Galgay, in recognizing that the courts have denied the application of equitable subordination even where a creditor exercises a significant degree of daily monitoring of its debtor, rejected objectants' argument on the theory that the actions taken by the debtor "reflected independent policy decisions and not rigid submission to the dictates of the Bank claimants." 4 B.R. at 77. In affirming Judge Galgay's decision, the Second Circuit found nothing improper about the banks' "careful watch" of the bankrupt's activities, and suggested that the banks indeed would have been derelict in their duty to their own creditors and equityholders if they had not done so:

The cases cited above strongly suggest that a non-insider creditor will be held to a fiduciary standard only where his ability to command the debtor's obedience to his policy directives is so overwhelming that there has been, to some extent, a merger of identity. Unless the debtor has become, in effect, the alter ego of the creditor, he will not be held to an ethical duty in excess of the morals of the marketplace.

In *In re Beverages International, Ltd.*, 50 B.R. 273 (Bankr.D.Mass.1985), the court subordinated the claim of a dominant creditor after finding that the creditor exercised control over the debtor. Evidence showed that the creditor required the debtor to change attorneys and accountants, participated in board meetings and engineered the sales of inferior inventory. The creditor also delayed in obtaining and recording a blanket security interest in all of the

Chapter 8. Equitable Subordination and Substantive Consolidation

debtor's assets in order to encourage third parties to extend credit to the debtor that they would not have given had they known of the security interest.

In the following case the decision by a bankruptcy court to subordinate the claim of a dominant creditor was initially affirmed by the Fifth Circuit which subsequently reconsidered the case, confessed error, and reversed itself in the opinion reproduced below.

Matter of Clark Pipe & Supply Co.
United States Court of Appeals, Fifth Circuit, 1990.
893 F.2d 693.

■ E. GRADY JOLLY, Circuit Judge:

Treating the suggestion for rehearing en banc filed in this case by Associates Commercial Corporation ("Associates"), as a petition for panel rehearing, we hereby grant the petition for rehearing. After re-examining the evidence in this case and the applicable law, we conclude that our prior opinion was in error. We therefore withdraw our prior opinion and substitute the following:

* * *

Clark Pipe and Supply Company, Inc., ("Clark") was in the business of buying and selling steel pipe used in the fabrication of offshore drilling platforms. In September 1980, Associates and Clark executed various agreements under which Associates would make revolving loans secured by an assignment of accounts receivable and an inventory mortgage. Under the agreements, Clark was required to deposit all collections from the accounts receivable in a bank account belonging to Associates. The amount that Associates would lend was determined by a formula, i.e., a certain percentage of the amount of eligible accounts receivable plus a certain percentage of the cost of inventory. The agreements provided that Associates could reduce the percentage advance rates at any time at its discretion.

When bad times hit the oil fields in late 1981, Clark's business slumped. In February 1982 Associates began reducing the percentage advance rates so that Clark would have just enough cash to pay its direct operating expenses. Clark used the advances to keep its doors open and to sell inventory, the proceeds of which were used to pay off the past advances from Associates. Associates did not expressly dictate to Clark which bills to pay. Neither did it direct Clark not to pay vendors or threaten Clark with a cutoff of advances if it did pay vendors. But Clark had no funds left over from the advances to pay vendors or other creditors whose services were not essential to keeping its doors open.

One of Clark's vendors, going unpaid, initiated foreclosure proceedings in February and seized the pipe it had sold Clark. Another attempted to do so in

March. * * * When a third unpaid creditor initiated foreclosure proceedings in May, Clark sought protection from creditors by filing for reorganization under Chapter 11 of the Bankruptcy Code.

The case was converted to a Chapter 7 liquidation on August 31, 1982, and a trustee was appointed. In 1983, the trustee brought this adversary proceeding against Clark's lender, Associates. The trustee sought * * * equitable subordination of Associates' claims. * * * The court * * * subordinated Associates' claims. The district court affirmed on May 24, 1988.

* * * This court has enunciated a three-pronged test to determine whether and to what extent a claim should be equitably subordinated: (1) the claimant must have engaged in some type of inequitable conduct, (2) the misconduct must have resulted in injury to the creditors of the bankrupt or conferred an unfair advantage on the claimant, and (3) equitable subordination of the claim must not be inconsistent with the provisions of the Bankruptcy Code. * * * Three general categories of conduct have been recognized as sufficient to satisfy the first prong of the three-part test: (1) fraud, illegality or breach of fiduciary duties; (2) undercapitalization; and (3) a claimant's use of the debtor as a mere instrumentality or alter ego.

In essence, the bankruptcy court found that once Associates realized Clark's desperate financial condition, Associates asserted total control and used Clark as a mere instrumentality to liquidate Associates' unpaid loans. Moreover, it did so, the trustee argues, to the detriment of the rights of Clark's other creditors.

Associates contends that its control over Clark was far from total. Associates says that it did no more than determine the percentage of advances as expressly permitted in the loan agreement; it never made or dictated decisions as to which creditors were paid. Thus, argues Associates, it never had the "actual, participatory, total control of the debtor" required to make Clark its instrumentality under *Krivo Industrial Supply Co. v. National Distillers & Chemical Corp.*, 483 F.2d 1098, 1105 (5th Cir. 1973) * * *. If it did not use Clark as an instrumentality or engage in any other type of inequitable conduct * * * argues Associates, then it cannot be equitably subordinated.

We first consider whether Associates asserted such control over the activities of Clark that we should consider that it was using Clark as its mere instrumentality. In our prior opinion, we agreed with the district court and the bankruptcy court that, as a practical matter, Associates asserted total control over Clark's liquidation, and that it used its control in a manner detrimental to the unsecured creditors. Upon reconsideration, we have concluded that we cannot say that the sort of control Associates asserted over Clark's financial affairs rises to the level of unconscionable conduct necessary to justify the application of the doctrine of equitable subordination. We have reached our revised conclusion primarily because we cannot escape the salient fact that, pursuant to its loan agreement with Clark, Associates had the right to reduce funding, just as it did, as Clark's sales slowed. We now conclude that there is no evidence that Associates exceeded its authority under the loan agreement, or that Associates acted inequitably in exercising its rights under that agreement.

We think it is important to note at the outset that the loan and security agreements between Associates and Clark, which are at issue here, were executed in 1980, at the inception of their relationship. There is no evidence that Clark was insolvent at the time the agreements were entered into. Clark was represented by counsel during the negotiations, and there is no evidence that the loan documents were negotiated at anything other than arm's length or that they are atypical of loan documents used in similar asset-based financings.

The loan agreement between Associates and Clark established a line of credit varying from $2.2 million to approximately $2.7 million over the life of the loan. The amount that Associates would lend was determined by a formula: 85% of the amount of eligible accounts receivables plus 60% of the cost of inventory. Under the agreement, Clark was required to deposit all collections from the accounts receivable in a bank account belonging to Associates. Associates would, in turn, readvance the agreed-upon portion of those funds to Clark on a revolving basis. The agreement provided that Associates could reduce the percentage advance rates at any time in its discretion.

When Clark's business began to decline, along with that of the oil patch generally, Associates advised Clark that it would reduce the advance ratio for the inventory loan by 5% per month beginning in January 1982. After that time, the company stopped buying new inventory and, according to the Trustee's expert witness, Clark's monthly sales revenues amounted to less than one-fifth of the company's outstanding accounts payable. Clark prepared a budget at Associates' request that indicated the disbursements necessary to keep the company operating. The budget did not include payment to vendors for previously shipped goods. Associates' former loan officer, Fred Slice, testified as to what he had in mind:

> If he [the comptroller of Clark] had had the availability [of funds to pay a vendor or other trade creditor] that particular day, I would have said, "Are you sure you've got that much availability, Jim," because he shouldn't have that much. The way I had structured it, he wouldn't have any money to pay his suppliers.

* * *

> But you know, the possibility that—this is all hypothetical. I had it structured so that there was no—there was barely enough money—

there was enough money, if I did it right, enough money to keep the doors open. Clark could continue to operate, sell the inventory, turn it into receivables, collect the cash, transfer that cash to me, and reduce my loans.

And, if he had ever had availability for other things, that meant I had done something wrong, and I would have been surprised. To ask me what I would have done is purely hypothetical[;] I don't think it would happen. I think it's so unrealistic, I don't know.

Despite Associates' motive, which was, according to Slice, "to get in the best position I can prior to the bankruptcy, i.e., I want to get the absolute amount of dollars as low as I can by hook or crook," the evidence shows that the amount of its advances continued to be based on the applicable funding formulas. Slice testified that the lender did not appreciably alter its original credit procedures when Clark fell into financial difficulty.

In our original opinion, we failed to focus sufficiently on the loan agreement, which gave Associates the right to conduct its affairs with Clark in the manner in which it did. In addition, we think that in our previous opinion we were overly influenced by the negative and inculpatory tone of Slice's testimony. Given the agreement he was working under, his testimony was hardly more than fanfaronading about the power that the agreement afforded him over the financial affairs of Clark. Although his talk was crass (e.g., "I want to get the absolute dollars as low as I can, by hook or crook"), our careful examination of the record does not reveal any conduct on his part that was inconsistent with the loan agreement, irrespective of what his personal motive may have been.

Through its loan agreement, every lender effectively exercises "control" over its borrower to some degree. A lender in Associates' position will usually possess "control" in the sense that it can foreclose or drastically reduce the debtor's financing. The purpose of equitable subordination is to distinguish between the unilateral remedies that a creditor may properly enforce pursuant to its agreements with the debtor and other inequitable conduct such as fraud, misrepresentation, or the exercise of such total control over the debtor as to have essentially replaced its decision-making capacity with that of the lender. The crucial distinction between what is inequitable and what a lender can reasonably and legitimately do to protect its interests is the distinction between the existence of "control" and the exercise of that "control" to direct the activities of the debtor. As the Supreme Court stated in *Comstock v. Group of Institutional Investors*, 335 U.S. 211, 229 (1948): "It is not mere existence of an opportunity to do wrong that brings the rule into play; it is the unconscionable use of the opportunity afforded by the domination to advantage itself at the injury of the subsidiary that deprives the wrongdoer of the fruits of his wrong."

In our prior opinion, we drew support from *In re American Lumber Co.* to reach our conclusion that Associates' claims should be equitably subordinated. Upon reconsideration, however, we find that the facts of that case are significantly more egregious than we have here. In that case, the court equitably subordinated the claims of a bank because the bank "controlled" the debtor through its right to a controlling interest in the debtor's stock. The bank forced the debtor to convey security interests in its remaining unencumbered assets to the bank after the borrower defaulted on an existing debt. Immediately thereafter, the bank foreclosed on the borrower's accounts receivable, terminated the borrower's employees, hired its own skeleton crew to conduct a liquidation, and selectively honored the debtor's payables to improve its own position. The bank began receiving and opening all incoming mail at the borrower's office, and it established a bank account into which all amounts received by the borrower were deposited and over which the bank had sole control. The bankruptcy court found that the bank exercised control over all aspects of the debtor's finances and operation including: payments of payables and wages, collection and use of accounts receivable and contract rights, purchase and use of supplies and materials, inventory sales, a lumber yard, the salaries of the principals, the employment of employees, and the receipt of payments for sales and accounts receivable.

Despite its decision to prohibit further advances to the debtor, its declaration that the debtor was in default of its loans, and its decisions to use all available funds of the company to offset the company's obligations to it, the bank in *American Lumber* made two specific representations to the American Lumbermen's Credit Association that the debtor was not in a bankruptcy situation and that current contracts would be fulfilled. Two days after this second reassurance, the bank gave notice of foreclosure of its security interests in the company's inventory and equipment. Approximately two weeks later the bank sold equipment and inventory of the debtor amounting to roughly $450,000, applying all of the proceeds to the debtor's indebtedness to the bank.

Associates exercised significantly less "control" over the activities of Clark than did the lender in *American Lumber*. Associates did not own any stock of Clark, much less a controlling block. Nor did Associates interfere with the operations of the borrower to an extent even roughly commensurate with the degree of interference exercised by the bank in *American Lumber*. Associates made no management decisions for Clark, such as deciding which creditors to prefer with the diminishing amount of funds available. At no time did Associates place any of its employees as either a director or officer of Clark. Associates never influenced the removal from office of any Clark personnel, nor did Associates ever request Clark to take any particular action at a shareholders meeting. Associates did not expressly dictate to Clark which bills to pay, nor did it direct Clark not to pay vendors or threaten a cut-off of advances if it did pay vendors. Clark handled its own daily operations. The same basic procedures with respect to the reporting of collateral, the calculation of availability of funds, and the procedures for the advancement of funds were followed throughout the relationship between Clark and Associates. Unlike the lender in *American Lumber*, Associates did not mislead creditors to continue supplying Clark. Perhaps the most important fact that distinguishes this case from *American Lumber* is that Associates did not coerce Clark into executing the security agreements after Clark became insolvent. Instead, the loan and security agreements between Clark and Associates were entered into at arm's length prior to Clark's insolvency, and all of Associates' activities were conducted pursuant to those agreements.

Associates' control over Clark's finances, admittedly powerful and ultimately severe, was based solely on the exercise of powers found in the loan agreement. Associates' close watch over Clark's affairs does not, by itself, however, amount to such control as would justify equitable subordination. "There is nothing inherently wrong with a creditor carefully monitoring his debtor's financial situation or with suggesting what course of action the debtor ought to follow." *In re Teltronics Services, Inc.*, 29 B.R. 139, 172 (Bankr.E.D.N.Y.1983) (citations omitted). Although the terms of the agreement did give Associates potent leverage over Clark, that agreement did not give Associates total control over Clark's activities. At all material times Clark had the power to act autonomously and, if it chose, to disregard the advice of Associates; for example, Clark was free to shut its doors at any time it chose to do so and to file for bankruptcy.

Finally, on reconsideration, we are persuaded that the rationale of *In re W.T. Grant Co.* should control the case before us. In that case, the Second Circuit recognized that

> a creditor is under no fiduciary obligation to its debtor or to other creditors of the debtor in the collection of its claim. [citations omitted] The permissible parameters of a creditor's efforts to seek collection from a debtor are generally those with respect to voidable preferences and fraudulent conveyances proscribed by the Bankruptcy Act; apart from these there is generally no objection to a creditor's using his bargaining position, including his ability to refuse to make further loans needed by the debtor, to improve the status of his existing claims.

699 F.2d at 609–10. Associates was not a fiduciary of Clark, it did not exert improper control over Clark's financial affairs, and it did not act inequitably in exercising its rights under its loan agreement with Clark.

Finally, we should note that in our earlier opinion, we found that, in exercising such control over Clark, Associates engaged in other inequitable conduct that justified equitable subordination. Our re-examination of the record indicates, however, that there is not really any evidence that Associates engaged in such conduct. Our earlier opinion assumed that Associates knew that Clark was selling pipe to which the suppliers had a first lien, but the issue of whether the vendors had a first lien on the pipe was not decided by our court until a significantly later time. In addition, although the trustee made much of the point on appeal, after our re-study of the record, we conclude that it does not support the finding that Associates encouraged Clark to remove decals from pipe in its inventory.

We also note that the record is devoid of any evidence that Associates misled other Clark creditors to their detriment. *See, e.g., Matter of CTS Truss, Inc.*, 868 F.2d 146, 149 (5th Cir. 1989) (lender did not represent to third parties that additional financing was in place or that debtor was solvent, when the opposite was true).

When the foregoing factors are considered, there is no basis for finding inequitable conduct upon which equitable subordination can be based. We therefore conclude that the district court erred in affirming the bankruptcy court's decision to subordinate Associates' claims.

* * *

NOTES

1. In *Kham & Nate's Shoes No. 2, Inc. v. First Bank of Whiting*, 908 F.2d 1351 (7th Cir. 1990), Bank opened a $300,000 line of credit for Debtor that permitted Bank to cancel at its discretion. After advancing $75,000, of which Debtor repaid $10,000, Bank refused to make further advances. The lower court equitably subordinated Bank's $65,000 claim on the ground that Bank's refusal to extend further credit was inequitable conduct. In overruling the lower court, Judge Easterbrook, speaking for the court, stated:

> "Inequitable conduct" in commercial life means breach *plus* some advantage-taking, such as the star who agrees to act in a motion picture and then, after $20 million has been spent, sulks in his dressing room until the contract has been renegotiated.

* * *

Bank did not break a promise at a time Debtor was especially vulnerable, then use the costs and delay of obtaining legal enforcement of the contract as levers to a better deal. Debtor and Bank signed a contract expressly allowing the Bank to cease making further advances. The

$300,000 was the maximum loan, not a guarantee. The Bank exercised its contractual privilege after loaning Debtor $75,000; it made a clean break and did not demand improved terms. It had the right to do this for any reason satisfactory to itself.

* * *

Although Bank's decision left Debtor scratching for other sources of credit, Bank did not create Debtor's need for funds, and it was not contractually obliged to satisfy its customer's desires. The Bank was entitled to advance its own interest, and it did not need to put the interests of Debtor and Debtor's other creditors first. To the extent *K.M.C. Co., Inc. v. Irving Trust Co.*, 757 F.2d 752, 759–63 (6th Cir. 1985), holds that a bank must loan more money or give more advance notice of termination than its contract requires, we respectfully disagree. First Bank of Whiting is not an eleemosynary institution. It need not throw good money after bad, even if other persons would catch the lucre.

* * *

Debtor stresses, and the bankruptcy judge found, that Bank would have been secure in making additional advances. Perhaps so, but the contract did not oblige Bank to make all advances for which it could be assured of payment. *Ex post* assessments of a lender's security are no basis on which to deny it the negotiated place in the queue. Risk must be assessed *ex ante* by lenders, rather than *ex post* by judges. If a loan seems secure at the time, lenders will put up the money; their own interests are served by making loans bound to be repaid. What is more, the bankruptcy judge's finding that Bank would have been secure in making additional advances is highly questionable. The judgment of the market vindicates Bank. If more credit would have enabled Debtor to flourish, then other lenders should have been willing to supply it. Yet no one else, not even the SBA, would advance additional money to Debtor.

908 F.2d at 1357–1358.

2. Even if the claimant has not controlled the conduct of the debtor in the degree required by *Clark Pipe*, a noninsider claim may be subordinated in case of gross misconduct by the claimant. The court in *In re 604 Columbus Ave. Realty Trust*, 968 F.2d 1332, 1360 (1st Cir. 1992), observed: "Claims arising from dealings between a debtor and an insider are rigorously scrutinized by the court. * * * On the other hand, if the claimant is not an insider, 'then evidence of more egregious misconduct such as fraud, spoliation or overreaching is necessary.'"

In *In re Osborne*, 42 B.R. 988 (W.D.Wis.1984), Debtor was indebted to its principal lender, the Production Creditor Association (PCA), as well as to a bank and several trade creditors. When Debtor filed in bankruptcy, a dispute very familiar in agricultural financing arose: the other creditors asserted that the PCA, which was trying to keep Debtor afloat, had misled them about their prospect of being paid after it knew that Debtor was in serious financial trouble. At least with respect to one of the trade creditors, the court found PCA's remarks about the prospect of payment to be a knowingly false misrepresentation that amounted to gross misconduct. The court held that PCA's claim would be subordinated only with respect to the particular creditor who was injured by PCA's misconduct and only to the extent of that injury.

B. SUBSTANTIVE CONSOLIDATION

The priority and treatment of claims can be dramatically affected by the bankruptcy doctrine of substantive consolidation. Under this doctrine, the assets of several debtors, usually affiliated corporations in a family of corporations operated as a unit, are pooled in bankruptcy and the claims of creditors of any member of the corporate family are treated as claims against the consolidated assets of all members of the family. In a substantive consolidation, creditors of a debtor whose asset-to-liability ratio is higher than that of affiliated debtors will lose to the extent the asset-to-liability ratio of the pooled estates is lower. Hence, substantive consolidation is sparingly invoked. On the other hand procedural consolidation, which is authorized by Bankruptcy Rule 1015, is quite common. In procedural consolidation two or more bankruptcy estates are administered together, but the assets are not pooled and each creditor has a claim only against the assets of its debtor. The usual examples are husband and wife, debtor and affiliate, and two or more partners.

No Code provision specifically authorizes substantive consolidation. The general powers of a bankruptcy court under § 105(a) to issue orders "necessary or appropriate to carry out the provisions" of the Code constitute the authority to act in this area.

The following opinion is important not only for its apparently restricted view of substantive consolidation but also because it binds courts in Delaware where many large companies and their affiliates file for Chapter 11 protection.

In re Owens Corning, Inc.
United States Court of Appeals, Third Circuit, 2005.
419 F.3d 195.

■ AMBRO, Circuit Judge.

We consider under what circumstances a court exercising bankruptcy powers may substantively consolidate affiliated entities. Appellant Credit Suisse First Boston ("CSFB") is the agent for a syndicate of banks (collectively, the "Banks")[1] that extended in 1997 a $2 billion unsecured loan to Owens Corning, a Delaware corporation ("OCD"), and certain of its subsidiaries. This credit was enhanced in part by guarantees made by other OCD subsidiaries. The District Court granted a motion to consolidate the assets and liabilities of the OCD borrowers and guarantors in anticipation of a plan of reorganization.

The Banks appeal and argue that the Court erred by granting the motion, as it misunderstood the reasons for, and standards for considering, the extraordinary remedy of substantive consolidation, and in any event did not make factual determinations necessary even to consider its use. Though we reverse the ruling of the District Court, we do so aware that it acted on an issue with no opinion on point by our Court and differing rationales by other courts.

While this area of law is difficult and this case important, its outcome is easy with the facts before us. Among other problems, the consolidation sought is "deemed." Should we approve this non-consensual arrangement, the plan process would proceed as though assets and liabilities of separate entities were merged, but in fact they remain separate with the twist that the guarantees to the Banks are eliminated. From this we conclude that the proponents of substantive consolidation request it not to rectify the seldom-seen situations that call for this last-resort remedy but rather as a ploy to deprive one group of creditors of their rights while providing a windfall to other creditors.

I. Factual background and procedural history

A. Owens Corning Group of Companies

OCD and its subsidiaries (which include corporations and limited liability companies) comprise a multinational corporate group. Different entities within the group have different purposes. Some, for example, exist to limit liability concerns (such as those related to asbestos), others to gain tax benefits, and others have regulatory reasons for their formation.

---

[1] Though CSFB is the named appellant, the real parties in interest are the Banks (which include CSFB). Thus, unless the context requires otherwise, CSFB and the Banks are referred to interchangeably in this opinion.

Each subsidiary was a separate legal entity that observed governance formalities. Each had a specific reason to exist separately, each maintained its own business records, and intercompany transactions were regularly documented. Although there may have been some "sloppy" bookkeeping, two of OCD's own officers testified that the financial statements of all the subsidiaries were accurate in all material respects. Further, through an examination of the subsidiaries' books, OCD's postpetition auditors (Ernst & Young) have eliminated most financial discrepancies, particularly with respect to the larger guarantor subsidiaries.

B. The 1997 Credit Agreement

In 1997 OCD sought a loan to acquire Fibreboard Corporation. At this time OCD faced growing asbestos liability and a poor credit rating that hindered its ability to obtain financing. When CSFB was invited to submit a bid, it included subsidiary guarantees in the terms of its proposal. The guarantees gave the Banks direct claims against the guarantors for payment defaults. They were a "credit enhancement" without which the Banks would not have made the loan to OCD. All draft loan term sheets included subsidiary guarantees.

A $2 billion loan from the Banks to OCD closed in June 1997. The loan terms were set out primarily in a Credit Agreement. Among those terms were the guarantee provisions and requirements for guarantors, who were defined as "present or future Domestic Subsidiar[ies]... having assets with an aggregate book value in excess of $30,000,000." Section 10.07 of the Agreement provided that the guarantees were "absolute and unconditional" and each "constitute[d] a guarant[ee] of payment and not a guarant[ee] of collection."[4] A "No Release of Guarantor" provision in § 10.8 stated that "the obligations of each guarantor... shall not be reduced, limited or terminated, nor shall such guarantor be discharged from any such obligations, for any reason whatsoever," except payment and performance in full or through waiver or amendment of the Credit Agreement. Under § 13.05 of the Credit Agreement, a guarantor could be released only through (i) the unanimous consent of the Banks for the guarantees of Fibreboard subsidiaries or through the consent of Banks holding 51% of the debt for other subsidiaries, or (ii) a fair value sale of the guarantor if its cumulative assets totaled less than 10% of the book value of the aggregate OCD group of entities.

---

[4] This standard guarantee term means simply that, once the primary obligor (here OCD) defaults, the Banks can proceed against the guarantors directly and immediately without first obtaining a judgment against OCD and collecting against that judgment to determine if a shortfall from OCD exists.

CSFB negotiated the Credit Agreement expressly to limit the ways in which OCD could deal with its subsidiaries. For example, it could not enter into transactions with a subsidiary that would result in losses to that subsidiary. Importantly, the Credit Agreement contained provisions designed to protect the separateness of OCD and its subsidiaries. The subsidiaries agreed explicitly to maintain themselves as separate entities. To further this agreement, they agreed to keep separate books and financial records in order to prepare separate financial statements. The Banks were given the right to visit each subsidiary and discuss business matters directly with that subsidiary's management. The subsidiaries also were prohibited from merging into OCD because both entities were required to survive a transaction under § 8.09(a)(ii)(A) of the Credit Agreement. This provision also prohibited guarantor subsidiaries from merging with other subsidiaries unless there would be no effect on the guarantees' value.

C. Procedural History

On October 5, 2000, facing mounting asbestos litigation, OCD and seventeen of its subsidiaries (collectively, the "Debtors") filed for reorganization under Chapter 11 of the Bankruptcy Code, § 1101 *et seq* Twenty-seven months later, the Debtors and certain unsecured creditor groups (collectively, the "Plan Proponents") proposed a reorganization plan (as amended, the "Plan") predicated on obtaining "substantive consolidation" of the Debtors along with three non-Debtor OCD subsidiaries. Typically this arrangement pools all assets and liabilities of the subsidiaries into their parent and treats all claims against the subsidiaries as transferred to the parent. In fact, however, the Plan Proponents sought a form of what is known as a "deemed consolidation," under which a consolidation is deemed to exist[7] for purposes of valuing and satisfying creditor claims, voting for or against the Plan, and making distributions for allowed claims under it. Plan § 6.1. Yet "the Plan would not result in the merger of or the transfer or commingling of any assets of any of the Debtors or Non-Debtor Subsidiaries,... [which] will continue to be owned by the respective Debtors or Non-Debtors." Plan § 6.1(a). Despite this, on the Plan's effective date "all guarantees of the Debtors of the obligations of any other Debtor will be deemed eliminated, so that any claim against any such Debtor and any guarantee thereof... will be deemed to be one obligation of the Debtors with respect to the consolidated estate." Plan § 6.1(b). Put another way, "the Plan eliminates the separate obligations of the Subsidiary Debtors arising from the guarant[e]es of the 1997 Credit Agreement." Plan Disclosure Statement at A-9897.

---

[7] "[A]ll assets and liabilities of each Subsidiary Debtor... *will be treated as though they were merged into and with the assets and liabilities of OCD*...." Plan § 6.1(b) (emphasis added).

The Banks objected to the proposed consolidation. Judge John Fullam * * * granted the consolidation motion in an order accompanied by a short opinion. *In re Owens Corning*, 316 B.R. 168 (Bankr.D.Del.2004).

Judge Fullam concluded that there existed "substantial identity between... OCD and its wholly-owned subsidiaries." *Id.* at 171. He further determined that "there [was] simply no basis for a finding that, in extending credit, the Banks relied upon the separate credit of any of the subsidiary guarantors." *Id.* at 172. In Judge Fullam's view, it was "also clear that substantive consolidation would greatly simplify and expedite the successful completion of this entire bankruptcy proceeding. More importantly, it would be exceedingly difficult to untangle the financial affairs of the various entities." *Id.* at 171. As such, he held substantive consolidation should be permitted, as not only did it allow "obvious advantages... [, but was] a virtual necessity." *Id.* at 172. In any event, Judge Fullam wrote, "[t]he real issue is whether the Banks are entitled to participate, *pari passu*, with other unsecured creditors, or whether the Banks' claim is entitled to priority, in whole or in part, over the claims of other unsecured creditors." *Id.* But this issue, he stated, "cannot now be determined." *Id.*

CSFB appeals on the Banks' behalf. * * *

III. Substantive consolidation

Substantive consolidation, a construct of federal common law, emanates from equity. It "treats separate legal entities as if they were merged into a single survivor left with all the cumulative assets and liabilities (save for inter-entity liabilities, which are erased). The result is that claims of creditors against separate debtors morph to claims against the consolidated survivor." *Genesis Health Ventures, Inc. v. Stapleton (In re Genesis Health Ventures, Inc.)*, 402 F.3d 416, 423 (3d Cir. 2005). Consolidation restructures (and thus revalues) rights of creditors and for certain creditors this may result in significantly less recovery.

While we have not fully considered the character and scope of substantive consolidation, we discussed the concept in *Nesbit,* 347 F.3d at 86-88 (surveying substantive consolidation case law for application by analogy to the Title VII inquiry of when to consolidate employers for the purpose of assessing a discrimination claim), and *In re Genesis Health Ventures,* 402 F.3d at 423-24 (examining, *inter alia,* whether a "deemed" consolidation for voting in connection with, and distribution under, a proposed plan of reorganization is a substantive consolidation for purposes of calculating U.S. Trustee quarterly fees under 28 U.S.C. § 1930(a)(6)). Other courts, including the Supreme Court itself in an opinion that spawned the concept of consolidation, have holdings more on point than heretofore have we. We begin with a survey of key cases, drawing from them when substantive consolidation may apply consistent with the principles we perceive as cabining its use, and apply those principles to this case.

A. History of Substantive Consolidation

The concept of substantively consolidating separate estates begins with a commonsense deduction. Corporate disregard[10] as a fault may lead to corporate disregard as a remedy.

Prior to substantive consolidation, other remedies for corporate disregard were (and remain) in place. For example, where a subsidiary is so dominated by its corporate parent as to be the parent's "alter ego," the "corporate veil" of the subsidiary can be ignored (or "pierced") under state law. Kors, *supra,* at 386-90 (citing as far back as I. Maurice Wormser, *Piercing the Veil of Corporate Entity,* 12 Colum. L.Rev. 496 (1912)). Or a court might mandate that the assets transferred to a corporate subsidiary be turned over to its parent's trustee in bankruptcy for wrongs such as fraudulent transfers, Kors, *supra,* at 391, in effect bringing back to the bankruptcy estate assets wrongfully conveyed to an affiliate. If a corporate parent is both a creditor of a subsidiary and so dominates the affairs of that entity as to prejudice unfairly its other creditors, a court may place payment priority to the parent below that of the other creditors, a remedy known as equitable subordination, which is now codified in § 510(c) of the Bankruptcy Code. *See generally id.* at 394-95.

Adding to these remedies, the Supreme Court, little more than six decades ago, approved (at least indirectly and perhaps inadvertently) what became known as substantive consolidation. *Sampsell v. Imperial Paper & Color Corp.,* 313 U.S. 215 (1941). In *Sampsell* an individual in bankruptcy had transferred assets prepetition to a corporation he controlled. (Apparently these became the corporation's sole assets.) When the bankruptcy referee ordered that the transferred assets be turned over by the corporation to the individual debtor's trustee, a creditor of the non-debtor corporation sought distribution priority with respect to that entity's assets. In deciding that the creditor should not be accorded priority (thus affirming the bankruptcy referee), the Supreme Court turned a typical turnover/fraudulent transfer case into the forebear of today's substantive consolidation by terming the bankruptcy referee's order (marshaling the corporation's assets for the benefit of the debtor's estate) as "consolidating the estates." *Id.* at 219.

---

[10] A term used by Mary Elisabeth Kors in her comprehensive and well-organized article entitled *Altered Egos: Deciphering Substantive Consolidation,* 59 U. Pitt. L.Rev. 381, 383 (1998) (hereinafter "Kors").

Each of these remedies has subtle differences. "Piercing the corporate veil" makes shareholders liable for corporate wrongs. Equitable subordination places bad-acting creditors behind other creditors when distributions are made. Turnover and fraudulent transfer bring back to the transferor debtor assets improperly transferred to another (often an affiliate). Substantive consolidation goes in a direction different (and in most cases further) than any of these remedies; it is not limited to shareholders, it affects distribution to innocent creditors, and it mandates more than the return of specific assets to the predecessor owner. It brings all the assets of a group of entities into a single survivor. Indeed, it merges liabilities as well. "The result," to repeat, "is that claims of creditors against separate debtors morph to claims against the consolidated survivor." *In re Genesis Health Ventures,* 402 F.3d at 423. The bad news for certain creditors is that, instead of looking to assets of the subsidiary with whom they dealt, they now must share those assets with all creditors of all consolidated entities, raising the specter for some of a significant distribution diminution.

Though the concept of consolidating estates had Supreme Court approval, Courts of Appeal (with one exception) were slow to follow suit. * * * Little occurred thereafter for more than two decades, until the Second Circuit issued several decisions * * * that brought substantive consolidation as a remedy back into play and premise its modern-day understanding.

Other Circuit Courts fell in line in acknowledging substantive consolidation as a possible remedy. * * *

The reasons of these courts for allowing substantive consolidation as a possible remedy span the spectrum and often overlap. * * *

Ultimately most courts slipstreamed behind two rationales-those of the Second Circuit in *In re Augie/Restivo Baking Co., Ltd.*, 860 F.2d 515 (2d Cir. 1988) and the D.C. Circuit in *In re Auto-Train Corp.*, 810 F.2d 270 (D.C.Cir. 1987). The former found that the competing "considerations are merely variants on two critical factors: (i) whether creditors dealt with the entities as a single economic unit and did not rely on their separate identity in extending credit, . . . or (ii) whether the affairs of the debtors are so entangled that consolidation will benefit all creditors. . . ." *In re Augie/Restivo,* 860 F.2d at 518 (internal quotation marks and citations omitted). *Auto-Train* touched many of the same analytical bases as the prior Second Circuit cases, but in the end chose as its overarching test the "substantial identity" of the entities and made allowance for consolidation in spite of creditor reliance on separateness when "the demonstrated benefits of consolidation 'heavily' outweigh the harm." *In re Auto-Train,* 810 F.2d at 276 (citation omitted).

Whatever the rationale, courts have permitted substantive consolidation as an equitable remedy in certain circumstances. No court has held that substantive consolidation is not authorized, though there appears nearly unanimous consensus that it is a remedy to be used "sparingly." *In re Augie/Restivo,* 860 F.2d at 518.

B. Our View of Substantive Consolidation

Substantive consolidation exists as an equitable remedy. But when should it be available and by what test should its use be measured? As already noted, we have commented on substantive consolidation only generally in *Nesbit,* 347 F.3d at 86-88, and *In re Genesis Health Ventures,* 402 F.3d at 423-24. The latter nonetheless left little doubt that, if presented with a choice of analytical avenues, we favor essentially that of *Augie/Restivo. Id.* at 423. The *Auto-Train* approach (requiring "substantial identity" of entities to be consolidated, plus that consolidation is "necessary to avoid some harm or realize some benefit," 810 F.2d at 276) adopts, we presume, one of the *Augie/Restivo* touchstones for substantive consolidation while adding the low bar of avoiding some harm or discerning some benefit by consolidation. To us this fails to capture completely the few times substantive consolidation may be considered and then, when it does hit one chord, it allows a threshold not sufficiently egregious and too imprecise for easy measure. For example, we disagree that "[i]f a creditor makes [a showing of reliance on separateness], the court may order consolidation... if it determines that the demonstrated benefits of consolidation 'heavily' outweigh the harm." *Id.* at 276 (citation omitted); *see also Eastgroup,* 935 F.2d at 249. If an objecting creditor relied on the separateness of the entities, consolidation cannot be justified *vis-à-vis* the claims of that creditor.

In assessing whether to order substantive consolidation, courts consider many factors * * *. Too often the factors in a check list fail to separate the unimportant from the important, or even to set out a standard to make the attempt. * * * This often results in rote following of a form containing factors where courts tally up and spit out a score without an eye on the principles that give the rationale for substantive consolidation (and why, as a result, it should so seldom be in play). *Id.* ("[D]iffering tests with... agreed... factors run the risk that courts will miss the forest for the trees. Running down factors as a check list can lead a court to lose sight of why we have substantive consolidation in the first instance... and often [to] fail [to] identify a metric by which [it] can... [assess] the relative importance among the factors. The... [result is] resort to ad hoc balancing without a steady eye on the... [principles] to be advanced....").

Chapter 8. Equitable Subordination and Substantive Consolidation 455

What, then, are those principles? We perceive them to be as follows.

(1) Limiting the cross-creep of liability by respecting entity separateness is a "fundamental ground rule[ ]." Kors, *supra,* at 410. As a result, the general expectation of state law and of the Bankruptcy Code, and thus of commercial markets, is that courts respect entity separateness absent compelling circumstances calling equity (and even then only possibly substantive consolidation) into play.

(2) The harms substantive consolidation addresses are nearly always those caused by *debtors* (and entities they control) who disregard separateness. Harms caused by creditors typically are remedied by provisions found in the Bankruptcy Code (*e.g.,* fraudulent transfers, §§ 548 and 544(b)(1), and equitable subordination, § 510(c)).

(3) Mere benefit to the administration of the case (for example, allowing a court to simplify a case by avoiding other issues or to make postpetition accounting more convenient) is hardly a harm calling substantive consolidation into play.

(4) Indeed, because substantive consolidation is extreme (it may affect profoundly creditors' rights and recoveries) and imprecise, this "rough justice" remedy should be rare and, in any event, one of last resort after considering and rejecting other remedies (for example, the possibility of more precise remedies conferred by the Bankruptcy Code).

(5) While substantive consolidation may be used defensively to remedy the identifiable harms caused by entangled affairs, it may not be used offensively (for example, having a primary purpose to disadvantage tactically a group of creditors in the plan process or to alter creditor rights).

The upshot is this. In our Court what must be proven (absent consent) concerning the entities for whom substantive consolidation is sought is that (i) prepetition they disregarded separateness so significantly their creditors relied on the breakdown of entity borders and treated them as one legal entity,[19] or (ii) postpetition their assets and liabilities are so scrambled that separating them is prohibitive and hurts all creditors.[20]

---

[19] This rationale is meant to protect in bankruptcy the prepetition expectations of those creditors. *Accord* Kors, *supra,* at 419. The usual scenario is that creditors have been misled by debtors' actions (regardless whether those actions were intentional or inadvertent) and thus perceived incorrectly (and relied on this perception) that multiple entities were one.

[20] This rationale is at bottom one of practicality when the entities' assets and liabilities have been "hopelessly commingled." *In re Gulfco Inv.,* 593 F.2d at 929; *In re Vecco,* 4 B.R. at 410. Without substantive consolidation all creditors will be worse off (as Humpty

Proponents of substantive consolidation have the burden of showing one or the other rationale for consolidation. The second rationale needs no explanation. The first, however, is more nuanced. A *prima facie* case for it typically exists when, based on the parties' prepetition dealings, a proponent proves corporate disregard creating contractual expectations of creditors that they were dealing with debtors as one indistinguishable entity. Kors, *supra,* at 417-18 * * *. Proponents who are creditors must also show that, in their prepetition course of dealing, they actually and reasonably relied on debtors' supposed unity. Kors, *supra,* at 418-19. Creditor opponents of consolidation can nonetheless defeat a *prima facie* showing under the first rationale if they can prove they are adversely affected and actually relied on debtors' separate existence.

C. Application of Substantive Consolidation to Our Case

With the principles we perceive underlie use of substantive consolidation, the outcome of this appeal is apparent at the outset. Substantive consolidation fails to fit the facts of our case and, in any event, a "deemed" consolidation cuts against the grain of all the principles.

To begin, the Banks did the "deal world" equivalent of "Lending 101." They loaned $2 billion to OCD and enhanced the credit of that unsecured loan indirectly by subsidiary guarantees covering less than half the initial debt. What the Banks got in lending lingo was "structural seniority"-a direct claim against the guarantors (and thus against their assets levied on once a judgment is obtained) that other creditors of OCD did not have. This kind of lending occurs every business day. To undo this bargain is a demanding task.

1. No Prepetition Disregard of Corporate Separateness.

Despite the Plan Proponents' pleas to the contrary, there is no evidence of the prepetition disregard of the OCD entities' separateness. To the contrary, OCD (no less than CSFB) negotiated the 1997 lending transaction premised on the separateness of all OCD affiliates. Even today no allegation exists of bad faith by anyone concerning the loan. In this context, OCD and the other Plan Proponents cannot now ignore, or have us ignore, the very ground rules OCD put in place. Playing by these rules means that obtaining the guarantees of separate entities, made separate by OCD's choice of how to structure the affairs of its affiliate group of companies, entitles a lender, in bankruptcy or out, to

---

Dumpty cannot be reassembled or, even if so, the effort will threaten to reprise *Jarndyce v. Jarndyce,* the fictional suit in Dickens' *Bleak House* where only the professionals profited). With substantive consolidation the lot of all creditors will be improved, as consolidation "advance[s] one of the primary goals of bankruptcy-enhancing the value of the assets available to creditors...-often in a very material respect." Kors, *supra,* at 417 (citation omitted).

look to any (or all) guarantor(s) for payment when the time comes. As such, the District Court's conclusions of "substantial identity" of OCD and its subsidiaries, and the Banks' reliance thereon, are incorrect. For example, testimony presented by both the Banks and the Debtors makes plain the parties' intention to treat the entities separately. CSFB presented testimony from attorneys and bankers involved in negotiating the Credit Agreement that reflected their assessment of the value of the guarantees as partially derived from the separateness of the entities. As OCD concedes, these representatives "testified that the guarant[e]es were... intended to provide 'structural seniority' to the banks," and were thus fundamentally premised on an assumption of separateness. Debtors Ans. Br. at 26.

In the face of this testimony, Plan Proponents nonetheless argue that the Banks intended to ignore the separateness of the entities. In support of this contention, they assert, *inter alia*, that because the Banks did not receive independent financial statements for each of the entities during the negotiating process, they must have intended to deal with them as a unified whole. Because the Banks were unaware of the separate financial makeup of the subsidiaries, the argument goes, they could not have relied on their separateness.

This argument is overly simplistic. Assuming the Banks did not obtain separate financial statements for each subsidiary, they nonetheless obtained detailed information about each subsidiary guarantor from OCD, including information about that subsidiary's assets and debt. Moreover, the Banks knew a great deal about these subsidiaries. For example, they knew that each subsidiary guarantor had assets with a book value of at least $30 million as per the terms of the Credit Agreement, that the aggregate value of the guarantor subsidiaries was over $900 million and that those subsidiaries had little or no debt. Additionally, the Banks knew that Fibreboard's subsidiaries (including the entities that became part of ESI) had no asbestos liability, would be debt-free post-acquisition and had assets of approximately $700 million.

Even assuming the Plan Proponents could prove prepetition disregard of Debtors' corporate forms, we cannot conceive of a justification for imposing the rule that a creditor must obtain financial statements from a debtor in order to rely reasonably on the separateness of that debtor. Creditors are free to employ whatever metrics they believe appropriate in deciding whether to extend credit free of court oversight. We agree with the Banks that "the reliance inquiry is not an inquiry into lenders' internal credit metrics. Rather, it is about the *fact* that the credit decision was made in reliance on the existence of separate entities. . . ." CSFB Opening Br. at 31 (emphasis in original). Here there is no serious dispute as to that fact.

2. No Hopeless Commingling Exists Postpetition.

There also is no meaningful evidence postpetition of hopeless commingling of Debtors' assets and liabilities. Indeed, there is no question which entity owns which principal assets and has which material liabilities. Likely for this reason little time is spent by the parties on this alternative test for substantive consolidation. It is similarly likely that the District Court followed suit.

The Court nonetheless erred in concluding that the commingling of assets will justify consolidation when "the affairs of the two companies are so entangled that consolidation *will be beneficial.*" *In re Owens Corning,* 316 B.R. at 171 (emphasis added). As we have explained, commingling justifies consolidation only when separately accounting for the assets and liabilities of the distinct entities will reduce the recovery of *every* creditor-that is, when every creditor will benefit from the consolidation. Moreover, the benefit to creditors should be from cost savings that make assets available rather than from the shifting of assets to benefit one group of creditors at the expense of another. Mere benefit to some creditors, or administrative benefit to the Court, falls far short. The District Court's test not only fails to adhere to the theoretical justification for "hopeless commingling" consolidation-that no creditor's rights will be impaired-but also suffers from the infirmity that it will almost always be met. That is, substantive consolidation will nearly always produce some benefit to some in the form of simplification and/or avoidance of costs. Among other things, following such a path misapprehends the degree of harm required to order substantive consolidation.

But no matter the legal test, a case for hopeless commingling cannot be made. Arguing nonetheless to the contrary, Debtors assert that "it would be practically impossible and prohibitively expensive in time and resources" to account for the voluntary bankruptcies of the separate entities OCD has created and maintained. Debtors Ans. Br. at 63. In support of this contention, Debtors rely almost exclusively on the District Court's findings that

> it would be exceedingly difficult to untangle the financial affairs of the various entities. . . [and] there are. . . many reasons for challenging the accuracy of the results achieved [in accounting efforts thus far]. For example, transfers of cash between subsidiaries and parent did not include any payment of interest; and calculations of royalties are subject to question.

In re Owens Corning, 316 B.R. at 171. Assuming *arguendo* that these findings are correct, they are simply not enough to establish that substantive consolidation is warranted.

Neither the impossibility of perfection in untangling the affairs of the entities nor the likelihood of some inaccuracies in efforts to do so is sufficient to justify consolidation. We find *R 2 Investments, LDC v. World Access, Inc.* (*In re World Access, Inc.*), 301 B.R. 217 (Bankr.N.D.Ill.2003), instructive on this point. In *World Access* the Court noted that the controlling entity "had no uniform guidelines for the recording of intercompany interest charges" and that the debtors failed to "allocate overhead charges amongst themselves." *Id.* at 234. The Court held, however, that those accounting shortcomings were "merely imperfections in a sophisticated system of accounting records that were conscientiously maintained." *Id.* at 279. It ultimately concluded that "all the relevant accounting data. . . still exist [ed]," that only a "reasonable review to make any necessary adjustments [was] required," and, thus, that substantive consolidation was not warranted. *Id.*

The record in our case compels the same conclusion. At its core, Debtors' argument amounts to the contention that because intercompany interest and royalty payments were not perfectly accounted for, untangling the finances of those entities is a hopeless endeavor. Yet imperfection in intercompany accounting is assuredly not atypical in large, complex company structures. For obvious reasons, we are loathe to entertain the argument that complex corporate families should have an expanded substantive consolidation option in bankruptcy. And we find no reason to doubt that "perfection is not the standard in the substantive consolidation context." *Id.* We are confident that a court could properly order and oversee an accounting process that would sufficiently account for the interest and royalty payments owed among the OCD group of companies for purposes of evaluating intercompany claims-dealing with inaccuracies and difficulties as they arise and not in hypothetical abstractions.

On the basis of the record before us, the Plan Proponents cannot fulfill their burden of demonstrating that Debtors' affairs are even tangled, let alone that the cost of untangling them is so high relative to their assets that the Banks, among other creditors, will benefit from a consolidation.

3. Other Considerations Doom Consolidation as Well.

Other considerations drawn from the principles we set out also counsel strongly against consolidation. First of all, holding out the possibility of later giving priority to the Banks on their claims does not cure an improvident grant of substantive consolidation. Among other things, the prerequisites for this last-resort remedy must still be met no matter the priority of the Banks' claims.

Secondly, substantive consolidation should be used defensively to remedy identifiable harms, not offensively to achieve advantage over one group in the plan negotiation process (for example, by deeming assets redistributed to negate plan voting rights), nor a "free pass" to spare Debtors or any other group from proving challenges, like fraudulent transfer claims, that are liberally brandished to scare yet are hard to show. If the Banks are so vulnerable to the fraudulent transfer challenges Debtors have teed up (but have not swung at for so long), then the game should be played to the finish in that arena.

But perhaps the flaw most fatal to the Plan Proponents' proposal is that the consolidation sought was "deemed" (*i.e.,* a pretend consolidation for all but the Banks). If Debtors' corporate and financial structure was such a sham before the filing of the motion to consolidate, then how is it that post the Plan's effective date this structure stays largely undisturbed, with the Debtors reaping all the liability-limiting, tax and regulatory benefits achieved by forming subsidiaries in the first place? In effect, the Plan Proponents seek to remake substantive consolidation not as a remedy, but rather a stratagem to "deem" separate resources reallocated to OCD to strip the Banks of rights under the Bankruptcy Code, favor other creditors, and yet trump possible Plan objections by the Banks. Such "deemed" schemes we deem not Hoyle.

IV. Conclusion

Substantive consolidation at its core is equity. Its exercise must lead to an equitable result. "Communizing" assets of affiliated companies to one survivor to feed all creditors of all companies may to some be equal (and hence equitable). But it is hardly so for those creditors who have lawfully bargained prepetition for unequal treatment by obtaining guarantees of separate entities. *Accord Chemical Bank New York Trust Co. v. Kheel,* 369 F.2d 845, 848 (Friendly, J., concurring) ("Equality among creditors who have lawfully bargained for different treatment is not equity but its opposite. . . ."). No principled, or even plausible, reason exists to undo OCD's and the Banks' arms-length negotiation and lending arrangement, especially when to do so punishes the very parties that conferred the prepetition benefit-a $2 billion loan unsecured by OCD and guaranteed by others only in part. To overturn this bargain, set in place by OCD's own pre-loan choices of organizational form, would cause chaos in the marketplace, as it would make this case the Banquo's ghost of bankruptcy.

With no meaningful evidence supporting either test to apply substantive consolidation, there is simply not the nearly "perfect storm" needed to invoke it. Even if there were, a "deemed" consolidation-"several zip (if not area) codes away from anything resembling substantive consolidation," *In re Genesis Health Ventures,* 402 F.3d at 424-fails even to qualify for consideration. Moreover, it is here a tactic used as a sword and not a shield.

We thus reverse and remand this case to the District Court.

NOTES

1. The most common use of substantive consolidation is in consensual cases in which the parties agree on the distribution of value in a reorganization plan approved by the court. "Deemed consolidation" in which a consolidation is deemed to exist for purposes of valuing creditor claims and voting on the plan

is commonly sought in these cases. But such a plan does not result in the merger of affiliates or commingling of assets of the different entities.

2. The question left by *Owens Corning* is what remains of nonconsensual substantive consolidation in the Third Circuit. Senior District Court Judge Fullam, sitting in bankruptcy, stated:

> I have no difficulty in concluding that there is indeed substantial identity between the parent debtor OCD and its wholly-owned subsidiaries. All of the subsidiaries were controlled by a single committee, from central headquarters, without regard to the subsidiary structure. Control was exercised on a product-line basis. For example, the president of the insulating systems business managed all aspects of the production, marketing, and distribution of insulation products, regardless of whether those products were manufactured in a factory owned by OCD or by a foreign subsidiary. The officers and directors of the subsidiaries did not establish business plans or budgets, and did not appoint senior management except at the direction of the central committee * * * Subsidiaries were established for the convenience of the parent company, primarily for tax reasons. All the subsidiaries were dependent upon the parent company for funding and capital. The financial management of the entire enterprise was conducted in an integrated manner. No subsidiary exercised control over its own finances.
>
> It is also clear that substantive consolidation would greatly simplify and expedite the successful completion of this entire bankruptcy proceeding. More importantly, it would be exceedingly difficult to untangle the financial affairs of the various entities. * * *
>
> There can be no doubt that the Banks relied upon the overall credit of the entire Owens Corning enterprise. Each Bank's commitment was to the entire enterprise. The decision as to whether funds would be borrowed by the parent company, or by one or more of the subsidiaries, was made by the borrowers, not by the lenders. All of Owens Corning's financial reporting was done on a consolidated basis, and only that consolidated information was provided to the Banks. * * *
>
> In short, there is simply no basis for a finding that, in extending credit, the Banks relied upon the separate credit of any of the subsidiary guarantors. This is not to say that the guarantees were not important to the Banks. * * *

In re Owens Corning, 316 B.R. 168, 171-172 (Bankr.D.Del.2004).

In view of these findings, why did the Third Circuit, in reversing, consider this an easy case for rejecting substantive consolidation?

3. After *Owens Corning*, one might conclude that, assuming formal corporate governance boundaries are observed, substantive consolidation in the Third Circuit is effectively limited to cases in which no objecting creditor is prejudiced by the consolidation.

Not according to *In re Lisanti Foods, Inc.*, 2006 WL 2927619 (D.N.J. 2006), in which the district court had no difficulty in approving a substantive consolidation plan under the first prong of the *Owens Corning* test (creditor reliance on prepetition disregard of separateness). The plan was proposed by the unsecured creditors' committee and was opposed by the debtors' owners. The three debtors that filed for Chapter 11 relief were engaged in operating wholesale distribution centers for specialty foods in several states. The bankruptcy court found that creditors viewed the debtors as a single entity when extending credit. The evidence showed that: all three debtors had the same officers, directors, and shareholders; they conducted virtually identical business operations under very similar names, and used the same general methods of operation; they performed all their accounting functions in one centralized location (New Jersey); the bulk of their administrative staff also worked out of New Jersey. The court found that these facts provided "ample support" for granting substantive consolidation under *Owens Corning*.

4. Although Courts of Appeals frequently repeat that use of substantive consolidation should be "sparing," hundreds of reported decisions approve Chapter 11 plans providing for substantive consolidation on a bewildering set of fact patterns. The authorities are collected and analyzed in Mary Elisabeth Kors, *Altered Egos: Deciphering Substantive Consolidation*, 59 U.Pitt.L.Rev. 381 (1998), which is cited in *Owens Corning*. Recent empirical work finds that large public companies that find themselves in Chapter 11 frequently employ substantive consolidation in their reorganization plans. William H. Widen, *The Reality of Substantive Consolidation*, 26 ABI J. 14 (2007) (157 substantive consolidations out of 283 large public company reorganizations filed between 2000 and 2004). Most of these were "deemed" consolidations. *Id.*

5. The doctrine of substantive consolidation may provide debtors' lawyers with a basis for attacking the increasingly common practice of segregating accounts receivable and other payment rights into "bankruptcy remote vehicles" through the process of "asset securitization." The history and nature of "asset securitization" or "structured finance" is described in two Reports of the Association of the Bar of the City of New York, *New Developments in Structured Finance*, 56 Bus. Law. 95 (2000), and *Structured Financing Techniques*, 50 Bus. Law. 527 (1995), which identifies the "one central, core principle" of asset securitization: "a defined group of assets can be structurally isolated and thus serve as the basis of a financing that is independent from the bankruptcy risks of the originator of the assets."

The proponents of asset securitization argue that by transferring assets to a trust or limited liability company that engages in no business activity other than the ownership and management of the segregated assets, the transferred assets are removed from the estate of the transferor. Credit rating agencies like Moody's and Standard and Poor's have agreed to rate securities issued by these trusts or limited liability companies based on the quality and value of the assets transferred rather than the general credit of the transferor. This enables a transferor with, say, a single A credit rating to obtain financing at AAA rates by segregating assets into "bankruptcy remote vehicles." Bankruptcy lawyers have long been skeptical of this stratagem, at least when the transferor remains heavily involved in the management of the assets after the transfer through ownership of the trust, or issued guarantees or similar "credit enhancement" activities or owned a residual interest in the entity holding the transferred assets.

In the *LTV Steel Co.* case, reported at 37 Bankr. Ct.Dec. 232 (2001), to the apparent horror of "the structured finance community," Bankruptcy Judge William T. Bodoh of the Northern District of Ohio, refused to consider the segregation of LTV's accounts receivables and inventory into bankruptcy remote vehicles a "true sale" and authorized the bankruptcy debtor to treat these assets as property of the estate, authorizing their use subject to an adequate protection order on an interim basis. The cash collateral litigation in *LTV Steel Co.* thereafter settled before a final order was entered on the question of the "true sale" nature of the securitization.

But attacking a securitization transaction as not a true sale is not the only possibility. If debtors could substantively consolidate the bankruptcy remote vehicle with the estate of the transferor, then presumably they could obtain use of the cash collateral and the protection of the automatic stay. This avenue of attack becomes more feasible the more intertwined the bankruptcy remote vehicle and the transferred assets are with the affairs of the bankruptcy debtor. Some law firms specialize in providing so-called "non-consolidation" opinions that analyze this risk in connection with the issuance of securities by "bankruptcy remote vehicles."

A third possibility is that the bankruptcy remote vehicle could itself initiate bankruptcy proceedings or suffer the filing of an involuntary bankruptcy. The structured finance community has developed elaborate forms to avoid this possibility, but it cannot be entirely eliminated. See *In re Kingston Square Associates*, 214 B.R. 713 (Bankr.S.D.N.Y.1997), which upheld an involuntary filing against a bankruptcy remote vehicle orchestrated by an insider of the debtor.

CHAPTER 9
THE CONSUMER DEBTOR IN CHAPTERS 7 AND 13

A. INTRODUCTION TO CONSUMER BANKRUPTCY

This chapter explores complex, and, in many instances, deeply flawed statutes that undertake to balance the competing interests of unpaid consumer lenders and insolvent consumer debtors. This subject involves complex policy choices relating to the proper scope of bankruptcy's fresh-start policy upon which we as a society have failed to develop any coherent or lasting consensus. When you reach the end of this chapter we expect that there will be no more consensus within your classroom than within the larger society on the fundamental policy choices. We do expect, however, that there will be a consensus that Congress has failed to coherently embody any workable policy concerning consumer bankruptcy in the Bankruptcy Code as it now stands. This reality makes study of consumer bankruptcy law inordinately challenging.

The most fundamental consumer bankruptcy policy choice is the extent to which a wide variety of debtors, in widely varying financial and moral circumstances, should be required to devote future earnings to the payment of past debts in order to obtain bankruptcy relief. In Chapter 7 cases, this balance is struck by defining the scope of discharge and in the treatment of secured claims. In Chapter 13 cases, the balance is struck by defining the "net disposable income" that is to be devoted to repayment of past obligations as well as by defining the scope of discharge and the treatment of secured claims. Determining whether a case belongs in Chapter 7 (more discharge) or Chapter 13 (more debt repayment) also involves striking this same balance.

Historically, the Bankruptcy Code afforded bankruptcy judges considerable discretion in drawing this balance in light of the circumstances of particular cases. In the perception of powerful consumer lending lobbies, however, this flexibility resulted in a systematic shift of the balance too far in favor of insolvent consumers.

In 2005, in enacting the "Bankruptcy Abuse Prevention and Consumer Protection Act" (BAPCPA), Congress attempted to drain discretion out of the system by imposing rigid "objective" tests while simultaneously shifting the balance decisively towards consumer lenders. Unfortunately, the "objective" standards chosen are arbitrary and in many cases bear no relation to the reality particular debtors, creditors and courts face. The story of this chapter is how courts are dealing with Congressionally-mandated standards that cannot be sensibly applied (indeed sometimes cannot be sensibly understood) in the cases before them.

Most consumer cases involve four key economic issues: (i) the consumer's home and related home mortgage, estimated at more than 70% of all household debts, (ii) the consumer's cars and related secured auto loans, (iii) the consumer's unsecured debts (often credit card obligations incurred for consumption), and (iv) the consumer's future earnings. After this brief introduction, we deal first with unsecured debts and future earnings in Parts A, B, C, and D. Claims secured by personal property (especially cars) are the subject of Parts E and F. The treatment of home mortgages and home equity loans is dealt with in Part G.

As you work through the difficult and frustrating material ahead, keep in mind the practical effects of the various statutory interpretation issues you face. Consider how you might sensibly apply a statute designed around an inflexible objective test that—while it might accord with some hypothetical consumers' objective circumstances—doesn't fit the situation before you.

1. BACKGROUND

As the volume of consumer credit grew rapidly in the last 50 years, Congress twice appointed commissions to study consumer bankruptcy reform. The Bankruptcy Law Revision Commission of the 1970s, on whose work the 1978 Bankruptcy Code was based, concluded that past bankruptcy laws inadequately addressed consumer debtor problems and proposed major reforms. The principal consumer reform in the 1978 Code was the strengthening of Chapter 13. H.R. Rep.No.95-595, 95th Cong., 1st Sess. (1977). The National Bankruptcy Review Commission (NBRC) of the 1990s concluded that the 1978 Code had also proved inadequate and proposed major changes, but no legislation resulted. *Report of the National Bankruptcy Review Commission (1997) (NBRC Rep.)*. In the late 1990s the consumer finance industry—banks, credit card issuers, finance companies, credit unions and retailers—took matters in its own hands and presented to Congress legislation that almost entirely ignored the recommendations of the NBRC. This measure became BAPCPA after eight years of legislative wrangling and lobbying. We will discuss in detail the provisions of this statute.

Efforts have been made to profile today's consumer bankruptcy debtor. If you seek the modern consumer debtor, look about you. Bankruptcy is a middle class phenomenon. Filers come from mid-level as well as from lower-level income groups, though on the whole their incomes tend to fall in the lower half. Many own their homes. They are as well educated as those who do not file. In short, they are a cross-section of society. What all these people have in common is that they are in financial trouble, usually big trouble. *See, e.g.,* Teresa A. Sullivan, Elizabeth Warren & Jay Lawrence Westbrook, *The Fragile Middle Class* 27 (2000); Kenneth N. Klee, *Restructuring Individual Debts,* 71 Am. Bankr. L.J. 431, 445-446 (1997).

2. PRIVATE SECTOR DEBT RELIEF

Under state law, the defaulting debtor is left to the tender mercies of collection agencies and, eventually, judgment creditors. Within the limits of state and federal exemptions, they can garnish her pay, seize her assets and stain her credit report. Consumers who are unemployed or otherwise generally unable to pay their monthly bills have few alternatives to bankruptcy. Creditors may, however, work with defaulting debtors on an informal basis so long as there is hope of repayment. For debtors with income, extensions and workout agreements may be reached and personal finance companies offer consolidation loans in which existing debts are paid off by a new loan and the debtor, closely monitored by the consolidator, makes single monthly payments on the consolidated debt. If a payment is late, their telephone—still the most effective collection device—begins to ring. In more recent years home equity lenders have moved into the debt-consolidation business by offering to consolidate debt at lower interest rates by offering loans secured by second mortgages against debtors' homes. *NBRC Rep.* at 93–94. As home values fell throughout the nation in 2007-2009, these home equity loans quickly turned into albatrosses around the necks of both homeowners and home lenders.

Various "credit repair" businesses have been spawned in recent years charging substantial fees to rehabilitate a debtor's credit. The latest iteration is "debt settlement" companies, which have clients make monthly payments into a special account rather than paying their creditors. The company promises to use the cash to settle debts for pennies on the dollar. They charge an upfront fee of 10% to 15% of the total amount owed and a back-end fee of 20% to 30% of the amount "saved" for clients in a settlement. Since creditors are not receiving payment while settlement negotiations proceed, interest and late fees accrue; collection agencies hassle the debtor; credit scores suffer. The FTC has brought a number of cases against these firms. *See* Eleanor Laise, *Debt-Relief Firms Attract Complaints,* Wall St. J., Oct. 14, 2008, at D1.

By 2006, low interest rates and lax mortgage lenders offering "exotic" loan terms had driven home values to unsustainable levels. When economic activity slowed and home prices crashed in 2007, borrowers were unable to make payments on their mortgages or to refinance their way out of their plight. Mortgage defaults reached recession levels and debtors cried out for help. The inadequacy of available nonbankruptcy remedies became glaringly apparent. In

2008, a presidential election year, candidates, legislators, and state and federal government officials demanded relief for mortgage debtors. We will discuss the bankruptcy ramifications of some of these developments later.

3. BANKRUPTCY RELIEF

The traditional remedy available to individual debtors in financial difficulty is discharge of their debts in bankruptcy at the cost of liquidation of their nonexempt assets for the benefit of their creditors. The discharge/liquidation bargain embodies a policy judgment that individual debtors should not be burdened perpetually by their debts; they should be given a "fresh start" and encouraged to resume their lives as productive members of society. It is sometimes said that bankruptcy is "bad debt insurance" for debtors: even if they cannot pay their debts, creditors cannot reach their future earnings. An even older principle is that creditors should share equitably in their bankrupt debtors' assets. Bankruptcy law replaces the race-to-the-courthouse, winner-take-all nature of state collection law with more efficient and fair collective procedures. Chapter 7 of the Bankruptcy Code is the modern process that offers a fresh-start discharge for debtors and equitable distribution of nonexempt assets of the debtor's estate for creditors.

B. THE CONSUMER DEBTOR IN CHAPTER 7 BEFORE BAPCPA

We have dealt extensively with some of the basic substantive issues that arise in Chapter 7 in the previous chapters of this book. In chapter 3 (Claims), we found that the Code sets out elaborate provisions on how debtor's assets are distributed among claimants in Chapter 7. In chapter 4 (Discharge), we visited the complex set of rules for determining when individual debtors in Chapter 7 may be discharged. But it turns out that in about 96% of the cases, Chapter 7 consumer debtors have no equity in nonexempt assets to liquidate, and, therefore, the provisions of the Code assuring equitable distribution of assets (except insofar as they relate to secured claims) are almost wholly irrelevant. Michelle J. White, *Abuse or Protection? Economics of Bankruptcy Reform under BAPCPA*, 2007 U. Ill. L. Rev. 275, 284. This means that in the vast majority of consumer cases Chapter 7 offers nothing to unsecured creditors but much to debtors: an automatic stay against creditor collection action and a discharge of prepetition debts, leaving the debtor's postpetition earnings free of prepetition claims.

1. ACCESS TO CHAPTER 7 UNDER THE 1978 CODE

The most contentious policy issue concerning consumer debtors has been the extent to which debtors should be allowed free access to Chapter 7 and its promise of a rapid discharge of unsecured claims. BAPCPA radically changed the Code's position on this issue. The 1978 Code offered two alternatives for consumer relief, Chapter 7 liquidation and Chapter 13 rehabilitation. In Chapter 7 the debtor surrendered all nonexempt assets to a trustee in bankruptcy who liquidated the assets for distribution to creditors; in turn, the debtor received a discharge of most of her unsecured debts. In Chapter 13 the debtor was allowed to retain her assets by undertaking a repayment plan under which she devoted a portion of her income over a three-year period to the payment of her debts. Upon completion of the plan, the debtor received a broad discharge, sometimes referred to as a super-discharge because it discharged some otherwise nondischargeable claims. The Chapter 13 debtor voluntarily traded a portion of her post-bankruptcy earnings for the right to retain her nonexempt property and the super-discharge.

Under the 1978 Code, a debtor had a virtually unfettered right to opt for Chapter 7 liquidation with its fresh-start discharge in preference to rehabilitation under Chapter 13. With respect to the choice between liquidation under Chapter 7, or repayment under Chapter 13, debtors did the choosing and they chose Chapter 7 in the great majority of cases. In the year ending in September 2004, immediately before passage of 2005 amendments, there were 1,153,865 Chapter 7 filings and 454,412 Chapter 13 filings. Administrative Office of U.S. Courts, *Judicial Business 2005,* p. 29, Table 7 (Bankruptcy Court Filings) (2005). This can be described as a regime of "debtor's choice." As Professor David A. Skeel, Jr. observed, no other country was as generous to debtors in bankruptcy. *Debt's Dominion: A History of Bankruptcy Law in America* 2 (2001). Even the United Kingdom, whose economy and legal culture resembles our own, has an administrative official determine the debtor's treatment in bankruptcy who may require further payments to creditors before discharge is granted.

2. THE 1984 SUBSTANTIAL ABUSE TEST

In the years immediately following enactment of the 1978 Code, the number of consumer bankruptcies rose substantially, and creditor groups contended that debtors were abusing the open access policy of Chapter 7, which allowed discharge of unsecured prepetition debts without regard to debtors' ability to pay these debts. Creditors argued that debtors with enough postpetition income to pay a significant part of their prepetition debts over a period of a few years should not be entitled to an immediate fresh-start discharge in Chapter 7. Rather they should be granted a discharge only through Chapter 13 in which they would have to make periodic payments on their prepetition debts over a period of years. Accordingly, creditors in the 1980s urged Congress to allow bankruptcy judges to convert, *sua sponte*, Chapter 7 cases filed by debtors with enough income to pay a substantial portion of their prepetition debts to Chapter 13. This would have introduced a regime of "judge's choice." In support of such a change, creditors complained that open access to Chapter 7 had altered the public perception of bankruptcy from a humiliating last resort for hard pressed debtors to a routine financial planning tool, increasingly free of moral stigma, which the public accepted as a normal alternative for financial woes that allowed debtors to move on with their lives at the expense of their creditors.

In 1984, the consumer finance industry clamored for a "means test," barring access to Chapter 7 for debtors who had sufficient excess income—the means—to pay a significant portion of their debts under a Chapter 13 plan. But in 1984 Congress flatly rejected a means test and renewed its traditional commitment to keep the door open to Chapter 7 for "honest debtors" seeking a "fresh start." However, as part of the legislative end game, Congress threw the credit industry a bone by enacting former § 707(b) that allowed dismissal of a Chapter 7 case for "substantial abuse."

Consumer advocates believed this to be an innocuous concession that finally put to rest any future means test. The undefined phrase was thought to be so vague as to be almost meaningless. As originally drafted, this provision seemed to offer creditors very little: only the court could move for dismissal for substantial abuse, and it was thought unlikely that overworked bankruptcy judges would expend additional time poring over a debtor's schedules to decide *sua sponte* that Chapter 7 should be denied the petitioner. Moreover, Congress showed its support for free access to Chapter 7 by adding to § 707(b): "There shall be a presumption in favor of granting the relief requested by the debtor." Nevertheless, in the years following 1984, creditors were able to snatch partial victory from the jaws of almost total defeat by persuading some judges to view the substantial abuse test as a proxy for a means test and by obtaining amendment of § 707(b) to allow U.S. Trustees, as well as courts, to move for dismissal for substantial abuse.

On the eve of BAPCPA in 2005, there were competing judicial views of the meaning of the substantial abuse test. (i) The "per se" rule of *In re Kelly*, 841 F.2d 908 (9th Cir. 1988): The debtor's ability to repay her debts is the principal factor to be considered in determining substantial abuse; having an income in excess of necessary expenses, standing alone, constitutes substantial abuse of Chapter 7 justifying dismissal. (ii) The "totality of circumstances" rule of *In re Green*, 934 F.2d 568 (4th Cir. 1991): The debtor's solvency is important but is not alone enough to constitute abuse. Courts, on a case-by-case basis, should consider a number of factors: whether the petition was filed because of sudden illness, calamity, disability or unemployment; whether the debtor incurred debts in excess of her ability to pay; whether the debtor's proposed budget was unreasonable; whether the debtor's schedules and statement of current income were honest; and whether the debtor filed in good faith. We will find later that the totality of circumstances view plays an important role under BAPCPA.

C. BAPCPA

In the later 1980s bankruptcy filings doubled, and in the 1990s filing rates exploded. Over a period of 20 years, consumer bankruptcy filings grew by 500%. Creditors redoubled their efforts to impose a means test: creditor lobbyists drafted preliminary versions of BAPCPA in the late 1990s. BAPCPA, containing a means test designed to make it more difficult for higher income debtors to file in Chapter 7, was met by a fusillade of criticism by the consumer bar and academic communities, as well as most bankruptcy professionals and judges. The ensuing debate has probed the economic and social bases of bankruptcy policy.

Opponents of a means test maintained that consumer bankruptcies are caused by adverse changes in household debt and income and that bankruptcy is a much needed safety net. Charles Jordan Tabb, *Consumer Filings: Trends and Indicators, Part II*, 25 Am. Bankr. Inst. J. 42 (2007) (finding a close relationship between the amount of revolving consumer credit and the consumer bankruptcy rate). Much of this growth was owing to lower credit standards for credit cards, and in home loans, featuring subprime loans, "teaser rate" periods, interest-only loans and the like. In Teresa A. Sullivan, Elizabeth Warren and Jay L. Westbrook in *The Fragile Middle Class* (2000), the authors see the rapid increase in the debt burden shouldered by consumers as making debtors increasingly vulnerable to disruptions in family income caused by illness, unemployment, divorce, and the like. Thus, increased bankruptcy filings correlate closely with the massive increase in consumer debt. Douglas G. Baird agrees: "Many assume that the recent growth in the number of bankruptcies is bad. But default and bankruptcy are the inevitable consequences of borrowing. Holding everything else constant, as consumers borrow more, defaults increase and bankruptcy filings rise." *Technology, Information, and Bankruptcy*, 2007 U. Ill. L. Rev. 305, 306.

Sullivan, Warren & Westbrook describe debtors as on the whole honest people who incur debt based on erroneous assumptions that their income will be maintained or grow over time, suffer a severe interruption of that income on account of the loss of employment, divorce, illness and the like, and desperately need the fresh start offered by a bankruptcy discharge to become productive members of society again. Sullivan-Warren-Westbrook's recommendation with respect to the great rise in consumer bankruptcies is to leave access to bankruptcy open and to allow the credit market to solve the problem. If there are too many bankruptcies, creditors can deal with the problem by tightening their credit standards and monitoring their debtors more effectively. *See* Susan Block-Lieb and Edward J. Janger, *The Myth of the Rational Borrower: Rationality, Behavioralism, and the Misguided "Reform" of Bankruptcy Law*, 84 Tex. L. Rev. 1481, 1496 (2006) (hereafter Block-Lieb & Janger).

Another empirical study, David Himmelstein, Elizabeth Warren, Deborah Thorne & Stephanie Woolhandler, *Illness and Injury as Contributors to Bankruptcy*, 24 Health Affairs, W5-63 (2005), concluded that medical problems contributed to about half of all consumer bankruptcies. Illness results in both high medical bills and lost income. Health insurance coverage tied to employment often lapses when employment terminates, and uninsured illness was ruinous for many families. From 1981 to 2001, the number of "medical bankruptcies" increased twenty-threefold.

However, some economists saw bankruptcy as a "tax" on consumers, arguing that a bankruptcy discharge for some increased the cost of credit for all. In this view, the free access regime of pre-BAPCPA law, with low cost bankruptcy discharges, encouraged opportunistic behavior on the part of debtors who sought discharge even though they had enough future income to pay significant amounts of their debts. If BAPCPA reduced bankruptcy discharges, so the argument went, interest rates would go down for all consumers. *See* Block-Lieb & Janger, at 1484. Such empirical data as exist, however, do not suggest that in fact BAPCPA has lowered interest rates for consumers. Michael Simkovic, *The Effect of BAPCPA on Credit Card Industry Profits and Prices*, 83 Am. Bankr. L. J. 1 (2009).

Proponents of a means test maintained that the findings of Sullivan, et al., cannot explain the great rise in bankruptcy filings during the 1990s on the ground of increased debtor distress because the decade was a period of great prosperity, very low unemployment, lower divorce rates, and health costs that fell during the introduction of managed care in the mid-90s. *See* Todd J. Zywicki, *An Economic Analysis of the Consumer Bankruptcy Crisis*, 99 Nw. U. L. Rev. 1463 (2005); Edith H. Jones & Todd J. Zywicki, *It's Time for Means-Testing*, 1999 B.Y.U. L. Rev. 177. Professor Zywicki, who participated in drafting BAPCPA, asserts that:

> [T]he foregoing discussion suggests that the rising consumer bankruptcy filing rate throughout the past several years is not the result of increasing household economic distress. Unemployment, divorce, health, and indebtedness have been a part of the human condition since human societies have existed and do not appear to be worsening over time. This suggests that the cause of the consumer bankruptcy crisis is not an increase in consumer financial vulnerability but rather an increase in consumers' propensity to respond to financial problems by filing bankruptcy and discharging their debts instead of reining in spending or

tapping accumulated wealth. The novelty, therefore, is not the underlying problems but rather the increasing willingness of individuals to use bankruptcy as a response to those underlying problems.

99 Nw. U. L. Rev. at 1525-1526.

1. INTRODUCTION

In BAPCPA the tables are decisively turned: an individual debtor seeking a discharge in Chapter 7 faces formidable barriers. In the following sections, we examine the complex series of barriers that an individual debtor encounters in filing for Chapter 7 bankruptcy under BAPCPA. The Chapter 7 filing fees have been increased to $299, and attorneys' charges are higher because of additional burdens that BAPCPA imposes on them. Moreover, the debtor must initially pay for credit counseling and ultimately a course in financial management. No doubt some debtors will no longer be able to afford bankruptcy in light of these additional costs.

One traditional barrier is the bar on repeat discharges. The waiting period between Chapter 7 discharges was six years under the 1978 Code. Under BAPCPA the Chapter 7 waiting period is increased to eight years by § 727(a)(8) and runs from the date the first case was filed. It precludes discharge in any subsequent Chapter 7 case filed within that period. *See In re Mayo*, 2007 WL 1074078 (Bankr.D.Md.2007). Section 727(a)(9) was not changed by BAPCPA. It prescribes a six-year waiting period in cases in which the debtor has previously received a Chapter 13 discharge unless payments under the Chapter 13 plan either paid 100% of the allowed secured claims or 70% of the claims and the plan was proposed by the debtor in good faith and was her best effort. We will see later in this chapter that under BAPCPA waiting periods for Chapter 13 discharges are imposed in § 1328(f).

2. THE MEANS TEST

The centerpiece of BAPCPA with respect to consumer bankruptcy reform is the means test, found in a complex series of amendments to § 707(b). Between the date of enactment of BAPCPA in April 2005 and its effective date of October 17, 2005, Interim Rules and Official Forms implementing BAPCPA were formulated. The new rules were finally approved by the Supreme Court and Congress and took effect on December 1, 2008. Official Forms 22A (Chapter 7), 22B (Chapter 11) and 22C (Chapter 13) must be completed by all consumer debtors filing under these chapters and are important in guiding debtors through the complexities of the means test. Since BAPCPA is a poorly drafted law, filled with uncertainties, in some instances the relevant forms go beyond the statute in resolving ambiguities and lacunae on the basis of implicit policy judgments. In most instances courts are content to rely on the interpretation of the statute found in the Official Forms, but when they disagree with the form's interpretation, they have no reluctance in holding that statutes trump forms, *e.g.*, *In re Lasowski*, 384 B.R. 205 (8th Cir. BAP 2008).

a. General Power to Dismiss

The organization of § 707(b) is confusing. Paragraph (1) states that: the bankruptcy court on its own motion or on that of the U.S. Trustee, the panel trustee or a party in interest (*e.g.* a creditor), may dismiss or, with the consent of the debtor, convert to Chapter 11 or 13, a case filed by an *individual* debtor whose debts are *primarily consumer debts* if it finds that granting relief "would be an abuse of the provisions of this chapter." Consumer debts are those incurred by an individual primarily for a personal, family or household purpose. § 101(8). There is no definition of "abuse," and the modifier "substantial" has been dropped. Also omitted is the provision in the former law that: "There shall be a presumption in favor of granting the relief requested by the debtor." The only limitation stated in paragraph (1) on the power of the court to limit access to Chapter 7 on the basis of abuse deals with charitable contributions, which we will discuss later. Form 22A requires all individuals filing in Chapter 7 to file Form 22A. If their debts are not primarily consumer debts, however, they may declare this fact and need complete only the verification at the end of the Form.

b. Presumption of Abuse

In BAPCPA, Congress moved decisively to limit the discretion of courts in the determination of credit abuse. It sought mechanical rules to identify the "can pays," debtors who have the means to pay a significant portion of their debts, and to deny them access to Chapter 7. The formula is set out in § 707(b)(2)(A)(i):

> In considering under paragraph [b](1) whether the granting of relief would be an abuse of the provisions of this chapter, the court shall presume abuse exists if the debtor's current monthly income reduced by the amounts determined under clauses (ii), (iii), and (iv), and multiplied by 60 is not less than the lesser of
>
> **(I)** 25 percent of the debtor's nonpriority unsecured claims in the case, or $6,575, whichever is greater; or
>
> **(II)** $10,950.

In discussing this provision, we will use the terminology of Form 22A, which is reprinted in the Appendix at p. 901, *infra*. The debtor's "current monthly income" reduced by the deductions set out in "clauses (ii), (iii), and (iv)" is the debtor's "monthly disposable income." This amount multiplied by 60 is the debtor's "60-month disposable income." The statute provides as a general rule that if a debtor's 60-month disposable income is at least 25% of her unsecured nonpriority debts existing at the time of filing, a presumption of abuse arises. But there are two major exceptions to this rule. Even if the calculation of the 60-month disposable income yields a figure that is less than 25% of the unsecured nonpriority debt a presumption of abuse still arises if the 60-month disposable income exceeds $10,950. On the other hand, if the debtor's 60-month disposable income is less than $6,575, the presumption of abuse does not arise, even though 60-month disposable income exceeds 25% of the unsecured non-priority debt. With respect to debtors having 60-month disposable income between $6,575 and $10,950, the 25% rule governs and the amount of the debt matters.

For example, if the debtor's 60-month disposable income is $8,000 and the debt is only $15,000, abuse is presumed because 60-month disposable income is more than 25% of $15,000, but if the amount of debt is $35,000 there is no presumed abuse because 25% of $35,000 is $8,750 and the 60-month disposable income of $8,000 is less than 25% of $35,000. A debtor with $50,000 in debt and a 60-month disposable income of $10,860 ($181 per month) is not a presumed credit abuser and has access to Chapter 7. Her 60-month disposable income is less than $10,950 and is less than 25% of $50,000 ($12,500). But a debtor with a 60-month disposable income of $10,980 ($183 per month) is presumed to be a credit abuser without respect to $50,000 of debt because her 60-month disposable income is more than $10,950. Her Chapter 7 case will be dismissed and she may seek a discharge in bankruptcy in Chapter 13 under which a three to five-year repayment plan will be prescribed. BAPCPA draws highly arbitrary lines and a few dollars more or less in monthly disposable income can have grave consequences in the lives of debtors. As we note later, Chapter 11 would also be available but is not commonly used by consumer debtors.

BAPCPA's means test compares the debtor's projected monthly disposable income over the next five years with unsecured debts at the time of filing. The income projection is not based on a snapshot of the debtor's monthly income at the time of filing but on the debtor's average monthly income over the six months before filing. This is the debtor's presumed "current monthly income" under § 101(10A), which is multiplied by 60, the length of a Chapter 13 repayment plan under BAPCPA, to find the debtor's 60-month disposable income. Thus, the debtor's projected income of the income for the five-year period ahead is based on the average income of the debtor over the six months preceding her filing, even though she might have little or no income at the time of filing or is unlikely to achieve that level of income over the term of her Chapter 13 plan. The assumption that a debtor's postpetition income over a five-year period will be similar to her prepetition income in the six months prior to filing has little basis under modern social and economic conditions.

Special circumstances.

Section 707(b)(2)(B)(i) provides: "In any proceeding brought under this subsection, the presumption of abuse may only be rebutted by demonstrating special circumstances, such as a serious medical condition or a call or order to active duty in the Armed Forces, to the extent such special circumstances that justify additional expenses or adjustments of current monthly income for which there is no reasonable alternative." The remainder of subparagraph (B) makes clear that the "special circumstances" provision was not intended to grant courts general equity powers to remedy injustices caused by the means test; rather, the debtor must be able to document each additional expense or adjustment to income allowed and the total must be great enough to exclude the case under the means test. Nevertheless, after Hurricanes Katrina and Rita in 2005, the Executive Office for U.S. Trustees (EOUST) announced enforcement guidelines providing that it will consider the adverse effects of natural disasters to constitute special circumstances. In 2008 Congress enacted the National Guard and Reservist Debt Relief Act, Pub. Law No. 110-438, suspending from the means test for 18 months members called to active duty after September 11, 2001 for not less than 90 days.

The EOUST reported that between October 1, 2006 and June 30, 2007, of the approximately 10 percent of above-median income debtors presumed abusive, U.S. Trustees declined to move to dismiss in about 30 percent of these cases on the ground of special circumstances, such as job loss, reduction in income, or medical condition. It contends that this shows that U.S. Trustees exercise their discretion generously and seek dismissal only in "meritorious cases."

An individual whose debts are primarily business debts is not subject to the means test. § 707(b)(1). Such a person may file in Chapter 7 whatever her income. Partnerships and corporations are also exempt, though they don't receive discharges in Chapter 7. Apparently business debtors may abuse credit with impunity unless a court is willing to find "cause" for dismissal under § 707(a), which sets out three nonexclusive procedural grounds.

It is unclear whether conversion from Chapter 13 to Chapter 7 may afford some debtors who would be presumed abusers under the means test, a back door into Chapter 7. According to *In re Fox*, 370 B.R. 639 (Bankr.D.N.J.2007), debtors who wish to voluntarily convert from Chapter 13 to Chapter 7 are not subject to the means test. In this case the debtor was seven months into a Chapter 13 plan when a reduction in income made it impossible for her to meet the payments under that plan. The court held that the means test applied only to cases "filed by an individual debtor under this chapter, (§ 707(b)(1))" and this case was not filed under Chapter 7. In *In re Perfetto*, 361 B.R. 27 (Bankr.D.R.I. 2007), the court disagreed: Interim Rule 1007(b)(4) requires debtors "in a chapter 7 case" to file a statement of current monthly income as prescribed in the appropriate Official Form (Form 22A). Debtors converting to Chapter 7 are in a Chapter 7 case. *Perfetto* probably reflects the commonsense assumption that debtors shouldn't be allowed to avoid the means test by entering Chapter 7 through the Chapter 13 back door, while *Fox* may have the better of the argument based on statutory "plain meaning."

c. Current Monthly Income

Current monthly income (CMI) is the key term in BAPCPA's means test provisions. Not only is it the basis for raising the presumption of credit abuse under § 707(b)(2)(A)(i), as we saw in the last section, but also, it determines whether debtors are exempt from the means test under the safe harbor provision in § 707(b)(7). Under that provision, if the debtor's CMI multiplied by 12 is below the state median family income the debtor is exempt from having her Chapter 7 filing dismissed on the basis of the means test.

The formula set out in § 707(b)(2)(A)(i) for determining abuse calls for an estimate of the debtor's income and expenses over a future five-year period, the length of a Chapter 13 repayment plan for debtors with above-median income. The income estimate is based solely on the debtor's CMI, defined in § 101(10A) as the debtor's average monthly income for a six-month period ending on the last day of the month before the petition is filed. The debtor's CMI includes the income the debtor receives from all sources, excluding Social Security benefits. In a joint case, the income of the debtor's spouse is included. A crude five-year projection is made by multiplying the CMI, less deductions, by 60. This method of estimating the debtor's future income is highly arbitrary. The debtor may have been unemployed during all or part of the six-month period prepetition period, or may have received a bonus during that period. Opportunism by debtors in the choice of the date of filing is to be expected. The assumption that a few months of prepetition income will predict the debtor's income over the next five years might have made some sense in an earlier age in which it was not unusual for a debtor to hold the same job for five years, but employees today are likely to hold several jobs, with intermittent times of unemployment, during any five-year period. Moreover, overwhelmingly, individuals file for bankruptcy after suffering a sudden and unexpected reduction in income.

When married debtors file in bankruptcy without their spouses, an adjustment in calculating income may be needed. For means test purposes, a debtor must include the income of the nonfiling spouse to determine whether the case is subject to dismissal for abuse and what the proper commitment period is. § 707(b)(7)(A). But before the final calculation of disposable income, the debtor is entitled to adjust the income by removing the portion of the nonfiling spouse's income not regularly used to pay household expenses or the debtor's dependents. This would often be true for married couples who are living apart.

d. Debtor's Monthly Expenses

Searching for uniform standards for household expenses, Congress turned to the Internal Revenue Service which had established categories of expenses that are used in determining payment plans for taxpayers with overdue taxes. Section 707(b)(2)(A)(ii) poses several difficult issues of interpretation with respect to deductions for monthly expenses.

Living expenses. Section 707(b)(2)(A)(ii)(I) adopts the IRS National Standards Allowable Living Expenses for monthly food, clothing, housekeeping supplies, personal care, apparel and services, and miscellaneous expenses. Allowable expenses are determined only by the size of debtor's family; the income level of the family does not matter. For example, in 2008 the monthly allowance for a four-person family was $1,331. The allowable amounts may bear no relationship to the debtor's actual living expenses, but, if proved "reasonable and necessary," the debtor's living expenses may include an additional allowance for food and clothing of up to five percent of the food and clothing categories specified in the IRS National Standards.

The IRS National Standards for Out-of-Pocket Health Care provides for monthly deductions of $54 for persons under 65 to cover co-payments, prescription drugs, eyeglasses, contact lenses and other medical supplies.

Housing and utilities standards. The IRS Local Housing and Utilities Standards prepared for use in completing bankruptcy forms are broken down into counties within states, family size and types of expense, that is whether mortgage/rent or non-mortgage. In California, a two-person family in San Francisco County that either rents or has a mortgage is allowed $1702 per month, but a two-person family in Modoc County is allowed only $505. For families who neither rent nor have mortgages, housing allowances are considerably less: for a two-person family in San Francisco County, $629; and in Modoc County, $417. A four-person family in these counties is allowed $739 and $490, respectively. Debtors may seek an additional allowance for "any additional amount to which you contend that you are entitled."

A controversial issue has arisen with respect to the disparate treatment of debtors who are renters and those who own their homes. Renters can deduct only the allowance set out in the IRS Local Housing and Utilities Standards even though the rent they pay is higher, but debtors who own their homes can deduct the amounts actually owing each month under the terms of the mortgage, including taxes and insurance required by the mortgage. See § 707(b)(2)(A)(iii)(I) (providing that the mortgage deduction is the average amount of payments actually owing in each of the 60 months following the date of the petition). If homeowners can deduct actual amounts of monthly payments, why shouldn't renters be able to deduct what they actually pay if it exceeds the Standards? The potentially unlimited mortgage debt deduction provision has also been criticized as offering opportunistic "can pay" debtors access to Chapter 7 if they load up on real property mortgage debt.

Transportation expenses standards. The IRS also publishes data relating to automobile operating (as opposed to ownership or lease) expenses on a regional basis and by major metropolitan areas. If the debtor has no car, a national standard of $163 monthly applies across the board whether or not the debtor actually uses public transportation or its actual monthly cost. Debtors who have cars but also use public transportation may contend that they are entitled to add the public transportation amount.

Transportation ownership/lease standards. The 2008 IRS National standard allowed $478 to be deducted for the cost of buying or leasing each of two cars. The debtor may not claim this allowance for additional cars. The same lease/mortgage distinction is found with respect to security interests in cars as for mortgages on real property. A debtor leasing a car may deduct only $478. But a debtor buying a car in which the seller retains a security interest may deduct the full amount due the secured creditor in the 60 months following the bankruptcy filing divided by 60. In a five-year secured car loan for the sale of a car, the deductible amount might be greater than $478. See Form 22C, Lines 28 and 29. The lease/mortgage distinction is even more irrational in this case than in the case of residences that we discussed earlier. In most cases car sales and car leases are functionally indistinguishable. Nearly all automobile financers offer both sales contracts and leases and all income levels of consumers use both. An opportunistic consumer filing in Chapter 7 may improve her chances of avoiding dismissal or conversion by buying rather than leasing before filing because her deductible expenses may substantially increase.

Section 707(b)(2)(A)(ii)(I) states: "The debtor's monthly expenses shall be the debtor's *applicable monthly expense amounts* specified under the National Standards and Local Standards, and the debtor's *actual monthly expenses* for the categories specified as Other Necessary Expenses issued by the Internal Revenue Service ..."(emphasis added). An issue that has been litigated in a host of decisions is whether a debtor may claim monthly expense amounts when she has a car on which no lease or secured claim payments are owing. The bankruptcy court opinions are almost equally divided on the issue and at the time of this writing only one court of appeals has spoken. In *In re Ross-Tousey*, 2008

WL 5234070 (7th Cir. 2008), the court held in a Chapter 7 case that an above-median income debtor who had no monthly vehicle loan or lease payment could claim a vehicle expense deduction when calculating his disposable income.

The court described its view as the "plain meaning" approach. The statute states that the deductions "shall be" the amounts specified in the local standards (currently $478) and there is nothing explicit in that statutory language that requires the debtor to have a debt or lease payment to deduct a vehicle ownership expense. The term "applicable" modifies the phrase "monthly expense amounts specified under the National Standards and Local Standards." This cannot mean the same thing as "actual monthly expenses," which is only relevant with respect to "Other Necessary Expenses." Thus, the statute allows the debtor to deduct the applicable ownership expenses monthly under the IRS Local Transportation Standard (currently $478) even if the debtor has no debt or lease expense. *See, e.g., In re Kimbro*, 389 B.R. 518 (6th Cir. BAP 2008).

Under the contrary view, the ownership deduction cannot be taken if the debtor has no car payment because the word "applicable" means "capable of being applied" and if the debtor has no such an expense the deduction is not capable of being applied. Congress must have merely intended to limit the ownership deduction by putting a cap on car payments deductions, some of which can far exceed $478. It's absurd to allow debtors who have *no* ownership expenses to increase their deduction by this "phantom" expense. *In re Ransom*, 380 B.R. 799 (9th Cir. BAP 2007), declared that both the "plain meaning" and the goals of the statute bar allowing a deduction in such a case. The debtor does not have "*applicable* monthly expense amounts" unless she has such an expense to begin with. "*Applicable*" modifies "monthly payments."

With both sides claiming their view is the "plain meaning" of the provision, it seems fair to conclude that there is no plain meaning of this poorly drafted statute. *See In re Pearson*, 390 B.R. 706 (10th Cir. BAP 2008), concurring opinion ("I cannot conclude that these statutes are either 'plain' or 'clear'.") 390 B.R. at 715. The vehicle expense amount issue is pending in several circuits and U.S. Trustee Program has intervened to assert the position that debtors cannot claim ownership expenses when they do not have actual loan or lease payments.

Secured Claims. Section 707(b)(2)(A)(iii) provides: "[t]he debtor's average monthly payments on account of secured debts shall be calculated as the sum of ...(I) the total of all amounts scheduled as contractually due to secured creditors in each month of the 60 months following the date of the petition...divided by 60." Form 22A directs that this sum be entered on the form for calculating disposable income for means test purposes. The issue that has been extensively litigated is how this language applies if the debtor has stated an intention to surrender the collateral. One view is that surrender eliminates the debtor's eligibility to claim secured debt payments on the means test. *In re Skaggs*, 349 B.R. 594 (Bankr.E.D.Mo.2006), is the leading case for this view. The contrary view is taken by *In re Rudler*, 388 B.R. 433 (1st Cir. BAP 2008) (debtors may deduct secured payments due at the time of filing the petition without respect to their intent concerning surrender or retention of the collateral). The case law is divided on the issue. The U. S. Trustee Program takes the view that *Rudler* should be overturned in the First Circuit.

Other necessary expenses. The "other necessary expenses" are based on the debtor's actual expenses: federal, state and local taxes; involuntary payroll deductions; life insurance; court ordered payments such as spousal or child support payments; education required for employment; education for a physically or mentally challenged dependent child; child care; health care premiums; and telecommunication services, including cell phone services, to the extent necessary for health and welfare of self or dependents. The necessary expenses listed in the previous sentence are taken from IRS regulations; however, Form 22A sets out additional expenses that are found in § 707(b). These include actual expenses for health and disability insurance premiums; health savings account expenses; payments for care and support of elderly, chronically ill or disabled members of debtor's household or family members; expenses incurred for family security; home energy costs; expenses for providing, at a private or public school, elementary and secondary education for dependent children under 18 years of age not to exceed $137.50 per child per month; and continued charitable contributions.

With respect to "Charitable Contributions," Form 22A ("Enter the amount that you will continue to contribute ... to a charitable organization") differs from Form 22C ("Enter the amount reasonably necessary for you to expend each month ... to a charitable organization. Do not include any amount in excess of 15% of your gross monthly income.") The treatment of charitable contributions in Forms 22A and 22C under "Subpart B: Additional Living Expense Deductions" is puzzling because no provision in § 707(b) expressly authorizes such a deduction. Its only reference to charitable contributions is found in the enigmatic second sentence of § 707(b)(1): "In making a determination whether to dismiss a case under this section, the court may not take into consideration whether a debtor has made, or continues to make charitable contributions * * * to any qualified religious or charitable entity* * *." The drafters of Forms 22A and 22C apparently rely on this provision as the statutory predicate for treating charitable contributions as living expense deductions. The question arises as to how big a loophole this creates for opportunistic debtors in avoiding the presumption of abuse. The only limitation in the Form 22A provision is that the debtor "will continue to contribute." And in Form 22C the 15% "of gross monthly income" limitation (for which we can find no statutory basis) seems quite large. Manifestly, the IRS "other necessary expenses" category and the deductions authorized in § 707(b) offer an affluent can pay debtor who is well represented ways of avoiding the presumption of abuse by reducing the size of her CMI. Income tax planning is analogous. The unlimited deductions for home mortgages and automobile finance payments, together with the generous charitable contributions deduction, invite opportunistic behavior on the part of the debtor.

In her article cited above, Michelle White, an economist, concludes that opportunistic debtors may avoid having to file under Chapter 13 even if their incomes are as high as $135,000 a year by careful planning of their deductions. 2007 U. of Ill. L. Rev. at 300. So much for Congress's objective standards in BAPCPA.

Payments for debts. A puzzling sentence appears in § 707(b)(2)(A)(ii)(I): "Notwithstanding any other provision of this clause [clause (ii)], the monthly expenses of the debtor shall not include any payments for debts." Assume that at the time of filing Chapter 7 the debtor who leases an apartment is entitled to a housing allowance deduction of $700 under the Local Housing and Utilities Standards for her home state. The question arises whether the quoted language means that the debtor cannot claim the $700 as an expense deduction on her Form 22A because her rental payments are "payments for debts." This would be absurd. The $700 deducted for her housing allowance is not payment of a debt; it is merely taking the housing allowance prescribed by the statute. If the quoted language has any utility, it might be an attempt to establish that the debtor cannot, in addition to her allowance, claim her obligation to pay her rent, which may be in excess of $700, as a housing expense. This would be double dipping. Form 22A identifies expenses that may be claimed as deductions; it says nothing about those that may not be claimed. Hence, it makes no reference to the quoted section. See Henry J. Sommer, *Trying to Make Sense Out of Nonsense: Representing Consumers under the "Bankruptcy Abuse Prevention and Consumer Protection Act of 2005,"* 79 Am. Bankr. L. J. 191, 199 at n.41 (2005).

Priority Debts. Section 707(b)(2)(A)(iv) allows debtors to deduct 1/60th of the total amount of debts entitled to priority. Common priority debts in consumer bankruptcies are domestic support obligations and taxes.

e. Residual Power of Court to Dismiss

Section 707(b)(3). As we have seen § 707(b)(2) poses a means test for the presumption of abuse. In cases in which no presumption of abuse has arisen or has been rebutted under (b)(2), paragraph (b)(3) provides that courts must consider whether granting relief would be an abuse because the debtor filed the petition in bad faith or, under the totality of circumstances, the debtor's financial situation demonstrates abuse. Much attention has been devoted to the means test under (b)(2), but as case law has developed under BAPCPA, (b)(3) is emerging as increasingly important. The statute provides:

> **(3)** In considering under paragraph (1) whether the granting of relief would be an abuse of the provisions of this chapter in a case in which the presumption in subparagraph (A)(i) of such paragraph does not apply or has been rebutted, the court *shall* consider—
>
> **(A)** whether the debtor filed the petition in bad faith; or
>
> **(B)** the totality of circumstances (including whether the debtor seeks to reject a personal services contract and the financial need for such rejection as sought by the debtor) of the debtor's financial situation demonstrates abuse.

One difficulty in construing paragraph (3) is that § 707(b)(**1**) has no subparagraph (A)(i). Congress must have intended to refer to § 707(b)(**2**)(A)(i). So read, paragraph (3) means that if no presumption of abuse arises under paragraph (2) (the means test) or the debtor has rebutted the presumption under the special circumstances set out in § 707(b)(2)(B)(i), the court "*shall* consider"(emphasis added) whether the debtor filed in bad faith or the totality of circumstances shows abuse, and dismiss or convert if it finds such conduct. In determining the existence of bad faith or totality of circumstances, courts may turn to the large body of pre-BAPCPA case law on these issues, of which *In re Green*, 934 F.2d 568 (4th Cir. 1991), is an example. Some courts have said that § 707(b)(3) is best understood as a codification of pre-BAPCPA law. *See, e.g., In re Oot*, 368 B.R. 662 (Bankr.N.D.Ohio2007).

U.S. Trustees use § 707(b)(3) in cases in which no presumption of abuse arises under the means test of § 707(b)(2) because, for instance, an above-median income debtor has planned her affairs so that most of her income is consumed by deductible expenses. If she is allowed to stay in Chapter 7 she may be able to obtain discharge of substantial credit card and other unsecured debts. The U.S. Trustee's weapon in such a case is a motion to dismiss under § 707(b)(3) on the basis of bad faith or totality of circumstances, or both. If the motion is granted, the debtor will receive a bankruptcy discharge only if she endures Chapter 13.

Section 707(b)(3)(A) (bad faith) and (B) (totality of circumstances) states these as separate grounds for dismissal under § 707(b)(3), but since the basis for each of these grounds is factual and, as some courts have conceded, subjective and ad hoc, it is difficult to draw clear lines distinguishing one from another. Indeed in one case examining whether there was a lack of "good faith" in a debtor's bankruptcy filing under § 707(a) (dismissal for cause) the court opined that "an inquiry into the totality of circumstances must be conducted." *In re Lombardo*, 370 B.R. 506, 511 (Bankr.E.D.N.Y.2007).

What the courts seem to be looking for under both the "bad faith" and "totality of circumstances" categories is whether debtors, who have enough income to make substantial payments on their debts, are intentionally manipulating the rules to deprive their creditors of payment. For instance in *In re O'Brien*, 373 B.R. 503 (Bankr.N.D.Ohio2007), three months before filing bankruptcy the debtors bought a home, incurring $265,000 in secured debt, and an automobile, incurring $24,900 in secured debt. In their petition they stated an intention to reaffirm these debts. They had $158,500 in unsecured debts and their combined monthly income was $13,000. After making large monthly payments on their secured obligations and household and other expenses, they had nothing left to pay their prepetition debts; hence, under the means test no presumption of abuse arose under § 707(b)(2). The court granted the U.S. Trustee's motion to dismiss on the basis of bad faith under § 707(b)(3)(A).

In *In re Wadsworth*, 383 B.R. 330 (Bankr.N.D.Ohio2007), Debtor filed in Chapter 7 and the U.S. Trustee moved to dismiss pursuant to § 707(b)(3)(B). Debtor's schedules showed secured debt of $342,639 (two real estate mortgages on his residence and an automobile loan on his large vehicle) and unsecured debt of $140,002. He planned to reaffirm his secured debts in bankruptcy. His monthly income was $8,000 and he had been employed as a nuclear specialist by the same employer for 19 years. Owing to the high cost of making his mortgage payments and paying for upkeep, his monthly housing costs were $2,646. Maintenance of his unnecessarily expensive car/truck was $833 monthly. He allocated $641 each month toward his 401(k) account and paid high utility costs. These expenses left no money to pay his unsecured debts of $140,002.

Relying on pre-BAPCPA authorities, the court stated that a principal issue under the totality-of-circumstances test is a debtor's ability to pay her debts. If she can do so, she has no need for relief under Chapter 7. In *Wadsworth*, Debtor had a stable source of income and would have been able to pay a substantial part of his debts under a Chapter 13 plan had he reduced his expenses to a reasonable level without depriving himself of adequate food, shelter and other necessities. The court observed, "Thus, when seeking bankruptcy relief, debtors may be expected to do some belt tightening, including, where necessary, foregoing the reaffirmation of those secured debts which are not reasonably necessary for the maintenance and support of the debtor and his family." 383 B.R. at 333.

Both *O'Brien* and *Wadsworth* were decided by the same judge in the same court. Although the facts were similar, *O'Brien* was decided under § 707(b)(3)(A) (bad faith) and *Wadsworth* was decided under § 707(b)(3)(B) (totality of circumstances). Apparently, the U.S. Trustee made the choice. A pre-BAPCPA case analyzed good faith under § 707(a) in this manner: "Whether the good faith requirement has been satisfied is a 'fact intensive inquiry' in which the court must examine the 'totality of facts and circumstances' and determine where a 'petition falls along the spectrum ranging from the clearly acceptable to the patently abusive.'" *In re Integrated Telecom Express, Inc.*, 384 F.3d 108, 118 (3d Cir. 2004).

Why paragraph (b)(3) is of growing importance. If a major factor in determining the existence of abuse under § 707(b)(3) is whether the debtor has the ability to pay her creditors over a period of time in the future, then the means test in § 707(b)(2) seems to be covering the same ground. But the means test uses an arbitrary historical test based on the debtor's average monthly earnings within six months before filing (current monthly income) to predict the debtor's capacity to pay creditors in the future. As we will see, the results under the means test are sometimes unreasonable, if not absurd. However, the ability-to-pay test under § 707(b)(3) frees the court to base its prediction of future income on the debtor's actual current income at the time of filing as stated in Schedule I (current income) and expenses as in Schedule J (current expenses). And under § 707(b)(3) judicial discretion exists to balance debtors' fresh start against creditors' entitlement to be paid something by debtors who can afford to do so. U.S. Trustees can ignore the debtor's attempts to make a facial compliance with the means test, which may involve quibbling with the debtor's attorney about the technicalities of the means test, and hit the debtor with (b)(3) which focuses on the debtor's real world ability to repay prepetition debt out of future income.

If motions to dismiss under the means test become less important than those under the bad faith or totality of circumstances tests, the means test goal of nationwide uniformity and limited judicial discretion would be frustrated. Nevertheless, the benefit of avoiding some of the arbitrary results under the means test may be worth the cost of some lack of uniformity.

Section 707(b)(3) and the below-median income debtor. In the next section, we will find that under § 707(b)(7), the "Safe Harbor" provision, debtors whose income is below the median state family income are, in effect, exempt from the means test. But below-median income debtors may be subject to review under § 707(b)(3) for bad faith or totality of circumstances abuse. *See, e.g., In re Pak*, 343 B.R. 239 (Bankr.N.D.Cal.2006). And the usual definition of totality of circumstances, including the debtor's ability to pay, applies.

Charitable contributions. The only limitation on the court's general power to dismiss under paragraph (b)(1) follows:

> ... In making a determination whether to dismiss a case under this section [§ 707], the court may not take into consideration whether a debtor

has made, or continues to make, charitable contributions (that meet the definition of "charitable contribution" under section 548(d)(3)) to any qualified religious or charitable entity or organization (as that term is defined in section 548(d)(4)).

Literally read, the provision says that making charitable contributions to qualified entities cannot be considered in deciding whether there is abuse under § 707(b). Thus, charitable contributions may not be relied on to show bad faith and should not be a factor in applying the "totality of circumstances" test under § 707(b)(3). Presumably, if in assessing good faith the court may not take into account the debtor's lack of any history of charitable giving, opportunistic debtors on a going forward basis might budget for substantial charitable giving to avoid dismissal based on a presumption of abuse. There does not appear to be any mechanism to compel a debtor who has received a Chapter 7 discharge to follow through on the projected charitable giving.

f. Safe Harbor

Paragraph 707(b)(7). This is one of the most important provisions in BAPCPA. It creates a safe harbor that exempts all debtors whose CMI, multiplied by 12, is at or below the state median family income from having their Chapter 7 filings dismissed on the basis of the means test under § 707(b)(2). Since most debtors who file in Chapter 7 earn less than the state median income standard, this important provision exempts the great bulk of cases filed in Chapter 7 from the presumption of abuse. But these debtors are not exempt from being screened under the means test, which requires filing the burdensome disclosure forms that we discuss in the next section.

Paragraph § 707(b)(6). This provision operates to limit the parties who may move for dismissal for abuse under § 707(b). Paragraph (6) provides that motions to dismiss for abuse under § 707(b) can be made only by judges and U.S. Trustees (including bankruptcy administrators) if the debtor's annualized CMI is at or below the state median family income. For instance, a motion to dismiss a case under paragraph (b)(3) on the basis of bad faith or one in which the totality of circumstances shows credit abuse can be made by judges and U.S. Trustees even though the debtor's income is below the state's median family income. These debtors are safe from being hassled by motions made by Chapter 7 panel trustees or creditors based on (b)(3).

In reconciling paragraphs (6) and (7), paragraph (7) totally bars dismissal on the basis of the means test in paragraph (2) if the debtor's annualized CMI is at or less than the state median. But paragraph (6) allows dismissal by the court sua sponte or upon motion of the U.S. Trustee for forms of abuse under § 707(b) even for below–median income debtors.

Median family income is reported from time to time for each state by the Census Bureau. § 101(39A). If no figures are reported for the current year, the figures last reported by the Census Bureau must be adjusted annually to reflect the change in the Consumer Price Index for All Urban Consumers during the period of years after the last report. Subparagraph 707(b)(7)(A) contemplates that the Census Bureau will report median incomes for 1 earner households, and families of 2, 3, and 4 individuals.

For purposes of this Casebook all amounts stated for median family income are those stated in the Census Bureau Median Income By Family Size for cases filed on and after February 1, 2008. For families of more than 4, $6,900 is added to the median income amounts for each additional dependent.

Preliminary data suggests the percentage of consumer debtors actually excluded by the means test from filing in Chapter 7 is less than 5% of those who would otherwise seek relief under Chapter 7. Culhane & White, *Catching Can-Pay Debtors: Is the Means Test The Only Way?* 13 Am. Bankr. Inst. L. Rev. 665 n.3 (2005). With respect to the safe harbor exclusion, state median incomes vary greatly: the median income for a family of four in Mississippi is $54,501, but in Connecticut it is $96,493. Moreover, residents of small urbanized states like New Jersey ($93,176) and Connecticut benefit from much higher state-wide medians than residents of large states with both urban and rural populations like New York ($77,664) and California ($76,931), even though incomes and costs of living in the urban centers of these large states are surely among the very highest in the country. And residents of adjoining states within the same metropolitan area may have very different access to bankruptcy even though they are otherwise similarly situated. For example, the state-wide median income applicable to a four person household in St. Louis, Missouri is $65,076, while the comparable median applicable to residents in (much poorer) East St. Louis, Illinois is $77,634.

The four rather stylized Problems below demonstrate the complexities of administering the means test in § 707(b)(2) and suggest the kinds of cases in which the formula does a better or worse job in selecting the parties who should be denied Chapter 7 access. Official Form 22A is assumed to be in effect during the relevant time period.

PROBLEMS

1. Paul is an unmarried 26-year old computer programmer who has been earning $5,000 per month for the past year and has no other income. He pays $2,000 monthly rental for an apartment in Los Angeles, pays $600 a month in lease payments on his 2006 BMW, owns negligible household furnishings (principally discarded milk cartons and a used waterbed), wears fashionable clothes, and impresses dates by taking them to expensive restaurants. He owes $40,000 in unsecured credit card debts. He is contemplating marriage and wants to clear up his debts before the wedding by filing in Chapter 7; he does so on August 1, 2008.

Form 22A states that amounts entered for income must reflect the average monthly income during the six months prior to the filing. Since Paul's monthly income has been $5,000 for the previous year, his current monthly income (CMI) is $5,000. In calculating his allowable deductions, assume the following: (1) under the National Standards for Allowable Living Expenses (Line 19A) (food, clothing, household supplies, etc.) his allowed deduction is $494 per month; (2) under the Local Housing and Utilities Standards (Line 20B), his allowed deduction for Los Angeles County is $1241 per month. (3) For transportation costs, Local Standards for Los Angeles for one car are $251 for operating costs (Line 22), and $478 for ownership costs (Line 23). (4) He pays $1,200 per month in federal and state taxes (Line 25). (5) He pays $500 per month for health and disability insurance (Line 34). (6) The monthly costs for his cell phone are $50. (7) He helps his impoverished, widowed mother with her living expenses by paying her rent of $200 each month (Line 35). Thus, the total amount of deductions from Paul's current monthly income of $5,000 is $4,414, leaving a balance of $586. The California median annual income for a one-earner household is $46,814.

    a. Does the § 707(b)(7) exclusion apply? See the calculations in Form 22A.

    b. Does a presumption of abuse arise under § 707(b)(2), subjecting Paul's Chapter 7 petition to dismissal or conversion?

2. Bridget is a third-year law student at Old Brigham Law School in Salt Lake City set to graduate in May, 2009. Last summer she worked for eight weeks at Cravath, Kirkland & Myers earning $3,000 weekly and received an offer of permanent employment at an annual salary of $160,000 beginning in September 2009. Since returning to law school in September 2008, she has earned no income. She has five credit cards all of which are maxed out with an aggregate outstanding balance of $75,000 on account of BAR-BRI tuition and materials, afternoons at the mall, ski trips to Park City, Christmas vacation in Las Vegas and a mid-February trip to Maui purchased with a credit card at a Public Interest Law Foundation fundraiser. She is making monthly payments of $750 on her credit cards from her savings. She lives in Salt Lake in a guest house rented from her generous parents for only $150 monthly; her utilities run $102 monthly. She has no automobile (though she is thinking of buying or leasing an expensive one before she starts at the firm) and uses public transportation to get around, if she can't beg a ride. Bridget wants a "fresh start" as she enters the legal profession and files in Chapter 7 on May 15, 2009.

Since Bridget has earned no income in the six months before she filed, her current monthly income is $0 (Line 18). Under the National Standards her "allowable living expenses" are $494 (Line 19A). Assume that the Local Standards for housing and utilities for a non-mortgage person in Salt Lake City allow her $525. (Line 20A). For transportation costs, the National Public Transportation Costs for a person without a car are $163 (Line 22A). She has no other expenses that are deductible on Lines 25-45. Thus, the total amount to be deducted from Bridget's current monthly income on Line 47 is $1182. The median income for a one-earner household in Utah is $45,724. Does the safe harbor provision of § 707(b)(7) apply to Bridget's case? If so, can her Chapter 7 petition be dismissed under § 707(b)(3)?

3. Marta's deadbeat ex-husband left her with $100,000 in debts, on which she is jointly liable, and $30,000 in unpaid legal bills from the divorce and related disputes. He has departed the state and failed to honor his child support obligation of $1,200 per month to assist her in raising their three-year old daughter. After her divorce, Marta moved to San Diego with her daughter to find employment in the telecommunications industry. She began working in January 2007 for Xpert, a placement agency for experienced personnel with unique high-tech skills, at $12,000 per month, which was at the time a market salary, given her experience in this highly specialized high demand area. On May 1, 2008, Xpert closed its doors and summarily discharged all its employees, leaving Marta with some worthless stock options. Marta's energetic, nationwide job search has been fruitless; at that time no one was hiring in the telecommunications industry, least of all in placement agencies serving that depressed industry. During May and June of 2008, she supported herself and her daughter by borrowing on her credit cards and by loans from her sister to pay for food, rent on her apartment, clothing, child care and travel expenses while she vainly sought employment. She cancelled her automobile lease and turned in her car.

Beset by collection agencies, she became despondent when she realized that she now had $200,000 in unsecured debts and no present prospect of employment for other than low or minimum wage jobs. The income she earned in the six months from January 1, 2008 until July 1, 2008, the date she filed in Chapter 7, was $48,000. The National Standards for Allowable Living Expenses for two people are $925 (Line 19A). The amounts under the Local Standards for housing and utilities in San Diego for a two-person rented apartment are $1569 (Line 20B). For transportation costs, the Local Standards for San Diego for a person without a car are $163 (Line 22A). Assume that her average monthly expenses for taxes (Line 25), payroll deductions (Line 26), life insurance (Line 27), and child care (Line 30) total $5,000. Hence, her total deductions for Line 47 are $7657, which deducted from her CMI of $8,000, leaves a monthly disposable income of $343 (Line 50). The median family income for a two-person household in California is $61,742 (Line 14).

    a. Does the safe harbor provision of § 707(b)(7) apply? Does a presumption of abuse arise in this case?

    b. If a presumption of abuse does arise in this case, does the bankruptcy court have discretion to allow her to file in Chapter 7 on equitable grounds to avoid hardship? Does the "special circumstances" exception under § 707(b)(2)(B) apply here? Later in this chapter, we will inquire whether Marta can obtain relief in Chapter 13 if she is denied access to Chapter 7.

4. Mark and Luke work for the same employer for the same annual salary of $48,000. Each receives a holiday bonus of 10% each December. After the first of the year, they both encountered serious financial problems. Mark files in Chapter 7 in May, but Luke, with better legal advice, waits until July. If the median income for one-earner households for the state in which they live is $50,000, does either of these debtors fall within the safe harbor provision of § 707(b)(7)?

g. Critique

Is the means test worth the costs it imposes on the bankruptcy system? Does it actually keep high-income deadbeats out of Chapter 7, as advertised? The EOUST states that between October 2006 and June 2007 only nine percent of Chapter 7 debtors had income above their state median, and of the cases filed by these debtors only about 10 percent were "presumed abusive." And U.S. Trustees exercised their statutory discretion to decline to file motions in about 30 percent of the "presumed abusive" cases that did not voluntarily convert or dismiss. They relied on special circumstances such as job loss, reduction in income or medical condition. However, U.S. Trustees are filing motions to dismiss at nearly three times the rate prior to enactment of BAPCPA. *See* Statement of Clifford J. White III, Director of the Executive Office for United States Trustees before House Judiciary Committee (Oct. 2007).

We saw in the Problems above that Congress's means-testing rules do not offer a coherent and reliable method of separating true credit abusers from honest debtors who need relief. As critics have noted, "[T]he rule focuses exclusively on the ability of the debtor to repay and not the circumstances that led to the debtor's present condition. The rule treats an abandoned spouse the same way it treats an MBA or lawyer who overspent on many vacations and fancy restaurants." National Bankruptcy Conference, *Analysis of Bankruptcy Legislation* 3 (2001). Creditors, Congress and, probably, the general public, agree that debtors who can afford to pay a significant amount of prepetition debt with postpetiton income should be allowed to obtain a discharge in bankruptcy only through performance of a Chapter 13 plan. However, in their quest to reach this goal, the drafters crafted an arbitrary and convoluted means test, often yielding anomalous results, that, considering the small number of cases dismissed or converted under the means test, appears to offer very modest benefits compared to the considerable costs it imposes on debtors, their attorneys, U.S. Trustees and the bankruptcy courts.

In our discussion of § 707(b)(3), we learned that even for those above-median debtors for whom no presumption of abuse arose under the means test of § 707(b)(2), U.S. Trustees could still find abuse under bad faith or totality of circumstances as set out in § 707(b)(3), which have been interpreted as merely codifications of pre-BAPCPA law. Under this view, the shrinking importance of the means test becomes evident. Not only does it limit access to Chapter 7 for only a comparatively small pool of above-median income debtors, but § 707(b)(3) may be more effective in excluding unworthy debtors from Chapter 7 in cases in which debtors are seen as really taking advantage of their creditors. In short, (i) the arbitrary means test of § 707(b)(2) does a poor job of selecting debtors who should be excluded from Chapter 7, and (ii) § 707(b)(3), with its flexibility, gives judges the power to make sensible choices on exclusion from Chapter 7. Is § 707(b)(2) needed?

The Effect of BAPCPA on Consumer Filings

Professor Tabb's extensive study of data on consumer filings following the effective date of BAPCPA concludes that there has been no major shift from Chapter 7 to Chapter 13 and the belief that a tougher law would discourage debtors from filing bankruptcy has not been borne out. He believes that whether debtors file in bankruptcy depends on how burdened they are by debt and not on what the bankruptcy law provides. Charles Jordan Tabb, *Consumer Filings: Trends and Indicators, Part II*, 25 Am. Bankr. Inst. J. 42 (Jan. 2007). The volume of filings has been consistent with his predictions.

The fiscal year for federal courts ends on September 30. Statistics reported by the Administrative Office for the U.S. Courts (AOUSC) for the period ending on September 30, 2008, (a recession year) reported bankruptcy filings of 1,042,993, an increase of over 30% from the 801,269 filings in FY 2007. Chapter 7 filings of 679,982 were up 40% over FY 2007. Chapter 13 filings were 353,828, up 14% during this period. Filings continued to increase dramatically in the first half of FY 2009 as economic conditions deteriorated further.

The first report of the 2007 Consumer Bankruptcy Project, Robert M. Lawless, et al., *Did Bankruptcy Reform Fail? An Empirical Study of Consumer Debtors*, 82 Am. Bankr. L. J. 349 (2008), studied bankruptcy filers in 2007, when, unforeseen by the investigators, the economy was on the precipice of a deep recession. The study's preliminary conclusions were that the assumption that the means test would drive can-pay debtors from bankruptcy has been proved wrong; the data show no change in income levels of bankruptcy filers in 2007 from those in 2001. But what has changed is that debtors have greater debt loads than before; debtors are waiting longer and running up larger balances before seeking bankruptcy relief.

These results tentatively confirm the theories of two scholars about the real effect of the means test. Professor Ronald J. Mann, in his book *Charging Ahead: The Growth and Regulation of Payment Card Markets* 177 (2007), and his article *Bankruptcy Reform and the "Sweat Box" of Credit Card Debt*, 2007 U. Ill. L. Rev. 375, contends that the true effect of BAPCPA was to delay bankruptcy filings and to "sweat" more payments out of debtors during the period before filing. This was accomplished by throwing up barriers to delay filing by increasing costs, requiring more documentation, and the like. Professor James J. White, *Abuse Prevention*, 71 Mo. L. Rev. 863 (2006), argues that by raising the costs of bankruptcy in many ways, BAPCPA makes bankruptcy unpalatable to all debtors, not just the rich—death by a thousand cuts. The true consequences of BAPCPA were hidden behind the appealing rhetoric of means test proponents who claimed that it was aimed at keeping high-income deadbeats out of bankruptcy.

The Congressional Budget Office estimates that BAPCPA will add $400 million to the federal budget deficit because more bankruptcy judges and U.S. Trustees and staff will have to be hired. James Flanigan, *Bankruptcy Bill Needs Reforming*, L.A. Times, April 10, 2005, at C1. No one can really know the long-term effect of BAPCPA on the behavior of consumers and creditors. Will creditors offer more credit on better terms because they are more sure of getting their money back? Will consumers become more prudent in taking on credit? The credit crunch of 2007-2009 (much of it the product of reckless lender behavior) has had far more effect on consumer credit than any countervailing tendency of BAPCPA's attempt to clamp down on debtor abuse. Consumer credit is far more restricted today than it ever was pre-BAPCPA.

h. A Chapter 11 Solution for a Consumer Debtor?

Some individual debtors who fall within the means test and cannot use Chapter 7 may not be eligible for Chapter 13 because their debt levels are too high under § 109(e), or for other reasons. With respect to Problem 3 on p. 489, we will find later in this chapter that Chapter 13 was probably not open to Marta because she was not an individual "with regular income" under § 109(e). The only avenue open to these individuals for bankruptcy relief is Chapter 11. Normally thought of as the means of reorganizing business entities, Chapter 11 is fully available to individual debtors whether or not they are in business, and without regard to income, assets or liabilities. *Toibb v. Radloff*, 501 U.S. 157 (1991).

The question posed is whether Chapter 11 offers a feasible solution to a consumer debtor like Marta who needs a bankruptcy discharge but can't qualify for one under either Chapter 7 or Chapter 13. Since we have not as yet studied either Chapter 13 or Chapter 11 in this course, a detailed answer to this question at this point would not be helpful. Suffice to say that Chapter 13 offers a simple process in which the debtor submits to the court a plan to pay her creditors out of her disposable income over a period of three to five years. A standing trustee supervises the payments and the court decides whether the plan should be confirmed. Creditors may object but cannot not vote on confirmation.

Chapter 11 is quite different. As we will see in the next chapter, there usually is no trustee in Chapter 11; the debtor, as debtor in possession, negotiates its own plan with creditor committees, with no statutorily prescribed payment period. Within limits, debtors retain much more control and flexibility than they enjoy in Chapter 13. With creditor consent, manifested by votes of creditor committees, debtors can make their own deals, and the automatic stay holds off creditors while this is being done.

Unless the debtor has considerable assets, consumer debtor cases are usually not a good fit with Chapter 11 procedures. Chapter 11 is more expensive than Chapter 13 as to filing fees ($1039 plus quarterly fees for Chapter 11; $274 for Chapter 13), and the proceedings are far more elaborate, involving more court and lawyer time. Consumer finance companies are unlikely to serve on creditors' committees. How creditor voting could be carried out is not at all clear. And these creditors would surely be uncomfortable with a consumer as a debtor in possession, wheeling and dealing with the assets of the estate without close supervision of a creditors' group. A trustee would probably have to be appointed, and if consumer cases came into Chapter 11 in volume, something resembling a Chapter 13 trustee would ultimately have to established.

A substantial number of individual debtors have been filing in Chapter 11 since BAPCPA, but no study has as yet reached conclusions about consumer use of Chapter 11. The consumer bankruptcy bar has historically dealt with Chapters 7 and 13. Whether it will turn to Chapter 11 in any significant way remains to be seen. The seminal work on individuals in Chapter 11 is Bruce A. Markell, *The Sub Rosa Subchapter: Individual Debtors in Chapter 11 After BAPCPA*, 2007 U. Ill. L. Rev. 67, in which Judge Markell argues convincingly for an individual debtor subchapter in Chapter 11.

3. DEBTOR'S DUTIES

Section 521(a) requires debtors to file schedules listing creditors, assets and liabilities, and current income and expenditures. These are found in Form 6

Summary of Schedules. Schedule I requires a statement of "Current Income of Individual Debtors" and Schedule J requires a statement of "Current Expenditures of Individual Debtors." Under § 521(i)(1), failure to file these schedules within 45 days after the date of filing the petition, causes the case to be automatically dismissed; however, the court may allow the debtor an additional 45 days if the court finds justification for extending the period. In order for the court and U.S. Trustee to administer the means test, detailed disclosures by the debtor are required under BAPCPA. Section 707(b)(2)(C) provides: "As part of the schedule of current income and expenditures required under § 521, the debtor shall include a statement of the debtor's current monthly income, and the calculations that determine whether a presumption arises under subparagraph (A)(i), that show how each such amount is calculated."

Section 521(e) requires the debtor, not later than seven days before the date first set for the first meeting of creditors, to provide a copy (or a transcript) of the debtor's federal tax return for the most recent tax year ending immediately before the commencement of the case to the panel trustee and to any creditor who requests a copy. Tax returns are based on annual, not monthly, income and may be of little assistance in determining the debtor's current monthly income. Whatever the benefit of requiring submission of tax returns, major privacy concerns arise.

In September 2005, the Director of the Administrative Office of the United States Courts issued an "Interim Guidance Regarding Tax Information" under § 521 that provides: (1) No tax information filed with the bankruptcy court or otherwise provided by the debtor will be available to the public via the Internet. (2) Debtors have the responsibility of redacting personal identifiers, such as Social Security Numbers (only last four digits may appear), names of minor children (only initials should be used), dates of birth (only years may appear), and financial account numbers (only the last four digits should appear). (3) Section 521(f) applies to cases in which the debtor files a tax return with the IRS while the bankruptcy case is pending, as in a Chapter 13 case. The Interim Guidance provides that in such a case, the U.S. Trustee, panel trustee or creditor may request that the debtor file a copy of the tax return with the court. In order to gain access to the debtor's tax information, the U.S. Trustee, panel trustee, or creditor must file a motion with the court describing the movant's status in the case, describing the information sought, indicating why the movant cannot obtain the information from other sources, and demonstrating a need for the tax information. The order granting a motion for access to tax information should include language advising the movant that the tax information obtained is confidential and should condition dissemination of the tax information as appropriate under the circumstances of the case. At the discretion of the court, the order may state that sanctions may be imposed for improper use, disclosure, or dissemination of the tax information.

4. DUTIES OF DEBTOR'S ATTORNEY AND U.S. TRUSTEE

a. Attorneys

The debtor's attorney's duties and liabilities under BAPCPA have been the subject of widespread criticism and are viewed as making consumer bankruptcies more hazardous for attorneys and more costly for debtors. We offer a brief summary of this subject. For a detailed treatment, see Henry J. Sommer, *Trying to Make Sense Out of Nonsense: Representing Consumers under the "Bankruptcy Abuse Prevention and Consumer Protection Act of 2005,"* 79 Am. Bankr. L.J. 191 (2005); Catherine E. Vance & Corinne Cooper, *Nine Traps and One Slap: Attorney Liability Under the New Bankruptcy Law,* 79 Am. Bankr. L.J. 283 (2005).

Under § 707(b)(1)(A) if an attorney files a debtor's case in Chapter 7 and a panel trustee's motion to convert or dismiss is granted on the ground that the case is an abuse under § 707(b), the attorney may be subject to sanctions if the court finds that the action of the attorney violated Rule 9011, which requires that legal contentions be warranted by the law and factual contentions have evidentiary support or are likely to have evidentiary support after a reasonable opportunity for further investigation or discovery. For sanctions, the court may order the attorney to reimburse the panel trustee for the reasonable costs and fees of prosecuting the motion to dismiss. This provision does not apply if the motion to convert or dismiss was brought by the U.S.Trustee. Section 707(b)(4)(B) authorizes the court, on its own initiative or on motion of a party in interest (creditor), to assess a civil penalty against the debtor's attorney if it finds a violation of Rule 9011. Section 707(b)(4)(C) broadly makes any attorney's signature on any petition, pleading or written motion a certification that the attorney has performed a reasonable investigation into the circumstances giving rise to the petition, pleading or motion and has determined that it is well grounded in fact and warranted by the law and "does not constitute an abuse under paragraph (1)" [of § 707(b)]. Section 707(b)(4)(D) adds that the attorney's signature also certifies that the attorney has no actual knowledge after inquiry that the information in the schedules is incorrect. These duties imposed on the debtor's attorney are heavy, but Mr. Sommer (no fan of BAPCPA) considers them only a moderate extension of a bankruptcy lawyer's obligations under the former law.

Bankruptcy attorneys report that more time is spent in preparing cases, and debtors are groaning under the increased fees they must pay for legal services. *See, e.g.,* BNA, 18 Bankr. L. Rep. 953 (2006). Michelle J. White, *Abuse or*

Protection? Economics of Bankruptcy Reform under BAPCPA, 2007 U. Ill. L. Rev. 275, 287, quotes a source saying that filing under Chapter 7 costs nearly $300 in filing fees and $1,500 to $2,500 for lawyers' charges, while under Chapter 13 these amounts are $189 and $2,500 to $3,500.

b. Debt Relief Agencies

Milavetz, Gallop & Milavetz, P.A. v. United States
United States Court of Appeals, Eighth Circuit, 2008.
541 F.3d 785.

■ SMITH, Circuit Judge.

Milavetz, Gallop & Milavetz, P.A., a law firm that practices bankruptcy law, the firm's president, a bankruptcy attorney within the firm, and two clients who sought bankruptcy advice from the firm brought suit against the United States seeking a declaratory judgment that certain provisions of the Bankruptcy Abuse Prevention and Consumer Protection Act of 2005 (BAPCPA)—11 U.S.C. §§ 526(a)(4) and 528(a)(4) and (b)(2)—did not apply to attorneys and law firms and are unconstitutional as applied to attorneys. The district court granted summary judgment to the plaintiffs and issued an order declaring that: (1) attorneys in the District of Minnesota were excluded from the definition of a "debt relief agency" as defined by BAPCPA; and (2) the challenged provisions were unconstitutional as applied to attorneys in the District of Minnesota. We affirm in part and reverse in part.

I. Background

On April 20, 2005, BAPCPA was signed into law, amending and adding multiple sections of the Bankruptcy Code ("the Code").

One BAPCPA amendment added a new term, "debt relief agency," which is defined in § 101(12A) of the Code. The amended Code restricts some actions of debt relief agencies, while requiring them to do others. *See* § 526 ("Restrictions on debt relief agencies"); § 528 ("Requirements for debt relief agencies"). For example, § 526(a)(4) bars a debt relief agency from advising a client "to incur more debt in contemplation" of a bankruptcy filing, § 526(a)(4), while §§ 528(a)(4) and (b)(2) require debt relief agencies to include a disclosure in their bankruptcy-related advertisements directed to the general public declaring: "'We are a debt relief agency. We help people file for bankruptcy relief under the Bankruptcy Code[,]'or a substantially similar statement." § 528(a)(4), (b)(2). The plaintiffs sought alternative remedies. First, plaintiffs requested a declaratory judgment that attorneys did not fall within the definition of "debt relief agency." If the court determined that attorneys fell within the definition of debt relief agency, they challenged the constitutionality of §§ 526(a)(4) and 528(a)(4) and (b)(2), as applied to attorneys.

II. Discussion

Initially, we address whether attorneys fall within the Code's definition of debt relief agencies. If they do not, we will have no need to address the constitutionality of §§ 526(a)(4) and 528(a)(4) and (b)(2), which only apply to debt relief agencies. * * *

The term "debt relief agency" means *any person* who provides *any bankruptcy assistance* to an *assisted person* in return for the payment of money or other valuable consideration, or who is a bankruptcy petition preparer under section 110 * * *

§ 101(12A) (emphasis added).

Further, the Code defines the term "bankruptcy assistance" to mean:

any goods or services sold or otherwise provided to an assisted person with the express or implied purpose of providing information, *advice, counsel,* document preparation, or filing, or attendance at a creditors' meeting or appearing in a case or proceeding on behalf of another *or providing legal representation* with respect to a case or proceeding under this title.

§ 101(4A) (emphasis added).

Additionally, the Code defines the term "assisted person" as "any person whose debts consist primarily of consumer debts and the value of whose nonexempt property is less than $164,250." *Id.* at § 101(3). * * *

Whether attorneys fall within the Code's definition of debt relief agencies is an issue of first impression among the Courts of Appeals. Although the plain language of the definition appears to include bankruptcy attorneys and does not appear to be ambiguous, lower "[c]ourts that have addressed the issue of whether attorneys are debt relief agencies have not been unanimous." *In re Irons,* 379 B.R. 680, 685 (Bankr.S.D.Tex.2007) (citing cases). Nevertheless, the majority of courts have held that compensated bankruptcy attorneys are debt relief agencies as that term is defined in the Code. * * *

The plain reading of the definition of debt relief agency, and the defined terms that make up that definition, leads us to conclude that attorneys who provide "bankruptcy assistance" to "assisted persons" are unambiguously included in the definition of "debt relief agencies." * * * The statutory language sweeps broadly and clearly covers the legal services provided by attorneys to debtors in bankruptcy unless excluded by another provision. * * *

Because attorneys were not specifically excluded from the definition of debt relief agencies, we hold that attorneys that provide "bankruptcy assistance" to "assisted persons" are "debt relief agencies" as that term is defined by the

Code. Interpreting the definition of "debt relief agency" to exclude bankruptcy attorneys would be contrary to Congress's intent.

B. Constitutionality of § 526(a)(4)

* * * [W]e now must determine whether the challenged provisions placing restrictions and requirements on debt relief agencies are unconstitutionally overbroad as applied to these types of attorneys. One of the sections challenged by the plaintiffs in this case is § 526(a)(4), which states:

> **(a)** A debt relief agency shall not-
>
> ...
>
> **(4)** advise an assisted person or prospective assisted person to incur more debt in contemplation of such person filing a case under this title or to pay an attorney or bankruptcy petition preparer fee or charge for services performed as part of preparing for or representing a debtor in a case under this title.

Plaintiffs assert that the prohibition against advising an assisted person or prospective assisted person to incur more debt in contemplation of bankruptcy violates the First Amendment. The parties disagree as to the level of scrutiny we apply to the constitutional analysis of this limitation on speech. Plaintiffs claim that we should review the constitutionality of § 526(a)(4) under the strict scrutiny standard as the restriction on attorney advice is content-based. *See Turner Broad. Sys., Inc. v. FCC*, 512 U.S. 622, 642 (1994) ("Our precedents thus apply the most exacting scrutiny to regulations that suppress, disadvantage, or impose differential burdens upon speech because of its content"). Under strict scrutiny review, the government has the burden to prove that the constraints on speech are supported by a compelling governmental interest and are narrowly tailored, such that the statutory effect does not prohibit any more speech than is necessary to serve the governmental interest.

In contrast, the government argues that § 526(a)(4)'s restrictions are a type of ethical regulation, invoking the more lenient standard outlined in *Gentile v. State Bar of Nev.*, 501 U.S. 1030 (1991). Under the *Gentile* standard, we would balance the First Amendment rights of the attorneys against the government's legitimate interest in regulating the activity in question—the prohibition of advising assisted persons to incur more debt in contemplation of bankruptcy—and then determine whether the regulations impose "only narrow and necessary limitations on lawyers' speech."*Id.* at 1075.

According to the government, § 526(a)(4) should be interpreted as merely preventing an attorney from advising an assisted person (or prospective assisted person) to take on more debt in contemplation of bankruptcy when the incurrence of such debt is done with the intent to manipulate the bankruptcy system, engage in abusive conduct, or take unfair advantage of the bankruptcy discharge. However, the plain language of the statute does not permit this narrow interpretation. Rather, § 526(a)(4) broadly prohibits a debt relief agency from advising an assisted person (or prospective assisted person) to incur *any* additional debt when the assisted person is contemplating bankruptcy. The statute's blanket prohibition applies even if the additional debt would not be discharged during the bankruptcy proceedings. § 526(a)(4).

Thus, regardless of whether the government's interest in prohibiting the speech was legitimate (*Gentile* standard) or compelling (strict scrutiny standard), § 526(a)(4) is unconstitutionally overbroad as applied to attorneys falling within the definition of debt relief agencies because it is not narrowly tailored, nor narrowly and necessarily limited, to restrict only that speech that the government has an interest in restricting. Instead, § 526(a)(4) prohibits attorneys classified as debt relief agencies from advising any assisted person to incur any additional debt in contemplation of bankruptcy; this prohibition would include advice constituting prudent prebankruptcy planning that is not an attempt to circumvent, abuse, or undermine the bankruptcy laws. Section 526(a)(4), as written, prevents attorneys from fulfilling their duty to clients to give them appropriate and beneficial advice not otherwise prohibited by the Bankruptcy Code or other applicable law.

There are certain situations where it would likely be in the assisted person's, and even the creditors', best interest for the assisted person to incur additional debt in contemplation of bankruptcy. However, under § 526(a)(4)'s plain language an attorney is prohibited from providing this beneficial advice—even if the advice could help the assisted person avoid filing for bankruptcy altogether. For instance, it may be in the assisted person's best interest to refinance a home mortgage in contemplation of bankruptcy to lower the mortgage payments. This could free up additional funds to pay off other debts and avoid the need for filing bankruptcy all together. Moreover, it may be in the client's best interest to incur additional debt to purchase a reliable automobile before filing for bankruptcy, so that the debtor will have dependable transportation to travel to and from work, which will likely be necessary to maintain the debtor's payments in bankruptcy. Incurring these types of additional secured debt, which would often survive or could be reaffirmed by the debtor, may be in the debtor's best interest without harming the creditors.

* * * Section 526(a)(4) is not narrowly tailored nor narrowly and necessarily limited to prevent only that speech which the government has an interest in restricting. Therefore, we hold that § 526(a)(4) is substantially overbroad, and unconstitutional as applied to attorneys who provide bankruptcy assistance to assisted persons, as those terms are defined in the Code.

C. Constitutionality of § 528(a)(4) and (b)(2)

The plaintiffs also challenged the constitutionality of §§ 528(a)(4) and (b)(2)(B), claiming that the advertising disclosure requirements mandated by those sections violate the First Amendment rights of bankruptcy attorneys through compelled speech. The disclosure requirements of § 528(a)(4) are supplemented by § 528(a)(3). These sections state:

(a) A debt relief agency shall-

...

(3) clearly and conspicuously disclose in any advertisement of bankruptcy assistance services or of the benefits of bankruptcy directed to the general public (whether in general media, seminars or specific mailings, telephonic or electronic messages, or otherwise) that the services or benefits are with respect to bankruptcy relief under this title; and

(4) clearly and conspicuously use the following statement in such advertisement: "We are a debt relief agency. We help people file for bankruptcy relief under the Bankruptcy Code." or a substantially similar statement.

Similarly, § 528(b)(2)(B) states:

(2) An advertisement, directed to the general public, indicating that the debt relief agency provides assistance with respect to credit defaults, mortgage foreclosures, eviction proceedings, excessive debt, debt collection pressure, or inability to pay any consumer debt shall-

...

(B) include the following statement: "We are a debt relief agency. We help people file for bankruptcy relief under the Bankruptcy Code." or a substantially similar statement.

As both §§ 528(a)(4) and (b)(2)(B) require debt relief agencies—which includes attorneys providing bankruptcy assistance to assisted persons—to disclose in their advertising that "'We are a debt relief agency. We help people file for bankruptcy relief under the Bankruptcy Code.' or some substantially similar statement," the statutes compel speech that, similar to a restriction on speech, receives constitutional protection under the First Amendment. *See Wooley v. Maynard,* 430 U.S. 705, 714 (1977) ("[T]he right of freedom of thought protected by the First Amendment against state action includes both the right to speak freely and the right to refrain from speaking at all"); *Turner Broad. Sys., Inc.,* 512 U.S. at 642 (stating that "[l]aws that compel speakers to utter or distribute speech bearing a particular message are subject to" constitutional scrutiny). * * *

By definition, debt relief agencies provide bankruptcy assistance to assisted persons (or prospective assisted persons) "with respect to a case or proceeding under [the Bankruptcy Code]." §§ 101(4A), (12A). Section 528 generally requires debt relief agencies to disclose on its advertisements of bankruptcy assistance services directed to the general public that their services do in fact relate to bankruptcy and that they assist people in filing for bankruptcy. § 528. As in *Zauderer v. Office of Disciplinary Counsel of the Supreme Court of Ohio*, 471 U.S. 626 (1985), the plaintiffs' "constitutionally protected interest in not providing [such] factual information in [their] advertising is minimal." 471 U.S. at 650. Further, the disclosure requirements are reasonably and rationally related to the government's interest in preventing the deception of consumer debtors, as the disclosure requirements are directed precisely at the problem targeted by Congress: ensuring that persons who advertise bankruptcy-related services to the general public make clear that their services do in fact involve filing for bankruptcy.

Section 528 requires debt relief agencies to disclose: "'We are a debt relief agency. We help people file for bankruptcy relief under the Bankruptcy Code.' or a substantially similar statement," in all of their bankruptcy-related advertising materials directed to the general public. §§ 528(a)(4), (b)(2). The requirement does not prevent those attorneys meeting the definition of debt relief agencies "from conveying information to the public; it ... only require[s] them to provide somewhat more information than they might otherwise be inclined to present." *Zauderer,* 471 U.S. at 650. Moreover, if any of these attorneys are concerned that the required disclosures will confuse the public, we note that nothing in the Code prevents them from identifying themselves in their advertisements as both attorneys and debt relief agencies. Simply put, attorneys that provide bankruptcy assistance to assisted persons are debt relief agencies under the Code, and the disclosure requirements of § 528 only require those attorneys to disclose factually correct statements on their advertising. This does not violate the First Amendment. * * *

The challenged sections of § 528 only require debt relief agencies to include a disclosure on certain advertisements. Although less intrusive means may be conceivable to prevent deceptive advertising, § 528's disclosure requirements are reasonably related to the government's interest in protecting consumer debtors from deceptive advertising, and thus the section passes constitutional muster.

III. Conclusion

In sum, attorneys who provide bankruptcy assistance to assisted persons are debt relief agencies under the Bankruptcy Code, and § 526(a)(4) is unconstitutional as applied to these attorneys, but §§ 528(a)(4) and (b)(2) are constitutional. Accordingly, we affirm in part and reverse in part.

JUDGE COLLOTON's opinion, concurring in part and dissenting in part, is omitted.

NOTES

1. The court in *Hersh v. United States*, 553 F.3d 743 (5th Cir. 2008), while agreeing that attorneys fall within the statutory definitions of "debt relief agency," took the position that the statutory limitation on advice should be interpreted to prohibit attorneys from counseling clients to incur debt only when doing so would entail abuse of the bankruptcy system, interpreting the provision narrowly in order to avoid constitutional concerns. See a critical analysis of these issues in Jean Braucher, *The Challenge to the Bench and Bar Presented by the 2005 Bankruptcy Act: Resistance Need Not Be Futile*, 2007 U. Ill. L. Rev. 93, 128. Attorneys performing services pro bono are not included in the definition of "debt relief agency."

2. BAPCPA regulates debt relief agencies in their dealings with assisted persons in great detail with respect to: advertising, failing to perform promised duties, making untrue or misleading statements in documents filed in a case, misrepresenting services promised or benefits or risks that may result, advising assisted persons to incur more debt to pay attorneys or bankruptcy petition preparers, and failure to comply with the disclosure provisions of § 527 and § 528. Section 527 requires debt relief agencies providing bankruptcy assistance services (attorneys) to give a large volume of disclosure to an assisted person, including what amounts to a short course in bankruptcy law. Section 528 calls for written contracts between debt relief agencies and assisted persons and regulates advertising by these agencies. In § 526(c), liabilities are set out and remedies are prescribed.

Section 527(a)(1) requires that the debt relief agency provide information involving the technical details of bankruptcy process as well as a rather lengthy statement, similar to the kind required by federal consumer protection laws, about services rendered by an attorney or bankruptcy petition preparer. Most of these disclosures are probably incomprehensible to almost all debtors.

Section 110 defines "bankruptcy petition preparer" as a person, other than an attorney or an attorney's employee (paralegal), who prepares for a fee documents for filing. This section regulates the activities of bankruptcy petition preparers in detail.

c. Advertising

The advertising provisions of the statute apply to statements "directed to the general public" that are made by debt relief agencies in the "general media, seminars or special mailings, telephonic or electronic messages, or otherwise...." § 528(a)(3). Advertising messages must "clearly and conspicuously" include the following statement: "We are a debt relief agency. We help people file for bankruptcy relief under the Bankruptcy Code" § 528(a)(4). Under § 528(b)(2), if its ads promise general nonbankruptcy debtor relief services, a debt relief agency must state clearly and conspicuously that its assistance may also involve bankruptcy relief and recite the legend quoted above. And this must be done even though the attorney does no bankruptcy work, making the representation false and misleading. An obvious difficulty with the legend is that it will mislead debtors into going to bankruptcy petition preparers when they need the services of an attorney.

Sections 526, 527 and 528 restrict what bankruptcy attorneys can tell their clients and advertise to the general public. Whether this infringement on lawyers' First Amendment rights is discussed in detail for the first time at the Court of Appeals level in *Milavetz, supra*. It is difficult to think of another area of activity in which attorneys are so heavily regulated with respect to their dealings with their clients. Each case file must contain a detailed compliance checklist with respect to meeting the numerous requirements of §§ 526, 527, and 528. The consumer protection benefits of these provisions, if any, are probably less significant than their effect in discouraging counsel from dealing with consumer debtors and driving up the cost of bankruptcy.

d. U.S. Trustee

Under BAPCPA, the U.S. Trustee is the enforcer of the means test and, as such, the gatekeeper to Chapter 7. Section 704(b)(1) provides that within 10 days after the first meeting of creditors, which must be held between 20 and 40 days after the order for relief (Rule 2003(a)), the U.S. Trustee must file a statement (the "10-Day Statement") that a case either is or is not presumptively an abuse under the means test, § 707(b). Case law has emphasized that the statement must be unequivocal. *See, e.g., In re Ansar*, 383 B.R. 344 (Bankr.D.Minn.2008), in which the U.S. Trustee's motion to dismiss failed because his statement indicated only that he did not have sufficient information to determine whether the presumption of abuse had arisen. The fact that the debtor subsequently provided the requested information did not change the result; the motion for dismissal was time-barred and had to be denied as a matter of law. Within 30 days after filing this statement, § 704(b)(2) requires the U.S. Trustee to file either a motion to dismiss or convert or a statement setting out the reasons why such a motion is not appropriate if the presumption of abuse applies. Thus, U.S. Trustees must review the hundreds of thousands of Chapter 7 filings by individual debtors and make the decision whether to move to dismiss or convert in 60-90 days. In short, the means test has raised the price of bankruptcy not only to debtors but also to the courts and U.S. Trustees. While means testing excludes only a small percentage of individual debtors who might have had access to Chapter 7 under the old rules, all individual debtors desiring bankruptcy relief from consumer debts must be screened for the applicability of the means test.

The U. S. Trustee Program (USTP) has been active in appellate courts to ensure that the law, as interpreted by USTP, is followed. It attempts to promote predictability and consistency in the bankruptcy system. References throughout this chapter have been made to instances in which USTP has taken a position on controversial issues. According to a recent article, USTP participated in more than 100 appeals in 2007. Mathew Sutko and Saleela Salahuddin, *U.S. Trustees: Bankruptcy Watchdogs and Appellate Advocates*, 27 Am. Bankr. Inst. J. 12 (2008).

BAPCPA has also increased the burdens of panel trustees. In addition to reviewing court documents including the debtor's petition and schedules and looking at liens and mortgages, they must now consider the debtor's status under the means test. Even seasoned trustees might spend two hours or more on a typical Chapter 7 no-asset case, for which they receive a flat fee of only $60. 20 BNA Bankr. L. Rep. 1086 (2008). Technology is their salvation.

e. Audits

Section 603(a) of the 2005 Act, Pub.L. 109-8, 119 Stat. 122, addresses concerns about the potential for cheating by debtors in their bankruptcy case submissions. Debtors' attorneys, panel trustees, U.S. Trustees and bankruptcy courts must rely on information given them by debtors in order to apply the means test and for other purposes under the Code, but heretofore there has been no systematic audit of this information for veracity. Section 603(a) requires the Attorney General to establish procedures for auditing the accuracy and completeness of petitions, schedules and other information that the debtor is required submit in a bankruptcy case. These procedures must call for random audits in not less than one out of every 250 cases, as well as audits of schedules that reflect certain variances in the statistical norms of income and expenses in the district. Section 603(b) adds 28 U.S.C. § 586(f), which authorizes the U.S. Trustee for each district to contract with auditors to perform audits in cases designated by the U.S. Trustee. The reports of audits will be filed with the court and transmitted to the U.S. Trustee.

Audits are conducted by CPAs and are "desk audits" with no personal contact with debtors. The auditors require documentary proof: pay stubs for six months, account statements (brokerage and financial), federal income tax returns for two years, divorce decrees, and property settlements.

If "material misstatement" of income, expenditures, or assets is reported by the audit, the U.S. Trustee shall take "appropriate action," which includes but is not restricted to seeking to revoke the debtor's discharge under § 727(d)(4). Other possible actions might include requiring the debtor to correct any misstatement, moving to dismiss the case, or objecting to plan confirmation. Ultimately, whether there is a material misstatement and the U.S. Trustee's proposed action is appropriate must be decided by the court upon motion brought by the U.S. Trustee or a party in interest. The U.S. Trustee may also report the misstatement to the U.S. Attorney for criminal proceedings. The U.S. Trustee Program reported that about 21 percent of individual bankruptcy cases selected for audit during the 2008 fiscal year contained material misstatements. United States Department of Justice, EOUST, Public Report: Debtor Audits by USTP FY 2008 (Mar. 2009). Just as tax audits give taxpayers incentive to file honest returns, bankruptcy audits should have a similar effect on bankruptcy debtors. *See* Clifford J. White III and Thomas C. Kearns, *BAPCPA Update: Debtor Audit Procedures and the Reporting of Material Misstatements*, 14 ABI J. 14 (Dec.–Jan. 2008); Kenneth N. Klee, *Restructuring Individual Debts,* in *Reforming Consumer Bankruptcy Law: Four Proposals*, 71 Am. Bankr. L.J. 431, 437, 442 (1997).

5. MANDATORY CREDIT COUNSELING

a. Credit Counseling

BAPCPA denies debtors of all income levels access to bankruptcy, except in emergency cases, unless they have "during the 180-day period before filing received from an approved nonprofit budget and credit counseling agency described in section 111(a) an individual or group briefing (including a briefing conducted by telephone or on the Internet) that outlined the opportunities for available credit counseling and assisted such individual in performing a related budget analysis." § 109(h)(1). The debtor must file with the court a certificate stating that an approved agency provided the debtor with the services described under § 109(h) and a copy of the repayment plan, if any, developed thereunder. § 521(b). BAPCPA says nothing about who pays for the mandated instruction; presumably the usually insolvent, sometimes indigent, debtor must foot the bill. A debtor need not complete an instructional course concerning personal financial management described in § 111 in order to be eligible for filing, but completion of such a course is a prerequisite for discharge in both Chapter 7, § 727(a)(11), and Chapter 13, § 1328(g).

Waiver

A prospective debtor may avoid compliance with the credit counseling requirement of § 109(h) for eligibility to file bankruptcy by obtaining a waiver from the court by proving the existence of "exigent circumstances that merit a waiver" and showing that the credit counseling agency could not provide the required services within five days after request was made. § 109(h)(3)(A). The U.S. Trustee may also exempt debtors who live in districts that do not have approved agencies able to provide the needed services. § 109(h)(2).

Prospective debtors who can show incapacity or disability are given a permanent waiver. § 109(h)(4). "Incapacity" is defined as mental deficiency; "disability" means physical impairment. A number of cases have dealt with whether the incarceration of the prospective debtor is a disability on the ground that the prisoner is physically prevented from receiving counseling. *See, e.g., In re Anderson*, 397 B.R. 363 (6th Cir. BAP 2008), in which the court took the view that the prospective debtor was not disabled even though prison policy prevented him from participating by telephone or the Internet without a court order.

Why mandatory credit counseling?

The argument for mandatory credit counseling is that bankruptcy lawyers have no financial incentive to encourage debtors to work their problems out with creditors informally or to seek formal credit counseling. This may lead them to take their clients into bankruptcy prematurely without fully explaining the consequences of filing or the alternatives to bankruptcy a debtor may have. Mandatory credit counseling is supposed to ensure that debtors receive advice from a party other than an attorney, creating an important gate-keeping function that may reduce the number of filings. The contention is that although mandatory credit counseling will increase the cost of filing bankruptcy, this cost may be outweighed by the effects of such a provision in keeping more debtors out of bankruptcy.

What mandatory credit counseling and financial management instruction has become under BAPCPA has been shaped largely by the U.S. Trustee Program which approves the agencies as satisfying the broad standards prescribed by the statute. To be approved, a credit counseling agency must be nonprofit and provide adequate counseling with respect to client credit problems that includes an analysis of their current situation, what brought them to that financial status, and how they can develop a plan to handle the problem without incurring negative amortization of their debts. § 111(c)(2)(A) and (E). These agencies may charge reasonable fees but must "provide services without regard to ability to pay the fee." § 111(c)(2)(B). The U.S. Trustee may approve financial management instructional courses only if the course provides "trained personnel with adequate experience and training in providing effective instruction and services." § 111(d)(1)(A). Courses may be offered by telephone or through the Internet. § 111(d)(1)(C). Agencies offering financial management courses must maintain records permitting auditors to evaluate whether the courses are effective. § 111(d)(1)(D).

At the time BAPCPA became effective, the credit counseling field was teeming with debt counselors hoping to be selected by the U.S. Trustee as approved agencies. The IRS was besieged by credit counseling businesses seeking nonprofit status so that they might qualify. The quality of these enterprises varies widely from established agencies affiliated with the National Foundation for Consumer Credit (NFCC), which limits the fees that its members may charge clients, to fly-by-night operators that advertise miraculous cures erasing debts and repairing credit records.

Will the pre-filing credit counseling prerequisite prescribed in BAPCPA in fact encourage debtors and creditors to reach extra-bankruptcy workout agreements or will the requirement amount to little more than an annoying obstruction that runs up the cost of bankruptcy for debtors—the equivalent of traffic school for debtors? The experience with mandatory credit counseling in the first year of BAPCPA was not encouraging. The great majority of counseling sessions were conducted either by telephone or the Internet. Face-to-face conferences occurred in no more than 15% of the cases. 18 BNA Bankr. L. Rep. 947 (2006). Apparently most sessions were conducted only a short time before the debtor filed, perhaps in the waiting room outside bankruptcy counsel's office, much too late to help the debtor deal with her present financial problems.

A much litigated issue, on which the bankruptcy courts are divided, is whether the statute requires that the debtor receive the counseling by at least the day before filing bankruptcy or merely by the same day. In *In re Gossett*, 369 B.R. 361 (Bankr.N.D.Ill.2007), the debtor admitted that she obtained the certificate "just minutes" prior to filing her petition. The court held that she was ineligible because "during the 180-day period preceding the date of filing" cannot include the date of filing. Many other cases disagree. *E.g,. In re Spears*, 355 B.R. 116 (Bankr.E.D.Wis.2006). Counselors report that the debtor is often in such hopeless economic distress that the counselors have a difficult time in filling the 90-minute period allotted for the session. A discussion of alternatives to bankruptcy would usually be useless because at that point the debtor has no alternatives. According to a survey of the first year of its experience under BAPCPA, the NFCC found that the average unsecured debt of debtors filing for bankruptcy was $11,599 more than their average annual income. The NFCC agencies waived fees for services for consumers unable to pay in 16 percent of the pre-filing sessions and 13 percent of the pre-discharge education classes. These agencies projected a loss of $7.52 million for their services offered in 2006.

b. Financial Management Instructional Courses

A debtor may not be discharged in Chapter 7, § 727(a)(11), or Chapter 13, § 1328(g), unless the debtor, after filing a petition, has completed an instructional course in personal financial management as required by § 111. Debtor education is a new field for EOUST, and Congress proceeded with caution in prescribing the form of the proposed educational programs. EOUST is required to develop financial management training curricula and materials after consulting with a wide rage of experts in debtor education, including Chapter 13 trustees and operators of financial management education programs. The curricula and materials must be tested in six judicial districts over an 18-month period beginning within 270 days of enactment of the Act. They will then be evaluated by Chapter 13 trustees and consumer counseling groups. These experts will also examine representative consumer education programs carried out by the credit industry.

The Director of EOUST reported to Congress in May 2008 on his findings regarding the effectiveness and cost of programs. He concluded that: "Almost all of the consumer debtors (97 percent) in the pilot study who took courses utilizing the financial management training curriculum and materials developed for EOUST expressed a high level of satisfaction with the curriculum. Further, almost half of the consumer bankruptcy debtors reported their intentions to change at least one financial practice. The pilot study did not, however, find substantial improvement in knowledge and financial practice, likely due to pre-existing knowledge regarding the topics measured." Almost all of the debtors reported that their ability to manage their finances had improved as a result of the class and that they would recommend the program to others. But only about a fifth reported that three months later they were still using a practice learned in the course.

D. CHAPTER 13 AS AN ALTERNATIVE FOR THE CONSUMER DEBTOR

1. AN OVERVIEW OF CHAPTER 13

Chapter 13 of the 1978 Code was enacted to offer an appealing alternative to debtors to induce them to voluntarily use future earnings to repay part or all of their debts rather than to opt for Chapter 7. But only approximately 30% of all debtors chose Chapter 13 over Chapter 7. On the eve of enactment of BAPCPA, Chapter 13 offered the following: The debtor could retain all her property. She was required to submit a plan in which she pledged to devote all her "disposable income" to debt repayment for three to five years. "Disposable income" was defined as all income projected by the debtor during the period of the plan that was not reasonably necessary for the maintenance and support of the debtor and her dependents. Former § 1325(b)(2). This plan had to be approved by the court; creditor approval was not required. There were two important additional limitations on this plan. The plan must return to each unsecured creditor at least what that creditor would have received in a Chapter 7 liquidation of debtor's nonexempt property, sometimes called the "best interests" test. § 1325(a)(4). And the plan must provide that each secured creditor receive deferred cash payments with sufficient interest to give that creditor present value equal to the allowed amount of that claim. § 1325(a)(5).

Requiring the debtor to devote future earnings to debt repayment, was intended to enhance the rights of both unsecured and secured creditors in comparison to what they would be in a Chapter 7 liquidation. And to some degree they did: in the years immediately preceding BAPCPA, Chapter 13 payments to creditors were substantially larger than those under Chapter 7. According to the U.S. Trustee, in 2003 creditors received only $1.5 billion in Chapter 7 cases and $4.2 billion in Chapter 13 cases. Michael Schroeder & Suein Hwang, *Sweeping New Bankruptcy Law to Make Life Harder for Debtors*, Wall St. J., April 6, 2005, at A1. But creditors wanted more.

Requiring the debtor to devote all disposable income to debt repayment for at least three years was not meaningful to unsecured creditors for those debtors that projected little income in excess of their living costs and secured debt obligations. Although some bankruptcy courts asserted the power to reject plans that do not call for reductions in living costs, there was no statutory requirement that a debtor reduce living expenses, and most courts were loathe to find expenses associated with an ordinary middle class standard of living unreasonable. Accordingly, many Chapter 13 plans provided for no or only very small payments to unsecured creditors. These plans could nevertheless be confirmed if the debtor could show that unsecured creditors would have received nothing in Chapter 7. In many cases, it was quite possible for the debtor to make this showing, and when this was so unsecured creditors did no better in Chapter 13 than in Chapter 7.

With respect to secured claims, each secured creditor must receive only the value of its interest in its collateral, usually not the full amount it was owed, in the form of deferred cash payments with interest. With the important exception of home mortgages, this provision allowed the debtor to "strip-down" the amount of her payment obligation to the value of the over-encumbered property she wished to retain. In effect, the debtor could "redeem" overencumbered property by paying to the creditor its value (as determined by the bankruptcy court) over time with interest. No comparable provision existed in Chapter 7. In that chapter, the debtor had to obtain the creditor's consent to any rescheduling of payments if she wished to remain in possession of encumbered property, while in Chapter 13 the debtor could impose a rescheduling based on judicial valuation of the collateral. Home mortgages were specially excepted from this power to modify the amount owed, although the debtor was permitted to pay out arrearages over the life of the plan with interest even in the case of home mortgages. § 1322(b).

Finally, former Chapter 13 permitted the discharge of some debts that could not be discharged in Chapter 7 cases. The only debts excepted from the super-discharge in Chapter 13 cases were claims for alimony and child support, criminal restitution orders, most educational loans, claims arising out of drunk driving accidents and long-term debts. § 1328(a). Moreover, some courts permitted debtors to separately classify and give preferred treatment to the holders of claims that were nondischargeable in Chapter 13. Allowing this discrimination in treatment was extremely favorable to debtors because it permitted them to devote all disposable income to the repayment of claims that in any event would survive the Chapter 13 plan while leaving nothing for the claims that would be discharged upon completion of the plan.

Unlike Chapter 7, which pre-BAPCPA had a six-year bar rule, nothing in Chapter 13 prevented repeated filings. This omission was deliberate, the assumption being that if a debtor was willing to subject all her disposable income to debt repayment for at least three years there was no harm in allowing her to re-enter Chapter 13. But filing under Chapter 13 (as in all bankruptcy filings) has the effect of automatically staying all nonbankruptcy debt collection proceedings, including foreclosures. A particular form of abuse of the bankruptcy process that frustrated mortgage lenders was repeated Chapter 13 filings intended to forestall foreclosure rather than confirm a debt repayment plan.

Experience showed that Chapter 13 plans were likely to fail. If the debtor's income fails to meet projections or her expenses exceed projections, she may be unable to make the payments called for under the plan. In these circumstances, it was common for the Chapter 13 case to be converted to Chapter 7 if no feasible plan remained possible. In these cases, the debtor generally forfeited whatever payments she had made under the plan to unsecured creditors and had to give up her nonexempt property in exchange for the more limited Chapter 7 discharge. There were provisions for a hardship discharge in Chapter 13 if the debtor had made enough payments under the plan to satisfy the best interests test and the plan nevertheless could not be completed on account of circumstances beyond her control. § 1328(b). In other cases, Chapter 13 plans could be modified in order to take into account changed circumstances. § 1329.

Some debtors had both large unsecured and secured debts and sought to take advantage of the most favorable aspects of both Chapters 7 and 13. By first invoking Chapter 7, the debtor could discharge her unsecured claims. The debtor could then file in Chapter 13 in order to deal with recalcitrant secured creditors or the holders of certain nondischargeable claims. The Supreme Court found that these "Chapter 20" cases (that is, *seriatim* Chapters 7 and 13 cases) were generally permitted under pre-BAPCPA law. *Johnson v. Home State Bank*, 501 U.S. 78 (1991).

Based on the above description of the differences between Chapter 7 and Chapter 13, one might predict that those debtors with relatively large unsecured debts, few secured debts, and little nonexempt property would disproportionately choose Chapter 7, while those with substantial nonexempt assets and secured debts would prefer Chapter 13. Teresa A. Sullivan, Elizabeth Warren & Jay Lawrence Westbrook, *Who Uses Chapter 13?* in *Consumer Bankruptcy in Global Perspective* 269 (2004), brings forward the work the authors commenced in their 1981 study (*As We Forgive Our Debtors: Bankruptcy and Consumer Credit in America* 236-238 (1989)). Their new findings, based on 1999 data, revealed that: (1) The proportion of consumer cases filed in Chapter 13 has remained stable from 1981 to 1999 at approximately 30%. (2) The strongest predictor of Chapter 13 filing was home ownership; homes are encumbered assets that debtors want to hold on to. (3) The second strongest predictor was local legal culture. (4) The total amount of debt was mildly negative correlated with filing in Chapter 13. (5) Demographic variables, such as sex, age, and ethnicity, were not significant.

In some jurisdictions, particularly in the Southeastern United States where the predecessor to Chapter 13 was developed in the Depression, bankruptcy courts and the local bar preferred Chapter 13, reasoning that debtors who can pay pre-bankruptcy debts out of future income ought to do so. Chapter 13s were disproportionately filed in those districts. Constance Mitchell Ford, *Creditor-Friendly South Offers Preview of Bankruptcy Changes*, Wall St. J., Mar. 10, 2005, at A1. In some districts, judges would dismiss Chapter 7 filings if the debtor appeared to have sufficient income to fund a Chapter 13 plan, making Chapter 13 virtually mandatory for those debtors. Still other jurisdictions, with judges who were either indifferent or hostile to Chapter 13 plans, tended to see disproportionately more Chapter 7 filings.

As we have seen earlier in this chapter, the principal thrust of BAPCPA with respect to consumer debtors is to employ a means test to restrict access to Chapter 7. If a debtor's case is excluded from Chapter 7 by the means test, the court may either dismiss the case or, with the consent of the debtor, convert the case to Chapter 13. § 707(b)(1). Even under the rather attractive regime offered debtors by pre-BAPCPA Chapter 13 described above, only about 30% of debtors opted for Chapter 13 in preference to Chapter 7, and in some regions significant numbers of those debtors were pushed into Chapter 13 filings. Of these, only about a third actually completed their plan. If, as is commonly assumed, a goal of BAPCPA is to reduce the number of consumer debtors availing themselves of Chapter 7 discharges, one might think that a step in this direction would be making Chapter 13 more appealing to consumer debtors, but as we see in the following sections Congress has most emphatically made Chapter 13 less friendly to consumer debtors than it was before. Nevertheless, the volume of Chapter 13 filings has remained about the same. Acccording to the ABI, U.S. consumer bankruptcy filings increased 29.2 percent in February 2009 over the same month in 2008, and Chapter 13 filings constituted 30.2 percent of all consumer cases during that month. ABI Update (Mar. 3, 2009). The ABI report relied on data from the National Bankruptcy Research Center.

2. ELIGIBILITY FOR CHAPTER 13

Chapter 13 has always been voluntary and under BAPCPA it remains so. If the debtor files in Chapter 7 and is excluded by the means test, the court may convert the case to Chapter 13 only with the debtor's consent. § 707(b)(1). The requirements for eligibility for Chapter 13 are set forth in § 109(e). The debtor must be a natural person. Even a one-stockholder corporation or family partnership is barred and may seek rehabilitation only in Chapter 11. The debtor must be an "individual with regular income," defined in § 101(30) as one with income "sufficiently stable and regular to enable such individual to make payments under a plan under chapter 13." The source of the income is not material. The drafters of the Code wanted to allow the small individual proprietorship to reorganize under Chapter 13 rather than under the more costly and burdensome procedures of Chapter 11. Hence, debtors may be self-employed as well as employees. Even unemployed or retired individuals are eligible so long as they receive regular income, which might be from investments, social security, private pensions, or other welfare or retirement programs. Spouses of debtors with regular income are eligible for Chapter 13 even though they have no income. The debtor must have noncontingent and liquidated debts of less than $336,900 of unsecured claims and $1,010,650 of secured claims. Pursuant to § 104(b), these amounts are adjusted every three years by the Judicial Conference to reflect changes in the Consumer Price Index; the levels were last adjusted in 2007. They were chosen to make Chapter 13 available to most consumer debtors and many small business debtors, leaving to Chapter 11 cases involving larger amounts of debt. The value of the debtor's assets is not relevant to her eligibility for Chapter 13. Rich people can use Chapter 13 so long as their debts are within the statutory limits.

Under § 109(h), added by BAPCPA, debtors are not eligible for Chapter 13 unless they have met the credit counseling requirements discussed above with respect to access to Chapter 7. Since a debtor doesn't have to meet the means test to file in Chapter 13, she doesn't have to file schedules containing the means test calculations that are required of a Chapter 7 filer, but, as in

Chapter 7, under § 521(e)(2) she must provide, not later than 7 days before the date first set for the first meeting of creditors, to the panel trustee, and to any creditor who timely requests a copy, a copy or transcript of her current federal income tax return. At the request of the court, U.S. Trustee or creditor, the debtor must file with the court tax returns for each tax year ending while the case is pending. § 521(f)(1). In addition, a Chapter 13 debtor must annually file a statement, under penalty of perjury, of the income and expenditures of the debtor that shows how income, expenditures and monthly income are calculated. § 521(f)(4) and (g)(1). The tax returns and statement of income and expenditures shall be available to the U.S. Trustee, the Chapter 13 trustee, and "any party in interest" for inspection and copying, subject to the privacy protection discussed previously with respect to Chapter 7. § 521(g)(2).

In *Marrama v. Citizens Bank of Massachusetts*, 549 U.S. 365 (2007), the Court held that a Chapter 7 debtor could not convert his case to Chapter 13 because he was found to be in bad faith. Section 706(a) appeared to give the debtor an unconditional right to convert to Chapter 13: "The debtor may convert a case under this chapter to a case under chapter 11, 12, or 13 of this title at any time... Any waiver of the right to convert a case under this section is unenforceable." Id. at 371. But in a 5-4 decision the Court denied the debtor the right to convert in *Marrama* on the following reasoning: Under § 706(d), a Chapter 7 debtor may not convert to another chapter "unless the debtor may be a debtor under such chapter." Under § 1307, a Chapter 13 case may be dismissed or converted to Chapter 7 "for cause" and bad faith is such a cause. Thus, a Chapter 7 debtor who has proceeded in bad faith and opts to convert the case to Chapter 13 is not eligible to "be a debtor" under Chapter 13 because the debtor's case would be subject to dismissal or reconversion to Chapter 7 under § 1307(c). The Court went further and recognized two alternative grounds for its holding: First, under the broad authority granted by § 105(a), bankruptcy courts may take any action that is necessary or appropriate "to prevent an abuse of process." The Court concluded that this provision is "surely adequate to authorize an immediate denial of a motion to conversion order that merely postpones the allowance of equivalent relief and may provide a debtor with an opportunity to take action prejudicial to creditors." Id. at 375. Second, the Court said that even without § 105(a), the bankruptcy court has "inherent power to sanction 'abusive litigation practices'" so as to deny a § 706(a) conversion request for bad faith.

The reliance of the Court on § 105(a) to modify a clear provision of the Code to control abuse may be of great importance. Some observers look upon the case as reviving the inherent and equitable powers of bankruptcy judges that had been curtailed in recent years. *See A Discourse of Marrama v. Citizens Bank of Massachusetts*, 16 Bankr. L. & Prac. 931 (2007). One of the judges participating in the discourse views *Marrama*'s holding on § 105(a) with enthusiasm and reports that other judges agree; he expects bankruptcy courts to apply the Court's holding to all manner of cases. The case encourages bankruptcy courts to look on § 105(a) as an independent provision, a view that was strongly challenged in Justice Alito's dissent. It will be interesting to see whether *Marrama* will be used in BAPCPA cases to extricate the parties from the clutches of some of the more irrational provisions of the statute. *See Matter of Rosson*, 545 F.3d 764 (9th Cir. 2008) (under *Marrama* debtor's right of voluntary dismissal under § 1307(b) is not absolute, but is qualified by the authority of a bankruptcy court to deny dismissal on grounds of bad faith conduct to prevent an abuse of process).

PROBLEMS

1. In Problem 3 on p. 489, will Marta be able to fund a repayment plan in Chapter 13? Is she even eligible for Chapter 13 given her current lack of regular income? Is it possible for a consumer debtor to be denied access both to Chapters 7 and 13?

2. Debtor mortgaged the family home to Bank to secure a debt of $600,000. Debtor has unsecured debts amounting to $50,000. Owing to a recession, Debtor's income was reduced, and he defaulted on the mortgage and other debts. Real estate values also plunged and the home is now valued at no more than $300,000. Debtor wishes to file in Chapter 13. Is Debtor eligible for Chapter 13 under § 109(e)? On the question of whether the deficiency portion of an undersecured claim counts an as an unsecured debt for Chapter 13 eligibility purposes, *see In re Scovis*, 249 F.3d 975 (9th Cir. 2001).

3. REPEATED DISCHARGES AND FILINGS

a. Repeated Discharges

Should a debtor be able to have the best of both worlds by first getting rid of ordinary debts in Chapter 7 and then filing in Chapter 13 to deal with nondischargeable debts and security interests? In *Johnson v. Home State Bank*, 501 U.S. 78 (1991), the Court answered in the affirmative, noting that Congress had expressly limited various forms of serial filings, *e.g.*, § 109(g), but did not categorically foreclose the power of a debtor to file in Chapter 13 subsequent to a Chapter 7 discharge. Lower courts imposed a good faith test to limit somewhat debtors' use of "Chapter 20." *See, e.g., In re Rasmussen*, 888 F.2d 703 (10th Cir. 1989) (nondischargeable debts); *In re Cushman*, 217 B.R. 470 (Bankr.E.D.Va.1998) (lien stripping).

BAPCPA § 1328(f)(1) addresses the "Chapter 20" strategem by barring a debtor who has previously received a discharge in Chapter 7 from receiving a Chapter 13 discharge in a case in which the Chapter 13 petition is filed within four years after the Chapter 7 petition was filed. *In re Sanders*, 551 F.3d 397 (6th Cir. 2008). Section 1328(f)(2) deals with successive Chapter 13 filings in a manner that has perplexed courts. It states that no discharge may be granted to a debtor in a Chapter 13 case if the debtor had received a discharge "in a case filed under chapter 13 of this title during the 2-year period preceding the date of such order." The issue is whether the 2-year period starts at the time the previous case was filed or at the time of discharge in that case. In the most authoritative case on the matter, *In re Bateman*, 515 F.3d 272 (4th Cir. 2008), the court held that the literal interpretation of the statute compelled a holding that the 2-year period ran from the time of filing in the first case to the time of filing in the second case.

In answer to the contention that this view essentially renders § 1328(f)(2) meaningless because Chapter 13 cases usually run from three to five years, the court held that § 1328(f)(2) is not an eligibility provision and the unavailability of a discharge does not preclude a good faith Chapter 13 filing. In the rare case in which a debtor has received a Chapter 13 discharge within the 2-year period after filing, she may file another Chapter 13 within the period if she does so in good faith and, by doing so, enjoy the protection of the automatic stay while paying off her creditors in an orderly manner under the plan, but she may not be discharged. In the common case in which the filing in the second case is to halt a foreclosure, as in *Bateman*, the debtor's immediate concern is not discharge but postponing the foreclosure. In *Bateman*, the court allowed the second filing only after the debtor demonstrated good faith by showing that her confirmed plan would pay all allowed claims in full. Both the debtor and her creditors should be pleased with this result. The next section deals with abusive repeated filings.

PROBLEM

Herman believes in paying his debts. When he found himself in financial difficulties, he filed in Chapter 13 in January 2007. His plan was confirmed and he completed it by paying all his creditors in full. He was discharged in January 2009. In June 2009 he was laid off from his job and was living on unemployment compensation while he searched for a new job. His mortgagee was threatening foreclosure on his residence, and he sought protection in Chapter 13 again so that he could retain his home and pay his creditors in an orderly manner.

What are Herman's rights to confirmation of a Chapter 13 plan under § 1328(f)(2)?

b. Repetitive Filings under BAPCPA

Some debtors have relied on repeated Chapter 13 filings to take advantage of the automatic stay to stave off foreclosure or eviction. After the creditor requests relief from the automatic stay under § 362(d) in order to foreclose or evict, the debtor dismisses under § 1307(b), only to file again when the mortgagee or landlord initiates another foreclosure or eviction. The bankruptcy court clerk is required to accept the bankruptcy petition of a debtor who files the correct papers and pays the fee. This process can go on indefinitely. Seeing the potential for abuse in this situation, Congress enacted § 109(g)(2) in 1984, which provides that an individual who has been a debtor at any time within the preceding 180-day period is ineligible to file in Chapter 13 if that individual had obtained voluntary dismissal of the prior case following the filing of a request for relief from the automatic stay by the creditor.

BAPCPA aggressively addressed the repeated filings issue in an elaborate set of provisions that should keep bankruptcy courts busy for years. The amendments adding § 362(c)(3) and (4) approach the problem of bad faith repeated filings by limiting the debtor's protection under the automatic stay against creditor collection actions. A superficial reading of (c)(3) is that a debtor, who files a Chapter 13 petition within a year after dismissal of a previous case, loses protection of the automatic stay 30 days after filing the later case unless the debtor is able to demonstrate to the court at a hearing completed within the 30-day period that the filing of the later case was in good faith as to the creditors to be stayed. And under (c)(4) if the debtor has had two or more cases dismissed that were pending the previous year, the stay does not go into effect at all upon the filing of a subsequent case, absent a showing of good faith. *See Dixon v. Federal National Mortgage Association*, 2006 WL 3371500 (S.D. Tex.2006). But a more careful reading of (c)(3) shows that "the stay ... shall terminate with *respect to the debtor*." A majority of cases have interpreted this language to lift the stay only with respect to the debtor and the debtor's property and not to the property of the estate. Since "property of the estate" includes virtually all the property except that abandoned or exempt, the literal reading of the statute effectively guts (c)(3). Thus, if a mortgagee attempts to foreclose on the mortgaged property, the stay remains in effect. *See, e.g.*, *In re Holcomb*, 380 B.R. 813 (10th Cir. BAP 2008). A minority of cases, noting that this reading renders (c)(3) meaningless, has interpreted "with respect to the debtor" to include property of the estate. *See, e.g.*, *In re Curry*, 362 B.R. 394 (Bankr.N.D.Ill.2007). Subsection (c)(4) is clear that the stay terminates entirely upon the happening of the enumerated events, absent a showing of good faith.

BAPCPA also added § 362(d)(4) aimed at curbing abusive filings calculated to forestall foreclosure. Mortgagees found the practice of debtors (often acting on the advice of unscrupulous "foreclosure consultants") of transferring title (or fractional interests in title) to other entities in order to frustrate foreclosure to be particularly troublesome. Section 362(d)(4) authorizes courts to grant a powerful new form of *in rem* relief from the stay "if the court finds that the filing of the petition was part of a scheme to delay, hinder and defraud creditors" that involved either transfer of the real property without the mortgagee's consent or multiple bankruptcy filings. The order lifting the stay may be recorded in the real property records and is binding for two years on any new bankruptcy cases affecting the real property. The provision is triggered only if the mortgagee can show that the mortgagor's activities were part of a fraudulent scheme.

Another species of bad faith filings relates to tenants who seek to delay eviction proceedings by filing in bankruptcy. Section 362(b)(22) excepts from the stay the continuation of eviction proceedings involving residential property if the lessor has obtained a judgment for possession before the tenant filed bankruptcy. The debtor can postpone the application of § 362(b)(22) until 30 days after her petition is filed by filing with her petition a certification that she has the right to cure her default and has deposited with the clerk any rent that would become due during the 30-day delay. If the lessor objects, a hearing must be held within 10 days after its objection is filed. § 362(*l*)(3).

4. COMMENCING A CHAPTER 13 CASE

Chapter 13 debtors retain their property and pay their debts out of future earnings pursuant to a plan confirmed by the court. At the time of filing, the debtor must file schedules with the petition in bankruptcy giving information about the debtor's employment, income, expenses, debts and property as well as estimates of future monthly income and expenses. § 521(a)(1). The debtor must file a plan with the petition or within 15 days thereafter unless an extension is granted for cause. Rule 3015(b). Debtors are not allowed to delay in commencing their payments under the plan. Under § 1326(a), the debtor "shall" commence payments proposed under the plan within 30 days after the plan is filed or the order for relief, whichever is earlier, even though the plan is not yet confirmed.

BAPCPA shores up the Chapter 13 position of lessors and secured creditors by providing in § 1326(a)(1) that the debtor must pay the trustee the amount "proposed by the plan" but, in addition, pay directly to any personal property lessor the amount of the rentals coming due after the case was filed (§ 1326(a)(1)(B)), and to any creditor having a purchase money security interest in personal property the amount of adequate protection payments coming due after filing (§ 1326(a)(1)(C)). The trustee must be provided with evidence of these payments. The debtor may reduce the amount of payments made to the trustee under the proposed plan by the amount of any payments made to lessors and secured creditors under these provisions. The payment provisions of § 1326(a)(1) are subject to the qualification "Unless the court orders otherwise..."

The meaning of these new provisions has divided the bankruptcy courts. For detailed discussions of these amendments, see David Gray Carlson, *Cars and Homes in Chapter 13 After the 2005 Amendments to the Bankrupcy Code*, 14 Am. Bankr. Inst. L. Rev. 301 (2006) and Henry Sommer, *supra*. The drafters apparently intended that lessors and secured creditors should be paid directly by the debtor at least during the period between filing and confirmation of the plan and that these payments should commence within 30 days of the petition date. Although lessors must receive the contract rent, secured creditors do not receive contractual monthly payments but rather adequate protection payments, presumably compensation for depreciation. Adequate protection payments will usually be less than the monthly payments under the loan agreement. The perceived evil giving rise to these provisions is that some "abusive" plans postponed payment to secured creditors until several months into the plan, leaving the secured creditor with uncompensated depreciation. See Richardo Kilpatrick, *Selected Creditor Issues Under the Bankruptcy Abuse Prevention and Consumer Protection Act of 2005*, 79 Am. Bankr. L.J. 817, 836 (2005). Now secured creditors and lessors come first and, in the view of some courts, even before the administrative claims of the debtor's attorney. *See, e.g., In re DeSardi*, 340 B.R. 790 (Bankr.S.D.Tex.2006). The statute does not say how long the direct payments to lessors and secured creditors by the debtor must continue. The general rule is that when the plan is confirmed, its terms determine how payments are to be directed. *See, e.g., In re Jones*, 2008 WL 5063809 (2d Cir. 2008) (a bankruptcy court's order that adequate protection payments be made to a creditor is not effective after the plan is confirmed; at that time the terms of the plan control). In order to deal with vagaries of the statute, bankruptcy districts, relying on the language in § 1326(a)(1) "Unless the court orders otherwise," have enacted local rules governing some of these issues. *E.g.*, the Southern District of Texas and Central District of California. *See In re Lopez*, 372 B.R. 40, 46 n.17 (9th Cir. BAP 2007). For instance, some reject direct payments by debtors and require that all adequate protection payments must go through the trustee; or fix presumed depreciation rates of 1% to 1.5%; or deal with the priority between adequate protection payments and administrative claims, such as the attorney's fee.

Another provision added by BAPCPA to aid secured creditors is § 1325(a)(5)(B)(iii)(I), which requires that periodic payments to secured creditors called for by the plan "shall be in equal monthly amounts" and "not be less than an amount sufficient to provide to the holder of such claim adequate protection during the period of the plan." Thus, balloon payments and other irregular payments are barred, and the payments must adequately protect the creditor against decline in value of the collateral. According to Professor William C. Whitford, *A History of the Automobile Lender Provisions of BAPCPA*, 2007 U. Ill. L. Rev. 143, 185, the equal payments provision was added at the behest of automobile financers to reverse cases that allowed debtors to delay making payments to secured creditors for a year or more after filing in Chapter 13.

Upon notice and hearing, the court may modify the amount of payments required by subsection (a) pending confirmation of the plan. Within 60 days after filing the plan, the debtor in possession of personal property subject to a lease or security interest must provide the lessor or secured creditor with evidence of insurance coverage on the property. Any payment received by the trustee before confirmation is to be held by the trustee until the plan is either confirmed or not confirmed. If the plan is confirmed, the trustee must distribute the money under the plan. If confirmation is denied, the trustee must give the money collected back to the debtor. Section 1302 requires the trustee to ensure that the debtor commences making timely payments under § 1302(b)(5). If the debtor fails to commence payments on time, the court may convert the case to Chapter 7 or dismiss it. § 1307(c)(4).

Within 20 to 50 days after the petition, the U.S. Trustee must call a meeting of creditors pursuant to § 341(a). Bankr. Rule 2003(a). Proofs of claim are to be filed within 90 days after the first date set for the meeting of creditors. Bankr. Rule 3002(c). The notice of confirmation hearing must include either the plan or a summary of it so that creditors can assess whether they wish to object to it at the confirmation hearing. Bankr. Rule 3015(d). Although the U.S. Trustee or a designee presides at the meeting of creditors (Bankr.Rule 2003(b)(1)), and the court ultimately decides whether to confirm the debtor's plan, the gatekeeper in the Chapter 13 confirmation process is the standing trustee. The trustee's staff examines the debtor's plan before the creditors' meeting and the trustee may use that meeting to raise with the debtor's counsel any deficiencies in the plan. Further information may be sought from the debtor who must be present at the meeting. § 343. If these problems can be worked out at the meeting, the trustee may place the debtor's case on what amounts to a consent calendar and allow the hearing on the confirmation of the plan to take place immediately.

BAPCPA validates this accelerated hearing practice in § 1324(b) if "the court determines that it would be in the best interests of the creditors and the estate to hold such hearing within 20 days of the § 341(a) meeting and there is no objection to such earlier date." Time and money are saved and the creditors receive distributions more promptly. Money to fund the plan may be paid to the trustee directly by the debtor or, pursuant to court order, by the debtor's employer or other source of income. § 1325(c). Upon completing all payments under the plan, the debtor is discharged. § 1328(a).

5. PROPERTY OF THE ESTATE

a. Role of Property of the Estate

In Chapter 7, property of the estate must be identified because it is the property the trustee liquidates and distributes to creditors. But in Chapter 13 the debtor usually retains the property and pays creditors out of future earnings. Nevertheless, identification of property of the estate is necessary in Chapter 13 because a plan may be confirmed only if each unsecured claim receives not less than it would in liquidation under Chapter 7. § 1325(a)(4). Thus, until a court knows the extent of the property of the estate, it cannot confirm a plan. The concept of property of the estate also determines the scope of the automatic stay. Preconfirmation the automatic stay operates in Chapter 13 much the same as in Chapter 7. Postconfirmation the automatic stay operates primarily to prevent creditors from disrupting execution of the plan by seizing postpetition income of the debtor to be distributed by the trustee. § 1306(a)(2); *Telfair v. First Union Mortgage Corp.*, 216 F.3d 1333 (11th Cir. 2000).

b. Conversion to Chapter 7

Section 1307 provides that "The debtor may convert a case under this chapter to a case under chapter 7 at any time." What is property of the estate in a case in which a Chapter 13 debtor converts to Chapter 7? Section 348(f) provides that upon conversion from Chapter 13 to Chapter 7, the property of the estate in the Chapter 7 case is only the property that the debtor had at the time of filing the Chapter 13 petition that is still under the control of the debtor on the conversion date. Thus, property acquired by the debtor after filing the Chapter 13 petition but before conversion to Chapter 7 is property of the debtor and not of the converted estate. The legislative history justifies this result to avoid creating disincentive for debtors to file in Chapter 13 by depriving them of their postpetition property if they later must convert to Chapter 7. The amendment rejects the concern of Judge Posner in *In re Lybrook*, 951 F.2d 136 (7th Cir. 1991), that to allow a Chapter 13 debtor to convert to Chapter 7 and keep all postpetition property encourages strategic conversions in cases in which the debtor, as in *Lybrook*, acquires substantial property after filing in Chapter 13.

6. THE PLAN

The requirements that the debtor must meet to confirm a Chapter 13 plan are, for the most part, found in § 1322 (contents of plan) and § 1325 (confirmation of plan). Before BAPCPA, § 1322(a) prescribed only three mandatory requirements: (1) the plan must provide for payment to the trustee of all or part of the debtor's future earnings or income "as is necessary for the execution of the plan;" (2) the plan must provide for full payment of priority claims in deferred payments unless the claimant agrees to different treatment; and (3) if the plan classifies claims, the plan must provide the same treatment for each claim within a class. BAPCPA added a fourth requirement regarding the duration of a plan involving DSO claims that is discussed below. § 1322(a)(4). A plan may not be confirmed under § 1325(a)(3) unless it has been proposed in good faith. Other provisions of § 1325 will be discussed in detail later.

a. Domestic Support Obligations

As we saw in chapter 3, women's and children's advocates urged Congress to shore up the position of children and spouses with respect to alimony, maintenance and support in BAPCPA. As the rights of credit card issuers, retailers, motor vehicle financers and other consumer creditors improved under early drafts of BAPCPA, less of the debtor's postpetition income remained to support children and ex-spouses. What these advocates wanted was, in substance, that bankruptcy not interfere with rights to collect support payments from debtors, that within the bankruptcy estate support obligations be given first dibs on the debtor's assets, and that a debtor not come out of Chapter 13 with a discharge unless current on support payments. Congress delivered in BAPCPA.

Since a number of provisions throughout BAPCPA are concerned with support provisions, the drafting approach was to define "domestic support obligations" ("DSO") in § 101(14A) as including alimony, maintenance or support payments owing to spouses, children and governmental units, as assignees for Social Security Act purposes, and to refer to the defined term in the substantive provisions of the Act.

Past due prepetition DSO balances are accorded a first priority under § 507(a)(1), even ahead of administrative expenses (including lawyers fees!). A Chapter 13 plan must provide for full payment in deferred cash payments of all priority claims, unless the holder of the claim agrees to a different treatment. § 1322(a)(2). DSO payments coming due after the filing must be paid in full before the plan can be confirmed (§ 1325(a)(8)), and failure to keep payments current on DSOs before or after confirmation is grounds for dismissal. § 1307(c)(11). In calculating the debtor's "disposable income," DSO claims are included as "reasonably necessary" expenses, thus reducing the amount payable to other creditors. § 1325(b)(2). DSO claimants may garnish the pay of debtors without violating the automatic stay. § 362(b)(2)(C). DSO claims are nondischargeable, (§ 523(a)(5), § 1328(a)(2)), and a discharge cannot be given in Chapter 13 unless the debtor certifies that all amounts payable under a DSO "that are due on or before the date of the certification (including amounts due before the petition was filed, but only to the extent provided for in the plan) have been paid." § 1328(a) (preamble). Debtors who are unable or unwilling to honor their DSOs will not find relief in Chapter 13.

b. Commitment Period

A major change under BAPCPA is lengthening the commitment period of Chapter 13 plans to five years for debtors whose annual incomes are above the state median family income. For debtors with incomes below the median, the commitment period of a plan may not exceed three years unless the court, for cause, approves a longer period not in excess of five years. §§ 1322(d), 1325(b)(4). The commitment period may be less than three or five years, whichever is applicable, only if the plan provides full payment for all allowed unsecured claims over a shorter period. § 1325(b)(4)(B). Thus, debtors whose Chapter 7 cases are dismissed because of application of the means test and have annual income above the state median family income will find that Chapter 13 relief is available to them only under a five-year plan. In one instance, a five-year commitment period is mandated without respect to the amount of the debtor's income: a plan may provide for less than full payment of a DSO priority claim owing to a governmental unit (§ 507(a)(1)(B)) only if all the debtor's projected disposable income for a five-year period is applied to payment of this claim. § 1322(a)(4). Given that only one-third of the plans were sustainable for the three-year duration under pre-BAPCPA law, there is no basis for optimism for the success of five-year plans under BAPCPA.

c. Disposable Income

(i) Before BAPCPA

The legislative history quoted below indicates that Congress, in exchange for allowing debtors to keep their property and enjoy a super-discharge, contemplated in the 1978 Code that Chapter 13 plans would result in some payment to unsecured creditors:

> The purpose of chapter 13 is to enable an individual, under court supervision and protection, to develop and perform under a plan for the repayment of his debts over an extended period. *In some cases, the plan will call for full repayment. In others, it may offer creditors a percentage of their claims in full settlement.* * * *

The benefit to the debtor of developing a plan of repayment under chapter 13, rather than opting for liquidation under chapter 7, is that it permits the debtor to protect his assets. In a liquidation case, the debtor must surrender his nonexempt assets for liquidation and sale by the trustee. *Under chapter 13, the debtor may retain his property by agreeing to repay his creditors.* Chapter 13 also protects a debtor's credit standing far better than a straight bankruptcy, because he is viewed by the credit industry as a better risk. In addition, it satisfies many debtors' desire to avoid the stigma attached to straight bankruptcy and to retain the pride attendant on being able to meet one's obligation. The benefit to creditors is self-evident: their losses will be significantly less than if their debtors opt for straight bankruptcy.

H.R. Rep. No.95-595, 95th Cong., 1st Sess., reprinted in 1978 U.S.C.C.A.N. 6079 (emphasis added).

Years of controversy have centered around how much the payment to unsecured creditors must be. The only guidance in the original Code was the "best-interests" test of § 1325(a)(4), which requires that unsecured creditors must receive as much in Chapter 13 as they would have received in a Chapter 7 liquidation, taking into account the fact that payment in Chapter 13 is on a deferred basis. However, in many cases, debtors, even those with substantial incomes, have no nonexempt assets, and in such cases, the best-interests test, literally read, is satisfied by a "zero payment" plan that pays off secured creditors and gives unsecured creditors nothing, even though the debtor could afford to pay more. In these cases, debtors seemed to be getting a free super discharge: they pay their secured creditors over time based on the current value of their encumbered property, and pay their unsecured creditors nothing. Judicial tolerance for zero payment plans has been low, and some courts rejected them as not being proposed in good faith under § 1325(a)(3). But judicial reaction was uneven and unpredictable.

Clearly, the best-interests test failed to assure unsecured creditors that they would receive payment under Chapter 13. Creditor discontent led in 1984 to the requirement, imposed by former § 1325(b)(1)(B), that the plan include "all of the debtor's projected disposable income to be received in the three-year period" of the plan. "Disposable income" was defined as "income which is * * * not reasonably necessary to be expended for the maintenance or support of the debtor or a dependent of the debtor." Former § 1325(b)(2). Far from resolving the "how-much" problem, this language dragged bankruptcy courts into a fact-intensive morass. Judges not only had to become prognosticators (how can income be reliably predicted three years ahead?) but, much worse, life-style arbiters (what expenses are reasonably necessary for the debtor's family?). The National Bankruptcy Review Commission viewed the test as so indeterminate that it recommended dropping it altogether.

> [I]t is all too clear that after thirteen years' experience with the disposable income requirement, courts seem no closer to sharing a collective view of what constitutes "reasonably necessary expenses" than they were at the inception. Some courts believe that private schools are necessary, while others do not. Orthodontia, piano lessons, college tuition, home repairs, dry cleaning, newspapers, tithing, utility payments, and food allocations are just a few of the expenses that are scrutinized in this context. Personal views of what is and what is not necessary for the family inescapably factor into the equation. The amount that debtors must pay to their unsecured creditors will differ from courtroom to courtroom not because of different circumstances, but because of divergent views on the expenses perceived to be reasonably necessary. Because the inquiry is so fact-specific and non-legal, published opinions have little precedential value. Any party can threaten to litigate, knowing that there is some case law to support any position. The confusion over standards increases the leverage of any party with the resources and the stamina to fight about disposable income.

NBRC Rep. at 263-265.

The "Religious Liberty and Charitable Donation Protection Act of 1998" (Donation Protection Act) introduced further complications by adding charitable contributions, up to 15% of the debtor's gross income for the year in which the contributions are made, to the amounts for maintenance and support that are considered reasonably necessary to be expended by the debtor. That Act says nothing about limiting the number of 15% gifts the debtor could make each year, nor is there a requirement that the debtor have a consistent practice of making charitable contributions, as would be true with debtors who tithe. Apparently, on the face of this provision, any debtor in Chapter 13 could make any number of annual gifts, each within the 15% ceiling, to a qualified charity at the expense of her creditors. But the first Court of Appeals case to consider the issue, *The Universal Church v. Geltzer*, 463 F.3d 218 (2d Cir. 2006), held that the aggregate annual transfers made by the debtor rather than each individual transfer determined whether the 15% safe harbor provision applies. According to the court, this holding safeguarded the right of Chapter 13 debtors to continue to tithe but avoided the possibility, described by the court as "absurd," that a debtor could contribute most of her assets by making several separate gifts, none larger than 15% of her gross income. Since the debtor in *Geltzer* tithed regularly, there was no occasion for the court to consider whether debtors must have a consistent practice of contributing to fall within the safe harbor. For an analysis of the Act, see Kenneth N. Klee, *Tithing and Bankruptcy*, 75 Am.

Bankr. L.J. 157, 186 (2001). The Donation Protection Act is also discussed in chapter 7 of the Casebook.

(ii) BAPCPA

Under the pre-BAPCPA disposable income test, the higher debtors lived the less their unsecured creditors were likely to be paid, and they had no incentive to lower their living standards because the money saved would go to their creditors. Experience showed that debtors with good legal advice had little disposable income. *NBRC Rep.* at 266. The National Bankruptcy Review Commission recommended that payments on unsecured debts be determined by guidelines based on a graduated percentage of the debtors' income. *NBRC Rep.* at 262-273. In a limited way, BAPCPA moves toward a more objective test for determining disposable income. Section § 1325(b) bifurcates debtors into those with annual incomes greater than the state median family income (§ 1325(b)(3)) and those with lesser income (§ 1325(b)(2)). For the lower income group, the much larger group in bankruptcy, the law remains much as it was: disposable income is determined by deducting "amounts reasonably necessary to be expended for the maintenance or support of the debtor or a dependent of the debtor" plus contributions to "qualified religious or charitable entities] or organization[s]" (§ 548(d)(4)) in an amount not to exceed 15% of the debtor's gross income. § 1325(b)(2)(A)(2). These debtors may deduct the amount of domestic support obligations. For the higher income group, BAPCPA standardizes the amounts necessary to be expended by adopting the IRS standards that are incorporated into § 707(b)(2)(A) and (B) for calculating the means test in Chapter 7. Now higher income debtors will have to commit all their income to Chapter 13 plans that is in excess of the IRS standards whatever the amount of their actual expenses unless they can show special circumstances that justify additional expenses. § 707(b)(2)(B). This could result in these debtors having to lower their standard of living. In 2008 Form 22C was amended to provide additional space for debtors to set out the details of special circumstances justifying additional expenses.

The two most important changes in Chapter 13 are the introduction of the 5-year commitment period and the imposition of "objective" standards for measuring income and expense based upon "current monthly income" and IRS guidelines for disposable income. Form 22C deals with disposable earnings and the commitment period in Parts I through V.

Part I. Income. Ironically, the statute projects the debtor's earnings over a 3- to 5-year period in the future based on the debtor's CMI, which, in turn, is based on an average of the debtor's monthly income during the 6-month period *before* the debtor files. Historical income is ascertainable and verifiable but may have nothing to do with future income. Indeed, bankruptcy debtors have usually suffered a drastic prebankruptcy interruption in income.

Part II. Commitment Period. In order to determine this period, the debtor's CMI is annualized by multiplying it by 12. If this amount is less than the applicable median family income, the commitment period is 3 years; if above the applicable median family income, the commitment period is 5 years. Two additional years of living under stingy IRS standards may prove a major deterrent to debtors otherwise disposed to file under Chapter 13.

Part III. Disposable Income. If the annualized CMI is more than the applicable median family income, disposable income is determined under § 1325(b)(3), which incorporates the same deductions allowed by § 707(b)(2) for application of the means test in Chapter 7. These deductions are set out in Part IV. If the annualized CMI is less than the applicable median family income, disposable income is determined by § 1325(b)(2), and the deductions are amounts reasonably necessary to be expended for the maintenance and support of the debtor or a dependent of the debtor or for a DSO.

Part IV. Deductions Allowed. Section § 1325(b)(2) incorporates the same deductions stated in § 707(b)(2) for means testing under Chapter 7 cases. DSOs, included in § 1325(b)(2)(A)(i), are priority payments. Charitable contributions, not mentioned in § 707(b)(2), are included in § 1325(b)(2)(A)(ii). Section 1325(b)(2)(A)(ii)(III) provides that the debtor's monthly expenses may include the actual expenses of administering a Chapter 13 plan, up to an amount of 10 percent of the projected plan payments.

Part V. DSO and Retirement Contributions. Since a debtor is required to count the child support payments, and the like, that she receives as income, she is allowed by § 1325(b)(2) to deduct from these payments amounts to the extent reasonably necessary to be expended for the child.

Section 541(b)(7) mandates that amounts withheld by employers as contributions to specified qualified retirement plans (e.g. § 401(k)) are not property of the employee's estate and not disposable earnings under § 1325. Under § 1322(f) amounts withheld by employers for the repayment of loans made to employees from such plans do not constitute disposable income under § 1325. In *In re Lasowski*, 384 B.R. 205 (8th Cir. BAP 2008), the court points out that under § 1322(f) a § 1325 plan cannot materially alter the terms of the loan repayment agreement, thus unsecured creditors may receive reduced payments under the plan until the loan repayment obligation to the debtor's own retirement account is paid off under its existing terms.

Before BAPCPA, debtors were ingenious in creating enough "reasonably necessary" expenses to limit the payout of disposable income to their creditors. Significant loopholes are still present under BAPCPA for the opportunistic debtor. Much turns on the amount of the debtor's CMI, a figure that can be affected by the timing of the debtor's date of filing. Deductions may be taken for life insurance payments, for telecommunication services, for the costs of private or public school education for dependent children, and for additional food and clothing expenses. Moreover, a debtor can reduce her disposable income substantially by deducting charitable donations under her Chapter 13 plan or getting divorced. It is difficult for standing trustees to monitor whether the debtor is really making charitable donations over the term of the plan.

Since those with incomes lower than the state median are not excluded from Chapter 7 by the means test, they have a choice between Chapters 7 and 13. With respect to the three-year commitment period plans and the amounts debtors must pay to fund these plans, the law remains largely unchanged. But members of the higher income group may find themselves excluded from Chapter 7 by the means test and left with only the alternatives of filing in Chapters 13 or 11 or facing their creditors under state collection law. BAPCPA has made Chapter 13 less attractive for this group by requiring them to submit to five-year plans and to devote all their income to funding the plan above the IRS levels for reasonable expenses, whatever their actual expenditures are. Use of the low IRS standards for family expenses under BAPCPA may endanger the viability of the plan by leaving the debtor with insufficient funds to meet her actual expenses and the demands of the plan over a five-year stretch. Given other barriers to completion of a Chapter 13 plan, discussed below, the harried higher income debtor may conclude that no feasible bankruptcy relief is available.

Nor, as we will see below, does much else in BAPCPA make Chapter 13 attractive to debtors. Changes in the treatment of secured creditors make it more difficult for Chapter 13 debtors to retain property subject to security interests, such as automobiles. The super-discharge is no longer very super, and in most cases is no broader than the discharge available in Chapter 7. The avowed thrust of BAPCPA is to induce debtors to pay more of their debts to earn a discharge, and Chapter 13 offers a process for debtors to pay their debts, while Chapter 7 is viewed as a method for avoiding such payment. But new Chapter 13 offers reduced benefits and increased burdens to debtors, and we are left with a paradox: debtors who might have preferred old Chapter 13 may be more likely to file in Chapter 7 under the new Act if they are eligible to do so. Although Chapter 13 never attained the popularity the drafters of the 1978 Code had hoped for, debtor payments under Chapter 13, as indicated earlier in the chapter, had risen to over $4 billion annually. Bankruptcy judges are concerned that the BAPCPA changes in Chapter 13 will undermine the very provision of the law in which debtors had been repaying significant amounts to their creditors. The leading authority on Chapter 13, Judge Keith Lundin, cautions: "The folks who brought you 'those who can pay, should pay' are pulling the stuffing out of the very part of the bankruptcy law where debtors do pay." Peter G. Gosselin, *Judges Say Overhaul Would Weaken Bankruptcy System*, L.A. Times, Mar. 29, 2005, at A1.

(iii) Does BAPCPA work?

Serious problems have emerged with the two most important changes made by BAPCPA in Chapter 13 bankruptcies: the imposition of objective standards in determining disposable income for above-median income debtors and the introduction of the five-year commitment period.

Disposable income

Section 1325(b)(1)(B) provides that if the trustee or holder of an allowed unsecured claim objects to confirmation of the plan, the court may not approve the plan unless the plan provides either for full payment of the objecting unsecured creditor's claim or that all of the debtor's "projected disposable income" is applied to make payments to unsecured creditors under the plan. Section 1325(b)(2) makes "disposable income" depend on a debtor's "current monthly income," as defined in § 101(10A), based on the debtor's income during the six-month period before filing. There is no definition of "projected disposable income" in § 1325(b)(1). Cases are sharply divided on the meaning of this term, which is central to the operation of Chapter 13 plans under BAPCPA. The dilemma facing courts is that "disposable income," based on the debtor's CMI, looks backward to the debtor's income during the six months before filing but the word "projected" looks forward to the debtor's anticipated income available to fund the plan.

The first three court of appeals decisions on the meaning of "projected disposable income" were decided within a few months of each other in 2008. The first to come down was *In re Kagenveama*, 527 F.3d 990 (9th Cir. 2008). In that case, Debtor's Schedule I listed monthly net income of $5,096, and her Schedule J listed monthly expenses of $2,572, leaving $2,523 in monthly income available to pay creditors. But as an above-median debtor, she had no "disposable income" because of her recalculated expenses under § 707(b)(2). Hence, under Form 22C, her plan left nothing for unsecured creditors. However, Debtor proposed a plan in which she would pay $1,000 per month with a commitment period of three years. This plan yielded $9,444 for unsecured creditors. The Chapter 13 Trustee objected to Debtor's plan because the plan duration was only three years rather than five. The bankruptcy court approved the plan and the Ninth Circuit affirmed. The court focused on two issues, the meaning of "projected disposable income" and the length of the "applicable commitment period" in a zero payment plan. We examine the court's views on projected disposable income first, followed by the commitment period of the plan in the following section.

The court calculated Debtor's "projected disposable income" under the formula prescribed by the statute: first, determine the amount of disposable income under the definition set out in § 1325(b)(2), which is based on a debtor's CMI, then project this amount forward for each month of the plan. This is the approach taken by Form 22C. Thus, a statute supposedly intended to make debtors with the means to do so pay their creditors in order to earn a discharge is interpreted by the Ninth Circuit court in *Kagenveama* to allow this debtor (whose own schedules show over $2500 per month in net income in excess of living expenses) to obtain a discharge without paying their unsecured creditors a cent. The court concludes, "If the changes imposed by BAPCPA arose from poor policy choices that produced undesirable results, it is up to Congress, not the courts, to amend the statute." At least, "the disposition required by the plain text of § 1325(b) is not absurd..." The court justifies its decision on the ground that the cold hand of the plain meaning rule leaves no alternative. But what is the plain meaning of § 1325(b)? As the court in *In re Kibbe* said, "Insofar as the term 'disposable income' demands a look back and the term 'projected' requires a look forward, the language is irreconcilable." 361 B.R. 302, 312 (1st Cir. BAP 2007).

In the second case, *In re Lanning*, 545 F.3d 1269 (10th Cir. 2008), the court rejected the "mechanical" approach of cases taking the *Kagenveama* view and adopted a "forward-looking" approach in which Debtor's projected disposable income is presumed to be determined by Debtor's current monthly income *subject to rebuttal by a showing of special circumstances at the time of plan confirmation.* Debtor's CMI was bloated by her receipt during the six-month period before filing of a large buyout amount from her ex-employer; hence, her monthly disposable income under the formula was $1,114. But her Income and Expenses schedules, speaking at the time of confirmation of the plan, showed that she would have monthly disposable income of only $144. Debtor contended that her repayment plan should be based on the $144 amount; the Chapter 13 trustee argued that the statute compelled the $1,114 figure to be be used, even though acknowledging that Debtor did not have the means to fund such a plan—leaving the plan unconfirmable under § 1325(a)(6) as infeasible.

The court's forward-looking view of the meaning of "projected disposable income" recognizes that the debtor's income must be used to fund the Chapter 13 plan. Hence, the debtor's actual circumstances at the time of plan confirmation must be taken into account in order to "project" how much income the debtor will actually receive during the commitment period. If the debtor's income during the six-month period before filing was unusually large, as in *Lanning*, it is unreasonable to require the debtor to have to meet a payment schedule beyond the her resources. By the same token, it would be unfair to deny payments to the unsecured creditors merely because the debtor's average income was substantially less over the six months preceding the debtor's date of filing.

The Eighth Circuit adopted the forward-looking view of "projected disposable income" in *In re Frederickson*, 545 F.3d 652 (8th Cir. 2008). The court noted that under this view bankruptcy courts will continue to have some discretion with the result that the debtor's projected disposable income "will end up more closely aligning with reality." By basing the meaning of the term merely on the statutory formula, the "outcome involves anomalous, and perhaps even absurd, results." The U.S. Trustee Program has taken the forward-looking view on the meaning of "projected disposable income" in those circuits that have the issue before their Courts of Appeals.

On December 1, 2007 the preambles of Schedules I and J were amended. Schedule I (Current Income of Individual Debtors) now states: "The average monthly income calculated on this form may differ from the current monthly income calculated on Form 22A, 22B or 22C." Schedule J (Current Expenditures of Individual Debtors) now provides similarly: "The average monthly expenses calculated on this form may differ from the deductions from income allowed on Form 22A or 22C." The fact that the amounts in the Schedules may differ from those in the Forms merely states the obvious: the amounts in the Forms are historic and those in the Schedules are prospective. Whether courts otherwise disposed to follow either *Kagenveama* or *Lanning* will be deterred by these ambiguous amendments to Schedules I and J is unclear.

PROBLEM

The court confirmed Debtor's Chapter 13 plan that proposed to pay 50% of the claims of unsecured creditors out of all her disposable income over a three-year period. Shortly after confirmation, Debtor sold real property that she owned at the time of her petition, and, after payment of all encumbrances, received $20,000 for the property. Trustee moved to modify Debtor's plan to include the proceeds of the sale as disposable income. Section 1325(b)(2) defines disposable income as meaning "income received by the debtor." Should the Trustee's motion be granted? *See In re Burgie*, 239 B.R. 406 (9th Cir. BAP 1999).

Five-year commitment period

Section 1325(b)(1)(B), states that if the trustee or a creditor objects to the plan the court may not approve the plan unless it provides that all the debtor's projected disposable income to be received in the *applicable commitment period* must be applied to make payments to unsecured creditors under the plan.

If the debtor has an above-median income, § 1325(b)(4) provides that the commitment period must be not less than five years; for other debtors the period is three years. The cases are divided on whether the applicable commitment period has a "temporal" function or merely serves as a "monetary multiplier."

Under the temporal view, if the debtor is an above-median debtor and has positive projected disposable income, the debtor's plan must call for 60 months of payments, however small the amount of the monthly payments, unless the plan calls for full payment of the claims of unsecured creditors in a shorter period. This line of cases holds that § 1325(b)(1)(B) and (4), in effect, impose the minimum length of any Chapter 13 plan that does not pay unsecured claims in full. These cases point out that "applicable commitment *period*" is *temporal*. Had Congress intended to allow debtors to cash-out and receive a discharge any time they pay the amount of disposable monthly income multiplied by 36 or 60, depending on whether the debtors are above or below median income, it would have said so. Presumably, under this view, debtors could be faced with nuisance payments of a few dollars over the life of the plan. Since debtors do not pay interest on the creditors' obligations, what interest could they have in prolonging payments when the debtor offers to cash-out the remaining balance of plan? One response is that holding the plan open for five years allows creditors to monitor the debtor's financial position over that period and to seek modification of the plan if the debtor's resources improve.

Courts taking the monetary multiplier view point out that the statute does not specify a minimum plan term. It merely states that, in order to be confirmed, a plan must apply all of a debtor's projected disposable income during the applicable commitment period. Since there is no minimum plan term in the law, the "total disposable monthly income" multiplied by 60, merely yields the *amount* that the debtor must pay its unsecured creditors during the applicable commitment period of the plan. There is no requirement in the statute that the payments must be spread over the entire 60-month period and it would make no sense to require that the plan be held open over that period if the debtor's plan calls for payment over a shorter period of the total disposable monthly income multiplied by 60. Judge Lundin, a leading authority on Chapter 13 bankruptcy, agrees with this view of the statute in his treatise, 5 *Lundin*, § 500.1.

The first two court of appeals decisions on applicable commitment period deal with cases in which the debtors had no projected disposable income under the statutory formula (CMI times 60), *Kagenveama* and *Frederickson*, both discussed above.

In *Kagenveama*, the Ninth Circuit stated that "applicable commitment period" mandates a temporal measurement. The plain meaning of the word "period" indicates a period of time. As a general rule, unless all unsecured creditor claims can be paid in full, anything less than a five-year commitment period cannot be confirmed. But in *Kagenveama* the bankruptcy court confirmed a three-year plan in which Debtor was to pay $1,000 per month, a total of $9,444, to her unsecured creditors. The Chapter 13 trustee challenged the bankruptcy court holding on the ground that since all unsecured creditors had not been paid, the five-year commitment period obtained. The Ninth Circuit affirmed on the ground that since Debtor had no "projected disposable income" to pay to her unsecured creditors, the requirement of an "applicable commitment period" had no relevance to the case. Subsection (b)(1)(B) states that "the debtor's 'projected disposable income' to be received in the 'applicable commitment period' ... will be applied to make payments under the plan." Since only "projected disposable income" has to be paid out over the "applicable commitment period," if there is no "projected disposable income," there is no "applicable commitment period" requirement. The term "applicable commitment period" does not set a minimum plan length, rather it refers only to period during which the debtor must pay "projected disposable income." Since there was no "projected disposable income" in this case, the $9,444 that Debtor agreed to pay does not have to be paid out over the five-year period. The court rejected the trustee's contention that if any unsecured claims were not paid the plan should be kept open for five years so that unsecured creditors could seek modification for any changes in the debtor's income.

In *Frederickson*, the debtor, who had no projected disposable income under the statutory formula, proposed a 48-month plan with payments of $600 per month. Under this plan unsecured creditors would receive about 61% of their claims; the bankruptcy court confirmed the plan. The Eighth Circuit court reversed. It agreed with *Kagenveama* that the temporal test applied, but disagreed on the meaning of projected disposable income. It concluded that the forward-looking view should prevail for the reasons discussed in the previous section, and that under this view the debtor had projected disposable income. Thus, the debtor's plan must have a 60-month duration in order to be confirmed. The realistic definition of projected disposable income prevents the temporal rule from producing anomalous results.

These two cases raise questions about what duration courts will approve for plans in the common situation in which the debtor actually does have no projected disposable income. In such cases would courts confirm plans filed for a period as short as 90-days or six-months if unsecured creditors received a 50% cash-out, financed from the debtor's savings or loans? Are short-term plans filed in good faith in view of the fact that when payments called for by the plan have been completed, no further modification can take place? If the debtor under the short-term plan wins the lottery a year after completion of the payments, the creditors are out of luck. One of the judges in *Kagenveama* dissented from the holding of the majority on the duration of the plan. He would hold the plan open for five years to give the creditors and trustee the opportunity to monitor the debtor's activities and to share in any windfalls.

What of cases in which the debtor's monthly disposable income is as low as $10? Must the plan be held open for five years during which the unsecured creditors would share a total of $600? Presumably, under the temporal view of the meaning of the applicable commitment period, the answer would be yes. Under the line of cases taking the monetary multiplier view, *see e.g., In re Swan*, 368 B.R. 12 (Bankr.N.D.Cal.2007), the court could approve a plan for a much shorter term upon adequate payment by the debtor.

Conclusion

The answer to the question posed at the beginning of this subsection— whether BAPCPA works with respect to its treatment of the two major changes it makes in Chapter 13 bankruptcies—must be no. In both instances the drafting is so imprecise as to breed a host of conflicting bankruptcy court decisions. Courts that have reached arbitrary or implausible results in some cases have justified their holdings as compelled by the "plain meaning rule." *See* Daniel J. Bussel, *Textualism's Failures: A Study of Overruled Bankruptcy Decisions*, 53 Vand. L. Rev. 885 (2000). Others that have reached more sensible results have concluded that the terms of the statute are so contradictory that they have no plain meaning. These courts endeavor to reach decisions in keeping with the purposes of Chapter 13. Meanwhile, debtors are using post-confirmation modification, discussed in the next section, to diminish the importance of BAPCPA's unworkable requirements for confirmation.

d. Modification of Plan

Modification issues in Chapter 13 cases continue to grow in importance. The volatile labor market, with plant closings, outsourcing of jobs, increased foreign competition, and resulting layoffs, makes maintenance of a stream of "regular income" (§ 109(e)) for a three to five-year plan highly uncertain. A further source of modification litigation has been fluctuation in residential real estate values in the first decade of the new century: unprecedented inflation in some areas followed by oversupply, defaults and foreclosures. The subprime market, combining unrealistic values with unrealistic loan-to-value and debt-to-income ratios in mortgage financing, together with seductive adjustable rate loans, has been especially hard hit. How well does Chapter 13 deal with these contemporary issues?

Section 1329(a) allows for postconfirmation modification of a plan upon request of the debtors, the unsecured creditors or the trustee, which may (1) increase or reduce the amounts of payments under the plan, (2) extend or reduce the term of the plan for such payments, and (3) alter the amount of the distribution to a creditor whose claim is provided for by the plan to the extent necessary to take account of any payment made other than under the plan. BAPCPA added a fourth ground for modification: (4) to reduce amounts paid under the plan by the amount expended by the debtor to purchase health insurance for the debtor and dependents if the cost of the plan is reasonable and necessary.

Section 1329(a) states the kinds of modifications that may be made but it doesn't say under what circumstances courts should approve a proposed modification of the kinds specified in § 1329(a). On this important threshold issue, the courts have long been divided and no reconciliation is in sight. For example, in *In re Murphy*, 474 F.3d 143 (4th Cir. 2007), the court stated that res judicata prevents modification of a confirmed plan under § 1329(a)(1) and (2) unless the party seeking modification demonstrates that the debtor has experienced a *substantial* and *unanticipated* postconfirmation change of financial condition. On the other hand, *In re Meza*, 467 F.3d 874 (5th Cir. 2006), finds no such conditions under the plain language of § 1329 and notes that an increasing number of courts are taking this view. *Collier* views the law as treating modifications at the request of the debtor very broadly; almost any modified plan that meets the requirements of Chapter 13 should be approved. But modifications at the request of the trustee or unsecured creditor should be allowed only when there has been an unanticipated substantial change in the debtor's income or expenses. *Collier on Bankruptcy* ¶ 1329.03 (15th ed. rev. 2008).

Section 1329(b) provides that the plan as modified must meet the same requirements as the original plan with respect to the contents of the plan (§ 1322(a) and (b)) and the provisions of § 1325(a), such as the value to be distributed to creditors and the good faith of the proponents. But nothing is said in the statute about whether the modified plan must meet the disposable income test of § 1325(b). The BAPCPA definition of disposable income greatly confuses this issue because the definition is based not on the debtor's actual income but on her CMI, which in turn is based on her prepetition income.

In *In re Kagenveama*, discussed in detail in the previous section, the Ninth Circuit held that even though the debtor's Schedules I and J showed that the debtor could make substantial payments to unsecured creditors over the period of her plan, her "projected disposable income" was a negative number and, under the court's "plain meaning" interpretation of § 1325(b), the creditors were entitled to no dividend. In ameliorating this result, the court suggested that the creditors might find succor in modification under § 1329.

The decision in *In re Ireland*, 366 B.R. 27 (Bankr.W.D.Ark.2007), gives the creditors in cases like *Kagenveama* hope. In that case, the debtors had suffered a substantial reduction in income since confirmation and sought modification lowering the payment to unsecured creditors from 100% to 19%. The trustee objected on the ground that the debtors were bound by the CMI as the minimum payment to unsecured creditors regardless of any change in actual income after confirmation. The court overruled the trustee's objection on the ground that § 1329 does not refer to § 1325(b) with respect to post-confirmation modifications. It quoted *Collier on Bankruptcy* ¶ 1329.03 (15th ed. rev. 2008): "It would be nonsensical to apply section 1325(b) to modifications and thereby require the use of [an] income figure that may differ greatly from the debtor's income at the time of the modification." *In re Girodes*, 350 B.R. 31 (Bankr.M.D.N.C.2006), is in accord. For modification purposes a more relevant source of income information is Schedule I, Current Income of Individual Debtors in Form 6 (Summary of Schedules).

Nor does § 1329(b)(1) refer to the provisions relating to the applicable commitment period under § 1325(b). A growing body of caselaw holds that § 1329(b) does not restrict modifications of the commitment periods set out in § 1325(b). In fact, § 1329(a)(2) specifically allows modifications that extend or reduce the time for payments. *See, e.g., In re Ewers*, 366 B.R. 139 (Bankr.D. Nev 2007), in which the debtors had above-median income at the time of confirmation of their five-year plan; soon after confirmation they retired and their income fell into the below-median level. Their were allowed to reduce the amount of their payments and to reduce the plan term to three years.

Pre-BAPCPA authorities held that the failure of § 1329 to refer to § 1325(b) meant that disposable income standards did not apply to modifications. Since the only change in § 1329 made by BAPCPA was the addition of § 1329(a)(4) referring to health insurance, the law should not have changed with respect to the inapplicability of § 1325(b). Thus, in a case in which the debtor's monthly disposable income was only $10, the debtor could, after confirmation, move to modify by paying the creditors $600 or more to end the plan. The view of the jurisdiction on whether change in circumstances was required for modification would presumably control the case. Since courts have, on the whole, been generous in allowing debtors to modify confirmed plans, modification is being used by debtors as an escape hatch from confirmed plans plans that have unworkable provisions required by the disposable earnings or five-year-duration requirements for confirmation. Once the plan is confirmed, the debtor, with the consent of the court, can adopt a modified plan—rid of the disposable income strictures or unreasonable duration—that is more workable. Through modification, Chapter 13 plans can become much more flexible.

e. Payments "Outside the Plan"

In "Commencing a Chapter 13 Case," Section 4 on p. 517, we discuss the BAPCPA provisions requiring direct payment to lessors and secured creditors in certain situations, § 1326(a)(1)(A) and (B). BAPCPA has not otherwise changed the pre-BAPCPA law on outside-the-plan payments discussed below. *See In re Lopez*, 372 B.R. 40 (9th Cir. BAP 2007).

Once a Chapter 13 plan is confirmed, the court may issue a payroll deduction order under which the debtor's employer must pay the required amount to the standing trustee for distribution to creditors entitled to payment under the plan. Or, the plan may provide for the debtor to pay the required amounts to the trustee. The advantage in having the trustee as the disbursing agent is that if the debtor were allowed to pay creditors directly without notifying the trustee, the trustee might not learn whether payments were being made unless creditors complained; the situation could become chaotic and difficult to administer.

In the case of a residential mortgage, however, the debtor is commonly allowed to make payments directly to the creditor. This is referred to as making payments "outside the plan." A justification for allowing a debtor to do this in the case of a residential mortgage is that the debtor usually owes the same payments on the mortgage after confirmation as before, and these payments will continue after the plan is completed because debtors are not discharged from long-term debts. § 1328(a)(1). The clear implication from § 1326(c) is that the court may approve a plan allowing the debtor to act as disbursing agent, and the residential mortgage case is an appropriate one for so designating the debtor. *In re Aberegg*, 961 F.2d 1307 (7th Cir. 1992).

Is the trustee entitled to claim a fee with respect to payments disbursed by the debtor in such cases? 28 U.S.C. § 586(e)(2) gives the trustee fees only on "payments received by [the trustee] under plans * * *." *Aberegg* concluded that under this provision the trustee is not entitled to a commission on funds disbursed by the debtor directly to a creditor. In deciding whether direct payments from the debtors to the creditor were appropriate, the court in *In re Slaughter*, 188 B.R. 29 (Bankr.D.N.D.1995), took into consideration the fact that if the debtors were required to pay the trustee's 10% fee, amounting to $1,700 annually, on payments made through the trustee, the plan would be infeasible for the debtors to carry out.

f. Classification of Unsecured Claims

Section 1322(b)(1) allows for classification of unsecured claims so long as all claims within each class are substantially similar (as required in § 1122(a)) and are treated the same (§ 1322(a)(3)), but the debtor's plan may not unfairly discriminate between the classes. We will find in the next chapter that creditors vote on a debtor's Chapter 11 plan by classes; hence, classification may play an important role in the debtor's strategy for gaining acceptance of the plan. In Chapter 13 debtors do not have to obtain the approval of creditors for the plan; the court confirms the plan if it meets the requirements of § 1325. Thus, the reason for a debtor to have separate classes of nonpriority unsecured claims in Chapter 13 is the desire to prefer one class over another in terms of how much the members of each class are paid. The only guidance offered by the Code to govern the degree of discrimination permitted is that it must not be unfair. There are innumerable bankruptcy court cases on the meaning of "discriminate unfairly" (§ 1322(b)(1)), and they differ widely in their interpretation of the term. Relatively few court of appeals decisions shed any light on the issue. The problem is treated in 2 *Lundin*, § 149.1.

Among the first cases on unfair discrimination in classification were those in which the debtor classified a debt separately on which there was a cosigner and proposed to pay the holder of the claim a greater percentage than that allocated to holders of other unsecured claims. In *Barnes v. Whelan*, 689 F.2d 193 (D.C.Cir. 1982), the debtor's plan called for 100% payment on a cosigned debt and only 1% on the other unsecured claims. The motive of debtors in these cosigner cases was to safeguard the cosigner, usually a family member or friend, from having to pay the debt, an obligation that the debtor would feel morally obligated to pay later. *Barnes* took the position that although there was a rational basis for classifying co-signed debts separately, still a 99% differential was unfair. Other cases disagreed, and Congress undertook to clarify the issue by the addition of the "however" clause to § 1322(b)(1).

The question left open by the amendment is how "differently" can Chapter 13 plans treat cosigned debts. May it pay them in full even though other classes of claims receive nothing, or may courts continue to examine the classification of cosigned claims on fairness grounds? In *In re Ramirez*, 204 F.3d 595 (5th Cir. 2000), the court denied confirmation of a plan that paid the cosigner debt in full plus 12% interest, prior to any payments to other unsecured claims. The court found no justification for "such a high and preferential interest rate." 204 F.3d at 596. Under § 502(b)(2), unsecured debts do not accrue interest after filing. The difficulty in determining when unfair discrimination is present is addressed in the following case.

In re Crawford
United States Court of Appeals, Seventh Circuit, 2003.
324 F.3d 539.

■ POSNER, Circuit Judge.

Wayne Crawford appeals from the district court's affirmance of the bankruptcy court's refusal to confirm his Chapter 13 plan. Chapter 13 is a counterpart to Chapter 11 (reorganization) but designed for individuals of modest means. It enables an individual, as an alternative to the liquidation of his assets, to submit for approval by the bankruptcy court a plan for paying his creditors as much as possible over a period of years, upon completion of which he is given a discharge of his remaining dischargeable debts. Crawford's appeal requires us to consider the circumstances in which and the degree to which a Chapter 13 debtor may shift the burden of a nondischargeable debt from his shoulders to those of his unsecured creditors by invocation of § 1322(b)(1), which provides that a Chapter 13 plan may "designate a class or class of unsecured claims . . . but may not discriminate unfairly against any class so designated." Classification is not unique to Chapter 13; it is available under other chapters of the Bankruptcy Code as well. *See* §§ 901(a), 1122(a), 1222(b)(1).

Crawford's nonpriority unsecured debts consist of some $19,000 owed the IRS; $18,000 owed the county as a result of Crawford's having been delinquent for a period in his child support payments (he is now current) and the county's having paid welfare to the mother and taken in exchange an assignment of her entitlement to child support; and $500 owed to a pair of trade creditors. The debt that Crawford owes the county is nondischargeable. § 523(a)(5)(A).

The plan proposed to divide Crawford's debts into two classes, one consisting of the debt to the county and the other of the other debts. The county debt would be paid first and only after it was paid in full would he begin to pay the debts of the second class. Originally the plan envisaged that over the course of its three years the county debt would be paid in full with enough left over to pay the other unsecured creditors between 3 and 6 percent of what they were owed. But this was contingent on Crawford's prevailing in a dispute he had with the IRS. He did not prevail and as a result the plan had to be amended. Under the amended plan, the county debt will not be paid in full but two-thirds of it will be paid, while the other unsecured creditors will get nothing at all, whereas without the preferred treatment of the county debt but with the same aggregate level of periodic payment as under the amended plan each unsecured creditor would receive roughly 32 cents on the dollar.

Section 1322(b) of the Bankruptcy Code, while forbidding as we have said classifications that discriminate unfairly against creditors, does not explain what "unfairly" means in this context. The courts have striven to formulate a more precise standard for determining the legitimacy of classifications proposed by Chapter 13 debtors, but without success.

A number of cases use a four-factor test: "1) whether the discrimination has a reasonable basis; 2) whether the debtor can carry out a plan without the discrimination; 3) whether the discrimination is proposed in good faith; and 4) whether the degree of discrimination is directly related to the basis or rationale for the discrimination." *In re Leser,* 939 F.2d 669, 672 (8th Cir. 1991) * * *. With respect, this test is empty except for point 2, which does identify an important factor bearing on the reasonableness of a classification, as we shall illustrate shortly.

Another test one finds in some cases is whether the debtor has a "legitimate" basis for the classification. *In re Brown,* 152 B.R. 232, 237-40

(Bankr.N.D.Ill.), reversed under the name *McCullough v. Brown,* 162 B.R. 506 (N.D. Ill. 1993) * * *. This, if it means anything, leans too far in favor of the debtor (as Judge Shadur explained in his opinion reversing the bankruptcy judge's decision in the *Brown* case), as it gives no consideration to the interest of creditors. The first test, the four-factor one, also fails to mention the creditors' interests, at least explicitly.

A third test insists that the classification presumptively give the disfavored creditors at least 80 percent of what they would get without the classification, *In re Sullivan,* 195 B.R. 649, 656 (Bankr.W.D.Tex.1996), and a fourth test adds a similar consideration as a fifth factor to the four-factor *Leser* test. * * * The third test is arbitrary, and the fourth test makes the first collapse of its own weight.

We haven't been able to think of a good test ourselves. We conclude, at least provisionally, that this is one of those areas of the law in which it is not possible to do better than to instruct the first-line decision maker, the bankruptcy judge, to seek a result that is reasonable in light of the purposes of the relevant law, which in this case is Chapter 13 of the Bankruptcy Code; and to uphold his determination unless it is unreasonable (an abuse of discretion). This approach has support in *In re Bentley,* 266 B.R. 229, 239-40 (1st Cir. BAP 2001), and 8 *Collier on Bankruptcy* ¶ 1322.05 (15th ed.2002), as well as in the statutory language of "unfair" discrimination against creditors. It is true that the use of "fair" in a statute or a legal doctrine need not preclude judicial development of a particularized standard; the "fair use" doctrine of copyright law and the "duty of fair representation" in labor law have considerable structure, and other examples could be given. But success has not attended efforts to give comparable structure to the classification provision of Chapter 13.

Mention of the statute's language should at least serve to remind bankruptcy judges that Chapter 13 is designed for the protection of creditors as well as debtors. * * * It is true that only the debtor can invoke Chapter 13. But he may not use it to deny consideration of the legitimate interest of creditors in repayment. * * * This point implies, however, that if without classification the debtor is unlikely to be able to fulfill a Chapter 13 plan and the result will be to make his creditors as a whole worse off than they would be with classification, then classification will be a win-win outcome. Suppose the debtor is a truck driver and one of his creditors is the state driver's license bureau which unless paid in full will yank his license, with the consequence that he won't have earnings out of which to make the payments called for in his plan. Or suppose the creditor is a supplier of the tools of the debtor's trade, and unless paid in full will cut him off and thereby prevent him from plying his trade, again with the result of depriving him of the earnings he needs to fund his plan. The creditor might be the supplier of the bottled gas that the debtor uses to heat his home, and if not paid in full will refuse to sell him more gas. (We use this example rather than that of natural gas or electricity because a public utility is not permitted to refuse to restore service because of nonpayment of fees incurred before the filing of a bankruptcy petition, § 366(a) (2003) * * *.) All these are substantial cases for a classification that will permit one creditor or class of creditors to be paid disproportionately to the rest because the creditors as a whole will be better off and so will the debtor. * * *

At the other extreme is a nondischargeable debt consisting of a fine imposed, or restitution ordered, in respect of a criminal fraud that the Chapter 13 debtor committed, together with other unsecured debts, and he proposes a classification under which the nondischargeable debt will be paid in full and the other creditors will receive nothing at all. Approval of such a plan would be unreasonable. * * * The effect of the plan if approved in such a case would be to make the debtor's other unsecured creditors pay his fine or restitution!

Crawford's rejected plan lies in between our examples, but it is closer to the second and close enough to require us to affirm its rejection. The nonpayment of child support is a serious matter and in fact a nationwide problem, which is why Congress has determined that child-support debts, of which the debt owed the county is a version, are nondischargeable. The retributive and deterrent interests are weaker than in the case of a deliberate criminal act, since nonpayment can be involuntary as well as voluntary; but no reason has been shown for allowing Crawford to shift two-thirds of this debt to his other unsecured creditors. Had he proposed to carve-down his nondischargeable debt to the principal owed on it (roughly $12,000), and had he shown that without such a carve-down he would be staggering under such a crushing load of undischarged debt as to make it inevitable or nearly so that he would soon be back in bankruptcy court, this time under Chapter 7, the bankruptcy court might deem such a plan reasonable and we presumably would affirm—especially if the unsecured creditors would do worse in Chapter 7 than they would do under Crawford's revised Chapter 13 plan. It is true that he has a previous Chapter 7 discharge and so must wait six years from the filing of his previous Chapter 7 petition before seeking another such discharge. 11 U.S.C. § 727(a). But although we don't know the exact date of his previous filing, we do know that he received his discharge in September 1997 and this means that he'll be eligible to file another Chapter 7 petition no later than September of this year—for all we know, he can do so right now.

We do not hold that child-support debts, or, as in this case, a debt arising from the assignment of the right to child support, cannot be classified. Nor do we hold that Crawford cannot formulate an acceptable plan that would involve an element of classification. We hold only that the bankruptcy court did not abuse its discretion in rejecting, as an unfair discrimination against his other creditors, the plan he proposed, which would if approved have shifted two-thirds of his nondischargeable debt to his other creditors, leaving them with nothing.

AFFIRMED.

NOTE

While Judge Posner forswears setting forth comprehensive standards for determining unfair discrimination, he does offer some baseline principles. How would you state those principles?

E. DISCHARGE

1. COMPLETE PAYMENT DISCHARGE

Although we discuss discharge issues throughout this chapter, we bring the discharge material together here in summary form. Under the 1978 Code, the super-discharge offered by § 1328(a) was viewed as an important incentive for debtors to choose Chapter 13. Under the original version, a debtor on completion of her plan was discharged from all debts provided for by the plan except obligations for alimony, maintenance or support of spouses and children, and those long term debts that cannot practicably be dealt by a three-year plan because the term of the obligation exceeds that of the plan. § 1322(b)(5). We discussed the nondischargeability of domestic support obligations in chapter 4 (Discharge). Section 1322(b)(5), discussed *infra* at p. 573, is unique to Chapter 13. It precludes discharge of debts that do not mature within the term of the plan. Obviously, a debtor cannot be expected to pay off a 25-year mortgage in a three-to-five-year Chapter 13 plan if the debtor files in the third year of the mortgage. Section 1322(a)(5) allows the debtor to propose the cure of arrearages and the maintenance of regular payments throughout the period of the plan; but the debtor remains liable on the mortgage obligation after the plan ends.

Hence, at its inception in 1978, Chapter 13 was an avenue for relief from a number of kinds of debts that were nondischargeable in Chapter 7 under § 523, such as claims arising from student loans, fraud, embezzlement, larceny, and willful and malicious injury, including, presumably, even intentional torts. In providing for the super-discharge, Congress offered debtors burdened by debts not dischargeable in Chapter 7 a fresh start in Chapter 13 so long as they were willing to make payments on their debts over the period of the plan.

Over the years, however, Congress has severely cut back on the expansive nature of the Chapter 13 discharge, and, culminating with BAPCPA, the super-discharge is no longer so super. Nondischargeable debts added to § 1328(a) include those for fraud, fiduciary defalcation, embezzlement, larceny, domestic support obligations, educational loans, drunk driving liability, criminal fines, and, under BAPCPA, obligations for liability in civil actions "as a result of willful or malicious injury by the debtor that caused personal injury to an individual or the death of an individual." § 1328(a)(4).

The latter provision was doubtless a reaction to cases like *In re LeMaire*, 898 F.2d 1346 (8th Cir. *en banc* 1990), in which the debtor fired nine rifle shots at another man, hitting him five times. The debtor admitted his intent to kill and served 27 months in prison. The victim obtained a civil judgment against the debtor, which created a debt that was nondischargeable in Chapter 7 under § 523 as arising from "willful and malicious injury." Since at that time § 1328(a) made no reference to willful and malicious injuries, the debtor filed in Chapter 13 and the bankruptcy court confirmed his plan. The Eighth Circuit, struggling to find a basis for denying discharge, held in an *en banc* 6-3 decision that the debtor's plan was not filed in good faith, even though it called for payment of 42% of his creditors' claims.

Plans that provide for the discharge of potentially non-dischargeable claims if confirmed may bind creditors absent timely objection and appeal. In *Espinosa v. United Student Aid Funds*, 545 F.3d 1193 (9th Cir. 2008), the court found that an otherwise nondischargeable student loan claim was discharged under the terms of an unobjected to Chapter 13. For a critique of this decision see Alane A. Becket, *Discharge by Declaration: Student Lender Dilemma*, 28 Am. Bankr. Inst. J. 24 (April 2009) (even creditors with knowledge of the case should have the right to assume that statutory reasonable notice will be given them before their claims are barred).

A § 1328(a) discharge applies to all debts provided for the plan or disallowed. Although the plan may call for unsecured claims to receive only nominal payment or no payment at all, the claims are treated as provided for by the plan and are discharged. Under most circumstances, post-confirmation debts cannot be paid under the plan and are not discharged upon completion of the plan. If, during the term of the plan, the debtor needs additional credit, two options may be open: First, modification of the plan under § 1329 may be available to the debtor. Under the modified plan, the new creditor may receive payment, and the debtor may be discharged of all debts included in the modified plan. Second, in the case of a consumer debt "for property or services necessary for the debtor's performance under the plan," § 1305 allows the creditor to share in the payments under the plan if the trustee approves the transaction in advance and the creditor manifests its consent to coming under the plan by filing a proof of claim. If prior approval by the trustee "was practicable and was not obtained," the post-confirmation debt is not discharged § 1328(d). The creditor's incentive to come under the plan is to receive payments immediately; the downside is that it will usually receive only partial payment and have the remainder of its claim discharged. If the creditor declines to file a claim, it cannot share under the plan and its claim will not be discharged.

BAPCPA erects several barriers to discharge. Under § 1328(a), the court cannot grant a discharge to a debtor unless the debtor certifies that all domestic support obligations due before the certification have been paid. Nor can a discharge be granted unless the debtor has completed an instructional course in personal financial management. § 1328(g). As discussed earlier in this chapter, limits are placed on successive discharges by § 1328(f). See Section F.3, *supra*, on Repeated Discharges and Filings. For analysis of discharge under BAPCPA, see 5 *Lundin*, § 542 *et seq.*

2. HARDSHIP DISCHARGE

Even before BAPCPA, about two-thirds of all confirmed Chapter 13 plans failed before the debtor completed payments; some debtors converted to Chapter 7, but others received no bankruptcy relief at all. A minor amelioration of this lamentable situation may be found in the "hardship" discharge offered by § 1328(b) to debtors whose "failure to complete such payments is due to circumstances for which the debtor should not justly be held accountable," but only if modification of the plan is not practicable. A third requirement, usually posing no difficulties, is that the debtor has satisfied the "best interests" test. The usual circumstances under which debtors are not responsible for failure to complete a plan are illness or loss of employment, but these are also the circumstances under which courts allow debtors to modify plans. The most obvious case in which modification is not practicable is that in which the debtor's misfortune has left inadequate income to complete a modified plan. In such a case, under § 1325(a)(6), the modified plan would not be feasible and thus not confirmable and, presumably, not practicable under § 1328(b).

Judge Lundin notes that courts have made hardship discharges difficult to obtain by insisting on proof of more permanent types of hardships than temporary job loss or illness. Catastrophe seems to be what they are looking for: permanent disability qualifies. 4 *Lundin*, § 352.1. The common case in which the debtor loses her job or falls ill within the early months of a Chapter 13 plan is not a likely candidate for a hardship discharge. And, even if a debtor scales the high wall that the courts have erected to qualify for a hardship discharge, she receives no better discharge, in terms of nondischargeable debts, than she would have received had she filed in Chapter 7 and not paid her creditors a cent. Section 1328(c)(1) excepts from a hardship discharge all the nondischargeable debts provided in § 523(a).

F. REAFFIRMATION OF DISCHARGED DEBTS

1. INTRODUCTION

Although the primary reason most individuals file bankruptcy is to discharge debts, creditors frequently induce debtors to "reaffirm" (agree to repay) otherwise dischargeable debts. Contract law enforces the agreement to pay the discharged debt. Restatement (Second) of Contracts § 83 (1981). "The rule of law is well-nigh universal that such a promise made has an obligating and validating consideration in the moral obligation of the debtor to pay. The debt is not paid by the discharge in bankruptcy. It is due in conscience, although discharged in law, and this moral obligation, uniting with the subsequent promise to pay, creates a right of action." *Herrington v. Davitt*, 115 N.E. 476, 477 (N.Y.1917).

Nothing in bankruptcy policy disfavors voluntary repayment by the debtor out of debtor's postpetition earnings, and § 524(f) allows voluntary repayment. It is a different matter, however, for the debtor to become obligated to repay. Since reaffirmation negates discharge, there is a prima facie conflict between reaffirmation and the bankruptcy policy of giving a fresh start to the debtor. The consequences of reaffirming a discharged debt are often more serious than incurring the original debt because the reaffirmed obligation cannot be discharged in a later Chapter 7 case for another eight years. § 727(a)(8).

In some cases reaffirmation is clearly against the debtor's self interest, but in others there may be a compelling reason to reaffirm. The compulsion can take various forms. The debtor may wish to reaffirm in order to protect the guarantor of the debtor's obligation who is a relative or close friend, or stay in the good graces of a creditor on whom the debtor is dependent. For example, the creditor may be the debtor's employer or a supplier of vital services. But the most common reason for reaffirming is to protect property such as the debtor's home, household goods or automobile that is collateral for the debt and that the secured creditor may seize absent reaffirmation. Discharge frees the debtor of personal liability on a secured debt, but it does not affect the secured creditor's right to collateral that secures the debt. Debtors often reaffirm to prevent seizure of household goods subject to indefeasible liens. *See* Marianne B. Culhane & Michaela M. White, *Debt After Discharge: An Empirical Study of Reaffirmation*, 73 Am. Bankr. L.J. 709, 713 (1999) (hereafter Culhane & White).

Section 522(f), which we have already examined, lessens the need for reaffirmation by avoiding nonpurchase-money security interests in the household goods cases. Purchase-money lien cases in household goods, as well as other secured transactions in consumer goods such as those involving automobiles, are covered by § 722, which allows the debtor to redeem the collateral by paying the value of the secured claim, *i.e.*, the value of the collateral. Since in many cases the amount of the discharged debt is substantially more than the value of the collateral, redemption may be a less onerous alternative to reaffirmation as a means of saving the collateral. But redemption under § 722 requires a lump-sum cash payment by the debtor. The creditor is not required to accept payment in installments. BAPCPA erased any doubt about this issue by adding at the end of § 722: "in full at the time of redemption."

2. BAPCPA

At the time Congress first addressed the subject in the eight-year long legislative process that eventually led to BAPCPA in 2005, reaffirmation was a hot potato. In the 1990s the National Bankruptcy Review Commission devoted a great deal of time and effort to its treatment of reaffirmation agreements. *NBRC Rep.* at 145 *et seq.* It found scandalous conditions existing. Some of the most reputable creditors in the country (*e.g.* Sears, GE Capital, Federated Department Stores, and AT&T) conceded in the mid-1990s that they had not been in compliance with the law in a significant percentage of their reaffirmation agreements. *NBRC Rep.* at 163-164. The most common violation was the failure of creditors to file agreements with the bankruptcy courts as required by § 524(c)(3). Research cited by the Commission suggests that as many as half of all reaffirmation agreements were unenforceable because they did not meet even this threshold test of validity. *NBRC Rep.* at 162. Debtors continued to pay under these agreements, unaware of their invalidity. Moreover, a significant percentage of reaffirmations were for totally unsecured debt in which debtors reaffirmed their debts but retained no property in exchange. *NBRC Rep.* at 153. It is questionable whether many of these reaffirmations were in the best interests of debtors.

Consumer representatives demanded that reaffirmations be banned; creditors strongly disagreed. In the face of a series of media exposes of creditor abuse, Congress apparently thought that it had to take some action to protect gullible consumers from giving away their bankruptcy discharges under pressure by creditors, but their response was modest.

The principal changes made by BAPCPA toward reducing abuses in reaffirmation cases are that:

(1) Pursuant to § 524(k), the debtor must be given a great deal of disclosure, including detailed Truth-in-Lending type disclosures concerning the reaffirmation transaction the debtor is entering into and information about how to enter into a reaffirmation agreement, the enforceability of the agreement, the consequences of reaffirmation, and the

debtor's right to rescind. This information should allow the debtor, her attorney and the court to decide whether the debtor can afford the reaffirmation.

(2) The bankruptcy court must intervene to invalidate reaffirmations that constitute undue hardship on the debtor, even in cases in which the debtor is represented by counsel.

Pursuant to § 524(k)(6)(A), the debtor must submit a "Statement in Support of Reaffirmation Agreement," which expresses the debtor's belief that the agreement will not impose an undue hardship and confirms the reasonableness of this belief by showing that the amount of income the debtor has left over after payment of expenses is adequate to meet the required payments on the reaffirmed debt. Section 524(m)(1) provides that for 60 days after a reaffirmation agreement is filed with the court there is a presumption that the reaffirmation agreement is an undue hardship on the debtor if the debtor's statement in support of reaffirmation shows that the debtor's income available to fund the reaffirmation agreement is less than the scheduled payments on the reaffirmed debt. "This presumption *shall* be reviewed by the court." § 524(m)(1) (emphasis added). The presumption may be rebutted in writing by the debtor if the statement identifies additional sources of funds to make the agreed payments. If the presumption is not rebutted to the satisfaction of the court, it may disapprove the agreement after notice and hearing.

(3) The U.S. Attorney and the FBI are brought in to address abusive reaffirmations. 18 U.S.C. § 158.

(4) Congress mandated a General Accounting Office study of the overall treatment of consumers in the reaffirmation process, with a report to Congress within one and one-half years after enactment making recommendations addressing any abusive or coercive tactics found.

A cynical view of BAPCPA's reaffirmation provisions might be that Congress has marshaled all the "usual suspects" of consumer protection: more disclosure, a GAO study, enforcement duties imposed on federal agencies that have better things to do, and more participation by the same judges that flatly ignored previous attempts to get them involved in reaffirmation matters. However, the BAPCPA reform provisions are similar to those proposed by Culhane & White who concluded on the basis of an empirical study made in the mid-1990s (i) that debtors and their counsel need more information to allow them to determine whether the debtors would have enough income to make the reaffirmation affordable and (ii) that the pre-BAPCPA practice of relying on debtor's counsel to determine whether the reaffirmation was fair and feasible doesn't work: the courts must be brought back into the process. Short of banning reaffirmations, perhaps this is all that a law can do.

Whether these reforms will be effective is yet to be seen. Modern consumer financers could probably get along without reaffirmations. In secured transactions, debtors who need the collateral can usually hold onto it by making voluntary payments: debtors have incentive to continue payments in order to keep the property; creditors have incentive to avoid being stuck with the repossessed goods. Informal arrangements of this sort are common.

G. Secured Claims in Personal Property

1. In Chapter 7

The treatment of secured claims in Chapter 13 is best understood by viewing it first in the context of the Chapter 7 alternative. Take as an example the most common, and usually the most valuable, piece of personal property owned by consumer debtors: a car. Suppose Debtor owns a car, subject to a perfected purchase money security interest held by Seller that secures an unpaid loan balance of $18,000. Assume the value of this hard-driven vehicle is now only $15,000. Debtor's financial condition is such that bankruptcy relief is imperative, but she wishes to retain the car, which she needs to drive to work because of the absence of public transportation. Since she has no equity in the car, a Chapter 7 trustee would likely abandon the vehicle to her (§ 554(a)), subject to Seller's security interest. Although she is behind on her large credit card debts, she has never missed a car payment and would like to work out a deal with Seller under which she could retain possession of the car after filing. What do Chapters 7 and 13 offer her?

If she files in Chapter 7, her alternatives are not inviting: she can either redeem the car pursuant to § 722 or reaffirm her obligation to Seller under § 524(c). In order to redeem she would have to pay Seller the amount of its allowed secured claim, which under § 506(a)(1) is $15,000, the value of the car. On its face, this is not a bad deal: she pays $15,000, gets to keep her car, and the $3,000 deficiency is discharged as an unsecured claim. But § 722 requires that the $15,000 must be paid in cash at the time of the redemption, and she doesn't have the money. Reaffirmation seems to be unappealing as well, for the Seller may insist that she be allowed to keep her car only by, in effect, waiving her discharge and assuming liability for the full $18,000 owed under the original obligation, but this may be the only way in which Debtor can retain possession of an indispensable car by making monthly payments. If she later faltered on her car payments, Seller could repossess and get a judgment against her for the deficiency remaining after foreclosure sale. Debtor could not obtain discharge of this judgment in a subsequent Chapter 7 for another eight years. § 727(a)(8).

Before BAPCPA, some courts allowed debtors to retain possession of their automobiles, without the consent of their secured creditors, without either redeeming or reaffirming merely by keeping their payments current after filing. This practice is referred to as "ride-through." *See, e.g.*, *In re Boodrow*, 126 F.3d 43 (2d Cir. 1997). BAPCPA was probably intended to end that practice. It provides that the automatic stay is terminated and the car is no longer property of the estate, unless she, within 45 days after the first meeting of creditors, both files a statement of intention indicating that Debtor either surrenders the property or, if retaining it, will either redeem or reaffirm, and follows the statement with timely action consistent with it. §§ 362(h)(1), 521(a)(6). However, terminating the stay merely allows Seller to proceed under nonbankruptcy law to enforce its security interest. Debtor may contend that Seller cannot repossess the car because she is not in default under the security agreement. Seller will point out to Debtor the clause in the security agreement that declares Debtor to be in default if she files in bankruptcy. Before BAPCPA some courts refused to enforce default-on-filing clauses, also known as bankruptcy or ipso facto clauses, even though no specific provision of the Code invalidated them in repossession cases. Under BAPCPA, § 521(d) specifically validates use of such clauses in cases in which a debtor fails to redeem or reaffirm within the statutory period. *See In re Dumont*, 383 B.R. 481 (9th Cir. BAP 2008) (collecting the authorities).

But a car is a necessity in many cases for a debtor seeking bankruptcy relief, and case law is emerging allowing debtors a limited right of ride-through. *See, e.g.*, *Costal Federal Credit Union v. Hardiman*, 398 B.R. 161 (E.D.N.C. 2008), which invokes a bewildering mismatch of statutes under BAPCPA to discover that the "plain meaning" of the several provisions relating to ride-through really is to revive the pre-BAPCPA law on the issue. Thus, it appears possible that there will be the same conflict in jurisdictions on ride-through that we had before BAPCPA. See, generally, Christopher M. Hogan, Note, *Will Ride-Through Ride Again?*, 108 Colum. L. Rev. 882 (2008). Whatever the law of the jurisdiction, in most cases debtors are likely to be allowed to continue to drive their cars as long as they are current on their payments; one more used car in a dealer's lot is hardly to be desired.

PROBLEM

Assume that Debtor in the case described above files in Chapter 7 and fails to redeem the car or reaffirm the car loan within the statutory period. In negotiations with Seller, she informally indicates that she will continue to make the regular payments under the contract if Seller allows her to retain possession of the collateral. She tells Seller that it has nothing to lose: if she makes all her payments, Seller wins, and if she later defaults, Seller can repossess the automobile. If Debtor receives a discharge in Chapter 7, what does Seller have to lose by allowing her to keep the car?

2. IN CHAPTER 13

a. The "Hanging Paragraph"

Under the fact situation stated at the beginning of the section (unpaid obligation of $18,000; present value of car $15,000), the 1978 version of Chapter 13 offered Debtor a favorable option. Her plan could, without Seller's consent, strip down Seller's lien to the amount of the allowed secured claim, which under § 506(a) is $15,000, and permit Debtor to pay off this amount in installments with interest. This "cramdown" was authorized by former § 1325(a)(5)(B)(ii), which stated that a plan modifying the rights of secured creditors could be confirmed if it provided that the secured party retains the lien and the plan provides for deferred payments over the life of the plan with a present value equal to the secured claim. The $3,000 unsecured deficiency claim could be classified with other unsecured claims and paid off pro rata over the life of the plan, usually at pennies on the dollar. One of the principal incentives for debtors to opt for Chapter 13 was to lien-strip and retain possession of automobiles and other items of personal property while shifting the costs of prepetition depreciation to the secured lender. It allowed debtors to do in Chapter 13 what they could not in Chapter 7: retain their property by paying in installments the present value of the property over the life of the plan.

Among the strongest supporters of BAPCPA were automobile finance companies that sponsored § 306 of the enacting statute, entitled "Giving Secured Creditors Fair Treatment in Chapter 13." This provision amended § 1325(a) to limit lien-stripping with respect to purchase money security interests in certain motor vehicles, as well as in other specified collateral. This was done by avoiding bifurcation under § 506(a), in which an undersecured claim is divided into a secured claim for the value of the collateral and an unsecured claim for the remainder of the debt. The following language was added in an unnumbered paragraph at the end of § 1325(a), after unrelated paragraph (9):

> For the purposes of paragraph (5), section 506 shall not apply to a claim described in that paragraph if the creditor has a purchase money security interest securing the debt that is the subject of the claim, the debt was incurred within the 910-day period preceding the filing of the petition, and the collateral for that debt consists of a motor vehicle * * * acquired for the personal use of the debtor, or if collateral for that debt

consists of any other thing of value, if the debt was incurred during the 1-year period preceding that filing.

After nearly three years of experience with BAPCPA, it is fair to conclude that in the poorly drafted grab bag of amendments that make up BAPCPA, no provision has engendered more consternation and litigation than has this one. Current judicial usage is to refer to this provision as the "hanging paragraph." Among the disputes about the interpretation of the hanging paragraph, the most important fall under four headings: Cramdown, Surrender, Interest and Refinancing Balances Due on Trade-in Vehicles.

b. Cramdown

Under the hanging paragraph, a "910" debt arises when a creditor makes a purchase money loan for a vehicle intended for the debtor's personal use within 910 days of the debtor's filing of a petition in bankruptcy, and the debt is secured by the purchased collateral. Reference to "910" loans, debts, debtors, creditors, claims, and collateral all refer to this transaction. After some early misinterpretations of the effect of the hanging paragraph, it is now generally accepted that a debtor can no longer bifurcate a 910 debt under a Chapter 13 cramdown plan; instead, the debtor must pay over the period of the plan the entire amount of the creditor's claim in order to retain the collateral. *See, e.g. In re Dean,* 537 F.3d 1315 (11th Cir. 2008). No longer can a 910 debtor retain a vehicle by paying the stripped-down value of the vehicle in installments.

Under the hypothetical facts set out above, if Debtor wishes to retain her car by making installment payments to Seller under her Chapter 13 cramdown plan, she must pay $18,000, with interest, over the life of the plan rather than $15,000, the value of the secured claim under § 506(a)(1). Paying off auto loans at the depreciated value of the vehicles allowed distressed debtors a reduction in their car payments and was a major attraction for debtors filing in Chapter 13.

"Personal use" is not defined and case law on the issue is scant. *Toyota Motor Credit Corp. v. John,* 2007 WL 2702193 (W.D.La.2007), a cramdown case, held that a car used merely to commute to work, even if the commute is lengthy, or run errands, is for personal use. If the car is used for the individual's job duties, however, the use is for a business purpose.

The language in the hanging paragraph that does not relate to motor vehicles is obscure. It abrogates lien-stripping with respect to purchase money security interests in "any other thing of value" if the debt secured was incurred within one year of filing. What Congress had in mind for this provision is unknown. The death of lien-stripping in automobile financing under the provision quoted above, which allocates more of a debtor's income to secured auto financiers and less to unsecured creditors, is a blow to credit card issuers, who were among the prime movers of BAPCPA. But, in recent years, credit card issuers have begun to require that holders grant security interests in the goods purchased with the card. The hanging paragraph gives retailers taking security interests in goods bought with credit cards an advantage over other unsecured creditors with respect to goods still unpaid for at the time of bankruptcy that had been purchased within one year of the bankruptcy. However, there are difficult operational problems in calculating the purchase money status of goods purchased under the open-end revolving charge accounts, and it may be that the amendment will be of little use to credit card issuers.

Section 1325(a)(5)(B)(i), requires that the Chapter 13 plan provide that the secured party retain a lien on the collateral until payment of the full amount of the underlying debt or until discharge of the debtor under § 1328, whichever is earlier. If the case is dismissed or converted before the plan is completed, Seller retains a lien in the full amount of the original debt. Assume that the original balance that Debtor owed Seller to finance the car was $18,000, but that at the time Debtor's case was dismissed Debtor had paid enough to reduce the balance owed to $15,000, and owing to further depreciation, the value of the car at that time was only $14,000. The creditor's lien on the car is for the amount of the full balance owed, $15,000. Thus, Debtor has paid $3,000 on a car now worth only $14,000, but the car is still subject to a lien for the full $15,000 amount of the unpaid balance.

c. Surrender

Section 1325(a)(5) offers the debtor two alternatives for dealing with nonconsenting holders of secured claims: retain the collateral (cramdown) under § 1325(a)(5)(B) or surrender the collateral to the creditor under § 1325(a)(5)(C). The majority of lower court took the view that since the hanging paragraph makes the amount of the 910 claim the full amount of the debtor's obligation, the debtor's surrender of the car must be considered full payment of that obligation. The creditor is left with no right to a deficiency judgment when it resells the car, even if it sells for much less than the balance of the obligation. *In re Ezell*, 338 B.R. 330 (Bankr.E.D.Tenn.2006), a much cited opinion, endorsed this view. The court found that the hanging paragraph applied equally to § 1325(a)(5)(B) and (C); therefore a creditor whose claim falls within the scope of paragraph (a)(5) is fully secured under (C) as well as (B), regardless of the amount the creditor might realize from liquidation of its collateral after the debtor's surrender. Since § 506(a) does not apply in such a case, there can be no deficiency balance and surrender satisfies the allowed secured claim in full.

Before BAPCPA, a Chapter 13 debtor had little incentive to surrender a car to the secured creditor; the creditor would sell the car and hold the debtor for the deficiency between the amount realized on resale and the unpaid obligation. After BAPCPA, under the *Ezell* view, surrender promised to be much more attractive to debtors; the debtor loses the use of the car but escapes any liability for the deficiency. This is a better deal for the debtor than cramdown, which would require the debtor in the earlier hypothetical to make installment payments totaling $18,000, plus interest, for a car worth $15,000 in order to retain the car. Rational debtors (at least those with other transportation options) will not make this choice. If *Ezell* were followed, debtors, armed with the right to surrender the car in full satisfaction, would have had bargaining power to force creditors into more advantageous cramdown deals. If the creditor would not deal, the debtor could buy a comparable car for $15,000. But the Courts of Appeal for the Fourth, Sixth, Seventh, Eighth, and Tenth circuits, invoking the *Butner* principle, have rejected *Ezell*. No court of appeal has endorsed it. The seminal opinion on the issue follows.

In re Wright
United States Court of Appeals, Seventh Circuit, 2007.
492 F.3d 829.

■ EASTERBROOK, chief judge.

Bankruptcy judges across the nation have divided over the effect of the unnumbered hanging paragraph that the Bankruptcy Abuse Prevention and Consumer Protection Act of 2005 added to § 1325(a) of the Bankruptcy Code, § 1325(a). Section 1325, part of Chapter 13, specifies the circumstances under which a consumer's plan of repayment can be confirmed. The hanging paragraph says that, for the purpose of a Chapter 13 plan, § 506 of the Code does not apply to certain secured loans.

Section 506(a) divides loans into secured and unsecured portions; the unsecured portion is the amount by which the debt exceeds the current value of the collateral. In a Chapter 13 bankruptcy, consumers may retain the collateral (despite contractual provisions entitling creditors to repossess) by making monthly payments that the judge deems equal to the market value of the asset, with a rate of interest that the judge will set (rather than the contractual rate). *See Associates Commercial Corp. v. Rash*, 520 U.S. 953 (1997); *Till v. SCS Credit Corp.*, 541 U.S. 465 (2004). This procedure is known as a "cramdown"—the court crams down the creditor's throat the substitution of money for the collateral, a situation that creditors usually oppose because the court may underestimate the collateral's market value and the appropriate interest rate, and the debtor may fail to make all promised payments, so that the payment stream falls short of the collateral's full value. (The effect is asymmetric: if a judge overestimates the collateral's value or the interest rate, the debtor will surrender the asset and the creditor will realize no more than the market price. When the judge errs in the debtor's favor, however, the debtor keeps the asset and pays at the reduced rate. Creditors systematically lose from this asymmetry—and in the long run solvent borrowers must pay extra to make up for creditors' anticipated loss in bankruptcy.)

The question we must decide is what happens when, as a result of the hanging paragraph, § 506 vanishes from the picture. The majority view among bankruptcy judges is that, with § 506(a) gone, creditors cannot divide their loans into secured and unsecured components. Because § 1325(a)(5)(C) allows a debtor to surrender the collateral to the lender, it follows (on this view) that surrender fully satisfies the borrower's obligations. If this is so, then many secured loans have been rendered non-recourse, no matter what the contract provides. * * * The minority view is that Article 9 of the Uniform Commercial Code plus the law of contracts entitle the creditor to an unsecured deficiency judgment after surrender of the collateral, unless the contract itself provides that the loan is without recourse against the borrower. That unsecured balance must be treated the same as other unsecured debts under the Chapter 13 plan.

Craig Wright and LaChone P. Giles-Wright, debtors in this proceeding, owe more on their purchase-money automobile loan than the car is worth. Because the purchase occurred within 910 days of the bankruptcy's commencement, the hanging paragraph in § 1325(a)(5) applies. This paragraph reads:

For purposes of paragraph (5), section 506 shall not apply to a claim described in that paragraph if the creditor has a purchase money security interest securing the debt that is the subject of the claim, the debt was incurred within the 910-day [sic] preceding the date of the filing of the petition, and the collateral for that debt consists of a motor vehicle (as defined in section 30102 of title 49) acquired for the personal use of the debtor, or if collateral for that debt consists of any other thing of value, if the debt was incurred during the 1-year period preceding that filing.

Debtors proposed a plan that would surrender the car to the creditor and pay nothing on account of the difference between the loan's balance and the collateral's market value. After taking the minority position on the effect of bypassing § 506, the bankruptcy judge declined to approve the Chapter 13 plan, because debtors did not propose to pay any portion of the shortfall.

Normally the next step would be an appeal to the district court, followed by an appeal to this court once a final decision had been rendered. But the 2005 Act amends 28 U.S.C. § 158 to allow a direct appeal from a bankruptcy court to the court of appeals, bypassing the expense and delay of litigation before a district judge. Section 158(d)(2)(A) now provides:

The appropriate court of appeals shall have jurisdiction of appeals described in the first sentence of subsection (a) if the bankruptcy court, the district court, or the bankruptcy appellate panel involved, acting on its own motion or on the request of a party to the judgment, order, or decree described in such first sentence, or all the appellants and appellees (if any) acting jointly, certify that—

(i) the judgment, order, or decree involves a question of law as to which there is no controlling decision of the court of appeals for the circuit or of the Supreme Court of the United States, or involves a matter of public importance;

(ii) the judgment, order, or decree involves a question of law requiring resolution of conflicting decisions; or

(iii) an immediate appeal from the judgment, order, or decree may materially advance the progress of the case or proceeding in which the appeal is taken; and if the court of appeals authorizes the direct appeal of the judgment, order, or decree.

The bankruptcy judge certified that this litigation satisfies both subparagraphs (i) and (ii). A motions panel of this court accepted the appeal because the issue not only has divided the bankruptcy courts but also arises in a large fraction of all consumer bankruptcy proceedings. A clear answer is needed-yet this issue appears to be "stuck" in the bankruptcy courts. No court of appeals has addressed the subject, and few district judges have done so. Lower litigation costs for thousands of debtors and creditors may be achieved by expediting appellate consideration of this case.

Like the bankruptcy court, we think that, by knocking out § 506, the hanging paragraph leaves the parties to their contractual entitlements. True enough, § 506(a) divides claims into secured and unsecured components. * * * Yet it is a mistake to assume, as the majority of bankruptcy courts have done, that § 506 is the *only* source of authority for a deficiency judgment when the collateral is insufficient. The Supreme Court held in *Butner v. United States,* 440 U.S. 48 (1979), that state law determines rights and obligations when the Code does not supply a federal rule. * * *

The contract between the Wrights and their lender is explicit: If the debt is not paid, the collateral may be seized and sold. Creditor "must account to Buyer for any surplus. Buyer shall be liable for any deficiency." In other words, the contract creates an ordinary secured loan with recourse against the borrower. Just in case there were doubt, the contract provides that the parties enjoy all of their rights under the Uniform Commercial Code. Section 9-615(d)(2) of the UCC, enacted in Illinois as 810 ILCS 5/9-615(d)(2), provides that the obligor must satisfy any deficiency if the collateral's value is insufficient to cover the amount due.

If the Wrights had surrendered their car the day before filing for bankruptcy, the creditor would have been entitled to treat any shortfall in the collateral's value as an unsecured debt. It is hard to see why the result should be different if the debtors surrender the collateral the day after filing for bankruptcy when, given the hanging paragraph, no operative section of the Bankruptcy Code contains any contrary rule. Section 306(b) of the 2005 Act, which enacted the hanging paragraph, is captioned "Restoring the Foundation for Secured Credit". This implies replacing a contract-defeating provision such as § 506 (which allows judges rather than the market to value the collateral and set an interest rate, and may prevent creditors from repossessing) with the agreement freely negotiated between debtor and creditor. Debtors do not offer any argument that "the Foundation for Secured Credit" could be "restored" by making all purchase-money secured loans non-recourse; they do not argue that non-recourse lending is common in consumer transactions, and it is hard to imagine that Congress took such an indirect means of making non-recourse lending *compulsory*.

Appearing as *amicus curiae*, the National Association of Consumer Bankruptcy Attorneys makes the bold argument that loans covered by the hanging paragraph cannot be treated as secured in any respect. Only § 506 provides for an "allowed secured claim," *amicus* insists, so the entire debt must be unsecured. This also would imply that a lender is not entitled to any post-petition interest. *Amicus* recognizes that § 502 rather than § 506 determines whether a claim should be "allowed" but insists that only § 506 permits an "allowed" claim to be a "secured" one.

This line of argument makes the same basic mistake as the debtors' position: it supposes that contracts and state law are irrelevant unless specifically implemented by the Bankruptcy Code. *Butner* holds that the presumption runs the other way: rights under state law count in bankruptcy unless the Code says otherwise. Creditors don't need § 506 to create, allow, or recognize security interests, which rest on contracts (and the UCC) rather than federal law. Section 502 tells bankruptcy courts to allow claims that stem from contractual debts; nothing in § 502 disfavors or curtails secured claims. Limitations, if any, depend on § 506, which the hanging paragraph makes inapplicable to purchase-money interests in personal motor vehicles granted during the 910 days preceding bankruptcy (and in other assets during the year before bankruptcy).

Both the debtors and the *amicus curiae* observe that many decisions, of which *United States v. Ron Pair Enterprises, Inc.*, 489 U.S. 235 (1989), is a good example, state that § 506 governs the treatment of secured claims in bankruptcy. No one doubts this, but the question at hand is what happens when § 506 does not apply. The fallback under *Butner* is the parties' contract (to the extent the deal is enforceable under state law), rather than non-recourse secured debt (the Wrights' position) or no security interest (the *amicus curiae*'s position). And there is no debate about how the parties' contract works: the secured lender is entitled to an (unsecured) deficiency judgment for the difference between the value of the collateral and the balance on the loan.

By surrendering the car, debtors gave their creditor the full market value of the collateral. Any shortfall must be treated as an unsecured debt. It need not be paid in full, any more than the Wrights' other unsecured debts, but it can't be written off *in toto* while other unsecured creditors are paid some fraction of their entitlements.

AFFIRMED

NOTES

1. In *Wright* Chief Judge Easterbrook invokes first principles: under *Butner*, state law governs the creditor's entitlements unless the Bankruptcy Code says otherwise. Under state law (the UCC), the creditor has recourse against the debtors for any deficiency remaining after the creditor's disposition of the collateral upon default. Thus, the creditor has an unsecured claim against debtor for the amount of any deficiency. According to the court, nothing in the Bankruptcy Code changes this result. Under § 502, the creditor's 910 claim is allowable. Section 506(a) bifurcates ordinary claims, but doesn't apply to the creditor's 910 claim because of the hanging paragraph. Hence, state law prevails and the creditor has recourse against the debtors for a deficiency. Section 1325(a)(5) goes unmentioned by the court.

The court reinforced its rather cavalier treatment of the issue by asserting that it would be "hard to imagine" that Congress had meant to change the long settled practice that consumer automobile financing is done on a recourse basis by adding an obscure provision like the hanging paragraph. If Congress had intended such a tectonic change as making automobile financing compulsorily nonrecourse, surely it would have done so in a direct manner, clearly evident to all parties concerned.

The court in *Capital One Auto Finance v. Osborn*, 515 F.3d 817 (8th Cir. 2008), agreed with *Wright*, but unlike the court in that case, the *Capital One* court carefully examined the effect of § 1325(a)(5). It reasoned that since nothing in § 1325(a)(5) says that the "allowed secured claim" is satisfied by the debtor's choosing the surrender option in subparagraph (C), the creditor retains its state law contractual right to a deficiency claim. Unlike the retention option in subparagraph (B) that requires full payment of the secured claim when the debtor retains the collateral ((B)(ii)), the surrender option in subparagraph (C) *does not speak to the satisfaction of a claim*. All subparagraph (C) means is that the debtor's plan can be confirmed upon surrender of the vehicle; the creditor's deficiency claim survives. Thus, no Bankruptcy Code provision bars the creditor's state law right to a deficiency claim. *In re Ballard*, 526 F.3d 634 (10th Cir. 2008), follows the *Capital One* analysis, while *Tidewater Finance Co. v. Kenney*, 531 F.3d. 312 (4th Cir. 2008), leans more to *Wright*. *In re Long*, 519 F.3d. 288 (6th Cir. 2008), reaches the same result using the common law principle of interpretation known as the "equity of the statute."

2. *Wright* reached the Seventh Circuit on direct appeal from the bankruptcy court under 28 USC § 158, which allows direct appeal to the court of appeals under the stated circumstances. The bankruptcy court certified that the *Wright* litigation satisfied both subparagraphs (i) and (ii). The surrender issue involved has been litigated in numerous bankruptcy courts, as well as a few district courts and bankruptcy appellate panels, with sharply divided holdings. The *Wright* court is one of the first Courts of Appeal to address jurisdiction to hear appeals directly from a bankruptcy court and it concluded that this is a strong case for direct appeal. It stated: "Lower litigation costs for thousands of debtors and creditors may be achieved by expediting appellate consideration of the case." The plethora of divergent bankruptcy court holdings on a number of BAPCPA issues suggests that it may become common for Courts of Appeals to resolve the meaning of BAPCPA through the direct appeal route, and there is a strong trend in this direction. Courts of Appeals can guard against becoming overburdened with certified appeals by rejecting the appeal in their discretion. In the course of declining to accept a direct appeal, *Weber v. U.S.*, 484 F.3d 154 (2d Cir. 2007), discussed in detail the background of direct appeal. *See* Christopher W. Frost, 27 *Bankruptcy Law Letter* No. 10 (Oct. 2007); Daniel J. Bussel, *Bankruptcy Appellate Reform: Issues and Options*, 1995-96 Ann. Survey Bankr. L. 257.

d. Interest

Section 1325(a)(5) allows the debtor three options for the treatment of "allowed secured claims." If the 910 debtor chooses to retain the collateral under a Chapter 13 cramdown plan, does she have to pay post-petition interest on the claim? Yes, § 1325(a)(5)(B)(ii) requires the debtor to distribute property of "value, as of the effective date of the plan" equal to the "allowed secured claim." Because a 910 car claim is not subject to bifurcation under § 506(a), the holder of the claim is entitled to the present value of the whole claim. Therefore, creditors are entitled to interest calculated to ensure that they receive the present value of their claims. The rate is the "prime plus" rate prescribed by *Till v. SCS Credit Corp.*, p. 722: *See, e.g., Drive Financial Services, L.L.P.v. Jordan*, 521 F.3d 343 (5th Cir. 2008).

e. Refinancing Balances Due on Trade-in Vehicles

At a time when auto loans are being stretched in some cases to as long as seven years, the trade-in of cars subject to unpaid loans is common. For instance, Dealer agrees to finance the sale to Buyer of a car for a price of $25,000 and to take as a trade-in Buyer's car, which has a value of $12,000. But Buyer still owes $3,000 on the trade-in. Dealer and Buyer enter into an installment sale contract for the new car that "rolls in" the $3,000 balance owing on the trade-in so that the amount financed is stated in the contract to be $16,000 plus interest, to be paid by Buyer to Dealer over a period of six years. Dealer retains a security interest in the new car for the amount of the unpaid obligation. Dealer pays Buyer's old lender $3,000 and takes ownership of the trade-in free and clear.

Under the hanging paragraph, Buyer's obligation to Dealer is a 910 claim only to the extent it is a purchase money loan. To what extent is Buyer's obligation to Dealer a 910 claim that cannot be bifurcated under § 506(a)? The Bankruptcy Code has no definition of "purchase money security interest." Bankruptcy courts usually look to the UCC definition that defines a "purchase money obligation" as "an obligation... incurred as all or part of the price of the collateral..." § 9-103(a)(2). The issue is whether Dealer has a purchase money security interest for only $13,000 (the amount owed on account of the new car) or whether the $3,000 owed on account of the trade-in should be added "as part of the price" of the new car. Courts usually refer to the balance due on the trade-in as "negative equity." The prevailing view is that if the buyer and seller agree to include the payoff of the outstanding balance due on the trade-in as an integral part of their transaction for the sale of the new car, the amount refinanced is a purchase money loan for the new car. *In re Graupner,* 537 F.3d 1295 (11th Cir. 2008), the first court of appeals decision in point, takes this view; the opinion inventories the scores of opinions on both sides of the issue. In a thoughtful opinion, Judge Bruce Markell disagrees with this view, *In re Penrod,* 392 B.R. 835 (9th Cir. BAP 2008), as does the court in *In re Callicott,* 396 B.R. 506 (E.D. Mo.2008) (money advanced to buyer to pay off the debt on her old car was not part of the price of the new car but was a loan to pay off an antecedent debt).

PROBLEM

Secured Party (SP) sold Debtor for family use a unit consisting of a computer, monitor and printer ("the unit") and retained a perfected security interest in the unit to secure $10,000, the unpaid portion of the purchase price. Two years later Debtor filed in Chapter 13. She wished to retain possession of these goods so that her children could continue to use them for school work. The value of the goods at the time of Debtor's filing was $6,000 as fixed by the bankruptcy court, and her remaining obligation to SP was $8,000. Debtor's plan proposed that: she pay SP $6,000 plus interest over the life of the plan, and the $2,000 unpaid balance be classified as an unsecured claim and paid off pro rata with other unsecured claims at 5% on the dollar. Debtor's disposable income was adequate to make the required payments over the three-year duration of the plan. The plan complied with § 1325(a)(5)(B)(i) in providing that SP retains a lien on the unit until the earlier of Debtor's discharge under § 1328 or payment of the underlying debt determined under nonbankruptcy law, and that if the case is dismissed or converted before completion, SP's lien shall be retained until the underlying debt is paid.

(a) Should the court confirm Debtor's plan under § 1325(a)(5)?

(b) Debtor was unable to complete her plan and her case was dismissed after she had paid SP $3,000 on the secured claim and $150 on the unsecured claim. SP claimed a lien on the unit in the amount of the remaining $5,850 unpaid on the original contract. Is SP correct? § 1325(a)(5)(B)(i)(II).

3. VALUATION OF COLLATERAL

As we have seen, if a Chapter 13 debtor wishes to retain collateral and the secured creditor will not consent, the debtor may "cramdown" the secured creditor's security interest under § 1325(a)(5). The debtor may retain the collateral only if the plan provides that the secured party receives the present value of the secured claim. § 1325(a)(5)(B)(ii). In order to determine this amount, the court must value the collateral and set an interest rate that will assure the creditor this value in deferred payments over the term of the plan. In giving directions for how to value the secured creditor's claim, § 506(a)(1) paints with a broad brush: "Such value shall be determined in the light of the purpose of the valuation and of the proposed disposition or use of such property * * *."

The two most common cases in which the amount of the creditor's secured claim had to be determined in consumer debtor cases under the 1978 Code were with respect to redemption in Chapter 7 under § 722 and cramdown in Chapter 13 under § 1325(a)(5)(B). Litigation on the valuation issue has centered on whether a retail or wholesale value is appropriate. Creditors, favoring a high valuation, contend that a retail valuation is appropriate because the debtor will continue to use the automobile and should have to pay its replacement cost—the retail price. Debtors, seeking a low valuation, assert that the value of the creditor's interest is what the creditor would receive for the automobile at a foreclosure sale of a repossessed automobile, often an auction sale to dealers. In *Associates Commercial Corp. v. Rash*, p. 109, the Supreme Court held that the "replacement value" (which it defined as retail value less costs of resale, warranties and accessions not subject to the lien) was the appropriate metric for valuing collateral to be retained under a Chapter 13 plan.

Under § 1325(a), Chapter 13 cramdown is no longer based on the value of the collateral in the case of 910 purchase money loans secured by motor vehicles and certain other property. In these cases, *Rash* has only limited applicability. Moreover, *Rash*'s replacement value interpretation of § 506(a) insofar as it still applies to individual debtors under Chapters 7 and 13 was further modified by BAPCPA by the addition of § 506(a)(2) as follows:

> **(2)** If the debtor is an individual in a case under chapter 7 or 13, such value with respect to personal property securing an allowed claim shall be determined based on the replacement value of such property as of the date of filing the petition without deduction for costs of sale or marketing. With respect to property acquired for personal, family, or household purpose, replacement value shall mean the price a retail merchant would charge for property of that kind considering the age and condition of the property at the time value is determined.

Even after *Rash* the view of the bankruptcy courts had consistently been that the § 722 redemption price was fixed by liquidation, not replacement value. *In re Weathington*, 254 B.R. 895 (6th Cir. BAP 2000). But § 506(a)(2) changed Chapter 7 law by requiring a modified "replacement value" standard for determining the value of a secured claim for redemption under § 722.

4. INTEREST RATE

The Code requires that a secured creditor receive under the plan property with a present value equal to the allowed amount of its secured claim, § 1325(a)(5)(B)(ii), but offers no specific guidance on the interest rate to be used in discounting future payments to arrive at the present value of a secured claim. 2 *Lundin*, § 112.1. Chapter 13 cases were sharply divided on the issue until *Till v. SCS Credit Corp.*, p. 722. The *Till* plurality adopted a rule that appears to require the bankruptcy court to use a market based rate (such as the "prime rate") that is current as of the time confirmation to compensate the secured creditor for delay in payment and adjust that rate upward to compensate the secured creditor for the risk of nonpayment. Dicta in *Till* appear to suggest that in most circumstances a risk adjustment in the range of 1-3% above the prime rate is appropriate, at least in the Chapter 13 car loan context.

H. SECURED CLAIMS IN DEBTOR'S RESIDENCE

1. MODIFICATION OF HOME MORTGAGES

In the Congressional debate on the 1978 Code, the provision allowing a Chapter 13 plan to modify the rights of holders of secured claims ran into stiff opposition from real estate mortgage lenders. Industry lobbyists predicted that the specter of home mortgages being subject to modification in bankruptcy by changing the amount or number of installment payments or by stripping down the mortgage debt to the value of the real property, would result in a drying up of home loans. Congress reacted to these predictions by amending the proposed § 1322(b)(2) to provide that the power of the debtor's plan to "modify the rights of holders of secured claims" was limited to claims "other than a claim secured only by a security interest in real property that is the debtor's principal residence." This language was intended to preclude debtors from using § 1325(a)(5)(B) to rewrite home mortgages in Chapter 13 plans. The plan may provide for cure of defaults, but the debtor could not otherwise modify debts secured by home mortgages.

The expectations of the real estate finance industry were undermined by a series of court decisions that applied the concept of "bifurcation" to the quoted language of § 1322(b)(2). Bifurcation is based on § 506(a) that relates to claims "secured by a lien on property." As we have seen, if the value of the property is less than the amount of the debt, § 506(a) bifurcates the claim into a secured claim to the extent of the value of the property and an unsecured claim for the remaining part of the debt. Hence, if the debt secured by a mortgage on the debtor's residence is $100,000 but the value of the residence has shrunk to $60,000, the mortgagee has a secured claim for $60,000 and an unsecured claim for $40,000. Four Courts of Appeals held that that under the literal wording of § 1322(b)(2) the phrase "other than a claim secured only by a security interest in real property that is the debtor's principal residence" immediately follows the part of § 1322(b)(2) that states that the plan may modify the rights of holders of "secured claims." Thus, the quoted phrase modifies the immediately preceding words "secured claims" and not the entire claim that is secured by the residence. Under this reading of § 1322(b)(2), only the $60,000 secured claim was immune from modification. To the extent the debt owed to the mortgagee was greater than the value of the residence, the mortgagee had only an unsecured claim that could be dealt with by the debtor's plan in the same way as other unsecured claims. In the following opinion, the Supreme Court rejected this interpretation.

Nobelman v. American Savings Bank
Supreme Court of the United States, 1993.
508 U.S. 324.

- Justice THOMAS delivered the opinion of the Court.

This case focuses on the interplay between two provisions of the Bankruptcy Code. The question is whether § 1322(b)(2) prohibits a Chapter 13 debtor from relying on § 506(a) to reduce an undersecured homestead mortgage to the fair market value of the mortgaged residence. We conclude that it does and therefore affirm the judgment of the Court of Appeals.

I.

In 1984, respondent American Savings Bank loaned petitioners Leonard and Harriet Nobelman $68,250 for the purchase of their principal residence, a condominium in Dallas, Texas. In exchange, petitioners executed an adjustable rate note payable to the bank and secured by a deed of trust on the residence. In 1990, after falling behind in their mortgage payments, petitioners sought relief under Chapter 13 of the Bankruptcy Code. The bank filed a proof of claim with the Bankruptcy Court for $71,335 in principal, interest, and fees owed on the note. Petitioners' modified Chapter 13 plan valued the residence at a mere $23,500—an uncontroverted valuation—and proposed to make payments pursuant to the mortgage contract only up to that amount (plus prepetition arrearages). Relying on § 506(a) of the Bankruptcy Code, petitioners proposed to treat the remainder of the bank's claim as unsecured. Under the plan, unsecured creditors would receive nothing.

The bank and the Chapter 13 trustee, also a respondent here, objected to petitioners' plan. They argued that the proposed bifurcation of the bank's claim into a secured claim for $23,500 and an effectively worthless unsecured claim modified the bank's rights as a homestead mortgagee, in violation of § 1322(b)(2). The Bankruptcy Court agreed with respondents and denied confirmation of the plan. The District Court affirmed, as did the Court of Appeals. We granted certiorari to resolve a conflict among the Courts of Appeals. * * *

II.

Under Chapter 13 of the Bankruptcy Code, individual debtors may obtain adjustment of their indebtedness through a flexible repayment plan approved by a bankruptcy court. Section 1322 sets forth the elements of a confirmable Chapter 13 plan. * * * Section 1322 (b)(2), the provision at issue here, allows modification of the rights of both secured and unsecured creditors, subject to special protection for creditors whose claims are secured only by a lien on the debtor's home. It provides that the plan may "modify the rights of holders of secured claims, *other than a claim secured only by a security interest in real property that is the debtor's principal residence*, or of holders of unsecured claims, or leave unaffected the rights of holders of any class of claims." § 1322(b)(2) (emphasis added).

The parties agree that the "other than" exception in § 1322 (b)(2) proscribes modification of the rights of a homestead mortgagee. Petitioners maintain, however, that their Chapter 13 plan proposes no such modification. They argue that the protection of § 1322(b)(2) applies only to the extent the mortgagee holds a "secured claim" in the debtor's residence and that we must look first to § 506(a) to determine the value of the mortgagee's "secured claim." Section 506(a) provides that an allowed claim secured by a lien on the debtor's property "is a secured claim to the extent of the value of [the] property"; to the extent the claim exceeds the value of the property, it "is an unsecured claim." Petitioners contend that the valuation provided for in § 506(a) operates automatically to adjust downward the amount of a lender's undersecured home mortgage before any disposition proposed in the debtor's Chapter 13 plan. Under this view, the bank is the holder of a "secured claim" only in the amount of $23,500—the value of the collateral property. Because the plan proposes to make $23,500 worth of payments pursuant to the monthly payment terms of the mortgage contract, petitioners argue, the plan effects no alteration of the bank's rights as the holder of that claim. Section 1322(b)(2), they assert, allows unconditional modification of the bank's leftover "unsecured claim."

This interpretation fails to take adequate account of § 1322(b)(2)'s focus on "rights." That provision does not state that a plan may modify "claims" or that the plan may not modify "a claim secured only by" a home mortgage. Rather, it focuses on the modification of the "*rights of holders*" of such claims. By virtue of its mortgage contract with petitioners, the bank is indisputably the holder of a claim secured by a lien on petitioners' home. Petitioners were correct in looking to § 506(a) for a judicial valuation of the collateral to determine the status of the bank's secured claim. It was permissible for petitioners to seek a valuation in proposing their Chapter 13 plan, since § 506(a) states that "[s]uch value shall be determined... in conjunction with any hearing... on a plan affecting such creditor's interest." But even if we accept petitioners' valuation, the bank is still the "holder" of a "secured claim," because petitioners' home retains $23,500 of value as collateral. The portion of the bank's claim that exceeds $23,500 is an "unsecured claim componen[t]" under § 506(a); however, that determination does not necessarily mean that the "rights" the bank enjoys as a mortgagee, which are protected by § 1322(b)(2), are limited by the valuation of its secured claim.

The term "rights" is nowhere defined in the Bankruptcy Code. In the absence of a controlling federal rule, we generally assume that Congress has "left the determination of property rights in the assets of a bankrupt's estate to state law," since such "[p]roperty interests are created and defined by state law." *Butner v. United States*, 440 U.S. 48, 54–55 (1979). * * * Moreover, we have specifically recognized that "[t]he justifications for application of state law are not limited to ownership interests," but "apply with equal force to security interests, including the interest of a mortgagee." *Butner, supra*, at 55. The bank's "rights," therefore, are reflected in the relevant mortgage instruments, which are enforceable under Texas law. They include the right to repayment of the principal in monthly installments over a fixed term at specified adjustable rates of interest, the right to retain the lien until the debt is paid off, the right to accelerate the loan upon default and to proceed against petitioners' residence by foreclosure and public sale, and the right to bring an action to recover any deficiency remaining after foreclosure. * * * These are the rights that were "bargained for by the mortgagor and the mortgagee," *Dewsnup v. Timm*, 502 U.S. 410, 417 (1992), and are rights protected from modification by § 1322(b)(2).

This is not to say, of course, that the contractual rights of a home mortgage lender are unaffected by the mortgagor's Chapter 13 bankruptcy. The lender's power to enforce its rights—and, in particular, its right to foreclose on the property in the event of default—is checked by the Bankruptcy Code's automatic stay provision. § 362. * * * In addition, § 1322(b)(5) permits the debtor to cure prepetition defaults on a home mortgage by paying off arrearages over the life of the plan "notwithstanding" the exception in § 1322(b)(2). These statutory limitations on the lender's rights, however, are independent of the debtor's plan or otherwise outside § 1322(b)(2)'s prohibition.

Petitioners urge us to apply the so-called "rule of the last antecedent," which has been relied upon by some Courts of Appeals to interpret § 1322(b)(2) the way petitioners favor. * * * According to this argument, the operative clause "other than a claim secured only by a security interest in... the debtor's principal residence" must be read to refer to and modify its immediate antecedent, "secured claims." Thus, § 1322(b)(2)'s protection would then apply only to that subset of allowed "secured claims," determined by application of § 506(a), that are secured by a lien on the debtor's home—including, with respect to the mortgage involved here, the bank's secured claim for $23,500. We acknowledge that this reading of the clause is quite sensible as a matter of grammar. But it is not compelled. Congress chose to use the phrase "claim secured... by" in § 1322(b)(2)'s exception, rather than repeating the term of art "secured claim." The unqualified word "claim" is broadly defined under the Code to encompass any "right to payment, whether... secure[d] or unsecured" or any "right to an equitable remedy for breach of performance if such breach gives rise to a right to payment, whether... secure[d] or unsecured." § 101(5). It is also plausible, therefore, to read "a claim secured only by a [homestead lien]" as referring to the lienholder's entire claim, including both the secured and the unsecured components of the claim. Indeed, § 506(a) itself uses the phrase "claim... secured by a lien" to encompass both portions of an undersecured claim.

This latter interpretation is the more reasonable one, since we cannot discern how § 1322(b)(2) could be administered under petitioners' interpretation. Petitioners propose to reduce the outstanding mortgage principal to the fair market value of the collateral, and, at the same time, they insist that they can do so without modifying the bank's rights "as to interest rates, payment amounts, and [other] contract terms." * * * That appears to be impossible. The bank's contractual rights are contained in a unitary note that applies at once to the bank's overall claim, including both the secured and unsecured components. Petitioners cannot modify the payment and interest terms for the unsecured component, as they propose to do, without also modifying the terms of the secured component. Thus, to preserve the interest rate and the amount of each monthly payment specified in the note after having reduced the principal to $23,500, the plan would also have to reduce the term of the note dramatically. That would be a significant modification of a contractual right. Furthermore, the bank holds an adjustable rate mortgage, and the principal and interest payments on the loan must be recalculated with each adjustment in the interest rate. There is nothing in the mortgage contract or the Code that suggests any basis for recalculating the amortization schedule whether by reference to the face value of the remaining principal or by reference to the unamortized value of the collateral. This conundrum alone indicates that § 1322(b)(2) cannot operate in combination with § 506(a) in the manner theorized by petitioners.

In other words, to give effect to § 506(a)'s valuation and bifurcation of secured claims through a Chapter 13 plan in the manner petitioners propose would require a modification of the rights of the holder of the security interest. Section 1322(b)(2) prohibits such a modification where, as here, the lender's claim is secured only by a lien on the debtor's principal residence.

The judgment of the Court of Appeals is therefore

Affirmed.

■ Justice STEVENS, concurring.

At first blush it seems somewhat strange that the Bankruptcy Code should provide less protection to an individual's interest in retaining possession of his or her home than of other assets. The anomaly is, however, explained by the legislative history indicating that favorable treatment of residential mortgagees was intended to encourage the flow of capital into the home lending market. *See Grubbs v. Houston First American Savings Assn.*, 730 F.2d 236, 245-246 (C.A.5 1984) (canvassing legislative history of Chapter 13 home mortgage provisions). It therefore seems quite clear that the Court's literal reading of the text of the statute is faithful to the intent of Congress. Accordingly, I join its opinion and judgment.

NOTES

1. As this Casebook went to press in June 2009, the Senate had, temporarily at least, killed a renewed effort to grant bankruptcy judges the power to modify home mortgages in Chapter 13. So far the real estate finance industry has been successful in opposing repeal largely on the ground that it would raise interest rates on home mortgage loans—the same argument that was successful in 1978. The limited empirical evidence available suggests that interest rates did not materially rise during the 15-year period in which § 1322(b)(2) was effectively gutted in several circuits by the "bifurcation" theory eventually rejected by *Nobelman* in 1993. *See* Adam Levitin & Joshua Goodman, *The Effect of Bankruptcy Strip Down on Mortgage Markets*, Georgetown Law & Economics Research Paper No. 1087816 (Feb. 6, 2008) (suggesting that lenders' losses upon strip down may be less than losses realized by foreclosure).

2. Section 1322(b)(2) bars modification of claims secured "only by a security interest in real property that is the debtor's principal residence." Hence, mortgages secured by vacation homes or covering other collateral in addition to the debtor's residence can be modified. In *Wilson v. Commonwealth Mortgage Corp.*, 895 F.2d 123, 124 (3d Cir. 1990), the mortgage included not only debtor's residence but also "any and all appliances, machinery, furniture and equipment (whether fixtures or not) of any nature whatsoever now or hereafter installed in or upon said premises." This was an easy case for allowing modification because a lien on both personal property and real property is not common in residential mortgages. But typical residential mortgages often contain boilerplate clauses that may cause unanticipated difficulty. For example, residential mortgages often grant the mortgagee a security interest in "rents, royalties, profits, and fixtures," even though there is no expectation that the property will ever be rented. This kind of clause has usually not been held to involve additional collateral because these benefits are merely incidental to an interest in real property. *In re Davis*, 989 F.2d 208 (6th Cir. 1993).

Another clause discussed in *Davis* is the common provision requiring the mortgagor to maintain fire insurance on improvements with the proceeds payable to the mortgagee. This clause has not usually been held to give rise to additional collateral. Since this provision is present in virtually all home mortgages, a contrary holding would allow nearly all home mortgages to be modified. Mortgagors sometimes buy optional credit life and disability insurance at the time of the loan, the proceeds of which are used to pay the balance of the loan if the mortgagor dies or is disabled. Although the cases are divided on the issue of whether such insurance allows the mortgagee's claim to be modified under § 1322(b)(2), the court in *In re Washington*, 967 F.2d 173 (5th Cir. 1992), views the trend of authority as holding that such clauses do not allow modification of the claim. Another boilerplate provision that raises problems for creditors is that granting mortgagees a security interest in funds held in an escrow account into which the mortgagor is required to pay sums each month to cover annual tax and insurance obligations. *In re Dent*, 130 B.R. 623 (Bankr.S.D.Ga.1991), held that the money in the escrow was separate from the real property and, therefore, the clause granted the mortgagee additional collateral. *Accord In re Reed*, 247 B.R. 618 (E.D.Pa.2000).

Courts have usually been reluctant to find additional collateral in cases involving the more common home mortgage boilerplate clauses, and BAPCPA gives real estate lenders still more protection from modification. "Debtor's principal residence" is defined in § 101(13A) to include mobile homes, thereby resolving a conflict in the decisions. The new definition also provides that a residential structure includes "incidental property," which is defined in § 101(27B) to make clear that familiar boilerplate provisions on easements, fixtures, rents, mineral rights, escrow funds or insurance proceeds are merely incidental to the residence.

The following Problem shows the kinds of troublesome questions the home mortgage provision in § 1332(b)(2) continues to raise.

PROBLEM

Debtor bought a multi-unit dwelling, with one apartment on the first floor and another on the second. She lived in the first floor apartment and rented out the second floor to a tenant. She granted a mortgage in the property to Bank in order to secure a purchase money loan. When she filed in Chapter 13, she still owed $90,000 on the mortgage debt, but the property was worth only $75,000. Her plan proposed to strip down Bank's secured claim to the value of the property and to pay it off over a 20-year period in accordance with the requirements of § 1325(a)(5)(B). The $15,000 unsecured deficiency claim was classified with other unsecured claims on which the plan proposed to pay 10% over a period of three years. Bank objected to the plan on the ground that it impermissibly modified the rights of the holder of a home mortgage under § 1322(b)(2). Is Bank correct in contending that this case involves a "claim secured only by a security interest in real property that is the debtor's principal residence"? *See In re Scarborough,* 461 F.3d 406 (3d Cir. 2006).

2. MODIFICATION OF WHOLLY UNSECURED HOME LOANS

PROBLEM

During the real estate "bubble" period, in which residential property values were inflated to unsustainable levels, a common transaction was for the home owner to obtain a "home equity" loan on the residence by granting a lender a second mortgage on the home as security for the loan. When the bubble burst, many second mortgagees found their security interest wholly under water. How does the *Nobelman* doctrine apply to such a case?

The following facts are based on *In re Tanner*, 217 F.3d 1357 (11th Cir. 2000). First Lender made a purchase money home loan to Debtor of $62,000 secured by a first mortgage. Later Second Lender made a home equity loan to Debtor of $23,000 secured by a second mortgage. After Debtor filed in Chapter 13, First Lender filed a secured claim for the $62,000 outstanding balance of the loan. Since the value of the property at that time was only $57,000, First Lender is an undersecured creditor but, under *Nobelman*, its secured claim could not be stripped down to $57,000 under § 1322(b)(2). Hence, the plan called for paying First Lender the full amount of its claim. Second Lender also filed a secured claim and contended that, even though its claim was completely under water, its security interest could not be stripped off under § 1322(b)(2). Debtor disagreed and argued that the plan could strip off Second Lender's claim because it was entirely unsecured under § 506(a); the holding of *Nobelman* extended only to undersecured claims not totally unsecured claims. Thus Debtor could classify Second Lender's entire claim as unsecured and pay it only a 6% dividend. Who is right? Does Second Lender have a secured claim under § 506(a)? Does *Nobelman* repeal § 506(a)?

NOTES

1. The Second, Third, Fifth, Ninth and Eleventh Circuits, as well as the First Circuit BAP, support the view that the anti-modification exception of § 1322(b)(2) does not apply to a mortgage loan that is wholly unsecured under § 506(a). *See, e.g., In re Zimmer*, 313 F.3d 1220 (9th Cir. 2002).

2. If the home is not the debtor's principal residence, the rights of mortgagees can be modified and the debtor's Chapter 13 plan can strip-down the mortgage to the current value of the home and deal with the deficiency as an unsecured claim. Section 1325(a)(5)(B)(i), on retention of liens, causes no difficulties: If the plan is completed, the debtor is discharged and the mortgage is extinguished. If the case is dismissed because the debtor failed to carry out the plan, the mortgagee retains its mortgage to secure the unpaid amount. If an underwater junior lien is involved, as in *Tanner*, the junior lien would also revive upon dismissal of the case, but the senior mortgagee could foreclose on the land under state law and cut off the rights of both the mortgagor and the junior lienholder. If the land appreciated to the extent of making the junior lien partially secured, foreclosure by the senior might produce a surplus, which under state law would be turned over to the junior creditor.

3. THE 2007 HOME LOAN CRISIS

Home mortgage lending used to mean consumers borrowing money from lenders to buy houses. And in the not-too-distant past, lenders would advance only 80% of the appraised value of the property. But in more recent years lenders offered lower income consumers as much as 95%-100% financing. Moreover, if the value of the property increased, consumers used their growing equity in the property as security for additional "home equity" loans. The home equity loan proceeds were often applied to home improvements but borrowers used them for a variety of other purposes as well. Consumers' homes became a source of funds for unrelated spending or investment But when the value of homes crashed, consumers had no equity in their property to support their existing home equity loans much less new loans. A major source of consumer credit had disappeared.

After the fall, many homeowner debtors of limited means who suffered financial setbacks found themselves faced with the problem of holding a costly and illiquid asset in which they had little or no equity. They cried out for help and both the federal government and the home lenders responded in various ways. The most tempting target for immediate relief was repeal of § 1322(b)(2), which would allow the debtor's Chapter 13 plan to reduce the secured loan balance to the market value of the property and relieve debtors of onerous interest rate terms by substituting an interest rate based on *Till*, p. 722. A dramatic reduction in the debtor's monthly payment would usually follow. Repeal would still give mortgagees the foreclosure value of the property but industry leaders contended that repeal would increase market mortgage rates from one to one and one-half percent or more because lenders and their assignees would discount the value of mortgages subject to being rewritten by bankruptcy courts. Attempts at enacting such a reform, however, including proposed compromises allowing stripped-down mortgages to share in future appreciation of the home, as of this writing remain stalled in the Congress owing to continuing opposition from home lenders.

The Emergency Economic Stabilization Act of 2008 (EESA), the 2008 $700 billion "bailout bill," neither required modification of mortgages nor provided for a moratorium on foreclosures. But it contained provisions designed to encourage the mortgage industry to voluntarily facilitate loan modifications to avoid foreclosures. The HOPE for Homeowners Act of 2008 is designed to assist debtors at risk of foreclosure to refinance into affordable 30-year, fixed rate FHA loans. But lender participation is voluntarily and has been disappointing. Other government programs are evolving; an example is an aggressive FDIC program that adjusts the debtors' payments to their income. In the private sector, several large banks have loan modification programs; some replace optional ARMs with fixed rate mortgages that the debtor can afford. For a helpful catalog of loan modification programs near the end of 2008, see Clarks' Secured Transactions Monthly, Vol. 24, No. 10, Oct. 2008. Nevertheless, the rate of home foreclosures remained at the highest level since the Great Depression.

A new chapter in the role played by courts in the foreclosure relief arena is heralded by *Com. v. Fremont Investment & Loan*, 897 N.E.2d 548 (Mass. Supp. 2008), in which the Supreme Judical Court of Massachusetts granted the Attorney General's motion for a preliminary injunction restricting the lender's ability to foreclose on a number of subprime real estate loans on the ground that the loans were "unfair" under the Unfair & Deceptive Practices Act (UDAP). The Act broadly states: "Unfair methods of competition and unfair or deceptive acts or practices in the conduct of any trade or commerce are hereby declared unlawful." Mass. Gen. Laws ch. 93A, section 2. The factors that led the court to grant the injunction were: (1) the loans were 30-year ARMs (adjustable rate mortgages) with an introductory period of two or three years at a low rate of interest, to reset at a higher rate; (2) the reset rate was more than 3% greater than the introductory rate; (3) after reset, the debtor's monthly payments when added to the debtor's other monthly obligations, exceeded 50% of his income; and (4) the loan-to-value ratio in most cases was 100%; thus the debtor had no equity in the property at the beginning of the loan, making refinancing possible only if real estate values increased.

The lower court injunction that was affirmed required the lender to work with the Attorney General to "resolve their differences" before foreclosure of any "presumptively unfair" loans (those bearing the four characteristics noted above). If agreement cannot be reached on restructuring the loan in a manner suitable to the Attorney General, the lender may have foreclosure only if a court approves. The UDAP provides a number of other remedies, including civil penalties. Since other states have statutes similar to the Massachusetts measure, *Fremont Investment* may become an important precedent in empowering courts and attorneys general to rewrite home mortgages.

4. CURE OF DEFAULTS

The desire to protect their homes from mortgage foreclosure is a major reason debtors opt for Chapter 13. Assume the common case in which Debtor is behind on her mortgage payments and the mortgage obligation on her home has 10 or 15 years left on the repayment schedule when Debtor files in Chapter 13. The mortgagee is threatening foreclosure. How can Debtor save her home? Under § 1322(b)(2), she cannot modify her obligation, but even if she could modify, she usually lacks the resources to pay off the entire obligation during the term of a three-to five-year plan. She finds her remedy in § 1322(b)(5), which allows her to maintain the current schedule of mortgage payments throughout the plan and cure her default by making up the arrearages in payments over the period of the plan. If she completes her plan, she is no longer in default and the mortgage is reinstated. Of course, the portion of the mortgage debt falling due in the years after her case is closed is not discharged, § 1328(a)(1), and the mortgagee retains a lien on the property until the remaining debt is paid. But if she cannot carry out the plan and converts to Chapter 7 before the default is cured, BAPCPA § 348(f)(1)(C)(ii) provides that the mortgage is in default to the same extent it would be outside bankruptcy.

Meaning of cure. The use in Chapter 13 of broad undefined terms like "cure" or "modify" has led to some confusion about the scope of each term. For example, if a debtor has been in default for an extended period, the mortgagee will commonly declare an acceleration of the entire unpaid balance of the loan before commencing foreclosure. After acceleration, is a proposal to pay the amounts in default at the time of acceleration a permissible cure or an impermissible modification? In a resolution of the issue that has been widely followed, the court in *In re Taddeo*, 685 F.2d 24 (2d Cir. 1982), held that it is a permissible cure:

> When Congress empowered Chapter 13 debtors to "cure defaults," we think Congress intended to allow mortgagors to "de-accelerate" their mortgage and reinstate its original payment schedule. We so hold for two reasons. First, we think that the power to cure must comprehend the power to "de-accelerate." This follows from the concept of "curing a default." A default is an event in the debtor-creditor relationship which triggers certain consequences—here, acceleration. Curing a default commonly means taking care of the triggering event and returning to pre-default conditions. The consequences are thus nullified. This is the concept of "cure" used throughout the Bankruptcy Code. * * *
>
> Secondly, we believe that the power to "cure any default" granted in § 1322(b)(3) and (b)(5) is not limited by the ban against "modifying" home mortgages in § 1322(b)(2) because we do not read "curing de-

faults" under (b)(3) or "curing defaults and maintaining payments" under (b)(5) to be *modifications* of claims.

It is true that § 1322(b)(5)'s preface, "notwithstanding paragraph (2)," seems to treat the power to cure in (b)(5) as a subset of the power to modify set forth in (b)(2), but that superficial reading of the statute must fall in the light of legislative history and legislative purpose. The "notwithstanding" clause was added to § 1322(b)(5) to emphasize that defaults in mortgages could be cured notwithstanding § 1322(b)(2).

685 F.2d at 26-27.

Case law after *Taddeo* has not been uniform on the reach of the cure remedy. Some cases denied debtors the right to cure after a judgment of foreclosure was entered, even though the property had not yet been sold under the judgment, e.g., *In re Roach*, 824 F.2d 1370 (3d Cir. 1987). Others allowed cure up to the point of the foreclosure sale. Still others allowed cure even after a foreclosure sale so long as the debtor had a right of redemption under state law. These views are discussed in *In re Glenn*, 760 F.2d 1428 (6th Cir. 1985), which adopted what is probably the majority view that cure is permissible under a Chapter 13 plan until the foreclosure sale but not after. The argument in favor of this view is that allowing cure to upset foreclosure sales during the post-sale redemption period would tend to chill bidding at the foreclosure sale, to the detriment of all involved. State post-sale redemption statutes require the debtor to pay the full unpaid balance before the end of the redemption period in order to redeem. If cure is permitted after the sale, the apparent effect would be to make the purchaser at the foreclosure sale an involuntary creditor who would have to accept repayment on the terms of the original mortgage. One court addressed this issue as follows: "A foreclosure sale * * * may introduce another party to the relationship—a good faith purchaser. We hesitate to further cloud the interests and expectations of a third party purchaser through an expansive right of bankruptcy cure." *In re Thompson*, 894 F.2d 1227, 1230 (10th Cir. 1990).

In 1994, § 1322(c)(1) was added, which states that "a lien on the debtor's principal residence may be cured under paragraph (3) or (5) of subsection (b) until such residence is sold at a foreclosure sale that is conducted in accordance with applicable non-bankruptcy law." The Section-by-Section Description § 301, 140 Cong.Rec. H10769 (1994), indicates that the intent was to overrule the *Roach* line of cases "by allowing the debtor to cure home mortgage defaults at least through completion of a foreclosure sale under applicable nonbankruptcy law. However, if the State provides the debtor more extensive 'cure' rights (through, for example, some later redemption period), the debtor would continue to enjoy such rights in bankruptcy."

The court in *Colon v. Option One Mortgage Corp.*, 319 F.3d 912, 920 (7th Cir. 2003), held that the phrase "applicable non-bankruptcy law" in § 1322(c)(1) "requires deference to state mortgage law on the scope of any right to cure after the sale." But *In re Cain*, 423 F.3d 617 (6th Cir. 2005), took the view that a mortgage may not be cured after a foreclosure sale regardless of whether a right of redemption survives the sale under state law.

Interest on arrearage. If a debtor who is delinquent on installments due on a mortgage debt may cure the default by spreading the amount of the arrearage over the period of the plan, is an oversecured mortgagee entitled to interest on the delayed payments on the arrearage? The language of § 1322 is not helpful in answering this question, and the Courts of Appeals were sharply divided on the issue until it was eventually resolved by the Supreme Court in *Rake v. Wade*, 508 U.S. 464 (1993), which held that § 506(b) applies to cure cases and allows oversecured creditors interest. After *Rake* was decided, § 1322 was amended in 1994 by adding a new subsection (e). According to the legislative history, Section-by-Section Description § 305, 140 Cong. Rec. H10770 (1994), this provision was intended to overturn *Rake*. But mortgagees can assure their right to interest on the arrearage by inserting a clause in the mortgage requiring the mortgagor to pay it, so long as the applicable state law would enforce such a promise.

5. THREE-TO-FIVE YEAR LIMITATION

Living under a Chapter 13 plan after BAPCPA is burdensome, and, unless some time limits are imposed, few would volunteer. Section 1322(d)(1) states for above-median debtors that "the plan may not provide for payments over a period that is longer than 5 years." And § 1322(d)(2) states for below-median debtors that "the plan may not provide for payments over a period that is longer than 3 years, unless the court, for cause, approves a longer period, but the court may not approve a period that is longer than 5 years." The issue these limits raise is how effective Chapter 13 plans can be in dealing with long-term obligations of debtors that extend beyond the three-to-five year duration of the plan. Assume an above-median income Debtor owns a home subject to a $400,000 mortgage that has a term extending beyond the duration of Debtors' Chapter 13 plan. The following Cases illustrate the application of these provisions.

> **Case #1.** Debtor is behind in her payments and Creditor is threatening foreclosure. Section 1322(b)(5) allows for a plan that proposes to cure a default in a mortgage that has a duration longer than five years, so long as the arrearage can be paid off within the period of the plan. The usual plan would provide (1) that the arrearage would be paid during the term of the plan, (2) Debtors would continue making contract pay-

ments on the mortgage throughout the plan, and (3) Debtors would continue making payments after the term of the plan.

Case # 2. The value of Debtor' home has declined to $300,000 and she wishes to modify the security interest by stripping down the principal balance of the secured claim to $300,000.

(a) If the home is Debtor's principal residence, *Nobelman* held that § 1322(b)(2) prevents modification without respect to the term of the indebtedness.

(b) If the home is not Debtor's principal residence, § 1322(b) provides no bar to modification of a mortgage. The question is whether the five-year limitation of § 1322(d) does so. What Debtors might desire in a case in which their mortgage is in default and the debt exceeds the value of the land is a plan that allows them (1) to cure the default within the term of the plan, (2) classify the $100,000 deficiency as an unsecured claim, to be paid off at a few cents on the dollar, and (3) maintain their regular payments until the $300,000 balance, with interest, is paid off. *In re Enewally*, 368 F.3d 1165 (9th Cir. 2004), denied this relief. It held that a modified secured debt cannot be paid off over a period in excess of the term of the plan. Thus, long-term mortgages may be cured but they may not be modified in a manner that requires payments to be made beyond the three-to-five year limit of the plan. Debtor's recourse is to Chapter 11. Judge Lundin, in § 202.1 of his treatise, reviews the authorities and concludes that *Enewally*, which states the majority view, is probably wrong. He sees nothing to indicate that § 1322(b)(2) and (5) are mutually exclusive.

CHAPTER 10
REORGANIZATION IN CHAPTER 11: OPERATING THE DEBTOR & PROPOSING A PLAN

A. INTRODUCTION

1. RATIONALE OF REORGANIZATION

The Supreme Court has described the purpose of Chapter 11 as follows:

> In proceedings under the reorganization provisions of the Bankruptcy Code, a troubled enterprise may be restructured to enable it to operate successfully in the future. * * * By permitting reorganization, Congress anticipated that the business would continue to provide jobs, to satisfy creditors' claims, and to produce a return for its owners. * * * Congress presumed that the assets of the debtor would be more valuable if used in a rehabilitated business than if "sold for scrap."

United States v. Whiting Pools, Inc., 462 U.S. 198, 203 (1983).

Reorganized debtors use their future earnings to repay prepetition creditors. Liquidated debtors' assets are sold to repay those claims. If the present value of a given firm's future earning power (the "going concern" value) is greater than the liquidation value of its assets, Chapter 11 reorganization is an attractive alternative to Chapter 7 liquidation. In this situation, creditors as a group are better off if the business continues to operate. And society is better off also when a firm that is worth more alive than dead is successfully rehabilitated.

In some cases, the debtor's prospects of generating additional value by continued operations are very remote. Consuming assets in continuing operations can, nevertheless, further the interests of managers, other employees, shareholders and postpetition suppliers at the expense of prepetition creditors. Accordingly, the interests of the debtor and those of creditors may conflict on the issue of whether continued operation is desirable. Section 1112(b)(1) mandates dismissal of a Chapter 11 case or its conversion to Chapter 7 upon a finding of "cause" which is defined to include among other things "substantial or continuing loss to or diminution of the estate." § 1112(b)(4)(A). Historically, courts have allowed debtors in possession to continue to operate for some period even in cases in which the enterprise is not economically viable. The *Eastern Airlines* debacle in which the doomed debtor, over the heated objection of creditors, spent $400 million in a futile continuation of operations was perhaps the high-water mark. Christie Harlan & Bridget O'Brian, *After Eastern, Debtors Face Bumpier Ride*, Wall St.J., Jan. 22, 1991, at B3. While the limited data that are available suggest that bankruptcy judges have become quite adept at dismissing or converting the cases of debtors that have little or no prospect of successful reorganization within the first few months of the Chapter 11 filing, so long as postpetition debts are being paid, debtors are generally given some time to attempt reorganization. Douglas Baird, *The New Face of Chapter 11*, 12 Am. Bankr. Instit. L. Rev. 69, 89 (2004) (citing study finding that of those businesses unable to reorganize, one-half are dismissed within three months and three-quarters are dismissed within five months).

Conflict between creditors and the debtor also occurs even when a business is clearly capable of successful reorganization under Chapter 11. Reorganizing an operating business in Chapter 11 usually requires cooperation from the debtor. The price of debtor cooperation may be a division of the value that is anticipated in the reorganization between creditors and ownership interests. If the anticipated reorganization value is not sufficient to pay all prepetition debt, all of that value, as a theoretical matter, belongs to creditors. But if that value cannot be obtained without the efforts or cooperation of the debtor, compensation of the ownership interests of the debtor may be in the interests of creditors. A successful reorganization is usually the product of a deal that is struck among secured creditors, unsecured creditors and the debtor. Bankruptcy reorganization can usefully be viewed from the perspective of the tension among the debtor and its creditors over the allocation of the reorganization value of the enterprise. Confirmation of a reorganization plan reflects an accommodation of this tension if it gives the debtor enough of this value to induce it to reorganize while, at the same time, according fair treatment to the claims of creditors.

For many years, Chapter 11 has been under attack by commentators. Over twenty years ago, Professor Douglas Baird challenged the assumption that the going concern value of a distressed business may commonly exceed its liquidation value. *The Uneasy Case for Corporate Reorganizations*, 15 J.Legal Stud. 127 (1986). Businesses are frequently sold as entities both inside and outside bankruptcy. Baird argued that if the best use of a company's assets lies in the continued operation of the business, assuming a properly functioning market, buyers will bid a price—the discounted value of future earnings—that equals the going concern value. Subsequently, two commentators called for the outright repeal of Chapter 11, arguing that Chapter 11 reorganizations provide less value for both equity and debt holders than the prior law and benefit principally corporate management. Michael Bradley & Michael Rosenzweig, *The Untenable Case for Chapter 11*, 101 Yale L.J. 1043 (1992). Replies to Bradley & Rosenzweig are found in Lynn M. LoPucki, *Strange Visions in a Strange World: A Reply to Professors Bradley and Rosenzweig*, 91 Mich.L.Rev. 79 (1992), and Elizabeth Warren, *The Untenable Case for Repeal of Chapter 11*, 102 Yale L.J. 437 (1992). Empirical work suggests that the direct costs of Chapter 11 reorganization of large public firms are a relatively modest 3% of the debtor's assets. Stephen J. Lubben, *The Direct Costs of Corporate Reorganization*, 74 Am. Bankr. L.J. 509 (2000). But Chapter 11's indirect costs in lost business opportunities, delays and strategic behavior have so far eluded measurement, and while varying greatly, undoubtedly loom large in some cases.

Chapter 11 practice has significantly evolved over the last thirty years. Increasingly, Chapter 11 cases do take the form of sales followed by liquidating plans, rather than traditional reorganizations or even sales under the terms of a plan. Often the sale transaction is negotiated pre-bankruptcy and the Chapter 11 case is simply the legal mechanism for implementing the pre-negotiated sale, subject to a court-approved overbid process. In a sale case, the main event is the sale of the company, not its plan of reorganization, and, if everything remains on track, the sale of the business can be completed within the first few months of the Chapter 11 filing, often within 60 days. Notwithstanding academic criticism of Chapter 11's reorganization premises, and the observed greater frequency of sales, traditional reorganizations remain an important component of Chapter 11 practice, and understanding how a traditional reorganization works an essential part of the bankruptcy lawyer's repertoire. Interestingly, a recent empirical study by our colleagues Joseph Doherty and Lynn LoPucki finds that traditional reorganizations return significantly more value to creditors than sales. *Bankruptcy Fire Sales*, 106 Mich. L. Rev. 1 (2007) (comparing recoveries from going-concern bankruptcy sales of 25 large, public companies with the recoveries from the bankruptcy reorganizations of 30 large, public companies in the same period, and finding that, controlling for asset size and pre-sale or pre-reorganization earnings, reorganization recoveries were more than double sale recoveries).

2. REORGANIZATION UNDER PREVIOUS LAW

The rich history of corporate reorganization law as it evolved from federal equity receivership law, the Bankruptcy Act of 1898, the 1933 and 1934 Amendments to the 1898 Act (§§ 77 and 77B), the 1938 Chandler Act (Chapters X, XI and XII), and the Bankruptcy Reform Act of 1978 (Chapter 11) is summarized in many places. The description below is drawn from Daniel J.

Bussel, *Coalition–Building Through Bankruptcy Creditors' Committees*, 43 UCLA L.Rev. 1547, 1552–58 (1996).

Reorganization law developed out of the federal courts' struggle to fashion an alternative to forced liquidation for large, financially distressed corporations in the late 19th and early 20th centuries. Statutory bankruptcy law provided no satisfactory alternative. Indeed from 1878 to 1898, the period of the birth and early development of United States corporate reorganization law, no federal bankruptcy statute existed. Even the Bankruptcy Act of 1898, the first comprehensive federal bankruptcy statute, was directed towards liquidation rather than reorganization of distressed firms.

The "equity receivership" arose first to deal with the problems of distressed railroads. The value of an operating railroad was almost always greater than that of an unwieldy liquidation of railroad property scattered across many jurisdictions. Moreover, there was a significant public interest in maintaining operating railroads throughout the country. The interests of the railroad's American managers, owners, employees, shippers (especially farmers) and passengers clearly favored reorganization. Liquidation might arguably have been in the interest of certain classes of debtholders, but American railroads in the 19th century were built primarily with European capital supplied through investment bankers in New York and London. Forced liquidation of American railroads in favor of these moneyed foreign interests was unlikely to be viewed with favor on this side of the Atlantic. Professors Baird and Rasmussen in *Control Rights, Priority Rights and the Conceptual Foundations of Corporate Reorganizations*, 87 Va.L.Rev. 921 (2001), have nevertheless suggested that the investment bankers who dominated the equity receivership process and who sometimes held significant equity stakes in the railroads, depended on their long-term relationships with these foreign investors and thus had incentives to balance these creditor interests against local interests. Arguably, the system's success in balancing creditor and debtor interests depended on these close interlocking relationships and thus equity receiverships did not benefit the relatively unsophisticated and unconnected public investors who had become common by the 1930's. Nevertheless Baird and Rasmussen point to evidence that even these later public investors, if they held diversified bond portfolios, in fact outperformed the market.

In the absence of a viable statutory procedure, federal courts and lawyers for distressed corporations and their creditors made up the rules as they played the game, which they called the "federal equity receivership." Eight key steps evolved:

First, subject to pre-arrangement with the debtor, a cooperative out-of-state creditor would sue under the federal diversity of citizenship jurisdiction in a venue of the debtor's liking. The creditor would seek appointment of a receiver (also of the debtor's liking) on the grounds of the debtor's equitable insolvency. The debtor would consent to the appointment of the receiver.

Second, pre-receivership management would continue to manage the company under the general supervision of the federal court while a plan was worked out.

Third, all creditor collection activity would be enjoined by the federal court during the receivership proceeding.

Fourth, committees representing each class of public debt would form. Each of these "protective" committees would solicit irrevocable proxies or the actual deposit of the securities for the particular class of debt that the committee purported to represent. The proxies and deposit agreements would give the protective committee broad discretion to negotiate a plan that would modify the rights of the securityholders it represented.

Fifth, the various protective committees would negotiate with each other and the debtor management over a plan. The plan would call for the surrender of old securities in exchange for new securities that would be allocated among creditors and shareholders in accordance with the terms of the plan. When a plan was agreed to, the protective committees and debtor management would join together and form a new "reorganization" committee.

Sixth, the court would then set rules for a foreclosure sale of all the debtor's property. Inevitably, the reorganization committee would be the only bidder, because the reorganization committee had the full cooperation of management and could use the securities controlled by the protective committees to "credit bid" for the firm's assets. Knowing there was only one likely bidder, the court would set a floor on the bidding, the "upset price." The "upset price" would generally be a low-end estimate of the value of the debtor's property. The court order authorizing the foreclosure sale would require notice and subsequent "confirmation" of the sale by the court. The negotiated reorganization plan would be disclosed to the court and subjected to a variable and uncertain degree of court scrutiny at this confirmation hearing. The sale of the debtor's property to the reorganization committee at the "upset price" would then be "confirmed" by the court.

Seventh, those creditors who chose not to participate in the reorganization would receive their pro rata share of the upset price in cash in accordance with the priority of their legal rights. This pro rata distribution would generally be a fraction of the amount owed on senior claims and nothing for junior claims—in both cases substantially less than the anticipated value of new securities distributed under the plan. The property purchased at the sale would be immediately transferred to a newly formed corporation and securities in that corporation would be distributed to participating creditors in accordance with the negotiated plan. Incumbent management would continue to operate the business under substantially the same ownership but with scaled down debt. The expenses of the proceeding (including the necessary cash payments to dissenters) would generally be funded by pre-receivership shareholders who would retain an equity interest in the new corporation in exchange for their cash contribution and the cancellation of their pre-receivership shares.

Finally, the whole process was constrained by the rule of *Northern Pacific Railway Co. v. Boyd*, 228 U.S. 482 (1913). *Boyd* held that a dissenting creditor could continue to assert its claims against the reorganized company notwithstanding the foreclosure sale if pre-receivership shareholders continued to hold an interest in the reorganized company, *unless* the dissenting creditor had refused a "fair offer" to participate in the reorganization. The practice developed that the court would make a specific finding that the reorganization plan was "fair" at the confirmation hearing or in connection with authorizing the foreclosure sale. A "fair offer" generally came to mean cash or securities of the reorganized company deemed by the court supervising the reorganization to be of a value equal to the face amount of the creditor's claim. *See Case v. Los Angeles Lumber Prods. Co.*, 308 U.S. 106 (1939). The *Boyd* rule became known variously as the "absolute priority rule" and the "fair and equitable rule," and in modified form is now codified in § 1129(b). The *Boyd* rule, though a significant obstacle, proved to be somewhat less onerous in practice than it might first appear. Courts proved reluctant to overturn plans as "unfair" when faced with substantial majorities of consenting creditors from all affected classes and no alternative but forced liquidation.

This odd little dance, a negotiated restructuring masquerading as a receivership and foreclosure, lent itself to various sorts of abuse. The most obvious abuses involved the unfair treatment of *dissenters*. Dissenters, a notoriously complaining and litigious breed, brought their problems to the attention of the federal courts, and the courts gave substantial, if imperfect, redress through the mechanisms of the upset price (protecting dissenting senior creditors) and the *Boyd* rule (protecting dissenting junior creditors). But the courts did little to protect uninformed or unsophisticated or powerless *consenters* who might be taken advantage of in the informal, ad hoc and extrajudicial process by which consent was obtained.

The Great Depression generated enormous pressure for the reform of this jerry-built system. The first reformers, however, were not the quiescent consenters but the reorganizers themselves. Reorganizers sought to preserve the substance of the equity receivership system by codifying, regularizing, and simplifying it. In 1934 Congress passed § 77B, the first statutory reorganization process for non-railroad corporations. Section 77B dispensed with the charade of the foreclosure sale altogether. With two-thirds of the amount of each affected class assenting to the plan, dissenters could be compelled to scale down their debts so long as the court found the plan was "fair and equitable," did not "discriminate unfairly," and was "feasible." These refinements obviated the need for the traditional foreclosure sale and more importantly the need to make pro rata cash distributions to dissenting senior creditors based upon the "upset price" bid at the sale.

Section 77B was relatively poorly drafted. The reorganization bar through the National Bankruptcy Conference undertook to make technical corrections and drafting improvements in the statute. Meanwhile William O. Douglas at the Securities and Exchange Commission launched a frontal assault on the reorganization processes born of equity receivership practice.

The essence of Douglas's attack was that the reorganization process was largely controlled by investment bankers, debtor management and their allies. These "insiders" generally created the protective committees and solicited the proxies and deposits of securityholders. Most often the insiders could control the reorganization process from beginning to end, perpetuating their control over the debtor corporation and realizing the "spoils" of the reorganization process—substantial fees of all kinds for legal, management and financial services and new securities to be issued by the reorganized company at discounts from their anticipated fair market value. More than occasionally sophisticated, noninsider interests would organize their own "protective" committees and contest with the insiders for control of the reorganization process and the reorganized company. Although public securityholders might incidentally benefit from such a contest, more often than not, insider committees and non-insider committees controlled by sophisticated investors would manage to negotiate a mutually satisfactory resolution whereby the spoils of the reorganization need not be too widely distributed.

Ample ammunition for the reform forces came in the form of the Securities and Exchange Commission monumental five volume Report on the Study and Investigation of the Work, Activities, Personnel and Functions of Protective and Reorganization Committees. Douglas's SEC investigated the most prominent reorganizations of the day. The picture of the reorganization process that emerged from this somewhat politicized account is of pervasive insider exploitation of the reorganization process. Insiders, in the SEC's account, converted their control over protective committees, the solicitation of proxies and deposits, and information into profit at the expense of public investors. The forces of reform (Douglas's SEC) and reaction (the National Bankruptcy Conference) collided and the result was the Chandler Act.

The Chandler Act provided for two very different types of reorganization procedures. One procedure, Chapter X directly addressed the perceived abuses of equity receivership practice as perpetuated in § 77B. Insider control of the process was diluted by the mandatory appointment of a disinterested trustee, SEC review of reorganization plans, a mandatory judicial hearing on the plan (requiring judicial valuation of the debtor) for compliance with the *Boyd* rule *before* the solicitation of consents to the plan, regulation of the solicitation of proxies, deposits and votes, and court supervision over compensation and fees.

The alternative reorganization procedure under the Chandler Act was Chapter XI. Secured debt and equity interests could not be directly restructured under Chapter XI. The proceedings under Chapter XI were far less formal. The debtor remained in possession of the property of the estate and had the exclusive right to file a plan of arrangement. The SEC had no official monitoring function. An official creditors' committee elected at the first meeting of creditors served as the only counterweight to the debtor. But the responsibilities and powers of the creditors' committee were unclear. The absolute priority rule was not applicable in Chapter XI arrangements, out-voted dissenters' only protection being that the plan had to be in "the best interests of creditors," that is provide each creditor with more value than a forced liquidation of the firm.

Although the Chandler Act did not specifically guide the debtor in deciding whether to file under Chapter X or Chapter XI, Congress intended Chapter X to be the normal procedure for reorganizing corporations having publicly held securities while Chapter XI was intended for small business arrangements in which the claims of trade creditors and unsecured lenders were scaled down or extended. But by the eve of the adoption of the Bankruptcy Code in 1978, Chapter XI, despite all of its limitations, was being used to reorganize corporations that were among the nation's largest and Chapter X was virtually a dead letter. The perceived reasons for the failure of Chapter X and the popularity of Chapter XI became guiding principles in the drafting of Chapter 11 of the Bankruptcy Code.

3. THE CHAPTER 11 APPROACH

Although Chapter 11 can be used by individuals who are not engaged in business, *Toibb v. Radloff*, 501 U.S. 157 (1991), the statute is clearly designed as a business reorganization procedure. Typically a Chapter 11 debtor is a business operated in the form of a corporation. The great majority of Chapter 11 cases are initiated by the debtor firm voluntarily filing a bankruptcy petition.

Chapter 11 fuses the Chandler Act's Chapter X and Chapter XI into a unitary reorganization procedure. Secured debt, unsecured debt and equity interests are all subject to restructuring under Chapter 11 reorganization plans. Unless a trustee is appointed or the court otherwise orders, for at least the first 120 days of the case and up to 18 months after commencement of the case, the debtor has the exclusive right to propose a plan. The plan must divide creditors and interest-holders into classes. Different classes may be treated differently under the plan, but all claimants within a class are entitled to identical treatment. After due disclosure regarding the plan is given, creditors and stockholders whose rights are altered by the plan vote by class on the plan. If all impaired classes approve the plan, confirmation by the court usually follows without the necessity for the Chapter X-style judicial valuation hearing. Dissenting minorities within a class are bound by a supermajority vote of the class. Even if all classes accept the plan, however, the court can not confirm a plan that does not meet certain minimum conditions that we will discuss later in the next chapter of the Casebook. If any class dissents the court can nevertheless confirm the plan if the minimum conditions and certain additional standards are met including a statutory version of the absolute priority rule. Confirmation over the objection of a dissenting class is usually referred to as "cramdown." Although it is important to understand each class's minimum legal entitlement in "cramdown," in fact most confirmed plans are "consensual" in the special bankruptcy sense that all impaired classes have accepted the plan by the requisite majorities. Most often the cramdown entitlements form a reference point in the bargaining that goes into formulating and confirming a consensual plan.

The actual process of formulating the consensus around a Chapter 11 plan remains mysterious, unregulated and irregular. Here Chapter 11 frankly rejects Douglas's reforms of mandatory trustees, SEC scrutiny of plans, and mandatory pre-solicitation judicial fairness hearings. Chapter 11 implicitly assumes that there is no one right plan for a particular case, or, if there is, courts and government agencies are not competent to discover it. Chapter 11 establishes a process and provides incentives to encourage the parties to negotiate a consensus around one of many plausible solutions, while seeking to control insider abuse. Except within broad limits, the Bankruptcy Code does not seek to determine the terms of the reorganization plan.

Debtors usually file Chapter 11 cases to deal with one of four types of business or legal problems:

1. To stop secured parties or judgment creditors from foreclosing or exercising other coercive debt collection measures authorized by state law.

2. To bind dissenting creditors or securityholders ("holdouts") to a generally consensual pre-negotiated debt restructuring.

3. To gain access to special bankruptcy powers not available under state law—for example to sell assets free and clear of adverse interests, estimate and discharge contingent claims, to avoid prebankruptcy transfers or resolve any potential avoidance claims, to appeal an adverse judgment without posting a supersedeas bond, or to reject, assume or assign defaulted leases.

4. To alleviate a liquidity crisis that immediately threatens the survival of the firm because it can not meet its financial obligations as they are maturing.

Notice that the asserted purpose of Chapter 11—the preservation of going concern value—is at best incidentally implicated in all these situations, with the possible exception of the use of Chapter 11 to deal with holdouts. Firms facing foreclosure or liquidity crises or that otherwise see advantage in exercising the powers of a bankruptcy trustee may or may not have any going concern value to protect.

Three distinctive types of firms make use of the unified Chapter 11 procedure: large operating businesses, small operating businesses, and "single asset real estate" debtors. Chapter 11 was designed with the large operating business principally in mind and it has proven to be best-suited for such cases. Procedures that are workable in such cases, prove much less suitable for small businesses and entities that do not operate businesses but simply own a particular piece of commercial real estate or raw land held for investment subject to a mortgage. Accordingly, though Chapter 11 is frequently the bankruptcy proceeding of first resort for financially troubled firms of all sizes, small businesses are notoriously unlikely to successfully reorganize.

Data on the rate of successful reorganization are surprisingly scarce, confused and contradictory. But there is little doubt that the great majority of firms filing for Chapter 11 reorganization do not successfully reorganize, however, one defines success. Small firms in Chapter 11 are unlikely to attract the necessary capital to fund reorganization and can ill afford the large expense associated with Chapter 11. Large firms that file under Chapter 11, on the other hand, do generally successfully reorganize, at least if success is defined in the minimal way of confirming a reorganization plan. The *NBRC Report* at 308 cites estimates that upwards of 95% of the largest firms in Chapter 11 confirm plans. The overall confirmation rate appears to be closer to 20–30%, with perhaps a third of all confirmed plans providing for some form of orderly liquidation rather than reorganization of the debtor.

In the year ending December 31, 2008, just over 10,000 debtors filed in Chapter 11, up more than 60% from 2007. Almost 20% of these cases were filed by individuals. Automated Access to Court Electronic Records (AACER). Although 2008 was a brutal recession year punctuated by the most severe financial panic since the Great Depression, only 39 large public companies filed Chapter 11 petitions, including, most notoriously, Lehman Brothers, by scheduled assets and liabilities, the largest bankruptcy case in history. The Chrysler Corporation filed under Chapter 11 on April 30, 2009 and no doubt 2009 will bring many more large Chapter 11 filings. In 2001 and 2002, also recession years 178 public companies with combined assets exceeding $615 billion filed, including 61 with more than $1 billion assets each and several of the largest cases ever filed, Pacific Gas & Electric, Enron, Worldcom, Adelphia, and United Air Lines. *See* Lynn M. LoPucki, WebBRD, at http: // lopucki.law.ucla.edu (Jan. 13, 2009).

The expense and delay that make Chapter 11 so unsuitable for small businesses produced calls for reform. Some bankruptcy courts instituted "fast-track" Chapter 11 procedures for small business bankruptcies that allowed these debtors to go though Chapter 11 on an accelerated basis. Some critics of Chapter 11 advocated a Chapter 13 type procedure that would allow small business debtors to keep their assets and to pay their creditors' claims out of disposable income over the period of the plan. Reformers in 1994 proposed a separate "Chapter 10," devoted to small business bankruptcies, which would speed the reorganization procedure and abolish some basic Chapter 11 creditor protections, considered later in this chapter, such as the absolute priority rule, the § 1111(b) election, and the creditors' right to vote on confirmation of the plan.

Creditor opposition defeated the ambitious "Chapter 10" proposal. Instead the 1994 amendments included a rather modest set of provisions that dealt with small business debtors within the familiar confines of Chapter 11. The modest procedural advantages of these amendments came at the cost to debtors of agreeing to further limit their exclusive right to file reorganization plans. The *NBRC Report* at 635 states, unsurprisingly in light of these considerations, that these small business provisions were "largely ignored." Congress responded in BAPCPA by making these specialized procedures mandatory for business debtors with less than $2,190,000 in liquidated debts, and coupling them with seemingly onerous reporting obligations and expanded grounds for dismissal and conversion, that promise to make small business reorganization in Chapter 11 even more difficult.

The single-asset real estate debtor raises another set of concerns. In such cases, "reorganization" in essence amounts to a contest between the debtor and the mortgage holder over who will own heavily encumbered real estate once the debtor has defaulted on its mortgage payments. There are generally no other creditors, no operating business, and no employees whose interests are implicated. Some theorists, and indeed some courts, question whether the use of Chapter 11 in these cases to merely stave off foreclosure and involuntarily restructure mortgage debt is appropriate. Although Chapter 11 remains open to single asset real estate debtors, over time, courts have grown increasingly hostile to their unfettered use (or abuse, depending upon one's view) of Chapter 11. Be aware as you work through the materials in this chapter of the difference in judicial attitude toward these debtors when you assess the construction placed upon generally applicable Chapter 11 provisions in single asset real estate cases. In a few areas, Congress has amended the Bankruptcy Code to place special limitations upon single asset real estate debtors. BAPCPA expanded these provisions and broadened their applicability to all single asset real estate debtors, by removing the $4 million statutory cap formerly limiting the definition of single asset real estate debtor.

B. MANAGEMENT AND CONTROL

1. ROLE OF DEBTOR IN POSSESSION

In Chapter 11 usually no bankruptcy trustee is appointed. The debtor (now called the "debtor-in-possession") succeeds to the trustee's rights, powers, and duties, and may operate its business without prior court approval. § 1107(a) and § 1108. One difference between the role of a bankruptcy trustee and that of the debtor in possession is that the debtor in possession does not investigate its own past conduct. § 1106(a)(3) and (4). Because it has the avoiding powers of the trustee, the debtor in possession may avoid preferential or fraudulent transfers that it made as debtor before bankruptcy.

In performing the trustee's duties, the debtor in possession is, under § 323(a), the "representative of the estate." In *Commodity Futures Trading Commission v. Weintraub*, 471 U.S. 343, 355 (1986), the Court said "* * * the willingness of courts to leave debtors in possession 'is premised upon an assurance that the officers and managing employees can be depended upon to carry out the fiduciary responsibilities of a trustee.'" Thus, the board of directors of a Chapter 11 debtor owes fiduciary obligations not only to its stockholders (as all corporate boards do) but also to creditors of the debtor. One must distinguish between situations in which the debtor's officers and directors act for the estate from those in which they act as the representative of the economic interests of stockholders. The Bankruptcy Code refers to "the debtor in possession" when the debtor acts as representative of the bankruptcy estate in continuing its business and otherwise exercising the powers of the trustee. In that role it has the responsibilities of a fiduciary. But § 1121, which deals with the issue of who can propose a plan of reorganization, uses the term "the debtor" to refer to the corporation being reorganized. Plans are negotiated between creditors and shareholders. To the extent creditors get more under the plan shareholders may get less. The use of "debtor" in § 1121 recognizes that in proposing and negotiating the plan of reorganization the corporation is not acting as a representative of the estate, but rather in the interests of itself and its stockholders.

Another dimension of the role of the debtor in possession is the fact that the debtor's management may have interests that differ from those of its stockholders. In many cases, professional turnaround management or other new management is brought into the firm either shortly before or during the Chapter 11 case. These new managers may have little incentive to advance the interests of shareholders or other "out-of-the-money" constituents; they may be engaged specifically for the purpose of preserving aggregate value while ensuring a smooth transition of the business to new ownership either through sale or reorganization. Even when incumbent pre-bankruptcy management remains in place, if at the end of the day, the plan of reorganization is likely to extinguish the interests of prebankruptcy shareholders, management may favor the interests of those creditors who are likely to end up with the stock of the reorganized corporation for it is they who will decide on the management for the reorganized business. If stockholders are dissatisfied with management's representation of their interests they can attempt to change the membership of the board of directors. However, courts have prevented stockholders from electing a new board in cases in which it appeared their intent was to block a viable plan. *In re Johns–Manville Corp.*, 801 F.2d 60 (2d Cir. 1986), discusses the authorities.

2. APPOINTMENT OF TRUSTEE IN BANKRUPTCY

The appointment of a trustee in bankruptcy in Chapter 11 occurs only in exceptional cases. The court may order the appointment of a trustee "for cause, including fraud, dishonesty, incompetence or gross mismanagement of the affairs of the debtor by current management * * * or similar cause." § 1104(a)(1). The court may also appoint a trustee or an examiner in lieu of dismissing or converting the case. § 1104(a)(3). It is also possible, under § 1104(a)(2), for the court to order appointment of a trustee "in the interests of creditors, any equity security holders, and other interests of the estate." The meaning of § 1104(a)(2) is unclear. It is apparently meant to apply to cases in which there is no gross misconduct by management, but in which there is some reason why the interests of everyone concerned would be better served by appointment of a trustee.

In the wake of the Chapter 11 cases involving Enron and Worldcom, which involved allegations of massive fraud in connection with accounting and financial reporting, Congress added § 1104(e) to the Code in BAPCPA. Section 1104(a)(1) continues to mandate appointment of a trustee "for cause, including fraud. . . by current management" on request of any party in interest or the U.S. Trustee. New § 1104(e) now requires the U.S. Trustee to move for the appointment of a trustee if there are "reasonable grounds to suspect" personal participation in fraud by the debtor's incumbent CEO, CFO or directors in connection with the debtor's management or financial reporting. Presumably, the U.S. Trustee's motion will be denied, notwithstanding its reasonable suspicions, if it cannot prove fraud by at least a preponderance of the admissible evidence introduced at the hearing. What is the point of requiring the

U.S. Trustee to move for a trustee based only on reasonable suspicion? Once having made the motion, is the U.S. Trustee required to prosecute it, rather than settle it?

In large Chapter 11 cases, it is far more common for the debtor to consensually replace management, frequently by installing a professional turnaround manager as "Chief Restructuring Officer" or CRO, than for the parties to seek a trustee. Indeed, in *Enron* itself the board appointed a mutually acceptable professional turnaround manager (CRO) rather than suffer the appointment of a trustee. Moreover, appointment of a trustee in most cases involving a small business debtor is overwhelmingly likely to preclude any result other than the liquidation or sale of the business. Small business debtors are generally closely identified with their owner-managers and displacement of that individual likely dooms any reorganization of the business.

If the court finds that exceptional circumstances do warrant appointment of a trustee, the appointing is done in the first instance by the U.S. Trustee unless a trustee is elected by creditors. To lawfully elect a trustee at least 20 percent of the creditors must vote and the trustee must receive the votes of creditors holding the majority in amount of claims who actually vote. § 702. Since Chapter 11 trustees are responsible for managing a distressed operating business, it is not uncommon to see the parties and the U.S. Trustee seek out specialized "turnaround" managers for this role rather than the lawyers and accountants who typically serve as Chapter 7 trustees.

If a trustee is appointed, the debtor's board of directors continues to exist after the appointment, but its powers are severely limited. In *Commodity Futures Trading Comm. v. Weintraub*, 471 U.S. 343, 352–53 (1985), the Court stated that upon appointment of a trustee: "[The board's] role is to turn over the corporation's property to the trustee and to provide certain information to the trustee and to the creditors. §§ 521, 343. Congress contemplated that when a trustee is appointed, he assumes control of the business, and the debtor's directors are 'completely ousted.'"

An important collateral consequence of the appointment of a Chapter 11 trustee is to terminate the debtor's exclusive right to file a reorganization plan, assuming that the statutory period has not otherwise expired. § 1121(c)(1).

3. EXAMINERS

The Bankruptcy Code provides for a middle ground between ousting the debtor by appointment of a trustee and leaving the debtor in possession subject to only general supervision by the court and any creditors' committee or other interested parties. The middle ground is the appointment of an examiner "to conduct such an investigation of the debtor as is appropriate, including an investigation of any allegations of fraud, dishonesty, incompetence, misconduct, mismanagement, or irregularity.... ." § 1104(c). Under § 1106(b) the examiner is given the investigatory powers of the trustee. In addition, the examiner is required to perform "any other duties of the trustee that the court orders the debtor in possession not to perform" unless the court orders otherwise. Thus, an examiner's functions can be limited to a particular investigatory role or can be expanded to include all of the functions of the trustee except those that the court allows the debtor in possession to perform.

Section 1104(c) states that on request of a party, the court "shall" appoint an examiner if (1) the appointment "is in the interests of creditors, any equity security holders, and other interests of the estate" or (2) the unsecured non-trade and non-insider claims exceed $5 million. § 1104(c). The language of § 1104(c) suggests that any party has the right to have an examiner appointed in any case involving more than $5 million in claims. But examiners are not routinely requested or appointed in such cases. Some courts refuse to read § 1104(c) literally and weigh the costs and benefits of appointing an examiner given the circumstances of the case or sharply limit the nature, extent, cost and duration of any investigation.

In some notable large cases including the *A.H. Robins* and *Olympia & York* cases, examiners were appointed to serve as mediators or facilitators when plan negotiations reached impasse.

4. CREDITORS' COMMITTEES

Section 1102(a)(1) requires the U.S. Trustee to promptly appoint a committee of creditors holding unsecured claims. This committee "shall ordinarily consist of the persons, willing to serve, that hold the seven largest claims against the debtor * * *." § 1102(b)(1). The "seven-largest" standard in the statute is merely precatory. H.R.Rep. No. 595, 95th Cong., 1st Sess. 401–02 (1977). Since the committees are intended to be the "primary negotiating bodies for the formulation of the plan of reorganization," the U.S. Trustee and bankruptcy courts have wide "latitude in appointing a committee that is manageable and representative in light of the circumstances of the case." Id. The debtor may have been negotiating a workout with a committee of its creditors before filing. If this committee is representative of the claims to be represented and was "fairly chosen," § 1102(b)(1) allows the U.S. Trustee to appoint its members as the creditors' committee.

What constitutes an adequately representative committee is unclear. One conception of the creditors' committee focuses on the need to control insider abuse and emphasizes committee members' undivided duty of loyalty to all unsecured creditors. A competing view focuses on the committee as an institutional device for building consensus around a plan and sees it as mediating and resolving conflicting interests among various constituencies of unsecured creditors. Daniel J. Bussel, *Coalition–Building Through Bankruptcy Creditors' Committees*, 43 UCLA L.Rev. 1547 (1996).

In complex cases either the U.S. Trustee or the court may cause additional committees of creditors or equity security holders to be appointed to ensure "adequate representation" of creditors or equity security holders. § 1102(a). "Equity security" is defined in § 101 to include a share in a corporation and the interest of a limited partner in a limited partnership. Committees of equity security holders are appropriate in cases in which the securities are publicly held and where they may arguably have rights to substantial reorganization value. A committee of equity security holders "shall ordinarily consist of the persons, willing to serve, that hold the seven largest amounts of equity securities of the debtor * * *." § 1102(b)(2).

Creditors' committees are given broad powers by § 1103(c). But the most important role of creditors' committees is to negotiate with the debtor in possession about the terms of the reorganization plan. In complex or contentious cases these negotiations may take years. If no agreement can be reached and the debtor exhausts its statutory exclusivity period, the creditors' committee may submit a rival plan.

In the usual case no trustee or examiner is appointed, and the creditors' committee is the only participant in the case that can carry out an investigation of the debtor's financial condition and of the debtor's chances for a successful reorganization. One of us has suggested that "the most sensible way to view these powers is as powers, not responsibilities. Their use, in the hands of a creditors' committee, is... the carrying on of plan negotiations by other means." Daniel J. Bussel, *Coalition–Building Through Bankruptcy Creditors' Committees*, 43 UCLA L.Rev. 1547, 1629 (1996). Committees on this view properly use their investigative powers strategically to advance their objectives in the plan formulation and confirmation processes.

Often debtors-in-possession are reluctant to press litigation against their own insiders or important constituents, such as significant continuing suppliers. Litigation recoveries generally accrue for the benefit of prepetition general creditors, and in those instances where the debtor-in-possession is reluctant or conflicted, and there is an active and well-represented creditors' committee, it is common for the committee to play an important role in the prosecution or settlement of estate litigation, such as the recovery of preferences or fraudulent transfers. *See Phar–Mor, Inc. v. Coopers & Lybrand*, 22 F.3d 1228 (3d Cir. 1994).

Often official committees, or less commonly other designated constituents, prosecute estate causes of action with specific bankruptcy court authorization. A few courts, in the light of *Hartford Underwriters*, p. 621, have questioned the source of the bankruptcy court's authority to designate committees as estate representatives for these purposes. For a fuller discussion and analysis of these issues, *see Official Committee of Unsecured Creditors of Cybergenics Corp. v. Chinery,* 330 F.3d 548 (3d Cir. *en banc* 2003) and Daniel J. Bussel, *Creditors' Committees as Estate Representatives in Bankruptcy Litigation,* 10 Stan. J.L. Bus. & Fin. 28 (2004).

It is difficult to appraise how well creditors' committees carry out the functions contemplated by Chapter 11. As a practical matter, the committee normally carries out its functions by employing professionals such as lawyers and financial advisors whose fees constitute expenses of administration under §§ 330(a) and 503(b). If a successful reorganization is a remote possibility or if the size of the debtor is not large enough to warrant the expense of professionals, a creditors' committee can do little to affect the outcome. Creditors' committees, however, have played prominent roles in Chapter 11 cases involving large debtors in which the financial stakes justified the expenditure of the time and money required to effectively investigate and negotiate on behalf of unsecured creditors. *See* Daniel J. Bussel, *Coalition–Building Through Bankruptcy Creditors' Committees,* 43 UCLA L.Rev. 1547 (1996) (studying 37 cases involving debtors with more than $50 million in assets filed in the Central District of California from 1986–1991 including 13 in which the creditors' committees played a major role in the case).

C. ADEQUATE PROTECTION FOR UNDERSECURED CREDITORS

Assume that a Chapter 11 debtor owns property encumbered by a mortgage and the value of the collateral is less than the amount of the debt it secures. If the collateral is necessary to operate the debtor's business, repossession and foreclosure is inconsistent with reorganization. Thus, the creditor is barred by the automatic stay, § 362(a), from seizing the collateral. But the creditor is entitled to relief from the stay under § 362(d)(1) unless adequate protection of the creditor's security interest is provided. It is common ground that adequate protection must include protection against or compensation for anticipated depreciation of the collateral during the reorganization. If the creditor's collateral is being used for the benefit of the debtor and other creditors, does adequate protection also require that the creditor be compensated for the loss resulting from delay in realizing upon its collateral—that is compensation for loss of its state law right to immediately seize and sell the collateral during the period from the filing of the petition until confirmation of the plan of reorganization? The House Report stated with respect to the meaning of adequate protection: "Secured creditors should not be deprived of the benefit of their bargain." 1978 U.S.C.C.A.N at 6295. The secured creditor's bargain is that upon default the creditor may immediately take possession of the collateral, sell it, and reinvest the proceeds. If there are to be any successful reorganizations under Chapter 11, creditors must be denied the right to seize collateral upon the debtor's filing in bankruptcy. But, perhaps, secured creditors should be compensated for the economic loss caused by the delay in repossession and foreclosure occasioned by the bankruptcy.

Professor Thomas Jackson, first in a law review article and later in his book, *The Logic and Limits of Bankruptcy Law* 189–190 (1986), argued that the creditor should be entitled to compensation. Costs of reorganization should not be imposed on secured creditors who do not benefit from reorganization. Rather, they should be borne by the debtor and unsecured creditors who may benefit from reorganization. Equity holders of an insolvent debtor gain by a successful reorganization and lose nothing if reorganization fails because their interests are, by definition, worthless in liquidation. Unsecured creditors may have something to gain from a successful reorganization and may have something to lose if it fails. An unsecured creditor who would have 35% of its claim satisfied in liquidation may lose it all if reorganization fails, or may receive 100% of the claim if the reorganization succeeds. But with respect to a secured claim, the creditor can receive no more than the amount of the claim if the reorganization succeeds and in this sense does not benefit from the reorganization. A rule requiring compensation for secured creditors for the interim loss of their collateral imposes costs; debtors may find it more difficult to reorganize and unsecured creditors may find their share of the estate reduced if liquidation ensues. But Professor Jackson contended that such a rule placed the costs of reorganization on the parties who stand to benefit from it.

Professor Jackson's reasoning was accepted in *In re American Mariner Industries, Inc.*, 734 F.2d 426 (9th Cir. 1984), but was rejected by the Fifth Circuit opinion in *Timbers*. In *Timbers* this conflict was resolved by the Supreme Court.

United Savings Assoc. of Texas v. Timbers of Inwood Forest Assoc., Ltd.
Supreme Court of the United States, 1988.
484 U.S. 365.

■   Justice SCALIA delivered the opinion of the Court.

* * *

I.

On June 29, 1982, respondent Timbers of Inwood Forest Associates, Inc. executed a note in the principal amount of $4,100,000. Petitioner is the holder of the note as well as of a security interest created the same day in an apartment project owned by respondent in Houston, Texas. The security interest included an assignment of rents from the project. On March 4, 1985, respondent filed a voluntary petition under Chapter 11 of the Bankruptcy Code * * *.

On March 18, 1985, petitioner moved for relief from the automatic stay of enforcement of liens triggered by the petition, see § 362(a), on the ground that there was lack of "adequate protection" of its interest within the meaning of § 362(d)(1). At a hearing before the Bankruptcy Court, it was established that respondent owed petitioner $4,366,388.77, and evidence was presented that the value of the collateral was somewhere between $2,650,000 and $4,250,000. The collateral was appreciating in value, but only very slightly. It was therefore undisputed that petitioner was an undersecured creditor. Respondent had agreed to pay petitioner the postpetition rents from the apartment project (covered by the after-acquired property clause in the security agreement), minus operating expenses. Petitioner contended, however, that it was entitled to additional compensation. The Bankruptcy Court agreed and on April 19, 1985, it conditioned continuance of the stay on monthly payments by respondent, at the market rate of 12% per annum, on the estimated amount realizable on foreclosure, $4,250,000—commencing six months after the filing of the bankruptcy petition, to reflect the normal foreclosure delays. * * * The court held that the postpetition rents could be applied to these payments. Respondent appealed to the District Court and petitioner cross-appealed on the amount of the adequate protection payments. The District Court affirmed but the Fifth Circuit en banc reversed.

We granted certiorari to determine whether undersecured creditors are entitled to compensation under § 362(d)(1) for the delay caused by the automatic stay in foreclosing on their collateral.

II.

When a bankruptcy petition is filed, § 362(a) of the Bankruptcy Code provides an automatic stay of, among other things, actions taken to realize the value of collateral given by the debtor. The provision of the Code central to the decision of this case is § 362(d), which reads as follows:

"On request of a party in interest and after notice and a hearing, the court shall grant relief from the stay provided under subsection (a) of this section, such as by terminating, annulling, modifying, or conditioning such stay—

"(1) for cause, including the lack of adequate protection of an interest in property of such party in interest; or

"(2) with respect to a stay of an act against property under subsection (a) of this section, if—

"(A) the debtor does not have an equity in such property; and

"(B) such property is not necessary to an effective reorganization."

The phrase "adequate protection" in paragraph (1) of the foregoing provision is given further content by § 361 of the Code * * *.

It is common ground that the "interest in property" referred to by § 362(d)(1) includes the right of a secured creditor to have the security applied in payment of the debt upon completion of the reorganization; and that that interest is not adequately protected if the security is depreciating during the term of the stay. Thus, it is agreed that if the apartment project in this case had been declining in value petitioner would have been entitled, under § 362(d)(1), to cash payments or additional security in the amount of the decline, as § 361 describes. The crux of the present dispute is that petitioner asserts, and respondent denies, that the phrase "interest in property" also includes the secured party's right (suspended by the stay) to take immediate possession of the defaulted security, and apply it in payment of the debt. If that right is embraced by the term, it is obviously not adequately protected unless the secured party is reimbursed for the use of the proceeds he is deprived of during the term of the stay.

The term "interest in property" certainly summons up such concepts as "fee ownership," "life estate," "co-ownership," and "security interest" more readily than it does the notion of "right to immediate foreclosure." Nonetheless, viewed in the isolated context of § 362(d)(1), the phrase could reasonably be given the meaning petitioner asserts. Statutory construction, however, is a holistic endeavor. A provision that may seem ambiguous in isolation is often clarified by the remainder of the statutory scheme—because the same terminology is used elsewhere in a context that makes its meaning clear, * * * or because only one of the permissible meanings produces a substantive effect that is compatible with the rest of the law * * *. That is the case here. Section 362(d)(1) is only one of a series of provisions in the Bankruptcy Code dealing with the rights of secured creditors. The language in those other provisions, and the substantive dispositions that they effect, persuade us that the "interest in property" protected by § 362(d)(1) does not include a secured party's right to immediate foreclosure.

Section 506 of the Code defines the amount of the secured creditor's allowed secured claim and the conditions of his receiving postpetition interest. In relevant part it reads as follows:

> "(a) An allowed claim of a creditor secured by a lien on property in which the estate has an interest * * * is a secured claim to the extent of the value of such creditor's interest in the estate's interest in such property, * * * and is an unsecured claim to the extent that the value of such creditor's interest * * * is less than the amount of such allowed claim * * *.

"(b) To the extent that an allowed secured claim is secured by property the value of which * * * is greater than the amount of such claim, there shall be allowed to the holder of such claim, interest on such claim, and any reasonable fees, costs, or charges provided for under the agreement under which such claim arose."

In subsection (a) of this provision the creditor's "interest in property" obviously means his security interest without taking account of his right to immediate possession of the collateral on default. If the latter were included, the "value of such creditor's interest" would increase, and the proportions of the claim that are secured and unsecured would alter, as the stay continues—since the value of the entitlement to use the collateral from the date of bankruptcy would rise with the passage of time. No one suggests this was intended. The phrase "value of such creditor's interest" in § 506(a) means "the value of the collateral." H.R.Rep. No. 95–595, pp. 181, 356 (1977) * * * We think the phrase "value of such entity's interest" in § 361(1) and (2), when applied to secured creditors, means the same.

Even more important for our purposes than § 506's use of terminology is its substantive effect of denying undersecured creditors postpetition interest on their claims—just as it denies *over*-secured creditors postpetition interest to the extent that such interest, when added to the principal amount of the claim, will exceed the value of the collateral. Section 506(b) provides that "*[t]o the extent that* an allowed secured claim is secured by property the value of which * * * is greater than the amount of such claim, there shall be allowed to the holder of such claim, interest on such claim." (Emphasis added.) Since this provision permits postpetition interest to be paid only out of the "security cushion," the undersecured creditor, who has no such cushion, falls within the general rule disallowing postpetition interest. See § 502(b)(2). If the Code had meant to give the undersecured creditor, who is thus denied interest on his *claim,* interest on the value of his *collateral,* surely this is where that disposition would have been set forth, and not obscured within the "adequate protection" provision of § 362(d)(1). Instead of the intricate phraseology set forth above, § 506(b) would simply have said that the secured creditor is entitled to interest "on his allowed claim, or on the value of the property securing his allowed claim, whichever is lesser." Petitioner's interpretation of § 362(d)(1) must be regarded as contradicting the carefully drawn disposition of § 506(b).

Petitioner seeks to avoid this conclusion by characterizing § 506(b) as merely an alternative method for compensating oversecured creditors, which does not imply that no compensation is available to undersecured creditors. This theory of duplicate protection for oversecured creditors is implausible even in the abstract, but even more so in light of the historical principles of bankruptcy law. Section 506(b)'s denial of postpetition interest to undersecured creditors merely codified pre-Code bankruptcy law, in which that denial was part of the conscious allocation of reorganization benefits and losses between undersecured and unsecured creditors. "To allow a secured creditor interest where his security was worth less than the value of his debt was thought to be inequitable to unsecured creditors." *Vanston Bondholders Protective Committee v. Green*, 329 U.S. 156, 164 (1946). It was considered unfair to allow an undersecured creditor to recover interest from the estate's unencumbered assets before unsecured creditors had recovered any principal. * * * We think it unlikely that § 506(b) codified the pre-Code rule with the intent, not of achieving the principal purpose and function of that rule, but of providing over-secured creditors an alternative method of compensation. Moreover, it is incomprehensible why Congress would want to favor undersecured creditors with interest if they move for it under § 362(d)(1) at the inception of the reorganization process—thereby probably pushing the estate into liquidation—but not if they forbear and seek it only at the completion of the reorganization.

Second, petitioner's interpretation of § 362(d)(1) is structurally inconsistent with § 552. Section 552(a) states the general rule that a prepetition security interest does not reach property acquired by the estate or debtor postpetition. Section 552(b) sets forth an exception, allowing postpetition "proceeds, product, offspring, rents, or profits" of the collateral to be covered only if the security agreement expressly provides for an interest in such property, and the interest has been perfected under "applicable nonbankruptcy law." * * * Section 552(b) therefore makes possession of a perfected security interest in postpetition rents or profits from collateral a condition of having them applied to satisfying the claim of the secured creditor ahead of the claims of unsecured creditors. Under petitioner's interpretation, however, the undersecured creditor who lacks such a perfected security interest in effect achieves the same result by demanding the "use value" of his collateral under § 362. It is true that § 506(b) gives the *oversecured* creditor, despite lack of compliance with the conditions of § 552, a similar priority over unsecured creditors; but that does not compromise the principle of § 552, since the interest payments come only out of the "cushion" in which the oversecured creditor *does have* a perfected security interest.

* * *

Section 362(d)(2) also belies petitioner's contention that undersecured creditors will face inordinate and extortionate delay if they are denied compensation for interest lost during the stay as part of "adequate protection" under § 362(d)(1). Once the movant under § 362(d)(2) establishes that he is an undersecured creditor, it is the burden of the *debtor* to establish that the collateral at issue is "necessary to an effective reorganization." See § 362(g). What this requires is not merely a showing that if there is conceivably to be an effective reorganization, this property will be needed for it; but that the property is essential for an effective reorganization *that is in prospect.* This means, as many lower courts, including the en banc court in this case, have properly said, that there must be "a reasonable possibility of a successful reorganization within a reasonable time." The cases are numerous in which § 362(d)(2) relief has been provided within less than a year from the filing of the bankruptcy petition. And while the bankruptcy courts demand less detailed showings during the four months in which the debtor is given the exclusive right to put together a plan, see § 1121(b), (c)(2), even within that period lack of any realistic prospect of effective reorganization will require § 362(d)(2) relief.

III.

A

Petitioner contends that denying it compensation under § 362(d)(1) is inconsistent with sections of the Code other than those just discussed. Petitioner principally relies on the phrase "indubitable equivalent" in § 361(3), which also appears in § 1129(b)(2)(A)(iii). Petitioner contends that in the latter context, which sets forth the standards for confirming a reorganization plan, the phrase has developed a well-settled meaning connoting the right of a secured creditor to receive present value of his security—thus requiring interest if the claim is to be paid over time. It is true that under § 1129(b) a secured claimant has a right to receive under a plan the present value of his collateral. This entitlement arises, however, not from the phrase "indubitable equivalent" in § 1129(b)(2)(A)(iii), but from the provision of § 1129(b)(2)(A)(i)(II) that guarantees the secured creditor "deferred cash payments * * * of a value, *as of the effective date of the plan,* of at least the value of such [secured claimant's] interest in the estate's interest in such property." (Emphasis added.) Under this formulation, even though the undersecured creditor's "interest" is regarded (properly) as solely the value of the collateral, he must be rendered payments that assure him that value *as of the effective date of the plan.* In § 361(3), by contrast, the relief pending the stay need only be such "*as will result in the realization* * * * of the indubitable equivalent" of the collateral. (Emphasis added.) It is obvious (since §§ 361 and 362(d)(1) do not entitle the secured creditor to immediate payment of the principal of his collateral) that this "realization" is to "result" not at once, but only upon completion of the reorganization. It is *then* that he must be assured "realization * * * of the indubitable equivalent" of his collateral. To put the point differently: similarity of outcome between § 361(3) and § 1129 would be demanded only if the former read "such other relief * * * as will give such entity, *as of the date of the relief,* the indubitable equivalent of such entity's interest in such property."

Nor is there merit in petitioner's suggestion that "indubitable equivalent" in § 361(3) connotes reimbursement for the use value of collateral because the phrase is derived from *In re Murel Holding Corp.*, 75 F.2d 941 (C.A.2 1935), where it bore that meaning. *Murel* involved a proposed reorganization plan that gave the secured creditor interest on his collateral for 10 years, with full payment of the secured principal due at the end of that term; the plan made no provision, however, for amortization of principal or maintenance of the collateral's value during the term. In rejecting the plan, *Murel* used the words "indubitable equivalence" with specific reference not to interest (which was assured), but to the jeopardized principal of the loan:

> "Interest is indeed the common measure of the difference [between payment now and payment 10 years hence], but a creditor who fears the safety of his principal will scarcely be content with that; he wishes to get his money or at least the property. We see no reason to suppose that the statute was intended to deprive him of that in the interest of junior holders, unless by a substitute of the most indubitable equivalence."

Of course *Murel*, like § 1129, proceeds from the premise that in the confirmation context the secured creditor is entitled to present value. But no more from *Murel* than from § 1129 can it be inferred that a similar requirement exists as of the time of the bankruptcy stay. The reorganized debtor is supposed to stand on his own two feet. The debtor in process of reorganization, by contrast, is given many temporary protections against the normal operation of the law.

* * *

B

Petitioner contends that its interpretation is supported by the legislative history of §§ 361 and 362(d)(1), relying almost entirely on statements that "[s]ecured creditors should not be deprived of the benefit of their bargain." H.R.Rep. No. 95–595, at 339; S.Rep. No. 95–989. Such generalizations are inadequate to overcome the plain textual indication in §§ 506 and 362(d)(2) of the Code that Congress did not wish the undersecured creditor to receive interest on his collateral during the term of the stay. If it is at all relevant, the legislative history tends to subvert rather than support petitioner's thesis, since it contains not a hint that § 362(d)(1) entitles the undersecured creditor to postpetition interest. Such a major change in the existing rules would not likely have been made without specific provision in the text of the statute * * * ; it is most improbable that it would have been made without even any mention in the legislative history.

* * *

The Fifth Circuit correctly held that the undersecured petitioner is not entitled to interest on its collateral during the stay to assure adequate protection under § 362(d)(1). Petitioner has never sought relief from the stay under § 362(d)(2) or on any ground other than lack of adequate protection. Accordingly, the judgment of the Fifth Circuit is

Affirmed.

NOTES

1. In *Timbers* the creditor contended that undersecured creditors would suffer "inordinate and extortionate delay" if they were denied compensation for postpetition interest as part of "adequate protection" under § 362(d)(1). In a famous dictum the Court answered that under § 362(d)(2), once the creditor establishes that the debtor has no equity in the collateral, the debtor has the burden of establishing that the collateral

> is "necessary to an effective reorganization." * * * What this requires is not merely a showing that if there is conceivably to be an effective reorganization, this property will be needed for it; but that the property is essential for an effective reorganization *that is in prospect*. This means, as many lower courts, including the en banc court in this case, have properly said, that there must be "a reasonable possibility of a successful reorganization within a reasonable time."

484 U.S. at 375–376.

There had been a split of authority on the meaning of "necessary to an effective reorganization" in § 362(d)(2)(B). Under the majority view (the "feasibility test") the debtor had to show that the property was necessary for a reorganization and that a reorganization was reasonably likely. The opposing view, referred to as the "necessity test," did not require a showing of a reasonable likelihood of a successful reorganization. *See, e.g., In re Koopmans*, 22 B.R. 395 (Bankr.D.Utah 1982). The Court's dictum in *Timbers* quoted above is looked upon as its approval of the feasibility test and it has been followed in the cases. *See, e.g., Matter of Canal Place Limited Partnership*, 921 F.2d 569 (5th Cir. 1991); *In re 8th Street Village Limited Partnership*, 94 B.R. 993, 996 (N.D.Ill.1988) ("even if the discussion of § 362(d)(2) [in *Timbers*] was *dictum*, that discussion of the Supreme Court should not be lightly ignored").

2. Section 361, stating ways in which adequate protection may be provided, was influenced by three decisions of the Second Circuit. *In re Murel Holding Corp.*, 75 F.2d 941 (2d Cir. 1935), which is discussed in *Timbers*, is the source of the term "indubitable equivalent" in § 361(3). *In re Yale Express System, Inc.*, 384 F.2d 990 (2d Cir. 1967), involved the question of how to compensate a creditor, Fruehauf, for the use of trucks and trailers in which it had a security interest. Yale Express, a Chapter X debtor, needed the equipment for its reorganization. The court declined to grant periodic payments to Fruehauf because "to grant rental payments or their equivalent to all such creditors would nullify the reorganization as effectively as granting the petition for reclamation." 384 F.2d at 992. The court concluded: "But to such extent as Fruehauf has been damaged by the use of its property pending the reorganization, it is entitled to equitable consideration in the reorganization plan." 384 F.2d at 992. The court probably meant that, to the extent damaged, Fruehauf would have a right to payment of an administrative expense. The third case, *In re Bermec,* 445 F.2d 367 (2d Cir. 1971), also concerned creditors with a security interest in the trucks of a Chapter X debtor that were necessary to the reorganization of the debtor's leasing business. The court stated that it was "conscious of the deep concern of the * * * secured creditors lest their security depreciate beyond adequate salvage, but we must balance that with the Congressional mandate to encourage attempts at corporate reorganization where there is a reasonable possibility of success." The court denied reclamation but the debtor was required to preserve the status quo by paying to the secured creditors amounts to cover the "economic depreciation" of the equipment it was using.

At a late stage in the legislative process, § 361 had four subsections illustrating forms of adequate protection: (1) periodic cash payments (*Bermec*); (2) additional or replacement liens; (3) administrative expense priority (*Yale Express*); and (4) other relief amounting to the indubitable equivalent of the entity's interest in the property (*Murel*). In the end the administrative priority illustration was deleted, and new subsection (3) provided that an administrative expense priority was not an acceptable means of adequate protection. Even though the administrative expense method of adequate protection espoused by *Yale Express* was rejected in § 361, Congress adopted the concept in § 507(b) by providing a super-priority administrative expense as back-up protection to a secured creditor who had been given an approved method of adequate protection that subsequently turned out not to be adequate in fact.

3. A question that courts have struggled with in trying to interpret § 507(b) (described by Judge Mabey in *In re Callister,* 15 B.R. 521, 526 (Bankr.D.Utah 1981), as "the proverbial prism in the fog") is the tension between § 507(b), which builds us up to expect that the creditor is going to be able to recover any loss it suffers on account of inadequate "adequate protection," and § 503(b) which lets us down by limiting recovery to the benefits conferred on the debtor's estate. Why should the creditor's loss owing to an error in determining that it is adequately protected under § 361 be limited to the estate's gain from having the stay remain in place? What's the connection? As Judge Mabey opines in *Callister*: "The language of 507(b), specially in relation to 503(b), is difficult to plumb. Indeed, 503(b) and 507(b) may be at odds. One is keyed to preserving the estate, the other is designed to protect secured creditors. * * * If 507(b) is faithful to one of these purposes, it may be untrue to the other." 15 B.R. at 528. *In re Carpet Center Leasing Co.*, 991 F.2d 682, *amended on reh'g*, 4 F.3d 940 (11th Cir. 1993), concludes: "Section 507(b) thus implies that an administrative expense claim under § 503(b) will be allowed where adequate protection payments prove insufficient to compensate a secured creditor for the diminution in the value of its collateral." But the court went on to show that the estate was in fact benefited in that case during the Debtor's failed attempt to reorganize. *Ford Motor Credit Company v. Dobbins*, 35 F.3d 860 (4th Cir. 1994), adopting a seemingly contrary approach, holds that a creditor cannot receive a superpriority administrative expense under § 507(b) unless it shows that the debtor's estate actually benefited from the stay. The fact that in *Dobbins* the estate depreciated in value during the period of the stay while the debtor was permitted to seek out a buyer, which it never found, was not enough to entitle the creditor to relief under § 507(b) because it does not qualify under § 503(b)(1)(A) as a legitimate administrative expense. "[W]e interpret the terms "actual" and "necessary" [in § 503(b)] with care and we require an *actual use* by (and therefore an actual benefit to) the estate for a creditor to have a § 503(b) claim." 35 F.3d at 868 n.7 (emphasis in original).

4. Does § 507(b) apply when there is no court order awarding adequate protection to the creditor? A secured creditor may withdraw its motion to lift the stay upon the debtor's undertaking to make periodic payments to compensate the creditor for the use of the collateral. If it turns out that these payments are inadequate to cover the depreciation in the value of the collateral, is the creditor entitled to invoke the super-priority of § 507(b) for the loss? Although prudent creditors can assure their recourse to § 507(b) by getting a court order for the protection to be provided by the debtor under § 361, the majority view appears to be that § 507(b) also applies to private adequate protection agreements for which no court approval has been obtained. Epstein, et al., *Bankruptcy* § 7–13 (1992). With respect to private agreements, some courts scrutinize the agreement to be sure that the creditor was not guilty of inequitable conduct in negotiating the agreement.

5. In the *Eastern Airlines* debacle discussed at p. 576, indenture trustees for secured bondholders failed to timely request adequate protection of their liens against certain airplanes. In defending claims for breach of duty, the indenture trustees asserted that moving for adequate protection would have accomplished nothing—such a motion would not have been granted and its denial would not have amounted to the "provision" of adequate protection that is the predicate for a superiority claim under § 507(b). The airplanes depreciated and the bondholders turned out to be undersecured. The district court judge found that the denial of the bondholders' adequate protection motion would not have been the "provision" of adequate protection and that accordingly no superpriority claim would have arisen under § 507(b). Leaving aside the question of the indenture trustees' liability for breach of duty, the court cannot be right that the § 507(b) superpriority claim in favor of the disappointed secured party can only arise if its motion for protection is granted, can it? *See LNC Investments, Inc. v. First Fidelity Bank*, 247 B.R. 38 (S.D.N.Y.2000), *aff'd sub nom. LNC Investments, Inc. v. National Westminister Bank*, 308 F.3d 169 (2d Cir. 2002).

NOTE: SINGLE ASSET REAL ESTATE

Timbers has been effectively limited with respect to cases involving what § 101 defines as "single asset real estate" ("SARE"). The commercial real estate depression of the 1980s filled the bankruptcy courts of the 1980s and 1990s with many cases in which single asset real estate enterprises struggled to reorganize. *Timbers* is such a case. Typically these are cases in which there is one large secured lender, whose claim is often undersecured, with a few small unsecured trade claims. Later in this chapter, we discuss some of the problems in classifying claims in debtors' plans in these cases. *Greystone*, p. 699. The debtor's objective is usually to hold on to the property for as long as possible in the forlorn hope that a market upturn will produce sufficient rents to enable the debtor to meet its mortgage payments, retain its interest in the property and avoid severe tax consequences associated with the recapture of past tax benefits upon foreclosure or other disposition of the property. Understandably, secured creditors view this conduct as stalling, and, after *Timbers* denied them compensation for the economic loss occasioned by the stay, they sought relief from Congress.

In 1994 § 362(d)(3) was added to provide that, with respect to single asset real estate cases, a court shall grant relief from the stay unless the debtor, within 90 days of entering Chapter 11, can either show that it has filed a plan of reorganization that has "a reasonable possibility of being confirmed within a reasonable time," or that it has commenced monthly payments equal to interest at "current fair market rate on the value of the creditor's interest in the real estate." The significance of § 362(d)(3) was initially limited because SARE was defined in § 101 as projects "having aggregate noncontingent, liquidated secured debts in an amount no more than $4,000,000." The dollar cap left a large number of properties owned by single purpose entities unaffected by the amendment. Research by our colleague Kenneth Klee indicates that the likelihood of successful reorganization in SARE cases varies directly with the debtor's value.

BAPCPA eliminated the $4 million cap from the definition of "single asset real estate." Now the SARE rules apply in large cases. Note however that the definition in § 101 still excludes real estate projects upon which the debtor operates a "real" business—marinas, hotels, farms, golf courses, and so forth. *See, e.g., In re Scotia Pacific Co., LLC*, 508 F.3d 214 (5th Cir. 2007) (debtor holding redwood forests for timbering not SARE); *In re Kemko, Inc.*, 181 B.R. 47 (Bankr.S.D.Ohio1995) (marina not SARE). Moreover, since entities with multiple projects are outside the SARE definition disputes are likely to arise over defining precisely the scope of a single "project" for purposes of application of the SARE rules.

Since 2005, § 362(d)(3) provides that in the event of a dispute over whether the debtor is subject to the SARE rules, monthly payments need not commence until 30 days after the bankruptcy court resolves the dispute. Especially in the larger cases, debtors may well take advantage of these provisions to defer payment. Monthly payments are based on the non-default rate of interest in the mortgage and the current value of the creditors's interest in the collateral. There had been a split of authority under pre-2005 law on whether rents may be a source of required adequate protection payments. Section 362(d)(3)(B) now clarifies that payments may come from pledged rents. Since rents are the only likely source of cash payments in a SARE case, this is a major concession to debtors. While the payments are measured as if they were interest, they are not interest payments. Whether they should be credited to interest or principal probably should depend on whether the property is over or undersecured.

There has been relatively little case law or experience with § 362(d)(3) because of the cap that existed under prior law. It remains to be seen how significant the SARE rules will be in practice in light of this limited experience. But at least in theory, SARE debtors must pay to play, that is stay current on monthly payments to secured creditors. Application of those monthly payments will depend on whether the creditor is over or undersecured. If the creditor is undersecured, under *Timbers*, the payments should be applied to reduce principal. Alternatively, the debtor can avoid foreclosure by getting a confirmable plan on file within 90 days.

D. Operating the Business From Petition to Confirmation

1. Introduction

In order to operate its business the debtor must be able to use its plant, equipment, inventory, and deposit accounts. It must be able to sell its product, pay its employees, and buy necessary services and supplies. But these needs of the debtor collide with the rights of secured creditors in the collateral that the debtor must use, and frustrate the demands of unsecured creditors to be paid out of the unencumbered assets of the estate. In this conflict between the debtor's need to use and sell the property of the estate and the interests of creditors with respect to this property, § 363(c) comes down resoundingly on the side of the debtor. So long as it is acting in the ordinary course of business, a debtor may use all property of the estate, except for cash collateral, and may sell or lease without prior notice and hearing. The debtor in possession, as well as any bankruptcy trustee, in operating the business must still obey otherwise applicable state laws and regulations. 28 U.S.C. § 959(b).

The interests of secured creditors are safeguarded by § 363(e) which instructs the court to prohibit or condition use, sale, or lease of the property of the estate "as is necessary to provide adequate protection of" the secured creditors' interests in this property. The rights of unsecured creditors to share in unencumbered assets find protection, such as it is, in § 1112(b) which allows the court to convert the case to Chapter 7 if there are "substantial and continuing" losses, gross mismanagement or a variety of other defaults by the debtor.

2. Use of Deposit Accounts and Other Cash Collateral

Whether a debtor in possession may continue to use property in which creditors have security interests is usually decided not under § 363 but under § 362 upon the creditor's motion for relief from the automatic stay. As we have seen, under appropriate circumstances relief from a stay may be obtained that allows secured creditors to foreclose against the property outside bankruptcy. § 362(d). The ultimate issue in deciding to lift the stay under § 362(d) and in determining the debtor's right to use the property under § 363(c) may often be the same: whether the debtor has provided the secured creditor "adequate protection." Compare § 362(d)(1) with § 363(e).

Section 363(c)(2) provides a special rule for "cash collateral," which, as defined in § 363(a), includes the cash or cash equivalent proceeds of prepetition collateral including, for example, inventory and accounts. With respect to cash collateral, the burden is on the debtor to obtain court authority to use (i.e. spend) the property rather than on the creditor to seek to limit or condition use based upon its right to adequate protection. Unless the secured creditor consents, the debtor may use cash collateral only if the court, after notice and hearing, authorizes the use first. The court may prohibit or condition the use of cash collateral on the debtor's providing adequate protection of the secured creditor's interest in its collateral.

A business can operate only a few days without cash. It must meet its payroll and buy vital services and supplies or close its doors. Given its often desperate need for cash, a debtor must have its cash collateral strategy worked out when it files. It must either have consents from creditors with security interests in its bank accounts and cash proceeds or have a request to use cash collateral ready to present to the court. Typically the debtor's motion to obtain interim approval of its agreement with its secured creditors over use of cash collateral or otherwise obtain interim court authority to use cash collateral is the first critical issue heard in the case at a "first day" hearing held within a few days of the commencement of the Chapter 11 case on an emergency basis on limited notice. The procedures for obtaining first interim and later final approval of these critical motions is governed by § 363(c)(3), Bankruptcy Rule 4001(b). The bankruptcy courts in several districts (including the District of Delaware and the Southern District of New York which are frequently the venues for the larger chapter 11 cases) have also attempted to indirectly regulate the substance of the relief available in this context, particularly on an interim basis, through elaborate General Orders and Local Rules that require heightened disclosure of controversial provisions in cash collateral agreements. *See, e.g.*, Local Rule 4001-2 (Bankr.D.Del.).

PROBLEM

Debtor Corporation manufactures widgets. Debtor finances its widget business with revolving loans from Bank. Over the past year, Debtor's sales have fallen and it has suffered $1 million in operating losses. Bank's loans are secured by a perfected first priority security interest in all Debtor's accounts, inventory, and general intangibles and their proceeds. Debtor has just filed a petition under Chapter 11. As of the petition date, Debtor's balance sheet reads:

ASSETS

Cash	$ 400,000
Accounts Receivable	5,000,000
Inventory (at cost)	6,500,000
Prepaid Expenses	100,000
Property & Plant (leasehold & improvements net of depreciation)	1,500,000
Equipment (net of depreciation)	2,500,000
Total Assets	**16,000,000**

LIABILITIES & NET WORTH (DEFICIT)

Accounts Payable	$ 7,500,000
Bank Debt	10,000,000
Capitalized Lease Obligations (discounted rent for leasehold expiring 2004)	1,000,000
Total Liabilities	**18,500,000**
Accumulated Capital Deficit	(2,500,000)
Total Liabilities and Deficit	**16,000,000**

Bank has prepared the following liquidation analysis:

DEBTOR CORPORATION—LIQUIDATION ANALYSIS

Cash	$ 400,000
Accounts Receivable (assumes collection costs and uncollectable accounts equal to 30% of receivables book value)	3,500,000
Inventory (assumes finished goods liquidated at 50% of cost and semifinished goods at 30% of cost)	2,600,000
Prepaid Expenses	—
Property, Plant & Equipment (assumes leasehold & improvements forfeited to landlord and equipment liquidated at 50% of book value)	1,250,000
Total Assets Forced Liquidation Value	**7,750,000**

Assume that all Debtor's existing cash, as well any cash that might be generated from collection of prepetition accounts and sales of prepetition inventory will be Bank's cash collateral under § 363(a) and subject to § 363(c)(2).

(a) Representing Bank what sort of conditions on the Debtor's use of cash collateral would you seek? § 363(c)(2)(A) & (e).

(b) Representing Debtor what alternatives do you have to acceding to the Bank's demands? § 363(c)(2)(B).

(c) Representing Debtor's general unsecured creditors what concerns might you have with an agreement between Bank and Debtor over the use of Bank's cash collateral? *See* Bankr.R. 4001(c).

(d) What are the critical legal, factual and business issues that will determine the provisions of any agreement between Bank and Debtor regarding postpetition use of Debtor's cash collateral? §§ 361, 363(e).

3. SALE OR LEASE OF PROPERTY IN ORDINARY COURSE

Under § 363(c)(1) a debtor in possession may sell or lease property of the estate without court approval if done in the ordinary course of the debtor's business. Ordinary course of business is not defined in the Bankruptcy Code. The court in *In re James A. Phillips, Inc.*, 29 B.R. 391, 394 (S.D.N.Y.1983), made the following comment on that term:

> The legislative history of § 363 provides no test or guideline concerning the scope of the "ordinary course of business" standard. * * * Nonetheless, the apparent purpose of requiring notice only where the use of property is extraordinary is to assure interested persons of an opportunity to be heard concerning transactions different from those that might be expected to take place so long as the debtor in possession is allowed to continue normal business operations under § 1107(a) & § 1108. The touchstone of "ordinariness" is thus the interested parties' reasonable expectations of what transactions the debtor in possession is likely to enter in the course of its business. So long as the transactions conducted are consistent with these expectations, creditors have no right to notice and hearing, because their objections to such transactions are likely to relate to the bankrupt's chapter 11 status, not the particular transactions themselves. Where the debtor in possession is merely exercising the privileges of its chapter 11 status, which include the right to operate the bankrupt business, there is no general right to notice and hearing concerning particular transactions. To preclude such transactions, interested parties must apply to the Bankruptcy Court for relief from the stay, § 362(d)(1), or for conversion or dismissal of the chapter 11 petition, § 1112(b).

Hence, a debtor in the business of selling goods or leasing equipment may continue to operate after filing with no notice to creditors or court authorization. The "ordinary course of business" language should allow the debtor to continue selling or leasing on the same terms it employed before filing or on terms generally followed in the business in which the debtor is engaged. Creditors or other parties in interest may request the court to place limits on the debtor's practices. § 363(c)(1).

4. OBTAINING CREDIT

a. Critical Vendors

Certainly obtaining use of cash collateral is necessary but it may not be sufficient. Upon filing in Chapter 11 debtors commonly need additional financing to obtain essential services or goods. Moreover, essential providers of those goods and services may hold prepetition claims and may refuse to deal with the debtor unless payment is made on account of those obligations, threatening the debtor's ability to continue to do business. Accordingly it is common for additional "first day" motions seeking emergency relief to be filed along with the Chapter 11 petition and the motion to obtain use of cash collateral. Generally speaking these motions seek authority to obtain "debtor-in-possession financing" from institutional lenders under § 364, discussed in the following section, and to pay certain prepetition debts to employees, customers, and "critical vendors" on the assumption that without the support of these critical constituents reorganization will be impossible. In the latter case, the debtor is asking the court to approve preferential postpetition payments to those prepetition creditors deemed critical to the continued operations of the debtor's enterprise outside of any plan of reorganization and inconsistently with the statutory priority scheme. While such payments to employees and customers on grounds of necessity frequently go unchallenged, *see infra* Note 4 at p. 613, "critical vendor" payments on account of ordinary prepetition trade claims are more controversial. In the following case, we see that the bankruptcy court treated the motion as routine even though it resulted in full payment of the prepetition debts of more than half of the debtor's vendors, leaving the other vendors only a 10% dividend on their claims mostly paid in reorganized Kmart stock. Judge Easterbrook examines both the legality of postpetition payments to prepetition critical vendors and, assuming payments to prepetition critical vendors are valid, how the determination is made that vendors are critical.

Matter of Kmart Corporation
United States Court of Appeals, Seventh Circuit, 2004.
359 F.3d 866.

- EASTERBROOK, Circuit Judge.

On the first day of its bankruptcy, Kmart sought permission to pay immediately, and in full, the prepetition claims of all "critical vendors." (Technically there are 38 debtors: Kmart Corporation plus 37 of its affiliates and subsidiaries. We call them all Kmart.) The theory behind the request is that some suppliers may be unwilling to do business with a customer that is behind in payment, and, if it cannot obtain the merchandise that its own customers have come to expect, a firm such as Kmart may be unable to carry on, injuring all of its creditors. Full payment to critical vendors thus could in principle make even the disfavored creditors better off: they may not be paid in full, but they will receive a greater portion of their claims than they would if the critical vendors cut off supplies and the business shut down. Putting the proposition in this way implies, however, that the debtor must *prove, and not just allege,* two things: that, but for immediate full payment, vendors *would* cease dealing; and that the business will gain enough from continued transactions with the favored vendors to provide some residual benefit to the remaining, disfavored creditors, or at least leave them no worse off.

Bankruptcy Judge SONDERBY entered a critical-vendors order just as Kmart proposed it, without notifying any disfavored creditors, without receiving any pertinent evidence (the record contains only some sketchy representations by counsel plus unhelpful testimony by Kmart's CEO, who could not speak for the vendors), and without making any finding of fact that the disfavored creditors would gain or come out even. The bankruptcy court's order declared that the relief Kmart requested-open-ended permission to pay any debt to any vendor it deemed "critical" in the exercise of unilateral discretion, provided that the vendor agreed to furnish goods on "customary trade terms" for the next two years-was "in the best interests of the Debtors, their estates and their creditors". The order did not explain why, nor did it contain any legal analysis, though it did cite § 105(a).

Kmart used its authority to pay in full the prepetition debts to 2,330 suppliers, which collectively received about $300 million. This came from the $2 billion in new credit (debtor-in-possession or DIP financing) that the bankruptcy judge authorized, granting the lenders super-priority in postpetition assets and revenues. * * * Another 2,000 or so vendors were not deemed "critical" and were not paid. They and 43,000 additional unsecured creditors eventually received about 10¢ on the dollar, mostly in stock of the reorganized Kmart. Capital Factors, Inc., appealed the critical-vendors order immediately after its entry on January 25, 2002. A little more than 14 months later, after all of the critical vendors had been paid and as Kmart's plan of reorganization was on the verge of approval, District Judge Grady reversed the order authorizing payment. 291 B.R. 818 (N.D.Ill.2003). He concluded that neither § 105(a) nor a "doctrine of necessity" supports the orders.

* * *

Section 105(a) allows a bankruptcy court to "issue any order, process, or judgment that is necessary or appropriate to carry out the provisions of" the Code. This does not create discretion to set aside the Code's rules about priority and distribution; the power conferred by § 105(a) is one to implement rather than override. * * * Every circuit that has considered the question has held that this statute does not allow a bankruptcy judge to authorize full payment of any unsecured debt, unless all unsecured creditors in the class are paid in full. * * * We agree with this view of § 105. "The fact that a [bankruptcy] proceeding is equitable does not give the judge a free-floating discretion to redistribute rights in accordance with his personal views of justice and fairness, however enlightened those views may be." *In re Chicago, Milwaukee, St. Paul & Pacific R.R.*, 791 F.2d 524, 528 (7th Cir. 1986).

A "doctrine of necessity" is just a fancy name for a power to depart from the Code. Although courts in the days before bankruptcy law was codified wielded power to reorder priorities and pay particular creditors in the name of "necessity"—see *Miltenberger v. Logansport Ry.*, 106 U.S. 286 (1882) ; *Fosdick v. Schall*, 99 U.S. 235 (1878)—today it is the Code rather than the norms of nineteenth century railroad reorganizations that must prevail. *Miltenberger* and *Fosdick* predate the first general effort at codification, the Bankruptcy Act of 1898. Today the Bankruptcy Code of 1978 supplies the rules. Congress did not in terms scuttle old common-law doctrines, because it did not need to; the Act curtailed, and then the Code replaced, the entire apparatus. Answers to contemporary issues must be found within the Code (or legislative halls). Older doctrines may survive as glosses on ambiguous language enacted in 1978 or later, but not as freestanding entitlements to trump the text.

So does the Code contain any grant of authority for debtors to prefer some vendors over others? Many sections require equal treatment or specify the details of priority when assets are insufficient to satisfy all claims. E.g., §§ 507, 1122(a), 1123(a)(4). Appellants rely on §§ 363(b), 364(b), and 503 as sources of authority for unequal treatment. Section 364(b) reads: "The court, after notice and a hearing, may authorize the trustee to obtain unsecured credit or to incur unsecured debt other than under subsection (a) of this section, allowable under section 503(b)(1) of this title as an administrative expense." This authorizes the debtor to obtain credit (as Kmart did) but has nothing to say about how the money will be disbursed or about priorities among creditors. * * * Section

503, which deals with administrative expenses, likewise is irrelevant. Pre-filing debts are not administrative expenses; they are the antithesis of administrative expenses. Filing a petition for bankruptcy effectively creates two firms: the debts of the pre-filing entity may be written down so that the post-filing entity may reorganize and continue in business if it has a positive cash flow. Treating pre-filing debts as "administrative" claims against the post-filing entity would impair the ability of bankruptcy law to prevent old debts from sinking a viable firm.

That leaves § 363(b)(1): "The trustee [or debtor in possession], after notice and a hearing, may use, sell, or lease, other than in the ordinary course of business, property of the estate." This is more promising, for satisfaction of a prepetition debt in order to keep "critical" supplies flowing is a use of property other than in the ordinary course of administering an estate in bankruptcy. Capital Factors insists that § 363(b)(1) should be limited to the commencement of capital projects, such as building a new plant, rather than payment of old debts-as paying vendors would be "in the ordinary course" but for the intervening bankruptcy petition. To read § 363(b)(1) broadly, Capital Factors observes, would be to allow a judge to rearrange priorities among creditors (which is what a critical-vendors order effectively does), even though the Supreme Court has cautioned against such a step. Yet what these decisions principally say is that priorities do not change unless a statute supports that step; and if § 363(b)(1) is such a statute, then there is no insuperable problem. If the language is too open-ended, that is a problem for the legislature. Nonetheless, it is prudent to read, and use, § 363(b)(1) to do the least damage possible to priorities established by contract and by other parts of the Bankruptcy Code. We need not decide whether § 363(b)(1) could support payment of some prepetition debts, because *this* order was unsound no matter how one reads § 363(b)(1).

The foundation of a critical-vendors order is the belief that vendors not paid for prior deliveries will refuse to make new ones. Without merchandise to sell, a retailer such as Kmart will fold. If paying the critical vendors would enable a successful reorganization and make even the disfavored creditors better off, then all creditors favor payment whether or not they are designated as "critical." ... For the premise to hold true, however, it is necessary to show not only that the disfavored creditors *will* be as well off with reorganization as with liquidation-a demonstration never attempted in this proceeding-but also that the supposedly critical vendors would have ceased deliveries if old debts were left unpaid while the litigation continued. If vendors will deliver against a promise of current payment, then a reorganization can be achieved, and all unsecured creditors will obtain its benefit, without preferring any of the unsecured creditors.

Some supposedly critical vendors will continue to do business with the debtor because they must. They may, for example, have long term contracts, and the automatic stay prevents these vendors from walking away as long as the debtor pays for new deliveries. See § 362. Fleming Companies, which received the largest critical-vendors payment because it sold Kmart between $70 million and $100 million of groceries and related goods weekly, was one of these. No matter how much Fleming would have liked to dump Kmart, it had no right to do so. It was unnecessary to compensate Fleming for continuing to make deliveries that it was legally required to make. Nor was Fleming likely to walk away even if it had a legal right to do so. Each new delivery produced a profit; as long as Kmart continued to pay for new product, why would any vendor drop the account? That would be a self-inflicted wound. To abjure new profits because of old debts would be to commit the sunk-cost fallacy; well-managed businesses are unlikely to do this. Firms that disdain current profits because of old losses are unlikely to stay in business. They might as well burn money or drop it into the ocean. Again Fleming illustrates the point. When Kmart stopped buying its products after the contract expired, Fleming collapsed (Kmart had accounted for more than 50% of its business) and filed its own bankruptcy petition. Fleming was hardly likely to have quit selling of its own volition, only to expire the sooner.

Doubtless many suppliers fear the prospect of throwing good money after bad. It therefore may be vital to assure them that a debtor will pay for new deliveries on a current basis. Providing that assurance need not, however, entail payment for prepetition transactions. Kmart could have paid cash or its equivalent. (Kmart's CEO told the bankruptcy judge that COD arrangements were not part of Kmart's business plan, as if a litigant's druthers could override the rights of third parties.) Cash on the barrelhead was not the most convenient way, however. Kmart secured a $2 billion line of credit when it entered bankruptcy. Some of that credit could have been used to assure vendors that payment would be forthcoming for all postpetition transactions. The easiest way to do that would have been to put some of the $2 billion behind a standby letter of credit on which the bankruptcy judge could authorize unpaid vendors to draw. That would not have changed the terms on which Kmart and any of its vendors did business; it just would have demonstrated the certainty of payment. If lenders are unwilling to issue such a letter of credit (or if they insist on a letter's short duration), that would be a compelling market signal that reorganization is a poor prospect and that the debtor should be liquidated post haste.

Yet the bankruptcy court did not explore the possibility of using a letter of credit to assure vendors of payment. The court did not find that any firm would have ceased doing business with Kmart if not paid for prepetition deliveries, and the scant record would not have supported such a finding had one been made. The court did not find that discrimination among unsecured creditors was the only way to facilitate a reorganization. It did not find that the disfavored creditors were at least as well off as they would have been had the critical-vendors order not been entered. For all the millions at stake, this proceeding looks much like the Chapter 13 reorganization that produced *In re Crawford,* 324 F.3d 539 (7th Cir. 2003). Crawford had wanted to classify his creditors in a way that would enable him to pay off those debts that would not be discharged, while stiffing the creditors whose debts were dischargeable. We replied that even though classification (and thus unequal treatment) is possible for Chapter 13 proceedings, see § 1322(b), the step would be proper only when the record shows that the classification would produce some benefit for the disfavored creditors. Just so here. Even if § 362(b)(1) allows critical-vendors orders in principle, preferential payments to a class of creditors are proper only if the record shows the prospect of benefit to the other creditors. This record does not, so the critical-vendors order cannot stand.

Affirmed.

NOTES

1. If Kmart had introduced sufficient evidence to support a factual finding that the vendors it sought to pay were critical to the success of the reorganization and would not ship to Kmart without receiving payment on their prepetition debts, is there a statutory basis to permit payment outside of a plan of reorganization?

2. Why would the court delegate to Kmart discretion to determine who was critical enough to receive early payment? Doesn't the bankruptcy court order authorize Kmart to pay vendors it likes or who cooperate with its reorganization effort in full while punishing troublemaking vendors by withholding payment? Would such orders ever be justifiable on grounds of "necessity"?

3. Note that the old caselaw "rule of necessity" doctrine justifying early priority payment of certain unsecured claims evolved in 19th century railroad equity receiverships and was codified with respect to railroad reorganizations in 11 U.S.C. § 1171(b). Does the existence of the special rule of § 1171(b) suggest that Chapter 11 does not authorize such payment in nonrailroad cases?

4. Reorganizing debtors typically seek special treatment for three types of creditors at the beginning of a Chapter 11 case: employees, customers and suppliers. Unless a special payroll was issued on the eve of the bankruptcy filing or employees were paid in advance, the employees of a chapter 11 debtor will be creditors to the extent of wages and benefits earned but not yet paid. Bankruptcy courts routinely allow ordinary course payment of these unsecured claims of continuing employees outside the plan, at least to the extent of the wage and benefit priority provided in § 507(a)(4)&(5). The tacit assumption has long been that essential employees must be paid for their work if there is to be any hope of reorganizing. Similarly, the unsecured claims of customers who have paid in advance or have returns or allowances coming to them are commonly honored in the ordinary course to maintain the reorganizing firm's goodwill, generally with little complaint from the parties or the courts. *Kmart* arises out of a more recent extension of these longstanding practices to trade suppliers that traditionally had to await confirmation of a plan for any payment on their prepetition claims. Predictably, as "critical vendor" status became a known possibility, demands for special treatment mushroomed. After the Seventh Circuit's decision in this case, critical vendor motions have become more narrowly drawn by debtors and more carefully scrutinized by the bankruptcy courts, but the practice has continued. Note that a "critical vendor" may actually be better off with critical vendor status post-bankruptcy than demanding payment prepetition. The prepetition payment might well be an avoidable preference, the critical vendor payment, if authorized, will not be subject to avoidance.

NOTE: RECLAMATION

BAPCPA sharply bolstered the position of trade vendors generally, whether or not such vendors would otherwise qualify for "critical vendor" status. Under state law, sellers of goods to insolvents may have the right to "reclaim" goods. *See e.g.* U.C.C. § 2-702(2). Before 2005 those "reclamation" rights were preserved only to a very limited extent in bankruptcy. After a bankruptcy filing a vendor asserting such a right could preserve it only with respect to goods shipped to the debtor within 10 days of bankruptcy by promptly serving a notice of reclamation under § 546(c). Under the majority view, the reclamation right could be extinguished by a prior lien in the debtor's inventory or by other disposition of the collateral prior to the serving of the notice under § 546(c), and the bankruptcy court would generally substitute an administrative claim for the value of any goods subject to reclamation for the reclamation right itself. Under BAPCPA a general administrative priority is created in favor of vendors for the value of all goods received by the debtor within 20 days of the bankruptcy filing whether or not there is any state law reclamation right with respect to such shipments or any notice served, § 503(b)(9), and reclamation rights are preserved with respect to goods shipped within 45 days of the bankruptcy filing, albeit subject to the rights of secured creditors and good faith purchasers for value in the goods sought to be reclaimed. At least arguably under the current Code the court is no longer authorized to substitute an administrative priority claim for the reclamation right. § 546(c). The new administrative priority for vendors of goods and the expansion of reclamation rights may well overwhelm any limitations on "critical vendor" orders based on the *Kmart Corporation* decision. If most prepetition vendor claims are entitled to administrative priority (that is, are based on shipment of goods received within 20 days of bankruptcy), critical vendor orders matter far less. For a fuller discussion of the rules relating to reclamation, *see* Richard Levin & Alesia Ranney-Marinelli, *The Creeping Repeal of Chapter 11*, 79 Am. Bankr. L. J. 603, 604-608 (2005) and *In re Dana Corp.*, 367 B.R. 409 (Bankr. S.D.N.Y.2007).

b. Rights of Administrative Claimants

In order to operate the business between petition and confirmation, the debtor in possession may have to borrow money or buy goods and services on unsecured credit. Section 364 gives the debtor this power. If the credit is obtained in the ordinary course of the debtor's business, no court approval is required. § 364(a). Otherwise, court approval must be obtained. § 364(b).

Under either § 364(a) or (b) the authorized credit is an administrative expense under § 503(b)(1) giving the creditor a second priority (behind only domestic support obligations) under § 507(a). The administrative expense priority is an incentive to deal with the debtor in possession in a Chapter 11 case. If a simple administrative expense priority will not induce a person to grant credit to the debtor in possession, § 364(c) allows the court to authorize (1) a priority over any or all of the other administrative expenses, (2) a lien on any unencumbered property of the estate, or (3) a junior lien on property already encumbered. If still no one is willing to grant credit, § 364(d) allows the court to authorize a lien senior or equal to an existing lien on property of the estate so long as adequate protection is given to the holder of the existing lien. Thus § 364 allows debtors to award priorities to postpetition lenders in an ascending order of attractiveness.

Suppose the bankruptcy court issues an order authorizing the debtor in possession to incur a debt on the basis of a priority or lien to the creditor under § 364. Other creditors appeal the order. While the appeal is pending, the debt is incurred. If the order is reversed or modified on appeal, what are the rights of the creditor that extended the credit in reliance on the order? Section 364(e) states that reversal or modification of the order does not affect the validity of the debt or the priority or lien granted to the creditor unless the incurring of the debt or the granting of the priority or lien was stayed pending the appeal. A creditor acting in good faith is protected even if the creditor had knowledge of the appeal. The apparent purpose is to stop other creditors from preventing an emergency extension of credit by simply filing an appeal. Without § 364(e), the creditor would have no assurance that the priority or lien would not be taken away by the appellate court after value was given to the debtor in possession.

Under § 364(e) the creditor is usually safe if no stay has been issued at the time it gave value to the debtor in possession, but in *Saybrook*, p. 628, we will see that an exception to § 364(e) may apply in some cases.

Section 364 creates risks as well as opportunities for postpetition creditors. Any creditor who deals with a Chapter 11 debtor and receives anything less than a lien as security is taking a risk that it may not be paid even if the court has approved the grant of credit. But even a postpetition secured lender may find its position substantially changed. It may have to share its collateral with a new lender or may even be subordinated to the lien of the new lender. The prior secured party is entitled only to adequate protection of its lien under § 364(d)(1)(B).

The plight of priority creditors under § 364 is illustrated by the case that follows.

General Electric Credit Corp. v. Levin & Weintraub
United States Court of Appeals, Second Circuit, 1984.
739 F.2d 73.

■ VAN GRAAFEILAND, Circuit Judge:

General Electric Credit Corporation (GECC) appeals from an order of the United States District Court for the Southern District of New York (Broderick, J.) which affirmed a bankruptcy court order awarding appellees interim compensation for professional services and disbursements and directing that payment thereof be made from assets of the debtors in possession in which GECC had a security interest. For reasons hereafter discussed, we reverse.

On July 21, 1981, Flagstaff Foodservice Corporation and its related companies (Flagstaff) filed petitions for reorganization under Chapter 11 of the Bankruptcy Reform Act of 1978 (the Code). As permitted by the Code, the companies continued to operate their businesses as debtors in possession.

GECC had been financing Flagstaff's operations since 1978 by making loans and advances on accounts receivable and inventory. As of July 21, 1981, Flagstaff owed GECC approximately $22 million, which was secured by assets worth $42 million. Shortly before commencement of the Chapter 11 proceedings, Flagstaff's attorneys met with representatives of GECC to obtain immediate short-term financing in order to maintain sufficient cash flow to support Flagstaff's operations. These negotiations resulted in an order which permitted Flagstaff to use up to $750,000 of GECC's collateral for the limited period of five days. Flagstaff's attorneys also prepared an application for a more permanent financing arrangement with GECC. An order (the "Financing Order") was issued by the bankruptcy court authorizing Flagstaff to borrow additional

Chapter 10. Operating the Debtor & Proposing a Plan 617

money from GECC, the loans to be secured by a super-priority interest in all present and future property of the estate. In pertinent part, the order provided that:

> any and all obligations and Liabilities of Borrowers and debtors in possession to GECC (as defined in the Loan Agreement and the Security Agreement) shall have priority in payment over any other debts or obligations now in existence or incurred hereafter of Borrowers and debtors in possession and over all administrative expenses of the kind specified in Sections 503(b) or 507(b) of the Bankruptcy Code, and said Liabilities and obligations of Borrowers and debtors in possession to GECC shall be secured by a first and prior lien on all property of whatever kind and nature of the Borrowers and debtors in possession, and proceeds thereof, until all such obligations and Liabilities of the Borrowers and debtors in possession to GECC shall have been paid in full.

By December 21, 1981, Flagstaff had generated enough income from its accounts receivable to pay all of GECC's prepetition liabilities. However, during the chapter 11 proceedings, GECC advanced an additional $9 million to Flagstaff pursuant to the Financing Order. Despite this infusion of funds, the Flagstaff reorganization ultimately failed. No chapter 11 plan ever was proposed; no bulk purchaser appeared; and no buyer emerged to take over any of the debtor companies. Accordingly, although Flagstaff's indebtedness to GECC had been reduced substantially, the realizable value of the collateral which remained was insufficient to satisfy the unpaid balance.

The issue before us is whether, despite the super-priority lien given GECC in the Financing Order, the bankruptcy court subsequently might direct that interim fees and disbursements of attorneys and accountants be paid from the encumbered collateral. The bankruptcy court awarded [almost $250,000 to attorneys and accountants]. In each instance, the award was 70% of the amount claimed. These awards were affirmed by the district court. We hold this to be error.

Section 364(c)(1) of the Code authorizes the issuance of a financing order, such as the one secured by Flagstaff, which will have "priority over any or all administrative expenses of the kind specified in section 503(b) or 507(b) of [the Code]." Among the administrative expenses listed in section 503(b), and thus reduced in priority by the Flagstaff Financing Order, are "compensation and reimbursement awarded under section 330 of [the Code]." Section 330 is the section that authorizes the bankruptcy court to make awards for services and expenses to attorneys and professional persons representing debtors or creditors' committees, which awards may be made on an interim basis pursuant to section 331.

Looking to the plain language of these sections, as we are bound to do, * * * we conclude that GECC's security interest has priority over appellees' claims for professional services * * *. To the extent that *In re Callister* * * *, relied upon by appellees, is to the contrary, we decline to follow it. Where, as here, the statutory language clearly expresses the congressional intent, a court may not read another meaning into the statute in order to arrive at a result which the court deems preferable. * * * Attorneys may * * * secure a portion of their fee in advance. * * * If attorneys need more encouragement than this to participate in chapter 11 proceedings, Congress, not the courts, must provide it. Under the law as it presently exists, knowledgeable bankruptcy attorneys must be aware that the priority ordinarily given to administration expenses may "prove illusive in light of the various provisions in the Code for competing or super-priorities." 2 Collier on Bankruptcy ¶ 364.02, at 364–6 (15th ed.1984). Section 364(c)(1) is such a provision.

We conclude that the district court erred in holding that section 330 "empower[ed] the Bankruptcy Judge to make awards without reference to any schedule of priorities, without reference to any contractual agreement with respect to those priorities and on the basis of his assessment in the course of supervising the bankruptcy proceeding that if actual and necessary services have been rendered, they should be compensated for." We hold, instead, that any fees payable from GECC's collateral must be for services which were for the benefit of GECC rather than the debtor or other creditors. * * * Provision for such allowance is made in section 506(c), which provides: "The trustee [debtor in possession] may recover from property securing an allowed secured claim the reasonable, necessary costs and expenses of preserving, or disposing of, such property to the extent of any benefit to the holder of such claim." Congress's express intent in enacting section 506(c) was to ensure that, any time a debtor in possession "expends money to provide for the reasonable and necessary cost and expenses of preserving or disposing of a secured creditor's collateral, the * * * debtor in possession is entitled to recover such expenses from the secured party or from the property securing an allowed secured claim held by such party." 124 Cong.Rec. H11089 (daily ed. Sept. 28, 1978) (Statement of Rep. Edwards) * * * * That is not the situation disclosed in appellees' affidavits.

It is undisputed that the chapter proceedings were initiated with the hope of effectuating Flagstaff's rehabilitation and with optimism that this could be accomplished. Indeed, a less forthright purpose in seeking chapter 11 relief might preclude the awarding of any fees at all. * * * Such benefits as might be said to have accrued to GECC from the attempt to reorganize were incidental to the reorganization efforts and did not fall within the intended scope of section 506(c). * * *

As a matter of fact, it requires rather strained logic to conclude that GECC actually benefited from appellees' services. At the outset of the chapter 11 proceedings, GECC's $22 million claim against Flagstaff was secured by $42 million in collateral. When the chapter 11 proceedings aborted, the indebtedness had been reduced to $4 million, but this balance was substantially undercollateralized. In return for this "benefit", appellees now seek to reduce the remaining collateral another quarter of a million dollars to pay their interim fee allowances.

Although GECC requested a hearing in connection with the fee applications, none was held, appellees being content to rest on their written applications. We are as well equipped as the district court to evaluate these documents. * * * Having done so, we are satisfied that, conclusory allegations aside, they do not justify the allowances made herein. For example [one] application, which is not atypical, states that "[a]ll of the professional services for which an interim allowance is being sought were rendered solely on behalf of the Committee in connection with the Debtors' Chapter 11 proceedings, pursuant to the responsibility of Applicant as attorneys for the Committee, and in accordance with the instructions of the Committee, and not on behalf of any other person, as such term is defined in Section 101(30) of the Code." The application then outlines the steps which [the attorneys] took to carry out their duties to the Committee, including, among other things, an extensive court challenge to the "validity, extent and priority" of GECC's security interest. [The attorneys] contend that they "performed services which benefited all creditors of the estate including GECC." The district court, whose opinion contains no reference whatever to section 506(c), adopted this argument, holding that the "context" of the case "necessarily imports" that appellees' services benefited GECC "by preserving or enhancing the bankrupt estate."

Approval of the fee award on this basis was error. Payment of administration expenses traditionally has been the responsibility of the debtor's estate, not its secured creditors. * * * However, if expenses for the preservation or disposition of property are incurred primarily for the benefit of a creditor holding a security interest in the property, such expenses, properly identified, may be charged against the secured creditor. * * * Appellees had the burden of proving that the administration expenses for which they sought recovery were covered by section 506(c). They failed to sustain that burden.

We find no merit in appellees' alternative argument that GECC impliedly consented to bearing the costs of their professional services by employing the chapter 11 procedure to effect the disposition of its collateral. * * * Appellees assert that GECC's active involvement in devising a program aimed at reducing its secured claims justified resorting to the secured assets for payment of the interim fees. Although a secured creditor may consent to bearing the costs of professional fees incurred by a debtor in possession, "such consent is not to be lightly inferred." *In re S & S Indus., Inc.*, 30 B.R. 395, 398 (Bankr.E.D.Mich.1983). "It is not to be inferred merely because a secured creditor cooperates with the debtor." Id. * * * We find no evidence of such consent in appellees' fee application. Moreover, the existence of consent is negatived by the provisions of the Financing Order.

Saddling unconsenting secured creditors with professional fees, such as are sought by appellees, would discourage those creditors from supporting debtors' reorganization efforts. "To hold that mere cooperation with the debtor exposes a secured creditor to payment of all expenses of administration would * * * make it difficult, if not impossible, to induce new lenders to finance a chapter 11 operation." *In re S & S Indus., Inc., supra.* The Financing Order granting GECC a super-priority position was intended to give GECC protection against the very awards made herein. The lack of sufficient unencumbered assets to pay appellees' fees is not an adequate basis for denying GECC its super-priority status. * * * Although it has been well said that "professionals should not be expected to finance the administration of liquidation or reorganization cases," 2 Collier on Bankruptcy ¶ 331.01, at 331–3 (15th ed.1984), "it does not follow that in the event the estate has no unencumbered funds from which to pay such expenses, the secured creditor becomes obligated to satisfy these obligations." *In re S & S Indus., Inc., supra.*

As stated above, GECC, alone, sought a hearing in connection with appellees' fee applications. Appellees have been content to rest on their written submissions. Because those documents do not warrant the allowances made herein, the order of the district court is reversed. The district court is instructed to direct the bankruptcy court to disallow payment of appellees' claims from the assets of the estate in which GECC has a security interest covered by the Financing Order.

NOTES

1. How can Chapter 11 professionals ensure payment of their postbankruptcy fees given the teaching of this case? Is it consistent with the debtor's attorney's professional obligations to insist that some property be left unencumbered to ensure payment of attorneys' fees if the debtor and the postpetition lender are otherwise prepared to agree to a postpetition secured loan needed to fund reorganization? Note that under current practice financing orders commonly approve negotiated "carve outs" that grant priority to a limited amount of professional fees for the debtors' and creditors' committee's professionals. The size and terms of the carve-outs can be one of the most contentious issues in negotiations between the debtor and its lenders.

2. Note that confirmation of the plan requires payment in full of all administrative expenses. § 1129(a)(9). So long as the lender prefers to exit the case through a reorganization plan rather than a Chapter 7 liquidation, administrative claimants retain significant leverage even if they are otherwise "out-of-the-money."

3. The cases are in conflict over the proper standard for determining when expenses benefit the holder of a secured claim. In a proceeding subsequent to *General Electric Credit,* Flagstaff attempted to use proceeds of GECC's collateral to pay payroll taxes incurred during Flagstaff's reorganization. Again the court held that § 506(c) did not permit use of the proceeds for this purpose. *In re Flagstaff Foodservice Corp.,* 762 F.2d 10 (2d Cir. 1985). In so holding the court rejected the assertion that payment of the taxes contributed to the reorganization and increased the going concern value of the assets and announced a narrow view of § 506(c): "The debtor in possession must show that its funds were expended primarily for the benefit of the creditor and that the creditor directly benefited from the expenditure." 762 F.2d at 12. A broader view of § 506(c) was embraced by *In re McKeesport Steel Castings Co.,* 799 F.2d 91 (3d Cir. 1986), in which the court allowed payments to a utility for providing natural gas to the debtor during its attempted reorganization to be paid out of the proceeds of collateral of a secured creditor. The court held that preservation of the going concern value of a business can constitute a benefit to a secured creditor under § 506(c). More recently, the Supreme Court narrowed the scope of recovery under § 506(c) in the following case.

Hartford Underwriters Ins. Co. v. Union Planters Bank, N.A.
Supreme Court of the United States, 2000.
530 U.S. 1.

- Justice SCALIA delivered the opinion of the Court.

In this case, we consider whether § 506(c) allows an administrative claimant of a bankruptcy estate to seek payment of its claim from property encumbered by a secured creditor's lien.

I.

This case arises out of the bankruptcy proceedings of Hen House Interstate, Inc., which at one time owned or operated several restaurants and service stations, as well as an outdoor-advertising firm. On September 5, 1991, Hen House filed a voluntary petition under Chapter 11 of the Bankruptcy Code in the United States Bankruptcy Court for the Eastern District of Missouri. As a Chapter 11 debtor-in-possession, Hen House retained possession of its assets and continued operating its business.

Respondent had been Hen House's primary lender. At the time the Chapter 11 petition was filed, it held a security interest in essentially all of Hen House's real and personal property, securing an indebtedness of over $4 million. After the Chapter 11 proceedings were commenced, it agreed to lend Hen House an additional $300,000 to help finance the reorganization. The Bankruptcy Court entered a financing order approving the loan agreement and authorizing Hen House to use loan proceeds and cash collateral to pay expenses, including workers' compensation expenses.

During the attempted reorganization, Hen House obtained workers' compensation insurance from petitioner Hartford Underwriters (which was unaware of the bankruptcy proceedings). Although the policy required monthly premium payments, Hen House repeatedly failed to make them; Hartford continued to provide insurance nonetheless. The reorganization ultimately failed, and on January 20, 1993, the Bankruptcy Court converted the case to a liquidation proceeding under Chapter 7 and appointed a trustee. At the time of the conversion, Hen House owed Hartford more than $50,000 in unpaid premiums. Hartford learned of Hen House's bankruptcy proceedings after the conversion, in March 1993.

Recognizing that the estate lacked unencumbered funds to pay the premiums, Hartford attempted to charge the premiums to respondent, the secured creditor, by filing with the Bankruptcy Court an "Application for Allowance of Administrative Expense, Pursuant to § 503 and Charge Against Collateral, Pursuant to § 506(c)." The Bankruptcy Court ruled in favor of Hartford, and the District Court and an Eighth Circuit panel affirmed. The Eighth Circuit subsequently granted en banc review, however, and reversed, concluding that § 506(c) could not be invoked by an administrative claimant.

* * *

III.

Because we believe that by far the most natural reading of § 506(c) is that it extends only to the trustee, petitioner's burden of persuading us that the section must be read to allow its use by other parties is "'exceptionally heavy.'" To support its proffered reading, petitioner advances arguments based on pre-Code practice and policy considerations. We address these arguments in turn.

A

Section 506(c)'s provision for the charge of certain administrative expenses against lienholders continues a practice that existed under the Bankruptcy Act of 1898. It was not to be found in the text of the Act, but traced its origin to early cases establishing an equitable principle that where a court has custody of property, costs of administering and preserving the property are a dominant charge. It was the norm that recovery of costs from a secured creditor would be sought by the trustee. Petitioner cites a number of lower court cases, however, in which–without meaningful discussion of the point–parties other than the trustee were permitted to pursue such charges under the Act, sometimes simultaneously with the trustee's pursuit of his own expenses, but sometimes independently. Petitioner also relies on early decisions of this Court allowing individual claimants to seek recovery from secured assets. *Wilson* and *Burnham* involved equity receiverships, and were not only pre-Code, but predate the Bankruptcy Act of 1898 that the Code replaced; while *New York Dock* was a case arising in admiralty.

It is questionable whether these precedents establish a bankruptcy practice sufficiently widespread and well recognized to justify the conclusion of implicit adoption by the Code. We have no confidence that the allowance of recovery from collateral by nontrustees is "the type of 'rule' that... Congress was aware of when enacting the Code." *United States v. Ron Pair Enterprises, Inc.* In any event, while pre-Code practice "informs our understanding of the language of the Code," *id.*, it cannot overcome that language. It is a tool of construction, not an extratextual supplement. We have applied it to the construction of provisions which were "subject to interpretation," *id.*, or contained "ambiguity in the text," *Dewsnup, supra*. "[W]here the meaning of the Bankruptcy Code's text is itself clear... its operation is unimpeded by contrary... prior practice," *BFP v. Resolution Trust Corporation*.

In this case, we think the language of the Code leaves no room for clarification by pre-Code practice. If § 506(c) provided only that certain costs and expenses could be recovered from property securing a secured claim, without specifying any particular party by whom the recovery could be pursued, the case would be akin to those in which we used prior practice to fill in the details of a pre-Code concept that the Code had adopted without elaboration. *See, e.g., United States v. Noland,* 517 U.S. 535, 539 (1996) (looking to pre-Code practice in interpreting Code's reference to "principles of equitable subordination"); *Midlantic Nat. Bank v. New Jersey Dept. of Environmental Protection,* 474 U.S. 494, 501 (1986) (codification of trustee's abandonment power held to incorporate established exceptions). Here, however, it is not the unelaborated concept but only a specifically narrowed one that has been adopted: a rule allowing the charge of costs to secured assets *by the trustee*. Pre–Code practice cannot transform § 506(c)'s reference to "the trustee" to "the trustee and other parties in interest."

B

Finally, petitioner argues that its reading is necessary as a matter of policy, since in some cases the trustee may lack an incentive to pursue payment.

Section 506(c) must be open to nontrustees, petitioner asserts, lest secured creditors enjoy the benefit of services without paying for them. Moreover, ensuring that administrative claimants are compensated may also serve purposes beyond the avoidance of unjust enrichment. To the extent that there are circumstances in which the trustee will not use the section although an individual creditor would,[4] allowing suits by nontrustees could encourage the provision of postpetition services to debtors on more favorable terms, which would in turn further bankruptcy's goals.

Although these concerns may be valid, it is far from clear that the policy implications favor petitioner's position. The class of cases in which § 506(c) would lie dormant without nontrustee use is limited by the fact that the trustee is obliged to seek recovery under the section whenever his fiduciary duties so require. And limiting § 506(c) to the trustee does not leave those who provide goods or services that benefit secured interests without other means of protecting themselves as against other creditors: They may insist on cash payment, or contract directly with the secured creditor, and may be able to obtain superpriority under § 364(c)(1) or a security interest under §§ 364(c)(2), (3) or § 364(d). And of course postpetition creditors can avoid unnecessary losses simply by paying attention to the status of their accounts, a protection which, by all appearances, petitioner neglected here.

On the other side of the ledger, petitioner's reading would itself lead to results that seem undesirable as a matter of policy. In particular, expanding the number of parties who could use § 506(c) would create the possibility of multiple administrative claimants seeking recovery under the section. Each such claim would require inquiry into the necessity of the services at issue and the

---

[4] The frequency with which such circumstances arise may depend in part on who ultimately receives the recovery obtained by a trustee under § 506(c). Petitioner argues that it goes to the party who provided the services that benefited collateral (assuming that party has not already been compensated by the estate). Respondent argues that this reading, like a reading that allows creditors themselves to use § 506(c), upsets the Code's priority scheme by giving administrative claimants who benefit collateral an effective priority over others–allowing, for example, a Chapter 11 administrative creditor (like petitioner) to obtain payment via § 506(c) while Chapter 7 administrative creditors remain unpaid, despite § 726(b)'s provision that Chapter 7 administrative claims have priority over Chapter 11 administrative claims. Thus, respondent asserts that a trustee's recovery under § 506(c) simply goes into the estate to be distributed according to the Code's priority provisions. Since this case does not involve a trustee's recovery under § 506(c), we do not address this question, or the related question whether the trustee may use the provision prior to paying the expenses for which reimbursement is sought, see In re K & L Lakeland, Inc., 128 F.3d 203, 207, 212 (C.A.4 1997).

degree of benefit to the secured creditor. Allowing recovery to be sought at the behest of parties other than the trustee could therefore impair the ability of the bankruptcy court to coordinate proceedings, as well as the ability of the trustee to manage the estate. Indeed, if administrative claimants were free to seek recovery on their own, they could proceed even where the trustee himself planned to do so.[5] Further, where unencumbered assets were scarce, creditors might attempt to use § 506(c) even though their claim to have benefited the secured creditor was quite weak. The possibility of being targeted for such claims by various administrative claimants could make secured creditors less willing to provide postpetition financing.

In any event, we do not sit to assess the relative merits of different approaches to various bankruptcy problems. It suffices that the natural reading of the text produces the result we announce. Achieving a better policy outcome—if what petitioner urges is that—is a task for Congress, not the courts.

* * *

We have considered the other points urged by petitioner and find them to be without merit. We conclude that 11 U.S.C. § 506(c) does not provide an administrative claimant an independent right to use the section to seek payment of its claim. The judgment of the Eighth Circuit is affirmed.

NOTE

Following the Supreme Court's decision in *Hartford Underwriters*, parties began to challenge the bankruptcy courts' power to authorize creditors' committees to prosecute estate causes of action, the question specifically reserved in footnote 5 of the decision. In *Official Committee of Unsecured Creditors of Cybergenics Corp. v. Chinery*, 330 F.3d 548 (3d Cir. *en banc* 2003), the Third

---

[5] We do not address whether a bankruptcy court can allow other interested parties to act in the trustee's stead in pursuing recovery under § 506(c). *Amici* American Insurance Association and National Union Fire Insurance Co. draw our attention to the practice of some courts of allowing creditors or creditors' committees a derivative right to bring avoidance actions when the trustee refuses to do so, even though the applicable Code provisions, see 11 U.S.C. §§ 544, 545, 547(b), 548(a), 549(a), mention only the trustee. See, *e.g., In re Gibson Group, Inc.*, 66 F.3d 1436, 1438 (C.A.6 1995). Whatever the validity of that practice, it has no analogous application here, since petitioner did not ask the trustee to pursue payment under § 506(c) and did not seek permission from the Bankruptcy Court to take such action in the trustee's stead. Petitioner asserted an independent right to use § 506(c), which is what we reject today. Cf. *In re Xonics Photochemical, Inc.*, 841 F.2d 198, 202-203 (C.A.7 1988) (holding that creditor had no right to bring avoidance action independently, but noting that it might have been able to seek to bring derivative suit).

Circuit, reversing an earlier panel decision, found that the Code did provide bankruptcy courts authority to designate official committees as estate representatives for the purpose of prosecuting lawsuits, relying upon §§ 105(a), 503(b) & 1103(c)(5) as well as pre-Code precedent and practice. *See also* Daniel J. Bussel, *Creditors' Committees as Estate Representatives in Bankruptcy Litigation*, 10 Stan. J.L. Bus. & Fin. 28 (2004).

c. Rights of Prepetition Creditors

Citing Woody Allen, the court in *In re Omegas Group, Inc.*, 16 F.3d 1443, 1445 (6th Cir. 1994), observed: "Understandably, creditors of bankrupt debtors often feel like restaurant patrons who not only hate the food, but think the portions are too small."

If the position of postpetition unsecured creditors under Chapter 11 is sometimes risky, that of prepetition unsecured creditors is always speculative and often bleak. The debtor's initial choice of Chapter 11—a choice prepetition creditors have virtually no power to influence—dictates that prepetition creditors will receive no payment on claims unless and until the debtor's reorganization plan is confirmed and becomes effective, months or years later. They will earn no interest on claims during this period. § 502(b)(2). Their right to share in a prompt Chapter 7 liquidation is taken away and in its stead they are given the hope, often unrealized, that the debtor will keep the business afloat and be able someday to pay part or all of the time-reduced claims. If the debtor fails in Chapter 11, liquidation in Chapter 7 usually follows, but the amount paid to prepetition creditors may be drastically less than the amount that would have been paid had the debtor originally filed in Chapter 7.

One of the principal reasons for a reduction in the liquidation value of a prepetition unsecured claim in Chapter 11 is the tendency of administrative expenses to balloon during the interim period during which the debtor is struggling to reorganize its business. Although prepetition creditors may eventually get to vote on the debtor's plan of reorganization, they have no effective voice in determining how much credit is approved as administrative expense having priority over their claims. They must sit back and wait while the court gives the debtor its run at a successful reorganization. Meanwhile prepetition creditors behold a growing number of postpetition creditors stepping ahead in line: lawyers, accountants, appraisers, examiners, trade creditors, tax collectors, and lenders.

Are there limits beyond which courts should not go in authorizing debtors to acquire postpetition credit? One restraint, is the fact that a plan cannot be confirmed unless all administrative expenses, which would include virtually all postpetition credit, can be paid in cash upon the effective date of the plan. § 1129(a)(9)(A). Before administrative expenses escalate to the point at which it is improbable that the debtor will be able to pay them in full and still carry out the plan, prepetition creditors should ask the court to convert the case to Chapter 7 or otherwise restrict the operation of the business by the debtor. The court should not allow further operation in Chapter 11 unless there is a reasonable probability of a successful reorganization and "administratively insolvent" debtors cannot reorganize.

Prepetition secured lenders are of course in a better position. But remarkably even a properly perfected and nonavoidable lien may be subordinated to postpetition lending under § 364(d), subject to the provision of "adequate protection" to the prepetition secured lenders. In *In re Swedeland Development Group, Inc.*, 16 F.3d 552 (3d Cir. 1994), the debtor was developing a residential community and adjacent golf course. By the time of the debtor's bankruptcy, it had borrowed $36 million from Carteret Federal Savings Bank, but its partly developed golf course and subdivision was worth only about $18 million. The debtor then sought to borrow an additional $4 million under § 364(d) to complete construction of 900 residences, to be secured by a first mortgage against the property senior to Carteret's prior perfected undersecured prepetition mortgage. The bankruptcy court approved the proposed § 364(d) credit on the ground that the likely increase in value in the property on account of the completion of the units meant that Carteret's subordinated lien would be adequately protected. As the completed residences were sold, Carteret would receive partial repayments from the proceeds, albeit at a lower rate than that contemplated by Carteret's original loan. The bankruptcy court found that, over time, if the debtor met its projections, that Carteret would eventually be repaid in full. The Third Circuit rejected the bankruptcy court's approval of this postpetitition financing arrangement:

> We cannot close this portion of our opinion without pointing out that what happened here is quite disturbing. There, of course, is no doubt that the policy underlying Chapter 11 is important. Nevertheless, Congress did not contemplate that a creditor could find its priority position eroded and, as compensation for the erosion, be offered an opportunity to recoup dependent upon the success of a business with inherently risky prospects. We trust that in the future bankruptcy judges in this circuit will require that adequate protection be demonstrated more tangibly than was done in this case.

16 F.3d at 567.

Nevertheless, the superpriority lien of the postpetition lender was held to be valid to the extent of monies that had already been advanced in reliance on the bankruptcy court's order approving the credit. § 364(e).

Section 364(d) embodies a paradox. It provides that "priming" liens that subordinate prepetition secured lenders are permitted only when two conditions are satisfied: first, that money necessary to fund reorganization is not otherwise available; and, second, that the subordinated prepetition lenders be "adequately protected." How can both conditions be simultaneously satisfied? If the protections being offered the prepetition lender are truly adequate, why aren't those same protections sufficient to induce a postpetition lender to provide credit without subordinating the prepetition lender?

d. Cross–Collateralization

Suppose a creditor with a prepetition claim is asked to grant postpetition credit. The creditor is willing so long as the creditor is given a lien on assets of the estate that secures not only payment of the postpetition credit but the prepetition claim as well. Is such a lien permissible? To the extent the lien secures payment of the prepetition claim, the granting of the lien amounts to a postpetition preference. The next case discusses the issue.

Matter of Saybrook Manufacturing Co.
United States Court of Appeals, Eleventh Circuit, 1992.
963 F.2d 1490.

■ COX, Circuit Judge:

Seymour and Jeffrey Shapiro, unsecured creditors, objected to the bankruptcy court's authorization for the Chapter 11 debtors to "cross–collateralize" their prepetition debt with unencumbered property from the bankruptcy estate. The bankruptcy court overruled the objection and also refused to grant a stay of its order pending appeal. The Shapiros appealed to the district court, which dismissed the case as moot under section 364(e) of the Bankruptcy Code because the Shapiros had failed to obtain a stay. We conclude that this appeal is not moot and that cross–collateralization is not authorized under the Bankruptcy Code. Accordingly, we reverse and remand.

I. Facts and procedural history

Saybrook Manufacturing Co., Inc., and related companies (the "debtors"), initiated proceedings seeking relief under Chapter 11 of the Bankruptcy Code on December 22, 1988. On December 23, 1988, the debtors filed a motion for the use of cash collateral and for authorization to incur secured debt. The bankruptcy court entered an emergency financing order that same day. At the time the bankruptcy petition was filed, the debtors owed Manufacturers Hanover approximately $34 million. The value of the collateral for this debt, however, was less than $10 million. Pursuant to the order, Manufacturers Hanover agreed to lend the debtors an additional $3 million to facilitate their reorganization. In exchange, Manufacturers Hanover received a security interest in all of the debtors' property—both property owned prior to filing the bankruptcy petition and that which was acquired subsequently. This security interest not only protected the $3 million of postpetition credit but also secured Manufacturers Hanover's $34 million prepetition debt.

This arrangement enhanced Manufacturers Hanover's position vis-a-vis other unsecured creditors, such as the Shapiros, in the event of liquidation. Because Manufacturers Hanover's prepetition debt was undersecured by approximately $24 million, it originally would have shared in a pro rata distribution of the debtors' unencumbered assets along with the other unsecured creditors. Under the financing order, however, Manufacturers Hanover's prepetition debt became fully secured by all of the debtors' assets. If the bankruptcy estate were liquidated, Manufacturers Hanover's entire debt—$34 million prepetition and $3 million postpetition—would have to be paid in full before any funds could be distributed to the remaining unsecured creditors.

Securing prepetition debt with pre-and postpetition collateral as part of a postpetition financing arrangement is known as cross–collateralization. The Second Circuit aptly defined cross–collateralization as follows:

> [I]n return for making new loans to a debtor in possession under Chapter XI, a financing institution obtains a security interest on all assets of the debtor, both those existing at the date of the order and those created in the course of the Chapter XI proceeding, not only for the new loans, the propriety of which is not contested, but [also] for existing indebtedness to it.

In re Texlon Corp., 596 F.2d 1092, 1094 (2d Cir. 1979).

Because the Second Circuit was the first appellate court to describe this practice in *Texlon*, it is sometimes referred to as *Texlon*-type cross–collateralization. Another form of cross–collateralization involves securing postpetition debt with prepetition collateral. * * * This form of non-*Texlon*-type cross–collateralization is not at issue in this appeal. * * * The Shapiros challenge only the cross–collateralization of the lenders' prepetition debt, not the propriety of collateralizing the postpetition debt.

The Shapiros filed a number of objections to the bankruptcy court's order on January 13, 1989. After a hearing, the bankruptcy court overruled the objections. The Shapiros then filed a notice of appeal and a request for the bankruptcy court to stay its financing order pending appeal. The bankruptcy court denied the request for a stay on February 23, 1989.

The Shapiros subsequently moved the district court to stay the bankruptcy court's financing order pending appeal; the court denied the motion on March

7, 1989. On May 20, 1989, the district court dismissed the Shapiros' appeal as moot under 11 U.S.C. § 364(e) because the Shapiros had failed to obtain a stay of the financing order pending appeal, rejecting the argument that cross–collateralization is contrary to the Code. The Shapiros then appealed to this court.

II. Issues on appeal

* * *

A. Mootness

We begin by addressing the lenders' claim that this appeal is moot under section 364(e) of the Bankruptcy Code. Section 364(e) provides that:

> The reversal or modification on appeal of an authorization under this section to obtain credit or incur debt, or of a grant under this section of a priority or a lien, does not affect the validity of any debt so incurred, or any priority or lien so granted, to an entity that extended such credit in good faith, whether or not such entity knew of the pendency of the appeal, unless such authorization and the incurring of such debt, or the granting of such priority or lien, were stayed pending appeal.

The purpose of this provision is to encourage the extension of credit to debtors in bankruptcy by eliminating the risk that any lien securing the loan will be modified on appeal.

The lenders suggest that we assume cross–collateralization is authorized under section 364 and then conclude the Shapiros' appeal is moot under section 364(e). This is similar to the approach adopted by the Ninth Circuit in *In re Adams Apple, Inc.*, 829 F.2d 1484 (9th Cir. 1987). That court held that cross–collateralization was "authorized" under section 364 for the purposes of section 364(e) mootness but declined to decide whether cross–collateralization was illegal per se under the Bankruptcy Code. * * * See also *In re Ellingsen MacLean Oil Co.*, 834 F.2d 599 (6th Cir. 1987) * * *.

We reject the reasoning of *Adams Apple* and *Ellingsen* because they "put the cart before the horse." By its own terms, section 364(e) is only applicable if the challenged lien or priority was authorized under section 364. See Charles J. Tabb, Lender Preference Clauses and the Destruction of Appealability and Finality: Resolving a Chapter 11 Dilemma, 50 Ohio St.L.J. 109, 116–35 (1989) (criticizing *Adams Apple, Ellingsen,* and the practice of shielding cross–collateralization from appellate review via mootness under section 364(e)); see also *Ellingsen,* 834 F.2d at 607 (Merritt, dissenting) (arguing that section 364(e) was not designed to prohibit creditors from challenging prepetition matters and that "[l]enders should not be permitted to use their leverage in making emergency loans in order to insulate their prepetition claims from attack"). We cannot determine if this appeal is moot under section 364(e) until we decide the central issue in this appeal—whether cross–collateralization is authorized under section 364. Accordingly, we now turn to that question.

B. Cross–Collateralization and Section 364

Cross–collateralization is an extremely controversial form of Chapter 11 financing. Nevertheless, the practice has been approved by several bankruptcy courts. *See, e.g., In re Vanguard Diversified, Inc.*, 31 B.R. 364 (Bankr.E.D.N.Y.1983) * * *. Even the courts that have allowed cross–collateralization, however, were generally reluctant to do so. * * *

In *Vanguard*, for example, the bankruptcy court noted that cross–collateralization is "a disfavored means of financing" that should only be used as a last resort. *Vanguard*, 31 B.R. at 366. In order to obtain a financing order including cross–collateralization, the court required the debtor to demonstrate (1) that its business operations would fail absent the proposed financing, (2) that it is unable to obtain alternative financing on acceptable terms, (3) that the proposed lender will not accept less preferential terms, and (4) that the proposed financing is in the general creditor body's best interest. This four-part test has since been adopted by other bankruptcy courts which permit cross–collateralization. * * *

The issue of whether the Bankruptcy Code authorizes cross–collateralization is a question of first impression in this court. Indeed, it is essentially a question of first impression before any court of appeals. Neither the lenders' brief nor our own research has produced a single appellate decision which either authorizes or prohibits the practice.

* * *

Cross–collateralization is not specifically mentioned in the Bankruptcy Code. * * * We conclude that cross–collateralization is inconsistent with bankruptcy law for two reasons. First, cross–collateralization is not authorized as a method of postpetition financing under section 364. Second, cross–collateralization is beyond the scope of the bankruptcy court's inherent equitable power because it is directly contrary to the fundamental priority scheme of the Bankruptcy Code. See generally Charles J. Tabb, A Critical Reappraisal of Cross–Collateralization in Bankruptcy, 60 S.Cal.L.Rev. 109 (1986).

Section 364 authorizes Chapter 11 debtors to obtain secured credit and incur secured debt as part of their reorganization. * * * By their express terms, sections 364(c) & (d) apply only to future—i.e., postpetition—extensions of credit. They do not authorize the granting of liens to secure prepetition loans.

* * *

Given that cross-collateralization is not authorized by section 364, we now turn to the lenders' argument that bankruptcy courts may permit the practice under their general equitable power. Bankruptcy courts are indeed courts of equity, * * * § 105(a), and they have the power to adjust claims to avoid injustice or unfairness. * * * This equitable power, however, is not unlimited.

> [T]he bankruptcy court has the ability to deviate from the rules of priority and distribution set forth in the Code in the interest of justice and equity. The Court cannot use this flexibility, however, merely to establish a ranking of priorities within priorities. Furthermore, absent the existence of some type of inequitable conduct on the part of the claimant, which results in injury to the creditors of the bankrupt or an unfair advantage to the claimant, the court cannot subordinate a claim to claims within the same class.

In re FCX, Inc., 60 B.R. 405, 409 (E.D.N.C.1986) (citations omitted).

Section 507 of the Bankruptcy Code fixes the priority order of claims and expenses against the bankruptcy estate. § 507. Creditors within a given class are to be treated equally, and bankruptcy courts may not create their own rules of superpriority within a single class. 3 Collier on Bankruptcy § 507.02[2] (15th ed.1992). Cross-collateralization, however, does exactly that. As a result of this practice, postpetition lenders' unsecured prepetition claims are given priority over all other unsecured prepetition claims. The Ninth Circuit recognized that "[t]here is no... applicable provision in the Bankruptcy Code authorizing the debtor to pay certain prepetition unsecured claims in full while others remain unpaid. To do so would impermissibly violate the priority scheme of the Bankruptcy Code." *In re Sun Runner*, 945 F.2d 1089, 1094 (9th Cir. 1991). * * *

The Second Circuit has noted that, if cross-collateralization were initiated by the bankrupt while insolvent and shortly before filing a petition, the arrangement "would have constituted a voidable preference." *Texlon,* 596 F.2d at 1097. The fundamental nature of this practice is not changed by the fact that it is sanctioned by the bankruptcy court. We disagree with the district court's conclusion that, while cross-collateralization may violate some policies of bankruptcy law, it is consistent with the general purpose of Chapter 11 to help businesses reorganize and become profitable. Rehabilitation is certainly the primary purpose of Chapter 11. This end, however, does not justify the use of any means. Cross-collateralization is directly inconsistent with the priority scheme of the Bankruptcy Code. Accordingly, the practice may not be approved by the bankruptcy court under its equitable authority.

VI. Conclusion

Cross-collateralization is not authorized by section 364. Section 364(e), therefore, is not applicable and this appeal is not moot. Because *Texlon*-type cross–collateralization is not explicitly authorized by the Bankruptcy Code and is contrary to the basic priority structure of the Code, we hold that it is an impermissible means of obtaining postpetition financing. The judgment of the district court is *Reversed* and the case is *Remanded* for proceedings not inconsistent with this opinion.

NOTE ON ROLL-UPS

Judicial resistance to *Texlon*-style cross–collateralization has resulted in increasing reliance on "roll-ups" which indirectly attempt to achieve many of the advantages of cross–collateralization (from the perspective of the secured creditor). In its original incarnation, the roll-up typically involved a senior secured creditor that had extended working capital loans pursuant to a revolving credit agreement secured by accounts receivable and inventory. Revolving credit lines involve daily repayments and advances as receivables are collected and new advances to fund working capital needs are made. Assuming that the secured creditor is willing to advance fresh working capital on the same basis postpetition, pursuant to a roll-up, the parties (subject to court approval) may agree that repayments are credited to prepetition claims while new advances are denominated post-petitition loans. Each day more of the outstanding prepetition debt is repaid and the postpetition loan balance grows, until over time the secured creditor's prepetition claims are entirely "rolled-up" into postpetition claims. See *In re General Oil Distributors, Inc.*, 20 B.R. 873 (Bankr.E.D.N.Y. 1982). This sort of roll-up is often justified as simplifying the task of accounting for and administering a revolving credit line by obviating the problems associated with segregating prepetition and postpetition receivables. But unlike prepetition claims which may be subject to avoidance or restructuring, postpetition loans are administrative liabilities that must be repaid in full in cash on confirmation and so the "roll-up" is more than merely an accounting convention: it improves the legal position of the (albeit generally fully secured) prepetition creditor by converting its debt into postpetition loans that are immune from avoidance and restructuring. This form of roll-up is commonly described as a "creeping roll" because it occurs slowly over time. Having grown accustomed to the advantages of the "creeping roll," more aggressive secured creditors have sought court approval of roll-ups that completely refinance prepetition secured claims early in the case rather than creep over time. Moreover secured creditors with term loans have also sought the advantage of roll-ups by offering postpetition financing on condition that their prepetition secured term loans also be refinanced into unavoidable postpetition loans similarly immune to restructuring—even though daily advances and repayments were never contemplated by their prepetition loan documents. Courts have sometimes approved such roll-ups subject to "clawback" provisions or "challenge rights" that preserve avoidance claims but nevertheless otherwise limit the ability of the debtor to restructure the indebtedness under a reorganization plan. Roll-ups in proposed postpetition financing arrangements are typically subject to heightened disclosure under applicable Local Rules and General Orders. *See e.g.*, Local Rule 4001-2 (Bankr.D.Del.).

5. SALES NOT IN ORDINARY COURSE: PARTIAL LIQUIDATION

If a debtor in possession wants to sell or lease property of the estate "other than in the ordinary course of business" it can do so "after notice and a hearing." §§ 102(1)(b), 363(b)(1). Under this provision and § 363(c)(1) a distinction is made between ordinary dispositions of property that are part of normal day-to-day business transactions that the debtor in possession may engage in without court supervision and those that are so unusual that judicial oversight is justified to protect the interests of creditors whose interests might be adversely affected by the transaction.

Under § 1123(b)(4), a Chapter 11 plan may provide for liquidation of all or part of the estate, but the plan is subject to acceptance by holders of claims and interests and confirmation by the bankruptcy court. § 1126 and § 1129. Is there a conflict with the voting and confirmation provisions if a sale of a major part of the assets of the estate is permitted under § 363(b)(1)? That question is considered in *Lionel* which follows.

In re Lionel Corp.
United States Court of Appeals, Second Circuit, 1983.
722 F.2d 1063.

■ CARDAMONE, Circuit Judge:

This expedited appeal is from an order of United States District Judge Dudley B. Bonsal dated September 7, 1983, approving an order entered earlier that day by the United States Bankruptcy Court for the Southern District of New York (Ryan, J.). The order authorized the sale by Lionel Corporation, a Chapter 11 debtor in possession, of its 82% common stock holding in Dale Electronics, Inc. to Peabody International Corporation for $50 million.

I. Facts

On February 19, 1982 the Lionel Corporation—toy train manufacturer of childhood memory—and two of its subsidiaries, Lionel Leisure, Inc. and Consolidated Toy Company, filed joint petitions for reorganization under Chapter 11 of the Bankruptcy Code. Resort to Chapter 11 was precipitated by losses totaling $22.5 million that Lionel incurred in its toy retailing operation during the two year period ending December 1982.

There are 7.1 million shares of common stock of Lionel held by 10,000 investors. Its consolidated assets and liabilities as of March 31, 1983 were $168.7 million and $191.5 million, respectively, reflecting a negative net worth of nearly $23 million. Total sales for 1981 and 1982 were $295.1 million and $338.6 million. Lionel's creditors hold approximately $135.6 million in prepetition claims, and they are represented in the ongoing bankruptcy proceedings by an Official Creditors' Committee whose 13 members hold $80 million of those claims. The remaining $55 million is scattered among thousands of small creditors.

Lionel continues to operate its businesses and manage its properties pursuant to §§ 1107–1108, primarily through its wholly-owned subsidiary, Leisure. Leisure operates Lionel's presently owned 56 specialty retail stores, which include a number of stores formerly managed by Lionel's other subsidiary, Consolidated Toy. In addition to the stock of Leisure and Consolidated Toy, Lionel has other assets such as the right to receive royalty payments relating to the manufacture of toy trains.

Lionel's most important asset and the subject of this proceeding is its ownership of 82% of the common stock of Dale, a corporation engaged in the manufacture of electronic components. Dale is not a party to the Lionel bankruptcy proceeding. Public investors own the remaining 18 percent of Dale's common stock, which is listed on the American Stock Exchange. Its balance sheet reflects assets and liabilities as of March 31, 1983 of $57.8 million and $29.8 million, respectively, resulting in shareholders equity of approximately $28.0 million. Lionel's stock investment in Dale represents approximately 34 percent of Lionel's consolidated assets, and its interest in Dale is Lionel's most valuable single asset. Unlike Lionel's toy retailing operation, Dale is profitable. For the same two-year period ending in December 1982 during which Lionel had incurred its substantial losses, Dale had an aggregate operating profit of $18.8 million.

On June 14, 1983 Lionel filed an application under section 363(b) seeking bankruptcy court authorization to sell its 82% interest in Dale to Acme–Cleveland Corporation for $43 million in cash. Four days later the debtor filed a plan of reorganization conditioned upon a sale of Dale with the proceeds to be distributed to creditors. Certain issues of the reorganization remain unresolved, and negotiations are continuing; however, a solicitation of votes on the plan has not yet begun. On September 7, 1983, following the Securities and Exchange Commission's July 15 filing of objections to the sale, Bankruptcy Judge RYAN held a hearing on Lionel's application. At the hearing, Peabody emerged as the successful of three bidders with an offer of $50 million for Lionel's interest in Dale.

The Chief Executive Officer of Lionel and a Vice–President of Salomon Brothers were the only witnesses produced and both testified in support of the application. Their testimony established that while the price paid for the stock was "fair," Dale is not an asset "that is wasting away in any sense." Lionel's Chief Executive Officer stated that there was no reason why the sale of Dale stock could not be accomplished as part of the reorganization plan, and that the sole reason for Lionel's application to sell was the Creditors' Committee's insistence upon it. The creditors wanted to turn this asset of Lionel into a "pot of cash," to provide the bulk of the $70 million required to repay creditors under the proposed plan of reorganization.

In confirming the sale, Judge Ryan made no formal findings of fact. He simply noted that cause to sell was sufficiently shown by the Creditors' Committee's insistence upon it. Judge Ryan further found cause—presumably from long experience—based upon his own opinion that a present failure to confirm would set the entire reorganization process back a year or longer while the parties attempted to restructure it.

The Committee of Equity Security Holders, statutory representatives of the 10,000 public shareholders of Lionel, appealed this order claiming that the sale, prior to approval of a reorganization plan, deprives the equity holders of the Bankruptcy Code's safeguards of disclosure, solicitation and acceptance and divests the debtor of a dominant and profitable asset which could serve as a cornerstone for a sound plan. The SEC also appeared and objected to the sale in the bankruptcy court and supports the Equity Committee's appeal, claiming that approval of the sale side-steps the Code's requirement for informed suffrage which is at the heart of Chapter 11.

The Creditors' Committee favors the sale because it believes it is in the best interests of Lionel and because the sale is expressly authorized by § 363(b) of the Code. Lionel tells us that its ownership of Dale, a non-operating asset, is held for investment purposes only and that its sale will provide the estate with the large block of the cash needed to fund its plan of reorganization.

From the oral arguments and briefs we gather that the Equity Committee believes that Chapter 11 has cleared the reorganization field of major pre-plan sales—somewhat like the way Minerva routed Mars—relegating § 363(b) to be used only in emergencies. The Creditors' Committee counters that a bankruptcy judge should have absolute freedom under § 363(b) to do as he thinks best. Neither of these arguments is wholly persuasive. Here, as in so many similar cases, we must avoid the extremes, for the policies underlying the Bankruptcy Reform Act of 1978 support a middle ground—one which gives the bankruptcy judge considerable discretion yet requires him to articulate sound business justifications for his decisions.

II. Discussion

The issue now before this Court is to what extent Chapter 11 permits a bankruptcy judge to authorize the sale of an important asset of the bankrupt's estate, out of the ordinary course of business and prior to acceptance and outside of any plan of reorganization. Section 363(b), the focal point of our analysis, provides that "[t]he trustee, after notice and a hearing, may use, sell, or lease, other than in the ordinary course of business, property of the estate."

On its face, section 363(b) appears to permit disposition of any property of the estate of a corporate debtor without resort to the statutory safeguards embodied in Chapter 11 of the Bankruptcy Code. Yet, analysis of the statute's history and over seven decades of case law convinces us that such a literal reading of section 363(b) would unnecessarily violate the congressional scheme for corporate reorganizations. * * *

B. Chandler Act of 1938—The "Upon Cause Shown" Standard

Section 116(3) of the 1938 Act, which was the immediate predecessor of § 363(b), was originally enacted as section 77B(c) in 1937. Section 116(3) provided:

> "Upon the approval of a petition, the judge may, in addition to the jurisdiction, powers and duties hereinabove and elsewhere in this chapter conferred and imposed upon him and the court * * * (3) authorize a receiver or a trustee or a debtor in possession, upon such notice as the judge may prescribe and upon cause shown, to lease or sell any property of the debtor, whether real or personal, upon such terms and conditions as the judge may approve."

This section applied in Chapter X proceedings, and a similar provision, § 313(2), pertained to Chapter XI cases. Thus, when reorganization became part of the bankruptcy law, the long established administrative powers of the court to sell a debtor's property prior to adjudication were extended to cover reorganizations with a debtor in possession under Chapter XI pursuant to § 313(2), as well as a trustee in control under Chapter X pursuant to § 116(3). These sections, as their predecessors, were designed to handle leases or sales required during the time lag between the filing of a petition for reorganization and the date when the plan was approved.[2]

---

[2] A letter from a district judge in California addressed to the House Committee holding hearings on these sections illustrates one of the reasons for the addition in 1937 of rules permitting pre-confirmation sales. The letter recounted the difficulty the writer had in a reorganization involving a California land company whose business consisted of selling real property. Because of the lack of clear authority to sell, title companies refused to certify title

The Rules of Bankruptcy Procedure applicable in Chapters X and XI, the Act's reorganization procedures, provided for a sale of all or part of a bankrupt's property after application to the court and "upon cause shown." * * * Despite the provisions of this Rule, the "perishable" concept, expressed in the view that a pre-confirmation or pre-adjudication sale was the exception and not the rule, persisted. As one commentator stated, "[o]rdinarily, in the absence of perishable goods, or depreciation of assets, or actual jeopardy of the estate, a sale will not be ordered, particularly prior to adjudication." 1 Collier on Bankruptcy ¶ 2.28(3) (14th ed.1978) (footnotes omitted).

* * * [I]n *Frank v. Drinc–O–Matic, Inc.*, we upheld the sale of a debtor's 19 vending machines that were subject to a vendor's lien and in the possession of their manufacturer. We noted that the trustee had no funds with which to redeem the machines and that six months had passed from the filing of the petition without proposal of a reorganization plan. Finally, we stated that appellate review of the power exercised by a lower court in directing a sale pursuant to § 116(3) was limited to whether the district court had abused its discretion.

Citing § 116(3) of the Act, we next affirmed an order of a sale of vats, kettles and other brewing machinery which, with "'the approach of warm weather * * * will, because of lack of use and refrigeration, deteriorate rapidly and lose substantially all their value.'" *In re V. Loewer's Gambrinus Brewery Co.*, 141 F.2d 747, 748 (2d Cir. 1944). While the court acknowledged the viability of the "perishable" property concept, it upheld the sale even though virtually all of the income producing assets of the debtor were involved. The same proceeding, then entitled *Patent Cereals v. Flynn*, 149 F.2d 711 (2d Cir. 1945), came before us the following year. We said it made no difference whether sale of a debtor's property preceded or was made part of a plan of reorganization. Nothing, we continued, in former section 216 (providing for the sale of a reorganizing debtor's property pursuant to a plan) precluded approval of a plan after a sale of all or a substantial part of the debtor's property. Section 216 merely permitted a plan providing for such sale and did not forbid a plan after such a sale has already taken place.

Judge Ryan, in authorizing the sale of the Dale stock cited *Patent Cereals* as his authority. Appellees here cite *Patent Cereals* for the proposition that this court has abandoned the perishable property or emergency concept. We reject

---

to the land during the time interval after a petition had been filed and prior to plan approval. The writer therefore recommended adoption of legislation that would grant the bankruptcy judge authority to issue orders during the time from filing to approval permitting the sale or lease of the debtor's property. * * *

such a broad reading of *Patent Cereals* for several reasons. First, the decision involved an appeal from a denial of confirmation of a plan of reorganization, i.e., the sale in that case was a *fait accompli,* it was not as here an appeal from an authorization of sale. Second, the earlier decision in *Loewer's Gambrinus Brewery* indicates that the court did view the original sale as involving perishable property. Third, subsequent cases in this Circuit confirm the misapprehension in appellees' and Judge Ryan's broad interpretation. * * *

The Third Circuit took an even stricter view in *In re Solar Mfg. Corp.*, 176 F.2d 493 (3d Cir. 1949). Acknowledging that a sale of corporate assets could occur outside and prior to a plan yet expressing concern that sales of that nature do not adequately "protect the interests of those whose money is tied up in the tottering enterprise," the court concluded that pre-confirmation sales should be "confined to emergencies where there is imminent danger that the assets of the ailing business will be lost if prompt action is not taken." This "emergency" approach was so appealing that our court cited *Solar Mfg. Corp.* with approval and held in *In re Pure Penn Petroleum Co.*, 188 F.2d 851 (2d Cir. 1951), that the debtor must plead and prove "the existence of an emergency involving imminent danger of loss of the assets if they were not promptly sold."

Finally, in *In re Sire Plan, Inc.*, 332 F.2d 497 (2d Cir. 1964), corporate owners of a seven-story skeletal building then under construction filed for reorganization under Chapter X of the Act. Because of the site's close proximity to the impending 1964 World's Fair, Holiday Inns felt it was a favorable location for a hotel and accordingly offered to purchase it. The sale to Holiday Inns was affirmed under the *Patent Cereals* rationale. The Court stated that there is no requirement that the sale be in aid of a reorganization; but we further noted, as in *Pure Penn,* that the evidence demonstrated that in its exposed state a "partially constructed building is a 'wasting asset' [that] can only deteriorate in value the longer it remains uncompleted."

More recently, other circuits have upheld sales prior to plan approval under the Bankruptcy Act where the bankruptcy court outlined the circumstances in its findings of fact indicating why the sale was in the best interest of the estate. * * * In essence, these cases evidence the continuing vitality under the old law of an "emergency" or "perishability" standard. As we shall see, the new Bankruptcy Code no longer requires such strict limitations on a bankruptcy judge's authority to order disposition of the estate's property; nevertheless, it does not go so far as to eliminate all constraints on that judge's discretion.

C. The Bankruptcy Reform Act of 1978

Section 363(b) of the Code seems on its face to confer upon the bankruptcy judge virtually unfettered discretion to authorize the use, sale or lease, other than in the ordinary course of business, of property of the estate. Of course, the statute requires that notice be given and a hearing conducted, but no reference is made to an "emergency" or "perishability" requirement nor is there an indication that a debtor in possession or trustee contemplating sale must show "cause." Thus, the language of § 363(b) clearly is different from the terms of its statutory predecessors. And, while Congress never expressly stated why it abandoned the "upon cause shown" terminology of § 116(3), arguably that omission permits easier access to § 363(b). * * * Various policy considerations lend some support to this view.

First and foremost is the notion that a bankruptcy judge must not be shackled with unnecessarily rigid rules when exercising the undoubtedly broad administrative power granted him under the Code. As Justice Holmes once said in a different context, "[s]ome play must be allowed for the joints of the machine * * *." To further the purposes of Chapter 11 reorganization, a bankruptcy judge must have substantial freedom to tailor his orders to meet differing circumstances. This is exactly the result a liberal reading of § 363(b) will achieve.

Support for this policy is found in the rationale underlying a number of earlier cases that had applied § 116(3) of the Act. In particular, this Court's decision in *Sire Plan* was not hinged on an "emergency" or "perishability" concept. Lip service was paid to the argument that a partially constructed building is a "wasting asset"; but the real justification for authorizing the sale was the belief that the property's value depended on whether a hotel could be built in time for the World's Fair and that an advantageous sale after the opening of the World's Fair seemed unlikely. Thus, the reason was not solely that a steel skeleton was deteriorating, but rather that a good business opportunity was presently available, so long as the parties could act quickly. In such cases therefore the bankruptcy machinery should not straightjacket the bankruptcy judge so as to prevent him from doing what is best for the estate.

Just as we reject the requirement that only an emergency permits the use of § 363(b), we also reject the view that § 363(b) grants the bankruptcy judge *carte blanche.* Several reasons lead us to this conclusion: the statute requires notice and a hearing, and these procedural safeguards would be meaningless absent a further requirement that reasons be given for whatever determination is made; similarly, appellate review would effectively be precluded by an irreversible order; and, finally, such construction of § 363(b) swallows up Chapter 11's safeguard. In fact, the legislative history surrounding the enactment of Chapter

11 makes evident Congress' concern with rights of equity interests as well as those of creditors.[3]

Chapter 5 of the House bill dealing with reorganizations states that the purpose of a business reorganization is to restructure a business' finances to enable it to operate productively, provide jobs for its employees, pay its creditors and produce a return for its stockholders. The automatic stay upon filing a petition prevents creditors from acting unilaterally or pressuring the debtor. * * * The plan of reorganization determines how much and in what form creditors will be paid, whether stockholders will continue to retain any interests, and in what form the business will continue. Requiring acceptance by a percentage of creditors and stockholders for confirmation forces negotiation among the debtor, its creditors and its stockholders. A fair analysis of the House bill reveals that reorganization under the 1938 Chandler Act, though designed to protect creditors had, over the years, often worked to their detriment and to the detriment of shareholders as well. The primary reason reorganization under the Act had not served well was that disclosure was minimal and reorganization under the Act was designed to deal with trade debt, not secured or public debt or equity. The present bill, it was believed, provides some form of investor protection to make it a "fairer reorganization vehicle." The key to the reorganization Chapter, therefore, is disclosure. To make disclosure effective, a provision was included that there be a disclosure statement and a hearing on the adequacy of the information it contains. The essential purpose served by disclosure is to ensure that public investors are not left entirely at the mercy of the debtor and its creditors. * * *

The Senate hearings similarly reflect a concern as to how losses are to be apportioned between creditors and stockholders in the reorganization of a public company. Noting that "the most vulnerable today are public investors," the Senate Judiciary Committee Report states that the bill is designed to counteract "the natural tendency of a debtor in distress to pacify large creditors with whom the debtor would expect to do business, at the expense of small and scattered public investors." * * *

---

[3] The Commission on the Bankruptcy Laws of the United States submitted a draft provision that would have permitted resort to section 363(b) in the absence of an emergency, even in the case of "all or substantially all the property of the estate." * * * Congress eventually deleted this provision without explanation, an action which we hardly consider dispositive of the issue before us here.

III. Conclusion

The history surrounding the enactment in 1978 of current Chapter 11 and the logic underlying it buttress our conclusion that there must be some articulated business justification, other than appeasement of major creditors, for using, selling or leasing property out of the ordinary course of business before the bankruptcy judge may order such disposition under section 363(b).

The case law under section 363's statutory predecessors used terms like "perishable," "deteriorating" and "emergency" as guides in deciding whether a debtor's property could be sold outside the ordinary course of business. The use of such words persisted long after their omission from newer statutes and rules. The administrative power to sell or lease property in a reorganization continued to be the exception, not the rule. In enacting the 1978 Code Congress was aware of existing case law and clearly indicated as one of its purposes that equity interests have a greater voice in reorganization plans—hence, the safeguards of disclosure, voting, acceptance and confirmation in present Chapter 11.

Resolving the apparent conflict between Chapter 11 and § 363(b) does not require an all or nothing approach. Every sale under § 363(b) does not automatically short-circuit or side-step Chapter 11; nor are these two statutory provisions to be read as mutually exclusive. Instead, if a bankruptcy judge is to administer a business reorganization successfully under the Code, then—like the related yet independent tasks performed in modern production techniques to ensure good results—some play for the operation of both § 363(b) and Chapter 11 must be allowed for.

The rule we adopt requires that a judge determining a § 363(b) application expressly find from the evidence presented before him at the hearing a good business reason to grant such an application. In this case the only reason advanced for granting the request to sell Lionel's 82 percent stock interest in Dale was the Creditors' Committee's insistence on it. Such is insufficient as a matter of fact because it is not a sound business reason and insufficient as a matter of law because it ignores the equity interests required to be weighed and considered under Chapter 11. The court also expressed its concern that a present failure to approve the sale would result in a long delay. As the Supreme Court has noted, it is easy to sympathize with the desire of a bankruptcy court to expedite bankruptcy reorganization proceedings for they are frequently protracted. "The need for expedition, however, is not a justification for abandoning proper standards." *Protective Committee for Independent Stockholders of TMT Trailer Ferry, Inc. v. Anderson*, 390 U.S. 414, 450 (1968). Thus, the approval of the sale of Lionel's 82 percent interest in Dale was an abuse of the trial court's discretion.

In fashioning its findings, a bankruptcy judge must not blindly follow the hue and cry of the most vocal special interest groups; rather, he should consider all salient factors pertaining to the proceeding and, accordingly, act to further the diverse interests of the debtor, creditors and equity holders, alike. He might, for example, look to such relevant factors as the proportionate value of the asset to the estate as a whole, the amount of elapsed time since the filing, the likelihood that a plan of reorganization will be proposed and confirmed in the near future, the effect of the proposed disposition on future plans of reorganization, the proceeds to be obtained from the disposition vis-a-vis any appraisals of the property, which of the alternatives of use, sale or lease the proposal envisions and, most importantly perhaps, whether the asset is increasing or decreasing in value. This list is not intended to be exclusive, but merely to provide guidance to the bankruptcy judge.

Finally, we must consider whether appellants opposing the sale produced evidence before the bankruptcy court that such sale was not justified. While a debtor applying under § 363(b) carries the burden of demonstrating that a use, sale or lease out of the ordinary course of business will aid the debtor's reorganization, an objectant, such as the Equity Committee here, is required to produce some evidence respecting its objections. Appellants made three objections below: First, the sale was premature because Dale is not a wasting asset and there is no emergency; second, there was no justifiable cause present since Dale, if anything, is improving; and third, the price was inadequate. No proof was required as to the first objection because it was stipulated as conceded. The second and third objections are interrelated. Following Judge Ryan's suggestion that objections could as a practical matter be developed on cross-examination, Equity's counsel elicited testimony from the financial expert produced by Lionel that Dale is less subject than other companies to wide market fluctuations. The same witness also conceded that he knew of no reason why those interested in Dale's stock at the September 7, 1983 hearing would not be just as interested six months from then.[4] The only other witness who testified was the Chief Executive Officer of Lionel, who stated that it was only at the insistence of the Creditors' Committee that Dale stock was being sold and that Lionel "would very much like to retain its interest in Dale." These uncontroverted statements of the two witnesses elicited by the Equity Committee on cross-examination were sufficient proof to support its objections to the present sale of Dale because this evidence demonstrated that there was no good business reason for the present sale. Hence, appellants satisfied their burden.

---

[4] As noted, the bidding for Dale started with a $43 million offer from Acme-Cleveland and has since jumped to $50 million. There is no indication that this trend will reverse itself.

Accordingly, the order appealed from is reversed and the matter remanded to the district court with directions to remand to the bankruptcy court for further proceedings consistent with this opinion.

■ WINTER, Circuit Judge, dissenting:

In order to expedite the decision in this matter, I set forth my dissenting views in summary fashion.

The following facts are undisputed as the record presently stands: (i) Lionel sought a buyer for the Dale stock willing to condition its purchase upon confirmation of a reorganization plan. It was unsuccessful since, in the words of the bankruptcy judge, "the confirmation of any plan is usually somewhat iffy," and few purchasers are willing to commit upwards of $50 million for an extended period without a contract binding on the other party; (ii) every feasible reorganization plan contemplates the sale of the Dale stock for cash; (iii) a reorganization plan may be approved fairly soon if the Dale stock is sold now. If the sale is prohibited, renewed negotiations between the creditors and the equity holders will be necessary, and the submission of a plan, if any, will be put off well into the future; and (iv) the Dale stock can be sold now at or near the same price as it can be sold later.

The effect of the present decision is thus to leave the debtor in possession powerless as a legal matter to sell the Dale stock outside a reorganization plan and unable as an economic matter to sell it within one. This, of course, pleases the equity holders who, having introduced no evidence demonstrating a disadvantage to the bankrupt estate from the sale of the Dale stock, are now given a veto over it to be used as leverage in negotiating a better deal for themselves in a reorganization.

The likely results of today's decision are twofold: (i) The creditors will at some point during the renewed protracted negotiations refuse to extend more credit to Lionel, thus thwarting a reorganization entirely; and (ii) notwithstanding the majority decision, the Dale stock will be sold under Section 363(b) for exactly the same reasons offered in support of the present proposed sale. However, the ultimate reorganization plan will be more favorable to the equity holders, and they will not veto the sale.

It seems reasonably obvious that result (i) is something that the statutory provisions governing reorganizations, including Section 363(b), are designed to avoid. Result (ii) not only is contrary to the purpose of the reorganization provisions in causing delay and further economic risk but also suffers from the legal infirmity which led the majority to reject the proposed sale, the only difference between the two sales being the agreement of the equity holders.

The equity holders offered no evidence whatsoever that the sale of Dale now will harm Lionel or that Dale can in fact be sold at a reasonable price as part of a reorganization plan. The courts below were quite right in not treating their arguments seriously for they are the legal equivalent of the "Hail Mary pass" in football.[5]

NOTES

1. Section 1123(b)(4) states that a plan may "provide for the sale of all or substantially all of the property of the estate, and the distribution of the proceeds of such sale among holders of claims or interests." Why would a debtor prefer to liquidate under Chapter 11 rather than under Chapter 7? Would creditors have the same preference? Note that by liquidating under a plan, the equity interest holders of an insolvent debtor are likely to do better in retaining some property or interest than under § 363 sales. After the property is reduced to cash, distribution must generally follow the Chapter 7 priorities, see § 1129(a)(7), rather than a negotiated solution that provides for sharing with equity. *See* Lee R. Bogdanoff, *Purchase and Sale of Assets in Reorganization*, 47 Bus. Law 1367, 1397-99 (1992).

In the common case in which the debtor has little or no unencumbered property, § 363 sales may primarily benefit the debtor's secured creditors and leave little or no proceeds for unsecured creditors. In recognition of this dynamic, some bankruptcy courts condition § 363 sales in Chapter 11 upon obtaining the consent of the general unsecured creditors' committee. These

---

[5] With due respect to my colleagues, the problem of statutory interpretation is entirely straightforward and not deserving of a lengthy exegesis into legal history. The language of Section 363(b) is about as plain as it could be and surely does not permit a judicial grafting of stringent conditions on the power of trustees. As for its legislative history, the words "upon cause shown" were dropped by the Congress from the predecessor to Section 363(b) in 1978, a signal clearly dictating that Congress meant what it said.

The equity holders argue that Chapter 11's provisions for disclosure, hearing and a vote before confirmation of a reorganization plan stringently limit the authority of trustees under § 363(b). However, a reorganization plan affects the rights of the parties as well as the disposition of assets, and there is no inconsistency in allowing the disposition of property outside the confirmation proceedings. Arguably, some transactions proposed under Section 363(b) would, if carried out, eliminate a number of options available for reorganization plans and thereby pre-ordain a particular kind of plan or preclude a reorganization entirely. In such a case, a colorable claim can be made for a limitation on a trustee's power under Section 363(b) narrowly tailored to prevent such a result in order to effectuate the core purposes of Chapter 11. However, it is not disputed that in the present case the final reorganization plan will include a sale of Dale stock. A sale now thus does not preclude any feasible reorganization plan.

courts effectively allow the committee to exact a "tax" (i.e., a distribution for unsecured creditors) on the debtor and secured lender's access to the § 363 process under Chapter 11. If the "tax" is too high, of course, the debtor and lender may prefer to liquidate under Chapter 7.

2. In *In re Braniff Airways, Inc.*, 700 F.2d 935 (5th Cir. 1983), the debtor Braniff, PSA, and certain secured and unsecured creditors agreed to a sale of a major part of Braniff's airline assets to PSA on certain conditions: (1) PSA would issue $7.5 million of scrip to Braniff entitling the holders to ride free on PSA's airline; (2) secured creditors were required to vote a portion of their deficiency claim in favor of any future reorganization plan approved by a majority of the unsecured creditors' committee; and (3) all claims against Braniff, its officers and directors, and its secured creditors would be released. The bankruptcy court approved the transaction under its authority to approve sales under § 363(b). The district court affirmed. The Fifth Circuit reversed:

> The courts below approved the PSA transaction pursuant to Section 363(b) of the Bankruptcy Code * * *.
>
> The appellants contend that § 363(b) is not applicable to sales or other dispositions of all the assets of a debtor, and that such a transaction must be effected pursuant to the voting, disclosure and confirmation requirements of the Code. * * * Braniff responds that cases decided before and after promulgation of the Code authorize a § 363(b) sale of all of a debtor's assets. * * *
>
> We need not express an opinion on this controversy because we are convinced that the PSA transaction is much more than the "use, sale or lease" of Braniff's property authorized by § 363(b). Reduced to its barest bones, the PSA transaction would provide for Braniff's transfer of cash, airplanes and equipment, terminal leases and landing slots to PSA in return for travel scrip, unsecured notes, and a profit participation in PSA's proposed operation. The PSA transaction would also require significant restructuring of the rights of Braniff creditors. Appellants raise a blizzard of objections to each of these elements of the deal. It is not necessary, however, to decide whether each individual component of the PSA transaction is or is not authorized by § 363 because the entire transaction was treated by both courts below as an integrated whole. Since certain portions of the transaction are clearly outside the scope of § 363, the district court was without power under that section to approve it. Its order must be reversed.
>
> Three examples will illustrate our rationale. The PSA Agreement provided that Braniff would pay $2.5 million to PSA in exchange for $7.5 million of scrip entitling the holder to travel on PSA. It further re-

quired that the scrip be used only in a future Braniff reorganization and that it be issued only to former Braniff employees or shareholders or, in a limited amount, to unsecured creditors. This provision not only changed the composition of Braniff's assets, the contemplated result under § 363(b), it also had the practical effect of dictating some of the terms of any future reorganization plan. The reorganization plan would have to allocate the scrip according to the terms of the PSA agreement or forfeit a valuable asset. The debtor and the Bankruptcy Court should not be able to short circuit the requirements of Chapter 11 for confirmation of a reorganization plan by establishing the terms of the plan *sub rosa* in connection with a sale of assets.

Second, under the agreement between Braniff and its creditors, the secured creditors were required to vote a portion of their deficiency claim in favor of any future reorganization plan approved by a majority of the unsecured creditors' committee. Again, such an action is not comprised by the term "use, sell, or lease," and it thwarts the Code's carefully crafted scheme for creditor enfranchisement where plans of reorganization are concerned. See § 1126.

Third, the PSA transaction also provided for the release of claims by all parties against Braniff, its secured creditors and its officers and directors. On its face, this requirement is not a "use, sale or lease" and is not authorized by § 363(b).

For these reasons, we hold that the district court was not authorized by § 363(b) to approve the PSA transaction and that its order is reversed. In any future attempts to specify the terms whereby a reorganization plan is to be adopted, the parties and the district court must scale the hurdles erected in Chapter 11. *See e.g.* § 1125 (disclosure requirements); § 1126 (voting); § 1129(a)(7) (best interest of creditors test); § 1129(b)(2)(B) (absolute priority rule). Were this transaction approved, and considering the properties proposed to be transferred, little would remain save fixed based equipment and little prospect or occasion for further reorganization. These considerations reinforce our view that this is in fact a reorganization.

700 F.2d at 939–940.

6. SALES FREE AND CLEAR OF INTERESTS

In re PW, LLC
United States Bankruptcy Appellate Panel, Ninth Circuit, 2008.
391 B.R. 25.

■ MARKELL, Bankruptcy Judge:

This appeal presents a simple issue: outside a plan of reorganization, does § 363(f) of the Bankruptcy Code permit a secured creditor to credit bid its debt and purchase estate property, taking title free and clear of valid, nonconsenting junior liens? We hold that it does not.

In reaching this conclusion, we reject the contention that once the sale is consummated, the appeal from the order stripping the junior creditor's liens is moot and immune from scrutiny, and we hold that, in the circumstances of this case, the junior lienholder's rights are preserved.

The debtor in this case, PW, LLC ("PW"), owned prime real estate in Burbank, California. DB Burbank, LLC ("DB"), an affiliate of a large public hedge fund, held a claim of more than $40 million secured by PW's property. But problems large and small plagued PW's development plan. These problems ultimately led to PW's chapter 11 bankruptcy and to the appointment of Nancy Knupfer as PW's chapter 11 trustee ("Trustee").

DB, working with the Trustee, organized a campaign to consolidate all of PW's property and development rights and to sell this package, free and clear of all claims and encumbrances, at a sale supervised by the bankruptcy court. At the sale, DB was the highest bidder, paying its consideration by credit-bidding the entire amount of its debt.

The only problem was the existence of a consensual lien securing a claim of approximately $2.5 million in favor of a junior creditor, Clear Channel Outdoor, Inc. ("Clear Channel"). Relying solely on § 363(f)(5), the bankruptcy court confirmed the sale to DB free and clear of Clear Channel's lien. The bankruptcy court then denied a stay of the sale pending appeal, as did our motions panel.

The first issue presented is whether the appeal is moot. We conclude that while any relief related to the transfer of title to DB is moot, stripping Clear Channel's lien and related state law rights present an issue that is discrete and separable from title transfer. That part of Clear Channel's appeal is not moot.

After reviewing applicable law, we conclude that § 363(f)(5) cannot support transfer of PW's property free and clear of Clear Channel's lien based on the existing record. We thus reverse that portion of the bankruptcy court's order authorizing the sale to DB free and clear of Clear Channel's lien, and we remand the matter to the bankruptcy court for further proceedings.

...

I. Facts

Before filing for bankruptcy, PW owned and was attempting to develop real property in Burbank, California. It had a development agreement with the City of Burbank ("Development Agreement") that provided entitlements for a mixed-use complex of luxury condominiums and retail space. In order to realize the value of the entitlements, however, PW had to acquire an assemblage of eighteen parcels of real estate by February 2009. When it filed bankruptcy, PW owned only fourteen of the necessary parcels. It had, however, entered into an agreement to acquire the final four parcels, which were occupied by a church ("Church Property"). Closing this agreement and the final purchase of the Church Property was conditioned on the church's finding another suitable location for its activities.

DB held a first-priority lien on substantially all of PW's assets. It began foreclosure proceedings in July 2006 and sought the appointment of a state court receiver. After the receiver was appointed, DB lent the receiver more money to buy additional parcels.

During this time, DB and PW tried to negotiate a chapter 11 plan. They had not reached an agreement when, on November 20, 2006, on the eve of a scheduled foreclosure sale, PW filed a chapter 11 case. DB immediately moved for, and the bankruptcy court granted, the appointment of a trustee, which was done on December 27. The receiver turned over all of PW's assets to the Trustee in January 2007.

The Trustee faced several immediate problems. These included obtaining and paying the cure amounts related to the contract to acquire the Church Property, and otherwise implementing the terms of the Development Agreement. In addition, as a "single asset real estate" case, *see* 11 U.S.C. § 101(51B), it was likely that DB would be granted relief from stay under § 362(d)(3).

In response, the Trustee proposed to sell PW's property and began discussions with DB to that end. With bankruptcy court authorization, the Trustee hired a real estate broker to market PW's property to others. In addition, to facilitate acquisition of the Church Property, the broker agreed to help the Trustee find a new location for the church.

After negotiation, the Trustee and DB entered into an agreement they called a "Binding Term Sheet," which established detailed sale procedures for an auction and sale of PW's assets. Under its terms, the Trustee gained time to market and sell PW's property and to resolve disputes that had arisen regarding the Church Property.

The Binding Term Sheet also provided that DB would serve as a stalking horse bidder for a sale of PW's property. If there were no qualified overbidders, DB would buy PW's property for $41,434,465, which the parties called the "Strike Price."[4] In addition, DB agreed to pay the Trustee a "Carve-Out Amount" of up to $800,000 for certain administrative fees and other expenses.[5] DB also agreed not to seek relief from the automatic stay and to refrain from communicating with third parties regarding the sale of PW's assets.

On March 20, 2007, the bankruptcy court entered an order establishing a procedure for the sale of PW's property. Two days later, the Trustee moved to approve the sale free and clear of liens under § 363(f)(3) and (f)(5).

Clear Channel opposed the motion, asserting that § 363(f) was not applicable. Over Clear Channel's objection, on April 26, 2007, the bankruptcy court entered a separate order authorizing the sale free and clear of Clear Channel's lien under § 363(f)(5) ("Sale Order").

The March 20 order set May 7 as the deadline for submitting written bids, and the same order set the minimum overbid at $43,618,048, plus whatever amount was necessary to cure defaults related to acquiring the Church Property. Only three bids were timely received, and none qualified. The highest was a nonconforming contingent bid of only $25.25 million.

With no qualified overbidders, the Binding Term Sheet required the Trustee to sell PW's property to DB at the Strike Price, DB to pay the Trustee the Carve-Out Amount, and DB to pay certain administrative fees, including the receiver's fees and other expenses.

On May 31, 2007, the bankruptcy court confirmed the sale to DB and found that DB was a purchaser in good faith. The court entered an order to this effect ("Confirmation Order"), and declined to stay that order pending appeal, as did a prior motions panel of this court.

The sale closed on June 15, 2007. Clear Channel received no payment under the terms of the sale because DB's credit bid meant that there were no proceeds to which Clear Channel's lien could attach. Since closing, DB has paid out more than $1.5 million, including $250,000 in final payment to the receiver for fees and expenses, $550,000 to the estate as the remaining Carve-Out Amount, $750,000 to a senior lienholder, and other amounts necessary to pay outstanding real estate taxes and other costs of closing. For her part, the

---

[4] The Strike Price equaled the amount due to DB plus a senior lien, less the negotiated minimum overbid amount.

[5] The Carve-Out Amount was to be reduced to $550,000 if DB paid the receiver's final fees.

Trustee has made payments out of the Carve-Out Amount to herself and her professionals on an interim basis.

Clear Channel filed a timely appeal on May 1, 2007, and seeks reversal of both the Sale Order and the Confirmation Order....[6]

...

III. Discussion

Before reaching the merits of Clear Channel's appeal, we must first determine whether it is moot. That determination requires us to examine what it means for an appeal from a sale order to be moot.

A. Mootness

In bankruptcy, mootness comes in a variety of flavors: constitutional, equitable, and statutory.

1. Constitutional Mootness

[omitted].

2. Equitable Mootness

[omitted].

3. Statutory Mootness Under § 363(m)

Sales of property of the estate under § 363(b) and (c) are protected by § 363(m), which states:

> The reversal or modification on appeal of an authorization under subsection (b) or (c) of this section of a sale or lease of property does not affect the validity of a sale or lease under such authorization to an entity that purchased or leased such property in good faith, whether or not such entity knew of the pendency of the appeal, unless such authorization and such sale or lease were stayed pending appeal.

Section 363(m) is a codification of some aspects of equitable mootness with respect to sales. Unlike equitable mootness, however, § 363(m) provides for specific procedures and findings in order to provide certainty for sales.

DB contends that this section deprives this court of the ability to affect the sale. It argues that Clear Channel did not obtain a stay pending appeal, and the bankruptcy court made findings that DB acted in good faith. These facts

---

[6] After the sale closed, DB and the Trustee moved to dismiss this appeal as moot. On September 11, 2007, a motions panel granted DB's motion as to the sale, citing § 363(m). But that motions panel left it to this merits panel to determine whether stripping Clear Channel's lien under § 363(f) was moot....

reinforce our decision not to tamper with transfer of title to DB. The appeal for that part of the transaction is equitably moot, as we noted above, and the facts establish that it is also protected by § 363(m).

But the Confirmation Order authorized both a sale of PW's property and lien-stripping. While the lack of a stay and a transfer of the property would be relevant to whether § 363(m) applies to a sale authorized by § 363(b), these facts continue to be relevant only if § 363(m) applies to lien-stripping authorizations under § 363(f). We do not consider these facts, however, because we conclude that § 363(m) does not apply to lien-stripping under § 363(f).

First, § 363(m) by its terms applies only to "an authorization under subsection (b) or (c) of this section...." Here, the remaining challenge is to the authorization under subsection (f) to sell the property free of Clear Channel's lien. Section 363(m) thus cleaves a distinction between authorizations to "use, sell or lease ... property of the estate" as set forth in § 363(b) and authorizations under § 363(f) to "sell property under subsection (b) or (c) of this section free and clear of any interest in such property...." Section 363(m) thus protects the court's authorization of a sale, in this case, out of the ordinary course of business, again making a distinction between the authorization of a sale and the terms under which the sale is to be made.

Second, the subsection limits only the ability to "affect the validity of a sale or lease under such authorization...." Here, the telling locution is the limitation of § 363(m) to "sale[s] or lease[s]" authorized under § 363(b) or (c). Omitted is the "use" prong of authorization. As a result, a plain-language reading of the section would not give § 363(m) protection to an out-of-the-ordinary-course use approved by a bankruptcy court. *See* Part III.B.1., *infra*.

This limitation leads us to conclude that Congress intended that § 363(m) address only changes of title or other essential attributes of a sale, together with the changes of authorized possession that occur with leases. The terms of those sales, including the "free and clear" term at issue here, are not protected.

Indeed, Congress could easily have broadened the protection of § 363(m) to include lien-stripping. As an example, it could have stated that all "transfers" were to be protected, as that term is broadly defined in § 101(54). It did not. Instead, it restricted the protection of § 363(m) to sales and leases.[9]

That § 363(m) is so limited can also be seen by comparing the language chosen-sales or leases-with Congress's efforts to protect liens and security

---

[9] As we point out later, the type of lien-stripping that PW and DB engaged in is specifically authorized in chapter 12 cases, and the relevant statute there does not contain any provisions similar to § 363(m). *See* 11 U.S.C. § 1206.

interests granted by the estate in § 364. Section 364 permits the estate to grant liens and security interests similar to those sought to be stripped here. To protect lenders' reliance of on such grants, Congress added § 364(e) to the Code. It states:

> (e) The reversal or modification on appeal of an authorization under this section to obtain credit or incur debt, or of a grant under this section of a priority or a lien, does not affect the validity of any debt so incurred, or any priority or lien so granted, to an entity that extended such credit in good faith, whether or not such entity knew of the pendency of the appeal, unless such authorization and the incurring of such debt, or the granting of such priority or lien, were stayed pending appeal.

In § 364(e), Congress chose words specific to the task-"debt," "lien," and "priority." That these types of words are absent from § 363(m) underscores congressional intent not to insulate and immunize lien-stripping actions from appellate review.

Not surprisingly, DB argues that its agreement to purchase the property was conditioned on receiving a free and clear title. For that reason, the Confirmation Order contained language both of sale and of lien-stripping. In DB's view, the sale language cannot be separated from the lien-stripping language because both sale and lien-stripping were integral to its decision to purchase the property. In short, DB contends that authorization for the sale also authorized the lien-stripping, and that one cannot be affected without necessarily affecting the other.

In response, we observe that in choosing the words it did in § 363(m), Congress did not intend the two types of actions to receive the same level of protection. That is, divesting the estate of property and vesting it in another is treated differently from stripping a lien. Put another way, stripping a lien is not a sale or a lease protected by the language of § 363(m), either directly or indirectly.

A more nuanced response is that a sophisticated lender such as DB knew of the risks inherent in relying solely on § 363(f)(5) to strip Clear Channel's lien. It could not have avoided these risks by, for example, insisting that the Confirmation Order contain an explicit contractual condition that there be no appellate review. That would have been rejected out of hand, as any other express condition that similarly violated law or public policy would have been. But a party ought not be able to do indirectly what it cannot do directly, and we are reluctant to interpret § 363(m) to give DB indirectly a review-free stripping of Clear Channel's nonbankruptcy property rights. DB cannot mask an improper condition of the transfer-avoiding appellate review-by cloaking it as an essential and inseparable part of a sale.

The response to this argument is that all that the Code and Rules provide for creditors such as Clear Channel is the ability to seek a stay pending appeal. But in these circumstances, when a bond staying the consummation of the deal would have been far in excess of the lien that Clear Channel is trying to protect, we question whether that remedy is exclusive.

In short, DB knew or should have known all along that lien-stripping might not work. So its assertion that the sale was inseparable from the lien-stripping rings hollow, as does its argument that a stay was required to avoid mootness. We conclude that, on these facts, lien-stripping under § 363(f)(5) is not protected under § 363(m).[10]

B. Statutory Interpretation of § 363(f)

Our holding that the appeal is not moot requires us to consider whether § 363(f) permits the stripping of Clear Channel's lien. Sales free and clear of interests are authorized under § 363(f).

Of the five paragraphs [in subsection 363(f)] that authorize a sale free and clear, three do not apply to this appeal. Paragraph (1) does not apply because applicable law-California real property law-does not permit a sale free and clear, and indeed would preserve Clear Channel's lien despite the transfer. Paragraph (2) is inapplicable as Clear Channel did not consent to the transfer free of its interest. Paragraph (4) applies only if the interest is in bona fide dispute, and no one disputes the validity of Clear Channel's lien. As a result, we need only analyze the bankruptcy court's ability to authorize a sale free and clear of Clear Channel's lien under paragraphs (3) and (5).

1. Guidance on Interpretation

We first review case law on statutory interpretation because paragraphs (3) and (5) of § 363(f) present legitimate and difficult questions of statutory interpretation. Paragraph (3), for example, uses a nonstandard term to refer to the claims held by creditors secured by the property being sold. It refers to the "aggregate value of all liens" on the property. The Code, however, tends to refer not to the economic value of the property secured by liens but to the value of claims secured by those liens. *See, e.g.,* 11 U.S.C. §§ 506(a); 1129(b)(2). If § 363(f)(3) had been worded to refer to the "aggregate value of all claims secured by liens on such property," it would have been in the mainstream of other

---

[10] Indeed, one commentator has decried the lack of doctrinal consistency in the § 363(f) area and has indicated that inconsistent and insufficiently justified applications of the mootness doctrine have been one cause. George W. Kuney, *Misinterpreting Bankruptcy Code Section 363(f) and Undermining the Chapter 11 Process,* 76 AM. BANKR. L.J. 235, 244 & n. 32 (2002).

provisions of the Code, and no real question would be presented. But it was not. This variant locution requires us to decide whether the unusual construction should be given special interpretive significance.

Paragraph (5) presents an even greater conundrum: the competing constructions seem either to render it so specialized as never to be invoked, or all-powerful, subsuming all the other paragraphs of § 363(f). Before launching into the task of interpreting these two paragraphs, we should first review applicable rules of construction for federal statutes.

When construing any federal statute, the presumption is that the accepted and plain meaning of the words used reflects the sense in which Congress used them. As the Supreme Court has stated:

The starting point in discerning congressional intent is the existing statutory text ... and not the predecessor statutes. It is well established that "when the statute's language is plain, the sole function of the courts-at least where the disposition required by the text is not absurd-is to enforce it according to its terms."

But there is more. Because the words of a statute are meant to be law, the legal background of the words used, as well as a lawyer's understanding of them, are also important. Part of the background relevant to this appeal is Congress's promulgation of federal bankruptcy law as a separate title of the United States Code. This separate title is organized as a cohesive code. For example, it groups similar topics together through the use of chapters, and it uses common, defined terms throughout. *See* 11 U.S.C. § 101. To aid in consistent application, the Code's terms are sometimes defined in ways that vary from standard English. A "custodian," for example, is not a janitor or building superintendent, but rather a receiver or trustee for the debtor's property. *See* 11 U.S.C. § 101(11).[11]

Further, the Supreme Court has acknowledged that even undefined words and phrases in the Bankruptcy Code should presumptively receive the same construction, even if found in different parts of the code.[12]

---

[11] This type of variance is not restricted to the Bankruptcy Code. In the Uniform Commercial Code, "afternoon" can mean one minute before midnight. *See* UCC § 4-104(a)(2) ("afternoon" is any time between noon and midnight).

[12] Even those who seek a strict reading of statutes embrace this contextual approach. As a leading proponent of the textualist school, Professor John Manning at Harvard Law School, states: "textualists further acknowledge that '[i]n textual interpretation, context is everything.'" John F. Manning, *What Divides Textualists From Purposivists?*, 106 COLUM. L.REV. 70, 79-80 (2006) (quoting Antonin Scalia). Put another way, "modern textualists urge judges to focus on what they consider the more realistic-and objective-

That brings us to § 363(f), and its proper interpretation.

2. Paragraph (3) and Sales for Less than the Amount of All Claims Secured by the Property

PW's property sold for less than the amount of claims secured by PW's property. DB and the Trustee contend that § 363(f)(3) authorizes the sale free and clear of the liens in this situation.[13] The bankruptcy court found, and we agree, that § 363(f)(3) cannot be so used.

The actual text of paragraph (3) permits a sale free and clear of an interest only if:

> **(3)** such interest is a lien and the price at which such property is to be sold is greater than the aggregate value of all liens on such property;....

The Trustee asserts that the "aggregate value of all liens" in this paragraph means the economic value of such liens, rather than their face value. This argument arises from § 363(f)(3)'s variance from general Code usage; that is, whether its reference to "value of all liens" is simply an unfortunate deviation from the Code's general preference to refer to claims, and not liens, or whether it has some other significance.

The Trustee and DB assert that, under conventional bankruptcy wisdom, supported by § 506(a), the amount of an allowed secured claim can never exceed the value of the property securing the claim. Since a secured claim is a form of "lien," *see* 11 U.S.C. § 101(37), some courts have found that an estate representative may use § 363(f)(3) to sell free and clear of the property rights of junior lienholders whose nonbankruptcy liens are not supported by the collateral's value. That is, there may be a sale free and clear of "out-of-the-money" liens.

We disagree. This reading expands § 363(f)(3) too far. It would essentially mean that an estate representative could sell estate property free and clear of any lien, regardless of whether the lienholder held an allowed secured claim. We think the context of paragraph (3) is inconsistent with this reading. If

---

measure of how 'a skilled, objectively-reasonable user of words' would have understood the statutory text in context." Manning, *supra*, 106 COLUM. L.REV. at 75 (quoting Frank H. Easterbrook).

[13] Although DB has not appealed the decision excluding § 363(f)(3) as a basis for selling PW's property free and clear of Clear Channel's lien, it does assert that § 363(f)(3) supports the bankruptcy court's decision. Under the rule that we may affirm a decision on any basis found in the record, we consider DB's arguments in this regard.

Congress had intended such a broad construction, it would have worded the paragraph very differently.[16]

But another reason, rooted in the text of the paragraph, exists to reject such an expansive reading. Paragraph (3) permits the sale free and clear only when "the price at which such property is to be sold *is greater than* the aggregate value of all liens...." 11 U.S.C. § 363(f)(3) (emphasis added). If, as DB and the Trustee assert, "aggregate value of all liens" means the aggregate amount of all allowed secured claims as used in § 506(a), then the paragraph could *never* be used to authorize a sale free and clear in circumstances like those present here; that is, when the claims exceed the value of the collateral that secures them. In any case in which the value of the property being sold is less than the total amount of claims held by secured creditors, the total of all allowed secured claims will *equal,* not exceed, the sales price, and the statute requires the price to be "greater than" the "value of all liens."

As a result, we join those courts cited above that hold that § 363(f)(3) does not authorize the sale free and clear of a lienholder's interest if the price of the estate property is equal to or less than the aggregate amount of all claims held by creditors who hold a lien or security interest in the property being sold.

3. Paragraph (5) and Sales for Less than the Lienholder's Claim

The parties' main dispute lies over the proper application of § 363(f)(5). The bankruptcy court, supported by the Trustee and DB, found that the plain meaning of that paragraph permitted a sale free and clear of Clear Channel's lien. On appeal, Clear Channel argues that the paragraph's plain meaning does not support the bankruptcy court's construction. Clear Channel has the best of this argument. We thus reverse on this point. Because the meaning of paragraph (5) is anything but plain, we must carefully consider the statute's wording and the competing interpretations.

We start with the text of the statute. Section 363(f)(5) permits an estate representative, such as the Trustee, to sell free of an entity's interest in estate property if:

> (5) such entity could be compelled, in a legal or equitable proceeding, to accept a money satisfaction of such interest.

---

[16] We also draw some interpretive comfort from Congress's 1984 amendment to § 363(f)(3). As noted in *Stroud Wholesale,* in 1984 Congress amended § 363(f)(3) to substitute "all liens on such property" for "such interest," which made "clear Congress' intention that sales free and clear of liens and interests may be justified by (f)(3) only if the sale price will exceed the aggregate value of all liens on the property."

We parse this paragraph to contain at least three elements: that (1) a proceeding exists or could be brought, in which (2) the nondebtor could be compelled to accept a money satisfaction of (3) its interest.

Courts are divided over the interpretation of each of these elements. We analyze these components in reverse order. We start first with an analysis of what Congress meant by an "interest," then move to the proper construction of a money satisfaction, and conclude with an examination of appropriate legal and equitable proceedings.

a. Lien as Interest

Clear Channel's primary contention is that the term "interest" must be read narrowly to exclude liens such as the one it holds. So read, § 363(f)(5) would be inapplicable, as a matter of law, to authorize the sale free and clear of Clear Channel's lien. *See, e.g., In re Canonigo,* 276 B.R. at 266. Clear Channel asserts that to do otherwise renders the other subsections under § 363(f) mere surplusage.

We reject Clear Channel's argument. We believe that Congress intended "interest" to have an expansive scope, as shown by *United States v. Knox-Schillinger (In re Trans World Airlines, Inc.),* 322 F.3d 283 (3d Cir. 2003). In *TWA,* the Third Circuit held that there were two "interests" subject to § 363(f)(5): 1) travel vouchers issued in connection with settlement of a discrimination action and 2) discrimination claims made by the EEOC. The court reasoned that, if the debtor-airline had liquidated its assets under Chapter 7 of the Bankruptcy Code, the claims at issue would have been converted to dollar amounts, and the claimants would have received the distribution provided to other general unsecured creditors on account of their claims. Similarly, the EEOC discrimination claims were reducible to, and could have been satisfied by, monetary awards even if injunctive relief was sought. *Id.* at 290-91. *See also P.K.R. Convalescent Ctrs., Inc. v. Virginia (In re P.K.R. Convalescent Ctrs., Inc.),* 189 B.R. 90, 94 (Bankr.E.D.Va.1995) (statutory right to recapture depreciation on sale of health facility an interest within meaning of § 363(f)(5)). *See also* Kuney, 76 Am. Bankr. L.J. at 257 (lien is a subset of interests).

Some cases, however, have adopted a restricted construction of "interest" in order to prevent needless overlap. In particular, cases such as *In re Canonigo* reason that the term "interest" must be read differently in (f)(5) from every other use of the term in § 363(f).

But the distinctions drawn by *Canonigo* are not supported by the plain reading we are required to give to the statute. It is telling that the introductory sentence to § 363(f) broadly refers to "any interest," and that four of the following paragraphs then refer back to "such interest." Within this group is

§ 363(f)(3), which explicitly states that it applies only if "such interest is a lien," making it apparent that Congress intended a lien to be a type of interest. Congress would not have used the language it did in paragraph (f)(3), or at least would have included additional language in paragraph (5), if it had intended to exclude liens from paragraph (f)(5).

In addition, though the Code does not define "interest,"[17] it does define "lien." Clear Channel's reading contradicts that definition in which lien "means charge against or *interest* in property." 11 U.S.C. § 101(37) (emphasis added). The definition of lien provides another inference consistent with the interpretation that a lien is but one type of interest. Clear Channel asserts that *Canonigo's* interpretation promotes the statutory purpose of avoiding the use of § 363(f) as a means of escaping the rigors of the chapter 11 plan confirmation process. Daniel J. Carragher, *Sales Free and Clear: Limits on § 363(f) Sales, ABI J.* at 16 (July/August 2007).[18]

Consistent with the plain reading of § 363(f) generally, and § 363(f)(5) in particular, we construe "interest" to include the type of lien at issue in this appeal.

b. Compelling Money Satisfaction

Clear Channel's alternative position is that if § 363(f)(5) does apply to authorize a sale free and clear of liens, then the bankruptcy court erred in holding that Clear Channel "could be compelled ... to accept a money satisfaction" of its interest.

i. Compelling Satisfaction for Less Than Full Payment

The bankruptcy court found paragraph(f)(5) applicable whenever a claim or interest can be paid with money.[19] We do not think that § 363(f)(5) is so simply analyzed. Although it is tautological that liens securing payment obligations can be satisfied by paying the money owed,[20] it does not necessarily

---

[17] Congress did refer to equity positions in partnerships as "interests," 11 U.S.C. § 101(16)(B), and did define a "security interest" as a lien created by agreement. *Id.* § 101(51).

[18] Some courts have reconciled the differences by simply stating that "[l]iens are addressed directly in § 363(f)(3) and it is that section which is to be applied." *Beker*, 63 B.R. at 478.

[19] The bankruptcy court stated at the hearing, "The question is, is it the kind of an interest that could be satisfied with money, and if so, then, you can sell free and clear." Hr'g. Tr. 99:1-3 (April 5, 2007).

[20] If the lien secured the faithful performance of a nonmonetary obligation, the generalization would not apply.

follow that such liens can be satisfied by paying *any* sum, however large or small. We assume that paragraph (5) refers to a legal and equitable proceeding in which the nondebtor could be compelled to take *less* than the value of the claim secured by the interest.

Other courts agree and hold that it is not the type of interest that matters, but whether monetary satisfaction may be compelled for less than full payment of the debt related to, or secured by, that interest. *In re Terrace Chalet Apts.,* 159 B.R. at 829 ("By its express terms, Section 363(f)(5) permits lien extinguishment if the trustee can demonstrate the existence of another legal mechanism by which a lien could be extinguished without full satisfaction of the secured debt."). If full payment were required, § 363(f)(5) would merely mirror § 363(f)(3) and render it superfluous.

Under the view that full payment is not necessary, it is not the amount of the payment that is at issue, but whether a "mechanism exists to address extinguishing the lien or interest without paying such interest in full." *In re Gulf States Steel,* 285 B.R. at 508. Other courts have required a showing of the basis that could be used to compel acceptance of less than full monetary satisfaction.

Although this view leads to a relatively small role for paragraph (5), we are not effectively writing it out of the Code. Paragraph (5) remains one of five different justifications for selling free and clear of interests, and its scope need not be expansive or all-encompassing. So long as its breadth complements the other four paragraphs consistent with congressional intent, without overlap, our narrow view is justified.

Examples can be formulated that demonstrate this complementary aspect of a narrow view of paragraph (5). One might be a buy-out arrangement among partners, in which the controlling partnership agreement provides for a valuation procedure that yields something less than market value of the interest being bought out. Another might be a case in which specific performance might normally be granted, but the presence of a liquidated-damages clause allows a court to satisfy the claim of a nonbreaching party in cash instead of a forced transfer of property. Yet another might be satisfaction of obligations related to a conveyance of real estate that normally would be specifically performed but for which the parties have agreed to a damage remedy. In these cases, a court could arguably compel the holders of the interest to take less than what their interest is worth.[22]

---

[22] A related example might be the ability to sell free and clear of a vendor's right to refuse to deliver except upon full cash payment, but the adequate protection required by § 363(e) for such a sale would likely be the full cash payment itself.

Of course, if the interest is such that it may be vindicated only by compelling or restraining some action, it does not qualify under this aspect of § 363(f)(5), and the estate cannot sell free and clear of that interest. *See, e.g., Gouveia v. Tazbir,* 37 F.3d 295 (7th Cir. 1994) (landowners whose land bordered on estate's land could not be compelled to accept money damages in lieu of equitable relief for violation of a reciprocal land covenant restricting the neighborhood to single-story, residential property; estate could therefore not sell the property free of the covenant under § 363(f)(5)). *See also In re WBQ P'ship,* 189 B.R. at 106 (finding § 363(f)(5) inapplicable to restrictive covenants without reference to specific state law governing monetary versus equitable satisfaction) (dicta); *In re 523 E. Fifth Street Hous. Pres. Dev. Fund Corp.,* 79 B.R. 568, 576 (Bankr.S.D.N.Y.1987) (court may not sell free and clear of covenant to provide low-income housing).

ii. Construction Consistent with §§ 363(f)(3) and 1206

While the bankruptcy court's reading is plausible if paragraph (5) is read in isolation, statutory interpretation requires a more detailed examination of the context of the statute. Put another way, any interpretation of paragraph (5) must satisfy the requirement that the various paragraphs of subsection (f) work harmoniously and with little overlap. The bankruptcy court's broad interpretation does not do this.

Initially, if the Trustee's and DB's interpretation were accepted, paragraph (5) would swallow and render superfluous paragraph (3), a provision directed specifically at liens. The specific provisions of paragraph (3) would never need to be used, since all liens would be covered, regardless of any negative or positive relationship between the value of a creditor's collateral and the amount of its claim. A result that makes one of five paragraphs redundant should be avoided.

A more narrow reading is also suggested by Congress's addition of § 1206 to the Code in 1986. Pre-BAPCPA section 1206 provided that:

> [a]fter notice and a hearing, *in addition to the authorization contained in section 363(f),* the trustee in a case under this chapter may sell property under section 363(b) and (c) free and clear of any interest in such property of an entity other than the estate if the property is farmland or farm equipment, except that the proceeds of such sale shall be subject to such interest.

11 U.S.C.A. § 1206 (West 2004) (emphasis added). Congress thus intended § 1206 to supplement an estate's rights. As a result, both § 363(f)(5) and § 1206 apply to sales of estate property in chapter 12.[23]

The interpretive challenge is to construe § 363(f)(5) in a way that complements § 1206. In this regard, the first difference between the two provisions is that, unlike § 363(f), § 1206 grants an absolute right to sell free and clear of an interest so long as the interest attaches to the proceeds. This absolute right does not exist in § 363(f)(5), requiring a more narrow interpretation.[24]

Congress added § 1206 in 1986. Its purpose was "to allow family farmers to sell assets not needed for the reorganization prior to confirmation without the consent of the secured creditor subject to the approval of the court." H.R.REP. NO. 958, 99th CONG., 2ND SESS. 50 (1986), U.S.Code Cong. & Admin.News 1986, pp. 5246, 5251. Significantly, Congress explicitly made it clear that an interest includes a lien. But § 1206 would be unnecessary with respect to liens if § 363(f)(5) already permitted a sale.

We follow this reasoning and hold that the bankruptcy court must make a finding of the existence of such a mechanism and the trustee must demonstrate how satisfaction of the lien "could be compelled." Here the bankruptcy court should not have explicitly dismissed the argument that any such finding or showing is required.[25]

c. Legal or Equitable Proceeding

Paragraph (5) requires that there be, or that there be the possibility of, some proceeding, either at law or at equity, in which the nondebtor could be

---

[23] Chapter 12 also permits confirmation over the dissent of a secured creditor, 11 U.S.C. § 1225(a)(5), and thus § 1206's existence belies the effort to select cramdown as a type of legal or equitable proceeding to which § 363(f)(5) refers.

[24] A sale under § 363(f) is subject to § 363(e), which also conditions the sale on the provision of adequate protection. "Most often, adequate protection in connection with a sale free and clear of other interests will be to have those interests attached to the proceeds of the sale." H.R.REP. NO. 595, 95th Cong., 1st Sess. 345 (1977). With respect to a lien, then, § 1206 provides no more than § 363(f)(5) if the availability of nonconsensual confirmation under § 1225(a)(5) is sufficient as a legal and equitable proceeding to trigger a sale free and clear under § 363(f)(5).

[25] The Trustee and DB attempt to resolve this dilemma by asserting that if (f)(5) is found to require full payment of the debt, then (f)(3) must require full payment of the economic value of the lien-the value of the property-rather than full payment of the debt itself. This interpretation, however, makes (f)(5) superfluous.

forced to accept money in satisfaction of its interest.[26] The bankruptcy court reasoned that there was no need to prove the existence or possibility of a qualifying legal or equitable proceeding when the interest at issue was a lien because all liens, by definition, are capable of being satisfied by money.[27]

The language of § 363(f)(5) indicates that compelling a nondebtor to accept a monetary satisfaction cannot be the sole focus of the inquiry under that paragraph. The statute additionally requires that "such entity could be compelled, *in a legal or equitable proceeding,* to accept" such a monetary satisfaction. 11 U.S.C. § 363(f)(5) (emphasis added). The question is thus whether there is an available type or form of legal or equitable proceeding in which a court could compel Clear Channel to release its lien for payment of an amount that was less than full value of Clear Channel's claim. Neither the Trustee nor DB has directed us to any such proceeding under nonbankruptcy law, and the bankruptcy court made no such finding.

The Trustee points out that courts have found that cramdown under § 1129(b)(2) is a qualifying legal or equitable proceeding.

We disagree with the reasoning of these courts. As a leading treatise recognizes, use of the cramdown mechanism to allow a sale free and clear under § 363(f)(5) uses circular reasoning-it sanctions the effect of cramdown without requiring any of § 1129(b)'s substantive and procedural protections. 3 COLLIER ON BANKRUPTCY, *supra,* at ¶ 363.06. If the proceeding authorizing the satisfaction was found elsewhere in the Bankruptcy Code, then an estate would not need § 363(f)(5) at all; it could simply use the other Code provision.

In addition, this reasoning undercuts the required showing of a separate proceeding. For example, it is correct that § 1129(b)(2) permits a cramdown of a lien to the value of the collateral, but it does so only in the context of plan confirmation. To isolate and separate the cramdown from the checks and balances inherent in the plan process undermines the entire confirmation process, and courts have been leery of using § 363(b) to gut plan confirmation or render it superfluous.

We thus hold that Congress did not intend under § 363(f)(5) that nonconsensual confirmation be a type of legal or equitable proceeding to which that

---

[26] We assume, but do not decide, that the appositive "in a legal or equitable proceeding" excludes the possibility of an administrative proceeding.

[27] The bankruptcy court stated at the hearing, "I don't even think they need to prove their cram-down scenario. I think ... that they could be made to go away if you wrote them a check.... The question is, is it the kind of an interest that could be satisfied with money, and if so, then, you can sell free and clear." Hr'g. Tr. 98:20-99:3 (April 5, 2007).

paragraph refers. As a result, the availability of cramdown under § 1129(b)(2) is not a legal or equitable proceeding to which § 363(f)(5) is applicable.

In short, for the reasons outlined above, § 363(f)(5) does not apply to the circumstances of this case.

...

IV. Conclusion

1. Considerations of equitable mootness and § 363(m) render moot Clear Channel's appeal of the validity of the sale of PW's property to DB. But Clear Channel's appeal of the lien-stripping is not ... [moot and] § 363(m) is inapplicable.

2. The bankruptcy court did not apply the correct legal standard under § 363(f)(5), and it therefore did not make the findings required by that paragraph. We therefore reverse that part of the bankruptcy court's order that held that, under § 363(f)(5), the sale was free and clear of Clear Channel's lien.

3. Further, because of the bankruptcy court's incorrect interpretation of the statute, we remand this case for further proceedings consistent with this disposition. This will allow the parties to attempt to identify a qualifying proceeding under nonbankruptcy law (if one exists) that would enable them to strip Clear Channel's lien and make the sale of PW's property to DB free and clear under § 363(f)(5).

NOTES

1. Subsection 363(f)(3) distinguishes between overencumbered property and property that has a value in excess of the liens against it. Overencumbered property may not be sold free and clear of liens under § 363(f)(3). The intuition that supports this result is that the bankruptcy estate has little economic incentive to maximize value of overencumbered property as all sale proceeds will be subject to the claims of the secured creditors. If the secured parties support the proposed sale, then the property can be sold free and clear subject to their consent, but there is little reason to allow a sale of overencumbered property over the objection of the primary parties in economic interest, the secured creditors. On the other hand, the bankruptcy estate has the proper incentive to maximize value if the sale price results in a surplus for the estate and there is little reason to allow a secured party to block a sale yielding an amount in excess of the secured debt so long as the secured claim is adequately protected by maintaining the lien in the sale proceeds. If § 363(f)(5) is read broadly enough to permit the sale of overecumbered property free and clear of liens over the secured creditor's objection, the distinction drawn in § 363(f)(3) would be meaningless. Judge Markell harmonizes § 363(f)(3) and § 363(f)(5) by

reading (f)(5) narrowly to require a full money satisfaction of the liens encumbering the property which effectively removes the sale of overencumbered property from the scope of that subsection. Note that if the secured party's liens are subject to bona fide dispute, the property may be sold free and clear of the disputed lien over the lienholder's objection under § 363(f)(4). Why should the bankruptcy estate be able to convey good title to property subject to a disputed lien without first resolving the dispute?

2. More troubling than Judge Markell's narrow construction of § 363(f)(5) to exclude sales of overencumbered property is his narrow construction of § 363(m). In this case, the secured creditor/purchaser, DB, wound up in a far worse position by virtue of the court's approval of the sale transaction than if the bankruptcy judge had denied the sale motion. After the BAP decision the sale cannot be unwound under § 363(m), but the lien of Clear Channel remains unaffected by the transfer and encumbers DB's property. In effect, Clear Channel's underwater junior lien has become the senior lien and DB's previously senior position is converted into equity ownership junior to Clear Channel's lien. If the sale motion had simply been denied at the outset, presumably the property would have been sold under a plan or foreclosed upon by DB, in either case extinguishing Clear Channel's lien, with all the value in the property up to the full amount of DB's claim going to DB. Isn't the potential for this kind of disaster based on the outcome of an appeal, precisely the reason Congress provided that sales to good faith purchasers could not be set aside unless the sale order is stayed pending appeal? Does Judge Markell's distinction between the sale itself (which is protected from reversal on appeal) and the provisions of the sale order ordering that the transfer be free and clear of liens make sense? Why is it relevant that DB should have known that its reliance on § 363(f)(5) to support the free and clear aspect of the transfer was questionable? Any appeal that has merit will involve issues that are doubtful. Absent a stay pending appeal, so long as the purchaser is acting in good faith § 363(m) shifts the risk that the bankruptcy court erred in resolving a doubtful question regarding the scope of § 363(f)(5) from the purchaser to the appellant doesn't it?

NOTE: PERSONAL INDENTIFIABLE INFORMATION

In the *Toysmart.com* Chapter 11 case the question arose whether the debtor Toysmart.com could sell its customer list (containing approximately 250,000 names, addresses, billing information, shopping preferences and family profiles) free of its contractual obligation to maintain customer privacy. Toysmart.com, a retailer of educational toys, was 60% owned by Buena Vista Internet Group, a subsidiary of Walt Disney. Shortly after the commencement of its Chapter 11 liquidating case, Toysmart.com filed a motion pursuant to

Bankruptcy Code section 363(b) seeking approval to motion pursuant to Bankruptcy Code section 363(b) seeking approval to sell substantially all of its assets, including its customer list. Several parties objected to the sale motion, including the Federal Trade Commission (the "FTC"), the attorneys general of 39 states and TRUSTe, an organization that certifies companies that adhere to online privacy guidelines. See *FTC v. Toysmart.com, LLC*, 2000 WL 1523287 (D.Mass.). Just before the hearing on the sale motion, Toysmart.com and the FTC reached a settlement, which would have allowed Toysmart.com to sell its customer list to a buyer that was willing to purchase Toysmart.com's entire Web site. The bankruptcy court did not approve the FTC settlement. The matter was eventually settled when Buena Vista Internet Group offered Toysmart.com $50,000 to destroy its customer list. 13 Bankr. L. Rep. 58 (Jan. 18, 2001). The *Toysmart.com* case began the debate over the protection of consumer privacy in the context of Bankruptcy Code § 363 asset sales. The consumer privacy issue raised many questions about how consumer privacy could be protected during the age of Internet bankruptcies, in which customer lists often constitute a major portion of the debtor's assets.

BAPCPA amended § 363(b) to prohibit a debtor from selling personally identifiable information in a manner that is inconsistent with its prepetition privacy policy (unless the court orders otherwise). In determining whether a debtor can sell personally identifiable information in a manner that is inconsistent with its prepetition privacy policy, the court is required to give due consideration to the facts and circumstances of the sale or lease. Ironically, these nominally privacy protective provisions appear to broaden the authority of the debtor to use, and the court to authorize the sale of, customer lists, in derogation of the debtor's prepetition contractual privacy obligations. In any event, following *Toysmart.com*, online retailers commonly modified their "privacy policies" to expressly permit the transfer of the customer information in bankruptcy.

7. BREAK–UP FEES AND BIDDING PROCEDURES

Negotiated sales of going concern businesses commonly occur in stages over time. Prudent buyers engage in thorough due diligence investigation, and it takes time to arrange financing, negotiate the details of transferring the business to the new owner and prepare the necessary legal documentation. Moreover, when public companies are involved shareholder approval is generally necessary. These processes cost money and more than occasionally deals are not successfully closed. In light of these realities, it is a commonplace business practice for parties to insist on a binding letter of intent prior closing the transaction that provides for some sum as liquidated damages if the transaction fails to close. In recent years, transactions involving public companies have generally included termination or "break-up" fees that average 2.5–3.0% of the transaction price. This represents a general increase in the frequency and amount of such fees. In the 1980s the average tended to be approximately 1%. John Coates IV & Guhan Subramian, *A Buy–Side Model of M & A Lockups: Theory and Evidence*, 53 Stan.L.Rev. 307 (2000).

Buyers demand break-up fees and other protections partly to compensate them for the substantial out-of-pocket and intangible costs associated with the failed transaction, but also to make it costly for the seller to back out of the deal. Buyers may also fear being used as a "stalking horse," that is incurring the costs of negotiating the transaction while the seller uses their bids to flush out other higher bids. Sellers commonly agree to such protections in order to induce buyers to enter into transactions. Strong initial bids are essential to starting the auction process for a going concern business and a strong initial bid may be unobtainable without some protections for the bidder. Such protections can be structured in a way that maximizes the efficiency of the auction process by setting orderly bid increments, screening out noncredible putative bidders and providing information and access to serious prospective bidders while protecting confidentiality. But in other situations, sellers may have special incentives to consummate the transaction without regard to higher competing bids. In these cases, the break-up fee and other protections may serve the function of chilling unwanted competing offers. This is particularly a problem when the persons negotiating the sale for the seller have interests in the transaction other than maximizing the sale's price. Management contracts, releases and other forms of consideration that are of no benefit to the estate are classic examples. See Coates & Subramian, *supra*.

Commonly, a letter of intent is agreed to between debtor and purchaser that contemplates a court supervised overbid procedure with agreed upon protections for the purchaser and rules for the auction. The buyer also has a strong incentive to lock-up the form of the bid, that is to preclude competing bids for some, but not all, of the assets or for additional assets or for different forms of consideration than those contemplated in the original bid. Presumably, buyer and debtor have configured buyer's bid, the assets being sold and the consideration being paid in a manner that is especially advantageous to this particular buyer. Forcing others to compete on those terms (rather than their own preferred terms) places those others at an immediate disadvantage. But buyers are infrequently content to rest on this advantage alone. Additional protections often demanded range from reimbursement of buyer's expenses in the event that the transaction does not close, to "break up fees" (payable if the transaction does not close for any reason), to "topping fees" (payable if the initial bidder does not end up being the high bidder), minimum overbid requirements, minimum bidding increments, bidders deposits, sealed or open bidding procedures, "no solicitation" clauses (barring the seller from soliciting competing bids) and even "no cooperation" clauses (barring the seller from cooperating with a competing bidder, except when necessary to avoid breach of fiduciary duty).

All of these devices have been used in ordinary out-of-court transactions. Even when public companies are involved, unless self-dealing by managers or directors is involved, the loose "business judgment" standard of judicial review, generally insulates them from legal attack except in cases where the protections are "draconian" or clearly and unreasonably chill competing offers. Courts have been loathe to strike such provisions as unlawful penalties in nonbankruptcy litigation. *See, e.g., St. Jude Medical, Inc. v. Medtronic, Inc.*, 536 N.W.2d 24 (Minn.App.1995). Beginning in the late 1980s and increasingly through the 1990s the bankruptcy sale practice has mimicked the out-of-court two-stage pattern. Bankruptcy courts are now accustomed to approving bidding procedures in advance of a final auction sale and parties frequently seek protections for the initial bidder at this stage. Although early cases seemed to passively accept the loose nonbankruptcy restrictions on bidder protections, bankruptcy courts have grown increasingly skeptical of substantial break fees and related protections in bankruptcy. An early critic of this passive acceptance of the nonbankruptcy business judgment standard was then-Professor Markell, the author of the *PW* decision at 648. *See* Bruce A. Markell, *The Case Against Breakup Fees In Bankruptcy*, 66 Am. Bankr. L.J. 349 (1992) (recommending that bankruptcy courts disallow all break-up fees in excess of the reimbursement of out-of-pocket marginal expenditures of the initial bidder).

The trend in the recent cases is to decisively reject the nonbankruptcy business judgment rule. Most cases apply a free-form balance-all-the-factors approach to determine whether the proposed bidding arrangements are in the best interests of the bankruptcy estate. Key considerations include the amount of the fees that will be paid if the transaction is not consummated, whether the procedures are well adapted to maximizing the price for the business being sold, whether the procedures seem more likely to catalyze or chill competing bids, and whether there is any hint of self dealing or collusion with the bidder by debtor management. The only court of appeals decision on point, *In re O'Brien Environmental Energy, Inc.*, 181 F.3d 527 (3d Cir. 1999), takes an even more restrictive view, finding that the disappointed buyer had to establish that the break-up fee was actually necessary to preserve the value of the estate. § 503(b). Since the disappointed buyer had continued to bid even though allowance of the break-up fee had been reserved by the bankruptcy court, the later award of the fee was not "necessary" to preserve the estate.

Skepticism increases as the protections proceed along a spectrum of increasingly onerous hurdles for competing bidders. Expense reimbursement is the most innocuous of the protections commonly offered to bidders and the most likely to be approved. Modest break-up fees are more likely to win court approval than large ones. No-solicitation clauses, and certainly non-cooperation clauses, on their face appear to be inconsistent with the fiduciary obligations of the debtor and are even less likely to win court approval.

E. Proposing the Plan

1. Introduction

In this section, we consider the court-supervised process under which a plan of reorganization is proposed by the debtor, negotiated amongst the parties in interest and accepted by holders of claims and interests. Under § 1121, for 120 days after the filing of the petition in bankruptcy, only the debtor may file a plan. If the debtor files a plan within 120 days, the debtor is given an additional period ending 180 days after the filing of the petition in bankruptcy to obtain acceptance of the plan by holders of claims and equity interests. The court may reduce or increase these periods, and in complex cases debtors have been granted protracted extensions. Since 2005, however, § 1121(d)(2) provides that in no event may the 120 and 180 exclusive periods be extended beyond 18 months and 20 months, respectively, from commencement of a voluntary Chapter 11 case. The debtor's exclusive right to file a plan also ends if a trustee in bankruptcy is appointed. § 1121(c)(1).

The plan is then presented to creditors and equity security holders whose rights are impaired by the plan. In drafting its plan the debtor may classify claims and interests and deal with the different classes in different ways. § 1122 and § 1123. The composition of the classes is important for they are the voting units for acceptance of the plan under § 1126. A class of creditors accepts a plan if two-thirds in amount and more than one-half in number of those claims voting have cast ballots accepting the plan. § 1126(c). A class of equity interests accepts if two-thirds of the shares (or other equity interests) voted have cast ballots accepting the plan. § 1126(d).

If any class impaired by the plan rejects it, § 1129(a)(8) is not met and the court cannot confirm the plan under § 1129(a). On request of the proponent of the plan, the court may, nevertheless, confirm the plan under § 1129(b) if the plan complies with all other requirements of § 1129(a) and "the plan does not discriminate unfairly and is fair and equitable" with respect to each nonconsenting class that is impaired. § 1129(b)(1). "Fair and equitable" is defined in § 1129(b)(2). We examine confirmation standards in detail in the next chapter of this Casebook. If the debtor is unable to confirm a plan and no other proponent steps forth, the case may be converted to Chapter 7 or may be dismissed. § 1112(b)(2).

2. EXCLUSIVITY

During the first 120 days of a Chapter 11 case only the debtor may formally propose a reorganization plan to the court. If the debtor files a plan within this "exclusivity period" the debtor has an additional 60 days of exclusivity during which it may proceed to solicit acceptances and confirm its plan without facing competing plans. Short of dismissal or conversion to Chapter 7, confirmation of a reorganization plan is the only exit to a Chapter 11 case. So long as "exclusivity" remains in place only the debtor holds the keys to the exit door. Limited exclusivity is thought to advance the reorganization goal of Chapter 11: the debtor is usually the most pro-reorganization constituent in the case. Moreover, by centralizing the plan process in the debtor, the reorganization effort can remain focused. Absent "exclusivity," it is argued, the case might quickly dissolve into chaos as each constituency independently seeks to promote its own plan. Moreover, "exclusivity" provides a procedural counterweight for the debtor to the substantive legal rights of creditors. The resulting balance of forces, it is hoped, will drive the parties towards a consensual rather than a litigated solution to the reorganization case. Under § 1121(d), the bankruptcy court may reduce or extend the initial exclusivity period "for cause." Early terminations of exclusivity, as one might surmise from the discussion above, are rare, but extensions have been extremely common. In general courts find cause in such factors as the size and complexity of the case, the progress the debtor is making toward reorganization, the extent to which exclusivity is being used to hold off other plans that would otherwise be in prospect and otherwise maintaining an appropriate balance between the debtor and its creditors. *See, e.g., In re Public Service of New Hampshire,* 88 B.R. 521 (Bankr.D.N.H.1988).

The debtor's exclusive right under § 1121 to propose a plan for the first 120 days of the Chapter 11 case and to obtain acceptance of it within an additional 60 days, together with the court's discretionary authority to grant extensions of those periods under § 1121(d), is of great strategic importance to the debtor in its plan negotiations. So long as exclusivity remains intact, time is on the side of the debtor. Since unsecured and undersecured creditors receive no postpetition interest on their claims, delay is very costly to them. Creditors normally want prompt confirmation. If there are lengthy extensions of exclusivity, creditors may feel they have little choice but to accept an unfavorable plan of the debtor when, absent exclusivity, they might have been able to propose their own plan—one more favorable to their interests.

On the other hand, the court's discretion to terminate exclusivity or to allow it to expire can be employed to motivate the debtor to make concessions it is not otherwise inclined to make. Debtors can be made to "pay" for exclusivity extensions in the coin of material progress towards confirming a consensual plan. Thus limited and contingent exclusivity extensions may be employed as a tool to push parties towards a negotiated solution.

Although large Chapter 11 cases commonly endure for two to three years or more, historically, creditors' plans or a lapse in exclusivity have been rare. Prior to 2005, courts repeatedly extended exclusivity if persuaded that the debtor was making reasonable progress towards reorganization. Even if a court refused to extend exclusivity, the most common consequence was simply to provoke the debtor into quickly filing a plan in order to retain control over the terms of reorganization. Alleged abuses by courts in extending the debtor's exclusivity period led to pressure on Congress to place an outside time limit beyond which the period of exclusivity could not be extended.

BAPCPA prohibits any further extension of the exclusive filing period beyond 18 months from the order of relief or of the exclusive solicitation period beyond 20 months from the order of relief. In small cases a lapse in exclusivity might be unimportant. No party other than the debtor is likely to be able to formulate other than a liquidating plan, and 18 months is probably about as long as any small debtor can remain in Chapter 11 and still be capable of successful reorganization. In large cases, however, it is possible that a non-extendable deadline on exclusivity would actually slow down cases as creditors have an incentive perhaps to wait out the exclusive period before making the concessions that might lead to a consensual plan. Also the deadline limits the bankruptcy court's ability to manipulate exclusivity extensions in order to encourage the parties to move plan negotiations along. *See e.g. In re Public Service of New Hampshire,* 88 B.R. 521, 539 n.17 (Bankr.D.N.H.1988) (quoting *In re United Press International, Inc.,* 60 B.R. 265 (Bankr.D.C.1986), which asserts a power to fashion a limited or partial termination of exclusivity in order to facilitate case administration. The 18-month deadline would seem to seriously limit the possibilities of this approach.

Can the court notwithstanding termination of the exclusive periods effectively prevent competing plans from proceeding to confirmation by deferring far into the future hearing dates on the proponent's plan and disclosure statement? Can the court choose to grant some plan proponents earlier hearing dates than others, effectively mooting disfavored competing plans?

3. ACCEPTANCE OF THE PLAN

a. Solicitation

Once a plan is filed with the court, impaired classes of claims or interests vote to accept or reject it. Before these votes can be solicited, a court-approved disclosure statement must be first given to the holders of the claims or interests. § 1125(b). The statement must contain "adequate information," defined in § 1125(a)(1), to allow the holder to make an informed judgment about the plan. The plan of reorganization is usually the product of negotiation between the debtor and creditors who may negotiate individually in some cases or may be represented by a creditors' committee. In cases in which the debtor has a large number of stockholders a committee representing stockholders may also participate in negotiations. In many cases, the negotiation process will result in a non-binding de facto acceptance of the plan before a disclosure statement is submitted to the court for its approval. That normally occurs if the debtor is a closely-held corporation with relatively few creditors. In those cases, the disclosure statement must be used to solicit binding acceptance, but it may amount to little more than a formality.

The disclosure statement is more than a formality in cases in which there are large numbers of creditors or stockholders whose rights will be impaired by the plan. If the plan involves the offering of securities by the reorganized debtor, the plan raises issues of disclosure and protection of investors that are normally dealt with by securities laws. By virtue of §§ 1125(d) and 1145, the adequacy of disclosure in the disclosure statement is governed by the Bankruptcy Code rather than securities laws that otherwise would be applicable. A discussion of the relationship between the Bankruptcy Code and the securities laws can be found in John C. Coffee, Jr. and Joel Seligman, *Securities Regulation* 506-514 (9th ed. 2003). The proper relationship between the negotiation, disclosure, solicitation and voting processes within a Chapter 11 case is the central issue in the following case.

Century Glove, Inc. v. First American Bank of New York
United States Court of Appeals, Third Circuit, 1988.
860 F.2d 94.

■ JAMES HUNTER, III, CIRCUIT JUDGE:

Century Glove, Inc. ("Century Glove"), a debtor seeking reorganization under the federal bankruptcy laws, seeks review of a district court order dismissing sanctions imposed on its creditors. Century Glove claims that one of its creditors, First American Bank ("FAB"), unlawfully solicited the votes of other creditors, in violation of Bankruptcy Code § 1125. The bankruptcy court agreed, imposing sanctions against FAB and invalidating another creditor's rejection of Century Glove's plan. On appeal, the district court reversed, holding FAB's action lawful. Century Glove now appeals to this court. We will affirm the order of the district court.

I.

Century Glove filed its petition seeking reorganization in bankruptcy on November 14, 1985. On August 1, 1986, Century Glove filed its reorganization plan, along with a draft of the disclosure statement to be presented along with the plan. Arguing that Century Glove's largest claimed assets are speculative lawsuits (including one against FAB), FAB presented a copy of an alternative plan to the unsecured creditors' committee. FAB advised that it would seek court approval to present its plan as soon as possible. The committee ultimately rejected the plan in favor of that of the debtor. On December 2, 1986, the bankruptcy court approved Century Glove's disclosure statement. A copy of the plan, the statement, and a sample ballot were then sent to Century Glove's creditors entitled to vote on the plan's acceptance.

Between December 12 and December 17, 1986, an attorney for FAB, John M. Bloxom, telephoned attorneys representing several of Century Glove's creditors. Among these creditors were Latham Four Partnerships ("Latham Four") and Bankers Trust New York Corporation ("BTNY"). Bloxom sought to find out what these creditors thought of the proposed reorganization, and to convince them to vote against the plan. He said that, while there was no other plan approved for presentation, and thus no other plan "on the table," FAB had drafted a plan and had tried to file it. The creditors' attorneys then asked for a copy of the plan, which FAB provided. The copies were marked "draft" and covering letters stated that they were submitted to the creditors for their comments. The draft did not contain certain information necessary for a proper disclosure statement, such as who would manage Century Glove after reorganization.

With a copy of its draft plan, FAB also sent to Latham Four a copy of a letter written to the unsecured creditors' committee by its counsel. In the letter, dated August 26, 1986, counsel questioned the committee's endorsement of the Century Glove plan, arguing that the lawsuits which Century Glove claims as assets are too speculative. As stated, the committee endorsed the plan anyway. Upset with this decision, one of its members sent a copy of the letter to a former officer of Century Glove. The officer then sent a copy, unsolicited, to FAB. Uncertain whether the letter was protected by an attorney-client privilege, FAB asked the committee member whether he had disclosed the letter voluntarily. He said that he had, and furnished a second copy directly to FAB. FAB attached this letter to a motion before the bankruptcy court seeking to have the committee replaced. The bankruptcy court later held the letter a privileged communication.

BTNY had made a preliminary decision on September 12, 1986, to reject Century Glove's plan. It reaffirmed this decision on December 15, when it received a copy of the plan and disclosure. Counsel for BTNY spoke with Bloxom the next day, December 16, 1986, and Bloxom mailed a letter confirming the call, but by mistake Bloxom did not send a draft of the alternate plan until December 17. On that day, counsel for BTNY prepared its ballot rejecting Century Glove's plan, and informed Bloxom of its vote.

After receiving the several rejections, Century Glove petitioned the bankruptcy court to designate, or invalidate, the votes of FAB, Latham Four and BTNY. Century Glove argued that FAB had acted in bad faith in procuring these rejections.

II.

The bankruptcy court held that FAB had violated § 1125(b), which allows solicitation of acceptance or rejections only after an approved disclosure statement has been provided the creditor. Though a statement had been filed and provided, the bankruptcy court stated that:

> solicitations * * * must be limited by the contents of the plan, the disclosure statement, and any other court-approved solicitation material. The solicitee may not be given information outside of these approved documents.

The bankruptcy court found that FAB violated the section by providing additional materials such as copies of its draft plan.

The bankruptcy court also concluded that FAB had violated "the spirit of § 1121(b), since FAB was apparently seeking approval of a plan which was not yet filed and which it could not file * * *." This "impropriety" was "heightened" by the absence from the FAB plan of such information as "who will manage the debtor." The bankruptcy court also found "improper" the disclosure by FAB of the August 26, 1986 letter to the creditors' committee. The court found that FAB's "machinations" in procuring a second copy of the letter showed that it was "obviously wary" that the letter might be privileged.

The bankruptcy court held invalid Latham Four's vote. It allowed the vote of BTNY, however, finding that the creditor had proved it had not relied on FAB's statements in deciding to reject Century Glove's plan. The court declined to bar FAB from participating further in the reorganization, finding such a sanction "too harsh," but instead, ordered FAB to pay for "all costs incurred by [Century Glove] in prosecuting" its motions. The amount of these damages was not specified. Both parties appealed the decision to the district court.

In a decision dated January 5, 1988, the district court affirmed the bankruptcy court rulings allowing BTNY's vote, but reversed the designation of Latham Four and the imposition of money sanctions against FAB. The district court disagreed that § 1125(b) requires approval for all materials accompanying a solicitation, and found such a reading in conflict with the bankruptcy code's policy of fostering free negotiation among creditors. The district court held that merely supplying additional information does not constitute "bad faith" or a violation of the bankruptcy rules. Therefore, the court concluded, the bankruptcy court had erred in finding that FAB had improperly solicited rejections of the Century Glove plan.

The district court next considered whether FAB had improperly sought acceptance of its own plan. The court found that, in order to facilitate negotiations, communications between creditors should not easily be read as solicitations. Because Bloxom did not make a "specific request for an official vote," *In re Snyder*, 51 B.R. 432, 437 (Bankr.D.Utah 1985), FAB's action "may only be fairly characterized as part of FAB's negotiations." Because FAB did not unlawfully solicit rejections, and did not solicit acceptances, the designation and sanction orders of the bankruptcy court were reversed. Century Glove appeals to this court.

* * *

IV.

Century Glove argues that the district court erred in holding FAB did not improperly solicit rejections of Century Glove's reorganization plan. Since a district court sits in an appellate capacity over bankruptcy decisions, our review of the district court's decision is plenary. * * * We should apply the same standard of review the district court should have applied. The bankruptcy court based its finding that FAB had violated § 1125(b) primarily on its determination that a solicitee may not be provided with materials not approved by the court. The district court disagreed with this reading of the law. As a question of the proper interpretation of the bankruptcy code, we have plenary review. However, we can reverse the factual findings of the bankruptcy court only if, applying the proper law, they are clearly erroneous.

Section 1125(b) states, in pertinent part, that:

> An acceptance or rejection of a plan may not be solicited after the commencement of the case under this title from a holder of a claim or interest with respect to such claim or interest, unless, at the time of or before such solicitation, there is transmitted to such holder the plan or summary of the plan, and a written disclosure statement approved, after notice and a hearing, by the court as containing adequate information.

There is no question that, at the time of FAB's solicitations, the solicitees had received a summary of the plan and a court-approved statement disclosing adequate information. Also, the bankruptcy court's factual conclusion that FAB was seeking rejections of Century Glove's plan is not clearly erroneous, and so must be assumed. Century Glove argues that FAB also was required to get court approval before it could disclose additional materials in seeking rejections.

Century Glove's interpretation of the section cannot stand. Century Glove argues, and the bankruptcy court assumed, that only approved statements may be communicated to creditors. The statute, however, never limits the facts which a creditor may receive, but only the time when a creditor may be solicited. Congress was concerned not that creditors' votes were based on misinformation, but that they were based on no information at all. * * * Rather than limiting the information available to a creditor, § 1125 seeks to guarantee a minimum amount of information to the creditor asked for its vote. See S.R. 95–989, at pp. 121 ("A plan is necessarily predicated on knowledge of the assets and liabilities being dealt with and on factually supported expectations as to the future course of the business * * *.") (*Senate Report*). The provision sets a floor, not a ceiling. Thus, we find that § 1125 does not on its face empower the bankruptcy court to require that all communications between creditors be approved by the court.

As the district court pointed out, allowing a bankruptcy court to regulate communications between creditors conflicts with the language of the statute. A creditor may receive information from sources other than the disclosure statement. Section 1125 itself defines "typical investor" of a particular class in part, as one having "such ability to obtain such information from sources other than the disclosure required by this section * * *." § 1125(a)(2)(C). In enacting the bankruptcy code, Congress contemplated that the creditors would be in active negotiations with the debtor over the plan. The necessity of "adequate information" was intended to help creditors in their negotiations. * * * Allowing the bankruptcy court to regulate communications between creditors under the guise of "adequate information" undercuts the very purpose of the statutory requirement.

Lastly, Century Glove's reading of § 1125 creates procedural difficulties. Century Glove provides this court no means to distinguish predictably between mere interpretations of the approved information, and additional information requiring separate approvals. Therefore, to be safe, the creditor must seek prior court approval for every communication with another creditor (or refrain from communication), whether soliciting a rejection or an acceptance. Congress can hardly have intended such a result. It would multiply hearings, hence expense and delay, at a time when efficiency is greatly needed.[7] We also note that, as expressed in the House Report, Congress evidently contemplated a single hearing on the adequacy of the disclosure statement.[8]

Century Glove argues that two additional instances show that FAB violated § 1125(b). First, it claims that FAB's draft plan contained material misrepresentations, mostly omissions. Second, it claims that FAB improperly disclosed to Latham Four a letter the bankruptcy court later found privileged. The bankruptcy court found both "improper" in support of its finding under § 1125(b), and Century Glove argues that the bankruptcy court's decision can be affirmed on these grounds. The problem with the argument is that it rests on an erroneous interpretation of the law. Once adequate information has been provided a creditor, § 1125(b) does not limit communication between creditors. It is not an anti-fraud device. Thus, the bankruptcy court erred in holding that FAB had violated § 1125(b) by communicating with other materials. The district court therefore properly reversed the bankruptcy court on this issue.

V.

Though FAB was not limited in its solicitation of rejections, § 1125 did prevent FAB from soliciting acceptances of its own plan. The bankruptcy court held that, "since FAB was apparently seeking approval of a plan which was not yet filed," FAB violated § 1125. The court also found that FAB's actions violated the spirit of § 1121, which provides the debtor with a limited, exclusive right to present a plan. Reversing, the district court held that solicitations barred by § 1125(b) include only the "specific request for an official vote," and not discussions of and negotiations over a plan leading up to its presentation. * * * Because Bloxom explained that he was sending the draft only for discussion purposes, the district court found that the transmittal "may only be fairly

---

[7] Expense was a prime reason Congress suspended the applicability of the securities laws to reorganizations. * * * The costs of delay was a prime reason the debtor was given a limited "exclusivity period" to present its reorganization plan.

* * *

[8] Century Glove relies for its interpretation of § 1125 entirely on statements in a bankruptcy treatise. See 5 Collier on Bankruptcy § 1125.03, at 1125–39 (15th ed.1987). The author found the provision ambiguous, and states only that a creditor "should" seek approval. As argued above, strong policy and administrative reasons—not to mention the likely intent of Congress—argue that this court should not impose any additional requirements on communications between creditors.

characterized as part of FAB's negotiations." We exercise plenary review over the proper interpretation of the legal term "solicitation."

We agree with the district court that "solicitation" must be read narrowly. A broad reading of § 1125 can seriously inhibit free creditor negotiations. All parties agree that FAB is not barred from honestly negotiating with other creditors about its unfiled plan. "Solicitations with respect to a plan do not involve mere requests for opinions." *Senate Report*, 1978 U.S.C.C.A.A.N. at 5907. The purpose of negotiations between creditors is to reach a compromise over the terms of a tentative plan. The purpose of compromise is to win acceptance for the plan. We find no principled, predictable difference between negotiation and solicitation of future acceptances. We therefore reject any definition of solicitation which might cause creditors to limit their negotiations.[9]

A narrow definition of "solicitation" does not offend the language or policy of § 1121(b). The section provides only that the debtor temporarily has the exclusive right to *file* a plan (and thus have it voted on). It does not state that the debtor has a right to have its plan *considered* exclusively.[10] A right of exclusive consideration is not warranted in the policy of the section. Congress believed that debtors often delay confirmation of a plan, while creditors want quick confirmation. Therefore, *unlimited* exclusivity gave a debtor "undue bargaining leverage," because it could use the threat of delay to force unfair concessions. House Report, 1978 U.S.C.C.A.A.N. at 6191. On the other hand, Congress evidently felt that creditors might not seek the plan fairest to the debtor. Therefore, Congress allowed a *limited* period of exclusivity, giving the debtor "adequate time to negotiate a settlement, without unduly delaying creditors." Id. Section 1121 allows a debtor the threat of limited delay to offset the creditors' voting power of approval. FAB did nothing to reduce Century's threat of limited delay, and so did not offend the balance of bargaining powers created by § 1121 or the "spirit" of the law.

On the contrary, Century Glove's reading of § 1121(b) would in fact give the debtor powers not contemplated by Congress. The ability of a creditor to compare the debtor's proposals against other possibilities is a powerful tool by which to judge the reasonableness of the proposals. A broad exclusivity provision, holding that only the debtor's plan may be "on the table," takes this tool from creditors. Other creditors will not have comparisons with which to

---

[9] Barring negotiations also would provide an unwarranted boon for the debtor: creditors wholly unable to be sure that an alternative plan can be agreed [to] are more likely to vote for the debtor's proposal rather than risk unknown delay.

[10] The bankruptcy court, perhaps recognizing this, found only that FAB violated the section's "spirit."

judge the proposals of the debtor's plan, to the benefit of the debtor proposing a reorganization plan. The history of § 1121 gives no indication that Congress intended to benefit the debtor in this way. The legislative history counsels a narrow reading of the section, one which FAB's actions do not violate.

We recognize that § 1125(b) bars the untimely solicitation of an "acceptance or rejection," indicating that the same definition applies to both. A narrow definition might allow a debtor to send materials seeking to prepare support for the plan, "for the consideration of the creditors," without adequate information approved by the court. Though such preparatory materials may undermine the purpose of adequate disclosure, the potential harm is limited in several ways. First, a creditor still must receive adequate information before casting a final vote, giving the creditor a chance to reconsider its preliminary decision. The harm is further limited by free and open negotiations between creditors. Last, because they are not "solicitations," pre-disclosure communications may still be subject to the stricter limitations of the securities laws. § 1125(e). Where, as here, the creditors are counseled and already have received disclosure about the debtor's business, there seems little need for additional procedural formalities. * * *

Therefore, we hold that a party does not solicit acceptances when it presents a draft plan for the consideration of another creditor, but does not request that creditor's vote. Applying this definition, FAB did not solicit acceptances of its plan. Century Glove does not dispute that FAB never asked for a vote, and clearly stated that the plan was not yet available for approval. Bloxom communicated with lawyers for the creditors, and there is no suggestion by Century that these lawyers did not understand the limitations. Also as Century argues, FAB never sent its plan to Hartford Insurance because Hartford firmly opposed Century's plan. Contrary to Century's conclusion, though, this fact argues that FAB sent copies of its plan because it was interested in obtaining rejections, not acceptances. (An opponent of Century's plan would be an ideal person to solicit for acceptances.) These undisputed facts require a finding that FAB did not "solicit" acceptances within the meaning of § 1125(b).

VI.

We hold that the district court correctly determined that Century Glove failed to show that FAB violated § 1125 by soliciting acceptances or improperly soliciting rejections. We therefore will affirm the district court's order reversing the imposition of costs against FAB. We do not decide, however, whether the circumstances merit designation of the votes of any creditors.

NOTE

Century Glove's narrow reading of solicitation has become the majority rule. However, in *In re Clamp–All Corp.*, 233 B.R. 198 (Bankr.D.Mass.1999), *Century Glove* was criticized for failing to "sufficiently recognize Congress' intention to allow the debtor a reasonable time to obtain confirmation of a plan without the threat of a competing plan." A § 1121(b) violation must be evaluated "not only in terms of its effect on the ability of a debtor to delay reorganization, but also in terms of its interference with the debtor's efforts to propose and confirm a plan of reorganization." The court then held that non-debtor parties are prohibited from circulating solicitation materials before a disclosure statement has been approved under § 1125(b). Therefore, two creditors, who had distributed their proposed competing plan of reorganization and unapproved disclosure statement to all other creditors during the exclusivity period and before the disclosure hearing, violated both §§ 1121(b) and 1125(b). Faced with the difficult task of finding a remedy for the creditors' irreversible acts, the court turned to § 510(c), subordinated their claims to all other non-insider claims, and required them to pay the debtor's attorney's fees.

In Robert Keach, *A Hole in the Glove: Why "Negotiation" Should Trump "Solicitation,"* 22-5 Am. Bankr. Inst. J. 22 (2003), the author criticizes two controversial unreported rulings of the Delaware Bankruptcy Court in the *Stations Holdings* and *NII Holdings* cases designating the votes of creditors that had signed a "lock-up agreement" after the petition date but before approval of a disclosure statement. Keech argues that since the parties in the Delaware cases were both sophisticated and well-informed, the decisions "had the effect of protecting parties who do not need protection from their own informed choices" and did not serve any of the purposes of §§ 1125 and 1126.

NOTE: PREPACKAGED BANKRUPTCIES

"Prepackaged bankruptcies" or "pre-packs" are Chapter 11 cases that are filed solely to implement an already fully negotiated restructuring that requires confirmation of a reorganization plan. In such cases, the debtor will solicit acceptances pre-bankruptcy using a prospectus that complies with applicable securities laws and regulations rather than a court-approved disclosure statement, and assuming sufficient acceptances are obtained will thereafter concurrently file a Chapter 11 petition, the preapproved plan and the pre-bankruptcy acceptances in order to finally implement the restructuring through confirmation of a Chapter 11 plan. Section 1126(b) specifically authorizes the court to rely upon pre-bankruptcy acceptances solicited in accordance with applicable nonbankruptcy law. What if the acceptances come in after the commencement of the prepackaged bankruptcy in light of the general rule that a debtor cannot solicit acceptances or rejections to a plan postpetition until the holders of each claim or interest have received a bankruptcy court-approved disclosure statement? Does the confirmation process need to be put on hold pending court approval of a disclosure statement and resolicitation? BAPCPA added § 1125(g), making it clear that "an acceptance or rejection of the plan may be solicited from a holder of a claim or interest if such solicitation complies with applicable nonbankruptcy law and if such holder was solicited before the commencement of the case in a manner complying with applicable nonbankruptcy law."

NOTE: SMALL BUSINESS CASES

Prior to 2005, small business debtors (of whom there were virtually none, since the prior small businesses provisions were both unattractive and elective) had the exclusive right to file a plan until 100 days after the date of the order for relief. The exclusivity deadline could be extended for cause under § 1121(e)(3)(B) if it were demonstrated that "[t]he need for an increase is caused by circumstances for which the debtor should not be held accountable."

Under BAPCPA, the small business provisions are no longer optional. All business debtors with less than $2,190,000 in debt (other than single asset real estate debtors who are treated separately) must comply with the special small business provision. § 101(51C) ("small business case") & (51D) ("small business debtor"). Section 1121(e) extends the small business debtor's exclusivity period to 180 days and the absolute plan-filing deadline to 300 days after the date of the order for relief. The court will not be permitted to extend those periods unless: (1) it is demonstrated by a preponderance of the evidence that it is more likely than not that the court will confirm the plan within a reasonable period of time; (2) a new deadline is imposed at the time the extension is granted; and (3) an order is signed before the existing deadline expires.

These provisons make it more difficult for the small business debtor to extend the exclusivity period. The preponderance of the evidence standard places the burden on the movant (usually the debtor in these instances) to show that it will propose a confirmable plan. The old standard only required the debtor to establish that it should not be held accountable for its failure to file a plan. Moreover, small business debtors will need to ensure that they move quickly to seek extensions so that the court has adequate time to enter any extension order before the expiration of the statutory periods.

Under pre-2005 law, a court could conditionally approve a disclosure statement in a small business case or combine the hearings on the disclosure statement and plan. The 2005 Act goes further by authorizing the court to determine that the plan itself provides adequate information, making it unnecessary to file a separate disclosure statement.

Small business debtors have significant additional reporting and record-keeping requirements, § 1116, and the U.S. Trustee has increased monitoring responsibilities in small business cases. 28 U.S.C. § 586(a). It is difficult to determine how the U.S. Trustee's increased monitoring function in small business cases affects a small business debtor's ability to conduct its normal business operations. However, many contend that requiring the U.S. Trustee involvement in a small business debtor's business affairs only hinders the small business debtor's reorganization efforts.

Finally, under § 362(n), serial filing of small business cases is discouraged by limiting the application of the automatic stay in subsequent cases. It is unclear why subsequent orderly liquidation under Chapter 11 in the event a small business reorganization effort fails should be discouraged.

b. Trading Claims

In *Century Glove*, the debtor and FAB are struggling over the solicitation of votes on the debtor's plan. FAB persuades other creditors to vote against the debtor's plan—in part by indicating a possible alternative—in order to defeat a plan it believes to be against its interests. The secured creditor in the following case follows a somewhat different strategy—buying the claims, rather than soliciting the votes of the holders. There is no requirement that a court-approved disclosure statement be delivered to the seller before a claim is purchased, but the effect of the transfer of the claim is to transfer the vote as well. Some of the issues raised by strategic claim-buying are discussed in the following case.

In re Figter Limited
United States Court of Appeals, Ninth Circuit, 1997.
118 F.3d 635.

■ FERNANDEZ, Circuit Judge.

Figter Limited, a Chapter 11 debtor and owner of Skyline Terrace, an apartment complex, appeals from the district court's affirmance of the bankruptcy court's decision that Teachers Insurance and Annuity Association of America (Teachers), the holder of a $15,600,000 promissory note secured by a first deed of trust on Skyline Terrace, bought twenty-one unsecured claims in good faith and that it could vote each one separately. We affirm.

Background

Figter filed a voluntary petition under Chapter 11 of the Bankruptcy Code. It owns Skyline Terrace, a 198–unit residential apartment complex located in

Los Angeles. Teachers is a creditor. It holds a $15,600,000 promissory note executed by Figter. The note is secured by a first deed of trust on Skyline Terrace and by $1,400,000 of cash on hand. In fact, Teachers is Figter's only secured creditor and is the only member of Class 2 in a reorganization plan proposed by Figter. The plan contemplates full payment of Teachers' secured claim, but at a disputed rate of interest. Thus, under Figter's plan, Teachers' claim is not impaired. The plan calls for the impairment of Class 3 unsecured claims by payment at only 80% of their face value.

Teachers has opposed Figter's reorganization plan from its inception because, among other things, that plan contemplates the conversion of Skyline Terrace Apartments into condominiums, with payment to and partial releases by Teachers as the units sell. That could easily result in a property that was part condominium and part rentals, if the plan ultimately fails in operation.

Teachers proposed a plan of its own, which provided for the transfer of Skyline Terrace and the cash collateral to Teachers in satisfaction of its secured claim, as well as a payment of Class 3 unsecured claims at 90%. Teachers' plan was premised on the assumption that its claim was partly unsecured. However, on May 31, 1994, before the purchases of other claims took place, the bankruptcy court determined that Skyline Terrace had a value of $19,300,000. Thus, Teachers' claim in the amount of $17,960,000 was fully secured. It did not thereafter pursue its plan. From October 27, 1994 until October 31, 1994, Teachers purchased twenty-one of the thirty-four unsecured claims in Class 3 at one hundred cents on the dollar, for a total purchase price of $14,588. Teachers had made the same offer to all of the Class 3 claim holders, but not all accepted it. The offer remained open. Teachers then filed notices of transfer of claims with the court, as is required under Bankruptcy Rule 3001(e)(2). Those notices were served on all affected parties, including Figter. No objections were filed by the unsecured creditors. The district court upheld the bankruptcy court's determination regarding Teachers' purchase of the unsecured claims. As a result, Figter's plan is unconfirmable because it is unable to meet the requirements of § 1129(a)(10); there will not be an impaired, consenting class of claims. That will preclude a "cram down" of Teachers' secured claim under § 1129(b). Figter has appealed in an attempt to avoid that result.

* * *

Discussion

Figter asserts that Teachers should be precluded from voting its purchased Class 3 claims because it did not buy them in good faith. Figter also asserts that even if the claims were purchased in good faith, Teachers cannot vote them separately, but is limited to one total vote as a Class 3 creditor. If Figter were correct in either of its assertions, it could obtain Class 3 approval of its plan and enhance its chances of cramming down Teachers' Class 2 claims. But Figter is not correct.

A. Good Faith.

The Bankruptcy Code provides that "[o]n request of a party in interest, and after notice and a hearing, the court may designate any entity whose acceptance or rejection of [a] plan was not in good faith, or was not solicited or procured in good faith or in accordance with the provisions of this title." 11 U.S.C. § 1126(e). In this context, designate means disqualify from voting. The Bankruptcy Code does not further define the rather murky term "good faith." That job has been left to the courts.

The Supreme Court brought some clarity to this area when it decided *Young v. Higbee Co.*, 324 U.S. 204 (1945). In *Young*, the Court was discussing the predecessor to § 1126(e) when it declared that if certain persons "had declined to accept [the] plan in bad faith, the court, under section 203 could have denied them the right to vote on the plan at all." Id. at 210–11. It went on to explain that the provision was intended to apply to those "whose selfish purpose was to obstruct a fair and feasible reorganization in the hope that someone would pay them more than the ratable equivalent of their proportionate part of the bankrupt assets." Id. at 211. In other words, the section was intended to apply to those who were not attempting to protect their own proper interests, but who were, instead, attempting to obtain some benefit to which they were not entitled. * * * While helpful, those reflections by the Court do not fully answer the question before us. Other courts have further illuminated the area.

If a person seeks to secure some untoward advantage over other creditors for some ulterior motive, that will indicate bad faith. * * * But that does not mean that creditors are expected to approach reorganization plan votes with a high degree of altruism and with the desire to help the debtor and their fellow creditors. Far from it.

> If a selfish motive were sufficient to condemn reorganization policies of interested parties, very few, if any, would pass muster. On the other hand, pure malice, "strikes" and blackmail, and the purpose to destroy an enterprise in order to advance the interests of a competing business, all plainly constituting bad faith, are motives which may be accurately described as ulterior.

In re Pine Hill Collieries Co., 46 F.Supp. 669, 671 (E.D.Pa.1942).

That is to say, we do not condemn mere enlightened self interest, even if it appears selfish to those who do not benefit from it. * * *

Thus, if Teachers acted out of enlightened self interest, it is not to be condemned simply because it frustrated Figter's desires. That is true, even if

Teachers purchased Class 3 claims for the very purpose of blocking confirmation of Figter's proposed plan. * * * That self interest can extend even further without being an ulterior motive. It has been held that a creditor commits no wrong when he votes against a plan of a debtor who has a lawsuit pending against the creditor, for that will not, by itself, show bad faith. * * * It has also been held that no bad faith is shown when a creditor chooses to benefit his interest as a creditor as opposed to some unrelated interest. * * * And the mere fact that a creditor has purchased additional claims for the purpose of protecting his own existing claim does not demonstrate bad faith or an ulterior motive. "As long as a creditor acts to preserve what he reasonably perceives as his fair share of the debtor's estate, bad faith will not be attributed to his purchase of claims to control a class vote." *In re Gilbert*, 104 B.R. 206, 217 (Bankr.W.D.Mo.1989).

Courts, on the other hand, have been sensitive to situations where a company, which was not a preexisting creditor, has purchased a claim for the purpose of blocking an action against it. They have seen that as an indication of bad faith. * * * The same has been true where creditors were associated with a competing business and desired to destroy the debtor's business in order to further their own. * * * And when the debtor had claims against itself purchased by an insider or affiliate for the purpose of blocking a plan, or fostering one, that was seen as a badge of bad faith. * * * Figter would have us add that in a single asset bankruptcy, claim purchasing activities, like those of Teachers, are in bad faith. It cites no authority for that, and we see no basis for establishing *that* as a per se rule.

In short, the concept of good faith is a fluid one, and no single factor can be said to inexorably demand an ultimate result, nor must a single set of factors be considered. It is always necessary to keep in mind the difference between a creditor's self interest as a creditor and a motive which is ulterior to the purpose of protecting a creditor's interest. Prior cases can offer guidance, but, when all is said and done, the bankruptcy court must simply approach each good faith determination with a perspicacity derived from the data of its informed practical experience in dealing with bankrupts and their creditors.

Here, the bankruptcy court did exactly that. It decided that Teachers was not, for practical purposes, the proponent of an alternate plan when it sought to purchase the Class 3 claims. Nor, it found, did Teachers seek to purchase a small number of claims for the purpose of blocking Figter's plan, while injuring other creditors, even if it could do that in some circumstances. Rather, Teachers offered to purchase all Class 3 claims, and only some of those claimants' refusals to sell precluded it from doing so. Moreover, Teachers was a lender, not a competing apartment owner. It acted to protect its interests as Figter's major creditor. It reasonably feared that it could be left with a very complex lien situation, if Figter went forward with its plan. Instead of holding a lien covering the whole of the property, it could have wound up with separate fractured liens on various parts of the property, while other parts were owned by others. That could create a very undesirable mix of owners and renters and of debtors and nondebtors. Added to that was the actual use of cash, which was collateral for the debt owed to Teachers. It cannot be said that Teachers' concerns were irrational.

Based on all that was before it, the bankruptcy court decided that in this case Teachers was a creditor which acted in a good faith attempt to protect its interests and not with some ulterior motive. We cannot say that it erred in making that ultimate determination.

B. Voting.

Figter's fallback position is that even if Teachers did act in good faith, it must be limited to one vote for its twenty-one claims. That assertion is answered by the language of the Bankruptcy Code, which provides that:

> A class of claims has accepted a plan if such plan has been accepted by creditors... that hold at least two-thirds in amount and *more than one-half in number of the allowed claims* of such class held by creditors... that have accepted or rejected such plan.

§ 1126(c) (emphasis added). That language was interpreted in *Gilbert*, 104 B.R. at 211, where the court reasoned:

> The formula contained in Section 1126(c) speaks in terms of the *number of claims*, not the number of creditors, that actually vote for or against the plan. . ... Each claim arose out of a separate transaction, evidencing separate obligations for which separate proofs of claim were filed. Votes of acceptance... are to be computed only on the basis of filed and allowed proofs of claim. . ... [The creditor] is entitled to one vote for each of his unsecured Class X claims.

That same view was iterated in *Concord Square Apartments of Wood Cty., Ltd. v. Ottawa Properties, Inc.*, 174 B.R. 71, 74 (Bankr.S.D.Ohio 1994), where the court held that a creditor with "multiple claims, has a voting right for each claim it holds." We agree. It would not make much sense to require a vote by creditors who held "more than one-half in number of the allowed claims" while at the same time limiting a creditor who held two or more of those claims to only one vote. If allowed claims are to be counted, they must be counted regardless of whose hands they happen to be in.

Figter seeks some succor from the Supreme Court's indication in *Dewsnup v. Timm* that ambiguous language in the Code should not be taken to effect a sea change in pre-Code practice. However, that does not help Figter's cause. In the first place, as we have indicated, the present language is not ambiguous. In the second place, the old law to which Figter refers relied upon a code section which required voting approval by a "majority in number of all creditors whose claims have been allowed." Bankruptcy Act of 1898, ch. 541, § 12 (repealed 1938). It is pellucid that "a majority in number of all creditors" is not at all like "more than one-half in number" of all claims. The former focuses on claimants; the latter on claims.

Nor is our conclusion affected by cases where other sections of the bankruptcy code, or other acts by creditors, were involved. For example, the predecessor to § 702 indicated that a creditor could vote for the trustee. In *In re Latham Lithographic Corp.*, 107 F.2d 749 (2d Cir. 1939), there was an attempt to split a single claim into multiple claims for the purpose of creating multiple creditors who could vote in a trustee election. It is not surprising that the court did not permit that. * * * And in *In re Gilbert*, 115 B.R. 458, 461 (Bankr.S.D.N.Y.1990), the court held that an involuntary petition in bankruptcy must be filed by three creditors, and a single creditor with three separate claims is still one creditor. * * * In fact, the involuntary petition section actually requires that there be three or more *entities*. See § 303(b). Certainly, a creditor with three claims is still a single entity.

Of course, that is not to say that a creditor can get away with splitting one claim into many, but that is not what happened here. Teachers purchased a number of separately incurred and separately approved claims (each of which carried one vote) from different creditors. There simply is no reason to hold that those separate votes suddenly became one vote, a result which would be exactly the opposite of claim splitting.

Therefore, the bankruptcy court did not err.

Conclusion

Figter hoped to obtain approval of a reorganization plan, which would require Teachers to thole what it saw as a diminution of its creditor's rights. Those hopes were dashed when Teachers bought up most of the Class 3 claims in an effort to protect its own Class 2 claim. Because the bankruptcy court determined that Teachers acted to protect its valid creditor's interest, rather than for ulterior motives, it held that Teachers had acted in good faith. That precluded designation of Teachers' purchased claims. The bankruptcy court also determined that Teachers could vote each of its twenty-one claims separately; it was not limited to a single vote. The district court affirmed those decisions. Because the bankruptcy court did not err in either its factual or its legal determinations, we agree with the district court and affirm the decision.

AFFIRMED.

NOTES

1. Note that debtors and their insiders cannot use the *Figter* claim buying strategy to confirm their plans. Debtors ordinarily cannot use estate funds to purchase claims outside of a plan. And if insiders do so using their own funds, the one-consenting-class requirement of § 1129(a)(10) must be determined "without including any acceptance of the plan by any insider."

2. In *Figter*, Teachers was able to buy sufficient claims to cause the unsecured class to reject the debtor's plan. Although Teachers was not seeking to confirm a competing plan in *Figter*, the Ninth Circuit's discussion of the majority-in-number requirement in § 1126(c) suggests that a claim buyer may not only be able to block opposing plans, but also affirmatively cause creditor classes to accept its own plan. If Teachers had acquired two-thirds in amount of the unsecured claims in addition to a majority in number (as well as the $17 million secured claim it began with), it presumably would have had the votes not only to reject the debtor's plan, but also to confirm its own plan. Does the Ninth Circuit's plain meaning interpretation of the majority-in-number requirement accord with the purpose of the requirement? Why do we measure the number as well as the dollar amount of the accepting claims? If one creditor holds a majority of the number of claims and two-thirds of the dollar amount, should it be able to impose a reorganization plan on all the other members of its class?

3. In *In re Allegheny Int'l, Inc.*, 118 B.R. 282 (Bankr.W.D.Pa.1990), after almost two years of extensive plan negotiations, the debtor filed an internal reorganization plan. After the debtor's disclosure statement had been approved, Japonica Partners, L.P. launched a hostile takeover bid by filing a competing reorganization plan calling for the distribution of the equity in Reorganized Allegheny to Japonica. Thereafter Japonica began to aggressively purchase bank claims until it held slightly more than one-third of the bank claims. In addition, Japonica purchased slightly less than one-third of the senior unsecured debt. When Japonica's no votes on the debtor's plan caused both the bank class and the senior unsecured class to reject the debtor's plan, the debtor sought to designate Japonica's votes under § 1126. The bankruptcy court found that Japonica acted in bad faith:

Under Chapter 11, creditors and interest holders vote for or against a plan of reorganization, after adequate disclosure, if such vote is in their best economic interests. If, as in the instant case, an outsider to the process can purchase a blocking position, those creditors and interest holders are disenfranchised. * * * Moreover, Japonica, who chose to become a creditor, should not have veto control over the reorganization process.

118 B.R. at 290.

As a footnote, although the *Allegheny* court confirmed the debtor's plan, when Japonica sought to appeal the confirmation order, the parties negotiated a settlement whereby Japonica acquired control of Allegheny. Is Teacher's strategic claim buying in *Figter* meaningfully distinguishable from Japonica's in *Allegheny*? The legal issues and risks associated with strategic claim-buying in Chapter 11 are discussed in a series of articles by Chaim J. Fortgang & Thomas Moers Mayer published at 12 Cardozo L.Rev. 1 (1990), 13 Cardozo L. Rev. 1 (1991), and 15 Cardozo L. Rev. 733 (1993).

4. Bankruptcy law's reliance on the consent of "similarly situated" class members to bind an entire class has become especially problematic in recent years as consent rights have increasingly been divorced from economic rights through modern "financial engineering," that is the emergence and manipulation of new financial instruments and markets. This separation is not an entirely new phenomenon: certainly the robber barons of old understood that in the reorganization context control of the vote of one constituency might advantage their other economic interests to the detriment of the voting class. But the ability to engage in undisclosed and nontransparent hedging transactions through derivatives has multiplied the opportunities for this sort of manipulation and degraded the ability of the courts to control abuse. Stephen Lubben, *Credit Derivatives and the Future of Chapter 11*, 81 AM. BANKR. L. J. 405 (2007). Thus bondholders may actually profit when "their" bonds lose value because they hold offsetting positions in credit-default swaps issued against those same securities. The notional value of credit default swaps are commonly many times greater than the aggregate amount of the bond issues upon which they are based. <www.isda.org> International Swaps & Derivatives Association 2008 Mid-Year Market Survey (total outstanding notional amount of credit default swaps as of July, 2008 $54.6 trillion). Through options, swaps, and participations, security holders can and do commonly acquire or dispose of substantially all the underlying economic interests (or even become "short" the relevant interest) without transferring the correlative right to vote on a reorganization plan or other legal consent rights. Bernard Black & Henry Hu, *Equity and Debt Decoupling and Empty Voting II: Importance and Extensions*, 156 U. PA. L. REV. 625 (2008); Iman Anabtawi & Lynn Stout, *Fiduciary Duties for*

Activist Shareholders, 60 STAN. L. REV. 1255 (2008); Stephen Lubben, *Credit Derivatives and the Future of Chapter 11*, 81 AM. BANKR. L. J. 405 (2007). Bankruptcy law will have to take account of these developments in determining whose consent is, or should be, relevant or transformative to avoid undermining public acceptance and credibility of bankruptcy processes. To date, the complexity of the issues, coupled with a general ideological commitment to deregulated financial markets, appears to have effectively deterred meaningful responses or changes in law to address these concerns. The dramatic financial crisis of 2008-09, and resulting disrepute into which financial deregulation has fallen both ideologically and politically, may open a window to begin to address this issue.

4. IMPAIRMENT OF CLAIMS OR INTERESTS

Only impaired classes vote. §§ 1126, 1129(a)(8). Unimpaired classes are deemed to have accepted the plan. § 1126(f). "Impairment" is defined in § 1124.

Under the Bankruptcy Act of 1898 a class of creditors was "affected" by a plan only if "its interest shall be materially and adversely affected thereby." The Code shifted from the standard of "materially and adversely affected" to the standard of § 1124(1) which states that impairment is present unless the plan leaves "unaltered" the rights of the holder of the claim or interest. Thus if stockholders are given nothing in a reorganization of an insolvent corporation they may not have been materially and adversely affected because they have lost nothing that had any present value. Nevertheless, under § 1124(1), they have been impaired because their rights as stockholders are being taken away by the plan. This is an important distinction. As an impaired class, they can effectively demand a valuation of the reorganizing firm before their interests can be eliminated without their consent. § 1129(b). Section 1124(1) makes it clear that an eliminated class is impaired even if that class would not be entitled to share in the reorganization in the event of cramdown, and, therefore, is a player in the negotiation process.

Since the § 1124(1) test of impairment is so broad, virtually all claims and interests are impaired in a Chapter 11 reorganization unless there is cure under § 1124(2). Under § 1124(2), the plan may effectively reinstate prepetition obligations on the prepetition terms. One reason to do so is to avoid soliciting votes and valuation hearings. Another may be to preserve for the reorganized firm favorable terms in the prebankruptcy loans, especially a below-market interest rate.

In *In re Southeast Co.*, 868 F.2d 335 (9th Cir. 1989), the issue raised was the scope of the cure necessary to effect reinstatement under § 1124(2) as an alternative to cramdown under § 1129(b). The note evidencing the mortgage loan in *Southeast* provided for current interest at 4% plus additional deferred interest, payable at maturity, of 2%. Upon default, the debtor obligated itself to pay current cash interest at 9%. The debtor defaulted prebankruptcy, and interest began to accrue at the default rate. The following year, the debtor filed in Chapter 11. Seeking to preserve the very favorable original loan terms on this secured claim, the debtor provided that the claim would be treated as unimpaired. The plan provided the debtor would bring the mortgage current by making the missed payments plus interest at 12% accruing from date due. The plan provided for future interest payments at the pre-default 6% rate, rather than the post-default 9% rate demanded by the mortgagee. The Ninth Circuit affirmed quoting *In re Entz–White Lumber and Supply, Inc.*, 850 F.2d 1338, 1342 (9th Cir. 1988): "[§ 1124] authorizes a plan to nullify all consequences of default, including avoidance of default penalties such as higher interest."

The Fifth Circuit in *In re Southland Corp.*, 160 F.3d 1054 (1998), was sharply critical of *Southeast* in rejecting the debtor's efforts to avoid default interest payments in that case. The bank demanded default interest for the period between the prebankruptcy default and the effective date of the reorganization plan. The court agreed with the bank's position and held that the "reinstatement" of the credit agreement under the reorganization plan did not automatically imply a "cure;" instead, the reinstatement simply returned the parties to their pre-bankruptcy status, not their pre-default status. Therefore, the debtor remained responsible for paying the default interest rate. Outside the context of reinstatement of a claim under § 1124 through a reorganization plan, even in the Ninth Circuit, postpetition interest may accrue on oversecured claims at the default rate under § 506(b). *GECC v. Future Media Productions, Inc.*, 536 F.3d 969 (9th Cir. 2008).

In 1994 § 1123(d) was added, ostensibly to prevent holders of residential mortgages from receiving the windfall of unbargained for interest-on-interest under *Rake v. Wade,* 508 U.S. 464 (1993). Section 1123(d) provides: "Notwithstanding subsection (a) of this section and sections 506(b), 1129(a)(7), and 1129(b) of this title, if it is proposed in a plan to cure a default the amount necessary to cure the default shall be determined in accordance with the underlying agreement and applicable nonbankruptcy law." Section 1123(d) can be read as requiring that the cure amount include default rate interest if "applicable nonbankruptcy law" would allow default rate interest. Compare *GECC v. Future Media Productions, supra* at 974 n.2 (noting plain language of § 1123(d) is consistent with a rule applying default rate).

Until 1994, § 1124 contained subsection (3), which provided that if the plan called for payment of a claim on the effective date of the plan by cash equal to "the allowed amount of such claim," the claim was not impaired. Thus, if the plan "cashed-out" a class of claims, under § 1126(f) the class, being unimpaired, was conclusively presumed to have accepted the plan. No solicitation of acceptances from that class was required because the class could not vote on confirmation of the plan. The most common application of the practice of cashing out classes under Chapter 11 plans is with respect to classes of small claims under § 1122(b) that are paid off to relieve the debtor of the burden of having to obtain the assent of what may be a host of small claims holders. According to the Section-by-Section Description § 213, 140 Cong.Rec. H10768 (1994), the reason for the deletion of § 1124(3) was to overrule *In re New Valley Corp.*, 168 B.R. 73 (Bankr.D.N.J.1994), which held that a claim cashed out under § 1124(3) was not entitled to postpetition interest even though the estate was solvent. This Section-by-Section Description contains a detailed explanation of how the deletion of § 1124(3) accomplishes the overruling of *New Valley*, but it gives no inkling that Congress grasped that the consequences of the amendment go far beyond the issue of postpetition interest. For example, it may no longer be possible to leave "convenience classes" of small claims, expressly authorized by § 1122(b), unimpaired. If so, there may be no administrative convenience in convenience classes since all impaired classes—convenience or not—must be solicited and vote in accordance with §§ 1125, 1126. Does the deletion of § 1124(3) de facto repeal § 1122(b) as well?

5. CLASSIFICATION OF CLAIMS

Since voting on acceptance or rejection of the plan is done by classes, the composition of the classes may have great strategic importance. If a class accepts the plan no member of that class not even those who reject the plan may assert rights under § 1129(b) including the absolute priority rule. The proponent of the plan normally knows in advance which creditors oppose the plan and are likely to reject it. The proponent may tailor the plan so that these claims are not impaired, or may provide in the plan for a classification of claims which puts dissenting creditors in a class in which it anticipates there will be sufficient favorable votes to assure approval by that class.

Two major questions arise with respect to classification. First, must the proponent place all similar claims and interests in the same class or may they be divided into more than one class? Section 1122(a) states that a claim or interest may be placed in a class "only if such claim or interest is substantially similar to other claims and interests of such class." Thus, claims that are not similar may not be classified together. But, except for a limited authorization of "convenience classes" of small claims, nothing in the Code either expressly authorizes or prohibits placing similar claims or interests in different classes.

Second, if the proponent can separate similar claims or interests into different classes, may the plan discriminate in the treatment accorded the different classes? Section 1123(a)(4) requires that the plan provide the same treatment for each claim or interest within the class. Thus, all claims classified together must be treated alike. There is no express requirement of equal treatment for similar claims in different classes, but § 1129(b)(1) mandates that the plan not "discriminate unfairly" against rejecting classes. Accepting classes waive their § 1129(b) objections, and so unfair discrimination is no more objectionable as to such classes than deviations from absolute priority. Moreover, as to dissenting classes, there is very little caselaw establishing the limits § 1129(b)(1) places on differential treatment of similar claims in different classes.

Bankruptcy Rule 3013 provides that on motion the court may determine classes of creditors and stockholders after notice and hearing. Hence, the proponent may obtain the court's approval of the makeup of the classes before acceptances of the plan are solicited.

Although § 1122(a) requires that claims and interests classified together be "substantially similar," the Code does not define "substantially similar." Claims or interests that are of unequal priority rank in liquidation are not similar. Thus, separate classification must be given to preferred stock and common stock, and perhaps to general unsecured debt and a debt that is subject to a clause subordinating it to all other debt of the debtor. Secured claims cannot be put into the same class if they are secured by different collateral. If there is more than one claim secured by the same collateral, separate classification is necessary if the claims have unequal priority, but a single class is appropriate if they have the same priority. For example, claims of bondholders secured by the same mortgage or deed of trust belong in the same class.

Unsecured debt of equal rank might be dissimilar because of the transaction out of which it grew or the identity of the creditor. Is it proper or necessary to separately classify debt owed to an insider and similar debt owed to other creditors? A 20-year debenture and a 30-day account payable are equal in priority if both are unsecured and there is no subordination clause in the debenture. Does the fact that the debenture represents a long-term investment and the account payable grew out of a nearly cash transaction justify separate classification and different treatment in the plan?

In re U.S. Truck Co.
United States Court of Appeals, Sixth Circuit, 1986.
800 F.2d 581.

- CORNELIA G. KENNEDY, Circuit Judge.

The Teamsters National Freight Industry Negotiating Committee (the Teamsters Committee), a creditor of U.S. Truck Company, Inc. (U.S. Truck)—the debtor-in-possession in this Chapter 11 bankruptcy proceeding—appeals the

District Court's order confirming U.S. Truck's Fifth Amended Plan of Reorganization. The Teamsters Committee complains that the plan does not satisfy three of the requirements of § 1129. The District Court, which presided over the matter after the resignation of Bankruptcy Judge STANLEY B. BERNSTEIN, held that the requirements of section 1129 had been satisfied. We agree.

I.

Underlying this appeal is the Teamsters Committee's claim that U.S. Truck is liable to its employees for rejecting a collective bargaining agreement between the local union and U.S. Truck. After filing its petition for relief under Chapter 11 of the Bankruptcy Code on June 11, 1982, U.S. Truck, a trucking company primarily engaged in intrastate shipping of parts and supplies for the automotive industry, sought to reject the collective bargaining agreement. U.S. Truck rejected the agreement with the approval of then-Bankruptcy Judge WOODS, in December 1982. Judge Woods found that rejection of the agreement was "absolutely necessary to save the debtor from collapse." New agreements have been negotiated to the satisfaction of each participating local union. Such agreements have been implemented over the lone dissent of the Teamsters Joint Area Rider Committee. Under the most recently mentioned agreement in the record (due to have expired in March 1985), U.S. Truck was able to record monthly profits in the range of $125,000 to $250,000. These new agreements achieved such results by reducing wages and requiring employees to buy their own trucking equipment, which the employees then leased to the company.

The parties agreed to an estimate of the size of the Teamsters Committee claim against U.S. Truck so that the confirmation plan could be considered. The District Court held a hearing to consider the plan on January 23, 1985. The court considered three objections by the Teamsters Committee to the plan. Consideration of the objections, and the court's treatment of them, requires an understanding of the statutory scheme for approval of a chapter 11 reorganization plan.

II.

Section 1129 contains two means by which a reorganization plan can be confirmed. The first way is to meet all eleven of the requirements of subsection (a), including (a)(8) which requires all impaired classes of claims or interests to accept the plan. The other way is to meet the requirements of subsection (b), which, first, incorporates all of the requirements of subsection (a), except for that contained in subsection (a)(8), and, second, imposes two additional requirements. Confirmation under subsection (b) is commonly referred to as a "cram down" because it permits a reorganization plan to go into effect over the objections of one or more impaired classes of creditors. In this case, U.S. Truck sought approval of its plan under this "cram down" provision.

III.

The Teamsters Committee's first objection is that the plan does not meet the requirement that at least one class of impaired claims accept the plan, see § 1129(a)(10), because U.S. Truck impermissibly gerrymandered the classes in order to neutralize the Teamsters Committee's dissenting vote. The reorganization plan contains twelve classes. The plan purports to impair five of these classes—Class VI (the secured claim of Manufacturer's National Bank of Detroit based on a mortgage); Class VII (the secured claim of John Graham, Trustee of Transportation Services, Inc., based on a loan); Class IX (the Teamsters Committee's claim based on rejection of the collective bargaining agreement); Class XI (all unsecured claims in excess of $200.00 including those arising from the rejection of executory contracts); and Class XII (the equity interest of the stockholder of the debtor). As noted above, § 1129(a)(10), as incorporated into subsection (b)(1), requires at least one of these classes of impaired claims to approve the reorganization plan before it can be confirmed. The parties agree that approval by Class XII would not count because acceptance must be determined without including the acceptance of the plan by any insider. See § 1129(a)(10). The Code's definition of "insider" clearly includes McKinlay Transport, Inc. * * * Thus, compliance with subsection (a)(10) depends on whether either of the other three classes that approved the plan—Class VI, Class VII, or Class XI—was a properly constructed impaired class. The Teamsters Committee argues that Classes VI and VII were not truly impaired classes and that Class XI should have included Class IX, and hence was an improperly constructed class.[6] Because we find that Class XI was a properly constructed class of impaired claims, we hold that the plan complies with subsection (a)(10).[7]

The issue raised by the Teamsters Committee's challenge is under what circumstances does the Bankruptcy Code permit a debtor to keep a creditor out of a class of impaired claims which are of a similar legal nature and are against the same property as those of the "isolated" creditor. The District Court held that the Code permits such action here because of the following circumstances: (1) the employees represented by the Teamsters Committee have a unique continued interest in the ongoing business of the debtor; (2) the mechanics of

---

[6] Had the debtor included the Teamsters Committee's claim in Class XI, the Committee's vote to reject the plan would have swung the results of the Class XI vote from an acceptance to a rejection. See § 1126(c) (setting forth the requirement that creditors holding at least two-thirds in amount of allowed claims of a class accept).

[7] For this reason, we need not decide the challenge to the status of Class VI and Class VII.

the Teamsters Committee's claim differ substantially from those of the Class XI claims; and (3) the Teamsters Committee's claim is likely to become part of the agenda of future collective bargaining sessions between the union and the reorganized company. Thus, according to the court, the interests of the Teamsters Committee are substantially dissimilar from those of the creditors in Class XI. We must decide whether the Code permits separate classification under such circumstances.

Congress has sent mixed signals on the issue that we must decide. Our starting point is § 1122.

* * *

The statute, by its express language, only addresses the problem of dissimilar claims being included in the same class. It does not address the correlative problem—the one we face here—of similar claims being put in different classes. Some courts have seized upon this omission, and have held that the Code does not require a debtor to put similar claims in the same class.

> We think the courts erred in holding that section 1122(a) prohibits classification based on the presence of a co-debtor. Section 1122(a) specifies that only claims which are "substantially similar" may be placed in the same class. It does not require that similar claims *must* be grouped together, but merely that any group created must be homogenous. * * * * Although some courts have held that section 1122(a) prohibits classification based on any criterion other than legal right to the debtor's assets, * * * the plain language of the statute contradicts such a construction. Moreover, section 1122(a) so interpreted would conflict with section 1322(b)(1), which specifically authorizes designation of more than one class of unsecured creditor, each presumably with equal legal rights to the debtor's estate.

Barnes v. Whelan, 689 F.2d 193, 201 (D.C.Cir. 1982) (emphasis in original) (holding that Chapter 13 debtor may group his unsecured creditors according to whether or not a co-debtor is present) * * *.

Further evidence that Congress intentionally failed to impose a requirement that similar claims be classified together is found by examining the "classification" sections of the former Bankruptcy Act. The applicable former provisions were 11 U.S.C., sections 597 (from former Chapter X) and 751 (from former Chapter XI).

> *§ 597. Classification of creditors and stockholders*
>
> For the purposes of the plan and its acceptance, the judge shall fix the division of creditors and stockholders into classes according to the nature of their respective claims and stock. For the purposes of such classification, the judge shall, if necessary, upon the application of the trus-

tee, the debtor, any creditor, or an indenture trustee, fix a hearing upon notice to the holders of secured claims, the debtor, the trustee, and such other persons as the judge may designate, to determine summarily the value of the security and classify as unsecured the amount in excess of such value.

§ 751. Classification of creditors

For the purposes of the arrangement and its acceptance, the court may fix the division of creditors into classes and, in the event of controversy, the court shall after hearing upon notice summarily determine such controversy.

Section 597 was interpreted to require all creditors of equal rank with claims against the same property to be placed in the same class. * * * Congress' switch to less restrictive language in section 1122 of the Code seems to warrant a conclusion that Congress no longer intended to impose the now-omitted requirement that similar claims be classified together. * * * However, the legislative history indicates that Congress may not have intended to change the prior rule. The Notes of the Senate Committee on the Judiciary state:

> This section [1122] codifies current case law surrounding the classification of claims and equity securities. It requires classification based on the nature of the claims or interests classified, and permits inclusion of claims or interests in a particular class only if the claim or interest being included is substantially similar to the other claims or interests of the class.

* * *

In this case, U.S. Truck is using its classification powers to segregate dissenting (impaired) creditors from assenting (impaired) creditors (by putting the dissenters into a class or classes by themselves) and, thus, it is assured that at least one class of impaired creditors will vote for the plan and make it eligible for cram down consideration by the court. We agree with the Teamsters Committee that there must be some limit on a debtor's power to classify creditors in such a manner. The potential for abuse would be significant otherwise. Unless there is some requirement of keeping similar claims together, nothing would stand in the way of a debtor seeking out a few impaired creditors (or even one such creditor) who will vote for the plan and placing them in their own class.[8]

---

[8] We need not speculate in this case whether the purpose of separate classification was to line up the votes in favor of the plan. The debtor admitted that to the District Court. * * *

We are unaware of any cases that deal with this problem as it arises in this case.[9] As we noted above, the legislative history of the Code provides little assistance in determining what limits there are to segregating similar claims. Nevertheless, we do find one common theme in the prior case law that Congress incorporated into section 1122. In those pre-Code cases, the lower courts were given broad discretion to determine proper classification according to the factual circumstances of each individual case.

* * *

The District Court noted three important ways in which the interests of the Teamsters Committee differ substantially from those of the other impaired creditors. Because of these differences, the Teamsters Committee has a different stake in the future viability of the reorganized company and has alternative means at its disposal for protecting its claim. The Teamsters Committee's claim is connected with the collective bargaining process. In the words of the Committee's counsel, the union employees have a "virtually unique interest." * * * These differences put the Teamsters Committee's claim in a different posture than the Class XI claims. The Teamsters Committee may choose to reject the plan not because the plan is less than optimal to it as a creditor, but because the Teamsters Committee has a noncreditor interest—e.g., rejection will benefit its members in the ongoing employment relationship. Although the Teamsters Committee certainly is not intimately connected with the debtor, to allow the Committee to vote with the other impaired creditors would be to allow it to prevent a court from considering confirmation of a plan that a significant group of creditors with similar interests have accepted. Permitting separate classification of the Teamsters Committee's claim does not automatically result in adoption of the plan. The Teamsters Committee is still protected by the provisions of subsections (a) and (b), particularly the requirements of subsection (b) that the plan not discriminate unfairly and that it be fair and equitable with respect to the Teamsters Committee's claim. In fact, the Teamsters Committee invokes those requirements, but as we note in the following sections, the plan does not violate them.

* * *

---

[9] In those cases where the courts have held that, as a general rule, similar claims need not be classified together, the debtor had not created the separate classes for the purpose of assuring acceptance * * * and the allegedly similar claims were treated differently under the plan * * *. In those cases where the courts have held that similar claims must be classified together, they have often faced problems of discriminatory treatment * * * and they have not had occasion to decide whether claims of the sort in this case are substantially similar * * *.

NOTE

Judge Kennedy states: "The Teamsters Committee's claim is connected with the collective bargaining process." 800 F.2d at 587. The district court opinion noted that the primary goal of the union was to restore, through the collective bargaining process, the terms of the labor contract which the debtor had rejected. In order to attain this end the union was willing to give up the damage claim that it was asserting in the bankruptcy. Apparently, the union believed that its opposition to the plan gave it leverage in the collective bargaining process. In an omitted portion of Judge Kennedy's opinion, she discussed the concern of the Teamsters that if the plan were confirmed the person taking control of the reorganized entity would liquidate the debtor and cause the loss of their jobs.

PROBLEM

Bank and various trade creditors held substantially all of the unsecured claims in Debtor's Chapter 11 bankruptcy. Bank held 60% in amount of the claims and opposed Debtor's plan. The trade creditors were willing to approve Debtor's plan. Debtor sought confirmation of its plan without approval of Bank by cramdown under § 1129(b). To that end Debtor placed Bank and the trade creditors in separate classes, anticipating that the trade creditor class would approve the plan and thus satisfy § 1129(a)(10). Debtor justified the classification on the ground that the trade creditors had advanced goods and services to Debtor in the past and would likely continue to do so in the future. Thus, their stake in the future viability of Debtor's business was different from that of Bank that wanted liquidation of Debtor's business. Would this classification meet the test of *U.S. Truck* for separate classes? *Hanson v. First Bank of South Dakota*, 828 F.2d 1310 (8th Cir. 1987).

Matter of Greystone III Joint Venture

United States Court of Appeals, Fifth Circuit, 1991.
995 F.2d 1274.

- EDITH H. JONES, Circuit Judge:

This appeal pits a debtor whose only significant asset is an office building in the troubled Austin, Texas real estate market against a lender who possesses a multi-million dollar lien on the property. After obtaining bankruptcy relief under Chapter 11, Greystone III proposed a "cramdown" plan of reorganization, hoping to force a write-down of over $3,000,000 on the secured lender's note and to retain possession and full ownership of the property. Over the secured lender's strenuous objections, the bankruptcy court confirmed the debtor's plan. On appeal, the district court upheld the bankruptcy court's judgment.

* * * [W]e must reverse. First, the Greystone plan impermissibly classified like creditors in different ways and manipulated classifications to obtain a favorable vote. Second, tenant security deposit holders were not properly deemed an "impaired" class under the circumstances of this plan. * * *

I.

Appellant Phoenix Mutual Life Insurance Corporation ("Phoenix") lent $8,800,000, evidenced by a non-recourse promissory note secured by a first lien, to Greystone to purchase the venture's office building. When Greystone defaulted on the loan, missing four payments, Phoenix posted the property for foreclosure. Greystone retaliated by filing a Chapter 11 bankruptcy reorganization petition.

At the date of bankruptcy Greystone owed Phoenix approximately $9,325,000, trade creditors approximately $10,000, and taxing authorities approximately $145,000. The bankruptcy court valued Phoenix's secured claim at $5,825,000, the appraised value of the office building, leaving Phoenix an unsecured deficiency of approximately $3,500,000—the difference between the aggregate owed Phoenix and its secured claim.

As filed, Greystone's Second Amended Plan of Reorganization (the "Plan"), the confirmation of which is challenged in this appeal, separately classified the Code-created unsecured deficiency claim of Phoenix Mutual, see § 1111(b), and the unsecured claims of the trade creditors. The Plan proposed to pay Phoenix and the trade creditors slightly less than four cents on the dollar for their unsecured claims, but it also provided that Greystone's general partner would satisfy the balance of the trade creditors' claims after confirmation of the Plan.

In a separate class, the Plan further provided for security deposit "claims" held by existing tenants of the office building. These claimants were promised, notwithstanding the debtor's eventual assumption of their leases * * *, 25% of their deposits upon approval of the Plan and 50% of their deposits at the expiration of their respective leases. The Plan stipulated that the general partner would "retain its legal obligations and... pay the [tenant]... creditors the balance of their claims upon confirmation."

Finally, Greystone's Plan contemplated a $500,000 capital infusion by the debtor's partners, for which they would reacquire 100% of the equity interest in the reorganized Greystone.

Unsurprisingly, Phoenix rejected this Plan, while the trade creditors and the class of holders of tenant security deposits voted to accept it. On January 27, 1989, the bankruptcy court held a confirmation hearing at which the Debtor orally modified its Plan to delete the statements that the general partner would pay the balance of trade debt and tenant security deposit claims after confirmation. A Phoenix representative testified that the insurance company was willing to fund its own plan of reorganization by paying off all unsecured creditors in cash in full after confirmation. The bankruptcy court refused to consider this proposal and then confirmed Greystone's modified Plan. The district court upheld the confirmation.

Phoenix Mutual now appeals on several grounds: (a) the plan classified Phoenix's unsecured deficiency claim separately from that of other unsecured creditors for no valid reason; * * * and (c) unpaid tenant security deposits were not impaired claims that could vote on the plan.

II.

Phoenix first attacks Greystone's classification of its unsecured deficiency claim in a separate class from that of the other unsecured claims against the debtor. This issue benefits from some background explanation.

Chapter 11 requires classification of claims against a debtor for two reasons. Each class of creditors will be treated in the debtor's plan of reorganization based upon the similarity of its members' priority status and other legal rights against the debtor's assets. § 1122. Proper classification is essential to ensure that creditors with claims of similar priority against the debtor's assets are treated similarly. Second, the classes must separately vote whether to approve a debtor's plan of reorganization. § 1129(a)(8), (10). A plan may not be confirmed unless either (1) it is approved by two-thirds in amount and more than one-half in number of each "impaired" class, §§ 1126(c), 1129(a)(8); or (2) at least one impaired class approves the plan, § 1129(a)(10), and the debtor fulfills the cramdown requirements of § 1129(b) to enable confirmation notwithstanding the plan's rejection by one or more impaired classes. Classification of claims thus affects the integrity of the voting process, for, if claims could be arbitrarily placed in separate classes, it would almost always be possible for the debtor to manipulate "acceptance" by artful classification.

In this case, Greystone's plan classified the Phoenix claim in separate secured and unsecured classes, a dual status afforded by § 1111(b) despite the nonrecourse nature of Phoenix's debt. Because of Phoenix's opposition to a reorganization, Greystone knew that its only hope for confirmation lay in the Bankruptcy Code's cramdown provision. § 1129(b). The substantive impact of cramdown will be discussed later. Procedurally, Greystone faced a dilemma in deciding how to obtain the approval of its cramdown plan by *at least one* class of "impaired" claims, as the Code requires.[3] § 1129(a)(10). Greystone anticipated an adverse vote of Phoenix's secured claim. If the Phoenix $3.5 million unsecured deficiency claim shared the same class as Greystone's other unsecured trade claims, it would swamp their $10,000 value in voting against confirmation. The only other arguably impaired class consisted of tenant security deposit claims, which, the bankruptcy court found, were not impaired at all.

Greystone surmounted the hurdle by classifying Phoenix's unsecured deficiency claim separately from the trade claims, although both classes were to be treated alike under the plan and would receive a cash payment equal to 3.42% of each creditor's claim. Greystone then achieved the required favorable vote of the trade claims class.

Phoenix contends that Greystone misapplied § 1122 by classifying its unsecured claim separately from those of trade creditors. The lower courts rejected Phoenix's argument in three steps. First, they held that § 1122 of the Code does not unambiguously prevent classification of like claims in separate classes. The only question is what types of class differentiations among like claims are acceptable. Second, Greystone's unsecured deficiency claim is "legally different" from that of the trade claims because it arises statutorily, pursuant to § 1111(b). Third, "good business reasons" justify the separate classification of these unsecured claims. We must address each of these arguments.

Section 1122 prescribes classification of claims for a reorganization as follows:

> **(a)** Except as provided in subsection (b) or this section, a plan may place a claim or an interest in a particular class only if such claim or interest is substantially similar to the other claims or interests of such claims.
>
> **(b)** A plan may designate a separate class of claims consisting only of every unsecured claim that is less than or reduced to an amount that the court approves as reasonable and necessary for administrative convenience.

We observe from this language that the lower courts' suggestion that § 1122 does not prevent classification of like claims in separate classes is oversimplified. It is true that § 1122(a) in terms only governs permissible *inclusions* of claims in a class rather requiring that all similar claims be grouped

---

[3] An impaired claim is defined at § 1124. For present purposes, it suffices to say that Phoenix was impaired both as a secured and unsecured creditor.

together. One cannot conclude categorically that § 1122(a) prohibits the formation of different classes from similar types of claims. But if § 1122(a) is wholly permissive regarding the creation of such classes, there would be no need for § 1122(b) specifically to authorize a class of smaller unsecured claims, a common feature of plans in reorganization cases past and present.[4] The broad interpretation of § 1122(a) adopted by the lower courts would render § 1122(b) superfluous, a result that is anathema to elementary principles of statutory construction.

Section 1122 consequently must contemplate some limits on classification of claims of similar priority. A fair reading of both subsections suggests that ordinarily "substantially similar claims," those which share common priority and rights against the debtor's estate, should be placed in the same class. Section 1122(b) expressly creates one exception to this rule by permitting small unsecured claims to be classified separately from their larger counterparts if the court so approves for administrative convenience. The lower courts acknowledged the force of this narrow rather than totally permissive construction of § 1122 by going on to justify Greystone's segregation of the Phoenix claim. Put otherwise, the lower courts essentially found that Phoenix's unsecured deficiency claim is not "substantially similar" to those of the trade creditors.

Those courts did not, however, adhere to the one clear rule that emerges from otherwise muddled caselaw on § 1122 claims classification: thou shalt not classify similar claims differently in order to gerrymander an affirmative vote on a reorganization plan. As the Sixth Circuit observed:

> [T]here must be some limit on a debtor's power to classify creditors in such a manner. . ... Unless there is some requirement of keeping similar claims together, nothing would stand in the way of a debtor seeking out a few impaired creditors (or even one such creditor) who will vote for the plan and placing them in their own class.

In re U.S. Truck Co., 800 F.2d 581, 586 (6th Cir. 1986). * * * We agree with this rule, and if Greystone's proffered "reasons" for separately classifying the Phoenix deficiency claim simply mask the intent to gerrymander the voting process, that classification scheme should not have been approved.

---

[4] Greystone has never sought to justify its separate class of trade creditors under § 1122(b), nor did the lower courts employ that provision in their analysis. There is no suggestion in the Code, however, that a class may be created under § 1122(b) in order to manipulate the outcome of the vote on a plan, rather than simply to enhance administration of the plan.

Greystone's reliance on *Brite v. Sun Country Development, Inc.*, 764 F.2d 406 (5th Cir. 1985), as an allegedly contrary rule is misplaced. That case allowed the debtor to impair a previously unimpaired class of creditors not for purposes of vote-getting but because the debtor belatedly discovered that it did not have sufficient funds to pay the creditors' claims in full. The court found that the debtor's decision to reclassify previously unimpaired creditors as impaired was necessary. * * * *Sun Country* does not support Greystone's argument that plan proponents possess unlimited discretion to classify unsecured claims separately. We conclude that if § 1122(a) permits classification of "substantially similar" claims in different classes, such classification may only be undertaken for reasons independent of the debtor's motivation to secure the vote of an impaired, assenting class of claims. To those proffered reasons we now turn.

Greystone contends that the "legal difference" between Phoenix's deficiency claim and the trade creditors' claims is sufficient to sustain its classification scheme. The alleged distinction between the legal attributes of the unsecured claims is that under state law Phoenix has no recourse against the debtor personally. However, state law is irrelevant where, as here, the Code has eliminated the legal distinction between non-recourse deficiency claims and other unsecured claims. See § 1111(b)(1)(A); * * *.[5]

The purpose of § 1111(b) is to provide an undersecured creditor an election with respect to the treatment of its deficiency claim. Generally, the creditor may elect recourse status and obtain the right to vote in the unsecured class, or it may elect to forego recourse to gain an allowed secured claim for the entire amount of the debt. If separate classification of unsecured deficiency claims arising from non-recourse debt were permitted solely on the ground that the claim is non-recourse under state law, the right to vote in the unsecured class would be meaningless. Plan proponents could effectively disenfranchise the holders of such claims by placing them in a separate class and confirming the plan over their objection by cramdown. With its unsecured voting rights effectively eliminated, the electing creditor's ability to negotiate a satisfactory settlement of either its secured or unsecured claims would be seriously undercut. It seems likely that the creditor would often have to "elect" to take an

---

[5] Greystone argues that *Hanson* is not controlling because the issue there was whether it was clearly erroneous for the bankruptcy court to *deny* separate classification whereas the issue here is whether it was clearly erroneous for the court to *approve* the classification. The clearly erroneous rule has no application in this context. Whether a deficiency claim is legally similar to an unsecured trade claim turns not on fact findings but on their legal characteristics. This is an issue of law, freely reviewable on appeal. * * * Subsidiary fact findings however, may be entitled to the deference of the clearly erroneous test.

allowed secured claim under § 1111(b)(2) in the hope that the value of the collateral would increase after the case is closed.[6] Thus, the election under § 1111(b) would be essentially meaningless. We believe Congress did not intend this result.

As the bankruptcy court viewed this issue, the debtor's ability to achieve a cramdown plan should be preferred over the creditor's § 1111(b) election rights because of the Code's policy of facilitating reorganization. The bankruptcy court resorted to policy considerations because it believed Congress did not foresee the potential impact of an electing creditor's deficiency claim on the debtor's aspiration to cramdown a plan. We disagree with this approach for three reasons. First, it results here in violating § 1122, by gerrymandering the plan vote, for the sake of allegedly effectuating a § 1129(b) cramdown. "Policy" considerations do not justify preferring one section of the Code, much less elevating its implicit "policies" over other sections, where the statutory language draws no such distinctions. Second, as shown, it virtually eliminates the § 1111(b) election for secured creditors in this type of case. Third, the bankruptcy court's concern for the viability of cramdown plans is overstated. If Phoenix's unsecured claim were lower and the trade debt were higher, or if there were other impaired classes that favored the plan, a cramdown plan would be more realistic. That Greystone's cramdown plan may not succeed on the facts before us does not disprove the utility of the cramdown provision. The state law distinction between Code-created unsecured deficiency claims and other unsecured claims does not alone warrant separate classification.

Greystone next argues that separate classification was justified for "good business reasons." The bankruptcy court found that the debtor "need[s] trade to maintain good will for future operations." * * * The court further reasoned:

> [I]f the expectation of trade creditors is frustrated... [they] have little recourse but to refrain from doing business with the enterprise. The resulting negative reputation quickly spreads in the trade community,

---

[6] In this case, for example, Greystone proposed to extinguish Phoenix's $3,500,000 deficiency claim by the promised payment of $140,000. Under the valuation process, it confined Phoenix's secured claim to $5.8 million, § 506(a). Phoenix obviously objects to this arrangement because, in the future, it might ultimately receive more than the written-down value of the office building in a liquidation following foreclosure. Yet, with its voting rights effectively eliminated by separate classification, Phoenix has no leverage to persuade the Debtor to consider a more reasonable settlement. Had this scenario triumphed, Phoenix's most realistic option might have been to take an allowed secured claim in the hope that eventually the market value of the office building will increase by more than $140,000 over the presently estimated value of the collateral.

making it difficult to obtain services in the future on any but the most onerous terms.

* * * Greystone argues that the "realities of business" more than justify separate classification of the trade debt from Phoenix's deficiency claim. This argument is specious, for it fails to distinguish between the *classification* of claims and the *treatment* of claims. Greystone's justification for separate classification of the trade claims might be valid if the trade creditors were to receive different treatment from Phoenix. Indeed, Greystone initially created a separate class of unsecured creditors that could be wooed to vote for the plan by the promise to pay their remaining claims in full *outside the plan*. Greystone then changed course and eliminated its promise. Because there is no separate treatment of the trade creditors in this case, we reject Greystone's "realities of business" argument.

Even if Greystone's Plan had treated the trade creditors differently from Phoenix, the classification scheme here is still improper. At the confirmation hearing, none of the Debtor's witnesses offered any reason for classifying the trade debt separately from Phoenix's unsecured deficiency claim. There is no evidence in the record of a limited market in Austin for trade goods and services. Nor is there any evidence that Greystone would be unable to obtain any of the trade services if the trade creditors did not receive preferential treatment under the Plan. Thus, the bankruptcy court's finding that there were good business reasons for separate classification is without support in the record and must be set aside as clearly erroneous.[7]

Phoenix's unsecured deficiency claim approximates $3,500,000, while the claims of the unsecured trade creditors who voted to accept the Plan total less than $10,000. Greystone's classification scheme, which effectively disenfranchised Phoenix's Code-created deficiency claim, is sanctioned neither by the Code nor by caselaw. The lower courts erred in approving it.

III.

As a fall-back position, Greystone argues that the office-building tenants constitute an impaired class whose votes for Greystone's Plan should have been considered for purposes of satisfying the pre-condition of cramdown that there be one assenting, impaired class. The bankruptcy court held that the tenants

---

[7] Two standards of appellate review apply to the debtor's classification of claims. Issues such as the similarity in priority and legal attributes and the ultimate question whether treatment in the same or separate classes is necessary, are legal issues reviewable by our court de novo. See n. 5 supra. Whether there were any good business reasons to support the debtor's separate classification of claims is a question of fact.

were not an impaired class and could not vote on the Plan because Greystone had assumed their leases. The district court disagreed and held that despite the Debtor's assumption of the leases, the tenants could be counted as an impaired accepting class. Phoenix argues this was error.

* * * Under the Code, only creditors are entitled to vote on a plan of reorganization. See § 1126(c). A party to a lease is considered a "creditor" who is allowed to vote, § 1126(c), only when the party has a claim against the estate that arises from *rejection* of a lease. * * * If, however, the debtor * * * assumes a lease, the lessee has no "claim" against the debtor under § 1126(a). See §§ 365(g), 502(g). The rights created by assumption of the lease constitute a postpetition administrative claim under § 503(b)(1)(A) of the Code. * * * The holder of such a claim is not entitled to vote on a plan of reorganization. § 1126(a); * * * *

Here, Greystone never rejected its leases with the tenants. There is thus no support for the assertion that the tenants' "claims" entitled them to vote on Greystone's Plan. The district court erred in alternatively permitting confirmation of the Plan based on the tenants' affirmative votes.

* * *

V.

For the foregoing reasons, the judgment of the district court affirming the bankruptcy court's confirmation of Greystone's plan of reorganization is REVERSED. The case is REMANDED for proceedings consistent with this opinion.

NOTES

1. How can *Greystone* be reconciled with *U.S. Truck*? In *U.S. Truck* the debtor concedes its intent to gerrymander. In both cases the two classes of unsecured claims are treated identically by the plan. Are single asset real estate cases treated differently from "operating" cases with respect to classification of claims?

2. *Greystone* is one of the many Chapter 11 single asset real estate cases resulting from the real estate recession of the 1980s. We discuss on p. 602 the impact on these cases of § 362(d)(3). *Greystone* is typical of these cases in that it involved an attempt to use § 1129(b)(2)(A) cramdown against an undersecured creditor with a mortgage on the debtor's real property. As *Greystone* demonstrates, one obstacle in the path to cramdown is the requirement of § 1129(a)(10) that there be at least one impaired class of creditors that will assent to the plan. Unsecured trade creditors to whom relatively small amounts are owed may be willing to agree to the debtor's plan, but the holding of

Greystone prevents the debtor from creating a separate class of trade creditors. The court's opinion implies that if the mortgagee loses on the classification issue, cramdown will necessarily follow with highly undesirable consequences for the mortgagee. It speaks of the effect of allowing the debtor to classify the creditor's deficiency claim separately as *disenfranchising* the holder of the deficiency claim. But we will see later that for the mortgagee loss of the classification battle is not necessarily defeat in the cramdown war, for § 1111(b) and the "fair and equitable" requirement of § 1129(b) were crafted to protect creditors like Phoenix from unfair treatment in cramdown plans.

3. The *Greystone* rule has been widely followed in single asset real estate reorganization cases. *E.g. In re Boston Post Road Limited Partnership*, 21 F.3d 477 (2d Cir. 1994); *John Hancock Mutual Life Insurance Co. v. Route 37 Business Park Assoc.*, 987 F.2d 154 (3d Cir. 1993); *In re Bryson Properties, XVIII*, 961 F.2d 496 (4th Cir. 1992); and *Matter of Lumber Exchange Building Ltd. Partnership*, 968 F.2d 647 (8th Cir. 1992). The Seventh Circuit was the first to take a contrary view in *Matter of Woodbrook Associates*, 19 F.3d 312 (7th Cir. 1994). In *Woodbrook* the undersecured mortgagee apparently made a loan to the debtor without recourse, i.e., the loan debt was secured by the real property but the debtor was not personally liable to pay the debt. But, in *Woodbrook* as in *Greystone* § 1111(b)(1)(A) accorded the undersecured mortgagee an unsecured claim for the amount of the deficiency which the debtor sought to classify in a separate class, leaving a class of trade creditors that would approve the debtor's plan. The mortgagee argued that separate classification violated the *Greystone* rule. The Seventh Circuit panel in *Woodbrook*, in refusing to follow *Greystone*, not only allowed separate classification but held that separate classification was required because § 1122(a) prohibits the inclusion of a claim in a class unless that claim "is substantially similar to the other claims" in the class. The *Woodbrook* court held that there were significant disparities between the legal rights of the holder of a claim arising under § 1111(b) and the holder of a general unsecured claim which precluded their classification in a single class. Judge Zagel stated:

> * * * These disparities in rights stem from the most obvious difference between the two claims: a general unsecured claim exists in all chapters of the Code, while a § 1111(b) claim exists only as long as the case remains in Chapter 11 and, once converted to a Chapter 7 case, recovery is limited to its collateral. * * * This difference is amplified when the debtor is a partnership (as in this case) and the creditors face possible failure of its Chapter 11 case. Under such circumstances, the general unsecured creditors can seek equitable relief to prevent dissipation of the assets of the general partners, who upon conversion to Chapter 7, are liable for the debts of the partnership. Such equitable relief is

not likely to be available to a § 1111(b) claimant, whose recovery is confined to its collateral.

This legal difference between the two claims also can lead to anomalous results when applying other sections of the Code to a class containing both § 1111(b) claimants and general unsecured claimants. First, § 1129(a)(7) requires that, for confirmation of a plan where a holder of a claim or interest in an impaired class rejects the plan, each claimant must "receive or retain... property of a value, as of the effective date of the plan, that is not less than the amount... receive[d] or retain[ed] if the debtor were liquidated under [C]hapter 7." A § 1111(b) claimant is not entitled to payment under Chapter 7. Yet, because the § 1111(b) claimant has been classified with other general unsecured creditors and because § 1123(a)(4) mandates the same treatment of all claims in the class, the § 1111(b) claimant can block confirmation unless it receives payment of an amount equal to that of the general unsecured creditors.

19 F.3d at 318–319.

The Ninth Circuit rejected the *Woodbrook* reasoning in *In re Barakat*, 99 F.3d 1520 (9th Cir. 1996), in denying separate classification of the secured creditor's deficiency claim in circumstances similar to *Greystone*.

4. What if the note in *Woodbrook* had been recourse so that the claim of the mortgagee had arisen under § 506(a) rather than under § 1111(b)(1)(A)? The disparities outlined in the quotation by Judge Zagel in *Woodbrook* would not apply. Nevertheless, is there sufficient disparity between the § 506(a) deficiency claim of an undersecured mortgagee and unsecured claims of trade creditors to preclude classification in a single class? In *Woodbrook*, Judge Zagel also discussed § 1111(b)(1)(A)(i). Under that provision, an undersecured mortgagee with a § 506(a) unsecured deficiency claim may elect under § 1111(b)(2) to have the entire mortgage debt treated as a secured claim notwithstanding § 506(a). The mortgagee has the option of waiving the unsecured deficiency claim and increasing the amount of the secured claim. That option is not available to holders of general unsecured claims. Thus, at the time of commencement of the Chapter 11 case, § 1122(a) would seem to prohibit putting the unsecured deficiency claim and general unsecured claims into one class because the various claims are not substantially similar. The § 1111(b) option is made by vote of the class of which the mortgagee's claim is a part. § 1111(b)(1)(A)(i). This provision clearly means that only "a claim secured by a lien on property of the estate" can be included in the class making the election. See Bankruptcy Rule 3014. In the usual case the mortgagee is the only member of the class. Thus, § 1111(b)(1)(A)(i) supports the conclusion in *Woodbrook* that a deficiency claim and general unsecured claims cannot be put into the same class. Courts following the *Greystone* rule seem to assume that

the requirements of § 1122(a) are to be applied after it is determined whether the § 1111(b) election is or is not made. They then treat the unsecured deficiency claim and the general unsecured claims as similar for the purposes of § 1122(a). On the other hand, in support of the *Woodbrook* rule, it can be argued that the special election available to deficiency claims in § 1111(b) demonstrates that the interests of holders of general unsecured claims and those of mortgagees cannot be considered to be substantially similar under § 1122(a).

5. Single asset Chapter 11 cases usually deal with *undersecured* creditors. As we have seen, under the *Greystone* line of cases, such a creditor may be able to prevent cramdown by insisting that its deficiency claim be classified with the other unsecured claims. Since its deficiency claim will usually be much larger than the other unsecured claims, its vote will prevent that class from assenting to the plan and may make it impossible for the debtor to fashion a consenting impaired class required by § 1129(a)(10) for confirmation. But an *oversecured* creditor has no deficiency claim and therefore cannot control the vote of the class of unsecured claims. If the debtor can formulate a plan that both impairs that class of claims and is attractive enough to the class to win its approval, § 1129(a)(10) has been satisfied and cramdown can ensue over the opposition of the oversecured creditor.

In *In re Windsor on the River Associates, Ltd.*, 7 F.3d 127 (8th Cir. 1993), the debtor, faced by a dissenting oversecured creditor whose claim amounted to $9.8 million, created a consenting impaired class of trade creditors by agreeing to pay them $13,000, the full amount of their claims, 60 days after the effective date of the plan. By postponing the date of payment by 60 days, the plan clearly impaired the rights of this class under the literal language of § 1124(1) which provides that impairment has occurred unless these rights have been left "unaltered." However, the court denied confirmation on the ground that the trade creditor class was only "artificially impaired." The court put a gloss on § 1124(1) as follows: if impairment of a class is discretionary on the part of the debtor and is done for the purpose of creating an impaired class that will provide the consenting class required by § 1129(a)(10), the impairment is artificial and that class will not be treated as impaired within the meaning of § 1124(1). In justifying its decision to ignore the words of § 1124(1), the court assimilates its views on artificial impairment to those of the courts that have rejected gerrymandering classes of claims to create a consenting class of impaired claims, e.g., the *Greystone* line of authority. One problem with this view is that while the statute is quite vague on what is proper classification of claims, it is crystal clear on what is impairment. The court goes on to say that allowing artificial impairment would result in undermining the policy of § 1129(a)(10) that there must be some showing of creditor support before a plan is crammed down. But the policy behind § 1129(a)(10) is very obscure. From a policy standpoint, why should the vote of $13,000 of trade claims be decisive with respect to the lawfulness of cramming down a plan on a separately classified and differently treated secured lender with a $9.8 million claim? *See* Gregory K. Jones, *The Classification and Cramdown Controversy in Single Asset Bankruptcy Cases: The Need For Repeal of § 1129(a)(10)*, 42 UCLA L. Rev. 623 (1994). Given the shaky premise of § 1129(a)(10) when applied to the facts of *Windsor on the River*, together with the clear wording of § 1124(1) on what constitutes impairment, the result in this case is questionable. As we shall see later, the oversecured creditor would still enjoy the protection of the absolute priority rule in the cramdown plan. The deletion of § 1124(3) in 1994 may have ended the unedifying debate over "artificial" impairment. If even claims paid in full on the effective date are impaired, and therefore may vote on the plan and constitute the required impaired accepting class, *Windsor on the River* may become irrelevant. *In re Atlanta–Stewart Partners*, 193 B.R. 79, 82 (Bankr.N.D.Ga.1996).

6. Although the requirement of one consenting impaired class may prevent cramdown of a debtor's plan, as in *Windsor on the River*, it is unlikely to bar cramdown of a plan proposed by a secured creditor if the view of *In re L & J Anaheim Associates*, 995 F.2d 940 (9th Cir. 1993), is followed. In that case, Debtor failed to propose a plan within the 120–day exclusivity period of § 1121(b). Secured Creditor then proposed a plan allowing it to sell the assets of the estate (a hotel and a cause of action for mismanagement of the property) and to use the proceeds to pay the outstanding liens in order of priority. Although Secured Creditor was the only class to vote to approve the plan, the court confirmed the plan over Debtor's contention that Secured Creditor's rights were not truly impaired because they were, in fact, improved under the plan. The court held that under § 1124(1) the issue is not whether rights are enhanced or reduced under the plan, it is whether the plan leaves rights "unaltered." Since the plan changed somewhat the rights Secured Creditor would have had under state law, its rights were altered and thus impaired. Under this holding, any secured creditor who proposes a plan can nominally impair its rights in order to ensure that there will be at least one impaired class that will consent to the plan. If a creditor class proposing a plan can comply with § 1129(a)(10) by nominal impairment of its rights, why shouldn't a debtor be able to do so by proposing a plan nominally impairing the rights of a creditor class that will consent to the plan?

CHAPTER 11
REORGANIZATION IN CHAPTER 11: CONFIRMING A PLAN

A. FEASIBILITY

Unless the proposed plan of reorganization is itself a plan of liquidation, § 1129(a)(11) requires the bankruptcy court to find the plan is not likely to be followed by liquidation or further financial reorganization of the debtor. Bankruptcy professionals refer to this as the "feasibility" requirement. Whether a particular plan is feasible is obviously a very fact-intensive inquiry and general rules are not very helpful. *Orfa*, the case that follows, illustrates the kind of factors that a bankruptcy judge must consider in evaluating feasibility.

Orfa involved three related corporations who filed in Chapter 11 in separate cases. A consolidated plan of reorganization, referred to in the case as "the Plan," was proposed for confirmation. The Plan was filed by two creditors, EAFC and Corsair, referred to in the case as the "Proponents." Debtors held valuable licenses to use a process for recycling solid waste. Confirmation of the Plan was opposed by two creditors, BEC and SPNB, and Licensors, the grantors of the licenses held by Debtors. The bankruptcy judge held that the Plan could not be confirmed for various reasons, but the court assumed that the defects in the Plan could be cured by amendment. In anticipation of the re-filing of the Plan, amended to cure the defects, the court addressed the issue of whether the Plan met the requirements of § 1129(a)(11). That part of the opinion follows.

In re Orfa Corp. of Philadelphia
United States Bankruptcy Court, E.D. Pennsylvania, 1991.
129 B.R. 404.

- DAVID A. SCHOLL, Bankruptcy Judge.

* * *

The most important "fact" at issue requiring some description is the Plan. Although the Debtors have never been formally consolidated, the Plan, for the most part, treats the creditors of each of the Debtors as one body, i.e., as if their cases were consolidated. Nevertheless, in a paragraph addressing "revesting of assets," the Plan provides that the Debtors will operate as separate entities post-petition.

All secured and unsecured claims of SPNB are placed into a single class. SPNB is to receive full payment on the effective date if the Proponents obtain financing sought from Chase Manhattan Bank, N.A. ("Chase"). If the Chase loan is not consummated, as has not occurred to date, the Proponents, who are investment brokers and counsellors by profession, will undertake a private placement of preferred stock of the Debtors. From the proceeds of this placement, which, according to the Proponents, cannot be effected until the plan is confirmed, SPNB will be paid interest "at the prime rate" and will receive a final balloon payment after ten years of $8,225,000, which is about $150,000 greater than SPNB's $8,072,065.76 Proofs of Claim as of the bankruptcy filings * * *

BEC's claim * * * is placed into a class (Class H) including unsecured noteholders and all other unsecured claims of the Debtors. Payment of twenty (20%) percent of such claims is contemplated on the effective date, with the remaining eighty (80%) percent to be paid in quarterly payments extending over five years.

The Debtors' licenses with the Licensors are to be assumed, and the Licensors are to be paid their claims in full on the effective date.

The Debtors' report of plan voting, as supplemented, although not having been formally introduced into the record, indicates that all classes have accepted the Plan except the class including SPNB. SPNB, BEC, and the Licensors all filed Objections to confirmation of the Plan.

* * *

All three objecting parties—SPNB, BEC, and the Licensors—contend that the Plan fails to meet the "feasibility" requirement of § 1129(a)(11), that confirmation is "not likely to be followed by liquidation, or the need for future financial reorganization,. . ." Of the three, only SPNB levels an attack at the technological backbone of the Plan, i.e., that the Orfa process merits development. However, on February 28, 1988, SPNB agreed to advance as much as $13.55 million to build the Philadelphia plant and thereby promulgate the Orfa process. Its own expert, Thomas Vence, a financial consultant who was involved in the process which led to the approval of the earlier loan, admitted that he did not question the viability of the technology behind the Orfa process.

The principal thrust of the criticisms of the technological feasibility of the Plan by SPNB emphasizes skepticism not with the process itself but with the facts that the Debtors' business has had little earning capacity in the past and that the Debtors have no outstanding written contracts by which they can generate the tipping fees and revenue from sales of the recycled end products which the Proponents' witnesses project will make its technology profitable in the future. The Philadelphia plant, built with SPNB's loan funds as a demonstration of the workability of the Orfa process, is of limited effectiveness due to defects in construction. Unless this plant is put into a better condition, the Proponents are capable of demonstrating only the Debtors' failure to transfer the Orfa process into a workable reality.

However, SPNB's purported contemporary skepticism is contrary to its own past behavior. In 1988, at a time when the Debtors' incumbent management, with a track record that all parties agree was unenviable, was in control, SPNB was willing to advance considerable funds to the Debtors. The Proponents are prepared to install, as President and Chief Executive Officer, Joseph G. Munisteri, who has a distinguished record in the engineering construction industry. Munisteri previously served as Chief Executive Officer and Board member of several engineering firms. Having testified at length in several hearings, Munisteri has impressed the court as knowledgeable and realistic in his assessment of the Debtors' prospects. He identified Lorin B. Ellison, a certified public accountant and previously Vice President of Finance of Bausch & Lomb, as the reorganized Debtors' proposed Secretary, Treasurer and Chief Financial Officer. The Board of Directors of the Debtors presently includes William F. Ballhaus, former Chief Executive Officer of Beckman Instruments; John Dutton, Corsair's Director of Corporate Finance and Senior Vice President of a large healthcare company; and R. Eric Miller, former President for Fluor Constructors, Inc. and Vice President of Bechtel Corporation. Ballhaus testified in prior proceedings and Dutton testified in December proceedings. Both have been optimistic, yet are tempered with a sense of realism, about the Debtors' prospects. This constellation of individuals is a vast improvement over the group of "dreamers" who were the Debtors' principals when SPNB made its loan in 1988.

Munisteri, Dutton, and Alexander Capello, EAFC's principal, acknowledged the basically inoperable status of the Debtors' Philadelphia plant. Their plan was to hire Fluor Daniel, Inc. and Thyssen AG, European companies of impeccable reputation, to repair and provide guarantees of the operation of the Philadelphia plant, at a cost of $4.5 million.

We accept Cappello's testimony that the private placement cannot be finalized until plan confirmation occurs. Unless the Chase loan materializes, the funds to repair the Philadelphia plant will therefore not appear until after the private placement is solicited. It is only after the repairs are made to the plant that it is realistic to expect contracts yielding tipping fees and end-product purchases to appear. This proposed progression of development of the Debtors by the Proponents appears reasonable. We accept the Proponents' assertions that it is unrealistic to expect definite commitments from investors and prospective customers at this juncture.

BEC and the Licensors voice little concern about the technology of the Orfa process. Indeed, BEC attempted several means of obtaining the Orfa license to incorporate it into a proposal for trash disposal in the City of Toronto, reflecting BEC's confidence in the efficacy of the process. Although the October 1, 1990, deadline by which BEC was compelled to make a presentation to the City of Toronto has passed, BEC has remained an active party in this case, either due to a hope that it can still compete in the Toronto process or a desire to develop the process in other Canadian municipalities. The Licensors of the process could hardly be expected to challenge its technological feasibility.

The thrust of the objection to feasibility from these parties is focused upon the use of the private placement as a means for raising capital. The effective date of the Plan is triggered by the Proponents' raising at least $7 million within 150 days after confirmation. The total debt of the three Debtors is $19.35 million, according to Dutton. The cost to repair the plant will be at least $4.5 million. Operating costs will result in a need for millions more, unless and until operations of the Debtors are profitable. The objectors are troubled because the Debtors have no funds and the Proponents themselves have insufficient resources to fund the Plan. Moreover, the source of the funds is not a recognizable financial institution, but an unidentified, amorphous group of individuals who have not been identified and indeed could not be identified because they do not yet exist.

Cappello and Dutton are aware of these aspects (drawbacks, if you will) of the Plan. However, they point out that solicitation of investors is unrealistic and perhaps illegal unless it is first backed by a confirmation order. Cappello points to his Companies' past success in raising $22 million on the Debtors' behalf. These funds were raised at a time when the incumbent management was in control. They reason, not illogically, that investments will be more readily obtainable with their proposed competent management team in place.

The standards for determining plan feasibility are not rigorous. *See, e.g., In re Temple Zion*, 125 B.R. 910, 914–15 (Bankr.E.D.Pa.1991) * * *

> Caselaw has established that bankruptcy court[s] must consider several factors in making a feasibility determination: (1) the adequacy of the debtor's capital structure; (2) the earning power of its business; (3) economic conditions; (4) the ability of the debtor's management; (5) the probability of the continuation of the same management; and (6) any other related matters which determine the prospects of a sufficiently successful operation to enable performance of the provisions of the plan. * * *

The Proponents have made a very strong showing of the fourth factor referenced supra. Since the management team which has been proven unable to accomplish the end of making the Debtors profitable is now out of the picture, the absence of probability that the same management will continue constitutes a positive showing of the fifth factor referenced supra.

The second factor referenced above is another strong element in the Proponents' favor. The possible earning power of the Debtors' business is very high. The Debtors' technology is highly regarded. The issue of waste disposal is very important and the prospect of a recycling process is a very attractive prospect at this stage in the history of our planet. In an era when many Chapter 11 cases present real estate developments which often have no upward potential or businesses engaged in industries in which growth potential is neither present nor likely, these Debtors stand out as presenting a relatively high probability of increased future earning power.

The third factor noted supra is difficult to measure, but appears to be positive in light of the type of financial plan offered by the Proponents. Loans from recognizable lending institutions are presently very difficult to obtain. However, the climate for new investments is positive, especially since alternatives such as real estate trusts have become less attractive investments. A plan which proposes a sale of stock is one of the few means of raising capital which has at least the potential for success in the current financial environment. The fact that the Proponents are professionals in the investment field who have not been tainted by past transactions renders them capable candidates to put together a private placement which can succeed. We therefore would classify current economic conditions as conducive to the plan proposed.

The first factor * * * recited above is, of course, not in the Proponents' favor. The Debtors have no capital at all, and the focus of the Plan is to provide them with capital. However, we believe that the Proponents' prospect of achieving that end are relatively bright.

No other parties have materialized who have been willing to invest the time, energy, and financial resources into the development of the Debtors that the Proponents have. The Proponents appear to have two strong incentives for doing so: (1) to prevent a loss of their prior investments in this venture; and (2) to obtain placement fees and future financial advantages from being on the ground floor of the Debtors' new financial life. These incentives, though selfish, assure that their participation will be ongoing. They provide the sort of "other related matters" within the scope of the sixth factor cited supra which are properly to be considered in determining plan feasibility.

The Proponents cite *In re American Solar King Corp.*, 90 B.R. 808, 831–33 (Bankr.W.D.Texas 1988), as an example of a Chapter 11 case in which a plan based upon funding from new investments was deemed feasible and was confirmed. SPNB and BES are quick to point out the distinctions between the instant case and that case. In *American Solar King,* two large potential investors in the debtor's private placement were identified, whereas here we have only the investment brokers identified and the large body of investors are faceless. However, the overall picture presented by the Proponents compares favorably with that in *American Solar King.* The very Proponents of the Plan are investment brokers, who, as we noted, appear quite capable of accomplishing a successful placement.

We therefore conclude that the weight of the factors relevant to a feasibility analysis supports the conclusion that the Plan is feasible.

* * *

NOTE

Although bankruptcy judges are required to find that even consensual plans are not likely to result in a need for further reorganization, refiling for reorganization (so-called "Chapter 22" cases) are actually quite common. Professor LoPucki in COURTING FAILURE (U. Mich. Press 2005) links the Chapter 22 phenomenon to bankruptcy court "competition" for large cases. Over the past 20 years a large proportion of those large Chapter 11 cases have been filed in New York City and Wilmington, Delaware. LoPucki and Sara Kalin and later Joseph Doherty demonstrated that the rate of refiling for firms reorganized in Delaware (30%) and New York (22%) in 1991-1996 far exceeded the 5% average refiling rate for other bankruptcy courts in comparable cases during the same period. LoPucki writes:

> Bankruptcy lawyers readily agreed that the Delaware judges were rubber-stamping plans (of course, the lawyers put it more delicately) but disagreed that the rubber-stamping made the judges responsible for ensuing refilings. Absent objection, the lawyers said, rubber-stamping the plans was what the judges were supposed to do. 'The court is permitting the parties-in-interest … to adjust their own debts.' … The debate quickly turned to whether it was even possible for judges to evaluate plans…. St. Louis bankruptcy lawyer David Lander put it more bluntly: "If nobody's complaining, the notion that the judge should do his or her own feasibility analysis is crazy." The reality, Harvey Miller said, was that "[i]f the banks say 'you have to carry so much debt' management will ultimately say okay…. Those deals go through. Whether those plans are feasible or not is not ever really subjected, in my view, to an objective analysis."

LoPucki, COURTING FAILURE at 104-106.

LoPucki goes on to note that from 1997 forward "refiling rates in the rest of the country jumped to roughly the same level as refiling rates in Delaware," and speculates that "other courts probably copied Delaware's practices thinking they would reproduce Delaware's success. Instead they reproduced Delaware's failure." Id. at 122.

Can judges meaningfully assess the likelihood of success of a plan in the absence of a well-funded opposition? Even if there is conflicting evidence or substantial doubt regarding the likelihood of a plan's success should judges substitute their judgment as to the plan's feasibility for that of the real parties in economic interest in the context of a consensual reorganization plan? If you were seeking to confirm a questionably feasible reorganization plan would you prefer a venue where only 5% of the confirmed plans resulted in Chapter 22s or one where the Chapter 22 rate was more like 30%?

B. Treatment of Priority Claims

Under § 1129(a)(9)(A) administrative expenses, having second priority under § 507(a), must be paid in full in cash on the effective date of the plan unless the claimant agrees to different treatment. Third priority "gap creditor" claims must also be fully paid in cash on the effective date of the plan. ("Gap creditors" exist only in involuntary cases and hold claims that arise between the filing of the involuntary petition and the court's adjudication that the filing was proper, the so-called "order for relief.") We saw earlier that administrative expenses can balloon as the debtor in possession borrows or buys on credit in an attempt to keep the business alive. If administrative expenses get too large the requirement that these expenses be paid in cash at the effective date of the plan may preclude confirmation of a plan.

A different rule applies to claims with first, fourth, fifth, sixth and seventh priority. The plan may provide for deferred payment of the amount of these claims with interest if the affected class accepts the plan. If the class does not accept, these claims must be fully paid in cash on the effective date of the plan. Any claimant can agree to different treatment for itself. § 1129(a)(9)(B).

Prior to 2005, the allowed priority prepetition tax claims of governmental units while entitled to payment in full with interest could be nonconsensually deferred for up to six years, even while lower priority claims received prompt payment. Secured tax claims could receive even less favorable treatment in a cramdown under § 1129(b)(2)(A). BAPCPA revised § 1129(a)(9)(C) to further improve the treatment of priority and secured tax claims.

First, priority tax claims must receive regular installment payments in cash "[o]f a total value, as of the effective date of the plan, equal to the allowed amount of such claim" within five years after the date of the entry of the order for relief.

Second, the priority tax claims must not be treated less favorably than non-priority unsecured claims. Thus, if a class (other than a convenience class) is paid on the effective date of the plan, it is arguable that the taxing agency must be paid on the effective date as well. On the other hand, if trade claims are paid at a discount on the effective date, perhaps the payment in full of the tax claim a few years later is not less favorable.

Third, § 511 now requires that tax claims bear postpetition and post-confirmation interest at the rates set by otherwise applicable nonbankruptcy law rather than (the generally lower) prevailing market rates applied to the restructuring of claims under § 1129.

Finally, secured tax claims which (but for the tax lien) would otherwise be priority tax claims are entitled to treatment no less favorable than unsecured priority tax claims.

C. TREATMENT OF SECURED CLAIMS

1. § 1129(b)(2)(A) STANDARDS FOR CRAMDOWN

The proponent of a reorganization plan may deal with a class of secured claims in one of three ways: (1) Leave the class unimpaired under § 1124; (2) Obtain acceptance of the plan by the class and qualify for a § 1129(a) consensual confirmation; or (3) Seek cramdown pursuant to § 1129(b)(2)(A).

Suppose Lender has a security interest in Debtor's property having a value of $150,000. The debt owed to Lender is $100,000 and it is now matured. How can Debtor restructure this secured obligation without Lender's consent?

By hypothesis Lender has rejected the plan so confirmation is not possible under § 1129(a) because all impaired classes have not accepted the plan. § 1129(a)(8). Moreover, restructuring the loan implies altering Lender's present legal rights and so Lender's class is impaired. § 1124(1). Confirmation, however, is still possible under § 1129(b)(1) if the plan is "fair and equitable" under one of the three subparagraphs of § 1129(b)(2)(A).

a. Deferred Cash Payments

Under the first alternative (subparagraph (i)) the plan could provide that Lender both retain its lien in the collateral *and* receive deferred cash payments having a value at the effective date of the plan of at least the amount of its secured claim.

This is the most common method for non-consensually restructuring a secured claim under § 1129(b) and it is the debtor's approach to cramdown against SPNB in *Orfa*. The creditor's right to "retain[] the lien" under § 1129(b)(2)(A)(i)(I) is usually understood as being limited to the essential attributes of the property interest of the secured party under otherwise applicable law—not necessarily all the rights created by the prepetition security agreement and certainly not the rights to a particular payment schedule or interest rate or covenant protections under the prepetition note or credit agreement. The present value requirement of § 1129(b)(2)(A)(i)(II) necessarily implies that if there is deferral of the payments on account of the secured claim past the plan's effective date fully compensatory interest at the then market rate must be paid as well. The Code offers no guidance on how to choose the appropriate interest rate, how long the payments may be deferred or when interest must be paid. *Collier on Bankruptcy* ¶ 1129.06[1][c][ii][A]-[C](15th ed. rev. 2008) describes three competing views on the question of the applicable rate of interest:

> One group of courts look at the creditor's costs in bearing the treatment provided for in the plan. These courts focus on the characteristics of the creditor, and its ability to obtain capital to lend. This inquiry, however, leads to diverse results based on the peculiarities of the secured creditor. * * *
>
> Some courts, however, treat any deferred payment of an obligation under a plan as a coerced loan and the rate of return with respect to such loan must correspond to the rate which would be charged or obtained by the creditor making a loan to a third party with similar terms, duration, collateral and risk. * * * Thus in determining the discount rate, the court must consider the prevailing market rate for a loan of a term equal to the payout period, with due consideration of the quality of the security and the risk of subsequent default.
>
> * * *
>
> A third group of courts * * * start[] with a baseline of a 'riskless' loan, and then [take] evidence on the risk presented by the loan proposed in the plan. In short, they have developed a formula for the discount rate required * * *.

The Supreme Court appears to have adopted a version of this third approach in the following Chapter 13 case. It remains a matter of debate whether the same principles for present valuing the secured creditor's payments under a plan apply in Chapter 11.

Till v. SCS Credit Corporation
Supreme Court of the United States, 2004.
541 U.S. 465.

■ Justice STEVENS announced the judgment of the Court and delivered an opinion, in which Justice SOUTER, Justice GINSBURG, and Justice BREYER join.

To qualify for court approval under Chapter 13 of the Bankruptcy Code, an individual debtor's proposed debt adjustment plan must accommodate each allowed, secured creditor in one of three ways: (1) by obtaining the creditor's acceptance of the plan; (2) by surrendering the property securing the claim; or (3) by providing the creditor both a lien securing the claim and a promise of future property distributions (such as deferred cash payments) whose total "value, as of the effective date of the plan,... is not less than the allowed amount of such claim." The third alternative is commonly known as the "cram down option" because it may be enforced over a claim holder's objection.[2]

Plans that invoke the cram down power often provide for installment payments over a period of years rather than a single payment. In such circumstances, the amount of each installment must be calibrated to ensure that, over time, the creditor receives disbursements whose total present value[4] equals or exceeds that of the allowed claim. The proceedings in this case that led to our grant of certiorari identified four different methods of determining the appropriate method with which to perform that calibration. Indeed, the Bankruptcy Judge, the District Court, the Court of Appeals majority, and the dissenting Judge each endorsed a different approach. We detail the underlying facts and describe each of those approaches before setting forth our judgment as to which approach best meets the purposes of the Bankruptcy Code.

I.

On October 2, 1998, petitioners Lee and Amy Till, residents of Kokomo, Indiana, purchased a used truck from Instant Auto Finance for $6,395 plus $330.75 in fees and taxes. They made a $300 down payment and financed the balance of the purchase price by entering into a retail installment contract that Instant Auto immediately assigned to respondent, SCS Credit Corporation. Petitioners' initial indebtedness amounted to $8,285.24—the $6,425.75 balance of the truck purchase plus a finance charge of 21% per year for 136 weeks, or

---

[2] As we noted in *Associates Commercial Corp. v. Rash,* 520 U.S. 953, 962 (1997), a debtor may also avail himself of the second option (surrender of the collateral) despite the creditor's objection.

[4] In the remainder of the opinion, we use the term "present value" to refer to the value as of the effective date of the bankruptcy plan.

$1,859.49. Under the contract, petitioners agreed to make 68 biweekly payments to cover this debt; Instant Auto—and subsequently respondent—retained a purchase money security interest that gave it the right to repossess the truck if petitioners defaulted under the contract.

On October 25, 1999, petitioners, by then in default on their payments to respondent, filed a joint petition for relief under Chapter 13 of the Bankruptcy Code. At the time of the filing, respondent's outstanding claim amounted to $4,894.89, but the parties agreed that the truck securing the claim was worth only $4,000. In accordance with the Bankruptcy Code, therefore, respondent's secured claim was limited to $4,000, and the $894.89 balance was unsecured. Petitioners' filing automatically stayed debt-collection activity by their various creditors, including the Internal Revenue Service (IRS), respondent, three other holders of secured claims, and unidentified unsecured creditors. In addition, the filing created a bankruptcy estate, administered by a trustee, which consisted of petitioners' property, including the truck.

Petitioners' proposed debt adjustment plan called for them to submit their future earnings to the supervision and control of the Bankruptcy Court for three years, and to assign $740 of their wages to the trustee each month. The plan charged the trustee with distributing these monthly wage assignments to pay, in order of priority: (1) administrative costs; (2) the IRS's priority tax claim; (3) secured creditors' claims; and finally, (4) unsecured creditors' claims.

The proposed plan also provided that petitioners would pay interest on the secured portion of respondent's claim at a rate of 9.5% per year. Petitioners arrived at this "prime-plus" or "formula rate" by augmenting the national prime rate of approximately 8% (applied by banks when making low-risk loans) to account for the risk of nonpayment posed by borrowers in their financial position. Respondent objected to the proposed rate, contending that the company was "entitled to interest at the rate of 21%, which is the rate... it would obtain if it could foreclose on the vehicle and reinvest the proceeds in loans of equivalent duration and risk as the loan" originally made to petitioners.

At the hearing on its objection, respondent presented expert testimony establishing that it uniformly charges 21% interest on so-called "subprime" loans, or loans to borrowers with poor credit ratings, and that other lenders in the subprime market also charge that rate. Petitioners countered with the testimony of an Indiana University-Purdue University Indianapolis economics professor, who acknowledged that he had only limited familiarity with the subprime auto lending market, but described the 9.5% formula rate as "very reasonable" given that Chapter 13 plans are "supposed to be financially feasible."[8] Moreover, the professor noted that respondent's exposure was "fairly limited because [petitioners] are under the supervision of the court." The bankruptcy trustee also filed comments supporting the formula rate as, among other things, easily ascertainable, closely tied to the "condition of the financial market," and independent of the financial circumstances of any particular lender. Accepting petitioners' evidence, the Bankruptcy Court overruled respondent's objection and confirmed the proposed plan.

The District Court reversed. It understood Seventh Circuit precedent to require that bankruptcy courts set cram down interest rates at the level the creditor could have obtained if it had foreclosed on the loan, sold the collateral, and reinvested the proceeds in loans of equivalent duration and risk. Citing respondent's unrebutted testimony about the market for subprime loans, the court concluded that 21% was the appropriate rate.

On appeal, the Seventh Circuit endorsed a slightly modified version of the District Court's "coerced" or "forced loan" approach. Specifically, the majority agreed with the District Court that, in a cram down proceeding, the inquiry should focus on the interest rate "that the creditor in question would obtain in making a new loan in the same industry to a debtor who is similarly situated, although not in bankruptcy." To approximate that new loan rate, the majority looked to the parties' prebankruptcy contract rate (21%). The court recognized, however, that using the contract rate would not "duplicat[e] precisely... the present value of the collateral to the creditor" because loans to bankrupt, court-supervised debtors "involve some risks that would not be incurred in a new loan to a debtor not in default" and also produce "some economies." To correct for these inaccuracies, the majority held that the original contract rate should "serve as a presumptive [cram down] rate," which either the creditor or the debtor could challenge with evidence that a higher or lower rate should apply. Accordingly, the court remanded the case to the Bankruptcy Court to afford petitioners and respondent an opportunity to rebut the presumptive 21% rate.[9]

Dissenting, Judge Rovner argued that the majority's presumptive contract rate approach overcompensates secured creditors because it fails to account for costs a creditor would have to incur in issuing a new loan. Rather than focusing on the market for comparable loans, Judge Rovner advocated either the Bank-

---

[8] The requirement of financial feasibility derives from 11 U.S.C. § 1325(a)(6), which provides that the bankruptcy court shall "confirm a plan if... the debtor will be able to make all payments under the plan and to comply with the plan."

[9] As 21% is the maximum interest rate creditors may charge for consumer loans under Indiana's usury statute, the remand presumably could not have benefited respondent.

ruptcy Court's formula approach or a "straightforward... cost of funds" approach that would simply ask "what it would cost the creditor to obtain the cash equivalent of the collateral from an alternative source." Although Judge Rovner noted that the rates produced by either the formula or the cost of funds approach might be "piddling" relative to the coerced loan rate, she suggested courts should "consider the extent to which the creditor has already been compensated for... the risk that the debtor will be unable to discharge his obligations under the reorganization plan... in the rate of interest that it charged to the debtor in return for the original loan." We granted certiorari and now reverse.

II.

The Bankruptcy Code provides little guidance as to which of the rates of interest advocated by the four opinions in this case—the formula rate, the coerced loan rate, the presumptive contract rate, or the cost of funds rate—Congress had in mind when it adopted the cram down provision. That provision, 11 U.S.C. § 1325(a)(5)(B), does not mention the term "discount rate" or the word "interest." Rather, it simply requires bankruptcy courts to ensure that the property to be distributed to a particular secured creditor over the life of a bankruptcy plan has a total "value, as of the effective date of the plan," that equals or exceeds the value of the creditor's allowed secured claim—in this case, $4,000.

That command is easily satisfied when the plan provides for a lump-sum payment to the creditor. Matters are not so simple, however, when the debt is to be discharged by a series of payments over time. A debtor's promise of future payments is worth less than an immediate payment of the same total amount because the creditor cannot use the money right away, inflation may cause the value of the dollar to decline before the debtor pays, and there is always some risk of nonpayment. The challenge for bankruptcy courts reviewing such repayment schemes, therefore, is to choose an interest rate sufficient to compensate the creditor for these concerns.

Three important considerations govern that choice. First, the Bankruptcy Code includes numerous provisions that, like the cram down provision, require a court to "discoun[t] ... [a] stream of deferred payments back to the[ir] present dollar value," *Rake v. Wade,* 508 U.S. 464, 472, n.8 (1993), to ensure that a creditor receives at least the value of its claim.[10] We think it likely that Con-

---

[10] See 11 U.S.C. § 1129(a)(7)(A)(ii) (requiring payment of property whose "value, as of the effective date of the plan" equals or exceeds the value of the creditor's claim); §§ 1129(a)(7)(B), 1129(a)(9)(B)(i), 1129(a)(9)(C), 1129(b)(2)(A)(ii), 1129(b)(2)(B)(i),

gress intended bankruptcy judges and trustees to follow essentially the same approach when choosing an appropriate interest rate under any of these provisions. Moreover, we think Congress would favor an approach that is familiar in the financial community and that minimizes the need for expensive evidentiary proceedings.

Second, Chapter 13 expressly authorizes a bankruptcy court to modify the rights of any creditor whose claim is secured by an interest in anything other than "real property that is the debtor's principal residence." 11 U.S.C. § 1322(b)(2). Thus, in cases like this involving secured interests in personal property, the court's authority to modify the number, timing, or amount of the installment payments from those set forth in the debtor's original contract is perfectly clear. Further, the potential need to modify the loan terms to account for intervening changes in circumstances is also clear: On the one hand, the fact of the bankruptcy establishes that the debtor is overextended and thus poses a significant risk of default; on the other hand, the postbankruptcy obligor is no longer the individual debtor but the court-supervised estate, and the risk of default is thus somewhat reduced.[12]

Third, from the point of view of a creditor, the cram down provision mandates an objective rather than a subjective inquiry.[13] That is, although § 1325(a)(5)(B) entitles the creditor to property whose present value objectively equals or exceeds the value of the collateral, it does not require that the terms of the cram down loan match the terms to which the debtor and creditor agreed prebankruptcy, nor does it require that the cram down terms make the creditor subjectively indifferent between present foreclosure and future payment.

1129(b)(2)(C)(i), 1173(a)(2), 1225(a)(4), 1225(a)(5)(B)(ii), 1228(b)(2), 1325(a)(4), 1228(b)(2) (same).

[12] Several factors contribute to this reduction in risk. First, as noted below, a court may only approve a cram down loan (and the debt adjustment plan of which the loan is a part) if it believes the debtor will be able to make all of the required payments. § 1325(a)(6). Thus, such loans will only be approved for debtors that the court deems creditworthy. Second, Chapter 13 plans must "provide for the submission" to the trustee "of all or such portion of [the debtor's] future... income... as is necessary for the execution of the plan," § 1322(a)(1), so the possibility of nonpayment is greatly reduced. Third, the Bankruptcy Code's extensive disclosure requirements reduce the risk that the debtor has significant undisclosed obligations. Fourth, as a practical matter, the public nature of the bankruptcy proceeding is likely to reduce the debtor's opportunities to take on additional debt.

[13] We reached a similar conclusion in *Associates Commercial Corp. v. Rash,* when we held that a creditor's secured interest should be valued from the debtor's, rather than the creditor's, perspective. *Id.,* at 963 ("[The debtor's] actual use, rather than a foreclosure sale that will not take place, is the proper guide...").

Indeed, the very idea of a "cram down" loan *precludes* the latter result: By definition, a creditor forced to accept such a loan would prefer instead to foreclose.[14] Thus, a court choosing a cram down interest rate need not consider the creditor's individual circumstances, such as its prebankruptcy dealings with the debtor or the alternative loans it could make if permitted to foreclose.[15] Rather, the court should aim to treat similarly situated creditors similarly, and to ensure that an objective economic analysis would suggest the debtor's interest payments will adequately compensate all such creditors for the time value of their money and the risk of default.

III.

These considerations lead us to reject the coerced loan, presumptive contract rate, and cost of funds approaches. Each of these approaches is complicated, imposes significant evidentiary costs, and aims to make each individual creditor whole rather than to ensure the debtor's payments have the required present value. For example, the coerced loan approach requires bankruptcy courts to consider evidence about the market for comparable loans to similar (though nonbankrupt) debtors—an inquiry far removed from such courts' usual task of evaluating debtors' financial circumstances and the feasibility of their debt adjustment plans. In addition, the approach overcompensates creditors because the market lending rate must be high enough to cover factors, like lenders' transaction costs and overall profits, that are no longer relevant in the context of court—administered and court—supervised cram down loans.

---

[14] This fact helps to explain why there is no readily apparent Chapter 13 "cram down market rate of interest": Because every cram down loan is imposed by a court over the objection of the secured creditor, there is no free market of willing cram down lenders. Interestingly, the same is *not* true in the Chapter 11 context, as numerous lenders advertise financing for Chapter 11 debtors in possession. See, *e.g.*, Balmoral Financial Corporation, http://www.balmoral.com/bdip.htm (all Internet materials as visited Mar. 4, 2004, and available in Clerk of Court's case file) (advertising debtor in possession lending); Debtor in Possession Financing: 1st National Assistance Finance Association DIP Division, http://www.loanmallusa.com/dip.htm (offering "to tailor a financing program... to your business' needs and... to work closely with your bankruptcy counsel"). Thus, when picking a cram down rate in a Chapter 11 case, it might make sense to ask what rate an efficient market would produce. In the Chapter 13 context, by contrast, the absence of any such market obligates courts to look to first principles and ask only what rate will fairly compensate a creditor for its exposure.

[15] See *supra* (noting that the District Court's coerced loan approach aims to set the cram down interest rate at the level the creditor could obtain from new loans of comparable duration and risk).

Like the coerced loan approach, the presumptive contract rate approach improperly focuses on the creditor's potential use of the proceeds of a foreclosure sale. In addition, although the approach permits a debtor to introduce some evidence about each creditor, thereby enabling the court to tailor the interest rate more closely to the creditor's financial circumstances and reducing the likelihood that the creditor will be substantially overcompensated, that right comes at a cost: The debtor must obtain information about the creditor's costs of overhead, financial circumstances, and lending practices to rebut the presumptive contract rate. Also, the approach produces absurd results, entitling "inefficient, poorly managed lenders" with lower profit margins to obtain higher cram down rates than "well managed, better capitalized lenders." 2 K. Lundin, Chapter 13 Bankruptcy § 112.1, p. 112-8 (3d ed.2000). Finally, because the approach relies heavily on a creditor's prior dealings with the debtor, similarly situated creditors may end up with vastly different cram down rates.[17]

The cost of funds approach, too, is improperly aimed. Although it rightly disregards the now-irrelevant terms of the parties' original contract, it mistakenly focuses on the creditworthiness of the *creditor* rather than the debtor. In addition, the approach has many of the other flaws of the coerced loan and presumptive contract rate approaches. For example, like the presumptive contract rate approach, the cost of funds approach imposes a significant evidentiary burden, as a debtor seeking to rebut a creditor's asserted cost of borrowing must introduce expert testimony about the creditor's financial condition. Also, under this approach, a creditworthy lender with a low cost of borrowing may obtain a lower cram down rate than a financially unsound, fly-by-night lender.

IV.

The formula approach has none of these defects. Taking its cue from ordinary lending practices, the approach begins by looking to the national prime rate, reported daily in the press, which reflects the financial market's estimate of the amount a commercial bank should charge a creditworthy commercial borrower to compensate for the opportunity costs of the loan, the risk of

---

[17] For example, suppose a debtor purchases two identical used cars, buying the first at a low purchase price from a lender who charges high interest, and buying the second at a much higher purchase price from a lender who charges zero-percent or nominal interest. Prebankruptcy, these two loans might well produce identical income streams for the two lenders. Postbankruptcy, however, the presumptive contract rate approach would entitle the first lender to a considerably higher cram down interest rate, even though the two secured debts are objectively indistinguishable.

inflation, and the relatively slight risk of default.[18] Because bankrupt debtors typically pose a greater risk of nonpayment than solvent commercial borrowers, the approach then requires a bankruptcy court to adjust the prime rate accordingly. The appropriate size of that risk adjustment depends, of course, on such factors as the circumstances of the estate, the nature of the security, and the duration and feasibility of the reorganization plan. The court must therefore hold a hearing at which the debtor and any creditors may present evidence about the appropriate risk adjustment. Some of this evidence will be included in the debtor's bankruptcy filings, however, so the debtor and creditors may not incur significant additional expense. Moreover, starting from a concededly *low* estimate and adjusting *upward* places the evidentiary burden squarely on the creditors, who are likely to have readier access to any information absent from the debtor's filing (such as evidence about the "liquidity of the collateral market," *post* (SCALIA, J., dissenting). Finally, many of the factors relevant to the adjustment fall squarely within the bankruptcy court's area of expertise.

Thus, unlike the coerced loan, presumptive contract rate, and cost of funds approaches, the formula approach entails a straightforward, familiar, and objective inquiry, and minimizes the need for potentially costly additional evidentiary proceedings. Moreover, the resulting "prime-plus" rate of interest depends only on the state of financial markets, the circumstances of the bankruptcy estate, and the characteristics of the loan, not on the creditor's circumstances or its prior interactions with the debtor. For these reasons, the prime-plus or formula rate best comports with the purposes of the Bankruptcy Code.[19]

We do not decide the proper scale for the risk adjustment, as the issue is not before us. The Bankruptcy Court in this case approved a risk adjustment of 1.5%, and other courts have generally approved adjustments of 1% to 3%. Respondent's core argument is that a risk adjustment in this range is entirely inadequate to compensate a creditor for the real risk that the plan will fail. There

---

[18] We note that, if the court could somehow be certain a debtor would complete his plan, the prime rate would be adequate to compensate any secured creditors forced to accept cram down loans.

[19] The fact that Congress considered but rejected legislation that would endorse the Seventh Circuit's presumptive contract rate approach, H.R. 1085, 98th Cong., 1st Sess., § 19(2)(A) (1983); H.R. 1169, 98th Cong., 1st Sess., § 19(2)(A) (1983); H.R. 4786, 97th Cong., 1st Sess., § 19(2)(A) (1981), lends some support to our conclusion. It is perhaps also relevant that our conclusion is endorsed by the Executive Branch of the Government and by the National Association of Chapter Thirteen Trustees. Brief for United States as *Amicus Curiae;* Brief for National Association of Chapter Thirteen Trustees as *Amicus Curiae.* If we have misinterpreted Congress' intended meaning of "value, as of the date of the plan," we are confident it will enact appropriate remedial legislation.

is some dispute about the true scale of that risk—respondent claims that more than 60% of Chapter 13 plans fail, Brief for Respondent 25, but petitioners argue that the failure rate for *approved* Chapter 13 plans is much lower, Tr. of Oral Arg. 9. We need not resolve that dispute. It is sufficient for our purposes to note that, under 11 U.S.C. § 1325(a)(6), a court may not approve a plan unless, after considering all creditors' objections and receiving the advice of the trustee, the judge is persuaded that "the debtor will be able to make all payments under the plan and to comply with the plan." Together with the cram down provision, this requirement obligates the court to select a rate high enough to compensate the creditor for its risk but not so high as to doom the plan. If the court determines that the likelihood of default is so high as to necessitate an "eye-popping" interest rate, the plan probably should not be confirmed.

V.

The dissent's endorsement of the presumptive contract rate approach rests on two assumptions: (1) "subprime lending markets are competitive and therefore largely efficient"; and (2) the risk of default in Chapter 13 is normally no less than the risk of default at the time of the original loan. Although the Bankruptcy Code provides little guidance on the question, we think it highly unlikely that Congress would endorse either premise.

First, the dissent assumes that subprime loans are negotiated between fully informed buyers and sellers in a classic free market. But there is no basis for concluding that Congress relied on this assumption when it enacted Chapter 13. Moreover, several considerations suggest that the subprime market is not, in fact, perfectly competitive. To begin with, used vehicles are regularly sold by means of tie-in transactions, in which the price of the vehicle is the subject of negotiation, while the terms of the financing are dictated by the seller.[20] In

---

[20] The dissent notes that "[t]ie-ins do not *alone* make financing markets noncompetitive; they only cause prices and interest rates to be considered *in tandem* rather than separately." This statement, while true, is nonresponsive. If a market prices the cost of goods and the cost of financing together, then even if that market is perfectly competitive, all we can know is that the *combined* price of the goods and the financing is competitive and efficient. We have no way of determining whether the allocation of that price between goods and financing would be the same if the two components were separately negotiated. But the only issue before us is the cram down interest rate (the cost of financing); the value of respondent's truck (the cost of the goods) is fixed. See *Rash*, 520 U.S. at 960 (setting the value of collateral in Chapter 13 proceedings at the "price a willing buyer in the debtor's trade, business, or situation would pay to obtain like property from a willing seller"). The competitiveness of the market for cost-*cum*-financing is thus irrelevant to our analysis.

addition, there is extensive federal[21] and state[22] regulation of subprime lending, which not only itself distorts the market, but also evinces regulators' belief that unregulated subprime lenders would exploit borrowers' ignorance and charge rates above what a competitive market would allow.[23] Indeed, Congress enacted the Truth in Lending Act in part because it believed "consumers would individually benefit not only from the more informed use of credit, but also from heightened competition which would result from more knowledgeable credit shopping." S.Rep. No. 96-368, p. 16 (1979).[24]

Second, the dissent apparently believes that the debtor's prebankruptcy default—on a loan made in a market in which creditors commonly charge the maximum rate of interest allowed by law, Brief for Respondent 16, and in which neither creditors nor debtors have the protections afforded by Chapter 13—translates into a high probability that the same debtor's confirmed Chapter 13 plan will fail. In our view, however, Congress intended to create a program under which plans that qualify for confirmation have a high probability of success. Perhaps bankruptcy judges currently confirm too many risky plans, but the solution is to confirm fewer such plans, not to set default cram down rates at absurdly high levels, thereby increasing the risk of default.

Indeed, as Justice THOMAS demonstrates, the text of § 1325(a)(5)(B)(ii) may be read to support the conclusion that Congress did not intend the cram down rate to include *any* compensation for the risk of default.[25] That reading is consistent with a view that Congress believed Chapter 13's protections to be so

---

[21] For example, the Truth in Lending Act regulates credit transactions and credit advertising.

[22] Usury laws provide the most obvious examples of state regulation of the subprime market.

[23] Lending practices in Mississippi, "where there currently is no legal usury rate," support this conclusion: in that State, subprime lenders charge rates "as high as 30 to 40%"—well above the rates that apparently suffice to support the industry in States like Indiana. Norberg, *Consumer Bankruptcy's New Clothes: An Empirical Study of Discharge and Debt Collection in Chapter 13*, 7 Am. Bankr. Inst. L.Rev. 415, 438-439 (1999).

[24] See also H.R.Rep. No. 1040, 90th Cong., 1st Sess., 17 (1967) ("The basic premise of the application of disclosure standards to credit advertising rests in the belief that a substantial portion of consumer purchases are induced by such advertising and that if full disclosure is not made in such advertising, the consumer will be deprived of the opportunity to effectively comparison shop for credit").

[25] The United States, too, notes that "[t]he text of Section 1325 is consistent with the view that the appropriate discount rate should reflect only the time value of money and not any risk premium." Brief for United States as *Amicus Curiae* 11, n.4. The remainder of the United States' brief, however, advocates the formula approach.

effective as to make the risk of default negligible. Because our decision in *Rash* assumes that cram down interest rates are adjusted to "offset," to the extent possible, the risk of default, and because so many judges who have considered the issue (including the authors of the four earlier opinions in this case) have rejected the risk-free approach, we think it too late in the day to endorse that approach now. Of course, if the text of the statute required such an approach, that would be the end of the matter. We think, however, that § 1325(a)(5)(B)(ii)'s reference to "value, as of the effective date of the plan, of property to be distributed under the plan" is better read to incorporate all of the commonly understood components of "present value," including any risk of nonpayment. Justice THOMAS' reading does emphasize, though, that a presumption that bankruptcy plans will succeed is more consistent with Congress' statutory scheme than the dissent's more cynical focus on bankrupt debtors' "financial instability and. . . proclivity to seek legal protection."

Furthermore, the dissent's two assumptions do not necessarily favor the presumptive contract rate approach. For one thing, the cram down provision applies not only to subprime loans but also to prime loans negotiated prior to the change in circumstance (job loss, for example) that rendered the debtor insolvent. Relatedly, the provision also applies in instances in which national or local economic conditions drastically improved or declined after the original loan was issued but before the debtor filed for bankruptcy. In either case, there is every reason to think that a properly risk-adjusted prime rate will provide a better estimate of the creditor's current costs and exposure than a contract rate set in different times.

Even more important, if all relevant information about the debtor's circumstances, the creditor's circumstances, the nature of the collateral, and the market for comparable loans were equally available to both debtor and creditor, then in theory the formula and presumptive contract rate approaches would yield the same final interest rate. Thus, we principally differ with the dissent not over what final rate courts should adopt but over which party (creditor or debtor) should bear the burden of rebutting the presumptive rate (prime or contract, respectively).

Justice SCALIA identifies four "relevant factors bearing on risk premium[:] (1) the probability of plan failure; (2) the rate of collateral depreciation; (3) the liquidity of the collateral market; and (4) the administrative expenses of enforcement." In our view, any information debtors have about any of these factors is likely to be included in their bankruptcy filings, while the remaining information will be far more accessible to creditors (who must collect information about their lending markets to remain competitive) than to individual debtors (whose only experience with those markets might be the single loan at issue in the case). Thus, the formula approach, which begins with a concededly low estimate of the appropriate interest rate and requires the creditor to present evidence supporting a higher rate, places the evidentiary burden on the more knowledgeable party, thereby facilitating more accurate calculation of the appropriate interest rate.

If the rather sketchy data uncovered by the dissent support an argument that Chapter 13 of the Bankruptcy Code should mandate application of the presumptive contract rate approach (rather than merely an argument that bankruptcy judges should exercise greater caution before approving debt adjustment plans), those data should be forwarded to Congress. We are not persuaded, however, that the data undermine our interpretation of the statutory scheme Congress has enacted.

The judgment of the Court of Appeals is reversed, and the case is remanded with instructions to remand the case to the Bankruptcy Court for further proceedings consistent with this opinion.

It is so ordered.

■ Justice THOMAS, concurring in the judgment.

[Omitted.]

■ Justice SCALIA, with whom the Chief Justice, Justice O'CONNOR, and Justice KENNEDY join, Dissenting.

My areas of agreement with the plurality are substantial. We agree that, although all confirmed Chapter 13 plans have been deemed feasible by a bankruptcy judge, some nevertheless fail. We agree that any deferred payments to a secured creditor must fully compensate it for the risk that such a failure will occur. Finally, we agree that adequate compensation may sometimes require an "'eye-popping'" interest rate, and that, if the rate is too high for the plan to succeed, the appropriate course is not to reduce it to a more palatable level, but to refuse to confirm the plan.

Our only disagreement is over what procedure will more often produce accurate estimates of the appropriate interest rate. The plurality would use the prime lending rate—a rate we *know* is too low—and require the judge in every case to determine an amount by which to increase it. I believe that, in practice, this approach will systematically undercompensate secured creditors for the true risks of default. I would instead adopt the contract rate—*i.e.*, the rate at which the creditor actually loaned funds to the debtor—as a presumption that the bankruptcy judge could revise on motion of either party. Since that rate is generally a good indicator of actual risk, disputes should be infrequent, and it will provide a quick and reasonably accurate standard.

I.

The contract-rate approach makes two assumptions, both of which are reasonable. First, it assumes that subprime lending markets are competitive and therefore largely efficient. If so, the high interest rates lenders charge reflect not extortionate profits or excessive costs, but the actual risks of default that subprime borrowers present. Lenders with excessive rates would be undercut by their competitors, and inefficient ones would be priced out of the market. We have implicitly assumed market competitiveness in other bankruptcy contexts. *See Bank of America Nat. Trust and Sav. Assn. v. 203 North LaSalle Street Partnership,* 526 U.S. 434, 456-458 (1999). Here the assumption is borne out by empirical evidence: One study reports that subprime lenders are nearly twice as likely to be unprofitable as banks, suggesting a fiercely competitive environment. *See* J. Lane, *A Regulator's View of Subprime Lending: Address at the National Automotive Finance Association Non-Prime Auto Lending Conference* 6 (June 18-19, 2002). By relying on the prime rate, the plurality implicitly assumes that the *prime* lending market is efficient; I see no reason not to make a similar assumption about the *sub*prime lending market.

The second assumption is that the expected costs of default in Chapter 13 are normally no less than those at the time of lending. This assumption is also reasonable. Chapter 13 plans often fail. I agree with petitioners that the relevant statistic is the percentage of *confirmed* plans that fail, but even resolving that issue in their favor, the risk is still substantial. The failure rate they offer—which we may take to be a conservative estimate, as it is doubtless the lowest one they could find—is 37%. *See* Girth, *The Role of Empirical Data in Developing Bankruptcy Legislation for Individuals,* 65 Ind. L.J. 17, 40-42 (1989) (reporting a 63.1% success rate).[1] In every one of the failed plans making up that 37%, a bankruptcy judge had found that "the debtor will be able to make all

---

[1] The true rate of plan failure is almost certainly much higher. The Girth study that yielded the 37% figure was based on data for a single division (Buffalo, New York) from over 20 years ago (1980-1982). *See* 65 Ind. L. J., at 41. A later study concluded that "the Buffalo division ha[d] achieved extraordinary results, far from typical for the country as a whole." Whitford, *The Ideal of Individualized Justice: Consumer Bankruptcy as Consumer Protection, and Consumer Protection in Consumer Bankruptcy,* 68 Am. Bankr. L.J. 397, 411, n. 50 (1994). Although most of respondent's figures are based on studies that do not clearly exclude unconfirmed plans, one study includes enough detail to make the necessary correction: It finds 32% of filings successful, 18% dismissed without confirmation of a plan, and 49% dismissed after confirmation, for a postconfirmation failure rate of 60% (*i.e.,* 49%/(32% + 49%)). *See* Norberg, *Consumer Bankruptcy's New Clothes: An Empirical Study of Discharge and Debt Collection in Chapter 13,* 7 Am. Bankr.Inst. L.Rev. 415, 440-441 (1999). This 60% failure rate is far higher than the 37% reported by Girth.

payments under the plan," § 1325(a)(6), and a trustee had supervised the debtor's compliance, § 1302. That so many nonetheless failed proves that bankruptcy judges are not oracles and that trustees cannot draw blood from a stone.

While court and trustee oversight may provide some marginal benefit to the creditor, it seems obviously outweighed by the fact that (1) an already-bankrupt borrower has demonstrated a financial instability and a proclivity to seek legal protection that other subprime borrowers have not, and (2) the costs of foreclosure are substantially higher in bankruptcy because the automatic stay bars repossession without judicial permission. It does not strike me as plausible that creditors would *prefer* to lend to individuals already in bankruptcy than to those for whom bankruptcy is merely a possibility—as if Chapter 13 were widely viewed by secured creditors as some sort of godsend. Certainly the record in this case contradicts that implausible proposition. *See* App. 48 (testimony of Craig Cook, sales manager of Instant Auto Finance) ("Q. Are you aware of how other lenders similar to Instant Auto Finance view credit applicants who appear to be candidates for Chapter 13 bankruptcy?" "A. Negative[ly] as well"). The better assumption is that bankrupt debtors are riskier than other subprime debtors—or, at the very least, not systematically *less* risky.

The first of the two assumptions means that the contract rate reasonably reflects actual risk at the time of borrowing. The second means that this risk persists when the debtor files for Chapter 13. It follows that the contract rate is a decent estimate, or at least the lower bound, for the appropriate interest rate in cramdown.[2]

The plurality disputes these two assumptions. It argues that subprime lending markets are not competitive because "vehicles are regularly sold by means of tie-in transactions, in which the price of the vehicle is the subject of negotiation, while the terms of the financing are dictated by the seller."[3] Tie-ins do not *alone* make financing markets noncompetitive; they only cause prices and interest rates to be considered *in tandem* rather than separately. The force of the plurality's argument depends entirely on its claim that "the terms of the financing are dictated by the seller." *Ibid.* This unsubstantiated assertion is contrary to

---

[2] The contract rate is only a presumption, however, and either party remains free to prove that a higher or lower rate is appropriate in a particular case. For example, if market interest rates generally have risen or fallen since the contract was executed, the contract rate could be adjusted by the same amount in cases where the difference was substantial enough that a party chose to make an issue of it.

[3] To the extent the plurality argues that subprime lending markets are not "*perfectly* competitive," (emphasis added), I agree. But there is no reason to doubt they are *reasonably* competitive, so that pricing in those markets is *reasonably* efficient.

common experience. Car sellers routinely advertise their interest rates, offer promotions like "zero-percent financing," and engage in other behavior that plainly assumes customers are sensitive to interest rates and not just price.[4]

The plurality also points to state and federal regulation of lending markets. It claims that state usury laws evince a belief that subprime lending markets are noncompetitive. While that is one *conceivable* explanation for such laws, there are countless others. One statistical and historical study suggests that usury laws are a "primitive means of social insurance" meant to ensure "low interest rates" for those who suffer financial adversity. Glaeser & Scheinkman, *Neither a Borrower Nor a Lender Be: An Economic Analysis of Interest Restrictions and Usury Laws*, 41 J. Law & Econ. 1, 26 (1998). Such a rationale does not reflect a belief that lending markets are inefficient, any more than rent controls reflect a belief that real estate markets are inefficient. Other historical rationales likewise shed no light on the point at issue here. The mere existence of usury laws is therefore weak support for any position.

The federal Truth in Lending Act not only fails to support the plurality's position; it positively refutes it. The plurality claims the Act reflects a belief that full disclosure promotes competition; the Act itself says as much. But that belief obviously *presumes* markets are competitive (or, at least, that they were noncompetitive only because of the absence of the disclosures the Act now requires). If lending markets were not competitive—if the terms of financing

---

[4] I confess that this is "nonresponsive" to the argument made in the plurality's footnote (that the contract interest rate may not accurately reflect risk when set jointly with a car's sale price), see *ante,* at n. 20; it is in response to the quite different argument made in the plurality's text (that joint pricing shows that the subprime lending market is not competitive). As to the *former* issue, the plurality's footnote makes a fair point. When the seller provides financing itself, there is a possibility that the contract interest rate might not reflect actual risk because a higher contract interest rate can be traded off for a lower sale price and vice versa. Nonetheless, this fact is not likely to bias the contract-rate approach in favor of creditors to any significant degree. If a creditor offers a promotional interest rate—such as "zero-percent financing"—in return for a higher sale price, the creditor bears the burden of showing that the true interest rate is higher than the contract rate. The opposite tactic—inflating the interest rate and decreasing the sale price—is constrained at some level by the buyer's option to finance through a third party, thus taking advantage of the lower price while avoiding the higher interest rate. (If a seller were to condition a price discount on providing the financing itself, the debtor should be entitled to rely on that condition to rebut the presumption that the contract rate reflects actual risk.) Finally, the debtor remains free to rebut the contract rate with any other probative evidence. While joint pricing may introduce some inaccuracy, the contract rate is still a far better initial estimate than the prime rate.

were indeed "dictated by the seller,"—disclosure requirements would be pointless, since consumers would have no use for the information.[5]

As to the second assumption (that the expected costs of default in Chapter 13 are normally no less than those at the time of lending), the plurality responds, not that Chapter 13 *as currently administered* is less risky than subprime lending generally, but that it *would* be less risky, if only bankruptcy courts would confirm fewer risky plans. *Ante,* at 1963. Of course, it is often quite difficult to predict which plans will fail. *See* Norberg, *Consumer Bankruptcy's New Clothes: An Empirical Study of Discharge and Debt Collection in Chapter 13*, 7 Am. Bankr.Inst. L.Rev. 415, 462 (1999). But even assuming the high failure rate primarily reflects judicial dereliction rather than unavoidable uncertainty, the plurality's argument fails for want of any reason to believe the dereliction will abate. While full compensation can be attained either by low-risk plans and low interest rates, or by high-risk plans and high interest rates, it cannot be attained by *high*-risk plans and *low* interest rates, which, absent cause to anticipate a change in confirmation practices, is precisely what the formula approach would yield.

The plurality also claims that the contract rate overcompensates creditors because it includes "transaction costs and overall profits." But the same is true of the rate the plurality prescribes: The prime lending rate includes banks' overhead and profits. These are necessary components of *any* commercial lending rate, since creditors will not lend money if they cannot cover their costs and return a level of profit sufficient to prevent their investors from going elsewhere. *See Koopmans v. Farm Credit Services of Mid-America, ACA,* 102 F.3d 874, 876 (C.A.7 1996). The plurality's criticism might have force if there were reason to believe subprime lenders made exorbitant profits while banks did not—but, again, the data suggest otherwise.[6]

---

[5] The plurality also argues that regulatory context is relevant because it "distorts the market." Federal disclosure requirements do not distort the market in any meaningful sense. And while state usury laws do, that distortion works only to the benefit of debtors under the contract-rate approach, since it keeps contract rates artificially low.

[6] Some transaction costs are avoided by the creditor in bankruptcy—for example, loan-origination costs such as advertising. But these are likely only a minor component of the interest rate. According to the record in this case, for example, the average interest rate on new-car loans was roughly 8.5%—only about 0.5% higher than the prime rate and 2.5% higher than the risk-free treasury rate. App. 43 (testimony of Professor Steve Russell). And the 2% difference between prime and treasury rates represented "mostly. . . risk [and] to some extent transaction costs." *Id.,* at 42. These figures suggest that loan-origination costs included in the new-car loan and prime rates but not in the treasury rate are likely only a fraction of a percent. There is no reason to think they are substantially higher in the

Finally, the plurality objects that similarly situated creditors might not be treated alike. But the contract rate is only a presumption. If a judge thinks it necessary to modify the rate to avoid unjustified disparity, he can do so. For example, if two creditors charged different rates solely because they lent to the debtor at different times, the judge could average the rates or use the more recent one. The plurality's argument might be valid against an approach that *irrebuttably* presumes the contract rate, but that is not what I propose.[7]

II.

The defects of the formula approach far outweigh those of the contract-rate approach. The formula approach starts with the prime lending rate—a number that, while objective and easily ascertainable, is indisputably too low. It then adjusts by adding a risk premium that, unlike the prime rate, is neither objective nor easily ascertainable. If the risk premium is typically small relative to the prime rate—as the 1.5% premium added to the 8% prime rate by the court below would lead one to believe—then this subjective element of the computation might be forgiven. But in fact risk premiums, if properly computed, would typically be substantial. For example, if the 21% contract rate is an accurate reflection of risk in this case, the risk premium would be 13%—nearly two-thirds of the total interest rate. When the risk premium is the greater part of the overall rate, the formula approach no longer depends on objective and easily ascertainable numbers. The prime rate becomes the objective tail wagging a dog of unknown size.

As I explain below, the most relevant factors bearing on risk premium are (1) the probability of plan failure; (2) the rate of collateral depreciation; (3) the liquidity of the collateral market; and (4) the administrative expenses of enforcement. Under the formula approach, a risk premium must be computed in every case, so judges will invariably grapple with these imponderables. Under

---

subprime auto lending market. Any transaction costs the creditor avoids in bankruptcy are thus far less than the additional ones he incurs.

[7] The plurality's other, miscellaneous criticisms do not survive scrutiny either. That the cramdown provision applies to prime as well as subprime loans, proves nothing. Nor is there any substance to the argument that the formula approach will perform better where "national or local economic conditions drastically improved or declined after the original loan was issued." To the extent such economic changes are reflected by changes in the prime rate, the contract rate can be adjusted by the same amount. See n. 2, *supra.* And to the extent they are not, they present the same problem under either approach: When a party disputes the presumption, the court must gauge the significance of the economic change and adjust accordingly. The difference, again, is that the contract-rate approach starts with a number that (but for the economic change) is reasonably accurate, while the formula approach starts with a number that (with or without the economic change) is not even close.

the contract-rate approach, by contrast, the task of assessing all these risk factors is entrusted to the entity most capable of undertaking it: the market. *See Bank of America,* 526 U.S., at 457 ("[T]he best way to determine value is exposure to a market"). All the risk factors are reflected (assuming market efficiency) in the debtor's contract rate—a number readily found in the loan document. If neither party disputes it, the bankruptcy judge's task is at an end. There are straightforward ways a debtor *could* dispute it—for example, by showing that the creditor is now substantially oversecured, or that some other lender is willing to extend credit at a lower rate. But unlike the formula approach, which requires difficult estimation in every case, the contract-rate approach requires it only when the parties choose to contest the issue.

The plurality defends the formula approach on the ground that creditors have better access to the relevant information. But this is not a case where we must choose between one initial estimate that is too low and another that is too high. Rather, the choice is between one that is far too low and another that is generally reasonably accurate (or, if anything, a bit too low). In these circumstances, consciously choosing the less accurate estimate merely because creditors have better information smacks more of policymaking than of faithful adherence to the statutory command that the secured creditor receive property worth "*not less than* the allowed amount" of its claim, § 1325(a)(5)(B)(ii) (emphasis added). Moreover, the plurality's argument assumes it is plausible—and desirable—that the issue will be litigated in most cases. But the costs of conducting a detailed risk analysis and defending it in court are prohibitively high in relation to the amount at stake in most consumer loan cases. Whatever approach we prescribe, the norm should be—and undoubtedly will be—that the issue is not litigated because it is not worth litigating. Given this reality, it is far more important that the initial estimate be accurate than that the burden of proving inaccuracy fall on the better informed party.

There is no better demonstration of the inadequacies of the formula approach than the proceedings in this case. Petitioners' economics expert testified that the 1.5% risk premium was "very reasonable" because Chapter 13 plans are "supposed to be financially feasible" and "the borrowers are under the supervision of the court." Nothing in the record shows how these two platitudes were somehow manipulated to arrive at a figure of 1.5%. It bears repeating that feasibility determinations and trustee oversight do not prevent at least 37% of confirmed Chapter 13 plans from failing. On cross-examination, the expert admitted that he had only limited familiarity with the subprime auto lending market and that he was not familiar with the default rates or the costs of collection in that market. In light of these devastating concessions, it is impossible to view the 1.5% figure as anything other than a smallish number picked out of a hat.

Based on even a rudimentary financial analysis of the facts of this case, the 1.5% figure is obviously wrong—not just off by a couple percent, but probably by roughly an order of magnitude. For a risk premium to be adequate, a hypothetical, rational creditor must be indifferent between accepting (1) the proposed risky stream of payments over time and (2) immediate payment of its present value in a lump sum. Whether he is indifferent—*i.e.*, whether the risk premium added to the prime rate is adequate—can be gauged by comparing benefits and costs: on the one hand, the expected value of the extra interest, and on the other, the expected costs of default.

Respondent was offered a risk premium of 1.5% on top of the prime rate of 8%. If that premium were fully paid as the plan contemplated, it would yield about $60.[8] If the debtor defaulted, all or part of that interest would not be paid, so the expected value is only about $50.[9] The prime rate itself already includes some compensation for risk; as it turns out, about the same amount, yielding another $50.[10] Given the 1.5% risk premium, then, the total expected benefit to respondent was about $100. Against this we must weigh the expected costs of default. While precise calculations are impossible, rough estimates convey a sense of their scale.

The first cost of default involves depreciation. If the debtor defaults, the creditor can eventually repossess and sell the collateral, but by then it may be substantially less valuable than the remaining balance due—and the debtor may stop paying long before the creditor receives permission to repossess. When petitioners purchased their truck in this case, its value was almost equal to the

---

[8] Given its priority, and in light of the amended plan's reduced debtor contributions, the $4,000 secured claim would be fully repaid by about the end of the second year of the plan. The average balance over that period would be about $2,000, *i.e.*, half the initial balance. The total interest premium would therefore be 1.5% x 2 x $2,000 = $60. In this and all following calculations, I do not adjust for time value, as timing effects have no substantial effect on the conclusion.

[9] Assuming a 37% rate of default that results on average in only half the interest's being paid, the expected value is $60 x (1—37%/2), or about $50.

[10] According to the record in this case, the prime rate at the time of filing was 2% higher than the risk-free treasury rate, and the difference represented "mostly... risk [and] to some extent transaction costs." App. 42 (testimony of Professor Steve Russell); see also Federal Reserve Board, Selected Interest Rates, http:// www.federalreserve.gov/releases/h15/data.htm (as visited Apr. 19, 2004) (available in Clerk of Court's case file) (historical data showing prime rate typically exceeding 3-month constant-maturity treasury rate by 2%- 3.5%). If "mostly" means about three-quarters of 2%, then the risk compensation included in the prime rate is 1.5%. Because this figure happens to be the same as the risk premium over prime, the expected value is similarly $50. See nn. 8-9, *supra*.

principal balance on the loan.[11] By the time the plan was confirmed, however, the truck was worth only $4,000, while the balance on the loan was $4,895. If petitioners were to default on their Chapter 13 payments and if respondent suffered the same relative loss from depreciation, it would amount to about $550.[12]

The second cost of default involves liquidation. The $4,000 to which respondent would be entitled if paid in a lump sum reflects the *replacement* value of the vehicle, *i.e.,* the amount it would cost the debtor to purchase a similar used truck. If the debtor defaults, the creditor cannot sell the truck for that amount; it receives only a lesser *foreclosure* value because collateral markets are not perfectly liquid and there is thus a spread between what a buyer will pay and what a seller will demand. The foreclosure value of petitioners' truck is not in the record, but, using the relative liquidity figures in *Rash* as a rough guide, respondent would suffer a further loss of about $450.[13]

The third cost of default consists of the administrative expenses of foreclosure. While a Chapter 13 plan is in effect, the automatic stay prevents secured creditors from repossessing their collateral, even if the debtor fails to pay. The creditor's attorney must move the bankruptcy court to lift the stay. In the District where this case arose, the filing fee for such motions is now $150. And the standard attorney's fee for such motions, according to one survey, is $350 in Indiana and as high as $875 in other States. *See* J. Cossitt, Chapter 13 Attorney Fee Survey, American Bankruptcy Institute Annual Spring Meeting (Apr. 10-13, 2003). Moreover, bankruptcy judges will often excuse first offenses, so foreclosure may require multiple trips to court. The total expected administrative expenses in the event of default could reasonably be estimated at $600 or more.

I have omitted several other costs of default, but the point is already adequately made. The three figures above total $1,600. Even accepting petitioners' low estimate of the plan failure rate, a creditor choosing the stream of future

---

[11] The truck was initially worth $6,395; the principal balance on the loan was about $6,426.

[12] On the original loan, depreciation ($6,395—$4,000, or $2,395) exceeded loan repayment ($6,426—$4,895, or $1,531) by $864, *i.e.,* 14% of the original truck value of $6,395. Applying the same percentage to the new $4,000 truck value yields approximately $550.

[13] The truck in *Rash* had a replacement value of $41,000 and a foreclosure value of $31,875, *i.e.,* 22% less. 520 U.S., at 957. If the market in this case had similar liquidity and the truck were repossessed after losing half its remaining value, the loss would be 22% of $2,000, or about $450.

payments instead of the immediate lump sum would be selecting an alternative with an expected cost of about $590 ($1,600 multiplied by 37%, the chance of failure) and an expected benefit of about $100 (as computed above). No rational creditor would make such a choice. The risk premium over prime necessary to make these costs and benefits equal is in the neighborhood of 16%, for a total interest rate of 24%.[14]

Of course, many of the estimates I have made can be disputed. Perhaps the truck will depreciate more slowly now than at first, perhaps the collateral market is more liquid than the one in *Rash,* perhaps respondent can economize on attorney's fees, and perhaps there is some reason (other than judicial optimism) to think the Tills were unlikely to default. I have made some liberal assumptions,[15] but also some conservative ones.[16] When a risk premium is off by an order of magnitude, one's estimates need not be very precise to show that it cannot possibly be correct.

In sum, the 1.5% premium adopted in this case is far below anything approaching fair compensation. That result is not unusual, *see, e.g., In re Valenti,* 105 F.3d 55, 64 (C.A.2 1997) (recommending a 1%-3% premium over the *treasury* rate—*i.e.,* approximately a 0% premium over prime); it is the entirely predictable consequence of a methodology that tells bankruptcy judges to set interest rates based on highly imponderable factors. Given the inherent uncertainty of the enterprise, what heartless bankruptcy judge can be expected to demand that the unfortunate debtor pay *triple* the prime rate as a condition of keeping his sole means of transportation? It challenges human nature.

III.

Justice THOMAS rejects both the formula approach and the contract-rate approach. He reads the statutory phrase "property to be distributed under the plan," § 1325(a)(5)(B)(ii), to mean the proposed payments *if made as the plan contemplates,* so that the plan need only pay the risk-free rate of interest. I would instead read this phrase to mean the right to receive payments that the

---

[14] A 1.5% risk premium plus a 1.5% risk component in the prime rate yielded an expected benefit of about $100, so, to yield $590, the total risk compensation would have to be 5.9 times as high, *i.e.,* almost 18%, or a 16.5% risk premium over prime.

[15] For example, by ignoring the possibility that the creditor might recover some of its undersecurity as an unsecured claimant, that the plan might fail only after full repayment of secured claims, or that an oversecured creditor might recover some of its expenses under 11 U.S.C. § 506(b).

[16] For example, by assuming a failure rate of 37%, cf. n. 1, *supra,* and by ignoring all costs of default other than the three mentioned.

plan vests in the creditor upon confirmation. Because there is no guarantee that the promised payments will in fact be made, the value of this property right must account for the risk of nonpayment.

Viewed in isolation, the phrase is susceptible of either meaning. Both the promise to make payments and the proposed payments themselves are property rights, the former "to be distributed under the plan" immediately upon confirmation, and the latter over the life of the plan. Context, however, supports my reading. The cramdown option which the debtors employed here is only one of three routes to confirmation. The other two—creditor acceptance and collateral surrender, § 1325(a)(5)(A), (C)—are both creditor protective, leaving the secured creditor roughly as well off as he would have been had the debtor not sought bankruptcy protection. Given this, it is unlikely the third option was meant to be substantially *under*protective; that would render it so much more favorable to debtors that few would ever choose one of the alternatives.

The risk-free approach also leads to anomalous results. Justice THOMAS admits that, if a plan distributes a note rather than cash, the value of the "property to be distributed" must reflect the risk of default on the note. But there is no practical difference between obligating the debtor to make deferred payments under a plan and obligating the debtor to sign a note that requires those same payments. There is no conceivable reason why Congress would give secured creditors risk compensation in one case but not the other.

Circuit authority uniformly rejects the risk-free approach. While Circuits addressing the issue are divided over *how* to calculate risk, to my knowledge all of them require some compensation for risk, either explicitly or implicitly. [citations omitted]. Justice THOMAS identifies no decision adopting his view.

Nor does our decision in *Rash* support the risk-free approach. There we considered whether a secured creditor's claim should be valued at what the debtor would pay to replace the collateral or at the lower price the creditor would receive from a foreclosure sale. Justice THOMAS contends that *Rash* selected the former in order to compensate creditors for the risk of plan failure, and that, having compensated them once in that context, we need not do so again here. I disagree with this reading of *Rash*. The Bankruptcy Code provides that "value shall be determined in light of the purpose of the valuation and of the proposed disposition or use of [the] property." 11 U.S.C. § 506(a). *Rash* held that the foreclosure-value approach failed to give effect to this language, because it assigned the same value whether the debtor surrendered the collateral or was allowed to retain it in exchange for promised payments. "From the creditor's perspective as well as the debtor's, surrender and retention are not equivalent acts." We did point out that retention entails risks for the creditor that surrender does not. But we made no effort to correlate that increased risk with the difference between replacement and foreclosure value. And we also pointed out that retention benefits the debtor by allowing him to continue to use the property—a factor we considered "[o]f prime significance." *Rash* stands for the proposition that surrender and retention are fundamentally different sorts of "disposition or use," calling for different valuations. Nothing in the opinion suggests that we thought the valuation difference reflected the degree of increased risk, or that we adopted the replacement-value standard *in order to compensate* for increased risk. To the contrary, we said that the debtor's "actual use. . . is the proper guide under a prescription hinged to the property's 'disposition or use.'"

If Congress wanted to compensate secured creditors for the risk of plan failure, it would not have done so by prescribing a particular method of valuing collateral. A plan may pose little risk even though the difference between foreclosure and replacement values is substantial, or great risk even though the valuation difference is small. For example, if a plan proposes immediate cash payment to the secured creditor, he is entitled to the higher replacement value under *Rash* even though he faces no risk at all. If the plan calls for deferred payments but the collateral consists of listed securities, the valuation difference may be trivial, but the creditor still faces substantial risks. And a creditor oversecured in even the slightest degree at the time of bankruptcy derives no benefit at all from *Rash*, but still faces some risk of collateral depreciation.[17]

There are very good reasons for Congress to prescribe full risk compensation for creditors. Every action in the free market has a reaction somewhere. If subprime lenders are systematically undercompensated in bankruptcy, they will charge higher rates or, if they already charge the legal maximum under state law, lend to fewer of the riskiest borrowers. As a result, some marginal but deserving borrowers will be denied vehicle loans in the first place. Congress evidently concluded that widespread access to credit is worth preserving, even if it means being ungenerous to sympathetic debtors.

* * *

Today's judgment is unlikely to burnish the Court's reputation for reasoned decisionmaking. Eight Justices are in agreement that the rate of interest set forth in the debtor's approved plan must include a premium for risk. Of those eight, four are of the view that beginning with the contract rate would

---

[17] It is true that, if the debtor defaults, one of the costs the creditor suffers is the cost of liquidating the collateral. But it is illogical to "compensate" for this risk by requiring all plans to pay the full cost of liquidation (replacement value minus foreclosure value), rather than an amount that reflects the possibility that liquidation will actually be necessary and that full payments will not be made.

most accurately reflect the actual risk, and four are of the view that beginning with the prime lending rate would do so. The ninth Justice takes no position on the latter point, since he disagrees with the eight on the former point; he would reverse because the rate proposed here, being above the risk-free rate, gave respondent no cause for complaint. Because I read the statute to require full risk compensation, and because I would adopt a valuation method that has a realistic prospect of enforcing that directive, I respectfully dissent.

NOTES

1. In his omitted concurrence Justice Thomas interpreted § 1325(a)(5) to require payment of interest at the "risk-free" rate. Since the plan's 9.5% rate exceeded the risk-free rate, he joined the plurality in affirming. The *Till* plurality opinion at n.10 and accompanying text goes out of its way to note that nonconsensual deferred payment of secured claims under Chapter 11 and Chapter 12 reorganization plans ("cramdown") requires the bankruptcy court to fix a risk-adjusted interest rate based on statutory provisions that are parallel to § 1325(a)(5). But Justice Thomas and the four dissenting Justices made no direct reference to Chapter 11, and the plurality also notes at n.14 that in Chapter 11 cases there may exist an efficient debtor-in-possession lending market that distinguishes corporate Chapter 11 cases from this case involving a treatment of a used car loan in Chapter 13. After *Till*, is the secured creditor cramdown standard the same in Chapter 11 as in Chapter 13? *See In re Prussia Associates*, 322 B.R. 572 (Bankr.E.D.Pa.2005) (*Till* is persuasive not controlling authority in Chapter 11 cases) and *In re Cook*, 322 B.R. 336 (Bankr.N.D.Ohio2005) (finding no opinion in *Till* whose reasoning commanded a majority of the Court or otherwise established controlling precedent). The Sixth Circuit, the first Court of Appeals to directly address the applicability of *Till* in Chapter 11, ambivalently found that its pre-*Till* coerced loan approach rather than *Till*'s formula approach continued to apply in Chapter 11 cases, while affirming confirmation of a Chapter 11 plan incorporating a cramdown interest rate consistent with *Till*'s prime plus 1%-3% formula. *In re American HomePatient*, 420 F.3d 559 (6th Cir. 2005); *compare In re Northwest Timberline Enter.*, 348 B.R. 412 (Bankr.N.D.Tex.2006) (criticizing *American HomePatient* and applying *Till* in Chapter 11).

2. Assuming arguendo that the *Till* plurality establishes a rule applicable in Chapter 11 cases what is the content of that rule? Is it that secured claims under feasible reorganization plans may be restructured at an interest rate equal to prime plus 1-3%, and that plans that would require higher (*i.e.* "eye-popping") rates should not be confirmed? Or is that the court should apply whatever risk-adjustment it believes is appropriate based on the evidence presented at trial?

Or is it that the current market rate should be used so long as there is sufficient evidence of an "efficient market"?

3. Why does it matter that one establishes "present value" by starting with the contract rate and adjusting upward or downward based on changes in market interest rates, rather than by starting with the current "prime rate" and adjusting upward for risk? Shouldn't you end up in the same place—the current market rate for comparable loans?

4. Justice Thomas's view that the plain language of § 1325 does not authorize risk adjustment but rather only authorizes compensation for the time value of money, if applied to § 1129(b)(2), would be inconsistent with essentially all reorganization practice and caselaw developed under the absolute priority rule since *Northern Pacific Railway Co. v. Boyd*, 228 U.S. 482 (1913). Note that if Justice Thomas were to determine that risk adjustment is appropriate in Chapter 11 notwithstanding his construction of § 1325, and further that Justice Scalia's "presumptive contract rate" approach were the proper methodology, and if Chief Justice Roberts and Justice Alito were to agree with that methodology, Justice Scalia's position would command a majority of the current Justices.

NOTE: CHAPTER 12—FAMILY FARMERS

The agricultural depression of the 1980s had roots in the inflation of the 1960s and 1970s when American farmers reacted to higher commodity prices by greatly increasing production. Production increases required additional capital and farm debt went from about $80 billion in 1960 to nearly $220 billion by the early 1980s. 1987 U.S.C.C.A.N. 2725. When commodity prices dropped in the 1980s, many farmers could not pay their debts and farm foreclosures were widespread. Congress reacted to the plight of over-extended farmers with the addition to the Bankruptcy Code of Chapter 12 on family farmer debt adjustment, effective November 26, 1986, and the enactment of the Agricultural Credit Act ("the ACA"), effective January 6, 1988, Public Law 100–233, 12 U.S.C. § 2001 et seq. One of the avowed objectives of the ACA is to keep farmers on the land. Among the ACA's debtor-protection provisions is one requiring federal farm credit system lenders to restructure loans of financially distressed farmers instead of foreclosing on collateral if the restructuring will produce more return to the creditor than will foreclosure. 12 U.S.C. § 2202(a). This provision requires these lenders, in appropriate cases, to meet with the debtor and attempt to effectuate a workout before foreclosing. *In re Hilton Land & Cattle Co.*, 101 B.R. 604 (D.Neb.1989), held that the restructuring requirement applies even if the debtor is in bankruptcy. In that case the debtor had filed a petition in Chapter 11 before the effective date of the ACA and the case was pending on the effective date. Courts of Appeal have uniformly held that there is no private right of action under the ACA. E.g., *Wagner v. PennWest Farm Credit, ACA*, 109 F.3d 909 (3d Cir. 1997). Some courts, nevertheless, permit farmers to block foreclosure by asserting that the creditor has failed to comply with the provisions of the ACA. Grant Nelson & Dale Whitman, *Real Estate Finance Law* § 7.7 at 594 (5th ed. 2007).

According to the Administrative Office of the United States Courts, over 6,000 Chapter 12 cases were filed in 1987, but this number dropped to 2,034 in 1988, and has continued to decrease since. In 2008, only 314 Chapter 12 cases were filed throughout the United States. Clearly the decrease in filings reflects better economic times in the farm belt and decreasing importance of family farms in agricultural production, but the ACA's restructuring requirements, which became effective in 1988, may have been a factor as well.

Chapter 12 was thought necessary because neither Chapter 11 nor Chapter 13 met the needs of the financially distressed farmer. Farmers usually were not eligible for Chapter 13 because their secured debts exceeded the limits of § 109(e). The absolute priority rule of Chapter 11 deprived insolvent family farmers of any ownership interest in the farm unless unsecured creditors as a class consented (including mortgagees holding unsecured deficiency claims). In *In re Ahlers*, 794 F.2d 388 (8th Cir. 1986), the court attempted to alter the absolute priority rule by allowing farmers to count the promise of future services as value for the purpose of applying the *Los Angeles Lumber* exception to that rule. As we will see, p. 783, the Supreme Court squelched this attempt.

Chapter 12 is largely based on Chapter 13, but incorporates some elements of Chapter 11. The debtor operates the farm as a debtor in possession and can be removed only for cause. § 1203 and § 1204. Unlike Chapter 11, however, there is always a trustee in bankruptcy in Chapter 12 serving alongside the debtor in possession. The Chapter 12 trustee's duties are similar to those of a Chapter 13 trustee. The trustee disburses part or all of the payments required by the plan. In the unlikely event that the debtor is removed as debtor in possession, the trustee can operate the business. § 1202(b)(5). The plan must be filed not later than 90 days after the petition unless an extension is granted, and only the debtor can file a plan—there is no provisions in Chapter 12 for terminating exclusivity and the filing of creditor plans. § 1221. Normally the confirmation hearing must be concluded not later than 45 days after the plan is filed. § 1224. As is true in Chapter 13, creditors do not vote on the plan.

The plan may modify the rights of the holders of both secured and unsecured claims and may provide for curing prepetition defaults. § 1222(b). Chapter 12, like Chapter 13, allows secured claims to be written down to the value of the collateral and paid off with interest over a period of time. § 1225(a)(5). But there is a fundamental difference between the two chapters with respect to long-term secured debt. Long-term mortgage debt cannot be effectively restructured in Chapter 13 except for curing of defaults. But a primary purpose of Chapter 12 is to allow the family farmer to deal with long-term secured debt on the farm and farm equipment. This debt can be written down, restructured and paid off over a period of time that may exceed the normal three-year period for other payments under the plan. § 1222(b)(9). The period is not specifically limited by Chapter 12. There is no provision like § 1111(b) in Chapter 12. Unsecured claims are protected only by the best interests rule and discharged to the extent they are not paid from the debtor's disposable income over the three-year term of the plan. There is no absolute priority rule in Chapter 12—the debtor may retain ownership of the farm even if unsecured claims are not paid or receive property worth only a fraction of the claims and do not consent to the plan.

A discharge comparable to that available in Chapter 13 is granted when the debtor completes the plan. § 1228(a). Hardship discharge is also provided for on terms similar to those stated in Chapter 13. § 1228(b) and (c). In recognition of the emergency nature of Chapter 12, Congress originally provided a seven-year sunset provision for the statute. Political interests serving the farm belt successfully ensured that the sun never set on Chapter 12 and it is now a permanent feature of the Code.

b. Sale of Property

Rather than allow Lender to retain its lien and make deferred payments, Debtor's plan might provide that the property be sold free and clear of Lender's lien and Lender's secured claim paid out of the proceeds. § 1129(b)(2)(A)(ii). This sale free and clear may be imposed upon a non-consenting Lender, however, it must be subject to § 363(k) which allows Lender to protect its interest in its collateral by credit-bidding the amount of its claim. If no one bids a higher amount than Lender, Lender can acquire the collateral by offsetting the bid against its claim. If the collateral is purchased by someone other than Lender who bids a higher amount, Lender obtains a lien in the cash proceeds that could be satisfied by payment in cash equal to the lesser of the total amount of proceeds or Lender's secured claim. Given these protections there is little reason for Lender to object to this sort of "cramdown" at least so long as the winning bid produces cash proceeds. On the other hand, after selling property pursuant to these provisions, the plan might further provide that Lender's lien continues in non-cash proceeds or other substitute collateral to serve as security for deferred cash payments stated in subparagraph (i). The substitute lien would have to meet the requirement of indubitable equivalence in subparagraph (iii) discussed below.

c. Indubitable Equivalence

Could Debtor's plan, in lieu of selling the property or making deferred payments with interest secured by Lender's pre-petition lien against all the property, surrender 2/3 of the property to Lender, judicially valued at $100,000 in full satisfaction of the secured claim? Under subparagraph (iii) the plan could provide "for the realization by [Lender] of the indubitable equivalent of [the secured claim]." The meaning of "indubitable equivalence" in a "dirt for debt" plan is discussed in the following case.

In re Arnold & Baker Farms
United States Court of Appeals, Ninth Circuit, 1996.
85 F.3d 1415.

■ WILLIAM A. NORRIS, Circuit Judge:

Debtor Arnold and Baker Farms petitioned for relief under Chapter 11 and filed a plan of reorganization which proposed to satisfy the claims of the creditors by transferring real property to them—colloquially known as a "dirt for debt" plan. When Arnold and Baker's largest creditor, the Farmers Home Administration (FmHA), objected to the plan, Arnold and Baker invoked the "cram down" provision of the Bankruptcy Code, § 1129(b). The question presented is whether the plan's proposal to transfer to FmHA a portion of the collateral securing FmHA's claim will provide FmHA with the "indubitable equivalent" of its secured claim, as required by the "cram down" provision. See § 1129(b)(2)(A)(iii).

I.

We adopt and quote verbatim the statement of facts set forth by the Bankruptcy Appellate Panel:

> The debtor Arnold and Baker Farms is an Arizona general partnership. The partnership was formed... for the purpose of farming and the sale and lease of farmland. Arnold and Baker purchased 1120 acres from Philip and Dorothy Ladra in 1975 and an additional 320 acres in 1979. The Ladras were given a first deed of trust on the property. In 1977, the farm began to experience financial difficulties.
>
> [FmHA] and Western Cotton Services Corporation, a wholly owned subsidiary of Anderson Clayton Company, financed certain crops for the years 1978 through 1981. Additionally, FmHA lent Arnold and Baker sufficient funds to make the annual payments on the installments due to the Ladras in the years 1979, 1980, and 1983. In return, FmHA held a second deed of trust on Arnold and Baker's real proper-

ty. . ... Western Cotton held a third deed of trust on Arnold and Baker's real property.

The Ladras ultimately instituted a judicial foreclosure proceeding against Arnold and Baker's real property. Subsequently, in April 1984, the Bakers individually filed a voluntary petition for relief under Chapter 11 of the Bankruptcy Code. The Ladras obtained relief from the automatic stay and continued their judicial foreclosure proceedings. Arnold and Baker, the partnership, filed a voluntary petition for relief under Chapter 11 of the Bankruptcy Code in April 1986.

In May 1986, the bankruptcy court approved the sale of two pieces of real property free and clear of liens: 360 acres of real property to Cardon Oil Company and 480 acres to the entity known as the Corks. From the net proceeds of the sale and the payment of annual installments, Arnold and Baker satisfied the secured claim of the Ladras in the amount of $1,650,000. FmHA thereafter held a first priority and Western Cotton held a second priority lien in the property.

Arnold and Baker subsequently formulated two plans based on the income generated from the Cardon and Cork sales which proposed to pay in full the allowed claims of all creditors. The first plan was withdrawn when the Corks defaulted on their note and the other, a revised plan, was withdrawn when Cardon Oil defaulted on its note. With respect to the Corks' default, Arnold and Baker negotiated a settlement pursuant to which the Corks tendered 360 acres to Arnold and Baker in lieu of foreclosure. With respect to the Cardon default, Arnold and Baker ultimately purchased the 320 acre parcel at a nonjudicial foreclosure.

In January 1991, Arnold and Baker filed a second amended plan and disclosure statement. The second amended plan proposed to pay FmHA's $3,837,618 note and Western Cotton's $565,044 note in full. The plan proposed to transfer a proportionate fee simple interest in the 635 acre parcel of real property to FmHA and Western Cotton. FmHA was earmarked to receive 515 acres of real property and Western Cotton was earmarked to receive 77 acres. Arnold and Baker was earmarked to retain ownership of 48 of the 640 acres scheduled for distribution. Arnold and Baker proposed to sell the adjoining 360 acre parcel of real property in order to pay the administrative claims, United States Trustee's fees, attorney fees, accountant fees, postpetition taxes, the real estate commission due and owing to Walter Arnold, and use the remainder to pay the unsecured creditors. Arnold and Baker retained an interest in the property remaining after distribution and sale.

Both FmHA and Western Cotton initially objected to confirmation of Arnold and Baker's second amended plan. However, during the course of the confirmation hearing, Western Cotton reached a settlement with Arnold and Baker pursuant to which Western Cotton agreed to accept 130 acres of real property in full satisfaction of its debt. Western subsequently withdrew its objection to confirmation and voted to accept the plan.

For purposes of the confirmation hearing, the parties stipulated that the second amended plan met all the requirements of § 1129(a)(1–13) with the exception of subsections (a)(3), (7), and (8). Additionally, FmHA objected to being crammed down pursuant to § 1129(b)(2). The principal factual issue concentrated on the fair market value of Arnold and Baker's 1320 acres of land. Arnold and Baker estimated the per acre value to be $7,322 for the 640 acre lot, $8,300 for the 360 acre lot, and $8,631 for the 320 acre lot. FmHA estimated the per acre value for the entire 1320 acres at $1,381.

On May 5, 1993, the bankruptcy court confirmed the plan finding that the property had an estimated value of $7,300 per acre. However, the bankruptcy court modified the transfer to FmHA in the plan by ordering an additional 10% transfer to FmHA in order to compensate it for the costs associated with a sale [resulting in a total of 566.5 acres].

FmHA appealed to the Bankruptcy Appellate Panel ("BAP"), which reversed the bankruptcy court's order confirming the plan. In consolidated appeals, Arnold and Baker and Western Cotton appeal the BAP's reversal.

* * *

III.

* * * Appellant Arnold and Baker argues that the BAP erred in reversing the confirmation of the plan on the ground that the proposed transfer of 566.5 acres to FmHA would not provide "for the realization by [FmHA] of the indubitable equivalent" of its secured claim, as required by § 1129(b)(2)(A)(iii).

Because FmHA objected to confirmation of the plan, Arnold and Baker invoked the "cram down" provision of Chapter 11, which provides that the court, on request of the proponent of the plan, shall confirm the plan notwithstanding the objection of an impaired creditor "if the plan does not discriminate unfairly, and is fair and equitable, with respect to each class of claims or interests that is impaired under, and has not accepted, the plan." § 1129(b)(1). To be "fair and equitable" the plan must satisfy, with respect to secured claims, one of the following three tests:

(1) The creditor is to retain the lien securing its claim and is to receive deferred cash payments with a present value at least equal to the claim;

(2) The property securing the claim is to be sold and the lien is to attach to the proceeds of the sale; the lien on the proceeds is then to be treated as described in test (1) or (3);

(3) The creditor is to realize the indubitable equivalent of its secured claim. * * *

The bankruptcy court confirmed the plan on the ground that the plan satisfied the third requirement. After an evidentiary hearing on the issue of valuation, the court found that the property was worth $7,300 per acre. It then concluded that the receipt of 566.5 acres at $7,300 per acre would provide for FmHA to realize the indubitable equivalent of its secured claim.

As an initial matter, we must address the appropriate standard of review of such a determination. Arnold and Baker argues that the question of indubitable equivalence is a question of fact to be reviewed under the clearly erroneous standard. We disagree. Although the value of the land is a finding of fact which we review for clear error, the ultimate conclusion of indubitable equivalence is a question of law which we review de novo because it requires analysis of the meaning of the statutory language in the context of the Bankruptcy Code's "cram down" scheme. *In re Pine Mountain*, 80 B.R. 171, 172 (9th Cir. BAP 1987) ("Whether a plan provides a secured creditor with the indubitable equivalent of its claim is... a mixed question of law and fact. Although the facts underlying such a determination are reviewed under the clearly erroneous standard, the question of whether the legal standard has been satisfied is reviewed de novo.") * * * *But see Matter of James Wilson Assocs.*, 965 F.2d 160, 172 (7th Cir. 1992) (holding that indubitable equivalence is a question of fact reviewed for clear error).

The BAP reviewed de novo the bankruptcy court's determination that the proposed transfer would provide FmHA with the indubitable equivalent of its secured claim, and reversed. Stressing that "[t]he determination of whether a partial dirt for debt distribution will provide the creditor with the indubitable equivalence of its secured claim must be made on a case-by-case basis," the BAP reasoned that the bankruptcy court's valuation of the property was an insufficient basis on which to conclude that the property was the indubitable equivalent of FmHA's secured claim. Again, we adopt and quote verbatim from the BAP's opinion:

The finding of a trial court of a particular value of real property... will not necessarily determine whether the creditor will receive the indubitable equivalent of its secured claim. Experience has taught us that determining the value of real property at any given time is not an exact science. Because each parcel of real property is unique, the precise value of land is difficult, if not impossible, to determine until it is actually sold. Nevertheless, bankruptcy courts have traditionally been requested, out of necessity, to determine the value of various types of property, including real property, and yet courts have recognized the difficulty of being able to determine accurately the value of land. For instance, in *In re Walat Farms, Inc.*, 70 B.R. 330 (Bankr.E.D.Mich.1987), the court stated:

> Similarly, we concede to doubts about our ability to fix the "value" of the land in question. We need not make a pronouncement that no plan proposing the surrender of a portion of mortgaged land to a mortgagee in return for a compelled release of the lien on the remainder of the property will ever be confirmed. Suffice it to say, however, that no matter how hot the market for real estate may become in the future, the market for farm real estate here and now is not such which would permit us to hold that the value of the land being offered is the indubitable equivalent of [the mortgagee]'s claim. "Indubitable" means "too evident to be doubted." Webster's Ninth New Collegiate Dictionary (1985). We profess doubt on the facts of this case.

[T]he determination of whether a dirt for debt distribution provides a secured creditor with the indubitable equivalent of its secured claim must be made on a case-by-case basis, and we must decide whether the bankruptcy court's finding with respect to the value of the real property for the purpose of determining the amount of the creditor's secured claim provided the secured creditor with the indubitable equivalent of its claim. In addition, we conclude that in order for a partial distribution to constitute the most "indubitable equivalence," the partial distribution must insure the safety of or prevent jeopardy to the principal.

Although we conclude that the bankruptcy court's valuation in this case is not clearly erroneous, we are not convinced that its finding regarding the value of the real property provided the indubitable equivalence of the particular secured claim in question, nor are we convinced that the partial distribution of 566.5 acres to FmHA will insure the safety of or prevent jeopardy to the principal.

The evidence at trial demonstrated that the value of the real property was far from certain. The Arnold and Baker appraisal admitted that due to unfavorable market conditions, including the fact that the [Resolution Trust Company had acquired 19,000 acres near Arnold and Baker's property and was considering bulk sale offers at no more than $2,105 per acre], the normal one year marketing period for the property would be extended by another two years [by which time the appraisal estimated that the Resolution Trust Company's activities would have ceased affecting the market]. The bankruptcy court agreed with Arnold and Baker's valuation of $7,300 per acre. FmHA, however, proffered a valuation of $1,381 per acre.[7] The large disparity in the parties' valuation of the same property illustrates the obvious uncertainty in attempting to forecast the price at which real property will sell at some uncertain future date.

The bankruptcy court found the value of each acre to be $7,300, and thus the value of the 566.5 acres to be transferred to FmHA to be $4,135,450 ($7,300 x 566.5). We must decide, therefore, whether a distribution of land with an estimated value of $4,135,450 constitutes the indubitable equivalent of a $3,837,618 claim secured by 1,320 acres. Under the circumstances of this case, we conclude that it does not.

The partial distribution of 566.5 acres to FmHA will not insure the safety of or prevent jeopardy to the principal. FmHA originally lent funds to Arnold and Baker secured by 1320 acres of land. If Arnold and Baker defaulted on the terms of the note, FmHA bargained for the right to foreclose on the entire 1320 acres of land in order to satisfy the outstanding obligation. In this situation, the principal is protected to the extent of the entire 1320 acres held as security. . ..

If FmHA subsequently sells the property for less than the value calculated by the bankruptcy court, FmHA has no recourse to the remaining collateral to satisfy the deficiency. As a result, the distribution to FmHA may not be "completely compensatory." *See In re Murel Holding Corp.*, 75 F.2d 941, 942 (2d Cir. 1935) (Learned Hand, J.).[8] FmHA is forced to assume the risk of receiving less on the sale without being able to look to the remaining undistributed collateral for security. "[T]o the extent a debtor seeks to alter the collateral securing a creditor's loan, providing the "indubitable equivalent' requires that the substitute collateral not increase the creditor's risk exposure." *In re Keller*, 157 B.R. 680, 683–84 (Bankr.E.D.Wash.1993); see also *Aetna Realty Investors,*

---

[7] The disparity was due in part to the parties' disagreement about the highest and best use of the property. Arnold and Baker argued that it was for land development, whereas FmHA maintained that it was for an irrigated farm.

[8] The legislative history of § 1129 indicates that *Murel Holding* was the source of the "indubitable equivalence" standard. * * *

Inc., v. Monarch Beach Venture, Ltd., 166 B.R. 428, 436 (C.D.Cal.1993) (fair and equitable prohibits a plan from unfairly shifting risk of plan failure to the creditor).

Arnold and Baker challenges the BAP's decision on the ground that it conflicts with *Matter of Sandy Ridge Development Corp.*,[9] in which the Fifth Circuit held that a "dirt for debt" plan satisfied the indubitable equivalence standard.[10] The BAP distinguished *Sandy Ridge* on the ground that the plan in that case provided for the transfer of all of the secured creditor's collateral, rather than only a portion of the collateral as in the present case. Arnold and Baker argues that even in the *Sandy Ridge* situation, the court's valuation of the collateral is critical to the creditor's substantive rights because the valuation directly impacts the creditor's rights regarding an unsecured deficiency claim, as was the case in *Sandy Ridge*.

However, this argument misapprehends the indubitable equivalence analysis. Section 1129(b)(2)(A)(iii) does not require that a creditor receive the indubitable equivalent of its entire claim, but only of its secured claim. *See Sandy Ridge*, 881 F.2d at 1350; 11 U.S.C. § 1129(b)(2)(A)(iii) ("With respect to a class of *secured claims*, the plan provides. . . (iii) for the realization by such holders of the indubitable equivalent of *such claims*.") (emphasis added). *Sandy Ridge* explained that, in the case of an undersecured creditor:

> [s]ection 506(a) of the Bankruptcy Code bifurcates. . . [the] total claim into secured and unsecured portions. . ... In situations involving only one creditor and one debtor, the value of the undersecured creditor's secured claim is simply the value of the underlying collateral. The difference between the collateral's value and the amount of the debt becomes an unsecured claim and is added to the existing pool of unsecured claims.

In other words, the value of the secured portion of an undersecured creditor's total claim is *by definition* equal to the value of the collateral securing it. Therefore, a creditor necessarily receives the indubitable equivalent of its secured claim when it receives the collateral securing that claim, regardless of how the court values the collateral. For this reason, the *Sandy Ridge* court did not need a judicial determination of value, explaining that "for the present

---

[9] Arnold and Baker also cites a number of decisions from bankruptcy courts approving dirt for debt plans. * * * However, none of the plans in these cases required a secured creditor to accept part of its collateral in full satisfaction of its secured claim.

[10] A subsequent opinion denying the petition for rehearing clarifies that this was the holding of *Sandy Ridge*.

analysis, the exact value of [the collateral] is unimportant." * * * The court's valuation of the collateral does, as Arnold and Baker observes, determine the amount of any remaining *unsecured* claim, but the Code requires only that the creditor receive the indubitable equivalent of its *secured* claim.

In this case, in contrast, the amount of collateral deemed to be the indubitable equivalent of FmHA's secured claim depends entirely on the court's valuation of the collateral. If the court had found that the land was worth more than $7,300 per acre, FmHA would receive correspondingly less land, and if the court had found that the land was worth less, FmHA would receive correspondingly more. Our holding that this plan does not satisfy the indubitable equivalent requirement is therefore entirely consistent with *Sandy Ridge*'s holding that the plan in that case did.

Conclusion

In conclusion, while we do not hold that the indubitable equivalent standard can never as a matter of law be satisfied when a creditor receives less than the full amount of the collateral originally bargained for, we do hold, as did the BAP, that the Arnold and Baker plan does not provide FmHA with the indubitable equivalent of its secured claim as required by the Bankruptcy Code.

The judgment of the BAP reversing the bankruptcy court's order confirming the plan is AFFIRMED.

NOTES

1. The meaning of indubitable equivalence is hardly clear, but that standard might be met if the plan provided for surrender of all the collateral to a secured party. As a practical matter, debtors do not surrender all the collateral if the collateral is worth more than secured claim—and secured creditors wouldn't object if they did. But what if the collateral is worth less than the secured creditor's claim? In that case, satisfying the secured claim through the surrender of the collateral is only the first step in determining the creditor's treatment. The court will have to fix the value of the collateral in order to determine the amount of the creditor's deficiency claim. Note that if the property is sold, the sale price (that is, the market) fixes the deficiency, but if it is surrendered to the secured creditor, the court does. Should debtors be permitted to use the power to cramdown under § 1129(b)(2)(A)(iii) to avoid market valuations of property they will not retain under the plan?

2. What if the plan proposes to extinguish Lender's secured claim and lien in exchange for common stock in the reorganized Debtor with an estimated value equal to the allowed amount of the secured claim? Lender wants cash or notes, not stock, and rejects the plan. Can Debtor cramdown under subparagraph (iii)? Arguably if the stock is actually worth the amount of the secured claim it is the equivalent of a payment in cash. That argument, however, will not persuade either the Lender or the court unless there is a ready market for the common stock that makes it a cash equivalent. Ownership of an equity interest in Debtor that is not a cash equivalent is not the indubitable equivalent of a secured claim against assets of Debtor. Senator DeConcini, the Senate manager of the Bankruptcy Reform Act of 1978, stated:

> Abandonment of the collateral to the creditor would clearly satisfy indubitable equivalence, as would a lien on similar collateral. * * * Unsecured notes as to the secured claim or equity securities of the debtor would not be the indubitable equivalent. * * *

1978 U.S.C.C.A.N. 6544.

2. § 1129(b)(1) "Fairness" and Negative Amortization

Great Western Bank v. Sierra Woods Group
United States Court of Appeals, Ninth Circuit, 1992.
953 F.2d 1174.

■ FERNANDEZ, Circuit Judge:

Sierra Woods Group (Sierra Woods) appeals the district court's decision that Sierra Woods' proposed reorganization plan, which included negative amortization, was not "fair and equitable" under § 1129(b). The bankruptcy court did not make specific factual findings regarding the fairness of the proposed deferral of interest, but rather adopted a per se rule against negative amortization. The district court did not address the legal permissibility of negative amortization, but concluded based upon a review of the record that the proposed plan was not fair and equitable. We hold that the fairness of a reorganization plan that includes the deferral of interest must be determined on a case-by-case basis. Therefore we reverse the district court's decision and remand to the district court for further remand to the bankruptcy court so that the bankruptcy court may make factual findings concerning the fairness of the proposed plan.

Factual and procedural background

This dispute centers on the Chapter 11 reorganization plan proposed by Sierra Woods. Its only asset is a ten-year-old apartment complex located in Sparks, Nevada. Bank of America owns a note secured by a first deed of trust on the property. As of April 17, 1989, Bank of America was owed $4,098,000. Great Western Bank (Great Western) owns a note secured by a second deed of trust, and was owed $3,845,124.47 plus $103,124.47 in interest as of April 17,

1989. The terms of Great Western's note called for an adjustable interest rate 3% over the Federal Home Loan Bank of San Francisco Eleventh District Cost of Funds Rate. The note was fully amortized over 30 years and was to mature in the year 2015.

Originally Sierra Woods proposed a reorganization plan under which it would make interest-only payments of 8% to Great Western for the first three years, and would then make interest-only payments at the prevailing note rate for the remaining term. The deferred interest and principal payments would be capitalized and would incur interest at the existing note rate. Sierra Woods later modified this proposal to include interest-only payments for the first five years. For the first three years, Sierra Woods proposed to pay interest of 8% and allow interest in excess of that amount to accrue and be added to principal. After five years, the note would fully amortize over the balance of the term at the adjustable note rate. The result would be negative amortization for three years because during that time the debt would increase rather than decrease.

Sierra Woods presented its modified proposal at a bankruptcy court hearing. Great Western cited *In re McCombs Properties VIII, Ltd.,* 91 B.R. 907, 911 (Bankr.C.D.Cal.1988), for the proposition that the promise to make up lost interest payments is not the legal equivalent of having those interest payments today. Sierra Woods told the court that its accountants were prepared to testify that the stream of payments under its proposal was equivalent to the stream of payments under the original note. Great Western responded that the permissibility of negative amortization was a "legal issue," and argued that interest deferral was not appropriate "under any circumstances."

The bankruptcy judge ruled in favor of Great Western. He said:

> I read the Code, and it's very clear, and I've always applied it in this manner. . . . [§ 1129(b)(2)(A)(i)(II) requires that] Mr. Beesley's client receive, on account of his claim, deferred cash payments totaling at least the amount of this claim as of the debt on the effective date of the plan. And that means a payment today, the next deferred payment, and next deferred payment, and the next. That's all it's ever meant. And I'm interpreting it that way. And I don't think negative amortization even—it just doesn't comply with that. . ..

Thereafter, the bankruptcy court confirmed a reorganization plan that required Sierra Woods to make timely interest payments at the market rate of interest. Sierra Woods appealed the bankruptcy court's ruling against deferral of interest to the district court. The district court examined the record and concluded that Sierra Woods had not honored its previous promises to pay Great Western, that the negative amortization proposal required a 100–percent value loan from Great Western to Sierra Woods, and that Great Western was in a secondary position to Bank of America on the loan. According to the district court, "the bankruptcy court properly determined that the deferral proposed in the plan... did not under the circumstances provide Great Western Bank with the equivalent of the present value of its claim...."

* * *

Discussion

Under § 1129(b), the bankruptcy court can confirm a plan of reorganization without creditor approval if the plan "does not discriminate unfairly, and is fair and equitable...." § 1129(b)(1). The "fair and equitable" condition includes the requirement that the holder of a secured claim receive "deferred cash payments totaling at least the allowed amount of such claim, of a value, as of the effective date of the plan, of at least the value of such holder's interest in the estate's interest in such property." § 1129(b)(2)(A)(i)(II).

Sierra Woods argues that § 1129(b) permits the deferral of interest, or negative amortization. Negative amortization refers to "a provision wherein part or all of the interest on a secured claim is not paid currently but instead is deferred and allowed to accrue," with the accrued interest added to the principal and paid when income is higher. *In re Club Associates*, 107 B.R. 385, 398 (Bankr.N.D.Ga.1989). The extent of negative amortization depends upon the difference between the "accrual rate," or the overall rate of interest to be paid on a claim, and the "pay rate," or the rate of interest to be paid on a monthly basis. Even when a debtor defers payments of interest on its debt obligation, the deferred amount can be capitalized at a rate of interest which enables the deferred amount to equal the present value of the creditor's allowed secured claim. * * * *See also In re Memphis Partners*, L.P., 99 B.R. 385, 388 (Bankr.M.D.Tenn.1989) (with an appropriate interest rate, a negative amortization plan can mathematically provide present value).

A. The Bankruptcy Court Ruling and District Court Review

The bankruptcy court did not make specific findings regarding the fairness of the proposed deferral of interest under § 1129(b), but rather objected to negative amortization on legal grounds. The bankruptcy court rejected appellant's proposal for the deferred payment of interest because, in that court's view, deferral of interest does not comport with the statutory requirement that secured creditors receive the present value of their claims.

The district court did not address the legal argument against negative amortization, but rather found support in the record for the proposition that in the context of this particular case the deferral of interest would not be fair and equitable. We have held, however, that the district court may not make its own factual findings when reviewing a decision of the bankruptcy court. * * * The question of whether a reorganization plan is fair and equitable involves questions of fact. * * * Because the bankruptcy court did not make factual findings on this issue, the district court erred when it independently determined that appellant's proposed plan was not fair and equitable. The district court should have decided whether the bankruptcy judge erred in adopting a blanket prohibition of negative amortization. If so, the district court should have remanded the case to the bankruptcy court for the making of necessary findings regarding the fairness of the plan, rather than conducting its own review of the record. * * *

B. The Fairness of Negative Amortization under § 1129(b)

We have not previously decided whether negative amortization is permissible under § 1129(b). *See In re Fowler*, 903 F.2d 694, 699 n.6 (9th Cir. 1990), where we noted the existence of the issue. One court has ruled that deferral of interest is not fair and equitable under section 1129(b) if the payment rate falls below the market rate of interest. *In re McCombs*, 91 B.R. at 911. In *McCombs*, the debtor sought to "cram down" a reorganization plan under which interest would accrue at the market rate of 10.5%, but the debtor would make payments of 9% and accrue the difference until sufficient funds were available. The court indicated a willingness to accept deferral of interest only if the debtor's payments at least equaled the market interest rate. * * * The court stated that even if it could adjust the interest rate to reflect "this accrual concept," it would only be guessing at the proper adjustment. * * *

As the *McCombs* court seemed to acknowledge, even when the payment rate falls below market rate, the accrual rate can be adjusted in order to give creditors the present value of their claims. * * * Assuming that such an adjustment is possible, the *McCombs* court offered no reason why negative amortization should be deemed impermissible under § 1129(b) whenever the payment rate on a secured claim falls below the market rate.

Our research has discovered no other court which has accepted the reasoning of the *McCombs* court. Rather, courts have decided on a case-by-case basis whether negative amortization under a given plan was fair and equitable, and have treated the market rate of interest as a necessary, but not sufficient, factor in that alchemy. * * *

In all of the above cases, save one, the court concluded that negative amortization was not fair and equitable under the circumstances, and the case approving of the deferral of interest concerned a contract that already provided for negative amortization. Thus while most courts have been reluctant to adopt a per se rule against negative amortization, there are commonly held reservations about the practice. That is not surprising because plans of that type tend to be fraught with pitfalls that unfairly endanger creditors. Even so, we see no reason to conclude that negative amortization is per se impermissible under § 1129(b). We hold that the fairness of a reorganization plan that includes negative amortization should be determined on a case-by-case basis. *In re Apple Tree Partners* contains a list of some of the factors that are relevant to this determination:

1. Does the plan offer a market rate of interest and present value of the deferred payments;

2. Is the amount and length of the proposed deferral reasonable;

3. Is the ratio of debt to value satisfactory throughout the plan;

4. Are the debtor's financial projections reasonable and sufficiently proven, or is the plan feasible;

5. What is the nature of the collateral, and is the value of the collateral appreciating, depreciating, or stable;

6. Are the risks unduly shifted to the creditor;

7. Are the risks borne by one secured creditor or class of secured creditors;

8. Does the plan preclude the secured creditor's foreclosure;

9. Did the original loan terms provide for negative amortization; and

10. Are there adequate safeguards to protect the secured creditor against plan failure.

We agree with that listing, without intending to limit consideration to those factors alone, and without intending to require courts to expressly refer to each one of them when considering proposed plans

Conclusion

Because the bankruptcy court erroneously concluded that negative amortization is per se impermissible and failed to make findings concerning the fairness of the proposed reorganization plan, we REVERSE the decision of the district court and REMAND to the district court for further remand to the bankruptcy court for further proceedings.

■ POOLE, Circuit Judge, concurring in part and dissenting in part:

I agree with the majority that negative amortization is not always disallowed by the bankruptcy code, and I concur in that part of the opinion. I write separately, however, because I do not believe it is either necessary or appropriate to reverse and remand in this case.

* * * The district court had, and this Court has, sufficient factual findings by the bankruptcy court to draw the legal conclusion that the "negative amortization" plan, as proposed by the debtor, was not fair and equitable. The plan rejected by the bankruptcy court originally called for three years of interest-only payments at 8%, followed by two years of interest-only payments at the prevailing adjustable note rate of 3% over the Eleventh District Cost of Funds Rate, after which the claim would fully amortize over the balance of the term at the adjustable note rate. Following the bankruptcy court's denial of this plan because of its provision for negative amortization, Sierra Woods filed a First Amended Plan of Reorganization proposing payments to Great Western Bank over five years at interest-only payments based on the prevailing note rate (3% over Eleventh District Cost of Funds Rate), after which the claim would fully amortize over a period of time extending ten years beyond the present maturity date of the note. The bankruptcy court found, however, that even this plan would not give Great Western Bank value, and thus provided Great Western with an interest rate of 4.5% over the 11th District Cost of Funds. The increased rate was necessary because the court found that:

> Great Western's second position is inherently at greater risk. The equity cushion ahead of it is approximately 10% and risk of default and failure to consummate the plan will bear the heaviest on it. Also to be considered is that the physical deterioration of the apartment complex has been significantly arrested and improved since the petition has been filed. However, the debtor's cash flow projection only covers current maintenance and no provision is made therein for deferred maintenance and repairs.

Thus the rejected plan, less favorable to Great Western than the First Amended Plan of Reorganization, would certainly have also been rejected by the court for failing to return present value.

Even had the interest rate in the original plan been set at market rate, that would only have aggravated the deferral and accrual of interest, resulting effectively in a full value loan to Sierra Woods, and have ultimately led to a deficiency which would have entirely consumed Great Western's equity cushion. Approval of a plan calling for negative amortization under such circumstances might itself constitute an abuse of discretion. Analyzed under the ten factors listed in the majority opinion, such a plan would (3) not have a satisfactory debt-to-value for a significant portion of the life of the loan, (4) not have reasonable financial projections in light of the inability to provide for deferred maintenance and repairs, (6) unduly shift the risks to Great Western, (7) cause Great Western to bear the risks, and (9) contravene the original loan terms which did not provide for negative amortization. Furthermore, the court could reasonably find that (2) the amount of the proposed deferral is not reasonable.

Based on the findings of fact made by the bankruptcy court, the district court was correct in concluding that the original plan calling for negative amortization would not have been fair and equitable. As a result, the failure of the bankruptcy court to conduct a hearing on the plan constituted harmless error. * * * Because reversing and remanding now would unnecessarily prolong the bankruptcy proceedings to the prejudice of the creditor, I respectfully dissent.

3. THE § 1111(b) ELECTION

Section 1111(b) is best understood by first considering the problem it is meant to solve. At the time § 1111(b) was enacted, § 1124(3) provided that a claim was not impaired if the claimant was paid cash equal to the allowed amount of the claim on the effective date of the plan. In 1994 § 1124(3) was deleted from the Code for reasons having nothing to do with § 1111(b). First we shall examine § 1111(b) against the Code background that existed when it was enacted, as though § 1124(3) were still in effect; then, at the end of this discussion, we will comment on the effect of the deletion of § 1124(3).

Assume Debtor borrowed money from Lender to buy an apartment building. As is frequently the case in commercial real property financing, the loan was nonrecourse, i.e., the loan was secured by a mortgage against the real property but Debtor was not personally liable on the loan. If Debtor defaulted, Lender's rights were limited to foreclosing on the property. If the property were worth more than the outstanding debt at the time of foreclosure, Lender would either be paid in full from the proceeds of a sale to a third party, or, in the absence of a higher third party bid, Lender could buy the property for a price equal to the amount of the debt; Lender pays for the property by simply canceling the debt. If the property were worth less than the debt at the time of foreclosure, Lender, by taking over the property, gets whatever speculative value the property has.

Assume further that because of a large increase in interest rates that reduced demand for real property, Debtor was unable to sell the building for what it considered a reasonable price. Debtor defaulted on Lender's loan. When Lender commenced foreclosure proceedings, Debtor filed in Chapter 11. Lender is the only secured creditor and the real property is Debtor's principal asset. Assume that at the time of bankruptcy the debt owed to Lender was $1,000,000 and the value of the property, based on the net proceeds that would be received if the property were sold at that time, was $750,000.

Both Debtor and Lender believe the property will increase substantially in value within 18 months owing to a likely decline in interest rates. There are no other creditors except for a class of impaired unsecured claims of trade creditors totaling less than $50,000. Debtor's Chapter 11 plan calls for a cash payment to that class that complies with the best interests rule. That class will consent to the plan. Debtor's plan provides that Debtor keeps the property and pays Lender $750,000 on the effective date of the plan.

Can Lender prevent confirmation of the plan in the absence of § 1111(b)? Lender has a claim against Debtor (§ 102(2)) and, under § 506(a), it is a secured claim of $750,000. Lender does not have an allowable unsecured claim because Debtor was not personally liable on the $1,000,000 debt. To be allowable a claim must be enforceable either against the debtor or against property of the debtor. Lender's claim is enforceable against the property to the extent of the $750,000 value of the property. It is not enforceable with respect to the remaining $250,000. Lender is a separate class and that class is not impaired because the plan provides for a cash payment to Lender on the effective date of the plan equal to the amount of Debtor's claim. Former § 1124(3). Since the class is not impaired it is deemed to have accepted the plan. § 1126(f). Since the only impaired class, the trade creditors, will accept the plan, the plan can be confirmed under § 1129(a). There is compliance with both § 1129(a)(8) and (10). Thus, if these sections are the only sections that apply to the case, Lender is powerless to prevent Debtor from imposing a forced redemption of the property at the depressed $750,000 value if that value is used to determine the amount of Lender's secured claim. Outside of bankruptcy Lender would have been able to foreclose and to buy the property at the foreclosure sale by credit bidding the amount of the $1,000,000 debt. In that case Lender would own the property and get the benefit of any rise in value. In bankruptcy Lender loses this benefit under the provisions which we have just examined. But § 1111(b) changes this result.

The facts in the hypothetical case resemble those in *In re Pine Gate Associates, Ltd.*, 2 B.C.D. 1478 (Bankr.N.D.Ga.1976), decided under Chapter XII of the 1898 Bankruptcy Act. There the court allowed the debtor to keep the property by paying the nonrecourse creditor the depressed value of the property. Hence, the creditor lost its expectation either of being paid in full or of getting the property to hold in anticipation of an economic upturn. In the familiar metaphor, the debtor used bankruptcy as a sword and not a shield. Section 1111(b) was added in large part as a reaction to *Pine Gate*. Section 1111(b) changes the rights of Lender in the hypothetical case.

First, assume that Lender does not make the election provided by § 1111(b)(1)(A)(i) to have its rights determined under § 1111(b)(2). Under § 1111(b)(1)(A) Lender is treated as having a secured claim for $750,000 and an unsecured claim for $250,000. Under former § 1124(3) the plan does not impair Lender's secured claim because Lender is receiving cash equal to the allowed amount of that claim. But the plan impairs Lender's unsecured claim because that claim will not be paid in full. Lender's unsecured claim will either be separately classified or it will be classified with the unsecured trade creditor claims. In the latter case Lender would control the class because other claims in the class are less than $50,000. Lender can cause that class to reject the plan, thereby making confirmation impossible. Confirmation requires that at least one class of impaired claims accept the plan. § 1129(a)(10) and § 1129(b)(1).

If Lender's unsecured claim is separately classified, § 1129(a)(10) will be satisfied because the trade creditors will accept the plan. But the absolute priority rule applies under § 1129(b). If Lender is not paid the full amount of the $250,000 unsecured claim under the plan, the equity security holders of Debtor cannot receive or retain any property under the plan. § 1129(b)(2)(B). Thus, confirmation cannot occur if the equity security holders are allowed to retain any interest in Debtor under the plan.

Second, assume that Lender makes the § 1111(b)(2) election. Under that provision, Lender is treated as having a secured claim in the amount of $1,000,000. The reference to "claim" in § 1111(b)(2) is to "claim secured by a lien on property of the estate" in § 1111(b)(1)(A). Lender has a claim of $1,000,000 against Debtor even though Debtor is not personally liable. § 101 ("claim"), § 101 ("creditor"), and § 102(2). We saw earlier that $250,000 of that claim is not allowable in the absence of § 1111(b), but it is allowable under § 1111(b)(1)(A). By electing application of § 1111(b)(2), Lender waives the unsecured claim that it has under § 1111(b)(1)(A) and receives instead a $1,000,000 secured claim. That claim is impaired. Former § 1124(3) is not satisfied because the plan gives Lender less than the full amount of the claim. The plan would have to be revised to meet the cramdown requirements of § 1129(b)(2)(A). The plan could allow Debtor to keep the property if Lender's lien is preserved and Lender is given deferred payments of at least $1,000,000 having a present value of at least "the value of [Lender's] interest in the estate's interest" in the property. Since that value can't be higher than the value of the property, it is $750,000 in this case. If the plan is so revised, it might not be favorable to Lender. Lender is assured of eventually receiving $1,000,000 but the amount over $750,000 may simply represent interest to reflect deferred payment. Lender has no assurance under § 1129(b)(2)(A) of receiving economic value beyond the present value of the property which in this case is $750,000.

But Lender obtains another benefit by electing § 1111(b)(2). The primary purpose of that section is to allow Lender to have a lien in the real property measured by the full value of Lender's claim rather than the value of the property. Debtor wants to be free to sell the property after confirmation of the plan in order to capture the anticipated appreciation in value of the property. This goal is denied to Debtor because the property is encumbered with Lender's lien and the lien secures the entire $1,000,000 claim of Lender. If Debtor sells the property it would have to satisfy that claim. Thus, Lender gets the economic benefit of a rise in value of the property if the property is sold.

As best we can tell, creditors rarely make the § 1111(b)(2) election. However, according to the court in *In re Cook*, 126 B.R. 575, 581–582

(Bankr.D.S.D.1991), before enactment of Chapter 12 the Farmers Home Administration (FmHA) routinely made the election in Chapter 11 cases involving farm land during the depression of the mid–1980s under plans allowing the farmer to retain the land. The FmHA anticipated that market value of the land was likely to increase during the payment period and, if the reorganization failed and the land was sold, the FmHA's lien would be enforceable against the appreciated value to the full extent of the original debt. By electing, the FmHA effectively permitted the family farmer to capture future appreciation but only to the extent he retained ownership of the farm rather than sell it.

In Chapter 11 cases, the undersecured creditor may not elect to have its claim treated as fully secured in two instances. The first is when the creditor's interest "is of inconsequential value." § 1111(b)(1)(B)(i). An example is a case in which liens having priority over the lien of the creditor exhaust all or almost all of the collateral, leaving the creditor functionally unsecured. The second is when there is recourse against the debtor and the property is sold under § 363 or is to be sold under the plan. § 1111(b)(1)(B)(i). If the property is sold pursuant to § 363(b), the creditor can protect itself by credit bidding the full amount of its claim. § 363(k). If there is a higher third party bid, the creditor will be paid in full; if not, the creditor will take the property. In either case the expectations of the undersecured creditor are realized and it has no need of the § 1111(b) protection.

Similarly, in Chapter 7 cases, since the real property will be sold or foreclosed upon, the expectations of the undersecured party are realized and there is no need for § 1111(b) protection. Accordingly, § 1111(b) does not apply in Chapter 7 cases. § 103(f).

What are the consequences on the above analysis of § 1111(b) of the repeal in 1994 of § 1124(3)? After this amendment, secured claims are impaired even though they are cashed out under the plan on its effective date. In the hypothetical case discussed above, Lender's $750,000 secured claim is impaired and Lender can vote to reject the plan. If Lender does so, Debtor can achieve confirmation of the plan only through cramdown under § 1129(b). Debtor can comply with this provision only if it can create at least one consenting class under § 1129(a)(10), and comply with the absolute priority rule as set out above. Without § 1111(b), cashing out Lender for $750,000 while leaving Lender technically impaired appears to comply with § 1129(b)(2)(A)(i), making the plan confirmable, even though Lender votes to reject the plan. With § 1111(b), however, Debtor's plan must provide either for Lender's $250,000 deficiency claim or, if the § 1111(b)(2) election is made, for a full $1 million secured claim. Hence, after the 1994 amendment deleting § 1124(3), creditors in *Pine Gate* type cases may still need § 1111(b) as a shield against an unwanted cash-out.

PROBLEM

Debtor filed in Chapter 11. Its sole asset was an apartment building worth $3.3 million. Creditor has a lien on the property securing nonrecourse debt of $6.6 million. Debtor's plan provided for the sale of the property to a new corporate entity in exchange for all its capital stock which would be distributed to the owners of Debtor. Creditor's secured claim would be paid by periodic cash payments having a present value equal to the value of the building as determined by the bankruptcy court. Creditor would be paid nothing for the portion of its debt that was not covered by the value of the building. Creditor argued that under § 1111(b)(1)(A) it had an unsecured claim to the extent the $6.6 million nonrecourse debt was not covered by the value of the building. Since the plan did not provide for the payment of this unsecured claim in full, it contended that the plan could not be crammed down because the old owners would receive value under the plan and, therefore, the absolute priority rule of § 1129(b)(2)(B)(ii) was not satisfied. Debtor answered that the normal rule of § 1111(b)(1)(A) did not apply in this case because the building would be "sold under the plan" and thus § 1111(b)(1)(A)(ii) applied and the nonrecourse debt could not be treated as recourse under § 1111(b)(1); therefore, Creditor had no unsecured claim in bankruptcy. Does Creditor have an unsecured claim in this case? What is the reason for the exception in § 1111(b)(1)(A)(ii)? Would this purpose be frustrated if Creditor were not awarded an unsecured claim in this case? *See In re Woodridge North Apts., Ltd.*, 71 B.R. 189 (Bankr.N.D.Cal.1987).

D. TREATMENT OF UNSECURED CLAIMS AND OWNERSHIP INTERESTS

1. BEST INTERESTS TEST

If a plan of reorganization is approved by all impaired classes of claims and interests as provided in § 1126(c) and (d), dissenting members of each class are bound so long as the best interests rule is met. Within each class dissenters must receive at least as much under the plan as they would have received under a Chapter 7 liquidation. § 1129(a)(7). With respect to § 1129(a)(7) Richard Broude, an experienced bankruptcy lawyer, has observed:

> Subsection 1129(a)(7) thus requires that the proponent of the plan present an appraisal demonstrating that, if the debtor were liquidated under Chapter 7, each of the creditors and holders of interest in each of the classes of claims or interests would receive no more than it will receive under the plan. Testimony about this hypothetical liquidation might be provided by auctioneers and other experts who could testify

about the liquidation value of the receivables, inventory, equipment, and other assets of the debtor. It is important to include a valuation of off-balance sheet assets such as patents, trade secrets, and other like intangibles. In addition, the hypothetical Chapter 7 analysis will have to take into account the increase in unsecured claims which would inevitably occur in Chapter 7. For example, secured creditors generally would receive less from foreclosure than they would receive under the plan. Therefore, the liquidation analysis under section 1129(a)(7) would require that any estimated deficiency of the secured creditors be added to the class of unsecured claims. Similarly, where a lease is being assumed in the Chapter 11 plan, it might logically be concluded that the lease would be rejected in a Chapter 7 case, and the damages that would be allowed the landlord under the rejected lease would be added to the body of unsecured claims. Thus, the best interests test of section 1129(a)(7) requires an analysis not only of the value of the assets of the debtor upon liquidation but also of the unsecured claims among which the proceeds of the liquidation (after deducting the expenses of the Chapter 7 liquidation) would be distributed.

Richard F. Broude, Cramdown and Chapter 11 of the Bankruptcy Code: The Settlement Imperative, 39 Bus.Law. 441, 448–449 (1984).

2. ABSOLUTE PRIORITY RULE

PROBLEMS

The following problems illustrating application of the absolute priority rule are taken from Kenneth N. Klee, *All You Ever Wanted to Know About Cram Down Under the New Bankruptcy Code*, 53 Am. Bankr. L.J. 133, 146–150 (1979).

1. Suppose an insolvent corporation has assets with a going concern value of $2 million, $1 million face amount in secured debt and $1.2 million face amount in unsecured debt. If the plan leaves the secured debt and shareholders unaffected and proposes to pay $1 million cash to unsecured creditors, can the plan be confirmed over the objection of the unsecured class?

2. What if the debtor in Problem 1 proposes to distribute non-interest bearing notes payable in three years at a face amount of $1.5 million in lieu of cash and the unsecured class still rejects the plan?

3. Suppose the shareholders reject the plan proposed by the corporation in Problem 1. What must the plan proponents establish at the confirmation hearing to confirm the plan?

4. Suppose a solvent corporation with cash-flow problems, $2 million going concern value, $1.2 million in unsecured claims and no other liabilities. The plan proposes to issue notes with a present value of $1 million and 100,000 common shares to unsecured creditors pro rata. Old shareholders retain their 100,000 common shares. The unsecured class accepts the plan and the old shareholders reject it. Can the plan be confirmed?

5. Formulate a different plan for the corporation in Problem 4 that (i) leaves old shareholders with their 100,000 shares, (ii) issues 100,000 new shares to the unsecured class and (iii) can be confirmed over the objection of the old shareholder class.

Chapter X of the 1898 Bankruptcy Act failed as a means of voluntary reorganization because it gave the management of the debtor too little incentive to use it. One disincentive was caused by the "fair and equitable" or "absolute priority" rule imposed under Chapter X. The absolute priority rule, required that each member of a senior class of claims or interests must receive full compensation before members of a junior class could receive anything. If there was a senior and junior class of unsecured creditors, the junior class could not share under a reorganization plan unless the senior class had been provided for to the full extent of its claims. Since creditor claims have priority over ownership interests, the most devastating impact of the absolute priority rule was to deprive stockholders of any interest in the reorganized entity unless the plan paid all creditors in full.

On its face the absolute priority rule appears to be one of elemental fairness. Seniors bargained for a priority position in any liquidation of the company. Juniors accepted the risk that the business might not prosper and that its assets might not cover both their claims and those of the seniors. Owners always understand that debt must come before equity. But in operation, the absolute priority rule, though seemingly "fair and equitable," often meant that an insolvent debtor had no incentive to reorganize under Chapter X because its shareholders could not gain a share in the reorganized business.

One problem with the absolute priority rule is that it is difficult to apply in some cases. Suppose the most junior class of unsecured claims will not receive full payment in cash under the plan of reorganization. Rather, that class will receive stock in the reorganized corporation. Suppose the plan provides that the reorganized corporation will be a new entity created to carry out the plan. The reorganized corporation will acquire all of the assets of the debtor corporation and all of the obligations to creditors under the plan. The debtor corporation becomes an empty shell when the plan goes into effect. The reorganized corporation will issue common stock and the junior class of unsecured claims will receive half of that stock. The other half of the common stock will be issued to the former stockholders of the debtor corporation. The absolute priority rule requires that the creditor class be compensated in full before the former stockholders of the debtor receive anything, but the issue of whether the creditor class is compensated in full depends upon the value of the reorganized corporation as a going concern. This valuation was done under the Bankruptcy Act by making estimates of the future earnings of the reorganized corporation and applying a multiple to them. The multiple was determined by considering the risk factors for the reorganized corporation and for the industry in which the corporation was competing. On the basis of expert testimony the court might decide that the appropriate multiple was, say, five under then-current market conditions for a firm of this type in that industry. Future annual earnings were then estimated. If the appropriate earnings figure was $1,000,000 the value of the reorganized corporation was $5,000,000. Professors Walter Blum and Stanley Kaplan made the following comment on the valuation procedure in their article, *The Absolute Priority Doctrine in Corporate Reorganizations*, 41 U. Chi.L.Rev. 651, 656–657 (1974):

> The valuation procedure always produces a dollars and cents figure. Although that figure looks mathematically exact, it actually reflects in a single number a whole series of highly conjectural and even speculative judgments concerning long-range business expectations and hazards as well as future social and general economic conditions. To exclude a class of creditors or investors from participation in a reorganization plan based upon so illusory a figure is criticized as capricious. The process is said to deceive by treating "soft" information as if it were "hard" and by cloaking predictions in the guise of mathematical certainty, under circumstances where consequences are drastic and final.
>
> Dependency of the valuation process upon the future outlook as of a particular moment adds to this dissatisfaction. The resultant value figure is inextricably related to the then accepted set of expectations and assumptions. If the situation improves shortly after the reorganization proceedings have been terminated (so that the risk factor used in determining valuation may appear to have been too high and the valuation too low), the elimination of certain investors from participation in the plan might be regarded as having been unwarranted and unduly harsh. Valuation is also considered somewhat arbitrary; values are always in flux because relevant conditions are always changing. A particular valuation figure, obtained at a given instant on the basis of the special circumstances of that moment, may well not be the same figure that would be obtained by the same process at a later date when circumstances

have changed. Pushed to an extreme, the position suggests that no valuation should ever take place because any valuation is always subject to attack as evanescent—the valuation figure would always be different if it had been made either earlier or later. Thus, criticism of valuation on the basis of changing conditions can prove too much, undermining the entire concept.

The imprecision of the valuation process has also led to the argument that valuation is so malleable that the entire process is perverse—that, in actuality, it is the reverse of what it seems to be. On this view, valuation is not an objective process by which projected earnings are capitalized to reach an ultimate figure under a procedure that has admitted infirmities. Instead, these critics assert, the trustees or the courts first determine the classes of claimants that should participate in the reorganization plan—on the basis of rough judgment or visceral reactions or other unexpressed or even unexpressable criteria—and then select the projection of earnings or the capitalization ratio necessary to reach a valuation figure that will include the preselected groups. The valuation process is not viewed as unduly harsh or rigid, but rather as so flexible that it is subject to abuse.

Moreover, valuation hearings could be expensive, protracted and rancorous. To the extent they were resorted to for purposes of delay and to obtain a better bargaining position they frequently were wasteful and counterproductive to a successful reorganization.

A second and even greater objection to the absolute priority rule under Chapter X of the Bankruptcy Act was that the rule could not be altered without unanimous consent. Even if creditors, voting by large majorities, were willing to grant stockholders a share of the reorganization value to induce them to reorganize, they often could not do so if there were dissenting creditor claims. Unless these claims were paid off, the plan could be confirmed only if claims and equity interests were treated in the plan according to what the absolute priority rule gave them; no more and no less. Bankruptcy Act § 221(2). This "hold-out" problem has been eliminated in the Bankruptcy Code. Dissenters in a class that accepts a Chapter 11 plan are protected only to the extent they have rights under the best interests rule of § 1129(a)(7). But the absolute priority rule continues to apply in Chapter 11 to a class of claims or interests that rejects the plan.

If an impaired class of unsecured claims does not accept the plan, confirmation of the plan is possible only if cramdown under § 1129(b)(2)(B) (the absolute priority rule) is permitted. If a creditor class is not fully paid no junior class can receive anything under the plan. Since any class of stockholder interests is junior to any class of claims the effect is to bar participation by stockholders in the reorganized corporation unless the nonconsenting class of claims is paid in full. The absolute priority rule is a powerful incentive to the debtor to offer a plan that unsecured creditors will accept.

3. INTER-CLASS "GIVE-UPS"

A line of authority stemming from *In re SPM Mfg.Corp.*, 984 F.2d 1305 (1st Cir. 1993), has emerged which suggests that a secured class may assign distributions to junior classes in ways that appear inconsistent with the traditional understanding of the absolute priority rule. The justification for this practice is said to be that a creditor may give its property to another as it chooses. But when that "gift" is implemented through or in connection with a reorganization plan, the absolute priority rule may be implicated. The following case is a good analysis of this emerging practice in confirmation strategy.

In re Armstrong World Industries, Inc.
United States Court of Appeals, Third Circuit, 2005.
432 F.3d 507.

■ ANNE E. THOMPSON, District Judge.

This matter is before the Court on Armstrong Worldwide Industries, Inc.'s ("AWI") appeal of the District Court's decision to deny confirmation of AWI's bankruptcy reorganization plan. In its decision, the District Court concluded that the plan could not be confirmed because the distribution of warrants to AWI's equity interest holders over the objection of the class of unsecured creditors violated the absolute priority rule, as codified in § 1129(b)(2)(B). AWI filed a timely appeal, contending that (1) the issuance of warrants does not violate the absolute priority rule, and (2) an equitable exception to the absolute priority rule applies. For the following reasons, we affirm the judgment of the District Court.

I. Facts and procedural history

AWI designs, manufactures, and sells flooring products, kitchen and bathroom cabinets, and ceiling systems. Due to asbestos litigation liabilities, AWI and two of its subsidiaries filed for Chapter 11 bankruptcy in the United States Bankruptcy Court for the District of Delaware on December 6, 2000. The United States Trustee for the District of Delaware appointed two committees to represent AWI's unsecured creditors: (1) the Official Committee of Asbestos Personal Injury Claimants ("APIC"), and (2) the Official Committee of Unsecured Creditors ("UCC"). The Bankruptcy Court appointed Dean M. Trafelet as the Future Claimants' Representative ("FCR").

After holding negotiations with APIC, UCC, and FCR, AWI filed its Fourth Amended Plan of Reorganization (the "Plan") and Amended Disclosure Statement with the Bankruptcy Court in May 2003. Under the Plan, AWI's creditors were divided into eleven classes, and AWI's equity interest holders were placed into a twelfth class. Relevant to this appeal are Class 6, a class of unsecured creditors; Class 7, a class of present and future asbestos-related personal injury claimants; and Class 12, the class of equity interest holders who own AWI's common stock. The only member of Class 12 is Armstrong Worldwide, Inc. ("AWWD"), the parent company of AWI, which is in turn wholly owned by Armstrong Holdings, Inc. ("Holdings"). Classes 6 and 7 hold equal priority, and have interests senior to those of Class 12. All three are impaired classes because their claims or interests would be altered by the Plan.

The Plan provided that AWI would place approximately $1.8 billion of its assets into a trust for Class 7 pursuant to 11 U.S.C. § 524(g). Class 7's members would be entitled to an initial payment percentage from the trust of 20% of their allowed claims. Meanwhile, Class 6 would recover about 59.5% of its $1.651 billion in claims. The Plan would also issue new warrants to purchase AWI's new common stock, estimated to be worth $35 to $40 million, to AWWD or Holdings (Class 12). If Class 6 rejected the Plan, then the Plan provided that Class 7 would receive the warrants.) However, the Plan also provided that Class 7 would automatically waive receipt of the warrants, which would then be issued to AWWD or Holdings (Class 12).

The Bankruptcy Court set September 22, 2003 as the deadline for voting on the Plan and for the parties to object to the Plan's confirmation. Because the Plan would distribute property to AWI's equity interest holders without fully paying off the unsecured creditors' claims, all impaired unsecured creditor classes were required to approve the Plan under 11 U.S.C. § 1129(a)(8). If any impaired class objected to the Plan, then the Plan could only be "crammed down" if it was "fair and equitable" to the objecting class. See § 1129(b)(1).

UCC represented all of the classes of unsecured creditors, including Class 6, during the negotiations that led to the Plan. Although UCC initially approved of the Plan in May 2003, it later filed a conditional objection to the Plan's confirmation [] based on (1) the greater potential distribution to creditors that would result if federal asbestos legislation was passed (namely, the FAIR Act), and (2) the possible applicability of the absolute priority rule, as codified in § 1129(b), if the Plan was not accepted by all classes.

As indicated in its conditional objection, UCC's reservations about the Plan were prompted in part by the proposal of the FAIR Act, which was reported out of the Senate Judiciary Committee in July 2003. If passed, the FAIR Act would remove asbestos-related personal injury claims from the courts and absolve asbestos defendants of liability in return for mandatory contributions to a federally supervised trust. AWI's contribution to the FAIR Act trust was estimated to range from $520 to $805 million, far less than the $1.8 billion it would put in trust for the Class 7 asbestos claimants under the Plan. Thus, if the FAIR Act passed, approximately $1 billion could be freed up for distribution among AWI's other creditors, including the class of unsecured creditors. [Editors' Note: The FAIR Act was not, in fact, ever enacted].

In response to UCC's concerns about the FAIR Act, the Bankruptcy Court extended the final deadline for voting to October 31, 2003. To accept the Plan, class members holding at least fifty percent of the number of claims and two-thirds of the amount of the claims would need to vote for the Plan. Although 88.03% of Class 6 claim holders voted for the Plan, only 23.21% of the amount of the claims voted to accept the Plan. As a result, Class 6 rejected the Plan. Classes 7 and 12 accepted the Plan, but Class 12's acceptance was rescinded under the Plan due to Class 6's rejection.

Following a hearing on November 17 and 18, 2003, the Bankruptcy Court recommended confirmation of the Plan to the District Court in its December 19, 2003 Proposed Findings and Conclusions. The Bankruptcy Court found that the absolute priority rule, as codified in section 1129(b)(2) of the Bankruptcy Code, was satisfied because the warrants were distributed to the holder of equity interests because of the waiver by Class 7, citing *In re Genesis Health Ventures, Inc.*, 266 B.R. 591 (Bkrtcy. D.Del.2001), and *In re SPM Mfg. Corp.*, 984 F.2d 1305 (1st Cir. 1993). In addition, the Bankruptcy Court found that UCC had waived its right to object to the Plan when it "entered into a consensual plan encompassing" the Plan provisions. Because the Plan included a channeling injunction under section 524(g) of the Bankruptcy Code, the District Court was required to affirm the Bankruptcy Court's Proposed Findings and Conclusions before the Plan could go into effect.

UCC filed objections to the Bankruptcy Court's Proposed Findings and Conclusions with the United States District Court for the District of Delaware. … The District Court found that (1) the issuance of warrants to the equity interest holders violated the absolute priority rule, and (2) no equitable exception to the absolute priority rule applied.

AWI now appeals the District Court's decision, and is joined by Appellees APIC and FCR, who jointly submitted a brief adopting and supporting AWI's arguments.

II. Discussion

…

C. Confirmation of a Reorganization Plan

Confirmation of a proposed Chapter 11 reorganization plan is governed by 11 U.S.C. § 1129. A court will confirm a plan if it meets all of the requirements set out in section 1129(a). Only one of these requirements concerns us in this appeal, and that is the requirement that the plan be consensual, with unanimous acceptance by all of the impaired classes. 11 U.S.C. § 1129(a)(8). If the plan is not consensual, a court may still confirm as long as the plan meets the other requirements of section 1129(a), and "does not discriminate unfairly, and is fair and equitable" as to any dissenting impaired class. 11 U.S.C. § 1129(b)(1); *see Bank of Am. Nat'l Trust & Sav. Ass'n v. 203 N. LaSalle St. P'ship* [hereinafter *LaSalle*]. The latter type of confirmation is also called a "cram down," as the court can cram a plan down over the objection of an impaired class. See generally Kenneth N. Klee, *All You Ever Wanted to Know About Cram Down Under the New Bankruptcy Code*, 53 Am. Bankr. L.J. 133 (1979).

1. The Absolute Priority Rule

The issues in this case require us to examine the "fair and equitable" requirement for a cram down, which invokes the absolute priority rule. The absolute priority rule is a judicial invention that predated the Bankruptcy Code. It arose from the concern that because a debtor proposed its own reorganization plan, the plan could be "too good a deal" for that debtor's owners. *LaSalle*. In its initial form, the absolute priority rule required that "creditors ... be paid before the stockholders could retain [equity interests] for any purpose whatever." Id. (*quoting N. Pac. Ry. Co. v. Boyd*).

The absolute priority rule was later codified as part of the "fair and equitable" requirement of § 1129(b). Under the statute, a plan is fair and equitable with respect to an impaired, dissenting class of unsecured claims if (1) it pays the class's claims in full, or if (2) it does not allow holders of any junior claims or interests to receive or retain any property under the plan "on account of" such claims or interests. § 1129(b)(2)(B)(i)-(ii).

At the heart of this appeal is the Plan provision that distributes warrants to AWI's equity interest holders (Class 12) through Class 7 in the event that Class 6 rejects the Plan. Appellant AWI argues that this provision does not violate the absolute priority rule because (1) legislative history and historical context indicate that the rule does not prohibit the transfer of warrants to the equity interest holders under the current circumstances; (2) case law establishes that Class 7 can transfer part of its distribution under the Plan to another claimant; and (3) the Plan did not give the warrants to Class 12 "on account of" its equity interests. We address each of these contentions in turn.

a. Interpreting the Absolute Priority Rule

First, AWI suggests that this Court should apply a flexible interpretation of the absolute priority rule based on its legislative history and historical context. Because the absolute priority rule is now codified as part of the Bankruptcy Code, we will interpret it using standard principles of statutory construction.

We begin by looking at the plain language of the statute. If the meaning is plain, we will make no further inquiry unless the literal application of the statute will end in a result that conflicts with Congress's intentions. In such a case, the intentions of Congress will control.

AWI contends that application of the absolute priority rule would be contrary to Congress's intentions because the rule was designed to prevent the "'squeezing out' [of] intermediate unsecured creditors." *See In re Wabash Valley Power Ass'n*, 72 F.3d 1305, 1314 (7th Cir. 1995) (citing *N. Pac. Ry. Co.[v. Boyd]* (emphasis added). AWI supports its claim with floor statements by Representative Don Edwards and Senator Dennis DeConcini, key legislators of the Bankruptcy Code. These statements indicate that "a senior class will not be able to give up value to a junior class over the dissent of an intervening class unless the intervening class receives the full amount, as opposed to value, of its claims or interests." 124 Cong. Rec. 32,408 & 34,007 (1978) (remarks of Rep. Edwards and remarks of Sen. DeConcini) (emphasis added). AWI argues that this language demonstrates that the absolute priority rule was not meant to apply to the situation before us because Class 6 is not an intervening (or intermediate) class, and is not being squeezed out by Class 7's transfer of warrants to Class 12 under the Plan.

The absolute priority rule, as codified, ensures that "the holder of any claim or interest that is junior to the claims of [an impaired dissenting] class will not receive or retain under the plan on account of such junior claim or interest any property." § 1129(b)(2)(B)(ii). The plain language of the statute makes it clear that a plan cannot give property to junior claimants over the objection of a more senior class that is impaired, but does not indicate that the objecting class must be an intervening class.

We find that the plain meaning of the statute does not conflict with Congress's intent. The legislative history shows that section 1129(b) was at least designed to address "give-up" situations where a senior class gave property to a class junior to the dissenting class. Other statements in the legislative history of section 1129(b), however, appear to apply the statute more broadly. For example, the House Report for H.R. 8200, the bill that was eventually enacted, states that section 1129(b) "codifies the absolute priority rule from the dissenting class on down." Despite amendments to the original version of H.R. 8200, the House Report has been considered an authoritative source of legislative history for section 1129(b). *See* 124 Cong. Rec. 32,408 & 34,007 (1978) (remarks of Rep. Edwards and remarks of Sen. DeConcini) ("[T]he House report remains an accurate description of confirmation of section 1129(b)."). In addition, the floor statements of Representative Edwards and Senator DeConcini do not rule out the possibility that an impaired class may object to a co-equal class's distribution of property to a junior class. *See id.* ("As long as senior creditors have not been paid more than in full, and classes of equal claims are being treated so that the dissenting class of impaired unsecured claims is not being discriminated against unfairly, the plan may be confirmed if the impaired class of unsecured claims receives less than 100 cents on the dollar (or nothing at all) as long as no class junior to the dissenting class receives anything at all."). As a result, we will apply the plain meaning of the statute. Under this reading, the statute would be violated because the Plan would give property to Class 12, which has claims junior to those of Class 6. This finding does not end our consideration of this appeal, as AWI makes further arguments regarding exceptions to the absolute priority rule.

b. Transfers of Bankruptcy Distributions Between Creditors and Equity Interest Holders

Second, AWI contends that Class 7 may distribute the property it will receive under the Plan to Class 12 without violating the absolute priority rule. AWI derives this result from application of the so-called "*MCorp-Genesis*" rule, which is based on a line of cases where creditors were allowed to distribute their proceeds from the bankruptcy estate to other claimants without offending section 1129(b). See SPM (permitting senior secured creditors to share bankruptcy proceeds with junior unsecured creditors while skipping over priority tax creditors in a Chapter 7 liquidation); Genesis Health, 266 B.R. at 602, 617-18 (allowing senior secured lenders to (1) give up a portion of their proceeds under the reorganization plan to holders of unsecured and subordinated claims, without including holders of punitive damages claims in the arrangement, and (2) allocate part of their value under the plan to the debtor's officers and directors as an employment incentive package); *In re MCorp Fin., Inc.*, 160 B.R. 941, 948 (S.D.Tex.1993) (permitting senior unsecured bondholders to allocate part of their claim to fund a settlement with the FDIC over the objection of the junior subordinated bondholders).

The District Court rejected this argument, and found that the *MCorp-Genesis* line of cases was distinguishable. It began its analysis with *SPM*, a First Circuit opinion cited by both the *MCorp* and *Genesis Health* courts to support the legality of the distribution schemes presented to them. The District Court differentiated *SPM* from the current case in three ways: (1) *SPM* involved a distribution under Chapter 7, which did not trigger § 1129(b)(2)(B)(ii); (2) the senior creditor had a perfected security interest, meaning that the property was not subject to distribution under the Bankruptcy Code's priority scheme; and (3) the distribution was a "carve out," a situation where a party whose claim is secured by assets in the bankruptcy estate allows a portion of its lien proceeds to be paid to others. See generally Richard B. Levin, *Almost All You Ever Wanted to Know About Carve Out*, 76 Am. Bankr. L.J. 445 (2002). Similarly, *Genesis Health* involved property subject to the senior creditors' liens that was "carved out" for the junior claimants. In addition, the District Court found *MCorp* distinguishable on its facts because the senior unsecured creditor transferred funds to the FDIC to settle pre-petition litigation.

We adopt the District Court's reading of these cases, and agree that they do not stand for the unconditional proposition that creditors are generally free to do whatever they wish with the bankruptcy proceeds they receive. Creditors must also be guided by the statutory prohibitions of the absolute priority rule, as codified in § 1129(b)(2)(B). Under the plan at issue here, an unsecured creditor class would receive and automatically transfer warrants to the holder of equity interests in the event that its co-equal class rejects the reorganization plan. We conclude that the absolute priority rule applies and is violated by this distribution scheme.

In addition, the structure of the Plan makes plain that the transfer between Class 7 and Class 12 was devised to ensure that Class 12 received the warrants, with or without Class 6's consent. The distribution of the warrants was only made to Class 7 if Class 6 rejected the Plan. In turn, Class 7 automatically waived the warrants in favor of Class 12, without any means for dissenting members of Class 7 to protest. Allowing this particular type of transfer would encourage parties to impermissibly sidestep the carefully crafted strictures of the Bankruptcy Code, and would undermine Congress's intention to give unsecured creditors bargaining power in this context. See H.R.Rep. No. 95-595, at 416 ("[Section 1129(b)(2)(B)(ii)] gives intermediate creditors a great deal of leverage in negotiating with senior or secured creditors who wish to have a plan that gives value to equity.").

c. On Account of

Third, AWI argues that the warrants would not be distributed to Class 12 on account of their equity interests, but rather would be given as consideration for settlement of their intercompany claims. UCC disputes the existence of any such settlement, alleging that such an arrangement should have been brought to the attention of the Bankruptcy Court. In response, AWI indicates that the settlement was detailed in the Plan's Disclosure Statement, which the Bankruptcy Court approved on June 2, 2003. The relevant portion of the Disclosure Statement reads as follows:

> In the ordinary course of business, such intercompany claims have been recorded on the books and records of Holdings, AWWD and AWI, and, assuming that all such intercompany claims are valid, the net intercompany claim so recorded is in favor of Holdings in the approximate amount of $12 million. In consideration of, among other things, AWI's agreement under the Plan to fund the reasonable fees and expenses associated with the Holdings Plan of Liquidation, the treatment of Holdings, AWWD, and their respective

officers and directors as PI Protected Parties under the Asbestos PI Permanent Channeling Injunction, the simultaneous release by AWI of any claims (known and unknown) AWI has against Holdings and AWWD, and the issuance of the New Warrants to AWWD, and to avoid potentially protracted and complicated proceedings to determine the exact amounts, nature and status under the Plan of all such claims and to facilitate the expeditious consummation of the Plan and the completion of Holdings' winding up, Holdings and AWWD will, effective upon and subject to the occurrence of the Effective Date, release all such intercompany claims (known and unknown) against AWI or any of AWI's subsidiaries[.]

As stated earlier, section 1129(b)(2)(B)(ii) provides that holders of junior claims or interests "will not receive or retain [any property] under the plan on account of such junior claim or interest." § 1129(b)(2)(B)(ii) (emphasis added). In LaSalle, the Supreme Court interpreted "on account of" to mean "because of," or a "causal relationship between holding the prior claim or interest and receiving and retaining property." Although the Supreme Court did not decide what degree of causation would be necessary, its discussion on that topic revealed that the absolute priority rule, as codified, was not in fact absolute. First, it indicated that the "on account of" language would be redundant if section 1129(b) was read as a categorical prohibition against transfers to prior equity. Second, it noted that a "less absolute prohibition" stemming from the "on account of language" would "reconcile the two recognized policies underlying Chapter 11, of preserving going concerns and maximizing property available to satisfy creditors."

In keeping with these observations, we noted in *PWS* that the "on account of" language "confirms that there are some cases in which property can transfer to junior interests not 'on account of' those interests but for other reasons." 228 F.3d at 238 (discussing LaSalle). In *PWS*, the debtors released their legal claims against various parties to facilitate their reorganization, including an avoidance claim that would have allowed them to avoid certain aspects of a previous recapitalization. The appellants in PWS argued that releasing the avoidance claim resulted in a prohibited transfer of value to equity interest holders who had participated in the recapitalization. We held that "without direct evidence of causation, releasing potential claims against junior equity does not violate the absolute priority rule in the particular circumstance [where] the claims are of only marginal viability and could be costly for the reorganized entity to pursue."

AWI would analogize AWWD and Holdings's release of intercompany claims in exchange for warrants to the release of claims in PWS. We disagree. According to the Disclosure Statement, the warrants have an estimated value of $35 to $40 million. In contrast, the intercompany claims were valued at approximately $12 million. This settlement would amount to a substantial benefit for Class 12, especially as the warrants were only part of the consideration for which the intercompany claims were released. Among other things, the intercompany claims were also ostensibly released in exchange for the simultaneous release of any claims by AWI against AWWD or Holdings and facilitation of the reorganization process. AWI gives no adequate explanation for this difference in value, leading us to conclude that AWWD or Holdings (Class 12) would receive the warrants on account of their status as equity interest holders.

d. Equity

1. Applicability of *Penn Central*

Appellant AWI further contends that this Court should apply equitable considerations to allow an exception to the absolute priority rule. It finds such an exception in the case of *In re Penn Central Transportation Co.*, 596 F.2d 1127, 1142 (3d Cir. 1979), and points to language in *Norwest Bank Worthington v. Ahlers*, 485 U.S. 197 (1988), that indicates that exceptions to the absolute priority rule may indeed exist. *See id.* (stating that the enactment of section 1129(b) "bar[s] any expansion of any exception to the absolute priority rule beyond that recognized" in pre-1978 Bankruptcy Code cases).

Penn Central involved a "monumental [reorganization] plan designed to resolve what [at the time was] the most complex set of interrelated and conflicting claims ever addressed under ... the Bankruptcy Act." Penn Central Transportation Company, which was formed in 1968 by the merger of the Pennsylvania Railroad Company and the New York Central Railroad Company, filed a petition for reorganization under the Bankruptcy Code in 1970. Thereafter, to prevent a rail transportation crisis and to address the particular difficulties of that reorganization, Congress passed the Regional Rail Reorganization Act of 1973, which directed that major portions of Penn Central's rail assets be conveyed to Conrail, a new company formed under the Act to continue operation of some of the routes served by Penn Central. In light of these exceptional circumstances, we found that "[o]ur construction and application of precedents such as the absolute priority rule must necessarily take account of the unique facts of this Plan and proceed in an environment pervaded more by relativity than by absolutes."

AWI argues that the facts of the case before us are similarly unique, and also warrant a more equitable and flexible application of the absolute priority rule. Among the facts that AWI finds unique are: (1) the involvement of UCC in the negotiation and drafting of the Plan; (2) UCC's endorsement of the Plan, as indicated by its signature on the cover letter accompanying the disclosure statement; (3) the lack of a negative effect on Class 6's distribution from the granting of warrants to Class 7; (4) the relatively small value of the warrants compared to the entire bankruptcy estate; (5) the acceptance of the Plan by the majority in number of UCC's constituents; and (6) the delay caused by UCC's objection, which was primarily lodged in anticipation of the passage of the FAIR Act. We do not find these facts to be as compelling as those that led us to apply a more flexible absolute priority rule in the past. AWI's bankruptcy due to asbestos liabilities simply does not involve the kind of exigent circumstances present in Penn Central, where Congress intervened in the reorganization process to avoid a rail transportation crisis of national import.

In addition, our application of equitable considerations in Penn Central did not mean that the absolute priority rule was abandoned. Rather, we held firm to the idea that the rule still "required ... that provision be made for satisfaction of senior claims prior to satisfaction of junior claims."

2. Judicial Estoppel

[Omitted].

III. Conclusion

We recognize that the longer that the reorganization process takes, the less likely that the purposes of Chapter 11 (preserving the business as a going concern and maximizing the amount that can be paid to creditors) will be fulfilled. Nevertheless, we conclude that the absolute priority rule applies in this case. We will accordingly affirm the District Court's decision to deny confirmation of AWI's Plan.

NOTES

1. How do you square this case with *In re Figter Limited*, p. 682 in which the Ninth Circuit held that a debtor's mortgagee could purchase the claims of the debtor's unsecured creditors?

2. Notwithstanding the apparently binding decision from its Court of Appeals in *Armstrong*, the Delaware bankruptcy court subsequently approved a pre-plan settlement in *In re World Health Alternatives, Inc.*, 344 B.R. 291 (Bankr.D.Del.2006), that involved a secured party "gifting" collateral to unsecured creditors without providing for prior payment in full of priority tax claims. It distinguished *Armstrong* on the grounds that the settlement (i) did not involve a plan confirmation proceeding and therefore the absolute priority rule was not applicable, (ii) in the circumstances of the *World Health* case no plan would ever be confirmed and that conversion to Chapter 7 was inevitable, and (iii) the *World Health* settlement contemplated distribution of collateral that was property of the secured party to unsecured creditors rather than distribution of property of the estate. In *Motorola, Inc. v. Official Committee of Unsecured Creditors (In re Iridium Operating LLC)*, 478 F.3d 452 (2d Cir. 2007), however, the Second Circuit was troubled by the implications for the absolute priority rule of a similar attempt to distribute settlement proceeds claimed as collateral by a secured bank group to fund a litigation trust for general unsecured creditors. The Second Circuit wrote:

> [w]hether a particular settlement's distribution scheme complies with the Code's priority scheme must be the most important factor for the bankruptcy court to consider when determining whether a settlement is 'fair and equitable' under Rule 9019. The court must be certain that parties to a settlement have not employed a settlement as a means to avoid the priority strictures of the Bankruptcy Code. In the Chapter 11 context, whether a settlement's distribution plan complies with Bankruptcy Code's priority scheme will often be the dispositive factor. However, where the remaining factors weigh heavily in favor of approving a settlement, the bankruptcy court, in its discretion, could endorse a settlement that does not comply in some minor respects with the priority rule if the parties to the settlement justify, and the reviewing court clearly articulates the reasons for approving, a settlement that deviates from the priority rule.

The Second Circuit then remanded for "clarification" of why the settlement before it required deviation from the absolute priority rule. Why would a settling defendant condition its willingness to settle on distribution of the settlement inconsistently with the Code's priority scheme? Why should the rights of nonconsenting senior claimholders ever be subordinated to the desire of the holders of junior claims and interests to condition settlement on deviations from absolute priority? *Id.* at 464-65.

4. NEW VALUE RULE

If the debtor cannot offer creditors a plan that all classes will accept, the debtor must conceive a plan that will meet the absolute priority standard of § 1129(b)(2)(B)(ii). A familiar tactic for otherwise out-of-the money equity is for the debtor to propose a plan that allows the debtor's stockholders to retain part or all of the ownership of the reorganized corporation based on their contributing new money equivalent to the value of the ownership interest they will retain under the plan. Judicial support for this procedure is found in *Case v. Los Angeles Lumber Products Co.*, 308 U.S. 106 (1939), an opinion of Justice Douglas discussed in *203 North LaSalle,* which follows. *Los Angeles Lumber* concerned the reorganization under § 77B of the Bankruptcy Act of a corporation whose assets were worth approximately $840,000 while its liabilities, mostly claims of first mortgage bondholders, totaled more than $3.8 million. Under § 77B a plan of reorganization could not be confirmed, even if all classes approved, unless the plan was "fair and equitable." Justice Douglas's opinion for the Court held that this requirement adopted the "full" or "absolute" priority rule. The plan provided for creation of a new corporation with new preferred stock issued to bondholders and new common stock issued to stockholders of the old corporation without any new contribution of money by those stockholders. The plan was approved by both bondholders and stockholders by majorities of over 90%. Confirmation of the plan was challenged by some dissenting bondholders on the ground that the plan did not satisfy the absolute priority rule. The stockholders attempted to justify their participation in the ownership of the new corporation by asserting that their commitment to continue as managers of the new corporation was a contribution of new value to the enterprise. They pointed to the fact that their experience and standing in the community would benefit the new corporation. The Court declared that it would be an evasion of the absolute priority rule to allow the owners of an insolvent business to take a share of the reorganized entity on the basis of intangibles like a promise to continue to provide management services that cannot be translated into money's worth reasonably equivalent to the value of the new stock. But Justice Douglas's opinion for the Court also said, in a much-discussed dictum, that the owners of an insolvent corporation can take ownership interests in a reorganized corporation to the extent they contribute money or money's worth.

In *Norwest Bank Worthington v. Ahlers*, 485 U.S. 197 (1988), the Supreme Court reaffirmed the principle that the equityholders' promise to provide future services to the reorganized debtor could not be used as a justification for passing value down to equity over the objections of dissenting classes of creditors. Such a plan violated the absolute priority rule as codified in § 1129(b)(2)(B). But in a startling footnote the Supreme Court went on to suggest that perhaps the codification of the rule in § 1129(b)(2)(B) was also inconsistent with Douglas's dictum in *Los Angeles Lumber* that the distribution of value to equity holders in exchange for "money or money's worth" might comply with the rule.

Though startling to bankruptcy specialists, the cloud the *Ahlers* court cast over the continued viability of the new value rule was supported by serious policy concerns with how the new value rule might be manipulated unfairly by the debtor. The kind of case that draws criticism of the new value rule is *In re Potter Material Service, Inc.*, 781 F.2d 99 (7th Cir. 1986), in which the sole stockholder of Debtor proposed in a cramdown plan to retain the full ownership interest in the reorganized corporation by contributing $14,800 to fund a 3% payout to the class of unsecured creditors and $20,000 to pay debtor's attorneys. A previous version of the plan had proposed a 40% payout to the unsecured creditors. The stockholder also agreed to renew his personal guaranty of Debtor's $600,000 obligation to the bank on which, apparently, the stockholder was already liable. The court determined that Debtor's going concern value was between $10,000 and $15,000 and confirmed the plan. The court based its valuation on evidence of Debtor's past earnings record, the state of the economy, the highly competitive nature of Debtor's business, the current financial position of Debtor, and projections of Debtor's future earnings. There is no indication that the court allowed any third party to bid for the firm or considered any plan but Debtor's.

In the post-*Ahlers* dispute about whether the new value rule survived enactment of the Bankruptcy Code, three views emerged which, for convenience, we can discuss as the Reinhardt view in *Bonner Mall*, the Easterbrook view in *Kham & Nate's*, and the market approach. In *In re Bonner Mall Partnership*, 2 F.3d 899 (9th Cir. 1993), Judge Reinhardt joined with some commentators and courts in rejecting the terminology "new value *exception*." He concludes that there is no exception in the Code to the absolute priority rule of § 1129(b)(2)(B)(ii). All classes of creditors must be fully paid before the old equity can retain any "property" under the reorganization plan "on account of such junior claim or interest." For the answer to the question whether old owners are in fact retaining property in a reorganized entity on account of their prior interest in the old entity, Judge Reinhardt turns to the traditional formulation of the new value rule which he describes as "an established pre-Code bankruptcy practice." Under this principle an old owner was allowed to retain an interest in the new entity if it makes a capital contribution to the new entity that is (1) new, (2) substantial, (3) money or money's worth, (4) necessary for a successful reorganization and (5) reasonably equivalent to the value or interest received. Moreover, the debtor's plan may designate the old owners as having the exclusive right to purchase the ownership interest in the new entity so long as the new contribution is "necessary for a successful reorganization and in the best interest of all concerned." All this can be done in a cramdown plan over the opposition of classes of creditors holding impaired claims who believe the old equity is not making a contribution commensurate with the participation it is taking in the new entity.

The Easterbrook view was expressed in *Kham & Nate's Shoes No. 2, Inc. v. First Bank of Whiting*, 908 F.2d 1351 (7th Cir. 1990), in which the court declined to confirm a cramdown plan under which the debtor's two stockholders proposed to retain ownership in exchange for their personal guaranties of a $435,000 loan to be made to the debtor corporation under the plan. Without deciding whether the new value rule was still in effect, the court held that the guaranties were not new value. Judge Easterbrook questioned the wisdom of the new value rule in the following paragraph:

> In principle, then, the exchange of stock for new value may make sense. When it does, the creditors should be willing to go along. Credi-

tors effectively own bankrupt firms. They may find it worthwhile, as owners, to sell equity claims to the managers; they may even find it worthwhile to give the equity away in order to induce managers to stay on and work hard. Because the Code allows creditors to consent to a plan that impairs their interests, voluntary transactions of this kind are possible. Only collective action problems could frustrate beneficial arrangements. If there are many creditors, one may hold out, seeking to engross a greater share of the gains. But the Code deals with holdups by allowing half of a class by number (two-thirds by value) to consent to a lower class's retention of an interest. § 1126(c). Creditors not acting in good faith do not count toward the one-third required to block approval, § 1126(e). When there is value to be gained by allowing a lower class to kick in new value and keep its interest, the creditors should be willing to go along. A "new value exception" means a power in the *judge* to "sell" stock to the managers even when the creditors believe that this transaction will *not* augment the value of the firm.

908 F.2d at 1360. In stating that "[c]reditors effectively own bankrupt firms," Judge Easterbrook means that if the value of the bankrupt business is not sufficient to pay in full the claims of the creditors, all of the value of the business equitably belongs to the creditors. If there is one dissenting class of claims, the class may argue that to the extent their claims are not paid in full any residual value of the business belongs to that class. That is the effect of the absolute priority rule. The ownership interest in the business represents the residual value. Presumably, Judge Easterbrook would not find it to be fair and equitable to allow the ownership interest to be sold to somebody else without the consent of the dissenting class of claims. If somebody is willing to pay for the ownership interest, that interest must have some value. To the extent the dissenting class is not paid in full, it follows that the payment for that interest should be for the benefit of the dissenting class and that class should have the right to decide whether the amount offered for the ownership interest is adequate.

Fundamental to the difference of opinion between Judge Easterbrook and Judge Reinhardt is *who* decides whether the new value contribution is, in fact, equal to the ownership interest retained in the new entity. Judge Easterbrook would have the creditors make that determination. If they believe the contribution is worth the interest taken, they will consent to the plan and confirmation can go forward under § 1129(a). Judge Reinhardt would have the court value the ownership interest in deciding whether to confirm the plan.

In terms of the pre-Code background of the new value rule, Judge Easterbrook seems to have the better of this argument. Judge Reinhardt resolves the contemporary problem of the terms on which old ownership interests can participate in a new entity by reference to a pre-Code common law rule that he holds was not abolished by enactment of the Code. What he does not disclose is that the legal regime in which the new value rule operated before the Code was quite different from that after the Code. Although Chapter X of the Act allowed two-thirds of a creditor class to accept a plan and bind dissenters, still the court could not confirm the plan over the objection of a single creditor unless it was "fair and equitable." *Case v. Los Angeles Lumber Products Co.*, 308 U.S. 106 (1939), held that the quoted phrase meant that the plan had to meet the absolute priority rule: old equity could retain nothing in the plan unless all creditors were fully paid or all of the value in the entity had passed to them. Thus, before the Code, creditors—even by a two-thirds vote—could not waive the absolute priority rule and allow old equity to participate. This rigidity could lead to extreme situations in which the reorganization plan of a company that had to have new capital to survive could not award the old owners an equity interest in the new entity even though the old owners were the only source of new capital and all creditor classes consented to the plan. In such a case the *Los Angeles Lumber* dictum offered a sensible safety valve by recognizing an "exception" to the absolute priority rule which permitted the old owners to participate in the reorganized entity if they gave new value reasonably equivalent to the participation they received in the new entity.

The common law rule that Judge Reinhardt brings into post-Code law was one that was carefully tailored to meet the extraordinary situation spelled out above: the contribution must not only be commensurate with the interest taken but it must also be "necessary for a successful reorganization." Moreover, before the Code, all classes of creditors had to agree to the plan before it could be confirmed, an act that indicated their satisfaction with the equivalence of the old owners' new capital infusion. Hence, the court's view that the new value rule was an established common law rule that Congress must have intended to continue under the Code seems undercut by the difference in function performed by the rule in the pre-Code era, when the new value rule operated as a means of saving a debtor under a plan approved by the creditors, as contrasted with the use the courts have made of it in cases like *Bonner Mall* and *Potter* in which a plan rejected by creditors is used to squeeze out the claims of those creditors. What is more, since § 1129(a) now allows creditor classes to waive the absolute priority rule by a vote of two-thirds in amount and one-half in number (§ 1126(c)) and to permit the old owners to retain their interests on almost any terms on which agreement can be reached, the emergency situation that the *Los Angeles Lumber* formulation of the new value rule was designed to address is now easily dealt with in a § 1129(a) consensual plan. Bruce A. Markell, *Owners, Auctions, and Absolute Priority in Bankruptcy Reorganiza-*

tions, 44 Stan.L.Rev. 69, 75–90 (1991), discusses the pre-Code legal regime under which the new value rule was developed.

A third view of the new value rule taken by some courts and commentators essentially denies the existence of or need for a new value rule in its classic pre-Code formulation under the Code. They agree with Judge Reinhardt that, without violating the absolute priority rule, a cramdown plan can be confirmed under which old owners take an ownership interest in the reorganized entity so long as they contribute new capital of value equal to the interest taken. But they disagree with his decision to permit a plan to give the old equity the exclusive right to buy the new equity. A technical argument against the Reinhardt view is that an exclusive right to buy the stock in a new company amounts to a warrant given to the old owners and is, within § 1129(b)(2)(B)(ii), "property" having some value (why else would they want it?) given them "on account of" their previous ownership interest. A more basic criticism of exclusivity relates to the question of who is to value the ownership interest in the reorganized entity which the old owners wish to buy.

Searching for a solution to the valuation problem in a case in which the owners of shares in a business trust proposed retention of their interest in exchange for a capital contribution, the court in *In re Bjolmes Realty Trust*, 134 B.R. 1000 (Bankr.D.Mass.1991), held that a "fresh contribution" of capital did not "dilute" § 1129(b)(2)(B)(ii) but that market forces should be allowed to determine the value of the residual interest by having the court hold an auction sale of that interest at which the shareholders and creditors of the debtor could bid. The court said "The decisions are particularly troubling in their handling of valuation of the retained stock interest. * * * And they do nothing to allay the suspicion that a court, intent on promoting reorganization, will gear the valuation to equal the contribution." 134 B.R. at 1008. The *Bjolmes* court saw the temptation for self-dealing on the part of the debtor in proposing a new value plan, in which only the old owners may participate, that places a low valuation on the new stock, as not adequately redressed by having the valuation decision made by a busy court "intent on promoting reorganization." Judge Easterbrook acidly comments that this, in effect, gives the *judge* the right to sell the stock to the insiders. The reaction to these concerns by critics is to urge that if stock in a new entity is to be sold for a new infusion of capital, market forces, rather than courts, should be relied on to fix the value of the stock to be sold. The *Bjolmes* holding ordered that the stock be sold on an auction basis at which the creditors could bid.

Our colleague, Kenneth Klee, observes:

> The vice of the new value exception is that it enables the debtor's owners to purchase an ownership interest based on a court-approved valuation without validation of the price in the market place. Valuation

by the court is, of course the norm for distribution of reorganization securities under the fair and equitable test. But when a reorganization security is to be sold, in effect, for a new contribution, rather than distributed in satisfaction of claims or interests to a class of creditors or owners under a plan, perhaps a market test should be applied as would be done with the sale of any other asset of the estate. At the very least, to maintain the balance of relative right, chapter 11 creditors who argue that the proposed capital contribution is too low should have the opportunity to match or exceed the pending offer.

Kenneth N. Klee, *Cram Down II*, 64 Am. Bankr. L.J. 229, 244 (1990).

What these views have in common is the simple tenet that the old owners should have no better or worse rights to buy into the reorganized entity than other investors. Elizabeth Warren, *A Theory of Absolute Priority*, 1991 Ann.Surv.Am.L. 9. If this principle is sound, then the classic formulation of the new value rule resurrected in *Bonner Mall* is an anachronism. Whether the contribution the old owners make is "substantial" or "necessary for a successful reorganization" should be irrelevant so long as they pay what the ownership interest in the new entity is worth in the market.

After doubt was cast on the new value rule in *Ahlers*, the continued viability of the new value exception became the most controversial and important unsettled issue of reorganization law. The Supreme Court seemed finally poised to resolve the issue in *In re Bonner Mall Partnership*, 2 F.3d 899 (9th Cir. 1993), *cert. granted*, 510 U.S. 1039 (1994), but later dismissed *Bonner Mall* on procedural grounds. Finally, in 1999, the Supreme Court reached the new value issue in the following case.

Bank of America v. 203 North LaSalle Street Partnership

Supreme Court of the United States, 1999.
526 U.S. 434.

■ Justice SOUTER delivered the opinion of the Court.

The issue in this Chapter 11 reorganization case is whether a debtor's pre-bankruptcy equity holders may, over the objection of a senior class of impaired creditors, contribute new capital and receive ownership interests in the reorganized entity, when that opportunity is given exclusively to the old equity holders under a plan adopted without consideration of alternatives. We hold that old equity holders are disqualified from participating in such a "new value" transaction by the terms of 11 U.S.C. § 1129(b)(2)(B)(ii), which in such circumstances bars a junior interest holder's receipt of any property on account of his prior interest.

I.

Petitioner, Bank of America National Trust and Savings Association (Bank), is the major creditor of respondent, 203 North LaSalle Street Partnership (Debtor or Partnership), an Illinois real estate limited partnership. The Bank lent the Debtor some $93 million, secured by a nonrecourse first mortgage[3] on the Debtor's principal asset, 15 floors of an office building in downtown Chicago. In January 1995, the Debtor defaulted, and the Bank began foreclosure in a state court.

In March, the Debtor responded with a voluntary petition for relief under Chapter 11 of the Bankruptcy Code which automatically stayed the foreclosure proceedings, see § 362(a). The Debtor's principal objective was to ensure that its partners retained title to the property so as to avoid roughly $20 million in personal tax liabilities, which would fall due if the Bank foreclosed. The Debtor proceeded to propose a reorganization plan during the 120 day period when it alone had the right to do so, see 11 U.S.C. § 1121(b); see also § 1121(c) (exclusivity period extends to 180 days if the debtor files plan within the initial 120 days).[4] The Bankruptcy Court rejected the Bank's motion to terminate the period of exclusivity to make way for a plan of its own to liquidate the property, and instead extended the exclusivity period for cause shown, under § 1121(d).

The value of the mortgaged property was less than the balance due the Bank, which elected to divide its undersecured claim into secured and unsecured deficiency claims under § 506(a) and § 1111(b).[6] Under the plan, the Debtor separately classified the Bank's secured claim, its unsecured deficiency claim, and unsecured trade debt owed to other creditors. See § 1122(a).[7] The

---

[3] A nonrecourse loan requires the Bank to look only to the Debtor's collateral for payment. But see n. 6, *infra*.

[4] The Debtor filed an initial plan on April 13, 1995, and amended it on May 12, 1995. The Bank objected, and the Bankruptcy Court rejected the plan on the ground that it was not feasible. See § 1129(a)(11). The Debtor submitted a new plan on September 11, 1995.

[6] Having agreed to waive recourse against any property of the Debtor other than the real estate, the Bank had no unsecured claim outside of Chapter 11. Section 1111(b), however, provides that nonrecourse secured creditors who are undersecured must be treated in Chapter 11 as if they had recourse.

[7] Indeed, the Seventh Circuit apparently requires separate classification of the deficiency claim of an undersecured creditor from other general unsecured claims. Nonetheless, the Bank argued that if its deficiency claim had been included in the class of general unsecured creditors, its vote against confirmation would have resulted in the plan's rejection by that class. The Bankruptcy Court and the District Court rejected the contention that the classifications were gerrymandered to obtain requisite approval by a single class and the

Bankruptcy Court found that the Debtor's available assets were prepetition rents in a cash account of $3.1 million and the 15 floors of rental property worth $54.5 million. The secured claim was valued at the latter figure, leaving the Bank with an unsecured deficiency of $38.5 million.

So far as we need be concerned here, the Debtor's plan had these further features:

(1) The Bank's $54.5 million secured claim would be paid in full between 7 and 10 years after the original 1995 repayment date.[8]

(2) The Bank's $38.5 million unsecured deficiency claim would be discharged for an estimated 16% of its present value.[9]

(3) The remaining unsecured claims of $90,000, held by the outside trade creditors, would be paid in full, without interest, on the effective date of the plan.[10]

(4) Certain former partners of the Debtor would contribute $6.125 million in new capital over the course of five years (the contribution being worth some $4.1 million in present value), in exchange for the Partnership's entire ownership of the reorganized debtor.

The last condition was an exclusive eligibility provision: the old equity holders were the only ones who could contribute new capital.[11]

The Bank objected and, being the sole member of an impaired class of creditors, thereby blocked confirmation of the plan on a consensual basis. See § 1129(a)(8). The Debtor, however, took the alternate route to confirmation of a reorganization plan, forthrightly known as the judicial "cramdown" process for imposing a plan on a dissenting class. § 1129(b). *See generally* Klee, *All You*

Court of Appeals agreed. The Bank sought no review of that issue, which is thus not before us.

[8] Payment consisted of a prompt cash payment of $1,149,500 and a secured, 7–year note, extendable at the Debtor's option.

[9] This expected yield was based upon the Bankruptcy Court's projection that a sale or refinancing of the property on the 10th anniversary of the plan confirmation would produce a $19–million distribution to the Bank.

[10] The Debtor originally owed $160,000 in unsecured trade debt. After filing for bankruptcy, the general partners purchased some of the trade claims. Upon confirmation, the insiders would waive all general unsecured claims they held.

[11] The plan eliminated the interests of noncontributing partners. More than 60% of the Partnership interests would change hands on confirmation of the plan. The new Partnership, however, would consist solely of former partners, a feature critical to the preservation of the Partnership's tax shelter.

Ever Wanted to Know About Cram Down Under the New Bankruptcy Code, 53 Am. Bankr. L.J. 133 (1979).

There are two conditions for a cramdown. First, all requirements of § 1129(a) must be met (save for the plan's acceptance by each impaired class of claims or interests, see § 1129(a)(8)). Critical among them are the conditions that the plan be accepted by at least one class of impaired creditors, and satisfy the "best-interest-of-creditors" test. Here, the class of trade creditors with impaired unsecured claims voted for the plan, and there was no issue of best interest. Second, the objection of an impaired creditor class may be overridden only if "the plan does not discriminate unfairly, and is fair and equitable, with respect to each class of claims or interests that is impaired under, and has not accepted, the plan." § 1129(b)(1). As to a dissenting class of impaired unsecured creditors, such a plan may be found to be "fair and equitable" only if the allowed value of the claim is to be paid in full, § 1129(b)(2)(B)(i), or, in the alternative, if "the holder of any claim or interest that is junior to the claims of such [impaired unsecured] class will not receive or retain under the plan on account of such junior claim or interest any property," § 1129(b)(2)(B)(ii). That latter condition is the core of what is known as the "absolute priority rule."

The absolute priority rule was the basis for the Bank's position that the plan could not be confirmed as a cramdown. As the Bank read the rule, the plan was open to objection simply because certain old equity holders in the Debtor Partnership would receive property even though the Bank's unsecured deficiency claim would not be paid in full. The Bankruptcy Court approved the plan nonetheless, and accordingly denied the Bank's pending motion to convert the case to Chapter 7 liquidation, or to dismiss the case. The District Court affirmed, as did the Court of Appeals.

The majority of the Seventh Circuit's divided panel found ambiguity in the language of the statutory absolute priority rule, and looked beyond the text to interpret the phrase "on account of" as permitting recognition of a "new value corollary" to the rule. According to the panel, the corollary, as stated by this Court in *Case v. Los Angeles Lumber Products Co.*, provides that the objection of an impaired senior class does not bar junior claim holders from receiving or retaining property interests in the debtor after reorganization, if they contribute new capital in money or money's worth, reasonably equivalent to the property's value, and necessary for successful reorganization of the restructured enterprise. The panel majority held that

> "when an old equity holder retains an equity interest in the reorganized debtor by meeting the requirements of the new value corollary, he is not receiving or retaining that interest "on account of" his prior equitable ownership of the debtor. Rather, he is allowed to participate in the

reorganized entity "on account of "a new, substantial, necessary and fair infusion of capital."

In the dissent's contrary view, there is nothing ambiguous about the text: the "plain language of the absolute priority rule... does not include a new value exception." Since "[t]he Plan in this case gives [the Debtor's] partners the exclusive right to retain their ownership interest in the indebted property *because of* their status as... prior interest holder[s]," the dissent would have reversed confirmation of the plan.

We granted certiorari to resolve a Circuit split on the issue. The Seventh Circuit in this case joined the Ninth in relying on a new value corollary to the absolute priority rule to support confirmation of such plans. The Second and Fourth Circuits, by contrast, without explicitly rejecting the corollary, have disapproved plans similar to this one.[15] We do not decide whether the statute includes a new value corollary or exception, but hold that on any reading respondent's proposed plan fails to satisfy the statute, and accordingly reverse.

II.

The terms "absolute priority rule" and "new value corollary" (or "exception") are creatures of law antedating the current Bankruptcy Code, and to understand both those terms and the related but inexact language of the Code some history is helpful. The Bankruptcy Act preceding the Code contained no such provision as subsection (b)(2)(B)(ii), its subject having been addressed by two interpretive rules. The first was a specific gloss on the requirement of § 77B (and its successor, Chapter X) of the old Act, that any reorganization plan be "fair and equitable." The reason for such a limitation was the danger inherent in any reorganization plan proposed by a debtor, then and now, that the plan will simply turn out to be too good a deal for the debtor's owners. *See* H.R. Doc. No. 93–137, pt. I, p. 255 (1973) (discussing concern with "the ability of a few insiders, whether representatives of management or major creditors, to use the reorganization process to gain an unfair advantage"); *ibid.* ("[I]t was believed that creditors, because of management's position of dominance, were not able to bargain effectively without a clear standard of fairness and judicial control"); Ayer, *Rethinking Absolute Priority After* Ahlers, 87 Mich. L.Rev. 963, 969–973 (1989). Hence the pre-Code judicial response known as the absolute priority rule, that fairness and equity required that "the creditors... be paid before the stockholders could retain [equity interests] for any purpose whatever." *Northern Pacific R. Co. v. Boyd,* 228 U.S. 482, 508 (1913).

---

[15] All four of these cases arose in the single-asset real estate context, the typical one in which new value plans are proposed. * * *

The second interpretive rule addressed the first. Its classic formulation occurred in *Case v. Los Angeles Lumber Products Co.*, in which the Court spoke through Justice DOUGLAS in this dictum:

> "It is, of course, clear that there are circumstances under which stockholders may participate in a plan of reorganization of an insolvent debtor.... Where th[e] necessity [for new capital] exists and the old stockholders make a fresh contribution and receive in return a participation reasonably equivalent to their contribution, no objection can be made....
>
> "[W]e believe that to accord 'the creditor his full right of priority against the corporate assets' where the debtor is insolvent, the stockholder's participation must be based on a contribution in money or in money's worth, reasonably equivalent in view of all the circumstances to the participation of the stockholder." 308 U.S., at 121–122.

Although counsel for one of the parties here has described the *Case* observation as "'black letter' principle," it never rose above the technical level of dictum in any opinion of this Court, which last addressed it in *Norwest Bank Worthington v. Ahlers,* holding that a contribution of "'labor, experience, and expertise'" by a junior interest holder was not in the "'money's worth'" that the *Case* observation required. Nor, prior to the enactment of the current Bankruptcy Code, did any court rely on the *Case* dictum to approve a plan that gave old equity a property right after reorganization. Hence the controversy over how weighty the *Case* dictum had become, as reflected in the alternative labels for the new value notion: some writers and courts (including this one, see *Ahlers, supra*) have spoken of it as an exception to the absolute priority rule, while others have characterized it as a simple corollary to the rule, *see, e.g., In re Bonner Mall Partnership.*

Enactment of the Bankruptcy Code in place of the prior Act might have resolved the status of new value by a provision bearing its name or at least unmistakably couched in its terms, but the Congress chose not to avail itself of that opportunity. In 1973, Congress had considered proposals by the Bankruptcy Commission that included a recommendation to make the absolute priority rule more supple by allowing nonmonetary new value contributions. Although Congress took no action on any of the ensuing bills containing language that would have enacted such an expanded new value concept, each of them was reintroduced in the next congressional session. See H.R. 31, 94th Cong., 1st

Sess., §§ 7–303(4),[17] 7–310(d)(2)(B) (1975).[18] * * * After extensive hearings, a substantially revised House bill emerged, but without any provision for nonmonetary new value contributions. See H.R. 6, 95th Cong., 1st Sess., §§ 1123, 1129(b) (1977).[19] After a lengthy mark-up session, the House produced [the bill] which would eventually become the law. It had no explicit new value language, expansive or otherwise, but did codify the absolute priority rule in nearly its present form. See H.R. 8200, *supra,* § 1129(b)(2)(B)(iv) ("[T]he holders of claims or interests of any class of claims or interests, as the case may be, that is junior to such class will not receive or retain under the plan on account of such junior claims or interests any property").[20]

For the purpose of plumbing the meaning of subsection (b)(2)(B)(ii) in search of a possible statutory new value exception, the lesson of this drafting history is equivocal. Although hornbook law has it that Congress does not intend *sub silentio* to enact statutory language that it has earlier discarded, the phrase "on account of "is not *silentium,* and the language passed by in this instance had never been in the bill finally enacted, but only in predecessors that died on the vine. None of these contained an explicit codification of the absolute priority rule, and even in these earlier bills the language in question stated an expansive new value concept, not the rule as limited in the *Case* dictum. The

---

[17] Section 7–303(4) read: "[W]hen the equity security holders retain an interest under the plan, the individual debtor, certain partners or equity security holders will make a contribution which is important to the operation of the reorganized debtor or the successor under the plan, for participation by the individual debtor, such partners, or such holders under the plan on a basis which reasonably approximates the value, if any, of their interests, and the additional estimated value of such contribution."

[18] Section 7–310(d)(2)(B) read: "Subject to the provisions of section 7–303(3) and (4) and the court's making any findings required thereby, there is a reasonable basis for the valuation on which the plan is based and the plan is fair and equitable in that there is a reasonable probability that the securities issued and other consideration distributed under the plan will fully compensate the respective classes of creditors and equity security holders of the debtor for their respective interests in the debtor or his property."

[19] Section 1129(b) of H.R. 6 read, in relevant part: "[T]he court, on request of the proponent of such plan, shall confirm such plan. . . if such plan is fair and equitable with respect to all classes except any class that has accepted the plan and that is comprised of claims or interests on account of which the holders of such claims or interests will receive or retain under the plan not more than would be so received or retained under a plan that is fair and equitable with respect to all classes."

[20] While the earlier proposed bills contained provisions requiring as a condition of confirmation that a plan be "fair and equitable," none of them contained language explicitly codifying the absolute priority rule.

equivocal note of this drafting history is amplified by another feature of the legislative advance toward the current law. Any argument from drafting history has to account for the fact that the Code does not codify any authoritative pre-Code version of the absolute priority rule. Compare § 1129(b)(2)(B)(ii) ("[T]he holder of any claim or interest that is junior to the claims of such [impaired unsecured] class will not receive or retain under the plan on account of such junior claim or interest any property") with *Boyd,* 228 U.S., at 508 ("[T]he creditors were entitled to be paid before the stockholders could retain [a right of property] for any purpose whatever"), and *Case,* 308 U.S., at 116 ("'[C]reditors are entitled to priority over stockholders against all the property of an insolvent corporation.'" See H.R.Rep. No. 95–595, *supra,* at 414 (characterizing § 1129(b)(2)(B)(ii) as a "partial codification of the absolute priority rule"); *ibid.* ("The elements of the [fair and equitable] test are new[,] departing from both the absolute priority rule and the best interests of creditors tests found under the Bankruptcy Act").

The upshot is that this history does nothing to disparage the possibility apparent in the statutory text, that the absolute priority rule now on the books as subsection (b)(2)(B)(ii) may carry a new value corollary. Although there is no literal reference to "new value" in the phrase "on account of such junior claim," the phrase could arguably carry such an implication in modifying the prohibition against receipt by junior claimants of any interest under a plan while a senior class of unconsenting creditors goes less than fully paid.

III.

Three basic interpretations have been suggested for the "on account of" modifier. The first reading is proposed by the Partnership, that "on account of" harks back to accounting practice and means something like "in exchange for," or "in satisfaction of." On this view, a plan would not violate the absolute priority rule unless the old equity holders received or retained property in exchange for the prior interest, without any significant new contribution; if substantial money passed from them as part of the deal, the prohibition of subsection (b)(2)(B)(ii) would not stand in the way, and whatever issues of fairness and equity there might otherwise be would not implicate the "on account of" modifier.

This position is beset with troubles, the first one being textual. Subsection (b)(2)(B)(ii) forbids not only receipt of property on account of the prior interest but its retention as well. A common instance of the latter would be a debtor's retention of an interest in the insolvent business reorganized under the plan. Yet it would be exceedingly odd to speak of "retain[ing]" property in exchange for the same property interest, and the eccentricity of such a reading is underscored by the fact that elsewhere in the Code the drafters chose to use the very phrase "in exchange for," § 1123(a)(5)(J) (a plan shall provide adequate means for implementation, including "issuance of securities of the debtor... for cash, for property, for existing securities, or in exchange for claims or interests"). It is unlikely that the drafters of legislation so long and minutely contemplated as the 1978 Bankruptcy Code would have used two distinctly different forms of words for the same purpose.

The second difficulty is practical: the unlikelihood that Congress meant to impose a condition as manipulable as subsection (b)(2)(B)(ii) would be if "on account of "meant to prohibit merely an exchange unaccompanied by a substantial infusion of new funds but permit one whenever substantial funds changed hands. "Substantial" or "significant" or "considerable" or like characterizations of a monetary contribution would measure it by the Lord Chancellor's foot, and an absolute priority rule so variable would not be much of an absolute. Of course it is true (as already noted) that, even if old equity holders could displace the rule by adding some significant amount of cash to the deal, it would not follow that their plan would be entitled to adoption; a contested plan would still need to satisfy the overriding condition of fairness and equity. But that general fairness and equity criterion would apply in any event, and one comes back to the question why Congress would have bothered to add a separate priority rule without a sharper edge.

Since the "in exchange for" reading merits rejection, the way is open to recognize the more common understanding of "on account of" to mean "because of." This is certainly the usage meant for the phrase at other places in the statute, see § 1111(b)(1)(A) (treating certain claims as if the holder of the claim "had recourse against the debtor on account of such claim"); § 522(d)(10)(E) (permitting debtors to exempt payments under certain benefit plans and contracts "on account of illness, disability, death, age, or length of service"); § 547(b)(2) (authorizing trustee to avoid a transfer of an interest of the debtor in property "for or on account of an antecedent debt owed by the debtor"); § 547(c)(4)(B) (barring trustee from avoiding a transfer when a creditor gives new value to the debtor "on account of which new value the debtor did not make an otherwise unavoidable transfer to... such creditor"). So, under the commonsense rule that a given phrase is meant to carry a given concept in a single statute the better reading of subsection (b)(2)(B)(ii) recognizes that a causal relationship between holding the prior claim or interest and receiving or retaining property is what activates the absolute priority rule.

The degree of causation is the final bone of contention. We understand the Government, as *amicus curiae,* to take the starchy position not only that any degree of causation between earlier interests and retained property will activate the bar to a plan providing for later property but also that whenever the holders of equity in the Debtor end up with some property there will be some causation; when old equity, and not someone on the street, gets property the reason is *res ipsa loquitur.* An old equity holder simply cannot take property under a plan if creditors are not paid in full.[23]

There are, however, reasons counting against such a reading. If, as is likely, the drafters were treating junior claimants or interest holders as a class at this point (see *Ahlers,* 485 U.S., at 202),[24] then the simple way to have prohibited the old interest holders from receiving anything over objection would have been to omit the "on account of" phrase entirely from subsection (b)(2)(B)(ii). On this assumption, reading the provision as a blanket prohibition would leave "on account of" as a redundancy, contrary to the interpretive obligation to try to give meaning to all the statutory language.[25] One would also have to ask why Congress would have desired to exclude prior equity categorically from the class of potential owners following a cramdown. Although we have some doubt about the Court of Appeals's assumption that prior equity is often the only source of significant capital for reorganizations, *see, e.g.,* Blum & Kaplan, *The Absolute Priority Doctrine in Corporate Reorganizations,* 41 U. Chi. L.Rev. 651, 672 (1974); Mann, *Strategy and Force in the Liquidation of Secured Debt,* 96 Mich. L.Rev. 159, 182–183, 192–194, 208–209 (1997), old equity may well

---

[23] Our interpretation of the Government's position in this respect is informed by its view as *amicus curiae* in the *Bonner Mall* case: "the language and structure of the Code prohibit in all circumstances confirmation of a plan that grants the prior owners an equity interest in the reorganized debtor over the objection of a class of unpaid unsecured claims."

The Government conceded that, in the case before us, it had no need to press this more stringent view, since "whatever [the] definition of 'on account of,' a 100 percent certainty that junior equit[y] obtains property because they're junior equity will satisfy that."

[24] It is possible, on the contrary, to argue on the basis of the immediate text that the prohibition against receipt of an interest "on account of "a prior unsecured claim or interest was meant to indicate only that there is no *per se* bar to such receipt by a creditor holding both a senior secured claim and a junior unsecured one, when the senior secured claim accounts for the subsequent interest. This reading would of course eliminate the phrase "on account of "as an express source of a new value exception, but would leave open the possibility of interpreting the absolute priority rule itself as stopping short of prohibiting a new value transaction.

[25] Given our obligation to give meaning to the "on account of "modifier, we likewise do not rely on various statements in the House Report or by the bill's floor leaders, which, when read out of context, imply that Congress intended an emphatic, unconditional absolute priority rule. See, *e.g.,* H.R.Rep. No. 95-595, p. 224 (1977). ("[T]he bill requires that the plan pay any dissenting class in full before any class junior to the dissenter may be paid at all"); *id.,* at 413 ("[I]f [an impaired class is] paid less than in full, then no class junior may receive anything under the plan"); 124 Cong. Rec. 32408 (1978) (statement of Rep. Edwards) (cramdown plan confirmable only "as long as no class junior to the dissenting class receives anything at all"); *id.,* at 34007 (statement of Sen. DeConcini) (same).

be in the best position to make a go of the reorganized enterprise and so may be the party most likely to work out an equity-for-value reorganization.

A less absolute statutory prohibition would follow from reading the "on account of" language as intended to reconcile the two recognized policies underlying Chapter 11, of preserving going concerns and maximizing property available to satisfy creditors. Causation between the old equity's holdings and subsequent property substantial enough to disqualify a plan would presumably occur on this view of things whenever old equity's later property would come at a price that failed to provide the greatest possible addition to the bankruptcy estate, and it would always come at a price too low when the equity holders obtained or preserved an ownership interest for less than someone else would have paid.[26] A truly full value transaction, on the other hand, would pose no threat to the bankruptcy estate not posed by any reorganization, provided of course that the contribution be in cash or be realizable money's worth, just as *Ahlers* required for application of *Case*'s new value rule.

IV.

Which of these positions is ultimately entitled to prevail is not to be decided here, however, for even on the latter view the Bank's objection would require rejection of the plan at issue in this case. It is doomed, we can say without necessarily exhausting its flaws, by its provision for vesting equity in the reorganized business in the Debtor's partners without extending an opportunity to anyone else either to compete for that equity or to propose a competing reorganization plan. Although the Debtor's exclusive opportunity to propose a plan under § 1121(b) is not itself "property" within the meaning of subsection (b)(2)(B)(ii), the respondent partnership in this case has taken advantage of this opportunity by proposing a plan under which the benefit of equity ownership may be obtained by no one but old equity partners. Upon the court's approval

---

[26] Even when old equity would pay its top dollar and that figure was as high as anyone else would pay, the price might still be too low unless the old equity holders paid more than anyone else would pay, on the theory that the "necessity" required to justify old equity's participation in a new value plan is a necessity for the participation of old equity as such. On this interpretation, disproof of a bargain would not satisfy old equity's burden; it would need to show that no one else would pay as much. See, *e.g., In re Coltex Loop Central Three Partners, L. P.*, 138 F.3d 39, 45 (C.A.2 1998) ("[O]ld equity must be willing to contribute more money than any other source"); Strub, 111 Banking L. J., at 243 (old equity must show that the reorganized entity "needs funds *from the prior owner-managers* because no other source of capital is available"). No such issue is before us, and we emphasize that our holding here does not suggest an exhaustive list of the requirements of a proposed new value plan.

of that plan, the partners were in the same position that they would have enjoyed had they exercised an exclusive option under the plan to buy the equity in the reorganized entity, or contracted to purchase it from a seller who had first agreed to deal with no one else. It is quite true that the escrow of the partners' proposed investment eliminated any formal need to set out an express option or exclusive dealing provision in the plan itself, since the court's approval that created the opportunity and the partners' action to obtain its advantage were simultaneous. But before the Debtor's plan was accepted no one else could propose an alternative one, and after its acceptance no one else could obtain equity in the reorganized entity. At the moment of the plan's approval the Debtor's partners necessarily enjoyed an exclusive opportunity that was in no economic sense distinguishable from the advantage of the exclusively entitled offeror or option holder. This opportunity should, first of all, be treated as an item of property in its own right. *Cf.* * * * D. Baird, *The Elements of Bankruptcy* 261 (rev. ed. 1993) ("The right to get an equity interest for its fair market value is "property' as the word is ordinarily used. Options to acquire an interest in a firm, even at its market value, trade for a positive price."). While it may be argued that the opportunity has no market value, being significant only to old equity holders owing to their potential tax liability, such an argument avails the Debtor nothing, for several reasons. It is to avoid just such arguments that the law is settled that any otherwise cognizable property interest must be treated as sufficiently valuable to be recognized under the Bankruptcy Code. Even aside from that rule, the assumption that no one but the Debtor's partners might pay for such an opportunity would obviously support no inference that it is valueless, let alone that it should not be treated as property. And, finally, the source in the tax law of the opportunity's value to the partners implies in no way that it lacks value to others. It might, indeed, be valuable to another precisely as a way to keep the Debtor from implementing a plan that would avoid a Chapter 7 liquidation.

Given that the opportunity is property of some value, the question arises why old equity alone should obtain it, not to mention at no cost whatever. The closest thing to an answer favorable to the Debtor is that the old equity partners would be given the opportunity in the expectation that in taking advantage of it they would add the stated purchase price to the estate. But this just begs the question why the opportunity should be exclusive to the old equity holders. If the price to be paid for the equity interest is the best obtainable, old equity does not need the protection of exclusiveness (unless to trump an equal offer from someone else); if it is not the best, there is no apparent reason for giving old equity a bargain. There is no reason, that is, unless the very purpose of the whole transaction is, at least in part, to do old equity a favor. And that, of course, is to say that old equity would obtain its opportunity, and the resulting benefit, because of old equity's prior interest within the meaning of subsection (b)(2)(B)(ii). Hence it is that the exclusiveness of the opportunity, with its protection against the market's scrutiny of the purchase price by means of competing bids or even competing plan proposals, renders the partners' right a property interest extended "on account of" the old equity position and therefore subject to an unpaid senior creditor class's objection.

It is no answer to this to say that the exclusive opportunity should be treated merely as a detail of the broader transaction that would follow its exercise, and that in this wider perspective no favoritism may be inferred, since the old equity partners would pay something, whereas no one else would pay anything. If this argument were to carry the day, of course, old equity could obtain a new property interest for a dime without being seen to receive anything on account of its old position. But even if we assume that old equity's plan would not be confirmed without satisfying the judge that the purchase price was top dollar, there is a further reason here not to treat property consisting of an exclusive opportunity as subsumed within the total transaction proposed. On the interpretation assumed here, it would, of course, be a fatal flaw if old equity acquired or retained the property interest without paying full value. It would thus be necessary for old equity to demonstrate its payment of top dollar, but this it could not satisfactorily do when it would receive or retain its property under a plan giving it exclusive rights and in the absence of a competing plan of any sort.[27] Under a plan granting an exclusive right, making no provision for competing bids or competing plans, any determination that the price was top dollar would necessarily be made by a judge in bankruptcy court, whereas the best way to determine value is exposure to a market. *See* Baird, Elements of Bankruptcy at 262; Bowers, *Rehabilitation, Redistribution or Dissipation: The Evidence for Choosing Among Bankruptcy Hypotheses,* 72 Wash. U.L.Q. 955, 959, 963 n.34, 975 (1994); Markell, 44 Stan. L.Rev., at 73 ("Reorganization practice illustrates that the presence of competing bidders for a debtor, whether they are owners or not, tends to increase creditor dividends"). This is a point of some significance, since it was, after all, one of the Code's innovations to narrow the occasions for courts to make valuation judgments, as shown by its preference for the supramajoritarian class creditor voting scheme in § 1126(c),

---

[27] The dissent emphasizes the care taken by the Bankruptcy Judge in examining the valuation evidence here, in arguing that there is no occasion for us to consider the relationship between valuation process and top-dollar requirement. While we agree with the dissent as to the judge's conscientious handling of the matter, the ensuing text of this opinion sets out our reasons for thinking the Act calls for testing valuation by a required process that was not followed here.

see *Ahlers, supra,* at 207 ("[T]he Code provides that it is up to the creditors–and not the courts–to accept or reject a reorganization plan which fails to provide them adequate protection or fails to honor the absolute priority rule").[28] In the interest of statutory coherence, a like disfavor for decisions untested by competitive choice ought to extend to valuations in administering subsection (b)(2)(B)(ii) when some form of market valuation may be available to test the adequacy of an old equity holder's proposed contribution.

Whether a market test would require an opportunity to offer competing plans or would be satisfied by a right to bid for the same interest sought by old equity, is a question we do not decide here. It is enough to say, assuming a new value corollary, that plans providing junior interest holders with exclusive opportunities free from competition and without benefit of market valuation fall within the prohibition of § 1129(b)(2)(B)(ii).

The judgment of the Court of Appeals is accordingly reversed, and the case is remanded for further proceedings consistent with this opinion.

It is so ordered.

■ Justice THOMAS with whom Justice SCALIA joins, concurring in the judgment.

[Omitted.]

■ Justice STEVENS, dissenting.

Prior to the enactment of the Bankruptcy Reform Act of 1978, this Court unequivocally stated that there are circumstances under which stockholders may participate in a plan of reorganization of an insolvent debtor if their participation is based on a contribution in money, or in money's worth, reason-

---

[28] In *Ahlers,* we explained: "The Court of Appeals may well have believed that petitioners or other unsecured creditors would be better off if respondents' reorganization plan was confirmed. But that determination is for the creditors to make in the manner specified by the Code. § 1126(c). Here, the principal creditors entitled to vote in the class of unsecured creditors (*i.e.,* petitioners) objected to the proposed reorganization. This was their prerogative under the Code, and courts applying the Code must effectuate their decision." 485 U.S., at 207. The voting rules of Chapter 11 represent a stark departure from the requirements under the old Act. "Congress adopted the view that creditors and equity security holders are very often better judges of the debtor's economic viability and their own economic self-interest than courts, trustees, or the SEC.... Consistent with this new approach, the Chapter 11 process relies on creditors and equity holders to engage in negotiations toward resolution of their interests." Brunstad, Sigal, & Schorling, *Review of the Proposals of the National Bankruptcy Review Commission Pertaining to Business Bankruptcies: Part One,* 53 Bus. Law. 1381, 1406, n. 136 (1998).

ably equivalent in view of all the circumstances to their participation.[1] As we have on two prior occasions, we granted certiorari in this case to decide whether § 1129(b)(2)(B)(ii) of the 1978 Act preserved or repealed this "new value" component of the absolute priority rule. I believe the Court should now definitively resolve the question and state that a holder of a junior claim or interest does not receive property "on account of" such a claim when its participation in the plan is based on adequate new value.

The Court today wisely rejects the Government's "starchy" position that an old equity holder can never receive an interest in a reorganized venture as a result of a cramdown unless the creditors are first paid in full.[3] Nevertheless, I find the Court's objections to the plan before us unsupported by either the text of 11 U.S.C. § 1129(b)(2)(B)(ii) or the record in this case. I would, therefore, affirm the judgment of the Court of Appeals.

---

[1] As Justice Douglas explained in *Case v. Los Angeles Lumber Products Co.*: "It is, of course, clear that there are circumstances under which stockholders may participate in a plan of reorganization of an insolvent debtor. This Court, as we have seen, indicated as much in *Northern Pacific Ry. Co.* v. *Boyd* and *Kansas City Terminal Ry. Co. v. Central Union Trust Co.* Especially in the latter case did this Court stress the necessity, at times, of seeking new money 'essential to the success of the undertaking' from the old stockholders. Where that necessity exists and the old stockholders make a fresh contribution and receive in return a participation reasonably equivalent to their contribution, no objection can be made. . . .

"In view of these considerations we believe that to accord 'the creditor his full right of priority against the corporate assets' where the debtor is insolvent, the stockholder's participation must be based on a contribution in money or in money's worth, reasonably equivalent in view of all the circumstances to the participation of the stockholder."

[3] As I noted earlier, Justice Douglas made this proposition clear in *Case v. Los Angeles, supra.* Justice Douglas was a preeminent bankruptcy scholar, well known for his views on the dangers posed by management-controlled corporate reorganizations. Both his work on the Protective Committee Study for the Securities and Exchange Commission and on Chapter X of the Bankruptcy Act sought to "restore the integrity of the reorganization process" which "too often [was] masterminded from behind the scenes by reorganization managers allied with the corporation's management or its bankers." Jennings, *Mr. Justice Douglas: His Influence on Corporate and Securities Regulation*, 73 Yale L.J. 920, 935–937 (1964). To this end, Douglas placed special emphasis on the protection of creditors' rights in reorganizations. I find it implausible that Congress, in enacting the Bankruptcy Code, intended to be even more strict than Justice Douglas in limiting the ability of debtors to participate in reorganizations.

I.

Section 1129 of Chapter 11 sets forth in detail the substantive requirements that a reorganization plan must satisfy in order to qualify for confirmation.[4] In the case of dissenting creditor classes, a plan must conform to the dictates of § 1129(b). With only one exception, the requirements of §§ 1129(a) and 1129(b) are identical for plans submitted by stockholders or junior creditors and plans submitted by other parties. That exception is the requirement in § 1129(b)(2)(B)(ii) that no holder of a junior claim or interest may receive or retain any property "on account of such junior claim or interest."

When read in the light of Justice DOUGLAS' opinion in *Case v. Los Angeles Lumber Products Co.*, the meaning of this provision is perfectly clear. Whenever a junior claimant receives or retains an interest for a bargain price, it does so "on account of" its prior claim. On the other hand, if the new capital that it invests has an equivalent or greater value than its interest in the reorganized venture, it should be equally clear that its participation is based on the fair price being paid and that it is not "on account of" its old claim or equity.

Of course, the fact that the proponents of a plan offer to pay a fair price for the interest they seek to acquire or retain does not necessarily mean that the bankruptcy judge should approve their plan. Any proposed cramdown must satisfy all of the requirements of § 1129 including, most notably, the requirement that the plan be "fair and equitable" to all creditors whose claims are impaired. Moreover, even if the old stockholders propose to buy the debtor for a fair price, presumably their plan should not be approved if a third party, perhaps motivated by unique tax or competitive considerations, is willing to pay an even higher price.

In every reorganization case, serious questions concerning the value of the debtor's assets must be resolved.[5] Nevertheless, for the purpose of answering the legal question presented by the parties to this case, I believe that we should assume that all valuation questions have been correctly answered. If, for example, there had been a widely advertised auction in which numerous bidders participated, and if the plan proposed by respondents had been more favorable by a wide margin than any competing proposal, would § 1129(b)(2)(B)(ii)

---

[4] "Confirmation of a plan of reorganization is the statutory goal of every chapter 11 case. Section 1129 provides the requirements for such confirmation, containing Congress' minimum requirements for allowing an entity to discharge its unpaid debts and continue its operations." 7 Collier on Bankruptcy ¶ 1129.01 (rev. 15th ed.1998).

[5] See Warren, *A Theory of Absolute Priority*, 1991 Ann. Survey Am. L. 9, 13 ("In practice, no problem in bankruptcy is more vexing than the problem of valuation").

require rejection of their plan simply because it provides that they shall retain 100% of the equity?

Petitioner and the Government would reply "yes" because they think § 1129(b)(2)(B)(ii) imposes an absolute ban on participation by junior claimants without the consent of all senior creditors. The Court correctly rejects this extreme position because it would make the words "on account of" superfluous, and because there is no plausible reason why Congress would have desired such a categorical exclusion, given that in some cases old equity may be the most likely source of new capital. Indeed, the dissenting judge in the Court of Appeals thought "such a result would border on the absurd."[6] Thus, neither the dissenting judge in the Court of Appeals nor the Court appears to be in doubt about the proper answer to my hypothetical question. Instead, the decision is apparently driven by doubts concerning the procedures followed by the Bankruptcy Judge in making his value determinations, implicitly suggesting that the statute should be construed to require some form of competitive bidding in cases like this.[7]

Perhaps such a procedural requirement would be a wise addition to the statute, but it is surely not contained in the present text of § 1129(b)(2)(B)(ii). Indeed, that subsection is not a procedural provision at all. Section 1129 defines the substantive elements that must be met to render plans eligible for confirmation by the bankruptcy judge after all required statutory procedures have been completed. Cf. § 1121 (Who may file a plan); § 1122 (Classification of claims

---

[6] Judge KANNE wrote in dissent: "Perhaps the majority's reasoning is driven by the fear that a 'but for' interpretation would prevent old equity from ever participating in a reorganized entity-something Congress could never have intended. Indeed, such a result would border on the absurd, but a simpler, 'but for' causation requirement would not preclude junior interests from participating in a reorganized entity. If prior equity holders earn their shares in an open auction, for example, their received interests would not be 'on account of 'their junior interests but 'on account of 'their capital contributions." It would seem logical for adherents of this view also to find participation by junior interests in the new entity not "on account of "their prior interest, if it were stipulated that old equity's capital contributions exceeded the amount attainable in an auction, or if findings to that effect were not challenged.

[7] This doubt is unwarranted in this case. The bank does not challenge the Bankruptcy Court's finding that the 15 floors of office space had a market value of $55.8 million. The bank's original expert testimony on the value of the property differed from the Bankruptcy Judge's finding by only 2.8%. Therefore, although the bank argues that the policy implications of the "new value debate" revolve around judicial determinations of the valuation of the relevant collateral this concern was neither squarely presented in this case nor preserved for our review.

or interests); § 1125 (Postpetition disclosure and solicitation); § 1126 (Acceptance of plan); § 1127 (Modification of plan). Because, as I discuss below, petitioner does not now challenge either the procedures followed by the Bankruptcy Judge or any of his value determinations, neither the record nor the text of § 1129(b)(2)(B)(ii) provides any support for the Court's disposition of this case.

II.

As I understand the Court's opinion, it relies on two reasons for refusing to approve the plan at this stage of the proceedings: one based on the plan itself and the other on the confirmation procedures followed before the plan was adopted. In the Court's view, the fatal flaw in the plan proposed by respondent was that it vested complete ownership in the former partners immediately upon confirmation, and the defect in the process was that no other party had an opportunity to propose a competing plan.

These requirements are neither explicitly nor implicitly dictated by the text of the statute. As for the first objection, if we assume that the partners paid a fair price for what the Court characterizes as their "exclusive opportunity," I do not understand why the retention of a 100% interest in assets is any more "on account of" their prior position than retaining a lesser percentage might have been. Surely there is no legal significance to the fact that immediately after the confirmation of the plan "the partners were in the same position that they would have enjoyed had they exercised an exclusive option under the plan to buy the equity in the reorganized entity, or contracted to purchase it from a seller who had first agreed to deal with no one else."

As to the second objection, petitioner does not challenge the Bankruptcy Judge's valuation of the property or any of his other findings under § 1129 (other than the plan's compliance with § 1129(b)(2)(B)(ii)). Since there is no remaining question as to value, both the former partners (and the creditors, for that matter) are in the same position that they would have enjoyed if the Bankruptcy Court had held an auction in which this plan had been determined to be the best available. That the court did not hold such an auction should not doom this plan, because no such auction was requested by any of the parties, and the statute does not require that an auction be held. As with all the provisions of § 1129, the question of compliance with § 1129(b)(2)(B)(ii) turns on the substantive content of the plan, not on speculation about the procedures that might have preceded its confirmation.

In this case, the partners had the exclusive right to propose a reorganization plan during the first 120 days after filing for bankruptcy. See § 1121(b). No one contends that that exclusive right is a form of property that is retained by the debtor "on account of" its prior status.[8] The partners did indeed propose a plan which provided for an infusion of $6.125 million in new capital in exchange for ownership of the reorganized debtor. Since the tax value of the partnership depended on their exclusive participation, it is unsurprising that the partners' plan did not propose that unidentified outsiders should also be able to own an unspecified portion of the reorganized partnership. It seems both practically and economically puzzling to assume that Congress would have expected old equity to provide for the participation of unknown third parties, who would have interests different (and perhaps incompatible) with the partners', in order to comply with § 1129(b)(2)(B)(ii).[9]

Nevertheless, even after proposing their plan, the partners had no vested right to purchase an equity interest in the post-reorganization enterprise until the Bankruptcy Judge confirmed the plan. They also had no assurance that the court would refuse to truncate the exclusivity period and allow other interested parties to file competing plans. As it turned out, the Bankruptcy Judge did not allow respondent to file its proposed plan, but the bank did not appeal that issue, and the question is not before us.[10]

The moment the judge did confirm the partners' plan, the old equity holders were required by law to implement the terms of the plan.[11] It was then, and only then, that what the Court characterizes as the critical "exclusive opportuni-

---

[8] Indeed, as the Court acknowledges it is not "property" within the meaning of the Act.

[9] It goes without saying that Congress could not have expected the partners' plan to include a provision that would allow for the Bankruptcy Judge to entertain competing plans, since that is a discretionary decision exclusively within the province of the court. See § 1121(d).

[10] Apparently, the bank's plan called for liquidation of the property. In order to flesh out all facts bearing on value, perhaps the Bankruptcy Judge should have terminated the exclusivity period and allowed the bank to file its plan. That the bank's plan called for liquidation of the property in a single-asset context does not necessarily contravene the purposes of Chapter 11.

[11] In this case, the plan provided: "The general partners and limited partners of the Reorganized Debtor shall contribute or cause to be contributed $6.125 million of new capital (the "New Capital") to the Reorganized Debtor as follows: $3.0 million in cash ("Initial Capital") on the first business banking day after the Effective Date, and $625,000 on each of the next five anniversaries of the Effective Date." The "Effective Date" of the plan was defined as "[t]he first business day after the Confirmation Order is entered on the docket sheet maintained for the Case."

ty" came into existence. What the Court refuses to recognize, however, is that this "exclusive opportunity" is the function of the procedural features of this case: the statutory exclusivity period, the Bankruptcy Judge's refusal to allow the bank to file a competing plan, and the inescapable fact that the judge could confirm only one plan.

The Court's repeated references to the partners' "opportunity," is potentially misleading because it ignores the fact that a plan is binding upon all parties once it is confirmed. One can, of course, refer to contractual rights and duties as "opportunities," but they are not separate property interests comparable to an option which gives its holder a legal right either to enter into a contract or not to do so. They are simply a part of the bundle of contractual terms that have legal significance when a plan is confirmed.

When the court approved the plan, it accepted an offer by old equity. If the value of the debtor's assets has been accurately determined, the fairness of such an offer should be judged by the same standard as offers made by newcomers. Of course, its offer should not receive more favorable consideration "on account of "their prior ownership. But if the debtor's plan would be entitled to approval if it had been submitted by a third party, it should not be disqualified simply because it did not include a unique provision that would not be required in an offer made by any other party, including the creditors.

Since the Court of Appeals correctly interpreted § 1129(b)(2)(B)(ii), its judgment should be affirmed.

Accordingly, I respectfully dissent.

NOTES

1. Among the proposals made to amend the Code to prevent debtors from taking unfair advantage of the new value exception in squeezing out creditors, perhaps the simplest is to terminate the debtor's exclusive right to propose a plan if the debtor proposes to cramdown a plan in which ownership interests are retained upon a contribution of new value. In *Owners, Auctions and Absolute Priority in Bankruptcy Reorganizations*, 44 Stan.L.Rev. 69 (1991), Professor (now Judge) Markell has proposed this reform. This would allow creditors the option either to consent to the debtor's plan or to propose their own plans which might terminate the interests of the old owners.

2. After more than ten years of suspense, the Supreme Court finally reached the question of whether bankruptcy debtors can impose new value reorganization plans on creditors in Chapter 11 cramdowns without distributing reorganization value to creditors that equal their claims in *203 North LaSalle Street Partnership*. Unfortunately, after careful reading of the Supreme Court's

LaSalle opinions, it is still not apparent what the answer is, although the Supreme Court majority appears to fall generally in the camp of the "market test" view.

The Supreme Court majority does decisively reject the "traditional" new value exception to the absolute priority rule that had previously been the law of the Seventh and Ninth Circuits. *Bonner Mall* and cases like it, had authorized courts to consider and confirm debtor proposed cramdown plans within the exclusivity period that permitted pre-bankruptcy equity holders to retain ownership in the reorganized firm if the retained interest was judicially determined to be equivalent in value to a fresh contribution of capital from the equity holders that was substantial, new, in the form of money or money's worth, and necessary for successful reorganization. This "traditional" new value exception did not, we now learn twenty years later, survive the enactment of the 1978 Bankruptcy Code.

The *LaSalle* court, however, also refused to absolutely forbid old equity from retaining an interest in the reorganized firm in violation of the absolute priority rule absent acceptance from all impaired classes of creditors. The prohibitionist position, advocated by the Solicitor General, was dismissed as "starchy" by the majority, and "almost absurd" by Justice Stevens, the lone dissenter.

The majority goes on to discuss why on historical, structural, precedent and policy bases, it was troubled by the confluence of judicial valuation, debtor exclusivity in determining the extent of the retained interest and the amount of the new value contribution, and the possibility of nonconsensual confirmation of the new value plan. It suggests that "some form" of market valuation was required before confirming a nonconsensual new value plan. But after alluding to the alternatives of competitive bidding and competing plans it expressly refuses to state whether either or both was required and what form the competition was supposed to take. Even this meager degree of guidance was considered injudicious and excessive by Justice Thomas and Justice Scalia in their omitted concurrence which, after finding the phrase "on account of" in the Random House and Webster's Third New International dictionaries determined that the dictionary definitions sufficed to establish that the *LaSalle* plan was unconfirmable, declared "speculations about the desirability of a market test... are dicta binding neither this Court nor the lower federal courts." (Talk about starchy!)

"Some form of market valuation" has an Alice-in-Wonderland quality in cases like *LaSalle*. There are exactly two bidders for the equity interest in real estate subject to a restructured secured claim measured by the present value of the real estate–the bank holding the mortgage and the old equity holders who for tax and speculative reasons wish to retain their ownership interest. A negotiation between these two parties, not an auction or competing "reorganization" plans is the answer. In many cases there will be some price at which a rational bank and debtor will agree to restructure the defaulted loan with continuing participation by old equity. If those parties cannot agree on a price for equity's continuing participation, then the holder of a defaulted mortgage of overencumbered real estate ought to be able to conduct a foreclosure sale.

In the context of the single asset real estate case like *LaSalle* there is nothing at all "starchy" much less "absurd" about this result. Indeed *any genuine* "form of market valuation" collapses into this result. If the bank can freely bid, the bank always has the capacity to overbid the old equity holders for the equity in real estate subject to its unsecured senior claim. Up until the point at which its bid exceeds both its secured claim and its unsecured deficiency claim, none of the proceeds of the winning bid will be distributable to old equity. And so the money the bank invests if its bid prevails will either go into real estate it will thereafter own or will be returned to it as distributions on account of its claims. A bank bidding on overencumbered real estate subject to its own mortgage is playing a shell game. The old equity can only win if the bank likes the price the old equity is bidding. In which case there should be a consensual new value plan, not an auction or a cramdown. The result of requiring true competitive bidding is that no new value plan can be confirmed unless the bank consents.

Terminating exclusivity or requiring auctions of the reorganized firm's equity as a condition of debtor proposed new value plans would have real bite in a case involving an operating firm with significant third party unsecured claims and a genuine need for working capital–if there were such cases. In fact, as the Supreme Court noted in footnote 15, the new value plans are almost always proposed in single-asset real estate cases. In large operating cases with widely dispersed public shareholders, new value plans are generally impractical and public shareholders have no incentive to propose them anyway. In smaller cases with concentrated ownership by the managers, new value plans may be unnecessary–if there is genuine going concern value to the enterprise old equity may participate on a negotiated basis without making new capital contributions, notwithstanding insolvency and absolute priority because the owners are managers essential to the preservation of that going concern value. *LaSalle* may be more relevant in cases involving concentrated ownership and hired management, for example portfolio companies held by private equity funds. There are no published decisions, however, applying *LaSalle* in this scenario, perhaps because such cases are generally resolved consensually rather than through cramdown.

Real estate is different, of course, precisely because the old owner-managers are ordinarily not essential to the continued economic viability of a commercial real estate project. In the single-asset real estate case, the underwater mortgagee, as senior claim holder, is effectively the seller as well as a potential bidder for the property. It is also the only potential bidder for the interest other than the prebankruptcy equityholders. Only when the mortgagee consents to a plan transferring that equity to another has some form of market valuation taken place. Practically and theoretically, no market transaction to which the mortgagee is not a willing party can occur. If the old equity retains an interest over the mortgagee's objection, the bankruptcy judge, not any market transaction, is fixing the price. *LaSalle*'s rejection of the noncompetitive debtor-exclusive new value plan effectively prohibits *any* nonconsensual new value plan. *LaSalle*, starchily or not, on this reading, precludes involuntary restructuring of defaulted mortgage debt on overencumbered real estate and significantly shifts the balance of power in such cases towards the mortgagee. In this light, the dearth of published decisions over the past decade confirming cramdown plans in single-asset real estate is unsurprising. *See Wilkow v. Forbes, Inc.*, 241 F.3d 552, 554 (7th Cir. 2001), characterizing *LaSalle* as having "hog-tied the [new value] doctrine."

Nevertheless, secured parties that fail to make competing offers for the property or submit competing reorganization plans may still find themselves stuck with judicial valuations of equity retained interests under debtor proposed plans. See *Cypresswood Land Partners I*, 2009 WL 136021 (Bankr.S.D.Tex.2009) (confirming new value plan over objections of disputed second lien creditor that failed to make competing bid or introduce evidence in support of objection, noting "[t]his case illustrates the risk that litigants take in opposing confirmation of a plan 'on the cheap.'")

E. EVOLVING NORMS IN LARGE CHAPTER 11 REORGANIZATIONS

We have seen the legal background against which bargaining between the debtor and its creditors is carried on in the adoption of a consensual plan. But other factors are involved in the bargaining process that are not easily discernible from the Code or the cases. Professors Lynn LoPucki and William Whitford in their article, *Bargaining Over Equity's Share in the Bankruptcy Reorganization of Large, Publicly Held Companies*, 139 U.Pa.L.Rev. 125 (1990), surveyed 43 Chapter 11 reorganizations involving debtors with declared assets exceeding $100 million (1990 dollars) in which consensual plans were confirmed. Their objective was to determine the frequency with which the parties were able to settle large bankruptcy reorganization cases, the degree to which the settlements deviated from the absolute priority rule, and the causes of the deviations. Among their conclusions were the following:

a. A § 1129(b) contested cramdown was a rare event. If a plan was confirmed it was usually the result of bargaining and settlement.

b. The size of the case was a major factor in the extent to which the plan varied from the absolute priority rule. They observed:

As has been reported in other studies, in the reorganization cases of small businesses in which managers are also the principal shareholders, equity frequently dominates the bargain to such an extent that the absolute priority rule is virtually stood on its head. In such cases, the claims of creditors are compromised, but shareholder-managers usually retain their shares without dilution. The dependence of the business upon the continuing services of the shareholder-manager is the primary bargaining leverage used to accomplish this feat. The dependence may result from the need to maintain personal relations with suppliers, customers, and key employees, the need for unique services that only the shareholder-manager can provide, or from the shareholder-manager's willingness to work for less than the economy generally pays for such effort. Unsecured creditors are willing to waive their right to priority in order to create a incentive for the shareholder-manager to continue her participation in the business. They realize that without such participation, the business will fail, and the assets will be liquidated for the benefit of the secured creditors, leaving nothing for the unsecured creditors.

139 U.Pa.L.Rev. at 149.

c. In large cases, their study showed that equity nearly always shared in distribution under the plan even though application of the absolute priority rule would have precluded their participation, but their share was almost invariably small when measured as a percentage of the total distributed. However, with one exception, equity took nothing in cases in which the company was so insolvent that its creditors received less than 14 cents on the dollar.

d. Perhaps their most controversial conclusion was that:

Within the category of large cases, the relative size of equity's recovery appeared to be not so much a product of the financial conditions of the company as it was a product of the quality and aggressiveness of equity's representation.

* * * [T]he observed deviations from absolute priority were not to any significant degree the product of difficulties in valuation. In nearly every case, the negotiators knew the company was insolvent and that equity would be entitled to nothing in an adjudication. Equity was allowed to share in the distribution for a wide variety of reasons. Central among them was a generalized desire to have a consensual plan—one supported by the debtor, the official committees, and major creditors. Part of the reason for seeking such a plan was a concern that equity might make trouble if there was an attempt to exclude it. Yielding to such a fear was easier for creditors because the cost of a distribution to equity was spread among so many creditors that the portion borne by each one was too small to justify resistance. To a large degree, however, the preference for a consensual plan rather than an adjudication was a matter of legal culture. Although these cases were spread throughout the United States, most of the lawyers who played key roles in them were members of the same legal community. They could expect to be involved in future cases with their current adversaries and were to various degrees dependent on those adversaries for professional respect and advancement. They were not entirely free to ignore the conventional wisdom that consensual plans were the responsible, appropriate means for accomplishing reorganization and that despite the absolute priority rule, everyone at the bargaining table was entitled to a share.

139 U.Pa.L.Rev. at 195.

The LoPucki-Whitford study pre-dates current trends toward going concern sales and greater creditor control over the Chapter 11 process. Creditor plans and sales, especially sales, are far more common today than during the period of the LoPucki-Whitford study. And internal reorganizations, especially internal reorganizations of insolvent large publicly traded firms with significant continuing participation of prepetition shareholders in the reorganized firm, are significantly less common. Professor Douglas Baird remarks on this shift in the balance of power in Chapter 11 in *The New Face of Chapter 11*, 12 Am. Bankr. Instit. L. Rev. 69 (2004):

Chapter 11 is performing a new role. During the 1980s, nine of ten large businesses entering chapter 11, crafted a plan of reorganization there, and then emerged intact. In 2002, this was true in fewer than one in four. Today the vast majority of the cases—three-quarters or more—fit the two patterns I have identified. Most often, chapter 11 is merely one way in which a business is sold. It is liquidated or merged with or acquired by another. Alternatively, the bankruptcy judge merely puts in place a restructuring of debt that the major investors have settled upon outside of bankruptcy and the chapter 11 is over within a few months.

Nearly every chapter 11 raises its own set of distinctive issues, but a number of patterns frequently recur. Features commonly found in large financially distressed businesses en route to chapter 11s include the following:

1. As the firm encounters financial distress, creditors realign themselves and shore up their positions. If the business's fortunes continue to decline, a major lender emerges with a security interest in all the business's assets. The board of the corporation may have been largely asleep as conditions declined, but when the picture becomes sufficiently grim, the independent directors wake up. When they do, they are attuned to the fiduciary duties they owe to the creditors. Whatever loyalty they once might have shown to the CEO who picked them quickly evaporates. The senior lenders assess the condition of the business. In many instances, new managers are needed to put the business's affairs in order. The first step is often hiring a Chief Restructuring Officer. Several businesses (including Alvarez & Marsal or AlixPartners) specialize in providing such personnel. Once hired, the CRO often goes on to replace the CEO.

2. When the business enters chapter 11, a senior lender becomes the post-petition lender. Covenants in the loan further tighten control over the debtor and the course of the chapter 11. Events of defaults include failure to meet specified financial targets, failure to sell the assets by a specified date, and sometimes even the filing of any motion in the bankruptcy court without its blessing.

3. The sale of the business is the benchmark by which all other options are assessed.

4. Once the restructuring is complete, the senior lenders or the new buyers replace the old board.

Id. at 80-81.

More recent work by Professor LoPucki and Dr. Joseph Doherty, *Bankruptcy Fire Sales*, 106 Mich. L. Rev. 1, 44-45 (2007) suggests that the trends towards sales and senior creditor control may not be altogether healthy:

Bankruptcy going-concern sales can provide a substitute for bankruptcy reorganization only if, for a given company, the sale can realize at least as much value as a reorganization. Otherwise, reorganization should continue in order to maximize value.

We found that, on average, reorganizations yielded 80% or 91% of book value, while sales yielded only 35% of book value. Those findings warrant the conclusion that, on average, companies sell for less than would be realized in their reorganizations. To reach a contrary conclusion, one might suppose that the best and strongest companies were reorganized while the worst and weakest were sold. But if debtors could sell their companies for as much as they would bring in reorganization, the statistically significant difference in sale and reorganization recoveries would never have arisen. Sale or reorganization would have been equally likely for each company and the pattern of sale or reorganization choices random. That the difference arose demonstrates at minimum that reorganization was sufficiently preferable to sale in high-recovery cases to warrant the cost of sorting the cases. If the reorganized companies had to be sold in some new regime, whatever reorganization advantage caused them to sort themselves under the old regime would be lost.

Our finding that the choice between sale and reorganization remains highly significant, even when we control for the financial condition of the company, suggests considerably more. It is theoretically possible that large differences in value existed among the companies studied; that those differences were not reflected in either book values or EBITDA; and that, for some reason not yet explained, those differences were highly correlated with the choice between sale and reorganization, with the weaker companies choosing sale. But barring such unlikely, unidentified differences, our findings demonstrate that large public companies were sold in bankruptcy going-concern sales for less than half what they would have been worth in reorganization.

Possible explanations for this market failure are not in short supply. The managers who decided to sell these companies rather than reorganize them frequently had conflicts of interest. So did the investment bankers who advised the managers and solicited bids. The stalking-horse bidders received protections in the form of breakup fees and substantial minimum bid increments that discouraged other bidders. The costs of participating in the bidding were high because the companies' situations were complex and changed rapidly. Bidders other than the stalking horse had little chance of winning. As a result, only a single bidder appeared at most bankruptcy auctions. The process from the hiring of the financial advisor to the court's order approving the sale was generally leisurely, averaging just under a year. In only five of twenty-nine cases (17%) did it take less than 180 days. But once the stalking horse was selected, the cases were fast tracked. The average time from execution of the stalking horse contract to the auction was only 41 days, giving competing bidders little time to organize. Together, these findings demonstrate, and at least partially explain, the failure of going-concern sales as an alternative to reorganization.

Why would a process increasingly controlled by key creditors result in sales that produce inferior returns to creditors as a whole? Under what circumstances is it in the interest of creditors (or at least some powerful creditors) to see that the debtor firm is sold quickly and cheaply rather than maximize the value of the estate?

F. EFFECT OF CONFIRMATION OF PLAN

Upon confirmation of a Chapter 11 plan the property of the estate vests in the reorganized debtor unless the plan provides for sale or transfer to another entity. After confirmation the debtor may deal with that property in any manner consistent with the plan. § 1141(b) and § 1142. Confirmation of a plan results in discharge of the debtor from preconfirmation debts in most cases (§ 1141(d)) and in termination of the automatic stay. § 362(c). The bankruptcy court retains jurisdiction to aid in the implementation of the plan, the resolution of disputes regarding interpretation of the plan, modification of the plan, and for various other purposes. § 1142 and 28 U.S.C. § 1334(b). The jurisdiction of the bankruptcy court is not exclusive, however, and the debtor may be sued in other courts for breach of its obligations under the plan as well as for breach of obligations incurred after confirmation. *In re Paradise Valley Country Club*, 31 B.R. 613 (D.Colo.1983). Some of the jurisdictional puzzles that may arise post confirmation are discussed at length in Frank Kennedy & Gerald Smith, *Post Confirmation Issues: The Effect of Confirmation and Post Confirmation Proceedings*, 44 S.C.L. Rev. 621 (1993).

Confirmation of a Chapter 11 plan not only discharges individuals, as in Chapter 7, but corporations and partnerships as well. § 1141(d). Discharge for a liquidating corporation under Chapter 7 is of no importance because of the ability of the entity to dissolve after liquidation. But discharge of preconfirmation debts is essential to the Chapter 11 process. If creditors can assert claims against the reorganized debtor other than as provided in the plan, then, in effect, those creditors are not bound by the plan, and the plan is not a full and final settlement of claims. Moreover, allowing creditors to assert claims outside the plan threatens both plan feasibility and the value of securities distributed to creditors and interest holders pursuant to the plan. Congressman Edwards made this point in rejecting a limitation on the scope of the § 1141 discharge in favor of tax claims:

> It is necessary for a corporation or partnership undergoing reorganization to be able to present its creditors with a fixed list of liabilities upon which the creditors or third parties can make intelligent decisions. Retaining an exception for discharge with respect to nondischargeable taxes would leave an undesirable uncertainty surrounding reorganizations that is unacceptable.

Cong.Rec. (Sept. 28, 1978) reprinted in *Collier on Bankruptcy*, Vol. D App.Pt. 4–2474.

BAPCPA added a new paragraph (6) to § 1141(d) to circumscribe the scope of the corporate debtor's Chapter 11 discharge:

> **(6)** Notwithstanding paragraph (1), the confirmation of a plan does not discharge a debtor that is a corporation from any debt—
>
> > **(A)** of a kind specified in paragraph (2)(A) or (2)(B) of section 523(a) that is owed to a domestic governmental unit, or owed to a person as the result of an action filed under subchapter III of chapter 37 of title 31 or any similar State statute; or
> >
> > **(B)** for a tax or customs duty with respect to which the debtor
> >
> > > **(i)** made a fraudulent return; or
> > >
> > > **(ii)** willfully attempted in any manner to evade or to defeat such tax or customs duty.

While seemingly limited to government claims for fraud, the reference to Subchapter III of chapter 37 to title 31 is to so-called *qui tam* actions or "whistleblower" suits brought under the federal False Claims Act. These actions may be brought by private persons, subject to the right of the Department of Justice to intervene and control the litigation. By opening the door to limitations on the scope of the Chapter 11 discharge, new paragraph (6) sets a troubling precedent. If tax fraud, government fraud and *qui tam* actions are now excepted from the corporate Chapter 11 discharge, why not the claims of other defrauded parties? Given the large number of bankruptcies where credible allegations of fraud are made, § 1141(d)(6) may represent the beginning of an erosion of the Chapter 11 discharge that may be difficult to contain.

Debtors may not use Chapter 11 with its broad discharge provisions to evade the limitations on discharge set out in § 727. A corporation or partnership cannot be discharged in a Chapter 7 liquidation (§ 727(a)(1)), and they cannot subvert this rule by liquidating under a plan in Chapter 11. § 1141(d)(3). By the same token, an individual debtor who is barred from discharge in Chapter 7 by the provisions of § 727 cannot obtain a discharge in Chapter 11 by a liquidation plan. Nor may an individual debtor evade the limitations on discharge in § 523 by filing under Chapter 11.

The scope of the Chapter 11 discharge raises critical constitutional due process issues. It is common ground that parties who are given actual notice of the Chapter 11 case are bound by § 1141 discharge. But the discharge is deliberately cast in terms broader than this and persistent questions arise about the binding effect of the Chapter 11 plan with respect to those who either did not have or could not be given notice. The seminal decision is *Mullane v. Central Hanover Bank & Trust Co.*, 339 U.S. 306 (1950), where the Supreme Court held that constitutional due process was satisfied by giving known claimants actual notice of the proceeding and an opportunity to be heard and by giving unknown claimants notice by publication in a manner reasonably calculated to apprise them of the pending action.

In *Reliable Electric Co. v. Olson*, 726 F.2d 620 (10th Cir. 1984), relying on *Mullane*, the court found that a known creditor who had knowledge of the pending Chapter 11 case but did not receive actual notice of the confirmation hearing was not bound by the discharge. Accord *In re Arch Wireless, Inc.*, 534 F.3d 76 (3d Cir. 2008); *In re Maya Constr. Co.*, 78 F.3d 1395 (9th Cir. 1996). How would the *Reliable* doctrine apply to a case in which Creditor's claim is postpetition, Debtor knows that Creditor is a potential creditor, and Creditor knows that Debtor has filed in Chapter 11? The court in *In re Unioil*, 948 F.2d 678 (10th Cir. 1991), held that Debtor had the burden of providing formal notice of its bankruptcy to Creditor; failure to do so meant that Creditor's claim was not discharged. *In re Christopher*, 28 F.3d 512 (5th Cir. 1994), takes a different view. The court believed that nothing in the Code or Rules requires a debtor to serve notice of a Chapter 11 proceeding on postpetition creditors. Under § 101 ("creditor"), a claimant is not a creditor unless its claim arose prepetition. In absence of a statutory requirement to give notice, the issue is whether Creditor's receipt of actual notice about the existence of Debtor's filing was sufficient to satisfy the due process requirements of *Mullane*. The court concluded that it was:

> Thus, given the actual notice of [Debtor's] bankruptcy proceeding possessed by [Creditors], we conclude that due process is not offended in this case by requiring postpetition claimants in [Creditors'] position to come forward and protect their enhanced rights [the court is referring to the likelihood that they can assert that their claims are administrative expenses] under the Code or else lose their rights through the sweeping discharge of Chapter 11.

28 F.3d at 519.

Christopher is criticized in *Arch Wireless*, 534 F.3d at 85 n.4, as being insufficiently sensitive to constitutional due process concerns.

Chemetron Corp. v. Jones, 72 F.3d 341 (3d Cir. 1995), dealt with the critical question of how "unknown" a creditor must be in order to be bound to the Chapter 11 discharge by publication notice. The debtor had been the owner of environmentally contaminated property and the claims were based on occupancy and visitation to homes adjacent to the contaminated site. The claimants argued that had Chemetron conducted a reasonable investigation it could have ascertained their identities and given them actual notice. The bankruptcy court agreed holding that the debtor could have reasonably foreseen that individuals living near the dumpsite might have toxic tort claims. The Third Circuit rejected this reasoning:

> A review of the facts in this case at bar reveals why the bankruptcy court's standard should not be followed. None of the claimants involved currently resides near either site. The claimants instead are scattered across Ohio and as far away as Texas. We are hard-pressed to conceive of any way the debtor could identify, locate, and provide actual notice to these claimants.
>
> It has been suggested that Chemetron could have conducted a title search on all properties surrounding the sites to determine all persons who might have lived in the area during the twenty years between Chemetron's operation of the sites and the Chapter 11 proceeding. We decline to chart a jurisprudential course through a Scylla of causational difficulties and a Charybdis of practical concerns.
>
> * * *
>
> * * * Debtors cannot be required to provide actual notice to anyone who potentially could have been affected by their actions; such a requirement would completely vitiate the important goal of prompt and effectual administration and settlement of debtors' estates.

72 F.3d at 347–348.

G. MODIFICATION OF PLAN

A debtor that is unable to carry out a confirmed plan may propose a modification of the plan. § 1127(b). But modification must occur before "substantial consummation" of the plan, a term defined in § 1101(2). Each of the three subparagraphs of § 1101(2) must be satisfied before the plan is substantially consummated. A Chapter 11 plan will always provide for payments to claimants and, under subparagraph (C), the plan is substantially consummated when those payments commence if the requirements of subparagraphs (A) and (B) are also satisfied. Subparagraph (A) refers to "transfer of all or substantially all of the property proposed by the plan to be transferred." Since any payment to a claimant is a transfer of property, subparagraph (A) might seem to refer to distributions under the plan. That reading, however, is not reasonable because it nullifies subparagraph (C). The latter provision specifically refers to distribution under the plan and the relevant time for determining substantial consummation of the plan is when distribution is commenced, not when it is substantially completed.

Subparagraph (A) is intended to refer to a plan providing for a liquidation of assets of the estate. The typical case is a plan calling for a partial liquidation by sale of some assets and a continuation of the business with the remaining assets. In such a case the plan is not substantially consummated until sale of substantially all of the assets to be liquidated is completed. Section 1101(2)(A) is based on 1898 Bankruptcy Act § 229(a)(1). The latter provision more clearly referred to assets to be sold under the plan by its reference to "transfer, sale or other disposition of all or substantially all of the property dealt with by the plan." There is no evidence that Congress intended to change the law by adoption of the slightly different language of § 1101(2)(A). Thus, if the plan does not call for liquidation of assets or if any required liquidation is completed, modification cannot occur once distribution to creditors under the plan is commenced.

In some instances the plan may provide for subsequent alterations in the operation of the plan. In the *Manville* asbestos case the plan called for a property damage trust fund and a personal injury fund. Since it was contemplated that changes might have to be made in the system for paying claims, the trustees were given the power to make changes in the property damage trust fund. The trustees eventually agreed to suspend payments from the property damage trust fund because of exhaustion of funding and to reinstitute payments at a later date when additional funding was contemplated. This action was challenged as an impermissible modification of the plan under § 1127(b). The court upheld the action of the trustees even though the plan had been substantially consummated. *In re Johns–Manville Corp.*, 920 F.2d 121 (2d Cir. 1990). The court viewed the alterations as procedural in nature and not as changes in substantive rights. It relied on the authority given the trustees in the plan to adjust the procedural aspects of payment of claims and noted the need for flexibility in dealing with the largely unexplored area of mass tort claims resolution. However, in a subsequent *Manville* case, *Findley v. Blinken*, 982 F.2d 721 (2d Cir. 1992), the court held a substantive change in the personal injury trust fund, not authorized by the plan or the trust, to be an impermissible modification.

If a modification is permissible under § 1127, § 1127(c) requires that disclosure with respect to the plan as modified must be given as required by § 1125. But Rule 3019 ameliorates this requirement by providing that if the court finds that a proposed pre-confirmation modification does not "adversely change" the rights of creditors or equity owners who have not accepted the modification, the modified plan will be deemed accepted by all creditors and equity owners who have previously accepted the plan. In *In re American Solar King Corp.*, 90 B.R. 808 (Bankr.W.D.Tex.1988), the modification brought into the plan a creditor previously excluded. Since the result of the modification was to dilute the equity shares distributed under the plan by less than one percent the court held that the change, though adverse to other recipients of equity shares, was not sufficiently material to call for further disclosure. A modification is material only if it would likely lead those who voted for the plan to reconsider their vote.

If a modification is not possible and the debtor cannot carry out the plan, the debtor can convert to Chapter 7 and liquidate. But the effect of a postconfirmation conversion is at best unclear given revesting of property of the estate in the debtor under § 1141. Some courts have held the revested property does not revert to the estate upon conversion but remains property of the debtor. *In re Lacy*, 304 B.R. 439 (D. Colo.2004); *In re K & M Printing, Inc.*, 210 B.R. 583 (Bankr.D.Ariz.1997). Others disagree. *In re Smith*, 201 B.R. 267 (D.Nev.1996), aff'd mem., 141 F.3d 1179 (9th Cir. 1998). One commentator suggests amending the Code to make clear that the bankruptcy trustee may liquidate revested property after postconfirmation conversion. See Sean P. Gates, *Conversion of the Post–Confirmation Chapter 11 Case: Selected Problems, Needed Reforms and Proposed Amendments*, 6 Bankr.L. & Prac. 3 (1997). Does such a debtor have the option of filing a new Chapter 11 to alter its obligations instead of converting to Chapter 7? In *In re Northampton Corp.*, 39 B.R. 955 (Bankr.E.D.Pa.1984), Debtor defaulted in its obligation under the substantially consummated plan to pay the amount of a secured claim to Bank. Debtor filed a second Chapter 11 plan which, by reason of the automatic stay, halted Bank's foreclosure. The court converted Debtor's case to Chapter 7 for cause under § 1112(b), stating: "The filing of a chapter 11 petition, with an eye toward curing defaults arising under a previously confirmed chapter 11 plan, is so akin to modifying the previous plan within the meaning of § 1127(b) that we deemed the filing of a new chapter 11 petition an attempted modification under that section." 39 B.R. at 956. But is a second Chapter 11 filing precluded in a case in which new debts incurred after confirmation of the earlier plan are dealt with as well as debts arising from the earlier plan? Or in which circumstances have changed since confirmation of the first plan?

Nothing in the Code prohibits the serial filing of Chapter 11 cases concerning corporate debtors; compare § 109(g)'s restrictions on serial filing under Chapters 12 and 13. Indeed as noted above at p. 718, "Chapter 22" cases have become quite common in some jurisdictions. The accepted view is that the serial filing of Chapter 11 cases is not per se grounds for dismissal. In *In re Jartran, Inc.*, 886 F.2d 859 (7th Cir. 1989), the court upheld a liquidating Chapter 11 following a failed reorganization Chapter 11 plan and stated, rather broadly: "Once a bankruptcy plan is effectuated, all indications from the Code would incline us to treat the reorganized entity as we would any other company." 886 F.2d at 870. The only limitation the court recognizes is a requirement that the subsequent plan be filed in good faith. The court in *In re Casa Loma Associates*, 122 B.R. 814 (Bankr.N.D.Ga.1991), found the requisite good faith to uphold the second Chapter 11, which in substance modified the plan confirmed and substantially consummated under the first Chapter 11, because unanticipated changes in circumstances made it impossible to carry out the earlier plan. The court cautioned that mere change in market conditions would not be enough to justify the new Chapter 11 but found additional unanticipated changed circumstances in enactment of a new federal regulatory law and in discovery of fire damage and structural defects in Debtor's apartment units.

CHAPTER 12
THE BANKRUPTCY COURTS

A. ORIGINAL JURISDICTION

1. INTRODUCTION

History, politics and Article III of the federal constitution have combined to create a bankruptcy jurisdiction framework of staggering complexity. This chapter describes how the existing system functions under the constraints imposed by Congress and the Supreme Court. It does not attempt to fully explore the history, rationale and soundness of those constraints. That subject is better suited for an advanced course in Federal Jurisdiction. A good starting place for most of these very complex issues is 1 *Collier on Bankruptcy* ¶¶ 3.01–5.11 (15th ed. rev. 2008).

As an initial matter, original federal bankruptcy jurisdiction is vested in the federal district courts. 28 U.S.C. § 1334(a). With respect to bankruptcy *cases* that jurisdiction is exclusive. In addition to exclusive jurisdiction over bankruptcy *cases*, the federal district courts have original but non-exclusive jurisdiction over *proceedings* that arise in or are related to bankruptcy cases. 28 U.S.C. § 1334(b).

The federal district courts do not exercise this extensive grant of jurisdiction directly. While the jurisdiction is formally vested in the district courts, cases arising under the grant are automatically referred to the United States Bankruptcy Court for that district. The bankruptcy court is staffed by bankruptcy judges appointed to fourteen year terms by the United States Court of Appeals for the circuit. 28 U.S.C. § 152(a)(1). Congress has authorized from one to twenty-one bankruptcy judges in the various districts. 28 U.S.C. § 1582(a)(2). Each bankruptcy judge sits as a single-judge trial court.

Bankruptcy judges are not appointed in accordance with the requirements of Article III of the Constitution: the President does not nominate bankruptcy judges, the Senate does not confirm them, and the bankruptcy judges do not have life tenure. Because bankruptcy judges are not appointed under Article III, the Supreme Court has held that they may not exercise the full judicial power of the United States. *Northern Pipeline Constr. Co. v. Marathon Pipe Line Co.*, 458 U.S. 50, 71 (1982). *Marathon* stunned the world of bankruptcy judges, lawyers and litigants: in a set of complex and confusing opinions none of which commanded a majority, the Supreme Court declared that the then existing jurisdictional statutes vesting the full breadth of the bankruptcy jurisdiction created by 28 U.S.C. § 1334 in non-Article III judges were unconstitutional. The case was not well received by scholars. *E.g.,* Erwin Chemerinsky, *Ending the Marathon: It Is Time to Overrule Northern Pipeline,* 65 Am. Bankr. L.J. 311 (1991) ("It is time for the Supreme Court to recognize that *Northern Pipeline* was a mistake and to allow bankruptcy courts the authority accorded them under the 1978 Act.").

The most logical response to *Marathon* would have been to create a free-standing Article III bankruptcy court. Such a court would be able to exercise the full breadth of the federal judicial power and would avoid the great jurisdictional complexity and uncertainty implicit in maintaining an Article I bankruptcy court. Expert panels and commentators continue to recommend this simple solution. *See NBRC Rep.* at 718 (Recommendation 3.1.1 is "[t]he bankruptcy court should be established under Article III. . ..").

Congress, however, while unable to ignore *Marathon,* has been unwilling to either create Article III bankruptcy judgeships or limit the bankruptcy jurisdiction in part owing to strong pressure from the Article III judiciary. Lawrence P. King, *The Unmaking of a Bankruptcy Court: Aftermath of Northern Pipeline v. Marathon,* 40 Wash. & Lee L.Rev. 99, 108–111 (1983). NBRC Recommendation 3.1.1 was no more appealing to Congress than the numerous similar prior expert recommendations.

Rather than reconstitute the bankruptcy court under Article III, the current jurisdictional statutes deal with the constitutional limitations on the Article I bankruptcy courts by dividing the full bankruptcy jurisdiction created by 28 U.S.C. § 1334 into "core" and "non-core" components, restricting the role of the bankruptcy courts in "non-core" matters, and otherwise placing bankruptcy courts under the supervision of the Article III district courts in various ways. 28 U.S.C. § 157(b). These additional complexities are piled upon other notoriously difficult jurisdictional limitations that apply to the Article III courts as well the bankruptcy courts.

Although the Supreme Court has never decided whether the revised system meets constitutional requirements, the lower federal courts have unanimously found that it does and later Supreme Court cases support a narrow reading of *Marathon. See Thomas v. Union Carbide Agricultural Products Co.,* 473 U.S. 568 (1985); *Commodity Futures Trading Commission v. Schor,* 478 U.S. 833 (1986). For a discussion of the impact of these two cases on *Marathon,* see George D. Brown, *Article III as a Fundamental Value—The Demise of Northern Pipeline and its Implications for Congressional Power,* 49 Ohio St. L.J. 55 (1988).

Assuming (as everyone does) the existing system is constitutional, bankruptcy lawyers and litigants still face daunting problems in determining which court system (the state courts, the bankruptcy court or the federal district court) has original jurisdiction to determine their disputes.

Four sets of questions regularly emerge from the complex existing framework governing the original jurisdiction of the bankruptcy court:

(1) What are the limits of the "related-to" jurisdiction under 28 U.S.C. § 1334? That is, which matters are excluded from the bankruptcy jurisdiction altogether without regard to whether that jurisdiction is exercised by the bankruptcy court or the federal district court?

(2) What are the limits of the "core" jurisdiction under 28 U.S.C. § 157? That is, which matters may be finally determined by the bankruptcy court and which must be subject to *de novo* review by the federal district court?

(3) What matters within the federal bankruptcy jurisdiction can not be adjudicated in the bankruptcy court on account of withdrawal of the reference, mandatory or permissive abstention, the policy favoring arbitration of certain matters, sovereign immunity, and comity with foreign courts?

(4) What are the scope of Seventh Amendment jury trial rights in both core and non-core matters?

We will explore each of these questions in this chapter and briefly touch on questions of venue and the bankruptcy appellate process as well. The first two sets of questions—the scope of related-to, core and non-core jurisdiction—are dealt with in the following section. Further limits on original jurisdiction and jury trial issues are discussed later in this chapter. Comity with foreign courts is the subject of the final section on Transnational Bankruptcy.

2. "RELATED-TO," "CORE" AND "NON-CORE" JURISDICTION

28 U.S.C. § 157(b)(1) provides that for "core" cases, bankruptcy judges may "hear and determine" the matter and enter final judgment subject only to appeal under 28 U.S.C. § 158. However, for matters that are not core proceedings but are "otherwise related" to bankruptcy cases, 28 U.S.C. § 157(c)(1) provides that the bankruptcy judge acts as a kind of special master. In that role the bankruptcy judge submits proposed findings of fact and conclusions of law to the district court which reviews *de novo* any "matters to which any party has timely and specifically objected." Furthermore, if the parties consent, the bankruptcy judge can enter a final order in an "otherwise related case" as well. 28 U.S.C. § 157(c)(1).

The nonexclusive enumeration of core proceedings in 28 U.S.C. § 157(b)(2) includes administering the estate and adjudicating the debtor's rights and liabilities vis-a-vis creditors in such matters as the allowance of claims, counterclaims against persons filing claims, motions affecting stays, confirmation of plans, and the like. It also extends to some proceedings that involve recovery of money damages or property from third parties such as preference or fraudulent conveyance suits. Expressly excluded from the core proceedings category are claims against the estate for personal injury tort or wrongful death. 28 U.S.C. § 157(b)(2)(B). These claims must be tried in the district court. 28 U.S.C. § 157(b)(5). A jury may be demanded in such a case. 28 U.S.C. § 1411.

Bankruptcy courts, however, may estimate such claims for purposes other than distribution (*e.g.*, voting on a reorganization plan or assessing feasibility in a Chapter 11 case), 28 U.S.C. § 157(b)(2)(B), and have conducted dispositive pretrial proceedings, in some cases, including summary judgment, in such matters. *See, e.g., In re UAL Corp.*, 310 B.R. 373 (Bankr.N.D.Ill.2004) (disallowing personal injury claims as a matter of law).

The following case deals with the questions of the limits of the "related-to" jurisdiction under § 1334 and the line between core and non-core matters.

In re Toledo
United States Court of Appeals, Eleventh Circuit, 1999.
170 F.3d 1340.

■ ANDERSON, Circuit Judge:

Carmen Sanchez filed the instant adversary proceeding against the trustee of the bankruptcy estate ("Estate") of Orlando and Maria Toledo, the debtors themselves, and the Continental National Bank of Miami ("Bank"). The bankruptcy court invalidated the Bank's mortgage on real estate owned by a partnership of which the debtors and Sanchez were the partners. The district court affirmed the bankruptcy court, applying the deferential standards of review applicable to "core" proceedings under the Bankruptcy Code. The Bank appeals. The issues presented for review are (i) whether the bankruptcy court had jurisdiction to hear this adversary proceeding, and (ii) if so, whether the district court was correct in treating it as a core proceeding rather than as a non-core proceeding requiring de novo, plenary review. For the reasons stated below, we hold that the bankruptcy court had jurisdiction, but that this was a non-core matter necessitating plenary review by the district court.

I. Facts

In 1988, Orlando and Maria Toledo, debtors in the underlying bankruptcy case, formed a partnership with Tomas and Carmen Sanchez called the Latin Quarter Center Partnership ("Partnership"). Each of the four partners held an equal one-fourth share. The purpose of the partnership was to hold, develop, and deal in certain contiguous parcels of real estate in downtown Miami ("Partnership Property"). No formal partnership agreement was ever entered into, but Orlando Toledo, acting alone, generally managed and acted on behalf of the partnership. Shortly after the Partnership came into being, Tomas Sanchez died, and his wife Carmen Sanchez (plaintiff in the instant adversary proceeding) succeeded to his 25% share, so that she then owned a total 50% interest in the Partnership. Orlando Toledo continued to act as managing partner and Carmen Sanchez was uninvolved in Partnership affairs.

In April of 1989, Orlando Toledo encountered personal financial difficulties. In order to assuage the Bank's concern about its position as one of his creditors and to induce it not to foreclose on a mortgage it held on his Key Biscayne personal residence, Toledo purported to convey a mortgage on the Partnership Property to the Bank to secure Toledo's personal indebtedness to the Bank in the approximate amount of $1,100,000. This was done without Sanchez' consent or knowledge. In taking this action, Toledo claimed to be acting in the capacity of a general partner as an agent for the Partnership. If the mortgage was valid, the Partnership Property thereby became a guarantee for Toledo's personal debt. Toledo also convinced McDonald's Corp., which had a $275,000 pre-existing purchase money mortgage on the Partnership Property, to subordinate its mortgage to the one newly granted to the Bank.

Orlando Toledo's financial outlook did not improve, and the Bank eventually obtained a judgment of foreclosure on both the Partnership Property and Toledo's Key Biscayne personal residence (which secured the same indebtedness) in Dade County circuit court in November 1992. Despite her status as 50% partner, Sanchez was not served with the notice of foreclosure and therefore was not a party to these Florida state court proceedings; the Bank apparently relied on Florida law allowing service on a partnership to be effected by serving a single general partner. The circuit court rendering the foreclosure judgment held that Toledo's residence would be sold first, and if the debt to the Bank (now, including interest, real estate taxes, and subsequent advances, at some $1.8 million) was still unsatisfied thereafter, it would schedule sale of the Partnership Property. On January 11, 1993, the day before the scheduled foreclosure sale of the Key Biscayne residence, Orlando and Maria Toledo filed for Chapter 11 and thereby averted the sale.

Soon after the commencement of the bankruptcy case, a private sale of the Partnership Property to McDonald's Corp. was negotiated by Toledo, the

Estate, and the Bank under supervision of the bankruptcy court. The terms of this sale, which the record indicates were favorable to the sellers, were that McDonald's Corp. would purchase the Partnership Property for an agreed sale price of $825,000. Of that $825,000, approximately $474,000 would go to satisfy amounts due under McDonald's Corp.'s purchase money mortgage (plus past real estate taxes paid by McDonald's and other costs), and about $351,000 would go to the Bank and/or the Partnership.[2] The parties, apparently assuming that the bankruptcy court's stamp of approval was necessary in order to consummate the sale, applied to the court for approval even though the Partnership Property was not property of the Estate. Acting under purported authority of 11 U.S.C. § 363(f), Judge Weaver approved the sale in an order dated April 12, 1993 (and modified in respects not material on June 4, 1993).[3] In that same sale order, Judge Weaver directed that of the proceeds of the sale of the Partnership Property, $200,000 be disbursed to the Bank in satisfaction of its mortgage.[4] The sale was carried out and the Bank was so paid. Sanchez, as a 50% partner, consented to the terms of sale but asked that the proceeds be placed in escrow rather than being distributed immediately; Judge Weaver refused to consider the escrow proposal because Sanchez' counsel filed a pleading by facsimile transmission rather than appearing personally in court. Later, Sanchez signed a closing statement reflecting that the proceeds would be distributed in accordance with the sale order.

---

[2] For reasons not clear on this record, the Bank apparently was satisfied to receive $200,000 of the proceeds of the sale, even though its mortgage on the Partnership Property secured Toledo's personal debts in excess of $1.8 million.

[3] Section 363(f) of the Bankruptcy Code provides that "the trustee may sell property under subsections (b) and (c) of this section free and clear of any interest in such property of an entity other than the state" upon certain conditions. It is questionable whether § 363(f) gives a bankruptcy court power to order or approve a sale of property that belongs only to an entity in which the estate holds an interest, and not to the estate itself. However, the validity of the sale order is not presently before this Court, and at any rate, it appears that the sale of the Partnership Property was a voluntary transaction, on favorable terms to the seller, to which all of the parties consented. Thus, we do not consider any issues relating to Judge Weaver's sale order.

[4] The sale price to McDonald's Corp. was $825,000. These proceeds were distributed as follows: (i) $200,000 to the Bank pursuant to its mortgage securing Toledo's personal indebtedness, (ii) $450,000 to McDonald's Corp. pursuant to its purchase money mortgage which had been contractually subordinated to the Bank's mortgage (since McDonald's was the purchaser, this amount was simply set off against the purchase price), and (iii) the remaining $175,000, less real estate taxes that had been paid by McDonald's Corp. as mortgagee over the course of the Partnership's ownership, to the Partnership (i.e., ultimately to Sanchez and/or the Toledos and the Estate).

Meanwhile, Sanchez filed the instant adversary complaint in the bankruptcy court against the trustee of the Estate, the debtors themselves, and the Bank (i) to determine entitlement to the proceeds of the sale of the Partnership Property to McDonald's Corp., and (ii) to contest the validity of the Bank's lien (formerly on the Partnership Property, and now on $200,000 of the proceeds therefrom). The action was styled as a "Complaint to Determine Validity, Priority, and Extent of Lien and Ownership Interest." After four evidentiary hearings in which extensive testimony was taken from Orlando Toledo, employees of the Bank, and others, Judge Cristol of the bankruptcy court accepted Sanchez' argument and ordered that (i) the Bank had had no valid lien on the Partnership Property because it knew Toledo was conveying the mortgage for improper, non-partnership purposes, and (ii) the Bank must pay to Sanchez the $200,000 it had previously received from the sale of the Partnership Property. The bankruptcy court noted that it had jurisdiction under 28 U.S.C. § 1334, but never specifically confronted the question whether the adversary proceeding was core or non-core under 28 U.S.C. § 157. By issuing an order that purported to be final and binding, rather than submitting proposed findings of fact and conclusions of law to the district court, the bankruptcy court indicated that it viewed the proceeding as a core one of which it had full, plenary authority to dispose.

Appealing to the district court, the Bank argued that (i) the bankruptcy court lacked subject matter jurisdiction to hear the adversary proceeding filed by Sanchez; (ii) the bankruptcy court erred in finding that the Bank knew Toledo lacked authority to mortgage the Partnership Property for personal purposes; and (iii) the doctrines of waiver or estoppel should have precluded the bankruptcy court from granting Sanchez relief. The district court held that the bankruptcy court had subject matter jurisdiction and that the matter was a core matter. It then found, applying the "clearly erroneous" standard of review to the bankruptcy court's fact findings (the appropriate standard of review for bankruptcy court orders regarding core matters), that Toledo lacked authority to mortgage the Partnership Property for his personal purposes, and that the Bank was aware thereof. The district court also held that the bankruptcy court did not abuse its discretion by not applying the doctrines of waiver or estoppel to bar relief invalidating the Bank's mortgage. Consequently, the district court affirmed the bankruptcy court's judgment.

On appeal to this court, the Bank argues first that the bankruptcy court lacked jurisdiction to entertain the adversary proceeding under 28 U.S.C. § 1334. Second, it argues that, even if the bankruptcy court had jurisdiction, such jurisdiction was in the nature of a non-core proceeding limiting the bankruptcy court's adjudicative powers. Third, the Bank reiterates its various substantive arguments as to why the bankruptcy court erred in its determination of the merits under Florida law; however, in light of our conclusion that this was a non-core proceeding, it is unnecessary for us to reach those issues.

II. Discussion

A. Jurisdiction under 28 U.S.C. § 1334

The first question is whether the bankruptcy court had jurisdiction to entertain the instant adversary proceeding under 28 U.S.C. § 1334. Section 1334(b) provides that "the district courts shall have original but not exclusive jurisdiction of all civil proceedings arising under title 11, or arising in or related to cases under title 11." This provision creates jurisdiction in three categories of proceedings: those that "arise under title 11," those that "arise in cases under title 11," and those "related to cases under title 11." The bankruptcy court's jurisdiction is derivative of and dependent upon these three bases. *Celotex Corp. v. Edwards*, 514 U.S. 300 (1995); 1 Lawrence P. King, *Collier on Bankruptcy* ¶ 3.01[4] (15th ed.1998) [hereinafter *Collier on Bankruptcy*]. The instant adversary proceeding did not "arise under" or "arise in" a case under the Bankruptcy Code. "Arising under" proceedings are matters invoking a substantive right created by the Bankruptcy Code. *In re Wood*, 825 F.2d 90, 97 (5th Cir. 1987); 1 *Collier on Bankruptcy* ¶ 3.01[4][c][i]. The "arising in a case under" category is generally thought to involve administrative-type matters, 1 *Collier on Bankruptcy* ¶ 3.01[4][c][iv], or as the *Wood* court put it, "matters that could arise only in bankruptcy." Hence, the only one of the three categories of proceedings over which the district court is granted jurisdiction in § 1334(b) that is potentially relevant to the instant case is proceedings "related to cases under title 11." The "related to" connection has been described as "the minimum for bankruptcy jurisdiction." E. Scott Fruehwald, *The Related to Subject Matter Jurisdiction of Bankruptcy Courts*, 44 Drake L.Rev. 1, 7 (1995).

The Bank claims that the dispute between Sanchez and the Bank over entitlement to the proceeds of the Partnership Property was not related to Toledo's underlying bankruptcy case and had no effect on Toledo or the Estate, and therefore the bankruptcy court had no jurisdiction to adjudicate that dispute. Blending the concepts of jurisdiction and the core versus non-core dichotomy, the district court held that the bankruptcy court had jurisdiction because the dispute was a "core proceeding" under 28 U.S.C. § 157(b)(2)(K).[6]

---

[6] Although whether something is a core proceeding is analytically separate from whether there is jurisdiction, by definition all core proceedings are within the bankruptcy court's jurisdiction. Core proceedings are defined in 28 U.S.C. § 157(b)(1) as "proceedings arising under title 11, or arising in a case under title 11," which is a subset of the cases over which jurisdiction is granted in § 1334(b).

As both parties acknowledge, *In re Lemco Gypsum, Inc.*, 910 F.2d 784 (11th Cir. 1990), is the seminal case in this Circuit on the scope of the bankruptcy court's "related to" jurisdiction. In *Lemco Gypsum*, this Court adopted the following liberal test from *Pacor, Inc. v. Higgins*, 743 F.2d 984 (3d Cir. 1984), for determining jurisdiction over an adversary proceeding:

> The usual articulation of the test for determining whether a civil proceeding is related to bankruptcy is whether the outcome of the proceeding could conceivably have an effect on the estate being administered in bankruptcy. The proceeding need not necessarily be against the debtor or the debtor's property. An action is related to bankruptcy if the outcome could alter the debtor's rights, liabilities, options, or freedom of action (either positively or negatively) and which in any way impacts upon the handling and administration of the bankrupt estate.

Lemco Gypsum, 910 F.2d at 788 (quoting *Pacor*); *see also Celotex Corp.*, 115 S. Ct. at 1499 & n.6 (expressing approval of the *Pacor* test). The key word in the *Lemco Gypsum/Pacor* test is "conceivable," which makes the jurisdictional grant extremely broad.

In the instant case, Sanchez was seeking a judicial determination of the extent and priority of liens and other interests in the Partnership Property so that the proceeds of the sale earlier approved by Judge Weaver's order could be distributed appropriately. The nexus with the bankruptcy estate contemplated by the *Lemco Gypsum/Pacor* test was present in two ways. First, if the Bank's mortgage were adjudged valid, its $1.8 million claim against the Estate (partially secured by the Key Biscayne residence) would be reduced by the $200,000 due and paid to the Bank out of the proceeds of the sale of the Partnership Property. Thus, the payment of these $200,000 to the Bank from non-Estate property would ultimately free up an additional $200,000 for distribution to unsecured creditors.[7] In contrast, if the Bank's mortgage was held invalid, as

---

[7] Because additional collateral (the Toledos' Key Biscayne residence) and an additional creditor (BankAtlantic) on that collateral were involved, the logical chain is fairly complicated and deserves some explanation. The Toledos owed the Bank about $1.8 million. Their residence was encumbered first by a BankAtlantic mortgage, then by the Bank's mortgage securing the $1.8 million indebtedness, then by a third mortgage also belonging to BankAtlantic. If $200,000 of the Toledos' indebtedness to the Bank were satisfied out of the proceeds of the sale of the Partnership Property, the Bank's "intermediate" mortgage on the Key Biscayne residence would secure only $1.6 million, i.e., $200,000 less than it would otherwise have secured. Put differently, the value of the residence would be exhausted more slowly and either the Bank or BankAtlantic (pursuant to its third mortgage) would be undersecured to a lesser extent than before. Consequently, depending on the value of the residence, more funds would be available either to satisfy

actually occurred, the Bank would have to look entirely to the Key Biscayne residence (or, more precisely, to what remained from the proceeds of the residence after satisfaction of BankAtlantic's first mortgage thereon) for satisfaction of its $1.8 million indebtedness. To the extent the value to which it was entitled from the residence was insufficient to satisfy this debt, the Bank would become an unsecured creditor causing the funds available for unsecured claims to be spread more thinly. A conceivable effect on the Estate thus exists in the possible partial satisfaction and consequent downward adjustment of the claim filed against the Estate by the Bank.

The second connection to the Estate stems from the fact that if the mortgage were adjudged invalid, there would be more equity in the Partnership Property and an additional $200,000 would be freed up to go to the Partnership. Whatever interest the Toledos had in the Partnership at the time the petition was filed became part of the Estate. Under the terms of the sale order, approximately $151,000 already was available for distribution to the Partnership. It was originally contemplated that these proceeds would be split 50/50 between Sanchez and the Estate, according to Sanchez' and the Toledos' respective 50% interests in the Partnership. Under this arrangement, if the Bank's mortgage were held invalid, the Estate might have been enriched by $100,000 (one-half of $200,000)–clearly a "conceivable effect" on the Estate that would support "related to" jurisdiction. *Cf. Wood*, 825 F.2d at 93–94 (holding that relatedness existed where an action against the debtor personally for post-petition misappropriation of corporate assets would "resolve the disputed allocation of interest in the [corporation]" and where the debtor's stock holdings in the corporation were property of the estate so that their value would affect the estate).[8]

BankAtlantic's third mortgage, or to go into the Estate to pay off unsecured creditors. General creditors of the Estate would ultimately benefit, either because (i) their claims were not diluted or were less diluted by the presence of the Bank as a competing unsecured creditor, (ii) their claims were not diluted or were less diluted by the presence of BankAtlantic (to the extent of its debt secured by the third mortgage on the Key Biscayne residence) as a competing unsecured creditor, or (iii) if the value of the residence was sufficient to satisfy both mortgages, the excess value that constituted equity in the property would go into the Estate.

[8] * * * [T]he bankruptcy court ultimately determined that the Estate's and the debtors' interests in the Partnership were worthless. Thus, the additional $200,000 flowing to the Partnership by virtue of the invalidity of the Bank's mortgage did not ultimately benefit the Estate. However, it is clear that the issue of the validity of the Bank's mortgage could conceivably have had an effect on the Estate, thus satisfying the test. *See Wood*, 825 F.2d at 94 ("Although we acknowledge the possibility that this suit may ultimately have no effect on the bankruptcy, we cannot conclude, on the facts before us, that it will have no *conceiv-*

The instant case is distinguishable from a recent case in which we determined that the essential "related to" nexus under § 1334(b) was not present. In *In re Boone* this Court determined that the bankruptcy court lacked jurisdiction over a lawsuit by Chapter 7 debtors against a creditor for tortious interference with contract. The rationale was that the conduct giving rise to the claim occurred after the date of the bankruptcy petition; the cause of action therefore belonged to the debtors themselves rather than to the estate, and consequently any recovery in the lawsuit would not inure to the benefit of the estate. In the instant adversary proceeding, the property interest whose value would be affected by the outcome of the proceeding (the Toledos' interest in the Partnership) was a pre-petition property interest and therefore belonged to the Estate. Unlike in *Boone*, the value and extent of the Estate's indirect interest in the Partnership Property would necessarily be affected by the outcome of the adversary proceeding. Also, unlike in *Boone*, we have an additional connection with the estate inasmuch that resolution of the dispute over the validity of the mortgage ultimately affects whether the creditor whose mortgage is invalidated must look to other collateral or compete with general unsecured creditors to satisfy the debt it is owed.

B. Core Versus Non–Core

Having found that the district court had jurisdiction over the adversary proceeding, we turn next to the question whether the district court correctly referred to it as a core proceeding under 28 U.S.C. § 157(b). If it was a core proceeding, the district court correctly applied normal, deferential standards of appellate review to the bankruptcy court's disposition of it. *See* 28 U.S.C. § 158(a); Fed. R. Bankr.P. 8013. If it was a noncore proceeding, the bankruptcy court could only submit proposed findings of fact and conclusions of law, not a final order or judgment, and the district court was obligated to conduct a de novo review of those matters to which the Bank objected. *See* 28 U.S.C. § 157(c)(1) ("In [a non-core] proceeding, the bankruptcy judge shall submit proposed findings of fact and conclusions of law to the district court, and any final order or judgment shall be entered by the district judge after considering the bankruptcy judge's proposed findings and conclusions and after reviewing de novo those matters to which any party has timely and specifically objected."); Fed. R. Bankr.P. 9033 (specifying the exact procedures to be followed by the district court in such cases).

---

able effect.") (emphasis in original). The presence or absence of jurisdiction must be evaluated based on the state of affairs existing at the time the adversary complaint was filed not at some later time when, for example, it was ultimately determined here that the Estate had no interest in the sale proceeds.

Congress created the distinction between core and non-core proceedings in... 1984 in order to avoid the constitutional problems, identified in *Northern Pipeline Constr. Co. v. Marathon Pipe Line Co.*, associated with the expansive bankruptcy court jurisdiction permitted under prior law. 28 U.S.C. § 157(b)(2) lists fourteen specific types of actions that are considered core proceedings, and provides a fifteenth, catch-all category for "other proceedings affecting the liquidation of the assets of the estate or the adjustment of the debtor-creditor or the equity security holder relationship," 28 U.S.C. § 157(b)(2)(O). The statutory list provides that it is not intended to be exhaustive of the entire universe of core proceedings.

The district court held that the instant case was a core proceeding under 28 U.S.C. § 157(b)(2)(K), which applies to "determinations of the validity, extent, or priority of liens." This reliance on § 157(b)(2)(K) was misplaced. The district court apparently reasoned that since the purpose of the instant adversary proceeding was to obtain a judicial determination of the validity of the Bank's mortgage, which is a lien on real estate, it fit the language of subsection (b)(2)(K). However, the case law on (b)(2)(K) indicates that it encompasses only proceedings to determine the validity, extent, or priority of liens on the estate's or the debtor's property. "Otherwise, [bankruptcy courts] would be asserting a form of jurisdiction ferae naturae, capable of the adjudication of property rights wherever found and by whomever owned." *In re Dr. C. Huff Co.*, 44 B.R. 129, 134 (Bankr.W.D.Ky.1984). Here, the real property on which the disputed mortgage existed belonged to the non-debtor Partnership, not to the Toledos or the Estate. The Estate owned a 50% interest in the Partnership, but no direct interest in the Partnership Property. Thus, § 157(b)(2)(K) is no basis for calling the instant proceeding a "core proceeding." *Cf. In re Guild & Gallery Plus, Inc.*, 72 F.3d 1171, 1179 (3d Cir. 1996) (holding that the § 157(b)(2)(A) core proceeding category for "matters concerning the administration of the estate" did not apply to an action concerning goods with respect to which the debtor was bailee but not owner).

The distinction between property belonging to a partnership of which the debtor was partner, and property belonging to the debtor-partner, is well-established in bankruptcy law. * * * *In re Palumbo*, 154 B.R. 357, 358 (Bankr.S.D.Fla.1992) (noting, with regard to a partner who had a 97% interest in a partnership and claimed that foreclosure on the partnership property violated the automatic stay, that "it is firmly established that the assets of a partnership are not to be administered in a partner's bankruptcy proceeding since a partnership is a separate entity from its partners under bankruptcy law"); *In re Funneman*, 155 B.R. 197, 199 (Bankr.S.D.Ill.1993) ("It is well settled that assets owned by a partnership are not included in the bankruptcy estate of the individual partner. The only partnership property before the court during an individual's bankruptcy is the partner's personal property interest in the partnership, which consists of the individual's interest, if any, in the partnership assets after an accounting and payment of partnership debts out of the property belonging to the partnership."). The Partnership Property never entered the Estate in the instant case.

Nor do any of the other types of core proceedings appearing in § 157(b)'s list fit the instant adversary proceeding, especially in light of the fact that they are to be construed in light of the constitutional limitations that prompted their enactment. To the extent that the literal wording of some of the types of proceedings might conceivably seem to apply,[10] it should be remembered that engrafted upon all of them is an overarching requirement that property of the estate under § 541 be involved. *In re Gallucci*, 931 F.2d 738, 742 (11th Cir. 1991) (noting that § 157(b)(2)(E) category for turnover actions applies only to orders to turn over property of the estate). Here, of course, the property in question was owned by the Partnership, not by Toledo himself.

Because the list in the statute is non-exhaustive, it is not the end of our inquiry whether the adversary proceeding was core. The most helpful explanation of what is a core proceeding, accepted almost universally by the courts, is found in the Fifth Circuit's decision in *Wood*:

> If the proceeding involves a right created by the federal bankruptcy law, it is a core proceeding; for example, an action by the trustee to avoid a preference. If the proceeding is one that would arise only in bankruptcy, it is also a core proceeding; for example, the filing of a proof of claim or an objection to the discharge of a particular debt. If the proceeding does not invoke a substantive right created by the federal bankruptcy law and is one that could exist outside of bankruptcy it is not a core proceeding; it may be *related to* the bankruptcy because of its potential effect, but under section 157(c)(1) it is an "otherwise related" or non-core proceeding.

825 F.2d at 97 (emphasis in original). In *Wood*, the adversary proceeding in question was an action by a shareholder of a corporation of which the bankruptcy debtor was the only other shareholder, to obtain redress for allegedly improper stock issued to and dividends received by the debtor-shareholder or the estate. The Fifth Circuit held that under the above test this adversary proceeding was not a core proceeding because it was "simply a state contract action that, had there been no bankruptcy, could have proceeded in state court."

---

[10] For example, "matters concerning the administration of the estate," § 157(b)(2)(A).

Id. Although the court had subject matter jurisdiction pursuant to the "related to" prong of § 1334(b), it was not a core proceeding.

Wood's interpretation of § 157 rested heavily on the ostensible purpose of the 1984 Act, i.e., "to conform the bankruptcy statutes to the dictates of *Marathon*." The Fifth Circuit's test breathes life into the terms "core" and "non-core" by construing them in light of the constitutional concerns that prompted the enactment of the statute. In fact, it appears that the use of the word "core" was itself borrowed from Justice Brennan's reference in the plurality opinion to "the core of the federal bankruptcy power." What the Supreme Court, and by extension Congress, was concerned about was the plenary adjudication by bankruptcy courts of proceedings "related only peripherally to an adjudication of bankruptcy." *Northern Pipeline*, 458 U.S. at 92 (Burger, C.J., dissenting). Hence, the issue before us ultimately depends on whether the instant case was of the type with respect to which the *Northern Pipeline* Court rejected giving bankruptcy courts full adjudicative power.

We are mindful that the dependence of the merits of an action on state law (as the instant case turns on various partnership law and real estate finance law issues) does not, in and of itself, mean that the action is non-core. 28 U.S.C. § 157(b)(3); see also *Wood*, 825 F.2d at 96, 97 n.4; *Northern Pipeline*, 458 U.S. at 96–97, 102 S. Ct. 2858 (White, J., dissenting) ("The distinction between claims based on state law and those based on federal law disregards the real character of bankruptcy proceedings. . . .. The bankruptcy judge is constantly enmeshed in state-law issues."). Nevertheless, based on the *Wood* test as well as the constitutional concerns expressed in *Northern Pipeline*, we conclude that the instant case was not a core proceeding. Sanchez' action to determine the validity, priority, and extent of liens on the Partnership Property did not invoke a substantive right created by bankruptcy law, and could clearly occur outside of bankruptcy.[11] Indeed, actions similar to the instant case are filed in state court all the time.

---

[11] *Wood* is especially instructive because its facts are roughly analogous to those in the instant case. In *Wood*, the complaint filed in the bankruptcy court concerned the debtors' post-petition wrongful issuance of stock and payment of dividends (the debtors were controlling shareholders and directors of the corporation) to themselves, which violated the plaintiff's right as an equal shareholder. By comparison, the instant case concerns a debtor-partner's alleged manipulation of a partnership to exploit its property to secure personal debts, to the detriment of the other partner. In both cases, the right that the plaintiffs sought to vindicate involved a wrongful manipulation of the property of an entity other than the debtor (i.e., a corporation or partnership), and was essentially a state-law right based on principles of contract and/or fiduciary duty. Neither case is one involving a right

The linguistic structure of § 157 lends further support to this conclusion. Subsection (b)(1) equates core proceedings with those "arising under title 11, or arising in a case under title 11," whereas subsection (c)(1) makes "non-core" proceedings synonymous with "otherwise related to" proceedings. "The phrases 'arising under' and 'arising in' are helpful indicators of the meaning of core proceedings." *Wood*, 825 F.2d at 97; *see also* 1 *Collier on Bankruptcy*, ¶ 3.01[4][c]. "Arising under" means that a proceeding invokes a cause of action, or substantive right, created by a specific section of the Bankruptcy Code. *Celotex Corp. v. Edwards*, 115 S. Ct. at 1506 & n.13 (Stevens, J., dissenting); 1 *Collier on Bankruptcy* ¶ 3.01[4][c][I] . "Arising in" describes administrative matters unique to the management of a bankruptcy estate. 1 *Collier on Bankruptcy* ¶ 3.01[4][c][iv]. For example, as the *Wood* court explained, the filing of a claim against a bankruptcy estate triggers a core proceeding under § 157(b)(2)(B), but only because it "invokes the peculiar powers of the bankruptcy court." However, the administrative act of filing such a claim must be distinguished from the state-law right underlying the claim, which "could be enforced in a state court proceeding absent the bankruptcy" and is non-core. In the instant case, the adversary proceeding sought to vindicate state-created common-law rights but did not utilize any process specially established by the Bankruptcy Code. Clearly, Sanchez' adversary proceeding neither "arose under" nor "arose in" the Bankruptcy Code as those terms of art have been understood, and therefore it must necessarily fall within the residual category of "otherwise related," i.e., non-core matters.

III. Conclusion

In conclusion, we hold that there was "related to" jurisdiction over the adversary proceeding under 28 U.S.C. § 1334, but that it was a non-core proceeding under 28 U.S.C. § 157. Because the district court mistook it for a core proceeding, it exercised only "clearly erroneous" review of the bankruptcy court's findings of fact and "abuse of discretion" review of the bankruptcy court's application of waiver and estoppel, despite the Bank's specific objections to those findings and applications.[12] We remand with instructions to the district court to treat the bankruptcy court's findings of fact and conclusions of

---

created by bankruptcy law, or one which would arise only in bankruptcy. Rather, both cases invoke purely state-law rights and could exist outside bankruptcy.

[12] It is evident from the tone of the district court's opinion that its review of certain issues was highly deferential to the bankruptcy court. For example, it stated that "there is a valid basis for the relief granted by the bankruptcy court to avoid an injustice to override the application of res judicata and collateral estoppel." On remand, the district court should undertake a fresh, independent analysis of these issues.

law and "judgments" granting Sanchez relief, as merely proposed findings of fact and conclusions of law, and to conduct the *de novo* review contemplated by § 157(c)(1) and Bankruptcy Rule 9033. The judgment of the district court is
VACATED AND REMANDED.

NOTES

1. The *Pacor* test for "related to" jurisdiction (whether the proceeding could have any conceivable effect on the estate), adopted in *Toledo*, has been widely followed. Judge Posner comments on the scope of "related to" jurisdiction in *Zerand-Bernal Group, Inc. v. Cox*, 23 F.3d 159 (7th Cir. 1994). There Zerand bought the debtor's assets at a bankruptcy sale free and clear of liens. All property of the estate was subsequently distributed and the debtor went out of business. Four and a half years after the sale to Zerand, Cox, who was injured by a machine that debtor had sold to Cox's employer before the asset sale to Zerand, brought a products liability suit in federal district court against Zerand on the theory of successor liability. Zerand sought to reopen the bankruptcy case and asked that Cox be enjoined from proceeding with his products liability suit. The bankruptcy court held that it lacked jurisdiction over the proceeding brought by Cox because it was not related to the bankruptcy case within the meaning of 28 U.S.C. § 1334(b). In affirming the decision, Posner conceded that the "related to" language was probably broad enough to encompass Zerand's proceeding because it related to the bankruptcy sale at which Zerand acquired the debtor's assets and thereby exposed itself to Cox's suit.

> But the language should not be read so broadly. The reference to cases related to bankruptcy cases is primarily intended to encompass tort, contract, and other legal claims by and against the debtor, claims that, were it not for bankruptcy, would be ordinary stand-alone lawsuits between the debtor and others but that section 1334(b) allows to be forced into bankruptcy court so that all claims by and against the debtor can be determined in the same forum. * * * A secondary purpose is to force into the bankruptcy court suits to which the debtor need not be a party but which may affect the amount of property in the bankrupt estate.

23 F.3d at 161–162. Cox's suit was not covered by either test. The debtor company no longer exists and all its assets have been distributed to creditors; Cox's suit could not affect the amount of property available to creditors.

In *In re Johns–Manville Corp.*, 517 F.3d 52 (2d Cir. 2008), cert. granted, 77 U.S.L.W. 3358 (2008), the Second Circuit determined that the bankruptcy court lacked even related-to jurisdiction over claims against Manville's liability insurers based on the insurers' own independently wrongful conduct in handling asbestos claims. That decision testing the boundaries of the related-to jurisdiction in the mass tort context is before the Supreme Court as of this writing and may provide a vehicle for the Court to weigh in on the scope of the jurisdictional grant in § 1334 and proper application of the *Pacor* test.

2. In 28 U.S.C. § 157(b)(2)(A) and (O), Congress has included two catch-all categories that give bankruptcy courts flexibility in identifying matters as core proceedings. The wording of § 157(b)(2)(O) is so broad that it could be interpreted to make the matter in *Marathon* a core proceeding. In adopting the view that a court should avoid characterizing a proceeding as core if to do so would raise constitutional problems, *In re Castlerock Properties,* 781 F.2d 159 (9th Cir. 1986), held that state law contract claims that do not specifically fall within § 157(b)(2)(B)-(N) are noncore proceedings under § 157(c) even if they fall within the literal wording of § 157(b)(2)(A) or (O).

3. The prevailing view is that a claim by a trustee or debtor in possession arising from a postpetition contract is a core matter. The court in *In re Arnold Print Works, Inc.*, 815 F.2d 165 (1st Cir. 1987) (Breyer, J.), held that such a suit falls within 28 U.S.C. § 157(b)(2)(A) because it concerns the administration of the estate and within § 157(b)(2)(O) because the claim arose out of the debtor's efforts to liquidate estate assets. Can this case be reconciled with *Castlerock Properties* in Note 2? In *Arnold Print Works* the court asserts that its interpretation of § 157(b) is constitutional under *Marathon* because under the 1898 Bankruptcy Act bankruptcy courts had jurisdiction over postpetition contract claims on the fiction that a contract with a trustee is a contract with the court. The court said, "Quite apart from the force of the fiction, the history of bankruptcy court jurisdiction means that a post-petition contract made with a debtor-in-possession cannot be called a "'traditional' state contract action." 815 F.2d at 170. Several Courts of Appeal have also held that professional malpractice claims by trustees or debtors against court-appointed professionals are core proceedings. *See In re Southmark Corp.*, 193 F.3d 925 (5th Cir. 1999) (accountants); *Billing v. Ravin, Greenberg, & Zackin, P.A.*, 22 F.3d 1242 (3d Cir. 1994) (lawyers). Some courts have extended *Arnold Print Works* to find that postpetition causes of action arising under pre-petition contracts are also "core" proceedings. *In re Kids World of Am., Inc.*, 349 B.R. 152 (Bankr.W.D. Ky.2006); *In re Columbia Gas Sys.*, 164 B.R. 883, 885 (Bankr.D.Del 1994).

4. More surprising than the *Arnold Print Works* holding with respect to claims under postpetition contracts is that, despite *Marathon*, bankruptcy courts have split over whether the right of the trustee or debtor in possession to collect a prepetition debt is a core proceeding. One view reads Bankruptcy Code § 542(b) as authorizing a turnover order in cases in which a defendant owes the debtor a matured debt and sees 28 U.S.C. § 157(b)(2)(E) as making a proceeding under § 542(b) a core proceeding. For example, *In re Leco Enterprises, Inc.*,

125 B.R. 385 (S.D.N.Y.1991), holds that an action to collect a disputed account receivable is a core proceeding under § 157(b)(A), (E) and (O) because it sought an order to turn over property that would inure to the benefit of the estate and was, therefore, inextricably linked to the administration of the estate. Most cases reject the *Leco* approach as creating an exception to *Marathon* that would swallow the rule of the case. See, *e.g.*, *In re Apex Express Corp.*, 190 F. 3d 624 (4th Cir. 1999). *In re Orion Pictures Corp.*, 4 F.3d 1095, 1102 (2d Cir. 1993); *Beard v. Braunstein*, 914 F.2d 434 (3d Cir. 1990), (holding action by Chapter 7 trustee to recover prepetition and postpetition rents from a tenant under a prepetition lease was a noncore proceeding); 1 Collier on Bankruptcy ¶ 3.02[4] (*Leco* and progeny "should not be followed").

5. As *Toledo* indicates, 28 U.S.C. § 157(c)(1) requires that in a non-core proceeding the bankruptcy judge must submit proposed findings of fact and conclusions of law to the district court. The district court will enter a final order after reviewing *de novo* those matters to which any party has objected. Under Rule 9033(d) the district judge may accept, reject, or modify the proposed findings of fact or conclusions of law, receive further evidence or recommit the matter to the bankruptcy judge with instructions. In *In re Castro*, 919 F.2d 107 (9th Cir. 1990), the circuit court remanded to the district court a case in which the district court had entered its order before it had a transcript of the testimony given in the bankruptcy court. The circuit court observed that for *de novo* review the district court need not hold new hearings but must review the record. Note that given the busy dockets of district judges, the bankruptcy judge's ability to manage and shape the proceedings through interlocutory rulings that are never reviewed, and the relative expertise of bankruptcy judges even with respect to non-core matters that arise in bankruptcy, there may be precious little practical difference in the bankruptcy judge's role as trial court, or in the amount of district judge scrutiny between non-core matters and core matters. *See* Daniel J. Bussel, *Power, Authority and Precedent in Interpreting the Bankruptcy Code*, 41 UCLA L. Rev. 1063, 1068 n.28 (1994).

3. FURTHER LIMITS ON ORIGINAL JURISDICTION

The problems inherent in defining the scope of § 157(b) and § 1334(b) do not exhaust the legal limits on the original federal bankruptcy jurisdiction. Bankruptcy courts may also be precluded from adjudicating claims otherwise within the original federal bankruptcy jurisdiction under § 1334(b) for the following reasons:

(a) withdrawal of the reference under 28 U.S.C. § 157(d);

(b) abstention under 28 U.S.C. § 1334(c);

(c) enforcement of arbitration clauses; and

(d) state sovereign immunity under the Eleventh Amendment.

a. Withdrawal of the Reference

Whether or not a matter is "core," a district court *may* withdraw a case or proceeding from a bankruptcy court "for cause." The district court *must* withdraw a matter "if the court determines that resolution of the proceeding requires consideration of both title 11 and other laws of the United States regulating organizations or activities affecting interstate commerce." 28 U.S.C. § 157(d). Nothing in *Marathon* requires withdrawal if nonbankruptcy federal law is implicated; Congress, nevertheless, favored adjudication of rights under nonbankruptcy federal laws in federal district courts. Mandatory withdrawal applies when "substantial and material consideration" of federal statutes, in addition to the Bankruptcy Code, is required. See, *e.g., In re Chateaugay Corp.,* 108 B.R. 17 (S.D.N.NY 1989). "Substantial and material" is generally construed to require that substantial issues of interpretation (as opposed to mere application) of federal nonbankruptcy law be present. *City of New York v. Exxon Corp.,* 932 F.2d 1020, 1026 (2d Cir. 1991). Even when withdrawal is mandatory, the actual hearing may still be in the bankruptcy court. In *Chateaugay,* the district court referred the proceedings to the bankruptcy court for findings of fact and conclusions of law under § 157(c)(1). In general, district courts are far less likely to withdraw the reference for "core" matters than they are for "non-core" matters unless the "core" matter involves a right to trial by jury. *In re Orion Pictures Corp.,* 4 F.3d 1095 (2d Cir. 1993). Even if there is a jury trial right, however, pretrial proceedings are generally conducted in the bankruptcy court.

b. Abstention

In 1978, Senate conservatives wanted bankruptcy courts to abstain from adjudicating state law causes of action, whether the debtor was plaintiff or defendant. The compromise result was 28 U.S.C. § 1334(c)(2). This provision is only an attenuated version of what these Senators sought. Section 1334(c)(2) requires district courts to abstain from hearing a state cause of action over which they have jurisdiction solely because the claim is "related to a case under title 11" when the action on the claim "is commenced, and can be timely adjudicated, in a State forum of appropriate jurisdiction." The majority view is that a state court proceeding must be pending at the time the order to abstain is entered. *In re West Coast Video Enterprises, Inc.,* 145 B.R. 484, 486 (Bankr.E.D.Pa.1992). This interpretation would usually restrict § 1334(c)(2) mandatory abstention to suits brought by debtors against third parties before bankruptcy. Mandatory abstention does not apply to a case in which the "related to" action could have been commenced in a federal court under diversity jurisdiction or under any other nonbankruptcy federal jurisdiction (although permissive abstention or withdrawal of the reference may apply in these cases).

In 1994, § 1334(d) was added to provide that decisions either to abstain or not to abstain under (c)(1) (discretionary abstention) and decisions *to* abstain under (c)(2) (mandatory abstention) are not reviewable by the court of appeals or Supreme Court; decisions *not* to abstain under (c)(2) are reviewable by these courts. Under Rule 5011(b) the motion to abstain is heard by the bankruptcy court. The bankruptcy court order determining the abstention motion remains appealable to the district court or BAP by leave of court, but further appeals are barred by § 1334(d) as are any appeals of district court abstention orders in withdrawn matters.

State court actions pending against the debtor at the time of bankruptcy are normally claims in the bankruptcy. The action would be automatically stayed by § 362 and, if the stay is not lifted, the claimant would have to file a proof of claim in the bankruptcy court which would then allow or disallow it. The proceeding to collect the claim in bankruptcy is one "arising in a case under title 11" rather than one "related to a case under title 11" and is a core proceeding. 28 U.S.C. § 157(b)(1). Thus § 1334(c)(2) doesn't apply. Although § 1334(c)(2) refers to "the district court," that reference must also apply to the bankruptcy court which is treated as a unit of the district court. 28 U.S.C. § 151.

c. Arbitration

Many commercial and consumer contracts provide for mandatory arbitration of disputes. At common law agreements to arbitrate future disputes were generally unenforceable. The Federal Arbitration Act of 1925 reversed this common law rule and requires federal courts to compel arbitration if the parties have agreed in writing to arbitrate a matter otherwise within the federal court's jurisdiction. Over 50 years later, Congress passed the Bankruptcy Code which on its face stays arbitration proceedings, § 362(a)(1), and, subject to relief from stay "for cause," § 362(d)(1) and discretionary abstention, 28 U.S.C. § 1334(d), centralizes all dispute resolution in the federal bankruptcy court, particularly with respect to "core matters" as defined in 28 U.S.C. § 157(b).

Until the mid–1980s, it was accepted that bankruptcy courts had broad discretion with respect to whether to stay proceedings in the bankruptcy case properly falling within their jurisdiction and enforce contractual arbitration clauses. *Zimmerman v. Continental Airlines, Inc.*, 712 F.2d 55 (3d Cir. 1983).

In two Securities Act cases, *Shearson/American Express, Inc. v. McMahon*, 482 U.S. 220 (1987) and *Rodriguez de Quijas v. Shearson/American Express, Inc.*, 490 U.S. 477 (1989), however, the Supreme Court strongly endorsed the general policy in favor of arbitration indicating that even in matters involving statutory schemes providing for judicial enforcement, written arbitration agreements should be enforced unless the party opposing arbitration could show that "Congress did intend to limit or prohibit waiver of a judicial forum for a particular claim... [as] 'deducible from [the statute's] text or legislative history' or from an inherent conflict between arbitration and the statute's underlying purposes." *McMahon*, 482 U.S. at 227.

In the wake of these securities law cases and the 1984 amendments to the bankruptcy jurisdictional statutes, there has been considerable disagreement over the scope of bankruptcy courts' discretion to refuse to enforce arbitration clauses. In *Hays & Co. v. Merrill, Lynch, Pierce, Fenner & Smith, Inc.*, 885 F.2d 1149 (3d Cir. 1989), the Third Circuit overruled its own earlier decision in *Zimmerman* and held that the bankruptcy court had no discretion to refuse to enforce an arbitration clause in a non-core proceeding brought by the trustee under a prepetition agreement. *Hays* distinguished a related avoiding powers action brought under § 544(b), finding that although the claim of the estate based on the prepetition agreement had to be arbitrated, the avoiding power claim could be brought in the bankruptcy court.

Courts generally agree with *Hays* with respect to non-core claims based on prepetition agreements brought by trustees or debtors against third parties. The trustee or debtor is bound to arbitrate such claims if the agreement so provides. There is little agreement beyond this, however.

Some later courts interpret *Hays* to adopt a crucial distinction between core and non-core matters. These courts hold that *Hays* rule of no discretion applies only to non-core matters. As to core matters bankruptcy courts retain discretion to hear matters which would be otherwise subject to arbitration. *Selcke v. New England Ins. Co.*, 995 F.2d 688 (7th Cir. 1993); *In re American Freight Sys., Inc.*, 164 B.R. 341 (D.Kan.1994); *In re Spectrum Info. Tech., Inc.*, 183 B.R. 360 (Bankr.E.D.N.Y.1995). Other courts have found that arbitration clauses must be enforced—even in core matters—unless the legal right at issue arises from the Bankruptcy Code itself rather than the agreement. In *Matter of National Gypsum Co.*, 118 F.3d 1056 (5th Cir. 1997), the court adopted this narrower of view of the bankruptcy court's discretion, nevertheless holding that the arbitration agreement in that case would not be enforced because the legal questions at issue arose out of the effect of the debtor's confirmed plan of reorganization and the discharge provisions of the Code rather than from the prepetition agreement assumed in the plan. *National Gypsum* appears to draw the line between bankruptcy and arbitration at the nature of the rights asserted—that is whether "bankruptcy rights" or "contract rights" are at issue, not whether the matter is "core" or "non-core."

Whiting-Turner Contracting Co. v. Electric Machinery Enterprises, Inc., 479 F.3d 791 (11th Cir. 2007), is further evidence of the trend towards expanding the enforceability of contractual arbitration clauses into the domain of core bankruptcy matters. In this case the Eleventh Circuit compelled arbitration of a subcontractor-debtor's adversary proceeding to obtain turnover of funds held by a general contractor. The Eleventh Circuit reversed the finding that the turnover action was a core proceeding, but went on to declare that even if the matter were considered a core matter, arbitration would be required unless enforcement of the arbitration agreement "would inherently conflict with the underlying purposes of the Bankruptcy Code." Until the Supreme Court directly resolves the conflict between the Bankruptcy Code and the Federal Arbitration Act, continuing confusion in the lower federal courts and bankruptcy courts concerning bankruptcy court jurisdiction over matters that would be otherwise subject to arbitration will persist. Why should there be greater deference in bankruptcy to contractual arbitration clauses than other forum selection clauses?

d. Sovereign Immunity

Since the enactment of the 1978 Bankruptcy Code, the courts and Congress have struggled with the extent to which the Eleventh Amendment, which embodies a principle of state sovereign immunity, limits the ability of the federal bankruptcy courts to enforce the provisions of the Code against State governments and their agencies.

The threat posed by the Eleventh Amendment to important bankruptcy policies is well summarized in the *NBRC Rep.* at 898–902:

> Bankruptcy is a collective proceeding, providing a single forum for the resolution of claims against the debtor's property "wherever located.". . . By providing a single forum governed by a single set of procedural rules, the bankruptcy process ensures uniform procedural treatment for every type of claimant. . . . A single bankruptcy forum also advances a variety of fundamental policy goals, including, equal distribution and treatment for similarly situated creditors, promotion of a cost-effective and speedy process to minimize the cost to creditors, and the rehabilitation of individuals as well as business entities. Determining creditors' rights in the debtor's estate is a fundamental role of the bankruptcy court. A single forum for the resolution of claims against a bankruptcy estate is a critical component of the court's responsibility for a number of reasons.
>
> First, multiple proceedings in different courts may result in conflicting determinations. . . . Moreover, separate treatment in multiple courts may also result in unequal treatment of similarly-situated creditors. A creditor that is able to enforce its rights in a separate forum without consideration of other possible claims in the property will benefit to the detriment of other creditors.

Second, the ability of a bankruptcy court to quickly restructure a debtor's obligations enhances the likelihood of saving a business or giving a family a fresh start and increasing the distribution to creditors. The bankruptcy court has the ability to give notice to all parties with an interest in the debtor's property and to bring those persons or entities into the bankruptcy court for a final binding determination of the rights in the property....

Third, a single forum reduces the cost of collection for creditors....

Fourth, Chapter 11 of the Bankruptcy Code favors the reorganization of debtors in an effort to preserve going-concern value, retain jobs, and promote the efficient use of capital. A bankruptcy court that does not control all critical aspects of a debtor's business will be unable to achieve a reorganization....

Because the Eleventh Amendment protects *only* the states, the ability to bring actions against federal and municipal agencies remains unaffected [by the Eleventh Amendment].... As a result, states must be treated differently from all other creditors and parties in interest (including the federal government) in the bankruptcy process.

States play an important role in the bankruptcy process, appearing in many bankruptcy cases in a myriad of roles—as priority tax creditor, secured creditor, unsecured creditor, police and regulatory authority, environmental creditor, landlord, guarantor, bondholder, leaseholder, and equity interest holder. Similarly, a debtor may have a number of potential actions against a state, including a stay violation, preferences, turnover of property, and lien avoidance.... Different treatment of state entities will alter the statutory equilibrium struck in the Bankruptcy Code that balances the rights of creditors against each other as well as against the rights of the debtor.

Section 106 of the Bankruptcy Code dealt with this threat posed by the States' sovereign immunity by purporting to generally abrogate the sovereign immunity of any "governmental unit," which includes agencies of the United States, state governments, local governments and foreign governments. § 101(27). The unmistakable intent was to subject governmental units to the general provisions of the Bankruptcy Code, including for example the claims adjudication process, automatic stay, avoiding powers of the trustee and the discharge provisions, to the same extent as private parties.

The constitutionality of § 106 was drawn into doubt by *Seminole Tribe of Florida v. Florida*, 517 U.S. 44 (1996), where a closely divided Supreme Court overruled *Pennsylvania v. Union Gas Co.*, 491 U.S. 1 (1989), and found that the Eleventh Amendment precluded Congress from abrogating State sovereign immunity through the exercise of its commerce powers under Article I of the Constitution, no matter how clear its intention to do so. Though *Seminole Tribe* did not involve the bankruptcy power, there was no obvious basis for distinguishing the bankruptcy power from the other Article I powers at issue in that case, and the Court and the dissent, and most of the rest of the legal community, assumed that its holding would apply to § 106 and render it unconstitutional in part or in whole as applied to State governments.

Bankruptcy courts and the lower federal courts spent the next ten years struggling to limit the potential for havoc resulting from routine assertions of State sovereign immunity by State governments and their agencies whenever faced with a claim or defense based upon the Bankruptcy Code. Various tactics emerged for enforcing bankruptcy law against objecting State governments. These tactics generally focused on previously established exceptions to the Eleventh Amendment especially those involving *Ex parte Young* injunctions and *in rem* jurisdiction.

Under the doctrine of *Ex parte Young*, 209 U.S. 123 (1908), suits to prospectively enjoin state officials against violating federal law are not considered suits against the state for purposes of the Eleventh Amendment. Presumably, for example, the bankruptcy court could invoke *Ex parte Young* to enjoin state officials to desist from conduct that amounted to a continuing violation of the automatic stay notwithstanding the Eleventh Amendment, even though the State would be immune from suit for damages for the stay violation unless it had waived the Eleventh Amendment defense.

The Supreme Court also recognized in *Tennessee Student Assistance Corp. v. Hood*, 541 U.S. 440 (2004), that the *in rem* exception to the Eleventh Amendment had significant application in bankruptcy cases. Like *Ex parte Young* this exception depends upon a legal fiction. The fiction is that if the federal court has jurisdiction over certain property, then it may issue orders that relate to that property, orders with which State officers must comply. A particular application of this *in rem* jurisdiction theory of great practical importance is the binding effect of orders of confirmation in Chapter 11, 12 and 13 cases and discharge orders in Chapter 7 cases. In *Maryland v. Antonelli Creditors' Liquidating Trust*, 123 F.3d 777 (4th Cir. 1997), the Fourth Circuit found that the Eleventh Amendment did not insulate a non-consenting State seeking collection of postconfirmation taxes from the binding effect of a prior Chapter 11 discharge entered by the bankruptcy court properly vested with *in rem* jurisdiction over the property subject to the plan. *Hood* suggested that *Antonelli Creditors' Liquidating Trust* would become the general view, and debtors would be able to achieve through plan confirmation and discharge that which they might not be able to achieve through adversary proceedings against the State.

Most welcome relief from all of this uncertainty and complication relating to the effect of the Eleventh Amendment on bankruptcy cases came from an unexpected quarter—the Supreme Court itself. In *Central Virginia Community College v. Katz*, the Supreme Court found a unique bankruptcy exception to the Eleventh Amendment based upon a close reading of constitutional history. The "Plan of the Convention" was to subordinate State sovereign immunity in the interest of uniform enforcement of federal bankruptcy laws and, by ratifying the Constitution, the States forfeited their sovereign immunity to this extent.

Central Virginia Community College v. Katz
Supreme Court of the United States, 2006.
546 U.S. 356.

■ Justice STEVENS delivered the opinion of the Court.

Article I, § 8, cl. 4, of the Constitution provides that Congress shall have the power to establish "uniform Laws on the subject of Bankruptcies throughout the United States." In *Tennessee Student Assistance Corporation v. Hood*, we granted certiorari to determine whether this Clause gives Congress the authority to abrogate States' immunity from private suits. Without reaching that question, we upheld the application of the Bankruptcy Code to proceedings initiated by a debtor against a state agency to determine the dischargeability of a student loan debt. In this case we consider whether a proceeding initiated by a bankruptcy trustee to set aside preferential transfers by the debtor to state agencies is barred by sovereign immunity. Relying in part on our reasoning in *Hood*, we reject the sovereign immunity defense advanced by the state agencies.

I.

Petitioners are Virginia institutions of higher education that are considered "arm[s] of the State" entitled to sovereign immunity. Wallace's Bookstores, Inc. did business with petitioners before it filed a petition for relief under chapter 11 of the Bankruptcy Code in the United States Bankruptcy Court for the Eastern District of Kentucky. Respondent, Bernard Katz, is the court-appointed liquidating supervisor of the bankrupt estate. He has commenced proceedings in the Bankruptcy Court pursuant to §§ 547(b) and 550(a) to avoid and recover alleged preferential transfers to each of the petitioners made by the debtor when it was insolvent. Petitioners' motions to dismiss those proceedings on the basis of sovereign immunity were denied by the Bankruptcy Court.

The denial was affirmed by the District Court and the Court of Appeals for the Sixth Circuit on the authority of the Sixth Circuit's prior determination that Congress has abrogated the States' sovereign immunity in bankruptcy proceedings. We granted certiorari to consider the question left open by our opinion in *Hood:* whether Congress' attempt to abrogate state sovereign immunity in 11 U.S.C. § 106(a) is valid. As we shall explain, however, we are persuaded that the enactment of that provision was not necessary to authorize the Bankruptcy Court's jurisdiction over these preference avoidance proceedings.

Bankruptcy jurisdiction, at its core, is *in rem.* See *Gardner v. New Jersey* ("The whole process of proof, allowance, and distribution is, shortly speaking, an adjudication of interests claimed in a *res* "). As we noted in *Hood,* it does not implicate States' sovereignty to nearly the same degree as other kinds of jurisdiction. That was as true in the 18th century as it is today. Then, as now, the jurisdiction of courts adjudicating rights in the bankrupt estate included the power to issue compulsory orders to facilitate the administration and distribution of the res.

It is appropriate to presume that the Framers of the Constitution were familiar with the contemporary legal context when they adopted the Bankruptcy Clause[3]—a provision which, as we explain in Part IV, *infra,* reflects the States' acquiescence in a grant of congressional power to subordinate to the pressing goal of harmonizing bankruptcy law sovereign immunity defenses that might have been asserted in bankruptcy proceedings. The history of the Bankruptcy Clause, the reasons it was inserted in the Constitution, and the legislation both proposed and enacted under its auspices immediately following ratification of the Constitution demonstrate that it was intended not just as a grant of legislative authority to Congress, but also to authorize limited subordination of state sovereign immunity in the bankruptcy arena. Foremost on the minds of those who adopted the Clause were the intractable problems, not to mention the injustice, created by one State's imprisoning of debtors who had been discharged (from prison and of their debts) in and by another State. As discussed below, to remedy this problem, the very first Congresses considered, and the Sixth Congress enacted, bankruptcy legislation authorizing federal courts to, among other things, issue writs of habeas corpus directed at state officials ordering the release of debtors from state prisons.

We acknowledge that statements in both the majority and the dissenting opinions in *Seminole Tribe of Fla. v. Florida* reflected an assumption that the

---

[3] In *Cannon v. University of Chicago* we endorsed the presumption "that Congress was thoroughly familiar" with contemporary law when it enacted Title IX of the Civil Rights Act of 1964. It is equally proper to presume that the delegates to the Constitutional Convention were fully aware of the potential for injustice, discussed in Part II, *infra,* presented by the nonuniform state laws authorizing imprisonment as a remedy for the nonpayment of an insolvent's debts.

holding in that case would apply to the Bankruptcy Clause. Careful study and reflection have convinced us, however, that that assumption was erroneous. For the reasons stated by Chief Justice Marshall in *Cohens v. Virginia*, we are not bound to follow our dicta in a prior case in which the point now at issue was not fully debated.

II.

Critical features of every bankruptcy proceeding are the exercise of exclusive jurisdiction over all of the debtor's property, the equitable distribution of that property among the debtor's creditors, and the ultimate discharge that gives the debtor a "fresh start" by releasing him, her, or it from further liability for old debts. See, *e.g., Local Loan Co. v. Hunt*. "Under our longstanding precedent, States, whether or not they choose to participate in the proceeding, are bound by a bankruptcy court's discharge order no less than other creditors." *Hood*. Petitioners here, like the state agencies that were parties in *Hood*, have conceded as much.

The history of discharges in bankruptcy proceedings demonstrates that the state agencies' concessions, and *Hood's* holding, are correct. The term "discharge" historically had a dual meaning; it referred to both release of debts and release of the debtor from prison. Indeed, the earliest English statutes governing bankruptcy and insolvency authorized discharges of persons, not debts. One statute enacted in 1649 was entitled "An act for discharging Poor Prisoners unable to satisfy their creditors." The stated purpose of the Act was to "Discharge ... the person of [the] Debtor" "of and from his or her Imprisonment." *Ibid.* Not until 1705 did the English Parliament extend the discharge (and then only for traders and merchants) to include release of debts. *See* 4 Ann., ch. 17, § 7 (providing that upon compliance with the statute, "all and every person and persons so becoming bankrupt ... shall be discharged from all debts by him, her, or them due and owing at the time that he, she, or they did become bankrupt").

Well into the 18th century, imprisonment for debt was still ubiquitous in England and the American Colonies. Bankruptcy and insolvency laws remained as much concerned with ensuring full satisfaction of creditors (and, relatedly, preventing debtors' flight to parts unknown) as with securing new beginnings for debtors. Illustrative of bankruptcy laws' harsh treatment of debtors during this period was that debtors often fared worse than common criminals in prison; unfortunate insolvents, unlike criminals, were forced to provide their own food, fuel, and clothing while behind bars. See B. MANN, REPUBLIC OF DEBTORS: BANKRUPTCY IN THE AGE OF AMERICAN INDEPENDENCE 78-108 (2002).

Common as imprisonment itself was, the American Colonies, and later the several States, had wildly divergent schemes for discharging debtors and their debts. *Id.* ("The only consistency among debt laws in the eighteenth century was that every colony, and later every state, permitted imprisonment for debt—most on *mesne* process, and all on execution of a judgment"). At least four jurisdictions offered relief through private Acts of their legislatures. Those Acts released debtors from prison upon surrender of their property, and many coupled the release from prison with a discharge of debts. Other jurisdictions enacted general laws providing for release from prison and, in a few places, discharge of debt. Others still granted release from prison, but only in exchange for indentured servitude. Some jurisdictions provided no relief at all for the debtor.[6]

The difficulties posed by this patchwork of insolvency and bankruptcy laws were peculiar to the American experience. In England, where there was only one sovereign, a single discharge could protect the debtor from his jailer and his creditors. As two cases—one litigated before the Constitutional Convention in Philadelphia and one litigated after it—demonstrate, however, the uncoordinated actions of multiple sovereigns, each laying claim to the debtor's body and effects according to different rules, rendered impossible so neat a solution on this side of the Atlantic.

In the first case, *James v. Allen* (C.P. Phila.Cty.1786), Jared Ingersoll, an attorney who a year later would become a delegate to the Philadelphia Convention, represented a Pennsylvania creditor seeking recovery from a debtor who had been released from prison in New Jersey. Shortly after his release, the debtor traveled to Pennsylvania, where he was arrested for nonpayment of the Pennsylvania debt. In seeking release from the Pennsylvania prison, he argued that his debt had been discharged by the New Jersey court. Ingersoll responded that the order granting relief under New Jersey's insolvency laws "only discharged the person of the debtor from arrest within the State of New Jersey." *Id.* The court agreed: Whatever effect the order might have had in New Jersey, the court said, it "goes no further than to discharge [the debtor] from his imprisonment in the Gaol of Essex County in the State of New Jersey; which, if the fullest obedience were paid to it, could not authorize a subsequent discharge from imprisonment in another Gaol, in another State." *Id.* The court further observed that "[i]nsolvent laws subsist in every State in the Union, and are

---

[6] "At the time of the Revolution, only three of the thirteen colonies ... had laws discharging insolvents of their debts. No two of these relief systems were alike in anything but spirit. In four of the other ten colonies, insolvency legislation was either never enacted or, if enacted, never went into effect, and in the remaining six colonies, full relief was available only for scattered, brief periods, usually on an *ad hoc* basis to named insolvents." Coleman, DEBTORS AND CREDITORS IN AMERICA.

probably all different from each other. . . . Even the Bankrupt Laws of England, while we were the subjects of that country, were never supposed to extend here, so as to exempt the persons of the Bankrupts from being arrested." *Id.*

In the second case, *Millar v. Hall* (Pa.1788), which was decided the year after the Philadelphia Convention, Ingersoll found himself arguing against the principle announced in *James*. His client, a debtor named Hall, had been "discharged under an insolvent law of the state of Maryland, which is in the nature of a general bankrupt[cy] law." Prior to his discharge, Hall had incurred a debt to a Pennsylvanian named Millar. Hall neglected to mention that debt in his schedule of creditors presented to the Maryland court, or to personally notify Millar of the looming discharge. Following the Maryland court's order, Hall traveled to Pennsylvania and was promptly arrested for the unpaid debt to Millar.

Responding to Millar's counsel's argument that the holding of *James* controlled, Ingersoll urged adoption of a rule that "the discharge of the Defendant in one state ought to be sufficient to discharge [a debtor] in every state." Absent such a rule, Ingersoll continued, "perpetual imprisonment must be the lot of every man who fails; and all hope of retrieving his losses by honest and industrious pursuits, will be cut off from the unfortunate bankrupt." *Ibid.* The court accepted this argument. Allowing a creditor to execute "upon [a debtor's] person out of the state in which he has been discharged," the court explained, "would be giving a superiority to some creditors, and affording them a double satisfaction—to wit, a proportionable dividend of his property there, and the imprisonment of his person here." *Id.* Indeed, the debtor having already been obliged to surrender all of his effects, "to permit the taking [of] his person here, would be to attempt to compel him to perform an impossibility, that is, to pay a debt after he has been deprived of every means of payment—an attempt which would, at least, amount to perpetual imprisonment, unless the benevolence of his friends should interfere to discharge [his] account." *Ibid.*

These two cases illustrate the backdrop against which the Bankruptcy Clause was adopted. In both *James* and *Millar,* the debtors argued that the earlier discharge should be given preclusive effect pursuant to the Full Faith and Credit Clause of the Articles of Confederation. That possibility was the subject of discussion at the Constitutional Convention when a proposal to encompass legislative Acts, and insolvency laws in particular, within the coverage of the Full Faith and Credit Clause of the Constitution was committed to the Committee of Detail[8] together with a proposal "'[t]o establish uniform laws upon the subject of bankruptcies, and respecting the damages arising on the protest of foreign bills of exchange.'" See Nadelmann, *On the Origin of the Bankruptcy Clause*, 1 Am. J. Legal Hist. 215, 216-217, 219 (1957); see also Plank, *The Constitutional Limits of Bankruptcy*, 63 Tenn. L.Rev. 487, 527-528 (1996). A few days after this proposal was taken under advisement, the Committee of Detail reported that it had recommended adding the power "'[t]o establish uniform laws upon the subject of bankruptcies'" to the Naturalization Clause of what later became Article I.

The Convention adopted the Committee's recommendation with very little debate two days later. Roger Sherman of Connecticut alone voted against it, apparently because he was concerned that it would authorize Congress to impose upon American citizens the ultimate penalty for debt then in effect in England: death. See J. MADISON, NOTES OF DEBATES IN THE FEDERAL CONVENTION OF 1787. The absence of extensive debate over the text of the Bankruptcy Clause or its insertion indicates that there was general agreement on the importance of authorizing a uniform federal response to the problems presented in cases like *James* and *Millar*.[9]

III.

Bankruptcy jurisdiction, as understood today and at the time of the framing, is principally *in rem* jurisdiction. In bankruptcy, "the court's jurisdiction is premised on the debtor and his estate, and not on the creditors." *Hood*. As such, its exercise does not, in the usual case, interfere with state sovereignty even when States' interests are affected.

The text of Article I, § 8, cl. 4, of the Constitution, however, provides that Congress shall have the power to establish "uniform Laws on the subject of Bankruptcies throughout the United States." Although the interest in avoiding unjust imprisonment for debt and making federal discharges in bankruptcy

---

[8] The Committee of Detail was created by the Convention on July 25, 1787, to prepare a draft text of the Constitution based on delegates' proposals.

[9] Of course, the Bankruptcy Clause, located as it is in Article I, is "'intimately connected'" not just with the Full Faith and Credit Clause, which appears in Article IV of the Constitution, but also with the Commerce Clause. That does not mean, however, that the state sovereign immunity implications of the Bankruptcy Clause necessarily mirror those of the Commerce Clause. Indeed, the Bankruptcy Clause's unique history, combined with the singular nature of bankruptcy courts' jurisdiction, discussed *infra*, have persuaded us that the ratification of the Bankruptcy Clause does represent a surrender by the States of their sovereign immunity in certain federal proceedings. That conclusion is implicit in our holding in *Tennessee Student Assistance Corporation v. Hood.*

enforceable in every State was a primary motivation for the adoption of that provision, its coverage encompasses the entire "subject of Bankruptcies." The power granted to Congress by that Clause is a unitary concept rather than an amalgam of discrete segments.

The Framers would have understood that laws "on the subject of Bankruptcies" included laws providing, in certain limited respects, for more than simple adjudications of rights in the res. The first bankruptcy statute, for example, gave bankruptcy commissioners appointed by the district court the power, *inter alia,* to imprison recalcitrant third parties in possession of the estate's assets. See Bankruptcy Act of 1800, § 14 (repealed 1803). More generally, courts adjudicating disputes concerning bankrupts' estates historically have had the power to issue ancillary orders enforcing their *in rem* adjudications. See, *e.g.,* 2 W. BLACKSTONE, COMMENTARIES ON THE LAWS OF ENGLAND (noting that the assignees of the bankrupt's property—the 18th-century counterparts to today's bankruptcy trustees—could "pursue any *legal* method of recovering [the debtor's] property so vested in them," and could pursue methods in equity with the consent of the creditors); Plank, 63 Tenn. L. Rev., at 523 (discussing State insolvency and bankruptcy laws in the 18th century empowering courts to recover preferential transfers); see also *Ex parte Christy* (Story, J.) (describing bankruptcy jurisdiction under the 1841 Act in broad terms); *Wright v. Union Central Life Ins. Co.* (defining "bankruptcy" as the "'subject of the relations between an insolvent or nonpaying or fraudulent debtor and his creditors, *extending to his and their relief*" (emphasis added)).

Our decision in *Hood* illustrates the point. As the dissenters in that case pointed out, it was at least arguable that the particular procedure that the debtor pursued to establish dischargeability of her student loan could have been characterized as a suit against the State rather than a purely *in rem* proceeding. But because the proceeding was merely ancillary to the Bankruptcy Court's exercise of its *in rem* jurisdiction, we held that it did not implicate state sovereign immunity. The point is also illustrated by Congress' early grant to federal courts of the power to issue *in personam* writs of habeas corpus directing States to release debtors from state prisons, discussed in Part IV, *infra*. See *Braden v. 30th Judicial Circuit Court of Ky.,* ("The writ of habeas corpus does not act upon the prisoner who seeks relief, but upon the person who holds him in what is alleged to be unlawful custody").

The interplay between *in rem* adjudications and orders ancillary thereto is evident in the case before us. Respondent first seeks a determination under 11 U.S.C. § 547 that the various transfers made by the debtor to petitioners qualify as voidable preferences. The § 547 determination, standing alone, operates as a mere declaration of avoidance. That declaration may be all that the trustee wants; for example, if the State has a claim against the bankrupt estate, the avoidance determination operates to bar that claim until the preference is turned over. See § 502(d). In some cases, though, the trustee, in order to marshal the entirety of the debtor's estate, will need to recover the subject of the transfer pursuant to § 550(a). A court order mandating turnover of the property, although ancillary to and in furtherance of the court's *in rem* jurisdiction, might itself involve *in personam* process.

As we explain in Part IV, *infra*, it is not necessary to decide whether actions to recover preferential transfers pursuant to § 550(a) are themselves properly characterized as *in rem*.[10] Whatever the appropriate appellation, those who crafted the Bankruptcy Clause would have understood it to give Congress the power to authorize courts to avoid preferential transfers and to recover the transferred property. Petitioners do not dispute that that authority has been a core aspect of the administration of bankrupt estates since at least the 18th century. See, *e.g., Rust v. Cooper* (K.B.1777); *Alderson v. Temple* (K.B.1768); see also McCoid, *Bankruptcy, Preferences, and Efficiency: An Expression of Doubt*, 67 Va. L.Rev. 249, 251-253 (1981) (discussing English precedents, dating back to Sir Edward Coke's discussion in *The Case of Bankrupts*, addressing bankruptcy commissioners' power to avoid preferences). And it, like the authority to issue writs of habeas corpus releasing debtors from state prisons, see Part IV, *infra*, operates free and clear of the State's claim of sovereign immunity.

---

[10] The proper characterization of such actions is not as clear as petitioners suggest. The Court in *Nordic Village, Inc.* stated, as an alternative basis for rejecting a bankruptcy trustee's argument that a suit to avoid a preferential transfer made to the Internal Revenue Service was an action *in rem*, that any *in rem* "exception" to sovereign immunity was unavailable in that case because the trustee sought to recover a "sum of money, not 'particular dollars.'" There was, in the Court's view, "no *res* to which the [bankruptcy] court's *in rem* jurisdiction could have attached." *Ibid.* In making that determination, the Court distinguished our earlier decision in *United States v. Whiting Pools, Inc.* which held that the debtor's "estate," the res, "includes property of the debtor that has been seized by a creditor prior to the filing of a [bankruptcy] petition." *Id.*; see also *Begier v. IRS* ("'property of the debtor' subject to the preferential transfer provision is best understood as that property that would have been part of the estate had it not been transferred before the commencement of bankruptcy proceedings"). We observe that the trustee in this case, unlike the one in *Nordic Village*, seeks, in the alternative, both return of the "value" of the preference, see 11 U.S.C. § 550(a), and return of the actual "property transferred." See Brief for Respondent ("Respondent invokes the *in rem* jurisdiction of the bankruptcy court to recover under section 550 'the property transferred'").

IV.

Insofar as orders ancillary to the bankruptcy courts' *in rem* jurisdiction, like orders directing turnover of preferential transfers, implicate States' sovereign immunity from suit, the States agreed in the plan of the Convention not to assert that immunity. So much is evidenced not only by the history of the Bankruptcy Clause, which shows that the Framers' primary goal was to prevent competing sovereigns' interference with the debtor's discharge, see Part II, *supra,* but also by legislation considered and enacted in the immediate wake of the Constitution's ratification.

Congress considered proposed legislation establishing uniform federal bankruptcy laws in the first and each succeeding Congress until 1800, when the first Bankruptcy Act was passed. See C. WARREN, BANKRUPTCY IN UNITED STATES HISTORY ("[I]n the very first session of the 1st Congress, during which only the most necessary subjects of legislation were considered, bankruptcy was one of those subjects; and as early as June 1, 1789, a Committee of the House was named to prepare a bankruptcy bill"). The Bankruptcy Act of 1800 was in many respects a copy of the English bankruptcy statute then in force. It was, like the English law, chiefly a measure designed to benefit creditors. Like the English statute, its principal provisions permitted bankruptcy commissioners, on appointment by a federal district court, to arrest the debtor; to "cause the doors of the dwelling-house of [the] bankrupt to be broken"; to seize and collect the debtor's assets; to examine the debtor and any individuals who might have possession of the debtor's property; and to issue a "certificate of discharge" once the estate had been distributed.

The American legislation differed slightly from the English, however. That difference reflects both the uniqueness of a system involving multiple sovereigns and the concerns that lay at the core of the Bankruptcy Clause itself. The English statute gave a judge sitting on a court where the debtor had obtained his discharge the power to order a sheriff, "Bailiff or Officer, Gaoler or Keeper of any Prison" to release the "Bankrupt out of Custody" if he were arrested subsequent to the discharge. 5 Geo. 2, ch. 30, ¶ 13 (1732). The American version of this provision was worded differently; it specifically granted federal courts the authority to issue writs of habeas corpus effective to release debtors from state prisons. See also *In re Comstock* (Vt.1842) (observing that Bankruptcy Act of 1800, then repealed, would have granted a federal court the power to issue a writ of habeas corpus to release a debtor from state prison if he had been arrested following his bankruptcy discharge).

This grant of habeas power is remarkable not least because it would be another 67 years, after ratification of the Fourteenth Amendment, before the writ would be made generally available to state prisoners. See *Ex parte Royall*.[11] Moreover, the provision of the 1800 Act granting that power was considered and adopted during a period when state sovereign immunity could hardly have been more prominent among the Nation's concerns. *Chisholm v. Georgia*, the case that had so "shock[ed]" the country in its lack of regard for state sovereign immunity was decided in 1793. The ensuing five years that culminated in adoption of the Eleventh Amendment were rife with discussion of States' sovereignty and their amenability to suit. Yet there appears to be no record of any objection to the bankruptcy legislation or its grant of habeas power to federal courts based on an infringement of sovereign immunity.

This history strongly supports the view that the Bankruptcy Clause of Article I, the source of Congress' authority to effect this intrusion upon state sovereignty, simply did not contravene the norms this Court has understood the Eleventh Amendment to exemplify. Cf. *Blatchford v. Native Village of Noatak* ("[W]e have understood the Eleventh Amendment to stand not so much for what it says, but for the presupposition of our constitutional structure which it confirms...").[12] Petitioners, ignoring this history, contend that nothing in the *words* of the Bankruptcy Clause evinces an intent on the part of the Framers to

---

[11] The Judiciary Act of 1789 authorized issuance of the writ, but only to release those held in *federal* custody. Also, in the interim between 1800 and 1867, Congress authorized limited issuance of the writ in response to two crises it viewed as sufficiently pressing to warrant a federal response: The South Carolina nullification controversy of 1828-1833 and the imprisonment of a foreign national by New York State a few years later....

[12] Further evidence of the Framers' intent to exempt laws "on the subject of Bankruptcies" from the operation of state sovereign immunity principles can be gleaned from § 62 of the Bankruptcy Act of 1800. That section provided that "nothing contained in this law shall, in any manner, affect the right of preference to prior satisfaction of debts due to the United States as secured or provided by any law heretofore passed, nor shall be construed to lessen or impair any right to, or security for, money due to the United States or to any of them." That Congress felt the need to carve out an exception for States' preferences undermines any suggestion that it was operating against a background presumption of state sovereign immunity to bankruptcy laws. Indeed, one contemporary commentator read this section of the Act as requiring that the protected "priorit[ies]" would have to be "specifically given by some act of the Legislature of the Union" before they would be exempt from operation of the Act's provisions. See T. COOPER, THE BANKRUPT LAW OF AMERICA, COMPARED WITH THE BANKRUPT LAW OF ENGLAND (1801) ("But I do not apprehend [that] this extends to give any priority to the United States, not specifically given by some act of the Legislature of the Union; nor will the English doctrine of priorities in favour of the crown be extended by analogy into this country").

alter the "background principle" of state sovereign immunity. Specifically, they deny that the word "uniform" in the Clause implies anything about pre-existing immunities or Congress' power to interfere with those immunities. Whatever the merits of petitioners' argument,[13] it misses the point; text aside, the Framers, in adopting the Bankruptcy Clause, plainly intended to give Congress the power to redress the rampant injustice resulting from States' refusal to respect one another's discharge orders. As demonstrated by the First Congress' immediate consideration and the Sixth Congress' enactment of a provision granting federal courts the authority to release debtors from state prisons, the power to enact bankruptcy legislation was understood to carry with it the power to subordinate state sovereignty, albeit within a limited sphere.

The ineluctable conclusion, then, is that States agreed in the plan of the Convention not to assert any sovereign immunity defense they might have had

---

[13] Petitioners make much of precedents suggesting that the word "uniform" represents a limitation, rather than an expansion, of Congress' legislative power in the bankruptcy sphere. See, *e.g., Gibbons* ("Unlike the Commerce Clause, the Bankruptcy Clause itself contains an affirmative limitation or restriction upon Congress' power: bankruptcy laws must be uniform throughout the United States"). They also cite Justice Frankfurter's concurring opinion in *Vanston Bondholders Protective Comm. v. Green*, for the proposition that "[t]he Constitutional requirement of uniformity is a requirement of geographic uniformity." Based on these authorities, petitioners argue that the word "uniform" in the Bankruptcy Clause cannot be interpreted to confer upon Congress any greater authority to impinge upon state sovereign immunity than is conferred, for example, by the Commerce Clause.

Petitioners' logic is not persuasive. Although our analysis does not rest on the peculiar text of the Bankruptcy Clause as compared to other Clauses of Article I, we observe that, if anything, the mandate to enact "uniform" laws supports the historical evidence showing that the States agreed not to assert their sovereign immunity in proceedings brought pursuant to "Laws on the subject of Bankruptcies." That Congress is constrained to enact laws that are uniform in application, whether geographically or otherwise, cf. *Gibbons* (invalidating a bankruptcy law aimed at "one regional bankrupt railroad" and no one else), does not imply that it *lacks power* to enact bankruptcy legislation that is uniform in a more robust sense. As our holding today demonstrates, Congress has the power to enact bankruptcy laws the purpose and effect of which are to ensure uniformity in treatment of state and private creditors. See *Sturges v. Crowninshield* (Marshall, C.J.) ("The peculiar terms of the grant certainly deserve notice. Congress is not authorized merely to pass laws, the operation of which shall be uniform, but to *establish* uniform laws on the subject throughout the United States"); see also *In re Dehon, Inc.* (Bkrtcy. D.Mass.2005) (discussing THE FEDERALIST Nos. 32 and 81 (A.Hamilton) (pointing to the "uniform[ity]" language of the Naturalization Clause, which appears in the same clause of Article I as the bankruptcy provision, as an example of an instance where the Framers contemplated a "surrender of [States'] immunity in the plan of the convention").

in proceedings brought pursuant to "Laws on the subject of Bankruptcies." See *Blatchford* (observing that a State is not "subject to suit in federal court unless it has consented to suit, either expressly or in the 'plan of the convention'").[14] The scope of this consent was limited; the jurisdiction exercised in bankruptcy proceedings was chiefly *in rem*—a narrow jurisdiction that does not implicate state sovereignty to nearly the same degree as other kinds of jurisdiction. But while the principal focus of the bankruptcy proceedings is and was always the res, some exercises of bankruptcy courts' powers—issuance of writs of habeas corpus included—unquestionably involved more than mere adjudication of rights in a res. In ratifying the Bankruptcy Clause, the States acquiesced in a subordination of whatever sovereign immunity they might otherwise have asserted in proceedings necessary to effectuate the *in rem* jurisdiction of the bankruptcy courts.[15]

V.

Neither our decision in *Hood*, which held that States could not assert sovereign immunity as a defense in adversary proceedings brought to adjudicate the dischargeability of student loans, nor the cases upon which it relied rested on any statement Congress had made on the subject of state sovereign immunity. Nor does our decision today. The relevant question is not whether Congress has "abrogated" States' immunity in proceedings to recover preferential transfers. *See* 11 U.S.C. § 106(a).[16] The question, rather, is whether Congress' determination that States should be amenable to such proceedings is within the scope of its power to enact "Laws on the subject of Bankruptcies." We think it beyond peradventure that it is.

Congress may, at its option, either treat States in the same way as other creditors insofar as concerns "Laws on the subject of Bankruptcies" or exempt them from operation of such laws. Its power to do so arises from the

---

[14] One might object that the writ of habeas corpus was no infringement on state sovereignty, and would not have been understood as such, because that writ, being in the nature of an injunction against a state official, does not commence or constitute a suit against the State. See *Ex parte Young*. While that objection would be supported by precedent today, it would not have been apparent to the Framers. The *Ex parte Young* doctrine was not finally settled until over a century after the Framing and the enactment of the first bankruptcy statute. Indeed, we have recently characterized the doctrine as an expedient "fiction" necessary to ensure the supremacy of federal law.

[15] We do not mean to suggest that every law labeled a "bankruptcy" law could, consistent with the Bankruptcy Clause, properly impinge upon state sovereign immunity.

[16] Cf. *Hoffman* (holding that, in an earlier version of 11 U.S.C. § 106, Congress had failed to make sufficiently clear its intent to abrogate state sovereign immunity).

Bankruptcy Clause itself; the relevant "abrogation" is the one effected in the plan of the Convention, not by statute.

....

It is so ordered.

■ Justice THOMAS, with whom THE CHIEF JUSTICE, Justice SCALIA, and Justice KENNEDY join, dissenting.

[Omitted].

NOTE

Katz, removes much of the uncertainty in the enforcement of the Bankruptcy Code against the States and places States on the same footing as the federal and foreign governments as well as local governments that never benefited from the Eleventh Amendment.

Still caveats remain. Footnote 15 in the *Katz* majority opinion notes that the Court is not suggesting that "every law labeled a 'bankruptcy' law [can] ... properly impinge upon state sovereign immunity." This raises the question as to whether claims based on the Bankruptcy Code but dealing with matters further afield from the traditional core of bankruptcy law than ordinary automatic stay, discharge and preference litigation, can be enforced against States without running afoul of the Eleventh Amendment. Moreover, causes of action brought before bankruptcy courts that, unlike the preference suit at issue in *Katz*, are grounded on applicable nonbankruptcy law, may still be subject to the sovereign immunity defense. In particular it is unclear how broadly waivers of sovereign immunity in connection with counterclaims seeking affirmative recovery against States based upon nonbankruptcy causes of action will be applied.

As with any affirmative defense, States may waive their sovereign immunity. Indeed the waiver may be implied from such conduct as filing or asserting a claim in the bankruptcy proceeding, at least to the extent of counterclaims arising out of the same transaction or set-offs that reduce the estate's liability on the claim, and perhaps to a greater extent. The fullest recent statement of the scope of waiver occasioned by the State's filing of a proof of claim is *Arecibo Community Health Care, Inc. v. Puerto Rico*, 270 F.3d 17 (1st Cir. 2001) (on rehearing). In *Arecibo*, the First Circuit found that Puerto Rico's (Puerto Rico enjoys 11th Amendment immunity as if it were a State) decision to assert a claim for breach of contract in the amount of $1.65 million exposed it to the debtor in bankruptcy's compulsory counterclaim in excess of $8.2 million arising out of the same contract. As to reducing the debtor's liability on account of Puerto Rico's claim, the result upholding waiver was foreordained by pre-*Seminole Tribe* precedent at both the Supreme Court and Court of Appeals level. *See Gardner v. New Jersey*, 329 U.S. 565 (1947). More difficult was the question whether the filing of the claim exposed the State to net affirmative liability. The First Circuit acknowledged that the issue was unsettled in most of the circuits, but wrote:

> Where a state avails itself of the federal courts to protect a claim, we think it reasonable to consider that action to waive the state's immunity *in toto* and, therefore, to construe that waiver to encompass compulsory counterclaims, even though they could require affirmative recovery from the state. The alternative approach would have the unfortunate effect of preventing the complete adjudication of the claims in a single forum, undermining the principles that led the framers of the Federal Rules to compel the litigation of certain counterclaims as a part of a single lawsuit.

270 F.3d at 28.

B. Venue

1. Commencement of the Case

The Bankruptcy Code's venue provisions are found at 28 U.S.C. §§ 1408–1412. Under 28 U.S.C. § 1408(1), for a non-business individual the petition may be filed in the district in which the debtor has resided or was domiciled for the 180 days preceding the filing. An alternative basis for venue for such an individual would be the location of the debtor's principal assets, but in the typical case these would be in the same district as the residence.

For business debtors a petition may be filed under 28 U.S.C. § 1408 in any district where (1) the debtor resides or is domiciled (for an entity this is usually the state under whose laws the entity is organized); (2) the debtor's principal place of business (usually the company's headquarters); (3) the debtor's principal assets are located; (4) an affiliate's bankruptcy is pending; or (5) wherever the case has been filed if no one moves to transfer or dismiss the case as one filed in an improper venue under Rule 1014(a)(2). The combination of the affiliate rule and the state of incorporation rule provides great flexibility to a business operating through large numbers of affiliated entities. For example, searching for a basis for venue in the Southern District of New York, Eastern Airlines chose to file first a New York subsidiary operating its frequent flyer lounges in New York and then file the airline itself and its other subsidiaries under the affiliate rule, even though they were not New York corporations or otherwise eligible for venue there. Thus, all the reported decisions in the *Eastern Airlines* case carry the caption *In re Ionosphere Clubs, Inc.*

In their study of large Chapter 11 cases, Professors Lynn LoPucki and William Whitford found forum-shopping in a significant percentage of cases. *Venue Choice and Forum Shopping in The Bankruptcy Reorganization of Large, Publicly Held Companies*, 1991 Wis.L.Rev. 11. They found that some companies changed their corporate headquarters before filing. In a number of cases in which debtors filed in the district where their headquarters was located, the debtors had no significant assets or other operations in the district. Some corporations like Eastern Airlines filed in the affiliate's district after the affiliate had filed, often only minutes after the affiliate had filed. One may speculate on the reasons for forum-shopping. Debtors may prefer to file in jurisdictions thought to be more pro-debtor or at least avoid pro-creditor courts. New York may attract filings because of its large and high quality bankruptcy bar. In some cases debtors apparently choose a venue for their convenience or that of their attorneys. Sometimes forum-shopping may be driven by concerns about adverse appellate decisions in particular circuits on crucial issues. In recent years Delaware, the state of incorporation for many large corporations, as well as New York, has become a venue of choice in large Chapter 11 reorganizations. Probably the most important factor for large companies with a choice of venues is the major parties' (including the debtor, principal secured lenders and prospective purchasers) confidence that they understand (and can live with) the chosen venue's procedures and the substantive limitations the judges in that district are likely to impose on the major parties. Given the large number of New York and Delaware cases, the predilections of the judges in those districts with respect to the administration of large Chapter 11 cases are generally well known.

The large number of New York and Delaware filings that are clear examples of forum shopping by debtors has caused some to question the propriety of the liberal bankruptcy venue statutes. The National Bankruptcy Review Commission has recommended eliminating state of incorporation filing completely and affiliate filing unless debtor's corporate parent is a debtor in that forum. *NBRC Rep.* at 770–771 (Recommendation 3.1.5). There have been complaints that New York and Delaware bankruptcy judges have allowed their eagerness to maintain the flow of large Chapter 11 cases into their jurisdictions to cloud their judgment in confirming reorganization plans and perhaps in other matters affecting administration of debtors' estates. Lynn LoPucki and Sara Kalin have shown that the refiling rate for New York and Delaware Chapter 11 debtors is six to seven times as high as it is elsewhere for large public companies. Their controversial conclusion is: "Competing courts attract filings by applying lax standards for plan confirmation that lead to excessive refiling rates." Lynn M. LoPucki & Sara D. Kalin, *The Failure of Public Company Bankruptcies in Delaware and New York: Empirical Evidence of a "Race to the Bottom,"* 54

Vand.L.Rev. 231, 237 (2001). Professor LoPucki has expanded his analysis of the subject in his book, COURTING FAILURE (2005). Defenders of the status quo respond by suggesting that New York and Delaware courts are tackling more difficult reorganization cases, that bankruptcy courts generally are not well situated to scrutinize plan feasibility, that the virtues of having certain jurisdictions with wide experience in large Chapter 11 cases outweigh the resulting problems, and that to the extent there are problems the Delaware and New York bankruptcy courts can be expected to promptly correct them. David A. Skeel, *What's So Bad About Delaware?*, 54 Vand.L.Rev. 309 (2001). As a political matter, the New York reorganization bar and Delaware's small but tenacious Congressional delegation have been strongly committed to, and thus far entirely successful in, preserving liberal venue provisions against all objections.

Section 1412 states: "A district court may transfer a case or proceeding under title 11 to a district court for another district, in the interest of justice or for the convenience of the parties." The factors courts consider in deciding whether to transfer a case were stated in *In re Commonwealth Oil Refining Co.*, 596 F.2d 1239 (5th Cir. 1979), to be: (1) proximity of creditors; (2) proximity of debtor; (3) proximity of witnesses; (4) location of assets; and (5) promotion of the economic and efficient administration of the estate. Critics complain, however, that the venue chosen by the debtor is almost never successfully challenged in large Chapter 11 cases.

PROBLEM

Debtor filed a petition for voluntary bankruptcy in New Jersey where Debtor resides. Without knowledge of this petition, Debtor's creditors then filed an involuntary petition in New York where Debtor's principal place of business is located. How is the conflict resolved? Bankruptcy Rule 1014(b).

2. PROCEEDINGS IN THE CASE

Venue with respect to proceedings "arising under title 11 or arising in or related to a case under title 11" is governed by 28 U.S.C. § 1409. Subsection (a) states the general rule that these proceedings may be brought in the court where the case is pending, sometimes called the "home court." Subsection (b) carves out an exception for small claims. Trustees must sue nonresident non-insider defendants in the defendant's district if the claim is less than $10,950. Moreover, a trustee's claim to collect a consumer debt of less than $16,425 must be prosecuted in the nonresident defendant's district regardless of the debtor's insider status. In small transactions the inconvenience to nonresident defendants of defending outside their district is often greater than the value of the claim. These venue rules shift the burden of litigation to the trustee and make it impractical for trustees to collect small claims against nonresident defendants through litigation whatever the merits.

Subsection (c) offers an alternative to the home court rule of subsection (a) if the trustee is suing as a statutory successor to the debtor under § 541 or to a creditor under § 544(b). Under § 541 the bankruptcy estate may include causes of action and the trustee may be suing as the debtor's statutory successor. Section 544(b) allows the trustee to avoid transfers or obligations that are voidable by creditors having allowable unsecured claims. Taking 28 U.S.C. § 1409(a) and (c) together, the trustee has the alternative of suing either in the home court or in the district court of the district that would have had venue had the debtor or creditor brought suit under nonbankruptcy law. Subsection (c) is expressly made subject to subsection (b).

With respect to a postpetition claim by the trustee against others arising out of the operation of the debtor's business, subsection (d) provides that the trustee may sue only in a district in which the suit could have been brought under nonbankruptcy law. With respect to a postpetition cause of action against the bankruptcy estate arising out of the operation of the debtor's business, subsection (e) states that the suit may be brought either in the "home court" or in a district in which the suit could have been brought under nonbankruptcy law.

C. APPELLATE JURISDICTION

Perhaps the only set of jurisdictional statutes more complex and confusing than those vesting original bankruptcy jurisdiction are those vesting the appellate bankruptcy jurisdiction.

In the First, Sixth, Eighth, Ninth and Tenth Circuits both bankruptcy appellate panels (BAPs) and federal district courts may hear appeals from both interlocutory orders and final decisions of bankruptcy judges. Elsewhere all appeals are routed to the local district court (except in those few instances where a direct appeal from the bankruptcy court is certified and accepted by the Court of Appeals under 28 U.S.C. § 158(d)(2)). The bankruptcy appellate panels do not have regular full-time appellate judges. Rather they consist of three ordinary bankruptcy judges selected from districts within the circuit other than the district from which the appeal being heard arises. Appeals to the district courts are assigned to a single district judge on a rotating basis in accordance with local rules or practice.

The appellate jurisdiction statutes provide that in Circuits where a BAP is functioning and the local district court by majority vote of the local district judges has specifically authorized that appeals from that district may be heard by that BAP, unless one of the parties specifically demands that the appeal be routed to the local district court (or "opts-out"), the regional BAP hears the initial appeal. If the matter is "non-core" and the parties have not consented to entry of a final judgement by the bankruptcy judge, then in lieu of an initial appeal to the district court or BAP, there is a right of *de novo* review in the district court. *De novo* review may involve rehearing evidence but commonly it is limited to review of the recommended disposition of the bankruptcy court on the record created in the bankruptcy court.

In the Ninth Circuit, where BAPs have operated since 1979, the quality of work done by BAPs is well regarded, but controversy has surrounded the precedential weight to be accorded their decisions.

Of the 3210 appeals taken in 2007, 2290 were filed in district courts and 920 in BAPs. The Ninth Circuit BAP alone docketed 507 cases representing 60% of appeals from the bankruptcy courts of that Circuit. 2007 Annual Report of the Director of the Administrative Office of the US Courts, Tbl. B-1; <http://pacer.bap09.uscourts.gov>. The National Bankruptcy Review Commission found that "[t]he problems that arise from a lack of effective *stare decisis* in a two-tier appellate system can not be overestimated." *NBRC Rep.* at 754. Daniel J. Bussel, *Power, Authority, and Precedent in Interpreting the Bankruptcy Code*, 41 UCLA L.Rev. 1063, 1071–75, 1094 (1994) (footnotes omitted), discusses the precedential questions that have arisen with regard to both BAPs and district court decisions:

> [B]ankruptcy courts in several jurisdictions have expressly refused to follow both district court and Bankruptcy Appellate Panel (BAP) precedents.
>
> * * *
>
> Bankruptcy courts rejecting district court precedents offer two distinct sets of arguments: one formal and one policy-based. The formal argument, typified by *In re Rheuban* [128 B.R. 551 (Bankr.C.D. Cal.1991)], suggests that a bankruptcy court, as a "unit" of the district court, is not "inferior" to a single district judge in a multi-judge district. *Rheuban* and similar cases assume that the principle of stare decisis binds only "inferior" courts, and conclude that bankruptcy courts are therefore not bound by district court decisions. * * *
>
> * * *
>
> Other bankruptcy courts supplement the formal *Rheuban* argument with a more policy oriented one. For example, in *In re Gaylor* [123 B.R. 236 (Bankr.E.D.Mich.1991)], the court recognized that one benefit of stare decisis is limiting the number of appeals. Appeals are costly to litigants and society, and lower court departures from established reviewing court precedent would surely multiply appeals. Stare decisis discourages appeals, but this function is served only when litigants have

reason to believe that the reviewing court will adhere to its prior decisions. District judges, *Gaylor* notes, have no obligation to follow prior decisions of other judges even within the same district.

With respect to the non-binding effect of BAP decisions, bankruptcy courts [e.g., *In re Standard Brands Paint Co.*, 154 B.R. 563, 568 n.3 (Bankr.C.D.Cal.1993)] and commentators make an essentially derivative argument: The BAP sits "in lieu of" the district court, and its precedent-setting power is limited to that of the district court in lieu of which it sits. Early versions of this "in lieu" argument suggested that BAP opinions had stare decisis effect only within the district from whence appeal was taken, rather than circuit-wide. Later versions of the argument suggest that since district court opinions do not bind bankruptcy courts for the reasons described above, then neither can BAP opinions. Of course, if one adopts the view that district court opinions *do* have stare decisis effect, this technical argument falls on its own terms.

At least one bankruptcy court in the Central District of California has advanced a formal argument suggesting BAP precedents are binding [*In re Globe Illumination Co.*, 149 B.R. 614 (Bankr.C.D. Cal.1993)]. According to this court, the jurisdictional statutes and Ninth Circuit rules make the BAP an "adjunct" of the United States Court of Appeals, which all apparently concede has the power to bind the bankruptcy courts (and for that matter the federal district courts) within the geographic area of the Ninth Circuit. As an "adjunct" of the Court of Appeals, the BAP shares the Ninth Circuit's power to create binding precedents circuit-wide, presumably on district as well as bankruptcy courts.

These formal arguments for and against the BAPs' authoritativeness, regardless of their technical merit, all share the premises of the *Rheuban* and *Gaylor* courts: that the rule of stare decisis is a deduction from the hierarchical nature of the judicial system and a related interest in judicial economy.

* * *

* * * [S]tripping the BAP of its ability to make precedents leads one to question the BAP's institutional role as an expert appellate panel. If the BAP cannot assist in the orderly and coherent development of bankruptcy law, it serves no function beyond case-by-case error-correction, a function the federal district court can serve at less cost. Deploying three expert Article I bankruptcy judges with all the appellate formalities solely to correct errors in individual cases and not to clarify the law seems an oddly wasteful experiment to impute to the Congress. I am unaware of any evidence or plausible rationale suggesting that Congress in fact intended to so limit the Bankruptcy Appellate Panels.

* * *

Given the existing structure of the bankruptcy appellate system, if interstitial law is going to be made by appellate courts, the lion's share of the burden must fall on the first-tier court. Both the district court (acting in an appellate capacity) and the BAP are institutionally competent to assume the law-making function * * *. Allocating law-making authority to these appellate courts results in a reasonable division of authority and labor between the appellate and trial courts and appropriately dilutes and constrains the otherwise relatively uncabined power of the bankruptcy court. * * *

Although the bankruptcy jurisdictional statutes provide for district court and BAP jurisdiction over interlocutory appeals from bankruptcy court decisions, further appeals up the system to the Courts of Appeals lie only from final orders from either the BAPs or the district court or from those limited types of interlocutory orders reviewable under the general jurisdictional statutes of the Courts of Appeals—the grant or denial of injunctions, certified appeals and a special bankruptcy exception for interlocutory orders modifying the statutory period during which the debtor has the exclusive right to file a reorganization plan in Chapter 11 cases.

Because (i) the jurisdiction of the Courts of Appeals is limited to final orders, (ii) the bankruptcy case serves as an umbrella proceeding in which many discrete proceedings are litigated, (iii) initial appeals of interlocutory orders to BAP and district court are available and (iv) final orders entered at the bankruptcy court may be subject to further proceedings after the initial appeal to the BAP or district court, it becomes necessary to make difficult judgments about the meaning of finality in the context of a bankruptcy case at the Court of Appeals level. Most Courts of Appeals have tended to adopt a relatively loose "pragmatic" view of finality in bankruptcy cases in order to allow meaningful appellate review to occur on important questions. 16 Charles A. Wright, et al., *Federal Practice and Procedure: Jurisdiction* 2d § 3926.2 (2d ed.1996). But the "pragmatic" approach has led to substantial confusion and inconsistency in the caselaw and seems to turn primarily on the appellate court's perception of the importance of the issue and the effect of the lower court ruling on the parties. One of the most important unresolved questions is the appealability of district court's remand order from an appeal of an otherwise final bankruptcy court order. There is great disarray in the cases over the question of whether the fact that the remand requires substantial new proceedings in the bankruptcy court converts what was initially a final order into an interlocutory one.

In addition to the issue of finality, mootness is frequently a problem at the Court of Appeals level. Mootness commonly results when parties rely on unstayed orders of the bankruptcy court in a way that makes it impossible for an appellate court to fashion meaningful relief without creating injustice. The Courts of Appeals, of course, have no jurisdiction over moot cases and must dismiss appeals in these circumstances. 13A Charles A. Wright et al., *Federal Practice and Procedure: Jurisdiction* 2d § 3533 (2d ed.1996). In addition, the Bankruptcy Code itself precludes appellate review of postpetition financing orders and bankruptcy sales absent a stay. §§ 363(m) & 364(e). *But see Matter of Saybrook Mfg. Co.*, p. 628, and *In re PW, LLC*, p. 648. Traditional statements of the bankruptcy mootness doctrine can be found in *In re Continental Airlines*, 91 F.3d 553, 565 (3d Cir. *en banc* 1996) and *In re Roberts Farms, Inc.*, 652 F.2d 739 (9th Cir. 1981). Perhaps in recent years appellate courts have begun to exhibit more willingness to review appeals from unstayed confirmation orders. See, *e.g.*, *In re 203 North LaSalle Street Partnership*, 126 F.3d 955, 961 (7th Cir. 1997), *rev'd on other grounds*, 526 U.S. 434 (1999).

Given the intervening level of appellate review and the mootness and finality barriers to review, relatively few bankruptcy appeals reach the Courts of Appeals. Appeals from the Courts of Appeals are available as a matter of discretion in the Supreme Court on writ of certiorari under the Supreme Court's general jurisdictional statutes. But the Supreme Court reviews only a few bankruptcy cases each year.

Under 28 U.S. § 158(d)(1), the Courts of Appeals have jurisdiction over appeals from all final decisions, judgments, orders, and decrees of the district courts and BAPs entered under § 158(a) and (b). BAPCPA Act added § 158(d)(2), which allows direct appeal to the Courts of Appeals under certain circumstances, making it possible to bypass district court or BAP review and appeal orders and decrees of the bankruptcy court directly to the Courts of Appeal. A court of appeals may authorize an immediate appeal of an order or decree, if the bankruptcy court, the district court, the BAP or the parties acting jointly certify that:

(I) the judgment, order or decree involves a question of law as to which there is no controlling decision of the court of appeals for the circuit or of the Supreme Court or involves a matter of public importance;

(II) the judgment, order or decree involves a question of law requiring resolution of conflicting decisions; or

(III) an immediate appeal from the judgment, order or decree may materially advance the progress of the case or the proceeding in which the appeal is taken.

An unusual innovation in new § 158(d)(2)(A) requires the court from whence the appeal originates to certify the appeal for direct review if "a majority of the appellants" and a "majority of the appellees" request such certification. The requirement of specific authorization from the court of appeals remains notwithstanding certification by the bankruptcy court, BAP or district court whether upon such court's own motion or the request of a majority of both appellants and appellees. The certification standard is analogous to that authorizing certification of interlocutory appeals under the general jurisdictional statutes of the United States Courts of Appeals—28 U.S.C. § 1292(b). Direct appeal appears to be available in cases involving interlocutory as well as final orders if the requisite certification is obtained. *Matter of Oca, Inc.*, 552 F.3d 413 (5th Cir. 2008).

In general, courts impose a very high standard for certification of appeals under § 1292(b) and certification is rarely granted. Some district courts adopt the § 1292(b) standard for determining when "leave of court" is appropriate in hearing an interlocutory appeal from the bankruptcy court under 28 U.S.C. § 158(a)(3), *see* 1 *Collier On Bankruptcy* ¶ 5.07[4] (15th ed. rev. 2008), but some courts apply a less rigorous standard. The ability of the parties or the bankruptcy court (in lieu of the district court) to certify a direct appeal and the absence of § 1292(b)'s controlling question language in § 158(d) may allow a looser standard than that of § 1292(b) and more analogous to the leave of court standard to develop. Since October 2005, approximately twenty direct appeals have been authorized, suggesting that the reform has been at least a modest success in generating greater certainty within the circuits over issues deemed to be sufficiently important. *Compare* Daniel J. Bussel, *Bankruptcy Appellate Reform: Issues and Options*, 1995-96 Ann. Surv. of Bankr. L. 257 (1995).

D. RIGHT TO JURY TRIAL

As part of the 1984 post-*Marathon* amendments, Congress enacted 28 U.S.C. § 1411. Section 1411 is one of Congress' more Delphic contributions to bankruptcy law:

> **(a)** Except as provided in subsection (b) of this section, this chapter and title 11 do not affect any right to trial by jury that an individual has under applicable nonbankruptcy law with regard to a personal injury or wrongful death tort claim.

(b) The district court may order the issues arising under section 303 of title 11 to be tried without a jury.

28 U.S.C. § 157(b)(5) requires that district courts rather than bankruptcy judges hear personal injury tort and wrongful death claims against the estate. Section 1411(a) requires that in cases in which these kinds of claims are asserted, the parties have a right of jury trial if they would have had this right in a trial of such claims outside bankruptcy. Having said that, where does § 1411(a) leave the law of trial by jury on all the other issues that might arise in bankruptcy? In footnote 3 of *Granfinanciera,* the case that follows, the Supreme Court describes 28 U.S.C. § 1411 as "notoriously ambiguous." If § 1411(a) excludes jury trials in all cases except those involving personal injuries or wrongful death claims, § 1411(b) is unneeded.

In *Granfinanciera* the Supreme Court, in its first case concerning the right to jury trial in bankruptcy under the Code, prescribed a role for juries in bankruptcy proceedings grounded on the Seventh Amendment, thereby transcending the ambiguities of 28 U.S.C. § 1411 and plunging bankruptcy and district courts into a most difficult task of arcane historically-based line-drawing.

Granfinanciera, S.A. v. Nordberg
Supreme Court of the United States, 1989.
492 U.S. 33.

■ BRENNAN, J., delivered the opinion of the Court, in which REHNQUIST, C.J., and MARSHALL, STEVENS, and KENNEDY, JJ., joined, and in Parts I, II, III, and V, of which SCALIA, J., joined. SCALIA, J., filed an opinion concurring in part and concurring in the judgment. White, J., filed a dissenting opinion. BLACKMUN, J., filed a dissenting opinion, in which O'CONNOR, J., joined.

The question presented is whether a person who has not submitted a claim against a bankruptcy estate has a right to a jury trial when sued by the trustee in bankruptcy to recover an allegedly fraudulent monetary transfer. We hold that the Seventh Amendment entitles such a person to a trial by jury, notwithstanding Congress' designation of fraudulent conveyance actions as "core proceedings" in 28 U.S.C. § 157(b)(2)(H).

I.

The Chase & Sanborn Corporation filed a petition for reorganization under Chapter 11 in 1983. A Plan of Reorganization approved by the United States Bankruptcy Court for the Southern District of Florida vested in respondent Nordberg, the trustee in bankruptcy, causes of action for fraudulent conveyances. In 1985, respondent filed suit against petitioners Granfinanciera, S.A. and Medex, Ltda. in the United States District Court for the Southern District of

Florida. The complaint alleged that petitioners had received $1.7 million from Chase & Sanborn's corporate predecessor within one year of the date its bankruptcy petition was filed, without receiving consideration or reasonably equivalent value in return. Respondent sought to avoid what it alleged were constructively and actually fraudulent transfers and to recover damages, costs, expenses, and interest under §§ 548(a)(1) and (a)(2), 550(a)(1).

The District Court referred the proceedings to the Bankruptcy Court. Over five months later, and shortly before the Colombian Government nationalized Granfinanciera, respondent served a summons on petitioners in Bogota, Colombia. In their answer to the complaint following Granfinanciera's nationalization, both petitioners requested a "trial by jury on all issues so triable." The Bankruptcy Judge denied petitioners' request for a jury trial, deeming a suit to recover a fraudulent transfer "a core action that originally, under the English common law, as I understand it, was a non-jury issue." Following a bench trial, the court dismissed with prejudice respondent's actual fraud claim but entered judgment for respondent on the constructive fraud claim in the amount of $1,500,000 against Granfinanciera and $180,000 against Medex. The District Court affirmed, without discussing petitioners' claim that they were entitled to a jury trial.

The Court of Appeals for the Eleventh Circuit also affirmed. The court found that petitioners lacked a statutory right to a jury trial, because the constructive fraud provision under which suit was brought—§ 548(a)(2)—contains no mention of a right to a jury trial and 28 U.S.C. § 1411 "affords jury trials only in personal injury or wrongful death suits." The Court of Appeals further ruled that the Seventh Amendment supplied no right to a jury trial, because actions to recover fraudulent conveyances are equitable in nature, even when a plaintiff seeks only monetary relief, and because "bankruptcy itself is equitable in nature and thus bankruptcy proceedings are inherently equitable." The court read our opinion in *Katchen v. Landy*, 382 U.S. 323 (1966), to say that "Congress may convert a creditor's legal right into an equitable claim and displace any seventh amendment right to trial by jury," and held that Congress had done so by designating fraudulent conveyance actions "core proceedings" triable by bankruptcy judges sitting without juries.

We granted certiorari to decide whether petitioners were entitled to a jury trial * * * and now reverse.

* * *

III.

Petitioners rest their claim to a jury trial on the Seventh Amendment alone.[3] The Seventh Amendment provides: "In Suits at common law, where the value in controversy shall exceed twenty dollars, the right of trial by jury shall be preserved * * *." We have consistently interpreted the phrase "Suits at common law" to refer to "suits in which *legal* rights were to be ascertained and determined, in contradistinction to those where equitable rights alone were recognized, and equitable remedies were administered." *Parsons v. Bedford*, 3 Pet. 433, 447 (1830). Although "the thrust of the Amendment was to preserve the right to jury trial as it existed in 1791," the Seventh Amendment also applies to actions brought to enforce statutory rights that are analogous to common-law causes of action ordinarily decided in English law courts in the late 18th century, as opposed to those customarily heard by courts of equity or admiralty. * * *

The form of our analysis is familiar. "First, we compare the statutory action to 18th-century actions brought in the courts of England prior to the merger

---

[3] The current statutory provision for jury trials in bankruptcy proceedings—28 U.S.C. § 1411 enacted as part of the Bankruptcy Amendments and Federal Judgeship Act of 1984 (1984 Amendments)—is notoriously ambiguous. Section 1411(a) provides: "[T]his chapter and title 11 do not affect any right to trial by jury that an individual has under applicable non-bankruptcy law with regard to a personal injury or wrongful death tort claim." Although this section might suggest that jury trials are available only in personal injury and wrongful death actions, that conclusion is debatable. Section 1411(b) provides that "[t]he district court may order the issues arising [in connection with involuntary bankruptcy petitions] to be tried without a jury," suggesting that the court lacks similar discretion to deny jury trials on at least some issues presented in connection with voluntary petitions. The confused legislative history of these provisions has further puzzled commentators. See, *e.g.*, Gibson, Jury Trials in Bankruptcy: Obeying the Commands of Article III and the Seventh Amendment, 72 Minn.L.Rev. 967, 989–996 (1988) (hereinafter Gibson); * * * Whatever the proper construction of § 1411, petitioners concede that this section does not entitle them to a jury trial. Section 122(b) of the 1984 Amendments, 98 Stat. 346, bars application of § 1411 to "cases under title 11 of the United States Code that are pending on the date of enactment of this Act or to proceedings arising in or related to such cases," and Chase & Sanborn's petition for reorganization was pending on that date. Nor does § 1411's predecessor—28 U.S.C. § 1480(a), which stated that "this chapter and title 11 do not affect any right to trial by jury, in a case under title 11 or in a proceeding arising under title 11 or arising in or related to a case under title 11, that is provided by any statute in effect on September 30, 1979"—seem to afford petitioners a statutory basis for their claim. As they recognize, § 1480 was apparently repealed by the 1984 Amendments. Petitioners therefore appear correct in concluding that "absent any specific legislation in force providing jury trials for cases filed before July 10, 1984, but tried afterwards, [their] right to jury trial in this proceeding must necessarily be predicated entirely on the Seventh Amendment."

of the courts of law and equity. Second, we examine the remedy sought and determine whether it is legal or equitable in nature." *Tull v. United States*, 481 U.S. 412, 417–418 (1987) (citations omitted). The second stage of this analysis is more important than the first. If, on balance, these two factors indicate that a party is entitled to a jury trial under the Seventh Amendment, we must decide whether Congress may assign and has assigned resolution of the relevant claim to a non-Article III adjudicative body that does not use a jury as factfinder.[4]

A

There is no dispute that actions to recover preferential or fraudulent transfers were often brought at law in late 18th-century England. As we noted in *Schoenthal v. Irving Trust Co.*, 287 U.S. 92, 94 (1932), "[I]n England, long prior to the enactment of our first Judiciary Act, common law actions of trover and money had and received were resorted to for the recovery of preferential payments by bankrupts." * * * These actions, like all suits at law, were conducted before juries.

Respondent does not challenge this proposition or even contend that actions to recover fraudulent conveyances or preferential transfers were more than occasionally tried in courts of equity. He asserts only that courts of equity had concurrent jurisdiction with courts of law over fraudulent conveyance actions. While respondent's assertion that courts of equity sometimes provided relief in fraudulent conveyance actions is true, however, it hardly suffices to undermine petitioners' submission that the present action for *monetary* relief would not have sounded in equity two hundred years ago in England. In *Parsons v. Bedford,* 3 Pet., at 447 (emphasis added), we contrasted suits at law with "those where equitable rights *alone* were recognized" in holding that the Seventh Amendment right to a jury trial applies to all but the latter actions. Respondent adduces no authority to buttress the claim that suits to recover an allegedly fraudulent transfer of money, of the sort that he has brought, were typically or indeed ever entertained by English courts of equity when the Seventh Amendment was adopted. * * *

We therefore conclude that respondent would have had to bring his action to recover an alleged fraudulent conveyance of a determinate sum of money at

---

[4] * * * We consider this issue in Part IV, *infra*. Contrary to Justice White's contention, * * * we do not declare that the Seventh Amendment provides a right to a jury trial on all legal rather than equitable claims. If a claim that is legal in nature asserts a "public right," as we define that term in Part IV, then the Seventh Amendment does not entitle the parties to a jury trial if Congress assigns its adjudication to an administrative agency or specialized court of equity. * * * The Seventh Amendment protects a litigant's right to a jury trial only if a cause of action is legal in nature and it involves a matter of "private right."

law in 18th-century England, and that a court of equity would not have adjudicated it.

B

The nature of the relief respondent seeks strongly supports our preliminary finding that the right he invokes should be denominated legal rather than equitable. Our decisions establish beyond peradventure that "[i]n cases of fraud or mistake, as under any other head of chancery jurisdiction, a court of the United States will not sustain a bill in equity to obtain only a decree for the payment of money by way of damages, when the like amount can be recovered at law in an action sounding in tort or for money had and received." *Buzard v. Houston*, 119 U.S., at 352 * * *.

Indeed, in our view *Schoenthal v. Irving Trust Co.* removes all doubt that respondent's cause of action should be characterized as legal rather than as equitable. In *Schoenthal,* the trustee in bankruptcy sued in equity to recover alleged preferential payments, claiming that it had no adequate remedy at law. As in this case, the recipients of the payments apparently did not file claims against the bankruptcy estate. The Court held that the suit had to proceed at law instead, because the long-settled rule that suits in equity will not be sustained where a complete remedy exists at law, then codified at 28 U.S.C. § 384, "serves to guard the right of trial by jury preserved by the Seventh Amendment and to that end it should be liberally construed." 287 U.S. at 94. The Court found that the trustee's suit—indistinguishable from respondent's suit in all relevant respects—could not go forward in equity because an adequate remedy was available at law. There, as here, "[t]he preferences sued for were money payments of ascertained and definite amounts," and "[t]he bill discloses no facts that call for an accounting or other equitable relief." *Id.*, at 95. Respondent's fraudulent conveyance action plainly seeks relief traditionally provided by law courts or on the law side of courts having both legal and equitable dockets. Unless Congress may and has permissibly withdrawn jurisdiction over that action by courts of law and assigned it exclusively to non-Article III tribunals sitting without juries, the Seventh Amendment guarantees petitioners a jury trial upon request.

IV.

Prior to passage of the Bankruptcy Reform Act of 1978 * * * "[s]uits to recover preferences constitute[d] no part of the proceedings in bankruptcy." *Schoenthal v. Irving Trust Co., supra,* at 94–95. Although related to bankruptcy proceedings, fraudulent conveyance and preference actions brought by a trustee in bankruptcy were deemed separate, plenary suits to which the Seventh Amendment applied. While the 1978 Act brought those actions within the jurisdiction of the bankruptcy courts, it preserved parties' rights to trial by jury as they existed prior to the effective date of the 1978 Act. 28 U.S.C. § 1480(a) (repealed). The 1984 Amendments, however, designated fraudulent conveyance actions "core proceedings," 28 U.S.C. § 157(b)(2)(H), which bankruptcy judges may adjudicate and in which they may issue final judgments, § 157(b)(1), if a district court has referred the matter to them. § 157(a). We are not obliged to decide today whether bankruptcy courts may conduct jury trials in fraudulent conveyance suits brought by a trustee against a person who has not entered a claim against the estate, either in the rare procedural posture of this case * * * or under the current statutory scheme. * * * Nor need we decide whether, if Congress has authorized bankruptcy courts to hold jury trials in such actions, that authorization comports with Article III when non-Article III judges preside over them subject to review in, or withdrawal by, the district courts. We also need not consider whether jury trials conducted by a bankruptcy court would satisfy the Seventh Amendment's command that "no fact tried by a jury, shall be otherwise re-examined in any Court of the United States, than according to the rules of the common law," given that district courts may presently set aside clearly erroneous factual findings by bankruptcy courts. Bankr. Rule 8013. The sole issue before us is whether the Seventh Amendment confers on petitioners a right to a jury trial in the face of Congress' decision to allow a non-Article III tribunal to adjudicate the claims against them.

A

In *Atlas Roofing*, we noted that "when Congress creates new statutory "public rights,' it may assign their adjudication to an administrative agency with which a jury trial would be incompatible, without violating the Seventh Amendment's injunction that jury trial is to be 'preserved' in 'suits at common law.'" 430 U.S., at 455. We emphasized, however, that Congress' power to block application of the Seventh Amendment to a cause of action has limits. Congress may only deny trials by jury in actions at law, we said, in cases where "public rights" are litigated: "Our prior cases support administrative factfinding in only those situations involving "public rights,' *e.g.*, where the Government is involved in its sovereign capacity under an otherwise valid statute creating enforceable public rights. Wholly private tort, contract, and property cases, as well as a vast range of other cases, are not at all implicated." *Id.*, at 458.[8]

---

[8] Although we left the term "public rights" undefined in *Atlas Roofing*, we cited *Crowell v. Benson*, approvingly. In *Crowell*, 285 U.S. 22 (1932), we defined "private right" as "the liability of one individual to another under the law as defined," *id.*, at 51, in contrast to cases that "arise between the Government and persons subject to its authority in connection with the performance of the constitutional functions of the executive or legislative departments." *Id.*, at 50.

We adhere to that general teaching. As we said in *Atlas Roofing:* "'On the common law side of the federal courts, the aid of juries is not only deemed appropriate but is required by the Constitution itself.'" *Id.*, at 450, n.7, quoting *Crowell v. Benson*, 285 U.S. 22, 51 (1932). Congress may devise novel causes of action involving public rights free from the strictures of the Seventh Amendment if it assigns their adjudication to tribunals without statutory authority to employ juries as factfinders. But it lacks the power to strip parties contesting matters of private right of their constitutional right to a trial by jury. As we recognized in *Atlas Roofing,* to hold otherwise would be to permit Congress to eviscerate the Seventh Amendment's guarantee by assigning to administrative agencies or courts of equity all causes of action not grounded in state law, whether they originate in a newly fashioned regulatory scheme or possess a long line of common-law forebears. The Constitution nowhere grants Congress such puissant authority. "[L]egal claims are not magically converted into equitable issues by their presentation to a court of equity," *Ross v. Bernhard*, 396 U.S. 531, 538 (1970), nor can Congress conjure away the Seventh Amendment by mandating that traditional legal claims be brought there or taken to an administrative tribunal.

In certain situations, of course, Congress may fashion causes of action that are closely *analogous* to common-law claims and place them beyond the ambit of the Seventh Amendment by assigning their resolution to a forum in which jury trials are unavailable. See, *e.g., Atlas Roofing, supra,* at 450–461 (workplace safety regulations); *Block v. Hirsh*, 256 U.S. 135, 158 (1921) (temporary emergency regulation of rental real estate). * * * Congress' power to do so is limited, however, just as its power to place adjudicative authority in non-Article III tribunals is circumscribed. * * * Unless a legal cause of action involves "public rights," Congress may not deprive parties litigating over that right of the Seventh Amendment's guarantee to a jury trial.

In *Atlas Roofing,* we noted that Congress may effectively supplant a common-law cause of action carrying with it a right to a jury trial with a statutory cause of action shorn of a jury trial right if that statutory cause of action inheres in or lies against the Federal Government in its sovereign capacity. Our case law makes plain, however, that the class of "public rights" whose adjudication Congress may assign to administrative agencies or courts of equity sitting without juries is more expansive than *Atlas Roofing*'s discussion suggests. Indeed, our decisions point to the conclusion that, if a statutory cause of action is legal in nature, the question whether the Seventh Amendment permits Congress to assign its adjudication to a tribunal that does not employ juries as factfinders requires the same answer as the question whether Article III allows Congress to assign adjudication of that cause of action to a non-Article III tribunal. For if a statutory cause of action, such as respondent's right to recover a fraudulent conveyance under § 548(a)(2), is not a "public right" for Article III purposes, then Congress may not assign its adjudication to a specialized non-Article III court lacking "the essential attributes of the judicial power." *Crowell v. Benson, supra,* at 51. And if the action must be tried under the auspices of an Article III court, then the Seventh Amendment affords the parties a right to a jury trial whenever the cause of action is legal in nature. Conversely, if Congress may assign the adjudication of a statutory cause of action to a non-Article III tribunal, then the Seventh Amendment poses no independent bar to the adjudication of that action by a nonjury factfinder. * * * In addition to our Seventh Amendment precedents, we therefore rely as well on our decisions exploring the restrictions Article III places on Congress' choice of adjudicative bodies to resolve disputes over statutory rights to determine whether petitioners are entitled to a jury trial.

In our most recent discussion of the "public rights" doctrine as it bears on Congress' power to commit adjudication of a statutory cause of action to a non-Article III tribunal, we rejected the view that "a matter of public rights must at a minimum arise 'between the government and others.'" *Northern Pipeline Construction Co.*, [458 U.S.] at 69 (opinion of Brennan, J.), quoting *Ex parte* Bakelite Corp., 279 U.S. 438, 451 (1929). We held, instead, that the Federal Government need not be a party for a case to revolve around "public rights." The crucial question, in cases not involving the Federal Government, is whether "Congress, acting for a valid legislative purpose pursuant to its constitutional powers under Article I, [has] create[d] a seemingly "private' right that is so closely integrated into a public regulatory scheme as to be a matter appropriate for agency resolution with limited involvement by the Article III judiciary." [*Thomas*, 473 U.S.], at 593–594. *See id.*, at 600 (BRENNAN, J., concurring in judgment) (challenged provision involves public rights because "the dispute arises in the context of a federal regulatory scheme that virtually occupies the field"). If a statutory right is not closely intertwined with a federal regulatory program Congress has power to enact, and if that right neither belongs to nor exists against the Federal Government, then it must be adjudicated by an Article III court. If the right is legal in nature, then it carries with it the Seventh Amendment's guarantee of a jury trial.

B

Although the issue admits of some debate, a bankruptcy trustee's right to recover a fraudulent conveyance under § 548(a)(2) seems to us more accurately characterized as a private rather than a public right as we have used those terms in our Article III decisions. In *Northern Pipeline Construction Co.*, the plurality noted that the restructuring of debtor-creditor relations in bankruptcy "may well be a 'public right.'" But the plurality also emphasized that state-law causes of action for breach of contract or warranty are paradigmatic private rights, even when asserted by an insolvent corporation in the midst of Chapter 11 reorganization proceedings. The plurality further said that "matters from their nature subject to "a suit at common law or in equity or admiralty' lie at the "protected core" of Article III judicial power—a point we reaffirmed in *Thomas*. There can be little doubt that fraudulent conveyance actions by bankruptcy trustees—suits which, we said in *Schoenthal v. Irving Trust Co.*, 287 U.S., at 94–95, "constitute no part of the proceedings in bankruptcy but concern controversies arising out of it"—are quintessentially suits at common law that more nearly resemble state-law contract claims brought by a bankrupt corporation to augment the bankruptcy estate than they do creditors' hierarchically ordered claims to a pro rata share of the bankruptcy *res*. They therefore appear matters of private rather than public right.

Our decision in *Katchen v. Landy*, 382 U.S. 323 (1966), under the Seventh Amendment rather than Article III, confirms this analysis. Petitioner, an officer of a bankrupt corporation, made payments from corporate funds within four months of bankruptcy on corporate notes on which he was an accommodation maker. When petitioner later filed claims against the bankruptcy estate, the trustee counterclaimed, arguing that the payments petitioner made constituted voidable preferences because they reduced his potential personal liability on the notes. We held that the bankruptcy court had jurisdiction to order petitioner to surrender the preferences and that it could rule on the trustee's claim without according petitioner a jury trial. * * *

We read *Schoenthal* and *Katchen* as holding that, under the Seventh Amendment, a creditor's right to a jury trial on a bankruptcy trustee's preference claim depends upon whether the creditor has submitted a claim against the estate, not upon Congress' precise definition of the "bankruptcy estate" or upon whether Congress chanced to deny jury trials to creditors who have not filed claims and who are sued by a trustee to recover an alleged preference. Because petitioners here, like the petitioner in *Schoenthal,* have not filed claims against the estate, respondent's fraudulent conveyance action does not arise "as part of the process of allowance and disallowance of claims." Nor is that action integral to the restructuring of debtor-creditor relations. Congress therefore cannot divest petitioners of their Seventh Amendment right to a trial by jury. *Katchen* thus supports the result we reach today; it certainly does not compel its opposite.

The 1978 Act abolished the statutory distinction between plenary and summary bankruptcy proceedings, on which the Court relied in *Schoenthal* and *Katchen.* Although the 1978 Act preserved parties' rights to jury trials as they existed prior to the day it took effect, 28 U.S.C. § 1480(a) (repealed), in the 1984 Amendments Congress drew a new distinction between "core" and "non-core" proceedings and classified fraudulent conveyance actions as core proceedings triable by bankruptcy judges. 28 U.S.C. § 157(b)(2)(H). Whether 28 U.S.C. § 1411 purports to abolish jury trial rights in what were formerly plenary actions is unclear, and at any rate is not a question we need decide here. * * * The decisive point is that in neither the 1978 Act nor the 1984 Amendments did Congress "creat[e] a new cause of action, and remedies therefor, unknown to the common law," because traditional rights and remedies were inadequate to cope with a manifest public problem. *Atlas Roofing,* 430 U.S., at 461. Rather, Congress simply reclassified a pre-existing common-law cause of action that was not integrally related to the reformation of debtor-creditor relations and that apparently did not suffer from any grave deficiencies. This purely taxonomic change cannot alter our Seventh Amendment analysis. Congress cannot eliminate a party's Seventh Amendment right to a jury trial merely by relabeling the cause of action to which it attaches and placing exclusive jurisdiction in an administrative agency or a specialized court of equity. * * *

Nor can Congress' assignment be justified on the ground that jury trials of fraudulent conveyance actions would "go far to dismantle the statutory scheme," *Atlas Roofing,* 430 U.S., at 454 n.11, or that bankruptcy proceedings have been placed in "an administrative forum with which the jury would be incompatible." *Id.*, at 450. To be sure, we owe some deference to Congress' judgment after it has given careful consideration to the constitutionality of a legislative provision. But respondent has adduced no evidence that Congress considered the constitutional implications of its designation of all fraudulent conveyance actions as core proceedings. Nor can it seriously be argued that permitting jury trials in fraudulent conveyance actions brought by a trustee against a person who has not entered a claim against the estate would "go far to dismantle the statutory scheme," as we used that phrase in *Atlas Roofing,* when our opinion in that case, following *Schoenthal,* plainly assumed that such claims carried with them a right to a jury trial. In addition, one cannot easily say that "the jury would be incompatible" with bankruptcy proceedings, in view of Congress' express provision for jury trials in certain actions arising out of bankruptcy litigation. *See* 28 U.S.C. § 1411 * * * And Justice WHITE's claim that juries may serve usefully as checks only on the decisions of judges who enjoy life tenure overlooks the extent to which judges who are appointed for fixed terms may be beholden to Congress or executive officials, and thus ignores the potential for juries to exercise beneficial restraint on their decisions.

It may be that providing jury trials in some fraudulent conveyance actions—if not in this particular case, because respondent's suit was commenced after the bankruptcy court approved the debtor's plan of reorganization—would impede swift resolution of bankruptcy proceedings and increase the expense of Chapter 11 reorganizations. But "these considerations are insufficient to overcome the clear command of the Seventh Amendment." *Curtis v. Loether,*

415 U.S., at 198. *See also Bowsher v. Synar*, 478 U.S. 714, 736 (1986) ("'[T]he fact that a given law or procedure is efficient, convenient, and useful in facilitating functions of government, standing alone, will not save it if it is contrary to the Constitution'"), quoting *INS v. Chadha*, 462 U.S. 919, 944 (1983); *Pernell v. Southall Realty*, 416 U.S., at 383–384 (discounting arguments that jury trials would be unduly burdensome and rejecting "the notion that there is some necessary inconsistency between the desire for speedy justice and the right to jury trial").

V.

We do not decide today whether the current jury trial provision—28 U.S.C. § 1411—permits bankruptcy courts to conduct jury trials in fraudulent conveyance actions like the one respondent initiated. Nor do we express any view as to whether the Seventh Amendment or Article III allows jury trials in such actions to be held before non-Article III bankruptcy judges subject to the oversight provided by the district courts pursuant to the 1984 Amendments. We leave those issues for future decisions. We do hold, however, that whatever the answers to these questions, the Seventh Amendment entitles petitioners to the jury trial they requested. Accordingly, the judgment of the Court of Appeals is reversed, and the case is remanded for further proceedings consistent with this opinion.

It is so ordered.

[The opinions of Justices Blackmun, Scalia, and White are omitted.]

NOTES

1. In *Langenkamp v. Culp*, 498 U.S. 42 (1990), the Court held that if a creditor who files a claim is sued by the trustee to recover a voidable preference, the creditor is not entitled to a jury trial on the preference question under the Seventh Amendment. "In *Granfinanciera* we recognized that by filing a claim against a bankruptcy estate the creditor triggers the process of 'allowance and disallowance of claims,' thereby subjecting himself to the bankruptcy court's equitable power. * * * If the creditor is met, in turn, with a preference action from the trustee, that action becomes part of the claims-allowance process which is triable only in equity. * * * In other words, the creditor's claim and the ensuing preference action by the trustee become integral to the restructuring of the debtor-creditor relationship through the bankruptcy court's *equity jurisdiction.* * * * As such, there is no Seventh Amendment right to a jury trial. If the party does *not* submit a claim against the bankruptcy estate, however, the trustee can recover allegedly preferential transfers only by filing what amounts to a legal action to recover a monetary transfer. In those circumstances the preference defendant is entitled to a jury trial." 498 U.S. at 44–45 (emphasis in original).

2. An issue on which the circuits are divided is whether a debtor, who has a cause of action on which it would be entitled to a jury trial under the *Granfinanciera* test, is deprived of that right if the person against whom the action is brought files a claim in the debtor's bankruptcy. In *In re Hallahan*, 936 F.2d 1496 (7th Cir. 1991), a creditor filed a claim for willful violation of a contract and tortious interference with business expectations and filed a complaint requesting a nondischargeability hearing under § 523(a)(6). The debtor requested a jury trial on the nondischargeability issue, arguing that the creditor's underlying breach of contract action was a suit at common law even though it was being tried as a part of an equitable bankruptcy proceeding. The court rejected the debtor's demand for a jury trial. Even assuming that a nondischargeability hearing is a legal matter (which the court thought it was not), by voluntarily filing its petition in bankruptcy, the debtor submitted to the equitable jurisdiction of the bankruptcy court and, in effect, waived its right to a jury trial. If the creditor lost its right to a jury trial by filing a claim, the debtor "cannot be endowed with any stronger right." 936 F.2d at 1505. *In re McLaren*, 3 F.3d 958, 960–61 (6th Cir. 1993), is in accord.

Several courts hold that *Hallahan* went too far with its theory that a debtor's act in filing a petition in bankruptcy waives its right to a jury trial. In *In re Jensen*, 946 F.2d 369 (5th Cir. 1991), the debtors filed suit against several third parties for prepetition breach of fiduciary duty, fraud and tortious interference with business relations and conspiracy having to do with the development and marketing of an invention of the debtors. The third parties were not creditors and did not file a claim in the debtors' bankruptcy. The court granted the debtors a jury trial on their claims over the objection that under *Hallahan* the debtors had waived their right to a jury trial by filing a petition in bankruptcy. "As we see it, the debtor was not entitled to a jury trial in *Hallahan*, not because the debtor had filed a petition in bankruptcy, but because the plaintiff had submitted his claim against the debtor to the equitable jurisdiction of the bankruptcy court. Filing a proof of claim denied both the plaintiff and the defendant, debtor, any right to a jury trial that they otherwise might have had on that claim." 946 F.2d at 374.

In *Germain v. Connecticut National Bank*, 988 F.2d 1323 (2d Cir. 1993), the court thoroughly analyzed the issue and rejected both *Hallahan* and *Jensen*. In that case Bank filed a claim in the debtor's bankruptcy; later the trustee brought suit for money damages against Bank on an array of lender liability claims, all arising out of Bank's alleged postpetition misconduct. The court found that the trustee's suit was on a legal claim and granted the trustee a trial by jury. The trustee's postpetition lender liability claims against Bank had no relation to Bank's claim against the debtor. The court saw *Hallahan*'s waiver theory as unjustified and viewed *Jensen* as going too far in stating that *any* dispute between a debtor and a creditor who has filed a claim is equitable in nature. The question should be whether the trustee's claim has become a part of the equitable process of allowing claims. In *Germain* the trustee's claims may enhance the *amount* of the debtor's estate but they have nothing to do with the *allowance* of Bank's claim; thus the trustee's claims have not become a part of the equitable claims allowance process. *Billing v. Ravin, Greenberg & Zackin, P.A.*, 22 F.3d 1242 (3d Cir. 1994), presents an extremely close case on that point. In *Billing* the law firm which advised the debtor filed a claim for postpetition legal fees. The debtor filed an objection to the fees and brought a separate action for malpractice. The majority opinion held that the debtor was not entitled to a jury trial on its malpractice claim because it was so closely related to the fee objection that the malpractice claim became part of the equitable process of allowance of claims. A strong dissenting opinion characterized the malpractice action as a separate proceeding to recover damages which was not closely related to the objection to the fee application, hence, the malpractice action had not been converted to an equitable dispute as part of the process of allowance of claims.

Contrast this approach with *In re Weinstein*, 237 B.R. 567 (Bankr.E.D. N.Y.1999), where the court bifurcated a dischargeability determination under § 523(a)(2)(A) from the question of the debtor's underlying liability for fraud, distinguishing between the "foundational" determination of liability and damages for fraud and the ultimate exercise of the bankruptcy court's "equitable jurisdiction" in establishing whether the claim should be excepted from the scope of the discharge. As a result, the creditor-plaintiff was entitled to receive a jury trial for the foundational determination only. The court refused to find a waiver of jury trial by the creditor by seeking a bankruptcy court determination of nondischargeability, arguing that there was no other court from which the creditor could have sought this relief. Acknowledging that demands for jury trials were usually "asserted for strategic leverage," the court nevertheless recognized that "many creditors perceive, rightly or wrongly, that bankruptcy judges tend to be more personally and institutionally sympathetic to debtors.... In this respect, the demand for a jury trial is intended to protect the creditor against the adverse impact of that perceived bias." 237 B.R. at 574. Relying on both *Billing* and *Weinstein*, the court in *In re Hechinger Investment Co. of Delaware*, 327 B.R. 537 (D.Del.2005), refused the Hechinger liquidating trust's request for a jury trial on fraudulent transfer claims against the debtor's primary secured creditors on the ground that lien and claim avoidance issues were inextricably intertwined with the claims allowance process. The court went on to dismiss the avoidance claims against the lenders on the merits by summary judgment.

3. Assume the debtor in possession in a Chapter 11 case sues Bank to recover property as a preference or a fraudulent transfer. Under *Granfinanciera* and *Langenkamp,* Bank would have been entitled to a jury trial unless it filed a proof of claim. Since Bank had a large claim against Debtor, it wished both to file a claim and to preserve its right to jury trial. When Debtor filed a request that an order be entered barring all claims filed thereafter, Bank sought a modification of the order that would allow Bank to postpone the filing of its claim until after the adversary proceedings had been concluded. The court in *In re Hooker Investments, Inc.*, 937 F.2d 833 (2d Cir. 1991), denied Bank's modification and stated that it would set a dangerous precedent to have to draft a bar order to preserve rights for anybody who believed that they would be prejudiced by filing a proof of claim. In *Travellers International AG v. Robinson,* 982 F.2d 96, 97 (3d Cir. 1992), a creditor submitted a proof of claim stating: "claimant does not, by filing this claim, waive its demand for a jury trial * * *." It didn't work. Neither does withdrawing the proof of claim. *Smith v. Dowden,* 47 F.3d 940 (8th Cir. 1995).

4. In *Granfinanciera* the Court expressly declined to decide whether bankruptcy judges can conduct jury trials. If they cannot, district courts must do so in those instances in which the parties in bankruptcy are entitled to a jury trial. The first circuit court opinion decided after *Granfinanciera* held that bankruptcy judges may conduct jury trials in core proceedings under their 28 U.S.C. § 157(b) authority to hear and determine these proceedings. *In re Ben Cooper, Inc.*, 896 F.2d 1394 (2d Cir. 1990). Since then six circuits have disagreed. These courts rely on the fact that there is no express statutory grant to bankruptcy judges of the power to conduct jury trials and there are constitutional problems with implying such a power. The Supreme Court granted certiorari in *Ben Cooper,* but before oral argument the Court vacated the Second Circuit decision and remanded the case to the Second Circuit to determine whether it had jurisdiction. The Second Circuit held that it had jurisdiction and reinstated its prior decision. Inexplicably, the Supreme Court subsequently denied certiorari. 500 U.S. 928 (1991).

In 1994 Congress added 28 U.S.C. § 157(e) which provides: "If the right to a jury trial applies in a proceeding that may be heard under this section by a bankruptcy judge, the bankruptcy judge may conduct the jury trial if specially designated to exercise such jurisdiction by the district court and with the express consent of all the parties." District courts may be willing to designate bankruptcy judges to conduct jury trials, but it is unlikely that the parties will always consent. If one party wishes to delay the proceeding or to have a different judge, this party can achieve these ends by withholding consent.

Of course, this statute cannot solve the constitutional problems inherent in delegating one of the essential attributes of the judicial power of the United States—the authority to conduct a jury trial—to an Article I judge. Several of the courts, enumerated above, which deny bankruptcy judges the power to conduct jury trials, harbor grave concerns about the constitutionality of allowing them to do so. But in patterning § 157(e) after 28 U.S.C. § 636(c)(1), which authorizes U.S. magistrates to conduct jury trials when the parties consent and the district court specially designates, Congress has made its strongest case for the constitutionality of the statute. The court in *In re Clay*, 35 F.3d 190, 196 (5th Cir. 1994) stated: "* * * consent matters. Because one function of Article III is to protect litigants, courts have accorded significant if not dispositive weight to consent and waiver. * * * Consent is a key factor empowering magistrates to conduct jury proceedings." A number of court of appeals decisions have upheld the constitutionality of § 636(c), e.g., *Pacemaker Diagnostic Clinic of America, Inc. v. Instromedix, Inc.*, 725 F.2d 537 (9th Cir. 1984) (Kennedy, J.). A question that arises with respect to § 157(e) is whether Congress can constitutionally authorize bankruptcy judges to conduct jury trials in noncore cases. The Second Circuit, which allows bankruptcy judges to conduct jury trials under *Ben Cooper*, has barred them from doing so with respect to noncore matters because the Seventh Amendment permits only appellate review of facts tried by juries; the de novo review provided in § 157(c) for noncore matters does not meet this requirement. *In re Orion Pictures Corp.*, 4 F.3d 1095, 1101 (2d Cir. 1993).

E. TRANSNATIONAL BANKRUPTCY

In theory, bankruptcy laws provide a single collective proceeding to consistently and comprehensively solve the problems arising out of a given debtor's insolvency. But in an age in which economic activity to an ever increasing extent is not limited by national borders, one inherent limitation of the United States Bankruptcy Code is that it is domestic United States law. While the theory of the Code is that its reach is extraterritorial, *see e.g.* § 541 (property of estate includes property "wherever located and by whomever held") enforcement of the Code as to property located abroad and as to foreign parties as a practical matter often requires cooperation from foreign nations. The general problem of international coordination of laws governing international commercial activity has proven especially difficult in the bankruptcy field.

Historically, in bankruptcy matters, nations insisted on the "territorial principle": each nation uses its insolvency laws to administer assets within that jurisdiction according to the procedures and priorities of that nation's laws. Critics of the territorial principle note that it can lead to multiple inconsistent proceedings, dissipation of assets, inequality of distribution, debtor abuse, and de facto discrimination against foreign debtors and creditors. It also may adversely affect the debtor's prospects for successful reorganization. To some degree these problems can be ameliorated by the sort of "cooperative territoriality" and general principles of comity illustrated below by *Maxwell Communication*, p. 885.

Unfortunately, achieving consensus on a broader principle allowing for unified or coordinated proceedings has proved exceedingly difficult. One possibility would be harmonization of different nations' insolvency laws. Thus in the United States we have a uniform federal bankruptcy law and the same Bankruptcy Code applies to insolvencies in all fifty states. One could imagine a treaty imposing a uniform international bankruptcy law among the various signatory nations. Given the complexity and idiosyncratic nature of existing national laws—embedded as they are in distinct legal and economic systems—and the disagreement over bankruptcy policy even among the economically developed nations—this approach has proved infeasible so far, even for nations such as the United States and Canada that share many common legal traditions and whose markets and societies are well-integrated.

Another approach would be a comprehensive principle governing conflict of laws. If nations agreed that the insolvency law of the jurisdiction where the debtor's principal place of business (in the argot of transnational bankruptcy practice the "home country" or "the debtor's center of main interests") was located would govern all the property and all the creditors and interest holders wherever located, then at least there might be harmony within a particular bankruptcy case. This approach is sometimes referred to as "universalism." The European Union adopted a universalist approach (subject to a public policy exception) in Council Regulation 1346/00, Insolvency Proceedings, 2000 O.J. (L160) 1 (EC). The first major test of that regulation involved the transnational insolvency arising out of the Paramalat accounting fraud. Applying the regulation, over significant political and legal opposition from Italy, the European Court of Justice in *Eurofood IFSC Ltd*, 2006 E.C.R. 1-3813, upheld the jurisdiction of the Irish courts as the home court under the applicable regulation. The EC's universalist approach has engendered criticism that the regulation facilitates forum-shopping. London, in particular, has become the venue of choice within the European Union for insolvency matters. Moreover, unlike forum-shopping within the United States (where the United States Bankruptcy Code, subject to the vagaries of inter-circuit conflicts, applies in all jurisdictions), forum-shopping in Europe allows the debtor to select among varying national insolvency laws after it has become apparent that it will seek insolvency protection. Notwithstanding such concerns, non-EU nations (including the United States), in adopting the United Nations Commission on International

Trade Law (UNCITRAL) Model Law on Cross-Border Insolvency (which itself was significantly shaped by the experience of *Maxwell Communication*), have also begun to make some significant progress towards systematic coordination of proceedings through comprehensive choice of law provisions, a kind of cooperative territorialism that is pointing towards universalism. As discussed in the notes following *Maxwell Communication*, in 2005 the United States Congress enacted this Model Law as Chapter 15 of the United States Bankruptcy Code. Chapter 15 is discussed in the notes following *Maxwell Communication*, reprinted below.

In re Maxwell Communication Corporation

United States Court of Appeals, Second Circuit, 1996.
93 F.3d 1036.

■ CARDAMONE, Circuit Judge:

The demise of the late British media magnate Robert Maxwell and that of the corporation bearing his name, the Maxwell Communication Corporation plc, followed a similar and scandalous path, spawning civil and criminal litigation in England and around the world. This case illustrates that some positive consequences have resulted from these parallel demises. From Maxwell's mysterious death, which forced his international corporation into bankruptcy, was born a unique judicial administration of the debtor corporation by parallel and cooperative proceedings in the courts of the United States and England aimed at harmonizing the laws of both countries and also aimed at maximizing the benefits to creditors and the prospects of rehabilitation.

We have before us a small but significant piece of the swirling legal controversy that followed the collapse of Robert Maxwell's media empire. The question to be addressed is whether Maxwell Communication, as a debtor estate in Chapter 11, may recover under American law millions of dollars it transferred to three foreign banks shortly before declaring bankruptcy. It has sought such relief in adversary proceedings in the bankruptcy court under those sections of the United States Bankruptcy Code, 11 U.S.C. §§ 101–1330 (1994) (Bankruptcy Code or Code), providing for what is known as "avoidance" of pre-petition transactions. Because, in our view, the doctrine of international comity supports deferring to the courts and laws of England, we affirm the dismissal of the Chapter 11 debtor's complaints.

Background

* * *

A. Events Preceding the Dual Filings

The debtor was originally incorporated in England over 60 years ago as a limited company. Robert Maxwell acquired control of this limited company 15 years ago. The following year, the company was re-registered under English law as a public limited company and, in 1987, it became Maxwell Communication Corporation plc (hereafter Maxwell or the debtor). Before filing for bankruptcy protection, Maxwell functioned as a holding company for Robert Maxwell's "public side" holdings—as distinguished from Maxwell's private holdings, which at one time included the *New York Daily News*—and controlled a variety of media-related companies. Although Maxwell was headquartered and managed in England and incurred most of its debt there, approximately 80 percent of its assets were located in the United States, most notably its subsidiaries Macmillan, Inc. and Official Airlines Guide, Inc.

Maxwell alleges that in the fall of 1991, less than 90 days before its Chapter 11 filing, it made several transfers—transfers it now seeks to avoid—to three European banks (collectively, the banks) with whom it had credit arrangements. Two of these banks are Barclays Bank plc (Barclays) and National Westminster Bank plc (National Westminster), both of which have their headquarters in London and maintain an international presence, with branches in New York and elsewhere. The other bank is Société Générale, a French Bank headquartered in Paris with offices, among other places, in London and New York.

From 1985 until 1991 Maxwell obtained credit from Barclays under the terms of a credit arrangement known in England as an "overdraft facility." This written agreement, negotiated in London, stated that any disputes arising under it would be governed by English law. Maxwell drew $30 million under the overdraft facility, none of which had been repaid on November 24, 1991, the agreed-upon maturity date. Two days later, under pressure from Barclays' banking director in London, Maxwell repaid the $30 million from the proceeds of the sale of Que Computer Books, Inc. (Que), a subsidiary of Macmillan in New York. The Que proceeds had originally been deposited in a Maxwell account at the New York branch of National Westminster and subsequently credited to Maxwell's U.S. dollar account with National Westminster in London. On November 26, 1991 repayment was effected by transferring $30 million from Maxwell's dollar account in London to Barclays' New York branch, which was then credited the following day against the balance in the appropriate Maxwell overdraft account at Barclays in London. In addition to this transfer from the Que proceeds, Maxwell alleged in its amended complaint that 11 other transfers of funds were made to Barclays during the 90 days preceding Maxwell's bankruptcy filing, amounting to a total of £2,110,970 (net of various payments by Barclays to or on behalf of Maxwell during the same period). No connection between these other transfers and the United States was alleged in the complaint.

National Westminster's relationship with the debtor began in the 1930s and continued through the bankruptcy filing. As of late 1991 Maxwell maintained several accounts with National Westminster, with overdraft facilities to help it meet its cash needs. These arrangements were similar to those it had with Barclays in that they were negotiated in England and provided for the governance of English law. In October 1991 Maxwell received $145 million from the sale of Macmillan Directories, Inc. (another Macmillan subsidiary in the United States) and used the proceeds—which had been paid into a Maxwell account at Citibank in New York and thereafter credited to an account at Citibank in London—to purchase British pounds. Maxwell then paid £15 million from these proceeds to an account it maintained at National Westminster's London branch. Maxwell then applied the £15 million to satisfy an overdraft balance with National Westminster.

In November 1991 Maxwell converted a portion of the $157.5 million of Que proceeds (originally deposited in National Westminster's New York branch but then transferred to its London branch) into £27.5 million. It used this sum to cover its overdraft balances in National Westminster's London branch. The purchase of pounds sterling and subsequent credits to the National Westminster overdraft accounts occurred in London. Maxwell also alleges it made eight other transfers to National Westminster from accounts at Midland Bank in London shortly before Maxwell's bankruptcy filing, payments which amounted to £29,046,738 (net of payments by National Westminster to Maxwell during the same period).

Société Générale also extended credit to Maxwell under an agreement negotiated and administered in England. On October 7, 1991, in satisfaction of principal and interest on a $10 million loan extended under that credit arrangement, Maxwell made a payment of roughly £5.765 million to Société Générale. The funds were transferred from an account Maxwell maintained at Marine Midland Bank in London to Société Générale's London branch. Although the debtor did not allege that the transfer was connected to the United States, the district court assumed for purposes of its decision that the funds came from the sale of Macmillan Directories because that sale also occurred on October 7, 1991.

B. The Dual Insolvency Proceedings

On December 16, 1991 Maxwell filed a petition for reorganization under Chapter 11 of the United States Bankruptcy Code in the Bankruptcy Court for the Southern District of New York. The next day, it petitioned the High Court of Justice in London for an administration order. Administration, introduced by the Insolvency Act 1986, is the closest equivalent in British law to Chapter 11 relief. Acting under the terms of the Insolvency Act, Justice HOFFMAN, then of the High Court (now a member of the House of Lords), appointed members of the London office of the accounting firm of Price Waterhouse as administrators to manage the affairs and property of the corporation.

Simultaneous proceedings in different countries, especially in multi-party cases like bankruptcies, can naturally lead to inconsistencies and conflicts. To minimize such problems, Judge Brozman appointed Richard A. Gitlin, Esq. as examiner, pursuant to 11 U.S.C. § 1104(c), in the Chapter 11 proceedings. The order of appointment required the examiner, inter alia, to investigate the debtor's financial condition, to function as a mediator among the various parties, and to "act to harmonize, for the benefit of all of [Maxwell's] creditors and stockholders and other parties in interest, [Maxwell's] United States chapter 11 case and [Maxwell's] United Kingdom administration case so as to maximize [the] prospects for rehabilitation and reorganization."

Judge Brozman and Justice HOFFMAN subsequently authorized the examiner and the administrators to coordinate their efforts pursuant to a so-called Protocol, an agreement between the examiner and the administrators. In approving the Protocol, Judge Brozman recognized the English administrators as the corporate governance of the debtor-in-possession. As the bankruptcy judge later explained, this recognition was motivated not only by the need for coordination but also because Maxwell was "incorporated in England and run. . . by [Maxwell] executives out of Maxwell House in London subject to the direction of an English board of directors." [*Maxwell Communication Corp. v. Barclays Bank plc*, 170 B.R. 800, 817 (Bankr.S.D.N.Y.1994) (Maxwell I)] * * * Justice HOFFMAN reciprocated, granting the examiner leave to appear before the High Court in England.

These joint efforts resulted in what has been described as a "remarkable sequence of events leading to perhaps the first world-wide plan of orderly liquidation ever achieved." Jay Lawrence Westbrook, *The Lessons of Maxwell Communication*, 64 Fordham L.Rev. 2531, 2535 (1996). The administrators, the examiner, and other interested parties worked together to produce a common system for reorganizing Maxwell by disposing of assets as going concerns and distributing the proceeds to creditors. The mechanism for accomplishing this is embodied in a plan of reorganization and a scheme of arrangement, which are interdependent documents and were filed by the administrators in the United States and English courts respectively.

The reorganization plan incorporates the scheme and makes it binding on Maxwell and its creditors. The plan and scheme thus constitute a single and integrated system for realizing the value of Maxwell's assets and paying its creditors. As was set forth in a letter from the administrators to Maxwell's creditors, the proposal was to pay in full all holders of secured claims and of claims enjoying preferential status under United States or English law. The plan and scheme treat all of Maxwell's assets as a single pool and leave them under Maxwell's control for distribution to claimants. They allow any creditor to submit a claim in either jurisdiction. And, in addition to overcoming many of the substantive differences in the insolvency laws of the two jurisdictions, the plan and scheme resolve many procedural differences, such as the time limits for submitting claims.

Following the requisite creditor voting in the United States and England, the plan was approved in the United States and the scheme was approved in England. Judge Brozman entered an order confirming the plan—and, by implication, the scheme incorporated therein—on July 14, 1993. Justice HOFFMAN thereafter entered an order sanctioning the scheme under § 425 of the Companies Act 1985 on July 21, 1993. Barclays, National Westminster, and Société Générale each filed a notice of claim with the administrators, seeking pro rata distributions on various unsecured claims against Maxwell.

Despite the unusual degree of cooperation and reconciliation of the laws of the two forums, the plan and scheme predictably did not resolve all the problems that might arise from the concurrent proceedings. For example, these documents did not specify which substantive law would govern the resolution of disputed claims by creditors. More importantly, they did not address the instant dispute regarding the debtor's ability to set aside pre-petition transfers to certain creditors.

C. British Denial of Anti–Suit Injunction

In July 1992 Barclays faced the possibility that the administrators would institute litigation in the bankruptcy court to recover the $30 million it had received from Maxwell on November 26, 1991. Barclays therefore obtained an ex parte order in the High Court (not from Justice HOFFMAN) barring the commencement of such an action. In seeking to prevent litigation in the bankruptcy court, Barclays was apparently motivated by a difference in the American and British "avoidance" rules. Rules governing avoidance generally allow the estate to recover certain pre-petition transfers of property to creditors occurring within a defined period of time. Such rules are sometimes referred to as the law of preferences because such transfers, left unchecked, may put transferees in a better position than other creditors if the debtor becomes insolvent.

Thus, under § 547(b), a trustee may avoid certain transfers to outside creditors made within 90 days before the filing of the petition. The corresponding provision in English law is § 239 of the Insolvency Act 1986. That section is in many respects similar to the American law, but the British law imposes an additional condition—it limits avoidance to those situations where placing the transferee in a better position was something the debtor intended. See Insolvency Act 1986 § 239(5). This seemingly innocuous subjective intent requirement in English law apparently would be a significant or insurmountable obstacle for the administrators were they to litigate the preferences question in London under English law. For obvious reasons, they opposed the anti-suit injunction sought by Barclays, that is, they wanted this issue litigated in the Southern District bankruptcy court.

Following a hearing, Justice HOFFMAN vacated the ex parte order Barclays had obtained. The British judge declined to interfere with the American court's determination of the reach of our avoidance law. He cited the British presumption that in such a situation the foreign judge is normally in the best position to decide whether proceedings are to go forward in the foreign court, and the rule that anti-suit injunctions will issue only where an assertion of jurisdiction in the foreign court would be "unconscionable."

In so doing, Justice HOFFMAN noted the cooperative course of the parallel insolvency proceedings. He distinguished recent cases involving the extraterritorial application of American antitrust law, reasoning that injunctive relief is available only if it appears that a foreign court is likely to assert jurisdiction in a manner "contrary to accepted principles of international law." The High Court's decision did not pass judgment on the merits of whether the application of American law would violate such norms. It did assume, however, that the bankruptcy court would dismiss the anticipated suit if it found that there was an insufficient connection with the United States. This ruling was affirmed by the Court of Appeal, and leave for further review by the House of Lords was denied.

D. The Adversary Complaints and the Bankruptcy and District Court Decisions

Freed from the constraints of an anti-suit injunction, the administrators commenced adversary proceedings in the bankruptcy court against Barclays, National Westminster, and Société Générale. The complaints sought the recovery of the above-described transfers to the banks on the theory that they were avoidable preferences under § 547(b) and therefore recoverable under § 550(a)(1). In addition, each complaint sought the disallowance under § 502(d) of any claims made by the defendant, unless the defendant first returns to the debtor the transferred funds, with interest. This subject is discussed and resolved in Part IV, *infra*. The examiner joined the administrators in instituting these adversary proceedings against National Westminster and intervened in the proceeding against Barclays; he is not a party in Maxwell's suit against Société Générale.

Defendants filed motions for dismissal under Fed.R.Civ.P. 12(b)(6) asserting, inter alia, that applying § 547 of the Bankruptcy Code to these transactions would violate the "presumption against extraterritoriality" and that dismissal was also warranted on grounds of international comity. The bankruptcy court granted the motions, holding that the transfers were extraterritorial and that the Bankruptcy Code does not apply to these transfers, whose "center of gravity" lies outside the United States and, in the alternative, that international comity precluded the application of the Code in this instance.

Treating comity as a "canon of statutory construction," the bankruptcy court emphasized choice-of-law principles and asked "which jurisdiction's laws and policies are implicated to the greatest extent." The answer, the court found, was England. It also noted Maxwell's insolvency did not jeopardize United States interests because its holdings were sold as going businesses, because most of its creditors were not residents of the United States, and because the two countries' preference laws in any event serve similar ends, and that England had a greater interest in applying its own laws.

The district court affirmed on both the extraterritoriality and comity grounds. On the latter question, it held that the "bankruptcy court did not abuse its discretion in finding that traditional choice of law principles 'point decidedly towards the application of U.K. law.'" *Maxwell II*, 186 B.R. at 822. The district court's analysis of the relative interests was substantially similar to that of the bankruptcy court, but it also underscored the cooperation between the courts of the two countries and found that deference would comport with the previous efforts by both courts to harmonize the dual proceedings. Judge Scheindlin believed this to be "the unique aspect and the most important feature of this case." Id., at 813.

Maxwell and the examiner appealed. We consolidated the three cases on January 15, 1996 and now address the merits.

Discussion

* * *

III. Propriety of dismissal by the bankruptcy court

A. Standard of Review

Having established that the doctrine of comity applies, we now explain why we think dismissal was warranted, that is to say, why the statute was properly construed not to reach the pre-petition fund transfers to the defendant banks. * * *

* * *

B. Primacy of English Law

England has a much closer connection to these disputes than does the United States. The debtor and most of its creditors—not only the beneficiaries of the pre-petition transfers—are British. Maxwell was incorporated under the laws of England, largely controlled by British nationals, governed by a British board of directors, and managed in London by British executives. These connecting factors indicated what the bankruptcy judge called the "Englishness" of the debtor, which was one reason for recognizing the administrators—who are officers of the High Court—as Maxwell's corporate governance. These same factors, particularly the fact that most of Maxwell's debt was incurred in England, show that England has the strongest connection to the present litigation.

Although an avoidance action concededly affects creditors other than the transferee, because scrutiny of the transfer is at the heart of such a suit it is assuredly most relevant that the transfers in this case related primarily to England. The $30 million received by Barclays came from an account at National Westminster in London and, while it was routed through Barclays' New York branch like all payments received in U.S. dollars, it was immediately credited to an overdraft account maintained in England. Plaintiffs claim no particular United States connection to the other alleged transfers to Barclays, all of which were denominated in the amended complaint in pounds sterling. Similarly, the transfers to National Westminster and Société Générale were made to and from accounts maintained in Great Britain.

Further, the overdraft facilities and other credit transactions between the transferee banks and the debtor resulted from negotiations that took place in England and were administered primarily there. English law applied to the resolution of disputes arising under such agreements. We recognize that some of the money transferred to the banks came from the proceeds of the sale of Maxwell subsidiaries in the United States, which is a subject we discuss in a moment. In almost all other respects, however, the credit transactions were centered in London and the fund transfers occurred there.

C. Relative Interests of Forum and Foreign States

Given the considerably lesser American connection to the dispute, the bankruptcy court believed its forum's interests were "not very compelling." *Maxwell I*, 170 B.R. at 814. Virtually the only factor linking the transfers to the United States—that the sale of certain Maxwell subsidiaries in the United States provided the source of some of the funds—is not particularly weighty because those companies were sold as going concerns. Hence, the potential effect that such sales might have had on local economies is not here implicated.

The examiner warns that dire consequences would result from a failure to enforce the Code's avoidance provision. The first one he mentions is that such a course ignores § 103(a) of the Code. This contention is one we have already addressed and rejected. The examiner next urges that the purposes underlying § 547 and § 502(d) would be thwarted unless both of these provisions were applied in all Chapter 11 proceedings. Although the non-application of these or other Bankruptcy Code provisions certainly might detract from the Code's policies in other cases, here the negative effects are insubstantial. The principal policies underlying the Code's avoidance provisions are equal distribution to creditors and preserving the value of the estate through the discouragement of aggressive pre-petition tactics causing dismemberment of the debtor. *Wolas*, 502 U.S. at 161. These policies are effectuated, although in a somewhat different way, by the provisions' British counterpart.

In the present case, in which there is a parallel insolvency proceeding taking place in another country, failure to apply § 547 and § 502(d) does not free creditors from the constraints of avoidance law, nor does it severely undercut the policy of equal distribution. All avoidance laws are necessarily limited in scope because time limits and other conditions are imposed on the voidability of transactions. Although a different result might be warranted were there no parallel proceeding in England—and, hence, no alternative mechanism for voiding preferences—we cannot say the United States has a significant interest in applying its avoidance law. Moreover, as noted, international comity is a policy that Congress expressly made part of the Bankruptcy Code, and a decision consistent with comity therefore furthers the Code's policy.

Because of the strong British connection to the present dispute, it follows that England has a stronger interest than the United States in applying its own avoidance law to these actions. Its law implicates that country's interest in promoting what Parliament apparently viewed as the appropriate compromise between equality of distribution and other important commercial interests, for instance, ensuring potentially insolvent debtors' ability to secure essential ongoing financing. In addition, although complexity in the conduct of transnational insolvencies makes choice-of-law prognostication imprecise, we agree with the lower courts that English law could have been expected to apply. [S]ee also *Canada S. Ry. v. Gebhard*, 109 U.S. 527, 537 38 (1883) (domestic creditors of foreign bankrupts "presumed to have contracted with a view to. . . laws of th[e] [foreign] government").

The administrators further declare that the English court's decision vacating the ex parte anti-avoidance suit order established that the application of our preference law by the Southern District courts would not violate the law of nations, and that American courts should not use comity as a reason to decline to assert jurisdiction under section § 547. The decision in the English court implied nothing of the kind. Instead, that court ruled that Barclays could not obtain an injunction because an expression of the principle of comity that relied on the good sense of the bankruptcy court outweighed the risk that it would assume jurisdiction in violation of international law.

Rather than take a confrontational posture by enjoining this litigation and prejudice the cooperation which has thus far prevailed between the Chapter 11 and the English administration, the High Court left the merits of the question for the American courts to decide. Thus, the English court's decision affords no basis for concluding that England's interests are insubstantial.

D. Cooperation and Harmonization: Systemic Interest

In addition to the relative strength of the respective jurisdictional interests of England and the United States, there is a compelling systemic interest pointing in this instance against the application of the Bankruptcy Code. These parallel proceedings in the English and American courts have resulted in a high level of international cooperation and a significant degree of harmonization of the laws of the two countries. The affected parties agreed to the plan and scheme despite differences in the two nations' bankruptcy laws. The distribution mechanism established by them—beyond addressing some of the most obvious substantive and procedural incongruities—allowed Maxwell's assets to be pooled together and sold as going concerns, maximizing the return to creditors. And, by not requiring a creditor to file its claim in both forums, the arrangement eliminated many of the inefficiencies usually attendant in multi-jurisdiction proceedings.

Taken together, these accomplishments—which, we think, are attributable in large measure to the cooperation between the two courts overseeing the dual proceedings—are well worth preserving and advancing. This collaborative effort exemplifies the "spirit of cooperation" with which tribunals, guided by comity, should approach cases touching the laws and interests of more than one country. Where a dispute involving conflicting avoidance laws arises in the context of parallel bankruptcy proceedings that have already achieved substantial reconciliation between the two sets of laws, comity argues decidedly against the risk of derailing that cooperation by the selfish application of our law to circumstances touching more directly upon the interests of another forum.

It should be remembered that the interest of the system as a whole—that of promoting "a friendly intercourse between the sovereignties," *Hilton*, 159 U.S. at 165—also furthers American self-interest, especially where the workings of international trade and commerce are concerned. * * *

We recognize that forbearance and goodwill in the conduct of international bankruptcies is an ideal not easily achieved in the near-term. Many commentators advocate centralized administration of each insolvency under one country's laws, which could require a multi-lateral treaty or, even, a greater degree of harmonization of the commercial laws throughout the world. *See, e.g.,* Douglass G. Boshkoff, *Some Gloomy Thoughts Concerning Cross–Border Insolvencies*, 72 Wash.U.L.Q. 931, 931–36 (1994). In the meanwhile, bankruptcy courts may best be able to effectuate the purposes of the bankruptcy law by cooperating with foreign courts on a case-by-case basis. Congress contemplated this approach when it provided for "ancillary" proceedings under § 304. Although comity analysis admittedly does not yield the commercial predictability that might eventually be achieved through uniform rules, it permits the courts to reach workable solutions and to overcome some of the problems of a disordered international system. Given that the scheme and plan in this case did not clearly address the choice-of-law and choice-of-forum questions that have generated this litigation, resort to comity and choice-of-law principles should naturally have been foreseen. Consequently, the interests of the affected forums and the mutual interest of all nations in smoothly functioning international law counsel against the application of United States law in the present case.

IV. Denial of distributions under § 502

The final issue to be resolved is the plaintiffs' contention that even if the pre-petition transfers to the banks may not be recovered under § 547 for comity reasons or otherwise, the administrators are nevertheless entitled under § 502(d) to deny distributions to the banks as unsecured creditors. Section 502(d) provides in relevant part that "the court shall disallow any claim of any entity... that is a transferee of a transfer avoidable under section... 547 of this title."

The district court turned this challenge aside on two separate grounds. It held that § 502 is inapplicable because § 547 does not govern the avoidance action by the administrators and the transfers are therefore not "avoidable" under § 547. Further, it stated that the banks have not filed "claims" under § 502(d) because they have never submitted themselves to the bankruptcy court's jurisdiction. Defendants declare that this argument was waived because it was not submitted to the bankruptcy court. We nonetheless exercise our appellate discretion to entertain the issue because it is one of law, it was clearly presented in the adversary complaints, it was argued before and decided by the district court, and the transcript of hearing on the Rule 12(b)(6) motions indicates the bankruptcy court was quite aware of the relevant statute.

We hold that § 502(d) does not apply, but for reasons slightly different than those expressed by the district court. The plaintiffs strongly urge that the district court conflated § 547 and § 502(d) by reading the words "transfer avoidable" in the latter to mean any transfer that actually could be recovered by the estate under the former. They rely on cases holding that disallowance is required under § 502(d) even where a transfer may not affirmatively be recovered because the limitations period for such recovery has expired. * * *

The rule that § 502(d) disallowance is not precluded by the expiration of the limitations period governing recovery under § 547, however sound it may be, does not control in this case. Where a transfer could be avoided under § 547 but for the running of the statute of limitations, disallowance may be warranted because the substantive provisions of § 547, as opposed to the time-limit set forth in § 546(a), still apply to the transfer at issue. See *McLean*, 184 B.R. at 15 (§ 502(d) refers to § 547, not § 546). But in the present case, the doctrine of comity leads to the conclusion that § 547 does not apply to the pre-petition transfers at all. Consequently, the transfers cannot in any way be included among the "transfers avoidable" listed in § 502(d). In addition, because § 502(d) and § 547 apply to the same types of transfers and serve similar purposes, the former is inapplicable to the present case for the reasons discussed in Part III of this opinion.

With respect to the district court's alternative ground for denying relief under § 502(d), we must agree with the administrators that the banks' decision to lodge notices of claim in England, rather than filing proofs of claim with the bankruptcy court, cannot be construed to mean that they have not submitted "claims" for purposes of the Bankruptcy Code. To be eligible for distributions under the plan, the banks had to submit "claims," which must be "allowed." See § 726(a).

* * * [B]y requiring the administrators to pass along to the bankruptcy court notices of claim filed in England, the plan and scheme comply with the Code's requirement that a proof of claim be filed with the bankruptcy court. Such claims are "allowed" under the Code, see § 502(a), if they are accepted without objection by the administrators or liability is established by adjudication in the appropriate court, which may be the bankruptcy court or the English court depending upon the circumstances. We are therefore unable to agree with the district court's conclusion that § 502(d) is inapplicable because the banks have not submitted "claims."

Conclusion

In sum, we hold that the binding effect of the confirmation order does not preclude the banks from challenging the applicability of the Bankruptcy Code's avoidance rules to these actions brought by the administrators. Further, in this unique case involving cooperative parallel bankruptcy proceedings seeking to harmonize two nations' insolvency laws for the common benefit of creditors, the doctrine of international comity precludes application of the American avoidance law to transfers in which England's interest has primacy. We decline to decide whether, setting aside considerations of comity, the "presumption against extraterritoriality" would compel a conclusion that the Bankruptcy Code does not reach the pre-petition transfers at issue. Thus, we express no view regarding the banks' contention that the Bankruptcy Code never applies to non-domestic conduct or conditions. Finally, we reject plaintiffs' argument that the defendant banks' claims against the estate must be disallowed under § 502(d) notwithstanding the non-applicability of § 547.

Accordingly, for the reasons stated, the order appealed from is affirmed.

NOTES

1. The history and significance of the *Maxwell Communication* case is discussed in Jay L. Westbrook, *The Lessons of Maxwell Communication*, 64 Fordham L.Rev. 2531 (1996). *In re Treco*, 240 F.3d 148 (2d Cir. 2001), suggests some of the limits to comity and international cooperation. In *Treco*, the Bank of New York asserted that certain funds sought by the Bahamian liquidators of the Meridien International Bank Ltd. (MIBL) were subject to setoff under United States law and accordingly refused to turnover the funds. The Second Circuit refused to require turnover because Bahamian insolvency law (unlike the United States Bankruptcy Code) might subordinate the Bank of New York's secured claim to administrative expenses that threatened to consume the MIBL estate. It wrote:

> The principle of comity has never meant categorical deference to foreign proceedings. It is implicit in the concept that deference should be withheld where appropriate to avoid the violation of the laws, public policies or rights of citizens of the United States.

240 F.3d at 157.

2. The bankruptcy court in a Chapter 15 proceeding has discretion to issue stays, enforce judgments and order turnover of property to the foreign representative and issue other relief in its discretion. Fundamentally, Chapter 15 seeks to ensure that foreign representatives of insolvent estates and foreign insolvency proceedings receive recognition in United States courts, §§ 1509-1524 and that formal and informal mechanisms of cooperation and comity (like the *Maxwell Communication* protocol) receive official sanction and encouragement. §§ 1525-1532. The seeds of a broader conflict of laws principle, that all courts defer to the "main proceeding" taking place in "the center of the debtor's main interests," § 1502(4), are planted, but not implemented in Chapter 15, which presumes that existing United States bankruptcy law, subject to already recognized principles of conflicts of laws and comity, will continue to govern all United States bankruptcy proceedings. Moreover, even the limited provisions of Chapter 15 remain subject to an overall public policy exception, § 1506, and the mandate for international cooperation is conditioned on the

United States courts finding that "the interests of creditors in the United States are sufficiently protected." § 1521(b).

Forum-shopping remains a concern under Chapter 15. Lynn M. LoPucki, *Universalism Unravels*, 79 Am. Bankr. L. J. 143 (2005). Recognition of a foreign proceeding implies some degree of (albeit discretionary) deference to foreign insolvency law in the adjustment of debtor-creditor relations and administration of bankruptcy estates. This feature of Chapter 15 raises the specter of debtors manipulating venue in order to avoid application of United States law. Chapter 15 appears to limit the parties' choice of venue for "foreign main proceedings" to the debtor's "center of main interests." § 1517(b)(1). "Foreign non-main proceedings" may be commenced in jurisdictions where the debtor maintains an "establishment." § 1517(b)(2). In *In re Bear Stearns High Grade Structured Credit Strategies Master Fund Ltd*, 389 B.R. 325 (S.D.N.Y. 2008), the Cayman Islands representative of a New York based investment fund organized under the laws of the Cayman Islands sought recognition of its Cayman Islands insolvency proceeding as either a "foreign main proceeding" or a "foreign non-main proceeding." The Southern District of New York declined both invitations, finding that the debtor had only superficial connections to the Cayman Islands. *Bear Stearns* reflects a reluctance to grant forum-shopping Chapter 15 debtors the benefits of a United States bankruptcy filing while avoiding its burdens by filing first in off-shore havens like the Cayman Islands.

Notably, many Chapter 15 filings, like *Bear Stearns*, appear to fall into the forum-shopping category. The most prominent cases requiring extensive coordination of proceedings in two or more countries typically involve massive fraud such as *Maxwell Communication, Eurofood* (*Parmalat*) and *Bank of Credit and Commerce International (BCCI)*. In general, at least in the absence of massive fraud, United States firms with far flung operations can reorganize under Chapter 11 without commencing insolvency proceedings in foreign jurisdictions for themselves or on behalf of their foreign subsidiaries. Robert K. Rasmussen, *Where are All the Transnational Bankruptcies: The Puzzling Case for Universalism*, 32 Brooklyn J. Int'l L. 983 (2007). In addition to forming the basis for Chapter 15 in the United States, the UNCITRAL Model Law has (in various permutations) been adopted by Australia (2008), British Virgin Islands (2005), Colombia (2006), Eritrea (1998), Great Britain (2006), Japan (2000), Mexico (2000), Montenegro (2002), New Zealand (2006), Poland (2003), Republic of Korea (2006), Romania (2003), Serbia (2004), South Africa (2000).

3. Venue within the United States for Chapter 15 cases is prescribed by 28 U.S.C. § 1410, which directs filing to the district in the United States where the debtor maintains its principal place of business or principal assets. If the debtor has no such domestic location or assets, then the district in which the debtor is defending lawsuits is proper. Otherwise, the case may be filed anywhere consistent with the interests of justice. Notwithstanding, these apparently restrictive venue provisions, of the 42 Chapter 15 cases filed in 2007, 31 were filed in the Southern District of New York, and three in Delaware. No other district docketed more than a single Chapter 15 case.

4. What if a Chapter 11 case is pending in the United States, but there are foreign assets or parties and a concurrently pending foreign insolvency proceeding? The Bankruptcy Code asserts extraterritorial reach over all the debtor's "property wherever located and by whomever held. . ." § 541(a). One issue in *Maxwell Communication* not reached by the Second Circuit was the extraterritorial reach of § 547 in connection with the preferential transfers to foreign parties that was deemed to have occurred in London. In a controversial holding, the bankruptcy court and district court found that § 547 did not reach these transfers. *Maxwell Communication Corp. plc v. Société Générale PLC*, 186 B.R. 807 (S.D.N.Y.1995). Should a preferential transfer made by a United States debtor through a foreign bank account be subject to avoidance (if at all) only in accordance with the law of the country within which the bank account is located?

5. Beginning in the 1990s some nations, see *Barclays Bank PLC v. Homan*, BCLC 680 (1993) (UK law), and *Roberts v. Picture Butte Municipal Hospital* [1998], 227 A.R. 308 (Canada law), made significant steps towards greater formal recognition of foreign bankruptcy cases in their domestic insolvency law. Canada, in particular, has embraced a kind of cooperative territorialism it describes as "pluralist," and, as in *Roberts, supra*, has demonstrated a willingness in appropriate cases to defer to Chapter 11 proceedings in the United States in light of the similarities in the two nations' insolvency laws. Absent a foreign court's decision to defer to the United States bankruptcy proceeding, however, notwithstanding the extraterritorial reach of the Code, as a practical matter, some creditors may be able to achieve more favorable treatment in a foreign proceeding where the local court asserts control over property within the foreign jurisdiction. Section 1532 (derived from former 508(a)), the "hotch-pot rule," provides some relief in this situation by reducing a creditor's distributions under the Bankruptcy Code by the amount the creditor receives in any foreign proceeding. The hotch-pot rule seeks to put all claimants in the United States bankruptcy case on as equal a footing as possible in light of the reality that some creditors may be able to gain special advantages in foreign bankruptcy proceedings.

As we begin the 21st century, neither the United States nor the other commercial nations of the world are ready to unequivocally accept the principle that one uniform law should govern the rights and liabilities of parties to an insolvent estate throughout the world. In contrast, the 220 year-old American Constitution's Art. I, § 8 provision that Congress may establish "uniform laws on the subject of Bankruptcies throughout the United States" seems remarkably farsighted and non-parochial.

APPENDIX
SELECTED OFFICIAL CONSUMER BANKRUPTCY FORMS

Form 22A

B22A (Official Form 22A) (Chapter 7) (12/08)

In re _____
     Debtor(s)

Case Number: _____
              (If known)

According to the information required to be entered on this statement (check one box as directed in Part I, III, or VI of this statement):

☐ The presumption arises.
☐ The presumption does not arise.
☐ The presumption is temporarily inapplicable.

CHAPTER 7 STATEMENT OF CURRENT MONTHLY INCOME AND MEANS-TEST CALCULATION

In addition to Schedules I and J, this statement must be completed by every individual chapter 7 debtor, whether or not filing jointly. Unless the exclusion in Line 1C applies, joint debtors may complete a single statement. If the exclusion in Line 1C applies, each joint filer must complete a separate statement.

	Part I. MILITARY AND NON-CONSUMER DEBTORS
1A	**Disabled Veterans.** If you are a disabled veteran described in the Declaration in this Part 1A, (1) check the box at the beginning of the Declaration, (2) check the box for "The presumption does not arise" at the top of this statement, and (3) complete the verification in Part VIII. Do not complete any of the remaining parts of this statement. ☐ **Declaration of Disabled Veteran.** By checking this box, I declare under penalty of perjury that I am a disabled veteran (as defined in 38 U.S.C. § 3741(1)) whose indebtedness occurred primarily during a period in which I was on active duty (as defined in 10 U.S.C. § 101(d)(1)) or while I was performing a homeland defense activity (as defined in 32 U.S.C. §901(1)).
1B	**Non-consumer Debtors.** If your debts are not primarily consumer debts, check the box below and complete the verification in Part VIII. Do not complete any of the remaining parts of this statement. ☐ **Declaration of non-consumer debts.** By checking this box, I declare that my debts are not primarily consumer debts.

1C	**Reservists and National Guard Members; active duty or homeland defense activity.** Members of a reserve component of the Armed Forces and members of the National Guard who were called to active duty (as defined in 10 U.S.C. § 101(d)(1)) after September 11, 2001, for a period of at least 90 days, or who have performed homeland defense activity (as defined in 32 U.S.C. § 901(1)) for a period of at least 90 days, are excluded from all forms of means testing during the time of active duty or homeland defense activity and for 540 days thereafter (the "exclusion period"). If you qualify for this temporary exclusion, (1) check the appropriate boxes and complete any required information in the Declaration of Reservists and National Guard Members below, (2) check the box for "The presumption is temporarily inapplicable" at the top of this statement, and (3) complete the verification in Part VIII. **During your exclusion period you are not required to complete the balance of this form, but you must complete the form no later than 14 days after the date on which your exclusion period ends, unless the time for filing a motion raising the means test presumption expires in your case before your exclusion period ends.**
	
	☐ **Declaration of Reservists and National Guard Members.** By checking this box and making the appropriate entries below, I declare that I am eligible for a temporary exclusion from means testing because, as a member of a reserve component of the Armed Forces or the National Guard
	
	    a. ☐ I was called to active duty after September 11, 2001, for a period of at least 90 days and
	        ☐ I remain on active duty /or/
	        ☐ I was released from active duty on _____, which is less than 540 days before this bankruptcy case was filed;
	    OR
	    b. ☐ I am performing homeland defense activity for a period of at least 90 days /or/
	        ☐ I performed homeland defense activity for a period of at least 90 days, terminating on _____, which is less than 540 days before this bankruptcy case was filed.

B22A (Official Form 22A) (Chapter 7) (12/08)

Part II. CALCULATION OF MONTHLY INCOME FOR § 707(b)(7) EXCLUSION

2	**Marital/filing status.** Check the box that applies and complete the balance of this part of this statement as directed. a. ☐ Unmarried. **Complete only Column A ("Debtor's Income") for Lines 3-11.** b. ☐ Married, not filing jointly, with declaration of separate households. By checking this box, debtor declares under penalty of perjury: "My spouse and I are legally separated under applicable non-bankruptcy law or my spouse and I are living apart other than for the purpose of evading the requirements of § 707(b)(2)(A) of the Bankruptcy Code." **Complete only Column A ("Debtor's Income") for Lines 3-11.** c. ☐ Married, not filing jointly, without the declaration of separate households set out in Line 2.b above. **Complete both Column A ("Debtor's Income") and Column B ("Spouse's Income") for Lines 3-11.** d. ☐ Married, filing jointly. **Complete both Column A ("Debtor's Income") and Column B ("Spouse's Income") for Lines 3-11.**				
	All figures must reflect average monthly income received from all sources, derived during the six calendar months prior to filing the bankruptcy case, ending on the last day of the month before the filing. If the amount of monthly income varied during the six months, you must divide the six-month total by six, and enter the result on the appropriate line.			**Column A** Debtor's Income	**Column B** Spouse's Income
3	**Gross wages, salary, tips, bonuses, overtime, commissions.**			$	$
4	**Income from the operation of a business, profession or farm.** Subtract Line b from Line a and enter the difference in the appropriate column(s) of Line 4. If you operate more than one business, profession or farm, enter aggregate numbers and provide details on an attachment. Do not enter a number less than zero. **Do not include any part of the business expenses entered on Line b as a deduction in Part V.**				
	a.	Gross receipts	$		
	b.	Ordinary and necessary business expenses	$		
	c.	Business income	Subtract Line b from Line a	$	$
5	**Rent and other real property income.** Subtract Line b from Line a and enter the difference in the appropriate column(s) of Line 5. Do not enter a number less than zero. **Do not include any part of the operating expenses entered on Line b as a deduction in Part V.**				
	a.	Gross receipts	$		
	b.	Ordinary and necessary operating expenses	$		
	c.	Rent and other real property income	Subtract Line b from Line a	$	$
6	**Interest, dividends and royalties.**			$	$
7	**Pension and retirement income.**			$	$
8	Any amounts paid by another person or entity, on a regular basis, for the household expenses of the debtor or the debtor's dependents, including child support paid for that purpose. Do not include alimony or separate maintenance payments or amounts paid by your spouse if Column B is completed.			$	$
9	**Unemployment compensation.** Enter the amount in the appropriate column(s) of Line 9. However, if you contend that unemployment compensation received by you or your spouse was a benefit under the Social Security Act, do not list the amount of such compensation in Column A or B, but instead state the amount in the space below: Unemployment compensation claimed to be a benefit under the Social Security Act Debtor $ _____ Spouse $ _____			$	$

B22A (Official Form 22A) (Chapter 7) (12/08)

10	**Income from all other sources.** Specify source and amount. If necessary, list additional sources on a separate page. **Do not include alimony or separate maintenance payments paid by your spouse if Column B is completed, but include all other payments of alimony or separate maintenance.** Do not include any benefits received under the Social Security Act or payments received as a victim of a war crime, crime against humanity, or as a victim of international or domestic terrorism.		
	a.	$	
	b.	$	
	Total and enter on Line 10	$	$
11	**Subtotal of Current Monthly Income for § 707(b)(7).** Add Lines 3 thru 10 in Column A, and, if Column B is completed, add Lines 3 through 10 in Column B. Enter the total(s).	$	$
12	**Total Current Monthly Income for § 707(b)(7).** If Column B has been completed, add Line 11, Column A to Line 11, Column B, and enter the total. If Column B has not been completed, enter the amount from Line 11, Column A.	$	

Part III. APPLICATION OF § 707(b)(7) EXCLUSION

13	**Annualized Current Monthly Income for § 707(b)(7).** Multiply the amount from Line 12 by the number 12 and enter the result.	$
14	**Applicable median family income.** Enter the median family income for the applicable state and household size. (This information is available by family size at www.usdoj.gov/ust/ or from the clerk of the bankruptcy court.) a. Enter debtor's state of residence: _____ b. Enter debtor's household size: _____	$
15	**Application of Section 707(b)(7).** Check the applicable box and proceed as directed. ☐ **The amount on Line 13 is less than or equal to the amount on Line 14.** Check the box for "The presumption does not arise" at the top of page 1 of this statement, and complete Part VIII; do not complete Parts IV, V, VI or VII. ☐ **The amount on Line 13 is more than the amount on Line 14.** Complete the remaining parts of this statement.	

Complete Parts IV, V, VI, and VII of this statement only if required. (See Line 15.)

Part IV. CALCULATION OF CURRENT MONTHLY INCOME FOR § 707(b)(2)

16	Enter the amount from Line 12.	$
17	**Marital adjustment.** If you checked the box at Line 2.c, enter on Line 17 the total of any income listed in Line 11, Column B that was NOT paid on a regular basis for the household expenses of the debtor or the debtor's dependents. Specify in the lines below the basis for excluding the Column B income (such as payment of the spouse's tax liability or the spouse's support of persons other than the debtor or the debtor's dependents) and the amount of income devoted to each purpose. If necessary, list additional adjustments on a separate page. If you did not check box at Line 2.c, enter zero.	
	a.	$
	b.	$
	c.	$
	Total and enter on Line 17.	$
18	**Current monthly income for § 707(b)(2).** Subtract Line 17 from Line 16 and enter the result.	$

Part V. CALCULATION OF DEDUCTIONS FROM INCOME

Subpart A: Deductions under Standards of the Internal Revenue Service (IRS)

19A	**National Standards: food, clothing and other items.** Enter in Line 19A the "Total" amount from IRS National Standards for Food, Clothing and Other Items for the applicable household size. (This information is available at www.usdoj.gov/ust/ or from the clerk of the bankruptcy court.)	$

B22A (Official Form 22A) (Chapter 7) (12/08)

19B	**National Standards: health care.** Enter in Line a1 below the amount from IRS National Standards for Out-of-Pocket Health Care for persons under 65 years of age, and in Line a2 the IRS National Standards for Out-of-Pocket Health Care for persons 65 years of age or older. (This information is available at www.usdoj.gov/ust/ or from the clerk of the bankruptcy court.) Enter in Line b1 the number of members of your household who are under 65 years of age, and enter in Line b2 the number of members of your household who are 65 years of age or older. (The total number of household members must be the same as the number stated in Line 14b.) Multiply Line a1 by Line b1 to obtain a total amount for household members under 65, and enter the result in Line c1. Multiply Line a2 by Line b2 to obtain a total amount for household members 65 and older, and enter the result in Line c2. Add Lines c1 and c2 to obtain a total health care amount, and enter the result in Line 19B.				
	Household members under 65 years of age		Household members 65 years of age or older		
	a1. Allowance per member		a2. Allowance per member		
	b1. Number of members		b2. Number of members		
	c1. Subtotal		c2. Subtotal		$
20A	**Local Standards: housing and utilities; non-mortgage expenses.** Enter the amount of the IRS Housing and Utilities Standards; non-mortgage expenses for the applicable county and household size. (This information is available at www.usdoj.gov/ust/ or from the clerk of the bankruptcy court).				$
20B	**Local Standards: housing and utilities; mortgage/rent expense.** Enter, in Line a below, the amount of the IRS Housing and Utilities Standards; mortgage/rent expense for your county and household size (this information is available at www.usdoj.gov/ust/ or from the clerk of the bankruptcy court); enter on Line b the total of the Average Monthly Payments for any debts secured by your home, as stated in Line 42; subtract Line b from Line a and enter the result in Line 20B. **Do not enter an amount less than zero.**				
	a.	IRS Housing and Utilities Standards; mortgage/rental expense	$		
	b.	Average Monthly Payment for any debts secured by your home, if any, as stated in Line 42	$		
	c.	Net mortgage/rental expense	Subtract Line b from Line a.		$
21	**Local Standards: housing and utilities; adjustment.** If you contend that the process set out in Lines 20A and 20B does not accurately compute the allowance to which you are entitled under the IRS Housing and Utilities Standards, enter any additional amount to which you contend you are entitled, and state the basis for your contention in the space below:				$
22A	**Local Standards: transportation; vehicle operation/public transportation expense.** You are entitled to an expense allowance in this category regardless of whether you pay the expenses of operating a vehicle and regardless of whether you use public transportation. Check the number of vehicles for which you pay the operating expenses or for which the operating expenses are included as a contribution to your household expenses in Line 8. ☐ 0 ☐ 1 ☐ 2 or more. If you checked 0, enter on Line 22A the "Public Transportation" amount from IRS Local Standards: Transportation. If you checked 1 or 2 or more, enter on Line 22A the "Operating Costs" amount from IRS Local Standards: Transportation for the applicable number of vehicles in the applicable Metropolitan Statistical Area or Census Region. (These amounts are available at www.usdoj.gov/ust/ or from the clerk of the bankruptcy court.)				$
22B	**Local Standards: transportation; additional public transportation expense.** If you pay the operating expenses for a vehicle and also use public transportation, and you contend that you are entitled to an additional deduction for your public transportation expenses, enter on Line 22B the "Public Transportation" amount from IRS Local Standards: Transportation. (This amount is available at www.usdoj.gov/ust/ or from the clerk of the bankruptcy court.)				$

B22A (Official Form 22A) (Chapter 7) (12/08)

23	**Local Standards: transportation ownership/lease expense; Vehicle 1.** Check the number of vehicles for which you claim an ownership/lease expense. (You may not claim an ownership/lease expense for more than two vehicles.) ☐ 1 ☐ 2 or more. Enter, in Line a below, the "Ownership Costs" for "One Car" from the IRS Local Standards: Transportation (available at www.usdoj.gov/ust/ or from the clerk of the bankruptcy court); enter in Line b the total of the Average Monthly Payments for any debts secured by Vehicle 1, as stated in Line 42; subtract Line b from Line a and enter the result in Line 23. **Do not enter an amount less than zero.**			
	a.	IRS Transportation Standards, Ownership Costs	$	
	b.	Average Monthly Payment for any debts secured by Vehicle 1, as stated in Line 42	$	
	c.	Net ownership/lease expense for Vehicle 1	Subtract Line b from Line a.	$
24	**Local Standards: transportation ownership/lease expense; Vehicle 2.** Complete this Line only if you checked the "2 or more" Box in Line 23. Enter, in Line a below, the "Ownership Costs" for "One Car" from the IRS Local Standards: Transportation (available at www.usdoj.gov/ust/ or from the clerk of the bankruptcy court); enter in Line b the total of the Average Monthly Payments for any debts secured by Vehicle 2, as stated in Line 42; subtract Line b from Line a and enter the result in Line 24. **Do not enter an amount less than zero.**			
	a.	IRS Transportation Standards, Ownership Costs	$	
	b.	Average Monthly Payment for any debts secured by Vehicle 2, as stated in Line 42	$	
	c.	Net ownership/lease expense for Vehicle 2	Subtract Line b from Line a.	$
25	**Other Necessary Expenses: taxes.** Enter the total average monthly expense that you actually incur for all federal, state and local taxes, other than real estate and sales taxes, such as income taxes, self-employment taxes, social-security taxes, and Medicare taxes. **Do not include real estate or sales taxes.**			$
26	**Other Necessary Expenses: involuntary deductions for employment.** Enter the total average monthly payroll deductions that are required for your employment, such as retirement contributions, union dues, and uniform costs. **Do not include discretionary amounts, such as voluntary 401(k) contributions.**			$
27	**Other Necessary Expenses: life insurance.** Enter total average monthly premiums that you actually pay for term life insurance for yourself. **Do not include premiums for insurance on your dependents, for whole life or for any other form of insurance.**			$
28	**Other Necessary Expenses: court-ordered payments.** Enter the total monthly amount that you are required to pay pursuant to the order of a court or administrative agency, such as spousal or child support payments. **Do not include payments on past due obligations included in Line 44.**			$
29	**Other Necessary Expenses: education for employment or for a physically or mentally challenged child.** Enter the total average monthly amount that you actually expend for education that is a condition of employment and for education that is required for a physically or mentally challenged dependent child for whom no public education providing similar services is available.			$
30	**Other Necessary Expenses: childcare.** Enter the total average monthly amount that you actually expend on childcare—such as baby-sitting, day care, nursery and preschool. **Do not include other educational payments.**			$
31	**Other Necessary Expenses: health care.** Enter the total average monthly amount that you actually expend on health care that is required for the health and welfare of yourself or your dependents, that is not reimbursed by insurance or paid by a health savings account, and that is in excess of the amount entered in Line 19B. **Do not include payments for health insurance or health savings accounts listed in Line 34.**			$
32	**Other Necessary Expenses: telecommunication services.** Enter the total average monthly amount that you actually pay for telecommunication services other than your basic home telephone and cell phone service—such as pagers, call waiting, caller Id, special long distance, or internet service—to the extent necessary for your health and welfare or that of your dependents. **Do not include any amount previously deducted.**			$
33	**Total Expenses Allowed under IRS Standards.** Enter the total of Lines 19 through 32.			$

B22A (Official Form 22A) (Chapter 7) (12/08)

	Subpart B: Additional Living Expense Deductions Note: Do not include any expenses that you have listed in Lines 19-32			
34	**Health Insurance, Disability Insurance, and Health Savings Account Expenses.** List the monthly expenses in the categories set out in lines a-c below that are reasonably necessary for yourself, your spouse, or your dependents.			
	a.	Health Insurance	$	
	b.	Disability Insurance	$	
	c.	Health Savings Account	$	
	Total and enter on Line 34			$
	If you do not actually expend this total amount, state your actual total average monthly expenditures in the space below: $ _____			
35	**Continued contributions to the care of household or family members.** Enter the total average actual monthly expenses that you will continue to pay for the reasonable and necessary care and support of an elderly, chronically ill, or disabled member of your household or member of your immediate family who is unable to pay for such expenses.			$
36	**Protection against family violence.** Enter the total average reasonably necessary monthly expenses that you actually incurred to maintain the safety of your family under the Family Violence Prevention and Services Act or other applicable federal law. The nature of these expenses is required to be kept confidential by the court.			$
37	**Home energy costs.** Enter the total average monthly amount, in excess of the allowance specified by IRS Local Standards for Housing and Utilities, that you actually expend for home energy costs. **You must provide your case trustee with documentation of your actual expenses, and you must demonstrate that the additional amount claimed is reasonable and necessary.**			$
38	**Education expenses for dependent children less than 18.** Enter the total average monthly expenses that you actually incur, not to exceed $137.50 per child, for attendance at a private or public elementary or secondary school by your dependent children less than 18 years of age. **You must provide your case trustee with documentation of your actual expenses, and you must explain why the amount claimed is reasonable and necessary and not already accounted for in the IRS Standards.**			$
39	**Additional food and clothing expense.** Enter the total average monthly amount by which your food and clothing expenses exceed the combined allowances for food and clothing (apparel and services) in the IRS National Standards, not to exceed 5% of those combined allowances. (This information is available at www.usdoj.gov/ust/ or from the clerk of the bankruptcy court.) **You must demonstrate that the additional amount claimed is reasonable and necessary.**			$
40	**Continued charitable contributions.** Enter the amount that you will continue to contribute in the form of cash or financial instruments to a charitable organization as defined in 26 U.S.C. § 170(c)(1)-(2).			$
41	**Total Additional Expense Deductions under § 707(b).** Enter the total of Lines 34 through 40			$

B22A (Official Form 22A) (Chapter 7) (12/08)

	Subpart C: Deductions for Debt Payment		
42	**Future payments on secured claims.** For each of your debts that is secured by an interest in property that you own, list the name of the creditor, identify the property securing the debt, state the Average Monthly Payment, and check whether the payment includes taxes or insurance. The Average Monthly Payment is the total of all amounts scheduled as contractually due to each Secured Creditor in the 60 months following the filing of the bankruptcy case, divided by 60. If necessary, list additional entries on a separate page. Enter the total of the Average Monthly Payments on Line 42. <table><tr><th></th><th>Name of Creditor</th><th>Property Securing the Debt</th><th>Average Monthly Payment</th><th>Does payment include taxes or insurance?</th></tr><tr><td>a.</td><td></td><td></td><td>$</td><td>☐ yes ☐ no</td></tr><tr><td>b.</td><td></td><td></td><td>$</td><td>☐ yes ☐ no</td></tr><tr><td>c.</td><td></td><td></td><td>$</td><td>☐ yes ☐ no</td></tr><tr><td></td><td></td><td></td><td colspan="2">Total: Add Lines a, b and c.</td></tr></table>		$
43	**Other payments on secured claims.** If any of debts listed in Line 42 are secured by your primary residence, a motor vehicle, or other property necessary for your support or the support of your dependents, you may include in your deduction 1/60th of any amount (the "cure amount") that you must pay the creditor in addition to the payments listed in Line 42, in order to maintain possession of the property. The cure amount would include any sums in default that must be paid in order to avoid repossession or foreclosure. List and total any such amounts in the following chart. If necessary, list additional entries on a separate page. <table><tr><th></th><th>Name of Creditor</th><th>Property Securing the Debt</th><th>1/60th of the Cure Amount</th></tr><tr><td>a.</td><td></td><td></td><td>$</td></tr><tr><td>b.</td><td></td><td></td><td>$</td></tr><tr><td>c.</td><td></td><td></td><td>$</td></tr><tr><td></td><td></td><td></td><td>Total: Add Lines a, b and c</td></tr></table>		$
44	**Payments on prepetition priority claims.** Enter the total amount, divided by 60, of all priority claims, such as priority tax, child support and alimony claims, for which you were liable at the time of your bankruptcy filing. **Do not include current obligations, such as those set out in Line 28.**		$
45	**Chapter 13 administrative expenses.** If you are eligible to file a case under chapter 13, complete the following chart, multiply the amount in line a by the amount in line b, and enter the resulting administrative expense. <table><tr><td>a.</td><td>Projected average monthly chapter 13 plan payment.</td><td>$</td></tr><tr><td>b.</td><td>Current multiplier for your district as determined under schedules issued by the Executive Office for United States Trustees. (This information is available at www.usdoj.gov/ust/ or from the clerk of the bankruptcy court.)</td><td>x</td></tr><tr><td>c.</td><td>Average monthly administrative expense of chapter 13 case</td><td>Total: Multiply Lines a and b</td></tr></table>		$
46	**Total Deductions for Debt Payment.** Enter the total of Lines 42 through 45.		$
	Subpart D: Total Deductions from Income		
47	**Total of all deductions allowed under § 707(b)(2).** Enter the total of Lines 33, 41, and 46.		$

B22A (Official Form 22A) (Chapter 7) (12/08)

	Part VI. DETERMINATION OF § 707(b)(2) PRESUMPTION	
48	Enter the amount from Line 18 (Current monthly income for § 707(b)(2))	$
49	Enter the amount from Line 47 (Total of all deductions allowed under § 707(b)(2))	$
50	**Monthly disposable income under § 707(b)(2).** Subtract Line 49 from Line 48 and enter the result	$
51	**60-month disposable income under § 707(b)(2).** Multiply the amount in Line 50 by the number 60 and enter the result.	$
52	**Initial presumption determination.** Check the applicable box and proceed as directed. ☐ **The amount on Line 51 is less than $6,575** Check the box for "The presumption does not arise" at the top of page 1 of this statement, and complete the verification in Part VIII. Do not complete the remainder of Part VI. ☐ **The amount set forth on Line 51 is more than $10,950.** Check the box for "The presumption arises" at the top of page 1 of this statement, and complete the verification in Part VIII. You may also complete Part VII. Do not complete the remainder of Part VI. ☐ **The amount on Line 51 is at least $6,575, but not more than $10,950.** Complete the remainder of Part VI (Lines 53 through 55).	
53	Enter the amount of your total non-priority unsecured debt	$
54	**Threshold debt payment amount.** Multiply the amount in Line 53 by the number 0.25 and enter the result.	$
55	**Secondary presumption determination.** Check the applicable box and proceed as directed. ☐ **The amount on Line 51 is less than the amount on Line 54.** Check the box for "The presumption does not arise" at the top of page 1 of this statement, and complete the verification in Part VIII. ☐ **The amount on Line 51 is equal to or greater than the amount on Line 54.** Check the box for "The presumption arises" at the top of page 1 of this statement, and complete the verification in Part VIII. You may also complete Part VII.	
	Part VII: ADDITIONAL EXPENSE CLAIMS	
56	**Other Expenses.** List and describe any monthly expenses, not otherwise stated in this form, that are required for the health and welfare of you and your family and that you contend should be an additional deduction from your current monthly income under § 707(b)(2)(A)(ii)(I). If necessary, list additional sources on a separate page. All figures should reflect your average monthly expense for each item. Total the expenses. 		Expense Description	Monthly Amount
a.		$
b.		$
c.		$
	Total: Add Lines a, b and c	$		
	Part VIII: VERIFICATION	
57	I declare under penalty of perjury that the information provided in this statement is true and correct. *(If this is a joint case, both debtors must sign.)* Date: _____ Signature: _____ *(Debtor)* Date: _____ Signature: _____ *(Joint Debtor, if any)*	

Appendix: Selected Official Consumer Bankruptcy Forms   909

Form 22B

B 22B (Official Form 22B) (Chapter 11) (01/08)

In re _____
         Debtor(s)

Case Number: _____
              (If known)

CHAPTER 11 STATEMENT OF CURRENT MONTHLY INCOME

In addition to Schedules I and J, this statement must be completed by every individual chapter 11 debtor, whether or not filing jointly. Joint debtors may complete one statement only.

	Part I. CALCULATION OF CURRENT MONTHLY INCOME		
1	**Marital/filing status.** Check the box that applies and complete the balance of this part of this statement as directed. a. ☐ Unmarried. **Complete only Column A ("Debtor's Income") for Lines 2-10.** b. ☐ Married, not filing jointly. **Complete only Column A ("Debtor's Income") for Lines 2-10.** c. ☐ Married, filing jointly. **Complete both Column A ("Debtor's Income") and Column B ("Spouse's Income") for Lines 2-10.**		
	All figures must reflect average monthly income received from all sources, derived during the six calendar months prior to filing the bankruptcy case, ending on the last day of the month before the filing. If the amount of monthly income varied during the six months, you must divide the six-month total by six, and enter the result on the appropriate line.	Column A Debtor's Income	Column B Spouse's Income
2	**Gross wages, salary, tips, bonuses, overtime, commissions.**	$	$
3	**Net income from the operation of a business, profession, or farm.** Subtract Line b from Line a and enter the difference in the appropriate column(s) of Line 3. If more than one business, profession or farm, enter aggregate numbers and provide details on an attachment. Do not enter a number less than zero. a. Gross receipts — $ b. Ordinary and necessary business expenses — $ c. Business income — Subtract Line b from Line a.	$	$
4	**Net rental and other real property income.** Subtract Line b from Line a and enter the difference in the appropriate column(s) of Line 4. Do not enter a number less than zero. a. Gross receipts — $ b. Ordinary and necessary operating expenses — $ c. Rent and other real property income — Subtract Line b from Line a.	$	$
5	**Interest, dividends, and royalties.**	$	$
6	**Pension and retirement income.**	$	$
7	**Any amounts paid by another person or entity, on a regular basis, for the household expenses of the debtor or the debtor's dependents, including child support paid for that purpose.** Do not include alimony or separate maintenance payments or amounts paid by the debtor's spouse if Column B is completed.	$	$
8	**Unemployment compensation.** Enter the amount in the appropriate column(s) of Line 8. However, if you contend that unemployment compensation received by you or your spouse was a benefit under the Social Security Act, do not list the amount of such compensation in Column A or B, but instead state the amount in the space below: Unemployment compensation claimed to be a benefit under the Social Security Act Debtor $ _____ Spouse $ _____	$	$

B 22B (Official Form 22B) (Chapter 11) (01/08)

9	**Income from all other sources.** Specify source and amount. If necessary, list additional sources on a separate page. Total and enter on Line 9. **Do not include alimony or separate maintenance payments paid by your spouse if Column B is completed, but include all other payments of alimony or separate maintenance. Do not include** any benefits received under the Social Security Act or payments received as a victim of a war crime, crime against humanity, or as a victim of international or domestic terrorism.			
	a.		$	
	b.		$	$	$
10	**Subtotal of current monthly income.** Add Lines 2 thru 9 in Column A, and, if Column B is completed, add Lines 2 through 9 in Column B. Enter the total(s).		$	$
11	**Total current monthly income.** If Column B has been completed, add Line 10, Column A to Line 10, Column B, and enter the total. If Column B has not been completed, enter the amount from Line 10, Column A.		$	

Part II: VERIFICATION

12	I declare under penalty of perjury that the information provided in this statement is true and correct. *(If this a joint case, both debtors must sign.)* Date: _____ Signature: _____ (Debtor) Date: _____ Signature: _____ (Joint Debtor, if any)

Form 22C

B 22C (Official Form 22C) (Chapter 13) (01/08)

In re _____
      Debtor(s)

Case Number: _____
             (If known)

According to the calculations required by this statement:
☐ The applicable commitment period is 3 years.
☐ The applicable commitment period is 5 years.
☐ Disposable income is determined under § 1325(b)(3).
☐ Disposable income is not determined under § 1325(b)(3).
(Check the boxes as directed in Lines 17 and 23 of this statement.)

CHAPTER 13 STATEMENT OF CURRENT MONTHLY INCOME AND CALCULATION OF COMMITMENT PERIOD AND DISPOSABLE INCOME

In addition to Schedules I and J, this statement must be completed by every individual chapter 13 debtor, whether or not filing jointly. Joint debtors may complete one statement only.

	Part I. REPORT OF INCOME			
1	**Marital/filing status.** Check the box that applies and complete the balance of this part of this statement as directed. a. ☐ **Unmarried. Complete only Column A ("Debtor's Income") for Lines 2-10.** b. ☐ **Married. Complete both Column A ("Debtor's Income") and Column B ("Spouse's Income") for Lines 2-10.**			
	All figures must reflect average monthly income received from all sources, derived during the six calendar months prior to filing the bankruptcy case, ending on the last day of the month before the filing. If the amount of monthly income varied during the six months, you must divide the six-month total by six, and enter the result on the appropriate line.		**Column A** Debtor's Income	**Column B** Spouse's Income
2	**Gross wages, salary, tips, bonuses, overtime, commissions.**		$	$
3	**Income from the operation of a business, profession, or farm.** Subtract Line b from Line a and enter the difference in the appropriate column(s) of Line 3. If you operate more than one business, profession or farm, enter aggregate numbers and provide details on an attachment. Do not enter a number less than zero. **Do not include any part of the business expenses entered on Line b as a deduction in Part IV.**			
	a.	Gross receipts	$	
	b.	Ordinary and necessary business expenses	$	
	c.	Business income	Subtract Line b from Line a	$	$
4	**Rent and other real property income.** Subtract Line b from Line a and enter the difference in the appropriate column(s) of Line 4. Do not enter a number less than zero. **Do not include any part of the operating expenses entered on Line b as a deduction in Part IV.**			
	a.	Gross receipts	$	
	b.	Ordinary and necessary operating expenses	$	
	c.	Rent and other real property income	Subtract Line b from Line a	$	$
5	**Interest, dividends, and royalties.**		$	$
6	**Pension and retirement income.**		$	$
7	**Any amounts paid by another person or entity, on a regular basis, for the household expenses of the debtor or the debtor's dependents, including child support paid for that purpose.** Do not include alimony or separate maintenance payments or amounts paid by the debtor's spouse.		$	$
8	**Unemployment compensation.** Enter the amount in the appropriate column(s) of Line 8. However, if you contend that unemployment compensation received by you or your spouse was a benefit under the Social Security Act, do not list the amount of such compensation in Column A or B, but instead state the amount in the space below:			
	Unemployment compensation claimed to be a benefit under the Social Security Act	Debtor $ _____	Spouse $ _____	$	$

B 22C (Official Form 22C) (Chapter 13) (01/08) 2

9	**Income from all other sources.** Specify source and amount. If necessary, list additional sources on a separate page. Total and enter on Line 9. **Do not include alimony or separate maintenance payments paid by your spouse, but include all other payments of alimony or separate maintenance. Do not include** any benefits received under the Social Security Act or payments received as a victim of a war crime, crime against humanity, or as a victim of international or domestic terrorism.			
	a.		$	
	b.		$	
			$	$
10	**Subtotal.** Add Lines 2 thru 9 in Column A, and, if Column B is completed, add Lines 2 through 9 in Column B. Enter the total(s).		$	$
11	**Total.** If Column B has been completed, add Line 10, Column A to Line 10, Column B, and enter the total. If Column B has not been completed, enter the amount from Line 10, Column A.		$	

Part II. CALCULATION OF § 1325(b)(4) COMMITMENT PERIOD

12	Enter the amount from Line 11.		$
13	**Marital adjustment.** If you are married, but are not filing jointly with your spouse, AND if you contend that calculation of the commitment period under § 1325(b)(4) does not require inclusion of the income of your spouse, enter on Line 13 the amount of the income listed in Line 10, Column B that was NOT paid on a regular basis for the household expenses of you or your dependents and specify, in the lines below, the basis for excluding this income (such as payment of the spouse's tax liability or the spouse's support of persons other than the debtor or the debtor's dependents) and the amount of income devoted to each purpose. If necessary, list additional adjustments on a separate page. If the conditions for entering this adjustment do not apply, enter zero.		
	a.		$
	b.		$
	c.		$
	Total and enter on Line 13.		$
14	Subtract Line 13 from Line 12 and enter the result.		$
15	**Annualized current monthly income for § 1325(b)(4).** Multiply the amount from Line 14 by the number 12 and enter the result.		$
16	**Applicable median family income.** Enter the median family income for applicable state and household size. (This information is available by family size at www.usdoj.gov/ust/ or from the clerk of the bankruptcy court.) a. Enter debtor's state of residence: _____ b. Enter debtor's household size: _____		$
17	**Application of § 1325(b)(4).** Check the applicable box and proceed as directed. ☐ **The amount on Line 15 is less than the amount on Line 16.** Check the box for "The applicable commitment period is 3 years" at the top of page 1 of this statement and continue with this statement. ☐ **The amount on Line 15 is not less than the amount on Line 16.** Check the box for "The applicable commitment period is 5 years" at the top of page 1 of this statement and continue with this statement.		

Part III. APPLICATION OF § 1325(b)(3) FOR DETERMINING DISPOSABLE INCOME

18	Enter the amount from Line 11.		$

B 22C (Official Form 22C) (Chapter 13) (01/08) 3

19	**Marital adjustment.** If you are married, but are not filing jointly with your spouse, enter on Line 19 the total of any income listed in Line 10, Column B that was NOT paid on a regular basis for the household expenses of the debtor or the debtor's dependents. Specify in the lines below the basis for excluding the Column B income (such as payment of the spouse's tax liability or the spouse's support of persons other than the debtor or the debtor's dependents) and the amount of income devoted to each purpose. If necessary, list additional adjustments on a separate page. If the conditions for entering this adjustment do not apply, enter zero.	
	a. _____ $	
	b. _____ $	
	c. _____ $	
	Total and enter on Line 19.	$
20	**Current monthly income for § 1325(b)(3).** Subtract Line 19 from Line 18 and enter the result.	
21	**Annualized current monthly income for § 1325(b)(3).** Multiply the amount from Line 20 by the number 12 and enter the result.	$
22	**Applicable median family income.** Enter the amount from Line 16.	$
23	**Application of § 1325(b)(3).** Check the applicable box and proceed as directed. ☐ **The amount on Line 21 is more than the amount on Line 22.** Check the box for "Disposable income is determined under § 1325(b)(3)" at the top of page 1 of this statement and complete the remaining parts of this statement. ☐ **The amount on Line 21 is not more than the amount on Line 22.** Check the box for "Disposable income is not determined under § 1325(b)(3)" at the top of page 1 of this statement and complete Part VII of this statement. Do not complete Parts IV, V, or VI.	

Part IV. CALCULATION OF DEDUCTIONS FROM INCOME		
Subpart A: Deductions under Standards of the Internal Revenue Service (IRS)		
24A	**National Standards: food, apparel and services, housekeeping supplies, personal care, and miscellaneous.** Enter in Line 24A the "Total" amount from IRS National Standards for Allowable Living Expenses for the applicable household size. (This information is available at www.usdoj.gov/ust/ or from the clerk of the bankruptcy court.)	$
24B	**National Standards: health care.** Enter in Line a1 below the amount from IRS National Standards for Out-of-Pocket Health Care for persons under 65 years of age, and in Line a2 the IRS National Standards for Out-of-Pocket Health Care for persons 65 years of age or older. (This information is available at www.usdoj.gov/ust/ or from the clerk of the bankruptcy court.) Enter in Line b1 the number of members of your household who are under 65 years of age, and enter in Line b2 the number of members of your household who are 65 years of age or older. (The total number of household members must be the same as the number stated in Line 16b.) Multiply Line a1 by Line b1 to obtain a total amount for household members under 65, and enter the result in Line c1. Multiply Line a2 by Line b2 to obtain a total amount for household members 65 and older, and enter the result in Line c2. Add Lines c1 and c2 to obtain a total health care amount, and enter the result in Line 24B.	

	Household members under 65 years of age			Household members 65 years of age or older	
a1.	Allowance per member		a2.	Allowance per member	
b1.	Number of members		b2.	Number of members	
c1.	Subtotal		c2.	Subtotal	

25A	**Local Standards: housing and utilities; non-mortgage expenses.** Enter the amount of the IRS Housing and Utilities Standards; non-mortgage expenses for the applicable county and household size. (This information is available at www.usdoj.gov/ust/ or from the clerk of the bankruptcy court).	$

B 22C (Official Form 22C) (Chapter 13) (01/08) 4

25B	**Local Standards: housing and utilities; mortgage/rent expense.** Enter, in Line a below, the amount of the IRS Housing and Utilities Standards; mortgage/rent expense for your county and household size (this information is available at www.usdoj.gov/ust/ or from the clerk of the bankruptcy court); enter on Line b the total of the Average Monthly Payments for any debts secured by your home, as stated in Line 47; subtract Line b from Line a and enter the result in Line 25B. **Do not enter an amount less than zero.**		
	a.	IRS Housing and Utilities Standards; mortgage/rent expense	$
	b.	Average Monthly Payment for any debts secured by your home, if any, as stated in Line 47	$
	c.	Net mortgage/rental expense	Subtract Line b from Line a.	$
26	**Local Standards: housing and utilities; adjustment.** If you contend that the process set out in Lines 25A and 25B does not accurately compute the allowance to which you are entitled under the IRS Housing and Utilities Standards, enter any additional amount to which you contend you are entitled, and state the basis for your contention in the space below: _____ _____		$
27A	**Local Standards: transportation; vehicle operation/public transportation expense.** You are entitled to an expense allowance in this category regardless of whether you pay the expenses of operating a vehicle and regardless of whether you use public transportation. Check the number of vehicles for which you pay the operating expenses or for which the operating expenses are included as a contribution to your household expenses in Line 7. ☐ 0 ☐ 1 ☐ 2 or more. If you checked 0, enter on Line 27A the "Public Transportation" amount from IRS Local Standards: Transportation. If you checked 1 or 2 or more, enter on Line 27A the "Operating Costs" amount from IRS Local Standards: Transportation for the applicable number of vehicles in the applicable Metropolitan Statistical Area or Census Region. (These amounts are available at www.usdoj.gov/ust/ or from the clerk of the bankruptcy court.)		$
27B	**Local Standards: transportation; additional public transportation expense.** If you pay the operating expenses for a vehicle and also use public transportation, and you contend that you are entitled to an additional deduction for your public transportation expenses, enter on Line 27B the "Public Transportation" amount from IRS Local Standards: Transportation. (This amount is available at www.usdoj.gov/ust/ or from the clerk of the bankruptcy court.)		$
28	**Local Standards: transportation ownership/lease expense; Vehicle 1.** Check the number of vehicles for which you claim an ownership/lease expense. (You may not claim an ownership/lease expense for more than two vehicles.) ☐ 1 ☐ 2 or more. Enter, in Line a below, the "Ownership Costs" for "One Car" from the IRS Local Standards: Transportation (available at www.usdoj.gov/ust/ or from the clerk of the bankruptcy court); enter in Line b the total of the Average Monthly Payments for any debts secured by Vehicle 1, as stated in Line 47; subtract Line b from Line a and enter the result in Line 28. **Do not enter an amount less than zero.**		
	a.	IRS Transportation Standards, Ownership Costs	$
	b.	Average Monthly Payment for any debts secured by Vehicle 1, as stated in Line 47	$
	c.	Net ownership/lease expense for Vehicle 1	Subtract Line b from Line a.	$

B 22C (Official Form 22C) (Chapter 13) (01/08)

29	**Local Standards: transportation ownership/lease expense; Vehicle 2.** Complete this Line only if you checked the "2 or more" Box in Line 28. Enter, in Line a below, the "Ownership Costs" for "One Car" from the IRS Local Standards: Transportation (available at www.usdoj.gov/ust/ or from the clerk of the bankruptcy court); enter in Line b the total of the Average Monthly Payments for any debts secured by Vehicle 2, as stated in Line 47; subtract Line b from Line a and enter the result in Line 29. **Do not enter an amount less than zero.**		
	a.	IRS Transportation Standards, Ownership Costs	$
	b.	Average Monthly Payment for any debts secured by Vehicle 2, as stated in Line 47	$
	c.	Net ownership/lease expense for Vehicle 2	Subtract Line b from Line a.	$
30	**Other Necessary Expenses: taxes.** Enter the total average monthly expense that you actually incur for all federal, state, and local taxes, other than real estate and sales taxes, such as income taxes, self-employment taxes, social-security taxes, and Medicare taxes. **Do not include real estate or sales taxes.**		$
31	**Other Necessary Expenses: involuntary deductions for employment.** Enter the total average monthly deductions that are required for your employment, such as mandatory retirement contributions, union dues, and uniform costs. **Do not include discretionary amounts, such as voluntary 401(k) contributions.**		$
32	**Other Necessary Expenses: life insurance.** Enter total average monthly premiums that you actually pay for term life insurance for yourself. **Do not include premiums for insurance on your dependents, for whole life or for any other form of insurance.**		$
33	**Other Necessary Expenses: court-ordered payments.** Enter the total monthly amount that you are required to pay pursuant to the order of a court or administrative agency, such as spousal or child support payments. **Do not include payments on past due obligations included in Line 49.**		$
34	**Other Necessary Expenses: education for employment or for a physically or mentally challenged child.** Enter the total average monthly amount that you actually expend for education that is a condition of employment and for education that is required for a physically or mentally challenged dependent child for whom no public education providing similar services is available.		$
35	**Other Necessary Expenses: childcare.** Enter the total average monthly amount that you actually expend on childcare—such as baby-sitting, day care, nursery and preschool. **Do not include other educational payments.**		$
36	**Other Necessary Expenses: health care.** Enter the total average monthly amount that you actually expend on health care that is required for the health and welfare of yourself or your dependents, that is not reimbursed by insurance or paid by a health savings account, and that is in excess of the amount entered in Line 24B. **Do not include payments for health insurance or health savings accounts listed in Line 39.**		$
37	**Other Necessary Expenses: telecommunication services.** Enter the total average monthly amount that you actually pay for telecommunication services other than your basic home telephone and cell phone service—such as pagers, call waiting, caller id, special long distance, or internet service—to the extent necessary for your health and welfare or that of your dependents. **Do not include any amount previously deducted.**		$
38	**Total Expenses Allowed under IRS Standards.** Enter the total of Lines 24 through 37.		$
	Subpart B: Additional Living Expense Deductions **Note: Do not include any expenses that you have listed in Lines 24-37**		

B 22C (Official Form 22C) (Chapter 13) (01/08)

39		Health Insurance, Disability Insurance, and Health Savings Account Expenses. List the monthly expenses in the categories set out in lines a-c below that are reasonably necessary for yourself, your spouse, or your dependents.			
	a.	Health Insurance	$		
	b.	Disability Insurance	$		
	c.	Health Savings Account	$		
		Total and enter on Line 39			$
		If you do not actually expend this total amount, state your actual total average monthly expenditures in the space below: $ _____			
40		**Continued contributions to the care of household or family members.** Enter the total average actual monthly expenses that you will continue to pay for the reasonable and necessary care and support of an elderly, chronically ill, or disabled member of your household or member of your immediate family who is unable to pay for such expenses. **Do not include payments listed in Line 34.**			$
41		**Protection against family violence.** Enter the total average reasonably necessary monthly expenses that you actually incur to maintain the safety of your family under the Family Violence Prevention and Services Act or other applicable federal law. The nature of these expenses is required to be kept confidential by the court.			$
42		**Home energy costs.** Enter the total average monthly amount, in excess of the allowance specified by IRS Local Standards for Housing and Utilities, that you actually expend for home energy costs. **You must provide your case trustee with documentation of your actual expenses, and you must demonstrate that the additional amount claimed is reasonable and necessary.**			$
43		**Education expenses for dependent children under 18.** Enter the total average monthly expenses that you actually incur, not to exceed $137.50 per child, for attendance at a private or public elementary or secondary school by your dependent children less than 18 years of age. **You must provide your case trustee with documentation of your actual expenses, and you must explain why the amount claimed is reasonable and necessary and not already accounted for in the IRS Standards.**			$
44		**Additional food and clothing expense.** Enter the total average monthly amount by which your food and clothing expenses exceed the combined allowances for food and clothing (apparel and services) in the IRS National Standards, not to exceed 5% of those combined allowances. (This information is available at www.usdoj.gov/ust/ or from the clerk of the bankruptcy court.) **You must demonstrate that the additional amount claimed is reasonable and necessary.**			$
45		**Charitable contributions.** Enter the amount reasonably necessary for you to expend each month on charitable contributions in the form of cash or financial instruments to a charitable organization as defined in 26 U.S.C. § 170(c)(1)-(2). **Do not include any amount in excess of 15% of your gross monthly income.**			$
46		**Total Additional Expense Deductions under § 707(b).** Enter the total of Lines 39 through 45.			$

Subpart C: Deductions for Debt Payment

47		**Future payments on secured claims.** For each of your debts that is secured by an interest in property that you own, list the name of the creditor, identify the property securing the debt, state the Average Monthly Payment, and check whether the payment includes taxes or insurance. The Average Monthly Payment is the total of all amounts scheduled as contractually due to each Secured Creditor in the 60 months following the filing of the bankruptcy case, divided by 60. If necessary, list additional entries on a separate page. Enter the total of the Average Monthly Payments on Line 47.			
		Name of Creditor	Property Securing the Debt	Average Monthly Payment	Does payment include taxes or insurance?
	a.			$	☐ yes ☐ no
	b.			$	☐ yes ☐ no
	c.			$	☐ yes ☐ no
				Total: Add Lines a, b, and c	$

B 22C (Official Form 22C) (Chapter 13) (01/08)

48	**Other payments on secured claims.** If any of debts listed in Line 47 are secured by your primary residence, a motor vehicle, or other property necessary for your support or the support of your dependents, you may include in your deduction 1/60th of any amount (the "cure amount") that you must pay the creditor in addition to the payments listed in Line 47, in order to maintain possession of the property. The cure amount would include any sums in default that must be paid in order to avoid repossession or foreclosure. List and total any such amounts in the following chart. If necessary, list additional entries on a separate page.			
		Name of Creditor	Property Securing the Debt	1/60th of the Cure Amount
	a.			$
	b.			$
	c.			$
				Total: Add Lines a, b, and c $
49	**Payments on prepetition priority claims.** Enter the total amount, divided by 60, of all priority claims, such as priority tax, child support and alimony claims, for which you were liable at the time of your bankruptcy filing. **Do not include current obligations, such as those set out in Line 33.**			$
50	**Chapter 13 administrative expenses.** Multiply the amount in Line a by the amount in Line b, and enter the resulting administrative expense.			
	a.	Projected average monthly chapter 13 plan payment.		$
	b.	Current multiplier for your district as determined under schedules issued by the Executive Office for United States Trustees. (This information is available at www.usdoj.gov/ust/ or from the clerk of the bankruptcy court.)		x
	c.	Average monthly administrative expense of chapter 13 case		Total: Multiply Lines a and b $
51	**Total Deductions for Debt Payment.** Enter the total of Lines 47 through 50.			$

Subpart D: Total Deductions from Income

52	**Total of all deductions from income.** Enter the total of Lines 38, 46, and 51.	$

Part V. DETERMINATION OF DISPOSABLE INCOME UNDER § 1325(b)(2)

53	**Total current monthly income.** Enter the amount from Line 20.	$
54	**Support income.** Enter the monthly average of any child support payments, foster care payments, or disability payments for a dependent child, reported in Part I, that you received in accordance with applicable nonbankruptcy law, to the extent reasonably necessary to be expended for such child.	$
55	**Qualified retirement deductions.** Enter the monthly total of (a) all amounts withheld by your employer from wages as contributions for qualified retirement plans, as specified in § 541(b)(7) and (b) all required repayments of loans from retirement plans, as specified in § 362(b)(19).	$
56	**Total of all deductions allowed under § 707(b)(2).** Enter the amount from Line 52.	$

B 22C (Official Form 22C) (Chapter 13) (01/08) 8

57	**Deduction for special circumstances.** If there are special circumstances that justify additional expenses for which there is no reasonable alternative, describe the special circumstances and the resulting expenses in lines a-c below. If necessary, list additional entries on a separate page. Total the expenses and enter the total in Line 57. **You must provide your case trustee with documentation of these expenses and you must provide a detailed explanation of the special circumstances that make such expenses necessary and reasonable.**		
		Nature of special circumstances	Amount of expense
	a.		$
	b.		$
	c.		$
		Total: Add Lines a, b, and c	$
58	**Total adjustments to determine disposable income.** Add the amounts on Lines 54, 55, 56, and 57 and enter the result.		$
59	**Monthly Disposable Income Under § 1325(b)(2).** Subtract Line 58 from Line 53 and enter the result.		$

Part VI: ADDITIONAL EXPENSE CLAIMS

60	**Other Expenses.** List and describe any monthly expenses, not otherwise stated in this form, that are required for the health and welfare of you and your family and that you contend should be an additional deduction from your current monthly income under § 707(b)(2)(A)(ii)(I). If necessary, list additional sources on a separate page. All figures should reflect your average monthly expense for each item. Total the expenses.		
		Expense Description	Monthly Amount
	a.		$
	b.		$
	c.		$
		Total: Add Lines a, b, and c	$

Part VII: VERIFICATION

| 61 | I declare under penalty of perjury that the information provided in this statement is true and correct. *(If this is a joint case, both debtors must sign.)*

 Date: _____ Signature: _____
 (Debtor)

 Date: _____ Signature: _____
 (Joint Debtor, if any) |

INDEX

2005 ACT
See BAPCPA

ABSOLUTE PRIORITY
Evolving Norms in Large
   Reorganizations: 810-814
History: 580, 769-772
Inter-Class Give-Ups: 772-782
LoPucki-Whitford Survey: 810-812
New Value Exception: 782-810
Unsecured Claims and Equity Interests:
   768-772
Valuation: 769-772

ADEQUATE PROTECTION
Chapter 11 Reorganization
   Case Collateral: 604-607
   Chapter 13: 517-519
   Postpetition priming liens: 615-616
   Relief from stay: 591-600
   § 507(b) Superpriority: 600-602
   Single Asset Real Estate: 602-603
   Use of collateral: 604, 607-608

AUDITS
Generally: 504-505

AUTOMATIC STAY
   See STAYS AND INJUNCTIONS

AVOIDING POWERS
Asset Protection Trusts: 74-76
Avoiding Liens Under § 506(d):
   117-120

Fraudulent Transfers: 368-420
   See also FRAUDULENT
   TRANSFERS
Judicial Liens: 48-56
Liens in Household Goods: 46-48
Preferences: 323-362, 420-421
   See also PREFERENCES
Setoff: 362-368
Strong Arm Clause: 421-430
   See also STRONG ARM CLAUSE
Swaps and Derivatives: 418-420

BANKRUPTCY COURTS
Abstention: 841-842
Appellate Jurisdiction: 863-868
Arbitration: 842-844
Bankruptcy Appellate Panels: 863-866
Core and Non-Core: 825-840
Direct Appeals to Circuits: 557, 867-868
Districts: 21
Jurisdiction: 823-840
Jury Trials: 868-883
Sovereign Immunity: 844-860
Transnational Bankruptcy: 885
Venue: 860-863
Withdrawal of Reference: 841

BANKRUPTCY ESTATE
   See also EXEMPT PROPERTY
Asset Protection Trusts: 74-76
Avoidance of Judicial Liens: 48-56
Chapter 13: 520
Divided Property Interests: 36-38

BANKRUPTCY ESTATE (cont.)
Earmarking: 326-327
Exempt Property: 40-44, 56-59
Fraudulent Use of Exemptions: 59-74
Generally: 29-36
Impairment of Exemptions: 46-48
Possession and Turnover: 36-40
Post-Confirmation Issues: 820
Retirement Plans: 44-46

BAPCPA
Bankruptcy Estate
    Domicile: 58
    Homestead: 57-59
    Retirement Plans: 44-46
Chapter 11 Reorganization
    Discharge: 816
    Exclusivity Period Limited: 671
    Personally Identifiable Information Limitations: 665-666
    Prepackaged Bankruptcies: 680-681
    Reclamation: 614-615
    Single Asset Real Estate: 585-586, 602-603
    Small Business Cases: 681-682
Claims
    Domestic Support Obligations (DSO): 143-144, 521-522
    Valuing Secured Claims: 549-557, 559-560, 116-117
Consumer Debtor in Chapter 13
    Audits: 504-505
    Current Monthly Income (CMI): 477-478
    Disposable Income Test Tightened: 525-530
    Duration of Plan Increased: 530-533
    Lien-Stripping Limited: 549-551
    Means Test: 474-482, 490-492
    Modification: 533-535
    New Exceptions to Discharge: 541-543
    Repetitive Filings: 516-517
    Safe Harbor (Below Median Income Debtors): 486-490
Consumer Debtor in Chapter 7
    Increased Disclosures: 493-495, 502-503
    Increased Duties of Attorneys and U.S. Trustees: 495-505
    Mandatory Credit Counseling: 505-508
    Reaffirmation: 545-547
    Ride-Through: 547-549
Discharge
    Assumed Leases: 305
    Chapter 11 Discharge: 816
    DSOs Nondischargeable: 522
    Expanded Nondischargeability of Credit Card Debt: 162
    Nondischargeable Debts Expanded in Chapter 13: 541-543
Fraudulent Transfers
    Insider Transfers under Employment Contracts: 376-377
    Self-Settled Trusts: 76, 373
    Two-Year Lookback Period: 369, 370, 373
Leases
    Limits Administrative Expense Claims: 305
    Limits Time for Assumption / Rejection Decision: 292
Preferences
    Expands Ordinary Course Defense: 342, 346
    Extends Relation-Back Period: 361
    Small Transaction Defense: 352, 862-863

BEST INTERESTS TEST
Chapter 11: 767-768
Chapter 13: 523-524, 548-549

Index

BREAKUP FEES
Generally: 666-669

CASH COLLATERAL
Setoff: 362-366
Use: 604-607

CHAPTER 11
See REORGANIZATION IN CHAPTER 11

CHAPTER 12
See FAMILY FARMER

CHAPTER 13
See CONSUMER DEBTOR

"CHAPTER 20"
Filing Limitations: 514-515

"CHAPTER 22"
Refiling Rates: 718-719, 861
Good Faith Limitation: 820-821

CLAIMS
Administrative Expenses: 123-127, 615-626, 719
Classification: 692-710
    See also CLASSIFICATION
Estimation: 104-106
Generally: 77-78
Impairment: 690-692, 710-711
Mass Torts: 80-93
Priority Claims: 121-122, 719
    Administrative Expenses: 123-127
    Critical Vendor Orders: 608-614
    Domestic Support Obligations: 122-123
    Reclamation & Trade Priority: 614-615
    Surcharge Claims: 616-625

Proofs of Claim: 78-80
Rights to Payment
    Legal Rights: 80-93
    Equitable Rights: 93-104
Secured Claims: 106-117, 549-557, 559-560, 591-603, 720-767
    See also SECURED CLAIMS
    Lien Stripping: 117-120, 549-551
    Post-Filing Interest: 120-121
Trading: 682-688
Unsecured Claims: 760-782
    Assumed Leases: 294-305
    Claim Procedures: 78-80
    Determining Amount: 104-106
    Tax Claims: 167-168, 719-720

CLASSIFICATION
Chapter 11: 692-710
Unfair Discrimination in Chapter 13: 536-541

CONSENSUAL LIENS
Personal Property: 3-9
Real Property: 9-14

CONSUMER DEBTOR
Access to Chapter 7
    Substantial Abuse Test: 469-471
    Under 1978 Code: 468-469
    Under BAPCPA: 471-492
Adequate Protection: 517-519
Audits: 504
Chapter 11 as Alternative: 492-493
Chapter 13 as Alternative: 508-574
    Commencing Chapter 13 Case: 517-520
    Conversion to Chapter 7: 520
    Eligibility: 512-514
    Overview: 508-512
    Property of Estate and Automatic Stay: 520
    Repeated Discharges and Filings: 514-517

CONSUMER DEBTOR (cont.)
Chapter 13 Plan: 521-541
   Best Interests Test:
      523-524, 548-549
   Classification of Claims: 536-541
   Cramdown: 509-510, 550-551,
      568-569, 571-574
   Critique: 528-533
   Disposable Income:
      522-528, 528-530
   Domestic Support Obligations
      (DSO): 521-522
   Duration: 522, 530-533, 573-574
   Modification: 533-535
   Payments Outside of Plan: 535-536
   Religious and Charitable Donations:
      524-527, 481-482
Debtor's Disclosures: 493-495
Discharge in Chapter 13: 541-543
Duties of Debtor's Attorney: 495-503
Duties of U.S. Trustee: 503-505
Generally: 465-466
Mandatory Credit Counseling: 505-508
Means Test: 473-492
   Critique: 490-492
   Current Monthly Income (CMI):
      477-478
   Debtor's Monthly Expenses: 478-482
   Presumption of Abuse: 474-477
   Residual Power to Dismiss:
      474, 482-486
   Safe Harbor: 486-487
Nondischargeability: 132-168
   Credit card fraud: 156-163
   Domestic Support Obligations
      (DSO): 137-145, 521-522
   Educational loans: 151-155
   Fines, Penalties and Forfeitures:
      163-166
   Fraud: 155-156
   Intentional Torts: 145-151
   Unscheduled Debts: 132-137

Private-Sector Debt Relief: 467-468
Reaffirmation of Debts: 544-545
Ride-Through: 547-548
Secured Claims in Personal Property in
   Chapter 13: 547-560
   Chapter 7 Contrasted: 547
   Cramdown: 550-551
   Hanging Paragraph: 549-550
   Interest Rate: 557, 560
   Refinancing Balances Due: 558-559
   Surrender: 551-557
   Valuation of Collateral: 559-560
Secured Claims in Real Property in
   Chapter 13: 561-574
   2007 Home Loan Crisis: 569-570
   Cure of Defaults: 571-573
   Generally: 561-574
   Modification of Home Mortgages:
      561-568
   Three-to-Five Year Limitations:
      573-574
   Wholly Unsecured Home Loans:
      568-569
Restitution: 166
Spousal and child support:
   137-145, 521-522
Taxes: 167-168

CRAMDOWN
   See ABSOLUTE PRIORITY;
   CONSUMER DEBTOR;
   REORGANIZATION IN CHAPTER 11

DISCHARGE
Chapter 11 Discharge: 815-818
Chapter 13 Discharge: 541-543
Denial of Discharge: 130-132
Discrimination Against Debtors:
   171-178
Effect on Liens: 117-120, 170
Enforcement: 168-170
Generally: 129-130
Non-Dischargeability: 132-168

DISCHARGE (cont.)
Credit card fraud: 156-163
Domestic Support Obligations (DSO): 137-145, 521-522
Educational loans: 151-155
Fines, Penalties and Forfeitures: 163-166
Fraud: 155-156
Intentional Torts: 145-151
Restitution: 166
Taxes: 167-168
Unscheduled Debts: 132-137

EQUITABLE SUBORDINATION
Dominant Creditors: 436-447
Insiders: 431-436
Leveraged Buyout Participants: 415
Recharacterization: 435-436
Undercapitalization: 434-435

EQUITY RECEIVERSHIPS
Generally: 577-582

EXECUTORY CONTRACTS
Assignment: 258-267
Assumption: 229-232, 244-258
Contracts Nonassignable Under Non-bankruptcy Law: 244
Enforcement Before Assumption or Rejection: 267-274
Executoriness: 232-236
Licenses of Intellectual Property: 237-256
Nonmonetary Defaults: 256-258
Rejection: 229-232, 237-244

EXEMPT PROPERTY
Asset Protection Trusts: 74-76
Claiming Exemption: 41-44
Generally: 40-41
Homesteads: 57-59

Impairment of Exemptions: 46-56
　Avoidance of judicial liens: 48-56
　Avoidance of security interests: 46-48
Prebankruptcy Planning: 56-74
Retirement Plans: 44-46

FAMILY FARMER
Generally: 746-748

FEASIBILITY
Generally: 713-719

FRAUDULENT TRANSFERS
Actual Fraud: 368-373
Asset Protection Trusts: 74-76, 373
Constructive Fraud: 373-374
Corporate Distributions: 386-395
Discharge Limitations: 130-131
Employment Contracts: 376-377
Foreclosures: 377-386
Intercorporate Guarantees: 396-398
Leveraged Buyouts: 398-418
Religious and Charitable Donations: 374-376
Swaps & Derivatives: 418-420

HISTORY OF BANKRUPTCY
Fraudulent Transfer Law: 371-372
Generally: 18-20
Reorganization Law: 577-582

IMPAIRMENT
Exemptions: 46-49
Artificial Impairment: 710-711
Reinstatement in Chapter 11: 690-692
Cash-outs Plans (§ 1111(b)): 763-766

INDUBITABLE EQUIVALENCE
Adequate Protection: 597-598, 599-600
Dirt-for-Debt Plans: 749-757
Secured Creditor Cramdown: 749-757

INSOLVENCY
Absolute Priority: 769-772, 783
Fraudulent Transfers:
   374, 408-410, 415-416
Leveraged Buyouts: 408-410, 415-416
Not Required For Voluntary Debtors:
   24
Preferences: 323-325

INTEREST
Disallowance of Unmatured Postpetition
   Interest: 626
Postconfirmation Interest in
   Reorganization Cases
      Chapters 11 and 12: 720-748
      Chapter 13: 557, 560, 573, 722-746
Postpetition Interest and Fees on Secured
   Claims: 120-121, 591-603

JUDICIAL LIENS
Attachment Liens: 17-18
Avoidance: 48-56
Execution Liens: 14-15, 16-17
Generally: 2
Judgment Liens: 14-16

JURISDICTION
   See BANKRUPTCY COURTS

LEASES
Assignment: 306-322
      Anti assignment provisions: 312-314
      Use provisions: 306-312
Assumption: 294-312
Eviction: 292-293
Expiration: 293
Liability for use of Leased Property
   before Rejection: 285-290
Personal Property Leases: 290-291
Rejection: 274-290
      By lessee: 283-285
      By lessor: 274-283
      When rejection occurs: 285
Shopping Centers: 314-322
Termination: 293-294
Time in which to Assume or Reject:
   291-292

LIEN STRIPPING
Chapter 7: 108-109, 117-120
Chapter 13: 549-559, 566-569
   See also REORGANIZATION IN
   CHAPTER 11 and CONSUMER
   DEBTOR

LIENS
   See CONSENSUAL LIENS and
   JUDICIAL LIENS

MORTGAGES
   See also CONSENSUAL LIENS
2007 Home Loan Crisis: 569-570
Cure of Defaults: 571-574
Generally: 9-14
Home Mortgage Modification: 561-568
Underwater Junior Liens: 568-569

NEGATIVE AMORTIZATION
Generally: 757-763

Index

NEW VALUE
Exception to Absolute Priority: 782-810
Subsequent Advance Preference
 Defense: 346-347

ORDINARY COURSE OF BUSINESS
Preference Defense: 330-346
Sales and Leases: 607-608
Role of Debtor-in-Possession:
 586-587, 604, 615

OVERVIEW
Automatic Stay: 24
Claims: 27
Creditors' Meeting: 26-27
Discharge: 28
Distribution of Assets: 27-28
Eligibility: 23-24
Trustee in Bankruptcy: 24-26, 27
Types of Bankruptcy: 21-23

POSTPETITION FINANCING
Cash Collateral
 Setoff: 362-366
 Use: 604-607
Critical Vendors: 608-614
Cross–Collateralization: 628-633
Ordinary Course of Business: 615-616
Priming Liens: 615-616, 626-628
Roll-Ups: 633-634
Superpriority Claim: 615-621
Surcharge under § 506(c): 621-626

PREBANKRUPTCY PLANNING
Exempt Property: 56-74
Asset Protection Trusts: 74-76

PREFERENCES
Contemporaneous Exchanges: 328-330
Domestic Support Obligations (DSO):
 351-352
Earmarking: 326-327
Generally: 323-326
Improvement in Position Test
 Inventory and receivables: 349-351
 Setoff: 368
Insider Preferences: 420-421
Letters of Credit: 352-359
Ordinary Course Defense: 330-346
Preference Period: 328
Small Transactions: 352, 862-863
Subsequent Advance Defense (New
 Value): 346-347
Swaps & Derivatives: 418-420
Time of Transfer
 Calculating time: 328
 Checks: 347-349
 Late perfection: 360-362

PRIORITY CLAIMS
Administrative Expenses: 123-127, 615-626, 719
Assumed Leases: 294-305
Domestic Support Obligations (DSO):
 122-123
Reclamation & Vendor Priority: 614-615
Surcharge Claims: 616-625
Tax Claims: 167-168, 719-720

PROPERTY OF ESTATE
See BANKRUPTCY ESTATE

REAFFIRMATION
Generally: 544-547

RECHARACTERIZATION
Leases to Secured Transactions: 290-291, 479
Loans to Equity: 435-436

REDEMPTION
Chapter 7: 116-117
Generally: 547-548
Valuation: 560

RELIGIOUS AND CHARITABLE DONATIONS
Chapter 13 Plans: 524-527
Dismissal: 485-486
Fraudulent Transfers: 374-376
Means Test: 481-482

REORGANIZATION IN CHAPTER 11
Absolute Priority: 768-772
   History: 580, 769-772
   Inter-Class "Give-ups": 772-782
   LoPucki–Whitford survey: 810-812
   New value exception: 782-810
   Unsecured claims and equity interests: 768-772
Acceptance: 672-682, 669-670
Adequate Protection: 591-607, 615-616
Best Interests Rule: 767-768
Best Interests Test: 767-768
Break–Up Fees: 666-669
Cash Collateral: 604-607
Classification: 692-710
Cramdown
   Deferred cash payments: 720-476
   Dirt-for-debt plans: 479-756
   Indubitable Equivalent: 749-757
   Negative amortization plans: 757-763
   Sale of Property: 748
   Secured creditor cramdown generally: 720
   Unsecured claims and equity interests: 768-772
   Valuation: 109-116, 769-772
Creditors' Committees: 589-591
Critical Vendors: 608-614
Cross–Collateralization: 628-633
Debtors In Possession: 586-587
Discharge: 815-818
Election Under § 1111(b): 763-767
Evolving Norms: 810-814
Examiners: 588-589
Exclusivity: 670-672
Feasibility: 713-719
Generally: 582-586
History of Reorganization Law: 577-582
Impairment: 690-692
Personally Identifiable Information: 665-666
Postconfirmation Modification: 818-821
Postpetition Financing: 604-607, 608-634
Pre-Code Law: 577-582
Prepackaged Plans: 680-681
   See also SECURED CLAIMS
Prepetition Creditors: 626-628
Rationale: 575-577
Reclamation: 614-615
Rights of Administrative Claimants: 615-621, 719
Roll-Ups: 633-634
Sales: 607-608, 634-665, 812-814
Single Asset Real Estate Debtors: 585-586, 602-603, 699-711, 807-810
Small Business Debtors: 681-682
Solicitation: 672-682
Sub-Rosa Plan: 646-647
Trading Claims: 682-688
Trustees: 587-588

RIDE-THROUGH
Generally: 547-548

ROLL-UPS
Generally: 633-634

SALES
Increasing Frequency: 812-814
Nonordinary Course: 634-669
Ordinary Course: 604-608
Personal Identifiable Information: 665-666
Sales Free and Clear: 648-665
Sub Rosa Plan: 646-647
Substantially All Assets: 645-646

SECURED CLAIMS
Adequate Protection
    See ADEQUATE PROTECTION
After–Acquired Property: 29-35, 604-607
Avoiding Powers
    See AVOIDING POWERS
Chapter 13 Plans
    See CONSUMER DEBTOR
Cramdown in Chapter 11
    See REORGANIZATION IN CHAPTER 11
Impairment: 690-692, 763-766
Lien Stripping: 108-109, 117-120
Postfiling Interest: 120-121
Reaffirmation: 544-547
Relief from Stay: 591-600
Setoff: 362-368
Superpriority Under § 507: 600-602
Turnover: 36-40
Valuation: 109-117, 559-560
Roll-Ups: 633-634
Redemption: 116-117, 559-560

SECURITIZATION
Vulnerability to Substantive Consolidation: 462-463

SECURITY INTERESTS
    See CONSENSUAL LIENS

SETOFF
Administrative Freeze of Deposit Accounts: 362-368
Improvement in Position Test: 368

SINGLE ASSET REAL ESTATE
BAPCPA: 602-603, 585-586
Caselaw: 699-711, 807-810

STAYS AND INJUNCTIONS
Applicability of Stays: 180-182
Chapter 13 Stay: 36, 510, 520
Exceptions to Automatic Stay: 182-185
Generally: 24, 179-180
Nondebtors: 204-226
    Co-defendants: 204-212
    Guarantors: 213-217
    Insurers: 211-212, 226
    Letter of credit issuers: 217-218
    Officers and controlling shareholders: 206-217
    Partners: 218-222
Options: 204
Post-Foreclosure Right of Redemption: 197-204
Prebankruptcy Stay Waivers: 226-227
Property Protected: 181-182
Regulatory Powers Exception: 184-185
Relief from Stay: 222-226, 591-603
Remedies for Violation: 185-197
Repetitive Filings: 183, 516-517
Secured Claims: 197-204
Single Asset Real Estate: 602-603
Swaps & Derivatives: 182
Termination: 185

STRONG ARM CLAUSE
Constructive and Express Trusts: 427-430
Generally: 421-423
Knowledge of Debtor or Trustee: 423-427
Property Held by Debtor as Nominee: 427-430

SUBSTANTIVE CONSOLIDATION
Generally: 447-462
Securitization: 462-463

SWAPS AND DERIVATIVES
Automatic Stay Exemption: 182
Defense to Avoidance: 418-420
Plan Acceptance: 689-690

TRADE CREDITORS
Critical Vendors: 608-614
Reclamation: 614-615
Rights of Prepetition Creditors: 626-628

TRANSNATIONAL CASES
Chapter 15: 884-885, 897-898
Generally: 883-899
Hotch-pot Rule: 899
Venue: 898-899

TRUSTEES
Chapter 11 Trustees: 587-588
Chapter 12 Trustees: 747
Chapter 13 Trustees: 519
Chapter 7 Trustees: 24-27
Election: 26-27, 588
Generally: 24-27
United States Trustee: 21, 26, 503-505, 589

VALUATION
Absolute Priority: 769-772
  See also ABSOLUTE PRIORITY
Improvement in Position Test: 349-351
Secured Claims: 109-117, 559-560

VENUE
Chapter 11 Cases: 861-862
Generally: 860
Proceedings in Cases: 862-863
Transnational: 898-899

* * *